高等院校双语教材·经济系列

THE ECONOMICS OF MONEY, BANKING, AND FINANCIAL MARKETS
(Alternate Edition)

货币金融学
（商学院版）

弗雷德里克·S·米什金（Frederic S. Mishkin）著

中国人民大学出版社
·北京·

出版说明

中国的入世，使其真正融入到经济全球化的浪潮中。中国政府“引进来，走出去”战略，使得中国经济的发展需要大量的“国际化”人才储备。这就对我国一般本科院校多年来所采取的单一语言（母语）教学提出严峻挑战，财经院校涉外经济类专业实行双语教学改革迫在眉睫。

顺应这一潮流，中国人民大学出版社携手众多国际知名的大出版公司，如麦格劳-希尔、培生教育出版公司等，面向大学本科层次，遴选了一批国外最优秀的经济类原版教材，包括宏观经济学、微观经济学、计量经济学、金融学等经济类专业基础课。

我们在引进出版过程中，注重把好质量关，每一本书都经过该学科领域的专家审核选题和内容，争取做到把国外真正高水平的适合国内实际的优秀教材引进来。本套教材主要有以下特点：

第一，体系设计完整。本套教材精选了一批国外著名出版公司的优秀教材，基本上涵盖了经济学专业的核心课程。

第二，保持英文原版教材的特色。本套教材根据国内教学需要，对原书进行了一定的改编，主要删减了一些不适合和不符合我国国情的内容，但体系结构和内容方面都保持原版教材的特色。

第三，内容紧扣学科前沿。本套教材在原著选择上紧扣国外教学的前沿，基本上都选择国外最流行教材的最新版本，有利于老师和学生掌握国外教学研究的最新发展趋势。

第四，篇幅合理，价格适中。为适应国内双语教学内容和课时上的实际需要，本套教材在进行了删减改编后，篇幅更为合理。同时，考虑到学生实际的购买能力，我们采取低定价策略，这样，读者既能领略原版图书的风貌，又避免了高额的购买费用。

第五，提供强大的教学支持。依托国外大出版公司的力量，本套教材为教师提供了配套的教辅资料，如教师手册、PPT课堂演示文稿、试题库等，并配套有内容丰富的网络资源，从而使教学更为便利。

本套教材既适合高等院校经济类专业的本科教学使用，也适合从事经济类工作和研究的人员阅读和培训使用。我们在选书、改编过程中虽然全面听取了专家的意见，做到尽可能满足读者的需求，但由于各教材的作者所处的政治、经济和文化背景不同，书中内容仍可能有不妥之处，我们真诚希望广大读者提出宝贵意见和建议，以便我们在以后的版本中不断改进和完善。

中国人民大学出版社

目　录

第1篇　导　言

第1章　为什么研究货币、银行与金融市场 …… 3

第2章　金融体系概览 …… 23

第3章　什么是货币? …… 49

第2篇　金融市场

第4章　理解利率 …… 67

第5章　利率行为 …… 93

第6章　利率的风险结构与期限结构 …… 127

第7章　股票市场、理性预期理论与有效市场假定 …… 151

第3篇　金融机构

第8章　金融结构的经济学分析 …… 181

第9章　银行业与金融机构的管理 …… 219

第10章　银行业:结构与竞争 …… 247

第11章　银行监管的经济学分析 …… 279

第12章　非银行金融机构 …… 309

第13章　衍生金融工具 …… 333

第14章　金融行业的利率冲突 …… 361

第4篇　中央银行与货币政策操作

第15章　中央银行的结构与联邦储备体系 …… 383

第16章　多倍存款创造和货币供给过程 …… 405

第17章　货币供给的决定因素 …… 423

第18章　货币政策工具 …… 445

第19章　中央银行的职责是什么?货币政策目标、策略和战略 …… 465

第 5 篇　国际金融与货币政策

第 20 章　外汇市场 …… 503

第 21 章　国际金融体系 …… 531

第 6 篇　货币理论

第 22 章　货币需求 …… 565

第 23 章　总需求与总供给分析 …… 585

第 24 章　货币政策传导机制的实证分析 …… 607

第 25 章　货币与通货膨胀 …… 637

词汇表 …… G-1

部分问答题和思考题答案 …… A-1

CONTENTS

PART 1 Introduction 1

CHAPTER 1
Why Study Money, Banking, and Financial Markets? 3
Preview 3
Why Study Financial Markets? 3
Why Study Banking and Financial Institutions? 7
Why Study Money and Monetary Policy? 8
How We Will Study Money, Banking, and Financial Markets 13
Web Exercises 15
Concluding Remarks 16

APPENDIX TO CHAPTER 1
Defining Aggregate Output, Income, the Price Level, and the Inflation Rate 20
Aggregate Output and Income 20
Real Versus Nominal Magnitudes 20
Aggregate Price Level 21
Growth Rates and the Inflation Rate 22

CHAPTER 2
An Overview of the Financial System 23
Preview 23
Function of Financial Markets 23
Structure of Financial Markets 25
Financial Market Instruments 28
Internationalization of Financial Markets 33
Function of Financial Intermediaries: Indirect Finance 35
Types of Financial Intermediaries 39
Regulation of the Financial System 42

CHAPTER 3
What Is Money? 49
Preview 49
Meaning of Money 49
Functions of Money 50
Evolution of the Payments System 53
Measuring Money 56
How Reliable Are the Money Data? 59

PART 2 Financial Markets 65

CHAPTER 4
Understanding Interest Rates 67
Preview 67
Measuring Interest Rates 67
Application Simple Present Value 69
Application How Much Is That Jackpot Worth? 69
Application Yield to Maturity on a Simple Loan 71
Application Yield to Maturity and the Yearly Payment on a Fixed-Payment Loan 73
Application Yield to Maturity and the Bond Price for a Coupon Bond 74
Application Perpetuity 76
Yield on a Discount Basis 78
Application Reading the *Wall Street Journal*: The Bond Page 80
The Distinction Between Interest Rates and Returns 82
The Distinction Between Real and Nominal Interest Rates 87
Application Calculating Real Interest Rates 88

CHAPTER 5
The Behavior of Interest Rates 93
Preview 93
Determinants of Asset Demand 93
Supply and Demand in the Bond Market 95
Changes in Equilibrium Interest Rates 99
Application Changes in the Interest Rate Due to Expected Inflation: The Fisher Effect 105
Application Changes in the Interest Rate Due to a Business Cycle Expansion 106
Application Explaining Low Japanese Interest Rates 109
Application Reading the *Wall Street Journal* "Credit Markets" Column 109
Supply and Demand in the Market for Money: The Liquidity Preference Framework 111
Changes in Equilibrium Interest Rates in the Liquidity Preference Framework 113
Application Changes in the Equilibrium Interest Rate Due to Changes in Income, the Price Level, or the Money Supply 114
Application Money and Interest Rates 116

CHAPTER 6
The Risk and Term Structure of Interest Rates 127
Preview 127
Risk Structure of Interest Rates 127
Application The Enron Bankruptcy and the Baa-Aaa Spread 131
Application Effects of the Bush Tax Cut on Bond Interest Rates 134
Term Structure of Interest Rates 134
Application Interpreting Yield Curves, 1980–2006 145

CHAPTER 7
The Stock Market, the Theory of Rational Expectations, and the Efficient Market Hypothesis 151
Preview 151
Computing the Price of Common Stock 151
How the Market Sets Stock Prices 154
Application Monetary Policy and Stock Prices 155
Application The September 11 Terrorist Attacks, the Enron Scandal, and the Stock Market 156
The Theory of Rational Expectations 156
The Efficient Market Hypothesis: Rational Expectations in Financial Markets 160
Evidence on the Efficient Market Hypothesis 162
Application Should Foreign Exchange Rates Follow a Random Walk? 165
Application Practical Guide to Investing in the Stock Market 168
Evidence on Rational Expectations in Other Markets 171
Application What Do the Black Monday Crash of 1987 and the Tech Crash of 2000 Tell Us About Rational Expectations and Efficient Markets? 172
Behavioral Finance 173

PART 3 Financial Institutions 179

CHAPTER 8
An Economic Analysis of Financial Structure 181
Preview 181
Basic Facts About Financial Structure Throughout the World 181
Transaction Costs 186
Asymmetric Information: Adverse Selection and Moral Hazard 187
The Lemons Problem: How Adverse Selection Influences Financial Structure 188
How Moral Hazard Affects the Choice Between Debt and Equity Contracts 194
How Moral Hazard Influences Financial Structure in Debt Markets 197

Conflicts of Interest 201
Application Financial Development and Economic Growth 202
Application Is China a Counter-Example to the Importance of Financial Development? 203
Financial Crises and Aggregate Economic Activity 204
Application Financial Crises in the United States 207
Application Financial Crises in Emerging-Market Countries: Mexico, 1994–1995; East Asia, 1997–1998; and Argentina, 2001–2002 209

CHAPTER 9
Banking and the Management of Financial Institutions 219
Preview 219
The Bank Balance Sheet 219
Basic Banking 223
General Principles of Bank Management 226
Application Strategies for Managing Bank Capital 233
Application Did the Capital Crunch Cause a Credit Crunch in the Early 1990s? 234
Managing Credit Risk 234
Managing Interest-Rate Risk 238
Application Strategies for Managing Interest-Rate Risk 240
Off-Balance-Sheet Activities 241

CHAPTER 10
Banking Industry: Structure and Competition 247
Preview 247
Historical Development of the Banking System 247
Financial Innovation and the Evolution of the Banking Industry 250
Structure of the U.S. Commercial Banking Industry 261
Bank Consolidation and Nationwide Banking 263
Separation of the Banking and Other Financial Service Industries 268
Thrift Industry: Regulation and Structure 270
International Banking 271

CHAPTER 11
Economic Analysis of Banking Regulation 279
Preview 279
Asymmetric Information and Banking Regulation 279
International Banking Regulation 291
The 1980s U.S. Savings and Loan and Banking Crisis: Why? 292
Political Economy of the Savings and Loan Crisis 295
Savings and Loan Bailout: The Financial Institutions Reform, Recovery, and Enforcement Act of 1989 298

Federal Deposit Insurance Corporation Improvement Act of 1991 299
Banking Crises Throughout the World 300

CHAPTER 12
Nonbank Finance 309
Preview 309
Insurance 309
Application Insurance Management 313
Pension Funds 316
Finance Companies 320
Mutual Funds 320
Government Financial Intermediation 325
Securities Market Operations 326

CHAPTER 13
Financial Derivatives 333
Preview 333
Hedging 333
Interest-Rate Forward Contracts 334
Application Hedging with Interest-Rate Forward Contracts 334
Financial Futures Contracts and Markets 335
Application Hedging with Financial Futures 338
Application Hedging Foreign Exchange Risk 342
Options 344
Application Hedging with Futures Options 348
Swaps 351
Application Hedging with Interest-Rate Swaps 352
Credit Derivatives 354
Application Are Financial Derivatives a Worldwide Time Bomb? 355

CHAPTER 14
Conflicts of Interest in the Financial Industry 361
Preview 361
What Are Conflicts of Interest and Why are They Important? 362
Ethics and Conflicts of Interest 362
Types of Conflicts of Interest 363
Can the Market Limit Exploitation of Conflicts of Interest? 368
What Has Been Done to Remedy Conflicts of Interest? 371
A Framework for Evaluating Policies to Remedy Conflicts of Interest 372
Application Evaluating Sarbanes-Oxley and the Global Legal Settlement 375

PART 4 Central Banking and the Conduct of Monetary Policy 381

CHAPTER 15
Structure of Central Banks and the Federal Reserve System 383
Preview 383
Origins of the Federal Reserve System 383
Structure of the Federal Reserve System 384
How Independent Is the Fed? 393
Structure and Independence of the European Central Bank 394
Structure and Independence of other Foreign Central Banks 397
Explaining Central Bank Behavior 398
Should the Fed Be Independent? 400

CHAPTER 16
Multiple Deposit Creation and the Money Supply Process 405
Preview 405
Four Players in the Money Supply Process 405
The Fed's Balance Sheet 406
Control of the Monetary Base 407
Multiple Deposit Creation: A Simple Model 413

CHAPTER 17
Determinants of the Money Supply 423
Preview 423
The Money Supply Model and the Money Multiplier 424
Factors that Determine the Money Multiplier 427
Additional Factors That Determine the Money Supply 431
Overview of the Money Supply Process 432
Application Explaining Movements in the Money Supply, 1980–2005 434
Application The Great Depression Bank Panics, 1930–1933 436

APPENDIX TO CHAPTER 17
The M2 Money Multiplier 442
Factors that Determine the M2 Money Multiplier 443

CHAPTER 18
Tools of Monetary Policy 445
Preview 445
The Market for Reserves and the Federal Funds Rate 445
Open Market Operations 450
Discount Policy 452
Reserve Requirements 455

Application Why Have Reserve Requirements Been Declining Worldwide? 457

Application The Channel/Corridor System for Setting Interest Rates Used in Other Countries 458

Monetary Policy Tools of the European Central Bank 460

CHAPTER 19
What Should Central Banks Do? Monetary Policy Goals, Strategy, and Tactics 465

Preview 465
The Price Stability Goal and the Nominal Anchor 465
Other Goals of Monetary Policy 467
Should Price Stability be the Primary Goal of Monetary Policy? 469
Monetary Targeting 470
Inflation Targeting 474
Monetary Policy with an Implicit Nominal Anchor 480
Tactics: Choosing the Policy Instrument 484
The Taylor Rule, NAIRU, and the Phillips Curve 486

APPENDIX TO CHAPTER 19
Fed Policy Procedures: Historical Perspective 492

The Early Years: Discount Policy as the Primary Tool 492
Discovery of Open Market Operations 493
The Great Depression 493
Reserve Requirements as a Policy Tool 494
War Finance and the Pegging of Interest Rates: 1942–1951 495
Targeting Money Market Conditions: The 1950s and 1960s 495
Targeting Monetary Aggregates: The 1970s 496
New Fed Operating Procedures: October 1979–October 1982 497
De-Emphasis of Monetary Aggregates: October 1982–Early 1990s 498
Federal Funds Targeting Again: Early 1990s and Beyond 499
International Considerations 500

PART 5 International Finance and Monetary Policy 501

CHAPTER 20
The Foreign Exchange Market 503

Preview 503
Foreign Exchange Market 503
Exchange Rates in the Long Run 507
Exchange Rates in the Short Run 510
Explaining Changes in Exchange Rates 516

Application Changes in the Equilibrium Exchange Rate: Two Examples 519

Application Why Are Exchange Rates So Volatile? 523

Application The Dollar and Interest Rates, 1973–2005 524

Application The Euro's First Seven Years 525

Application Reading the *Wall Street Journal:* The "Currency Trading" Column 525

CHAPTER 21
The International Financial System 531

Preview 531
Intervention in the Foreign Exchange Market 531
Balance of Payments 536
Exchange Rate Regimes in the International Financial System 537
Application How Did China Accumulate Nearly $1 Trillion of International Reserves? 542
Application The Foreign Exchange Crisis of September 1992 544
Application Recent Foreign Exchange Crises in Emerging Market Countries: Mexico 1994, East Asia 1997, Brazil 1999, and Argentina 2002 546
Capital Controls 547
The Role of the IMF 548
International Considerations and Monetary Policy 551
To Peg or Not to Peg: Exchange-Rate Targeting as an Alternative Monetary Policy Strategy 553

PART 6 Monetary Theory 563

CHAPTER 22
The Demand for Money 565

Preview 565
Quantity Theory of Money 565
Is Velocity a Constant? 568
Keynes's Liquidity Preference Theory 569
Further Developments in the Keynesian Approach 573
Friedman's Modern Quantity Theory of Money 577
Distinguishing Between The Friedman and Keynesian Theories 579
Empirical Evidence on the Demand for Money 581

CHAPTER 23
Aggregate Demand and Supply Analysis 585

Preview 585
Aggregate Demand 585
Aggregate Supply 589
Equilibrium in Aggregate Supply and Demand Analysis 594

Application Explaining Past Business Cycle Episodes 601

CHAPTER 24
Transmission Mechanisms of Monetary Policy: The Evidence 607
Preview 607
Framework for Evaluating Empirical Evidence 607
Application The Debate on the Importance of Monetary Policy to Economic Fluctuations 611
Transmission Mechanisms of Monetary Policy 620
Application Corporate Scandals and the Slow Recovery from the March 2001 Recession 629
Lessons for Monetary Policy 630
Application Applying the Monetary Policy Lessons to Japan 631

CHAPTER 25
Money and Inflation 637
Preview 637
Money and Inflation: Evidence 637
Meaning of Inflation 639
Views of Inflation 640
Origins of Inflationary Monetary Policy 644
Application Explaining the Rise in U. S. Inflation, 1960–1980 651
Activist/NonActivist Policy Debate 654
Application Importance of Credibility to Volcker's Victory over Inflation 658

Glossary G-1
Answers to Selected Questions and Problems A-1
Credits C-1

PREFACE

A NOTE FROM THE AUTHOR

When I first wrote *The Economics of Money, Banking, and Financial Markets* seven editions ago I saw there was a true need for a contemporary approach to the study of this area of economics. At the time, the existing books offered only an institutional approach to the material. I knew that students would benefit from understanding the economics behind how money and banking institutions work, and that's what I set out to do. To this day, I remain committed to educating money and banking students. I am honored that each year tens of thousands of students throughout the world learn about the systems of money and banking by reading my book. With this honor comes a personal responsibility that I take very seriously. In every new edition, dedicated professors from around the world generously offer suggestions on how I might enhance the teaching and learning of money, banking, and financial markets through my book. I am deeply grateful for this feedback, and as with the First Edition, I take great care to craft a better book, page by page. While not typical of many textbook authors, I also write the Instructor's Manual so that I have the opportunity to share my teaching experiences with other professors teaching this course. This edition is another major revision that features substantial changes throughout the book, including new chapters, reorganization of old chapters, and much new material to keep the book current. I believe that this Alternate Edition of *The Economics of Money, Banking, and Financial Markets* will be as exciting as previous editions, if not more so, for students new to the subject.

May 2006

HALLMARKS

Although this text has undergone a major revision, it retains the basic hallmarks that have made it the best-selling textbook on money and banking over the past seven editions:

- A unifying, analytic framework that uses a few basic economic principles to organize students' thinking about the structure of financial markets, the foreign exchange markets, financial institution management, and the role of monetary policy in the economy
- A careful, step-by-step development of models (an approach found in the best principles of economics textbooks), which makes it easier for students to learn
- The complete integration of an international perspective throughout the text
- A thoroughly up-to-date treatment of the latest developments in monetary theory
- Special features called "Following the Financial News" and "Reading the *Wall Street Journal*" to encourage reading of a financial newspaper
- An applications-oriented perspective with numerous applications and special-topic boxes that increase students' interest by showing them how to apply theory to real-world examples

WHAT'S NEW IN THIS EDITION

In addition to the expected updating of all data through the end of 2005 whenever possible, there is major new material in every part of the text.

A New Alternative

One of my primary goals when writing *The Economics of Money, Banking, and Financial Markets* has always been to create a text that is both comprehensive and flexible. With this edition, I have chosen to respond to the varied and sometimes conflicting needs of professors by providing two versions of the text.

While both versions contain the core chapters that all professors will want to cover, *The Economics of Money, Banking, and Financial Markets*, Alternate Edition, is designed for those professors who teach at an institution that requires intermediate macroeconomics as a prerequisite, who prefer to focus more on finance, or who simply do not cover *ISLM*. The Alternate Edition includes not only chapters on nonbank finance and financial derivatives, but also an entire chapter on conflicts of interest in the financial industry; this chapter covers this important topic in detail with many examples. The Alternate Edition omits the two *ISLM* chapters and the chapter on the implications of rational expectations for policy. For those professors whose courses have less of an emphasis on monetary theory, *The Economics of Money, Banking, and Financial Markets*, Alternate Edition, will more closely fit your needs.

For those professors who want a comprehensive discussion of monetary theory and monetary policy, *The Economics of Money, Banking, and Financial Markets*, Eighth Edition, contains all of the chapters on monetary theory. Professors who do want this coverage are often hard-pressed to cover all the finance and institutions chapters. To that end, the Eighth Edition omits the chapters on nonbank finance, financial derivatives, and conflicts of interest. The MyEconLab Web site for each edition provides the omitted chapters, thus making them readily available for students to read online and for professors to photocopy should they prefer to include them in their course.

PEDAGOGICAL AIDS

In teaching theory or its applications, a textbook must be a solid motivational tool. To this end, I have incorporated a wide variety of pedagogical features to make the material easy to learn:

1. **Previews** at the beginning of each chapter tell students where the chapter is heading, why specific topics are important, and how they relate to other topics in the book.
2. **Applications**, numbering more than 50, demonstrate how the analysis in the book can be used to explain many important real-world situations. A special set of applications, called "Reading the *Wall Street Journal*," shows students how to read daily columns in this leading financial newspaper.
3. **Following the Financial News boxes** introduce students to relevant news articles and data that are reported daily in the press, and explain how to read them.
4. **Inside the Fed boxes** give students a feel for what is important in the operation and structure of the Federal Reserve System.
5. **Global boxes** include interesting material with an international focus.

6. **E-Finance boxes** relate how changes in technology have affected financial markets or institutions.
7. **Conflicts of Interest boxes** outline conflicts of interest in different financial service industries.
8. **FYI boxes** highlight dramatic historical episodes, interesting ideas, and intriguing facts related to the subject matter.
9. **Study Guides** are highlighted statements scattered throughout the text that provide hints to the student on how to think about or approach a topic.
10. **Summary tables** provide a useful study aid in reviewing material.
11. **Key statements** are important points set in boldface italic type so that students can easily find them for later reference.
12. **Graphs** with captions, numbering more than 150, help students clearly understand the interrelationship of the variables plotted and the principles of analysis.
13. **Summary** at the end of each chapter lists the main points covered.
14. **Key terms** are important words or phrases, boldfaced when they are defined for the first time and listed by page number at the end of the chapter.
15. **End-of-chapter questions and problems**, numbering more than 400, help students learn the subject matter by applying economic concepts, including a special class of problems that students find particularly relevant, under the heading "Using Economic Analysis to Predict the Future."
16. **Web Exercises** encourage students to collect information from online sources or use online resources to enhance their learning experience.
17. **Web Sources** report the Web URL source of the data used to create the many tables and charts.
18. **Web References** point the student to Web sites that provide information or data that supplement the text material.
19. **Glossary** at the back of the book provides definitions of all the key terms.
20. **Answers section** at the back of the book provides solutions to half of the questions and problems (marked by *).

AN EASIER WAY TO TEACH: SUPPLEMENTS TO ACCOMPANY THIS EDITION

The Economics of Money, Banking, and Financial Markets, Alternate Edition, includes the most comprehensive program of supplements of any money, banking, and financial markets textbook. These items are available to qualified domestic adopters, but in some cases may not be available to international adopters.

For the Professor

1. **Instructor's Manual**, a print supplement prepared by me and offering conventional elements such as sample course outlines, chapter outlines, and answers to questions and problems in the text.
2. **PowerPoint® Slides**. New to this edition is a far more comprehensive set of PowerPoint slides—greatly expanded from the previous edition and now numbering over 550—that provides not only all the tables and graphs in the text, but very detailed

lecture notes for all the material in the course. The basis of the lecture notes is, in fact, the notes I use in class—and they should help other instructors prepare their lectures as they have helped me. In this edition, Lori Bell of Blackburn College has enhanced the presentation by adding additional lecture notes. Some instructors might use these PowerPoint slides as their own class notes and prefer to teach with a blackboard. But for those who prefer to teach with visual aids, the PowerPoint slides, which are fully customizable, afford the flexibility to take this approach.

3. **Transparency Masters**, a print supplement, containing the same lecture notes as the PowerPoint presentation, along with all figures and tables from the text.
4. **Overhead Transparencies**, full-color acetates, numbering more than 150, for all of the figures and tables.
5. **Printed Test Bank** updated and revised by Richard Stahl of Louisiana State University and Kathy Kelly of the University of Texas at Arlington, comprising more than 2,500 multiple-choice and essay test items, many with graphs.
6. **Computerized Test Bank**, allowing the instructor to produce exams efficiently. This product consists of the multiple-choice and essay questions in the printed Test Bank and offers editing capabilities. It is available in Macintosh and Windows versions.
7. **Instructor's Resource CD-ROM**. This edition of the book comes with a powerful teaching tool: an Instructor's Resource CD-ROM. Fully compatible with Windows and Macintosh computers, the CD-ROM contains Word files for the entire contents of the *Instructor's Manual*, PowerPoint presentations, Computerized Test Bank files, and Word files of the Test Bank. Using this supplement, instructors can prepare student handouts such as solutions to problem sets made from end-of-chapter problems or the outline of the lecture of the day. I have used handouts of this type in my classes and have found them to be very effective. The Computerized Test Bank software (TestGen for Windows and Macintosh) is a valuable test preparation tool that allows professors to view, edit, and add questions. Instructors have our permission—and are encouraged—to reproduce all of the materials on the CD-ROM and use them as they see fit in class.
8. **Mishkin Web site**, located at www.myeconlab.com/mishkin, which features chapter synopses, student practice quizzes, appendices on a wide variety of topics (see "Appendices on the Web"), omitted chapters, links to the URLs that appear at the end of the chapters, and various resources for the instructors.

For the Student

1. **Study Guide**, fully revised and updated by David Hakes of University of Northern Iowa and Ed Gamber of Lafayette College, includes chapter synopses and completions, exercises, self-tests, and answers to the exercises and self-tests.
2. **Readings on Money, Banking, and Financial Markets**, edited by James W. Eaton of Bridgewater College and me, updated annually, with over half the articles new each year to enable instructors to keep the content of their course current throughout the life of an edition of the text. The readings are available within MyEconLab (see pages ii–iv).

FREDERIC S. MISHKIN

PART

1

Introduction

CHAPTER

1 Why Study Money, Banking, and Financial Markets?

Preview

On the evening news you have just heard that the Federal Reserve is raising the federal funds rate by $\frac{1}{2}$ of a percentage point. What effect might this have on the interest rate of an automobile loan when you finance your purchase of a sleek new sports car? Does it mean that a house will be more or less affordable in the future? Will it make it easier or harder for you to get a job next year?

This book provides answers to these and other questions by examining how financial markets (such as those for bonds, stocks, and foreign exchange) and financial institutions (banks, insurance companies, mutual funds, and other institutions) work and by exploring the role of money in the economy. Financial markets and institutions not only affect your everyday life but also involve flows of trillions of dollars of funds throughout our economy, which in turn affect business profits, the production of goods and services, and even the economic well-being of countries other than the United States. What happens to financial markets, financial institutions, and money is of great concern to politicians and can even have a major impact on elections. The study of money, banking, and financial markets will reward you with an understanding of many exciting issues. In this chapter we provide a road map of the book by outlining these issues and exploring why they are worth studying.

WHY STUDY FINANCIAL MARKETS?

Part II of this book focuses on **financial markets**, markets in which funds are transferred from people who have an excess of available funds to people who have a shortage. Financial markets such as bond and stock markets are crucial to promoting greater economic efficiency by channeling funds from people who do not have a productive use for them to those who do. Indeed, well-functioning financial markets are a key factor in producing high economic growth, and poorly performing financial markets are one reason that many countries in the world remain desperately poor. Activities in financial markets also have direct effects on personal wealth, the behavior of businesses and consumers, and the cyclical performance of the economy.

The Bond Market and Interest Rates

A **security** (also called a *financial instrument*) is a claim on the issuer's future income or **assets** (any financial claim or piece of property that is subject to ownership). A **bond** is a debt security that promises to make payments periodically for a specified period of time.[1] The bond market is especially important to economic activity because it enables corporations and governments to borrow to finance their activities and because it is where interest rates are determined. An **interest rate** is the cost of borrowing or the price paid for the rental of funds (usually expressed as a percentage of the rental of $100 per year). There are many interest rates in the economy—mortgage interest rates, car loan rates, and interest rates on many different types of bonds.

Interest rates are important on a number of levels. On a personal level, high interest rates could deter you from buying a house or a car because the cost of financing it would be high. Conversely, high interest rates could encourage you to save because you can earn more interest income by putting aside some of your earnings as savings. On a more general level, interest rates have an impact on the overall health of the economy because they affect not only consumers' willingness to spend or save but also businesses' investment decisions. High interest rates, for example, might cause a corporation to postpone building a new plant that would provide more jobs.

Because changes in interest rates have important effects on individuals, financial institutions, businesses, and the overall economy, it is important to explain fluctuations in interest rates that have been substantial over the past twenty years. For example, the interest rate on three-month Treasury bills peaked at over 16% in 1981. This interest rate fell to 3% in late 1992 and 1993, rose to above 5% in the mid- to late 1990s, and fell to below 1% in 2004, only to begin rising again.

Because different interest rates have a tendency to move in unison, economists frequently lump interest rates together and refer to "the" interest rate. As Figure 1 shows, however, interest rates on several types of bonds can differ substantially. The interest rate on three-month Treasury bills, for example, fluctuates more than the other interest rates and is lower, on average. The interest rate on Baa (medium-quality) corporate

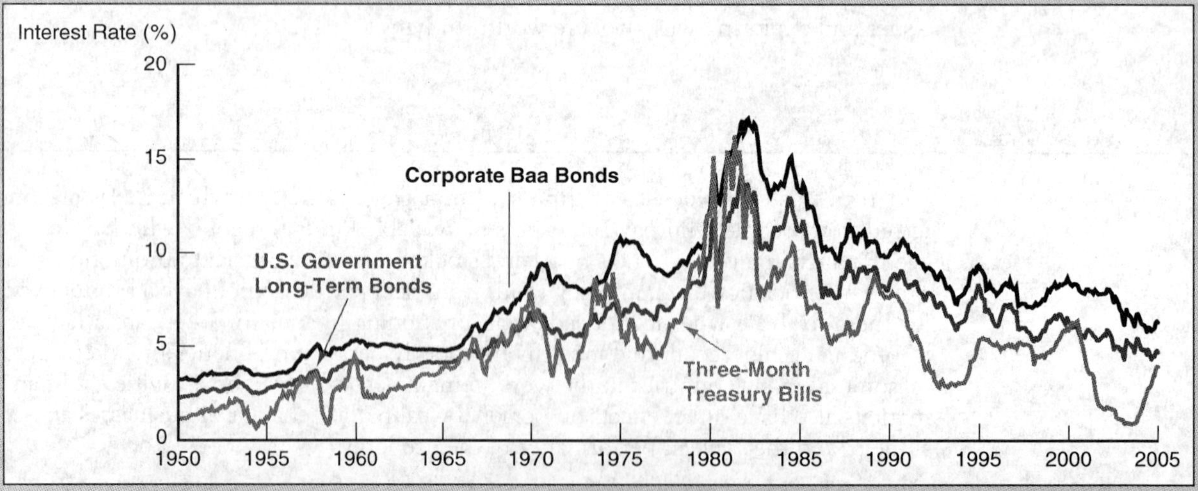

FIGURE 1 **Interest Rates on Selected Bonds, 1950–2005**

Sources: Federal Reserve *Bulletin*; www.federalreserve.gov/releases/H15/data.htm.

[1]The definition of *bond* used throughout this book is the broad one in common use by academics, which covers both short- and long-term debt instruments. However, some practitioners in financial markets use the word *bond* to describe only specific long-term debt instruments such as corporate bonds or U.S. Treasury bonds.

bonds is higher, on average, than the other interest rates, and the spread between it and the other rates became larger in the 1970s, narrowed in the 1990s, and rose briefly in the early 2000s, before narrowing again.

In Chapter 2 we study the role of bond markets in the economy, and in Chapters 4 through 6 we examine what an interest rate is, how the common movements in interest rates come about, and why the interest rates on different bonds vary.

The Stock Market

A **common stock** (typically just called a **stock**) represents a share of ownership in a corporation. It is a security that is a claim on the earnings and assets of the corporation. Issuing stock and selling it to the public is a way for corporations to raise funds to finance their activities. The stock market, in which claims on the earnings of corporations (shares of stock) are traded, is the most widely followed financial market in almost every country that has one; that's why it is often called simply "the market." A big swing in the prices of shares in the stock market is always a major story on the evening news. People often speculate on where the market is heading and get very excited when they can brag about their latest "big killing," but they become depressed when they suffer a big loss. The attention the market receives can probably be best explained by one simple fact: It is a place where people can get rich—or poor—quickly.

As Figure 2 indicates, stock prices are extremely volatile. After the market rose in the 1980s, on "Black Monday," October 19, 1987, it experienced the worst one-day drop in its entire history, with the Dow Jones Industrial Average (DJIA) falling by 22%. From then until 2000, the stock market experienced one of the great bull markets in its history, with the Dow climbing to a peak of over 11,000. With the collapse of the high-tech bubble in 2000, the stock market fell sharply, dropping by over 30% by late 2002. It then recovered again to over the 10,000 level in 2004–2005. These considerable fluctuations in stock prices affect the size of people's wealth and as a result may affect their willingness to spend.

The stock market is also an important factor in business investment decisions, because the price of shares affects the amount of funds that can be raised by selling newly issued stock to finance investment spending. A higher price for a firm's shares means that it can raise a larger amount of funds, which can be used to buy production facilities and equipment.

In Chapter 2 we examine the role that the stock market plays in the financial system, and we return to the issue of how stock prices behave and respond to information in the marketplace in Chapter 7.

The Foreign Exchange Market

For funds to be transferred from one country to another, they have to be converted from the currency in the country of origin (say, dollars) into the currency of the country they are going to (say, euros). The **foreign exchange market** is where this conversion takes place, so it is instrumental in moving funds between countries. It is also important because it is where the **foreign exchange rate**, the price of one country's currency in terms of another's, is determined.

Figure 3 shows the exchange rate for the U.S. dollar from 1970 to 2005 (measured as the value of the U.S. dollar in terms of a basket of major foreign currencies). The fluctuations in prices in this market have also been substantial: The dollar's value weakened considerably from 1971 to 1973, rose slightly until 1976, and then reached a low point in the 1978–1980 period. From 1980 to early 1985, the dollar's value appreciated

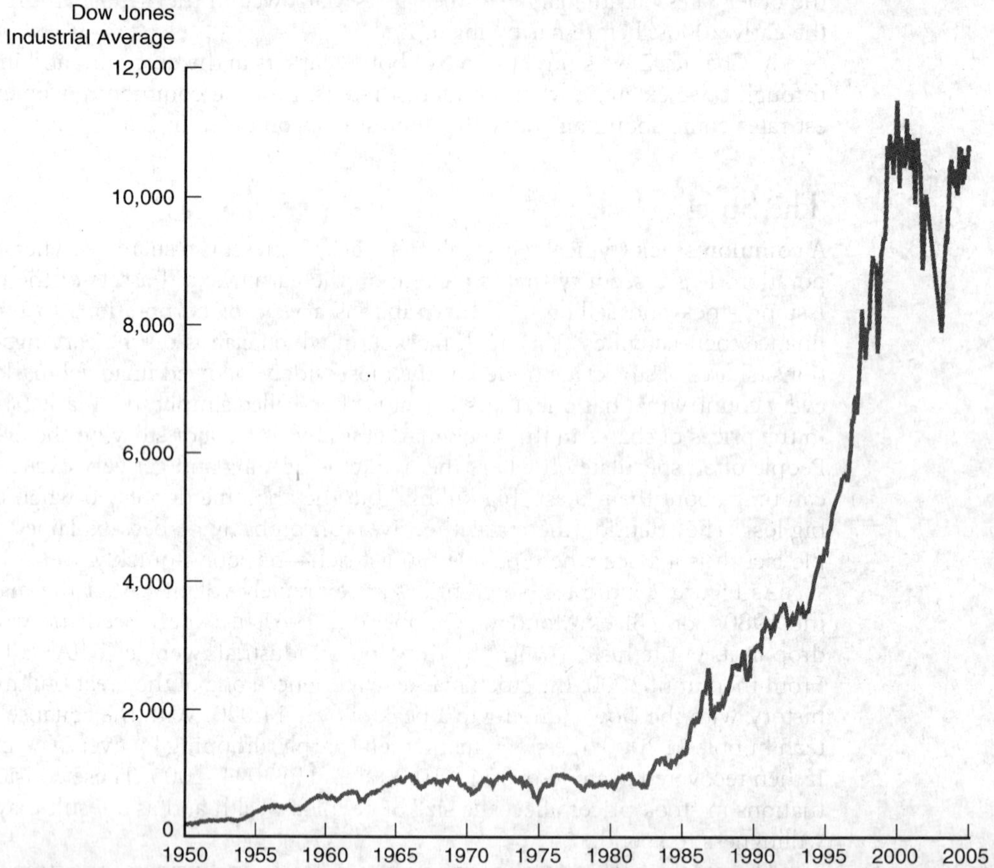

FIGURE 2 **Stock Prices as Measured by the Dow Jones Industrial Average, 1950–2005**

Source: Dow Jones Indexes: http://finance.yahoo.com/?u.

dramatically, and then declined again reaching another low in 1995. The dollar appreciated from 1995 to 2000, only to depreciate thereafter.

What have these fluctuations in the exchange rate meant to the American public and businesses? A change in the exchange rate has a direct effect on American consumers because it affects the cost of imports. In 2001 when the euro was worth around 85 cents, 100 euros of European goods (say, French wine) cost $85. When the dollar subsequently weakened, raising the cost of a euro near $1.20, the same 100 euros of wine now cost $120. Thus a weaker dollar leads to more expensive foreign goods, makes vacationing abroad more expensive, and raises the cost of indulging your desire for imported delicacies. When the value of the dollar drops, Americans decrease their purchases of foreign goods and increase their consumption of domestic goods (such as travel in the United States or American-made wine).

Conversely, a strong dollar means that U.S. goods exported abroad will cost more in foreign countries, and hence foreigners will buy fewer of them. Exports of steel, for example, declined sharply when the dollar strengthened in the 1980–1985 and 1995–2001 periods. A strong dollar benefited American consumers by making foreign

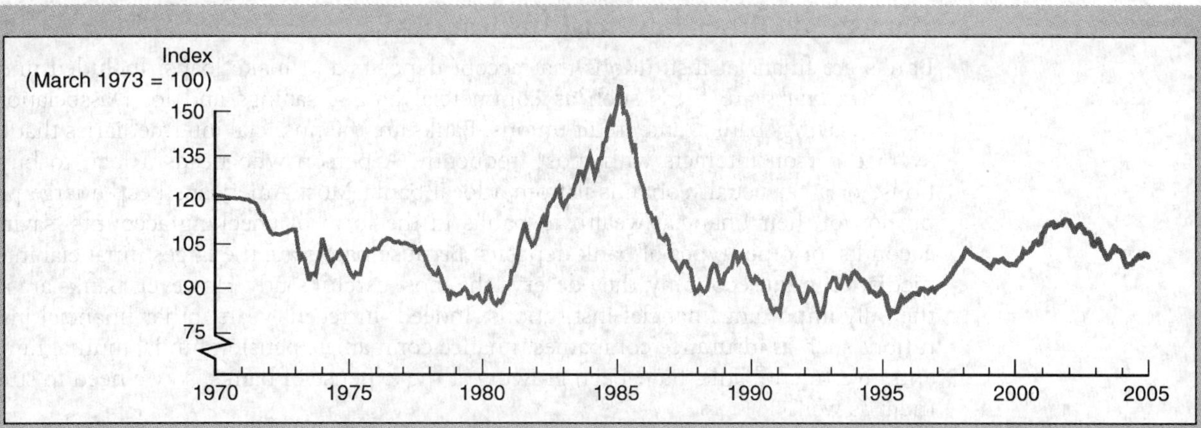

FIGURE 3 **Exchange Rate of the U.S. Dollar, 1970–2005**

Source: Federal Reserve: www.federalreserve.gov/releases/H10/summary/indexbc_m.txt/.

goods cheaper but hurt American businesses and eliminated some jobs by cutting both domestic and foreign sales of their products. The decline in the value of the dollar from 1985 to 1995 and 2001 to 2005 had the opposite effect: It made foreign goods more expensive, but made American businesses more competitive. Fluctuations in the foreign exchange markets have major consequences for the American economy.

In Chapter 20 we study how exchange rates are determined in the foreign exchange market in which dollars are bought and sold for foreign currencies.

WHY STUDY BANKING AND FINANCIAL INSTITUTIONS?

Part III of this book focuses on financial institutions and the business of banking. Banks and other financial institutions are what make financial markets work. Without them, financial markets would not be able to move funds from people who save to people who have productive investment opportunities. Thus they play a crucial role in the economy.

Structure of the Financial System

The financial system is complex, comprising many different types of private sector financial institutions, including banks, insurance companies, mutual funds, finance companies, and investment banks, all of which are heavily regulated by the government. If an individual wanted to make a loan to IBM or General Motors, for example, he or she would not go directly to the president of the company and offer a loan. Instead, he or she would lend to such companies indirectly through **financial intermediaries**, institutions that borrow funds from people who have saved and in turn make loans to others.

Why are financial intermediaries so crucial to well-functioning financial markets? Why do they extend credit to one party but not to another? Why do they usually write complicated legal documents when they extend loans? Why are they the most heavily regulated businesses in the economy?

We answer these questions in Chapter 8 by developing a coherent framework for analyzing financial structure in the United States and in the rest of the world.

Banks and Other Financial Institutions

Banks are financial institutions that accept deposits and make loans. Included under the term *banks* are firms such as commercial banks, savings and loan associations, mutual savings banks, and credit unions. Banks are the financial intermediaries that the average person interacts with most frequently. A person who needs a loan to buy a house or a car usually obtains it from a local bank. Most Americans keep a large proportion of their financial wealth in banks in the form of checking accounts, savings accounts, or other types of bank deposits. Because banks are the largest financial intermediaries in our economy, they deserve the most careful study. However, banks are not the only important financial institutions. Indeed, in recent years, other financial institutions such as insurance companies, finance companies, pension funds, mutual funds, and investment banks have been growing at the expense of banks, so we need to study them as well.

In Chapter 9, we examine how banks and other financial institutions manage their assets and liabilities to make profits. In Chapter 10, we look at the banking industry; we examine how the competitive environment has changed in this industry and learn why some financial institutions have been growing at the expense of others. In Chapters 11 and 12, we extend the economic analysis in Chapter 8 to understand why bank regulation takes the form it does and what can go wrong in the regulatory process.

Financial Innovation

In the good old days, when you took cash out of the bank or wanted to check your account balance, you got to say hello to a friendly human teller. Nowadays you are more likely to interact with an automatic teller machine (ATM) when withdrawing cash, and you can get your account balance from your home computer. To see why these options have developed, in Chapter 10 we study why and how financial innovation takes place, with particular emphasis on how the dramatic improvements in information technology have led to new means of delivering financial services electronically, in what has become known as **e-finance**. We also study financial innovation, because it shows us how creative thinking on the part of financial institutions can lead to higher profits. By seeing how and why financial institutions have been creative in the past, we obtain a better grasp of how they may be creative in the future. This knowledge provides us with useful clues about how the financial system may change over time and will help keep our knowledge about banks and other financial institutions from becoming obsolete.

WHY STUDY MONEY AND MONETARY POLICY?

Money, also referred to as the **money supply**, is defined as anything that is generally accepted in payment for goods or services or in the repayment of debts. Money is linked to changes in economic variables that affect all of us and are important to the health of the economy. The final two parts of the book examine the role of money in the economy.

Money and Business Cycles

In 1981–1982, total production of goods and services (called **aggregate output**) in the U.S. economy fell and the **unemployment rate** (the percentage of the available labor force unemployed) rose to over 10%. After 1982, the economy began to expand rapidly, and by 1989 the unemployment rate had declined to 5%. In 1990, the eight-year expansion came to an end, with the unemployment rate rising above 7%. The economy bottomed out in 1991, and the subsequent recovery was the longest in U.S. history, with the unemployment rate falling to around 4%. A mild economic downturn began in March 2001, with unemployment rising to 6%; the economy began to recover in November 2001 with unemployment eventually declining to below 5%.

Why did the economy expand from 1982 to 1990, contract in 1990 to 1991, boom again from 1991 to 2001, contract again in 2001 and recover thereafter? Evidence suggests that money plays an important role in generating **business cycles**, the upward and downward movement of aggregate output produced in the economy. Business cycles affect all of us in immediate and important ways. When output is rising, for example, it is easier to find a good job; when output is falling, finding a good job might be difficult. Figure 4 shows the movements of the rate of money growth over the 1950–2005 period, with the shaded areas representing **recessions**, periods of declining aggregate output. What we see is that the rate of money growth has declined before every recession, indicating that changes in money might be a driving force behind business cycle fluctuations. However, not every decline in the rate of money growth is followed by a recession.

We explore how money might affect aggregate output in Chapters 22 through 25, where we study **monetary theory**, the theory that relates changes in the quantity of money to changes in aggregate economic activity and the price level.

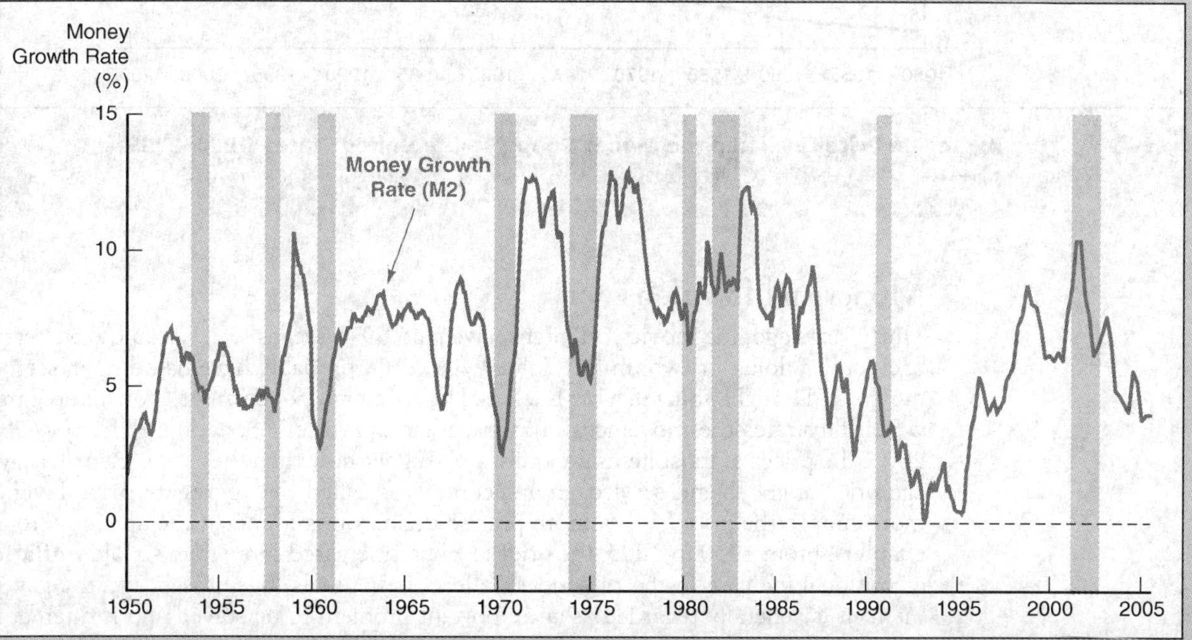

FIGURE 4 **Money Growth (M2 Annual Rate) and the Business Cycle in the United States, 1950–2005**

Note: Shaded areas represent recessions.

Source: Federal Reserve *Bulletin*, p. A4, Table 1.10; www.federalreserve.gov/releases/h6/hist/h6hist1.txt.

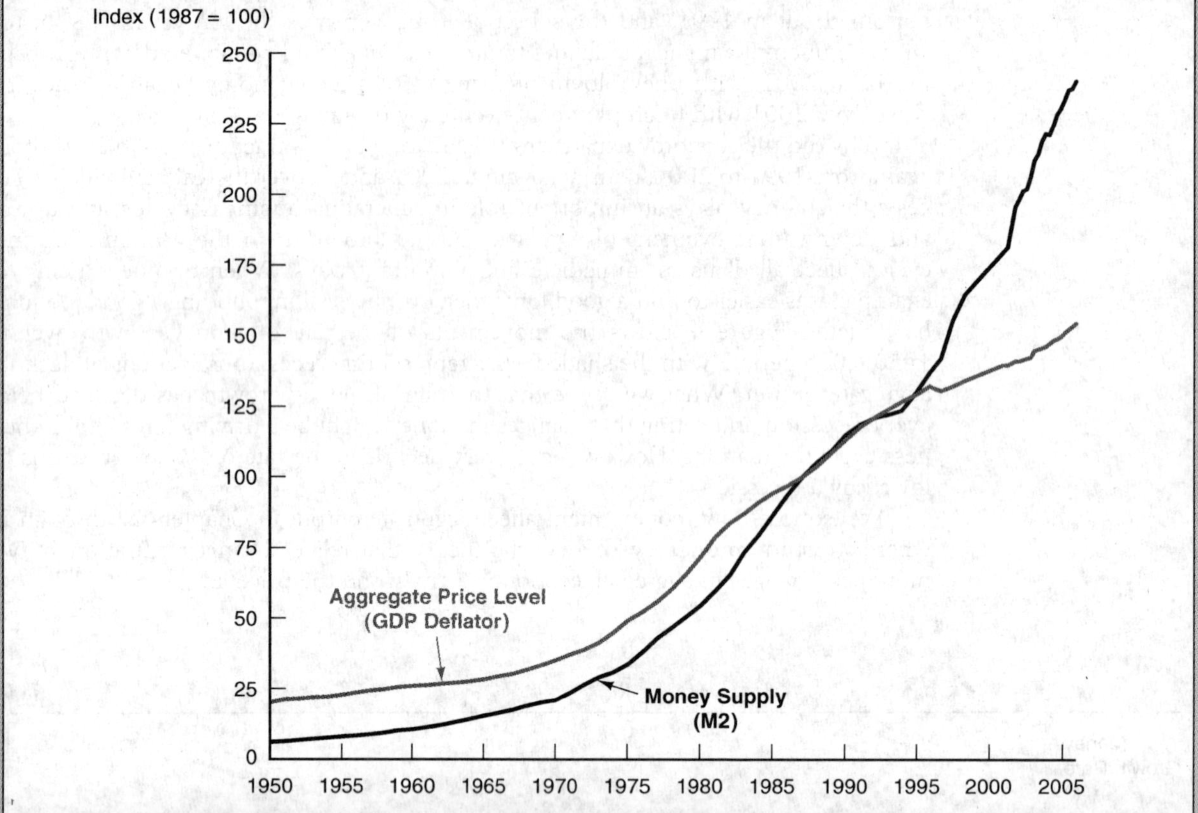

FIGURE 5 Aggregate Price Level and the Money Supply in the United States, 1950–2005
Sources: www.stls.frb.org/fred/data/gdp/gdpdef; www.federalreserve.gov/releases/h6/hist/h6hist10.txt.

Money and Inflation

Thirty years ago, the movie you might have paid $9 to see last week would have set you back only a dollar or two. In fact, for $9 you could probably have had dinner, seen the movie, and bought yourself a big bucket of hot buttered popcorn. As shown in Figure 5, which illustrates the movement of average prices in the U.S. economy from 1950 to 2005, the prices of most items are quite a bit higher now than they were then. The average price of goods and services in an economy is called the **aggregate price level**, or, more simply, the *price level* (a more precise definition is found in the appendix to this chapter). From 1950 to 2005, the price level has increased more than sixfold. **Inflation**, a continual increase in the price level, affects individuals, businesses, and the government. It is generally regarded as an important problem to be solved and is often at the top of the political and policymaking agendas. To solve the inflation problem, we need to know something about its causes.

What explains inflation? One clue to answering this question is found in Figure 5, which plots the money supply and the price level. As we can see, the price level and the money supply generally rise together. These data seem to indicate that a continuing

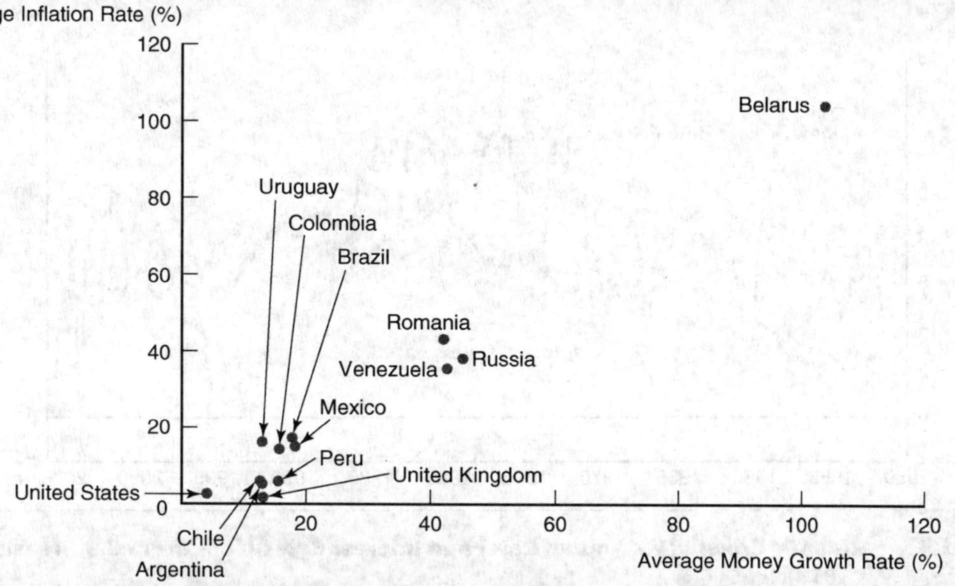

FIGURE 6 **Average Inflation Rate Versus Average Rate of Money Growth for Selected Countries, 1995–2004**

Source: International Financial Statistics.

increase in the money supply might be an important factor in causing the continuing increase in the price level that we call inflation.

Further evidence that inflation may be tied to continuing increases in the money supply is found in Figure 6. For a number of countries, it plots the average **inflation rate** (the rate of change of the price level, usually measured as a percentage change per year) over the ten-year period 1995–2004 against the average rate of money growth over the same period. As you can see, there is a positive association between inflation and the growth rate of the money supply: The countries with the highest inflation rates are also the ones with the highest money growth rates. Belarus, Brazil, Romania, and Russia, for example, experienced high inflation during this period, and their rates of money growth were high. By contrast, the United Kingdom and the United States had low inflation rates over the same period, and their rates of money growth have been low. Such evidence led Milton Friedman, a Nobel laureate in economics, to make the famous statement, "Inflation is always and everywhere a monetary phenomenon."[2] We look at money's role in creating inflation in Chapter 24.

Money and Interest Rates

In addition to other factors, money plays an important role in interest-rate fluctuations, which are of great concern to businesses and consumers. Figure 7 shows the changes in the interest rate on long-term Treasury bonds and the rate of money growth. As the

[2]Milton Friedman, *Dollars and Deficits* (Upper Saddle River, N.J.: Prentice Hall, 1968), p. 39.

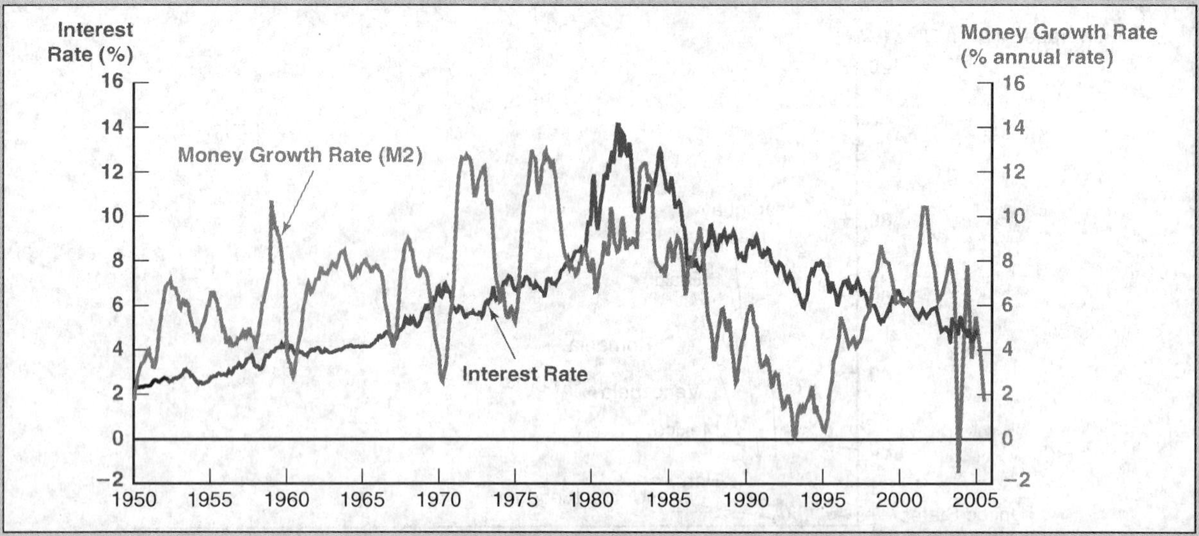

FIGURE 7 **Money Growth (M2 Annual Rate) and Interest Rates (Long-Term U.S. Treasury Bonds), 1950–2005**

Sources: Federal Reserve *Bulletin*, p. A4, Table 1.10; www.federalreserve.gov/releases/h6/hist/h6hist1.txt.

money growth rate rose in the 1960s and 1970s, the long-term bond rate rose with it. However, the relationship between money growth and interest rates has been less clear-cut since 1980. We analyze the relationship between money and interest rates when we examine the behavior of interest rates in Chapter 5.

Conduct of Monetary Policy

Because money can affect many economic variables that are important to the well-being of our economy, politicians and policymakers throughout the world care about the conduct of **monetary policy**, the management of money and interest rates. The organization responsible for the conduct of a nation's monetary policy is the **central bank**. The United States' central bank is the **Federal Reserve System** (also called simply **the Fed**). In Chapters 15–19, we study how central banks like the Federal Reserve System can affect the quantity of money and interest rates in the economy and then look at how monetary policy is actually conducted in the United States and elsewhere.

Fiscal Policy and Monetary Policy

Fiscal policy involves decisions about government spending and taxation. A **budget deficit** is the excess of government expenditures over tax revenues for a particular time period, typically a year, while a **budget surplus** arises when tax revenues exceed government expenditures. The government must finance any deficit by borrowing, while a budget surplus leads to a lower government debt burden. As Figure 8 shows, the budget deficit, relative to the size of the U.S. economy, peaked in 1983 at 6% of national output (as calculated by the **gross domestic product**, or *GDP*, a measure of aggregate output described in the appendix to this chapter). Since then, the budget deficit at first

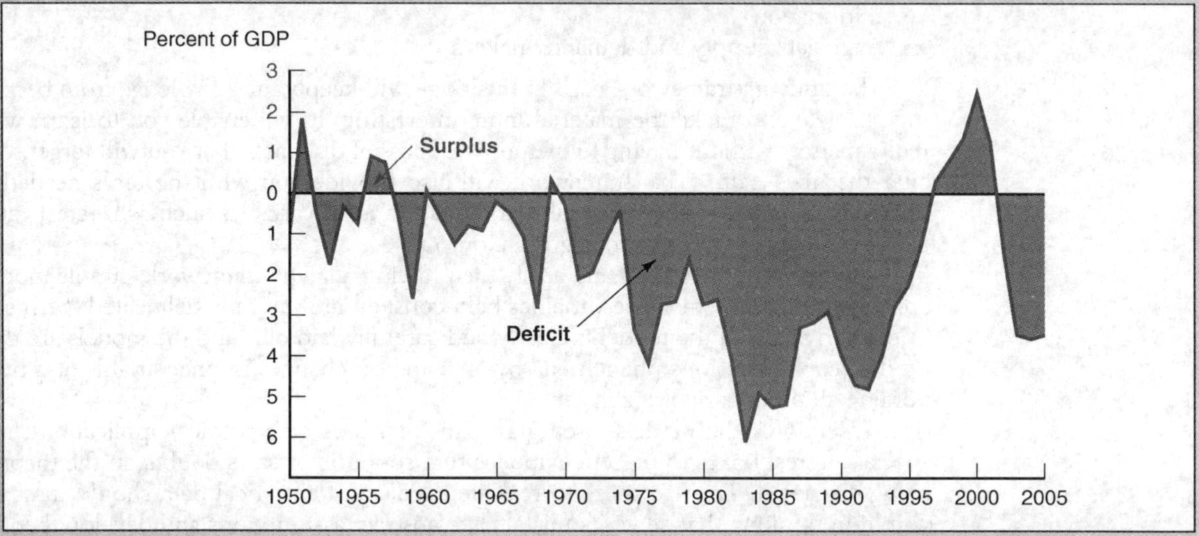

FIGURE 8 **Government Budget Surplus or Deficit as a Percentage of Gross Domestic Product, 1950–2005**

Source: www.gpoaccess.gov/usbudget/fy06/sheets/hist01z2.xls.

declined to less than 3% of GDP, rose again to over 5% by 1989, and fell subsequently, leading to budget surpluses from 1999 to 2001. In the aftermath of the terrorist attacks of September 11, 2001, and the war in Iraq that began in March 2003, the budget has swung back again into deficit. What to do about budget deficits and surpluses has been the subject of legislation and bitter battles between the president and Congress in recent years.

You may have heard statements in newspapers or on TV that budget surpluses are a good thing while deficits are undesirable. We explore the accuracy of such claims in Chapters 8 and 21 by seeing how budget deficits might lead to a financial crisis as they did in Argentina in 2001. In Chapter 25, we examine why deficits might result in a higher rate of money growth, a higher rate of inflation, and higher interest rates.

HOW WE WILL STUDY MONEY, BANKING, AND FINANCIAL MARKETS

This textbook stresses the economic way of thinking by developing a unifying framework to study money, banking, and financial markets. This analytic framework uses a few basic economic concepts to organize your thinking about the determination of asset prices, the structure of financial markets, bank management, and the role of money in the economy. It encompasses the following basic concepts:

- A simplified approach to the demand for assets
- The concept of equilibrium
- Basic supply and demand to explain behavior in financial markets
- The search for profits

- An approach to financial structure based on transaction costs and asymmetric information
- Aggregate supply and demand analysis

The unifying framework used in this book will keep your knowledge from becoming obsolete and make the material more interesting. It will enable you to learn what *really* matters without having to memorize a mass of dull facts that you will forget soon after the final exam. This framework will also provide you with the tools needed to understand trends in the financial marketplace and in variables such as interest rates, exchange rates, inflation, and aggregate output.

To help you understand and apply the unifying analytic framework, simple models are constructed in which the variables held constant are carefully delineated, each step in the derivation of the model is clearly and carefully laid out, and the models are then used to explain various phenomena by focusing on changes in one variable at a time, holding all other variables constant.

To reinforce the models' usefulness, this text uses case studies, applications, and special-interest boxes to present evidence that supports or casts doubts on the theories being discussed. This exposure to real-life events and empirical data should dissuade you from thinking that all economists make abstract assumptions and develop theories that have little to do with actual behavior.

To function better in the real world outside the classroom, you must have the tools to follow the financial news that appears in leading financial publications such as the *Wall Street Journal*. To help and encourage you to read the financial section of the newspaper, this book contains two special features. The first is a set of special boxed inserts titled Following the Financial News that contain actual columns and data from the *Wall Street Journal* that typically appear daily or periodically. These boxes give you the detailed information and definitions you need to evaluate the data being presented. The second feature is a set of special applications titled "Reading the *Wall Street Journal*" that expand on the Following the Financial News boxes. These applications show you how the analytic framework in the book can be used directly to make sense of the daily columns in the United States' leading financial newspaper. In addition to these applications, this book also contains nearly 400 end-of-chapter problems that ask you to apply the analytic concepts you have learned to other real-world issues. Particularly relevant is a special class of problems headed "Predicting the Future." So that you can work on many of these problems on your own, answers to half of them are found at the end of the book. These give you an opportunity to review and apply many of the important financial concepts and tools presented throughout the book.

Exploring the Web

The World Wide Web has become an extremely valuable and convenient resource for financial research. We emphasize the importance of this tool in several ways. First, wherever we utilize the Web to find information to build the charts and tables that appear throughout the text, we include the source site's URL. These sites often contain additional information and are updated frequently. Second, we have added Web exercises to the end of each chapter. These exercises prompt you to visit sites related to the chapter and to work with real-time data and information. We have also added Web references to the end of each chapter that list the URLs of sites related to the material being discussed. Visit these sites to further explore a topic you find of particular interest. Web site URLs are subject to frequent change. We have tried to select stable sites, but we realize that even government URLs change. The publisher's web site (www.myeconlab.com/mishkin) will maintain an updated list of current URLs for your reference.

Collecting and Graphing Data

The following Web exercise is especially important because it demonstrates how to export data from a web site into Microsoft® Excel for further analysis. We suggest you work through this problem on your own so that you will be able to perform this activity when prompted in subsequent Web exercises.

WEB EXERCISES

You have been hired by Risky Ventures, Inc., as a consultant to help the company analyze interest-rate trends. Your employers are initially interested in determining the historical relationship between long- and short-term interest rates. The biggest task you must immediately undertake is collecting market interest-rate data. You know the best source of this information is the Web.

1. You decide that your best indicator of long-term interest rates is the ten-year U.S. Treasury note. Your first task is to gather historical data.
   Go to www.federalreserve.gov/releases/H15. The site should look like Figure 9.
   a. At the top click on Historical Data. Now scroll down to "Treasury Constant Maturities" and click on the annual tag to the right of the 10 Year category.
   b. While you have located an accurate source of historical interest rate data, getting it onto a spreadsheet will be very tedious. You recall that Excel will let you convert text data into columns. Begin by highlighting the two columns of data (the year and rate).

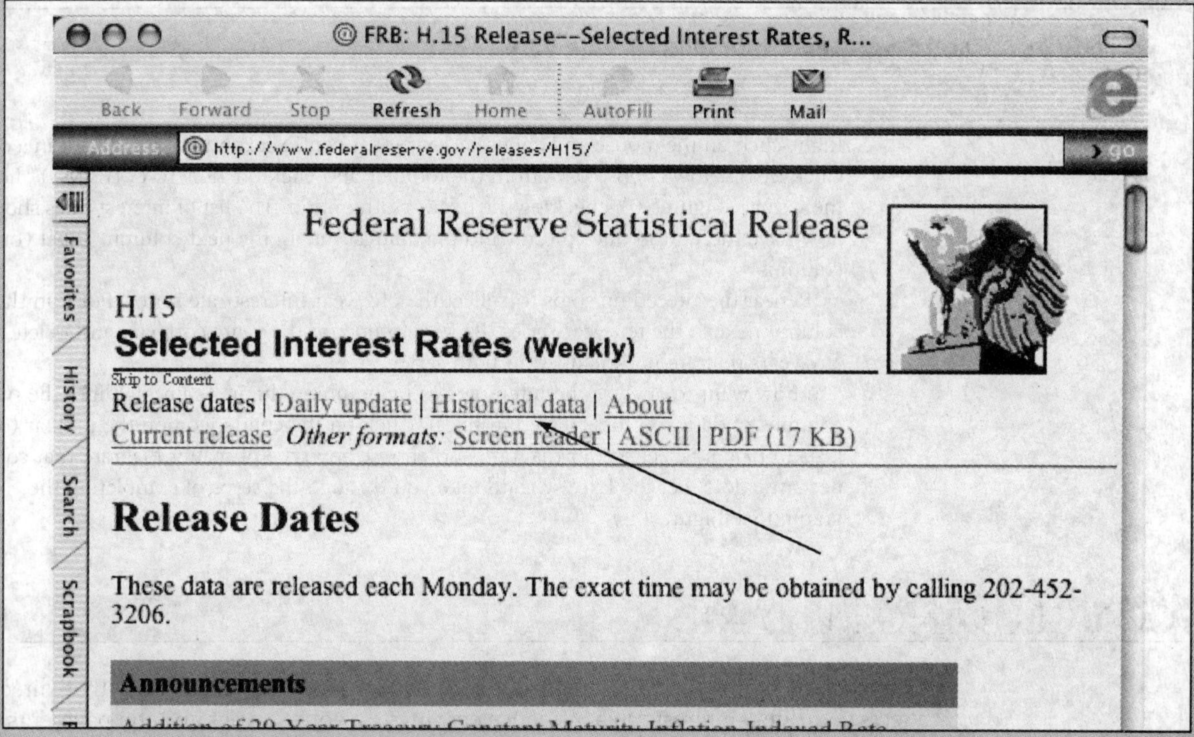

FIGURE 9 **Federal Reserve Board Web Site**

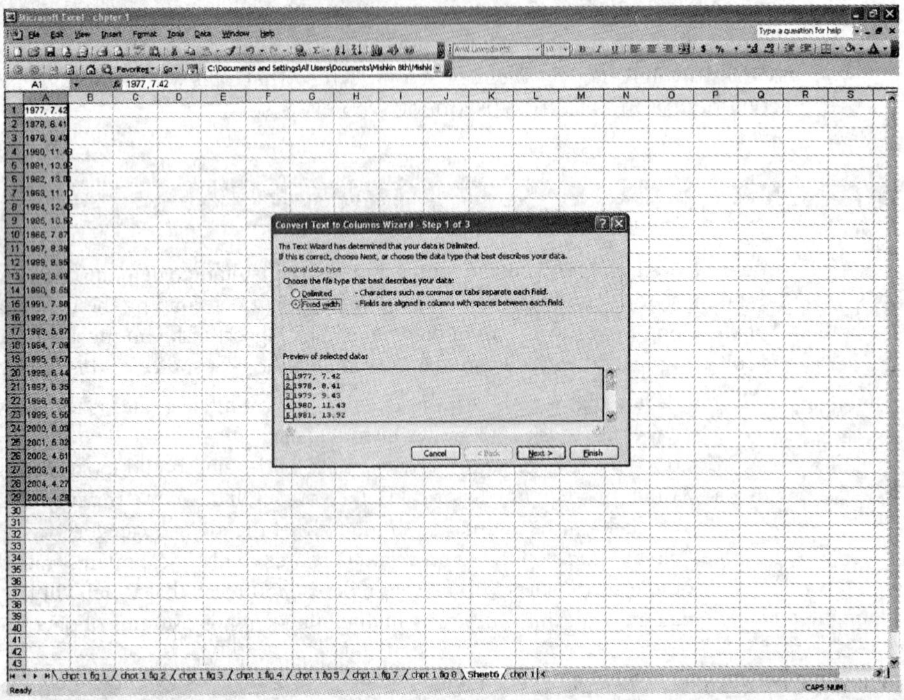

FIGURE 10 **Excel Spreadsheet with Interest-Rate Data**

Right-click on the mouse and choose COPY. Now open Excel and put the cursor in a cell. Click PASTE. Now choose DATA from the tool bar and click on TEXT TO COLUMNS. Follow the wizard (Figure 10), checking the fixed-width option. The list of interest rates should now have the year in one column and the interest rate in the next column. Label your columns.

Repeat the preceding steps to collect the one-year interest rate series. Put it in the column next to the ten-year series. Be sure to line up the years correctly and delete any years that are not included in both series.

c. You now want to analyze the interest rates by graphing them. Again highlight the two columns of data you just created in Excel. Click on the charts icon on the toolbar (or INSERT/CHART). Select scatter diagram and choose any type of scatter diagram that connects the dots. Let the Excel wizard take you through the steps of completing the graph. (See Figure 11.)

CONCLUDING REMARKS

The topic of money, banking, and financial markets is an exciting field that directly affects your life—interest rates influence earnings on your savings and the payments on loans you may seek on a car or a house, and monetary policy may affect your job prospects and the prices of goods in the future. Your study of money, banking, and

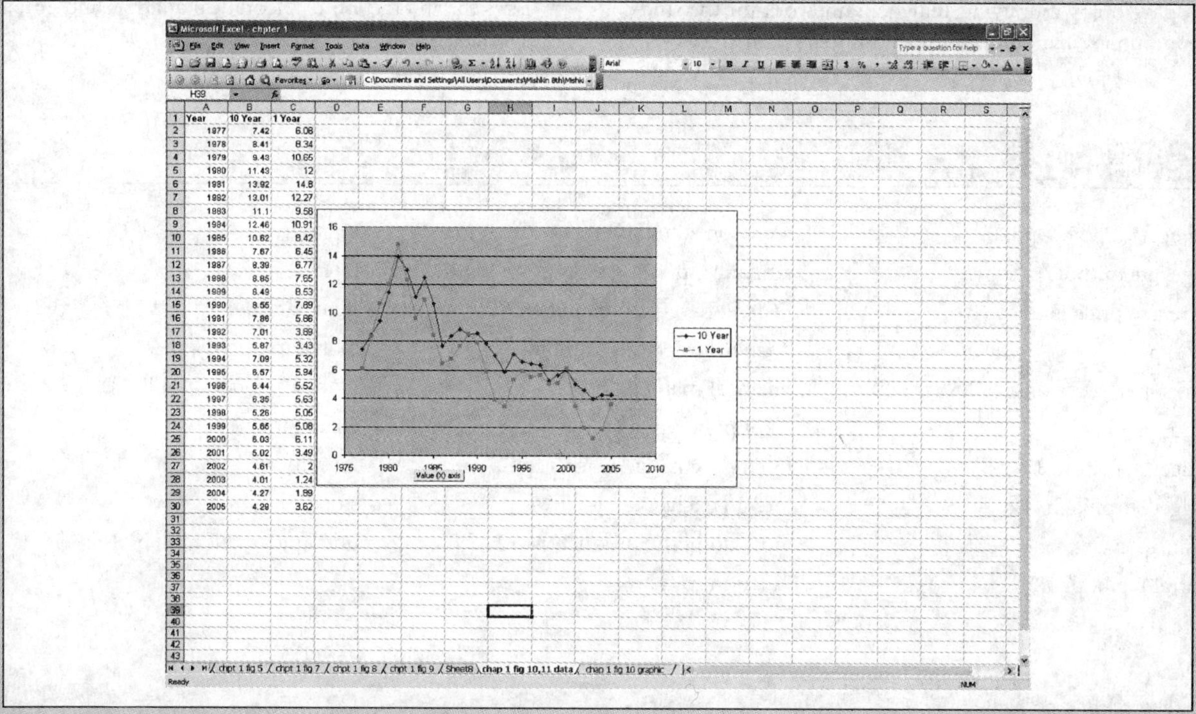

FIGURE 11 **Excel Graph of Interest-Rate Data**

financial markets will introduce you to many of the controversies about the conduct of economic policy that are hotly debated in the political arena and will help you gain a clearer understanding of economic phenomena you hear about in the news media. The knowledge you gain will stay with you and benefit you long after the course is done.

SUMMARY

1. Activities in financial markets have direct effects on individuals' wealth, the behavior of businesses, and the efficiency of our economy. Three financial markets deserve particular attention: the bond market (where interest rates are determined), the stock market (which has a major effect on people's wealth and on firms' investment decisions), and the foreign exchange market (because fluctuations in the foreign exchange rate have major consequences for the U.S. economy).
2. Banks and other financial institutions channel funds from people who might not put them to productive use to people who can do so and thus play a crucial role in improving the efficiency of the economy.
3. Money appears to be a major influence on inflation, business cycles, and interest rates. Because these economic variables are so important to the health of the economy, we need to understand how monetary policy is and should be conducted. We also need to study government fiscal policy because it can be an influential factor in the conduct of monetary policy.

4. This textbook stresses the economic way of thinking by developing a unifying analytic framework for the study of money, banking, and financial markets using a few basic economic principles. This textbook also emphasizes the interaction of theoretical analysis and empirical data.

KEY TERMS

aggregate income, p. 20
aggregate output, p. 8
aggregate price level, p. 10
asset, p. 3
banks, p. 8
bond, p. 3
budget deficit, p. 12
budget surplus, p. 12
business cycles, p. 9
central bank, p. 12
common stock, p. 5
e-finance, p. 8
Federal Reserve System (the Fed), p. 12
financial intermediaries, p. 7
financial markets, p. 3
fiscal policy, p. 12
foreign exchange market, p. 5
foreign exchange rate, p. 5
gross domestic product, p. 12, 20
inflation, p. 10
inflation rate, p. 11
interest rate, p. 4
monetary policy, p. 12
monetary theory, p. 9
money (money supply), 8
recession, p. 9
security, p. 3
stock, p. 5
unemployment rate, p. 8

QUESTIONS AND PROBLEMS

Questions marked with an asterisk are answered at the end of the book in an appendix, "Answers to Selected Questions and Problems." Questions marked with a blue circle indicate the question is available in MyEconLab at www.myeconlab.com/mishkin.

1. Has the inflation rate in the United States increased or decreased in the past few years? What about interest rates?
*2. If history repeats itself and we see a decline in the rate of money growth, what might you expect to happen to
   a. real output?
   b. the inflation rate?
   c. interest rates?
3. When was the most recent recession?
*4. When interest rates fall, how might you change your economic behavior?
5. Can you think of any financial innovation in the past ten years that has affected you personally? Has it made you better off or worse off? Why?
*6. Is everybody worse off when interest rates rise?
7. What is the basic activity of banks?
*8. Why are financial markets important to the health of the economy?
9. What is the typical relationship between interest rates on three-month Treasury bills, long-term Treasury bonds, and Baa corporate bonds?
*10. What effect might a fall in stock prices have on business investment?
11. What effect might a rise in stock prices have on consumers' decisions to spend?
*12. How does a fall in the value of the pound sterling affect British consumers?
13. How does an increase in the value of the pound sterling affect American businesses?
*14. Looking at Figure 3, in which years would you have chosen to visit the Grand Canyon in Arizona rather than the Tower of London?
15. When the dollar is worth more in relation to currencies of other countries, are you more likely to buy American-made or foreign-made jeans? Are U.S. companies that manufacture jeans happier when the dollar is strong or when it is weak? What about an American company that is in the business of importing jeans into the United States?

WEB EXERCISES

1. In this exercise we will practice collecting data from the Web and graphing it using Excel. Use the example on page 17 as a guide. Go to www.forecasts.org/data/index.htm, click on "stock index data" at the top of the page then choose the U.S. Stock indices—monthly option. Finally, choose the Dow Jones Industrial Average option.
   a. Using the method presented in this chapter, move the data into an Excel spreadsheet.
   b. Using the data from part a, prepare a graph. Use the graphing wizard to properly label your axes.
2. In Web Exercise 1 you collected and graphed the Dow Jones Industrial Average. This same site reports forecast values of the DJIA. Go to www.forecasts.org/data/index.htm and click on "FFC Home" at the top of the page. Click on the Dow Jones Industrial link under Forecasts in the far left column.
   a. What is the Dow forecast to be in three months?
   b. What percentage increase is forecast for the next three months?

WEB REFERENCES

www.federalreserve.gov/releases/

Daily, weekly, monthly, quarterly, and annual releases and historical data for selected interest rates, foreign exchange rates, and so on.

http://stockcharts.com/charts/historical/

Historical charts of various stock indexes over differing time periods.

www.federalreserve.gov

General information, monetary policy, banking system, research, and economic data of the Federal Reserve.

www.newsengin.com /neFreeTools.nsf/CPIcalc

Calculator lets you compute how the dollar's buying power has changed since 1913.

www.kowaldesign.com/budget/

This site reports the current federal budget deficit or surplus and how it has changed since the 1950s. It also reports how the federal budget isspent.

www.brillig.com/debt_clock/

National debt clock. This site reports the exact national debt at each point in time.

MyEconLab CAN HELP YOU GET A BETTER GRADE

If your exam were tomorrow, would you be ready? For each chapter, MyEconLab Practice Tests and Study Plans pinpoint which sections you have mastered and which ones you need to study. That way, you are more efficient with your study time, and you are better prepared for your exams.

Here's how it works:

1. Register and log in at www.myeconlab.com/mishkin
2. Click on "Take a Test" and select Sample Test A for this chapter.
3. Take the diagnostic test. MyEconLab will grade it automatically and create a personalized Study Plan so you see which sections of the chapter you should study further.
4. The Study Plan will serve up additional practice problems and tutorials to help you master the specific areas where you need to focus. By practicing online, you can track your progress in the Study Plan.
5. After you have mastered the sections, go to "Take a Test" and select Sample Test B for this chapter. Take the test and see how you do!

APPENDIX TO CHAPTER

1 Defining Aggregate Output, Income, the Price Level, and the Inflation Rate

Because these terms are used so frequently throughout the text, we need to have a clear understanding of the definitions of *aggregate output*, *income*, the *price level*, and the *inflation rate*.

AGGREGATE OUTPUT AND INCOME

The most commonly reported measure of aggregate output, the **gross domestic product (GDP)**, is the market value of all final goods and services produced in a country during the course of the year. This measure excludes two sets of items that at first glance you might think would be included. Purchases of goods that have been produced in the past, whether a Rembrandt painting or a house built twenty years ago, are not counted as part of GDP, nor are purchases of stocks or bonds. None of these enter into GDP because they are not goods and services produced during the course of the year. Intermediate goods, which are used up in producing final goods and services, such as the sugar in a candy bar or the energy used to produce steel, are also not counted separately as part of GDP. Because the value of the final goods already includes the value of the intermediate goods, to count them separately would be to count them twice.

Aggregate income, the total income of *factors of production* (land, labor, and capital) from producing goods and services in the economy during the course of the year, is best thought of as being equal to aggregate output. Because the payments for final goods and services must eventually flow back to the owners of the factors of production as income, income payments must equal payments for final goods and services. For example, if the economy has an aggregate output of $10 trillion, total income payments in the economy (aggregate income) are also $10 trillion.

REAL VERSUS NOMINAL MAGNITUDES

When the total value of final goods and services is calculated using current prices, the resulting GDP measure is referred to as *nominal GDP*. The word *nominal* indicates that values are measured using current prices. If all prices doubled but actual production of goods and services remained the same, nominal GDP would double even though people would not enjoy the benefits of twice as many goods and services. As a result, nominal variables can be misleading measures of economic well-being.

A more reliable measure of economic production expresses values in terms of prices for an arbitrary base year, currently 2000. GDP measured with constant prices is referred to as *real GDP*, the word *real* indicating that values are measured in terms of fixed prices. Real variables thus measure the quantities of goods and services and do not change because prices have changed, but rather only if actual quantities have changed.

A brief example will make the distinction clearer. Suppose that you have a nominal income of $30,000 in 2007 and that your nominal income was $15,000 in 2000. If all prices doubled between 2000 and 2007, are you better off? The answer is no: Although your income has doubled, your $30,000 buys you only the same amount of goods because prices have also doubled. A real income measure indicates that your income in terms of the goods it can buy is the same. Measured in 2000 prices, the $30,000 of nominal income in 2007 turns out to be only $15,000 of real income. Because your real income is actually the same in the two years, you are no better or worse off in 2007 than you were in 2000.

Because real variables measure quantities in terms of real goods and services, they are typically of more interest than nominal variables. In this text, discussion of aggregate output or aggregate income always refers to real measures (such as real GDP).

AGGREGATE PRICE LEVEL

In this chapter, we defined the aggregate price level as a measure of average prices in the economy. Three measures of the aggregate price level are commonly encountered in economic data. The first is the *GDP deflator*, which is defined as nominal GDP divided by real GDP. Thus, if 2007 nominal GDP is $10 trillion but 2007 real GDP in 2000 prices is $9 trillion,

$$\text{GDP deflator} = \frac{\$10 \text{ trillion}}{\$9 \text{ trillion}} = 1.11$$

The GDP deflator equation indicates that, on average, prices have risen 11% since 2000. Typically, measures of the price level are presented in the form of a price index, which expresses the price level for the base year (in our example, 2000) as 100. Thus the GDP deflator for 2007 would be 111.

Another popular measure of the aggregate price level (which officials in the Fed frequently focus on) is the *PCE deflator*, which is similar to the GDP deflator and is defined as nominal personal consumption expenditures (PCE) divided by real PCE.

The measure of the aggregate price level that is most frequently reported in the press is the ***consumer price index (CPI)***. The CPI is measured by pricing a "basket" of goods and services bought by a typical urban household. If over the course of the year, the cost of this basket of goods and services rises from $500 to $600, the CPI has risen by 20%. The CPI is also expressed as a price index with the base year equal to 100.

The CPI, the PCE deflator, and the GDP deflator measures of the price level can be used to convert or deflate a nominal magnitude into a real magnitude. This is accomplished by dividing the nominal magnitude by the price index. In our example, in which the GDP deflator for 2007 is 1.11 (expressed as an index value of 111), real GDP for 2007 equals

$$\frac{\$10 \text{ trillion}}{1.11} = \$9 \text{ trillion in 2000 prices}$$

which corresponds to the real GDP figure for 2007 assumed earlier.

GROWTH RATES AND THE INFLATION RATE

The media often talk about the economy's growth rate, and particularly the growth rate of real GDP. A growth rate is defined as the percentage change in a variable, i.e.,

$$\text{growth rate} = \frac{x_t - x_{t-1}}{x_{t-1}} \times 100$$

where t indicates today and $t - 1$ a year earlier.

For example, if real GDP grew from \$9 trillion in 2007 to \$9.5 trillion in 2008, then the GDP growth rate for 2008 would be 5.6%:

$$\text{GDP growth rate} = \frac{\$9.5\ \text{trillion} - \$9\ \text{trillion}}{\$9\ \text{trillion}} \times 100 = 5.6\%$$

The inflation rate is defined as the growth rate of the aggregate price level. Thus, if the GDP deflator rose from 111 in 2007 to 113 in 2008, the inflation rate using the GDP deflator would be 1.8%:

$$\text{inflation rate} = \frac{113 - 111}{111} \times 100 = 1.8\%$$

If the growth rate is for a period less than one year, it is usually reported on an annualized basis; that is, it is converted to the growth rate over a year's time, assuming that the growth rate remains constant. For GDP, which is reported quarterly, the annualized growth rate would be approximately four times the percentage change in GDP from the previous quarter. For example, if GDP rose $\frac{1}{2}$% from the first quarter of 2007 to the second quarter of 2007, then the annualized GDP growth rate for the second quarter of 2007 would be reported as 2% ($= 4 \times \frac{1}{2}$%). (A more accurate calculation would be 2.02%, because a precise quarterly growth rate should be compounded on a quarterly basis.)

CHAPTER

2 An Overview of the Financial System

Preview

Inez the Inventor has designed a low-cost robot that cleans house (even does windows), washes the car, and mows the lawn, but she has no funds to put her wonderful invention into production. Walter the Widower has plenty of savings, which he and his wife accumulated over the years. If Inez and Walter could get together so that Walter could provide funds to Inez, Inez's robot would see the light of day, and the economy would be better off: We would have cleaner houses, shinier cars, and more beautiful lawns.

Financial markets (bond and stock markets) and financial intermediaries (banks, insurance companies, pension funds) have the basic function of getting people like Inez and Walter together by moving funds from those who have a surplus of funds (Walter) to those who have a shortage of funds (Inez). More realistically, when Apple invents a better iPod, it may need funds to bring its new product to market. Similarly, when a local government needs to build a road or a school, it may need more funds than local property taxes provide. Well-functioning financial markets and financial intermediaries are crucial to economic health.

To study the effects of financial markets and financial intermediaries on the economy, we need to acquire an understanding of their general structure and operation. In this chapter, we learn about the major financial intermediaries and the instruments that are traded in financial markets as well as how these markets are regulated.

This chapter presents an overview of the fascinating study of financial markets and institutions. We return to a more detailed treatment of the regulation, structure, and evolution of the financial system in Chapters 8 through 14.

FUNCTION OF FINANCIAL MARKETS

Financial markets perform the essential economic function of channeling funds from households, firms, and governments that have saved surplus funds by spending less than their income to those that have a shortage of funds because they wish to spend more than their income. This function is shown schematically in Figure 1. Those who have saved and are lending funds, the lender-savers, are at the left, and those who must borrow funds to finance their spending, the borrower-spenders, are at the right. The principal lender-savers are households, but business enterprises and the government (particularly state and local government), as well as foreigners and their governments, sometimes also find themselves with excess funds and so lend them out. The most important borrower-spenders are businesses and the government (particularly the federal government), but

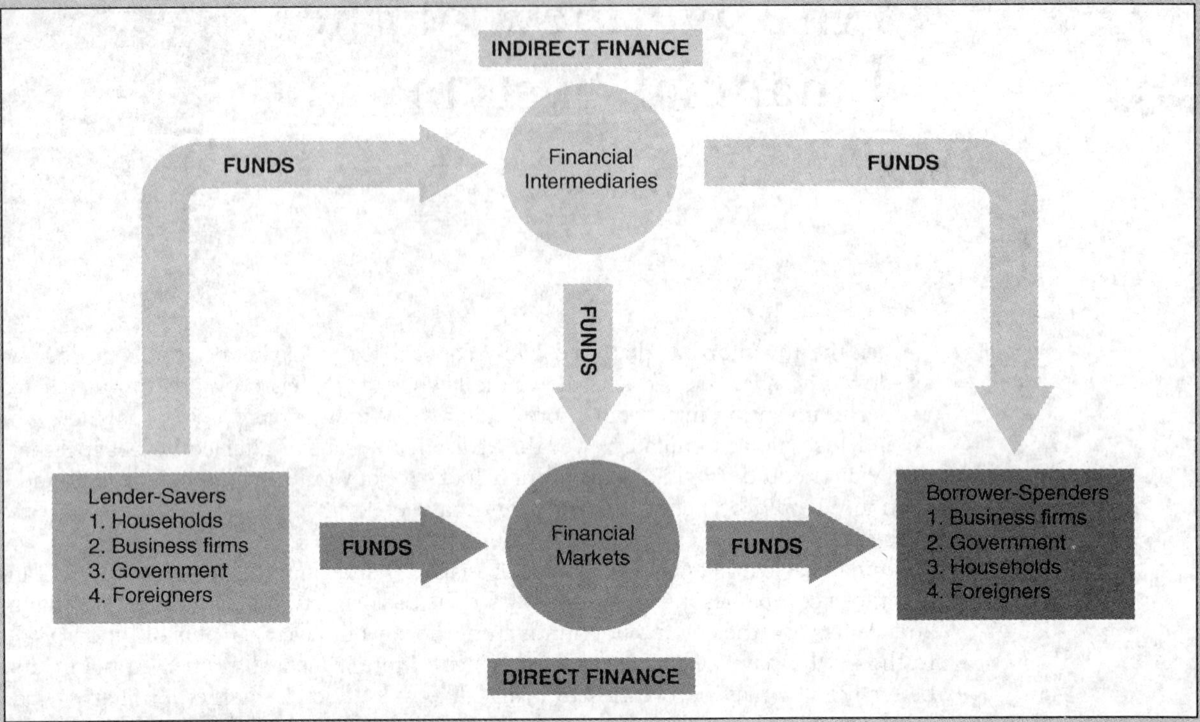

FIGURE 1 **Flows of Funds Through the Financial System**

households and foreigners also borrow to finance their purchases of cars, furniture, and houses. The arrows show that funds flow from lender-savers to borrower-spenders via two routes.

In *direct finance* (the route at the bottom of Figure 1), borrowers borrow funds directly from lenders in financial markets by selling them *securities* (also called *financial instruments*), which are claims on the borrower's future income or assets. Securities are assets for the person who buys them but **liabilities** (IOUs or debts) for the individual or firm that sells (issues) them. For example, if General Motors needs to borrow funds to pay for a new factory to manufacture electric cars, it might borrow the funds from savers by selling them *bonds*, debt securities that promise to make payments periodically for a specified period of time.

Why is this channeling of funds from savers to spenders so important to the economy? The answer is that the people who save are frequently not the same people who have profitable investment opportunities available to them, the entrepreneurs. Let's first think about this on a personal level. Suppose that you have saved $1,000 this year, but no borrowing or lending is possible because there are no financial markets. If you do not have an investment opportunity that will permit you to earn income with your savings, you will just hold on to the $1,000 and will earn no interest. However, Carl the Carpenter has a productive use for your $1,000: He can use it to purchase a new tool that will shorten the time it takes him to build a house, thereby earning an extra $200 per year. If you could get in touch with Carl, you could lend him the $1,000 at a rental fee (interest) of $100 per year, and both of you would be better off. You would earn

$100 per year on your $1,000, instead of the zero amount that you would earn otherwise, while Carl would earn $100 more income per year (the $200 extra earnings per year minus the $100 rental fee for the use of the funds).

In the absence of financial markets, you and Carl the Carpenter might never get together. You would both be stuck with the status quo, and both of you would be worse off. Without financial markets, it is hard to transfer funds from a person who has no investment opportunities to one who has them. Financial markets are thus essential to promoting economic efficiency.

The existence of financial markets is beneficial even if someone borrows for a purpose other than increasing production in a business. Say that you are recently married, have a good job, and want to buy a house. You earn a good salary, but because you have just started to work, you have not saved much. Over time, you would have no problem saving enough to buy the house of your dreams, but by then you would be too old to get full enjoyment from it. Without financial markets, you are stuck; you cannot buy the house and must continue to live in your tiny apartment.

If a financial market were set up so that people who had built up savings could lend you the funds to buy the house, you would be more than happy to pay them some interest so that you could own a home while you are still young enough to enjoy it. Then, over time, you would pay back your loan. If this loan could occur, you would be better off, as would the persons who made you the loan. They would now earn some interest, whereas they would not if the financial market did not exist.

Now we can see why financial markets have such an important function in the economy. They allow funds to move from people who lack productive investment opportunities to people who have such opportunities. Financial markets are critical for producing an efficient allocation of capital, which contributes to higher production and efficiency for the overall economy. Indeed, as we will explore in Chapter 8, when financial markets break down during financial crises, as they have in Mexico, East Asia, and Argentina in recent years, severe economic hardship results, which can even lead to dangerous political instability.

Well-functioning financial markets also directly improve the well-being of consumers by allowing them to time their purchases better. They provide funds to young people to buy what they need and can eventually afford without forcing them to wait until they have saved up the entire purchase price. Financial markets that are operating efficiently improve the economic welfare of everyone in the society.

STRUCTURE OF FINANCIAL MARKETS

Now that we understand the basic function of financial markets, let's look at their structure. The following descriptions of several categorizations of financial markets illustrate essential features of these markets.

Debt and Equity Markets

A firm or an individual can obtain funds in a financial market in two ways. The most common method is to issue a debt instrument, such as a bond or a mortgage, which is a contractual agreement by the borrower to pay the holder of the instrument fixed dollar amounts at regular intervals (interest and principal payments) until a specified date (the maturity date), when a final payment is made. The **maturity** of a debt instrument is the number of years (term) until that instrument's expiration date. A debt instrument is **short-term** if its maturity is less than a year and **long-term** if its maturity is ten years or longer. Debt instruments with a maturity between one and ten years are said to be **intermediate-term**.

The second method of raising funds is by issuing **equities**, such as common stock, which are claims to share in the net income (income after expenses and taxes) and the assets of a business. If you own one share of common stock in a company that has issued one million shares, you are entitled to 1 one-millionth of the firm's net income and 1 one-millionth of the firm's assets. Equities often make periodic payments (**dividends**) to their holders and are considered long-term securities because they have no maturity date. In addition, owning stock means that you own a portion of the firm and thus have the right to vote on issues important to the firm and to elect its directors.

The main disadvantage of owning a corporation's equities rather than its debt is that an equity holder is a *residual claimant*; that is, the corporation must pay all its debt holders before it pays its equity holders. The advantage of holding equities is that equity holders benefit directly from any increases in the corporation's profitability or asset value because equities confer ownership rights on the equity holders. Debt holders do not share in this benefit, because their dollar payments are fixed. We examine the pros and cons of debt versus equity instruments in more detail in Chapter 8, which provides an economic analysis of financial structure.

The total value of equities in the United States has typically fluctuated between $4 and $20 trillion since the early 1990s, depending on the prices of shares. Although the average person is more aware of the stock market than any other financial market, the size of the debt market is often larger than the size of the equities market: The value of debt instruments was $41 trillion at the end of 2005, while the value of equities was $18 trillion at the end of 2005.

Primary and Secondary Markets

A **primary market** is a financial market in which new issues of a security, such as a bond or a stock, are sold to initial buyers by the corporation or government agency borrowing the funds. A **secondary market** is a financial market in which securities that have been previously issued can be resold.

The primary markets for securities are not well known to the public because the selling of securities to initial buyers often takes place behind closed doors. An important financial institution that assists in the initial sale of securities in the primary market is the **investment bank**. It does this by **underwriting** securities: It guarantees a price for a corporation's securities and then sells them to the public.

The New York and American stock exchanges and NASDAQ (National Association of Securities Dealers Automated Quotation System), in which previously issued stocks are traded, are the best-known examples of secondary markets, although the bond markets, in which previously issued bonds of major corporations and the U.S. government are bought and sold, actually have a larger trading volume. Other examples of secondary markets are foreign exchange markets, futures markets, and options markets. Securities brokers and dealers are crucial to a well-functioning secondary market. **Brokers** are agents of investors who match buyers with sellers of securities; **dealers** link buyers and sellers by buying and selling securities at stated prices.

When an individual buys a security in the secondary market, the person who has sold the security receives money in exchange for the security, but the corporation that issued the security acquires no new funds. A corporation acquires new funds only when its securities are first sold in the primary market. Nonetheless, secondary markets serve two important functions. First, they make it easier and quicker to sell these financial instruments to raise cash; that is, they make the financial instruments more **liquid**. The increased liquidity of these instruments then makes them more desirable and thus easier for the issuing firm to sell in the primary market. Second, they determine the price of the security that the issuing firm sells in the primary market. The investors who buy securities in the primary market will pay the issuing corporation no more than the price they think the secondary market will set for this security. The higher the security's price in the secondary market, the higher the price that the issuing firm will receive for a new security in the primary market, and hence the greater the amount of financial capital it can raise. Conditions in the secondary market are therefore the most relevant to corporations issuing securities. It is for this reason that books like this one, which deal with financial markets, focus on the behavior of secondary markets rather than primary markets.

Exchanges and Over-the-Counter Markets

Secondary markets can be organized in two ways. One method is to organize **exchanges**, where buyers and sellers of securities (or their agents or brokers) meet in one central location to conduct trades. The New York and American Stock Exchanges for stocks and the Chicago Board of Trade for commodities (wheat, corn, silver, and other raw materials) are examples of organized exchanges.

The other method of organizing a secondary market is to have an **over-the-counter (OTC) market**, in which dealers at different locations who have an inventory of securities stand ready to buy and sell securities "over the counter" to anyone who comes to them and is willing to accept their prices. Because over-the-counter dealers are in computer contact and know the prices set by one another, the OTC market is very competitive and not very different from a market with an organized exchange.

Many common stocks are traded over-the-counter, although a majority of the largest corporations have their shares traded at organized stock exchanges. The U.S. government bond market, with a larger trading volume than the New York Stock Exchange, by contrast, is set up as an over-the-counter market. Forty or so dealers establish a "market" in these securities by standing ready to buy and sell U.S. government bonds. Other over-the-counter markets include those that trade other types of financial instruments such as negotiable certificates of deposit, federal funds, banker's acceptances, and foreign exchange.

Money and Capital Markets

Another way of distinguishing between markets is on the basis of the maturity of the securities traded in each market. The **money market** is a financial market in which only short-term debt instruments (generally those with original maturity of less than one year) are traded; the **capital market** is the market in which longer-term debt (generally those with original maturity of one year or greater) and equity instruments are traded. Money market securities are usually more widely traded than longer-term securities and so tend to be more liquid. In addition, as we will see in Chapter 4, short-term securities have smaller fluctuations in prices than long-term securities, making them safer investments. As a result, corporations and banks actively use the money market to earn interest on surplus funds that they expect to have only temporarily. Capital market securities, such as stocks and long-term bonds, are often held by financial intermediaries such as insurance companies and pension funds, which have little uncertainty about the amount of funds they will have available in the future.

FINANCIAL MARKET INSTRUMENTS

To complete our understanding of how financial markets perform the important role of channeling funds from lender-savers to borrower-spenders, we need to examine the securities (instruments) traded in financial markets. We first focus on the instruments traded in the money market and then turn to those traded in the capital market.

Money Market Instruments

Because of their short terms to maturity, the debt instruments traded in the money market undergo the least price fluctuations and so are the least risky investments. The money market has undergone great changes in the past three decades, with the amount of some financial instruments growing at a far more rapid rate than others.

The principal money market instruments are listed in Table 1 along with the amount outstanding at the end of 1980, 1990, 2000, and 2005. The Following the Financial News box illustrates how the interest rates on many of the insturments are reported.

United States Treasury Bills. These short-term debt instruments of the U.S. government are issued in one-, three-, and six-month maturities to finance the federal government. They pay a set amount at maturity and have no interest payments, but they effectively pay interest by initially selling at a discount, that is, at a price lower than the set amount paid at maturity. For instance, in May 2007 you might buy a one-year Treasury bill for $9,000 that can be redeemed in May 2008 for $10,000.

TABLE 1 Principal Money Market Instruments

	Amount Outstanding ($ billions, end of year)			
Type of Instrument	**1980**	**1990**	**2000**	**2005**
U.S. Treasury bills	216	527	647	923
Negotiable bank certificates of deposit (large denominations)	317	543	1053	1742
Commercial paper	122	557	1619	1544
Banker's acceptances	42	52	8	4
Repurchase agreements	57	144	366	518
Federal funds	18	61	60	83
Eurodollars	55	92	195	438

Sources: Federal Reserve Flow of Funds Accounts; Federal Reserve *Bulletin*; *Economic Report of the President.*

U.S. Treasury bills are the most liquid of all the money market instruments because they are the most actively traded. They are also the safest of all money market instruments because there is almost no possibility of **default**, a situation in which the party issuing the debt instrument (the federal government in this case) is unable to make interest payments or pay off the amount owed when the instrument matures. The federal government is always able to meet its debt obligations because it can raise taxes or issue **currency** (paper money or coins) to pay off its debts. Treasury bills are held mainly by banks, although small amounts are held by households, corporations, and other financial intermediaries.

Negotiable Bank Certificates of Deposit. A *certificate of deposit (CD)* is a debt instrument sold by a bank to depositors that pays annual interest of a given amount and at maturity pays back the original purchase price. Negotiable CDs are CDs that are sold in secondary markets, with the amount outstanding currently around $1.7 trillion. Negotiable CDs are an extremely important source of funds for commercial banks, from corporations, money market mutual funds, charitable institutions, and government agencies.

Commercial Paper. *Commercial paper* is a short-term debt instrument issued by large banks and well-known corporations, such as Microsoft and General Motors. Growth of the commercial paper market has been substantial: The amount of commercial paper outstanding has increased by over 1,200% (from $122 billion to $1,544 billion) in the period 1980–2005. We will discuss why the commercial paper market has had such tremendous growth in Chapter 10.

Banker's Acceptances. These money market instruments are created in the course of carrying out international trade and have been in use for hundreds of years. A *banker's acceptance* is a bank draft (a promise of payment similar to a check) issued by a firm, payable at some future date, and guaranteed for a fee by the bank that stamps it "accepted." The firm issuing the instrument is required to deposit the required funds into its account to cover the draft. If the firm fails to do so, the bank's guarantee means that it is obligated to make good on the draft. The advantage to the firm is that the draft is more likely to be accepted when purchasing goods abroad because the foreign exporter knows that even if the company purchasing the goods goes bankrupt, the bank draft will still be paid off. These "accepted" drafts are often resold in a secondary market at a discount and so are similar in function to Treasury bills. Typically, they are held by many of the same parties that hold Treasury bills, and the amount outstanding declined ($42 billion to $4 billion) from 1980 to 2005.

Repurchase Agreements. *Repurchase agreements (repos)* are effectively short-term loans (usually with a maturity of less than two weeks) for which Treasury bills serve as *collateral,* an asset that the lender receives if the borrower does not pay back the loan. Repos are made as follows: A large corporation, such as Microsoft, may have some idle funds in its bank account, say $1 million, which it would like to lend for a week. Microsoft uses this excess $1 million to buy Treasury bills from a bank, which agrees to repurchase them the next week at a price slightly above Microsoft's purchase price. The effect of this agreement is that Microsoft makes a loan of $1 million to the bank and holds $1 million of the bank's Treasury bills until the bank repurchases the bills to pay off the loan. Repurchase agreements are now an important source of bank funds (over $500 billion). The most important lenders in this market are large corporations.

Following the Financial News Money Market Rates

The *Wall Street Journal* publishes daily a listing of interest rates on many different financial instruments in its "Money Rates" column. (See "Today's Contents" on page 1 of the *Journal* for the location.)

The four interest rates in the "Money Rates" column that are discussed most frequently in the media are these:

Prime rate: The base interest rate on corporate bank loans, an indicator of the cost of business borrowing from banks

Federal funds rate: The interest rate charged on overnight loans in the federal funds market, a sensitive indicator of the cost to banks of borrowing funds from other banks and the stance of monetary policy

Treasury bill rate: The interest rate on U.S. Treasury bills, an indicator of general interest-rate movements

Federal Home Loan Mortgage Corporation rates: Interest rates on "Freddie Mac"–guaranteed mortgages, an indicator of the cost of financing residential housing purchases

Money Rates

Thursday, January 12, 2006

The key U.S. and foreign annual interest rates below are a guide to general levels but don't always represent actual transactions.

Prime Rate: 7.25% (effective 12/13/05). The base rate on corporate loans posted by at least 75% of the nation's 30 largest banks.

Discount Rate (Primary): 5.25% (effective 12/13/05).

Federal Funds: 4.438% high, 4.230% low, 4.250% near closing bid, 4.313% offered. Effective rate: 4.28%. Source; Tullett Prebon Information, Ltd. Federal-funds target rate: 4.250% (effective 12/13/05).

Call Money: 6.00% (effective 12/13/05).

Commercial Paper: Placed directly by General Electric Capital Corp.: 4.34% 30 to 42 days; 4.39% 43 to 59 days; 4.41% 60 to 89 days; 4.47% 90 to 119 days; 4.50% 120 to 149 days; 4.53% 150 to 179 days; 4.55% 180 to 209 days; 4.56% 210 to 239 days; 4.57% 240 to 270 days.

Euro Commercial Paper: Placed directly by General Electric Capital Corp.: 2.35% 30 days; 2.40% two months; 2.47% three months; 2.52% four months; 2.56% five months; 2.61% six months.

Dealer Commercial Paper: High-grade unsecured notes sold through dealers by major corporations: 4.39% 30 days; 4.45% 60 days; 4.53% 90 days.

Certificates of Deposit: 4.42% one month; 4.56% three months; 4.68% six months.

Bankers Acceptances: 4.41% 30 days; 4.47% 60 days; 4.55% 90 days; 4.61% 120 days; 4.65% 150 days; 4.68% 180 days. Source: Tullett Prebon Information, Ltd.

Eurodollars: 4.44%-4.42% one month; 4.48%-4.46% two months; 4.58%-4.56% three months; 4.62%-4.59% four months; 4.66%-4.63% five months; 4.70%-4.67% six months. Source: Tullett Prebon Information, Ltd.

London Interbank Offered Rates (Libor): 4.4700% one month; 4.6000% three months; 4.73875% six months; 4.8600% one year. Effective rate for contracts entered into two days from datt appearing at top of this column.

Euro Libor: 2.39200% one month; 2.51644% three months 2.65856% six months; 2.84713% one year. Effective rate for contracts entered into two days from date appearing at top of this column.

Euro Interbank Offered Rates (Euribor): 2.396% one month; 2.514% three months; 2.661% six months; 2.847% one year. Source: Reuters.

Foreign Prime Rates: Canada 5.00%; European Central Bank 2.25%; Japan 1.375%; Switzerland 2.41%; Britain 4.50%.

Treasury Bills: Results of the Monday, January 9, 2006, auction of short-term U.S. government bills, sold at a discount from face value in units of $1,000 to $1 million: 4.150% 13 weeks; 4.250% 26 weeks. Tuesday, January 10, 2006 auction: 4.070% 4 weeks.

Overnight Repurchase Rate: 4.21%. Source: Garban Intercapital.

Freddie Mac: Posted yields on 30-year mortgage commitments. Delivery within 30 days 5.93%, 60 days 5.96%, standard conventional fixed-rate mortgages: 3.375%, 2% rate capped one-year adjustable rate mortgages.

Fannie Mae: Posted yields on 30 year mortgage commitments (priced at par) for delivery within 30 days 6.021%, 60 days 6.058%, standard conventional fixed-rate mortgages. Constant Maturity Debt Index: 4.487% three months; 4.647% six months; 4.708% one year.

Merrill Lynch Ready Assets Trust: 3.57%.

Consumer Price Index: November, 197.6, up 3.5% from a year ago. Bureau of Labor Statistics.

Source: Wall Street Journal, Friday, January 13, 2006, p. C12.

Federal (Fed) Funds. These instruments are typically overnight loans between banks of their deposits at the Federal Reserve. The *federal funds* designation is somewhat confusing because these loans are not made by the federal government or by the Federal Reserve but rather by banks to other banks. One reason why a bank might borrow in the federal funds market is that it might find it does not have enough deposits at the Fed to meet the amount required by regulators. It can then borrow these deposits from another bank, which transfers them to the borrowing bank using the Fed's wire transfer system. This market is very sensitive to the credit needs of the banks, so the interest rate on these loans, called the **federal funds rate**, is a closely watched barometer of the tightness of credit market conditions in the banking system and the stance of monetary policy. When it is high, it indicates that the banks are strapped for funds; when it is low, banks' credit needs are low.

Capital Market Instruments

Capital market instruments are debt and equity instruments with maturities of greater than one year. They have far wider price fluctuations than money market instruments and are considered to be fairly risky investments. The principal capital market instruments are listed in Table 2, which shows the amount outstanding at the end of 1980, 1990, 2000, and 2005.

Stocks. *Stocks* are equity claims on the net income and assets of a corporation. Their value of $18 trillion at the end of 2005 exceeds that of any other type of security in the capital market. The amount of new stock issues in any given year is typically quite small, less than 1% of the total value of shares outstanding. Individuals hold around half of the value of stocks; the rest are held by pension funds, mutual funds, and insurance companies.

Mortgages. *Mortgages* are loans to households or firms to purchase housing, land, or other real structures, where the structure or land itself serves as collateral for the loans. The mortgage market is the largest debt market in the United States, with the amount of residential mortgages (used to purchase residential housing) outstanding more than quadruple the amount of commercial and farm mortgages. Savings and loan associations and mutual savings banks have been the primary lenders in the residential mortgage

TABLE 2 Principal Capital Market Instruments

	Amount Outstanding ($ billions, end of year)			
Type of Instrument	**1980**	**1990**	**2000**	**2005**
Corporate stocks (market value)	1,601	4,146	17,627	17,853
Residential mortgages	1,106	2,886	5,463	9,436
Corporate bonds	366	1,008	2,230	2,983
U.S. government securities (marketable long-term)	407	1,653	2,184	2,803
U.S. government agency securities	193	435	1,616	2,696
State and local government bonds	310	870	1,192	1,807
Bank commercial loans	459	818	1,091	1,031
Consumer loans	355	813	536	710
Commercial and farm mortgages	352	829	1,214	1,919

Sources: Federal Reserve Flow of Funds Accounts; Federal Reserve *Bulletin*.

market, although commercial banks have started to enter this market more aggressively. The majority of commercial and farm mortgages are made by commercial banks and life insurance companies. The federal government plays an active role in the mortgage market via the three government agencies—the Federal National Mortgage Association (FNMA, "Fannie Mae"), the Government National Mortgage Association (GNMA, "Ginnie Mae"), and the Federal Home Loan Mortgage Corporation (FHLMC, "Freddie Mac")—that provide funds to the mortgage market by selling bonds and using the proceeds to buy mortgages.

Corporate Bonds. These long-term bonds are issued by corporations with very strong credit ratings. The typical *corporate bond* sends the holder an interest payment twice a year and pays off the face value when the bond matures. Some corporate bonds, called *convertible bonds,* have the additional feature of allowing the holder to convert them into a specified number of shares of stock at any time up to the maturity date. This feature makes these convertible bonds more desirable to prospective purchasers than bonds without it and allows the corporation to reduce its interest payments because these bonds can increase in value if the price of the stock appreciates sufficiently. Because the outstanding amount of both convertible and nonconvertible bonds for any given corporation is small, they are not nearly as liquid as other securities such as U.S. government bonds.

Although the size of the corporate bond market is substantially smaller than that of the stock market, with the amount of corporate bonds outstanding less than one-fifth that of stocks, the volume of new corporate bonds issued each year is substantially greater than the volume of new stock issues. Thus the behavior of the corporate bond market is probably far more important to a firm's financing decisions than the behavior of the stock market. The principal buyers of corporate bonds are life insurance companies; pension funds and households are other large holders.

U.S. Government Securities. These long-term debt instruments are issued by the U.S. Treasury to finance the deficits of the federal government. Because they are the most widely traded bonds in the United States (the volume of transactions on average exceeds $100 billion daily), they are the most liquid security traded in the capital market. They are held by the Federal Reserve, banks, households, and foreigners.

U.S. Government Agency Securities. These long-term bonds are issued by various government agencies such as Ginnie Mae, the Federal Farm Credit Bank, and the Tennessee Valley Authority to finance such items as mortgages, farm loans, or power-generating equipment. Many of these securities are guaranteed by the federal government. They function much like U.S. government bonds and are held by similar parties.

State and Local Government Bonds. State and local bonds, also called *municipal bonds,* are long-term debt instruments issued by state and local governments to finance expenditures on schools, roads, and other large programs. An important feature of these bonds is that their interest payments are exempt from federal income tax and generally from state taxes in the issuing state. Commercial banks, with their high income tax rate, are the biggest buyers of these securities, owning over half the total amount outstanding. The next biggest group of holders consists of wealthy individuals in high income tax brackets, followed by insurance companies.

Consumer and Bank Commercial Loans. These loans to consumers and businesses are made principally by banks but, in the case of consumer loans, also by finance companies.

INTERNATIONALIZATION OF FINANCIAL MARKETS

The growing internationalization of financial markets has become an important trend. Before the 1980s, U.S. financial markets were much larger than financial markets outside the United States, but in recent years the dominance of U.S. markets has been disappearing. The extraordinary growth of foreign financial markets has been the result of both large increases in the pool of savings in foreign countries such as Japan and the deregulation of foreign financial markets, which has enabled foreign markets to expand their activities. American corporations and banks are now more likely to tap international capital markets to raise needed funds, and American investors often seek investment opportunities abroad. Similarly, foreign corporations and banks raise funds from Americans, and foreigners have become important investors in the United States. A look at international bond markets and world stock markets will give us a picture of how this globalization of financial markets is taking place.

International Bond Market, Eurobonds, and Eurocurrencies

The traditional instruments in the international bond market are known as **foreign bonds**. Foreign bonds are sold in a foreign country and are denominated in that country's currency. For example, if the German automaker Porsche sells a bond in the United States denominated in U.S. dollars, it is classified as a foreign bond. Foreign bonds have been an important instrument in the international capital market for centuries. In fact, a large percentage of U.S. railroads built in the nineteenth century were financed by sales of foreign bonds in Britain.

A more recent innovation in the international bond market is the **Eurobond**, a bond denominated in a currency other than that of the country in which it is sold—for example, a bond denominated in U.S. dollars sold in London. Currently, over 80% of the new issues in the international bond market are Eurobonds, and the market for these securities has grown very rapidly. As a result, the Eurobond market is now larger than the U.S. corporate bond market.

A variant of the Eurobond is **Eurocurrencies**, which are foreign currencies deposited in banks outside the home country. The most important of the Eurocurrencies are **Eurodollars**, which are U.S. dollars deposited in foreign banks outside the United States or in foreign branches of U.S. banks. Because these short-term deposits earn interest, they are similar to short-term Eurobonds. American banks borrow Eurodollar deposits from other banks or from their own foreign branches, and Eurodollars are now an important source of funds for American banks (over $190 billion outstanding).

Note that the new currency, the euro, can create some confusion about the terms Eurobond, Eurocurrencies, and Eurodollars. A bond denominated in euros is called a Eurobond only *if it is sold outside the countries that have adopted the euro.* In fact, most Eurobonds are not denominated in euros but are instead denominated in U.S. dollars. Similarly, Eurodollars have nothing to do with euros, but are instead U.S. dollars deposited in banks outside the United States.

World Stock Markets

Until recently, the U.S. stock market was by far the largest in the world, but foreign stock markets have been growing in importance, with the United States not always being number one. The increased interest in foreign stocks has prompted the

Following the Financial News Foreign Stock Market Indexes

Foreign stock market indexes are published daily in the *Wall Street Journal* next to the "World Markets" column, which reports developments in foreign stock markets.

The first column identifies the market of the foreign stock exchange followed by the market index; for example, the circled entry is for the Nikkei 300 Average in Japan. The third column, "CLOSE," gives the closing value of the index, which was 320.65 for the Nikkei 300 Average on January 1, 2006. The "NET CHG" column indicates the change in the index from the previous trading day, +1.96, and the "% CHG" column indicates the percentage change in the index, +0.62%. The "YTD NET CHG" column indicates the change in the index from the beginning of the year (year to date), +5.13, and the "YTD % CHG" column indicates the percentage change in the index from the beginning of the year, +1.63%.

International Stock Market Indexes

Market	INDEX	1/12/06 CLOSE	NET CHG	% CHG	YTD NET CHG	YTD % CHG	P/E
World	DJ World Index	244.17	-0.52	-0.21	+10.03	+4.28	17
World ex-US	DJ World ex-US	207.84	+0.36	+0.17	+10.26	+5.19	17
Argentina	Merval	1638.09	-11.58	-0.70	+94.78	+6.14	...
Australia	S&P/ASX 200	4836.90	-1.20	-0.02	+73.50	+1.54	16
Belgium	Bel-20	3676.23	+13.08	+0.36	+126.98	+3.58	12
Brazil	Sao Paulo Bovespa	35779.30	-172.94	-0.48	+2323.36	+6.94	9
Canada	S&P/TSX Composite	11595.18	-25.85	-0.22	+322.92	+2.86	19
Chile	Santiago IPSA	2061.28	-16.68	-0.80	+96.81	+4.93	18
China	Dow Jones CBN China 600	8980.28	+109.88	+1.24	+519.31	+6.14	17
China	Dow Jones China 88	100.53	+0.60	+0.60	+4.83	+5.05	15
Europe	DJ STOXX 600	318.68	+1.13	+0.36	+8.65	+2.79	13
Europe	DJ STOXX 50	3444.10	+12.48	+0.36	+95.00	+2.84	12
Euro Zone	DJ Euro STOXX	338.60	+0.43	+0.13	+9.68	+2.94	15
Euro Zone	DJ Euro STOXX 50	3670.20	+1.59	+0.04	+91.27	+2.55	13
EAFE	MSCI EAFE	1763.95	+1.75	+0.10	+83.82	+4.99	16
France	Paris CAC 40	4890.24	-0.25	-0.01	+175.01	+3.71	12
Germany	Frankfurt Xetra DAX	5542.13	+9.24	+0.17	+133.87	+2.48	15
Hong Kong	Hang Seng	15719.37	+68.49	+0.44	+842.94	+5.67	14
India	Bombay Sensex	9380.88	-64.42	-0.68	-17.05	-0.18	19
Israel	Tel Aviv 25	825.69	+1.24	+0.15	+2.27	+0.28	...
Italy	S&P/MIB	36661	+113	+0.31	+957	+2.68	19
Japan	Tokyo Nikkei Stock Average	16445.19	+81.60	+0.50	+333.76	+2.07	...
Japan	Tokyo Nikkei 300	320.65	+1.96	+0.62	+5.13	+1.63	...
Japan	Tokyo Topix Index	1684.34	+11.90	+0.71	+34.58	+2.10	115
Mexico	I.P.C. All-Share	18925.01	-235.43	-1.23	+1122.30	+6.30	13
Netherlands	Amsterdam AEX	447.40	+1.09	+0.24	+10.62	+2.43	12
Russia	DJ Russia Titans 10	4552.37	+239.08	+5.54	+574.36	+14.44	73
Singapore	Straits Times	2407.38	-11.27	-0.47	+60.04	+2.56	9
South Africa	Johannesburg All Share	18577.00	-17.16	-0.09	+480.46	+2.65	13
South Korea	KOSPI	1402.58	+8.49	+0.61	+23.21	+1.68	10
Spain	IBEX 35	10955.80	-10.40	-0.09	+221.90	+2.07	18
Sweden	SX All Share	308.37	-0.61	-0.20	+5.46	+1.80	20
Switzerland	Zurich Swiss Market	7798.10	+46.04	+0.59	+214.17	+2.82	19
Taiwan	Weighted	6725.61	-10.28	-0.15	+177.27	+2.71	13
Turkey	Istanbul National 100	41905.41	Closed	...	+2127.71	+5.35	19
U.K.	London FTSE 100-share	5735.10	+3.60	+0.06	+116.30	+2.07	14
U.K.	London FTSE 250-share	8938.90	+10.90	+0.12	+144.60	+1.64	17

Source: Wall Street Journal, Friday, January 13, 2006, p. C16.

development in the United States of mutual funds that specialize in trading in foreign stock markets. American investors now pay attention not only to the Dow Jones Industrial Average but also to stock price indexes for foreign stock markets such as the Nikkei 300 Average (Tokyo) and the Financial Times Stock Exchange (FTSE) 100-Share Index (London).

The internationalization of financial markets is having profound effects on the United States. Foreigners, particularly Japanese investors, are not only providing funds to corporations in the United States, but are also helping finance the federal government. Without these foreign funds, the U.S. economy would have grown far less rapidly in the last twenty years. The internationalization of financial markets is also leading the way to a more integrated world economy in which flows of goods and technology between countries are more commonplace. In later chapters, we will encounter many examples of the important roles that international factors play in our economy (see the Following the Financial News box).

FUNCTION OF FINANCIAL INTERMEDIARIES: INDIRECT FINANCE

As shown in Figure 1 (p. 26), funds can move from lenders to borrowers by a second route, called *indirect finance* because it involves a financial intermediary that stands between the lender-savers and the borrower-spenders and helps transfer funds from one to the other. A financial intermediary does this by borrowing funds from the lender-savers and then using these funds to make loans to borrower-spenders. For example, a bank might acquire funds by issuing a liability to the public (an asset for the public) in the form of savings deposits. It might then use the funds to acquire an asset by making a loan to General Motors or by buying a U.S. Treasury bond in the financial market. The ultimate result is that funds have been transferred from the public (the lender-savers) to GM or the U.S. Treasury (the borrower-spender) with the help of the financial intermediary (the bank).

The process of indirect finance using financial intermediaries, called **financial intermediation**, is the primary route for moving funds from lenders to borrowers. Indeed, although the media focus much of their attention on securities markets, particularly the stock market, financial intermediaries are a far more important source of financing for corporations than securities markets are. This is true not only for the United States but for other industrialized countries as well (see the Global box). Why are financial intermediaries and indirect finance so important in financial markets? To answer this question, we need to understand the role of transaction costs, risk sharing, and information costs in financial markets.

Transaction Costs

Transaction costs, the time and money spent in carrying out financial transactions, are a major problem for people who have excess funds to lend. As we have seen, Carl the Carpenter needs $1,000 for his new tool, and you know that it is an excellent investment opportunity. You have the cash and would like to lend him the money, but to protect your investment, you have to hire a lawyer to write up the loan contract that specifies how much interest Carl will pay you, when he will make these interest payments, and when he will repay you the $1,000. Obtaining the contract will cost you $500. When you figure in this transaction cost for making the loan, you realize that you can't earn enough from the deal (you spend $500 to make perhaps $100) and reluctantly tell Carl that he will have to look elsewhere.

This example illustrates that small savers like you or potential borrowers like Carl might be frozen out of financial markets and thus be unable to benefit from them. Can anyone come to the rescue? Financial intermediaries can.

Financial intermediaries can substantially reduce transaction costs because they have developed expertise in lowering them; and because their large size allows them to take advantage of **economies of scale**, the reduction in transaction costs per dollar of transactions as the size (scale) of transactions increases. For example, a bank knows how to find a good lawyer to produce an airtight loan contract, and this contract can be used

Global The Importance of Financial Intermediaries Relative to Securities Markets: An International Comparison

Patterns of financing corporations differ across countries, but one key fact emerges: Studies of the major developed countries, including the United States, Canada, the United Kingdom, Japan, Italy, Germany, and France, show that when businesses go looking for funds to finance their activities, they usually obtain them indirectly through financial intermediaries and not directly from securities markets.* Even in the United States and Canada, which have the most developed securities markets in the world, loans from financial intermediaries are far more important for corporate finance than securities markets are. The countries that have made the least use of securities markets are Germany and Japan; in these two countries, financing from financial intermediaries has been almost ten times greater than that from securities markets. However, after the deregulation of Japanese securities markets in recent years, the share of corporate financing by financial intermediaries has been declining relative to the use of securities markets.

Although the dominance of financial intermediaries over securities markets is clear in all countries, the relative importance of bond versus stock markets differs widely across countries. In the United States, the bond market is far more important as a source of corporate finance: On average, the amount of new financing raised using bonds is ten times the amount raised using stocks. By contrast, countries such as France and Italy make more use of equities markets than of the bond market to raise capital.

*See, for example, Colin Mayer, "Financial Systems, Corporate Finance, and Economic Development," in *Asymmetric Information, Corporate Finance, and Investment*, ed. R. Glenn Hubbard (Chicago: University of Chicago Press, 1990), pp. 307–332.

over and over again in its loan transactions, thus lowering the legal cost per transaction. Instead of a loan contract (which may not be all that well written) costing $500, a bank can hire a topflight lawyer for $5,000 to draw up an airtight loan contract that can be used for 2,000 loans at a cost of $2.50 per loan. At a cost of $2.50 per loan, it now becomes profitable for the financial intermediary to lend Carl the $1,000.

Because financial intermediaries are able to reduce transaction costs substantially, they make it possible for you to provide funds indirectly to people like Carl with productive investment opportunities. In addition, a financial intermediary's low transaction costs mean that it can provide its customers with **liquidity services**, services that make it easier for customers to conduct transactions. For example, banks provide depositors with checking accounts that enable them to pay their bills easily. In addition, depositors can earn interest on checking and savings accounts and yet still convert them into goods and services whenever necessary.

Risk Sharing

Another benefit made possible by the low transaction costs of financial institutions is that they can help reduce the exposure of investors to **risk**—that is, uncertainty about the returns investors will earn on assets. Financial intermediaries do this through the process known as **risk sharing**: They create and sell assets with risk characteristics that people are comfortable with, and the intermediaries then use the funds they acquire by selling these assets to purchase other assets that may have far more risk. Low transaction costs allow financial intermediaries to share risk at low cost, enabling them to earn a profit on the spread between the returns they earn on risky assets and the payments they make on the assets they have sold. This process of risk sharing is also sometimes referred to as **asset transformation**, because in a sense, risky assets are turned into safer assets for investors.

Financial intermediaries also promote risk sharing by helping individuals to diversify and thereby lower the amount of risk to which they are exposed. **Diversification** entails investing in a collection (**portfolio**) of assets whose returns do not always move together, with the result that overall risk is lower than for individual assets. (Diversification is just another name for the old adage, "You shouldn't put all your eggs in one basket.") Low transaction costs allow financial intermediaries to do this by pooling a collection of assets into a new asset and then selling it to individuals.

Asymmetric Information: Adverse Selection and Moral Hazard

The presence of transaction costs in financial markets explains, in part, why financial intermediaries and indirect finance play such an important role in financial markets. An additional reason is that in financial markets, one party often does not know enough about the other party to make accurate decisions. This inequality is called **asymmetric information**. For example, a borrower who takes out a loan usually has better information about the potential returns and risk associated with the investment projects for which the funds are earmarked than the lender does. Lack of information creates problems in the financial system on two fronts: before the transaction is entered into and after.[1]

Adverse selection is the problem created by asymmetric information *before* the transaction occurs. Adverse selection in financial markets occurs when the potential borrowers who are the most likely to produce an undesirable (*adverse*) outcome—the bad credit risks—are the ones who most actively seek out a loan and are thus most likely to be selected. Because adverse selection makes it more likely that loans might be made to bad credit risks, lenders may decide not to make any loans even though there are good credit risks in the marketplace.

To understand why adverse selection occurs, suppose that you have two aunts to whom you might make a loan—Aunt Louise and Aunt Sheila. Aunt Louise is a conservative type who borrows only when she has an investment she is quite sure will pay off. Aunt Sheila, by contrast, is an inveterate gambler who has just come across a get-rich-quick scheme that will make her a millionaire if she can just borrow $1,000 to invest in it. Unfortunately, as with most get-rich-quick schemes, there is a high probability that the investment won't pay off and that Aunt Sheila will lose the $1,000.

Which of your aunts is more likely to call you to ask for a loan? Aunt Sheila, of course, because she has so much to gain if the investment pays off. You, however, would not want to make a loan to her because there is a high probability that her investment will turn sour and she will be unable to pay you back.

If you knew both your aunts very well—that is, if your information were not asymmetric—you wouldn't have a problem, because you would know that Aunt Sheila is a bad risk and so you would not lend to her. Suppose, though, that you don't know your aunts well. You are more likely to lend to Aunt Sheila than to Aunt Louise because Aunt Sheila would be hounding you for the loan. Because of the possibility of adverse selection, you might decide not to lend to either of your aunts, even though there are times when Aunt Louise, who is an excellent credit risk, might need a loan for a worthwhile investment.

---

[1]Asymmetric information and the adverse selection and moral hazard concepts are also crucial problems for the insurance industry. (see Chapter 12).

Moral hazard is the problem created by asymmetric information *after* the transaction occurs. Moral hazard in financial markets is the risk (*hazard*) that the borrower might engage in activities that are undesirable (*immoral*) from the lender's point of view, because they make it less likely that the loan will be paid back. Because moral hazard lowers the probability that the loan will be repaid, lenders may decide that they would rather not make a loan.

As an example of moral hazard, suppose that you made a $1,000 loan to another relative, Uncle Melvin, who needs the money to purchase a computer so he can set up a business typing students' term papers. Once you have made the loan, however, Uncle Melvin is more likely to slip off to the track and play the horses. If he bets on a 20-to-1 long shot and wins with your money, he is able to pay you back your $1,000 and live high off the hog with the remaining $19,000. But if he loses, as is likely, you don't get paid back, and all he has lost is his reputation as a reliable, upstanding uncle. Uncle Melvin therefore has an incentive to go to the track because his gains ($19,000) if he bets correctly are much greater than the cost to him (his reputation) if he bets incorrectly. If you knew what Uncle Melvin was up to, you would prevent him from going to the track, and he would not be able to increase the moral hazard. However, because it is hard for you to keep informed about his whereabouts—that is, because information is asymmetric—there is a good chance that Uncle Melvin will go to the track and you will not get paid back. The risk of moral hazard might therefore discourage you from making the $1,000 loan to Uncle Melvin, even if you were sure that you would be paid back if he used it to set up his business.

STUDY GUIDE

Because the concepts of adverse selection and moral hazard are extremely useful in understanding the behavior we examine in this and many of the later chapters (and in life in general), you must understand them fully. One way to distinguish between them is to remember that adverse selection is a problem of asymmetric information *before* entering into a transaction, whereas moral hazard is a problem of asymmetric information *after* the transaction has occurred. A helpful way to nail down these concepts is to think of other examples, for financial or other types of transactions, in which adverse selection or moral hazard plays a role. Several problems at the end of the chapter provide additional examples of situations involving adverse selection and moral hazard.

The problems created by adverse selection and moral hazard are an important impediment to well-functioning financial markets. Again, financial intermediaries can alleviate these problems.

With financial intermediaries in the economy, small savers can provide their funds to the financial markets by lending these funds to a trustworthy intermediary—say, the Honest John Bank—which in turn lends the funds out either by making loans or by buying securities such as stocks or bonds. Successful financial intermediaries have higher earnings on their investments than small savers, because they are better equipped than individuals to screen out bad credit risks from good ones, thereby reducing losses due to adverse selection. In addition, financial intermediaries have high earnings because they develop expertise in monitoring the parties they lend to, thus reducing losses due to moral hazard. The result is that financial intermediaries can afford to pay lender-savers interest or provide substantial services and still earn a profit.

As we have seen, financial intermediaries play an important role in the economy because they provide liquidity services, promote risk sharing, and solve information problems, thereby allowing small savers and borrowers to benefit from the existence of financial markets. The success of financial intermediaries in performing this role is evidenced by the fact that most Americans invest their savings with them and obtain loans from them. Financial intermediaries play a key role in improving economic efficiency because they help financial markets channel funds from lender-savers to people with productive investment opportunities. Without a well-functioning set of financial intermediaries, it is very hard for an economy to reach its full potential. We will explore further the role of financial intermediaries in the economy in Part III.

TYPES OF FINANCIAL INTERMEDIARIES

We have seen why financial intermediaries play such an important role in the economy. Now we look at the principal financial intermediaries themselves and how they perform the intermediation function. They fall into three categories: depository institutions (banks), contractual savings institutions, and investment intermediaries. Table 3 provides a guide to the discussion of the financial intermediaries that fit into these three categories by describing their primary liabilities (sources of funds) and assets (uses of funds). The relative size of these intermediaries in the United States is indicated in Table 4, which lists the amount of their assets at the end of 1980, 1990, 2000, and 2005.

Depository Institutions

Depository institutions (for simplicity, we refer to these as *banks* throughout this text) are financial intermediaries that accept deposits from individuals and institutions and make loans. The study of money and banking focuses special attention on this group of financial institutions, because they are involved in the creation of deposits, an important component of the money supply. These institutions include commercial banks and the so-called **thrift institutions (thrifts)**: savings and loan associations, mutual savings banks, and credit unions.

Commercial Banks.

These financial intermediaries raise funds primarily by issuing checkable deposits (deposits on which checks can be written), savings deposits (deposits that are payable on demand but do not allow their owner to write checks), and time deposits (deposits with fixed terms to maturity). They then use these funds to make commercial, consumer, and mortgage loans and to buy U.S. government securities and municipal bonds. There are slightly fewer than 7,500 commercial banks in the United States, and as a group, they are the largest financial intermediary and have the most diversified portfolios (collections) of assets.

Savings and Loan Associations (S&Ls) and Mutual Savings Banks.

These depository institutions, of which there are approximately 1,500, obtain funds primarily through savings deposits (often called *shares*) and time and checkable deposits. In the past, these institutions were constrained in their activities and mostly made mortgage loans for residential housing. Over time, these restrictions have been loosened so

TABLE 3 Primary Assets and Liabilities of Financial Intermediaries

Type of Intermediary	Primary Liabilities (Sources of Funds)	Primary Assets (Uses of Funds)
Depository institutions (banks)		
Commercial banks	Deposits	Business and consumer loans, mortgages, U.S. government securities and municipal bonds
Savings and loan associations	Deposits	Mortgages
Mutual savings banks	Deposits	Mortgages
Credit unions	Deposits	Consumer loans
Contractual savings institutions		
Life insurance companies	Premiums from policies	Corporate bonds and mortgages
Fire and casualty insurance companies	Premiums from policies	Municipal bonds, corporate bonds and stock, U.S. government securities
Pension funds, government retirement funds	Employer and employee contributions	Corporate bonds and stock
Investment intermediaries		
Finance companies	Commercial paper, stocks, bonds	Consumer and business loans
Mutual funds	Shares	Stocks, bonds
Money market mutual funds	Shares	Money market instruments

that the distinction between these depository institutions and commercial banks has blurred. These intermediaries have become more alike and are now more competitive with each other.

Credit Unions. These financial institutions, numbering about 8,900, are typically very small cooperative lending institutions organized around a particular group: union members, employees of a particular firm, and so forth. They acquire funds from deposits called *shares* and primarily make consumer loans.

Contractual Savings Institutions

Contractual savings institutions, such as insurance companies and pension funds, are financial intermediaries that acquire funds at periodic intervals on a contractual basis. Because they can predict with reasonable accuracy how much they will have to pay out in benefits in the coming years, they do not have to worry as much as depository institutions about losing funds quickly. As a result, the liquidity of assets is not as important a consideration for them as it is for depository institutions, and they tend to invest their funds primarily in long-term securities such as corporate bonds, stocks, and mortgages.

TABLE 4 Principal Financial Intermediaries and Value of Their Assets

	Value of Assets ($ billions, end of year)			
Type of Intermediary	**1980**	**1990**	**2000**	**2005**
Depository institutions (banks)				
Commercial banks	1,481	3,334	6,469	9,156
Savings and loan associations and mutual savings banks	792	1,365	1,218	1,750
Credit unions	67	215	441	688
Contractual savings institutions				
Life insurance companies	464	1,367	3,136	4,351
Fire and casualty insurance companies	182	533	862	1,242
Pension funds (private)	504	1,629	4,355	4,527
State and local government retirement funds	197	737	2,293	2,661
Investment intermediaries				
Finance companies	205	610	1,140	1,439
Mutual funds	70	654	4,435	5,882
Money market mutual funds	76	498	1,812	1,877

Source: Federal Reserve Flow of Funds Accounts: www.federalreserve.gov/releases/Z1/.

Life Insurance Companies. Life insurance companies insure people against financial hazards following a death and sell annuities (annual income payments upon retirement). They acquire funds from the premiums that people pay to keep their policies in force and use them mainly to buy corporate bonds and mortgages. They also purchase stocks, but are restricted in the amount that they can hold. Currently, with $4.4 trillion in assets, they are among the largest of the contractual savings institutions.

Fire and Casualty Insurance Companies. These companies insure their policyholders against loss from theft, fire, and accidents. They are very much like life insurance companies, receiving funds through premiums for their policies, but they have a greater possibility of loss of funds if major disasters occur. For this reason, they use their funds to buy more liquid assets than life insurance companies do. Their largest holding of assets is municipal bonds; they also hold corporate bonds and stocks and U.S. government securities.

Pension Funds and Government Retirement Funds. Private pension funds and state and local retirement funds provide retirement income in the form of annuities to employees who are covered by a pension plan. Funds are acquired by contributions from employers and from employees, who either have a contribution automatically deducted from their paychecks or contribute voluntarily. The largest asset holdings of pension funds are corporate bonds and stocks. The establishment of pension funds has been actively encouraged by the federal government, both through legislation requiring pension plans and through tax incentives to encourage contributions.

Investment Intermediaries

This category of financial intermediaries includes finance companies, mutual funds, and money market mutual funds.

Finance Companies. Finance companies raise funds by selling commercial paper (a short-term debt instrument) and by issuing stocks and bonds. They lend these funds to consumers, who make purchases of such items as furniture, automobiles, and home improvements, and to small businesses. Some finance companies are organized by a parent corporation to help sell its product. For example, Ford Motor Credit Company makes loans to consumers who purchase Ford automobiles.

Mutual Funds. These financial intermediaries acquire funds by selling shares to many individuals and use the proceeds to purchase diversified portfolios of stocks and bonds. Mutual funds allow shareholders to pool their resources so that they can take advantage of lower transaction costs when buying large blocks of stocks or bonds. In addition, mutual funds allow shareholders to hold more diversified portfolios than they otherwise would. Shareholders can sell (redeem) shares at any time, but the value of these shares will be determined by the value of the mutual fund's holdings of securities. Because these fluctuate greatly, the value of mutual fund shares will, too; therefore, investments in mutual funds can be risky.

Money Market Mutual Funds. These financial institutions have the characteristics of a mutual fund but also function to some extent as a depository institution because they offer deposit-type accounts. Like most mutual funds, they sell shares to acquire funds that are then used to buy money market instruments that are both safe and very liquid. The interest on these assets is paid out to the shareholders.

A key feature of these funds is that shareholders can write checks against the value of their shareholdings. In effect, shares in a money market mutual fund function like checking account deposits that pay interest. Money market mutual funds have experienced extraordinary growth since 1971, when they first appeared. By 2005, their assets had climbed to nearly $1.9 trillion.

Investment Banks. Despite its name, an investment bank is not a bank or a financial intermediary in the ordinary sense; that is, it does not take in deposits and then lend them out. Instead, an investment bank is a different type of intermediary that helps a corporation issue securities. First it advises the corporation on which type of securities to issue (stocks or bonds); then it helps sell (**underwrite**) the securities by purchasing them from the corporation at a predetermined price and reselling them in the market. Investment banks also act as deal makers and earn enormous fees by helping corporations acquire other companies through mergers or acquisitions.

REGULATION OF THE FINANCIAL SYSTEM

The financial system is among the most heavily regulated sectors of the American economy. The government regulates financial markets for two main reasons: to increase the information available to investors and to ensure the soundness of the financial system. We will examine how these two reasons have led to the present regulatory environment. As a study aid, the principal regulatory agencies of the U.S. financial system are listed in Table 5.

TABLE 5 Principal Regulatory Agencies of the U.S. Financial System

Regulatory Agency	Subject of Regulation	Nature of Regulations
Securities and Exchange Commission (SEC)	Organized exchanges and financial markets	Requires disclosure of information, restricts insider trading
Commodities Futures Trading Commission (CFTC)	Futures market exchanges	Regulates procedures for trading in futures markets
Office of the Comptroller of the Currency	Federally chartered commercial banks	Charters and examines the books of federally chartered commercial banks and imposes restrictions on assets they can hold
National Credit Union Administration (NCUA)	Federally chartered credit unions	Charters and examines the books of federally chartered credit unions and imposes restrictions on assets they can hold
State banking and insurance commissions	State-chartered depository institutions	Charter and examine the books of state-chartered banks and insurance companies, impose restrictions on assets they can hold, and impose restrictions on branching
Federal Deposit Insurance Corporation (FDIC)	Commercial banks, mutual savings banks, savings and loan associations	Provides insurance of up to $100,000 for each depositor at a bank, examines the books of insured banks, and imposes restrictions on assets they can hold
Federal Reserve System	All depository institutions	Examines the books of commercial banks that are members of the system, sets reserve requirements for all banks
Office of Thrift Supervision	Savings and loan associations	Examines the books of savings and loan associations, imposes restrictions on assets they can hold

Increasing Information Available to Investors

Asymmetric information in financial markets means that investors may be subject to adverse selection and moral hazard problems that may hinder the efficient operation of financial markets. Risky firms or outright crooks may be the most eager to sell securities to unwary investors, and the resulting adverse selection problem may keep investors out of financial markets. Furthermore, once an investor has bought a security, thereby lending money to a firm, the borrower may have incentives to engage in risky activities or to commit outright fraud. The presence of this moral hazard problem may also keep investors away from financial markets. Government regulation can reduce adverse selection and moral hazard problems in financial markets and increase their efficiency by increasing the amount of information available to investors.

As a result of the stock market crash in 1929 and revelations of widespread fraud in the aftermath, political demands for regulation culminated in the Securities Act of 1933 and the establishment of the Securities and Exchange Commission (SEC). The SEC requires corporations issuing securities to disclose certain information about their sales, assets, and earnings to the public and restricts trading by the largest stockholders (known as *insiders*) in the corporation. By requiring disclosure of this information and by discouraging insider trading, which could be used to manipulate security prices, the SEC hopes that investors will be better informed and protected from some of the abuses in financial markets that occurred before 1933. Indeed, in recent years, the SEC has been particularly active in prosecuting people involved in insider trading.

Ensuring the Soundness of Financial Intermediaries

Asymmetric information can lead to the widespread collapse of financial intermediaries, referred to as a **financial panic**. Because providers of funds to financial intermediaries may not be able to assess whether the institutions holding their funds are sound, if they have doubts about the overall health of financial intermediaries, they may want to pull their funds out of both sound and unsound institutions. The possible outcome is a financial panic that produces large losses for the public and causes serious damage to the economy. To protect the public and the economy from financial panics, the government has implemented six types of regulations.

Restrictions on Entry. State banking and insurance commissions, as well as the Office of the Comptroller of the Currency (an agency of the federal government), have created tight regulations governing who is allowed to set up a financial intermediary. Individuals or groups that want to establish a financial intermediary, such as a bank or an insurance company, must obtain a charter from the state or the federal government. Only if they are upstanding citizens with impeccable credentials and a large amount of initial funds will they be given a charter.

Disclosure. There are stringent reporting requirements for financial intermediaries. Their bookkeeping must follow certain strict principles, their books are subject to periodic inspection, and they must make certain information available to the public.

Restrictions on Assets and Activities. There are restrictions on what financial intermediaries are allowed to do and what assets they can hold. Before you put your funds into a bank or some other such institution, you would want to know that your funds are safe and that the bank or other financial intermediary will be able to meet its obligations to you. One way of doing this is to restrict the financial intermediary from engaging in certain risky activities. Legislation passed in 1933 (repealed in 1999) separated commercial banking from the securities industry so that banks could not engage in risky ventures associated with this industry. Another way to limit a financial intermediary's risky behavior is to restrict it from holding certain risky assets, or at least from holding a greater quantity of these risky assets than is prudent. For example, commercial banks and other depository institutions are not allowed to hold common stock because stock prices experience substantial fluctuations. Insurance companies are allowed to hold common stock, but their holdings cannot exceed a certain fraction of their total assets.

Deposit Insurance. The government can insure people's deposits so that they do not suffer great financial loss if the financial intermediary that holds these deposits should fail. The most important government agency that provides this type of insurance is the Federal Deposit Insurance Corporation (FDIC), which insures each depositor at a commercial bank or mutual savings bank up to a loss of $100,000 per account. All commercial and mutual savings banks, with a few minor exceptions, are contributers to the FDIC's Bank Insurance Fund, which is used to pay off depositors in the case of a bank's failure. The FDIC was created in 1934 after the massive bank failures of 1930–1933, in which the savings of many depositors at commercial banks were wiped out. Similar government agencies exist for other depository institutions: The Savings Association Insurance Fund (part of the FDIC) provides deposit insurance for savings and loan associations, and the National Credit Union Share Insurance Fund (NCUSIF) does the same for credit unions.

Limits on Competition. Politicians have often declared that unbridled competition among financial intermediaries promotes failures that will harm the public. Although the evidence that competition has this effect is extremely weak, it did not stop the state and federal governments from imposing restrictions on the opening of additional locations (branches). In the past, banks were not allowed to open up branches in other states, and in some states, banks were restricted from opening branches in additional locations.

Restrictions on Interest Rates. Competition has also been inhibited by regulations that impose restrictions on interest rates that can be paid on deposits. For decades after 1933, banks were prohibited from paying interest on checking accounts. In addition, until 1986, the Federal Reserve System had the power under *Regulation Q* to set maximum interest rates that banks could pay on savings deposits. These regulations were instituted because of the widespread belief that unrestricted interest-rate competition helped encourage bank failures during the Great Depression. Later evidence does not seem to support this view, and Regulation Q has been abolished (although there are still restrictions on paying interest on checking accounts held by businesses).

In later chapters, we will look more closely at government regulation of financial markets and will see whether it has improved their functioning.

Financial Regulation Abroad

Not surprisingly, given the similarity of the economic system here and in Japan, Canada, and the nations of Western Europe, financial regulation in these countries is similar to financial regulation in the United States. The provision of information is improved by requiring corporations issuing securities to report details about assets and liabilities, earnings, and sales of stock, and by prohibiting insider trading. The soundness of intermediaries is ensured by licensing, periodic inspection of financial intermediaries' books, and the provision of deposit insurance (although its coverage is smaller than in the United States and its existence is often intentionally not advertised).

The major differences between financial regulation in the United States and abroad relate to bank regulation. In the past, the United States was the only industrialized country to subject banks to restrictions on branching, which limited banks' size and restricted them to certain geographic regions. (These restrictions were abolished by legislation in 1994.) U.S. banks are also the most restricted in the range of assets they may hold. Banks abroad frequently hold shares in commercial firms; in Japan and Germany, those stakes can be sizable.

SUMMARY

1. The basic function of financial markets is to channel funds from savers who have an excess of funds to spenders who have a shortage of funds. Financial markets can do this either through direct finance, in which borrowers borrow funds directly from lenders by selling them securities, or through indirect finance, which involves a financial intermediary that stands between the lender-savers and the borrower-spenders and helps transfer funds from one to the other. This channeling of funds improves the economic welfare of everyone in the society. Because they allow funds to move from people who have no productive investment opportunities to those who have such opportunities, financial markets contribute to economic efficiency. In addition, channeling of funds directly benefits consumers by allowing them to make purchases when they need them most.
2. Financial markets can be classified as debt and equity markets, primary and secondary markets, exchanges and over-the-counter markets, and money and capital markets.
3. The principal money market instruments (debt instruments with maturities of less than one year) are U.S. Treasury bills, negotiable bank certificates of deposit, commercial paper, banker's acceptances, repurchase agreements, federal funds, and Eurodollars. The principal capital market instruments (debt and equity instruments with maturities greater than one year) are stocks, mortgages, corporate bonds, U.S. government securities, U.S. government agency securities, state and local government bonds, and consumer and bank commercial loans.
4. An important trend in recent years is the growing internationalization of financial markets. Eurobonds, which are denominated in a currency other than that of the country in which they are sold, are now the dominant security in the international bond market and have surpassed U.S. corporate bonds as a source of new funds. Eurodollars, which are U.S. dollars deposited in foreign banks, are an important source of funds for American banks.
5. Financial intermediaries are financial institutions that acquire funds by issuing liabilities and, in turn, use those funds to acquire assets by purchasing securities or making loans. Financial intermediaries play an important role in the financial system because they reduce transaction costs, allow risk sharing, and solve problems created by adverse selection and moral hazard. As a result, financial intermediaries allow small savers and borrowers to benefit from the existence of financial markets, thereby increasing the efficiency of the economy.
6. The principal financial intermediaries fall into three categories: (a) banks—commercial banks, savings and loan associations, mutual savings banks, and credit unions; (b) contractual savings institutions—life insurance companies, fire and casualty insurance companies, and pension funds; and (c) investment intermediaries—finance companies, mutual funds, and money market mutual funds.
7. The government regulates financial markets and financial intermediaries for two main reasons: to increase the information available to investors and to ensure the soundness of the financial system. Regulations include requiring disclosure of information to the public, restrictions on who can set up a financial intermediary, restrictions on what assets financial intermediaries can hold, the provision of deposit insurance, and reserve requirements.

KEY TERMS

adverse selection, p. 37
asset transformation, p. 37
asymmetric information, p. 37
brokers, p. 26
capital market, p. 27
currency, p. 29
dealers, p. 26
default, p. 29
diversification, p. 37
dividends, p. 26
economies of scale, p. 35
equities, p. 26
Eurobond, p. 33
Eurocurrencies, p. 33
Eurodollars, p. 33
exchanges, p. 27
federal funds rate, p. 31
financial intermediation, p. 35
financial panic, p. 44
foreign bonds, p. 33
intermediate-term, p. 26
investment bank, p. 26
liabilities, p. 24
liquid, p. 27
liquidity services, p. 36
long-term, p. 26
maturity, p. 25
money market, p. 27
moral hazard, p. 38
over-the-counter (OTC) market, p. 27
portfolio, p. 37
primary market, p. 26
risk, p. 36
risk sharing, p. 36
secondary market, p. 26
short-term, p. 26
thrift institutions (thrifts), p. 39
transaction costs, p. 35
underwriting, p. 26

QUESTIONS AND PROBLEMS

Questions marked with an asterisk are answered at the end of the book in an appendix, "Answers to Selected Questions and Problems." Questions marked with a blue circle indicate the question is available in MyEconLab at www.myeconlab.com/mishkin.

*1. Why is a share of Microsoft common stock an asset for its owner and a liability for Microsoft?

2. If I can buy a car today for $5,000 and it is worth $10,000 in extra income next year to me because it enables me to get a job as a traveling anvil seller, should I take out a loan from Larry the Loan Shark at a 90% interest rate if no one else will give me a loan? Will I be better or worse off as a result of taking out this loan? Can you make a case for legalizing loan-sharking?

*3. Some economists suspect that one of the reasons that economies in developing countries grow so slowly is that they do not have well-developed financial markets. Does this argument make sense?

4. The U.S. economy borrowed heavily from the British in the nineteenth century to build a railroad system. What was the principal debt instrument used? Why did this make both countries better off?

*5. "Because corporations do not actually raise any funds in secondary markets, they are less important to the economy than primary markets." Comment.

6. If you suspect that a company will go bankrupt next year, which would you rather hold, bonds issued by the company or equities issued by the company? Why?

*7. How can the adverse selection problem explain why you are more likely to make a loan to a family member than to a stranger?

8. Think of one example in which you have had to deal with the adverse selection problem.

*9. Why do loan sharks worry less about moral hazard in connection with their borrowers than some other lenders do?

10. If you are an employer, what kinds of moral hazard problems might you worry about with your employees?

*11. If there were no asymmetry in the information that a borrower and a lender had, could there still be a moral hazard problem?

12. "In a world without information and transaction costs, financial intermediaries would not exist." Is this statement true, false, or uncertain? Explain your answer.

*13. Why might you be willing to make a loan to your neighbor by putting funds in a savings account earning a 5% interest rate at the bank and having the bank lend her the funds at a 10% interest rate rather than lend her the funds yourself?

14. How does risk sharing benefit both financial intermediaries and private investors?

*15. Discuss some of the manifestations of the globalization of world capital markets.

WEB EXERCISES

1. One of the single best sources of information about financial institutions is the U.S. Flow of Funds report produced by the Federal Reserve. This document contains data on most financial intermediaries. Go to www.federalreserve.gov/releases/Z1/. Go to the most current release. You may have to load Acrobat Reader if your computer does not already have it; the site has a link for a free patch. Go to the Level Tables and answer the following.
   a. What percentage of assets do commercial banks hold in loans? What percentage of assets are held in mortgage loans?
   b. What percentage of assets do savings and loans hold in mortgage loans?
   c. What percentage of assets do credit unions hold in mortgage loans and in consumer loans?
2. The most famous financial market in the world is the New York Stock Exchange. Go to www.nyse.com.
   a. What is the mission of the NYSE?
   b. Firms must pay a fee to list their shares for sale on the NYSE. What would be the fee for a firm with five million common shares outstanding?

WEB REFERENCES

http://stockcharts.com/def/servlet/Favorites.CServlet?obj=msummary&cmd=show&disp=SXA

This site contains historical stock market index charts for many countries around the world.

www.nyse.com

New York Stock Exchange. Find listed companies, quotes, company historical data, real-time market indices, and more.

www.nasdaq.com

Detailed market and security information for the Nasdaq OTC stock exchange.

http://quote.yahoo.com/m2?u

Major world stock indexes, with charts, news, and components.

www.sec.gov

The United States Securities and Exchange Commission home page. It contains vast SEC resources, laws and regulations, investor information, and litigation.

CHAPTER

3 What Is Money?

Preview

If you had lived in America before the Revolutionary War, your money might have consisted primarily of Spanish doubloons (silver coins that were also called *pieces of eight*). Before the Civil War, the principal forms of money in the United States were gold and silver coins and paper notes, called *banknotes*, issued by private banks. Today, you use not only coins and dollar bills issued by the government as money, but also checks written on accounts held at banks. Money has been different things at different times, but it has *always* been important to people and to the economy.

To understand the effects of money on the economy, we must understand exactly what money is. In this chapter, we develop precise definitions by exploring the functions of money, looking at why and how it promotes economic efficiency, tracing how its forms have evolved over time, and examining how money is currently measured.

MEANING OF MONEY

As the word *money* is used in everyday conversation, it can mean many things, but to economists, it has a very specific meaning. To avoid confusion, we must clarify how economists' use of the word *money* differs from conventional usage.

Economists define *money* (also referred to as the *money supply*) as anything that is generally accepted in payment for goods or services or in the repayment of debts. Currency, consisting of dollar bills and coins, clearly fits this definition and is one type of money. When most people talk about money, they're talking about **currency** (paper money and coins). If, for example, someone comes up to you and says, "Your money or your life," you should quickly hand over all your currency rather than ask, "What exactly do you mean by 'money'?"

To define money merely as currency is much too narrow for economists. Because checks are also accepted as payment for purchases, checking account deposits are considered money as well. An even broader definition of money is often needed, because other items such as savings deposits can in effect function as money if they can be quickly and easily converted into currency or checking account deposits. As you can see, there is no single, precise definition of money or the money supply, even for economists.

To complicate matters further, the word *money* is frequently used synonymously with *wealth*. When people say, "Joe is rich—he has an awful lot of money," they probably mean that Joe not only has a lot of currency and a high balance in his checking account but also has stocks, bonds, four cars, three houses, and a yacht. Thus, while "currency" is too narrow a definition of money, this other popular usage is much too broad. Economists make a distinction between money in the form of currency, demand deposits, and other items that are used to make purchases and **wealth**, the total collection of pieces of property that serve to store value. Wealth includes not only money but also other assets such as bonds, common stock, art, land, furniture, cars, and houses.

People also use the word *money* to describe what economists call *income*, as in the sentence "Sheila would be a wonderful catch; she has a good job and earns a lot of money." **Income** is a *flow* of earnings per unit of time. Money, by contrast, is a *stock*: It is a certain amount at a given point in time. If someone tells you that he has an income of $1,000, you cannot tell whether he earned a lot or a little without knowing whether this $1,000 is earned per year, per month, or even per day. But if someone tells you that she has $1,000 in her pocket, you know exactly how much this is.

Keep in mind that the money discussed in this book refers to anything that is generally accepted in payment for goods and services or in the repayment of debts and is distinct from income and wealth.

FUNCTIONS OF MONEY

Whether money is shells or rocks or gold or paper, it has three primary functions in any economy: as a medium of exchange, as a unit of account, and as a store of value. Of the three functions, its function as a medium of exchange is what distinguishes money from other assets such as stocks, bonds, and houses.

Medium of Exchange

In almost all market transactions in our economy, money in the form of currency or checks is a **medium of exchange**; it is used to pay for goods and services. The use of money as a medium of exchange promotes economic efficiency by minimizing the time spent in exchanging goods and services. To see why, let's look at a *barter economy*, one without money, in which goods and services are exchanged directly for other goods and services.

Take the case of Ellen the Economics Professor, who can do just one thing well: give brilliant economics lectures. In a barter economy, if Ellen wants to eat, she must find a farmer who not only produces the food she likes but also wants to learn economics. As you might expect, this search will be difficult and time-consuming, and Ellen might spend more time looking for such an economics-hungry farmer than she will teaching. It is even possible that she will have to quit lecturing and go into farming herself. Even so, she may still starve to death.

The time spent trying to exchange goods or services is called a *transaction cost*. In a barter economy, transaction costs are high because people have to satisfy a "double coincidence of wants"—they have to find someone who has a good or service they want and who also wants the good or service they have to offer.

Let's see what happens if we introduce money into Ellen the Economics Professor's world. Ellen can teach anyone who is willing to pay money to hear her lecture. She can then go to any farmer (or his representative at the supermarket) and buy the food she needs with the money she has been paid. The problem of the double coincidence of wants is avoided, and Ellen saves a lot of time, which she may spend doing what she does best: teaching.

As this example shows, money promotes economic efficiency by eliminating much of the time spent exchanging goods and services. It also promotes efficiency by allowing people to specialize in what they do best. Money is therefore essential in an economy: It is a lubricant that allows the economy to run more smoothly by lowering transaction costs, thereby encouraging specialization and the division of labor.

The need for money is so strong that almost every society beyond the most primitive invents it. For a commodity to function effectively as money, it has to meet several criteria: (1) It must be easily standardized, making it simple to ascertain its value; (2) it must be widely accepted; (3) it must be divisible, so that it is easy to "make change"; (4) it must be easy to carry; and (5) it must not deteriorate quickly. Forms of money that have satisfied these criteria have taken many unusual forms throughout human history, ranging from wampum (strings of beads) used by Native Americans, to tobacco and whiskey, used by the early American colonists, to cigarettes, used in prisoner-of-war camps during World War II.[1] The diversity of forms of money that have been developed over the years is as much a testament to the inventiveness of the human race as the development of tools and language.

Unit of Account

The second role of money is to provide a **unit of account**; that is, it is used to measure value in the economy. We measure the value of goods and services in terms of money, just as we measure weight in terms of pounds or distance in terms of miles. To see why this function is important, let's look again at a barter economy where money does not perform this function. If the economy has only three goods—say, peaches, economics lectures, and movies—then we need to know only three prices to tell us how to exchange one for another: the price of peaches in terms of economics lectures (that is, how many economics lectures you have to pay for a peach), the price of peaches in terms of movies, and the price of economics lectures in terms of movies. If there were ten goods, we would need to know 45 prices to exchange one good for another; with 100 goods, we would need 4,950 prices; and with 1,000 goods, 499,500 prices.[2]

Imagine how hard it would be in a barter economy to shop at a supermarket with 1,000 different items on its shelves, having to decide whether chicken or fish is a better buy if the price of a pound of chicken were quoted as 4 pounds of butter and the price of a pound of fish as 8 pounds of tomatoes. To make it possible to compare prices, the tag on each item would have to list up to 999 different prices, and the time spent reading them would result in very high transaction costs.

The solution to the problem is to introduce money into the economy and have all prices quoted in terms of units of that money, enabling us to quote the price of

---

[1]An extremely entertaining article on the development of money in a prisoner-of-war camp during World War II is R. A. Radford, "The Economic Organization of a P.O.W. Camp," *Economica* 12 (November 1945): 189–201.

[2]The formula for telling us the number of prices we need when we have N goods is the same formula that tells us the number of pairs when there are N items. It is

$$\frac{N(N-1)}{2}$$

In the case of ten goods, for example, we would need

$$\frac{10(10-1)}{2} = \frac{90}{2} = 45$$

economics lectures, peaches, and movies in terms of, say, dollars. If there were only three goods in the economy, this would not be a great advantage over the barter system, because we would still need three prices to conduct transactions. But for ten goods we now need only ten prices; for 100 goods, 100 prices; and so on. At the 1,000-good supermarket, there are now only 1,000 prices to look at, not 499,500!

We can see that using money as a unit of account reduces transaction costs in an economy by reducing the number of prices that need to be considered. The benefits of this function of money grow as the economy becomes more complex.

Store of Value

Money also functions as a **store of value**; it is a repository of purchasing power over time. A store of value is used to save purchasing power from the time income is received until the time it is spent. This function of money is useful, because most of us do not want to spend our income immediately upon receiving it, but rather prefer to wait until we have the time or the desire to shop.

Money is not unique as a store of value; any asset—whether money, stocks, bonds, land, houses, art, or jewelry—can be used to store wealth. Many such assets have advantages over money as a store of value: They often pay the owner a higher interest rate than money, experience price appreciation, and deliver services such as providing a roof over one's head. If these assets are a more desirable store of value than money, why do people hold money at all?

The answer to this question relates to the important economic concept of **liquidity**, the relative ease and speed with which an asset can be converted into a medium of exchange. Liquidity is highly desirable. Money is the most liquid asset of all because it *is* the medium of exchange; it does not have to be converted into anything else to make purchases. Other assets involve transaction costs when they are converted into money. When you sell your house, for example, you have to pay a brokerage commission (usually 5% to 7% of the sales price), and if you need cash immediately to pay some pressing bills, you might have to settle for a lower price if you want to sell the house quickly. Because money is the most liquid asset, people are willing to hold it even if it is not the most attractive store of value.

How good a store of value money is depends on the price level, because its value is fixed in terms of the price level. A doubling of all prices, for example, means that the value of money has dropped by half; conversely, a halving of all prices means that the value of money has doubled. During inflation, when the price level is increasing rapidly, money loses value rapidly, and people will be more reluctant to hold their wealth in this form. This is especially true during periods of extreme inflation, known as **hyperinflation**, in which the inflation rate exceeds 50% per month.

Hyperinflation occurred in Germany after World War I, with inflation rates sometimes exceeding 1,000% per month. By the end of the hyperinflation in 1923, the price level had risen to more than 30 billion times what it had been just two years before. The quantity of money needed to purchase even the most basic items became excessive. There are stories, for example, that near the end of the hyperinflation, a wheelbarrow of cash would be required to pay for a loaf of bread. Money was losing its value so rapidly that workers were paid and given time off several times during the day to spend their wages before the money became worthless. No one wanted to hold on to money, so the use of money to carry out transactions declined and barter became more and more dominant. Transaction costs skyrocketed, and as we would expect, output in the economy fell sharply.

EVOLUTION OF THE PAYMENTS SYSTEM

We can obtain a better picture of the functions of money and the forms it has taken over time by looking at the evolution of the **payments system**, the method of conducting transactions in the economy. The payments system has been evolving over centuries, and with it the form of money. At one point, precious metals such as gold were used as the principal means of payment and were the main form of money. Later, paper assets such as checks and currency began to be used in the payments system and viewed as money. Where the payments system is heading has an important bearing on how money will be defined in the future.

Commodity Money

To obtain perspective on where the payments system is heading, it is worth exploring how it has evolved. For any object to function as money, it must be universally acceptable; everyone must be willing to take it in payment for goods and services. An object that clearly has value to everyone is a likely candidate to serve as money, and a natural choice is a precious metal such as gold or silver. Money made up of precious metals or another valuable commodity is called **commodity money**, and from ancient times until several hundred years ago, commodity money functioned as the medium of exchange in all but the most primitive societies. The problem with a payments system based exclusively on precious metals is that such a form of money is very heavy and is hard to transport from one place to another. Imagine the holes you'd wear in your pockets if you had to buy things only with coins! Indeed, for large purchases such as a house, you'd have to rent a truck to transport the money payment.

Fiat Money

The next development in the payments system was *paper currency* (pieces of paper that function as a medium of exchange). Initially, paper currency carried a guarantee that it was convertible into coins or into a fixed quantity of precious metal. However, currency has evolved into **fiat money**, paper currency decreed by governments as legal tender (meaning that legally it must be accepted as payment for debts) but not convertible into coins or precious metal. Paper currency has the advantage of being much lighter than coins or precious metal, but it can be accepted as a medium of exchange only if there is some trust in the authorities who issue it and if printing has reached a sufficiently advanced stage that counterfeiting is extremely difficult. Because paper currency has evolved into a legal arrangement, countries can change the currency that they use at will. Indeed, this is what many European countries did when they abandoned their currencies for the euro in 2002.

Major drawbacks of paper currency and coins are that they are easily stolen and can be expensive to transport in large amounts because of their bulk. To combat this problem, another step in the evolution of the payments system occurred with the development of modern banking: the invention of *checks*.

Checks

A check is an instruction from you to your bank to transfer money from your account to someone else's account when she deposits the check. Checks allow transactions to take place without the need to carry around large amounts of currency. The introduction of checks was a major innovation that improved the efficiency of the payments system. Frequently, payments made back and forth cancel each other; without checks, this would involve the movement of a lot of currency. With checks, payments that cancel each other can be settled by canceling the checks, and no currency need be moved. The use of checks thus reduces the transportation costs associated with the payments system and improves economic efficiency. Another advantage of checks is that they can be written for any amount up to the balance in the account, making transactions for large amounts much easier. Checks are also advantageous in that loss from theft is greatly reduced, and because they provide convenient receipts for purchases.

There are, however, two problems with a payments system based on checks. First, it takes time to get checks from one place to another, a particularly serious problem if you are paying someone in a different location who needs to be paid quickly. In addition, if you have a checking account, you know that it usually takes several business days before a bank will allow you to make use of the funds from a check you have deposited. If your need for cash is urgent, this feature of paying by check can be frustrating. Second, all the paper shuffling required to process checks is costly; it is estimated that it currently costs over $10 billion per year to process all the checks written in the United States.

Electronic Payment

The development of inexpensive computers and the spread of the Internet now make it cheap to pay bills electronically. In the past, you had to pay your bills by mailing a check, but now banks provide Web sites at which you just log on, make a few clicks, and thereby transmit your payment electronically. Not only do you save the cost of the stamp, but paying bills becomes (almost) a pleasure, requiring little effort. Electronic payment systems provided by banks now even spare you the step of logging on to pay the bill. Instead, recurring bills can be automatically deducted from your bank account. Estimated cost savings when a bill is paid electronically rather than by a check exceed one dollar per transaction. Electronic payment is thus becoming far more common in the United States, but Americans lag considerably behind Europeans, particularly Scandinavians, in their use of electronic payments (see the E-Finance box, "Why Are Scandinavians So Far Ahead of Americans in Using Electronic Payments?").

E-Money

Electronic payments technology can substitute not only for checks, but also for cash, in the form of **electronic money** (or **e-money**)—money that exists only in electronic form. The first form of e-money was the *debit card*. Debit cards, which look like credit cards, enable consumers to purchase goods and services by electronically transferring funds directly from their bank accounts to a merchant's account. Debit cards are used in many of the same places that accept credit cards and are now often becoming faster to use than cash. At most supermarkets, for example, you can swipe your debit card through the card reader at the checkout station, press a button, and the amount of your purchases is deducted from your bank account. Most banks and companies such as Visa and MasterCard issue debit cards, and your ATM card typically can function as a debit card.

A more advanced form of e-money is the *stored-value card*. The simplest form of stored-value card is purchased for a preset dollar amount that the consumer pays up front, like a prepaid phone card. The more sophisticated stored-value card is known as

E-Finance Why Are Scandinavians So Far Ahead of Americans in Using Electronic Payments?

Americans are the biggest users of checks in the world. Close to 100 billion checks are written every year in the United States, and over three-quarters of noncash transactions are conducted with paper. In contrast, in most countries of Europe, more than two-thirds of noncash transactions are electronic, with Finland and Sweden having the greatest proportion of online banking customers of any countries in the world. Indeed, if you were Finnish or Swedish, instead of writing a check, you would be far more likely to pay your bills online, using a personal computer or even a mobile phone. Why do Europeans and especially Scandinavians so far outpace Americans in the use of electronic payments?

First, Europeans got used to making payments without checks even before the advent of the personal computer. Europeans have long made use of *giro* payments, in which banks and post offices transfer funds for customers to pay bills. Second, Europeans—and particularly Scandinavians—are much greater users of mobile phones and the Internet than are Americans. Finland has the highest per capita use of mobile phones in the world, and Finland and Sweden lead the world in the percentage of the population that accesses the Internet. Maybe these usage patterns stem from the low population densities of these countries and the cold and dark winters that keep Scandinavians inside at their PCs. For their part, Scandinavians would rather take the view that their high-tech culture is the product of their good education systems and the resulting high degree of computer literacy, the presence of top technology companies such as Finland's Nokia and Sweden's Ericsson, and government policies promoting the increased use of personal computers, such as Sweden's tax incentives for companies to provide their employees with home computers. The wired populations of Finland and Sweden are (percentage-wise) the biggest users of online banking in the world.

Americans are clearly behind the curve in their use of electronic payments, which has imposed a high cost on the U.S. economy. Switching from checks to electronic payments might save the U.S. economy tens of billions of dollars per year, according to some estimates. Indeed, the U.S. federal government is trying to switch all its payments to electronic ones by directly depositing them into bank accounts, in an effort to reduce its expenses. Can Americans be weaned from paper checks and fully embrace the world of high-tech electronic payments?

a **smart card**. It contains a computer chip that allows it to be loaded with digital cash from the owner's bank account whenever needed. In Asian countries, such as Japan and Korea, cell phones now have a smart card feature that raises the expression, "pay by phone," to a new level. Smart cards can be loaded from ATM machines, personal computers with a smart card reader, or specially equipped telephones.

A third form of electronic money is often referred to as **e-cash**, which is used on the Internet to purchase goods or services. A consumer gets e-cash by setting up an account with a bank that has links to the Internet and then has the e-cash transferred to her PC. When she wants to buy something with e-cash, she surfs to a store on the Web and clicks the "buy" option for a particular item, whereupon the e-cash is automatically transferred from her computer to the merchant's computer. The merchant can then have the funds transferred from the consumer's bank account to his before the goods are shipped.

Given the convenience of e-money, you might think that we would move quickly to a cashless society in which all payments are made electronically. However, this hasn't happened, as discussed in the E-Finance box, "Are We Headed for a Cashless Society?"

E-Finance Are We Headed for a Cashless Society?

Predictions of a cashless society have been around for decades, but they have not come to fruition. For example, *Business Week* predicted in 1975 that electronic means of payment "would soon revolutionize the very concept of money itself," only to reverse itself several years later. Pilot projects in recent years with smart cards to convert consumers to the use of e-money have not been a success. Mondex, one of the widely touted, early stored-value cards that was launched in Great Britain in 1995, is only used on a few British university campuses. In Germany and Belgium, millions of people carry bank cards with computer chips embedded in them that enable them to make use of e-money, but very few use them. Why has the movement to a cashless society been so slow in coming?

Although e-money might be more convenient and may be more efficient than a payments system based on paper, several factors work against the disappearance of the paper system. First, it is very expensive to set up the computer, card reader, and telecommunications networks necessary to make electronic money the dominant form of payment. Second, electronic means of payment raise security and privacy concerns. We often hear media reports that an unauthorized hacker has been able to access a computer database and to alter information stored there. Because this is not an uncommon occurrence, unscrupulous persons might be able to access bank accounts in electronic payments systems and steal funds by moving them from someone else's accounts into their own. The prevention of this type of fraud is no easy task, and a whole new field of computer science has developed to cope with security issues. A further concern is that the use of electronic means of payment leaves an electronic trail that contains a large amount of personal data on buying habits. There are worries that government, employers, and marketers might be able to access these data, thereby encroaching on our privacy.

The conclusion from this discussion is that although the use of e-money will surely increase in the future, to paraphrase Mark Twain, "the reports of cash's death are greatly exaggerated."

MEASURING MONEY

The definition of money as anything that is generally accepted in payment for goods and services tells us that money is defined by people's behavior. What makes an asset money is that people believe it will be accepted by others when making payment. As we have seen, many different assets have performed this role over the centuries, ranging from gold to paper currency to checking accounts. For that reason, this behavioral definition does not tell us which assets in our economy should be considered money. To measure money, we need a precise definition that tells us exactly which assets should be included.

The Federal Reserve's Monetary Aggregates

The Federal Reserve System (the Fed), the central banking authority responsible for monetary policy in the United States, has conducted many studies on how to measure money. The problem of measuring money has recently become especially crucial because extensive financial innovation has produced new types of assets that might properly belong in a measure of money. Since 1980, the Fed has modified its measures

TABLE 1 Measures of the Monetary Aggregates

	Value as of December 2005 ($ billions)
M1 = Currency	725.2
+ Traveler's checks	7.3
+ Demand deposits	338.8
+ Other checkable deposits	317.8
Total M1	1,389.1
M2 = M1	
+ Small-denomination time deposits	968.8
+ Savings deposits and money market deposit accounts	3626.5
+ Money market mutual fund shares (retail)	723.9
Total M2	5,319.2

Source: www.federalreserve.gov/releases/h6/hist.

of money several times and has settled on the following measures of the money supply, which are also referred to as **monetary aggregates** (see Table 1 and the Following the Financial News box).

The narrowest measure of money that the Fed reports is **M1**, which includes currency, checking account deposits, and traveler's checks. The components of M1 are shown in Table 1. The *currency* component of M1 includes only paper money and coins in the hands of the nonbank public and does not include cash that is held in ATMs or banks vaults. Suprisingly, there is more than $2,000 cash in circulation for each person in the United States (see the FYI box). The *traveler's checks* component of M1 includes only traveler's checks not issued by banks. The *demand deposits* component includes business checking accounts that do not pay interest as well as traveler's checks issued by banks. The *other checkable deposits* item includes all other checkable deposits, particularly checking accounts held by households that pay interest. These assets are clearly money, because they can be used directly as a medium of exchange.

Until the mid-1970s, only commercial banks were permitted to establish checking accounts, and they were not allowed to pay interest on them. With the financial innovation that has occurred (discussed more extensively in Chapter 10), regulations have changed so that other types of banks, such as savings and loan associations, mutual savings banks, and credit unions, can also offer checking accounts. In addition, banking institutions can offer other checkable deposits, such as NOW (negotiated order of withdrawal) accounts and ATS (automatic transfer from savings) accounts, that do pay interest on their balances.

The **M2** monetary aggregate adds to M1 other assets that have check-writing features (money market deposit accounts and money market mutual fund shares) and other assets (savings deposits and small-denomination time deposits) that are extremely liquid, because they can be turned into cash quickly at very little cost. *Small-denomination time deposits* are certificates of deposit with a denomination of less than

Following the Financial News The Monetary Aggregates

Data for the Federal Reserve's monetary aggregates (M1 and M2) are published every Friday. In the *Wall Street Journal*, the data are found in the "Federal Reserve Data" column, an example of which is presented here.

The third entry indicates that the money supply (M2) averaged $6,725.1 billion for the week ending January 2, 2006. The notation "sa" for this entry indicates that the data are seasonally adjusted; that is, seasonal movements, such as those associated with Christmas shopping, have been removed from the data. The notation "nsa" indicates that the data have not been seasonally adjusted.

Federal Reserve Data

MONETARY AGGREGATES

(daily average in billions)

	1 WEEK ENDED: Jan. 2	Dec. 26
Money supply (M1) sa	1387.7	1388.9
Money supply (M1) nsa	1458.4	1459.8
Money supply (M2) sa	6725.1	6711.5
Money supply (M2) nsa	6733.9	6715.9
	4 WEEKS ENDED: Jan. 2	**Dec. 5**
Money supply (M1) sa	1375.2	1372.8
Money supply (M1) nsa	1410.8	1375.6
Money supply (M2) sa	6699.8	6651.7
Money supply (M2) nsa	6717.6	6670.6
	MONTH Dec.	**Nov.**
Money supply (M1) sa	1372.3	1372.7
Money supply (M2) sa	6691.5	6652.9

nsa-Not seasonally adjusted. sa-Seasonally adjusted.

Source: Wall Street Journal, January 13, 2006, p. C12.

$100,000 that can only be redeemed at a fixed maturity date without a penalty. *Savings deposits* are non-transactions deposits that can be added to or taken out at any time. *Money market deposit accounts* are similar to money market mutual funds, but are issued by banks. The *money market mutual fund shares* are retail accounts on which households can write checks.

Because we cannot be sure which of the monetary aggregates is the true measure of money, it is logical to wonder if their movements closely parallel one another. If they do, then using one monetary aggregate to predict future economic performance and to conduct policy will be the same as using another, and it does not matter much that we are not sure of the appropriate definition of money for a given policy decision. However, if the monetary aggregates do not move together, then what one monetary aggregate tells us is happening to the money supply might be quite different from what another monetary aggregate would tell us. The conflicting stories might present a confusing picture that would make it hard for policymakers to decide on the right course of action.

FYI Where Are All the U.S. Dollars?

The more than $2,000 of U.S. currency held per person in the United States is a surprisingly large number. U.S. currency is bulky, can be easily stolen, and pays no interest, so it doesn't make sense for most of us to keep a lot of it. Do you know anyone who carries $2,000 in his or her pockets? We have a puzzle: Where are all these dollars and who is holding them?

Criminals are one group who hold a lot of dollars. If you were engaged in illegal activity, you would not conduct your transactions with checks because they are traceable and therefore a potentially powerful piece of evidence against you. That explains why Tony Soprano has so much cash in his backyard. Some businesses also like to retain a lot of cash because if they operate as a cash business that makes their transactions less traceable; thus they can avoid declaring income on which they would have to pay taxes.

Foreigners are the other group who routinely hold U.S. dollars. In many countries, people do not trust their own currency because they often experience high inflation, which erodes the value of that currency; these people hold U.S. dollars as a hedge against this inflation risk. Lack of trust in the ruble, for example, has led Russians to hoard enormous amounts of U.S. dollars. More than half the quantity of U.S. dollars are held abroad.

Figure 1 plots the growth rates of M1 and M2 from 1960 to 2005. The growth rates of these two monetary aggregates do tend to move together; the timing of their rise and fall is roughly similar until the 1990s, and they both show a higher growth rate on average in the 1970s than in the 1960s.

Yet some glaring discrepancies exist in the movements of these aggregates. According to M1, the growth rate of money did not accelerate between 1968, when it was in the 6–7% range, and 1971, when it was at a similar level. In the same period, the M2 measure tells a different story; it shows a marked acceleration from the 8–10% range to the 12–15% range. Similarly, while the growth rate of M1 actually increased from 1989 to 1992, the growth rate of M2 in this same period instead showed a downward trend. Furthermore, from 1992 to 1998, the growth rate of M1 fell sharply while the growth rate of M2 rose substantially; from 1998 to 2002, M1 growth generally remained well below M2 growth. Thus, the different measures of money tell a very different story about the course of monetary policy in recent years.

From the data in Figure 1, you can see that obtaining a single precise, correct measure of money does seem to matter and that it does make a difference which monetary aggregate policymakers and economists choose as the true measure of money.

HOW RELIABLE ARE THE MONEY DATA?

The difficulties of measuring money arise not only because it is hard to decide what is the best definition of money, but also because the Fed frequently later revises earlier estimates of the monetary aggregates by large amounts. There are two reasons why the Fed revises its figures. First, because small depository institutions need to report the amounts of their deposits only infrequently, the Fed has to estimate these amounts until

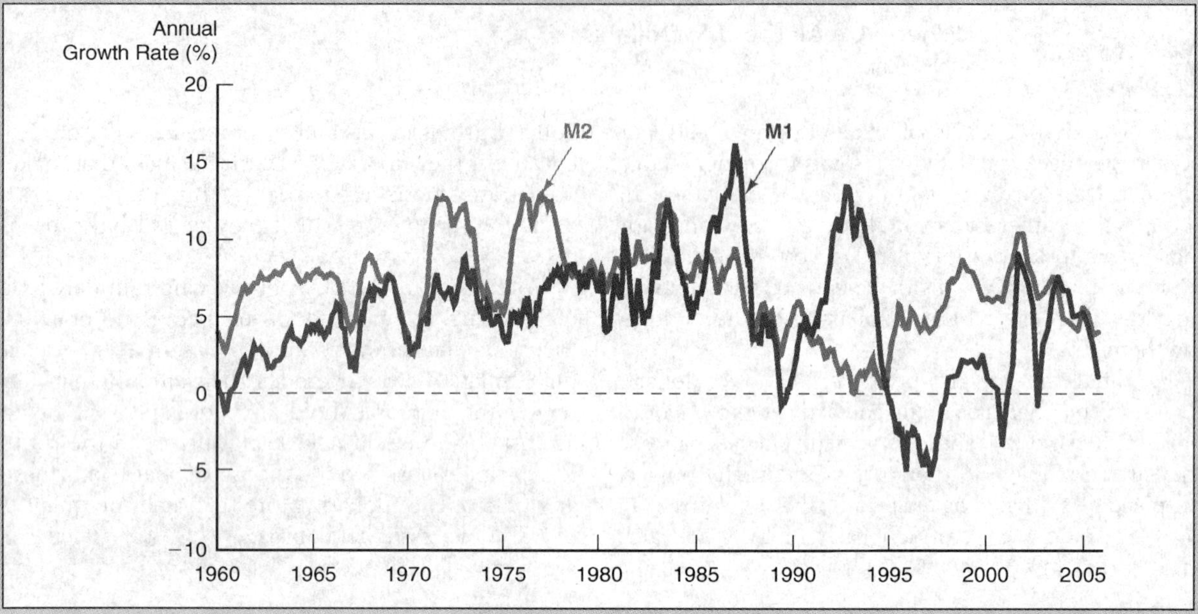

FIGURE 1 **Growth Rates of the M1 and M2 Aggregates, 1960–2005**

Sources: Federal Reserve *Bulletin*, p. A4, Table 1.10, various issues; Citibase databank; www.federalreserve.gov/releases/h6/hist/h6hist1.txt.

these institutions provide the actual figures at some future date. Second, the adjustment of the data for seasonal variation is revised substantially as more data become available. To see why this happens, let's look at an example of the seasonal variation of the money data around Christmastime. The monetary aggregates always rise around Christmas because of increased spending during the holiday season; the increase is greater in some years than in others. This means that the factor that adjusts the data for the seasonal variation due to Christmas must be estimated from several years of data, and the estimates of this seasonal factor become more precise only as more data become available. When the data on the monetary aggregates are revised, the seasonal adjustments often change dramatically from the initial calculation.

Table 2 shows how severe a problem these data revisions can be. It provides annual rates of money growth for one-month periods calculated from initial estimates of the M2 monetary aggregate, along with the rates of money growth calculated from a major revision of the M2 numbers. As the table shows, for one-month periods the initial versus the revised data can give a different picture of what is happening to monetary policy. For January 2005, for example, the initial data indicated that the growth rate of M2 at an annual rate was 6.1%, whereas the revised data indicate a much lower growth rate of 2.7%.

A distinctive characteristic shown in Table 2 is that the differences between the initial and revised M2 series tend to cancel out. You can see this by looking at the last row of the table, which shows the average rate of M2 growth for the two series and the average difference between them. The average M2 growth for the initial calculation of M2 is 4.5%, and the revised number is 3.9%, a difference of 0.6%. The conclusion we can draw is that the initial data on the monetary aggregates reported by the Fed are not a

TABLE 2 Growth Rate of M2: Initial and Revised Series, 2005 (percent, compounded annual rate)

Period	Initial Rate	Revised Rate	Difference (Revised Rate − Initial Rate)
January	6.1	2.7	−3.4
February	2.5	3.6	1.1
March	5.9	3.6	−2.3
April	−1.0	1.1	2.1
May	−1.0	1.6	2.6
June	7.2	4.9	−2.3
July	1.4	3.7	2.3
August	7.3	5.5	−1.7
September	6.9	5.5	−1.4
October	7.0	5.3	−1.7
November	4.7	3.9	−0.8
December	7.0	5.1	−1.9
Average	4.5	3.9	−0.6

Source: Federal Reserve Statistical Release H.6: www.federalreserve.gov/releases/h6.

reliable guide to what is happening to short-run movements in the money supply, such as the one-month growth rates. However, the initial money data are reasonably reliable for longer periods, such as a year. The moral is that ***we probably should not pay much attention to short-run movements in the money supply numbers, but should be concerned only with longer-run movements.***

SUMMARY

1. To economists, the word *money* has a different meaning from *income* or *wealth*. Money is anything that is generally accepted as payment for goods or services or in the repayment of debts.
2. Money serves three primary functions: as a medium of exchange, as a unit of account, and as a store of value. Money as a medium of exchange avoids the problem of double coincidence of wants that arises in a barter economy, and thus lowers transaction costs and encouraging specialization and the division of labor. Money as a unit of account reduces the number of prices needed in the economy, which also reduces transaction costs. Money also functions as a store of value, but performs this role poorly if it is rapidly losing value due to inflation.
3. The payments system has evolved over time. Until several hundred years ago, the payments system in all but the most primitive societies was based primarily on precious metals. The introduction of paper currency lowered the cost of transporting money. The next major advance was the introduction of checks, which lowered transaction costs still further. We are currently moving toward an electronic payments system in which paper is eliminated and all transactions are handled by computers. Despite the potential efficiency of such a system, obstacles are slowing the movement to the checkless society and the development of new forms of electronic money.

4. The Federal Reserve System has defined two different measures of the money supply—M1 and M2. These measures are not equivalent and do not always move together, so they cannot be used interchangeably by policymakers. Obtaining the precise, correct measure of money does seem to matter and has implications for the conduct of monetary policy.

5. Another problem in the measurement of money is that the data are not always as accurate as we would like. Substantial revisions in the data do occur; they indicate that initially released money data are not a reliable guide to short-run (say, month-to-month) movements in the money supply, although they are more reliable over longer periods of time, such as a year.

KEY TERMS

commodity money, p. 53
currency, p. 49
e-cash, p. 55
electronic money (e-money), p. 54
fiat money, p. 53
hyperinflation, p. 52
income, p. 50
liquidity, p. 52
M1, p. 57
M2, p. 57
medium of exchange, p. 50
monetary aggregates, p. 57
payments system, p. 53
smart card, p. 55
store of value, p. 52
unit of account, p. 51
wealth, p. 50

QUESTIONS AND PROBLEMS

Questions marked with an asterisk are answered at the end of the book in an appendix, "Answers to Selected Questions and Problems." Questions marked with a blue circle indicate the question is available in MyEconLab at www.myeconlab.com/mishkin.

1. Which of the following three expressions uses the economists' definition of money?
   a. "How much money did you earn last week?"
   b. "When I go to the store, I always make sure that I have enough money."
   c. "The love of money is the root of all evil."

*2. There are three goods produced in an economy by three individuals:

Good	*Producer*
Apples	Orchard owner
Bananas	Banana grower
Chocolate	Chocolatier

If the orchard owner likes only bananas, the banana grower likes only chocolate, and the chocolatier likes only apples, will any trade between these three persons take place in a barter economy? How will introducing money into the economy benefit these three producers?

3. Why did cavemen not need money?

*4. Why were people in the United States in the nineteenth century sometimes willing to be paid by check rather than with gold, even though they knew that there was a possibility that the check might bounce?

5. In ancient Greece, why was gold a more likely candidate for use as money than wine was?

*6. Was money a better store of value in the United States in the 1950s than it was in the 1970s? Why or why not? In which period would you have been more willing to hold money?

7. Would you be willing to give up your checkbook and instead use an electronic means of payment if it were made available? Why or why not?

8. Rank the following assets from most liquid to least liquid:
   a. Checking account deposits
   b. Houses
   c. Currency
   d. Washing machines
   e. Savings deposits
   f. Common stock

*9. Why have some economists described money during a hyperinflation as a "hot potato" that is quickly passed from one person to another?

10 In Brazil, a country that was undergoing a rapid inflation before 1994, many transactions were conducted in dollars rather than in reals, the domestic currency. Why?

*11. Suppose that a researcher discovers that a measure of the total amount of debt in the U.S. economy over the past twenty years was a better predictor of inflation and the business cycle than M1 or M2. Does this discovery mean that we should define money as equal to the total amount of debt in the economy?

12 Look up the M1 and M2 numbers in the Federal Reserve *Bulletin* for the most recent one-year period. Have their growth rates been similar? What implications do their growth rates have for the conduct of monetary policy?

*13 Which of the Federal Reserve's measures of the monetary aggregates—M1 or M2—is composed of the most liquid assets? Which is the largest measure?

14 For each of the following assets, indicate which of the monetary aggregates (M1 and M2) includes them:
a. Currency
b. Money market mutual funds
c. Small-denomination time deposits
d. Checkable deposits

*15. Why are revisions of monetary aggregates less of a problem for measuring long-run movements of the money supply than they are for measuring short-run movements?

WEB EXERCISES

1. Go to www.federalreserve.gov/releases/h6/Current/.
   a. What has been the growth rate in M1 and M2 over the last twelve months?
   b. From what you know about the state of the economy, does this seem expansionary or restrictive?
2. Go to www.federalreserve.gov/paymentsys.htm and select one topic on which the Federal Reserve has a written policy. Write a one-paragraph summary of this policy.

WEB REFERENCES

www.federalreserve.gov/paymentsys.htm

This site reports on the Federal Reserve's policies regarding payments systems.

www.federalreserve.gov/releases/h6/Current/

The Federal Reserve reports the current levels of M1 and M2 on its web site.

PART

2

Financial Markets

CHAPTER

4 Understanding Interest Rates

Preview

Interest rates are among the most closely watched variables in the economy. Their movements are reported almost daily by the news media, because they directly affect our everyday lives and have important consequences for the health of the economy. They affect personal decisions such as whether to consume or save, whether to buy a house, and whether to purchase bonds or put funds into a savings account. Interest rates also affect the economic decisions of businesses and households, such as whether to use their funds to invest in new equipment for factories or to save their money in a bank.

Before we can go on with the study of money, banking, and financial markets, we must understand exactly what the phrase *interest rates* means. In this chapter, we see that a concept known as the *yield to maturity* is the most accurate measure of interest rates; the yield to maturity is what economists mean when they use the term *interest rate*. We discuss how the yield to maturity is measured and examine alternative (but less accurate) ways in which interest rates are quoted. We'll also see that a bond's interest rate does not necessarily indicate how good an investment the bond is because what it earns (its rate of return) does not necessarily equal its interest rate. Finally, we explore the distinction between real interest rates, which are adjusted for inflation, and nominal interest rates, which are not.

Although learning definitions is not always the most exciting of pursuits, it is important to read carefully and understand the concepts presented in this chapter. Not only are they continually used throughout the remainder of this text, but a firm grasp of these terms will give you a clearer understanding of the role that interest rates play in your life as well as in the general economy.

MEASURING INTEREST RATES

Different debt instruments have very different streams of cash payments to the holder (known as **cash flows**) with very different timing. Thus we first need to understand how we can compare the value of one kind of debt instrument with another before we see how interest rates are measured. To do this, we make use of the concept of *present value*.

Present Value

The concept of **present value** (or **present discounted value**) is based on the commonsense notion that a dollar paid to you one year from now is less valuable to you than a dollar paid to you today: This notion is true because you can deposit a dollar today in a savings account that earns interest and have more than a dollar in one year. Economists use a more formal definition, as explained in this section.

Let's look at the simplest kind of debt instrument, which we will call a **simple loan.** In this loan, the lender provides the borrower with an amount of funds (called the *principal*) that must be repaid to the lender at the *maturity date*, along with an additional payment for the interest. For example, if you made your friend, Jane, a simple loan of $100 for one year, you would require her to repay the principal of $100 in one year's time along with an additional payment for interest—say, $10. In the case of a simple loan like this one, the interest payment divided by the amount of the loan is a natural and sensible way to measure the interest rate. This measure of the so-called *simple interest rate*, i, is

$$i = \frac{\$10}{\$100} = 0.10 = 10\%$$

If you make this $100 loan, at the end of the year you would have $110, which can be rewritten as

$$\$100 \times (1 + 0.10) = \$110$$

If you then lent out the $110, at the end of the second year you would have

$$\$110 \times (1 + 0.10) = \$121$$

or, equivalently,

$$\$100 \times (1 + 0.10) \times (1 + 0.10) = \$100 \times (1 + 0.10)^2 = \$121$$

Continuing with the loan again, you would have at the end of the third year

$$\$121 \times (1 + 0.10) = \$100 \times (1 + 0.10)^3 = \$133$$

Generalizing, we can see that at the end of n years, your $100 would turn into

$$\$100 \times (1 + i)^n$$

The amounts you would have at the end of each year by making the $100 loan today can be seen in the following timeline:

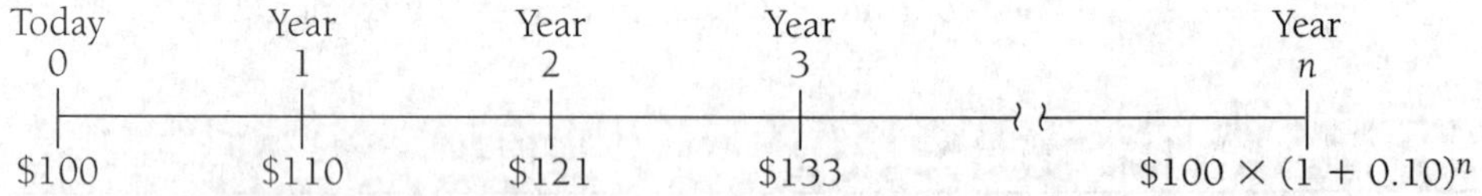

This timeline immediately tells you that you are just as happy having $100 today as having $110 a year from now (of course, as long as you are sure that Jane will pay you back). You are also just as happy having $100 today as having $121 two years from now, or $133 three years from now or $\$100 \times (1 + 0.10)^n$ n years from now. The timeline tells us that we can also work backward from future amounts to the present. For example, $\$133 = \$100 \times (1 + 0.10)^3$ three years from now is worth $100 today, so that

$$\$100 = \frac{\$133}{(1 + 0.10)^3}$$

The process of calculating today's value of dollars received in the future, as we have done above, is called *discounting the future*. We can generalize this process by writing today's (present) value of \$100 as *PV*, the future cash flow (payment) of \$133 as *CF*, and replacing 0.10 (the 10% interest rate) by *i*. This leads to the following formula:

$$PV = \frac{CF}{(1 + i)^n} \tag{1}$$

Intuitively, Equation 1 tells us that if you are promised \$1 of cash flow for certain ten years from now, this dollar would not be as valuable to you as \$1 is today because if you had the \$1 today, you could invest it and end up with more than \$1 in ten years.

The concept of present value is extremely useful, because it allows us to figure out today's value (price) of a credit (debt) market instrument at a given simple interest rate *i* by just adding up the individual present values of all the future payments received. This information allows us to compare the values of two or more instruments with very different timing of their payments.

APPLICATION Simple Present Value

What is the present value of \$250 to be paid in two years if the interest rate is 15%?

Solution

The present value would be \$189.04. Using Equation 1

$$PV = \frac{CF}{(1 + i)^n}$$

where

$$\begin{aligned} CF &= \text{cash flow in two years} &&= \$250 \\ i &= \text{annual interest rate} &&= 0.15 \\ n &= \text{number of years} &&= 2 \end{aligned}$$

Thus

$$PV = \frac{\$250}{(1 + 0.15)^2} = \frac{\$250}{1.3225} = \$189.04$$

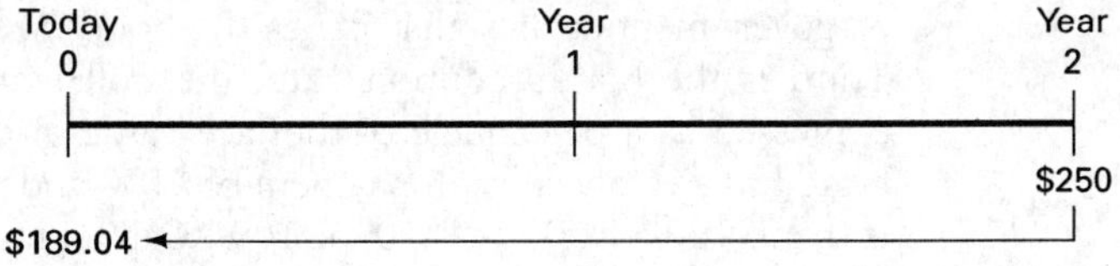

APPLICATION How Much Is That Jackpot Worth?

Assume that you just hit the \$20 million jackpot in the New York State Lottery, which promises you a payment of \$1 million for the next twenty years. You are clearly excited, but have you really won \$20 million?

Solution

No, not in the present value sense. In today's dollars, that \$20 million is worth a lot less. If we assume an interest rate of 10% as in the earlier examples, the first payment of \$1 million is clearly worth \$1 million today, but the next payment next year is only worth \$1 million/(1 + 0.10) = \$909,090, a lot less than \$1 million. The following year the payment is worth \$1 million/$(1 + 0.10)^2$ = \$826,446 in today's dollars, and so on. When you add all these up, they come to \$9.4 million. You are still pretty excited (who wouldn't be?), but because you understand the concept of present value, you recognize that you are the victim of false advertising. In present value terms, you didn't really win \$20 million, but instead won less than half as much.

Four Types of Credit Market Instruments

In terms of the timing of their cash flow payments, there are four basic types of credit market instruments.

1. A simple loan, which we have already discussed, in which the lender provides the borrower with an amount of funds, which must be repaid to the lender at the maturity date along with an additional payment for the interest. Many money market instruments are of this type—for example, commercial loans to businesses.

2. A **fixed-payment loan** (which is also called a **fully amortized loan**) in which the lender provides the borrower with an amount of funds, which must be repaid by making the same payment every period (such as a month), consisting of part of the principal and interest for a set number of years. For example, if you borrowed \$1,000, a fixed-payment loan might require you to pay \$126 every year for 25 years. Installment loans (such as auto loans) and mortgages are frequently of the fixed-payment type.

3. A **coupon bond** pays the owner of the bond a fixed interest payment (coupon payment) every year until the maturity date, when a specified final amount (**face value** or **par value**) is repaid. (The coupon payment is so named because the bondholder used to obtain payment by clipping a coupon off the bond and sending it to the bond issuer, who then sent the payment to the holder. Nowadays, it is no longer necessary to send in coupons to receive these payments.) A coupon bond with \$1,000 face value, for example, might pay you a coupon payment of \$100 per year for ten years, and at the maturity date repay you the face value amount of \$1,000. (The face value of a bond is usually in \$1,000 increments.)

A coupon bond is identified by three pieces of information. First is the corporation or government agency that issues the bond. Second is the maturity date of the bond. Third is the bond's **coupon rate,** the dollar amount of the yearly coupon payment expressed as a percentage of the face value of the bond. In our example, the coupon bond has a yearly coupon payment of \$100 and a face value of \$1,000. The coupon rate is then \$100/\$1,000 = 0.10, or 10%. Capital market instruments such as U.S. Treasury bonds and notes and corporate bonds are examples of coupon bonds.

4. A **discount bond** (also called a **zero-coupon bond**) is bought at a price below its face value (at a discount), and the face value is repaid at the maturity date. Unlike a coupon bond, a discount bond does not make any interest payments; it just pays off the face value. For example, a one-year discount bond with a face value of \$1,000 might be bought for \$900; in a year's time the owner would be repaid the face value of \$1,000. U.S. Treasury bills, U.S. savings bonds, and long-term zero-coupon bonds are examples of discount bonds.

These four types of instruments require payments at different times: Simple loans and discount bonds make payment only at their maturity dates, whereas fixed-payment loans and coupon bonds have payments periodically until maturity. How would you decide which of these instruments provides you with more income? They all seem so different because they make payments at different times. To solve this problem, we use the concept of present value, explained earlier, to provide us with a procedure for measuring interest rates on these different types of instruments.

Yield to Maturity

Of the several common ways of calculating interest rates, the most important is the **yield to maturity**, the interest rate that equates the present value of cash flow payments received from a debt instrument with its value today.[1] Because the concept behind the calculation of the yield to maturity makes good economic sense, economists consider it the most accurate measure of interest rates.

To understand the yield to maturity better, we now look at how it is calculated for the four types of credit market instruments.

Simple Loan. Using the concept of present value, the yield to maturity on a simple loan is easy to calculate. For the one-year loan we discussed, today's value is \$100, and the payments in one year's time would be \$110 (the repayment of \$100 plus the interest payment of \$10). We can use this information to solve for the yield to maturity i by recognizing that the present value of the future payments must equal today's value of a loan.

APPLICATION Yield to Maturity on a Simple Loan

If Pete borrows \$100 from his sister and next year she wants \$110 back from him, what is the yield to maturity on this loan?

Solution

The yield to maturity on the loan is 10%.

$$PV = \frac{CF}{(1+i)^n}$$

where

$$\begin{aligned} PV &= \text{amount borrowed} &&= \$100 \\ CF &= \text{cash flow in one year} &&= \$110 \\ n &= \text{number of years} &&= 1 \end{aligned}$$

Thus

$$\$100 = \frac{\$110}{(1+i)}$$

$$(1+i)\$100 = \$110$$

$$(1+i) = \frac{\$110}{\$100}$$

$$i = 1.10 - 1 = 0.10 = 10\%$$

[1]In other contexts, it is also called the *internal rate of return*.

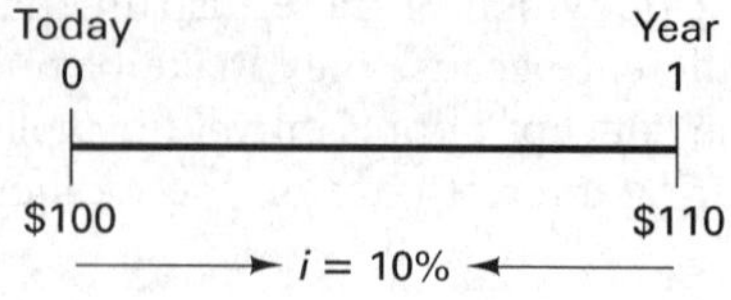

This calculation of the yield to maturity should look familiar, because it equals the interest payment of $10 divided by the loan amount of $100; that is, it equals the simple interest rate on the loan. An important point to recognize is that ***for simple loans, the simple interest rate equals the yield to maturity.*** Hence the same term i is used to denote both the yield to maturity and the simple interest rate.

STUDY GUIDE

The key to understanding the calculation of the yield to maturity is equating today's value of the debt instrument with the present value of all of its future cash flow payments. The best way to learn this principle is to apply it to other specific examples of the four types of credit market instruments in addition to those we discuss here. See if you can develop the equations that would allow you to solve for the yield to maturity in each case.

Fixed-Payment Loan. Recall that this type of loan has the same cash flow payment every period throughout the life of the loan. On a fixed-rate mortgage, for example, the borrower makes the same payment to the bank every month until the maturity date, when the loan will be completely paid off. To calculate the yield to maturity for a fixed-payment loan, we follow the same strategy we used for the simple loan—we equate today's value of the loan with its present value. Because the fixed-payment loan involves more than one cash flow payment, the present value of the fixed-payment loan is calculated as the sum of the present values of all cash flow payments (using Equation 1).

In the case of our earlier example, the loan is $1,000 and the yearly payment is $126 for the next 25 years. The present value is calculated as follows: At the end of one year, there is a $126 payment with a *PV* of $\$126/(1 + i)$; at the end of two years, there is another $126 payment with a *PV* of $\$126/(1 + i)^2$; and so on until at the end of the twenty-fifth year, the last payment of $126 with a *PV* of $\$126/(1 + i)^{25}$ is made. Making today's value of the loan ($1,000) equal to the sum of the present values of all the yearly payments gives us

$$\$1{,}000 = \frac{\$126}{1 + i} + \frac{\$126}{(1 + i)^2} + \frac{\$126}{(1 + i)^3} + \cdots + \frac{\$126}{(1 + i)^{25}}$$

More generally, for any fixed-payment loan,

$$LV = \frac{FP}{1 + i} + \frac{FP}{(1 + i)^2} + \frac{FP}{(1 + i)^3} + \cdots + \frac{FP}{(1 + i)^n} \qquad (2)$$

where LV = loan value
FP = fixed yearly payment
n = number of years until maturity

For a fixed-payment loan amount, the fixed yearly payment and the number of years until maturity are known quantities, and only the yield to maturity is not. So we can solve this equation for the yield to maturity i. Because this calculation is not easy, many pocket calculators have programs that allow you to find i given the loan's numbers for LV, FP, and n. For example, in the case of a 25-year loan with yearly payments of \$85.81, the yield to maturity that solves Equation 2 is 7%. Real estate brokers always have a pocket calculator that can solve such equations so that they can immediately tell the prospective house buyer exactly what the yearly (or monthly) payments will be if the house purchase is financed by taking out a mortgage.

APPLICATION Yield to Maturity and the Yearly Payment on a Fixed-Payment Loan

You decide to purchase a new home and need a \$100,000 mortgage. You take out a loan from the bank that has an interest rate of 7%. What is the yearly payment to the bank to pay off the loan in twenty years?

Solution

The yearly payment to the bank is \$9,439.29.

$$LV = \frac{FP}{1+i} + \frac{FP}{(1+i)^2} + \frac{FP}{(1+i)^3} + \cdots + \frac{FP}{(1+i)^n}$$

where LV = loan value amount = \$100,000
i = annual interest rate = 0.07
n = number of years = 20

Thus

$$\$100{,}000 = \frac{FP}{1+0.07} + \frac{FP}{(1+0.07)^2} + \frac{FP}{(1+0.07)^3} + \cdots + \frac{FP}{(1+0.07)^{20}}$$

To find the monthly payment for the loan using a financial calculator:

n = number of years = 20
PV = amount of the loan (LV) = −100,000
FV = amount of the loan after 20 years = 0
i = annual interest rate = .07

Then push the *PMT* button = fixed yearly payment (FP) = \$9,439.29.

Coupon Bond. To calculate the yield to maturity for a coupon bond, follow the same strategy used for the fixed-payment loan: Equate today's value of the bond with its present value. Because coupon bonds also have more than one cash flow payment, the present value of the bond is calculated as the sum of the present values of all the coupon payments plus the present value of the final payment of the face value of the bond.

The present value of a $1,000-face-value bond with ten years to maturity and yearly coupon payments of $100 (a 10% coupon rate) can be calculated as follows: At the end of one year, there is a $100 coupon payment with a *PV* of $\$100/(1 + i)$; at the end of the second year, there is another $100 coupon payment with a *PV* of $\$100/(1 + i)^2$; and so on until at maturity, there is a $100 coupon payment with a *PV* of $\$100/(1 + i)^{10}$ plus the repayment of the $1,000 face value with a *PV* of $\$1{,}000/(1 + i)^{10}$. Setting today's value of the bond (its current price, denoted by *P*) equal to the sum of the present values of all the cash flow payments for this bond gives

$$P = \frac{\$100}{1+i} + \frac{\$100}{(1+i)^2} + \frac{\$100}{(1+i)^3} + \cdots + \frac{\$100}{(1+i)^{10}} + \frac{\$1{,}000}{(1+i)^{10}}$$

More generally, for any coupon bond,[2]

$$P = \frac{C}{1+i} + \frac{C}{(1+i)^2} + \frac{C}{(1+i)^3} + \cdots + \frac{C}{(1+i)^n} + \frac{F}{(1+i)^n} \tag{3}$$

where P = price of coupon bond
C = yearly coupon payment
F = face value of the bond
n = years to maturity date

In Equation 3, the coupon payment, the face value, the years to maturity, and the price of the bond are known quantities, and only the yield to maturity is not. Hence we can solve this equation for the yield to maturity *i*. Just as in the case of the fixed-payment loan, this calculation is not easy, so business-oriented software and pocket calculators have built-in programs that solve this equation for you.

APPLICATION Yield to Maturity and the Bond Price for a Coupon Bond

Find the price of a 10% coupon bond with a face value of $1000, a 12.25% yield to maturity, and eight years to maturity.

Solution

The price of the bond is $889.20. To solve using a financial calculator:

n = years to maturity = 8
FV = face value of the bond (F) = 1,000
i = annual interest rate = 12.25%
PMT = yearly coupon payments (C) = 100

Then push the *PV* button = price of the bond = $889.20.

Alternatively, you could solve for the yield to maturity given the bond price by putting in $889.20 for *PV* and pushing the *i* button to get a yield to maturity of 12.25%.

[2]Most coupon bonds actually make coupon payments on a semiannual basis rather than once a year as assumed here. The effect on the calculations is only very slight and will be ignored here.

TABLE 1 **Yields to Maturity on a 10%-Coupon-Rate Bond Maturing in Ten Years (Face Value = $1,000)**

Price of Bond ($)	Yield to Maturity (%)
1,200	7.13
1,100	8.48
1,000	10.00
900	11.75
800	13.81

Table 1 shows the yields to maturity calculated for several bond prices. Three interesting facts emerge:

1. When the coupon bond is priced at its face value, the yield to maturity equals the coupon rate.
2. The price of a coupon bond and the yield to maturity are negatively related; that is, as the yield to maturity rises, the price of the bond falls. As the yield to maturity falls, the price of the bond rises.
3. The yield to maturity is greater than the coupon rate when the bond price is below its face value.

These three facts are true for any coupon bond and are really not surprising if you think about the reasoning behind the calculation of the yield to maturity. When you put $1,000 in a bank account with an interest rate of 10%, you can take out $100 every year and you will be left with the $1,000 at the end of ten years. This is similar to buying the $1,000 bond with a 10% coupon rate analyzed in Table 1, which pays a $100 coupon payment every year and then repays $1,000 at the end of ten years. If the bond is purchased at the par value of $1,000, its yield to maturity must equal 10%, which is also equal to the coupon rate of 10%. The same reasoning applied to any coupon bond demonstrates that if the coupon bond is purchased at its par value, the yield to maturity and the coupon rate must be equal.

It is straightforward to show that the bond price and the yield to maturity are negatively related. As i, the yield to maturity, increases, all denominators in the bond price formula (equation 3) must necessarily increase. Hence a rise in the interest rate as measured by the yield to maturity means that the price of the bond must fall. Another way to explain why the bond price falls when the interest rate rises is that a higher interest rate implies that the future coupon payments and final payment are worth less when discounted back to the present; hence the price of the bond must be lower.

The third fact, that the yield to maturity is greater than the coupon rate when the bond price is below its par value, follows directly from facts 1 and 2. When the yield to maturity equals the coupon rate, then the bond price is at the face value; when the yield to maturity rises further, the bond price necessarily falls and so must be below the face value of the bond.

There is one special case of a coupon bond that is worth discussing because its yield to maturity is particularly easy to calculate. This bond is called a **consol** or a **perpetuity**; it is a perpetual bond with no maturity date and no repayment of principal that makes fixed coupon payments of $\$C$ forever. Consols were first sold by the British Treasury during the Napoleonic Wars and are still traded today; they are quite rare, however, in American capital markets. The formula in Equation 3 for the price of the consol P_c simplifies to the following:[3]

$$P_c = \frac{C}{i_c} \tag{4}$$

where P_c = price of the perpetuity (consol)
C = yearly payment
i_c = yield to maturity of the perpetuity (consol)

One nice feature of perpetuities is that you can immediately see that as i_c increases, the price of the bond falls. For example, if a perpetuity pays \$100 per year forever and the interest rate is 10%, its price will be \$1,000 = \$100/0.10. If the interest rate rises to 20%, its price will fall to \$500 = \$100/0.20. We can also rewrite this formula as

$$i_c = \frac{C}{P_c} \tag{5}$$

APPLICATION Perpetuity

What is the yield to maturity on a bond that has a price of \$2,000 and pays \$100 of interest annually forever?

Solution

The yield to maturity would be 5%.

$$i_c = \frac{C}{P_c}$$

where C = yearly payment = \$100
P_c = price of perpetuity (consol) = \$2,000

---

[3]The bond price formula for a consol is

$$P = \frac{C}{1+i} + \frac{C}{(1+i)^2} + \frac{C}{(1+i)^3} + \cdots$$

which can be written as

$$P = C(x + x^2 + x^3 + \cdots)$$

in which $x = 1/(1+i)$. The formula for an infinite sum is:

$$1 + x + x^2 + x^3 + \cdots = \frac{1}{1-x} \quad \text{for } x < 1$$

and so

$$P = C\left(\frac{1}{1-x} - 1\right) = C\left[\frac{1}{1 - 1/(1+i)} - 1\right]$$

which by suitable algebraic manipulation becomes

$$P = C\left(\frac{1+i}{i} - \frac{i}{i}\right) = \frac{C}{i}$$

Thus

$$i_c = \frac{\$100}{\$2{,}000}$$

$$i_c = 0.05 = 5\%$$

The formula in Equation 5, which describes the calculation of the yield to maturity for a perpetuity, also provides a useful approximation for the yield to maturity on coupon bonds. When a coupon bond has a long term to maturity (say, twenty years or more), it is very much like a perpetuity, which pays coupon payments forever. This is because the cash flows more than twenty years in the future have such small present discounted values that the value of a long-term coupon bond is very close to the value of a perpetuity with the same coupon rate. Thus i_c in Equation 5 will be very close to the yield to maturity for any long-term bond. For this reason, i_c, the yearly coupon payment divided by the price of the security, has been given the name **current yield** and is frequently used as an approximation to describe interest rates on long-term bonds.

Discount Bond. The yield-to-maturity calculation for a discount bond is similar to that for the simple loan. Let us consider a discount bond such as a one-year U.S. Treasury bill, which pays a face value of \$1,000 in one year's time. If the current purchase price of this bill is \$900, then equating this price to the present value of the \$1,000 received in one year, using Equation 1, gives

$$\$900 = \frac{\$1{,}000}{1 + i}$$

Solving for *i*,

$$(1 + i) \times \$900 = \$1{,}000$$

$$\$900 + \$900i = \$1{,}000$$

$$\$900i = \$1{,}000 - \$900$$

$$i = \frac{\$1{,}000 - \$900}{\$900} = 0.111 = 11.1\%$$

More generally, for any one-year discount bond, the yield to maturity can be written as

$$i = \frac{F - P}{P} \tag{6}$$

where F = face value of the discount bond
P = current price of the discount bond

In other words, the yield to maturity equals the increase in price over the year $(F - P)$ divided by the initial price (P). In normal circumstances, investors earn positive returns from holding these securities and so they sell at a discount, meaning that the current price of the bond is below the face value. Therefore, $F - P$ should be positive, and the yield to maturity should be positive as well. However, this is not always the case, as recent extraordinary events in Japan indicate (see the Global box).

Global Negative T-Bill Rates? Japan Shows the Way

We normally assume that interest rates must always be positive. Negative interest rates would imply that you are willing to pay more for a bond today than you will receive for it in the future (as our formula for yield to maturity on a discount bond demonstrates). Negative interest rates therefore seem like an impossibility because you would do better by holding cash that has the same value in the future as it does today.

The Japanese have demonstrated that this reasoning is not quite correct. In November 1998, interest rates on Japanese six-month Treasury bills became negative, yielding an interest rate of –0.004%, with investors paying more for the bills than their face value. This is an extremely unusual event—no other country in the world has seen negative interest rates during the last 50 years. How could this happen?

As we will see in Chapter 5, the weakness of the Japanese economy and a negative inflation rate drove Japanese interest rates to low levels, but these two factors can't explain the negative rates. The answer is that large investors found it more convenient to hold these six-month bills as a store of value rather than holding cash because the bills are denominated in larger amounts and can be stored electronically. For that reason, some investors were willing to hold them, despite their negative rates, even though in monetary terms the investors would be better off holding cash. Clearly, the convenience of T-bills goes only so far, and thus their interest rates can go only a little bit below zero.

An important feature of this equation is that it indicates that for a discount bond, the yield to maturity is negatively related to the current bond price. This is the same conclusion that we reached for a coupon bond. For example, Equation 6 shows that a rise in the bond price, say from \$900 to \$950, means that the bond will have a smaller increase in its price at maturity, and the yield to maturity falls, from 11.1% to 5.3%. Similarly, a fall in the yield to maturity means that the price of the discount bond has risen.

Summary. The concept of present value tells you that a dollar in the future is not as valuable to you as a dollar today because you can earn interest on this dollar. Specifically, a dollar received n years from now is worth only $\$1/(1 + i)^n$ today. The present value of a set of future cash flow payments on a debt instrument equals the sum of the present values of each of the future payments. The yield to maturity for an instrument is the interest rate that equates the present value of the future payments on that instrument to its value today. Because the procedure for calculating the yield to maturity is based on sound economic principles, this is the measure that economists think most accurately describes the interest rate.

Our calculations of the yield to maturity for a variety of bonds reveal the important fact that ***current bond prices and interest rates are negatively related: When the interest rate rises, the price of the bond falls, and vice versa.***

YIELD ON A DISCOUNT BASIS

The yield to maturity is the most accurate measure of interest rates; this is what economists mean when they use the term *interest rate*. Unless otherwise specified, the terms *interest rate* and *yield to maturity* are used synonymously in this book. However, because the yield to maturity is sometimes difficult to calculate, another, less accurate measure of interest rates has come into common use in bond markets, the *yield on a discount basis*. When reading the newspaper, it is important for you to understand what it means and how it differs from the more accurate measure of interest rates, the yield to maturity.

Before the advent of calculators and computers, dealers in U.S. Treasury bills found it difficult to calculate interest rates as a yield to maturity. Instead, they quoted the interest rate on bills as a **yield on a discount basis** (or **discount yield**), and they still do so today. Formally, the yield on a discount basis is defined by the following formula:

$$i_{db} = \frac{F - P}{F} \times \frac{360}{\textit{days to maturity}} \tag{7}$$

where i_{db} = yield on a discount basis
F = face value of the Treasury bill (discount bond)
P = purchase price of the discount bond

This method for calculating interest rates has two peculiarities. First, it uses the percentage gain on the face value of the bill, $(F - P)/F$, rather than the percentage gain on the purchase price of the bill, $(F - P)/P$, used in calculating the yield to maturity. Second, it puts the yield on an annual basis by considering the year to be 360 days long rather than 365 days.

Because of these peculiarities, the discount yield understates the interest rate on bills as measured by the yield to maturity. On a one-year bill, which is selling for \$900 and has a face value of \$1,000, the yield on a discount basis would be as follows:

$$i_{db} = \frac{\$1{,}000 - \$900}{\$1{,}000} \times \frac{360}{365} = 0.099 = 9.9\%$$

The yield to maturity for this bill, which we calculated before, is 11.1%. The discount yield understates the yield to maturity by a factor of over 10%. A little more than 1% ([365 − 360]/360 = 0.014 = 1.4%) can be attributed to the understatement of the length of the year: When the bill has one year to maturity, the second term on the right-hand side of the formula is 360/365 = 0.986 rather than 1.0, as it should be.

The more serious source of the understatement, however, is the use of the percentage gain on the face value rather than on the purchase price. Because, by definition, the purchase price of a discount bond is always less than the face value, the percentage gain on the face value is necessarily smaller than the percentage gain on the purchase price. The greater the difference between the purchase price and the face value of the discount bond, the more the discount yield understates the yield to maturity. Because the difference between the purchase price and the face value gets larger as maturity gets longer, we can draw the following conclusion about the relationship of the yield on a discount basis to the yield to maturity: The yield on a discount basis always understates the yield to maturity, and this understatement becomes more severe the longer the maturity of the discount bond.

Another important feature of the discount yield is that, like the yield to maturity, it is negatively related to the price of the bond. For example, when the price of the bond rises from \$900 to \$950, the formula indicates that the yield on a discount basis declines from 9.9% to 4.9%. At the same time, the yield to maturity declines from 11.1% to 5.3%. Here we see another important factor about the relationship of yield on a discount basis to yield to maturity: They always move together. That is, a rise in the discount yield always means that the yield to maturity has risen, and a decline in the discount yield means that the yield to maturity has declined as well.

The characteristics of the yield on a discount basis can be summarized as follows: Yield on a discount basis understates the more accurate measure of the interest rate, the yield to maturity; and the longer the maturity of the discount bond, the greater this understatement becomes. Even though the discount yield is a somewhat misleading measure of the interest rates, a change in the discount yield always indicates a change in the same direction for the yield to maturity.

APPLICATION Reading the *Wall Street Journal*: The Bond Page

Now that we understand the different interest-rate definitions, let's apply our knowledge and take a look at what kind of information appears on the bond page of a typical newspaper, in this case the *Wall Street Journal*. The Following the Financial News box contains the *Journal*'s listing for three different types of bonds on Thursday, January 12, 2006. Panel (a) contains the information on U.S. Treasury bonds and notes. Both are coupon bonds, the only difference being their time to maturity from when they were originally issued: Notes have a time to maturity of less than ten years; bonds have a time to maturity of more than ten years.

The information found in the "Rate" and "Maturity" columns identifies the bond by coupon rate and maturity date. For example, T-bond 1 has a coupon rate of 1.875%, indicating that it pays out $18.75 per year on a $1,000-face-value bond and matures in January 2006. In bond market parlance, it is referred to as the Treasury's $1\frac{7}{8}$s of 2006. The next three columns tell us about the bond's price. By convention, all prices in the bond market are quoted per $100 of face value. Furthermore, the numbers after the colon represent thirty-seconds ($^{x}/_{32}$, or 32nds). In the case of T-bond 1, the first price of 99:28 represents $99\frac{28}{32} = 99.875$, or an actual price of $998.75 for a $1,000-face-value bond. The bid price tells you what price you will receive if you sell the bond, and the asked price tells you what you must pay for the bond. (You might want to think of the bid price as the "wholesale" price and the asked price as the "retail" price.) The "Chg." column indicates how much the bid price has changed in 32nds (in this case, $\frac{1}{32}$) from the previous trading day.

Notice that for all the bonds and notes, the asked price is more than the bid price. Can you guess why this is so? The difference between the two (the *spread*) provides the bond dealer who trades these securities with a profit. For T-bond 1, the dealer who buys it at 99:28, and sells it for 99:29, makes a profit of $\frac{1}{32}$. This profit is what enables the dealer to make a living and provide the service of allowing you to buy and sell bonds at will.

The "Ask Yld." column provides the yield to maturity, which is 3.76% for T-bond 1. It is calculated with the method described earlier in this chapter (in equation 3) using the asked price as the price of the bond. The asked price is used in the calculation because the yield to maturity is most relevant to a person who is going to buy and hold the security and thus earn the yield. The person selling the security is not going to be holding it and hence is less concerned with the yield.

Two other categories of bonds are reported much like the Treasury bonds and notes in the newspaper. Government agency and miscellaneous securities include securities issued by U.S. government agencies such as the Government National Mortgage Association, which makes loans to savings and loan institutions, and international agencies

Following the Financial News **Bond Prices and Interest Rates**

Bond prices and interest rates are published daily. In the *Wall Street Journal*, they can be found in the "NYSE/AMEX Bonds" and "Treasury/Agency Issues" section of the paper. Three basic formats for quoting bond prices and yields are illustrated here.

TREASURY BONDS, NOTES AND BILLS

January 12, 2006

Representative Over-the-Counter quotation based on transactions of $1 million or more. Treasury bond, note and bill quotes are as of mid-afternoon. Colons in bid-and-asked quotes represent 32nds; 101:01 means 101 1/32. Net changes in 32nds. n-Treasury note. i-Inflation-Indexed issue. Treasury bill quotes in hundredths, quoted on terms of a rate of discount. Days to maturity calculated from settlement date. All yields are to maturity and based on the asked quote. Latest 13-week and 26-week bills are boldfaced. For bonds callable prior to maturity, yields are computed to the earliest call date for issues quoted above par and to the maturity date for issues below par. *When issued.

Source: eSpeed/Cantor Fitzgerald

U.S. Treasury strips as of 3 p.m. Eastern time, also based on transactions of $1 million or more. Colons in bid and asked quotes represent 32nds; 99:01 means 99 1/32. Net changes in 32nds. Yields calculated on the asked quotation. ci-stripped coupon interest. bp-Treasury bond, stripped principal. np-Treasury note, stripped principal. For bonds callable prior to maturity, yields are computed to the earliest call date for issues quoted above par and to the maturity date for issues below par.

Source: Bear, Stearns & Co. via Street Software Technology, Inc.

(a) Treasury bonds and notes

GOVT. BONDS & NOTES

	Rate	Maturity Mo/Yr	Bid	Asked	Chg.	Ask Yld.
T-bond 1	1.875	Jan 06n	99:28	99:29	1	3.76
	5.625	Feb 06n	100:03	100:04	. . .	3.96
	9.375	Feb 06	100:14	100:15	. . .	3.98
	1.625	Feb 06n	99:21	99:22	. . .	4.07
	1.500	Mar 06n	99:12	99:13	. . .	4.24
	2.250	Apr 06n	99:11	99:12	. . .	4.32
	2.000	May 06n	99:06	99:07	1	4.34
	4.625	May 06n	100:01	100:02	. . .	4.36

(b) Treasury bills

TREASURY BILLS

	Maturity	Days to Mat.	Bid	Asked	Chg.	Ask Yld.	Maturity	Days to Mat.	Bid	Asked	Chg.	Ask Yld.
	Jan 19 06	6	4.01	4.00	–0.08	4.06	Apr 20 06	97	4.22	4.21	0.01	4.32
	Jan 26 06	13	4.01	4.00	–0.04	4.06	Apr 27 06	104	4.23	4.22	0.01	4.33
T-bill 1	Feb 02 06	20	4.04	4.03	–0.03	4.10	May 04 06	111	4.23	4.22	0.01	4.34
	Feb 09 06	27	4.06	4.05	–0.02	4.12	May 11 06	118	4.23	4.22	. . .	4.34
	Feb 16 06	34	4.05	4.04	–0.02	4.11	May 18 06	125	4.23	4.22	. . .	4.34
	Feb 23 06	41	4.06	4.05	–0.02	4.13	May 25 06	132	4.23	4.22	–0.01	4.35
	Mar 02 06	48	4.12	4.11	0.01	4.19	Jun 01 06	139	4.24	4.23	. . .	4.36
	Mar 09 06	55	4.13	4.12	0.01	4.20	Jun 08 06	146	4.25	4.24	. . .	4.37
	Mar 16 06	62	4.11	4.10	–0.01	4.19	Jun 15 06	153	4.25	4.24	–0.01	4.38
	Mar 23 06	69	4.17	4.16	0.01	4.25	Jun 22 06	160	4.24	4.23	–0.02	4.37
	Mar 30 06	76	4.19	4.18	0.02	4.28	Jun 29 06	167	4.26	4.25	. . .	4.40
	Apr 06 06	83	4.20	4.19	0.02	4.29	Jul 06 06	174	4.26	4.25	. . .	4.40
	Apr 13 06	**90**	**4.21**	**4.20**	**0.01**	**4.30**	Jul 13 06	181	4.28	4.27	–0.01	4.42

Source: *Wall Street Journal*, Thursday, January 13, 2006.

(c) New York Stock Exchange bonds

CORPORATE BONDS

Thursday, January 12, 2006

Forty most active fixed-coupon corporate bonds

Company (TICKER)	Coupon	Maturity	Last Price	Last Yield	*Est Spread	Ust†	Est $ Vol (000's)
Tyco International Group (TYC)	6.000	Nov 15, 2013	103.104	5.505	110	10	143,116
HSBC Finance Corp (HSBC)	5.250	Jan 14, 2011	100.169	5.211	83	5	101,312
Wells Fargo (WFC)	4.875	Jan 12, 2011	99.851	4.909	54	5	94,719
Bank of America Corp (BAC)	4.875	Sep 15, 2012	99.217	5.014	57	5	93,623
Verizon New York Inc (VZ)	7.000	Dec 01, 2033	97.625	7.198	261	30	85,530

Volume represents total volume for each issue; price/yield data are for trades of $1 million and greater. *Estimated spreads, in basis points (100 basis points is one percentage point), over the 2, 3, 5, 10, or 30-year hot run Treasury note/bond. 2-year: 4.375 12/07; 3-year: 4.375 11/08; 5-year: 4.375 12/10; 10-year: 4.500 11/15; 30-year: 5.375 02/31. †Comparable U.S. Treasury issue.

Source: MarketAxess Corporate BondTicker

such as the World Bank. Tax-exempt bonds are the other category reported in a manner similar to panel (a), except that yield-to-maturity calculations are not usually provided. Tax-exempt bonds include bonds issued by local government and public authorities whose interest payments are exempt from federal income taxes.

Panel (b) quotes yields on U.S. Treasury bills, which, as we have seen, are discount bonds. Because there is no coupon, these securities are identified solely by their maturity dates, which you can see in the first column. The next column, "Days to Mat.," provides the number of days to maturity of the bill. Dealers in these markets always refer to prices by quoting the yield on a discount basis. The "Bid" column gives the discount yield for people selling the bills to dealers (4.04% for T-bill 1), and the "Asked" column gives the discount yield for people buying the bills from dealers (4.03%). As with bonds and notes, the dealers' profits are made by the asked price being higher than the bid price, leading to the asked discount yield being lower than the bid discount yield.

The "Chg." column indicates how much the asked discount yield changed from the previous day. When financial analysts talk about changes in the yield, they frequently describe the changes in terms of **basis points**, which are hundredths of a percentage point. For example, a financial analyst would describe the −0.03 change in the asked discount yield for the February 02, 2006, T-bill 1 by saying that it had fallen by three basis points.

As we learned earlier, the yield on a discount basis understates the yield to maturity, which is reported in the column of panel (b) headed "Ask Yld." This is evident from a comparison of the "Ask Yld." and "Asked" columns. As we would also expect from our discussion of the calculation of yields on a discount basis, the understatement grows as the maturity of the bill lengthens.

Panel (c) has quotations for the five most active fixed-coupon corporate bonds. The first column identifies the issuing company. In our example, we see that Tyco Int'l was the most actively traded bond that day. The second column reports the coupon rate (6.00 for Tyco). The maturity date of the bond is reported in the next column. The Tyco bond matures on Nov. 15, 2013. The last price the bond sold for that day and the last yield are reported in the next two columns. Note that the Tyco bond is selling for a premium, so the yield is below the coupon rate. The "Est Spread" column reports the number of basis points between the corporate bond and the comparable-maturity Treasury bond. The "Ust" column gives the term of the Treasure security used for computing the "Est Spread." For example, Tyco bonds are selling for 110 basis points above the 10-year Treasury bond. The last column reports the volume traded in thousands.

THE DISTINCTION BETWEEN INTEREST RATES AND RETURNS

Many people think that the interest rate on a bond tells them all they need to know about how well off they are as a result of owning it. If Irving the Investor thinks he is better off when he owns a long-term bond yielding a 10% interest rate and the interest rate rises to 20%, he will have a rude awakening: As we will shortly see, if he has to sell the bond, Irving has lost his shirt! How well a person does by holding a bond or any other security over a particular time period is accurately measured by the **return**, or, in more precise terminology, the **rate of return**. For any security, the rate of return is defined as the payments to the owner plus the change in its value, expressed as a fraction of its purchase price. To make this definition clearer, let us see what the return would look like for a \$1,000-face-value coupon bond with a coupon rate of 10% that is bought for \$1,000, held for one year, and then sold for \$1,200. The payments to the owner are the yearly coupon payments of \$100, and the change in its value is \$1,200 − \$1,000 = \$200. Adding these together and expressing them as a fraction of the purchase price of \$1,000 gives us the one-year holding-period return for this bond:

$$\frac{\$100 + \$200}{\$1{,}000} = \frac{\$300}{\$1{,}000} = 0.30 = 30\%$$

You may have noticed something quite surprising about the return that we have just calculated: It equals 30%, yet as Table 1 indicates, initially the yield to maturity was only 10%. This demonstrates that ***the return on a bond will not necessarily equal the yield to maturity on that bond***. We now see that the distinction between interest rate and return can be important, although for many securities the two may be closely related.

STUDY GUIDE

The concept of *return* discussed here is extremely important because it is used continually throughout the book. Make sure that you understand how a return is calculated and why it can differ from the interest rate. This understanding will make the material presented later in the book easier to follow.

More generally, the return on a bond held from time t to time $t + 1$ can be written as

$$R = \frac{C + P_{t+1} - P_t}{P_t} \tag{8}$$

where

R = return from holding the bond from time t to time $t + 1$
P_t = price of the bond at time t
P_{t+1} = price of the bond at time $t + 1$
C = coupon payment

A convenient way to rewrite the return formula in Equation 8 is to recognize that it can be split into two separate terms:

$$R = \frac{C}{P_t} + \frac{P_{t+1} - P_t}{P_t}$$

The first term is the current yield i_c (the coupon payment over the purchase price):

$$\frac{C}{P_t} = i_c$$

The second term is the **rate of capital gain**, or the change in the bond's price relative to the initial purchase price:

$$\frac{P_{t+1} - P_t}{P_t} = g$$

where g is the rate of capital gain. Equation 8 can then be rewritten as

$$R = i_c + g \tag{9}$$

which shows that the return on a bond is the current yield i_c plus the rate of capital gain g. This rewritten formula illustrates the point we just discovered: Even for a bond for which the current yield i_c is an accurate measure of the yield to maturity, the return can differ substantially from the interest rate. Returns will differ from the interest rate, especially if there are sizable fluctuations in the price of the bond that produce substantial capital gains or losses.

To explore this point even further, let's look at what happens to the returns on bonds of different maturities when interest rates rise. Table 2 calculates the one-year return on several 10%-coupon-rate bonds all purchased at par when interest rates on all these bonds rise from 10% to 20%. Several key findings in this table are generally true of all bonds:

- The only bond whose return equals the initial yield to maturity is one whose time to maturity is the same as the holding period (see the last bond in Table 2).
- A rise in interest rates is associated with a fall in bond prices, resulting in capital losses on bonds whose terms to maturity are longer than the holding period.
- The more distant a bond's maturity, the greater the size of the percentage price change associated with an interest-rate change.
- The more distant a bond's maturity, the lower the rate of return that occurs as a result of the increase in the interest rate.
- Even though a bond has a substantial initial interest rate, its return can turn out to be negative if interest rates rise.

At first it frequently puzzles students (as it puzzles poor Irving the Investor) that a rise in interest rates can mean that a bond has been a poor investment. The trick to understanding this is to recognize that a rise in the interest rate means that the price of

TABLE 2 One-Year Returns on Different-Maturity 10%-Coupon-Rate Bonds When Interest Rates Rise from 10% to 20%

(1) Years to Maturity When Bond Is Purchased	(2) Initial Current Yield (%)	(3) Initial Price ($)	(4) Price Next Year* ($)	(5) Rate of Capital Gain (%)	(6) Rate of Return (2 + 5) (%)
30	10	1,000	503	−49.7	−39.7
20	10	1,000	516	−48.4	−38.4
10	10	1,000	597	−40.3	−30.3
5	10	1,000	741	−25.9	−15.9
2	10	1,000	917	−8.3	+1.7
1	10	1,000	1,000	0.0	+10.0

*Calculated using Equation 3.

FYI Helping Investors to Select Desired Interest-Rate Risk

Because many investors want to know how much interest-rate risk they are exposed to, some mutual fund companies try to educate investors about the perils of interest-rate risk, as well as to offer investment alternatives that match their investors' preferences.

Vanguard Group, for example, offers eight separate high-grade bond mutual funds. In its prospectus, Vanguard separates the funds by the average maturity of the bonds they hold and demonstrates the effect of interest-rate changes by computing the percentage change in bond value resulting from a 1% increase and decrease in interest rates. Three of the bond funds invest in bonds with average maturities of one to three years, which Vanguard rates as having the lowest interest-rate risk. Three other funds hold bonds with average maturities of five to ten years, which Vanguard rates as having medium interest-rate risk. Two funds hold long-term bonds with maturities of 15 to 30 years, which Vanguard rates as having high interest-rate risk.

By providing this information, Vanguard hopes to increase its market share in the sales of bond funds. Not surprisingly, Vanguard is one of the most successful mutual fund companies in the business.

a bond has fallen. A rise in interest rates therefore means that a capital loss has occurred. If this loss is large enough, the bond can be a poor investment indeed. For example, we see in Table 2 that the bond that has 30 years to maturity when purchased has a capital loss of 49.7% when the interest rate rises from 10% to 20%. This loss is so large that it exceeds the current yield of 10%, resulting in a negative return (loss) of −39.7%. If Irving does not sell the bond, his capital loss is often referred to as a "paper loss." This is a loss nonetheless because if he had not bought this bond and had instead put his money in the bank, he would now be able to buy more bonds at their lower price than he presently owns.

Maturity and the Volatility of Bond Returns: Interest-Rate Risk

The finding that the prices of longer-maturity bonds respond more dramatically to changes in interest rates helps explain an important fact about the behavior of bond markets: ***Prices and returns for long-term bonds are more volatile than those for shorter-term bonds***. Price changes of +20% and −20% within a year, with corresponding variations in returns, are common for bonds more than twenty years away from maturity.

We now see that changes in interest rates make investments in long-term bonds quite risky. Indeed, the riskiness of an asset's return that results from interest-rate changes is so important that it has been given a special name, **interest-rate risk**.[4] Dealing with interest-rate risk is a major concern of managers of financial institutions and investors, as we will see in later chapters (see also the FYI box).

Although long-term debt instruments have substantial interest-rate risk, short-term debt instruments do not. Indeed, bonds with a maturity that is as short as the holding

[4]Interest-rate risk can be quantitatively measured using the concept of *duration*. This concept and its calculation are discussed in an appendix to this chapter, which can be found on this book's web site at www.myeconlab.com/mishkin.

period have no interest-rate risk.[5] We see this for the coupon bond at the bottom of Table 2, which has no uncertainty about the rate of return because it equals the yield to maturity, which is known at the time the bond is purchased. The key to understanding why there is no interest-rate risk for *any* bond whose time to maturity matches the holding period is to recognize that (in this case) the price at the end of the holding period is already fixed at the face value. The change in interest rates can then have no effect on the price at the end of the holding period for these bonds, and the return will therefore be equal to the yield to maturity known at the time the bond is purchased.[6]

Summary

The return on a bond, which tells you how good an investment it has been over the holding period, is equal to the yield to maturity in only one special case: when the holding period and the maturity of the bond are identical. Bonds whose term to maturity is longer than the holding period are subject to interest-rate risk: Changes in interest rates lead to capital gains and losses that produce substantial differences between the return and the yield to maturity known at the time the bond is purchased. Interest-rate risk is especially important for long-term bonds, where the capital gains and losses can be substantial. This is why long-term bonds are not considered to be safe assets with a sure return over short holding periods.

---

[5]The statement that there is no interest-rate risk for any bond whose time to maturity matches the holding period is literally true only for discount bonds and zero-coupon bonds that make no intermediate cash payments before the holding period is over. A coupon bond that makes an intermediate cash payment before the holding period is over requires that this payment be reinvested. Because the interest rate at which this payment can be reinvested is uncertain, there is some uncertainty about the return on this coupon bond even when the time to maturity equals the holding period. However, the riskiness of the return on a coupon bond from reinvesting the coupon payments is typically quite small, so the basic point that a coupon bond with a time to maturity equaling the holding period has very little risk still holds true.

[6]In the text, we are assuming that all holding periods are short and equal to the maturity on short-term bonds and are thus not subject to interest-rate risk. However, if an investor's holding period is longer than the term to maturity of the bond, the investor is exposed to a type of interest-rate risk called *reinvestment risk.* Reinvestment risk occurs because the proceeds from the short-term bond need to be reinvested at a future interest rate that is uncertain.

To understand reinvestment risk, suppose that Irving the Investor has a holding period of two years and decides to purchase a $1,000 one-year bond at face value and will then purchase another one at the end of the first year. If the initial interest rate is 10%, Irving will have $1,100 at the end of the year. If the interest rate rises to 20%, as in Table 2, Irving will find that buying $1,100 worth of another one-year bond will leave him at the end of the second year with $\$1{,}100 \times (1 + 0.20) = \$1{,}320$. Thus Irving's two-year return will be $(\$1{,}320 - \$1{,}000)/1{,}000 = 0.32 = 32\%$, which equals 14.9% at an annual rate. In this case, Irving has earned more by buying the one-year bonds than if he had initially purchased the two-year bond with an interest rate of 10%. Thus, when Irving has a holding period that is longer than the term to maturity of the bonds he purchases, he benefits from a rise in interest rates. Conversely, if interest rates fall to 5%, Irving will have only $1,155 at the end of two years: $\$1{,}100 \times (1 + 0.05)$. His two-year return will be $(\$1{,}155 - \$1{,}000)/1{,}000 = 0.155 = 15.5\%$, which is 7.2% at an annual rate. With a holding period greater than the term to maturity of the bond, Irving now loses from a decline in interest rates.

We have thus seen that when the holding period is longer than the term to maturity of a bond, the return is uncertain because the future interest rate when reinvestment occurs is also uncertain—in short, there is reinvestment risk. We also see that if the holding period is longer than the term to maturity of the bond, the investor benefits from a rise in interest rates and is hurt by a fall in interest rates.

THE DISTINCTION BETWEEN REAL AND NOMINAL INTEREST RATES

So far in our discussion of interest rates, we have ignored the effects of inflation on the cost of borrowing. What we have up to now been calling the interest rate makes no allowance for inflation, and it is more precisely referred to as the **nominal interest rate**, which is distinguished from the **real interest rate**, the interest rate that is adjusted by subtracting expected changes in the price level (inflation) so that it more accurately reflects the true cost of borrowing. The real interest rate defined in the text is more precisely referred to as the *ex ante real interest rate* because it is adjusted for *expected* changes in the price level. This is the real interest rate that is most important to economic decisions, and typically it is what economists mean when they make reference to the "real" interest rate. The interest rate that is adjusted for *actual* changes in the price level is called the *ex post real interest rate.* It describes how well a lender has done in real terms *after the fact.*

The real interest rate is more accurately defined by the *Fisher equation*, named for Irving Fisher, one of the great monetary economists of the twentieth century. The Fisher equation states that the nominal interest rate i equals the real interest rate i_r plus the expected rate of inflation π^e:[7]

$$i = i_r + \pi^e \tag{10}$$

Rearranging terms, we find that the real interest rate equals the nominal interest rate minus the expected inflation rate:

$$i_r = i - \pi^e \tag{11}$$

To see why this definition makes sense, let us first consider a situation in which you have made a one-year simple loan with a 5% interest rate ($i = 5\%$) and you expect the price level to rise by 3% over the course of the year ($\pi^e = 3\%$). As a result of making the loan, at the end of the year you will have 2% more in **real terms**—that is, in terms of real goods and services you can buy. In this case, the interest rate you have earned in terms of real goods and services is 2%:

$$i_r = 5\% - 3\% = 2\%$$

as indicated by the Fisher definition.

---

[7]A more precise formulation of the Fisher equation is

$$i = i_r + \pi^e + (i_r \times \pi^e)$$

because

$$1 + i = (1 + i_r)(1 + \pi^e) = 1 + i_r + \pi^e + (i_r \times \pi^e)$$

and subtracting 1 from both sides gives us the first equation. For small values of i_r and π^e, the term $i_r \times \pi^e$ is so small that we ignore it, as in the text.

APPLICATION Calculating Real Interest Rates

What is the real interest rate if the nominal interest rate is 8% and the expected inflation rate is 10% over the course of a year?

Solution

The real interest rate is −2%. Although you will be receiving 8% more dollars at the end of the year, you will be paying 10% more for goods. The result is that you will be able to buy 2% fewer goods at the end of the year, and you are 2% worse off in real terms.

$$i_r = i - \pi^e$$

where i = nominal interest rate = 0.08

π^e = expected inflation rate = 0.10

Thus

$$i_r = 0.08 - 0.10 = -0.02 = -2\%$$

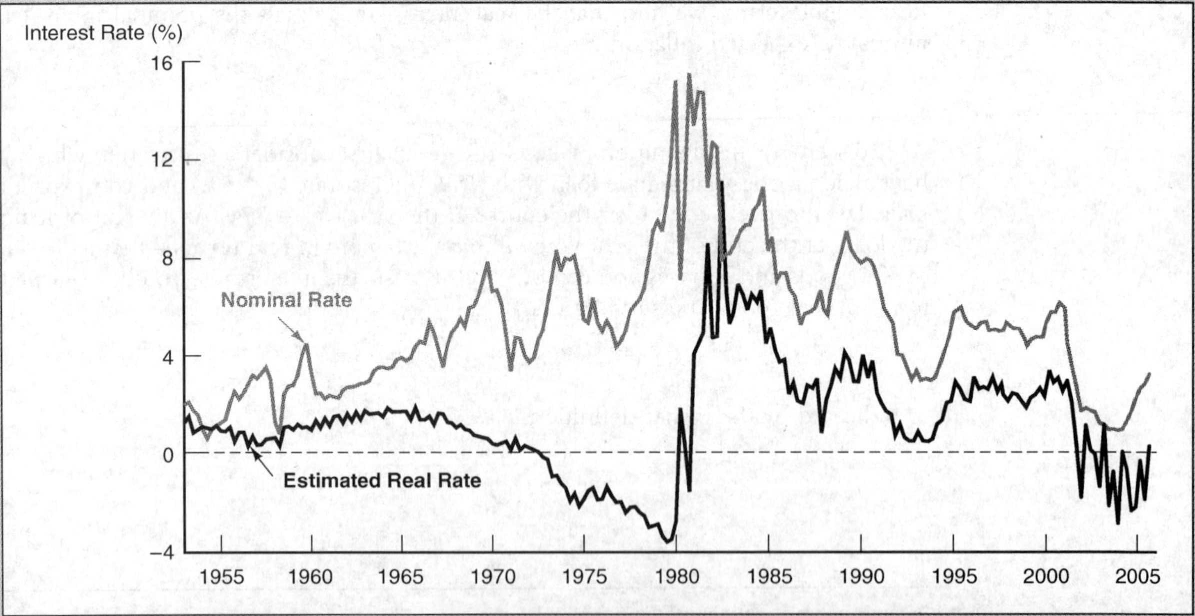

FIGURE 1 **Real and Nominal Interest Rates (Three-Month Treasury Bill), 1953–2005**

Sources: Nominal rates from www.federalreserve.gov/releases/H15. The real rate is constructed using the procedure outlined in Frederic S. Mishkin, "The Real Interest Rate: An Empirical Investigation," *Carnegie-Rochester Conference Series on Public Policy* 15 (1981): 151–200. This procedure involves estimating expected inflation as a function of past interest rates, inflation, and time trends and then subtracting the expected inflation measure from the nominal interest rate.

As a lender, you are clearly less eager to make a loan in this case, because in terms of real goods and services you have actually earned a negative interest rate of 2%. By contrast, as the borrower, you fare quite well because at the end of the year, the amounts you will have to pay back will be worth 2% less in terms of goods and services—you as the borrower will be ahead by 2% in real terms. ***When the real interest rate is low, there are greater incentives to borrow and fewer incentives to lend.***

A similar distinction can be made between nominal returns and real returns. Nominal returns, which do not allow for inflation, are what we have been referring to as simply "returns." When inflation is subtracted from a nominal return, we have the real return, which indicates the amount of extra goods and services that can be purchased as a result of holding the security.

The distinction between real and nominal interest rates is important because the real interest rate, which reflects the real cost of borrowing, is likely to be a better indicator of the incentives to borrow and lend. It appears to be a better guide to how people will be affected by what is happening in credit markets. Figure 1, which presents estimates from 1953 to 2005 of the real and nominal interest rates on three-month U.S. Treasury bills, shows us that nominal and real rates often do not move together. (This is also true for nominal and real interest rates in the rest of the world.) In particular, when nominal rates in the United States were high in the 1970s, real rates were actually extremely low—often negative. By the standard of nominal interest rates, you would have thought that credit market conditions were tight in this period, because it was expensive to borrow. However, the estimates of the real rates indicate that you would have been mistaken. In real terms, the cost of borrowing was actually quite low.[8]

Until recently, real interest rates in the United States were not observable; only nominal rates were reported. This all changed when, in January 1997, the U.S. Treasury began to issue **indexed bonds**, whose interest and principal payments are adjusted for changes in the price level (see the FYI box on TIPS).

---

[8]Because most interest income in the United States is subject to federal income taxes, the true earnings in real terms from holding a debt instrument are not reflected by the real interest rate defined by the Fisher equation but rather by the *after-tax real interest rate,* which equals the nominal interest rate *after income tax payments have been subtracted,* minus the expected inflation rate. For a person facing a 30% tax rate, the after-tax interest rate earned on a bond yielding 10% is only 7% because 30% of the interest income must be paid to the Internal Revenue Service. Thus the after-tax real interest rate on this bond when expected inflation is 5% equals 2% (= 7% − 5%). More generally, the after-tax real interest rate can be expressed as

$$i(1 - \tau) - \pi^e$$

where τ = the income tax rate.

This formula for the after-tax real interest rate also provides a better measure of the effective cost of borrowing for many corporations and homeowners in the United States because in calculating income taxes, they can deduct interest payments on loans from their income. Thus, if you face a 30% tax rate and take out a mortgage loan with a 10% interest rate, you are able to deduct the 10% interest payment and lower your taxes by 30% of this amount. Your after-tax nominal cost of borrowing is then 7% (10% minus 30% of the 10% interest payment), and when the expected inflation rate is 5%, the effective cost of borrowing in real terms is again 2% (= 7% − 5%).

As the example (and the formula) indicates, after-tax real interest rates are always below the real interest rate defined by the Fisher equation. For a further discussion of measures of after-tax real interest rates, see Frederic S. Mishkin, "The Real Interest Rate: An Empirical Investigation," *Carnegie-Rochester Conference Series on Public Policy* 15 (1981): 151–200.

FYI With TIPS, Real Interest Rates Have Become Observable in the United States

When the U.S. Treasury decided to issue TIPS (Treasury Inflation Protection Securities), a version of indexed Treasury coupon bonds, in January 1997, it was somewhat late in the game. Other countries such as the United Kingdom, Canada, Australia, and Sweden had already beaten the United States to the punch. (In September 1998, the U.S. Treasury also began issuing the Series I savings bond, which provides inflation protection for small investors.)

These indexed securities have successfully carved out a niche in the bond market, enabling governments to raise more funds. In addition, because their interest and principal payments are adjusted for changes in the price level, the interest rate on these bonds provides a direct measure of a real interest rate. These indexed bonds are very useful to policymakers, especially monetary policymakers, because by subtracting their interest rate from a nominal interest rate on a nonindexed bond, they generate more insight into expected inflation, a valuable piece of information. For example, on January 12, 2006, the interest rate on the ten-year Treasury bond was 4.48%, while that on the ten-year TIPS was 2.01%. Thus, the implied expected inflation rate for the next ten years, derived from the difference between these two rates, was 2.47%. The private sector finds the information provided by TIPS very useful: Many commercial and investment banks routinely publish the expected U.S. inflation rates derived from these bonds.

SUMMARY

1. The yield to maturity, which is the measure that most accurately reflects the interest rate, is the interest rate that equates the present value of future payments of a debt instrument with its value today. Application of this principle reveals that bond prices and interest rates are negatively related: When the interest rate rises, the price of the bond must fall, and vice versa.
2. Two less accurate measures of interest rates are commonly used to quote interest rates on coupon and discount bonds. The current yield, which equals the coupon payment divided by the price of a coupon bond, is a less accurate measure of the yield to maturity the shorter the maturity of the bond. The yield on a discount basis (also called the discount yield) understates the yield to maturity on a discount bond, and the understatement worsens with the distance from maturity of the discount security. Even though these measures are misleading guides to the size of the interest rate, a change in them always signals a change in the same direction for the yield to maturity.
3. The return on a security, which tells you how well you have done by holding this security over a stated period of time, can differ substantially from the interest rate as measured by the yield to maturity. Long-term bond prices have substantial fluctuations when interest rates change and thus bear interest-rate risk. The resulting capital gains and losses can be large, which is why long-term bonds are not considered to be safe assets with a sure return.
4. The real interest rate is defined as the nominal interest rate minus the expected rate of inflation. It is a better measure of the incentives to borrow and lend than the nominal interest rate, and it is a more accurate indicator of the tightness of credit market conditions than the nominal interest rate.

KEY TERMS

basis point, p. 82
cash flows, p. 67
consol or perpetuity, p. 75
coupon bond, p. 70
coupon rate, p. 70
current yield, p. 77
discount bond (zero-coupon bond), p. 70
face value (par value), p. 70
fixed-payment loan (fully amortized loan), p. 70
indexed bond, p. 89
interest-rate risk, p. 85
nominal interest rate, p. 87
present discounted value, p. 67
present value, p. 67
rate of capital gain, p. 83
real interest rate, p. 87
real terms, p. 87
return (rate of return), p. 82
simple loan, p. 68
yield on a discount basis (discount yield), p. 79
yield to maturity, p. 71

QUESTIONS AND PROBLEMS

Questions marked with an asterisk are answered at the end of the book in an appendix, "Answers to Selected Questions and Problems." Questions marked with a blue circle indicate the question is available in MyEconLab at www.myeconlab.com/mishkin.

*1. Would a dollar tomorrow be worth more to you today when the interest rate is 20% or when it is 10%?

2. You have just won $10 million in the state lottery, which promises to pay you $1 million (tax free) every year for the next ten years. Have you really won $10 million?

*3. If the interest rate is 10%, what is the present value of a security that pays you $1,100 next year, $1,210 the year after, and $1,331 the year after that?

4. If the security in Problem 3 sold for $3,500, is the yield to maturity greater or less than 10%? Why?

*5. Write down the formula that is used to calculate the yield to maturity on a twenty-year 10% coupon bond with $1,000 face value that sells for $2,000.

6. What is the yield to maturity on a $1,000-face-value discount bond maturing in one year that sells for $800?

*7. What is the yield to maturity on a simple loan for $1 million that requires a repayment of $2 million in five years' time?

8. To pay for college, you have just taken out a $1,000 government loan that makes you pay $126 per year for 25 years. However, you don't have to start making these payments until you graduate from college two years from now. Why is the yield to maturity necessarily less than 12%, the yield to maturity on a normal $1,000 fixed-payment loan in which you pay $126 per year for 25 years?

*9. Which $1,000 bond has the higher yield to maturity, a twenty-year bond selling for $800 with a current yield of 15% or a one-year bond selling for $800 with a current yield of 5%?

10. Pick five U.S. Treasury bonds from the bond page of the newspaper, and calculate the current yield. Note when the current yield is a good approximation of the yield to maturity.

*11. You are offered two bonds, a one-year U.S. Treasury bond with a yield to maturity of 9% and a one-year U.S. Treasury bill with a yield on a discount basis of 8.9%. Which would you rather own?

12. If there is a decline in interest rates, which would you rather be holding, long-term bonds or short-term bonds? Why? Which type of bond has the greater interest-rate risk?

*13. Francine the Financial Advisor has just given you the following advice: "Long-term bonds are a great investment because their interest rate is over 20%." Is Francine necessarily right?

14. If mortgage rates rise from 5% to 10% but the expected rate of increase in housing prices rises from 2% to 9%, are people more or less likely to buy houses?

*15. Interest rates were lower in the mid-1980s than they were in the late 1970s, yet many economists have commented that real interest rates were actually much higher in the mid-1980s than in the late 1970s. Does this make sense? Do you think that these economists are right?

WEB EXERCISES

1. Investigate the data available from the Federal Reserve at www.federalreserve.gov/releases/. Answer the following questions:
   a. What is the difference in the interest rates on commercial paper for financial firms when compared to nonfinancial firms?
   b. What was the interest rate on the one-month Eurodollar at the end of 2002?
   c. What is the most recent interest rate report for the 30-year Treasury note?
2. Figure 1 in the text shows the estimated real and nominal rates for three-month Treasury bills. Go to www.martincapital.com/charts.htm and click on "interest rates and yields," then on "real interest rates."
   a. Compare the three-month real rate to the long-term real rate. Which is greater?
   b. Compare the short-term nominal rate to the long-term nominal rate. Which appears most volatile?
3. In this chapter we discussed long-term bonds as if there were only one type, coupon bonds. In fact, there are also long-term discount bonds. A discount bond is sold at a low price and the whole return comes in the form of a price appreciation. You can easily compute the current price of a discount bond using the financial calculator at www.publicdebt.treas.gov/sav/savcalc.htm.

   To compute the redemption values for savings bonds, fill in the information at the site and click the Compute Values button. A maximum of five years of data will be displayed for each computation.

WEB REFERENCES

www.bloomberg.com/markets/

Under "Rates & Bonds," you can access information on key interest rates, U.S. Treasuries, government bonds, and municipal bonds.

www.teachmefinance.com

A review of the key financial concepts: time value of money, annuities, perpetuities, and so on.

www.martincapital.com/charts.htm

Go to charts of real versus nominal rates to view 30 years of nominal interest rates compared to real rates for the 30-year T-bond and 90-day T-bill.

CHAPTER

5 The Behavior of Interest Rates

Preview

In the early 1950s, nominal interest rates on three-month Treasury bills were about 1% at an annual rate; by 1981, they had reached over 15%; in the early 2000s they fell below 2%. What explains these substantial fluctuations in interest rates? One reason why we study money, banking, and financial markets is to provide some answers to this question.

In this chapter, we examine how the overall level of *nominal* interest rates (which we refer to as simply "interest rates") is determined and which factors influence their behavior. We learned in Chapter 4 that interest rates are negatively related to the price of bonds, so if we can explain why bond prices change, we can also explain why interest rates fluctuate. We make use of supply and demand analysis for bond markets and money markets to examine how interest rates change.

To derive a demand curve for assets such as money or bonds, the first step in our analysis, we must first understand what determines the demand for these assets. We do this by examining the *theory of asset demand*, an economic theory that outlines criteria that are important when deciding how much of an asset to buy. Armed with this theory, we can then go on to derive the demand curve for bonds or money. After deriving supply curves for these assets, we develop the concept of *market equilibrium*, the point at which the quantity supplied equals the quantity demanded. Then we use this model to explain changes in equilibrium interest rates.

Because interest rates on different securities tend to move together, in this chapter we will proceed as if there were only one type of security and one interest rate in the entire economy. In the following chapter, we expand our analysis to look at why interest rates on different types of securities differ.

DETERMINANTS OF ASSET DEMAND

Before going on to our supply and demand analysis of the bond market and the market for money, we must first understand what determines the quantity demanded of an asset. Recall that an asset is a piece of property that is a store of value. Items such as money, bonds, stocks, art, land, houses, farm equipment, and manufacturing machinery are all assets. Facing the question of whether to buy and hold an asset or whether to buy one asset rather than another, an individual must consider the following factors:

1. **Wealth**, the total resources owned by the individual, including all assets
2. **Expected return** (the return expected over the next period) on one asset relative to alternative assets

3. **Risk** (the degree of uncertainty associated with the return) on one asset relative to alternative assets
4. **Liquidity** (the ease and speed with which an asset can be turned into cash) relative to alternative assets

STUDY GUIDE

As we discuss each factor that influences asset demand, remember that we are always holding all the other factors constant. Also, think of additional examples of how changes in each factor would influence your decision to purchase a particular asset—say, a house or a share of common stock. This intuitive approach will help you understand how the theory works in practice.

Wealth

When we find that our wealth has increased, we have more resources available with which to purchase assets, and so, not surprisingly, the quantity of assets we demand increases. Therefore, the effect of changes in wealth on the quantity demanded of an asset can be summarized as follows: ***Holding everything else constant, an increase in wealth raises the quantity demanded of an asset.***

Expected Returns

In Chapter 4, we saw that the return on an asset (such as a bond) measures how much we gain from holding that asset. When we make a decision to buy an asset, we are influenced by what we expect the return on that asset to be. If an Exxon Mobil Corporation bond, for example, has a return of 15% half the time and 5% the other half of the time, its expected return (which you can think of as the average return) is 10% ($= 0.5 \times 15\% + 0.5 \times 5\%$).[1] If the expected return on the Exxon Mobil bond rises relative to expected returns on alternative assets, holding everything else constant, then it becomes more desirable to purchase it, and the quantity demanded increases. This can occur in either of two ways: (1) when the expected return on the Exxon Mobil bond rises while the return on an alternative asset—say, stock in Google—remains unchanged or (2) when the return on the alternative asset, the Google stock, falls while the return on the Exxon Mobil bond remains unchanged. To summarize, ***an increase in an asset's expected return relative to that of an alternative asset, holding everything else unchanged, raises the quantity demanded of the asset.***

[1]If you are interested in finding out more information on how to calculate expected returns, as well as standard deviations of returns that measure risk, you can look at an appendix to this chapter describing models of asset pricing that is on this book's web site at www.myeconlab.com/mishkin. This appendix also describes how diversification lowers the overall risk of a portfolio and has a discussion of systematic risk and basic asset pricing models such as the capital asset pricing model and arbitrage pricing theory.

Risk

The degree of risk or uncertainty of an asset's returns also affects the demand for the asset. Consider two assets, stock in Fly-by-Night Airlines and stock in Feet-on-the-Ground Bus Company. Suppose that Fly-by-Night stock has a return of 15% half the time and 5% the other half of the time, making its expected return 10%, while stock in Feet-on-the-Ground has a fixed return of 10%. Fly-by-Night stock has uncertainty associated with its returns and so has greater risk than stock in Feet-on-the-Ground, whose return is a sure thing.

A *risk-averse* person prefers stock in Feet-on-the-Ground (the sure thing) to Fly-by-Night stock (the riskier asset), even though the stocks have the same expected return, 10%. By contrast, a person who prefers risk is a *risk preferrer* or *risk lover*. Most people are risk-averse, especially in their financial decisions: Everything else being equal, they prefer to hold the less risky asset. Hence, ***holding everything else constant, if an asset's risk rises relative to that of alternative assets, its quantity demanded will fall.***

Liquidity

Another factor that affects the demand for an asset is how quickly it can be converted into cash at low costs—its liquidity. An asset is liquid if the market in which it is traded has depth and breadth; that is, if the market has many buyers and sellers. A house is not a very liquid asset, because it may be hard to find a buyer quickly; if a house must be sold to pay off bills, it might have to be sold for a much lower price. And the transaction costs in selling a house (broker's commissions, lawyer's fees, and so on) are substantial. A U.S. Treasury bill, by contrast, is a highly liquid asset. It can be sold in a well-organized market where there are many buyers, so it can be sold quickly at low cost. ***The more liquid an asset is relative to alternative assets, holding everything else unchanged, the more desirable it is, and the greater will be the quantity demanded.***

Theory of Asset Demand

All the determining factors we have just discussed can be assembled into the **theory of asset demand**, which states that, holding all of the other factors constant:

1. The quantity demanded of an asset is positively related to wealth.
2. The quantity demanded of an asset is positively related to its expected return relative to alternative assets.
3. The quantity demanded of an asset is negatively related to the risk of its returns relative to alternative assets.
4. The quantity demanded of an asset is positively related to its liquidity relative to alternative assets.

These results are summarized in Table 1.

SUPPLY AND DEMAND IN THE BOND MARKET

Our first approach to the analysis of interest-rate determination looks at supply and demand in the bond market to see how the price of bonds is determined. Thanks to our understanding of how interest rates are measured from Chapter 4, we know that each

SUMMARY TABLE 1 Response of the Quantity of an Asset Demanded to Changes in Wealth, Expected Returns, Risk, and Liquidity

Variable	Change in Variable	Change in Quantity Demanded
Wealth	↑	↑
Expected return relative to other assets	↑	↑
Risk relative to other assets	↑	↓
Liquidity relative to other assets	↑	↑

Note: Only increases in the variables are shown. The effect of decreases in the variables on the change in quantity demanded would be the opposite of those indicated in the rightmost column.

bond price is associated with a particular level of the interest rate. Specifically, the negative relationship between bond prices and interest rates means that when a bond price rises, its interest rate falls, and vice versa.

The first step in the analysis is to obtain a bond **demand curve**, which shows the relationship between the quantity demanded and the price when all other economic variables are held constant (that is, values of other variables are taken as given). You may recall from previous economics courses that the assumption that all other economic variables are held constant is called *ceteris paribus*, which means "other things being equal" in Latin.

Demand Curve

To clarify our analysis, let us consider the demand for one-year discount bonds, which make no coupon payments but pay the owner the $1,000 face value in a year. If the holding period is one year, then as we have seen in Chapter 4, the return on the bonds is known absolutely and is equal to the interest rate as measured by the yield to maturity. This means that the expected return on this bond is equal to the interest rate i, which, using Equation 6 in Chapter 4, is

$$i = R^e = \frac{F - P}{P}$$

where
i = interest rate = yield to maturity
R^e = expected return
F = face value of the discount bond
P = initial purchase price of the discount bond

This formula shows that a particular value of the interest rate corresponds to each bond price. If the bond sells for $950, the interest rate and expected return are

$$\frac{\$1{,}000 - \$950}{\$950} = 0.053 = 5.3\%$$

At this 5.3% interest rate and expected return corresponding to a bond price of $950, let us assume that the quantity of bonds demanded is $100 billion, which is plotted as point A in Figure 1.

FIGURE 1
Supply and Demand for Bonds
Equilibrium in the bond market occurs at point C, the intersection of the demand curve B^d and the bond supply curve B^s. The equilibrium price is $P^* = \$850$, and the equilibrium interest rate is $i^* = 17.6\%$.

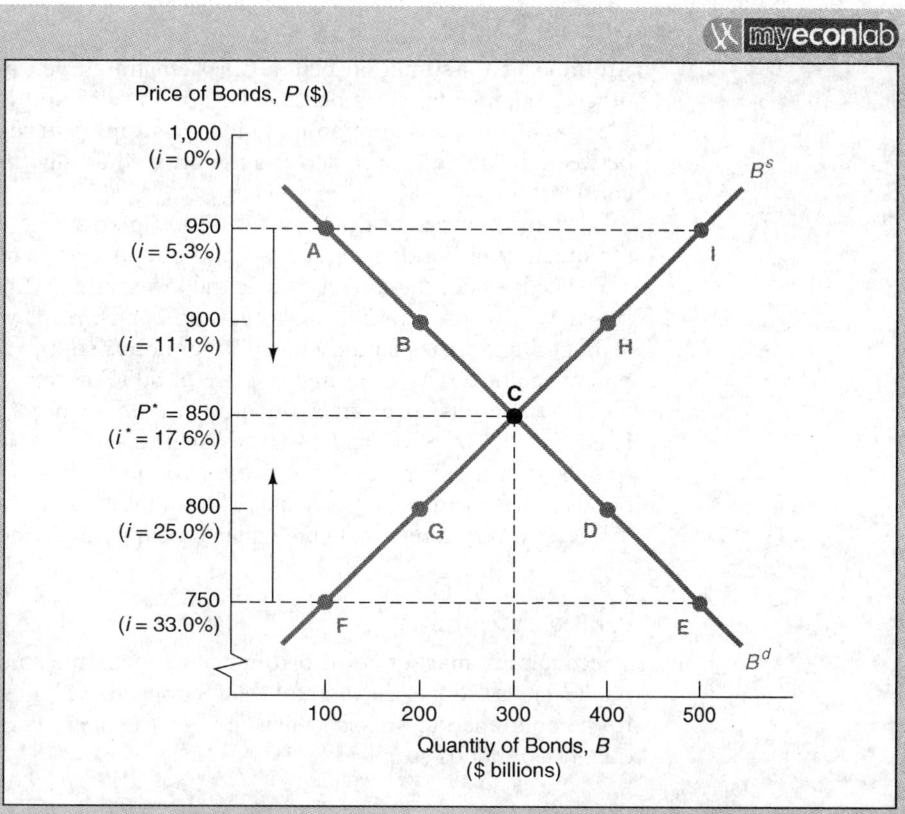

At a price of $900, the interest rate and expected return is

$$\frac{\$1{,}000 - \$900}{\$900} = 0.111 = 11.1\%$$

Because the expected return on these bonds is higher, with all other economic variables (such as income, expected returns on other assets, risk, and liquidity) held constant, the quantity demanded of bonds will be higher as predicted by the theory of asset demand. Point B in Figure 1 shows that the quantity of bonds demanded at the price of $900 has risen to $200 billion. Continuing with this reasoning, if the bond price is $850 (interest rate and expected return = 17.6%), the quantity of bonds demanded (point C) will be greater than at point B. Similarly, at the lower prices of $800 (interest rate = 25%) and $750 (interest rate = 33.3%), the quantity of bonds demanded will be even higher (points D and E). The curve B^d, which connects these points, is the demand curve for bonds. It has the usual downward slope, indicating that at lower prices of the bond (everything else being equal), the quantity demanded is higher.[2]

[2]Although our analysis indicates that the demand curve is downward-sloping, it does not imply that the curve is a straight line. For ease of exposition, however, we will draw demand curves and supply curves as straight lines.

Supply Curve

An important assumption behind the demand curve for bonds in Figure 1 is that all other economic variables besides the bond's price and interest rate are held constant. We use the same assumption in deriving a **supply curve**, which shows the relationship between the quantity supplied and the price when all other economic variables are held constant.

When the price of the bonds is $750 (interest rate = 33.3%), point F shows that the quantity of bonds supplied is $100 billion for the example we are considering. If the price is $800, the interest rate is the lower rate of 25%. Because at this interest rate it is now less costly to borrow by issuing bonds, firms will be willing to borrow more through bond issues, and the quantity of bonds supplied is at the higher level of $200 billion (point G). An even higher price of $850, corresponding to a lower interest rate of 17.6%, results in a larger quantity of bonds supplied of $300 billion (point C). Higher prices of $900 and $950 result in even greater quantities of bonds supplied (points H and I). The B^s curve, which connects these points, is the supply curve for bonds. It has the usual upward slope found in supply curves, indicating that as the price increases (everything else being equal), the quantity supplied increases.

Market Equilibrium

In economics, **market equilibrium** occurs when the amount that people are willing to buy (*demand*) equals the amount that people are willing to sell (*supply*) at a given price. In the bond market, this is achieved when the quantity of bonds demanded equals the quantity of bonds supplied:

$$B^d = B^s \tag{1}$$

In Figure 1, equilibrium occurs at point C, where the demand and supply curves intersect at a bond price of $850 (interest rate of 17.6%) and a quantity of bonds of $300 billion. The price of $P^* = \$850$, where the quantity demanded equals the quantity supplied, is called the *equilibrium* or *market-clearing* price. Similarly, the interest rate of $i^* = 17.6\%$ that corresponds to this price is called the equilibrium or market-clearing interest rate.

The concepts of market equilibrium and equilibrium price or interest rate are useful, because there is a tendency for the market to head toward them. We can see that it does in Figure 1 by first looking at what happens when we have a bond price that is above the equilibrium price. When the price of bonds is set too high, at, say, $950, the quantity of bonds supplied at point I is greater than the quantity of bonds demanded at point A. A situation like this, in which the quantity of bonds supplied exceeds the quantity of bonds demanded, is called a condition of **excess supply**. Because people want to sell more bonds than others want to buy, the price of the bonds will fall, which is why the downward arrow is drawn in the figure at the bond price of $950. As long as the bond price remains above the equilibrium price, there will continue to be an excess supply of bonds, and the price will continue to fall. This decline will stop only when the price has reached the equilibrium price of $850, where the excess supply of bonds has been eliminated.

Now let's look at what happens when the price of bonds is below the equilibrium price. If the price of the bonds is set too low, at, say, $750, the quantity demanded at point E is greater than the quantity supplied at point F. This is called a condition of **excess demand**. People now want to buy more bonds than others are willing to sell, so the price of bonds will be driven up. This is illustrated by the upward arrow drawn in the figure at the bond price of $750. Only when the excess demand for bonds is eliminated by the price rising to the equilibrium level of $850 is there no further tendency for the price to rise.

We can see that the concept of equilibrium price is a useful one because it indicates where the market will settle. Because each price on the left vertical axis of Figure 1 corresponds to a particular value of the interest rate, the same diagram also shows that the interest rate will head toward the equilibrium interest rate of 17.6%. When the interest rate is below the equilibrium interest rate, as it is when it is at 5.3%, the price of the bond is above the equilibrium price, and there will be an excess supply of bonds. The price of the bond then falls, leading to a rise in the interest rate toward the equilibrium level. Similarly, when the interest rate is above the equilibrium level, as it is when it is at 33.3%, there is excess demand for bonds, and the bond price will rise, driving the interest rate back down to the equilibrium level of 17.6%.

Supply and Demand Analysis

Our Figure 1 is a conventional supply and demand diagram with price on the vertical axis and quantity on the horizontal axis. Because the interest rate that corresponds to each bond price is also marked on the vertical axis, this diagram allows us to read the equilibrium interest rate, giving us a model that describes the determination of interest rates. It is important to recognize that a supply and demand diagram like Figure 1 can be drawn for *any* type of bond because the interest rate and price of a bond are *always* negatively related for any type of bond, whether a discount bond or a coupon bond.

An important feature of the analysis here is that supply and demand are always in terms of *stocks* (amounts at a given point in time) of assets, not in terms of *flows*. The **asset market approach** for understanding behavior in financial markets—which emphasizes stocks of assets rather than flows in determining asset prices—is the dominant methodology used by economists, because correctly conducting analyses in terms of flows is very tricky, especially when we encounter inflation.[3]

CHANGES IN EQUILIBRIUM INTEREST RATES

We will now use the supply and demand framework for bonds to analyze why interest rates change. To avoid confusion, it is important to make the distinction between *movements along* a demand (or supply) curve and *shifts in* a demand (or supply) curve. When quantity demanded (or supplied) changes as a result of a change in the price of the bond (or, equivalently, a change in the interest rate), we have a *movement along* the demand (or supply) curve. The change in the quantity demanded when we move from point A to B to C in Figure 1, for example, is a movement along a demand curve. A *shift in* the demand (or supply) curve, by contrast, occurs when the quantity demanded (or

---

[3]The asset market approach developed in the text is useful in understanding not only how interest rates behave but also how any asset price is determined. A second appendix to this chapter, which is on this book's web site at www.myeconlab.com/mishkin, shows how the asset market approach can be applied to understanding the behavior of commodity markets; in particular, the gold market. The analysis of the bond market that we have developed here has another interpretation using a different terminology and framework involving the supply and demand for loanable funds. This loanable funds framework is discussed in a third appendix to this chapter, which is also on the book's web site.

supplied) changes *at each given price (or interest rate)* of the bond in response to a change in some other factor besides the bond's price or interest rate. When one of these factors changes, causing a shift in the demand or supply curve, there will be a new equilibrium value for the interest rate.

In the following pages, we will look at how the supply and demand curves shift in response to changes in variables, such as expected inflation and wealth, and what effects these changes have on the equilibrium value of interest rates.

Shifts in the Demand for Bonds

The theory of asset demand demonstrated at the beginning of the chapter provides a framework for deciding which factors cause the demand curve for bonds to shift. These factors include changes in four parameters:

1. Wealth
2. Expected returns on bonds relative to alternative assets
3. Risk of bonds relative to alternative assets
4. Liquidity of bonds relative to alternative assets

To see how a change in each of these factors (holding all other factors constant) can shift the demand curve, let us look at some examples. (As a study aid, Table 2 summarizes the effects of changes in these factors on the bond demand curve.)

Wealth.

When the economy is growing rapidly in a business cycle expansion and wealth is increasing, the quantity of bonds demanded at each bond price (or interest rate) increases as shown in Figure 2. To see how this works, consider point B on the initial demand curve for bonds B_1^d. With higher wealth, the quantity of bonds demanded at the same price must rise, to point B′. Similarly, for point D the higher wealth causes the quantity demanded at the same bond price to rise to point D′. Continuing with this reasoning for every point on the initial demand curve B_1^d, we can see that the demand curve shifts to the right from B_1^d to B_2^d as is indicated by the arrows.

The conclusion we have reached is that ***in a business cycle expansion with growing wealth, the demand for bonds rises and the demand curve for bonds shifts to the right.*** Using the same reasoning, ***in a recession, when income and wealth are falling, the demand for bonds falls, and the demand curve shifts to the left.***

Another factor that affects wealth is the public's propensity to save. If households save more, wealth increases and, as we have seen, the demand for bonds rises and the demand curve for bonds shifts to the right. Conversely, if people save less, wealth and the demand for bonds will fall and the demand curve shifts to the left.

Expected Returns.

For a one-year discount bond and a one-year holding period, the expected return and the interest rate are identical, so nothing besides today's interest rate affects the expected return.

For bonds with maturities of greater than one year, the expected return may differ from the interest rate. For example, we saw in Chapter 4, Table 2, that a rise in the interest rate on a long-term bond from 10% to 20% would lead to a sharp decline in price and a very large negative return. Hence, if people began to think that interest rates would be higher next year than they had originally anticipated, the expected return today on long-term bonds would fall, and the quantity demanded would fall at each interest rate. ***Higher expected interest rates in the future lower the expected return for long-term bonds, decrease the demand, and shift the demand curve to the left.***

SUMMARY TABLE 2 Factors That Shift the Demand Curve for Bonds

Variable	Change in Variable	Change in Quantity Demanded at Each Bond Price	Shift in Demand Curve
Wealth	↑	↑	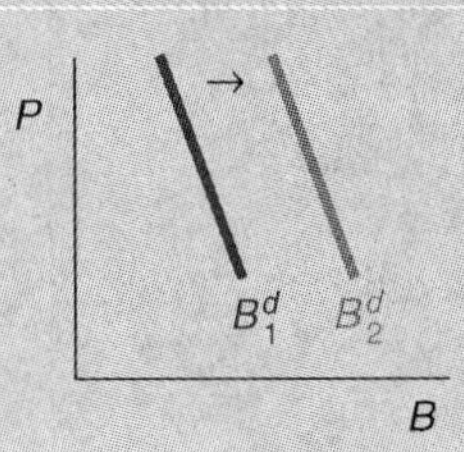
Expected interest rate	↑	↓	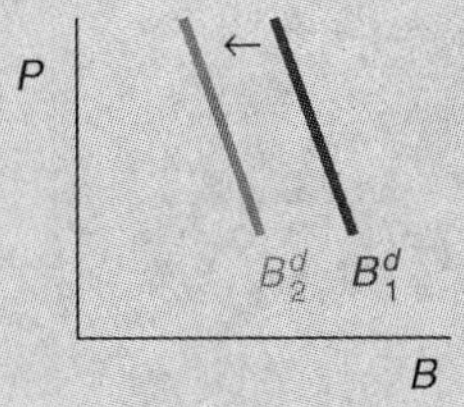
Expected inflation	↑	↓	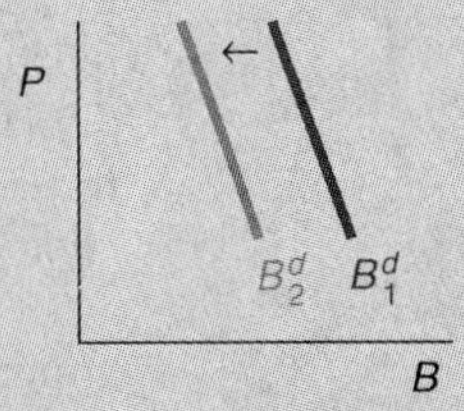
Riskiness of bonds relative to other assets	↑	↓	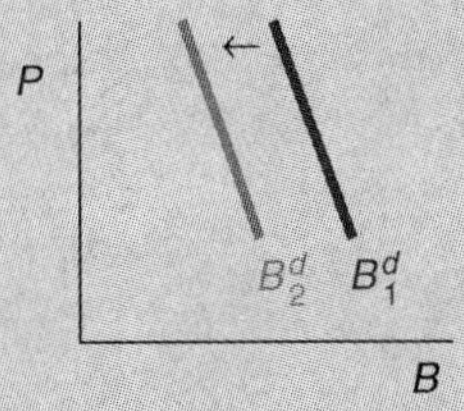
Liquidity of bonds relative to other assets	↑	↑	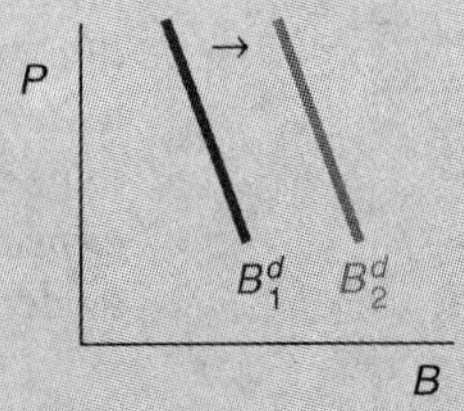

Note: Only increases in the variables are shown. The effect of decreases in the variables on the change in demand would be the opposite of those indicated in the remaining columns.

FIGURE 2
Shift in the Demand Curve for Bonds
When the demand for bonds increases, the demand curve shifts to the right as shown.

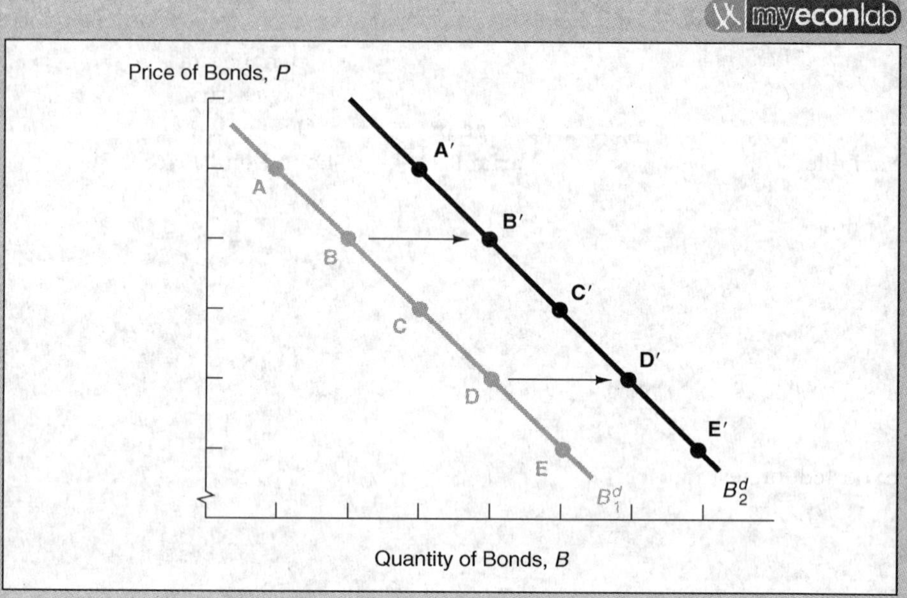

By contrast, a revision downward of expectations of future interest rates would mean that long-term bond prices would be expected to rise more than originally anticipated, and the resulting higher expected return today would raise the quantity demanded at each bond price and interest rate. ***Lower expected interest rates in the future increase the demand for long-term bonds and shift the demand curve to the right*** (as in Figure 2).

Changes in expected returns on other assets can also shift the demand curve for bonds. If people suddenly became more optimistic about the stock market and began to expect higher stock prices in the future, both expected capital gains and expected returns on stocks would rise. With the expected return on bonds held constant, the expected return on bonds today relative to stocks would fall, lowering the demand for bonds and shifting the demand curve to the left.

A change in expected inflation is likely to alter expected returns on physical assets (also called *real assets*) such as automobiles and houses, which affect the demand for bonds. An increase in expected inflation, say, from 5% to 10%, will lead to higher prices on cars and houses in the future and hence higher nominal capital gains. The resulting rise in the expected returns today on these real assets will lead to a fall in the expected return on bonds relative to the expected return on real assets today and thus cause the demand for bonds to fall. Alternatively, we can think of the rise in expected inflation as lowering the real interest rate on bonds, and the resulting decline in the relative expected return on bonds will cause the demand for bonds to fall. ***An increase in the expected rate of inflation lowers the expected return for bonds, causing their demand to decline and the demand curve to shift to the left.***

Risk. If prices in the bond market become more volatile, the risk associated with bonds increases, and bonds become a less attractive asset. ***An increase in the riskiness of bonds causes the demand for bonds to fall and the demand curve to shift to the left.***

Conversely, an increase in the volatility of prices in another asset market, such as the stock market, would make bonds more attractive. ***An increase in the riskiness of alternative assets causes the demand for bonds to rise and the demand curve to shift to the right*** (as in Figure 2).

Liquidity. If more people started trading in the bond market, and as a result it became easier to sell bonds quickly, the increase in their liquidity would cause the quantity of bonds demanded at each interest rate to rise. ***Increased liquidity of bonds results in an increased demand for bonds, and the demand curve shifts to the right*** (see Figure 2). ***Similarly, increased liquidity of alternative assets lowers the demand for bonds and shifts the demand curve to the left.*** The reduction of brokerage commissions for trading common stocks that occurred when the fixed-rate commission structure was abolished in 1975, for example, increased the liquidity of stocks relative to bonds, and the resulting lower demand for bonds shifted the demand curve to the left.

Shifts in the Supply of Bonds

Certain factors can cause the supply curve for bonds to shift, among them these:

1. Expected profitability of investment opportunities
2. Expected inflation
3. Government budget

We will look at how the supply curve shifts when each of these factors changes (all others remaining constant). (As a study aid, Table 3 summarizes the effects of changes in these factors on the bond supply curve.)

Expected Profitability of Investment Opportunities. The more profitable plant and equipment investments that a firm expects it can make, the more willing it will be to borrow to finance these investments. When the economy is growing rapidly, as in a business cycle expansion, investment opportunities that are expected to be profitable abound, and the quantity of bonds supplied at any given bond price will increase (see Figure 3). ***Therefore, in a business cycle expansion, the supply of bonds increases, and the supply curve shifts to the right. Likewise, in a recession, when there are far fewer expected profitable investment opportunities, the supply of bonds falls, and the supply curve shifts to the left.***

Expected Inflation. As we saw in Chapter 4, the real cost of borrowing is more accurately measured by the real interest rate, which equals the (nominal) interest rate minus the expected inflation rate. For a given interest rate (and bond price), when expected inflation increases, the real cost of borrowing falls; hence the quantity of bonds supplied increases at any given bond price. ***An increase in expected inflation causes the supply of bonds to increase and the supply curve to shift to the right*** (see Figure 3).

Government Budget. The activities of the government can influence the supply of bonds in several ways. The U.S. Treasury issues bonds to finance government deficits, the gap between the government's expenditures and its revenues. When these deficits are large, the Treasury sells more bonds, and the quantity of bonds supplied at each

SUMMARY TABLE 3 Factors That Shift the Supply of Bonds

Variable	Change in Variable	Change in Quantity Supplied at Each Bond Price	Shift in Supply Curve
Profitability of investments	↑	↑	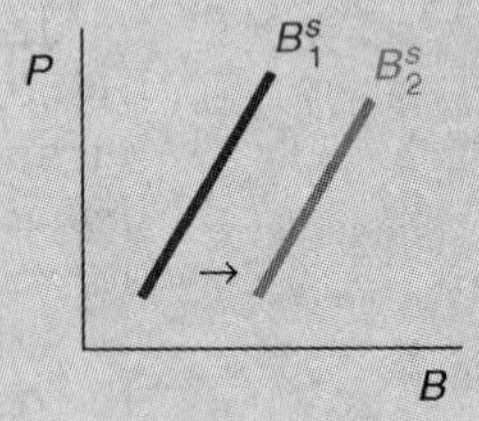
Expected inflation	↑	↑	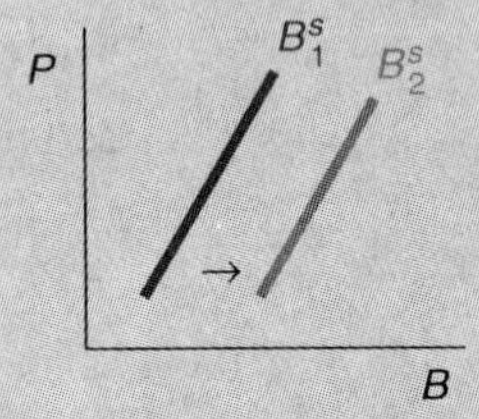
Government deficit	↑	↑	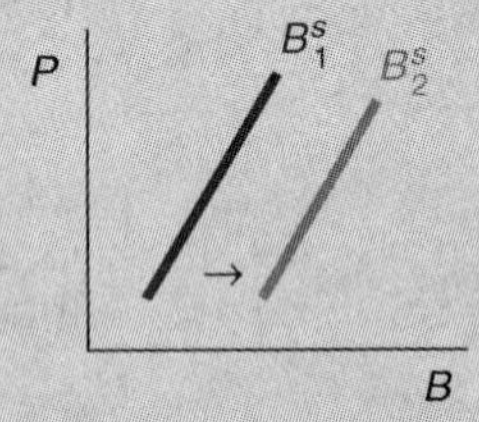

Note: Only increases in the variables are shown. The effect of decreases in the variables on the change in supply would be the opposite of those indicated in the remaining columns.

bond price increases. ***Higher government deficits increase the supply of bonds and shift the supply curve to the right*** (see Figure 3). ***On the other hand, government surpluses, as occurred in the late 1990s, decrease the supply of bonds and shift the supply curve to the left.***

State and local governments and other government agencies also issue bonds to finance their expenditures, and this can also affect the supply of bonds. We will see in later chapters that the conduct of monetary policy involves the purchase and sale of bonds, which in turn influences the supply of bonds.

We now can use our knowledge of how supply and demand curves shift to analyze how the equilibrium interest rate can change. The best way to do this is to pursue several applications that are particularly relevant to our understanding of how monetary policy affects interest rates.

FIGURE 3
Shift in the Supply Curve for Bonds
When the supply of bonds increases, the supply curve shifts to the right.

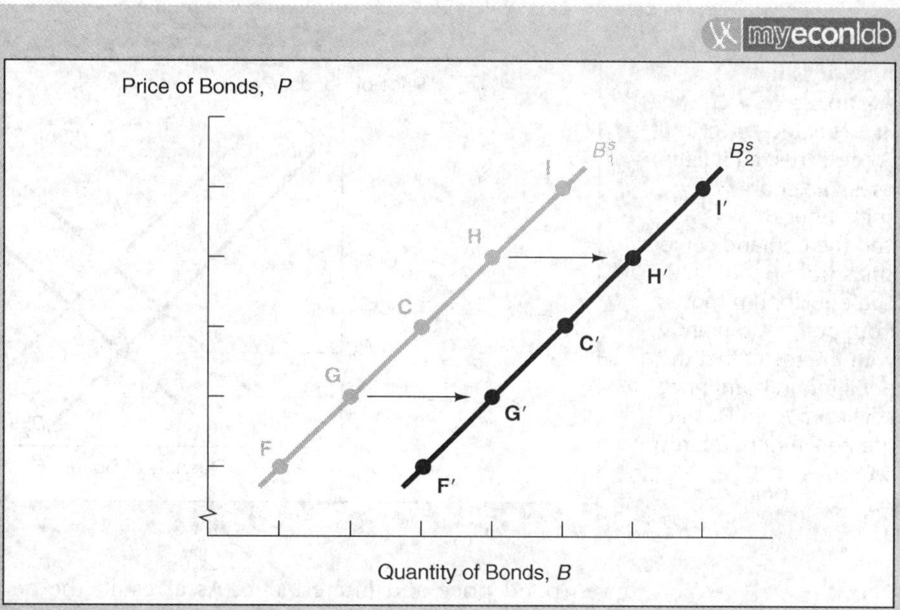

STUDY GUIDE

Supply and demand analysis for the bond market is best learned by practicing applications. When there is an application in the text and we look at how the interest rate changes because some economic variable increases, see if you can draw the appropriate shifts in the supply and demand curves when this same economic variable decreases. While you are practicing applications, keep two things in mind:

1. *When you examine the effect of a variable change, remember that we are assuming that all other variables are unchanged; that is, we are making use of the ceteris paribus assumption.*
2. *Remember that the interest rate is negatively related to the bond price, so when the equilibrium bond price rises, the equilibrium interest rate falls. Conversely, if the equilibrium bond price moves downward, the equilibrium interest rate rises.*

APPLICATION Changes in the Interest Rate Due to Expected Inflation: The Fisher Effect

We have already done most of the work to evaluate how a change in expected inflation affects the nominal interest rate, in that we have already analyzed how a change in expected inflation shifts the supply and demand curves. Figure 4 shows the effect on the equilibrium interest rate of an increase in expected inflation.

Suppose that expected inflation is initially 5% and the initial supply and demand curves B_1^s and B_1^d intersect at point 1, where the equilibrium bond price is P_1. If expected inflation rises to 10%, the expected return on bonds relative to real assets falls for any

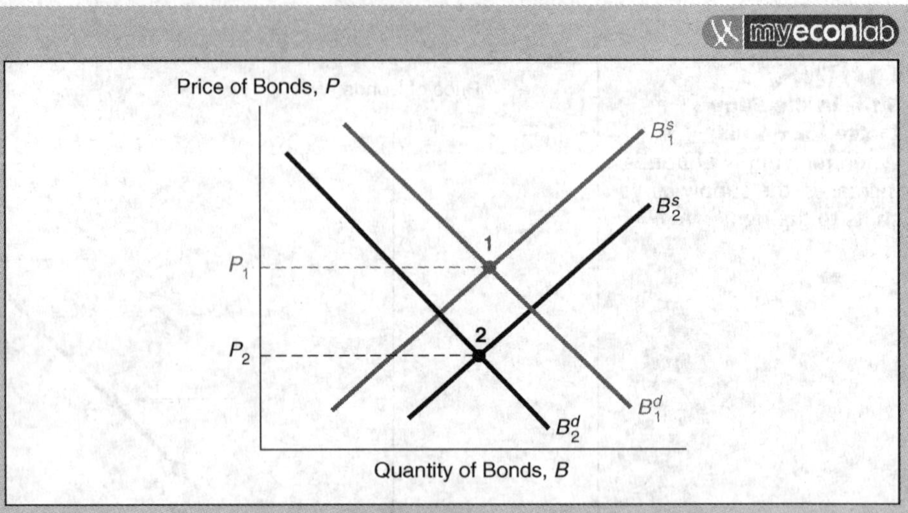

FIGURE 4
Response to a Change in Expected Inflation
When expected inflation rises, the supply curve shifts from B_1^s to B_2^s, and the demand curve shifts from B_1^d to B_2^d. The equilibrium moves from point 1 to point 2, with the result that the equilibrium bond price falls from P_1 to P_2 and the equilibrium interest rate rises.

given bond price and interest rate. As a result, the demand for bonds falls, and the demand curve shifts to the left from B_1^d to B_2^d. The rise in expected inflation also shifts the supply curve. At any given bond price and interest rate, the real cost of borrowing has declined, causing the quantity of bonds supplied to increase, and the supply curve shifts to the right, from B_1^s to B_2^s.

When the demand and supply curves shift in response to the change in expected inflation, the equilibrium moves from point 1 to point 2, the intersection of B_2^d and B_2^s. The equilibrium bond price has fallen from P_1 to P_2, and because the bond price is negatively related to the interest rate, this means that the interest rate has risen. Note that Figure 4 has been drawn so that the equilibrium quantity of bonds remains the same for both point 1 and point 2. However, depending on the size of the shifts in the supply and demand curves, the equilibrium quantity of bonds could either rise or fall when expected inflation rises.

Our supply and demand analysis has led us to an important observation: ***When expected inflation rises, interest rates will rise.*** This result has been named the **Fisher effect**, after Irving Fisher, the economist who first pointed out the relationship of expected inflation to interest rates. The accuracy of this prediction is shown in Figure 5. The interest rate on three-month Treasury bills has usually moved along with the expected inflation rate. Consequently, it is understandable that many economists recommend that inflation must be kept low if we want to keep nominal interest rates low.

APPLICATION Changes in the Interest Rate Due to a Business Cycle Expansion

Figure 6 analyzes the effects of a business cycle expansion on interest rates. In a business cycle expansion, the amounts of goods and services being produced in the economy increase, so national income increases. When this occurs, businesses will be more willing to borrow, because they are likely to have many profitable investment opportunities for which they need financing. Hence at a given bond price, the quantity of bonds that firms want to sell (that is, the supply of bonds) will increase. This means that in a business cycle expansion, the supply curve for bonds shifts to the right (see Figure 6) from B_1^s to B_2^s.

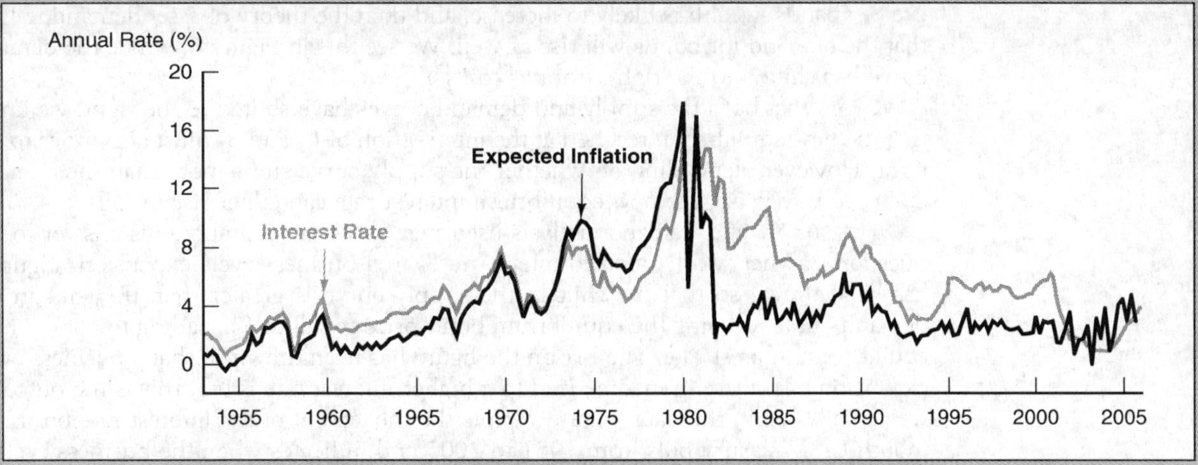

FIGURE 5 **Expected Inflation and Interest Rates (Three-Month Treasury Bills), 1953–2005**

Source: Expected inflation calculated using procedures outlined in Frederic S. Mishkin, "The Real Interest Rate: An Empirical Investigation," *Carnegie-Rochester Conference Series on Public Policy* 15 (1981): 151–200. These procedures involve estimating expected inflation as a function of past interest rates, inflation, and time trends.

FIGURE 6

Response to a Business Cycle Expansion

In a business cycle expansion, when income and wealth are rising, the demand curve shifts rightward from B_1^d to B_2^d, and the supply curve shifts rightward from B_1^s to B_2^s. If the supply curve shifts to the right more than the demand curve, as in this figure, the equilibrium bond price moves down from P_1 to P_2, and the equilibrium interest rate rises.

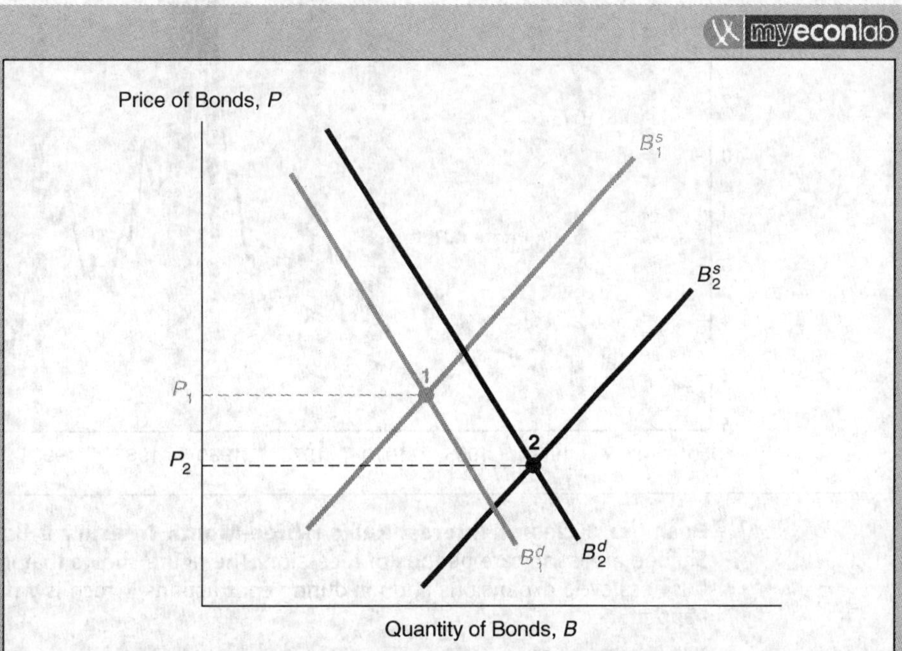

Expansion in the economy will also affect the demand for bonds. As the business cycle expands, wealth is likely to increase, and then the theory of asset demand tells us that the demand for bonds will rise as well. We see this in Figure 6, where the demand curve has shifted to the right, from B_1^d to B_2^d.

Given that both the supply and demand curves have shifted to the right, we know that the new equilibrium reached at the intersection of B_2^d and B_2^s must also move to the right. However, depending on whether the supply curve shifts more than the demand curve, or vice versa, the new equilibrium interest rate can either rise or fall.

The supply and demand analysis used here gives us an ambiguous answer to the question of what will happen to interest rates in a business cycle expansion. Figure 6 has been drawn so that the shift in the supply curve is greater than the shift in the demand curve, causing the equilibrium bond price to fall to P_2, leading to a rise in the equilibrium interest rate. The reason the figure has been drawn so that a business cycle expansion and a rise in income lead to a higher interest rate is that this is the outcome we actually see in the data. Figure 7 plots the movement of the interest rate on three-month U.S. Treasury bills from 1951 to 2005 and indicates when the business cycle is undergoing recessions (shaded areas). As you can see, the interest rate rises during business cycle expansions and falls during recessions, which is what the supply and demand diagram indicates.

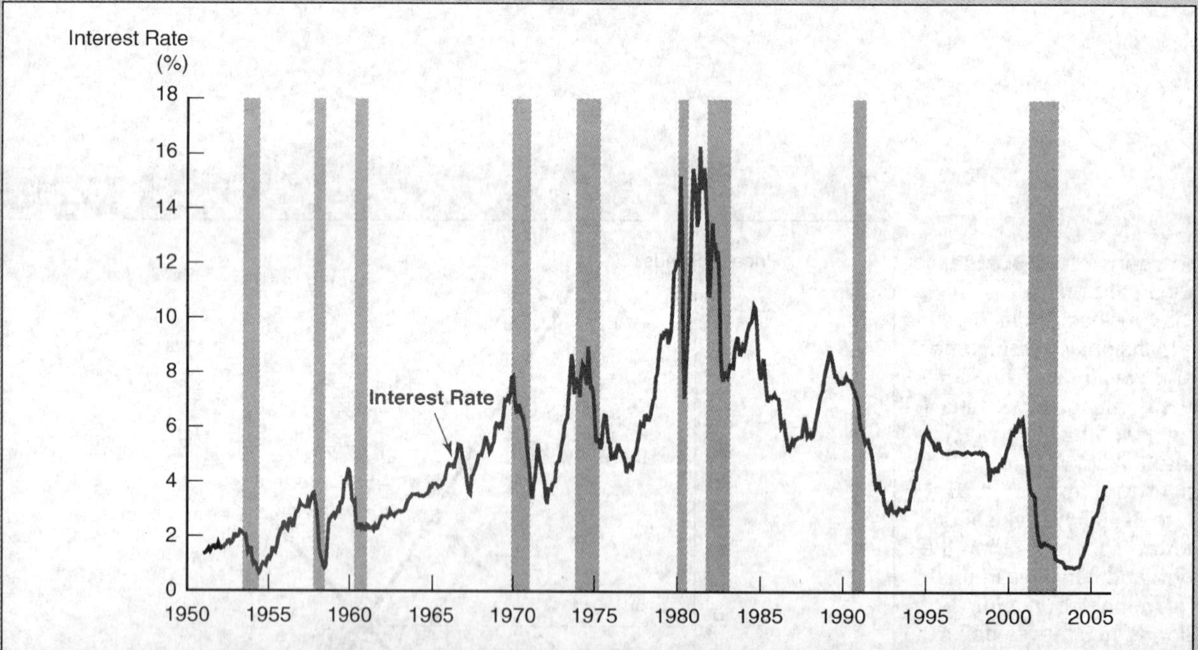

FIGURE 7 **Business Cycle and Interest Rates (Three-Month Treasury Bills), 1951–2005**
Shaded areas indicate periods of recession. The figure shows that interest rates rise during business cycle expansions and fall during contractions, which is what Figure 6 suggests would happen.

Source: Federal Reserve: www.federalreserve.gov/releases/H15/data.htm.

APPLICATION Explaining Low Japanese Interest Rates

In the 1990s and early 2000s, Japanese interest rates became the lowest in the world. Indeed, in November 1998, an extraordinary event occurred: Interest rates on Japanese six-month Treasury bills turned slightly negative (see Chapter 4). Why did Japanese rates drop to such low levels?

In the late 1990s and early 2000s, Japan experienced a prolonged recession, which was accompanied by deflation, a negative inflation rate. Using these facts, analysis similar to that used in the preceding application explains the low Japanese interest rates.

Negative inflation caused the demand for bonds to rise because the expected return on real assets fell, thereby raising the relative expected return on bonds and in turn causing the demand curve to shift to the right. The negative inflation also raised the real interest rate and therefore the real cost of borrowing for any given nominal rate, thereby causing the supply of bonds to contract and the supply curve to shift to the left. The outcome was then exactly the opposite of that graphed in Figure 4: The rightward shift of the demand curve and leftward shift of the supply curve led to a rise in the bond price and a fall in interest rates.

The business cycle contraction and the resulting lack of profitable investment opportunities in Japan also led to lower interest rates, by decreasing the supply of bonds and shifting the supply curve to the left. Although the demand curve also would shift to the left because wealth decreased during the business cycle contraction, we have seen in the preceding application that the demand curve would shift less than the supply curve. Thus, the bond price rose and interest rates fell (the opposite outcome to that in Figure 6).

Usually, we think that low interest rates are a good thing, because they make it cheap to borrow. But the Japanese example shows that just as there is a fallacy in the adage, "You can never be too rich or too thin" (maybe you can't be too rich, but you can certainly be too thin and do damage to your health), there is a fallacy in always thinking that lower interest rates are better. In Japan, the low and even negative interest rates were a sign that the Japanese economy was in real trouble, with falling prices and a contracting economy. Only when the Japanese economy returns to health will interest rates rise back to more normal levels.

APPLICATION Reading the *Wall Street Journal* "Credit Markets" Column

Now that we have an understanding of how supply and demand determine prices and interest rates in the bond market, we can use our analysis to understand discussions about bond prices and interest rates appearing in the financial press. Every day, the *Wall Street Journal* reports on developments in the bond market on the previous business day in its "Credit Markets" column, an example of which is found in the Following the Financial News box on the next page. Let's see how statements in the "Credit Markets" column can be explained using our supply and demand framework.

The column describes how the price of Treasury bonds rose when the stock market faltered. This is exactly what our supply and demand analysis predicts would happen.

The weakness in stocks suggests a decline in the expected return on these securities, thus raising the relative expected return on bonds. The higher relative expected returns on bonds would then cause the quantity demanded to rise at each price, shifting the demand curve to the right. The outcome is a rise in the equilibrium price and a fall in interest rates.

Following the Financial News The "Credit Markets" Column

The "Credit Markets" column appears daily in the *Wall Street Journal*; an example is presented here. It is found in the third section, "Money and Investing."

Treasury Prices Edge Higher Amid Stock-Market Weakness

By Shayna Stoyko
Dow Jones Newswires

Treasurys prices ended slightly higher Friday as a late bid emerged amid weakness in equities, the pricing of some commercial mortgage-bond deals and position-squaring ahead of the weekend.

The upturn came at the end of a session in which prices moved between positive and negative territory as the market tried to determine the course of interest rates.

Analysts said there is little reason for Treasurys to break out of recent ranges until there are clearer signs that either growth is faltering for inflation is picking up.

CREDIT MARKETS

Looking at recent data, "nothing fundamental has changed," said Alex Li, strategist at Credit Suisse in New York.

At 4 p.m., the benchmark 10-year note was up 6/32 point, or $1.875 per $1,000 face value, at 101 5/32. Its yield fell to 4.355% from 4.377% Thursday, as yields move inversely to prices. The two-year bond was up 1/32 point at 100 1/32 to yield 4.357%, leaving the benchmark yield curve, the gap between the two-year and the 10-year notes, slightly inverted. The 30-year bond rose 11/32 to 112 21/32 to yield 4.525%.

With a massive amount of supply set to enter the market over the next month, some say there is a bias for Treasury prices to head lower. Next week's $10 billion sale of 20-year inflation-protected securities kicks off a five-week period in which the government will issue some $112 billion in supply over seven auctions, according to estimates by Barclays Capital strategists.

"This glut of supply is likely to weigh heavily on a Treasury market that we already find rich from a fundamental standpoint," said Barclays strategist Michael Pond.

The supply surge will include the reintroduction of the 30-year bond, which the Treasury Department last issued in late 2001. Friday, the Treasury Department asked bond dealers for input on the size of the 30-year bond offering it will announce Feb. 1 and reaffirmed plans to sell between $20 billion and $30 billion in 30-year bonds each year.

"Please elaborate on the factors that influenced your estimate of the appropriate size of the 30-year bond offering and describe market conditions in the long-end of the market," the Treasury asked in its agenda for meetings with 11 of the 22 primary dealers slated for next week ahead of the Feb. 1 quarterly refunding.

Yield Comparisons

Based on Merrill Lynch Bond indexes, priced as of midafternoon Eastern time.

	1/20	1/19	52-week HIGH	52-week LOW
Corp. Govt. Master	4.81%	4.83%	5.02%	4.04%
Treasury				
1-10 yr	4.37	4.38	4.54	3.39
10+ yr	4.56	4.57	4.93	4.18
Agencies				
1-10 yr	4.73	4.74	4.84	3.65
10+ yr	4.99	5.01	5.28	4.49
Corporate				
1-10 yr High Quality	4.94	4.95	5.11	4.03
Medium Quality	5.24	5.26	5.52	4.40
10+ yr High Quality	5.59	5.61	5.87	5.08
Medium Quality	5.92	5.94	6.18	5.48
Yankee bonds (1)	5.17	5.19	5.38	4.43
Current-coupon mortgages (2)				
GNMA 5.49% (3)	5.30	5.33	5.65	4.74
FNMA 5.49%	5.55	5.58	5.90	4.83
FHLMC 5.49%	5.56	5.59	5.93	4.89
High-yield corporates	8.04	8.03	8.51	6.82
Tax-Exempt Bonds				
7-12 yr G.O. (AA)	3.76	3.76	4.02	3.33
12-22 yr G.O. (AA)	4.08	4.08	4.42	3.63
22+ yr revenue (A)	4.50	4.50	4.75	4.22

Note: High quality rated AAA-AA; medium quality A-BBB/Baa; high yield, BB/Ba-C.
(1) Dollar-denominated, SEC-registered bonds of foreign issuers sold in the U.S. (2) Reflects the 52-week high and low of mortgage-backed securities indexes rather than the individual securities shown. (3) Government guaranteed.

Source: *Wall Street Journal*, Saturday/Sunday, January 21-22, 2006, p. B6.

The column also mentions that for Treasurys to break out of recent ranges, there would have to be clearer signs of lower growth or higher inflation. Our analysis also comes to a similar conclusion because, as we have seen in Figures 6 and 7, changes in inflation expectations or economic growth are key determinants of bond prices. The column also points out that a massive amount of supply of bonds is set to enter the market over the next month, leading some analysts to suggest that there is a bias for Treasury bond prices to head lower. This is consistent with our supply and demand analysis of the bond market. The increase in supply would shift the supply curve to the right, causing the equilibrium price to fall.

SUPPLY AND DEMAND IN THE MARKET FOR MONEY: THE LIQUIDITY PREFERENCE FRAMEWORK

Instead of determining the equilibrium interest rate using the supply of and demand for bonds, an alternative model developed by John Maynard Keynes, known as the **liquidity preference framework**, determines the equilibrium interest rate in terms of the supply of and demand for money. Although the two frameworks look different, the liquidity preference analysis of the market for money is closely related to the supply and demand framework of the bond market.[4]

The starting point of Keynes's analysis is his assumption that there are two main categories of assets that people use to store their wealth: money and bonds. Therefore, total wealth in the economy must equal the total quantity of bonds plus money in the economy, which equals the quantity of bonds supplied (B^s) plus the quantity of money supplied (M^s). The quantity of bonds (B^d) and money (M^d) that people want to hold and thus demand must also equal the total amount of wealth, because people cannot purchase more assets than their available resources allow. The conclusion is that the quantity of bonds and money supplied must equal the quantity of bonds and money demanded:

$$B^s + M^s = B^d + M^d \tag{2}$$

Collecting the bond terms on one side of the equation and the money terms on the other, this equation can be rewritten as

$$B^s - B^d = M^d - M^s \tag{3}$$

The rewritten equation tells us that if the market for money is in equilibrium ($M^s = M^d$), the right-hand side of Equation 3 equals zero, implying that $B^s = B^d$, meaning that the bond market is also in equilibrium.

Thus it is the same to think about determining the equilibrium interest rate by equating the supply and demand for bonds or by equating the supply and demand for money. In this sense, the liquidity preference framework, which analyzes the market for money, is equivalent to a framework analyzing supply and demand in the bond market. In practice, the approaches differ, because by assuming that there are only two kinds of assets, money and bonds, the liquidity preference approach implicitly ignores any effects on interest rates that arise from changes in the expected returns on real assets such as automobiles and houses. In most instances, however, both frameworks yield the same predictions.

The reason that we approach the determination of interest rates with both frameworks is that the bond supply and demand framework is easier to use when analyzing the effects from changes in expected inflation, whereas the liquidity preference framework provides a simpler analysis of the effects from changes in income, the price level, and the supply of money.

Because the definition of money that Keynes used includes currency (which earns no interest) and checking account deposits (which in his time typically earned little or no interest), he assumed that money has a zero rate of return. Bonds, the only alternative

[4]Note that the term *market for money* refers to the market for the medium of exchange, money. This market differs from the *money market* referred to by finance practitioners, which, as discussed in Chapter 2, is the financial market in which short-term debt instruments are traded.

FIGURE 8
Equilibrium in the Market for Money

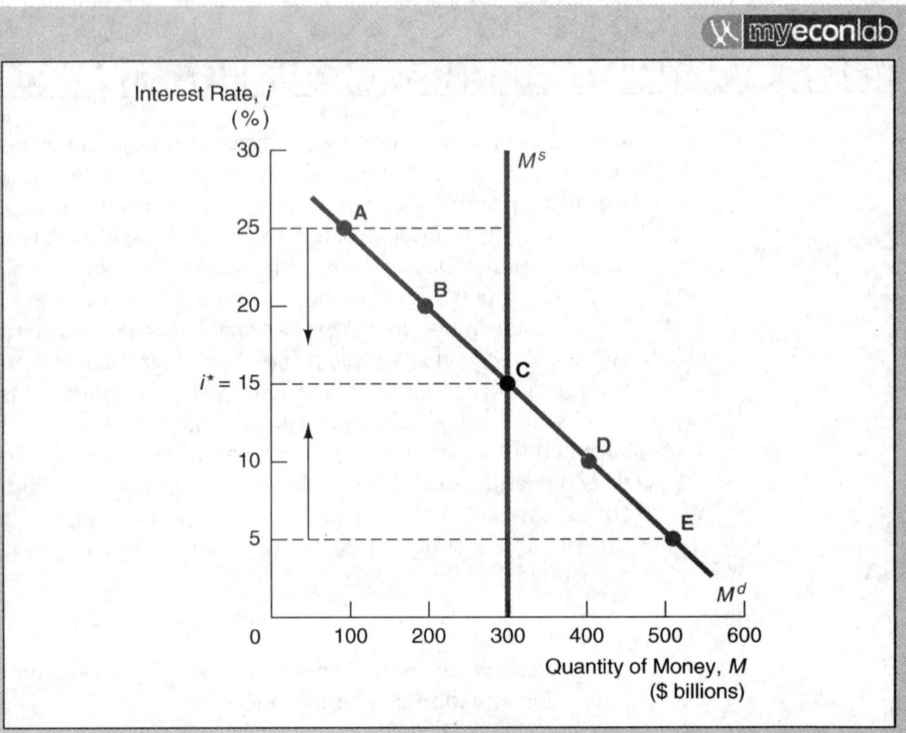

asset to money in Keynes's framework, have an expected return equal to the interest rate i.[5] As this interest rate rises (holding everything else unchanged), the expected return on money falls relative to the expected return on bonds, and as the theory of asset demand tells us, this causes the quantity of money demanded to fall.

We can also see that the quantity of money demanded and the interest rate should be negatively related by using the concept of **opportunity cost**, the amount of interest (expected return) sacrificed by not holding the alternative asset—in this case, a bond. As the interest rate on bonds, i, rises, the opportunity cost of holding money rises; thus money is less desirable and the quantity of money demanded must fall.

Figure 8 shows the quantity of money demanded at a number of interest rates, with all other economic variables, such as income and the price level, held constant. At an interest rate of 25%, point A shows that the quantity of money demanded is $100 billion. If the interest rate is at the lower rate of 20%, the opportunity cost of holding money is lower, and the quantity of money demanded rises to $200 billion, as indicated by the move from point A to point B. If the interest rate is even lower, the quantity of money demanded is even higher, as is indicated by points C, D, and E. The curve M^d connecting these points is the demand curve for money, and it slopes downward.

At this point in our analysis, we will assume that a central bank controls the amount of money supplied at a fixed quantity of $300 billion, so the supply curve for money M^s in the figure is a vertical line at $300 billion. The equilibrium where the

[5]Keynes did not actually assume that the expected returns on bonds equaled the interest rate but rather argued that they were closely related. This distinction makes no appreciable difference in our analysis.

quantity of money demanded equals the quantity of money supplied occurs at the intersection of the supply and demand curves at point C, where

$$M^d = M^s \tag{4}$$

The resulting equilibrium interest rate is at $i^* = 15\%$.

We can again see that there is a tendency to approach this equilibrium by first looking at the relationship of money demand and supply when the interest rate is above the equilibrium interest rate. When the interest rate is 25%, the quantity of money demanded at point A is \$100 billion, yet the quantity of money supplied is \$300 billion. The excess supply of money means that people are holding more money than they desire, so they will try to get rid of their excess money balances by trying to buy bonds. Accordingly, they will bid up the price of bonds. As the bond price rises, the interest rate will fall toward the equilibrium interest rate of 15%. This tendency is shown by the downward arrow drawn at the interest rate of 25%.

Likewise, if the interest rate is 5%, the quantity of money demanded at point E is \$500 billion, but the quantity of money supplied is only \$300 billion. There is now an excess demand for money because people want to hold more money than they currently have. To try to obtain more money, they will sell their only other asset—bonds—and the price will fall. As the price of bonds falls, the interest rate will rise toward the equilibrium rate of 15%. Only when the interest rate is at its equilibrium value will there be no tendency for it to move further, and the interest rate will settle to its equilibrium value.

CHANGES IN EQUILIBRIUM INTEREST RATES IN THE LIQUIDITY PREFERENCE FRAMEWORK

Analyzing how the equilibrium interest rate changes using the liquidity preference framework requires that we understand what causes the demand and supply curves for money to shift.

STUDY GUIDE

Learning the liquidity preference framework also requires practicing applications. When there is an application in the text to examine how the interest rate changes because some economic variable increases, see if you can draw the appropriate shifts in the supply and demand curves when this same economic variable decreases. And remember to use the *ceteris paribus* assumption: When examining the effect of a change in one variable, hold all other variables constant.

Shifts in the Demand for Money

In Keynes's liquidity preference analysis, two factors cause the demand curve for money to shift: income and the price level.

Income Effect. In Keynes's view, there were two reasons why income would affect the demand for money. First, as an economy expands and income rises, wealth increases and people will want to hold more money as a store of value. Second, as the economy expands and income rises, people will want to carry out more transactions using money, with the result that they will also want to hold more money. The conclusion is that ***a higher level of income causes the demand for money at each interest rate to increase and the demand curve to shift to the right.***

Price-Level Effect. Keynes took the view that people care about the amount of money they hold in real terms—that is, in terms of the goods and services that it can buy. When the price level rises, the same nominal quantity of money is no longer as valuable; it cannot be used to purchase as many real goods or services. To restore their holdings of money in real terms to its former level, people will want to hold a greater nominal quantity of money, so ***a rise in the price level causes the demand for money at each interest rate to increase and the demand curve to shift to the right.***

Shifts in the Supply of Money

We will assume that the supply of money is completely controlled by the central bank, which in the United States is the Federal Reserve. (Actually, the process that determines the money supply is substantially more complicated, involving banks, depositors, and borrowers from banks. We will study it in more detail later in the book.) For now, all we need to know is that ***an increase in the money supply engineered by the Federal Reserve will shift the supply curve for money to the right.***

APPLICATION Changes in the Equilibrium Interest Rate Due to Changes in Income, the Price Level, or the Money Supply

To see how the liquidity preference framework can be used to analyze the movement of interest rates, we will again look at several applications that will be useful in evaluating the effect of monetary policy on interest rates. (As a study aid, Table 4 summarizes the shifts in the demand and supply curves for money.)

Changes in Income

When income is rising during a business cycle expansion, we have seen that the demand for money will rise, shown in Figure 9 by the shift rightward in the demand curve from M_1^d to M_2^d. The new equilibrium is reached at point 2 at the intersection of the M_2^d curve with the money supply curve M^s. As you can see, the equilibrium interest rate rises from i_1 to i_2. The liquidity preference framework thus generates the conclusion that ***when income is rising during a business cycle expansion (holding other economic variables constant), interest rates will rise.*** This conclusion is unambiguous when contrasted to the conclusion reached about the effects of a change in income on interest rates using the bond supply and demand framework.

Changes in the Price Level

When the price level rises, the value of money in terms of what it can purchase is lower. To restore their purchasing power in real terms to its former level, people will want to

SUMMARY TABLE 4 Factors That Shift the Demand for and Supply of Money

Variable	Change in Variable	Change in Money Demand (M^d) or Supply (M^s) at Each Interest Rate	Change in Interest Rate	
Income	↑	M^d↑	↑	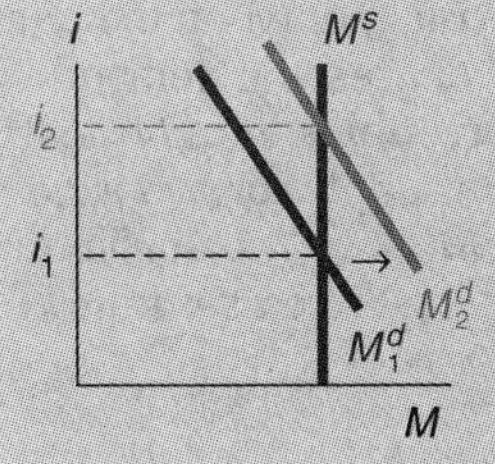
Price level	↑	M^d↑	↑	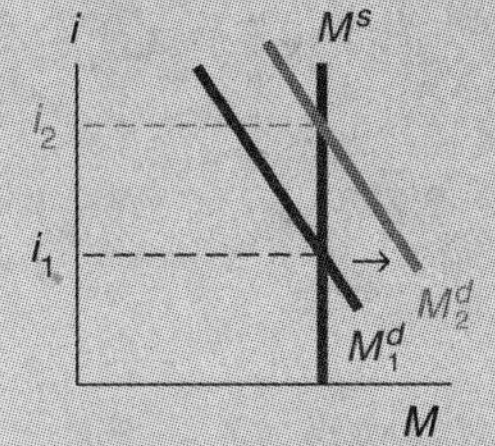
Money supply	↑	M^s↑	↓	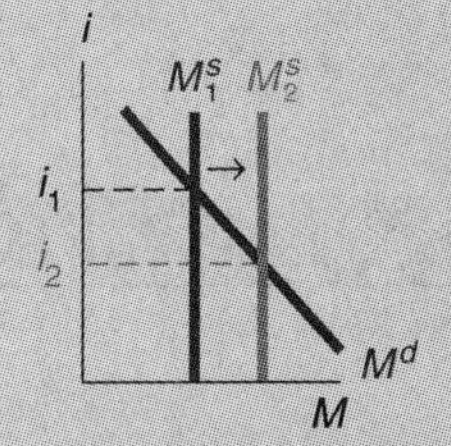

Note: Only increases in the variables are shown. The effect of decreases in the variables on the change in demand would be the opposite of those indicated in the remaining columns.

hold a greater nominal quantity of money. A higher price level shifts the demand curve for money to the right from M^d_1 to M^d_2 (see Figure 9). The equilibrium moves from point 1 to point 2, where the equilibrium interest rate has risen from i_1 to i_2, illustrating that ***when the price level increases, with the supply of money and other economic variables held constant, interest rates will rise.***

Changes in the Money Supply

An increase in the money supply due to expansionary monetary policy by the Federal Reserve implies that the supply curve for money shifts to the right. As is shown in Figure 10 by the movement of the supply curve from M^s_1 to M^s_2, the equilibrium moves

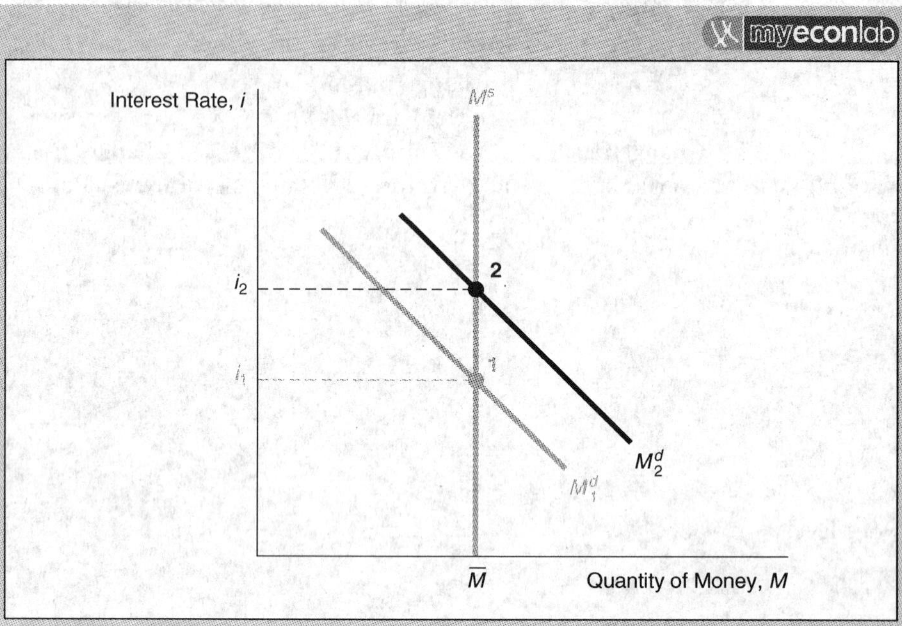

FIGURE 9
Response to a Change in Income or the Price Level
In a business cycle expansion, when income is rising, or when the price level rises, the demand curve shifts from M_1^d to M_2^d. The supply curve is fixed at $M^s = \overline{M}$. The equilibrium interest rate rises from i_1 to i_2.

from point 1 down to point 2, where the M_2^s supply curve intersects with the demand curve M^d and the equilibrium interest rate has fallen from i_1 to i_2. ***When the money supply increases (everything else remaining equal), interest rates will decline.***[6]

APPLICATION Money and Interest Rates

The liquidity preference analysis in Figure 10 seems to lead to the conclusion that an increase in the money supply will lower interest rates. This conclusion has important policy implications because it has frequently caused politicians to call for a more rapid growth of the money supply in an effort to drive down interest rates.

But is this conclusion that money and interest rates should be negatively related correct? Might there be other important factors left out of the liquidity preference analysis in Figure 10 that would reverse this conclusion? We will provide answers to these questions by applying the supply and demand analysis we have used in this chapter to obtain a deeper understanding of the relationship between money and interest rates.

An important criticism of the conclusion that an increase in the money supply lowers interest rates has been raised by Milton Friedman, a Nobel laureate in economics. He acknowledges that the liquidity preference analysis is correct and calls the result—

[6]This same result can be generated using the bond supply and demand framework. As we will see in Chapters 16 and 17, the primary way that a central bank produces an increase in the money supply is by buying bonds and thereby decreasing the supply of bonds to the public. The resulting shift to the left of the supply curve for bonds will lead to a decline in the equilibrium interest rate.

FIGURE 10
Response to a Change in the Money Supply
When the money supply increases, the supply curve shifts from M_1^s to M_2^s, and the equilibrium interest rate falls from i_1 to i_2.

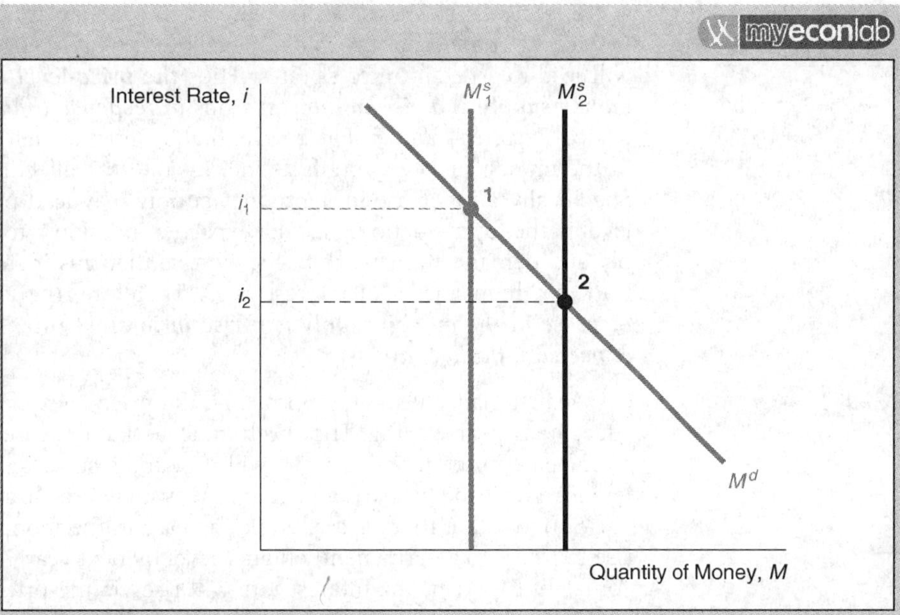

that an increase in the money supply (*everything else remaining equal*) lowers interest rates—the *liquidity effect*. However, he views the liquidity effect as merely part of the story: An increase in the money supply might not leave "everything else equal" and will have other effects on the economy that may make interest rates rise. If these effects are substantial, it is entirely possible that when the money supply increases, interest rates may also increase.

We have already laid the groundwork to discuss these other effects because we have shown how changes in income, the price level, and expected inflation affect the equilibrium interest rate.

STUDY GUIDE

To get further practice with the bond supply and demand and liquidity preference frameworks, show how the effects discussed here work by drawing the supply and demand diagrams that explain each effect. This exercise will also improve your understanding of the effect of money on interest rates.

1. *Income Effect*. Because an increasing money supply is an expansionary influence on the economy, it should raise national income and wealth. Both the liquidity preference and bond supply and demand frameworks indicate that interest rates will then rise (see Figures 6 and 9). Thus ***the income effect of an increase in the money supply is a rise in interest rates in response to the higher level of income.***

2. *Price-Level Effect.* An increase in the money supply can also cause the overall price level in the economy to rise. The liquidity preference framework predicts that this will lead to a rise in interest rates. Thus ***the price-level effect from an increase in the money supply is a rise in interest rates in response to the rise in the price level.***

3. *Expected-Inflation Effect.* The higher inflation rate that results from an increase in the money supply also affects interest rates by affecting the expected inflation rate. Specifically, an increase in the money supply may lead people to expect a higher price level in the future—and hence the expected inflation rate will be higher. The bond supply and demand framework has shown us that this increase in expected inflation will lead to a higher level of interest rates. Therefore, ***the expected-inflation effect of an increase in the money supply is a rise in interest rates in response to the rise in the expected inflation rate.***

At first glance it might appear that the price-level effect and the expected-inflation effect are the same thing. They both indicate that increases in the price level induced by an increase in the money supply will raise interest rates. However, there is a subtle difference between the two, and this is why they are discussed as two separate effects.

Suppose that there is a onetime increase in the money supply today that leads to a rise in prices to a permanently higher level by next year. As the price level rises over the course of this year, the interest rate will rise via the price-level effect. Only at the end of the year, when the price level has risen to its peak, will the price-level effect be at a maximum.

The rising price level will also raise interest rates via the expected-inflation effect, because people will expect that inflation will be higher over the course of the year. However, when the price level stops rising next year, inflation and the expected inflation rate will return to zero. Any rise in interest rates as a result of the earlier rise in expected inflation will then be reversed. We thus see that in contrast to the price-level effect, which reaches its greatest impact next year, the expected-inflation effect will have its smallest impact (zero impact) next year. The basic difference between the two effects, then, is that the price-level effect remains even after prices have stopped rising, whereas the expected-inflation effect disappears.

An important point is that the expected-inflation effect will persist only as long as the price level continues to rise. As we will see in our discussion of monetary theory in subsequent chapters, a one-time increase in the money supply will not produce a continually rising price level; only a higher rate of money supply growth will. Thus a higher rate of money supply growth is needed if the expected-inflation effect is to persist.

Does a Higher Rate of Growth of the Money Supply Lower Interest Rates?

We can now put together all the effects we have discussed to help us decide whether our analysis supports the politicians who advocate a greater rate of growth of the money supply when they feel that interest rates are too high. Of all the effects, only the liquidity effect indicates that a higher rate of money growth will cause a decline in interest rates. In contrast, the income, price-level, and expected-inflation effects indicate that interest rates will rise when money growth is higher. Which of these effects are largest, and how quickly do they take effect? The answers are critical in determining whether interest rates will rise or fall when money supply growth is increased.

Generally, the liquidity effect from the greater money growth takes effect immediately, because the rising money supply leads to an immediate decline in the equilibrium interest rate. The income and price-level effects take time to work, because it takes time for the increasing money supply to raise the price level and income, which in turn raise interest rates. The expected-inflation effect, which also raises interest rates, can be slow or fast, depending on whether people adjust their expectations of inflation slowly or quickly when the money growth rate is increased.

Three possibilities are outlined in Figure 11; each shows how interest rates respond over time to an increased rate of money supply growth starting at time T. Panel (a) shows a case in which the liquidity effect dominates the other effects so that the interest rate falls from i_1 at time T to a final level of i_2. The liquidity effect operates quickly to lower the interest rate, but as time goes by, the other effects start to reverse some of the decline. Because the liquidity effect is larger than the others, however, the interest rate never rises back to its initial level.

Panel (b) has a smaller liquidity effect than the other effects, with the expected-inflation effect operating slowly because expectations of inflation are slow to adjust upward. Initially, the liquidity effect drives down the interest rate. Then the income, price-level, and expected-inflation effects begin to raise it. Because these effects are dominant, the interest rate eventually rises above its initial level to i_2. In the short run, lower interest rates result from increased money growth, but eventually they end up climbing above the initial level.

Panel (c) has the expected-inflation effect dominating as well as operating rapidly because people quickly raise their expectations of inflation when the rate of money growth increases. The expected-inflation effect begins immediately to overpower the liquidity effect, and the interest rate immediately starts to climb. Over time, as the income and price-level effects start to take hold, the interest rate rises even higher, and the eventual outcome is an interest rate that is substantially higher than the initial interest rate. The result shows clearly that increasing money supply growth is not the answer to reducing interest rates; rather, money growth should be reduced to lower interest rates!

An important issue for economic policymakers is which of these three scenarios is closest to reality. If a decline in interest rates is desired, then an increase in money supply growth is called for when the liquidity effect dominates the other effects, as in panel (a). A decrease in money growth is appropriate when the other effects dominate the liquidity effect and expectations of inflation adjust rapidly, as in panel (c). If the other effects dominate the liquidity effect but expectations of inflation adjust only slowly, as in panel (b), then whether you want to increase or decrease money growth depends on whether you care more about what happens in the short run or the long run.

Which scenario is supported by the evidence? The relationship of interest rates and money growth from 1950 to 2005 is plotted in Figure 12. When the rate of money supply growth began to climb in the mid-1960s, interest rates rose, indicating that the liquidity effect was dominated by the price-level, income, and expected-inflation effects. By the 1970s, interest rates reached levels unprecedented in the post–World War II period, as did the rate of money supply growth.

The scenario depicted in panel (a) of Figure 11 seems doubtful, and the case for lowering interest rates by raising the rate of money growth is much weakened. Looking back at Figure 5, which shows the relationship between interest rates and expected inflation, you should not find this too surprising. The rise in the rate of money supply growth in the 1960s and 1970s is matched by a large rise in expected inflation, which

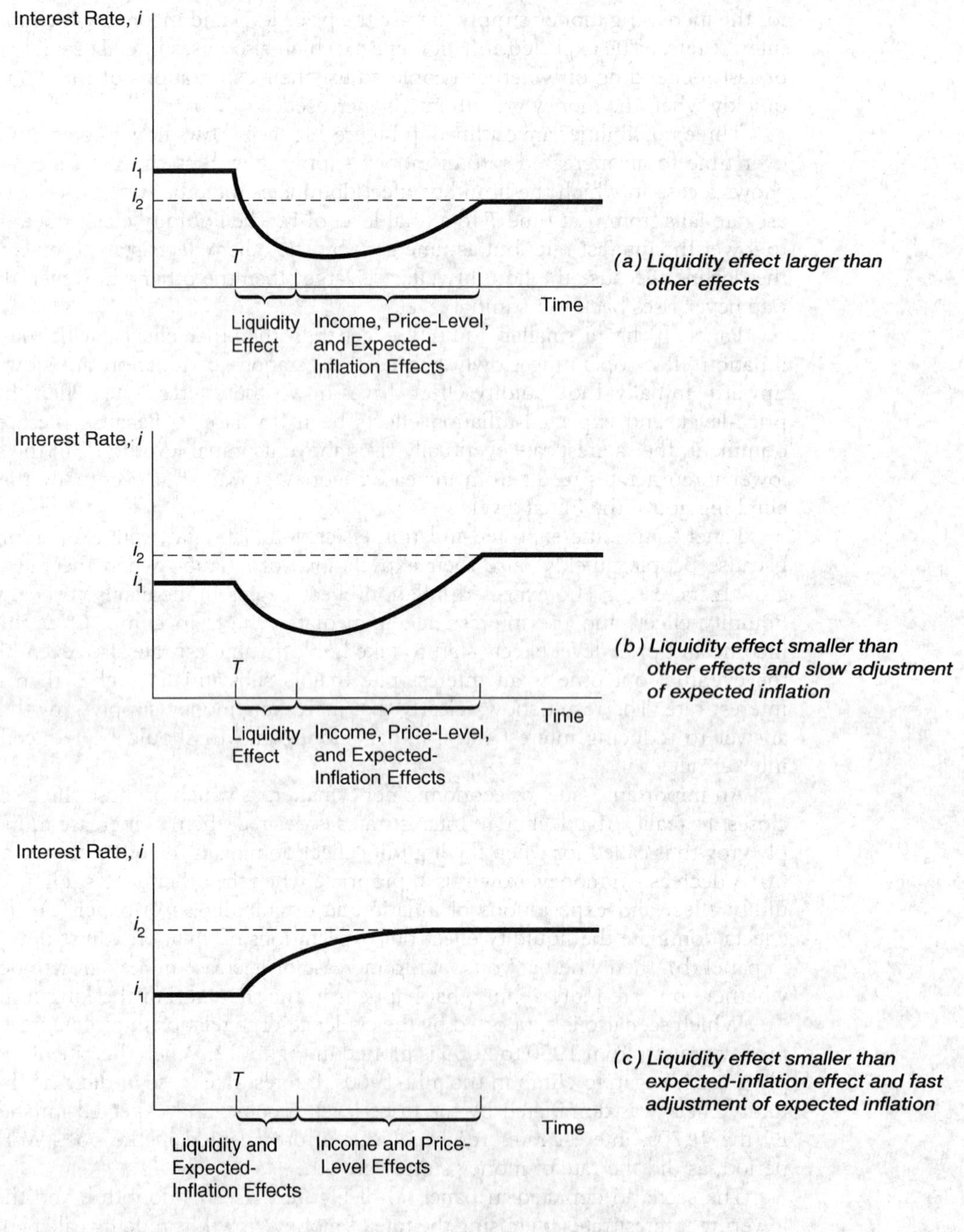

FIGURE 11 **Response Over Time to an Increase in Money Supply Growth**

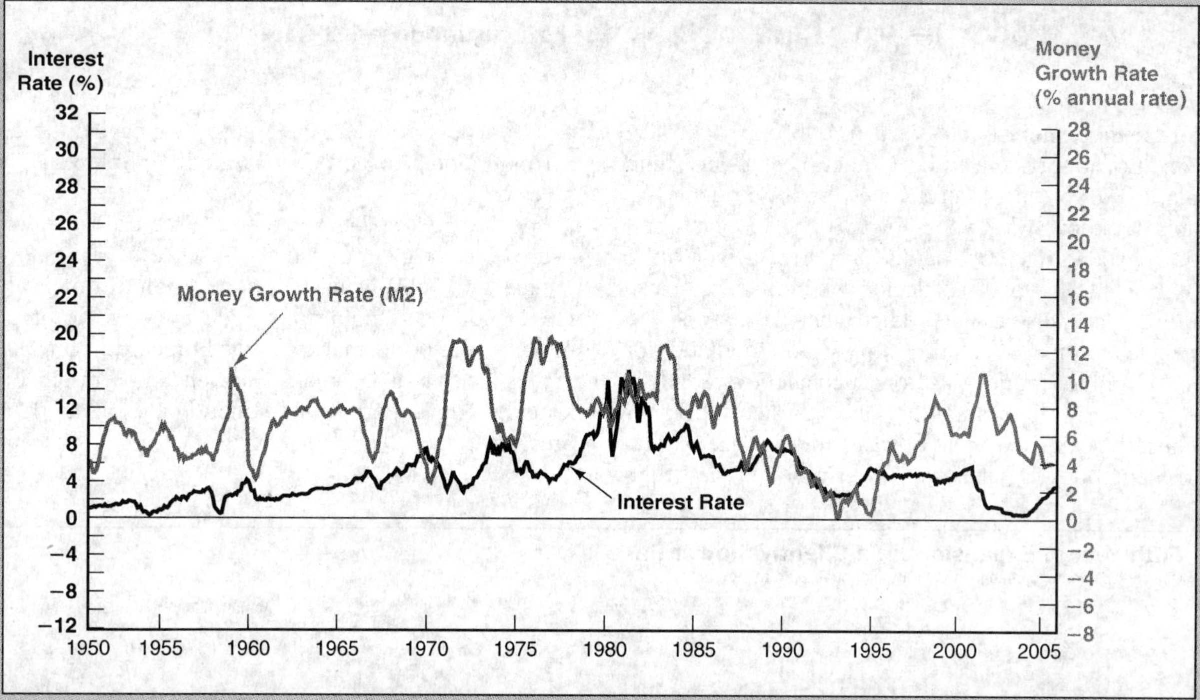

FIGURE 12 **Money Growth (M2, Annual Rate) and Interest Rates (Three-Month Treasury Bills), 1950–2005**

Sources: Federal Reserve: www.federalreserve.gov/releases/h6/hist/h6hist1.txt.

would lead us to predict that the expected-inflation effect would be dominant. It is the most plausible explanation for why interest rates rose in the face of higher money growth. However, Figure 12 does not really tell us which one of the two scenarios, panel (b) or panel (c) of Figure 11, is more accurate. It depends critically on how fast people's expectations about inflation adjust. However, recent research using more sophisticated methods than just looking at a graph like Figure 12 do indicate that increased money growth temporarily lowers short-term interest rates.[7]

[7]See Lawrence J. Christiano and Martin Eichenbaum, "Identification and the Liquidity Effect of a Monetary Policy Shock," in *Business Cycles, Growth, and Political Economy*, ed. Alex Cukierman, Zvi Hercowitz, and Leonardo Leiderman (Cambridge, Mass.: MIT Press, 1992), pp. 335–370; Eric M. Leeper and David B. Gordon, "In Search of the Liquidity Effect," *Journal of Monetary Economics* 29 (1992): 341–370; Steven Strongin, "The Identification of Monetary Policy Disturbances: Explaining the Liquidity Puzzle," *Journal of Monetary Economics* 35 (1995): 463–497; Adrian Pagan and John C. Robertson, "Resolving the Liquidity Effect," *Federal Reserve Bank of St. Louis Review* 77 (May–June 1995): 33–54; and Ben S. Bernanke and Ilian Mihov, "Measuring Monetary Policy," *Quarterly Journal of Economics* 113, 3 (August 1998), pp. 869–902.

Following the Financial News Forecasting Interest Rates

Forecasting interest rates is a time-honored profession. Economists are hired (sometimes at very high salaries) to forecast interest rates, because businesses need to know what the rates will be to plan their future spending, and banks and investors require interest-rate forecasts to decide which assets to buy. Interest-rate forecasters predict what will happen to the factors that affect the supply and demand for bonds and for money—factors such as the strength of the economy, the profitability of investment opportunities, the expected inflation rate, and the size of government budget deficits and borrowing. They then use the supply and demand analysis we have outlined in this chapter to come up with their interest-rate forecasts.

The *Wall Street Journal* reports interest-rate forecasts by leading prognosticators twice a year (early January and July) in its "Economy" column or in its "Credit Markets" column, which surveys developments in the bond market daily. Forecasting interest rates is a perilous business. To their embarrassment, even the top experts are frequently far off in their forecasts.

Fifth Year of Expansion, at a Slightly Slower Pace

Quarterly percentage change in GDP at an annualized rate

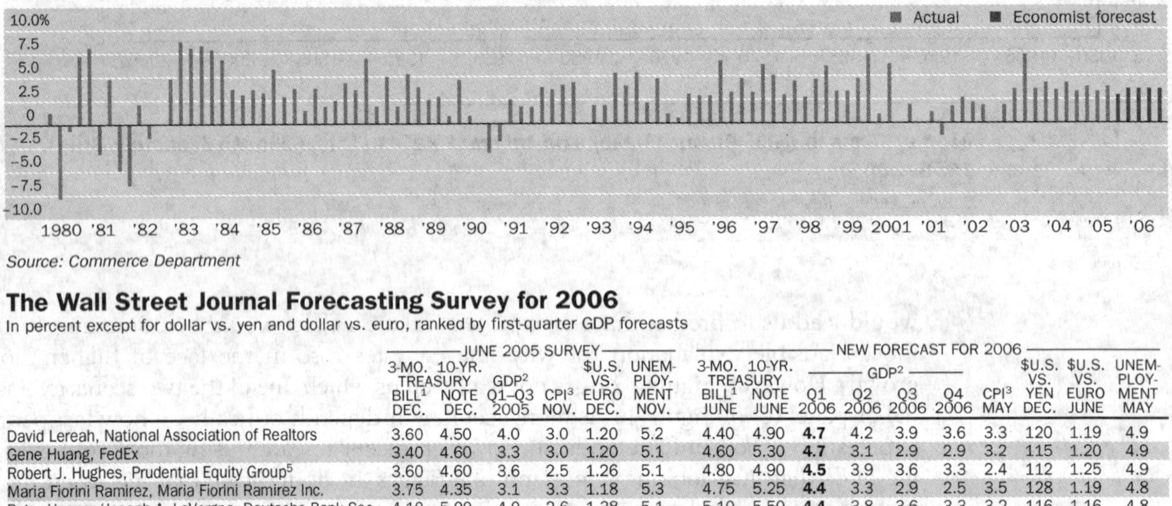

Source: Commerce Department

The Wall Street Journal Forecasting Survey for 2006

In percent except for dollar vs. yen and dollar vs. euro, ranked by first-quarter GDP forecasts

	JUNE 2005 SURVEY						NEW FORECAST FOR 2006									
	3-MO. TREASURY BILL[1] DEC.	10-YR. TREASURY NOTE DEC.	GDP[2] Q1–Q3 2005	CPI[3] NOV.	$U.S. VS. EURO DEC.	UNEMPLOYMENT NOV.	3-MO. TREASURY BILL[1] JUNE	10-YR. TREASURY NOTE JUNE	GDP[2] Q1 2006	GDP[2] Q2 2006	GDP[2] Q3 2006	GDP[2] Q4 2006	CPI[3] MAY	$U.S. VS. YEN DEC.	$U.S. VS. EURO JUNE	UNEMPLOYMENT MAY
David Lereah, National Association of Realtors	3.60	4.50	4.0	3.0	1.20	5.2	4.40	4.90	**4.7**	4.2	3.9	3.6	3.3	120	1.19	4.9
Gene Huang, FedEx	3.40	4.60	3.3	3.0	1.20	5.1	4.60	5.30	**4.7**	3.1	2.9	2.9	3.2	115	1.20	4.9
Robert J. Hughes, Prudential Equity Group[5]	3.60	4.60	3.6	2.5	1.26	5.1	4.80	4.90	**4.5**	3.9	3.6	3.3	2.4	112	1.25	4.9
Maria Fiorini Ramirez, Maria Fiorini Ramirez Inc.	3.75	4.35	3.1	3.3	1.18	5.3	4.75	5.25	**4.4**	3.3	2.9	2.5	3.5	128	1.19	4.8
Peter Hooper/Joseph A. LaVorgna, Deutsche Bank Sec.	4.10	5.00	4.0	2.6	1.38	5.1	5.10	5.50	**4.4**	3.8	3.6	3.3	3.2	116	1.16	4.8
Joel Prakken/Chris Varvares, Macroeconomic Advisers	4.00	4.80	3.8	2.8	1.27	5.0	4.56	5.05	**4.2**	3.6	3.4	3.3	3.3	N.A.	N.A.	4.9
Brian S. Wesbury, Claymore Securities	4.20	5.20	4.2	3.4	1.10	4.9	4.95	5.50	**4.1**	3.5	4.1	4.4	3.3	122	1.15	4.7
David Malpass/John Ryding, Bear Stearns	4.30	5.10	4.1	2.8	1.20	4.9	5.00	5.60	**4.1**	3.7	3.6	3.8	3.1	124	1.16	4.8
David Resler, Nomura Securities International	3.40	4.50	3.6	2.7	1.15	5.0	4.65	4.85	**4.1**	4.0	3.2	3.3	3.1	118	1.18	4.9
Mickey D. Levy, Bank of America	3.85	4.50	3.7	3.0	1.21	5.2	4.80	4.90	**4.1**	4.0	3.6	3.0	3.1	113	1.24	4.9
Saul Hymans/Joan Crary/Janet Wolfe, RSQE, U. of Mich	3.60	5.10	3.5	2.9	1.32	5.2	4.50	5.30	**4.1**	3.6	2.9	2.5	3.0	113	1.21	4.8
Richard DeKaser, National City	3.80	4.75	4.1	2.7	1.24	5.0	4.30	5.20	**4.1**	3.6	3.4	3.0	2.9	115	1.21	4.8
Ian Shepherdson, High Frequency Economics	4.25	5.50	4.2	3.0	1.15	4.7	4.75	5.00	**4.0**	3.5	2.0	0.0	2.8	124	1.13	4.5
Ram Bhagavatula, Combinatorics Capital	4.20	5.50	4.0	2.9	1.18	4.8	4.65	5.40	**4.0**	4.0	3.5	3.2	2.8	112	1.18	4.7
David W. Berson, Fannie Mae	3.80	4.25	3.8	2.5	1.18	5.1	4.60	4.79	**3.9**	3.6	3.4	3.4	2.9	118	1.15	5.0
Douglas Duncan, Mortgage Bankers Association	3.85	4.60	3.3	2.7	1.24	5.1	4.60	5.00	**3.9**	3.6	3.5	3.2	3.0	125	1.15	4.9
James F. Smith U. of North Carolina and SIOR	3.41	4.49	4.3	1.1	1.04	4.7	4.73	4.53	**3.9**	3.5	3.5	4.1	–0.9	123	1.11	4.6
Allen Sinai, Decision Economics	3.97	4.53	3.5	2.7	1.14	4.9	4.88	5.14	**3.8**	2.9	3.4	2.7	3.5	109	1.26	4.8
Nariman Behravesh, Global Insight	3.90	4.90	3.5	2.5	1.31	5.1	4.50	5.10	**3.8**	3.2	3.1	2.9	2.9	110	1.26	4.8
Richard Berner/David Greenlaw, Morgan Stanley	4.10	4.75	3.5	2.6	1.19	5.0	4.75	4.90	**3.8**	3.4	3.9	4.2	3.2	122	1.20	4.9
Robert T. McGee, U.S. Trust Co.	4.25	3.95	3.7	2.7	1.18	4.9	4.41	4.15	**3.8**	3.2	3.2	3.2	2.4	115	1.19	4.8
William T. Wilson, Keystone Bus. Intelligence India	3.30	4.50	3.7	2.6	1.16	5.1	4.30	5.30	**3.8**	3.8	3.7	3.5	3.3	110	1.17	5.0
Neal Soss, CSFB	N.A.	4.00	3.7	2.8	1.15	5.1	N.A.	5.20	**3.7**	3.7	3.4	3.3	3.2	125	1.12	5.0

Source: Wall Street Journal, Tuesday, January 3, 2006, p. A2.

Following the Financial News Forecasting Interest Rates (continued)

David Wyss, Standard & Poor's	3.90	4.70	3.6	2.6	1.25	5.0	4.70	4.90	**3.7**	3.1	2.9	2.8	2.9	116	1.22	4.8
Lou Crandall, Wrightson ICAP	New Participant						5.00	5.25	**3.7**	3.7	3.3	3.3	2.9	110	1.25	4.7
Stuart Hoffman, PNC Financial Services Group	3.68	4.35	3.2	2.8	1.21	5.0	4.68	4.70	**3.7**	3.2	2.8	2.7	3.2	118	1.19	4.9
Jim Meil/Arun Raha, Eaton	3.75	4.50	4.0	2.5	1.20	5.1	4.96	4.55	**3.6**	3.3	2.1	2.4	3.4	114	1.21	4.8
Diane Swonk, Mesirow Financial	3.60	4.20	3.6	2.8	1.22	5.2	4.80	5.30	**3.6**	3.5	3.1	3.4	3.5	119	1.17	5.0
John Lonski, Moody's Investors Service	3.90	4.75	3.5	2.8	1.20	4.9	4.75	5.20	**3.6**	4.2	3.2	3.0	3.3	112	1.20	4.8
Maury Harris, UBS	4.20	5.00	3.1	2.3	1.30	5.0	4.50	4.50	**3.6**	2.8	2.5	2.5	3.0	111	1.23	4.8
Dean Maki, Barclays Capital	4.00	4.85	4.0	2.6	1.25	5.0	N.A.	4.55	**3.5**	3.0	3.0	3.5	3.3	115	1.23	4.8
Donald H. Straszheim, Straszheim Global Advisors	3.50	4.25	3.3	2.5	1.18	5.0	4.00	4.50	**3.5**	3.0	3.0	3.0	3.0	120	1.14	4.9
Ethan S. Harris, Lehman Brothers	3.80	4.70	3.3	3.1	1.30	5.0	5.20	5.20	**3.5**	3.2	2.8	2.5	3.2	115	1.18	4.8
Jan Hatzius, Goldman Sachs & Co.[5]	4.00	4.90	3.2	2.9	1.25	5.0	4.60	5.00	**3.5**	4.0	3.5	2.5	3.1	102	1.25	4.8
Stephen Gallagher, Société Générale	3.25	4.00	3.7	2.7	1.20	5.1	4.70	4.60	**3.5**	3.0	3.0	3.0	3.1	110	1.22	4.8
Tracy Herrick, Private Bank	4.30	4.00	2.8	3.2	1.20	5.0	5.10	4.60	**3.4**	3.0	1.9	1.2	3.1	125	1.12	4.7
William B. Hummer, Wayne Hummer Investments	3.75	4.70	3.9	2.9	1.15	5.0	4.40	4.80	**3.4**	3.3	3.0	3.1	2.5	115	1.13	4.9
J. Dewey Daane, Vanderbilt University	3.75	4.50	3.1	3.5	1.15	5.2	5.00	5.00	**3.3**	3.1	2.9	2.7	3.5	118	1.22	5.0
Nicholas S. Perna, Perna Associates	4.17	4.84	3.3	3.2	1.25	5.0	4.39	5.01	**3.3**	3.2	2.9	3.3	3.4	114	1.22	5.0
Paul Kasriel, Northern Trust	3.05	4.15	3.2	2.8	1.25	5.3	4.10	4.50	**3.3**	3.3	2.7	2.7	3.6	114	1.22	5.1
Sung Won Sohn, Hanmi Financial	3.90	4.50	3.8	3.6	1.20	5.1	4.50	4.80	**3.3**	3.4	3.4	3.4	3.0	114	0.85	5.0
Daniel Laufenberg, American Express	4.00	4.95	3.5	2.9	1.23	5.0	4.45	4.85	**3.1**	2.4	3.7	3.8	3.4	105	1.23	5.0
Lawrence Kudlow, Kudlow & Co.	3.40	3.95	3.7	2.7	1.10	5.0	4.25	4.50	**3.1**	2.9	2.9	2.9	2.9	125	1.12	4.9
Robert DiClemente, Citigroup	3.75	4.35	4.0	2.4	1.34	5.1	4.25	4.35	**3.1**	3.3	3.0	3.6	3.2	110	1.34	5.3
Scott Anderson, Wells Fargo & Co.	3.70	4.40	3.6	2.5	1.27	5.1	4.70	4.80	**3.1**	3.2	3.2	3.2	3.5	120	1.22	5.0
Gary Thayer, A.G. Edwards	3.50	4.70	3.4	2.4	1.16	5.0	4.60	4.70	**3.0**	3.2	3.0	3.5	3.0	122	1.14	4.9
John Silvia, Wachovia	3.85	4.20	3.0	2.9	1.24	5.1	4.85	5.10	**3.0**	3.0	3.1	3.3	3.0	108	1.26	5.0
Michael P. Niemira, Int'l Council of Shopping Centers	New Participant						4.85	5.00	**3.0**	2.5	2.3	2.5	4.3	120	1.15	5.2
Mike Cosgrove, Econoclast	3.30	4.25	3.2	2.7	1.15	5.1	4.25	4.20	**3.0**	3.0	2.5	2.5	2.8	120	1.15	5.0
Susan M. Sterne, Economic Analysis	3.90	4.75	3.1	2.8	1.18	5.0	4.80	4.80	**2.8**	3.0	2.1	3.6	3.0	118	1.14	5.1
Dana Johnson, Economic Analysis	3.65	4.85	3.6	2.7	1.20	5.1	4.45	4.55	**2.7**	3.2	3.4	3.4	3.3	115	1.22	4.9
Edward Leamer, UCLA Anderson Forecast	3.60	4.90	3.0	2.8	N.A.	5.4	4.48	4.90	**2.7**	2.5	2.5	2.5	3.2	N.A.	N.A.	5.1
Joseph Carson, AllianceBernstein	4.00	4.75	4.3	3.6	1.23	5.0	4.45	4.85	**2.7**	2.8	2.9	3.1	3.1	110	1.23	5.0
Kurt Karl, Swiss Re	4.10	4.90	3.1	2.4	1.27	4.9	4.95	5.20	**2.5**	2.6	2.9	3.0	3.2	108	1.21	4.8
David Rosenberg, Merrill Lynch	3.45	3.80	2.7	2.5	N.A.	5.4	4.40	4.25	**2.2**	2.0	2.5	3.0	2.6	N.A.	N.A.	5.3
Gail Fosler, Conference Board	4.00	4.50	4.7	3.4	1.18	5.1	4.50	4.60	**2.2**	3.2	2.3	3.0	3.5	120	1.15	5.2
AVERAGES[4]	3.81	4.60	3.6	2.8	1.21	5.1	4.63	4.90	**3.6**	3.3	3.1	3.0	3.1	116	1.19	4.9
ACTUAL Numbers on Dec. 31	4.07	4.39	3.7	3.5	1.18	5.0										

Note: Forecasters are listed from most bullish first-quarter forecast to least bullish N.A.=Not Available
[1]Treasury-bill rates are on a bond-equivalent basis [2]Real gross domestic product, average growth rate for Q1 through Q3 [3]Year–to-year change in the consumer price index [4]Averages are for economists who were participants at time of survey [5]Replace William Dudley from Goldman Sachs and Richard Rippe from Prudential

Source: Wall Street Journal, Tuesday, January 3, 2006, p. A2.

SUMMARY

1. The theory of asset demand tells us that the quantity demanded of an asset is (a) positively related to wealth, (b) positively related to the expected return on the asset relative to alternative assets, (c) negatively related to the riskiness of the asset relative to alternative assets, and (d) positively related to the liquidity of the asset relative to alternative assets.
2. The supply and demand analysis for bonds provides one theory of how interest rates are determined. It predicts that interest rates will change when there is a change in demand because of changes in income (or wealth), expected returns, risk, or liquidity or when there is a change in supply because of changes in the attractiveness of investment opportunities, the real cost of borrowing, or the government budget.
3. An alternative theory of how interest rates are determined is provided by the liquidity preference framework, which analyzes the supply of and demand for money. It shows that interest rates will change when there is a change in the demand for money because of changes in income or the price level or when there is a change in the supply of money.

4. There are four possible effects of an increase in the money supply on interest rates: the liquidity effect, the income effect, the price-level effect, and the expected-inflation effect. The liquidity effect indicates that a rise in money supply growth will lead to a decline in interest rates; the other effects work in the opposite direction. The evidence seems to indicate that the income, price-level, and expected-inflation effects dominate the liquidity effect such that an increase in money supply growth leads to higher—rather than lower—interest rates.

KEY TERMS

asset market approach, p. 99
demand curve, p. 96
excess demand, p. 98
excess supply, p. 98
expected return, p. 93
Fisher effect, p. 106
liquidity, p. 94
liquidity preference framework, p. 111
market equilibrium, p. 98
opportunity cost, p. 112
risk, p. 94
supply curve, p. 98
theory of asset demand, p. 95
wealth, p. 93

QUESTIONS AND PROBLEMS

Questions marked with an asterisk are answered at the end of the book in an appendix, "Answers to Selected Questions and Problems." Questions marked with a blue circle indicate the question is available in MyEconLab at www.myeconlab.com/mishkin.

1. Explain why you would be more or less willing to buy a share of Microsoft stock in the following situations:
   a. Your wealth falls.
   b. You expect the stock to appreciate in value.
   c. The bond market becomes more liquid.
   d. You expect gold to appreciate in value.
   e. Prices in the bond market become more volatile.

*2. Explain why you would be more or less willing to buy a house under the following circumstances:
   a. You just inherited $100,000.
   b. Real estate commissions fall from 6% of the sales price to 5% of the sales price.
   c. You expect Microsoft stock to double in value next year.
   d. Prices in the stock market become more volatile.
   e. You expect housing prices to fall.

3. Explain why you would be more or less willing to buy gold under the following circumstances:
   a. Gold again becomes acceptable as a medium of exchange.
   b. Prices in the gold market become more volatile.
   c. You expect inflation to rise, and gold prices tend to move with the aggregate price level.
   d. You expect interest rates to rise.

*4. Explain why you would be more or less willing to buy long-term AT&T bonds under the following circumstances:
   a. Trading in these bonds increases, making them easier to sell.
   b. You expect a bear market in stocks (stock prices are expected to decline).
   c. Brokerage commissions on stocks fall.
   d. You expect interest rates to rise.
   e. Brokerage commissions on bonds fall.

5. What would happen to the demand for Rembrandt paintings if the stock market undergoes a boom? Why?

Answer each question by drawing the appropriate supply and demand diagrams.

*6. An important way in which the Federal Reserve decreases the money supply is by selling bonds to the public. Using a supply and demand analysis for bonds, show what effect this action has on interest rates. Is your answer consistent with what you would expect to find with the liquidity preference framework?

7. Using both the liquidity preference framework and the supply and demand for bonds framework, show why interest rates are procyclical (rising when the economy is expanding and falling during recessions).

*8. Why should a rise in the price level (but not in expected inflation) cause interest rates to rise when the nominal money supply is fixed?

9. Find the "Credit Markets" column in the *Wall Street Journal*. Underline the statements in the column that explain bond price movements, and draw the appropriate supply and demand diagrams that support these statements.

10. What effect will a sudden increase in the volatility of gold prices have on interest rates?

*11. How might a sudden increase in people's expectations of future real estate prices affect interest rates?

12. Explain what effect a large federal deficit might have on interest rates.

*13. Using both the supply and demand for bonds and liquidity preference frameworks, show what the effect is on interest rates when the riskiness of bonds rises. Are the results the same in the two frameworks?

14. If the price level falls next year, remaining fixed thereafter, and the money supply is fixed, what is likely to happen to interest rates over the next two years? (*Hint:* Take account of both the price-level effect and the expected-inflation effect.)

*15. Will there be an effect on interest rates if brokerage commissions on stocks fall? Explain your answer.

Using Economic Analysis to Predict the Future

16. The president of the United States announces in a press conference that he will fight the higher inflation rate with a new anti-inflation program. Predict what will happen to interest rates if the public believes him.

*17. The chairman of the Fed announces that interest rates will rise sharply next year, and the market believes him. What will happen to today's interest rate on AT&T bonds, such as the $8\frac{1}{8}$s of 2022?

18. Predict what will happen to interest rates if the public suddenly expects a large increase in stock prices.

*19. Predict what will happen to interest rates if prices in the bond market become more volatile.

20. If the next chair of the Federal Reserve Board has a reputation for advocating an even slower rate of money growth than the current chair, what will happen to interest rates? Discuss the possible resulting situations.

WEB EXERCISES

1. One of the largest single influences on the level of interest rates is inflation. There are a number of sites that report inflation over time. Go to ftp://ftp.bls.gov/pub/special.requests/cpi/cpiai.txt and review the data available. Note that the last columns report various averages. Move these data into a spreadsheet using the method discussed in the Web exploration at the end of Chapter 1. What has the average rate of inflation been since 1950, 1960, 1970, 1980, and 1990? Which year had the lowest level of inflation? Which year had the highest level of inflation?

2. Increasing prices erode the purchasing power of the dollar. It is interesting to compute what goods would have cost at some point in the past after adjusting for inflation. Go to http://minneapolisfed.org/Research/data/us/calc/. What would a car that cost $22,000 today have cost the year that you were born?

3. One of the points made in this chapter is that inflation erodes investment returns. Go to www.moneychimp.com/articles/econ/inflation_calculator.htm and review how changes in inflation alter your real return. What happens to the difference between the adjusted value of an investment compared to its inflation-adjusted value as
   a. Inflation increases?
   b. The investment horizon lengthens?
   c. Expected returns increase?

WEB REFERENCES

ftp://ftp.bls.gov/pub/special.requests/cpi/cpiai.txt

Contains historical information about inflation.

www.federalreserve.gov/releases/H6/Current

The Federal Reserve reports money supply data at 4:30 p.m. every Thursday.

CHAPTER

6 The Risk and Term Structure of Interest Rates

Preview

In our supply and demand analysis of interest-rate behavior in Chapter 5, we examined the determination of just one interest rate. Yet we saw earlier that there are enormous numbers of bonds on which the interest rates can and do differ. In this chapter, we complete the interest-rate picture by examining the relationship of the various interest rates to one another. Understanding why they differ from bond to bond can help businesses, banks, insurance companies, and private investors decide which bonds to purchase as investments and which ones to sell.

We first look at why bonds with the same term to maturity have different interest rates. The relationship among these interest rates is called the **risk structure of interest rates**, although risk, liquidity, and income tax rules all play a role in determining the risk structure. A bond's term to maturity also affects its interest rate, and the relationship among interest rates on bonds with different terms to maturity is called the **term structure of interest rates**. In this chapter, we examine the sources and causes of fluctuations in interest rates relative to one another and look at a number of theories that explain these fluctuations.

RISK STRUCTURE OF INTEREST RATES

Figure 1 shows the yields to maturity for several categories of long-term bonds from 1919 to 2005. It shows us two important features of interest-rate behavior for bonds of the same maturity: Interest rates on different categories of bonds differ from one another in any given year, and the spread (or difference) between the interest rates varies over time. The interest rates on municipal bonds, for example, are higher than those on U.S. government (Treasury) bonds in the late 1930s but lower thereafter. In addition, the spread between the interest rates on Baa corporate bonds (riskier than Aaa corporate bonds) and U.S. government bonds is very large during the Great Depression years 1930–1933, is smaller during the 1940s–1960s, and then widens again afterward. Which factors are responsible for these phenomena?

Default Risk

One attribute of a bond that influences its interest rate is its risk of **default**, which occurs when the issuer of the bond is unable or unwilling to make interest payments when promised or pay off the face value when the bond matures. A corporation suffering big losses, such as the major airline companies like United, Delta, US Airways, and Northwest in the mid-2000s, might be more likely to suspend interest payments on its

FIGURE 1
Long-Term Bond Yields, 1919–2005

Sources: Board of Governors of the Federal Reserve System, *Banking and Monetary Statistics, 1941–1970*; Federal Reserve: www.federalreserve.gov/releases/h15/data.htm.

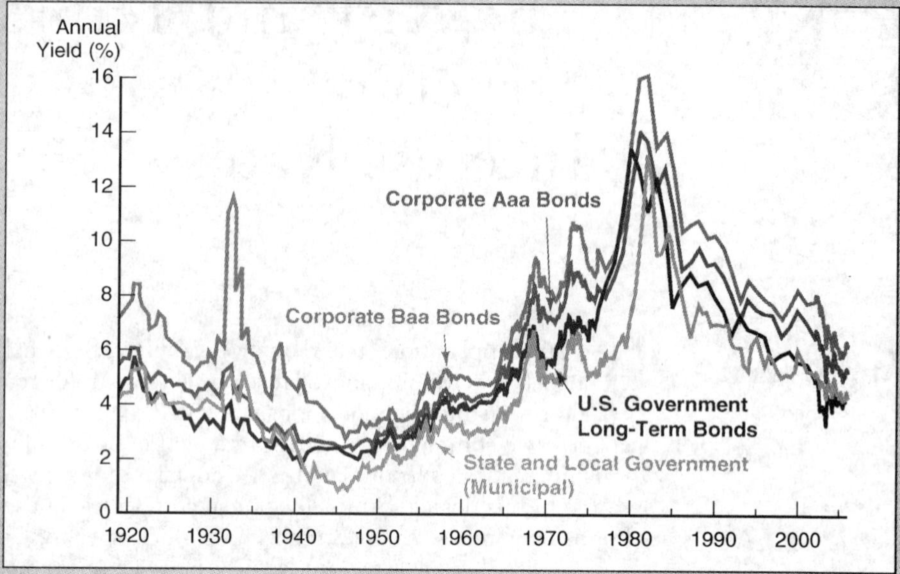

bonds. The default risk on its bonds would therefore be quite high. By contrast, U.S. Treasury bonds have usually been considered to have no default risk because the federal government can always increase taxes to pay off its obligations. Bonds like these with no default risk are called **default-free bonds**. (However, during the budget negotiations in Congress in 1995 and 1996, the Republicans threatened to let Treasury bonds default, and this had an impact on the bond market, as one application following this section indicates.) The spread between the interest rates on bonds with default risk and default-free bonds, both of the same maturity, called the **risk premium**, indicates how much additional interest people must earn to be willing to hold that risky bond. Our supply and demand analysis of the bond market in Chapter 5 can be used to explain why a bond with default risk always has a positive risk premium and why the higher the default risk is, the larger the risk premium will be.

To examine the effect of default risk on interest rates, let us look at the supply and demand diagrams for the default-free (U.S. Treasury) and corporate long-term bond markets in Figure 2. To make the diagrams somewhat easier to read, let's assume that initially corporate bonds have the same default risk as U.S. Treasury bonds. In this case, these two bonds have the same attributes (identical risk and maturity); their equilibrium prices and interest rates will initially be equal ($P_1^c = P_1^T$ and $i_1^c = i_1^T$), and the risk premium on corporate bonds ($i_1^c - i_1^T$) will be zero.

STUDY GUIDE

Two exercises will help you gain a better understanding of the risk structure:

1. Put yourself in the shoes of an investor—see how your purchase decision would be affected by changes in risk and liquidity.

2. Practice drawing the appropriate shifts in the supply and demand curves when risk and liquidity change. For example, see if you can draw the appropriate shifts in the supply and demand curves when, in contrast to the examples in the text, a corporate bond has a decline in default risk or an improvement in its liquidity.

If the possibility of a default increases because a corporation begins to suffer large losses, the default risk on corporate bonds will increase, and the expected return on these bonds will decrease. In addition, the corporate bond's return will be more uncertain. The theory of asset demand predicts that because the expected return on the corporate bond falls relative to the expected return on the default-free Treasury bond while its relative riskiness rises, the corporate bond is less desirable (holding everything else equal), and demand for it will fall. The demand curve for corporate bonds in panel (a) of Figure 2 then shifts to the left, from D_1^c to D_2^c.

At the same time, the expected return on default-free Treasury bonds increases relative to the expected return on corporate bonds, while their relative riskiness declines. The Treasury bonds thus become more desirable, and demand rises, as shown in panel (b) by the rightward shift in the demand curve for these bonds from D_1^T to D_2^T.

As we can see in Figure 2, the equilibrium price for corporate bonds falls from P_1^c to P_2^c, and since the bond price is negatively related to the interest rate, the equilibrium

myeconlab

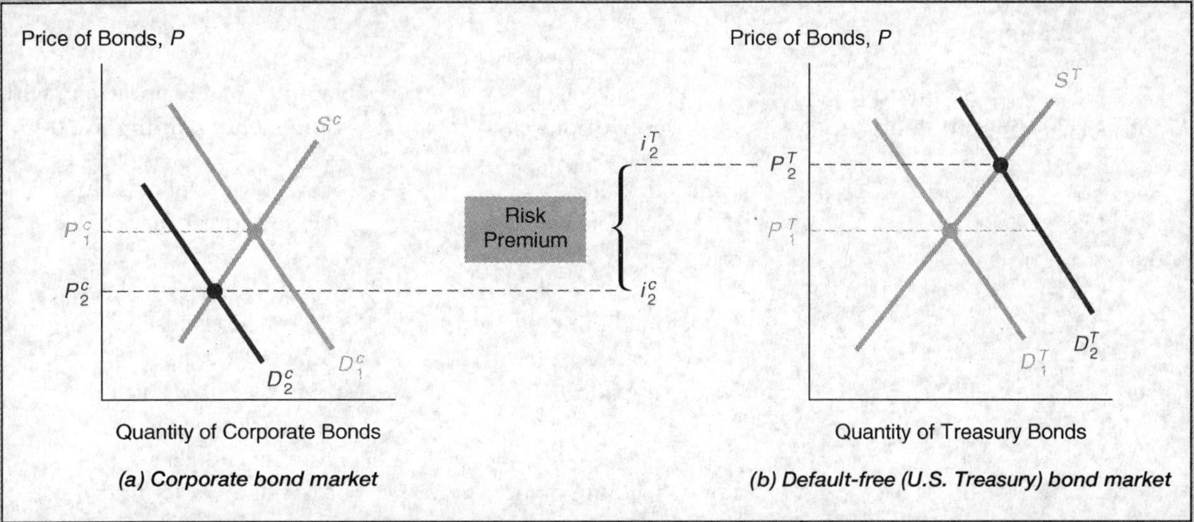

FIGURE 2 **Response to an Increase in Default Risk on Corporate Bonds**
An increase in default risk on corporate bonds shifts the demand curve from D_1^c to D_2^c. Simultaneously, it shifts the demand curve for Treasury bonds from D_1^T to D_2^T. The equilibrium price for corporate bonds falls from P_1^c to P_2^c, and the equilibrium interest rate on corporate bonds rises to i_2^c. In the Treasury market, the equilibrium bond price rises from P_1^T to P_2^T, and the equilibrium interest rate falls to i_2^T. The brace indicates the difference between i_2^c and i_2^T, the risk premium on corporate bonds. (Note that becasue P_2^c is lower than P_2^T, i_2^c is greater than i_2^T.)

interest rate on corporate bonds rises to i_2^c. At the same time, however, the equilibrium price for the Treasury bonds rises from P_1^T to P_2^T, and the equilibrium interest rate falls to i_2^T. The spread between the interest rates on corporate and default-free bonds—that is, the risk premium on corporate bonds—has risen from zero to $i_2^c - i_2^T$. We can now conclude that ***a bond with default risk will always have a positive risk premium, and an increase in its default risk will raise the risk premium.***

Because default risk is so important to the size of the risk premium, purchasers of bonds need to know whether a corporation is likely to default on its bonds. This information is provided by **credit-rating agencies**, investment advisory firms that rate the quality of corporate and municipal bonds in terms of the probability of default. Table 1 provides the ratings and their description for the two largest credit-rating agencies, Moody's Investor Service and Standard and Poor's Corporation. Bonds with relatively low risk of default are called *investment-grade* securities and have a rating of Baa (or BBB) and above. Bonds with ratings below Baa (or BBB) have higher default risk and have been aptly dubbed speculative-grade or **junk bonds**. Because these bonds always have higher interest rates than investment-grade securities, they are also referred to as high-yield bonds.

Next let's look at Figure 1 at the beginning of the chapter and see if we can explain the relationship between interest rates on corporate and U.S. Treasury bonds. Corporate bonds always have higher interest rates than U.S. Treasury bonds because they always have some risk of default, whereas U.S. Treasury bonds do not. Because Baa-rated corporate bonds have a greater default risk than the higher-rated Aaa bonds, their

TABLE 1 Bond Ratings by Moody's and Standard and Poor's

Rating			
Moody's	Standard and Poor's	Descriptions	Examples of Corporations with Bonds Outstanding in 2006
Aaa	AAA	Highest quality (lowest default risk)	General Electric, Pfizer, Inc. United Parcel Service, Inc.
Aa	AA	High quality	Wal-Mart, PepsiCo, Credit Suisse First Boston
A	A	Upper medium grade	Dell, Anheuser-Busch, McDonald's, Boeing
Baa	BBB	Medium grade	Motorola, FedEx Corp., Royal Caribbean, Tommy Hilfiger
Ba	BB	Lower medium grade	Ford, Allied Waste Industries, Jack in the Box, Inc.
B	B	Speculative	Rite Aid, General Motors, Levi Strauss
Caa	CCC, CC	Poor (high default risk)	Revlon, Fedders Corp., Integrated Electrical Services, Inc.
C	D	Highly speculative	United Airlines Corp., Pliont Corp., Northwest Airlines, Corp.

risk premium is greater, and the Baa rate therefore always exceeds the Aaa rate. We can use the same analysis to explain the huge jump in the risk premium on Baa corporate bond rates during the Great Depression years 1930–1933 and the rise in the risk premium after 1970 (see Figure 1). The depression period saw a very high rate of business failures and defaults. As we would expect, these factors led to a substantial increase in the default risk for bonds issued by vulnerable corporations, and the risk premium for Baa bonds reached unprecedentedly high levels. Since 1970, we have again seen higher levels of business failures and defaults, although they were still well below Great Depression levels. Again, as expected, both default risks and risk premiums for corporate bonds rose, widening the spread between interest rates on corporate bonds and Treasury bonds.

APPLICATION The Enron Bankruptcy and the Baa–Aaa Spread

In December 2001, Enron Corporation, a firm specializing in trading in the energy market and once the seventh-largest corporation in the United States, was forced to declare bankruptcy after it became clear that it had used shady accounting to hide its financial problems. (The Enron bankruptcy, the largest ever in the United States, will be discussed further in Chapter 8.) Because of the scale of the bankruptcy and the questions it raised about the quality of the information in accounting statements, the Enron collapse had a major impact on the corporate bond market. Let's see how our supply and demand analysis explains the behavior of the spread between interest rates on lower quality (Baa-rated) and highest quality (Aaa-rated) corporate bonds in the aftermath of the Enron failure.

As a consequence of the Enron bankruptcy, many investors began to doubt the financial health of corporations with lower credit ratings such as Baa. The increase in default risk for Baa bonds made them less desirable at any given interest rate, decreased the quantity demanded, and shifted the demand curve for Baa bonds to the left. As shown in panel (a) of Figure 2, the interest rate on Baa bonds should have risen, which is indeed what happened. Interest rates on Baa bonds rose by 24 basis points (0.24 percentage point) from 7.81% in November 2001 to 8.05% in December 2001. But the increase in the perceived default risk for Baa bonds after the Enron bankruptcy made the highest-quality (Aaa) bonds relatively more attractive and shifted the demand curve for these securities to the right—an outcome described by some analysts as a "flight to quality." Just as our analysis predicts in Figure 2, interest rates on Aaa bonds fell by 20 basis points, from 6.97% in November to 6.77% in December. The overall outcome was that the spread between interest rates on Baa and Aaa bonds rose by 44 basis points from 0.84% before the bankruptcy to 1.28% afterward.

Liquidity

Another attribute of a bond that influences its interest rate is its liquidity. As we learned in Chapter 4, a liquid asset is one that can be quickly and cheaply converted into cash if the need arises. The more liquid an asset is, the more desirable it is (holding everything else constant). U.S. Treasury bonds are the most liquid of all long-term bonds, because they are so widely traded that they are the easiest to sell quickly and the cost of selling them is low. Corporate bonds are not as liquid, because fewer bonds for any one corporation are traded; thus it can be costly to sell these bonds in an emergency, because it might be hard to find buyers quickly.

How does the reduced liquidity of the corporate bonds affect their interest rates relative to the interest rate on Treasury bonds? We can use supply and demand analysis with the same figure that was used to analyze the effect of default risk, Figure 2, to show that the lower liquidity of corporate bonds relative to Treasury bonds increases the spread between the interest rates on these two bonds. Let us start the analysis by assuming that initially corporate and Treasury bonds are equally liquid and all their other attributes are the same. As shown in Figure 2, their equilibrium prices and interest rates will initially be equal: $P_1^c = P_1^T$ and $i_1^c = i_1^T$. If the corporate bond becomes less liquid than the Treasury bond because it is less widely traded, then (as the theory of asset demand indicates) demand for it will fall, shifting its demand curve from D_1^c to D_2^c as in panel (a). The Treasury bond now becomes relatively more liquid in comparison with the corporate bond, so its demand curve shifts rightward from D_1^T to D_2^T as in panel (b). The shifts in the curves in Figure 2 show that the price of the less liquid corporate bond falls and its interest rate rises, while the price of the more liquid Treasury bond rises and its interest rate falls.

The result is that the spread between the interest rates on the two bond types has risen. Therefore, the differences between interest rates on corporate bonds and Treasury bonds (that is, the risk premiums) reflect not only the corporate bond's default risk but also its liquidity. This is why a risk premium is more accurately a "risk and liquidity premium," but convention dictates that it is called a *risk premium*.

Income Tax Considerations

Returning to Figure 1, we are still left with one puzzle—the behavior of municipal bond rates. Municipal bonds are certainly not default-free: State and local governments have defaulted on the municipal bonds they have issued in the past, particularly during the Great Depression and even more recently in the case of Orange County, California, in 1994 (more on this in Chapter 13). Also, municipal bonds are not as liquid as U.S. Treasury bonds.

Why is it, then, that these bonds have had lower interest rates than U.S. Treasury bonds for at least 40 years, as indicated in Figure 1? The explanation lies in the fact that interest payments on municipal bonds are exempt from federal income taxes, a factor that has the same effect on the demand for municipal bonds as an increase in their expected return.

Let us imagine that you have a high enough income to put you in the 35% income tax bracket, where for every extra dollar of income you have to pay 35 cents to the government. If you own a \$1,000-face-value U.S. Treasury bond that sells for \$1,000 and has a coupon payment of \$100, you get to keep only \$65 of the payment after taxes. Although the bond has a 10% interest rate, you actually earn only 6.5% after taxes.

Suppose, however, that you put your savings into a \$1,000-face-value municipal bond that sells for \$1,000 and pays only \$80 in coupon payments. Its interest rate is only 8%, but because it is a tax-exempt security, you pay no taxes on the \$80 coupon payment, so you earn 8% after taxes. Clearly, you earn more on the municipal bond after taxes, so you are willing to hold the riskier and less liquid municipal bond even though it has a lower interest rate than the U.S. Treasury bond. (This was not true before World War II, when the tax-exempt status of municipal bonds did not convey much of an advantage because income tax rates were extremely low.)

Another way of understanding why municipal bonds have lower interest rates than Treasury bonds is to use the supply and demand analysis depicted in Figure 3. We

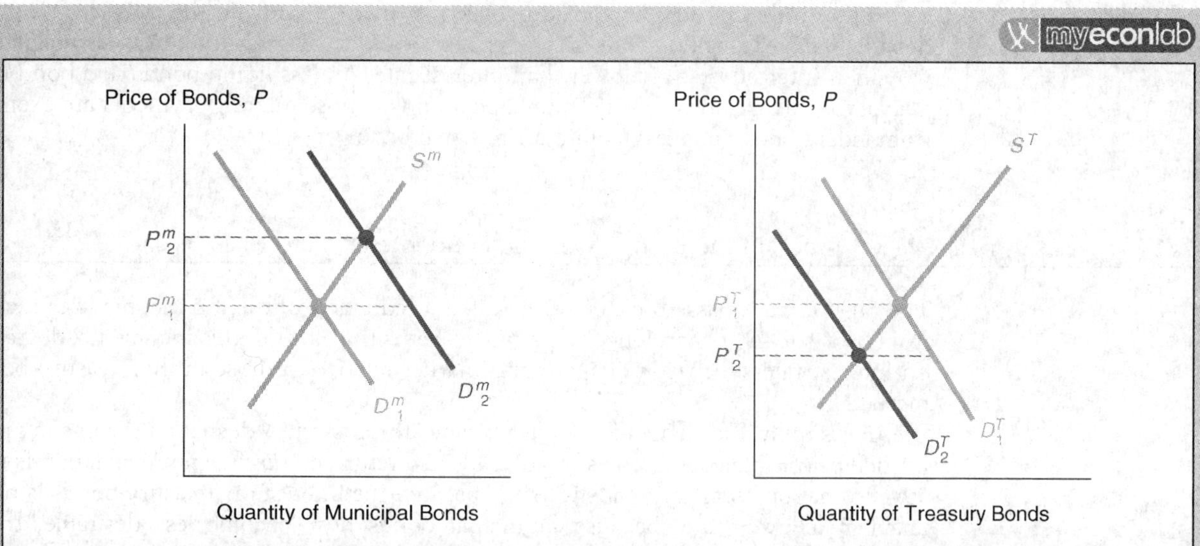

(a) Market for municipal bonds　　*(b) Market for Treasury bonds*

FIGURE 3 **Interest Rates on Municipal and Treasury Bonds**
When the municipal bond is given tax-free status, demand for the municipal bond shifts rightward from D^m_1 to D^m_2 and demand for the Treasury bond shifts leftward from D^T_1 to D^T_2. The equilibrium price of the municipal bond rises from P^m_1 to P^m_2, so its interest rate falls, while the equilibrium price of the Treasury bond falls from P^T_1 to P^T_2 and its interest rate rises. The result is that municipal bonds end up with lower interest rates than those on Treasury bonds.

assume that municipal and Treasury bonds have identical attributes and so have the same bond prices as drawn in the figure: $P^m_1 = P^T_1$, and the same interest rates. Once the municipal bonds are given a tax advantage that raises their after-tax expected return relative to Treasury bonds and makes them more desirable, demand for them rises, and their demand curve shifts to the right, from D^m_1 to D^m_2. The result is that their equilibrium bond price rises from P^m_1 to P^m_2, and their equilibrium interest rate falls. By contrast, Treasury bonds have now become less desirable relative to municipal bonds; demand for Treasury bonds decreases, and D^T_1 shifts to D^T_2. The Treasury bond price falls from P^T_1 to P^T_2, and the interest rate rises. The resulting lower interest rates for municipal bonds and higher interest rates for Treasury bonds explain why municipal bonds can have interest rates below those of Treasury bonds.[1]

Summary

The risk structure of interest rates (the relationship among interest rates on bonds with the same maturity) is explained by three factors: default risk, liquidity, and the income tax treatment of a bond's interest payments. As a bond's default risk increases, the risk

[1]In contrast to corporate bonds, Treasury bonds are exempt from state and local income taxes. Using the analysis in the text, you should be able to show that this feature of Treasury bonds provides an additional reason why interest rates on corporate bonds are higher than those on Treasury bonds.

premium on that bond (the spread between its interest rate and the interest rate on a default-free Treasury bond) rises. The greater liquidity of Treasury bonds also explains why their interest rates are lower than interest rates on less liquid bonds. If a bond has a favorable tax treatment, as do municipal bonds, whose interest payments are exempt from federal income taxes, its interest rate will be lower.

APPLICATION Effects of the Bush Tax Cut on Bond Interest Rates

The Bush tax cut passed in 2001 scheduled a reduction of the top income tax bracket from 39% to 35% over a ten-year period. What is the effect of this income tax decrease on interest rates in the municipal bond market relative to those in the Treasury bond market?

Our supply and demand analysis provides the answer. A decreased income tax rate for rich people means that the after-tax expected return on tax-free municipal bonds relative to that on Treasury bonds is lower, because the interest on Treasury bonds is now taxed at a lower rate. Because municipal bonds now become less desirable, their demand decreases, shifting the demand curve to the left, which lowers their price and raises their interest rate. Conversely, the lower income tax rate makes Treasury bonds more desirable; this change shifts their demand curve to the right, raises their price, and lowers their interest rates.

Our analysis thus shows that the Bush tax cut raised the interest rates on municipal bonds relative to interest rates on Treasury bonds.

TERM STRUCTURE OF INTEREST RATES

We have seen how risk, liquidity, and tax considerations (collectively embedded in the risk structure) can influence interest rates. Another factor that influences the interest rate on a bond is its term to maturity: Bonds with identical risk, liquidity, and tax characteristics may have different interest rates because the time remaining to maturity is different. A plot of the yields on bonds with differing terms to maturity but the same risk, liquidity, and tax considerations is called a **yield curve**, and it describes the term structure of interest rates for particular types of bonds, such as government bonds. The "Following the Financial News" box shows several yield curves for Treasury securities that were published in the *Wall Street Journal*. Yield curves can be classified as upward-sloping, flat, and downward-sloping (the last sort is often referred to as an **inverted yield curve**). When yield curves slope upward, the most usual case, the long-term interest rates are above the short-term interest rates; when yield curves are flat, as in the Following the Financial News box, short- and long-term interest rates are the same; and when yield curves are inverted, long-term interest rates are below short-term interest rates. Yield curves can also have more complicated shapes in which they first slope up and then down, or vice versa. Why do we usually see upward slopes of the yield curve but sometimes other shapes?

Besides explaining why yield curves take on different shapes at different times, a good theory of the term structure of interest rates must explain the following three important empirical facts:

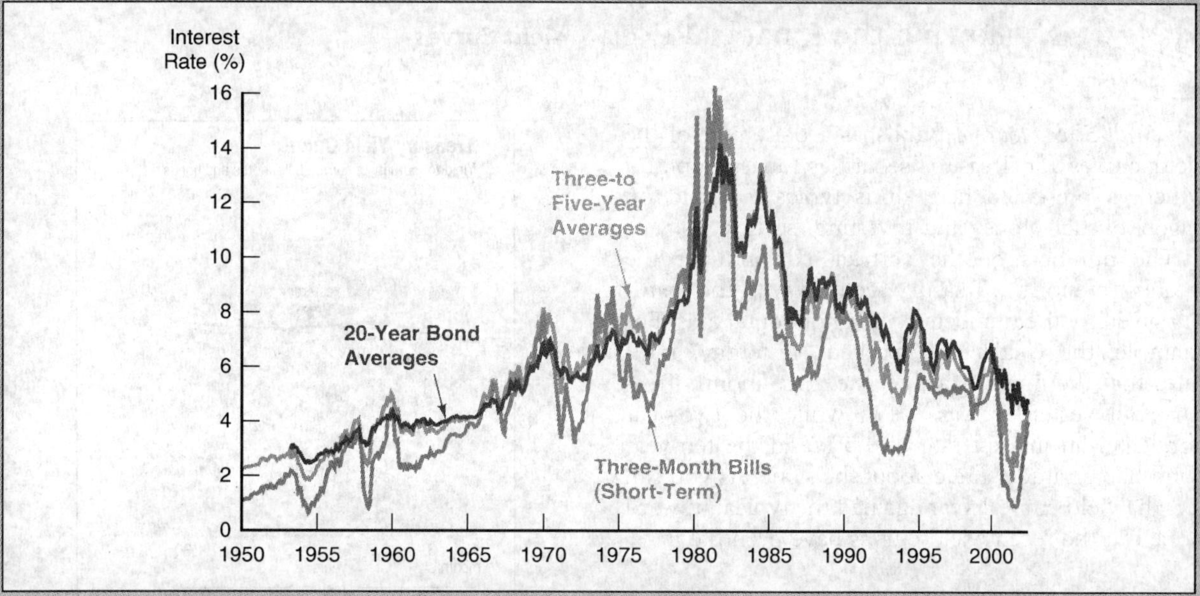

FIGURE 4 **Movements over Time of Interest Rates on U.S. Government Bonds with Different Maturities**

Sources: Federal Reserve: www.federalreserve.gov/releases/h15/data.htm.

1. As we see in Figure 4, interest rates on bonds of different maturities move together over time.
2. When short-term interest rates are low, yield curves are more likely to have an upward slope; when short-term interest rates are high, yield curves are more likely to slope downward and be inverted.
3. Yield curves almost always slope upward, as in the Following the Financial News box.

Three theories have been put forward to explain the term structure of interest rates—that is, the relationship among interest rates on bonds of different maturities reflected in yield curve patterns: (1) the expectations theory, (2) the segmented markets theory, and (3) the liquidity premium theory, each of which is described in the following sections. The expectations theory does a good job of explaining the first two facts on our list, but not the third. The segmented markets theory can explain fact 3 but not the other two facts, which are well explained by the expectations theory. Because each theory explains facts that the other cannot, a natural way to seek a better understanding of the term structure is to combine features of both theories, which leads us to the liquidity premium theory, which can explain all three facts.

If the liquidity premium theory does a better job of explaining the facts and is hence the most widely accepted theory, why do we spend time discussing the other two theories? There are two reasons. First, the ideas in these two theories lay the groundwork for the liquidity premium theory. Second, it is important to see how economists modify theories to improve them when they find that the predicted results are inconsistent with the empirical evidence.

Following the Financial News Yield Curves

The *Wall Street Journal* publishes a daily plot of the yield curves for Treasury securities, an example of which is presented here. It is typically found on page 2 of the "Money and Investing" section.

The numbers on the vertical axis indicate the interest rate for the Treasury security, with the maturity given by the numbers on the horizontal axis. For example, the yield curve marked "Yesterday" indicates that the interest rate on the three-month Treasury bill yesterday was 4.4%, while the two-year bond had an interest rate of 4.5% and the ten-year bond had an interest rate about the same. As you can see, the yield curve 1 year ago had the typical upward slope but the recent yield curves have been flat.

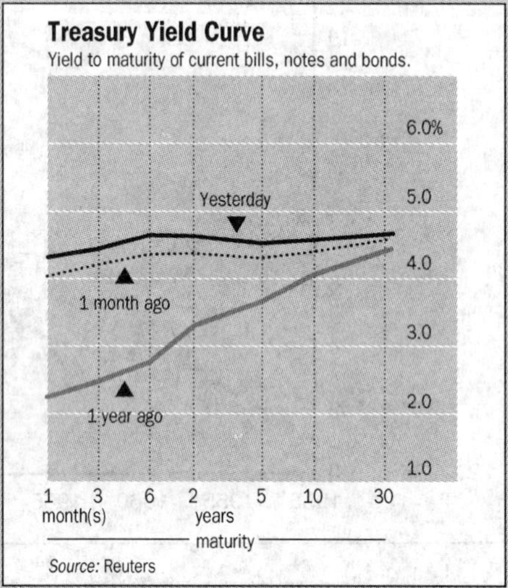

Source: Wall Street Journal, Tuesday, February 7, 2006, p. C2.

Expectations Theory

The **expectations theory** of the term structure states the following commonsense proposition: The interest rate on a long-term bond will equal an average of the short-term interest rates that people expect to occur over the life of the long-term bond. For example, if people expect that short-term interest rates will be 10% on average over the coming five years, the expectations theory predicts that the interest rate on bonds with five years to maturity will be 10%, too. If short-term interest rates were expected to rise even higher after this five-year period, so that the average short-term interest rate over the coming 20 years is 11%, then the interest rate on 20-year bonds would equal 11% and would be higher than the interest rate on five-year bonds. We can see that the explanation provided by the expectations theory for why interest rates on bonds of different maturities differ is that short-term interest rates are expected to have different values at future dates.

The key assumption behind this theory is that buyers of bonds do not prefer bonds of one maturity over another, so they will not hold any quantity of a bond if its expected return is less than that of another bond with a different maturity. Bonds that have this characteristic are said to be *perfect substitutes*. What this means in practice is that if bonds with different maturities are perfect substitutes, the expected return on these bonds must be equal.

To see how the assumption that bonds with different maturities are perfect substitutes leads to the expectations theory, let us consider the following two investment strategies:

1. Purchase a one-year bond, and when it matures in one year, purchase another one-year bond.
2. Purchase a two-year bond and hold it until maturity.

Because both strategies must have the same expected return if people are holding both one- and two-year bonds, the interest rate on the two-year bond must equal the average of the two one-year interest rates. For example, let's say that the current interest rate on the one-year bond is 9% and you expect the interest rate on the one-year bond next year to be 11%. If you pursue the first strategy of buying the two one-year bonds, the expected return over the two years will average out to be (9% + 11%)/2 = 10% per year. You will be willing to hold both the one- and two-year bonds only if the expected return per year of the two-year bond equals this return. Therefore, the interest rate on the two-year bond must equal 10%, the average interest rate on the two one-year bonds.

We can make this argument more general. For an investment of $1, consider the choice of holding, for two periods, a two-period bond or two one-period bonds. Using the definitions

i_t = today's (time t) interest rate on a one-period bond
i^e_{t+1} = interest rate on a one-period bond expected for next period (time $t + 1$)
i_{2t} = today's (time t) interest rate on the two-period bond

the expected return over the two periods from investing $1 in the two-period bond and holding it for the two periods can be calculated as

$$(1 + i_{2t})(1 + i_{2t}) - 1 = 1 + 2i_{2t} + (i_{2t})^2 - 1 = 2i_{2t} + (i_{2t})^2$$

After the second period, the $1 investment is worth $(1 + i_{2t})(1 + i_{2t})$. Subtracting the $1 initial investment from this amount and dividing by the initial $1 investment gives the rate of return calculated in the previous equation. Because $(i_{2t})^2$ is extremely small—if $i_{2t} = 10\% = 0.10$, then $(i_{2t})^2 = 0.01$—we can simplify the expected return for holding the two-period bond for the two periods to

$$2i_{2t}$$

With the other strategy, in which one-period bonds are bought, the expected return on the $1 investment over the two periods is

$$(1 + i_t)(1 + i^e_{t+1}) - 1 = 1 + i_t + i^e_{t+1} + i_t(i^e_{t+1}) - 1 = i_t + i^e_t + i_t(i^e_{t+1})$$

This calculation is derived by recognizing that after the first period, the $1 investment becomes $1 + i_t$, and this is reinvested in the one-period bond for the next period, yielding an amount $(1 + i_t)(1 + i^e_{t+1})$. Then subtracting the $1 initial investment from this amount and dividing by the initial investment of $1 gives the expected return for the strategy of holding one-period bonds for the two periods. Because $i_t(i^e_{t+1})$ is also extremely small—if $i_t = i^e_{t+1} = 0.10$, then $i_t(i^e_{t+1}) = 0.01$—we can simplify this to

$$i_t + i^e_{t+1}$$

Both bonds will be held only if these expected returns are equal—that is, when

$$2i_{2t} = i_t + i^e_{t+1}$$

Solving for i_{2t} in terms of the one-period rates, we have

$$i_{2t} = \frac{i_t + i^e_{t+1}}{2} \qquad (1)$$

which tells us that the two-period rate must equal the average of the two one-period rates. Graphically, this can be shown as

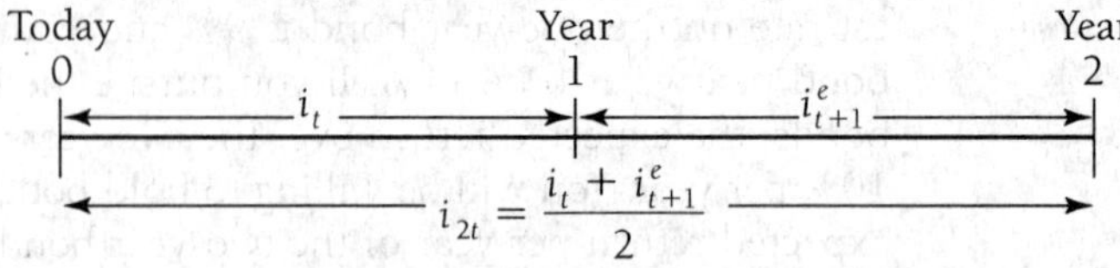

We can conduct the same steps for bonds with a longer maturity so that we can examine the whole term structure of interest rates. Doing so, we will find that the interest rate of i_{nt} on an n-period bond must be

$$i_{nt} = \frac{i_t + i^e_{t+1} + i^e_{t+2} + \cdots + i^e_{t+(n-1)}}{n} \tag{2}$$

Equation 2 states that the n-period interest rate equals the average of the one-period interest rates expected to occur over the n-period life of the bond. This is a restatement of the expectations theory in more precise terms.[2]

A simple numerical example might clarify what the expectations theory in Equation 2 is saying. If the one-year interest rate over the next five years is expected to be 5%, 6%, 7%, 8%, and 9%, Equation 2 indicates that the interest rate on the two-year bond would be

$$\frac{5\% + 6\%}{2} = 5.5\%$$

For the five-year bond it would be

$$\frac{5\% + 6\% + 7\% + 8\% + 9\%}{5} = 7\%$$

Doing a similar calculation for the one-, three-, and four-year interest rates, you should be able to verify that the one- to five-year interest rates are 5.0%, 5.5%, 6.0%, 6.5%, and 7.0%, respectively. Thus we see that the rising trend in expected short-term interest rates produces an upward-sloping yield curve along which interest rates rise as maturity lengthens.

The expectations theory is an elegant theory that explains why the term structure of interest rates (as represented by yield curves) changes at different times. When the yield curve is upward-sloping, the expectations theory suggests that short-term interest rates are expected to rise in the future, as we have seen in our numerical example. In this situation, in which the long-term rate is currently higher than the short-term rate, the average of future short-term rates is expected to be higher than the current short-term rate, which can occur only if short-term interest rates are expected to rise. This is what we see in our numerical example. When the yield curve is inverted (slopes downward), the average of future short-term interest rates is expected to be lower than the current short-term rate, implying that short-term interest rates are expected to fall, on average, in the future. Only when the yield curve is flat does the expectations theory suggest that short-term interest rates are not expected to change, on average, in the future.

---

[2]The analysis here has been conducted for discount bonds. Formulas for interest rates on coupon bonds would differ slightly from those used here, but would convey the same principle.

The expectations theory also explains fact 1, which states that interest rates on bonds with different maturities move together over time. Historically, short-term interest rates have had the characteristic that if they increase today, they will tend to be higher in the future. Hence a rise in short-term rates will raise people's expectations of future short-term rates. Because long-term rates are the average of expected future short-term rates, a rise in short-term rates will also raise long-term rates, causing short- and long-term rates to move together.

The expectations theory also explains fact 2, which states that yield curves tend to have an upward slope when short-term interest rates are low and are inverted when short-term rates are high. When short-term rates are low, people generally expect them to rise to some normal level in the future, and the average of future expected short-term rates is high relative to the current short-term rate. Therefore, long-term interest rates will be substantially higher than current short-term rates, and the yield curve would then have an upward slope. Conversely, if short-term rates are high, people usually expect them to come back down. Long-term rates would then drop below short-term rates because the average of expected future short-term rates would be lower than current short-term rates and the yield curve would slope downward and become inverted.[3]

The expectations theory is an attractive theory because it provides a simple explanation of the behavior of the term structure, but unfortunately it has a major shortcoming: It cannot explain fact 3, which says that yield curves usually slope upward. The typical upward slope of yield curves implies that short-term interest rates are usually expected to rise in the future. In practice, short-term interest rates are just as likely to fall as they are to rise, and so the expectations theory suggests that the typical yield curve should be flat rather than upward-sloping.

Segmented Markets Theory

As the name suggests, the **segmented markets theory** of the term structure sees markets for different-maturity bonds as completely separate and segmented. The interest rate for each bond with a different maturity is then determined by the supply of and demand for that bond, with no effects from expected returns on other bonds with other maturities.

The key assumption in the segmented markets theory is that bonds of different maturities are not substitutes at all, so the expected return from holding a bond of one maturity has no effect on the demand for a bond of another maturity. This theory of the term structure is at the opposite extreme to the expectations theory, which assumes that bonds of different maturities are perfect substitutes.

The argument for why bonds of different maturities are not substitutes is that investors have strong preferences for bonds of one maturity but not for another, so they will be concerned with the expected returns only for bonds of the maturity they prefer.

---

[3]The expectations theory explains another important fact about the relationship between short-term and long-term interest rates. As you can see in Figure 4, short-term interest rates are more volatile than long-term rates. If interest rates are *mean-reverting*—that is, if they tend to head back down after they are at unusually high levels or go back up when they are at unusually low levels—then an average of these short-term rates must necessarily have less volatility than the short-term rates themselves. Because the expectations theory suggests that the long-term rate will be an average of future short-term rates, it implies that the long-term rate will have less volatility than short-term rates.

This might occur because they have a particular holding period in mind, and if they match the maturity of the bond to the desired holding period, they can obtain a certain return with no risk at all.[4] (We have seen in Chapter 4 that if the term to maturity equals the holding period, the return is known for certain because it equals the yield exactly, and there is no interest-rate risk.) For example, people who have a short holding period would prefer to hold short-term bonds. Conversely, if you were putting funds away for your young child to go to college, your desired holding period might be much longer, and you would want to hold longer-term bonds.

In the segmented markets theory, differing yield curve patterns are accounted for by supply and demand differences associated with bonds of different maturities. If, as seems sensible, investors have short desired holding periods and generally prefer bonds with shorter maturities that have less interest-rate risk, the segmented markets theory can explain fact 3, which states that yield curves typically slope upward. Because in the typical situation the demand for long-term bonds is relatively lower than that for short-term bonds, long-term bonds will have lower prices and higher interest rates, and hence the yield curve will typically slope upward.

Although the segmented markets theory can explain why yield curves usually tend to slope upward, it has a major flaw in that it cannot explain facts 1 and 2. First, because it views the market for bonds of different maturities as completely segmented, there is no reason for a rise in interest rates on a bond of one maturity to affect the interest rate on a bond of another maturity. Therefore, it cannot explain why interest rates on bonds of different maturities tend to move together (fact 1). Second, because it is not clear how demand and supply for short- versus long-term bonds change with the level of short-term interest rates, the theory cannot explain why yield curves tend to slope upward when short-term interest rates are low and to be inverted when short-term interest rates are high (fact 2).

Because each of our two theories explains empirical facts that the other cannot, a logical step is to combine the theories, which leads us to the liquidity premium theory.

Liquidity Premium and Preferred Habitat Theories

The **liquidity premium theory** of the term structure states that the interest rate on a long-term bond will equal an average of short-term interest rates expected to occur over the life of the long-term bond plus a liquidity premium (also referred to as a term premium) that responds to supply and demand conditions for that bond.

The liquidity premium theory's key assumption is that bonds of different maturities are substitutes, which means that the expected return on one bond *does* influence the expected return on a bond of a different maturity, but it allows investors to prefer one bond maturity over another. In other words, bonds of different maturities are assumed to be substitutes but not perfect substitutes. Investors tend to prefer shorter-term bonds because these bonds bear less interest-rate risk. For these reasons, investors must be offered a positive liquidity premium to induce them to hold longer-term bonds. Such an outcome would modify the expectations theory by adding a positive liquidity pre-

[4]The statement that there is no uncertainty about the return if the term to maturity equals the holding period is literally true only for a discount bond. For a coupon bond with a long holding period, there is some risk because coupon payments must be reinvested before the bond matures. Our analysis here is thus being conducted for discount bonds. However, the gist of the analysis remains the same for coupon bonds because the amount of this risk from reinvestment is small when coupon bonds have the same term to maturity as the holding period.

mium to the equation that describes the relationship between long- and short-term interest rates. The liquidity premium theory is thus written as

$$i_{nt} = \frac{i_t + i^e_{t+1} + i^e_{t+2} + \cdots + i^e_{t+(n-1)}}{n} + l_{nt} \qquad (3)$$

where l_{nt} is the liquidity (term) premium for the n-period bond at time t, which is always positive and rises with the term to maturity of the bond, n.

Closely related to the liquidity premium theory is the **preferred habitat theory**, which takes a somewhat less direct approach to modifying the expectations hypothesis but comes to a similar conclusion. It assumes that investors have a preference for bonds of one maturity over another, a particular bond maturity (preferred habitat) in which they prefer to invest. Because they prefer bonds of one maturity over another, they will be willing to buy bonds that do not have the preferred maturity only if they earn a somewhat higher expected return. Because investors are likely to prefer the habitat of short-term bonds over that of longer-term bonds, they are willing to hold long-term bonds only if they have higher expected returns. This reasoning leads to the same Equation 3 implied by the liquidity premium theory with a term premium that typically rises with maturity.

The relationship between the expectations theory and the liquidity premium and preferred habitat theories is shown in Figure 5. There we see that because the liquidity premium is always positive and typically grows as the term to maturity increases, the yield curve implied by the liquidity premium theory is always above the yield curve implied by the expectations theory and generally has a steeper slope.

A simple numerical example similar to the one we used for the expectations hypothesis further clarifies what the liquidity premium and preferred habitat theories in Equation 3 are saying. Again suppose that the one-year interest rate over the next five years is expected to be 5%, 6%, 7%, 8%, and 9%, while investors' preferences for holding

FIGURE 5

The Relationship Between the Liquidity Premium (Preferred Habitat) and Expectations Theory

Because the liquidity premium is always positive and grows as the term to maturity increases, the yield curve implied by the liquidity premium and preferred habitat theories is always above the yield curve implied by the expectations theory and has a steeper slope. For simplicity the yield curve implied by the expectations theory is drawn under the scenario of unchanging future one-year interest rates.

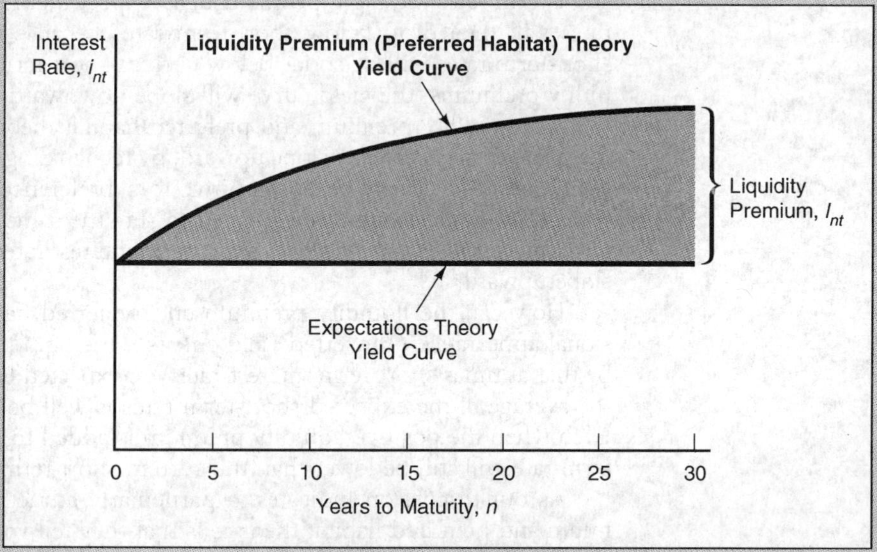

short-term bonds means that the liquidity premiums for one- to five-year bonds are 0%, 0.25%, 0.5%, 0.75%, and 1.0%, respectively. Equation 3 then indicates that the interest rate on the two-year bond would be

$$\frac{5\% + 6\%}{2} + 0.25\% = 5.75\%$$

For the five-year bond it would be

$$\frac{5\% + 6\% + 7\% + 8\% + 9\%}{5} + 1\% = 8\%$$

Doing a similar calculation for the one-, three-, and four-year interest rates, you should be able to verify that the one- to five-year interest rates are 5.0%, 5.75%, 6.5%, 7.25%, and 8.0%, respectively. Comparing these findings with those for the expectations theory, we see that the liquidity premium and preferred habitat theories produce yield curves that slope more steeply upward because of investors' preferences for short-term bonds.

Let's see if the liquidity premium and preferred habitat theories are consistent with all three empirical facts we have discussed. They explain fact 1, which states that interest rates on different-maturity bonds move together over time: A rise in short-term interest rates indicates that short-term interest rates will, on average, be higher in the future, and the first term in Equation 3 then implies that long-term interest rates will rise along with them.

They also explain why yield curves tend to have an especially steep upward slope when short-term interest rates are low and to be inverted when short-term rates are high (fact 2). Because investors generally expect short-term interest rates to rise to some normal level when they are low, the average of future expected short-term rates will be high relative to the current short-term rate. With the additional boost of a positive liquidity premium, long-term interest rates will be substantially higher than current short-term rates, and the yield curve will then have a steep upward slope. Conversely, if short-term rates are high, people usually expect them to come back down. Long-term rates will then drop below short-term rates because the average of expected future short-term rates will be so far below current short-term rates that despite positive liquidity premiums, the yield curve will slope downward.

The liquidity premium and preferred habitat theories explain fact 3, which states that yield curves typically slope upward, by recognizing that the liquidity premium rises with a bond's maturity because of investors' preferences for short-term bonds. Even if short-term interest rates are expected to stay the same on average in the future, long-term interest rates will be above short-term interest rates, and yield curves will typically slope upward.

How can the liquidity premium and preferred habitat theories explain the occasional appearance of inverted yield curves if the liquidity premium is positive? It must be that at times short-term interest rates are expected to fall so much in the future that the average of the expected short-term rates is well below the current short-term rate. Even when the positive liquidity premium is added to this average, the resulting long-term rate will still be lower than the current short-term interest rate.

As our discussion indicates, a particularly attractive feature of the liquidity premium and preferred habitat theories is that they tell you what the market is predicting about future short-term interest rates just from the slope of the yield curve. A steeply rising yield curve, as in panel (a) of Figure 6, indicates that short-term interest rates are expected to rise in the future. A moderately steep yield curve, as in panel (b), indicates

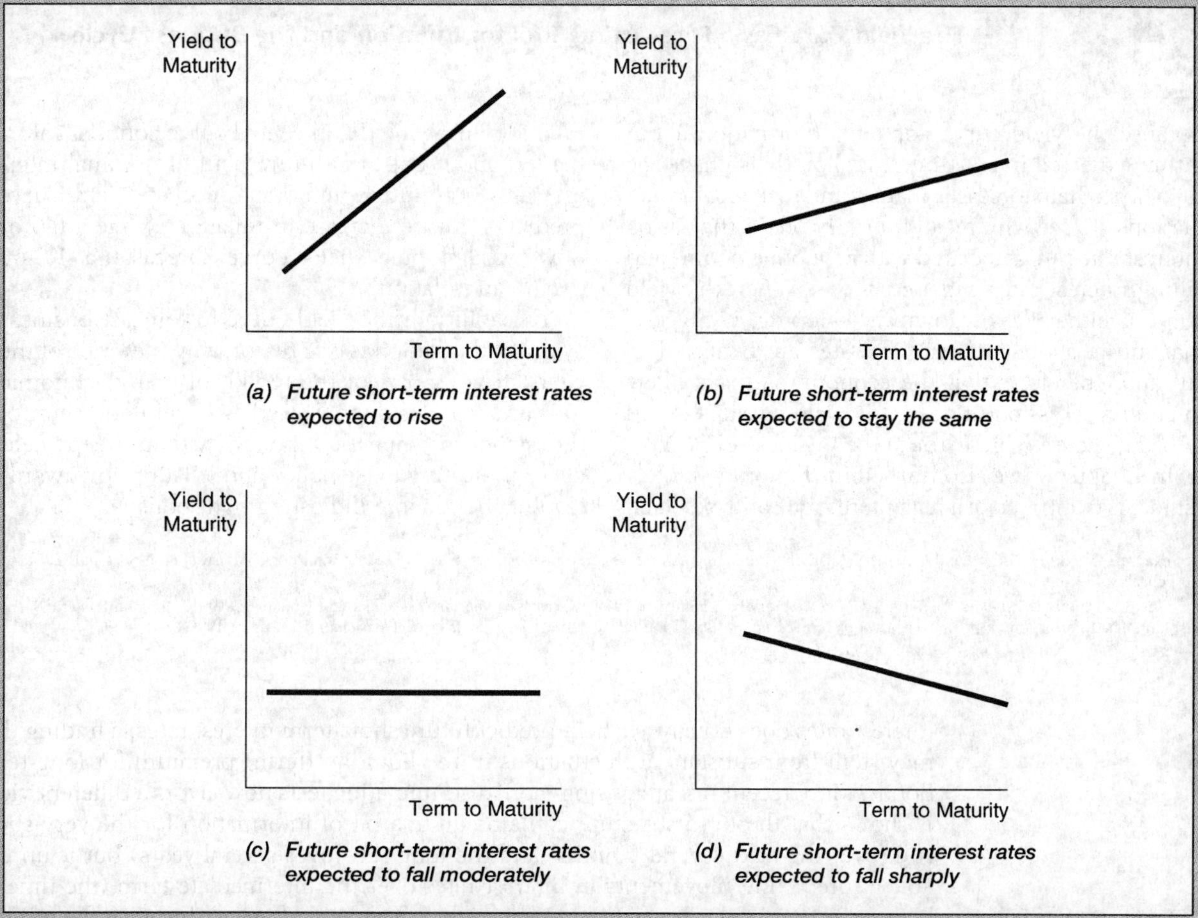

FIGURE 6 **Yield Curves and the Market's Expectations of Future Short-Term Interest Rates According to the Liquidity Premium (Preferred Habitat) Theory**

that short-term interest rates are not expected to rise or fall much in the future. A flat yield curve, as in panel (c), indicates that short-term rates are expected to fall moderately in the future. Finally, an inverted yield curve, as in panel (d), indicates that short-term interest rates are expected to fall sharply in the future.

Evidence on the Term Structure

In the 1980s, researchers examining the term structure of interest rates questioned whether the slope of the yield curve provides information about movements of future short-term interest rates.[5] They found that the spread between long- and short-term

[5]Robert J. Shiller, John Y. Campbell, and Kermit L. Schoenholtz, "Forward Rates and Future Policy: Interpreting the Term Structure of Interest Rates," *Brookings Papers on Economic Activity* 1 (1983): 173–217; N. Gregory Mankiw and Lawrence H. Summers, "Do Long-Term Interest Rates Overreact to Short-Term Interest Rates?" *Brookings Papers on Economic Activity* 1 (1984): 223–242.

FYI The Yield Curve as a Forecasting Tool for Inflation and the Business Cycle

Because the yield curve contains information about future expected interest rates, it should also have the capacity to help forecast inflation and real output fluctuations. To see why, recall from Chapter 5 that rising interest rates are associated with economic booms and falling interest rates with recessions. When the yield curve is either flat or downward-sloping, it suggests that future short-term interest rates are expected to fall and, therefore, that the economy is more likely to enter a recession. Indeed, the yield curve is found to be an accurate predictor of the business cycle.[a]

In Chapter 4, we also learned that a nominal interest rate is composed of a real interest rate and expected inflation, implying that the yield curve contains information about both the future path of nominal interest rates and future inflation. A steep yield curve predicts a future increase in inflation, while a flat or downward-sloping yield curve forecasts a future decline in inflation.[b]

The ability of the yield curve to forecast business cycles and inflation is one reason why the slope of the yield curve is part of the toolkit of many economic forecasters and is often viewed as a useful indicator of the stance of monetary policy, with a steep yield curve indicating loose policy and a flat or downward-sloping yield curve indicating tight policy.

[a]For example, see Arturo Estrella and Frederic S. Mishkin, "Predicting U.S. Recessions: Financial Variables as Leading Indicators," *Review of Economics and Statistics*, 80 (February 1998): 45–61.

[b]Frederic S. Mishkin, "What Does the Term Structure Tell Us About Future Inflation?" *Journal of Monetary Economics* 25 (January 1990): 77–95; and Frederic S. Mishkin, "The Information in the Longer-Maturity Term Structure About Future Inflation," *Quarterly Journal of Economics* 55 (August 1990): 815–828.

interest rates does not always help predict future short-term interest rates, a finding that may stem from substantial fluctuations in the liquidity (term) premium for long-term bonds. More recent research using more discriminating tests now favors a different view. It shows that the term structure contains quite a bit of information for the very short run (over the next several months) and the long run (over several years) but is unreliable at predicting movements in interest rates over the intermediate term (the time in between).[6] Research also finds that the yield curve helps forecast future inflation and business cycles (see the FYI box).

Summary

The liquidity premium and preferred habitat theories are the most widely accepted theories of the term structure of interest rates because they explain the major empirical facts about the term structure so well. They combine the features of both the expectations theory and the segmented markets theory by asserting that a long-term interest rate will be the sum of a liquidity (term) premium and the average of the short-term interest rates that are expected to occur over the life of the bond.

The liquidity premium and preferred habitat theories explain the following facts: (1) Interest rates on bonds of different maturities tend to move together over time,

[6]Eugene Fama, "The Information in the Term Structure," *Journal of Financial Economics* 13 (1984): 509–528; Eugene Fama and Robert Bliss, "The Information in Long-Maturity Forward Rates," *American Economic Review* 77 (1987): 680–692; John Y. Campbell and Robert J. Shiller, "Cointegration and Tests of the Present Value Models," *Journal of Political Economy* 95 (1987): 1062–1088; John Y. Campbell and Robert J. Shiller, "Yield Spreads and Interest Rate Movements: A Bird's Eye View," *Review of Economic Studies* 58 (1991): 495–514.

(2) yield curves usually slope upward, and (3) when short-term interest rates are low, yield curves are more likely to have a steep upward slope, whereas when short-term interest rates are high, yield curves are more likely to be inverted.

The theories also help us predict the movement of short-term interest rates in the future. A steep upward slope of the yield curve means that short-term rates are expected to rise, a mild upward slope means that short-term rates are expected to remain the same, a flat slope means that short-term rates are expected to fall moderately, and an inverted yield curve means that short-term rates are expected to fall sharply.

APPLICATION Interpreting Yield Curves, 1980–2006

Figure 7 illustrates several yield curves that have appeared for U.S. government bonds in recent years. What do these yield curves tell us about the public's expectations of future movements of short-term interest rates?

STUDY GUIDE

Try to answer the preceding question before reading further in the text. If you have trouble answering it with the liquidity premium and preferred habitat theories, first try answering it with the expectations theory (which is simpler because you don't have to worry about the liquidity premium). When you understand what the expectations of future interest rates are in this case, modify your analysis by taking the liquidity premium into account.

The steep inverted yield curve that occurred on January 15, 1981, indicated that short-term interest rates were expected to decline sharply in the future. For longer-term interest rates with their positive liquidity premium to be well below the short-term interest rate, short-term interest rates must be expected to decline so sharply that their average is far below the current short-term rate. Indeed, the public's expectations of sharply lower short-term interest rates evident in the yield curve were realized soon after January 15; by March, three-month Treasury bill rates had declined from the 16% level to 13%.

The steep upward-sloping yield curve on March 28, 1985 indicated that short-term interest rates would climb in the future. The long-term interest rate is higher than the short-term interest rate when short-term interest rates are expected to rise because their average plus the liquidity premium will be higher than the current short-term rate. The moderately upward-sloping yield curves on May 16, 1980, and March 3, 1997, indicated that short-term interest rates were expected neither to rise nor to fall in the near future. In this case, their average remains the same as the current short-term rate, and the positive liquidity premium for longer-term bonds explains the moderate upward slope of the yield curve. The flat yield curve of February 6, 2006 indicated that short-term interest rates were expected to fall slightly.

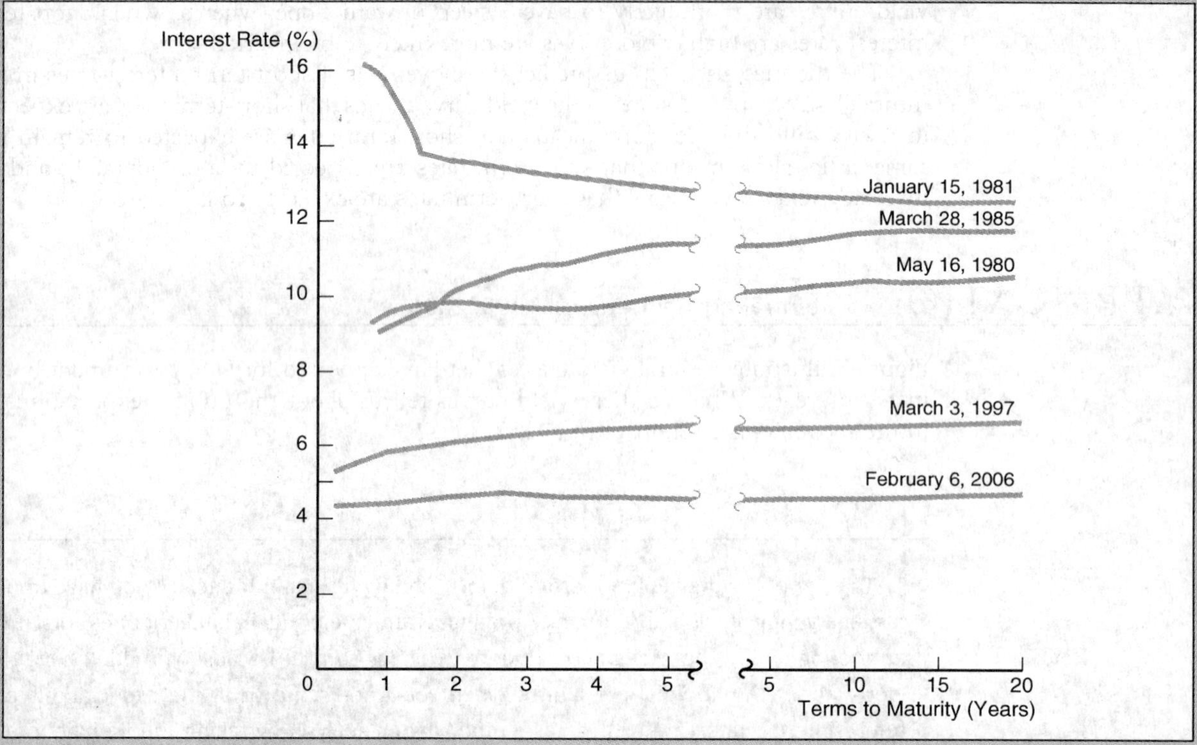

FIGURE 7 **Yield Curves for U.S. Government Bonds**

Sources: Federal Reserve Bank of St. Louis; *U.S. Financial Data*, various issues; *Wall Street Journal*, various dates.

SUMMARY

1. Bonds with the same maturity will have different interest rates because of three factors: default risk, liquidity, and tax considerations. The greater a bond's default risk, the higher its interest rate relative to other bonds; the greater a bond's liquidity, the lower its interest rate; and bonds with tax-exempt status will have lower interest rates than they otherwise would. The relationship among interest rates on bonds with the same maturity that arise because of these three factors is known as the *risk structure of interest rates*.

2. Four theories of the term structure provide explanations of how interest rates on bonds with different terms to maturity are related. The expectations theory views long-term interest rates as equaling the average of future short-term interest rates expected to occur over the life of the bond. By contrast, the segmented markets theory treats the determination of interest rates for each bond's maturity as the outcome of supply and demand in that market only. Neither of these theories by itself can explain the fact that interest rates on bonds of different maturities move together over time and that yield curves usually slope upward.

3. The liquidity premium and preferred habitat theories combine the features of the other two theories, and by so doing are able to explain the facts just mentioned. They view long-term interest rates as equaling the average of future short-term interest rates expected to occur over the life of the bond plus a liquidity premium. These theories allow us to infer the market's expectations about the movement of future short-term interest

rates from the yield curve. A steeply upward-sloping curve indicates that future short-term rates are expected to rise, a mildly upward-sloping curve indicates that short-term rates are expected to stay the same, a flat curve indicates that short-term rates are expected to decline slightly, and an inverted yield curve indicates that a substantial decline in short-term rates is expected in the future.

KEY TERMS

credit-rating agencies, p. 130
default, p. 127
default-free bonds, p. 128
expectations theory, p. 136
inverted yield curve, p. 130
junk bonds, p. 130
liquidity premium theory, p. 140
preferred habitat theory, p. 141
risk premium, p. 128
risk structure of interest rates, p. 127
segmented markets theory, p. 139
term structure of interest rates, p. 127
yield curve, p. 134

QUESTIONS AND PROBLEMS

Questions marked with an asterisk are answered at the end of the book in an appendix, "Answers to Selected Questions and Problems." Questions marked with a blue circle indicate the question is available in MyEconLab at www.myeconlab.com/mishkin.

1. Which should have the higher risk premium on its interest rates, a corporate bond with a Moody's Baa rating or a corporate bond with a C rating? Why?

*2. Why do U.S. Treasury bills have lower interest rates than large-denomination negotiable bank CDs?

3. Risk premiums on corporate bonds are usually *anti-cyclical*; that is, they decrease during business cycle expansions and increase during recessions. Why is this so?

*4. "If bonds of different maturities are close substitutes, their interest rates are more likely to move together." Is this statement true, false, or uncertain? Explain your answer.

5. If yield curves, on average, were flat, what would this say about the liquidity (term) premiums in the term structure? Would you be more or less willing to accept the expectations theory?

*6. Assuming that the expectations theory is the correct theory of the term structure, calculate the interest rates in the term structure for maturities of one to five years, and plot the resulting yield curves for the following series of one-year interest rates over the next five years:
   a. 5%, 7%, 7%, 7%, 7%
   b. 5%, 4%, 4%, 4%, 4%

   How would your yield curves change if people preferred shorter-term bonds over longer-term bonds?

7. Assuming that the expectations theory is the correct theory of the term structure, calculate the interest rates in the term structure for maturities of one to five years, and plot the resulting yield curves for the following paths of one-year interest rates over the next five years:
   a. 5%, 6%, 7%, 6%, 5%
   b. 5%, 4%, 3%, 4%, 5%

   How would your yield curves change if people preferred shorter-term bonds over longer-term bonds?

*8. If a yield curve looks like the one shown in figure (a) below, what is the market predicting about the movement of future short-term interest rates? What might the yield curve indicate about the market's predictions about the inflation rate in the future?

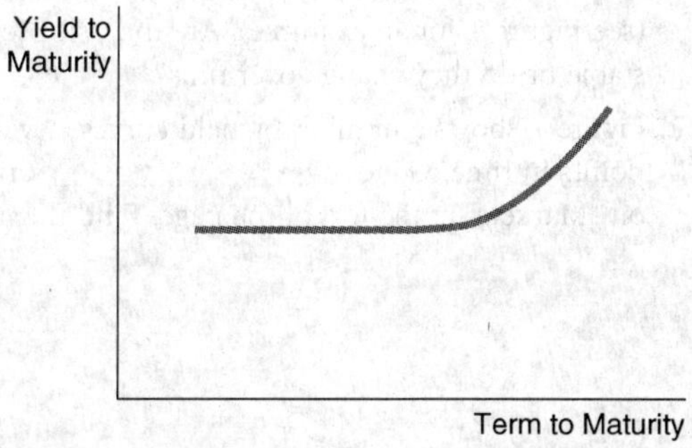

(a)

9. If a yield curve looks like the one shown in figure (b) below, what is the market predicting about the movement of future short-term interest rates? What might the yield curve indicate about the market's predictions about the inflation rate in the future?

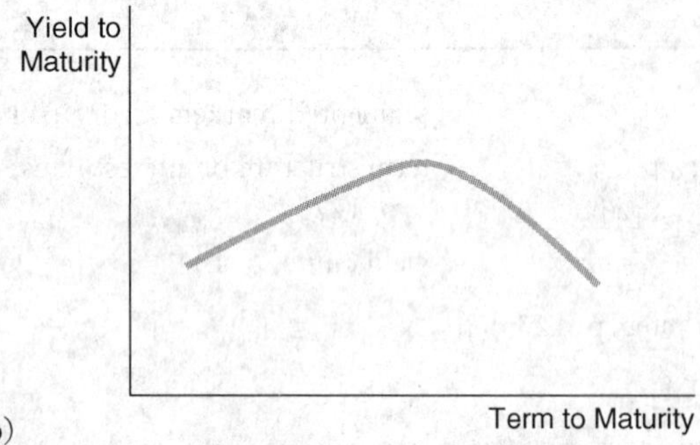

(b)

*10. What effect would reducing income tax rates have on the interest rates of municipal bonds? Would interest rates of Treasury securities be affected, and if so, how?

Using Economic Analysis to Predict the Future

11. Predict what will happen to interest rates on a corporation's bonds if the federal government guarantees today that it will pay creditors if the corporation goes bankrupt in the future. What will happen to the interest rates on Treasury securities?

*12. Predict what would happen to the risk premiums on corporate bonds if brokerage commissions were lowered in the corporate bond market.

13. If the income tax exemption on municipal bonds were abolished, what would happen to the interest rates on these bonds? What effect would the change have on interest rates on U.S. Treasury securities?

*14. If the yield curve suddenly becomes steeper, how would you revise your predictions of interest rates in the future?

15. If expectations of future short-term interest rates suddenly fall, what would happen to the slope of the yield curve?

WEB EXERCISES

1. The amount of additional interest investors receive due to the various risk premiums changes over time. Sometimes the risk premiums are much larger than at other times. For example, the default risk premium was very small in the late 1990s when the economy was so healthy that business failures were rare. This risk premium increases during recessions.

   Go to www.federalreserve.gov/releases/h15 (historical data) and find the interest rate listings for AAA- and Baa-rated bonds at three points in time: the most recent; June 1, 1995; and June 1, 1992. Prepare a graph that shows these three time periods (see Figure 1 for an example). Are the risk premiums stable or do they change over time?

2. Figure 7 shows a number of yield curves at various points in time. Go to www.bloomberg.com, and click on "Markets" at the top of the page. Find the Treasury yield curve. Does the current yield curve fall above or below the most recent one listed in Figure 7? Is the current yield curve flatter or steeper than the most recent one reported in Figure 7?

3. Investment companies attempt to explain to investors the nature of the risk the investor incurs when buying shares in their mutual funds. For example, Vanguard carefully explains interest-rate risk and offers alternative funds with different interest rate risks. Go to http://flagship5.vanguard.com/VGApp/hnw/FundsStocksOverview.

   a. Select the bond fund you would recommend to an investor who has a very low tolerance for risk and a short investment horizon. Justify your answer.

   b. Select the bond fund you would recommend to an investor who has a very high tolerance for risk and a long investment horizon. Justify your answer.

WEB REFERENCES

www.federalreserve.gov/Releases/h15/update/

The Federal Reserve reports the yields on different quality bonds. Look at the bottom of the listing of interest rates for AAA- and BBB-rated bonds.

http://stockcharts.com/charts/YieldCurve.html

This site lets you look at the dynamic yield curve at any point in time since 1995.

CHAPTER

7 The Stock Market, the Theory of Rational Expectations, and the Efficient Market Hypothesis

Preview

Rarely does a day go by that the stock market isn't a major news item. We have witnessed huge swings in the stock market in recent years. The 1990s were an extraordinary decade for stocks: The Dow Jones and S&P 500 indexes increased more than 400%, while the tech-laden NASDAQ index rose more than 1,000%. By early 2000, all three indexes had reached record highs. Unfortunately, the good times did not last, and many investors lost their shirts. Starting in early 2000, the stock market began to decline: The NASDAQ crashed, falling by more than 50%, while the Dow Jones and S&P 500 indexes fell by 30% through January 2003.

Because so many people invest in the stock market and the price of stocks affects the ability of people to retire comfortably, the market for stocks is undoubtedly the financial market that receives the most attention and scrutiny. In this chapter, we look first at how this important market works.

We begin by discussing the fundamental theories that underlie the valuation of stocks. These theories are critical to understanding the forces that cause the value of stocks to rise and fall minute by minute and day by day. Once we have learned the methods for stock valuation, we need to explore how expectations about the market affect its behavior. We do so by examining the *theory of rational expectations*. When this theory is applied to financial markets, the outcome is the *efficient market hypothesis*, which has some general implications for how markets in other securities besides stocks operate.

Theoretically, the theory of rational expectations should be a powerful tool for analyzing behavior. But to establish that it is *in reality* a useful tool, we must compare the outcomes predicted by the theory with empirical evidence. Although the evidence is mixed and controversial, it indicates that for many purposes, the theory of rational expectations is a good starting point for analyzing expectations.

COMPUTING THE PRICE OF COMMON STOCK

Common stock is the principal way that corporations raise equity capital. Holders of common stock own an interest in the corporation consistent with the percentage of outstanding shares owned. This ownership interest gives **stockholders**—those who hold stock in a corporation—a bundle of rights. The most important are the right to vote and to be the **residual claimant** of all funds flowing into the firm (known as **cash flows**), meaning that the stockholder receives whatever remains after all other claims against the firm's assets have been satisfied. Stockholders are paid dividends from the net earnings of the corporation. **Dividends** are payments made periodically, usually every quarter, to stockholders. The board of directors of the firm sets the level of the dividend, usually based on the recommendation of management. In addition, the stockholder has the right to sell the stock.

One basic principle of finance is that the value of any investment is found by computing the present value of all cash flows the investment will generate over its life. For example, a commercial building will sell for a price that reflects the net cash flows (rents—expenses) it is projected to have over its useful life. Similarly, we value common stock as the value in today's dollars of all future cash flows. The cash flows a stockholder might earn from stock are dividends, the sales price, or both.

To develop the theory of stock valuation, we begin with the simplest possible scenario: You buy the stock, hold it for one period to get a dividend, then sell the stock. We call this the *one-period valuation model*.

The One-Period Valuation Model

Suppose that you have some extra money to invest for one year. After a year, you will need to sell your investment to pay tuition. After watching *CNBC* or *Wall Street Week* on TV, you decide that you want to buy Intel Corp. stock. You call your broker and find that Intel is currently selling for $50 per share and pays $0.16 per year in dividends. The analyst on *Wall Street Week* predicts that the stock will be selling for $60 in one year. Should you buy this stock?

To answer this question, you need to determine whether the current price accurately reflects the analyst's forecast. To value the stock today, you need to find the present discounted value of the expected cash flows (future payments) using the formula in Equation 1 of Chapter 4. In this equation, the discount factor used to discount the cash flows is the required return on investments in equity rather than the interest rate. The cash flows consist of one dividend payment plus a final sales price. When these cash flows are discounted back to the present, the following equation computes the current price of the stock:

$$P_0 = \frac{Div_1}{(1 + k_e)} + \frac{P_1}{(1 + k_e)} \tag{1}$$

where P_0 = the current price of the stock. The zero subscript refers to time period zero, or the present.
Div_1 = the dividend paid at the end of year 1.
k_e = the required return on investments in equity.
P_1 = the price at the end of the first period; the assumed sales price of the stock.

To see how Equation 1 works, let's compute the price of the Intel stock if, after careful consideration, you decide that you would be satisfied to earn a 12% return on the investment. If you have decided that $k_e = 0.12$, are told that Intel pays $0.16 per year in dividends ($Div_1 = 0.16$), and forecast the share price of $60 for next year ($P_1 = \$60$), you get the following from Equation 1:

$$P_0 = \frac{0.16}{1 + 0.12} + \frac{\$60}{1 + 0.12} = \$0.14 + \$53.57 = \$53.71$$

Based on your analysis, you find that the present value of all cash flows from the stock is \$53.71. Because the stock is currently priced at \$50 per share, you would choose to buy it. However, you should be aware that the stock may be selling for less than \$53.71, because other investors place a different risk on the cash flows or estimate the cash flows to be less than you do.

The Generalized Dividend Valuation Model

Using the present value concept, the one-period dividend valuation model can be extended to any number of periods: The value of a stock today is the present value of all future cash flows. The only cash flows that an investor will receive are dividends and a final sales price when the stock is ultimately sold in period n. The generalized multi-period formula for stock valuation can be written as

$$P_0 = \frac{D_1}{(1+k_e)^1} + \frac{D_2}{(1+k_e)^2} + \cdots + \frac{D_n}{(1+k_e)^n} + \frac{P_n}{(1+k_e)^n} \qquad (2)$$

If you tried to use Equation 2 to find the value of a share of stock, you would soon realize that you must first estimate the value the stock will have at some point in the future before you can estimate its value today. In other words, you must find P_n before you can find P_0. However, if P_n is far in the future, it will not affect P_0. For example, the present value of a share of stock that sells for \$50 seventy-five years from now using a 12% discount rate is just one cent [$\$50/(1.12^{75}) = \$0.01$]. This reasoning implies that the current value of a share of stock can be calculated as simply the present value of the future dividend stream. The **generalized dividend model** is rewritten in Equation 3 without the final sales price:

$$P_0 = \sum_{t=1}^{\infty} \frac{D_t}{(1+k_e)^t} \qquad (3)$$

Consider the implications of Equation 3 for a moment. The generalized dividend model says that the price of stock is determined only by the present value of the dividends and that nothing else matters. Many stocks do not pay dividends, so how is it that these stocks have value? *Buyers of the stock expect that the firm will pay dividends someday*. Most of the time a firm institutes dividends as soon as it has completed the rapid growth phase of its life cycle.

The generalized dividend valuation model requires that we compute the present value of an infinite stream of dividends, a process that could be difficult, to say the least. Therefore, simplified models have been developed to make the calculations easier. One such model is the **Gordon growth model**, which assumes constant dividend growth.

The Gordon Growth Model

Many firms strive to increase their dividends at a constant rate each year. Equation 4 rewrites Equation 3 to reflect this constant growth in dividends:

$$P_0 = \frac{D_0 \times (1+g)^1}{(1+k_e)^1} + \frac{D_0 \times (1+g)^2}{(1+k_e)^2} + \cdots + \frac{D_0 \times (1+g)^\infty}{(1+k_e)^\infty} \qquad (4)$$

where

D_0 = the most recent dividend paid
g = the expected constant growth rate in dividends
k_e = the required return on an investment in equity

Equation 4 has been simplified to obtain Equation 5:[1]

$$P_0 = \frac{D_0 \times (1 + g)}{(k_e - g)} = \frac{D_1}{(k_e - g)} \tag{5}$$

This model is useful for finding the value of stock, given a few assumptions:

1. *Dividends are assumed to continue growing at a constant rate forever.* Actually, as long as they are expected to grow at a constant rate for an extended period of time, the model should yield reasonable results. This is because errors about distant cash flows become small when discounted to the present.
2. *The growth rate is assumed to be less than the required return on equity,* k_e. Myron Gordon, in his development of the model, demonstrated that this is a reasonable assumption. In theory, if the growth rate were faster than the rate demanded by holders of the firm's equity, in the long run the firm would grow impossibly large.

HOW THE MARKET SETS STOCK PRICES

Suppose you go to an auto auction. The cars are available for inspection before the auction begins, and you find a little Mazda Miata that you like. You test-drive it in the parking lot and notice that it makes a few strange noises, but you decide that you would still like the car. You decide \$5,000 would be a fair price that would allow you to pay some repair bills should the noises turn out to be serious. You see that the auction is ready to begin, so you go in and wait for the Miata to enter.

Suppose another buyer also spots the Miata. He test-drives the car and recognizes that the noises are simply the result of worn brake pads that he can fix himself at a nominal cost. He decides that the car is worth \$7,000. He also goes in and waits for the Miata to come up for auction.

Who will buy the car and for how much? Suppose only the two of you are interested in the Miata. You begin the bidding at \$4,000. Your competitor ups your bid to \$4,500. You bid your top price of \$5,000. He counters with \$5,100. The price is now higher than you are willing to pay, so you stop bidding. The car is sold to the more informed buyer for \$5,100.

---

[1] To generate Equation 5 from Equation 4, first multiply both sides of Equation 4 by $(1 + k_e)/(1 + g)$ and subtract Equation 4 from the result. This yields

$$\frac{P_0 \times (1 + k_e)}{(1 + g)} - P_0 = D_0 - \frac{D_0 \times (1 + g)^\infty}{(1 + k_e)^\infty}$$

Assuming that k_e is greater than g, the term on the far right will approach zero and can be dropped. Thus, after factoring P_0 out of the left-hand side,

$$P_0 \times \left[\frac{1 + k_e}{1 + g} - 1\right] = D_0$$

Next, simplify by combining terms:

$$P_0 \times \frac{(1 + k_e) - (1 + g)}{1 + g} = D_0$$

$$P_0 = \frac{D_0 \times (1 + g)}{k_e - g} = \frac{D_1}{k_e - g}$$

This simple example raises a number of points. First, the price is set by the buyer willing to pay the highest price. The price is not necessarily the highest price the asset could fetch, but it is incrementally greater than what any other buyer is willing to pay.

Second, the market price will be set by the buyer who can take best advantage of the asset. The buyer who purchased the car knew that he could fix the noise easily and cheaply. As a consequence, he was willing to pay more for the car than you were. The same concept holds for other assets. For example, a piece of property or a building will sell to the buyer who can put the asset to the most productive use.

Finally, the example shows the role played by information in asset pricing. Superior information about an asset can increase its value by reducing its risk. When you consider buying a stock, there are many unknowns about the future cash flows. The buyer who has the best information about these cash flows will discount them at a lower interest rate than will a buyer who is very uncertain.

Now let us apply these ideas to stock valuation. Suppose that you are considering the purchase of stock expected to pay a $2 dividend next year. Market analysts expect the firm to grow at 3% indefinitely. You are *uncertain* about both the constancy of the dividend stream and the accuracy of the estimated growth rate. To compensate yourself for this uncertainty (risk), you require a return of 15%.

Now suppose Jennifer, another investor, has spoken with industry insiders and feels more confident about the projected cash flows. Jennifer requires only a 12% return because her perceived risk is lower than yours. Bud, on the other hand, is dating the CEO of the company. He knows with more certainty what the future of the firm actually is, and thus requires only a 10% return.

What are the values each investor will give to the stock? Applying the Gordon growth model yields the following stock prices:

Investor	Discount Rate	Stock Price
You	15%	$16.67
Jennifer	12%	$22.22
Bud	10%	$28.57

You are willing to pay $16.67 for the stock. Jennifer would pay up to $22.22, and Bud would pay $28.57. The investor with the lowest perceived risk is willing to pay the most for the stock. If there were no other traders but these three, the market price would be between $22.22 and $28.57. If you already held the stock, you would sell it to Bud.

We thus see that the players in the market, bidding against one another, establish the market price. When new information is released about a firm, expectations change and with them, prices change. New information can cause changes in expectations about the level of future dividends or the risk of those dividends. Because market participants are constantly receiving new information and revising their expectations, it is reasonable that stock prices are constantly changing as well.

APPLICATION Monetary Policy and Stock Prices

Stock market analysts tend to hang on every word that the Chairman of the Federal Reserve utters because they know that an important determinant of stock prices is monetary policy. But how does monetary policy affect stock prices?

The Gordon growth model in Equation 5 explains this relationship. Monetary policy can affect stock prices in two ways. First, when the Fed lowers interest rates, the return on bonds (an alternative asset to stocks) declines, and investors are likely to accept a lower required rate of return on an investment in equity (k_e). The resulting decline in k_e would lower the denominator in the Gordon growth model (Equation 5), lead to a higher value of P_0, and raise stock prices. Furthermore, a lowering of interest rates is likely to stimulate the economy, so that the growth rate in dividends, g, is likely to be somewhat higher. This rise in g also causes the denominator in Equation 5 to decrease, which also leads to a higher P_0 and a rise in stock prices.

As we will see in Chapter 25, the impact of monetary policy on stock prices is one of the key ways in which monetary policy affects the economy.

APPLICATION The September 11 Terrorist Attacks, the Enron Scandal, and the Stock Market

In 2001, two big shocks hit the stock market: the September 11 terrorist attacks and the Enron scandal. Our analysis of stock price evaluation, again using the Gordon growth model, can help us understand how these events affected stock prices.

The September 11 terrorist attacks raised the possibility that terrorism against the United States would paralyze the country. These fears led to a downward revision of the growth prospects for U.S. companies, thus lowering the dividend growth rate (g) in the Gordon model. The resulting increase in the denominator in Equation 5 would lead to a decline in P_0 and hence a decline in stock prices.

Increased uncertainty for the U.S. economy would also raise the required return on investment in equity. A higher k_e also leads to an increase in the denominator in Equation 5, a decline in P_0, and a general fall in stock prices. As the Gordon model predicts, the stock market fell by more than 10% immediately after September 11.

Subsequently, the U.S. successes against the Taliban in Afghanistan and the absence of further terrorist attacks reduced market fears and uncertainty, causing g to recover and k_e to fall. The denominator in Equation 5 then decreased, leading to a recovery in P_0 and a rebound in the stock market in October and November. However, by the beginning of 2002, the Enron scandal and disclosures that many companies had overstated their earnings caused many investors to doubt the formerly rosy forecast of earnings and dividend growth for corporations. The resulting revision of g downward, and the rise in k_e because of increased uncertainty about the quality of accounting information, would lead to an increase in the denominator in the Gordon Equation 5, thereby lowering P_0 for many companies and hence the overall stock market. As predicted by our analysis, this is exactly what happened. The stock market recovery was aborted, and the market began a downward slide.

THE THEORY OF RATIONAL EXPECTATIONS

The analysis of stock price evaluation we outlined in the previous section depends on people's expectations—especially of cash flows. Indeed, it is difficult to think of any sector in the economy in which expectations are not crucial; this is why it is important to examine how expectations are formed. We do so by outlining the *theory of rational expectations*, currently the most widely used theory to describe the formation of business and consumer expectations.

In the 1950s and 1960s, economists regularly viewed expectations as formed from past experience only. Expectations of inflation, for example, were typically viewed as being an average of past inflation rates. This view of expectation formation, called **adaptive expectations**, suggests that changes in expectations will occur slowly over time as past data change.[2] So if inflation had formerly been steady at a 5% rate, expectations of future inflation would be 5%, too. If inflation rose to a steady rate of 10%, expectations of future inflation would rise toward 10%, but slowly: In the first year, expected inflation might rise only to 6%; in the second year, to 7%; and so on.

Adaptive expectations have been faulted on the grounds that people use more information than just past data on a single variable to form their expectations of that variable. Their expectations of inflation will almost surely be affected by their predictions of future monetary policy as well as by current and past monetary policy. In addition, people often change their expectations quickly in the light of new information. To meet these objections to adaptive expectations, John Muth developed an alternative theory of expectations, called **rational expectations**, which can be stated as follows: ***Expectations will be identical to optimal forecasts (the best guess of the future) using all available information.***[3]

What exactly does this mean? To explain it more clearly, let's use the theory of rational expectations to examine how expectations are formed in a situation that most of us encounter at some point in our lifetime: our drive to work. Suppose that when Joe Commuter travels when it is not rush hour, it takes an average of 30 minutes for his trip. Sometimes it takes him 35 minutes, other times 25 minutes, but the average non-rush-hour driving time is 30 minutes. If, however, Joe leaves for work during the rush hour, it takes him, on average, an additional 10 minutes to get to work. Given that he leaves for work during the rush hour, the best guess of the driving time—the **optimal forecast**—is 40 minutes.

If the only information available to Joe before he leaves for work that would have a potential effect on his driving time is that he is leaving during the rush hour, what does rational expectations theory allow you to predict about Joe's expectations of his driving time? Since the best guess of his driving time using all available information is 40 minutes, Joe's expectation should also be the same. Clearly, an expectation of 35 minutes would not be rational, because it is not equal to the optimal forecast, the best guess of the driving time.

Suppose that the next day, given the same conditions and the same expectations, it takes Joe 45 minutes to drive because he hits an abnormally large number of red lights, and the day after that he hits all the lights right and it takes him only 35 minutes. Do these variations mean that Joe's 40-minute expectation is irrational? No, an expectation of 40 minutes' driving time is still a rational expectation. In both cases, the forecast is

---

[2]More specifically, adaptive expectations—say, of inflation—are written as a weighted average of past inflation rates:

$$\pi_t^e = (1-\lambda)\sum_{j=0}^{\infty}\lambda^j\pi_{t-j}$$

where

π_t^e = adaptive expectation of inflation at time t

π_{t-j} = inflation at time $t-j$

λ = a constant between the values of 0 and 1

[3]John Muth, "Rational Expectations and the Theory of Price Movements," *Econometrica* 29 (1961): 315–335.

off by 5 minutes, so the expectation has not been perfectly accurate. However, the forecast does not have to be perfectly accurate to be rational—it need only be the *best possible* given the available information; that is, it has to be correct *on average*, and the 40-minute expectation meets this requirement. As there is bound to be some randomness in Joe's driving time regardless of driving conditions, an optimal forecast will never be completely accurate.

The example makes the following important point about rational expectations: ***Even though a rational expectation equals the optimal forecast using all available information, a prediction based on it may not always be perfectly accurate.***

What if an item of information relevant to predicting driving time is unavailable or ignored? Suppose that on Joe's usual route to work there is an accident that causes a two-hour traffic jam. If Joe has no way of ascertaining this information, his rush-hour expectation of 40 minutes' driving time is still rational, because the accident information is not available to him for incorporation into his optimal forecast. However, if there was a radio or TV traffic report about the accident that Joe did not bother to listen to or heard but ignored, his 40-minute expectation is no longer rational. In light of the availability of this information, Joe's optimal forecast should have been two hours and 40 minutes.

Accordingly, there are two reasons why an expectation may fail to be rational:

1. People might be aware of all available information but find it takes too much effort to make their expectation the best guess possible.
2. People might be unaware of some available relevant information, so their best guess of the future will not be accurate.

Nonetheless, it is important to recognize that if an additional factor is important but information about it is not available, an expectation that does not take account of it can still be rational.

Formal Statement of the Theory

We can state the theory of rational expectations somewhat more formally. If X stands for the variable that is being forecast (in our example, Joe Commuter's driving time), X^e for the expectation of this variable (Joe's expectation of his driving time), and X^{of} for the optimal forecast of X using all available information (the best guess possible of his driving time), the theory of rational expectations then simply says

$$X^e = X^{of} \tag{6}$$

That is, the expectation of X equals the optimal forecast using all available information.

Rationale Behind the Theory

Why do people try to make their expectations match their best possible guess of the future using all available information? The simplest explanation is that it is costly for people not to do so. Joe Commuter has a strong incentive to make his expectation of the time it takes him to drive to work as accurate as possible. If he underpredicts his driving time, he will often be late to work and risk being fired. If he overpredicts, he will, on average, get to work too early and will have given up sleep or leisure time unnecessarily. Accurate expectations are desirable, and there are strong incentives for people to try to make them equal to optimal forecasts by using all available information.

The same principle applies to businesses. Suppose that an appliance manufacturer—say, General Electric—knows that interest-rate movements are important to the sales of appliances. If GE makes poor forecasts of interest rates, it will earn less profit, because it might produce either too many appliances or too few. There are strong incentives for GE to acquire all available information to help it forecast interest rates and use the information to make the best possible guess of future interest-rate movements.

The incentives for equating expectations with optimal forecasts are especially strong in financial markets. In these markets, people with better forecasts of the future get rich. The application of the theory of rational expectations to financial markets (where it is called the **efficient market hypothesis** or the **theory of efficient capital markets**) is thus particularly useful.

Implications of the Theory

Rational expectations theory leads to two commonsense implications for the forming of expectations that are important in the analysis of both the stock market and the aggregate economy:

1. ***If there is a change in the way a variable moves, the way in which expectations of this variable are formed will change as well.*** This tenet of rational expectations theory can be most easily understood through a concrete example. Suppose that interest rates move in such a way that they tend to return to a "normal" level in the future. If today's interest rate is high relative to the normal level, an optimal forecast of the interest rate in the future is that it will decline to the normal level. Rational expectations theory would imply that when today's interest rate is high, the expectation is that it will fall in the future.

Suppose now that the way in which the interest rate moves changes so that when the interest rate is high, it stays high. In this case, when today's interest rate is high, the optimal forecast of the future interest rate, and hence the rational expectation, is that it will stay high. Expectations of the future interest rate will no longer indicate that the interest rate will fall. The change in the way the interest-rate variable moves has therefore led to a change in the way that expectations of future interest rates are formed. The rational expectations analysis here is generalizable to expectations of any variable. Hence, when there is a change in the way any variable moves, the way in which expectations of this variable are formed will change, too.

2. ***The forecast errors of expectations will, on average, be zero and cannot be predicted ahead of time.*** The forecast error of an expectation is $X - X^e$, the difference between the realization of a variable X and the expectation of the variable. That is, if Joe Commuter's driving time on a particular day is 45 minutes and his expectation of the driving time is 40 minutes, the forecast error is 5 minutes.

Suppose that in violation of the rational expectations tenet, Joe's forecast error is not, on average, equal to zero; instead, it equals 5 minutes. The forecast error is now predictable ahead of time because Joe will soon notice that he is, on average, 5 minutes late for work and can improve his forecast by increasing it by 5 minutes. Rational expectations theory implies that this is exactly what Joe will do because he will want his forecast to be the best guess possible. When Joe has revised his forecast upward by 5 minutes, on average, the forecast error will equal zero so that it cannot be predicted ahead of time. Rational expectations theory implies that forecast errors of expectations cannot be predicted.

THE EFFICIENT MARKET HYPOTHESIS: RATIONAL EXPECTATIONS IN FINANCIAL MARKETS

While the theory of rational expectations was being developed by monetary economists, financial economists were developing a parallel theory of expectations formation in financial markets. It led them to the same conclusion as that of the rational expectations theorists: Expectations in financial markets are equal to optimal forecasts using all available information.[4] Although financial economists gave their theory another name, calling it *the efficient market hypothesis,* in fact their theory is just an application of rational expectations to the pricing of stocks and also other securities.

The efficient market hypothesis is based on the assumption that prices of securities in financial markets fully reflect all available information. You may recall from Chapter 4 that the rate of return from holding a security equals the sum of the capital gain on the security (the change in the price), plus any cash payments, divided by the initial purchase price of the security:

$$R = \frac{P_{t+1} - P_t + C}{P_t} \tag{7}$$

where R = rate of return on the security held from time t to $t + 1$ (say, the end of 2007 to the end of 2008)
P_{t+1} = price of the security at time $t + 1$, the end of the holding period
P_t = price of the security at time t, the beginning of the holding period
C = cash payment (coupon or dividend payments) made in the period t to $t + 1$

Let's look at the expectation of this return at time t, the beginning of the holding period. Because the current price P_t and the cash payment C are known at the beginning, the only variable in the definition of the return that is uncertain is the price next period, P_{t+1}.[5] Denoting the expectation of the security's price at the end of the holding period as P^e_{t+1}, the expected return R^e is

$$R^e = \frac{P^e_{t+1} - P_t + C}{P_t}$$

The efficient market hypothesis views expectations of future prices as equal to optimal forecasts using all currently available information. In other words, the market's expectations of future securities prices are rational, so that

$$P^e_{t+1} = P^{of}_{t+1}$$

which in turn implies that the expected return on the security will equal the optimal forecast of the return:

$$R^e = R^{of} \tag{8}$$

Unfortunately, we cannot observe either R^e or P^e_{t+1}, so the rational expectations equations by themselves do not tell us much about how the financial market behaves. How-

---

[4]The development of the efficient market hypothesis was not wholly independent of the development of rational expectations theory, in that financial economists were aware of Muth's work.

[5]There are cases where C might not be known at the beginning of the period, but that does not make a substantial difference to the analysis. We would in that case assume that not only price expectations but also the expectations of C are optimal forecasts using all available information.

ever, if we can devise some way to measure the value of R^e, these equations will have important implications for how prices of securities change in financial markets.

The supply and demand analysis of the bond market developed in Chapter 5 shows us that the expected return on a security (the interest rate, in the case of the bond examined) will have a tendency to head toward the equilibrium return that equates the quantity demanded to the quantity supplied. Supply and demand analysis enables us to determine the expected return on a security with the following equilibrium condition: The expected return on a security R^e equals the equilibrium return R^*, which equates the quantity of the security demanded to the quantity supplied; that is,

$$R^e = R^* \tag{9}$$

The academic field of finance explores the factors (risk and liquidity, for example) that influence the equilibrium returns on securities. For our purposes, it is sufficient to know that we can determine the equilibrium return and thus determine the expected return with the equilibrium condition.

We can derive an equation to describe pricing behavior in an efficient market by using the equilibrium condition to replace R^e with R^* in the rational expectations equation (Equation 8). In this way, we obtain

$$R^{of} = R^* \tag{10}$$

This equation tells us that ***current prices in a financial market will be set so that the optimal forecast of a security's return using all available information equals the security's equilibrium return***. Financial economists state it more simply: In an efficient market, a security's price fully reflects all available information.

Rationale Behind the Hypothesis

Let's see what the efficient market condition means in practice and why it is a sensible characterization of pricing behavior. Suppose that the equilibrium return on a security—say, ExxonMobil common stock—is 10% at an annual rate, and its current price P_t is lower than the optimal forecast of tomorrow's price P^{of}_{t+1} so that the optimal forecast of the return at an annual rate is 50%, which is greater than the equilibrium return of 10%. We are now able to predict that, on average, ExxonMobil's return would be abnormally high. This situation is called an **unexploited profit opportunity** because, on average, people would be earning more than they should, given the characteristics of that security. Knowing that, on average, you can earn such an abnormally high rate of return on ExxonMobil because $R^{of} > R^*$, you would buy more, which would in turn drive up its current price P_t relative to the expected future price P^{of}_{t+1}, thereby lowering R^{of}. When the current price had risen sufficiently so that R^{of} equals R^* and the efficient market condition (Equation 10) is satisfied, the buying of ExxonMobil will stop, and the unexploited profit opportunity will have disappeared.

Similarly, a security for which the optimal forecast of the return is −5% and the equilibrium return is 10% ($R^{of} < R^*$) would be a poor investment, because, on average, it earns less than the equilibrium return. In such a case, you would sell the security and drive down its current price relative to the expected future price until R^{of} rose to the level of R^* and the efficient market condition is again satisfied. What we have shown can be summarized as follows:

$$R^{of} > R^* \rightarrow P_t\uparrow \rightarrow R^{of}\downarrow$$
$$R^{of} < R^* \rightarrow P_t\downarrow \rightarrow R^{of}\uparrow$$
$$\text{until}$$
$$R^{of} = R^*$$

Another way to state the efficient market condition is this: ***In an efficient market, all unexploited profit opportunities will be eliminated.***

An extremely important factor in this reasoning is that ***not everyone in a financial market must be well informed about a security or have rational expectations for its price to be driven to the point at which the efficient market condition holds***. Financial markets are structured so that many participants can play. As long as a few keep their eyes open for unexploited profit opportunities (often referred to as "smart money"), they will eliminate the profit opportunities that appear, because in so doing, they make a profit. The efficient market hypothesis makes sense, because it does not require everyone in a market to be cognizant of what is happening to every security.

Stronger Version of the Efficient Market Hypothesis

Many financial economists take the efficient market hypothesis one step further in their analysis of financial markets. Not only do they define efficient markets as those in which expectations are rational—that is, equal to optimal forecasts using all available information—but they also add the condition that an efficient market is one in which prices reflect the true fundamental (intrinsic) value of the securities. Thus, in an efficient market, all prices are always correct and reflect **market fundamentals** (items that have a direct impact on future income streams of the securities). This stronger view of market efficiency has several important implications in the academic field of finance. First, it implies that in an efficient capital market, one investment is as good as any other because the securities' prices are correct. Second, it implies that a security's price reflects all available information about the intrinsic value of the security. Third, it implies that security prices can be used by managers of both financial and nonfinancial firms to assess their cost of capital (cost of financing their investments) accurately and hence that security prices can be used to help them make the correct decisions about whether a specific investment is worth making. The stronger version of market efficiency is a basic tenet of much analysis in the finance field.

EVIDENCE ON THE EFFICIENT MARKET HYPOTHESIS

Early evidence on the efficient market hypothesis was quite favorable to it. In recent years, however, deeper analysis of the evidence suggests that the hypothesis may not always be entirely correct. Let's first look at the earlier evidence in favor of the hypothesis and then examine some of the more recent evidence that casts some doubt on it.

Evidence in Favor of Market Efficiency

Evidence in favor of market efficiency has examined the performance of investment analysts and mutual funds, whether stock prices reflect publicly available information, the random-walk behavior of stock prices, and the success of technical analysis.

Performance of Investment Analysts and Mutual Funds. We have seen that one implication of the efficient market hypothesis is that when purchasing a security, you cannot expect to earn an abnormally high return, a return greater than the equilibrium return. This implies that it is impossible to beat the market. Many studies shed light on whether investment advisers and mutual funds (some of which charge steep sales commissions to people who purchase them) beat the market. One common test that has been performed is to take buy and sell recommendations from a group of advisers or mutual funds and compare the performance of the resulting selection of stocks with the market as a whole. Sometimes the advisers' choices have even been compared to a group of stocks chosen by throwing darts at a copy of the financial page of the newspaper tacked to a dartboard. The *Wall Street Journal*, for example, has a regular feature called "Investment Dartboard" that compares how well stocks picked by investment advisers do relative to stocks picked by throwing darts. Do the advisers win? To their embarrassment, the dartboard beats them as often as they beat the dartboard. Furthermore, even when the comparison includes only advisers who have been successful in the past in predicting the stock market, the advisers still don't regularly beat the dartboard.

Consistent with the efficient market hypothesis, mutual funds also do not beat the market. Not only do mutual funds not outperform the market on average, but when they are separated into groups according to whether they had the highest or lowest profits in a chosen period, the mutual funds that did well in the first period do not beat the market in the second period.[6]

The conclusion from the study of investment advisers and mutual fund performance is this: ***Having performed well in the past does not indicate that an investment adviser or a mutual fund will perform well in the future.*** This is not pleasing news to investment advisers, but it is exactly what the efficient market hypothesis predicts. It says that some advisers will be lucky and some will be unlucky. Being lucky does not mean that a forecaster actually has the ability to beat the market.

Do Stock Prices Reflect Publicly Available Information? The efficient market hypothesis predicts that stock prices will reflect all publicly available information. Thus, if information is already publicly available, a positive announcement about a company will not, on average, raise the price of its stock because this information is already reflected in the stock price. Early empirical evidence also confirmed this conjecture from the efficient market hypothesis: Favorable earnings announcements or announcements of stock splits (a division of a share of stock into multiple shares, which is usually followed by higher earnings) do not, on average, cause stock prices to rise.[7]

Random-Walk Behavior of Stock Prices. The term **random walk** describes the movements of a variable whose future changes cannot be predicted (are random) because, given today's value, the variable is just as likely to fall as to rise. An important implication of the efficient market hypothesis is that stock prices should approximately follow a random walk; that is, ***future changes in stock prices should, for all practical***

---

[6]An early study that found that mutual funds do not outperform the market is Michael C. Jensen, "The Performance of Mutual Funds in the Period 1945–64," *Journal of Finance* 23 (1968): 389–416. Further studies on mutual fund performance are Mark Grimblatt and Sheridan Titman, "Mutual Fund Performance: An Analysis of Quarterly Portfolio Holdings," *Journal of Business* 62 (1989): 393–416; R. A. Ippolito, "Efficiency with Costly Information: A Study of Mutual Fund Performance, 1965–84," *Quarterly Journal of Economics* 104 (1989): 1–23; J. Lakonishok, A. Shleifer, and R. Vishny, "The Structure and Performance of the Money Management Industry," *Brookings Papers on Economic Activity, Microeconomics* (1992); and B. Malkiel, "Returns from Investing in Equity Mutual Funds, 1971–1991," *Journal of Finance* 50 (1995): 549–572.

[7]Ray Ball and Philip Brown, "An Empirical Evaluation of Accounting Income Numbers," *Journal of Accounting Research* 6 (1968):159–178, and Eugene F. Fama, Lawrence Fisher, Michael C. Jensen, and Richard Roll, "The Adjustment of Stock Prices to New Information," *International Economic Review* 10 (1969): 1–21.

purposes, be unpredictable. The random-walk implication of the efficient market hypothesis is the one most commonly mentioned in the press, because it is the most readily comprehensible to the public. In fact, when people mention the "random-walk theory of stock prices," they are in reality referring to the efficient market hypothesis.

The case for random-walk stock prices can be demonstrated. Suppose that people could predict that the price of Happy Feet Corporation (HFC) stock would rise 1% in the coming week. The predicted rate of capital gains and rate of return on HFC stock would then exceed 50% at an annual rate. Since this is very likely to be far higher than the equilibrium rate of return on HFC stock ($R^{of} > R^*$), the efficient market hypothesis indicates that people would immediately buy this stock and bid up its current price. The action would stop only when the predictable change in the price dropped to near zero so that $R^{of} = R^*$.

Similarly, if people could predict that the price of HFC stock would fall by 1%, the predicted rate of return would be negative ($R^{of} < R^*$), and people would immediately sell. The current price would fall until the predictable change in the price rose back to near zero, where the efficient market condition again holds. The efficient market hypothesis suggests that the predictable change in stock prices will be near zero, leading to the conclusion that stock prices will generally follow a random walk.[8]

Financial economists have used two types of tests to explore the hypothesis that stock prices follow a random walk. In the first, they examine stock market records to see if changes in stock prices are systematically related to past changes and hence could have been predicted on that basis. The second type of test examines the data to see if publicly available information other than past stock prices could have been used to predict changes. These tests are somewhat more stringent because additional information (money supply growth, government spending, interest rates, corporate profits) might be used to help forecast stock returns. Early results from both types of tests generally confirmed the efficient market view that stock prices are not predictable and follow a random walk.[9]

Technical Analysis. A popular technique used to predict stock prices, called *technical analysis*, is to study past stock price data and search for patterns such as trends and regular cycles. Rules for when to buy and sell stocks are then established on the basis of the patterns that emerge. The efficient market hypothesis suggests that technical analysis is a waste of time. The simplest way to understand why is to use the random-walk result derived from the efficient market hypothesis that holds that past stock

---

[8]Note that the random-walk behavior of stock prices is only an *approximation* derived from the efficient market hypothesis. It would hold exactly only for a stock for which an unchanged price leads to its having the equilibrium return. Then, when the predictable change in the stock price is exactly zero, $R^{of} = R^*$.

[9]The first type of test, using only stock market data, is referred to as a test of *weak-form efficiency*, because the information that can be used to predict stock prices is restricted to past price data. The second type of test is referred to as a test of *semistrong-form efficiency*, because the information set is expanded to include all publicly available information, not just past stock prices. A third type of test is called a test of *strong-form efficiency*, because the information set includes insider information, known only to the managers (directors) of the corporation, such as when they plan to declare a high dividend. Strong-form tests do sometimes indicate that insider information can be used to predict changes in stock prices. This finding does not contradict the efficient market hypothesis, because the information is not available to the market and hence cannot be reflected in market prices. In fact, there are strict laws against using insider information to trade in financial markets. For an early survey on the three forms of tests, see Eugene F. Fama, "Efficient Capital Markets: A Review of Theory and Empirical Work," *Journal of Finance* 25 (1970): 383–416.

price data cannot help predict changes. Therefore, technical analysis, which relies on such data to produce its forecasts, cannot successfully predict changes in stock prices.

Two types of tests bear directly on the value of technical analysis. The first performs the empirical analysis described earlier to evaluate the performance of any financial analyst, technical or otherwise. The results are exactly what the efficient market hypothesis predicts: Technical analysts fare no better than other financial analysts; on average, they do not outperform the market, and successful past forecasting does not imply that their forecasts will outperform the market in the future. The second type of test takes the rules developed in technical analysis for when to buy and sell stocks and applies them to new data.[10] The performance of these rules is then evaluated by the profits that would have been made using them. These tests also discredit technical analysis: It does not outperform the overall market.

APPLICATION Should Foreign Exchange Rates Follow a Random Walk?

Although the efficient market hypothesis is usually applied to the stock market, it can also be used to show that foreign exchange rates, like stock prices, should generally follow a random walk. To see why this is the case, consider what would happen if people could predict that a currency would appreciate by 1% in the coming week. By buying this currency, they could earn a greater than 50% return at an annual rate, which is likely to be far above the equilibrium return for holding a currency. As a result, people would immediately buy the currency and bid up its current price, thereby reducing the expected return. The process would stop only when the predictable change in the exchange rate dropped to near zero so that the optimal forecast of the return no longer differed from the equilibrium return. Likewise, if people could predict that the currency would depreciate by 1% in the coming week, they would sell it until the predictable change in the exchange rate was again near zero. The efficient market hypothesis therefore implies that future changes in exchange rates should, for all practical purposes, be unpredictable; in other words, exchange rates should follow random walks. This is exactly what empirical evidence finds.[11]

Evidence Against Market Efficiency

All the early evidence supporting the efficient market hypothesis appeared to be overwhelming, causing Eugene Fama, a prominent financial economist, to state in his famous 1970 survey of the empirical evidence on the efficient market hypothesis, "The

[10]Sidney Alexander, "Price Movements in Speculative Markets: Trends or Random Walks?" *Industrial Management Review,* May 1961, pp. 7–26; and Sidney Alexander, "Price Movements in Speculative Markets: Trends or Random Walks? No. 2," in *The Random Character of Stock Prices,* ed. Paul Cootner (Cambridge, Mass.: MIT Press, 1964), pp. 338–372. More recent evidence also seems to discredit technichal analysis—for example, F. Allen and R. Karjalainen, "Using Genetic Algorithms to Find Technical Trading Rules," *Journal of Financial Economics* 51 (1999): 245–271. However, some other research is more favorable to technical analysis—for example, R. Sullivan, A. Timmerman, and H. White, "Data-Snooping, Technical Trading Rule Performance and the Bootstrap," Centre for Economic Policy Research Discussion Paper No. 1976, 1998.

[11]See Richard A. Meese and Kenneth Rogoff, "Empirical Exchange Rate Models of the Seventies: Do They Fit Out of Sample?" *Journal of International Economics* 14 (1983): 3–24.

evidence in support of the efficient markets model is extensive, and (somewhat uniquely in economics) contradictory evidence is sparse."[12] However, in more recent years, the hypothesis has begun to show a few cracks, referred to as *anomalies*, and empirical evidence indicates that the efficient market hypothesis may not always be generally applicable.

Small-Firm Effect. One of the earliest reported anomalies in which the stock market did not appear to be efficient is called the *small-firm effect*. Many empirical studies have shown that small firms have earned abnormally high returns over long periods of time, even when the greater risk for these firms has been taken into account.[13] The small-firm effect seems to have diminished in recent years, but is still a challenge to the efficient market hypothesis. Various theories have been developed to explain the small-firm effect, suggesting that it may be due to rebalancing of portfolios by institutional investors, tax issues, low liquidity of small-firm stocks, large information costs in evaluating small firms, or an inappropriate measurement of risk for small-firm stocks.

January Effect. Over long periods of time, stock prices have tended to experience an abnormal price rise from December to January that is predictable and hence inconsistent with random-walk behavior. This so-called **January effect** seems to have diminished in recent years for shares of large companies but still occurs for shares of small companies.[14] Some financial economists argue that the January effect is due to tax issues. Investors have an incentive to sell stocks before the end of the year in December, because they can then take capital losses on their tax return and reduce their tax liability. Then when the new year starts in January, they can repurchase the stocks, driving up their prices and producing abnormally high returns. Although this explanation seems sensible, it does not explain why institutional investors such as private pension funds, which are not subject to income taxes, do not take advantage of the abnormal returns in January and buy stocks in December, thus bidding up their price and eliminating the abnormal returns.[15]

Market Overreaction. Research suggests that stock prices may overreact to news announcements and that the pricing errors are corrected only slowly.[16] When corporations announce a major change in earnings—say, a large decline—the stock price may overshoot, and after an initial large decline, it may rise back to more normal levels over

---

[12]Eugene F. Fama, "Efficient Capital Markets: A Review of Theory and Empirical Work," *Journal of Finance* 25 (1970): 383–416.

[13]For example, see Marc R. Reinganum, "The Anomalous Stock Market Behavior of Small Firms in January: Empirical Tests of Tax Loss Selling Effects," *Journal of Financial Economics* 12 (1983): 89–104; Jay R. Ritter, "The Buying and Selling Behavior of Individual Investors at the Turn of the Year," *Journal of Finance* 43 (1988): 701–717; and Richard Roll, "Vas Ist Das? The Turn-of-the-Year Effect: Anomaly or Risk Mismeasurement?" *Journal of Portfolio Management* 9 (1988): 18–28.

[14]For example, see Donald B. Keim, "The CAPM and Equity Return Regularities," *Financial Analysts Journal* 42 (May–June 1986): 19–34.

[15]Another anomaly that makes the stock market seem less than efficient is that the *Value Line Survey*, one of the most prominent investment advice newsletters, has produced stock recommendations that have yielded abnormally high returns on average. See Fischer Black, "Yes, Virginia, There Is Hope: Tests of the Value Line Ranking System," *Financial Analysts Journal* 29 (September–October 1973): 10–14; and Gur Huberman and Shmuel Kandel, "Market Efficiency and Value Line's Record," *Journal of Business* 63 (1990): 187–216. Whether the excellent performance of the *Value Line Survey* will continue in the future is, of course, a question mark.

[16]Werner De Bondt and Richard Thaler, "Further Evidence on Investor Overreaction and Stock Market Seasonality," *Journal of Finance* 62 (1987): 557–580.

a period of several weeks. This violates the efficient market hypothesis, because an investor could earn abnormally high returns, on average, by buying a stock immediately after a poor earnings announcement and then selling it after a couple of weeks when it has risen back to normal levels.

Excessive Volatility. A phenomenon closely related to market overreaction is that the stock market appears to display *excessive volatility*; that is, fluctuations in stock prices may be much greater than are warranted by fluctuations in their fundamental value. In an important paper, Robert Shiller of Yale University found that fluctuations in the S&P 500 stock index could not be justified by the subsequent fluctuations in the dividends of the stocks making up this index. There has been much subsequent technical work criticizing these results, but Shiller's work, along with research finding that there are smaller fluctuations in stock prices when stock markets are closed, has produced a consensus that stock market prices appear to be driven by factors other than fundamentals.[17]

Mean Reversion. Some researchers have also found that stock returns display **mean reversion**: Stocks with low returns today tend to have high returns in the future, and vice versa. Hence stocks that have done poorly in the past are more likely to do well in the future, because mean reversion indicates that there will be a predictable positive change in the future price, suggesting that stock prices are not a random walk. Other researchers have found that mean reversion is not nearly as strong in data after World War II and so have raised doubts about whether it is currently an important phenomenon. The evidence on mean reversion remains controversial.[18]

New Information Is Not Always Immediately Incorporated into Stock Prices. Although it is generally found that stock prices adjust rapidly to new information, as is suggested by the efficient market hypothesis, evidence suggests that, inconsistent with the efficient market hypothesis, stock prices do not instantaneously adjust to profit announcements. Instead, on average, stock prices continue to rise for some time after the announcement of unexpectedly high profits, and they continue to fall after surprisingly low profit announcements.[19]

---

[17]Robert Shiller, "Do Stock Prices Move Too Much to Be Justified by Subsequent Changes in Dividends?" *American Economic Review* 71 (1981): 421–436; and Kenneth R. French and Richard Roll, "Stock Return Variances: The Arrival of Information and the Reaction of Traders," *Journal of Financial Economics* 17 (1986): 5–26.

[18]Evidence for mean reversion has been reported by James M. Poterba and Lawrence H. Summers, "Mean Reversion in Stock Prices: Evidence and Implications," *Journal of Financial Economics* 22 (1988): 27–59; Eugene F. Fama and Kenneth R. French, "Permanent and Temporary Components of Stock Prices," *Journal of Political Economy* 96 (1988): 246–273; and Andrew W. Lo and A. Craig MacKinlay, "Stock Market Prices Do Not Follow Random Walks: Evidence from a Simple Specification Test," *Review of Financial Studies* 1 (1988): 41–66. However, Myung Jig Kim, Charles R. Nelson, and Richard Startz, in "Mean Reversion in Stock Prices? A Reappraisal of the Evidence," *Review of Economic Studies* 58 (1991): 515–528, question whether some of these findings are valid. For an excellent summary of this evidence, see Charles Engel and Charles S. Morris, "Challenges to Stock Market Efficiency: Evidence from Mean Reversion Studies," *Federal Reserve Bank of Kansas City Economic Review*, September–October 1991, pp. 21–35. See also N. Jegadeesh and Sheridan Titman, "Returns to Buying Winners and Selling Losers: Implications for Stock Market Efficiency," *Journal of Finance* 48 (1993): 65–92, which shows that mean reversion also occurs for individual stocks.

[19]For example, see R. Ball and P. Brown, "An Empirical Evaluation of Accounting Income Numbers," *Journal of Accounting Research* 6 (1968): 159–178; L. Chan, N. Jegadeesh, and J. Lakonishok, "Momentum Strategies," *Journal of Finance* 51 (1996): 1681–1713; and Eugene Fama, "Market Efficiency, Long-Term Returns and Behavioral Finance," *Journal of Financial Economics* 49 (1998): 283–306.

Overview of the Evidence on the Efficient Market Hypothesis

As you can see, the debate on the efficient market hypothesis is far from over. The evidence seems to suggest that the efficient market hypothesis may be a reasonable starting point for evaluating behavior in financial markets. However, there do seem to be important violations of market efficiency that suggest that the efficient market hypothesis may not be the whole story and so may not be generalizable to all behavior in financial markets.

APPLICATION Practical Guide to Investing in the Stock Market

The efficient market hypothesis has numerous applications to the real world. It is especially valuable because it can be applied directly to an issue that concerns many of us: how to get rich (or at least not get poor) in the stock market. (The Following the Financial News box shows how stock prices are reported daily.) A practical guide to investing in the stock market, which we develop here, provides a better understanding of the use and implications of the efficient market hypothesis.

How Valuable Are Published Reports by Investment Advisers?

Suppose you have just read in the "Heard on the Street" column of the *Wall Street Journal* that investment advisers are predicting a boom in oil stocks because an oil shortage is developing. Should you proceed to withdraw all your hard-earned savings from the bank and invest it in oil stocks?

The efficient market hypothesis tells us that when purchasing a security, we cannot expect to earn an abnormally high return, a return greater than the equilibrium return. Information in newspapers and in the published reports of investment advisers is readily available to many market participants and is already reflected in market prices. So acting on this information will not yield abnormally high returns, on average. As we have seen, the empirical evidence for the most part confirms that recommendations from investment advisers cannot help us outperform the general market. Indeed, as the FYI box suggests, human investment advisers in San Francisco do not, on average, even outperform an orangutan!

Probably no other conclusion is met with more skepticism by students than this one when they first hear it. We all know or have heard of someone who has been successful in the stock market for a period of many years. We wonder, "How could someone be so consistently successful if he or she did not really know how to predict when returns would be abnormally high?" The following story, reported in the press, illustrates why such anecdotal evidence is not reliable.

A get-rich-quick artist invented a clever scam. Every week, he wrote two letters. In letter A, he would pick team A to win a particular football game; in letter B, he would pick the opponent, team B. A mailing list would then be separated into two groups, and he would send letter A to the people in one group and letter B to the people in the other. The following week he would do the same thing but would send these letters only to the group who had received the first letter with the correct prediction. After doing this for ten games, he had a small cluster of people who had received letters predicting the correct winning team for every game. He then mailed a final letter to them, declaring that since he was obviously an expert predictor of the outcome of football games (he had picked winners ten weeks in a row) and since his predictions were profitable for

Following the Financial News **Stock Prices**

Stock prices are published daily, and in the *Wall Street Journal*, they are reported in the sections "NYSE—Composite Transactions," "Amex—Composite Transactions," and "NASDAQ National Market Issues." Stock prices are quoted in the following format:

52-week Hi	52-week LO	STOCK (DIV)	YLD %	PE	VOL 100s	CLOSE	NET CHG
41.30	30.25	IntAlum 1.20	3.1	13	40	38.60	0.02
94.97	71.85	IBM .80	1.0	16	75288	80.72	−0.19
13.10	8.72	IntCoalGp n	...	...	11700	9.85	−0.12
42.69	31.19	IntFlavor .74	2.2	17	8350	33.56	0.26

Source: *Wall Street Journal*, February 6, 2006, p. C6.

The following information is included in each column. International Business Machines (IBM) common stock is used as an example.

52 Week Hi: Highest price of a share in the past 52 weeks: 94.97 for IBM stock

52 Week Lo: Lowest price of a share in the past 52 weeks: 71.85 for IBM stock

Stock (Div): Company name: IBM for International Business Machines and the Annual Dividend ($0.80)

Yld %: Yield for stock expressed as annual dividends divided by today's closing price: 1.0% (= 0.8 ÷ 80.72) for IBM stock

PE: Price-earnings ratio; the stock price divided by the annual earnings per share: 16

Vol 100s: Number of shares (in hundreds) traded that day: 7,528,800 shares for IBM

Close: Closing price (last price) that day: 80.72

Net Chg: Change in the closing price from the previous day: −0.19

Prices quoted for shares traded over-the-counter (through dealers rather than on an organized exchange) are sometimes quoted with the same information, but in many cases only the bid price (the price the dealer is willing to pay for the stock) and the asked price (the price the dealer is willing to sell the stock for) are quoted.

the recipients who bet on the games, he would continue to send his predictions only if he were paid a substantial amount of money. When one of his clients figured out what he was up to, the con man was prosecuted and thrown in jail!

What is the lesson of the story? Even if no forecaster is an accurate predictor of the market, there will always be a group of consistent winners. A person who has done well regularly in the past cannot guarantee that he or she will do well in the future. Note that there will also be a group of persistent losers, but you rarely hear about them because no one brags about a poor forecasting record.

Should You Be Skeptical of Hot Tips?

Suppose your broker phones you with a hot tip to buy stock in the Happy Feet Corporation (HFC) because it has just developed a product that is completely effective in curing athlete's foot. The stock price is sure to go up. Should you follow this advice and buy HFC stock?

FYI Should You Hire an Ape as Your Investment Adviser?

The *San Francisco Chronicle* came up with an amusing way of evaluating how successful investment advisers are at picking stocks. They asked eight analysts to pick five stocks at the beginning of the year and then compared the performance of their stock picks to those chosen by Jolyn, an orangutan living at Marine World/Africa USA in Vallejo, California. Consistent with the results found in the "Investment Dartboard" feature of the *Wall Street Journal*, Jolyn beat the investment advisers as often as they beat her. Given this result, you might be just as well off hiring an orangutan as your investment adviser as you would hiring a human being!

The efficient market hypothesis indicates that you should be skeptical of such news. If the stock market is efficient, it has already priced HFC stock so that its expected return will equal the equilibrium return. The hot tip is not particularly valuable and will not enable you to earn an abnormally high return.

You might wonder, though, if the hot tip is based on new information and would give you an edge on the rest of the market. If other market participants have gotten this information before you, the answer is no. As soon as the information hits the street, the unexploited profit opportunity it creates will be quickly eliminated. The stock's price will already reflect the information, and you should expect to realize only the equilibrium return. But if you are one of the first to gain the new information, it can do you some good. Only then can you be one of the lucky ones who, on average, will earn an abnormally high return by helping eliminate the profit opportunity by buying HFC stock.

Do Stock Prices Always Rise When There Is Good News?

If you follow the stock market, you might have noticed a puzzling phenomenon: When good news about a stock, such as a particularly favorable earnings report, is announced, the price of the stock frequently does not rise. The efficient market hypothesis and the random-walk behavior of stock prices explain this phenomenon.

Because changes in stock prices are unpredictable, when information is announced that has already been expected by the market, the stock price will remain unchanged. The announcement does not contain any new information that should lead to a change in stock prices. If this were not the case and the announcement led to a change in stock prices, it would mean that the change was predictable. Because that is ruled out in an efficient market, ***stock prices will respond to announcements only when the information being announced is new and unexpected***. If the news is expected, there will be no stock price response. This is exactly what the evidence we described earlier, which shows that stock prices reflect publicly available information, suggests will occur.

Sometimes an individual stock price declines when good news is announced. Although this seems somewhat peculiar, it is completely consistent with the workings of an efficient market. Suppose that although the announced news is good, it is not as good as expected. HFC's earnings may have risen 15%, but if the market expected earnings to rise by 20%, the new information is actually unfavorable, and the stock price declines.

Efficient Market Prescription for the Investor

What does the efficient market hypothesis recommend for investing in the stock market? It tells us that hot tips, investment advisers' published recommendations, and technical analysis—all of which make use of publicly available information—cannot help an investor outperform the market. Indeed, it indicates that anyone without better information than other market participants cannot expect to beat the market. So what is an investor to do?

The efficient market hypothesis leads to the conclusion that such an investor (and almost all of us fit into this category) should not try to outguess the market by constantly buying and selling securities. This process does nothing but boost the income of brokers, who earn commissions on each trade.[20] Instead, the investor should pursue a "buy and hold" strategy—purchase stocks and hold them for long periods of time. This will lead to the same returns, on average, but the investor's net profits will be higher, because fewer brokerage commissions will have to be paid.

It is frequently a sensible strategy for a small investor, whose costs of managing a portfolio may be high relative to its size, to buy into a mutual fund rather than to buy individual stocks. Because the efficient market hypothesis indicates that no mutual fund can consistently outperform the market, an investor should not buy into one that has high management fees or that pays sales commissions to brokers, but rather should purchase a no-load (commission-free) mutual fund that has low management fees.

As we have seen, the evidence indicates that it will not be easy to beat the prescription suggested here, although some of the anomalies to the efficient market hypothesis suggest that an extremely clever investor (which rules out most of us) may be able to outperform a buy-and-hold strategy.

EVIDENCE ON RATIONAL EXPECTATIONS IN OTHER MARKETS

Evidence in other financial markets also supports the efficient market hypothesis and hence the rationality of expectations. For example, there is little evidence that financial analysts are able to outperform the bond market.[21] The returns on bonds appear to conform to the efficient market condition of Equation 10.

Rationality of expectations is, however, much harder to test in markets other than financial markets, because price data that reflect expectations are not as readily available. The most common tests of rational expectations in these markets make use of survey data on the forecasts of market participants. For example, one well-known study by James Pesando used a survey of inflation expectations collected from prominent economists and inflation forecasters.[22] In that survey, these people were asked what they

---

[20]The investor may also have to pay Uncle Sam capital gains taxes on any profits that are realized when a security is sold—an additional reason why continual buying and selling does not make sense.

[21]See the discussion in Frederic S. Mishkin, "Efficient Markets Theory: Implications for Monetary Policy," *Brookings Papers on Economic Activity* 3 (1978): 707–768, of the results in Michael J. Prell, "How Well Do the Experts Forecast Interest Rates?" *Federal Reserve Bank of Kansas City Monthly Review*, September–October 1973, pp. 3–15.

[22]James Pesando, "A Note on the Rationality of the Livingston Price Expectations," *Journal of Political Economy* 83 (1975): 845–858.

predicted the inflation rate would be over the next six months and over the next year. Because rational expectations theory implies that forecast errors should, on average, be zero and cannot be predicted tests of the theory involve asking whether the forecast errors in a survey could be predicted ahead of time using publicly available information. The evidence from Pesando's and subsequent studies is mixed. Sometimes the forecast errors cannot be predicted; at other times they can. The evidence is not as supportive of rational expectations theory as the evidence from financial markets.

Does the fact that forecast errors from surveys are often predictable suggest that we should reject rational expectations theory in these other markets? Not necessarily. One problem with this evidence is that the expectations data are obtained from surveys rather than from actual economic decisions of market participants. That is a serious criticism of this evidence. Survey responses are not always reliable, because there is little incentive for participants to tell the truth. For example, when people are asked in surveys how much television they watch, responses greatly underestimate the actual time spent. Neither are people very truthful about which shows they watch. They may say they watch ballet on public television, but we know they are actually watching *Desperate Housewives* instead, because it, not ballet, gets high Nielsen ratings. How many people will admit to being regular watchers of *Desperate Housewives*?

A second problem with survey evidence is that a market's behavior may not be equally influenced by the expectations of all the survey participants, making survey evidence a poor guide to market behavior. For example, we have already seen that prices in financial markets often *behave* as if expectations are rational even though many of the market participants do not have rational expectations.[23]

Proof is not yet conclusive on the validity of rational expectations theory in markets other than financial markets. One important conclusion, however, that is supported by the survey evidence is that ***if there is a change in the way a variable moves, there will be a change in the way expectations of this variable are formed as well***.

APPLICATION What Do the Black Monday Crash of 1987 and the Tech Crash of 2000 Tell Us About Rational Expectations and Efficient Markets?

On October 19, 1987, dubbed "Black Monday," the Dow Jones Industrial Average declined more than 20%, the largest one-day decline in U.S. history. The collapse of the high-tech companies' share prices from their peaks in March 2000 caused the heavily tech-laden NASDAQ index to fall from around 5,000 in March 2000 to around 1,500 in 2001 and 2002, a decline of well over 60%. These two crashes have caused many economists to question the validity of the efficient market and rational expectations. They do not believe that a rational marketplace could have produced such a massive swing in share prices. To what degree should these stock market crashes make us doubt the validity of rational expectations and the efficient market hypothesis?

Nothing in rational expectations theory rules out large changes in stock prices. A large change in stock prices can result from new information that produces a dramatic decline in optimal forecasts of the future valuation of firms. However, economists are hard pressed to come up with fundamental changes in the economy that can explain the

[23]There is some fairly strong evidence for this proposition. For example, Frederic S. Mishkin, "Are Market Forecasts Rational?" *American Economic Review* 71 (1981): 295–306, finds that although survey forecasts of short-term interest rates are not rational, the bond market *behaves* as if the expectations of these interest rates are rational.

Black Monday and tech crashes. One lesson from these crashes is that factors other than market fundamentals probably have an effect on stock prices. Hence these crashes have convinced many economists that the stronger version of the efficient market hypothesis, which states that asset prices reflect the true fundamental (intrinsic) value of securities, is incorrect. They attribute a large role in determination of stock prices to market psychology and to the institutional structure of the marketplace. However, nothing in this view contradicts the basic reasoning behind rational expectations or the efficient market hypothesis—that market participants eliminate unexploited profit opportunities. Even though stock market prices may not always solely reflect market fundamentals, this does not mean that rational expectations do not hold. As long as stock market crashes are unpredictable, the basic lessons of the theory of rational expectations hold.

Some economists have come up with theories of what they call *rational bubbles* to explain stock market crashes. A **bubble** is a situation in which the price of an asset differs from its fundamental market value. In a rational bubble, investors can have rational expectations that a bubble is occurring because the asset price is higher than its fundamental value but continue to hold the asset anyway. They might do so because they believe that someone else will buy the asset for a higher price in the future. In a rational bubble, asset prices can therefore deviate from their fundamental value for a long time because the bursting of the bubble cannot be predicted and so there are no unexploited profit opportunities.

However, other economists believe that the Black Monday crash of 1987 and the tech crash of 2000 suggest that there may be unexploited profit opportunities and that the theory of rational expectations and the efficient market hypothesis might be fundamentally flawed. The controversy over whether capital markets are efficient or expectations are rational continues.

BEHAVIORAL FINANCE

Doubts about the efficient market hypothesis, particularly after the stock market crash of 1987, have led to the emergence of a new field of study, **behavioral finance**. It applies concepts from other social sciences such as anthropology, sociology, and, particularly, psychology to understand the behavior of securities prices.[24]

As we have seen, the efficient market hypothesis assumes that unexploited profit opportunities are eliminated by "smart money" market participants. But can smart money dominate ordinary investors so that financial markets are efficient? Specifically, the efficient market hypothesis suggests that smart money participants will sell when a stock price goes up irrationally, with the result that the stock price falls back down to a level that is justified by fundamentals. For this to occur, smart money investors must be able to engage in **short sales**; that is, they must borrow stock from brokers and then sell it in the market, with the aim that they earn a profit by buying the stock back again ("covering the short") after it has fallen in price. Work by psychologists, however, suggests

[24]Surveys of this field can be found in Hersh Shefrin, *Beyond Greed and Fear: Understanding of Behavioral Finance and the Psychology of Investing* (Boston: Harvard Business School Press, 2000); Andrei Shleifer, *Inefficient Markets* (Oxford, U.K.: Oxford University Press, 2000); and Robert J. Shiller, "From Efficient Market Theory to Behavioral Finance," Cowles Foundation Discussion Paper No. 1385 (October 2002).

that people are subject to loss aversion: They are more unhappy when they suffer losses than they are happy when they achieve gains. Short sales can result in losses far in excess of an investor's initial investment if the stock price climbs sharply higher than the price at which the short sale is made (and losses have the possibility of being unlimited if the stock price climbs to astronomical heights).

Loss aversion can thus explain an important phenomenon: Very little short selling actually takes place. Short selling may also be constrained by rules restricting it because it seems unsavory for someone to make money from another person's misfortune. The existence of so little short selling can explain why stock prices are sometimes overvalued. That is, the lack of enough short selling means that smart money does not drive stock prices back down to their fundamental value.

Psychologists have also found that people tend to be overconfident in their own judgments. As a result, investors tend to believe that they are smarter than other investors. Because investors are willing to assume that the market typically doesn't get it right, they trade on their beliefs, rather than on pure facts. This theory may explain why securities markets have such a large trading volume—something that the efficient market hypothesis does not predict.

Overconfidence and social contagion (fads) provide an explanation for stock market bubbles. When stock prices go up, investors attribute their profits to their intelligence and talk up the stock market. This word-of-mouth enthusiasm and glowing media reports then can produce an environment in which even more investors think stock prices will rise in the future. The result is a positive feedback loop in which prices continue to rise, producing a speculative bubble, which finally crashes when prices get too far out of line with fundamentals.[25]

The field of behavioral finance is a young one, but it holds out hope that we might be able to explain some features of securities markets' behavior that are not well explained by the efficient market hypothesis.

---

[25]See Robert J. Shiller, *Irrational Exuberance* (New York: Broadway Books, 2001).

SUMMARY

1. Stocks are valued as the present value of future dividends. Unfortunately, we do not know very precisely what these dividends will be. This uncertainty introduces a great deal of error into the valuation process. The Gordon growth model is a simplified method of computing stock value that depends on the assumption that the dividends are growing at a constant rate forever. Given our uncertainty regarding future dividends, this assumption is often the best we can do.
2. The interaction among traders in the market is what actually sets prices on a day-to-day basis. The trader who values the security the most (either because of less uncertainty about the cash flows or because of greater estimated cash flows) will be willing to pay the most. As new information is released, investors will revise their estimates of the true value of the security and will either buy or sell it depending on how the market price compares to their estimated valuation. Because small changes in estimated growth rates or required return result in large changes in price, it is not surprising that the markets are often volatile.
3. The efficient market hypothesis states that current security prices will fully reflect all available information, because in an efficient market, all unexploited profit opportunities are eliminated. The elimination of unexploited profit opportunities necessary for a financial market to be efficient does not require that all market participants be well informed.

4. The evidence on the efficient market hypothesis is mixed. Early evidence on the performance of investment analysts and mutual funds, whether stock prices reflect publicly available information, the random-walk behavior of stock prices, and the lack of success of technical analysis was quite favorable to the efficient market hypothesis. However, in recent years, evidence on the small-firm effect, the January effect, market overreaction, excessive volatility, mean reversion, and evidence that new information is not always incorporated into stock prices, suggest that the hypothesis may not always be entirely correct. The evidence seems to suggest that the efficient market hypothesis may be a reasonable starting point for evaluating behavior in financial markets but may not be generalizable to all behavior in financial markets.

5. The efficient market hypothesis indicates that hot tips, investment advisers' published recommendations, and technical analysis cannot help an investor outperform the market. The prescription for investors is to pursue a buy-and-hold strategy—purchase stocks and hold them for long periods of time. Empirical evidence generally supports these implications of the efficient market hypothesis in the stock market.

6. The stock market crash of 1987 and the tech crash of 2000 have convinced many financial economists that the stronger version of the efficient market hypothesis, which states that asset prices reflect the true fundamental (intrinsic) value of securities, is not correct. It is less clear that these crashes show that the weaker version of the efficient market hypothesis is wrong. Even if the stock market was driven by factors other than fundamentals, these crashes do not clearly demonstrate that many of the basic lessons of the efficient market hypothesis are no longer valid, as long as these crashes could not have been predicted.

7. The new field of behavioral finance applies concepts from other social sciences such as anthropology, sociology, and psychology to understand the behavior of securities prices. Loss aversion, overconfidence, and social contagion can explain why trading volume is so high, stock prices become overvalued, and speculative bubbles occur.

KEY TERMS

adaptive expectations, p. 157
behavioral finance, p. 173
bubble, p. 173
cash flows, p. 151
dividends, p. 152
efficient market hypothesis, p. 159
generalized dividend model, p. 153
Gordon growth model, p. 153
January effect, p. 166
market fundamentals, p. 162
mean reversion, p. 167
optimal forecast, p. 157
random walk, p. 163
rational expectations, p. 157
residual claimant, p. 151
short sales, p. 173
stockholders, p. 151
theory of efficient capital markets, p. 159
unexploited profit opportunity, p. 161

QUESTIONS AND PROBLEMS

Questions marked with an asterisk are answered at the end of the book in an appendix, "Answers to Selected Questions and Problems." Questions marked with a blue circle indicate the question is available in MyEconLab at www.myeconlab.com/mishkin.

1 What basic principle of finance can be applied to the valuation of any investment asset?

*2 Identify the cash flows available to an investor in stock. How reliably can these cash flows be estimated? Compare the problem of estimating stock cash flows to estimating bond cash flows. Which security would you predict to be more volatile?

3 Compute the price of a share of stock that pays a $1 per year dividend and that you expect to be able to

sell in one year for $20, assuming you require a 15% return.

*4. After careful analysis, you have determined that a firm's dividends should grow at 7% on average in the foreseeable future. The firm's last dividend was $3. Compute the current price of this stock, assuming the required return is 18%.

5. Some economists think that the central banks should try to prick bubbles in the stock market before they get out of hand and cause later damage when they burst. How can monetary policy be used to prick a bubble? Explain how it can do this using the Gordon growth model.

*6. "Forecasters' predictions of inflation are notoriously inaccurate, so their expectations of inflation cannot be rational." Is this statement true, false, or uncertain? Explain your answer.

7. "Whenever it is snowing when Joe Commuter gets up in the morning, he misjudges how long it will take him to drive to work. Otherwise, his expectations of the driving time are perfectly accurate. Considering that it snows only once every ten years where Joe lives, Joe's expectations are almost always perfectly accurate." Are Joe's expectations rational? Why or why not?

*8. If a forecaster spends hours every day studying data to forecast interest rates but his expectations are not as accurate as predicting that tomorrow's interest rates will be identical to today's interest rate, are his expectations rational?

9. "If stock prices did not follow a random walk, there would be unexploited profit opportunities in the market." Is this statement true, false, or uncertain? Explain your answer.

*10. Suppose that increases in the money supply lead to a rise in stock prices. Does this mean that when you see that the money supply has had a sharp increase in the past week, you should go out and buy stocks? Why or why not?

11. If the public expects a corporation to lose $5 per share this quarter and it actually loses $4, which is still the largest loss in the history of the company, what does the efficient market hypothesis say will happen to the price of the stock when the $4 loss is announced?

*12. If you read in the *Wall Street Journal* that the "smart money" on Wall Street expects stock prices to fall, should you follow that lead and sell all your stocks?

13. If your broker has been right in her five previous buy and sell recommendations, should you continue listening to her advice?

*14. Can a person with rational expectations expect the price of a share of Google to rise by 10% in the next month?

15. "If most participants in the stock market do not follow what is happening to the monetary aggregates, prices of common stocks will not fully reflect information about them." Is this statement true, false, or uncertain? Explain your answer.

*16. "An efficient market is one in which no one ever profits from having better information than the rest." Is this statement true, false, or uncertain? Explain your answer.

17. If higher money growth is associated with higher future inflation, and if announced money growth turns out to be extremely high but is still less than the market expected, what do you think would happen to long-term bond prices?

*18. "Foreign exchange rates, like stock prices, should follow a random walk." Is this statement true, false, or uncertain? Explain your answer.

19. Can we expect the value of the dollar to rise by 2% next week if our expectations are rational?

*20. "Human fear is the source of stock market crashes, so these crashes indicate that expectations in the stock market cannot be rational." Is this statement true, false, or uncertain? Explain your answer.

WEB EXERCISES

1. Visit www.forecasts.org/data/index.htm. Click on "Stock Index" at the very top of the page. Now choose "U.S. Stock Indices—monthly." Review the indexes for the DJIA, the S&P 500, and the NASDAQ composite. Which index appears most volatile? In which index would you have rather invested in 1985 if the investment had been allowed to compound until now?

2. The Internet is a great source of information on stock prices and stock price movements. Yahoo Finance is a great source for stock market data. Go to http://finance.yahoo.com and click on the DOW ticker in the Market Summary section to view current data on the Dow Jones Industrial Average. Click on the chart to manipulate the different variables. Change the time range and observe the stock trend over various intervals. Have stock prices been going up or down over the last day, week, 3 months, and year?

WEB REFERENCES

http://stocks.tradingcharts.com
Access detailed stock quotes, charts, and historical stock data.

www.investorhome.com/emh.htm
Learn more about the efficient market hypothesis.

PART

3

Financial Institutions

CHAPTER

8 An Economic Analysis of Financial Structure

Preview

A healthy and vibrant economy requires a financial system that moves funds from people who save to people who have productive investment opportunities. But how does the financial system make sure that your hard-earned savings get channeled to Paula the Productive Investor rather than to Benny the Bum?

This chapter answers that question by providing an economic analysis of how our financial structure is designed to promote economic efficiency. The analysis focuses on a few simple but powerful economic concepts that enable us to explain features of our financial system, such as why financial contracts are written as they are and why financial intermediaries are more important than securities markets for getting funds to borrowers. The analysis also demonstrates the important link between the financial system and the performance of the aggregate economy, which is the subject of Part V of the book. The economic analysis of financial structure explains how the performance of the financial sector affects economic growth and why financial crises occur and have such severe consequences for aggregate economic activity.

BASIC FACTS ABOUT FINANCIAL STRUCTURE THROUGHOUT THE WORLD

The financial system is complex in structure and function throughout the world. It includes many different types of institutions: banks, insurance companies, mutual funds, stock and bond markets, and so on—all of which are regulated by government. The financial system channels trillions of dollars per year from savers to people with productive investment opportunities. If we take a close look at financial structure all over the world, we find eight basic facts, some of which are quite surprising, that we need to explain to understand how the financial system works.

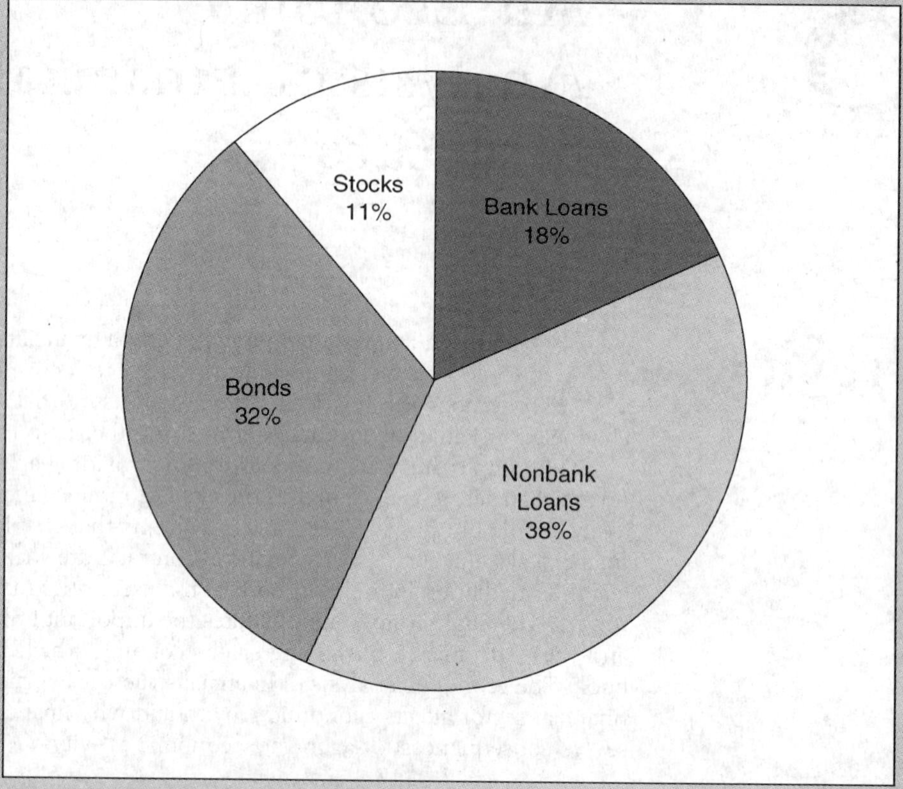

FIGURE 1 **Sources of External Funds for Nonfinancial Businesses in the United States**

Source: Andreas Hackethal and Reinhard H. Schmidt, "Financing Patterns: Measurement Concepts and Empirical Results," Johann Wolfgang Goethe-Universitat Working Paper No. 125, January 2004. The data are from 1970-2000 and are gross flows as percentage of the total, not including trade and other credit data, which are not available.

The pie chart in Figure 1 shows how American businesses financed their activities using external funds (those obtained from outside the business itself) in the period 1970–2000. The *Bank Loans* category is made up primarily of loans from depository institutions; *Nonbank Loans* is composed primarily of loans by other financial intermediaries; the *Bonds* category includes marketable debt securities such as corporate bonds and commercial paper; and *Stock* consists of new issues of new equity (stock market shares). Figure 2 uses the same classifications as Figure 1 and compares the U.S. data to those of Canada, Germany, and Japan.

Now let us explore the eight facts.

1. ***Stocks are not the most important source of external financing for businesses.*** Because so much attention in the media is focused on the stock market, many people have the impression that stocks are the most important sources of financing for American corporations. However, as we can see from the bar chart in Figure 2, the stock market accounted for only a small fraction of the external financing of American businesses in the 1970–2000 period: 11%.[1] Similarly small figures apply in the other countries presented in Figure 1 as well. Why is the stock market less important than other sources of financing in the United States and other countries?

2. ***Issuing marketable debt and equity securities is not the primary way in which businesses finance their operations.*** Figure 2 shows that bonds are a far more important source of financing than stocks in the United States (32% versus 11%). However, stocks and bonds combined (43%), which make up the total share of marketable securities, still supply less than one-half of the external funds corporations need to finance their activities. The fact that issuing marketable securities is not the most important source of financing is true elsewhere in the world as well. Indeed, as we see in Figure 2, other countries have a much smaller share of external financing supplied by marketable securities than the United States. Why don't businesses use marketable securities more extensively to finance their activities?

3. ***Indirect finance, which involves the activities of financial intermediaries, is many times more important than direct finance, in which businesses raise funds directly from lenders in financial markets.*** Direct finance involves the sale to households of marketable securities such as stocks and bonds. The 43% share of stocks and bonds as a source of external financing for American businesses actually greatly overstates the importance of direct finance in our financial system. Since 1970, less than 5% of newly issued corporate bonds and commercial paper and less than one-third of stocks have been sold directly to American households. The rest of these securities have been bought primarily by financial intermediaries such as insurance companies, pension funds, and mutual funds. These figures indicate that direct finance is used in less than 10% of the external funding of American business. Because in most countries marketable securities are an even less important source of finance than in the United States, direct finance is also far less important than indirect finance in the rest of the world. Why are financial intermediaries and indirect finance so important in financial markets? In recent years, indirect finance has been declining in importance. Why is this happening?

---

[1]The 11% figure for the percentage of external financing provided by stocks is based on the flows of external funds to corporations. However, this flow figure is somewhat misleading, because when a share of stock is issued, it raises funds permanently; whereas when a bond is issued, it raises funds only temporarily until they are paid back at maturity. To see this, suppose that a firm raises $1,000 by selling a share of stock and another $1,000 by selling a $1,000 one-year bond. In the case of the stock issue, the firm can hold on to the $1,000 it raised this way, but to hold on to the $1,000 it raised through debt, it has to issue a new $1,000 bond every year. If we look at the flow of funds to corporations over a 30-year period, as in Figure 1, the firm will have raised $1,000 with a stock issue only once in the 30-year period, while it will have raised $1,000 with debt 30 times, once in each of the 30 years. Thus it will look as though debt is 30 times more important than stocks in raising funds, even though our example indicates that they are actually equally important for the firm.

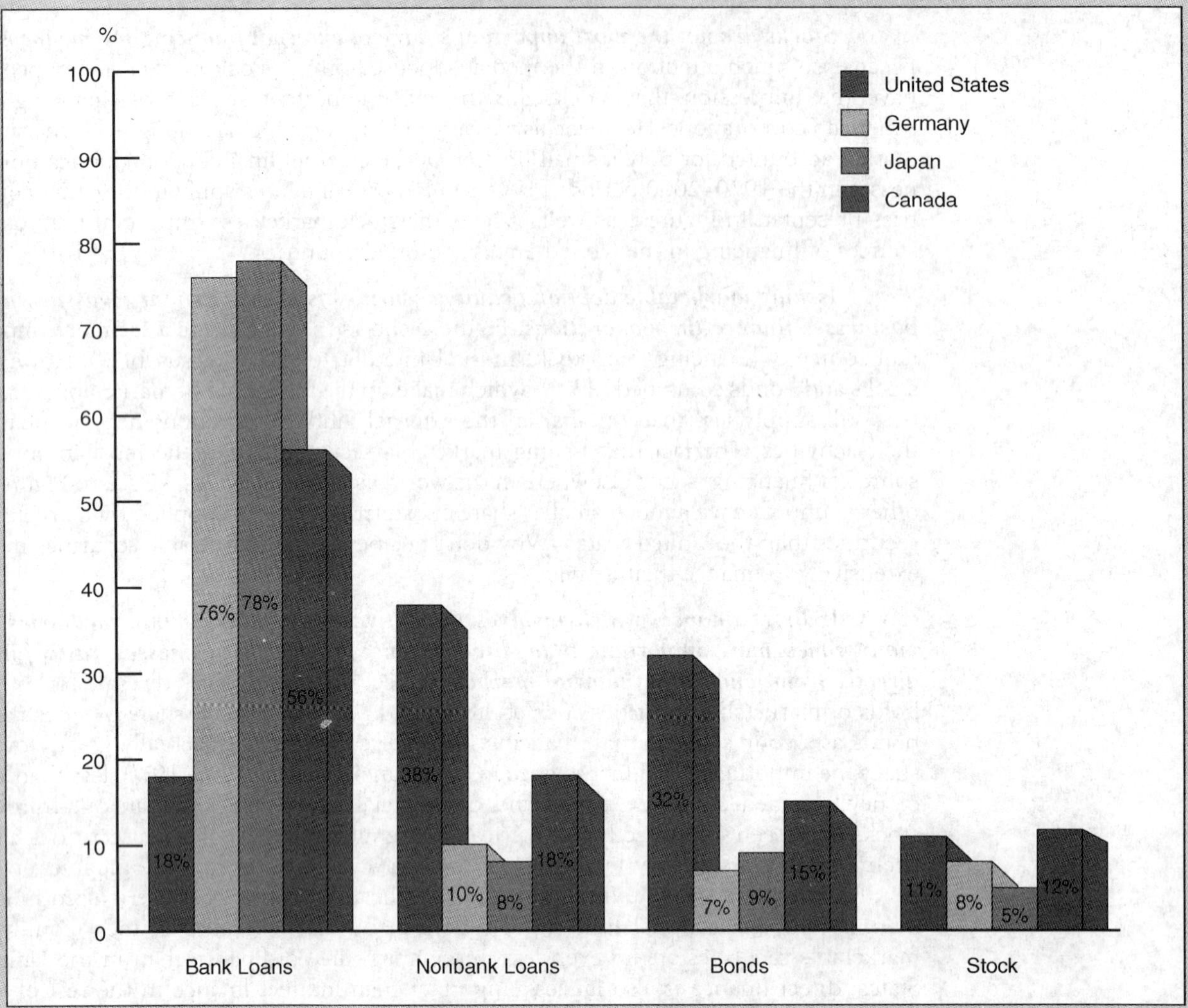

FIGURE 2 **Sources of External Funds for Nonfinancial Businesses: A Comparison of the United States with Germany, Japan, and Canada**

Source: Andreas Hackethal and Reinhard H. Schmidt, "Financing Patterns: Measurement Concepts and Empirical Results," Johann Wolfgang Goethe-Universitat Working Paper No. 125, January 2004. The data are from 1970–2000 and are gross flows as percentage of the total, not including trade and other credit data, which are not available.

4. ***Financial intermediaries, particularly banks, are the most important source of external funds used to finance businesses.*** As we can see in Figure 2, the primary source of external funds for businesses throughout the world comprises loans made by banks and other nonbank financial intermediaries (56% in the United States, but more than 70% in Germany, Japan, and Canada). In other industrialized countries, bank

loans are the largest category of sources of external finance (more than 70% in Germany and Japan and more than 50% in Canada). Thus the data suggest that banks in these countries have the most important role in financing business activities. In developing countries, banks play an even more important role in the financial system than they do in the industrialized countries. What makes banks so important to the workings of the financial system? Although banks remain important, their share of external funds for businesses has been declining in recent years. What is driving this decline?

5. ***The financial system is among the most heavily regulated sectors of the economy.*** The financial system is heavily regulated in the United States and all other developed countries. Governments regulate financial markets primarily to promote the provision of information, and to ensure the soundness (stability) of the financial system. Why are financial markets so extensively regulated throughout the world?

6. ***Only large, well-established corporations have easy access to securities markets to finance their activities.*** Individuals and smaller businesses that are not well established are less likely to raise funds by issuing marketable securities. Instead, they most often obtain their financing from banks. Why do only large, well-known corporations find it easier to raise funds in securities markets?

7. ***Collateral is a prevalent feature of debt contracts for both households and businesses.*** **Collateral** is property that is pledged to a lender to guarantee payment in the event that the borrower is unable to make debt payments. Collateralized debt (also known as **secured debt** to contrast it with **unsecured debt**, such as credit card debt, which is not collateralized) is the predominant form of household debt and is widely used in business borrowing as well. The majority of household debt in the United States consists of collateralized loans: Your automobile is collateral for your auto loan, and your house is collateral for your mortgage. Commercial and farm mortgages, for which property is pledged as collateral, make up one-quarter of borrowing by nonfinancial businesses; corporate bonds and other bank loans also often involve pledges of collateral. Why is collateral such an important feature of debt contracts?

8. ***Debt contracts typically are extremely complicated legal documents that place substantial restrictions on the behavior of the borrower.*** Many students think of a debt contract as a simple IOU that can be written on a single piece of paper. The reality of debt contracts is far different, however. In all countries, bond or loan contracts typically are long legal documents with provisions (called **restrictive covenants**) that restrict and specify certain activities that the borrower can engage in. Restrictive covenants are not just a feature of debt contracts for businesses; for example, personal automobile loan and home mortgage contracts have covenants that require the borrower to maintain sufficient insurance on the automobile or house purchased with the loan. Why are debt contracts so complex and restrictive?

As you may recall from Chapter 2, an important feature of financial markets is that they have substantial transaction and information costs. An economic analysis of how these costs affect financial markets provides us with explanations of the eight facts, which in turn provide us with a much deeper understanding of how our financial system works. In the next section, we examine the impact of transaction costs on the structure of our financial system. Then we turn to the effect of information costs on financial structure.

TRANSACTION COSTS

Transaction costs are a major problem in financial markets. An example will make this clear.

How Transaction Costs Influence Financial Structure

Say you have $5,000 you would like to invest, and you think about investing in the stock market. Because you have only $5,000, you can buy only a small number of shares. Even if you use online trading, your purchase is so small that the brokerage commission for buying the stock you picked will be a large percentage of the purchase price of the shares. If instead you decide to buy a bond, the problem is even worse, because the smallest denomination for some bonds you might want to buy is as much as $10,000, and you do not have that much to invest. You are disappointed and realize that you will not be able to use financial markets to earn a return on your hard-earned savings. You can take some consolation, however, in the fact that you are not alone in being stymied by high transaction costs. This is a fact of life for many of us: Only around one-half of American households own any securities.

You also face another problem because of transaction costs. Because you have only a small amount of funds available, you can make only a restricted number of investments because a large number of small transactions would result in very high transaction costs. That is, you have to put all your eggs in one basket, and your inability to diversify will subject you to a lot of risk.

How Financial Intermediaries Reduce Transaction Costs

This example of the problems posed by transaction costs and the example outlined in Chapter 2 when legal costs kept you from making a loan to Carl the Carpenter illustrate that small savers like you are frozen out of financial markets and are unable to benefit from them. Fortunately, financial intermediaries, an important part of the financial structure, have evolved to reduce transaction costs and allow small savers and borrowers to benefit from the existence of financial markets.

Economies of Scale. One solution to the problem of high transaction costs is to bundle the funds of many investors together so that they can take advantage of *economies of scale*, the reduction in transaction costs per dollar of investment as the size (scale) of transactions increases. Bundling investors' funds together reduces transaction costs for each individual investor. Economies of scale exist because the total cost of carrying out a transaction in financial markets increases only a little as the size of the transaction grows. For example, the cost of arranging a purchase of 10,000 shares of stock is not much greater than the cost of arranging a purchase of 50 shares of stock.

The presence of economies of scale in financial markets helps explain why financial intermediaries developed and have become such an important part of our financial structure. The clearest example of a financial intermediary that arose because of economies of scale is a mutual fund. A *mutual fund* is a financial intermediary that sells shares to individuals and then invests the proceeds in bonds or stocks. Because it buys large blocks of stocks or bonds, a mutual fund can take advantage of lower transaction costs. These cost savings are then passed on to individual investors after the mutual fund has taken its cut in the form of management fees for administering their accounts. An additional benefit for individual investors is that a mutual fund is large enough to purchase a widely diversified portfolio of securities. The increased diversification for individual investors reduces their risk, making them better off.

Economies of scale are also important in lowering the costs of things such as computer technology that financial institutions need to accomplish their tasks. Once a large mutual fund has invested a lot of money in setting up a telecommunications system, for example, the system can be used for a huge number of transactions at a low cost per transaction.

Expertise. Financial intermediaries are also better able to develop expertise to lower transaction costs. Their expertise in computer technology enables them to offer customers convenient services like being able to call a toll-free number for information on how well their investments are doing and to write checks on their accounts.

An important outcome of a financial intermediary's low transaction costs is the ability to provide its customers with *liquidity services*, services that make it easier for customers to conduct transactions. Money market mutual funds, for example, not only pay shareholders high interest rates, but also allow them to write checks for convenient bill-paying.

ASYMMETRIC INFORMATION: ADVERSE SELECTION AND MORAL HAZARD

The presence of transaction costs in financial markets explains in part why financial intermediaries and indirect finance play such an important role in financial markets (fact 3). To understand financial structure more fully, however, we turn to the role of information in financial markets.[2]

Asymmetric information—a situation that arises when one party's insufficient knowledge about the other party involved in a transaction makes it impossible to make accurate decisions when conducting the transaction—is an important aspect of financial markets. For example, managers of a corporation know whether they are honest or have better information about how well their business is doing than the stockholders do. The presence of asymmetric information leads to adverse selection and moral hazard problems, which were introduced in Chapter 2.

[2]An excellent survey of the literature on information and financial structure that expands on the topics discussed in the rest of this chapter is contained in Mark Gertler, "Financial Structure and Aggregate Economic Activity: An Overview," *Journal of Money, Credit and Banking* 20 (1988): 559–588.

Adverse selection is an asymmetric information problem that occurs *before* the transaction: Potential bad credit risks are the ones who most actively seek out loans. Thus the parties who are the most likely to produce an undesirable outcome are the ones most likely to want to engage in the transaction. For example, big risk takers or outright crooks might be the most eager to take out a loan because they know that they are unlikely to pay it back. Because adverse selection increases the chances that a loan might be made to a bad credit risk, lenders might decide not to make any loans, even though there are good credit risks in the marketplace.

Moral hazard arises *after* the transaction occurs: The lender runs the risk that the borrower will engage in activities that are undesirable from the lender's point of view because they make it less likely that the loan will be paid back. For example, once borrowers have obtained a loan, they may take on big risks (which have possible high returns but also run a greater risk of default) because they are playing with someone else's money. Because moral hazard lowers the probability that the loan will be repaid, lenders may decide that they would rather not make a loan.

The analysis of how asymmetric information problems affect economic behavior is called **agency theory**. We will apply this theory here to explain why financial structure takes the form it does, thereby explaining the facts outlined at the beginning of the chapter.

THE LEMONS PROBLEM: HOW ADVERSE SELECTION INFLUENCES FINANCIAL STRUCTURE

A particular aspect of the way the adverse selection problem interferes with the efficient functioning of a market was outlined in a famous article by Nobel prize winner George Akerlof. It is called the "lemons problem," because it resembles the problem created by lemons in the used-car market.[3] Potential buyers of used cars are frequently unable to assess the quality of the car; that is, they can't tell whether a particular used car is a car that will run well or a lemon that will continually give them grief. The price that a buyer pays must therefore reflect the *average* quality of the cars in the market, somewhere between the low value of a lemon and the high value of a good car.

The owner of a used car, by contrast, is more likely to know whether the car is a peach or a lemon. If the car is a lemon, the owner is more than happy to sell it at the price the buyer is willing to pay, which, being somewhere between the value of a lemon and a good car, is greater than the lemon's value. However, if the car is a peach, the owner knows that the car is undervalued at the price the buyer is willing to pay, and so the owner may not want to sell it. As a result of this adverse selection, few good used

[3]George Akerlof, "The Market for 'Lemons': Quality, Uncertainty and the Market Mechanism," *Quarterly Journal of Economics* 84 (1970): 488–500. Two important papers that have applied the lemons problem analysis to financial markets are Stewart Myers and N. S. Majluf, "Corporate Financing and Investment Decisions When Firms Have Information That Investors Do Not Have," *Journal of Financial Economics* 13 (1984): 187–221; and Bruce Greenwald, Joseph E. Stiglitz, and Andrew Weiss, "Information Imperfections in the Capital Market and Macroeconomic Fluctuations," *American Economic Review* 74 (1984): 194–199.

cars will come to the market. Because the average quality of a used car available in the market will be low and because few people want to buy a lemon, there will be few sales. The used-car market will function poorly, if at all.

Lemons in the Stock and Bond Markets

A similar lemons problem arises in securities markets—that is, the debt (bond) and equity (stock) markets. Suppose that our friend Irving the Investor, a potential buyer of securities such as common stock, can't distinguish between good firms with high expected profits and low risk and bad firms with low expected profits and high risk. In this situation, Irving will be willing to pay only a price that reflects the *average* quality of firms issuing securities—a price that lies between the value of securities from bad firms and the value of those from good firms. If the owners or managers of a good firm have better information than Irving and *know* that they are a good firm, they know that their securities are undervalued and will not want to sell them to Irving at the price he is willing to pay. The only firms willing to sell Irving securities will be bad firms (because his price is higher than the securities are worth). Our friend Irving is not stupid; he does not want to hold securities in bad firms, and hence he will decide not to purchase securities in the market. In an outcome similar to that in the used-car market, this securities market will not work very well because few firms will sell securities in it to raise capital.

The analysis is similar if Irving considers purchasing a corporate debt instrument in the bond market rather than an equity share. Irving will buy a bond only if its interest rate is high enough to compensate him for the average default risk of the good and bad firms trying to sell the debt. The knowledgeable owners of a good firm realize that they will be paying a higher interest rate than they should, so they are unlikely to want to borrow in this market. Only the bad firms will be willing to borrow, and because investors like Irving are not eager to buy bonds issued by bad firms, they will probably not buy any bonds at all. Few bonds are likely to sell in this market, so it will not be a good source of financing.

The analysis we have just conducted explains fact 2—why marketable securities are not the primary source of financing for businesses in any country in the world. It also partly explains fact 1—why stocks are not the most important source of financing for American businesses. The presence of the lemons problem keeps securities markets such as the stock and bond markets from being effective in channeling funds from savers to borrowers.

Tools to Help Solve Adverse Selection Problems

In the absence of asymmetric information, the lemons problem goes away. If buyers know as much about the quality of used cars as sellers, so that all involved can tell a good car from a bad one, buyers will be willing to pay full value for good used cars. Because the owners of good used cars can now get a fair price, they will be willing to sell them in the market. The market will have many transactions and will do its intended job of channeling good cars to people who want them.

Similarly, if purchasers of securities can distinguish good firms from bad, they will pay the full value of securities issued by good firms, and good firms will sell their securities in the market. The securities market will then be able to move funds to the good firms that have the most productive investment opportunities.

Private Production and Sale of Information. The solution to the adverse selection problem in financial markets is to eliminate asymmetric information by furnishing the people supplying funds with full details about the individuals or firms seeking to finance their investment activities. One way to get this material to saver-lenders is to have private companies collect and produce information that distinguishes good from bad firms and then sell it. In the United States, companies such as Standard and Poor's, Moody's, and Value Line gather information on firms' balance sheet positions and investment activities, publish these data, and sell them to subscribers (individuals, libraries, and financial intermediaries involved in purchasing securities).

The system of private production and sale of information does not completely solve the adverse selection problem in securities markets, however, because of the **free-rider problem**. The free-rider problem occurs when people who do not pay for information take advantage of the information that other people have paid for. The free-rider problem suggests that the private sale of information will be only a partial solution to the lemons problem. To see why, suppose that you have just purchased information that tells you which firms are good and which are bad. You believe that this purchase is worthwhile because you can make up the cost of acquiring this information, and then some, by purchasing the securities of good firms that are undervalued. However, when our savvy (free-riding) investor Irving sees you buying certain securities, he buys right along with you, even though he has not paid for any information. If many other investors act as Irving does, the increased demand for the undervalued good securities will cause their low price to be bid up immediately to reflect the securities' true value. Because of all these free riders, you can no longer buy the securities for less than their true value. Now because you will not gain any profits from purchasing the information, you realize that you never should have paid for this information in the first place. If other investors come to the same realization, private firms and individuals may not be able to sell enough of this information to make it worth their while to gather and produce it. The weakened ability of private firms to profit from selling information will mean that less information is produced in the marketplace, so adverse selection (the lemons problem) will still interfere with the efficient functioning of securities markets.

Government Regulation to Increase Information. The free-rider problem prevents the private market from producing enough information to eliminate all the asymmetric information that leads to adverse selection. Could financial markets benefit from government intervention? The government could, for instance, produce information to help investors distinguish good from bad firms and provide it to the public free of charge. This solution, however, would involve the government in releasing negative information about firms, a practice that might be politically difficult. A second possibility (and one followed by the United States and most governments throughout the world) is for the government to regulate securities markets in a way that encourages firms to reveal honest information about themselves so that investors can determine how good or bad the firms are. In the United States, the Securities and Exchange Commission (SEC) is the government agency that requires firms selling their securities to have independent audits, in which accounting firms certify that the firm is adhering to standard accounting principles and disclosing accurate information about sales, assets, and earnings. Similar regulations are found in other countries. However, disclosure requirements do not always work well, as the recent collapse of Enron and

FYI The Enron Implosion

Until 2001, Enron Corporation, a firm that specialized in trading in the energy market, appeared to be spectacularly successful. It had a quarter of the energy-trading market and was valued as high as $77 billion in August 2000 (just a little over a year before its collapse), making it the seventh-largest corporation in the United States at that time. However, toward the end of 2001, Enron came crashing down. In October 2001, Enron announced a third-quarter loss of $618 million and disclosed accounting "mistakes." The SEC then engaged in a formal investigation of Enron's financial dealings with partnerships led by its former finance chief. It became clear that Enron was engaged in a complex set of transactions by which it was keeping substantial amounts of debt and financial contracts off of its balance sheet. These transactions enabled Enron to hide its financial difficulties. Despite securing as much as $1.5 billion of new financing from J. P. Morgan Chase and Citigroup, the company was forced to declare bankruptcy in December 2001, the largest bankruptcy in U.S. history.

The Enron collapse illustrates that government regulation can lessen asymmetric information problems, but cannot eliminate them. Managers have tremendous incentives to hide their companies' problems, making it hard for investors to know the true value of the firm.

The Enron bankruptcy not only increased concerns in financial markets about the quality of accounting information supplied by corporations, but also led to hardship for many of the firm's former employees, who found that their pensions had become worthless. Outrage against the duplicity of executives at Enron has been high, and several have been indicted, with some being already convicted and sent to jail.

accounting scandals at other corporations, such as WorldCom and Parmalat (an Italian company) suggest (see the FYI box, "The Enron Implosion").

The asymmetric information problem of adverse selection in financial markets helps explain why financial markets are among the most heavily regulated sectors in the economy (fact 5). Government regulation to increase information for investors is needed to reduce the adverse selection problem, which interferes with the efficient functioning of securities (stock and bond) markets.

Although government regulation lessens the adverse selection problem, it does not eliminate it. Even when firms provide information to the public about their sales, assets, or earnings, they still have more information than investors: There is a lot more to knowing the quality of a firm than statistics can provide. Furthermore, bad firms have an incentive to make themselves look like good firms, because this would enable them to fetch a higher price for their securities. Bad firms will slant the information they are required to transmit to the public, thus making it harder for investors to sort out the good firms from the bad.

Financial Intermediation. So far we have seen that private production of information and government regulation to encourage provision of information lessen, but do not eliminate, the adverse selection problem in financial markets. How, then, can the financial structure help promote the flow of funds to people with productive investment opportunities when there is asymmetric information? A clue is provided by the structure of the used-car market.

An important feature of the used-car market is that most used cars are not sold directly by one individual to another. An individual considering buying a used car might pay for privately produced information by subscribing to a magazine like *Consumer Reports* to find out if a particular make of car has a good repair record. Nevertheless, reading *Consumer Reports* does not solve the adverse selection problem, because even if a particular make of car has a good reputation, the specific car someone is trying to sell could be a lemon. The prospective buyer might also bring the used car to a mechanic for a once-over. But what if the prospective buyer doesn't know a mechanic who can be trusted or if the mechanic would charge a high fee to evaluate the car?

Because these roadblocks make it hard for individuals to acquire enough information about used cars, most used cars are not sold directly by one individual to another. Instead, they are sold by an intermediary, a used-car dealer who purchases used cars from individuals and resells them to other individuals. Used-car dealers produce information in the market by becoming experts in determining whether a car is a peach or a lemon. Once they know that a car is good, they can sell it with some form of a guarantee: either a guarantee that is explicit, such as a warranty, or an implicit guarantee, in which they stand by their reputation for honesty. People are more likely to purchase a used car because of a dealer's guarantee, and the dealer is able to make a profit on the production of information about automobile quality by being able to sell the used car at a higher price than the dealer paid for it. If dealers purchase and then resell cars on which they have produced information, they avoid the problem of other people free-riding on the information they produced.

Just as used-car dealers help solve adverse selection problems in the automobile market, financial intermediaries play a similar role in financial markets. A financial intermediary, such as a bank, becomes an expert in producing information about firms, so that it can sort out good credit risks from bad ones. Then it can acquire funds from depositors and lend them to the good firms. Because the bank is able to lend mostly to good firms, it is able to earn a higher return on its loans than the interest it has to pay to its depositors. The resulting profit that the bank earns gives it the incentive to engage in this information production activity.

An important element in the bank's ability to profit from the information it produces is that it avoids the free-rider problem by primarily making private loans rather than by purchasing securities that are traded in the open market. Because a private loan is not traded, other investors cannot watch what the bank is doing and bid up the loan's price to the point that the bank receives no compensation for the information it has produced. The bank's role as an intermediary that holds mostly nontraded loans is the key to its success in reducing asymmetric information in financial markets.

Our analysis of adverse selection indicates that financial intermediaries in general—and banks in particular, because they hold a large fraction of nontraded loans—should play a greater role in moving funds to corporations than securities markets do. Our analysis thus explains facts 3 and 4: why indirect finance is so much more important than direct finance and why banks are the most important source of external funds for financing businesses.

Another important fact that is explained by the analysis here is the greater importance of banks in the financial systems of developing countries. As we have seen, when the quality of information about firms is better, asymmetric information problems will be less severe, and it will be easier for firms to issue securities. Information about private firms is harder to collect in developing countries than in industrialized countries;

therefore, the smaller role played by securities markets leaves a greater role for financial intermediaries such as banks. A corollary of this analysis is that as information about firms becomes easier to acquire, the role of banks should decline. A major development in the past twenty years in the United States has been huge improvements in information technology. Thus the analysis here suggests that the lending role of financial institutions such as banks in the United States should have declined, and this is exactly what has occurred (see Chapter 10).

Our analysis of adverse selection also explains fact 6, which questions why large firms are more likely to obtain funds from securities markets, a direct route, rather than from banks and financial intermediaries, an indirect route. The better known a corporation is, the more information about its activities is available in the marketplace. Thus it is easier for investors to evaluate the quality of the corporation and determine whether it is a good firm or a bad one. Because investors have fewer worries about adverse selection with well-known corporations, they will be willing to invest directly in their securities. Our adverse selection analysis thus suggests that there should be a pecking order for firms that can issue securities. Hence we have an explanation for fact 6: The larger and more established a corporation is, the more likely it will be to issue securities to raise funds.

Collateral and Net Worth. Adverse selection interferes with the functioning of financial markets only if a lender suffers a loss when a borrower is unable to make loan payments and thereby defaults. *Collateral*, property promised to the lender if the borrower defaults, reduces the consequences of adverse selection because it reduces the lender's losses in the event of a default. If a borrower defaults on a loan, the lender can sell the collateral and use the proceeds to make up for the losses on the loan. For example, if you fail to make your mortgage payments, the lender can take title to your house, auction it off, and use the receipts to pay off the loan. Lenders are thus more willing to make loans secured by collateral, and borrowers are willing to supply collateral because the reduced risk for the lender makes it more likely they will get the loan in the first place and perhaps at a better loan rate. The presence of adverse selection in credit markets thus provides an explanation for why collateral is an important feature of debt contracts (fact 7).

Net worth (also called **equity capital**), the difference between a firm's assets (what it owns or is owed) and its liabilities (what it owes), can perform a similar role to collateral. If a firm has a high net worth, then even if it engages in investments that cause it to have negative profits and so defaults on its debt payments, the lender can take title to the firm's net worth, sell it off, and use the proceeds to recoup some of the losses from the loan. In addition, the more net worth a firm has in the first place, the less likely it is to default, because the firm has a cushion of assets that it can use to pay off its loans. Hence, when firms seeking credit have high net worth, the consequences of adverse selection are less important and lenders are more willing to make loans. This analysis lies behind the often-heard lament, "Only the people who don't need money can borrow it!"

Summary. So far we have used the concept of adverse selection to explain seven of the eight facts about financial structure introduced earlier: The first four emphasize the importance of financial intermediaries and the relative unimportance of securities markets for the financing of corporations; the fifth, that financial markets are among the most heavily regulated sectors of the economy; the sixth, that only large, well-established corporations have access to securities markets; and the seventh, that collateral is an important feature of debt contracts. In the next section, we will see that the other asymmetric information concept of moral hazard provides additional reasons for the importance of financial intermediaries and the relative unimportance of securities markets for the financing of corporations, the prevalence of government regulation, and the importance of collateral in debt contracts. In addition, the concept of moral hazard can be used to explain our final fact (fact 8): why debt contracts are complicated legal documents that place substantial restrictions on the behavior of the borrower.

HOW MORAL HAZARD AFFECTS THE CHOICE BETWEEN DEBT AND EQUITY CONTRACTS

Moral hazard is the asymmetric information problem that occurs after the financial transaction takes place, when the seller of a security may have incentives to hide information and engage in activities that are undesirable for the purchaser of the security. Moral hazard has important consequences for whether a firm finds it easier to raise funds with debt than with equity contracts.

Moral Hazard in Equity Contracts: The Principal–Agent Problem

Equity contracts, such as common stock, are claims to a share in the profits and assets of a business. Equity contracts are subject to a particular type of moral hazard called the **principal–agent problem**. When managers own only a small fraction of the firm they work for, the stockholders who own most of the firm's equity (called the *principals*) are not the same people as the managers of the firm, who are the *agents* of the owners. This separation of ownership and control involves moral hazard, in that the managers in control (the agents) may act in their own interest rather than in the interest of the stockholder-owners (the principals) because the managers have less incentive to maximize profits than the stockholder-owners do.

To understand the principal–agent problem more fully, suppose that your friend Steve asks you to become a silent partner in his ice-cream store. The store requires an investment of $10,000 to set up and Steve has only $1,000. So you purchase an equity stake (stock shares) for $9,000, which entitles you to 90% of the ownership of the firm, while Steve owns only 10%. If Steve works hard to make tasty ice cream, keeps the store clean, smiles at all the customers, and hustles to wait on tables quickly, after all expenses (including Steve's salary), the store will have $50,000 in profits per year, of which Steve receives 10% ($5,000) and you receive 90% ($45,000).

But if Steve doesn't provide quick and friendly service to his customers, uses the $50,000 in income to buy artwork for his office, and even sneaks off to the beach while he should be at the store, the store will not earn any profit. Steve can earn the additional $5,000 (his 10% share of the profits) over his salary only if he works hard and forgoes unproductive investments (such as art for his office). Steve might decide that the extra $5,000 just isn't enough to make him expend the effort to be a good manager; he might decide that it would be worth his while only if he earned an extra $10,000. If Steve feels this way, he does not have enough incentive to be a good manager and will end up with a beautiful office, a good tan, and a store that doesn't show any profits. Because the store won't show any profits, Steve's decision not to act in your interest will cost you $45,000 (your 90% of the profits if he had chosen to be a good manager instead).

The moral hazard arising from the principal–agent problem might be even worse if Steve were not totally honest. Because his ice-cream store is a cash business, Steve has the incentive to pocket $50,000 in cash and tell you that the profits were zero. He now gets a return of $50,000, and you get nothing.

Further indications that the principal–agent problem created by equity contracts can be severe are provided by recent scandals in corporations such as Enron and Tyco International, in which managers have been accused of diverting funds for their own personal use. Besides pursuing personal benefits, managers might also pursue corporate strategies (such as the acquisition of other firms) that enhance their personal power but do not increase the corporation's profitability

The principal–agent problem would not arise if the owners of a firm had complete information about what the managers were up to and could prevent wasteful expenditures or fraud. The principal–agent problem, which is an example of moral hazard, arises only because a manager, such as Steve, has more information about his activities than the stockholder does—that is, there is asymmetric information. The principal–agent problem would also not arise if Steve alone owned the store and there were no separation of ownership and control. If this were the case, Steve's hard work and avoidance of unproductive investments would yield him a profit (and extra income) of $50,000, an amount that would make it worth his while to be a good manager.

Tools to Help Solve the Principal–Agent Problem

Production of Information: Monitoring.

You have seen that the principal–agent problem arises because managers have more information about their activities and actual profits than stockholders do. One way for stockholders to reduce this moral hazard problem is for them to engage in a particular type of information production, the monitoring of the firm's activities: auditing the firm frequently and checking on what the management is doing. The problem is that the monitoring process can be expensive in terms of time and money, as reflected in the name economists give it, **costly state verification**. Costly state verification makes the equity contract less desirable, and it explains, in part, why equity is not a more important element in our financial structure.

As with adverse selection, the free-rider problem decreases the amount of information production that would reduce the moral hazard (principal–agent) problem. In this example, the free-rider problem decreases monitoring. If you know that other stockholders are paying to monitor the activities of the company you hold shares in, you can take a free ride on their activities. Then you can use the money you save by not engaging in monitoring to vacation on a Caribbean island. If you can do this, though, so can other stockholders. Perhaps all the stockholders will go to the islands, and no one will spend any resources on monitoring the firm. The moral hazard problem for shares of common stock will then be severe, making it hard for firms to issue them to raise capital (providing an additional explanation for fact 1).

Government Regulation to Increase Information. As with adverse selection, the government has an incentive to try to reduce the moral hazard problem created by asymmetric information, which provides another reason why the financial system is so heavily regulated (fact 5). Governments everywhere have laws to force firms to adhere to standard accounting principles that make profit verification easier. They also pass laws to impose stiff criminal penalties on people who commit the fraud of hiding and stealing profits. However, these measures can be only partly effective. Catching this kind of fraud is not easy; fraudulent managers have the incentive to make it very hard for government agencies to find or prove fraud.

Financial Intermediation. Financial intermediaries have the ability to avoid the free-rider problem in the face of moral hazard, and this is another reason why indirect finance is so important (fact 3). One financial intermediary that helps reduce the moral hazard arising from the principal–agent problem is the **venture capital firm**. Venture capital firms pool the resources of their partners and use the funds to help budding entrepreneurs start new businesses. In exchange for the use of the venture capital, the firm receives an equity share in the new business. Because verification of earnings and profits is so important in eliminating moral hazard, venture capital firms usually insist on having several of their own people participate as members of the managing body of the firm, the board of directors, so that they can keep a close watch on the firm's activities. When a venture capital firm supplies start-up funds, the equity in the firm is not marketable to anyone *except* the venture capital firm. Thus other investors are unable to take a free ride on the venture capital firm's verification activities. As a result of this arrangement, the venture capital firm is able to garner the full benefits of its verification activities and is given the appropriate incentives to reduce the moral hazard problem. Venture capital firms have been important in the development of the high-tech sector in the United States, which has resulted in job creation, economic growth, and increased international competitiveness. However, these firms have made mistakes (see the E-Finance box, "Venture Capitalists and the High-Tech Sector").

Debt Contracts. Moral hazard arises with an equity contract, which is a claim on profits in all situations, whether the firm is making or losing money. If a contract could be structured so that moral hazard would exist only in certain situations, there would be a reduced need to monitor managers, and the contract would be more attractive than the equity contract. The debt contract has exactly these attributes because it is a contractual agreement by the borrower to pay the lender *fixed* dollar amounts at periodic intervals. When the firm has high profits, the lender receives the contractual payments and does not need to know the exact profits of the firm. If the managers are hiding profits or are pursuing activities that are personally beneficial but don't increase profitability, the lender doesn't care as long as these activities do not interfere with the ability of the firm to make its debt payments on time. Only when the firm cannot meet its debt payments, thereby being in a state of default, is there a need for the lender to verify the state of the firm's profits. Only in this situation do lenders involved in debt contracts need to act more like equity holders; now they need to know how much income the firm has to get their fair share.

E-Finance Venture Capitalists and the High-Tech Sector

Over the last half century, venture capital firms have nurtured the growth of America's high technology sector. Venture capitalists backed many of the most successful high-technology companies during the 1980s and 1990s, including Apple Computer, Cisco Systems, Genetech, Microsoft, Netscape, and Sun Microsystems.

Venture capital firms experienced explosive growth during the last half of the 1990s, with investments growing from $5.6 billion in 1995 to more than $103 billion by 2000, increasingly focused on investing in Internet "dot-com" companies. These two developments led to large losses for venture capitalists, for the following reasons.

First, it is likely that there are relatively few projects worthy of financing at any one time. When too much money chases too few deals, firms that would be rejected at other times will obtain financing. Second, the surge of money into venture capital funds reduced the ability of partners of venture capital firms to provide quality monitoring. Third, the infatuation with dot-com firms, many of which did not have adequately developed business plans, meant that too much investment was directed to this sector. Consequently, in the late 1990s, venture capital firms made many poor investments, which led to large losses by the early 2000s.

Consider the case of Webvan, an Internet grocer that received more than $1 billion in venture capital financing. Even though it was backed by a group of experienced financiers, including Goldman Sachs and Sequoia Capital, its business plan was fundamentally flawed. In its short life, Webvan spent more than $1 billion building automated warehouses and pricey tech gear. The resulting high overhead made it impossible to compete in the grocery business. Had the venture capitalists been actively monitoring the activities of Webvan, they might have balked at Webvan's plan to develop an infrastructure that requried 4,000 orders per day per warehouse just to break even. Not surprisingly, Webvan declared bankruptcy in July 2001.

The less frequent need to monitor the firm, and thus the lower cost of state verification, helps explain why debt contracts are used more frequently than equity contracts to raise capital. The concept of moral hazard thus helps explain fact 1, why stocks are not the most important source of financing for businesses.[4]

HOW MORAL HAZARD INFLUENCES FINANCIAL STRUCTURE IN DEBT MARKETS

Even with the advantages just described, debt contracts are still subject to moral hazard. Because a debt contract requires the borrowers to pay out a fixed amount and lets them keep any profits above this amount, the borrowers have an incentive to take on investment projects that are riskier than the lenders would like.

[4]Another factor that encourages the use of debt contracts rather than equity contracts in the United States is our tax code. Debt interest payments are a deductible expense for American firms, whereas dividend payments to equity shareholders are not.

For example, suppose that because you are concerned about the problem of verifying the profits of Steve's ice-cream store, you decide not to become an equity partner. Instead, you lend Steve the $9,000 he needs to set up his business and have a debt contract that pays you an interest rate of 10%. As far as you are concerned, this is a surefire investment because there is a strong and steady demand for ice cream in your neighborhood. However, once you give Steve the funds, he might use them for purposes other than you intended. Instead of opening up the ice-cream store, Steve might use your $9,000 loan to invest in chemical research equipment because he thinks he has a 1-in-10 chance of inventing a diet ice cream that tastes every bit as good as the premium brands but has no fat or calories.

Obviously, this is a very risky investment, but if Steve is successful, he will become a multimillionaire. He has a strong incentive to undertake the riskier investment with your money, because the gains to him would be so large if he succeeded. You would clearly be very unhappy if Steve used your loan for the riskier investment, because if he were unsuccessful, which is highly likely, you would lose most, if not all, of the money you gave him. And if he were successful, you wouldn't share in his success—you would still get only a 10% return on the loan because the principal and interest payments are fixed. Because of the potential moral hazard (that Steve might use your money to finance a very risky venture), you would probably not make the loan to Steve, even though an ice-cream store in the neighborhood is a good investment that would provide benefits for everyone.

Tools to Help Solve Moral Hazard in Debt Contracts

Net Worth and Collateral. When borrowers have more at stake because their net worth (the difference between their assets and their liabilities) is high or the collateral they have pledged to the lender is valuable, the risk of moral hazard—the temptation to act in a manner that lenders find objectionable—will be greatly reduced because the borrowers themselves have a lot to lose. Let's return to Steve and his ice-cream business. Suppose that the cost of setting up either the ice-cream store or the research equipment is $100,000 instead of $10,000. So Steve needs to put $91,000 of his own money into the business (instead of $1,000) in addition to the $9,000 supplied by your loan. Now if Steve is unsuccessful in inventing the no-calorie nonfat ice cream, he has a lot to lose—the $91,000 of net worth ($100,000 in assets minus the $9,000 loan from you). He will think twice about undertaking the riskier investment and is more likely to invest in the ice-cream store, which is more of a sure thing. Hence, when Steve has more of his own money (net worth) in the business, you are more likely to make him the loan. Similarly, if you have pledged your house as collateral, you are less likely to go to Las Vegas and gamble away your earnings that month because you might not be able to make your mortgage payments and might lose your house.

One way of describing the solution that high net worth and collateral provides to the moral hazard problem is to say that it makes the debt contract **incentive-compatible**; that is, it aligns the incentives of the borrower with those of the lender. The greater the borrower's net worth and collateral pledged, the greater the borrower's incentive to behave in the way that the lender expects and desires, the smaller the moral hazard problem in the debt contract, and the easier it is for the firm or household to borrow. Conversely, when the borrower's net worth and collateral are lower, the moral hazard problem is greater, and it is harder to borrow.

Monitoring and Enforcement of Restrictive Covenants. As the example of Steve and his ice-cream store shows, if you could make sure that Steve doesn't invest in anything riskier than the ice-cream store, it would be worth your while to make him the loan. You can ensure that Steve uses your money for the purpose *you* want it to be used for by writing provisions (restrictive covenants) into the debt contract that restrict his firm's activities. By monitoring Steve's activities to see whether he is complying with the restrictive covenants and enforcing the covenants if he is not, you can make sure that he will not take on risks at your expense. Restrictive covenants are directed at reducing moral hazard either by ruling out undesirable behavior or by encouraging desirable behavior. There are four types of restrictive covenants that achieve this objective:

1. ***Covenants to discourage undesirable behavior.*** Covenants can be designed to lower moral hazard by keeping the borrower from engaging in the undesirable behavior of undertaking risky investment projects. Some covenants mandate that a loan can be used only to finance specific activities, such as the purchase of particular equipment or inventories. Others restrict the borrowing firm from engaging in certain risky business activities, such as purchasing other businesses.

2. ***Covenants to encourage desirable behavior.*** Restrictive covenants can encourage the borrower to engage in desirable activities that make it more likely that the loan will be paid off. One restrictive covenant of this type requires the breadwinner in a household to carry life insurance that pays off the mortgage upon that person's death. Restrictive covenants of this type for businesses focus on encouraging the borrowing firm to keep its net worth high because higher borrower net worth reduces moral hazard and makes it less likely that the lender will suffer losses. These restrictive covenants typically specify that the firm must maintain minimum holdings of certain assets relative to the firm's size.

3. ***Covenants to keep collateral valuable.*** Because collateral is an important protection for the lender, restrictive covenants can encourage the borrower to keep the collateral in good condition and make sure that it stays in the possession of the borrower. This is the type of covenant ordinary people encounter most often. Automobile loan contracts, for example, require the car owner to maintain a minimum amount of collision and theft insurance and prevent the sale of the car unless the loan is paid off. Similarly, the recipient of a home mortgage must have adequate insurance on the home and must pay off the mortgage when the property is sold.

4. ***Covenants to provide information.*** Restrictive covenants also require a borrowing firm to provide information about its activities periodically in the form of quarterly accounting and income reports, thereby making it easier for the lender to monitor the firm and reduce moral hazard. This type of covenant may also stipulate that the lender has the right to audit and inspect the firm's books at any time.

We now see why debt contracts are often complicated legal documents with numerous restrictions on the borrower's behavior (fact 8): Debt contracts require complicated restrictive covenants to lower moral hazard.

Financial Intermediation. Although restrictive covenants help reduce the moral hazard problem, they do not eliminate it completely. It is almost impossible to write covenants that rule out *every* risky activity. Furthermore, borrowers may be clever enough to find loopholes in restrictive covenants that make them ineffective.

Another problem with restrictive covenants is that they must be monitored and enforced. A restrictive covenant is meaningless if the borrower can violate it knowing that the lender won't check up or is unwilling to pay for legal recourse. Because monitoring and enforcement of restrictive covenants are costly, the free-rider problem arises in the debt securities (bond) market just as it does in the stock market. If you know that other bondholders are monitoring and enforcing the restrictive covenants, you can free-ride on their monitoring and enforcement. But other bondholders can do the same thing, so the likely outcome is that not enough resources are devoted to monitoring and enforcing the restrictive covenants. Moral hazard therefore continues to be a severe problem for marketable debt.

As we have seen before, financial intermediaries—particularly banks—have the ability to avoid the free-rider problem as long as they make primarily private loans. Private loans are not traded, so no one else can free-ride on the intermediary's monitoring and enforcement of the restrictive covenants. The intermediary making private loans thus receives the benefits of monitoring and enforcement and will work to shrink the moral hazard problem inherent in debt contracts. The concept of moral hazard has provided us with additional reasons why financial intermediaries play a more important role in channeling funds from savers to borrowers than marketable securities do, as described in facts 3 and 4.

Summary

The presence of asymmetric information in financial markets leads to adverse selection and moral hazard problems that interfere with the efficient functioning of those markets. Tools to help solve these problems involve the private production and sale of information, government regulation to increase information in financial markets, the importance of collateral and net worth to debt contracts, and the use of monitoring and restrictive covenants. A key finding from our analysis is that the existence of the free-rider problem for traded securities such as stocks and bonds indicates that financial intermediaries—particularly banks—should play a greater role than securities markets in financing the activities of businesses. Economic analysis of the consequences of adverse selection and moral hazard has helped explain the basic features of our financial system and has provided solutions to the eight facts about our financial structure outlined at the beginning of this chapter.

STUDY GUIDE

To help you keep track of all the tools that help solve asymmetric information problems, Table 1 summarizes the asymmetric information problems and tools that help solve them. In addition, it notes how these tools and asymmetric information problems explain the eight facts of financial structure described at the beginning of the chapter.

SUMMARY TABLE 1 Asymmetric Information Problems and Tools to Solve Them

Asymmetric Information Problem	Tools to Solve It	Explains Fact Number
Adverse selection	Private production and sale of information	1, 2
	Government regulation to increase information	5
	Financial intermediation	3, 4, 6
	Collateral and net worth	7
Moral hazard in equity contracts (principal–agent problem)	Production of information: monitoring	1
	Government regulation to increase information	5
	Financial intermediation	3
	Debt contracts	1
Moral hazard in debt contracts	Collateral and net worth	
	Monitoring and enforcement of restrictive covenants	8
	Financial intermediation	3, 4

Note: List of facts:

1. Stocks are not the most important source of external financing.
2. Marketable securities are not the primary source of finance.
3. Indirect finance is more important than direct finance.
4. Banks are the most important source of external funds.
5. The financial system is heavily regulated.
6. Only large, well-established firms have access to securities markets.
7. Collateral is prevalent in debt contracts.
8. Debt contracts have numerous restrictive covenants.

CONFLICTS OF INTEREST

Earlier in this chapter, we saw how financial institutions play an important role in the financial system. They develop expertise in collecting, producing and distributing information and thereby not only gain a cost advantage in the production of information, but also can use the information over and over again in as many ways as they would like, thereby realizing economies of scale. In addition, by providing multiple financial services to their customers, such as offering them car loans as well as life insurance, they can also achieve **economies of scope**—that is, they can lower the cost of information production for each service by applying one information resource to many different services. An investment bank, for example, can evaluate how good a credit risk a corporation is and so arrange to market the corporation's bonds, but this information also can help the investment bank to decide whether it would be easy in addition to sell the corporation's stock to the public.

Although the presence of economies of scope may substantially benefit financial institutions, it also creates potential costs in terms of **conflicts of interest**. Conflicts of interest are a type of moral hazard problem that arise when a person or institution has multiple objectives (interests) and, as a result, has conflicts between these objectives. Conflicts of interest are especially likely to occur when a financial institution provides multiple services. The potentially competing interests of those services may lead an individual or firm to conceal information or disseminate misleading information. We care about these conflicts of interest because they can substantially reduce the quality of information in financial markets, which exacerbates asymmetric information problems and can make it harder for the financial system to carry out its essential function of channeling funds into productive investment opportunities. We examine conflicts of interest in great detail in Chapter 14, examining why they arise, why they are costly and what can be done about them.

APPLICATION Financial Development and Economic Growth

Recent research has found that an important reason why many developing countries or ex-communist countries like Russia (which are referred to as *transition countries*) experience very low rates of growth is that their financial systems are underdeveloped (a situation referred to as *financial repression*).[5] The economic analysis of financial structure helps explain how an underdeveloped financial system leads to a low state of economic development and economic growth.

The financial systems in developing and transition countries face several difficulties that keep them from operating efficiently. As we have seen, two important tools used to help solve adverse selection and moral hazard problems in credit markets are collateral and restrictive covenants. In many developing countries, the system of property rights (the rule of law, constraints on government expropriation, absence of corruption) functions poorly, making it hard to make effective use of these two tools. In these countries, bankruptcy procedures are often extremely slow and cumbersome. For example, in many countries, creditors (holders of debt) must first sue the defaulting debtor for payment, which can take several years; then, once a favorable judgment has been obtained, the creditor has to sue again to obtain title to the collateral. The process can take in excess of five years, and by the time the lender acquires the collateral, it well may have been neglected and thus have little value. In addition, governments often block lenders from foreclosing on borrowers in politically powerful sectors such as agriculture. Where the market is unable to use collateral effectively, the adverse selection problem will be worse, because the lender will need even more information about the quality of the borrower so that it can screen out a good loan from a bad one. The result is that it will be harder for lenders to channel funds to borrowers with the most productive investment opportunities. There will be less productive investment, and hence a slower-growing economy. Similarly, a poorly developed or corrupt legal system may make it extremely

[5]See World Bank, *Finance for Growth: Policy Choices in a Volatile World* (World Bank and Oxford University Press, 2001) for a survey of the literature linking economic growth with financial development and a list of additional references.

difficult for lenders to enforce restrictive covenants. Thus they may have a much more limited ability to reduce moral hazard on the part of borrowers and so will be less willing to lend. Again the outcome will be less productive investment and a lower growth rate for the economy.

Governments in developing and transition countries often use their financial systems to direct credit to themselves or to favored sectors of the economy by setting interest rates at artificially low levels for certain types of loans, by creating development finance institutions to make specific types of loans, or by directing existing institutions to lend to certain entities. As we have seen, private institutions have an incentive to solve adverse selection and moral hazard problems and lend to borrowers with the most productive investment opportunities. Governments have less incentive to do so because they are not driven by the profit motive and thus their directed credit programs may not channel funds to sectors that will produce high growth for the economy. The outcome is again likely to result in less efficient investment and slower growth.

In addition, banks in many developing and transition countries are owned by their governments. Again, because of the absence of the profit motive, these **state-owned banks** have little incentive to allocate their capital to the most productive uses. Not surprisingly, the primary loan customer of these state-owned banks is often the government, which does not always use the funds wisely.

We have seen that government regulation can increase the amount of information in financial markets to make them work more efficiently. Many developing and transition countries have an underdeveloped regulatory apparatus that retards the provision of adequate information to the marketplace. For example, these countries often have weak accounting standards, making it very hard to ascertain the quality of a borrower's balance sheet. As a result, asymmetric information problems are more severe, and the financial system is severely hampered in channeling funds to the most productive uses.

The institutional environment of a poor legal system, weak accounting standards, inadequate government regulation, and government intervention through directed credit programs and state ownership of banks all help explain why many countries stay poor while others grow richer.

APPLICATION Is China a Counter-Example to the Importance of Financial Development?

Although China appears to be on its way to becoming an economic powerhouse, its financial development remains in the early stages. The country's legal system is weak so that financial contracts are difficult to enforce, while accounting standards are lax so that high-quality information about creditors is hard to find. Regulation of the banking system is still in its formative stages, and the banking sector is dominated by large state-owned banks. Yet the Chinese economy has enjoyed one of the highest growth rates in the world over the last twenty years. How has China been able to grow so rapidly given its low level of financial development?

As noted above, China is in an early state of development, with a per capita income that is still less than $5,000, one-eighth of the per capita income in the United States. With an extremely high savings rate, averaging around 40% over the last two decades, the country has been able to rapidly build up its capital stock and shift a massive pool of underutilized labor from the subsistence-agriculture sector into higher-productivity activities that use capital. Even though available savings have not been allocated to their most productive uses, the huge increase in capital combined with the gains in productivity from moving labor out of low-productivity, subsistence agriculture have been enough to produce high growth.

As China gets richer, however, this strategy is unlikely to continue to work. The Soviet Union provides a graphic example. In the 1950s and 1960s, the Soviet Union shared many characteristics with modern-day China: high growth fueled by a high savings rate, a massive buildup of capital, and shifts of a large pool of underutilized labor from subsistence agriculture to manufacturing. During this high-growth phase, however, the Soviet Union was unable to develop the institutions needed to allocate capital efficiently. As a result, once the pool of subsistence laborers was used up, the Soviet Union's growth slowed dramatically and it was unable to keep up with the Western economies. Today no one considers the Soviet Union to have been an economic success story, and its inability to develop the institutions necessary to sustain financial development and growth was an important reason for the demise of this superpower.

To move into the next stage of development, China will need to allocate its capital more efficiently, which requires that it must improve its financial system. The Chinese leadership is well aware of this challenge: The government has announced that state-owned banks are being put on the path to privatization. In addition, the government is engaged in legal reform to make financial contracts more enforceable. New bankruptcy law is being developed so that lenders have the ability to take over the assets of firms that default on their loan contracts. Whether the Chinese government will succeed in developing a first-rate financial system, thereby enabling China to join the ranks of developed countries, is a big question mark.

FINANCIAL CRISES AND AGGREGATE ECONOMIC ACTIVITY

Agency theory, the economic analysis of the effects of adverse selection and moral hazard, can help us understand **financial crises**, major disruptions in financial markets that are characterized by sharp declines in asset prices and the failures of many financial and nonfinancial firms. Financial crises have been common in most countries throughout modern history. The United States has experienced major financial crises in the past, but has not had a full-scale financial crisis in recent times.[6] Studying financial crises is worthwhile because they have led to severe economic downturns in the past and have the potential for doing so in the future.

[6]Although those of us in the United States have not experienced any financial crises since the Great Depression, we have had several close calls—the October 1987 stock market crash, for example. An important reason why we have escaped financial crises is the timely action of the Federal Reserve to prevent them during episodes like that of October 1987. We look at the issue of the Fed's role in preventing financial crises in Chapter 18.

Financial crises occur when a disruption in the financial system causes such a sharp increase in adverse selection and moral hazard problems in financial markets that the markets are unable to channel funds efficiently from savers to people with productive investment opportunities. As a result of this inability of financial markets to function efficiently, economic activity contracts sharply.

Factors Causing Financial Crises

To understand why banking and financial crises occur and, more specifically, how they lead to contractions in economic activity, we need to examine the factors that cause them. Five categories of factors can trigger financial crises: increases in interest rates, increases in uncertainty, asset market effects on balance sheets, problems in the banking sector, and government fiscal imbalances.

Increases in Interest Rates. As we saw earlier, individuals and firms with the riskiest investment projects are those who are willing to pay the highest interest rates. If market interest rates are driven up sufficiently because of increased demand for credit or because of a decline in the money supply, good credit risks are less likely to want to borrow while bad credit risks are still willing to borrow. Because of the resulting increase in adverse selection, lenders will no longer want to make loans. The substantial decline in lending will lead to a substantial decline in investment and aggregate economic activity.

Increases in Uncertainty. A dramatic increase in uncertainty in financial markets, due perhaps to the failure of a prominent financial or nonfinancial institution, a recession, or a stock market crash, makes it harder for lenders to screen good from bad credit risks. The resulting inability of lenders to solve the adverse selection problem makes them less willing to lend, which leads to a decline in lending, investment, and aggregate economic activity.

Asset Market Effects on Balance Sheets. The state of firms' balance sheets has important implications for the severity of asymmetric information problems in the financial system. A sharp decline in the stock market is one factor that can cause a serious deterioration in firms' balance sheets. In turn, this deterioration can increase adverse selection and moral hazard problems in financial markets and provoke a financial crisis. A decline in the stock market means that the net worth of corporations has fallen, because share prices are the valuation of a corporation's net worth. The decline in net worth as a result of a stock market decline makes lenders less willing to lend because, as we have seen, the net worth of a firm plays a role similar to that of collateral. When the value of collateral declines, it provides less protection to lenders, meaning that losses on loans are likely to be more severe. Because lenders are now less protected against the consequences of adverse selection, they decrease their lending, which in turn causes investment and aggregate output to decline. In addition, the decline in corporate net worth as a result of a stock market decline increases moral hazard by providing incentives for borrowing firms to make risky investments, as they now have less to lose if their investments go sour. The resulting increase in moral hazard makes lending less attractive—another reason why a stock market decline and resultant decline in net worth leads to decreased lending and economic activity.

In economies in which inflation has been moderate, which characterizes most industrialized countries, many debt contracts are typically of fairly long maturity with fixed interest rates. In this institutional environment, unanticipated declines in the aggregate price level also decrease the net worth of firms. Because debt payments are contractually fixed in nominal terms, an unanticipated decline in the price level raises the value of firms' liabilities in *real* terms (increases the burden of the debt) but does not raise the real value of firms' assets. The result is that net worth in *real* terms (the difference between assets and liabilities in *real* terms) declines. A sharp drop in the price level therefore causes a substantial decline in real net worth and an increase in adverse selection and moral hazard problems facing lenders. An unanticipated decline in the aggregate price level thus leads to a drop in lending and economic activity.

Because of uncertainty about the future value of the domestic currency in developing countries (and in some industrialized countries), many nonfinancial firms, banks, and governments in these countries find it easier to issue debt denominated in foreign currencies. This can lead to a financial crisis in a similar fashion to an unanticipated decline in the price level. With debt contracts denominated in foreign currency, when there is an unanticipated decline in the value of the domestic currency, the debt burden of domestic firms increases. Since assets are typically denominated in domestic currency, there is a resulting deterioration in firms' balance sheets and a decline in net worth, which then increases adverse selection and moral hazard problems along the lines just described. The increase in asymmetric information problems leads to a decline in investment and economic activity.

Although we have seen that increases in interest rates have a direct effect on increasing adverse selection problems, increases in interest rates also play a role in promoting a financial crisis through their effect on both firms' and households' balance sheets. An increase in interest rates and therefore in households' and firms' interest payments decreases firms' **cash flow**, the difference between cash receipts and cash expenditures. The decline in cash flow causes a deterioration in the balance sheet because it decreases the liquidity of the household or firm and thus makes it harder for lenders to know whether the firm or household will be able to pay its bills. As a result, adverse selection and moral hazard problems become more severe for potential lenders to these firms and households, leading to a decline in lending and economic activity. There is thus an additional reason why sharp increases in interest rates can be an important factor leading to financial crises.

Problems in the Banking Sector. Banks play a major role in financial markets because they are well positioned to engage in information-producing activities that facilitate productive investment for the economy. The state of banks' balance sheets has an important effect on bank lending. If banks suffer a deterioration in their balance sheets and so have a substantial contraction in their capital, they will have fewer resources to lend, and bank lending will decline. The contraction in lending then leads to a decline in investment spending, which slows economic activity.

If the deterioration in bank balance sheets is severe enough, banks will start to fail, and fear can spread from one bank to another, causing even healthy banks to go under. The multiple bank failures that result are known as a **bank panic**. The source of the contagion is asymmetric information. In a panic, depositors, fearing for the safety of their deposits (in the absence of deposit insurance) and not knowing the quality of banks' loan portfolios, withdraw their deposits to the point that the banks fail. The failure of a large number of banks in a short period of time means that there is a loss of information production in financial markets and a direct loss of banks' financial intermediation.

The decrease in bank lending during a financial crisis decreases the supply of funds available to borrowers, which leads to higher interest rates. The outcome of a bank panic is an increase in adverse selection and moral hazard problems in credit markets: These problems produce an even sharper decline in lending to facilitate productive investments and lead to an even more severe contraction in economic activity.

Government Fiscal Imbalances. In emerging market countries (Argentina, Brazil, and Turkey are recent examples), government fiscal imbalances may create fears of default on the government debt. As a result, the government may have trouble getting people to buy its bonds and it might force banks to purchase them. If the debt then declines in price—which, as we have seen in Chapter 6, will occur if a government default is likely—bank balance sheets will weaken and their lending will contract for the reasons described earlier. Fears of default on the government debt can also spark a foreign exchange crisis in which the value of the domestic currency falls sharply because investors pull their money out of the country. The decline in the domestic currency's value will then lead to the destruction of the balance sheets of firms with large amounts of debt denominated in foreign currency. These balance sheet problems lead to an increase in adverse selection and moral hazard problems, a decline in lending, and a contraction of economic activity.

APPLICATION Financial Crises in the United States

The United States has a long history of banking and financial crises. Such crises occurred every twenty years or so in the nineteenth and early twentieth centuries—in 1819, 1837, 1857, 1873, 1884, 1893, 1907, and 1930–1933. Our analysis of the factors that lead to a financial crisis can explain why these crises took place and why they were so damaging to the U.S. economy.

STUDY GUIDE

To understand fully what took place in a U.S. financial crisis, make sure that you can state the reasons why each factor–increases in interest rates, increases in uncertainty, asset market effects on balance sheets, and problems in the banking sector–increases adverse selection and moral hazard problems, which in turn lead to a decline in economic activity. To help you understand these crises, you might want to refer to Figure 2, a diagram that traces the sequence of events in a U.S. financial crisis.

As shown in Figure 3, most financial crises in the United States have begun with a deterioration in banks' balance sheets, a sharp rise in interest rates (frequently stemming

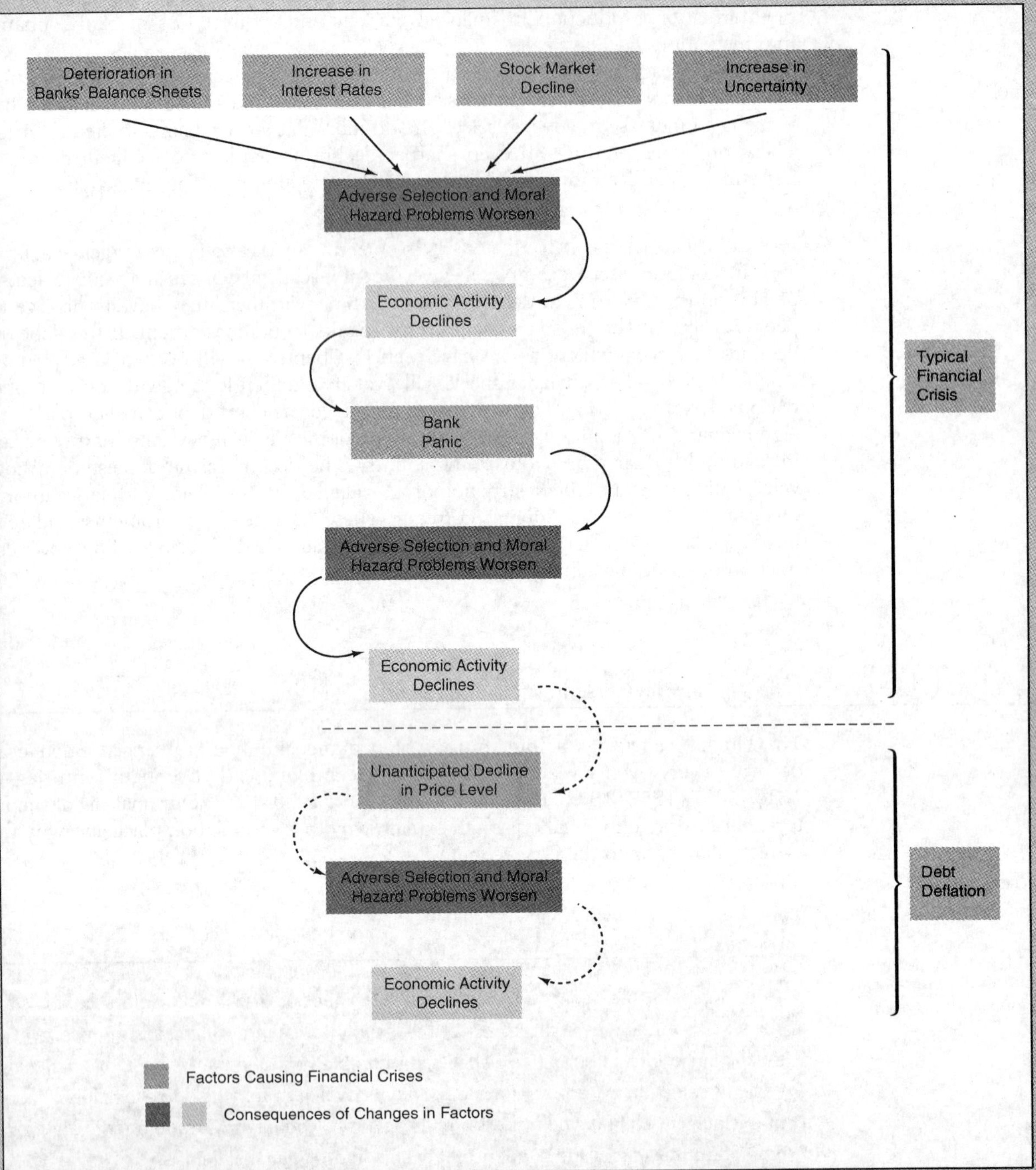

FIGURE 3 **Sequence of Events in U.S. Financial Crises**
The solid arrows trace the sequence of events in a typical financial crisis; the dotted arrows show the additional set of events that occur if the crisis develops into a debt deflation.

from increases in interest rates abroad), a steep stock market decline, and an increase in uncertainty resulting from a failure of major financial or nonfinancial firms (the Ohio Life Insurance & Trust Company in 1857, the Northern Pacific Railroad and Jay Cooke & Company in 1873, Grant & Ward in 1884, the National Cordage Company in 1893, the Knickerbocker Trust Company in 1907, and the Bank of United States in 1930). During these crises, deterioration in banks' balance sheets, the increase in uncertainty, the rise in interest rates, and the stock market decline increased the severity of adverse selection problems in credit markets; and the stock market decline, the deterioration in banks' balance sheets, and the rise in interest rates (which decreased firms' cash flow) also increased moral hazard problems. The rise in adverse selection and moral hazard problems then made it less attractive for lenders to lend, which led to a decline in investment and aggregate economic activity.

Because of the worsening business conditions and uncertainty about their bank's health (perhaps banks would go broke), depositors began to withdraw their funds from banks, which led to bank panics. The resulting decline in the number of banks raised interest rates even further and decreased the amount of financial intermediation by banks. Worsening of the problems created by adverse selection and moral hazard led to further economic contraction.

Finally, there was a sorting out of firms that were **insolvent** (had a negative net worth and hence were bankrupt) from healthy firms by bankruptcy proceedings. The same process occurred for banks, often with the help of public and private authorities. Once this sorting out was complete, uncertainty in financial markets declined, the stock market underwent a recovery, and interest rates fell. The overall result was that adverse selection and moral hazard problems diminished and the financial crisis subsided. With the financial markets able to operate well again, the stage was set for the recovery of the economy.

If, however, the economic downturn led to a sharp decline in prices, the recovery process was short-circuited. In this situation, shown in Figure 3, a process called **debt deflation** occurred, in which a substantial decline in the price level set in, leading to a further deterioration in firms' net worth because of the increased burden of indebtedness. When debt deflation set in, the adverse selection and moral hazard problems continued to increase so that lending, investment spending, and aggregate economic activity remained depressed for a long time. The most significant financial crisis that included debt deflation was the Great Depression, the worst economic contraction in U.S. history (see the FYI box, "Case Study of a Financial Crisis: The Great Depression").

APPLICATION Financial Crises in Emerging-Market Countries: Mexico, 1994–1995; East Asia, 1997–1998; and Argentina, 2001–2002

In recent years, many emerging-market countries have experienced financial crises, the most dramatic of which were the Mexican crisis, which started in December 1994; the East Asian crisis, which started in July 1997; and the Argentine crisis, which started in 2001. An important puzzle is how a developing country can shift dramatically from a path of high growth before a financial crisis—as was true for Mexico and particularly the East Asian countries of Thailand, Malaysia, Indonesia, the Philippines, and South Korea—to a sharp decline in economic activity. We can apply our asymmetric

FYI Case Study of a Financial Crisis: The Great Depression

In 1928 and 1929, prices doubled in the U.S. stock market. Federal Reserve officials viewed the stock market boom as excessive speculation. To curb it, they pursued a tight monetary policy to raise interest rates; the Fed got more than it bargained for when the stock market crashed in October 1929, falling by more than 60%.

Although the 1929 crash had a great impact on the minds of a whole generation, most people forget that by the middle of 1930, more than half of the stock market decline had been reversed. What might have been a normal recession turned into something far different, however, with adverse shocks to the agricultural sector, a continuing decline in the stock market after the middle of 1930, and a sequence of bank collapses from October 1930 until March 1933 in which more than one-third of the banks in the United States went out of business (events described in more detail in the appendix to Chapter 19).

The continuing decline in stock prices after mid-1930 (by mid-1932 stocks had declined to 10% of their value at the 1929 peak) and the increase in uncertainty from the unsettled business conditions created by the economic contraction made adverse selection and moral hazard problems worse in the credit markets. The loss of one-third of the banks reduced the amount of financial intermediation. This intensified adverse selection and moral hazard problems and decreased the ability of financial markets to channel funds to firms with productive investment opportunities. As our analysis predicts, the amount of outstanding commercial loans fell by half from 1929 to 1933, and investment spending collapsed, declining by 90% from its 1929 level.

The short-circuiting of the process that kept the economy from recovering quickly, which it does in most recessions, occurred because of a fall in the price level by 25% in the 1930–1933 period. This huge decline in prices triggered a debt deflation in which net worth fell because of the increased burden of indebtedness borne by firms. The decline in net worth and the resulting increase in adverse selection and moral hazard problems in the credit markets led to a prolonged economic contraction in which unemployment rose to 25% of the labor force. The financial crisis in the Great Depression was the worst ever experienced in the United States, and it explains why this economic contraction was also the most severe one ever experienced by the nation.*

*See Ben Bernanke, "Nonmonetary Effects of the Financial Crisis in the Propagation of the Great Depression," *American Economic Review* 73 (1983): 257–276, for a discussion of the role of asymmetric information problems in the Great Depression period.

information analysis of financial crises to explain this puzzle and to understand the Mexican, East Asian, and Argentine financial situations.[7]

Because of the different institutional features of emerging-market countries' debt markets, the sequence of events in the Mexican, East Asian, and Argentine crises differs from that occurring in the United States in the nineteenth and twentieth centuries. Figure 4 diagrams the sequence of events that occurred in Mexico, East Asia, and Argentina.

[7]This chapter does not examine two other recent crises, those in Brazil and Russia. Russia's financial crisis in August 1998 can also be explained with the asymmetric information story here, but it is more appropriate to view it as a symptom of a wider breakdown in the economy—and this is why we do not focus on it here. The Brazilian crisis in January 1999 has features of a more traditional balance-of-payments crisis (see Chapter 21), rather than a financial crisis.

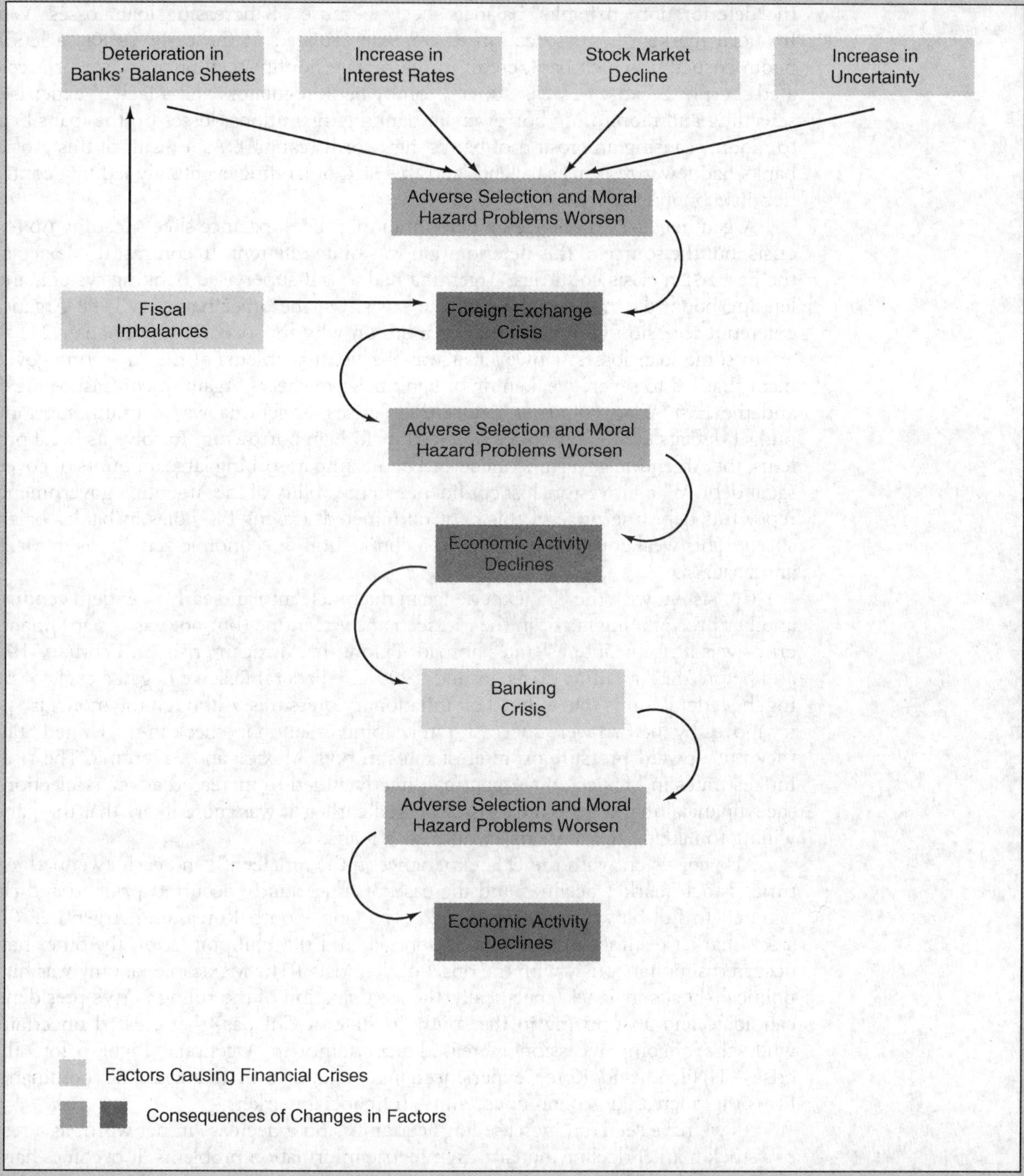

FIGURE 4 Sequence of Events in the Mexican, East Asian, and Argentine Financial Crises
The arrows trace the sequence of events during the financial crisis.

An important factor leading up to the financial crises in Mexico and East Asia was the deterioration in banks' balance sheets because of increasing loan losses. When financial markets in these countries were deregulated in the early 1990s, a lending boom ensued in which bank credit to the private nonfinancial business sector accelerated sharply. Because of weak supervision by bank regulators and a lack of expertise in screening and monitoring borrowers at banking institutions, losses on the loans began to mount, causing an erosion of banks' net worth (capital). As a result of this erosion, banks had fewer resources to lend, and this lack of lending eventually led to a contraction in economic activity.

Argentina also experienced a deterioration in bank balance sheets leading up to its crisis, but the source of this deterioration was quite different. In contrast to Mexico and the East Asian crisis countries, Argentina had a well-supervised banking system, and a lending boom did not occur before the crisis. On the other hand, in 1998 Argentina entered a recession (you can find out more on why this occurred in Chapter 21) that led to some loan losses. However, it was the fiscal problems of the Argentine government that led to severe weakening of bank balance sheets. Again in contrast to Mexico and the East Asian countries before their crises, Argentina was running substantial budget deficits that could not be financed by foreign borrowing. To solve its fiscal problems, the Argentine government coerced banks into absorbing large amounts of government debt. When investors lost confidence in the ability of the Argentine government to repay this debt, the price of this debt plummeted, leaving big holes in banks' balance sheets. This weakening helped lead to a contraction of economic activity, as in Mexico and East Asia.

Consistent with the U.S. experience in the nineteenth and early twentieth centuries, another precipitating factor in the Mexican and Argentine (but not East Asian) financial crises was a rise in interest rates abroad. Before the Mexican crisis, in February 1994, and before the Argentine crisis, in mid-1999, the Federal Reserve began a cycle of raising the federal funds rate to head off inflationary pressures. Although the monetary policy moves by the Fed were successful in keeping inflation in check in the United States, they put upward pressure on interest rates in both Mexico and Argentina. The rise in interest rates in Mexico and Argentina directly added to increased adverse selection in their financial markets because, as discussed earlier, it was more likely that the parties willing to take on the most risk would seek loans.

Also consistent with the U.S. experience in the nineteenth and early twentieth centuries, stock market declines and increases in uncertainty occurred prior to and contributed to full-blown crises in Mexico, Thailand, South Korea, and Argentina. (The stock market declines in Malaysia, Indonesia, and the Philippines, on the other hand, occurred simultaneously with the onset of the crisis.) The Mexican economy was hit by political shocks in 1994 (specifically, the assassination of the ruling party's presidential candidate and an uprising in the southern state of Chiapas) that created uncertainty, while the ongoing recession increased uncertainty in Argentina. Right before their crises, Thailand and Korea experienced major failures of financial and nonfinancial firms that increased general uncertainty in financial markets

As we have seen, an increase in uncertainty and a decrease in net worth as a result of a stock market decline increase asymmetric information problems. It becomes harder to screen out good from bad borrowers, and the decline in net worth decreases the value of firms' collateral and increases their incentives to make risky investments because there is less equity to lose if the investments are unsuccessful. The increase in uncertainty and stock market declines that occurred before the crisis, along with the deterioration in banks' balance sheets, worsened adverse selection and moral hazard problems (shown at the top of the diagram in Figure 4) and made the economies ripe for a serious financial crisis.

At this point, full-blown speculative attacks developed in the foreign exchange market, plunging these countries into a full-scale crisis. With the Colosio assassination, the Chiapas uprising, and the growing weakness in the banking sector, the Mexican peso came under attack. Even though the Mexican central bank intervened in the foreign exchange market and raised interest rates sharply, it was unable to stem the attack and was forced to devalue the peso on December 20, 1994. In the case of Thailand, concerns about the large current account deficit and weakness in the Thai financial system, culminating with the failure of a major finance company, Finance One, led to a successful speculative attack that forced the Thai central bank to allow the baht to float downward in July 1997. Soon thereafter, speculative attacks developed against the other countries in the region, leading to the collapse of the Philippine peso, the Indonesian rupiah, the Malaysian ringgit, and the South Korean won. In Argentina, a full-scale banking panic began in October–November 2001. This, along with realization that the government was going to default on its debt, also led to a speculative attack on the Argentine peso, resulting in its collapse on January 6, 2002.

The institutional structure of debt markets in Mexico and East Asia now interacted with the currency devaluations to propel the economies into full-fledged financial crises. Because so many firms in these countries had debt denominated in foreign currencies like the dollar and the yen, depreciation of their currencies resulted in increases in their indebtedness in domestic currency terms, even though the value of their assets remained unchanged. When the peso lost half its value by March 1995 and the Thai, Philippine, Malaysian, and South Korean currencies lost between a third and half of their value by the beginning of 1998, firms' balance sheets took a big negative hit, causing a dramatic increase in adverse selection and moral hazard problems. This negative shock was especially severe for Indonesia and Argentina, which saw the value of their currencies fall by more than 70%, resulting in insolvency for firms with substantial amounts of debt denominated in foreign currencies.

The collapse of currencies also led to a rise in actual and expected inflation in these countries, and market interest rates rose sky-high (to around 100% in Mexico and Argentina). The resulting increase in interest payments caused reductions in households' and firms' cash flow, which led to further deterioration in their balance sheets. A feature of debt markets in emerging-market countries, like those in Mexico, East Asia, and Argentina is that debt contracts have very short durations, typically less than one month. Thus the rise in short-term interest rates in these countries meant that the effect on cash flow and hence on balance sheets was substantial. As our asymmetric information analysis suggests, this deterioration in households' and firms' balance sheets increased adverse selection and moral hazard problems in the credit markets, making domestic and foreign lenders even less willing to lend.

Consistent with the theory of financial crises outlined in this chapter, the sharp decline in lending helped lead to a collapse of economic activity, with real GDP growth falling sharply.

As shown in Figure 4, further deterioration in the economy occurred because the collapse in economic activity and the deterioration in the cash flow and balance sheets of both firms and households led to worsening banking crises. The problems of firms and households meant that many of them were no longer able to pay off their debts, resulting in substantial losses for the banks. Even more problematic for the banks was that they had many short-term liabilities denominated in foreign currencies, and the sharp increase in the value of these liabilities after the devaluation led to a further deterioration in the banks' balance sheets. Under these circumstances, the banking system would have collapsed in the absence of a government safety net—as it did in the United States during the Great Depression—but with the assistance of the International Monetary Fund, these countries were in some cases able to protect depositors and avoid a bank panic. However, given the loss of bank capital and the need for the government to intervene to prop up the banks, the banks' ability to lend was nevertheless sharply curtailed. As we have seen, a banking crisis of this type hinders the ability of the banks to lend and also makes adverse selection and moral hazard problems worse in financial markets, because banks are less capable of playing their traditional financial intermediation role. The banking crisis, along with other factors that increased adverse selection and moral hazard problems in the credit markets of Mexico, East Asia, and Argentina, explains the collapse of lending and hence economic activity in the aftermath of the crisis.

Following their crises, Mexico began to recover in 1996, while the crisis countries in East Asia tentatively began their recovery in 1999, with a stronger recovery later. Argentina was still in a severe depression in 2003, but subsequently the economy has bounced back. In all these countries, the economic hardship caused by the financial crises was tremendous. Unemployment rose sharply, poverty increased substantially, and even the social fabric of the society was stretched thin. For example, Mexico City and Buenos Aires have become crime-ridden, while Indonesia has experienced waves of ethnic violence.

SUMMARY

1. There are eight basic facts about U.S. financial structure. The first four emphasize the importance of financial intermediaries and the relative unimportance of securities markets for the financing of corporations; the fifth recognizes that financial markets are among the most heavily regulated sectors of the economy; the sixth states that only large, well-established corporations have access to securities markets; the seventh indicates that collateral is an important feature of debt contracts; and the eighth presents debt contracts as complicated legal documents that place substantial restrictions on the behavior of the borrower.
2. Transaction costs freeze many small savers and borrowers out of direct involvement with financial markets. Financial intermediaries can take advantage of economies of scale and are better able to develop expertise to lower transaction costs, thus enabling their savers and borrowers to benefit from the existence of financial markets.
3. Asymmetric information results in two problems: adverse selection, which occurs before the transaction, and moral hazard, which occurs after the transaction. Adverse selection refers to the fact that bad credit risks are the ones most likely to seek loans, and moral hazard refers to the risk of the borrower's engaging in activities that are undesirable from the lender's point of view.
4. Adverse selection interferes with the efficient functioning of financial markets. Tools to help reduce the adverse selection problem include private production

and sale of information, government regulation to increase information, financial intermediation, and collateral and net worth. The free-rider problem occurs when people who do not pay for information take advantage of information that other people have paid for. This problem explains why financial intermediaries, particularly banks, play a more important role in financing the activities of businesses than securities markets do.

5. Moral hazard in equity contracts is known as the principal–agent problem, because managers (the agents) have less incentive to maximize profits than stockholders (the principals). The principal–agent problem explains why debt contracts are so much more prevalent in financial markets than equity contracts. Tools to help reduce the principal–agent problem include monitoring, government regulation to increase information, and financial intermediation.

6. Tools to reduce the moral hazard problem in debt contracts include net worth, monitoring and enforcement of restrictive covenants, and financial intermediaries.

7. Financial crises are major disruptions in financial markets. They are caused by increases in adverse selection and moral hazard problems that prevent financial markets from channeling funds to people with productive investment opportunities, leading to a sharp contraction in economic activity. The five types of factors that lead to financial crises are increases in interest rates, increases in uncertainty, asset market effects on balance sheets, problems in the banking sector, and government fiscal imbalances.

KEY TERMS

agency theory, pp. 188, 204
bank panic, p. 206
cash flow, p. 206
collateral, p. 185
conflicts of interest, p. 202
costly state verification, p. 195
debt deflation, p. 209
economies of scope, p. 201
financial crisis, p. 204
free-rider problem, p. 190
incentive-compatible, p. 198
insolvent, p. 209
net worth (equity capital), p. 193
principal–agent problem, p. 194
restrictive covenants, p. 185
secured debt, p. 185
state-owned banks, p. 203
unsecured debt, p. 185
venture capital firm, p. 196

QUESTIONS AND PROBLEMS

Questions marked with an asterisk are answered at the end of the book in an appendix, "Answers to Selected Questions and Problems." Questions marked with a blue circle indicate the question is available in MyEconLab at www.myeconlab.com/mishkin.

1. How can economies of scale help explain the existence of financial intermediaries?

*2. Describe two ways in which financial intermediaries help lower transaction costs in the economy.

3. Would moral hazard and adverse selection still arise in financial markets if information were not asymmetric? Explain.

*4. How do standard accounting principles help financial markets work more efficiently?

5. Do you think the lemons problem would be more severe for stocks traded on the New York Stock Exchange or those traded over-the-counter? Explain.

*6. Which firms are most likely to use bank financing rather than to issue bonds or stocks to finance their activities? Why?

7. How can the existence of asymmetric information provide a rationale for government regulation of financial markets?

*8. Would you be more willing to lend to a friend if she put all of her life savings into her business than you would if she had not done so? Why?

9. Rich people often worry that others will seek to marry them only for their money. Is this a problem of adverse selection?

*10. The more collateral there is backing a loan, the less the lender has to worry about adverse selection. Is this statement true, false, or uncertain? Explain your answer.

11. How does the free-rider problem aggravate adverse selection and moral hazard problems in financial markets?

*12. Explain how the separation of ownership and control in American corporations might lead to poor management.

13. Is a financial crisis more likely to occur when the economy is experiencing deflation or inflation? Explain.

*14. How can a stock market crash provoke a financial crisis?

15. How can a sharp rise in interest rates provoke a financial crisis?

WEB EXERCISES

1. In this chapter we discuss the lemons problem and its effect on the efficient functioning of a market. This theory was initially developed by George Akerlof. Go to www.nobel.se/economics/laureates/2001/public.html. This site reports that Akerlof, Spence, and Stiglitz were awarded the Nobel prize in economics in 2001 for their work. Read this report down through the section on George Akerlof. Summarize his research ideas in one page.

2. This chapter discusses how an understanding of adverse selection and moral hazard can help us better understand financial crises. The greatest financial crisis faced by the United States has been the Great Depression from 1929 to 1933. Go to www.amatecon.com/greatdepression.html. This site contains a brief discussion of the factors that led to the Great Depression. Write a one-page summary explaining how adverse selection and moral hazard contributed to the Great Depression.

WEB REFERENCES

www.nobel.se/economics/laureates/2001/public.html

A complete discussion of the lemons problem on a site dedicated to Nobel prize winners.

www.amatecon.com/gd/gdtimeline.html

A time line of the Great Depression.

CHAPTER

9 Banking and the Management of Financial Institutions

Preview

Because banking plays such a major role in channeling funds to borrowers with productive investment opportunities, this financial activity is important in ensuring that the financial system and the economy run smoothly and efficiently. In the United States, banks (depository institutions) supply more than \$6 trillion in credit annually. They provide loans to businesses, help us finance our college educations or the purchase of a new car or home, and provide us with services such as checking and savings accounts.

In this chapter, we examine how banking is conducted to earn the highest profits possible: how and why banks make loans, how they acquire funds and manage their assets and liabilities (debts), and how they earn income. Although we focus on commercial banking, because this is the most important financial intermediary activity, many of the same principles are applicable to other types of financial intermediation.

THE BANK BALANCE SHEET

To understand how banking works, we start by looking at the bank **balance sheet**, a list of the bank's assets and liabilities. As the name implies, this list balances; that is, it has the characteristic that

$$\text{total assets} = \text{total liabilities} + \text{capital}$$

A bank's balance sheet is also a list of its *sources* of bank funds (liabilities) and *uses* to which the funds are put (assets). Banks obtain funds by borrowing and by issuing other liabilities such as deposits. They then use these funds to acquire assets such as securities and loans. Banks make profits by charging an interest rate on their asset holdings of securities and loans that is higher than the expenses on their liabilities. The balance sheet of all commercial banks as of January 2006 appears in Table 1.

Liabilities

A bank acquires funds by issuing (selling) liabilities, such as deposits, which are the *sources of funds* the bank uses. The funds obtained from issuing liabilities are used to purchase income-earning assets.

TABLE 1 Balance Sheet of All Commercial Banks (items as a percentage of the total, January 2006)

Assets (Uses of Funds)*		Liabilities (Sources of Funds)	
Reserves and cash items	4%	Checkable deposits	7%
Securities		Nontransaction deposits	
U.S. government and agency	13	Small-denomination time deposits	
State and local government and		(< $100,000) + savings deposits	43
other securities	10	Large-denomination time deposits	16
Loans		Borrowings	26
Commercial and industrial	12	Bank capital	8
Real estate	34		
Consumer	8		
Interbank	3		
Other	9		
Other assets (for example,			
physical capital)	7		
Total	100	Total	100

*In order of decreasing liquidity.

Source: www.federalreserve.gov/releases/h8/current/.

Checkable Deposits. Checkable deposits are bank accounts that allow the owner of the account to write checks to third parties. Checkable deposits include all accounts on which checks can be drawn: non–interest-bearing checking accounts (demand deposits), interest-bearing NOW (negotiable order of withdrawal) accounts, and money market deposit accounts (MMDAs). Introduced with the Depository Institutions Act in 1982, MMDAs have features similar to those of money market mutual funds and are included in the checkable deposits category. However, MMDAs are not subject to reserve requirements (discussed later in the chapter) as checkable deposits are and are not included in the M1 definition of money. Table 1 shows that the category of checkable deposits is an important source of bank funds, making up 7% of bank liabilities. Once checkable deposits were the most important source of bank funds (more than 60% of bank liabilities in 1960), but with the appearance of new, more attractive financial instruments, such as money market deposit accounts, the share of checkable deposits in total bank liabilities has shrunk over time.

Checkable deposits and money market deposit accounts are payable on demand; that is, if a depositor shows up at the bank and requests payment by making a withdrawal, the bank must pay the depositor immediately. Similarly, if a person who receives a check written on an account from a bank, presents that check at the bank, it must pay the funds out immediately.

A checkable deposit is an asset for the depositor because it is part of his or her wealth. Because the depositor can withdraw funds and the bank is obligated to pay, checkable deposits are a liability for the bank. They are usually the lowest-cost source of bank funds because depositors are willing to forgo some interest to have access to a liquid asset that can be used to make purchases. The bank's costs of maintaining checkable deposits include interest payments and the costs incurred in servicing these accounts—processing, preparing, and sending out monthly statements, providing efficient tellers (human or otherwise), maintaining an impressive building and conveniently located branches, and advertising and marketing to entice customers to deposit their funds with a given bank. In recent years, interest paid on deposits (checkable and time) has accounted for around 25% of total bank operating expenses, while the costs involved in servicing accounts (employee salaries, building rent, and so on) have been approximately 50% of operating expenses.

Nontransaction Deposits. Nontransaction deposits are the primary source of bank funds (59% of bank liabilities in Table 1). Owners cannot write checks on nontransaction deposits, but the interest rates paid on these deposits are usually higher than those on checkable deposits. There are two basic types of nontransaction deposits: savings accounts and time deposits (also called certificates of deposit, or CDs).

Savings accounts were once the most common type of nontransaction deposit. In these accounts, to which funds can be added or from which funds can be withdrawn at any time, transactions and interest payments are recorded in a monthly statement or in a passbook held by the owner of the account.

Time deposits have a fixed maturity length, ranging from several months to over five years, and assess substantial penalties for early withdrawal (the forfeiture of several months' interest). Small-denomination time deposits (deposits of less than $100,000) are less liquid for the depositor than passbook savings, earn higher interest rates, and are a more costly source of funds for the banks.

Large-denomination time deposits (CDs) are available in denominations of $100,000 or more and are typically bought by corporations or other banks. Large-denomination CDs are negotiable; like bonds, they can be resold in a secondary market before they mature. For this reason, negotiable CDs are held by corporations, money market mutual funds, and other financial institutions as alternative assets to Treasury bills and other short-term bonds. Since 1961, when they first appeared, negotiable CDs have become an important source of bank funds (16%).

Borrowings. Banks also obtain funds by borrowing from the Federal Reserve System, the Federal Home Loan banks, other banks, and corporations. Borrowings from the Fed are called **discount loans** (also known as *advances*). Banks also borrow reserves overnight in the federal (fed) funds market from other U.S. banks and financial institutions. Banks borrow funds overnight to have enough deposits at the Federal Reserve to meet the amount required by the Fed. (The *federal funds* designation is somewhat confusing, because these loans are not made by the federal government or by the Federal Reserve, but rather by banks to other banks.) Other sources of borrowed funds are loans made to banks by their parent companies (bank holding companies), loan arrangements with corporations (such as repurchase agreements), and borrowings of Eurodollars (deposits denominated in U.S. dollars residing in foreign banks or foreign branches of U.S. banks). Borrowings have become a more important source of bank funds over time: In 1960, they made up only 2% of bank liabilities; currently, they are 26% of bank liabilities.

Bank Capital. The final category on the liabilities side of the balance sheet is bank capital, the bank's net worth, which equals the difference between total assets and liabilities (8% of total bank assets in Table 1). Bank capital is raised by selling new equity (stock) or from retained earnings. Bank capital is a cushion against a drop in the value of its assets, which could force the bank into insolvency (having liabilities in excess of assets, meaning that the bank can be forced into liquidation).

Assets

A bank uses the funds that it has acquired by issuing liabilities to purchase income-earning assets. Bank assets are thus naturally referred to as *uses of funds*, and the interest payments earned on them are what enable banks to make profits.

Reserves. All banks hold some of the funds they acquire as deposits in an account at the Fed. **Reserves** are these deposits plus currency that is physically held by banks (called **vault cash** because it is stored in bank vaults overnight). Although reserves currently do not pay any interest, banks hold them for two reasons. First, some reserves, called **required reserves**, are held because of **reserve requirements**, the regulation that for every dollar of checkable deposits at a bank, a certain fraction (10 cents, for example) must be kept as reserves. This fraction (10% in the example) is called the **required reserve ratio**. Banks hold additional reserves, called **excess reserves**, because they are the most liquid of all bank assets and can be used by a bank to meet its obligations when funds are withdrawn, either directly by a depositor or indirectly when a check is written on an account.

Cash Items in Process of Collection. Suppose that a check written on an account at another bank is deposited in your bank and the funds for this check have not yet been received (collected) from the other bank. The check is classified as a cash item in process of collection, and it is an asset for your bank because it is a claim on another bank for funds that will be paid within a few days.

Deposits at Other Banks. Many small banks hold deposits in larger banks in exchange for a variety of services, including check collection, foreign exchange transactions, and help with securities purchases. This is an aspect of a system called *correspondent banking*.

Collectively, reserves, cash items in process of collection, and deposits at other banks are referred to as *cash items*. In Table 1, they constitute only 4% of total assets, and their importance has been shrinking over time: In 1960, for example, they accounted for 20% of total assets.

Securities. A bank's holdings of securities are an important income-earning asset: Securities (made up entirely of debt instruments for commercial banks, because banks are not allowed to hold stock) account for 23% of bank assets in Table 1, and they provide commercial banks with about 10% of their revenue. These securities can be classified into three categories: U.S. government and agency securities, state and local government securities, and other securities. The U.S. government and agency securities are the most liquid because they can be easily traded and converted into cash with low transaction costs. Because of their high liquidity, short-term U.S. government securities are called **secondary reserves**.

Banks hold state and local government securities because state and local governments are more likely to do business with banks that hold their securities. State and local government and other securities are both less marketable (less liquid) and riskier than U.S. government securities, primarily because of default risk: There is some possibility that the issuer of the securities may not be able to make its interest payments or pay back the face value of the securities when they mature.

Loans. Banks make their profits primarily by issuing loans. In Table 1, some 66% of bank assets are in the form of loans, and in recent years they have generally produced more than half of bank revenues. A loan is a liability for the individual or corporation receiving it, but an asset for a bank, because it provides income to the bank. Loans are typically less liquid than other assets, because they cannot be turned into cash until the loan matures. If the bank makes a one-year loan, for example, it cannot get its funds back until the loan comes due in one year. Loans also have a higher probability of default than other assets. Because of the lack of liquidity and higher default risk, the bank earns its highest return on loans.

As you saw in Table 1, the largest categories of loans for commercial banks are commercial and industrial loans made to businesses and real estate loans. Commercial banks also make consumer loans and lend to each other. The bulk of these interbank loans are overnight loans lent in the federal funds market. The major difference in the balance sheets of the various depository institutions is primarily in the type of loan in which they specialize. Savings and loans and mutual savings banks, for example, specialize in residential mortgages, while credit unions tend to make consumer loans.

Other Assets. The physical capital (bank buildings, computers, and other equipment) owned by the banks is included in this category.

BASIC BANKING

Before proceeding to a more detailed study of how a bank manages its assets and liabilities to make the highest profit, you should understand the basic operation of a bank.

In general terms, banks make profits by selling liabilities with one set of characteristics (a particular combination of liquidity, risk, size, and return) and using the proceeds to buy assets with a different set of characteristics. This process is often referred to as *asset transformation*. For example, a savings deposit held by one person can provide the funds that enable the bank to make a mortgage loan to another person. The bank has, in effect, transformed the savings deposit (an asset held by the depositor) into a mortgage loan (an asset held by the bank). Another way this process of asset transformation is described is to say that the bank "borrows short and lends long" because it makes long-term loans and funds them by issuing short-dated deposits.

The process of transforming assets and providing a set of services (check clearing, record keeping, credit analysis, and so forth) is like any other production process in a firm. If the bank produces desirable services at low cost and earns substantial income on its assets, it earns profits; if not, the bank suffers losses.

To make our analysis of the operation of a bank more concrete, we use a tool called a **T-account**. A T-account is a simplified balance sheet, with lines in the form of a T, that lists only the changes that occur in balance sheet items starting from some initial balance sheet position. Let's say that Jane Brown has heard that the First National Bank provides excellent service, so she opens a checking account with a $100 bill. She now has a $100 checkable deposit at the bank, which shows up as a $100 liability on the bank's balance sheet. The bank now puts her $100 bill into its vault so that the bank's assets rise by the $100 increase in vault cash. The T-account for the bank looks like this:

First National Bank

Assets		Liabilities	
Vault cash	+$100	Checkable deposits	+$100

Because vault cash is also part of the bank's reserves, we can rewrite the T-account as follows:

Assets		Liabilities	
Reserves	+$100	Checkable deposits	+$100

Note that Jane Brown's opening of a checking account leads to *an increase in the bank's reserves equal to the increase in checkable deposits*.

If Jane had opened her account with a $100 check written on an account at another bank, say, the Second National Bank, we would get the same result. The initial effect on the T-account of the First National Bank is as follows:

Assets		Liabilities	
Cash items in process of collection	+$100	Checkable deposits	+$100

Checkable deposits increase by $100 as before, but now the First National Bank is owed $100 by the Second National Bank. This asset for the First National Bank is entered in the T-account as $100 of cash items in process of collection because the First National Bank will now try to collect the funds that it is owed. It could go directly to the Second National Bank and ask for payment of the funds, but if the two banks are in separate states, that would be a time-consuming and costly process. Instead, the First National Bank deposits the check in its account at the Fed, and the Fed collects the funds from the Second National Bank. The result is that the Fed transfers $100 of reserves from the Second National Bank to the First National Bank, and the final balance sheet positions of the two banks are as follows:

First National Bank				Second National Bank			
Assets		Liabilities		Assets		Liabilities	
Reserves	+$100	Checkable deposits	+$100	Reserves	−$100	Checkable deposits	−$100

The process initiated by Jane Brown can be summarized as follows: When a check written on an account at one bank is deposited in another, the bank receiving the deposit gains reserves equal to the amount of the check, while the bank on which the check is written sees its reserves fall by the same amount. Therefore, ***when a bank receives additional deposits, it gains an equal amount of reserves; when it loses deposits, it loses an equal amount of reserves.***

STUDY GUIDE

T-accounts are used to study various topics throughout this text. Whenever you see a T-account, try to analyze what would happen if the opposite action were taken; for example, what would happen if Jane Brown decided to close her $100 account at the First National Bank by writing a $100 check and depositing it in a new checking account at the Second National Bank?

Now that you understand how banks gain and lose reserves, we can examine how a bank rearranges its balance sheet to make a profit when it experiences a change in its deposits. Let's return to the situation when the First National Bank has just received the extra $100 of checkable deposits. As you know, the bank is obliged to keep a certain fraction of its checkable deposits as required reserves. If the fraction (the required reserve ratio) is 10%, the First National Bank's required reserves have increased by $10, and we can rewrite its T-account as follows:

First National Bank

Assets		Liabilities	
Required reserves	+$10	Checkable deposits	+$100
Excess reserves	+$90		

Let's see how well the bank is doing as a result of the additional checkable deposits. Because reserves pay no interest, it has no income from the additional $100 of assets. But servicing the extra $100 of checkable deposits is costly, because the bank must keep records, pay tellers, pay for check clearing, and so forth. The bank is taking a loss! The situation is even worse if the bank makes interest payments on the deposits, as with NOW accounts. If it is to make a profit, the bank must put to productive use all or part of the $90 of excess reserves it has available.

Let us assume that the bank chooses not to hold any excess reserves but to make loans instead. The T-account then looks like this:

Assets		Liabilities	
Required reserves	+$10	Checkable deposits	+$100
Loans	+$90		

The bank is now making a profit because it holds short-term liabilities such as checkable deposits and uses the proceeds to buy longer-term assets such as loans with higher interest rates. As mentioned earlier, this process of asset transformation is frequently described by saying that banks are in the business of "borrowing short and lending long." For example, if the loans have an interest rate of 10% per year, the bank earns $9 in income from its loans over the year. If the $100 of checkable deposits is in a NOW account with a 5% interest rate and it costs another $3 per year to service the account, the cost per year of these deposits is $8. The bank's profit on the new deposits is then $1 per year (a 1% return on assets).

GENERAL PRINCIPLES OF BANK MANAGEMENT

Now that you have some idea of how a bank operates, let's look at how a bank manages its assets and liabilities to earn the highest possible profit. The bank manager has four primary concerns. The first is to make sure that the bank has enough ready cash to pay its depositors when there are **deposit outflows**—that is, when deposits are lost because depositors make withdrawals and demand payment. To keep enough cash on hand, the bank must engage in **liquidity management**, the acquisition of sufficiently liquid assets to meet the bank's obligations to depositors. Second, the bank manager must pursue an acceptably low level of risk by acquiring assets that have a low rate of default and by diversifying asset holdings (**asset management**). The third concern is to acquire funds at low cost (**liability management**). Finally, the manager must decide the amount of capital the bank should maintain and then acquire the needed capital (**capital adequacy management**).

To understand bank and other financial institution management fully, we must go beyond the general principles of bank asset and liability management described next and look in more detail at how a financial institution manages its assets. The two sections following this one provide an in-depth discussion of how a financial institution manages **credit risk**, the risk arising because borrowers may default, and how it manages **interest-rate risk**, the riskiness of earnings and returns on bank assets that results from interest-rate changes.

Liquidity Management and the Role of Reserves

Let us see how a typical bank, the First National Bank, can deal with deposit outflows that occur when its depositors withdraw cash from checking or savings accounts or write checks that are deposited in other banks. In the example that follows, we assume that the bank has ample excess reserves and that all deposits have the same required reserve ratio of 10% (the bank is required to keep 10% of its time and checkable deposits as reserves). Suppose that the First National Bank's initial balance sheet is as follows:

Assets		Liabilities	
Reserves	$20 million	Deposits	$100 million
Loans	$80 million	Bank capital	$ 10 million
Securities	$10 million		

The bank's required reserves are 10% of $100 million, or $10 million. Given that it holds $20 million of reserves, the First National Bank has excess reserves of $10 million. If a deposit outflow of $10 million occurs, the bank's balance sheet becomes

Assets		Liabilities	
Reserves	$10 million	Deposits	$90 million
Loans	$80 million	Bank capital	$10 million
Securities	$10 million		

The bank loses $10 million of deposits *and* $10 million of reserves, but because its required reserves are now 10% of only $90 million ($9 million), its reserves still exceed this amount by $1 million. In short, ***if a bank has ample excess reserves, a deposit outflow does not necessitate changes in other parts of its balance sheet.***

The situation is quite different when a bank holds insufficient excess reserves. Let's assume that instead of initially holding $10 million in excess reserves, the First National Bank makes loans of $10 million, so that it holds no excess reserves. Its initial balance sheet would be

Assets		Liabilities	
Reserves	$10 million	Deposits	$100 million
Loans	$90 million	Bank capital	$ 10 million
Securities	$10 million		

When it suffers the $10 million deposit outflow, its balance sheet becomes

Assets		Liabilities	
Reserves	$ 0	Deposits	$90 million
Loans	$90 million	Bank capital	$10 million
Securities	$10 million		

After $10 million has been withdrawn from deposits and hence reserves, the bank has a problem: It has a reserve requirement of 10% of $90 million, or $9 million, but it has no reserves! To eliminate this shortfall, the bank has four basic options. One is to acquire reserves to meet a deposit outflow by borrowing them from other banks in the federal funds market or by borrowing from corporations.[1] If the First National Bank acquires the $9 million shortfall in reserves by borrowing it from other banks or corporations, its balance sheet becomes

Assets		Liabilities	
Reserves	$ 9 million	Deposits	$90 million
Loans	$90 million	Borrowings from other banks or corporations	$ 9 million
Securities	$10 million	Bank capital	$10 million

[1]One way that the First National Bank can borrow from other banks and corporations is by selling negotiable certificates of deposit. This method for obtaining funds is discussed in the section on liability management.

The cost of this activity is the interest rate on these borrowings, such as the federal funds rate.

A second alternative is for the bank to sell some of its securities to help cover the deposit outflow. For example, it might sell $9 million of its securities and deposit the proceeds with the Fed, resulting in the following balance sheet:

Assets		Liabilities	
Reserves	$ 9 million	Deposits	$90 million
Loans	$90 million	Bank capital	$10 million
Securities	$ 1 million		

The bank incurs some brokerage and other transaction costs when it sells these securities. The U.S. government securities that are classified as secondary reserves are very liquid, so the transaction costs of selling them are quite modest. However, the other securities the bank holds are less liquid, and the transaction cost can be appreciably higher.

A third way that the bank can meet a deposit outflow is to acquire reserves by borrowing from the Fed. In our example, the First National Bank could leave its security and loan holdings the same and borrow $9 million in discount loans from the Fed. Its balance sheet would be

Assets		Liabilities	
Reserves	$ 9 million	Deposits	$90 million
Loans	$90 million	Borrowings from the Fed	$ 9 million
Securities	$10 million	Bank capital	$10 million

The cost associated with discount loans is the interest rate that must be paid to the Fed (called the **discount rate**).

Finally, a bank can acquire the $9 million of reserves to meet the deposit outflow by reducing its loans by this amount and depositing the $9 million it then receives with the Fed, thereby increasing its reserves by $9 million. This transaction changes the balance sheet as follows:

Assets		Liabilities	
Reserves	$ 9 million	Deposits	$90 million
Loans	$81 million	Bank capital	$10 million
Securities	$10 million		

The First National Bank is once again in good shape because its $9 million of reserves satisfies the reserve requirement.

However, this process of reducing its loans is the bank's costliest way of acquiring reserves when there is a deposit outflow. If the First National Bank has numerous short-term loans renewed at fairly short intervals, it can reduce its total amount of loans outstanding fairly quickly by *calling in* loans—that is, by not renewing some loans when they come due. Unfortunately for the bank, this is likely to antagonize the customers whose loans are not being renewed because they have not done anything to deserve such treatment. Indeed, they are likely to take their business elsewhere in the future, a very costly consequence for the bank.

A second method for reducing its loans is for the bank to sell them off to other banks. Again, this is very costly because other banks do not personally know the customers who have taken out the loans and so may not be willing to buy the loans at their full value (This is just the lemons adverse selection problem described in Chapter 8.)

The foregoing discussion explains why banks hold excess reserves even though loans or securities earn a higher return. When a deposit outflow occurs, holding excess reserves allows the bank to escape the costs of (1) borrowing from other banks or corporations, (2) selling securities, (3) borrowing from the Fed, or (4) calling in or selling off loans. ***Excess reserves are insurance against the costs associated with deposit outflows. The higher the costs associated with deposit outflows, the more excess reserves banks will want to hold.***

Just as you and I would be willing to pay an insurance company to insure us against a casualty loss such as the theft of a car, a bank is willing to pay the cost of holding excess reserves (the opportunity cost, the earnings forgone by not holding income-earning assets such as loans or securities) to insure against losses due to deposit outflows. Because excess reserves, like insurance, have a cost, banks also take other steps to protect themselves; for example, they might shift their holdings of assets to more liquid securities (secondary reserves).

STUDY GUIDE

Bank management is easier to grasp if you put yourself in the banker's shoes and imagine what you would do in the situations described. To understand a bank's possible responses to deposit outflows, imagine how you as a banker might respond to two successive deposit outflows of $10 million.

Asset Management

Now that you understand why a bank has a need for liquidity, we can examine the basic strategy a bank pursues in managing its assets. To maximize its profits, a bank must simultaneously seek the highest returns possible on loans and securities, reduce risk, and make adequate provisions for liquidity by holding liquid assets. Banks try to accomplish these three goals in four basic ways.

First, banks try to find borrowers who will pay high interest rates and are unlikely to default on their loans. They seek out loan business by advertising their borrowing rates and by approaching corporations directly to solicit loans. It is up to the bank's loan officer to decide if potential borrowers are good credit risks who will make interest and principal payments on time (i.e., engage in screening to reduce the adverse selection problem). Typically, banks are conservative in their loan policies; the default rate is usually less than 1%. It is important, however, that banks not be so conservative that they miss out on attractive lending opportunities that earn high interest rates.

Second, banks try to purchase securities with high returns and low risk. Third, in managing their assets, banks must attempt to lower risk by diversifying. They accomplish this by purchasing many different types of assets (short- and long-term, U.S. Treasury, and municipal bonds) and approving many types of loans to a number of customers. Banks that have not sufficiently sought the benefits of diversification often come to regret it later. For example, banks that had overspecialized in making loans to energy companies, real estate developers, or farmers suffered huge losses in the 1980s with the slump in energy, property, and farm prices. Indeed, many of these banks went broke because they had "put too many eggs in one basket."

Finally, the bank must manage the liquidity of its assets so that it can satisfy its reserve requirements without bearing huge costs. This means that it will hold liquid securities even if they earn a somewhat lower return than other assets. The bank must decide, for example, how much in excess reserves must be held to avoid costs from a deposit outflow. In addition, it will want to hold U.S. government securities as secondary reserves so that even if a deposit outflow forces some costs on the bank, these will not be terribly high. Again, it is not wise for a bank to be too conservative. If it avoids all costs associated with deposit outflows by holding only excess reserves, the bank suffers losses because reserves earn no interest, while the bank's liabilities are costly to maintain. The bank must balance its desire for liquidity against the increased earnings that can be obtained from less liquid assets such as loans.

Liability Management

Before the 1960s, liability management was a staid affair: For the most part, banks took their liabilities as fixed and spent their time trying to achieve an optimal mix of assets. There were two main reasons for the emphasis on asset management. First, more than 60% of the sources of bank funds were obtained through checkable (demand) deposits that by law could not pay any interest. Thus banks could not actively compete with one another for these deposits by paying interest on them, and so their amount was effectively a given for an individual bank. Second, because the markets for making overnight loans between banks were not well developed, banks rarely borrowed from other banks to meet their reserve needs.

Starting in the 1960s, however, large banks (called **money center banks**) in key financial centers, such as New York, Chicago, and San Francisco, began to explore ways in which the liabilities on their balance sheets could provide them with reserves and liquidity. This led to an expansion of overnight loan markets, such as the federal funds market, and the development of new financial instruments such as negotiable CDs (first developed in 1961), which enabled money center banks to acquire funds quickly.[2]

This new flexibility in liability management meant that banks could take a different approach to bank management. They no longer needed to depend on checkable deposits as the primary source of bank funds and as a result no longer treated their sources of funds (liabilities) as given. Instead, they aggressively set target goals for their asset growth and tried to acquire funds (by issuing liabilities) as they were needed.

For example, today, when a money center bank finds an attractive loan opportunity, it can acquire funds by selling a negotiable CD. Or, if it has a reserve shortfall, it can bor-

---

[2]Because small banks are not as well known as money center banks and so might be a higher credit risk, they find it harder to raise funds in the negotiable CD market. Hence they do not engage nearly as actively in liability management.

row funds from another bank in the federal funds market without incurring high transaction costs. The federal funds market can also be used to finance loans. Because of the increased importance of liability management, most banks now manage both sides of the balance sheet together in an *asset–liability management (ALM) committee*.

The greater emphasis on liability management explains some of the important changes over the past three decades in the composition of banks' balance sheets. While negotiable CDs and bank borrowings have greatly increased in importance as a source of bank funds in recent years (rising from 2% of bank liabilities in 1960 to 42% by the end of 2005), checkable deposits have decreased in importance (from 61% of bank liabilities in 1960 to 7% in 2005). Newfound flexibility in liability management and the search for higher profits have also stimulated banks to increase the proportion of their assets held in loans, which earn higher income (from 46% of bank assets in 1960 to 66% in 2005).

Capital Adequacy Management

Banks have to make decisions about the amount of capital they need to hold for three reasons. First, bank capital helps prevents *bank failure*, a situation in which the bank cannot satisfy its obligations to pay its depositors and other creditors and so goes out of business. Second, the amount of capital affects returns for the owners (equity holders) of the bank. Third, a minimum amount of bank capital (bank capital requirements) is required by regulatory authorities.

How Bank Capital Helps Prevent Bank Failure.

Let's consider two banks with identical balance sheets, except that the High Capital Bank has a ratio of capital to assets of 10% while the Low Capital Bank has a ratio of 4%.

High Capital Bank

Assets		Liabilities	
Reserves	\$10 million	Deposits	\$90 million
Loans	\$90 million	Bank capital	\$10 million

Low Capital Bank

Assets		Liabilities	
Reserves	\$10 million	Deposits	\$96 million
Loans	\$90 million	Bank capital	\$ 4 million

Suppose that both banks get caught up in the euphoria of the telecom market, only to find that \$5 million of their telecom loans became worthless later. When these bad loans are written off (valued at zero), the total value of assets declines by \$5 million. As a consequence, bank capital, which equals total assets minus liabilities, also declines by \$5 million. The balance sheets of the two banks now look like this:

High Capital Bank

Assets		Liabilities	
Reserves	\$10 million	Deposits	\$90 million
Loans	\$85 million	Bank capital	\$ 5 million

Low Capital Bank

Assets		Liabilities	
Reserves	\$10 million	Deposits	\$96 million
Loans	\$85 million	Bank capital	−\$ 1 million

The High Capital Bank takes the \$5 million loss in stride because its initial cushion of \$10 million in capital means that it still has a positive net worth (bank capital) of \$5 million after the loss. The Low Capital Bank, however, is in big trouble. Now the value of its assets has fallen below its liabilities, and its net worth is now −\$1 million. Because the bank has a negative net worth, it is insolvent: It does not have sufficient assets to pay off all holders of its liabilities. When a bank becomes insolvent, government regulators close the bank, its assets are sold off, and its managers are fired. Because the owners of the Low Capital Bank will find their investment wiped out, they would clearly have preferred the bank to have had a large enough cushion of bank capital to absorb the losses, as was the case for the High Capital Bank. We therefore see an important rationale for a bank to maintain a sufficient level of capital: ***A bank maintains bank capital to lessen the chance that it will become insolvent.***

How the Amount of Bank Capital Affects Returns to Equity Holders. Because owners of a bank must know whether their bank is being managed well, they need good measures of bank profitability. A basic measure of bank profitability is the **return on assets (ROA)**, the net profit after taxes per dollar of assets:

$$\text{ROA} = \frac{\text{net profit after taxes}}{\text{assets}}$$

The return on assets provides information on how efficiently a bank is being run, because it indicates how much profits are generated on average by each dollar of assets.

However, what the bank's owners (equity holders) care about most is how much the bank is earning on their equity investment. This information is provided by the other basic measure of bank profitability, the **return on equity (ROE)**, the net profit after taxes per dollar of equity (bank) capital:

$$\text{ROE} = \frac{\text{net profit after taxes}}{\text{equity capital}}$$

There is a direct relationship between the return on assets (which measures how efficiently the bank is run) and the return on equity (which measures how well the owners are doing on their investment). This relationship is determined by the **equity multiplier (EM)**, the amount of assets per dollar of equity capital:

$$\text{EM} = \frac{\text{assets}}{\text{equity capital}}$$

To see this, we note that

$$\frac{\text{net profit after taxes}}{\text{equity capital}} = \frac{\text{net profit after taxes}}{\text{assets}} \times \frac{\text{assets}}{\text{equity capital}}$$

which, using our definitions, yields

$$\text{ROE} = \text{ROA} \times \text{EM} \qquad (1)$$

The formula in Equation 1 tells us what happens to the return on equity when a bank holds a smaller amount of capital (equity) for a given amount of assets. As we have seen, the High Capital Bank initially has \$100 million of assets and \$10 million of equity, which gives it an equity multiplier of 10 (= \$100 million/\$10 million). The Low Capital Bank, by contrast, has only \$4 million of equity, so its equity multiplier is higher, equaling 25 (= \$100 million/\$4 million). Suppose that these banks have been equally well run so that they both have the same return on assets, 1%. The return on equity for the High Capital Bank equals 1% × 10 = 10%, while the return on equity for the Low Capital Bank equals 1% × 25 = 25%. The equity holders in the Low Capital Bank are clearly a lot happier than the equity holders in the High Capital Bank because they are earning more than twice as high a return. We now see why owners of a bank may not want it to hold too much capital. ***Given the return on assets, the lower the bank capital, the higher the return for the owners of the bank.***

Trade-off Between Safety and Returns to Equity Holders. We now see that bank capital has both benefits and costs. Bank capital benefits the owners of a bank in that it makes their investment safer by reducing the likelihood of bankruptcy. But bank capital is costly because the higher it is, the lower will be the return on equity for a given return on assets. In determining the amount of bank capital, managers must decide how much of the increased safety that comes with higher capital (the benefit) they are willing to trade off against the lower return on equity that comes with higher capital (the cost).

In more uncertain times, when the possibility of large losses on loans increases, bank managers might want to hold more capital to protect the equity holders. Conversely, if they have confidence that loan losses won't occur, they might want to reduce the amount of bank capital, have a high equity multiplier, and thereby increase the return on equity.

Bank Capital Requirements. Banks also hold capital because they are required to do so by regulatory authorities. Because of the high costs of holding capital for the reasons just described, bank managers often want to hold less bank capital relative to assets than is required by the regulatory authorities. In this case, the amount of bank capital is determined by the bank capital requirements. We discuss the details of bank capital requirements and their important role in bank regulation in Chapter 11.

APPLICATION Strategies for Managing Bank Capital

Suppose that as the manager of the First National Bank, you have to make decisions about the appropriate amount of bank capital. Looking at the balance sheet of the bank, which like the High Capital Bank has a ratio of bank capital to assets of 10% ($10 million of capital and $100 million of assets), you are concerned that the large amount of bank capital is causing the return on equity to be too low. You conclude that the bank has a capital surplus and should increase the equity multiplier to increase the return on equity. What should you do?

To lower the amount of capital relative to assets and raise the equity multiplier, you can do any of three things: (1) You can reduce the amount of bank capital by buying back some of the bank's stock. (2) You can reduce the bank's capital by paying out higher dividends to its stockholders, thereby reducing the bank's retained earnings. (3) You can keep bank capital constant but increase the bank's assets by acquiring new funds—say, by issuing CDs—and then seeking out loan business or purchasing more securities with these new funds. Because you think that it would enhance your position with the stockholders, you decide to pursue the second alternative and raise the dividend on the First National Bank stock.

Now suppose that the First National Bank is in a similar situation to the Low Capital Bank and has a ratio of bank capital to assets of 4%. You now worry that the bank is short on capital relative to assets because it does not have a sufficient cushion to prevent bank failure. To raise the amount of capital relative to assets, you now have the following three choices: (1) You can raise capital for the bank by having it issue equity (common stock). (2) You can raise capital by reducing the bank's dividends to shareholders, thereby increasing retained earnings that it can put into its capital account. (3) You can keep capital at the same level but reduce the bank's assets by making fewer loans or by selling off securities and then using the proceeds to reduce its liabilities. Suppose that raising bank capital is not easy to do at the current time because capital markets are tight or because shareholders will protest if their dividends are cut. Then you might have to choose the third alternative and decide to shrink the size of the bank.

In past years, many banks experienced capital shortfalls and had to restrict asset growth, as you might have to do if the First National Bank were short of capital. The important consequences of this for the credit markets are discussed in the application that follows.

APPLICATION Did the Capital Crunch Cause a Credit Crunch in the Early 1990s?

During the 1990–1991 recession and the year following, there occurred a slowdown in the growth of credit that was unprecedented in the post–World War II era. Many economists and politicians have claimed that there was a "credit crunch" during this period in which credit was hard to get, and as a result the performance of the economy in 1990–1992 was very weak. Was the slowdown in credit growth a manifestation of a credit crunch, and if so, what caused it?

Our analysis of how a bank manages bank capital suggests that a credit crunch was likely to have occurred in 1990–1992 and that it was caused at least in part by the capital crunch, in which shortfalls of bank capital led to slower credit growth.

The period of the late 1980s saw a boom and then a major bust in the real estate market that led to huge losses for banks on their real estate loans. As our example of how bank capital helps prevent bank failures demonstrates, the loan losses caused a substantial fall in the amount of bank capital. At the same time, regulators were raising capital requirements (a subject discussed in Chapter 11). The resulting capital shortfalls meant that banks had to either raise new capital or restrict their asset growth by cutting back on lending. Because of the weak economy at the time, raising new capital was extremely difficult for banks, so they chose the latter course. Banks did restrict their lending, and borrowers found it harder to obtain loans, leading to complaints from banks' customers. Only with the stronger recovery of the economy in 1993, helped by a low-interest-rate policy at the Federal Reserve, did these complaints subside.

MANAGING CREDIT RISK

As seen in the earlier discussion of general principles of asset management, banks and other financial institutions must make successful loans that are paid back in full (and so subject the institution to little credit risk) if they are to earn high profits. The economic concepts of adverse selection and moral hazard (discussed in Chapters 2 and 8) provide a framework for understanding the principles that financial institutions have to follow to reduce credit risk and make successful loans.[3]

Adverse selection in loan markets occurs because bad credit risks (those most likely to default on their loans) are the ones who usually line up for loans; in other words, those who are most likely to produce an *adverse* outcome are the most likely to be *selected*. Borrowers with very risky investment projects have much to gain if their projects are successful, so they are the most eager to obtain loans. Clearly, however, they are the least desirable borrowers because of the greater possibility that they will be unable to pay back their loans.

Moral hazard exists in loan markets because borrowers may have incentives to engage in activities that are undesirable from the lender's point of view. In such situations, it is more likely that the lender will be subjected to the *hazard* of default. Once borrowers have obtained a loan, they are more likely to invest in high-risk investment projects—projects that pay high returns to the borrowers if successful. The high risk, however, makes it less likely that they will be able to pay the loan back.

To be profitable, financial institutions must overcome the adverse selection and moral hazard problems that make loan defaults more likely. The attempts of financial institutions to solve these problems help explain a number of principles for managing credit risk: screening and monitoring, establishment of long-term customer relationships, loan commitments, collateral and compensating balance requirements, and credit rationing.

Screening and Monitoring

Asymmetric information is present in loan markets because lenders have less information about the investment opportunities and activities of borrowers than borrowers do. This situation leads to two information-producing activities by banks and other financial institutions—screening and monitoring. Indeed, Walter Wriston, a former head of Citicorp, the largest bank corporation in the United States, was often quoted as stating that the business of banking is the production of information.

Screening. Adverse selection in loan markets requires that lenders screen out the bad credit risks from the good ones so that loans are profitable to them. To accomplish effective screening, lenders must collect reliable information from prospective borrowers. Effective screening and information collection together form an important principle of credit risk management.

When you apply for a consumer loan (such as a car loan or a mortgage to purchase a house), the first thing you are asked to do is fill out forms that elicit a great deal of information about your personal finances. You are asked about your salary, your bank accounts and other assets (such as cars, insurance policies, and furnishings), and your outstanding loans; your record of loan, credit card, and charge account repayments; the number of years you've worked and who your employers have been. You also are asked personal questions such as your age, marital status, and number of children. The lender uses this information to evaluate how good a credit risk you are by calculating your "credit score," a statistical measure derived from your answers that predicts whether you are likely to have trouble making your loan payments. Deciding on how good a risk you

---

[3]Other financial intermediaries, such as insurance companies, pension funds, and finance companies, also make private loans, and the credit risk management principles we outline here apply to them as well.

are cannot be entirely scientific, so the lender must also use judgment. The loan officer, whose job is to decide whether you should be given the loan, might call your employer or talk to some of the personal references you supplied. The officer might even make a judgment based on your demeanor or your appearance. (This is why most people dress neatly and conservatively when they go to a bank to apply for a loan.)

The process of screening and collecting information is similar when a financial institution makes a business loan. It collects information about the company's profits and losses (income) and about its assets and liabilities. The lender also has to evaluate the likely future success of the business. So in addition to obtaining information on such items as sales figures, a loan officer might ask questions about the company's future plans, the purpose of the loan, and the competition in the industry. The officer may even visit the company to obtain a firsthand look at its operations. The bottom line is that, whether for personal or business loans, bankers and other financial institutions need to be nosy.

Specialization in Lending. One puzzling feature of bank lending is that a bank often specializes in lending to local firms or to firms in particular industries, such as energy. In one sense, this behavior seems surprising, because it means that the bank is not diversifying its portfolio of loans and thus is exposing itself to more risk. But from another perspective, such specialization makes perfect sense. The adverse selection problem requires that the bank screen out bad credit risks. It is easier for the bank to collect information about local firms and determine their creditworthiness than to collect comparable information on firms that are far away. Similarly, by concentrating its lending on firms in specific industries, the bank becomes more knowledgeable about these industries and is therefore better able to predict which firms will be able to make timely payments on their debt.

Monitoring and Enforcement of Restrictive Covenants. Once a loan has been made, the borrower has an incentive to engage in risky activities that make it less likely that the loan will be paid off. To reduce this moral hazard, financial institutions must adhere to the principle for managing credit risk that a lender should write provisions (restrictive covenants) into loan contracts that restrict borrowers from engaging in risky activities. By monitoring borrowers' activities to see whether they are complying with the restrictive covenants and by enforcing the covenants if they are not, lenders can make sure that borrowers are not taking on risks at their expense. The need for banks and other financial institutions to engage in screening and monitoring explains why they spend so much money on auditing and information-collecting activities.

Long-Term Customer Relationships

An additional way for banks and other financial institutions to obtain information about their borrowers is through long-term customer relationships, another important principle of credit risk management.

If a prospective borrower has had a checking or savings account or other loans with a bank over a long period of time, a loan officer can look at past activity on the accounts and learn quite a bit about the borrower. The balances in the checking and savings accounts tell the banker how liquid the potential borrower is and at what time of year the borrower has a strong need for cash. A review of the checks the borrower has written reveals the borrower's suppliers. If the borrower has borrowed previously from the bank, the bank has a record of the loan payments. Thus long-term customer relationships reduce the costs of information collection and make it easier to screen out bad credit risks.

The need for monitoring by lenders adds to the importance of long-term customer relationships. If the borrower has borrowed from the bank before, the bank has already established procedures for monitoring that customer. Therefore, the costs of monitoring long-term customers are lower than those for new customers.

Long-term relationships benefit the customers as well as the bank. A firm with a previous relationship will find it easier to obtain a loan at a low interest rate because the bank has an easier time determining if the prospective borrower is a good credit risk and incurs fewer costs in monitoring the borrower.

A long-term customer relationship has another advantage for the bank. No bank can think of every contingency when it writes a restrictive covenant into a loan contract; there will always be risky borrower activities that are not ruled out. However, what if a borrower wants to preserve a long-term relationship with a bank because it will be easier to get future loans at low interest rates? The borrower then has the incentive to avoid risky activities that would upset the bank, even if restrictions on these risky activities are not specified in the loan contract. Indeed, if a bank doesn't like what a borrower is doing even when the borrower isn't violating any restrictive covenants, it has some power to discourage the borrower from such activity: The bank can threaten not to let the borrower have new loans in the future. Long-term customer relationships therefore enable banks to deal with even unanticipated moral hazard contingencies.

Loan Commitments

Banks also create long-term relationships and gather information by issuing **loan commitments** to commercial customers. A loan commitment is a bank's commitment (for a specified future period of time) to provide a firm with loans up to a given amount at an interest rate that is tied to some market interest rate. The majority of commercial and industrial loans are made under the loan commitment arrangement. The advantage for the firm is that it has a source of credit when it needs it. The advantage for the bank is that the loan commitment promotes a long-term relationship, which in turn facilitates information collection. In addition, provisions in the loan commitment agreement require that the firm continually supply the bank with information about the firm's income, asset and liability position, business activities, and so on. A loan commitment arrangement is a powerful method for reducing the bank's costs for screening and information collection.

Collateral and Compensating Balances

Collateral requirements for loans are important credit risk management tools. Collateral, which is property promised to the lender as compensation if the borrower defaults, lessens the consequences of adverse selection because it reduces the lender's losses in the case of a loan default. If a borrower defaults on a loan, the lender can sell the collateral and use the proceeds to make up for its losses on the loan. One particular form of collateral required when a bank makes commercial loans is called **compensating balances**: A firm receiving a loan must keep a required minimum amount of funds in a checking account at the bank. For example, a business getting a $10 million loan may be required to keep compensating balances of at least $1 million in its checking account at the bank. This $1 million in compensating balances can then be taken by the bank to make up some of the losses on the loan if the borrower defaults.

Besides serving as collateral, compensating balances help increase the likelihood that a loan will be paid off. They do this by helping the bank monitor the borrower and consequently reduce moral hazard. Specifically, by requiring the borrower to use a checking account at the bank, the bank can observe the firm's check payment practices, which may yield a great deal of information about the borrower's financial condition. For example, a sustained drop in the borrower's checking account balance may signal that the borrower is having financial trouble, or account activity may suggest that the borrower is engaging in risky activities; perhaps a change in suppliers means that the borrower is pursuing new lines of business. Any significant change in the borrower's payment procedures is a signal to the bank that it should make inquiries. Compensating balances therefore make it easier for banks to monitor borrowers more effectively and are another important credit risk management tool.

Credit Rationing

Another way in which financial institutions deal with adverse selection and moral hazard is through **credit rationing**: refusing to make loans even though borrowers are willing to pay the stated interest rate or even a higher rate. Credit rationing takes two forms. The first occurs when a lender refuses to make a loan *of any amount* to a borrower, even if the borrower is willing to pay a higher interest rate. The second occurs when a lender is willing to make a loan but restricts the size of the loan to less than the borrower would like.

At first you might be puzzled by the first type of credit rationing. After all, even if the potential borrower is a credit risk, why doesn't the lender just extend the loan but at a higher interest rate? The answer is that adverse selection prevents this solution. Individuals and firms with the riskiest investment projects are exactly those that are willing to pay the highest interest rates. If a borrower took on a high-risk investment and succeeded, the borrower would become extremely rich. But a lender wouldn't want to make such a loan precisely because the investment risk is high; the likely outcome is that the borrower will *not* succeed and the lender will not be paid back. Charging a higher interest rate just makes adverse selection worse for the lender; that is, it increases the likelihood that the lender is lending to a bad credit risk. The lender would therefore rather not make any loans at a higher interest rate; instead, it would engage in the first type of credit rationing and would turn down loans.

Financial institutions engage in the second type of credit rationing to guard against moral hazard: They grant loans to borrowers, but not loans as large as the borrowers want. Such credit rationing is necessary because the larger the loan, the greater the benefits from moral hazard. If a bank gives you a $1,000 loan, for example, you are likely to take actions that enable you to pay it back because you don't want to hurt your credit rating for the future. However, if the bank lends you $10 million, you are more likely to fly down to Rio to celebrate. The larger your loan, the greater your incentives to engage in activities that make it less likely that you will repay the loan. Because more borrowers repay their loans if the loan amounts are small, financial institutions ration credit by providing borrowers with smaller loans than they seek.

MANAGING INTEREST-RATE RISK

With the increased volatility of interest rates that occurred in the 1980s, banks and other financial institutions became more concerned about their exposure to interest-rate risk, the riskiness of earnings and returns that is associated with changes in interest rates. To see what interest-rate risk is all about, let's again take a look at the First National Bank, which has the following balance sheet:

First National Bank

Assets		Liabilities	
Rate-sensitive assets	$20 million	Rate-sensitive liabilities	$50 million
Variable-rate and short-term loans		Variable-rate CDs	
Short-term securities		Money market deposit accounts	
Fixed-rate assets	$80 million	Fixed-rate liabilities	$50 million
Reserves		Checkable deposits	
Long-term loans		Savings deposits	
Long-term securities		Long-term CDs	
		Equity capital	

A total of $20 million of its assets are rate-sensitive, with interest rates that change frequently (at least once a year), and $80 million of its assets are fixed-rate, with interest rates that remain unchanged for a long period (over a year). On the liabilities side, the First National Bank has $50 million of rate-sensitive liabilities and $50 million of fixed-rate liabilities. Suppose that interest rates rise by 5 percentage points on average, from 10% to 15%. The income on the assets increases by $1 million (= 5% × $20 million of rate-sensitive assets), while the payments on the liabilities increase by $2.5 million (= 5% × $50 million of rate-sensitive liabilities). The First National Bank's profits now decline by $1.5 million (= $1 million − $2.5 million). Conversely, if interest rates fall by 5 percentage points, similar reasoning tells us that the First National Bank's profits increase by $1.5 million. This example illustrates the following point: ***If a bank has more rate-sensitive liabilities than assets, a rise in interest rates will reduce bank profits and a decline in interest rates will raise bank profits.***

Gap and Duration Analysis

The sensitivity of bank profits to changes in interest rates can be measured more directly using **gap analysis**, in which the amount of rate-sensitive liabilities is subtracted from the amount of rate-sensitive assets. In our example, this calculation (called the "gap") is −$30 million (= $20 million − $50 million). By multiplying the gap times the change in the interest rate, we can immediately obtain the effect on bank profits. For example, when interest rates rise by 5 percentage points, the change in profits is 5% × −$30 million, which equals −$1.5 million, as we saw.

The analysis we just conducted is known as *basic gap analysis*, and it can be refined in two ways. Clearly, not all assets and liabilities in the fixed-rate category have the same maturity. One refinement, the *maturity bucket approach*, is to measure the gap for several maturity subintervals, called *maturity buckets*, so that effects of interest-rate changes over a multiyear period can be calculated. The second refinement, called *standardized gap analysis*, accounts for the differing degrees of rate sensitivity for different rate-sensitive assets and liabilities.

An alternative method for measuring interest-rate risk, called **duration analysis**, examines the sensitivity of the market value of the bank's total assets and liabilities to changes in interest rates. Duration analysis is based on what is known as Macaulay's concept of *duration*, which measures the average lifetime of a security's stream of payments.[4] Duration is a useful concept because it provides a good approximation of the sensitivity of a security's market value to a change in its interest rate:

$$\text{percent change in market value of security} \approx -\text{percentage-point change in interest rate} \times \text{duration in years}$$

where ≈ denotes "approximately equals."

Duration analysis involves using the average (weighted) duration of a financial institution's assets and of its liabilities to see how its net worth responds to a change in interest rates. Going back to our example of the First National Bank, suppose that the average duration of its assets is three years (that is, the average lifetime of the stream of payments is three years), while the average duration of its liabilities is two years. In addition, the First National Bank has $100 million of assets and, say, $90 million of liabilities, so its bank capital is 10% of assets. With a 5-percentage-point increase in interest rates, the market value of the bank's assets falls by 15% (= −5% × 3 years), a decline of $15 million on the $100 million of assets. However, the market value of the liabilities falls by 10% (= −5% × 2 years), a decline of $9 million on the $90 million of liabilities. The net result is that the net worth (the market value of the assets minus the liabilities) has declined by $6 million, or 6% of the total original asset value. Similarly, a 5-percentage-point decline in interest rates increases the net worth of the First National Bank by 6% of the total asset value.

As our example makes clear, both duration analysis and gap analysis indicate that the First National Bank will suffer if interest rates rise but will gain if they fall. Duration analysis and gap analysis are thus useful tools for telling a manager of a financial institution its degree of exposure to interest-rate risk.

APPLICATION Strategies for Managing Interest-Rate Risk

Suppose that as the manager of the First National Bank, you have done a duration and gap analysis for the bank as discussed in the text. Now you need to decide which alternative strategies you should pursue to manage the interest-rate risk.

If you firmly believe that interest rates will fall in the future, you may be willing to take no action because you know that the bank has more rate-sensitive liabilities than rate-sensitive assets and so will benefit from the expected interest-rate decline. However, you also realize that the First National Bank is subject to substantial interest-rate risk because there is always a possibility that interest rates will rise rather than fall. What should you do to eliminate this interest-rate risk? One thing you could do is to

---

[4]Algebraically, Macaulay's duration, D, is defined as

$$D = \sum_{\tau=1}^{N} \tau \frac{CP_\tau}{(1+i)^\tau} \Big/ \sum_{\tau=1}^{N} \frac{CP_\tau}{(1+i)^\tau}$$

where τ = time until cash payment is made
CP_τ = cash payment (interest plus principal) at time τ
i = interest rate
N = time to maturity of the security

For a more detailed discussion of duration gap analysis using the concept of Macaulay's duration, you can look at an appendix to this chapter that is on this book's web site at www.myeconlab.com/mishkin.

shorten the duration of the bank's assets to increase their rate sensitivity. Alternatively, you could lengthen the duration of the liabilities. By this adjustment of the bank's assets and liabilities, the bank's income will be less affected by interest-rate swings.

One problem with eliminating the First National Bank's interest-rate risk by altering the balance sheet is that doing so might be very costly in the short run. The bank may be locked in to assets and liabilities of particular durations because of where its expertise lies. Fortunately, recently developed financial instruments known as financial derivatives—financial forwards and futures, options, and swaps—can help the bank reduce its interest-rate risk exposure but do not require that the bank rearrange its balance sheet.

OFF-BALANCE-SHEET ACTIVITIES

Although asset and liability management has traditionally been the major concern of banks, in the more competitive environment of recent years banks have been aggressively seeking out profits by engaging in off-balance-sheet activities.[5] **Off-balance-sheet activities** involve trading financial instruments and generating income from fees and loan sales, activities that affect bank profits but do not appear on bank balance sheets. Indeed, off-balance-sheet activities have been growing in importance for banks: The income from these activities as a percentage of assets has nearly doubled since 1980.

Loan Sales

One type of off-balance-sheet activity that has grown in importance in recent years involves income generated by loan sales. A **loan sale**, also called a *secondary loan participation*, involves a contract that sells all or part of the cash stream from a specific loan and thereby removes the loan from the bank's balance sheet. Banks earn profits by selling loans for an amount slightly greater than the amount of the original loan. Because the high interest rate on these loans makes them attractive, institutions are willing to buy them, even though the higher price means that they earn a slightly lower interest rate than the original interest rate on the loan, usually on the order of 0.15 percentage point.

Generation of Fee Income

Another type of off-balance-sheet activity involves the generation of income from fees that banks receive for providing specialized services to their customers, such as making foreign exchange trades on a customer's behalf, servicing a mortgage-backed security by collecting interest and principal payments and then paying them out, guaranteeing debt securities such as banker's acceptances (by which the bank promises to make interest and principal payments if the party issuing the security cannot), and providing backup lines of credit. There are several types of backup lines of credit. We have already mentioned the most important, the loan commitment, under which for a fee the bank agrees

[5]Managers of financial institutions also need to know how well their banks are doing at any point in time. A second appendix to this chapter discusses how bank performance is measured; it can be found on the book's web site at www.myeconlab.com/mishkin.

to provide a loan at the customer's request, up to a given dollar amount, over a specified period of time. Credit lines are also now available to bank depositors with "overdraft privileges"—these bank customers can write checks in excess of their deposit balances and, in effect, write themselves a loan. Other lines of credit for which banks get fees include standby letters of credit to back up issues of commercial paper and other securities and credit lines (called *note issuance facilities*, NIFs, and *revolving underwriting facilities*, RUFs) for underwriting Euronotes, which are medium-term Eurobonds.

Off-balance-sheet activities involving guarantees of securities and backup credit lines increase the risk a bank faces. Even though a guaranteed security does not appear on a bank balance sheet, it still exposes the bank to default risk: If the issuer of the security defaults, the bank is left holding the bag and must pay off the security's owner. Backup credit lines also expose the bank to risk because the bank may be forced to provide loans when it does not have sufficient liquidity or when the borrower is a very poor credit risk.

Trading Activities and Risk Management Techniques

We have already mentioned that banks' attempts to manage interest-rate risk led them to trading in financial futures, options for debt instruments, and interest-rate swaps. Banks engaged in international banking also conduct transactions in the foreign exchange market. All transactions in these markets are off-balance-sheet activities because they do not have a direct effect on the bank's balance sheet. Although bank trading in these markets is often directed toward reducing risk or facilitating other bank business, banks also try to outguess the markets and engage in speculation. This speculation can be a very risky business and indeed has led to bank insolvencies, the most dramatic being the failure of Barings, a British bank, in 1995.

Trading activities, although often highly profitable, are dangerous because they make it easy for financial institutions and their employees to make huge bets quickly. A particular problem for management of trading activities is that the principal–agent problem, discussed in Chapter 8, is especially severe. Given the ability to place large bets, a trader (the agent), whether she trades in bond markets, in foreign exchange markets or in financial derivatives, has an incentive to take on excessive risks: If her trading strategy leads to large profits, she is likely to receive a high salary and bonuses, but if she takes large losses, the financial institution (the principal) will have to cover them. As the Barings Bank failure in 1995 so forcefully demonstrated, a trader subject to the principal–agent problem can take an institution that is quite healthy and drive it into insolvency very rapidly (see the Global box) .

To reduce the principal–agent problem, managers of financial institutions must set up internal controls to prevent debacles like the one at Barings. Such controls include the complete separation of the people in charge of trading activities from those in charge of the bookkeeping for trades. In addition, managers must set limits on the total amount of traders' transactions and on the institution's risk exposure. Managers must also scrutinize risk assessment procedures using the latest computer technology. One such method involves the value-at-risk approach. In this approach, the institution develops a statistical model with which it can calculate the maximum loss that its portfolio is likely to sustain over a given time interval, dubbed the value at risk, or VAR. For example, a bank might estimate that the maximum loss it would be likely to sustain over one day with a probability of 1 in 100 is $1 million; the $1 million figure is the bank's calculated value at risk. Another approach is called "stress testing." In this approach, a manager asks models what would happen if a doomsday scenario occurs; that is, she

Global Barings, Daiwa, Sumitomo, and Allied Irish: Rogue Traders and the Principal–Agent Problem

The demise of Barings, a venerable British bank more than a century old, is a sad morality tale of how the principal–agent problem operating through a rogue trader can take a financial institution that has a healthy balance sheet one month and turn it into an insolvent tragedy the next.

In July 1992, Nick Leeson, Barings's new head clerk at its Singapore branch, began to speculate on the Nikkei, the Japanese version of the Dow Jones stock index. By late 1992, Leeson had suffered losses of $3 million, which he hid from his superiors by stashing the losses in a secret account. He even fooled his superiors into thinking he was generating large profits, thanks to a failure of internal controls at his firm, which allowed him to execute trades on the Singapore exchange *and* oversee the bookkeeping of those trades. (As anyone who runs a cash business, such as a bar, knows, there is always a lower likelihood of fraud if more than one person handles the cash. Similarly for trading operations, you never mix management of the back room with management of the front room; this principle was grossly violated by Barings management.)

Things didn't get better for Leeson, who by late 1994 had losses exceeding $250 million. In January and February 1995, he bet the bank. On January 17, 1995, the day of the earthquake in Kobe, Japan, he lost $75 million, and by the end of the week had lost more than $150 million. When the stock market declined on February 23, leaving him with a further loss of $250 million, he called it quits and fled Singapore. Three days later, he turned himself in at the Frankfurt airport. By the end of his wild ride, Leeson's losses, $1.3 billion in all, ate up Barings's capital and caused the bank to fail. Leeson was subsequently convicted and sent to jail in Singapore for his activities. He was released in 1999 and apologized for his actions.

Our asymmetric information analysis of the principal–agent problem explains Leeson's behavior and the danger of Barings's management lapse. By letting Leeson control both his own trades and the back room, it increased asymmetric information, because it reduced the principal's (Barings's) knowledge about Leeson's trading activities. This lapse increased the moral hazard incentive for him to take risks at the bank's expense, as he was now less likely to be caught. Furthermore, once he had experienced large losses, he had even greater incentives to take on even higher risk because if his bets worked out, he could reverse his losses and keep in good standing with the company, whereas if his bets soured, he had little to lose because he was out of a job anyway. Indeed, the bigger his losses, the more he had to gain by bigger bets, which explains the escalation of the amount of his trades as his losses mounted. If Barings's managers had understood the principal–agent problem, they would have been more vigilant at finding out what Leeson was up to, and the bank might still be here today.

Unfortunately, Nick Leeson is no longer a rarity in the rogue traders' billionaire club, those who have lost more than $1 billion. Over eleven years, Toshihide Iguchi, an officer in the New York branch of Daiwa Bank, also had control of both the bond trading operation and the back room, and he racked up $1.1 billion in losses over the period. In July 1995, Iguchi disclosed his losses to his superiors, but the management of the bank did not disclose them to its regulators. The result was that Daiwa was slapped with a $340 million fine and the bank was thrown out of the country by U.S. bank regulators.

Yasuo Hamanaka is another member of the billionaire club. In July 1996, he topped Leeson's and Iguchi's record, losing $2.6 billion for his employer, the Sumitomo Corporation, one of Japan's top trading companies. John Rusnak lost *only* $691 million for his bank, Allied Irish Banks, over the period from 1997 until he was caught in February 2002.

The moral of these stories is that management of firms engaged in trading activities must reduce the principal–agent problem by closely monitoring their traders' activities, or the rogues' gallery will continue to grow.

looks at the losses the institution would sustain if an unusual combination of bad events occurred. With the value-at-risk approach and stress testing, a financial institution can assess its risk exposure and take steps to reduce it.

Because of the increased risk that banks are facing from their off-balance-sheet activities, U.S. bank regulators have become concerned about increased risk from banks' off-balance-sheet activities and, as we will see in Chapter 11, are encouraging banks to pay increased attention to risk management. In addition, the Bank for International Settlements is developing additional bank capital requirements based on value-at-risk calculations for a bank's trading activities.

SUMMARY

1. The balance sheet of commercial banks can be thought of as a list of the sources and uses of bank funds. The bank's liabilities are its sources of funds, which include checkable deposits, time deposits, discount loans from the Fed, borrowings from other banks and corporations, and bank capital. The bank's assets are its uses of funds, which include reserves, cash items in process of collection, deposits at other banks, securities, loans, and other assets (mostly physical capital).
2. Banks make profits through the process of asset transformation: They borrow short (accept deposits) and lend long (make loans). When a bank takes in additional deposits, it gains an equal amount of reserves; when it pays out deposits, it loses an equal amount of reserves.
3. Although more-liquid assets tend to earn lower returns, banks still desire to hold them. Specifically, banks hold excess and secondary reserves because they provide insurance against the costs of a deposit outflow. Banks manage their assets to maximize profits by seeking the highest returns possible on loans and securities while at the same time trying to lower risk and making adequate provisions for liquidity. Although liability management was once a staid affair, large (money center) banks now actively seek out sources of funds by issuing liabilities such as negotiable CDs or by actively borrowing from other banks and corporations. Banks manage the amount of capital they hold to prevent bank failure and to meet bank capital requirements set by the regulatory authorities. However, they do not want to hold too much capital because by so doing they will lower the returns to equity holders.
4. The concepts of adverse selection and moral hazard explain many credit risk management principles involving loan activities: screening and monitoring, establishment of long-term customer relationships and loan commitments, collateral and compensating balances, and credit rationing.
5. With the increased volatility of interest rates that occurred in the 1980s, financial institutions became more concerned about their exposure to interest-rate risk. Gap and duration analyses tell a financial institution if it has more rate-sensitive liabilities than assets (in which case a rise in interest rates will reduce profits and a fall in interest rates will raise profits). Financial institutions manage their interest-rate risk by modifying their balance sheets but can also use strategies involving financial derivatives.
6. Off-balance-sheet activities consist of trading financial instruments and generating income from fees and loan sales, all of which affect bank profits but are not visible on bank balance sheets. Because these off-balance-sheet activities expose banks to increased risk, bank management must pay particular attention to risk assessment procedures and internal controls to restrict employees from taking on too much risk.

KEY TERMS

asset management, p. 226
balance sheet, p. 219
capital adequacy management, p. 226
compensating balance, p. 237
credit rationing, p. 238
credit risk, p. 226
deposit outflows, p. 226
discount loans, p. 221
discount rate, p. 228

duration analysis, p. 239
equity multiplier (EM), p. 232
excess reserves, p. 222
gap analysis, p. 239
interest-rate risk, p. 226
liability management, p. 226
liquidity management, p. 226
loan commitment, p. 237
loan sale, p. 241
money center banks, p. 230
off-balance-sheet activities, p. 241
required reserve ratio, p. 222
required reserves, p. 222
reserve requirements, p. 222
reserves, p. 222
return on assets (ROA), p. 232
return on equity (ROE), p. 232
secondary reserves, p. 222
T-account, p. 223
vault cash, p. 222

QUESTIONS AND PROBLEMS

Questions marked with an asterisk are answered at the end of the book in an appendix, "Answers to Selected Questions and Problems." Questions marked with a blue circle indicate the question is available in MyEconLab at www.myeconlab.com/mishkin.

1. Why might a bank be willing to borrow funds from other banks at a higher rate than it can borrow from the Fed?

*2. Rank the following bank assets from most to least liquid:
   a. Commercial loans
   b. Securities
   c. Reserves
   d. Physical capital

3. Using the T-accounts of the First National Bank and the Second National Bank, describe what happens when Jane Brown writes a $50 check on her account at the First National Bank to pay her friend Joe Green, who in turn deposits the check in his account at the Second National Bank.

*4. What happens to reserves at the First National Bank if one person withdraws $1,000 of cash and another person deposits $500 of cash? Use T-accounts to explain your answer.

5. The bank you own has the following balance sheet:

Assets		Liabilities	
Reserves	$ 75 million	Deposits	$500 million
Loans	$525 million	Bank capital	$100 million

If the bank suffers a deposit outflow of $50 million with a required reserve ratio on deposits of 10%, what actions must you take to keep your bank from failing?

*6. If a deposit outflow of $50 million occurs, which balance sheet would a bank rather have initially, the balance sheet in Problem 5 or the following balance sheet? Why?

Assets		Liabilities	
Reserves	$100 million	Deposits	$500 million
Loans	$500 million	Bank capital	$100 million

7. Why has the development of overnight loan markets made it more likely that banks will hold fewer excess reserves?

*8. If the bank you own has no excess reserves and a sound customer comes in asking for a loan, should you automatically turn the customer down, explaining that you don't have any excess reserves to lend out? Why or why not? What options are available for you to provide the funds your customer needs?

9. If a bank finds that its ROE is too low because it has too much bank capital, what can it do to raise its ROE?

*10. If a bank is falling short of meeting its capital requirements by $1 million, what three things can it do to rectify the situation?

11. Why is being nosy a desirable trait for a banker?

*12. A bank almost always insists that the firms it lends to keep compensating balances at the bank. Why?

13. "Because diversification is a desirable strategy for avoiding risk, it never makes sense for a bank to specialize in making specific types of loans." Is this statement true, false, or uncertain? Explain your answer.

*14 Suppose that you are the manager of a bank whose $100 billion of assets have an average duration of four years and whose $90 billion of liabilities have an average duration of six years. Conduct a duration analysis for the bank, and show what will happen to the net worth of the bank if interest rates rise by 2 percentage points. What actions could you take to reduce the bank's interest-rate risk?

15 Suppose that you are the manager of a bank that has $15 million of fixed-rate assets, $30 million of rate-sensitive assets, $25 million of fixed-rate liabilities, and $20 million of rate-sensitive liabilities. Conduct a gap analysis for the bank, and show what will happen to bank profits if interest rates rise by 5 percentage points. What actions could you take to reduce the bank's interest-rate risk?

WEB EXERCISES

1. Table 1 reports the balance sheet of all commercial banks based on aggregate data found in the Federal Reserve *Bulletin*. Compare this table to the balance sheet reported by Wachovia found at www.wachovia.com/inside/page/0,,133_202,00.html. Does Wachovia have more or less of its portfolio in loans than the average bank? Which type of loan is most common?
2. It is relatively easy to find up-to-date information on banks because of their extensive reporting requirements. Go to www2.fdic.gov/qbp/. This site is sponsored by the Federal Deposit Insurance Corporation. You will find summary data on financial institutions. Go to the most recent Quarterly Banking Profile. Scroll to the bottom and open Table 1-A.
   a. Have banks' return on assets been increasing or decreasing over the last few years?
   b. Has the core capital been increasing, and how does it compare to the capital ratio reported in Table 1 in the text?
   c. How many institutions are currently reporting to the FDIC?

WEB REFERENCES

www.bankofamerica.com/investor/index.cfm?section=700

Click on Annual Reports to view balance sheet.

www.federalreserve.gov/boarddocs/SupManual/default.htm#trading

The Federal Reserve Bank Trading and Capital Market Activities Manual offers an in-depth discussion of a wide range of risk management issues encountered in trading operations.

CHAPTER

10 Banking Industry: Structure and Competition

Preview

The operations of individual banks (how they acquire, use, and manage funds to make a profit) are roughly similar throughout the world. In all countries, banks are financial intermediaries in the business of earning profits. When you consider the structure and operation of the banking industry as a whole, however, the United States is in a class by itself. In most countries, four or five large banks typically dominate the banking industry, but in the United States there are on the order of 7,500 commercial banks, 1,300 savings and loan associations, 400 mutual savings banks, and 8,900 credit unions.

Is more better? Does this diversity mean that the American banking system is more competitive and therefore more economically efficient and sound than banking systems in other countries? What in the American economic and political system explains this large number of banking institutions? In this chapter, we try to answer these questions by examining the historical trends in the banking industry and its overall structure.

We start by examining the historical development of the banking system and how financial innovation has increased the competitive environment for the banking industry and is causing fundamental changes in it. We go on to look at the commercial banking industry in detail and then discuss the thrift industry, which includes savings and loan associations, mutual savings banks, and credit unions. We spend more time on commercial banks because they are by far the largest depository institutions, accounting for more than two-thirds of the deposits in the banking system. In addition to looking at our domestic banking system, we examine the forces behind the growth in international banking to see how it has affected us in the United States.

HISTORICAL DEVELOPMENT OF THE BANKING SYSTEM

The modern commercial banking industry in the United States began when the Bank of North America was chartered in Philadelphia in 1782. With the success of this bank, other banks opened for business, and the American banking industry was off and running. (As a study aid, Figure 1 provides a time line of the most important dates in the history of American banking before World War II.)

A major controversy involving the industry in its early years was whether the federal government or the states should charter banks. The Federalists, particularly Alexander Hamilton, advocated greater centralized control of banking and federal chartering of banks. Their efforts led to the creation in 1791 of the Bank of the United States, which

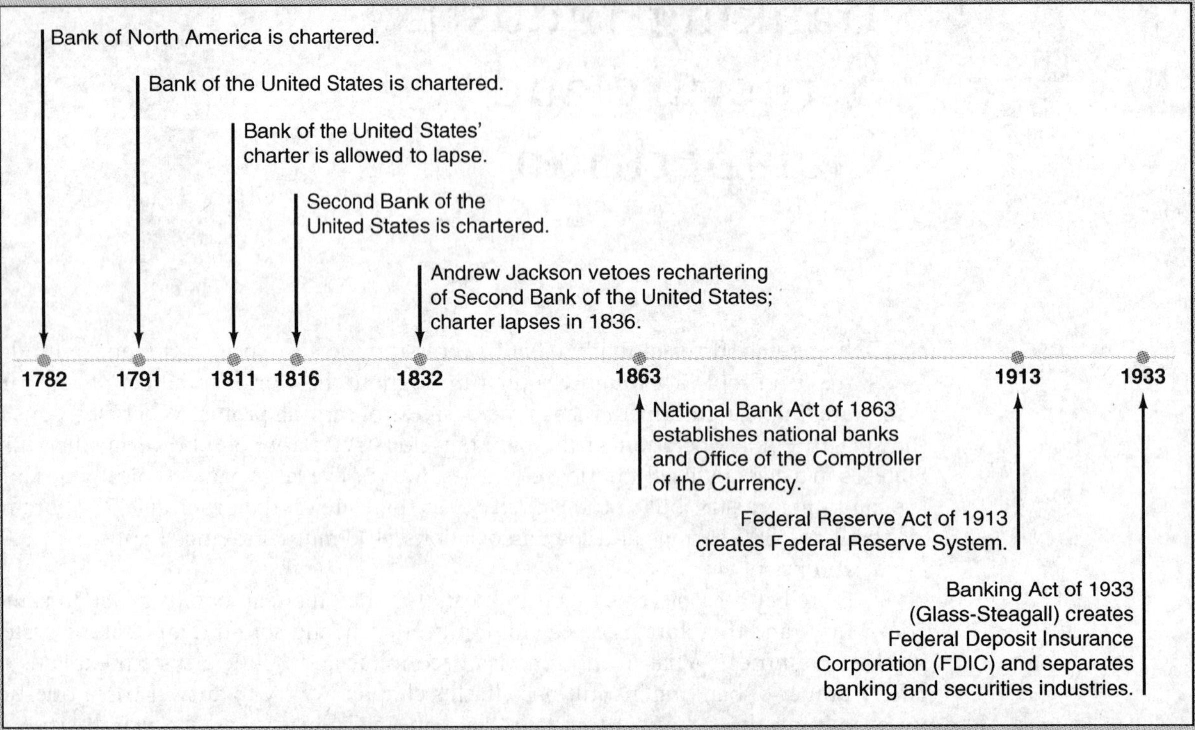

FIGURE 1 **Time Line of the Early History of Commercial Banking in the United States**

had elements of both a private bank and a **central bank**, a government institution that has responsibility for the amount of money and credit supplied in the economy as a whole. Agricultural and other interests, however, were quite suspicious of centralized power and hence advocated chartering by the states. Furthermore, their distrust of moneyed interests in the big cities led to political pressures to eliminate the Bank of the United States, and in 1811 their efforts met with success, when its charter was not renewed. Because of abuses by state banks and the clear need for a central bank to help the federal government raise funds during the War of 1812, Congress was stimulated to create the Second Bank of the United States in 1816. Tensions between advocates and opponents of centralized banking power were a recurrent theme during the operation of this second attempt at central banking in the United States, and with the election of Andrew Jackson, a strong advocate of states' rights, the fate of the Second Bank was sealed. After the election in 1832, Jackson vetoed the rechartering of the Second Bank of the United States as a national bank, and its charter lapsed in 1836.

Until 1863, all commercial banks in the United States were chartered by the banking commission of the state in which each operated. No national currency existed, and banks obtained funds primarily by issuing *banknotes* (currency circulated by the banks that could be redeemed for gold). Because banking regulations were extremely lax in many states, banks regularly failed due to fraud or lack of sufficient bank capital; their banknotes became worthless.

To eliminate the abuses of the state-chartered banks (called **state banks**), the National Bank Act of 1863 (and subsequent amendments to it) created a new banking system of federally chartered banks (called **national banks**), supervised by the Office of the Comptroller of the Currency, a department of the U.S. Treasury. This legislation was originally intended to dry up sources of funds to state banks by imposing a prohibitive tax on their banknotes while leaving the banknotes of the federally chartered banks untaxed. The state banks cleverly escaped extinction by acquiring funds through deposits. As a result, today the United States has a **dual banking system** in which banks supervised by the federal government and banks supervised by the states operate side by side.

Central banking did not reappear in this country until the Federal Reserve System (the Fed) was created in 1913 to promote an even safer banking system. All national banks were required to become members of the Federal Reserve System and became subject to a new set of regulations issued by the Fed. State banks could choose (but were not required) to become members of the system, and most did not because of the high costs of membership stemming from the Fed's regulations.

During the Great Depression years 1930–1933, some 9,000 bank failures wiped out the savings of many depositors at commercial banks. To prevent future depositor losses from such failures, banking legislation in 1933 established the Federal Deposit Insurance Corporation (FDIC), which provided federal insurance on bank deposits. Member banks of the Federal Reserve System were required to purchase FDIC insurance for their depositors, and non–Federal Reserve commercial banks could choose to buy this insurance (almost all of them did). The purchase of FDIC insurance made banks subject to another set of regulations imposed by the FDIC.

Because investment banking activities of the commercial banks were blamed for many bank failures, provisions in the banking legislation in 1933 (also known as the Glass-Steagall Act) prohibited commercial banks from underwriting or dealing in corporate securities (though allowing them to sell new issues of government securities) and limited banks to the purchase of debt securities approved by the bank regulatory agencies. Likewise, it prohibited investment banks from engaging in commercial banking activities. In effect, the Glass-Steagall Act separated the activities of commercial banks from those of the securities industry.

Under the conditions of the Glass-Steagall Act, which was repealed in 1999, commercial banks had to sell off their investment banking operations. The First National Bank of Boston, for example, spun off its investment banking operations into the First Boston Corporation, now part of one of the most important investment banking firms in America, Credit Suisse First Boston. Investment banking firms typically discontinued their deposit business, although J. P. Morgan discontinued its investment banking business and reorganized as a commercial bank; however, some senior officers of J. P. Morgan went on to organize Morgan Stanley, another one of the largest investment banking firms today.

Multiple Regulatory Agencies

Commercial bank regulation in the United States has developed into a crazy quilt of multiple regulatory agencies with overlapping jurisdictions. The Office of the Comptroller of the Currency has the primary supervisory responsibility for the 1,850 national banks which own more than half of the assets in the commercial banking system. The Federal Reserve and the state banking authorities have joint primary responsibility for the

900 state banks that are members of the Federal Reserve System. The Fed also has regulatory responsibility over companies that own one or more banks (called **bank holding companies**) and secondary responsibility for the national banks. The FDIC and the state banking authorities jointly supervise the 4,800 state banks that have FDIC insurance but are not members of the Federal Reserve System. The state banking authorities have sole jurisdiction over the fewer than 500 state banks without FDIC insurance. (Such banks hold less than 0.2% of the deposits in the commercial banking system.)

If you find the U.S. bank regulatory system confusing, imagine how confusing it is for the banks, which have to deal with multiple regulatory agencies. Several proposals have been raised by the U.S. Treasury to rectify this situation by centralizing the regulation of all depository institutions under one independent agency. However, none of these proposals has been successful in Congress, and whether there will be regulatory consolidation in the future is highly uncertain.

FINANCIAL INNOVATION AND THE EVOLUTION OF THE BANKING INDUSTRY

To understand how the banking industry has evolved over time, we must first understand the process of financial innovation, which has transformed the entire financial system. Like other industries, the financial industry is in business to earn profits by selling its products. If a soap company perceives that there is a need in the marketplace for a laundry detergent with fabric softener, it develops a product to fit the need. Similarly, to maximize their profits, financial institutions develop new products to satisfy their own needs as well as those of their customers; in other words, innovation—which can be extremely beneficial to the economy—is driven by the desire to get (or stay) rich. This view of the innovation process leads to the following simple analysis: ***A change in the financial environment will stimulate a search by financial institutions for innovations that are likely to be profitable.***

Starting in the 1960s, individuals and financial institutions operating in financial markets were confronted with drastic changes in the economic environment: Inflation and interest rates climbed sharply and became harder to predict, a situation that changed demand conditions in financial markets. The rapid advance in computer technology changed supply conditions. In addition, financial regulations became more burdensome. Financial institutions found that many of the old ways of doing business were no longer profitable; the financial services and products they had been offering to the public were not selling. Many financial intermediaries found that they were no longer able to acquire funds with their traditional financial instruments, and without these funds they would soon be out of business. To survive in the new economic environment, financial institutions had to research and develop new products and services that would meet customer needs and prove profitable, a process referred to as **financial engineering**. In their case, necessity was the mother of innovation.

Our discussion of why financial innovation occurs suggests that there are three basic types of financial innovation: responses to changes in demand conditions, responses to changes in supply conditions, and avoidance of regulations. Now that we have a framework for understanding why financial institutions produce innovations, let's look at examples of how financial institutions in their search for profits have produced financial innovations of the three basic types.

Responses to Changes in Demand Conditions: Interest Rate Volatility

The most significant change in the economic environment that altered the demand for financial products in recent years has been the dramatic increase in the volatility of interest rates. In the 1950s, the interest rate on three-month Treasury bills fluctuated between 1.0% and 3.5%; in the 1970s, it fluctuated between 4.0% and 11.5%; in the 1980s, it ranged from 5% to more than 15%. Large fluctuations in interest rates lead to substantial capital gains or losses and greater uncertainty about returns on investments. Recall that the risk that is related to the uncertainty about interest-rate movements and returns is called *interest-rate risk*, and high volatility of interest rates, such as we saw in the 1970s and 1980s, leads to a higher level of interest-rate risk.

We would expect the increase in interest-rate risk to increase the demand for financial products and services that could reduce that risk. This change in the economic environment would thus stimulate a search for profitable innovations by financial institutions that meet this new demand and would spur the creation of new financial instruments that help lower interest-rate risk. Two examples of financial innovations that appeared in the 1970s confirm this prediction: the development of adjustable-rate mortgages and financial derivatives.

Adjustable-Rate Mortgages. Like other investors, financial institutions find that lending is more attractive if interest-rate risk is lower. They would not want to make a mortgage loan at a 10% interest rate and two months later find that they could obtain 12% in interest on the same mortgage. To reduce interest-rate risk, in 1975 savings and loans in California began to issue adjustable-rate mortgages; that is, mortgage loans on which the interest rate changes when a market interest rate (usually the Treasury bill rate) changes. Initially, an adjustable-rate mortgage might have a 5% interest rate. In six months, this interest rate might increase or decrease by the amount of the increase or decrease in, say, the six-month Treasury bill rate, and the mortgage payment would change. Because adjustable-rate mortgages allow mortgage-issuing institutions to earn higher interest rates on mortgages when rates rise, profits remain high during these periods.

This attractive feature of adjustable-rate mortgages has encouraged mortgage-issuing institutions to issue adjustable-rate mortgages with lower initial interest rates than on conventional fixed-rate mortgages, making them popular with many households. However, because the mortgage payment on a variable-rate mortgage can increase, many households continue to prefer fixed-rate mortgages. Hence both types of mortgages are widespread.

Financial Derivatives. Given the greater demand for the reduction of interest-rate risk, commodity exchanges such as the Chicago Board of Trade recognized that if they could develop a product that would help investors and financial institutions to protect themselves from, or **hedge**, interest-rate risk, then they could make profits by selling this new instrument. **Futures contracts**, in which the seller agrees to provide a certain standardized commodity to the buyer on a specific future date at an agreed-on price, had been around for a long time. Officials at the Chicago Board of Trade realized that if they created futures contracts in financial instruments, which are called **financial derivatives** because their payoffs are linked to previously issued securities, they could be used to hedge risk. Thus, in 1975, financial derivatives were born. We will study financial derivatives later in the book, in Chapter 13.

Responses to Changes in Supply Conditions: Information Technology

The most important source of the changes in supply conditions that stimulate financial innovation has been the improvement in computer and telecommunications technology. This technology, called *information technology,* has had two effects. First, it has lowered the cost of processing financial transactions, making it profitable for financial institutions to create new financial products and services for the public. Second, it has made it easier for investors to acquire information, thereby making it easier for firms to issue securities. The rapid developments in information technology have resulted in many new financial products and services that we examine here.

Bank Credit and Debit Cards. Credit cards have been around since well before World War II. Many individual stores (Sears, Macy's, Goldwater's) institutionalized charge accounts by providing customers with credit cards that allowed them to make purchases at these stores without cash. Nationwide credit cards were not established until after World War II, when Diners Club developed one to be used in restaurants all over the country (and abroad). Similar credit card programs were started by American Express and Carte Blanche, but because of the high cost of operating these programs, cards were issued only to selected persons and businesses that could afford expensive purchases.

A firm issuing credit cards earns income from loans it makes to credit card holders and from payments made by stores on credit card purchases (a percentage of the purchase price, say 5%). A credit card program's costs arise from loan defaults, stolen cards, and the expense involved in processing credit card transactions.

Seeing the success of Diners Club, American Express, and Carte Blanche, bankers wanted to share in the profitable credit card business. Several commercial banks attempted to expand the credit card business to a wider market in the 1950s, but the cost per transaction of running these programs was so high that their early attempts failed.

In the late 1960s, improved computer technology, which lowered the transaction costs for providing credit card services, made it more likely that bank credit card programs would be profitable. The banks tried to enter this business again, and this time their efforts led to the creation of two successful bank credit card programs: BankAmericard (originally started by the Bank of America but now an independent organization called Visa) and MasterCharge (now MasterCard, run by the Interbank Card Association). These programs have become phenomenally successful; more than 200 million of their cards are in use. Indeed, bank credit cards have been so profitable that nonfinancial institutions such as Sears (which launched the Discover card), General Motors, and AT&T have also entered the credit card business. Consumers have benefited because credit cards are more widely accepted than checks to pay for purchases (particularly abroad), and they allow consumers to take out loans more easily.

The success of bank credit cards has led these institutions to come up with a new financial innovation, *debit cards.* Debit cards often look just like credit cards and can be used to make purchases in an identical fashion. However, in contrast to credit cards, which extend the purchaser a loan that does not have to be paid off immediately, a debit card purchase is immediately deducted from the card holder's bank account. Debit cards depend even more on low costs of processing transactions, because their profits are generated entirely from the fees paid by merchants on debit card purchases at their stores. Debit cards have grown extremely popular in recent years.

Electronic Banking. The wonders of modern computer technology have also enabled banks to lower the cost of bank transactions by having the customer interact with an electronic banking (e-banking) facility rather than with a human being. One important form of an e-banking facility is the **automated teller machine (ATM)**, an electronic machine that allows customers to get cash, make deposits, transfer funds from one account to another, and check balances. The ATM has the advantage that it does not have to be paid overtime and never sleeps, thus being available for use 24 hours a day. Not only does this result in cheaper transactions for the bank, but it also provides more convenience for the customer. Furthermore, because of their low cost, ATMs can be put at locations other than a bank or its branches, further increasing customer convenience. The low cost of ATMs has meant that they have sprung up everywhere and now number more than 250,000 in the United States alone. Furthermore, it is now as easy to get foreign currency from an ATM when you are traveling in Europe as it is to get cash from your local bank.

With the drop in the cost of telecommunications, banks have developed another financial innovation, *home banking*. It is now cost-effective for banks to set up an electronic banking facility in which the bank's customer is linked up with the bank's computer to carry out transactions by using either a telephone or a personal computer. Now a bank's customers can conduct many of their bank transactions without ever leaving the comfort of home. The advantage for the customer is the convenience of home banking, while banks find that the cost of transactions is substantially less than having the customer come to the bank. The success of ATMs and home banking has led to another innovation, the **automated banking machine (ABM)**, which combines in one location an ATM, an Internet connection to the bank's web site, and a telephone link to customer service.

With the decline in the price of personal computers and their increasing presence in the home, we have seen a further innovation in the home banking area, the appearance of a new type of banking institution, the **virtual bank**, a bank that has no physical location but rather exists only in cyberspace. In 1995, Security First Network Bank, based in Atlanta but now owned by Royal Bank of Canada, became the first virtual bank, offering an array of banking services on the Internet—accepting checking account and savings deposits, selling certificates of deposits, issuing ATM cards, providing bill-paying facilities, and so on. The virtual bank thus takes home banking one step further, enabling the customer to have a full set of banking services at home 24 hours a day. In 1996, Bank of America and Wells Fargo entered the virtual banking market, to be followed by many others, with Bank of America now being the largest Internet bank in the United States. Will virtual banking be the predominant form of banking in the future (see the E-Finance box, "Will 'Clicks' Dominate 'Bricks' in the Banking Industry?")?

Junk Bonds. Before the advent of computers and advanced telecommunications, it was difficult to acquire information about the financial situation of firms that might want to sell securities. Because of the difficulty in screening out bad from good credit risks, the only firms that were able to sell bonds were very well-established corporations that had high credit ratings.[1] Before the 1980s, then, only corporations that could issue bonds with ratings of Baa or above could raise funds by selling newly issued bonds. Some firms that had fallen on bad times, known as *fallen angels*, had previously issued

[1]The discussion of adverse selection problems in Chapter 8 provides a more detailed analysis of why only well-established firms with high credit ratings were able to sell securities.

E-Finance Will "Clicks" Dominate "Bricks" in the Banking Industry?

With the advent of virtual banks ("clicks") and the convenience they provide, a key question is whether they will become the primary form in which banks do their business, eliminating the need for physical bank branches ("bricks") as the main delivery mechanism for banking services. Indeed, will stand-alone Internet banks be the wave of the future?

The answer seems to be no. Internet-only banks such as Wingspan (owned by Bank One), First-e (Dublin-based), and Egg (a British Internet-only bank owned by Prudential) have had disappointing revenue growth and profits. The result is that pure online banking has not been the success that proponents had hoped for. Why has Internet banking been a disappointment?

There have been several strikes against Internet banking. First, bank depositors want to know that their savings are secure, and so are reluctant to put their money into new institutions without a long track record. Second, customers worry about the security of their online transactions and whether their transactions will truly be kept private. Traditional banks are viewed as being more secure and trustworthy in terms of releasing private information. Third, customers may prefer services provided by physical branches. For example, banking customers seem to prefer to purchase long-term savings products face-to-face. Fourth, Internet banking has run into technical problems—server crashes, slow connections over phone lines, mistakes in conducting transactions—that will probably diminish over time as technology improves.

The wave of the future thus does not appear to be pure Internet banks. Instead it looks like "clicks and bricks" will be the predominant form of banking, in which online banking is used to complement the services provided by traditional banks. Nonetheless, the delivery of banking services is undergoing massive changes, with more and more banking services delivered over the Internet and the number of physical bank branches likely to decline in the future.

long-term corporate bonds that now had ratings that had fallen below Baa, bonds that were pejoratively dubbed "junk bonds."

With the improvement in information technology in the 1970s, it became easier for investors to acquire financial information about corporations, making it easier to screen out bad from good credit risks. With easier screening, investors were more willing to buy long-term debt securities from less well-known corporations with lower credit ratings. With this change in supply conditions, we would expect that some smart individual would pioneer the concept of selling new public issues of junk bonds, not for fallen angels but for companies that had not yet achieved investment-grade status. This is exactly what Michael Milken of Drexel Burnham Lambert, an investment banking firm, started to do in 1977. Junk bonds became an important factor in the corporate bond market, with the amount outstanding exceeding $200 billion by the late 1980s. Although there was a sharp slowdown in activity in the junk bond market after Milken was indicted for securities law violations in 1989, it heated up again in the 1990s and 2000s.

Commercial Paper Market. *Commercial paper* is a short-term debt security issued by large banks and corporations. The commercial paper market has undergone tremendous growth since 1970, when there was $33 billion outstanding, to over $1.6 trillion outstanding at the end of 2005. Indeed, commercial paper has been one of the fastest-growing money market instruments.

Improvements in information technology also help provide an explanation for the rapid rise of the commercial paper market. We have seen that the improvement in information technology made it easier for investors to screen out bad from good credit risks, thus making it easier for corporations to issue debt securities. Not only did this make it easier for corporations to issue long-term debt securities as in the junk bond market, but it also meant that they could raise funds by issuing short-term debt securities such as commercial paper more easily. Many corporations that used to do their short-term borrowing from banks now frequently raise short-term funds in the commercial paper market instead.

The development of money market mutual funds has been another factor in the rapid growth in the commercial paper market. Because money market mutual funds need to hold liquid, high-quality, short-term assets such as commercial paper, the growth of assets in these funds to around $1.9 trillion has created a ready market in commercial paper. The growth of pension and other large funds that invest in commercial paper has also stimulated the growth of this market.

Securitization. An important example of a financial innovation arising from improvements in both transaction and information technology is securitization, one of the most important financial innovations in the past two decades. **Securitization** is the process of transforming otherwise illiquid financial assets (such as residential mortgages, auto loans, and credit card receivables), which have typically been the bread and butter of banking institutions, into marketable capital market securities. As we have seen, improvements in the ability to acquire information have made it easier to sell marketable capital market securities. In addition, with low transaction costs because of improvements in computer technology, financial institutions find that they can cheaply bundle together a portfolio of loans (such as mortgages) with varying small denominations (often less than $100,000), collect the interest and principal payments on the mortgages in the bundle, and then "pass them through" (pay them out) to third parties. By dividing the portfolio of loans into standardized amounts, the financial institution can then sell the claims to these interest and principal payments to third parties as securities. The standardized amounts of these securitized loans make them liquid securities, and the fact that they are made up of a bundle of loans helps diversify risk, making them desirable. The financial institution selling the securitized loans makes a profit by servicing the loans (collecting the interest and principal payments and paying them out) and charging a fee to the third party for this service.

Avoidance of Existing Regulations

The process of financial innovation we have discussed so far is much like innovation in other areas of the economy: It occurs in response to changes in demand and supply conditions. However, because the financial industry is more heavily regulated than other industries, government regulation is a much greater spur to innovation in this industry. Government regulation leads to financial innovation by creating incentives for firms to skirt regulations that restrict their ability to earn profits. Edward Kane, an economist at Boston College, describes this process of avoiding regulations as "loophole mining." The economic analysis of innovation suggests that when the economic environment changes such that regulatory constraints are so burdensome that large profits can be made by avoiding them, loophole mining and innovation are more likely to occur.

Because banking is one of the most heavily regulated industries in America, loophole mining is especially likely to occur. The rise in inflation and interest rates from the late 1960s to 1980 made the regulatory constraints imposed on this industry even more burdensome, leading to financial innovation.

Two sets of regulations have seriously restricted the ability of banks to make profits: reserve requirements that force banks to keep a certain fraction of their deposits as reserves (vault cash and deposits in the Federal Reserve System) and restrictions on the interest rates that can be paid on deposits. For the following reasons, these regulations have been major forces behind financial innovation.

1. *Reserve requirements.* The key to understanding why reserve requirements led to financial innovation is to recognize that they act, in effect, as a tax on deposits. Because the Fed does not pay interest on reserves, the opportunity cost of holding them is the interest that a bank could otherwise earn by lending the reserves out. For each dollar of deposits, reserve requirements therefore impose a cost on the bank equal to the interest rate, i, that could be earned if the reserves could be lent out times the fraction of deposits required as reserves, r. The cost of $i \times r$ imposed on the bank is just like a tax on bank deposits of $i \times r$ per dollar of deposits.

It is a great tradition to avoid taxes if possible, and banks also play this game. Just as taxpayers look for loopholes to lower their tax bills, banks seek to increase their profits by mining loopholes and by producing financial innovations that allow them to escape the tax on deposits imposed by reserve requirements.

2. *Restrictions on interest paid on deposits.* Until 1980, legislation prohibited banks in most states from paying interest on checking account deposits, and through Regulation Q, the Fed set maximum limits on the interest rate that could be paid on time deposits. To this day, banks are not allowed to pay interest on corporate checking accounts. The desire to avoid these **deposit rate ceilings** also led to financial innovations.

If market interest rates rose above the maximum rates that banks paid on time deposits under Regulation Q, depositors withdrew funds from banks to put them into higher-yielding securities. This loss of deposits from the banking system restricted the amount of funds that banks could lend (called **disintermediation**) and thus limited bank profits. Banks had an incentive to get around deposit rate ceilings, because by so doing, they could acquire more funds to make loans and earn higher profits.

We can now look at how the desire to avoid restrictions on interest payments and the tax effect of reserve requirements led to two important financial innovations.

Money Market Mutual Funds. Money market mutual funds issue shares that are redeemable at a fixed price (usually \$1) by writing checks. For example, if you buy 5,000 shares for \$5,000, the money market fund uses these funds to invest in short-term money market securities (Treasury bills, certificates of deposit, commercial paper) that provide you with interest payments. In addition, you are able to write checks up to the \$5,000 held as shares in the money market fund. Although money market fund shares effectively function as checking account deposits that earn interest, they are not legally deposits and so are not subject to reserve requirements or prohibitions on interest payments. For this reason, they can pay higher interest rates than deposits at banks.

The first money market mutual fund was created by two Wall Street mavericks, Bruce Bent and Henry Brown, in 1971. However, the low market interest rates from 1971 to 1977 (which were just slightly above Regulation Q ceilings of 5.25% to 5.5%) kept them from being particularly advantageous relative to bank deposits. In early 1978, the situation changed rapidly as inflation rose and market interest rates began to climb over 10%, well above the 5.5% maximum interest rates payable on savings accounts and time deposits under Regulation Q. In 1977, money market mutual funds had assets of less than \$4 billion; in 1978, their assets climbed to close to \$10 billion; in 1979, to more than \$40 billion; and in 1982, to \$230 billion. Currently, their assets are around $2 trillion. To say the least, money market mutual funds have been a successful financial innovation, which is exactly what we would have predicted to occur in the late 1970s and early 1980s when interest rates soared beyond Regulation Q ceilings.

Sweep Accounts. Another innovation that enables banks to avoid the "tax" from reserve requirements is the **sweep account**. In this arrangement, any balances above a certain amount in a corporation's checking account at the end of a business day are "swept out" of the account and invested in overnight securities that pay interest. Because the "swept out" funds are no longer classified as checkable deposits, they are not subject to reserve requirements and thus are not "taxed." They also have the advantage that they allow banks in effect to pay interest on these checking accounts, which otherwise is not allowed under existing regulations. Because sweep accounts have become so popular, they have lowered the amount of required reserves to the degree that most banking institutions do not find reserve requirements binding: In other words, they voluntarily hold more reserves than they are required to.

The financial innovation of sweep accounts is particularly interesting because it was stimulated not only by the desire to avoid a costly regulation, but also by a change in supply conditions—in this case, information technology. Without low-cost computers to process inexpensively the additional transactions required by these accounts, this innovation would not have been profitable and therefore would not have been developed. Technological factors often combine with other incentives, such as the desire to get around a regulation, to produce innovation.

Financial Innovation and the Decline of Traditional Banking

The traditional financial intermediation role of banking has been to make long-term loans and to fund them by issuing short-term deposits, a process of asset transformation commonly referred to as "borrowing short and lending long." Here we examine how financial innovations have created a more competitive environment for the banking industry, causing the industry to change dramatically, with its traditional banking business going into decline.

In the United States, the importance of commercial banks as a source of funds to nonfinancial borrowers has shrunk dramatically. As we can see in Figure 2, in 1974, commercial banks provided close to 40% of these funds; by 2005, their market share was down to below 30%. The decline in market share for thrift institutions has been even more precipitous, from more than 20% in the late 1970s to 6% today. Another way of viewing the declining role of banking in traditional financial intermediation is to look at the size of banks' balance sheet assets relative to those of other financial intermediaries (see Table 1 in Chapter 12). Commercial banks' share of total financial intermediary assets has fallen from about 40% in the 1960–1980 period to 30% by the end of 2005. Similarly, the share of total financial intermediary assets held by thrift institutions has declined even more from the 20% level of the 1960–1980 period to about 6% by 2005.

Clearly, the traditional financial intermediation role of banking, whereby banks make loans that are funded with deposits, is no longer as important in our financial system. However, the decline in the market share of banks in total lending and total financial intermediary assets does not necessarily indicate that the banking industry is in decline. There is no evidence of a declining trend in bank profitability. However, overall bank profitability is not a good indicator of the profitability of traditional banking, because it includes an increasing amount of income from nontraditional off-balance-sheet activities, discussed in Chapter 9. Noninterest income derived from

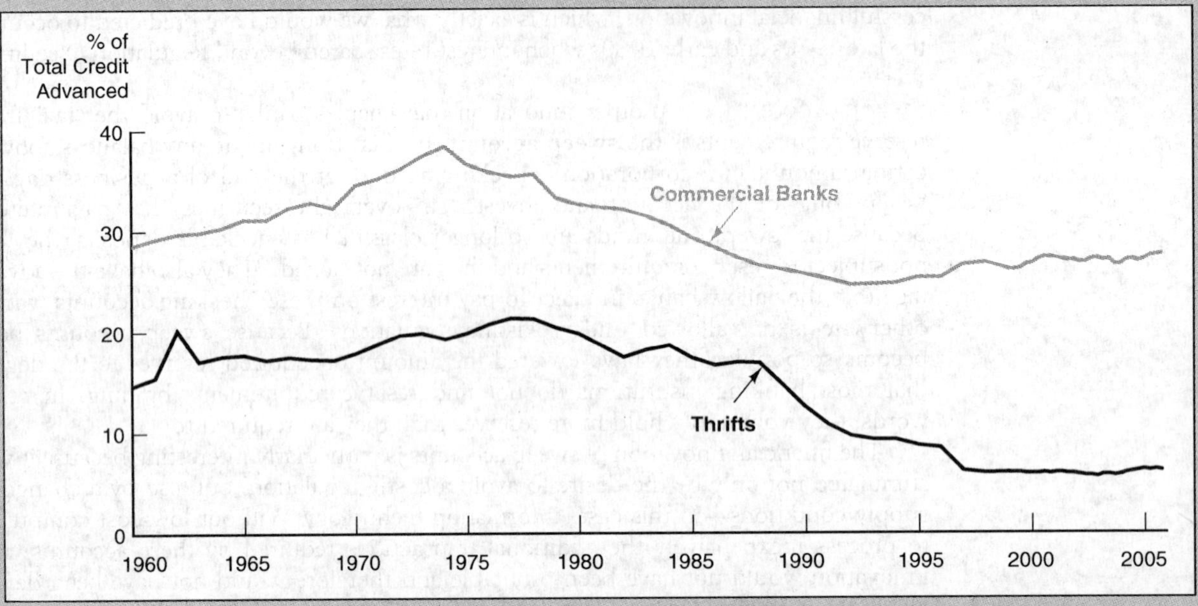

FIGURE 2 **Bank Share of Total Nonfinancial Borrowing, 1960–2005**

Source: Federal Reserve Flow of Funds Accounts; Federal Reserve Bulletin.

off-balance-sheet activities, as a share of total banking income, increased from around 7% in 1980 to more than 44% of total bank income today. Given that the overall profitability of banks has not risen, the increase in income from off-balance-sheet activities implies that the profitability of traditional banking business has declined. This decline in profitability explains why banks have been reducing their traditional business.

To understand why traditional banking business has declined in both size and profitability, we need to look at how the financial innovations described earlier have caused banks to suffer declines in their cost advantages in acquiring funds—that is, on the liabilities side of their balance sheet—while at the same time they have lost income advantages on the assets side of their balance sheet. The simultaneous decline of cost and income advantages has resulted in reduced profitability of traditional banking and an effort by banks to leave this business and engage in new and more profitable activities.

Decline in Cost Advantages in Acquiring Funds (Liabilities). Until 1980, banks were subject to deposit rate ceilings that restricted them from paying any interest on checkable deposits and (under Regulation Q) limited them to paying a maximum interest rate of a little more than 5% on time deposits. Until the 1960s, these restrictions worked to the banks' advantage because their major source of funds (in excess of 60%) was checkable deposits, and the zero interest cost on these deposits meant that the banks had a very low cost of funds. Unfortunately, this cost advantage for banks did not last. The rise in inflation beginning in the late 1960s led to higher interest rates, which made investors more sensitive to yield differentials on different assets. The result was the *disintermediation* process, in which people began to take their money out of banks, with their low interest rates on both checkable and time deposits, and began to seek out higher-yielding investments. At the same time, attempts to get around deposit rate ceilings and reserve requirements led to the financial innovation of money market mutual funds, which put the banks at an even further disadvantage because depositors could now obtain checking account-like services while earning high interest on their money market mutual fund accounts. One manifestation of these changes in the financial system was that the low-cost source of funds, checkable deposits, declined dramatically in importance for banks, falling from more than 60% of bank liabilities to less than 10% today.

The growing difficulty for banks in raising funds led to their supporting legislation in the 1980s that eliminated Regulation Q ceilings on time deposit interest rates and allowed checkable deposit accounts that paid interest. Although these changes in regulation helped make banks more competitive in their quest for funds, it also meant that their cost of acquiring funds had risen substantially, thereby reducing their earlier cost advantage over other financial institutions.

Decline in Income Advantages on Uses of Funds (Assets). The loss of cost advantages on the liabilities side of the balance sheet for American banks is one reason that they have become less competitive, but they have also been hit by a decline in income advantages on the assets side from the financial innovations we discussed earlier—junk bonds, securitization, and the rise of the commercial paper market.

We have seen that improvements in information technology have made it easier for firms to issue securities directly to the public. This has meant that instead of going to banks to finance short-term credit needs, many of the banks' best business customers now find it cheaper to go instead to the commercial paper market for funds. The loss of this competitive advantage for banks is evident in the fact that before 1970, nonfinancial commercial paper equaled less than 5% of commercial and industrial bank loans, whereas the figure has risen to 13% today. In addition, this growth in the commercial paper market has allowed finance companies, which depend primarily on commercial paper to acquire funds, to expand their operations at the expense of banks. Finance companies, which lend to many of the same businesses that borrow from banks, have increased their market share relative to banks: Before 1980, finance company loans to business equaled about 30% of commercial and industrial bank loans; currently, they account for more than 45%.

The emergence of the junk bond market has also eaten into banks' loan business. Improvements in information technology have made it easier for corporations to sell their bonds to the public directly, thereby bypassing banks. Although *Fortune* 500 companies started taking this route in the 1970s, now lower-quality corporate borrowers are using banks less often because they have access to the junk bond market.

We have also seen that improvements in computer technology have led to securitization, whereby illiquid financial assets such as bank loans and mortgages are transformed into marketable securities. Computers enable other financial institutions to originate loans because they can now accurately evaluate credit risk with statistical methods, while computers have lowered transaction costs, making it possible to bundle these loans and sell them as securities. When default risk can be easily evaluated with computers, banks no longer have an advantage in making loans. Without their former advantages, banks have lost loan business to other financial institutions even though the banks themselves are involved in the process of securitization. Securitization has been a particular problem for mortgage-issuing institutions such as S&Ls, because most residential mortgages are now securitized.

Banks' Responses. In any industry, a decline in profitability usually results in exit from the industry (often due to widespread bankruptcies) and a shrinkage of market share. This occurred in the banking industry in the United States during the 1980s via consolidations and bank failures (discussed in Chapter 11).

In an attempt to survive and maintain adequate profit levels, many U.S. banks face two alternatives. First, they can attempt to maintain their traditional lending activity by expanding into new and riskier areas of lending. For example, U.S. banks increased their risk taking by placing a greater percentage of their total funds in commercial real estate loans, traditionally a riskier type of loan. In addition, they increased lending for corporate takeovers and leveraged buyouts, which are highly leveraged transaction loans. The decline in the profitability of banks' traditional business may thus have helped lead to the crisis in banking in the 1980s and early 1990s that we discuss in the next chapter.

The second way banks have sought to maintain former profit levels is to pursue new off-balance-sheet activities that are more profitable. U.S. commercial banks did this during the early 1980s, more than doubling the share of their income coming from off-balance-sheet, non-interest-income activities. This strategy, however, has generated concerns about what activities are proper for banks and whether nontraditional activities might be riskier and, therefore, result in excessive risk taking by banks.

The decline of banks' traditional business has thus meant that the banking industry has been driven to seek out new lines of business. This could be beneficial because by so doing, banks can keep vibrant and healthy. Indeed, bank profitability has been high in recent years, and nontraditional, off-balance-sheet activities have been playing an important role in the resurgence of bank profits. However, there is a danger that the new directions in banking could lead to increased risk taking, and thus the decline in traditional banking requires regulators to be more vigilant. It also poses new challenges for bank regulators, who, as we will see in Chapter 11, must now be far more concerned about banks' off-balance-sheet activities.

Decline of Traditional Banking in Other Industrialized Countries. Forces similar to those in the United States have been leading to the decline of traditional banking in other industrialized countries. The loss of banks' monopoly power over depositors has occurred outside the United States as well. Financial innovation and deregulation are occurring worldwide and have created attractive alternatives for both depositors and borrowers. In Japan, for example, deregulation has opened a wide array of new financial instruments to the public, causing a disintermediation process similar to that in the United States. In European countries, innovations have steadily eroded the barriers that have traditionally protected banks from competition.

In other countries, banks have also faced increased competition from the expansion of securities markets. Both financial deregulation and fundamental economic forces in other countries have improved the availability of information in securities markets, making it easier and less costly for firms to finance their activities by issuing securities rather than going to banks. Further, even in countries where securities markets have not grown, banks have still lost loan business because their best corporate customers have had increasing access to foreign and offshore capital markets, such as the Eurobond market. In smaller economies, like Australia, which still do not have well-developed corporate bond or commercial paper markets, banks have lost loan business to international securities markets. In addition, the same forces that drove the securitization process in the United States are at work in other countries and will undercut the profitability of traditional banking in these countries as well. The United States is not unique in seeing its banks face a more difficult competitive environment. Thus, although the decline of traditional banking occurred earlier in the United States than in other countries, the same forces are causing a decline in traditional banking abroad.

STRUCTURE OF THE U.S. COMMERCIAL BANKING INDUSTRY

There are approximately 7,500 commercial banks in the United States, far more than in any other country in the world. As Table 1 indicates, we have an extraordinary number of small banks. Forty-seven percent of the banks have less than $100 million in assets. Far more typical is the size distribution in Canada or the United Kingdom, where five or fewer banks dominate the industry. In contrast, the ten largest commercial banks in the United States (listed in Table 2) together hold just 50% of the assets in their industry.

Most industries in the United States have far fewer firms than the commercial banking industry; typically, large firms tend to dominate these industries to a greater extent than in the commercial banking industry. (Consider the computer software industry, which is dominated by Microsoft, or the automobile industry, which is dominated by General Motors, Ford, Daimler-Chrysler, Toyota, and Honda.) Does the large number of banks in the commercial banking industry and the absence of a few dominant firms suggest that commercial banking is more competitive than other industries?

Restrictions on Branching

The presence of so many commercial banks in the United States actually reflects past regulations that restricted the ability of these financial institutions to open **branches** (additional offices for the conduct of banking operations). Each state had its own regulations on the type and number of branches that a bank could open. Regulations on both coasts, for example, tended to allow banks to open branches throughout a state; in the middle part of the country, regulations on branching were more restrictive. The McFadden Act of 1927, which was designed to put national banks and state banks on

TABLE 1 Size Distribution of Insured Commercial Banks, September 30, 2005

Assets	Number of Banks	Share of Banks (%)	Share of Assets Held (%)
Less than $100 million	3,523	46.72	1.92
$100 million–$1 billion	3,552	47.10	11.45
$1 billion–$10 billion	380	5.04	12.76
More than $10 billion	86	1.14	73.86
Total	7,541	100.00	100.00

Source: www2.fdic.gov/SDI/SOB/.

TABLE 2 Ten Largest U.S. Banks, September 30, 2005

Bank	Assets ($ millions)	Share of All Commercial Bank Assets (%)
1. Bank of America Corp., Charlotte, NC	1,057,298	12.19
2. J. P. Morgan Chase, Columbus, OH	1,008,426	11.63
3. Citibank, New York, NY	704,616	8.12
4. Wachovia Corp., Charlotte, NC	477,994	5.51
5. Wells Fargo, Sioux Falls, SD	380,109	4.38
6. U.S. Bancorp, Cincinnati, OH	206,667	2.38
7. SunTrust Bank, Atlanta, GA	170,774	1.97
8. HSBC Bank US, Wilmington, DE	145,949	1.68
9. State Street B & T Corp., Boston, MA	91,404	1.05
10. Keybank, Cleveland, OH	87,574	1.01
Total	4,330,811	49.93

Source: www.federalreserve.gov/releases/lbr/current/default.htm.

an equal footing (and the Douglas Amendment of 1956, which closed a loophole in the McFadden Act) effectively prohibited banks from branching across state lines and forced all national banks to conform to the branching regulations in the state of their location.

The McFadden Act and state branching regulations constituted strong anticompetitive forces in the commercial banking industry, allowing many small banks to stay in existence, because larger banks were prevented from opening a branch nearby. If competition is beneficial to society, why have regulations restricting branching arisen in America? The simplest explanation is that the American public has historically been hostile to large banks. States with the most restrictive branching regulations were typically ones in which populist antibank sentiment was strongest in the nineteenth century. (These states usually had large farming populations whose relations with banks periodically became tempestuous when banks would foreclose on farmers who couldn't pay their debts.) The legacy of nineteenth-century politics was a banking system with restrictive branching regulations and hence an inordinate number of small banks. However, as we will see later in this chapter, branching restrictions have been eliminated, and we are heading toward nationwide banking.

Response to Branching Restrictions

An important feature of the U.S. banking industry is that competition can be repressed by regulation but not completely quashed. As we saw earlier in this chapter, the existence of restrictive regulation stimulates financial innovations that get around these regulations in the banks' search for profits. Regulations restricting branching have stimulated similar economic forces and have promoted the development of two financial innovations: bank holding companies and automated teller machines.

Bank Holding Companies.

A holding company is a corporation that owns several different companies. This form of corporate ownership has important advantages for banks. It has allowed them to circumvent restrictive branching regulations, because the holding company can own a controlling interest in several banks even if branching is not permitted. Furthermore, a bank holding company can engage in other activities related to banking, such as the provision of investment advice, data processing and transmission services, leasing, credit card services, and servicing of loans in other states.

The growth of the bank holding companies has been dramatic over the past three decades. Today bank holding companies own almost all large banks, and more than 90% of all commercial bank deposits are held in banks owned by holding companies.

Automated Teller Machines. Another financial innovation that avoided the restrictions on branching is the automated teller machine (ATM). Banks realized that if they did not own or rent the ATM, but instead let it be owned by someone else and paid for each transaction with a fee, the ATM would probably not be considered a branch of the bank and thus would not be subject to branching regulations. This is exactly what the regulatory agencies and courts in most states concluded. Because they enable banks to widen their markets, a number of these shared facilities (such as Cirrus and NYCE) have been established nationwide. Furthermore, even when an ATM is owned by a bank, states typically have special provisions that allow wider establishment of ATMs than is permissible for traditional "brick and mortar" branches.

As we saw earlier in this chapter, avoiding regulation was not the only reason for the development of the ATM. The advent of cheaper computer and telecommunications technology enabled banks to provide ATMs at low cost, making them a profitable innovation. This example further illustrates that technological factors often combine with incentives such as the desire to avoid restrictive regulations like branching restrictions to produce financial innovation.

BANK CONSOLIDATION AND NATIONWIDE BANKING

As we can see in Figure 3, after a remarkable period of stability from 1934 to the mid-1980s, the number of commercial banks began to fall dramatically. Why has this sudden decline taken place?

The banking industry hit some hard times in the 1980s and early 1990s, with bank failures running at a rate of over 100 per year from 1985 to 1992 (more on this later in the chapter and in Chapter 11). But bank failures are only part of the story. In the years 1985–1992, the number of banks declined by 3,000—more than double the number of failures. And in the period 1992–2005, when the banking industry returned to health, the number of commercial banks declined by a little over 3,500, less than 5% of which were bank failures, and most of these were of small banks. Thus we see that bank failures played an important, though not predominant, role in the decline in the number of banks in the 1985–1992 period and an almost negligible role in the decline in the number of banks since then.

So what explains the rest of the story? The answer is bank consolidation. Banks have been merging to create larger entities or have been buying up other banks. This gives rise to a new question: Why has bank consolidation been taking place in recent years?

As we have seen, loophole mining by banks has reduced the effectiveness of branching restrictions, with the result that many states have recognized that it would be in their best interest if they allowed ownership of banks across state lines. The result has

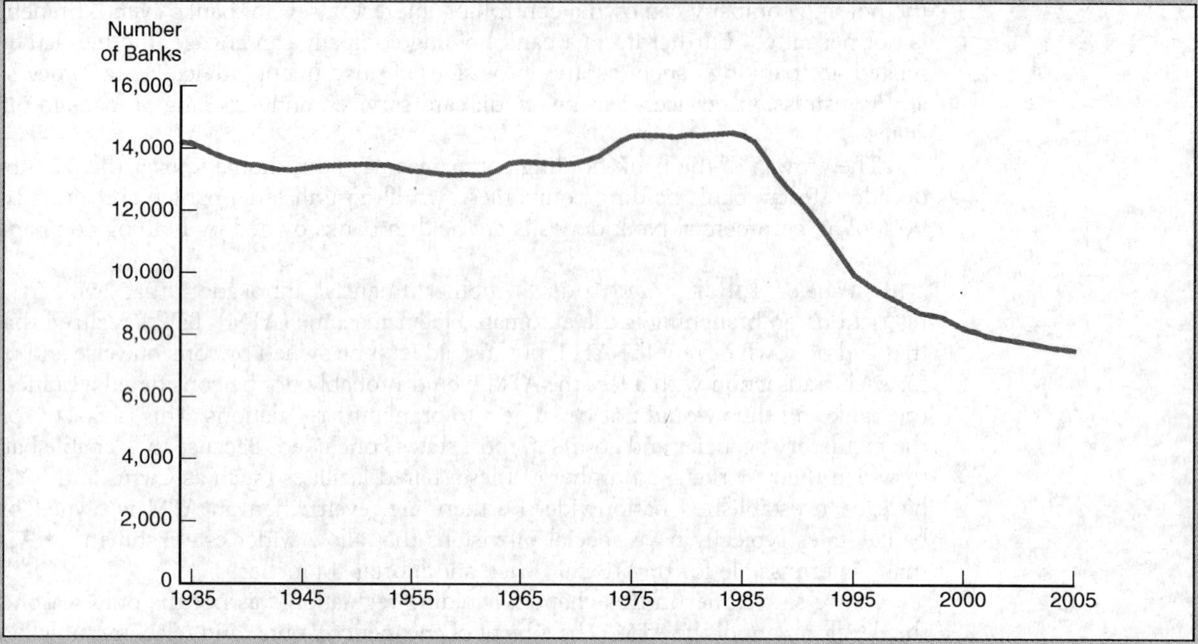

FIGURE 3 **Number of Insured Commercial Banks in the United States, 1934–2005**

Source: www2.fdic.gov/qbp/qbpSelect.asp?menuitem=STAT.

been the formation of reciprocal regional compacts in which banks in one state are allowed to own banks in other states in the region. In 1975, Maine enacted the first interstate banking legislation that allowed out-of-state bank holding companies to purchase banks in that state. In 1982, Massachusetts enacted a regional compact with other New England states to allow interstate banking, and many other regional compacts were adopted thereafter until by the early 1990s, almost all states allowed some form of interstate banking.

With the barriers to interstate banking breaking down in the early 1980s, banks recognized that they could gain the benefits of diversification because they would now be able to make loans in many states rather than just one. This gave them the advantage that if one state's economy was weak, another in which they operated might be strong, thus decreasing the likelihood that loans in different states would default at the same time. In addition, allowing banks to own banks in other states meant that they could take advantage of economies of scale by increasing their size through out-of-state acquisition of banks or by merging with banks in other states. Mergers and acquisitions explain the first phase of banking consolidation, which has played such an important role in the decline in the number of banks since 1985. Another result of the loosening of restrictions on interstate branching is the development of a new class of banks, the **superregional banks**, bank holding companies that have begun to rival the money center banks in size but whose headquarters are not in one of the money center cities (New York, Chicago, and San Francisco). Examples of these superregional banks are Bank of America of Charlotte, North Carolina, and Banc One of Columbus, Ohio.

Not surprisingly, the advent of the Web and improved computer technology is another factor driving bank consolidation. Economies of scale have increased, because

E-Finance **Information Technology and Bank Consolidation**

Achieving low costs in banking requires huge investments in information technology. In turn, such enormous investments require a business line of very large scale. This has been particularly true in the credit card business in recent years, in which huge technology investments have been made to provide customers with convenient web sites and to develop better systems to handle processing and risk analysis for both credit and fraud risk. The result has been substantial consolidation: As recently as 1995, the top five banking institutions issuing credit cards held less than 40% of total credit card debt, while today this number is more than 60%.

Information technology has also spurred increasing consolidation of the bank custody business. Banks hold the actual certificate for investors when they purchase a stock or bond and provide data on the value of these securities and the amount of risk an investor is facing. Because this business is also computer-intensive, it also requires very large-scale investments in computer technology for the bank to offer these services at competitive rates. The percentage of assets at the top ten custody banks has therefore risen from 40% in 1990 to more than 90% today.

The increasing importance of e-finance, in which the computer is playing a more central role in delivering financial services, is bringing tremendous changes to the structure of the banking industry. Although banks are more than willing to offer a full range of products to their customers, they no longer find it profitable to produce all of them. Instead, they are contracting out the business, a practice that will lead to further consolidation of technology-intensive banking businesses in the future.

large upfront investments are required to set up many information technology platforms for financial institutions (see the E-Finance box, "Information Technology and Bank Consolidation"). To take advantage of these economies of scale, banks have needed to get bigger, and this development has led to additional consolidation. Information technology has also been increasing **economies of scope**, the ability to use one resource to provide many different products and services. For example, details about the quality and creditworthiness of firms not only inform decisions about whether to make loans to them, but also can be useful in determining at what price their shares should trade. Similarly, once you have marketed one financial product to an investor, you probably know how to market another. Business people describe economies of scope by saying that there are "synergies" between different lines of business, and information technology is making these synergies more likely. The result is that consolidation is taking place not only to make financial institutions bigger, but also to increase the combination of products and services they can provide. This consolidation has had two consequences. First, different types of financial intermediaries are encroaching on each other's territory, making them more alike. Second, consolidation has led to the development of what the Federal Reserve has named **large, complex banking organizations (LCBOs)**. This development has been facilitated by the repeal of the Glass-Steagall restrictions on combinations of banking and other financial service industries discussed in the next section.

The Riegle-Neal Interstate Banking and Branching Efficiency Act of 1994

Banking consolidation was given further stimulus by the passage in 1994 of the Riegle-Neal Interstate Banking and Branching Efficiency Act. This legislation expands the regional compacts to the entire nation and overturns the McFadden Act and Douglas

Amendment's prohibition of interstate banking. Not only does this act allow bank holding companies to acquire banks in any other state, notwithstanding any state laws to the contrary, but bank holding companies can also merge the banks they own into one bank with branches in different states. States also have the option of opting out of interstate branching, a choice only Texas has made.

The Riegle-Neal Act finally established the basis for a true nationwide banking system. Although interstate banking was accomplished previously by out-of-state purchase of banks by bank holding companies, until 1994 interstate branching was virtually nonexistent, because very few states had enacted interstate branching legislation. Allowing banks to conduct interstate banking through branching is especially important, because many bankers feel that economies of scale cannot be fully exploited through the bank holding company structure, but only through branching networks in which all of the bank's operations are fully coordinated.

Nationwide banks are now emerging. With the merger in 1998 of Bank of America and NationsBank, which created the first bank with branches on both coasts, consolidation in the banking industry has led to banking organizations with operations in almost all of the fifty states.

What Will the Structure of the U.S. Banking Industry Look Like in the Future?

Now that true nationwide banking in the United States is a reality, the benefits of bank consolidation for the banking industry have increased substantially, driving the next phase of mergers and acquisitions and accelerating the decline in the number of commercial banks. With great changes occurring in the structure of this industry, the question naturally arises: What will the industry look like in ten years?

One view is that the industry will become more like that in many other countries (see the Global box, "Comparison of Banking Structure in the United States and Abroad") and we will end up with only a couple of hundred banks. A more extreme view is that the industry will look like that of Canada or the United Kingdom, with a few large banks dominating the industry. Research on this question, however, comes up with a different answer. The structure of the U.S. banking industry will still be unique, but not

Global Comparison of Banking Structure in the United States and Abroad

The structure of the commercial banking industry in the United States is radically different from that in other industrialized nations. The United States is the only country that is just now developing a true national banking system in which banks have branches throughout the country. One result is that there are many more banks in the United States than in other industrialized countries. In contrast to the United States, which has on the order of 7,500 commercial banks, every other industrialized country has far less than 1,000. Japan, for example, has fewer than 100 commercial banks—a mere fraction of the number in the United States, even though its economy and population are half the size of those of the United States. Another result of the past restrictions on branching in the United States is that our banks tend to be much smaller than those in other countries.

to the degree it once was. Most experts predict that the consolidation surge will settle down as the U.S. banking industry approaches several thousand, rather than several hundred, banks.[2]

Banking consolidation will result not only in a smaller number of banks, but as the mergers between Chase Manhattan Bank and Chemical Bank and between Bank of America and NationsBank suggest, a shift in assets from smaller banks to larger banks as well. Within ten years, the share of bank assets in banks with less than $100 million in assets is expected to halve, while the amount at the megabanks, those with more than $100 billion in assets, is expected to more than double. Indeed, the United States now has several trillion-dollar banks (e.g., Citibank, J. P. Morgan Chase, and Bank of America).

Are Bank Consolidation and Nationwide Banking Good Things?

Advocates of nationwide banking believe that it will produce more efficient banks and a healthier banking system less prone to bank failures. However, critics of bank consolidation fear that it will eliminate small banks, referred to as *community banks,* and that this will result in less lending to small businesses. In addition, they worry that a few banks will come to dominate the industry, making the banking business less competitive.

Most economists are skeptical of these criticisms of bank consolidation. As we have seen, research indicates that even after bank consolidation is completed, the United States will still have plenty of banks. The banking industry will thus remain highly competitive, probably even more so than now considering that banks that have been protected from competition from out-of-state banks will now have to compete with them vigorously to stay in business.

It also does not look as though community banks will disappear. When New York state liberalized its branching laws in 1962, there were fears that community banks upstate would be driven from the market by the big New York City banks. Not only did this not happen, but some of the big boys found that the small banks were able to run rings around them in the local markets. Similarly, California, which has had unrestricted statewide branching for a long time, continues to have a thriving population of community banks.

Economists see some important benefits from bank consolidation and nationwide banking. The elimination of geographic restrictions on banking will increase competition and drive inefficient banks out of business, increasing the efficiency of the banking sector. The move to larger banking organizations also means that there will be some increase in efficiency because they can take advantage of economies of scale and scope. The increased diversification of banks' loan portfolios may lower the probability of a banking crisis in the future. In the 1980s and early 1990s, bank failures were often concentrated in states with weak economies. For example, after the decline in oil prices in 1986, all of the major commercial banks in Texas, which had been very profitable, found themselves in trouble. At that time, banks in New England were doing fine. However, when the 1990–1991 recession hit New England hard, some New England banks started failing. With nationwide banking, a bank could make loans in both New England and

---

[2]For example, see Allen N. Berger, Anil K. Kashyap, and Joseph Scalise, "The Transformation of the U.S. Banking Industry: What a Long, Strange Trip It's Been," *Brookings Papers on Economic Activity* 2 (1995): 55–201; and Timothy Hannan and Stephen Rhoades, "Future U.S. Banking Structure, 1990–2010," *Antitrust Bulletin* 37 (1992) 737–798. For a more detailed treatment of the bank consolidation process taking place in the United States, see Frederic S. Mishkin, "Bank Consolidation: A Central Banker's Perspective," in *Mergers of Financial Institutions,* ed. Yakov Amihud and Geoffrey Wood (Boston: Kluwer Academic Publishers, 1998), pp. 3–19.

Texas and would thus be less likely to fail, because when loans go sour in one location, they would likely be doing well in the other. Thus nationwide banking is seen as a major step toward creating a banking system that is less vulnerable to banking crises.

Two concerns remain about the effects of bank consolidation—that it may lead to a reduction in lending to small businesses and that banks rushing to expand into new geographic markets may take increased risks leading to bank failures. The jury is still out on these concerns, but most economists see the benefits of bank consolidation and nationwide banking as outweighing the costs.

SEPARATION OF THE BANKING AND OTHER FINANCIAL SERVICE INDUSTRIES

Another important feature of the structure of the banking industry in the United States until recently was the separation of the banking and other financial services industries—such as securities, insurance, and real estate—mandated by the Glass-Steagall Act of 1933. As pointed out earlier in the chapter, Glass-Steagall allowed commercial banks to sell new offerings of government securities but prohibited them from underwriting corporate securities or from engaging in brokerage activities. It also prevented banks from engaging in insurance and real estate activities. In turn, it prevented investment banks and insurance companies from engaging in commercial banking activities and thus protected banks from competition.

Erosion of Glass-Steagall

Despite the Glass-Steagall prohibitions, the pursuit of profits and financial innovation stimulated both banks and other financial institutions to bypass the intent of the Glass-Steagall Act and encroach on each other's traditional territory. Brokerage firms engaged in the traditional banking business of issuing deposit instruments with the development of money market mutual funds and cash management accounts. After the Federal Reserve used a loophole in Section 20 of the Glass-Steagall Act in 1987 to allow bank holding companies to underwrite previously prohibited classes of securities, banks began to enter this business. The loophole allowed affiliates of approved commercial banks to engage in underwriting activities as long as the revenue didn't exceed a specified amount, which started at 10% but was raised to 25% of the affiliates' total revenue. After the U.S. Supreme Court validated the Fed's action in July 1988, the Federal Reserve allowed J. P. Morgan, a commercial bank holding company, to underwrite corporate debt securities (in January 1989) and to underwrite stocks (in September 1990), with the privilege later extended to other bank holding companies. The regulatory agencies also allowed banks to engage in some real estate and some insurance activities.

The Gramm-Leach-Bliley Financial Services Modernization Act of 1999: Repeal of Glass-Steagall

Because restrictions on commercial banks' securities and insurance activities put American banks at a competitive disadvantage relative to foreign banks, bills to overturn Glass-Steagall appeared in almost every session of Congress in the 1990s. With the merger in 1998 of Citicorp, the second-largest bank in the United States, and Travelers Group, an insurance company that also owned the third-largest securities firm in the country (Salomon Smith Barney), the pressure to abolish Glass-Steagall became overwhelming. Legislation to eliminate Glass-Steagall finally came to fruition in 1999. This legislation, the Gramm-Leach-Bliley Financial Services Modernization Act of 1999, allows securities firms and insurance companies to purchase banks, and allows banks to underwrite insurance and securities and engage in real estate activities. Under this legislation, states retain regulatory authority over insurance activities, while the Securities and Exchange Commission continues to have oversight of securities activities. The Office of the Comptroller of the Currency has the authority to regulate bank subsidiaries engaged in securities underwriting, but the Federal Reserve continues to have the authority to oversee the bank holding companies under which all real estate and insurance activities and large securities operations will be housed.

Implications for Financial Consolidation

As we have seen, the Riegle-Neal Interstate Banking and Branching Efficiency Act of 1994 has stimulated consolidation of the banking industry. The financial consolidation process will be further hastened by the Gramm-Leach-Bliley Act of 1999, because the way is now open to consolidation in terms not only of the number of banking institutions, but also across financial service activities. Given that information technology is increasing economies of scope, mergers of banks with other financial service firms like that of Citicorp and Travelers should become increasingly common, and more mega-mergers are likely to be on the way. Banking institutions are becoming not only larger, but also increasingly complex organizations, engaging in the full gamut of financial service activities.

Separation of Banking and Other Financial Services Industries Throughout the World

Not many other countries in the aftermath of the Great Depression followed the lead of the United States in separating the banking and other financial services industries. In fact, in the past this separation was the most prominent difference between banking regulation in the United States and in other countries. Around the world, there are three basic frameworks for the banking and securities industries.

The first framework is *universal banking,* which exists in Germany, the Netherlands, and Switzerland. It provides no separation at all between the banking and securities industries. In a universal banking system, commercial banks provide a full range of banking, securities, real estate, and insurance services, all within a single legal entity. Banks are allowed to own sizable equity shares in commercial firms, and often they do.

The *British-style universal banking system,* the second framework, is found in the United Kingdom and countries with close ties to it, such as Canada and Australia, and now the United States. The British-style universal bank engages in securities underwriting, but it differs from the German-style universal bank in three ways: Separate legal subsidiaries are more common, bank equity holdings of commercial firms are less common, and combinations of banking and insurance firms are less common.

The third framework features some legal separation of the banking and other financial services industries, as in Japan. A major difference between the U.S. and Japanese banking systems is that Japanese banks are allowed to hold substantial equity stakes in commercial firms, whereas American banks cannot. In addition, most American banks use a bank-holding-company structure, but bank holding companies are illegal in Japan. Although the banking and securities industries are legally separated in Japan under Section 65 of the Japanese Securities Act, commercial banks are increasingly being allowed to engage in securities activities and like U.S. banks are becoming more like British-style universal banks.

THRIFT INDUSTRY: REGULATION AND STRUCTURE

Not surprisingly, the regulation and structure of the thrift industry (savings and loan associations, mutual savings banks, and credit unions) closely parallels the regulation and structure of the commercial banking industry.

Savings and Loan Associations

Just as there is a dual banking system for commercial banks, savings and loan associations (S&Ls) can be chartered either by the federal government or by the states. Most S&Ls, whether state or federally chartered, are members of the Federal Home Loan Bank System (FHLBS). Established in 1932, the FHLBS was styled after the Federal Reserve System. It has 12 district Federal Home Loan banks, which are supervised by the Office of Thrift Supervision.

Federal deposit insurance (up to $100,000 per account) for S&Ls is provided by the Savings Association Insurance Fund, a subsidiary of the FDIC. The Office of Thrift Supervision regulates federally insured S&Ls by setting minimum capital requirements, requiring periodic reports, and examining the S&Ls. It is also the chartering agency for federally chartered S&Ls, and for these S&Ls it approves mergers and sets the rules for branching.

The branching regulations for S&Ls were more liberal than for commercial banks: In the past, almost all states permitted branching of S&Ls, and since 1980, federally chartered S&Ls were allowed to branch statewide in all states. Since 1981, mergers of financially troubled S&Ls were allowed across state lines, and nationwide branching of S&Ls is now a reality.

The FHLBS, like the Fed, makes loans to the members of the system (obtaining funds for this purpose by issuing bonds). However, in contrast to the Fed's discount loans, which are expected to be repaid quickly, the loans from the FHLBS often need not be repaid for long periods of time. In addition, the rates charged to S&Ls for these loans are often below the rates that the S&Ls must pay when they borrow in the open market. In this way, the FHLBS loan program provides a subsidy to the savings and loan industry (and implicitly to the housing industry, since most of the S&L loans are for residential mortgages).

As we will see in the next chapter, the savings and loans experienced serious difficulties in the 1980s. Because savings and loans now engage in many of the same activities as commercial banks, many experts view having a separate charter and regulatory apparatus for S&Ls an anachronism that no longer makes sense.

Mutual Savings Banks

Of the 400 or so mutual savings banks, which are similar to S&Ls but are jointly owned by the depositors, approximately half are chartered by states. Although the mutual savings banks are primarily regulated by the states in which they are located, the majority have their deposits insured by the FDIC up to the limit of $100,000 per account; these banks are also subject to many of the FDIC's regulations for state-chartered banks. As a rule, the mutual savings banks whose deposits are not insured by the FDIC have their deposits insured by state insurance funds.

The branching regulations for mutual savings banks are determined by the states in which they operate. Because these regulations are not particularly restrictive, there are few mutual savings banks with assets of less than $25 million.

Credit Unions

Credit unions are small cooperative lending institutions organized around a particular group of individuals with a common bond (e.g., union members or employees of a particular firm). They are the only depository institutions that are tax-exempt and can be chartered either by the states or by the federal government; more than half are federally chartered. The National Credit Union Administration (NCUA) issues federal charters and regulates federally chartered credit unions by setting minimum capital requirements, requiring periodic reports, and examining the credit unions. Federal deposit insurance (up to the $100,000-per-account limit) is provided to both federally chartered and state-chartered credit unions by a subsidiary of the NCUA, the National Credit Union Share Insurance Fund (NCUSIF). Because the majority of credit union lending is for consumer loans with fairly short terms to maturity, these institutions did not suffer the financial difficulties of the S&Ls and mutual savings banks.

Because their members share a common bond, credit unions are typically quite small; most hold less than $10 million of assets. In addition, their ties to a particular industry or company make them more likely to fail when large numbers of workers in that industry or company are laid off and have trouble making loan payments. Recent regulatory changes allow individual credit unions to cater to a more diverse group of people by interpreting the common bond requirement less strictly, and this has encouraged an expansion in the size of credit unions that may help reduce credit union failures in the future.

Often a credit union's shareholders are dispersed over many states, and sometimes even worldwide, so branching across state lines and into other countries is permitted for federally chartered credit unions. The Navy Federal Credit Union, for example, whose shareholders are members of the U.S. Navy and Marine Corps, has branches throughout the world.

INTERNATIONAL BANKING

In 1960, only eight U.S. banks operated branches in foreign countries, and their total assets were less than $4 billion. Currently, around 100 American banks have branches abroad, with assets totaling more than $1.5 trillion. The spectacular growth in international banking can be explained by three factors.

First is the rapid growth in international trade and multinational (worldwide) corporations that has occurred since 1960. When American firms operate abroad, they need banking services in foreign countries to help finance international trade. For example, they might need a loan in a foreign currency to operate a factory abroad. And when they sell goods abroad, they need to have a bank exchange the foreign currency they have received for their goods into dollars. Although these firms could use foreign banks to provide them with these international banking services, many of them prefer to do business with the U.S. banks with which they have established long-term relationships and which understand American business customs and practices. As international trade has grown, international banking has grown with it.

Second, American banks have been able to earn substantial profits by being very active in global investment banking, in which they underwrite foreign securities. They also sell insurance abroad, and they derive substantial profits from these investment banking and insurance activities.

Third, American banks have wanted to tap into the large pool of dollar-denominated deposits in foreign countries known as Eurodollars. To understand the structure of U.S. banking overseas, let us first look at the Eurodollar market, an important source of growth for international banking.

Eurodollar Market

Eurodollars are created when deposits in accounts in the United States are transferred to a bank outside the country and are kept in the form of dollars. (For a discussion of the birth of the Eurodollar, see the Global box, "Ironic Birth of the Eurodollar Market".) For example, if Rolls-Royce PLC deposits a $1 million check, written on an account at an American bank, in its bank in London—specifying that the deposit is payable in dollars—$1 million in Eurodollars is created.[3] More than 90% of Eurodollar deposits are time deposits, more than half of them certificates of deposit with maturities of 30 days or more. The total amount of Eurodollars outstanding is on the order of $5.2 trillion, making the Eurodollar market one of the most important financial markets in the world economy.

Why would companies such as Rolls-Royce want to hold dollar deposits outside the United States? First, the dollar is the most widely used currency in international trade, so Rolls-Royce might want to hold deposits in dollars to conduct its international transactions. Second, Eurodollars are "offshore" deposits—they are held in countries that will not subject them to regulations such as reserve requirements or restrictions (called *capital controls*) on taking the deposits outside the country.[4]

The main center of the Eurodollar market is London, a major international financial center for hundreds of years. Eurodollars are also held outside Europe in locations that provide offshore status to these deposits—for example, Singapore, the Bahamas, and the Cayman Islands.

The minimum transaction in the Eurodollar market is typically $1 million, and approximately 75% of Eurodollar deposits are held by banks. Plainly, you and I are unlikely to come into direct contact with Eurodollars. The Eurodollar market is, however, an important source of funds to U.S. banks, whose borrowing of these deposits is more than $700 billion. Rather than using an intermediary and borrowing all the deposits from foreign banks, American banks decided that they could earn higher profits by opening their own branches abroad to attract these deposits. Consequently, the Eurodollar market has been an important stimulus to U.S. banking overseas.

---

[3]Note that the London bank keeps the $1 million on deposit at the American bank, so the creation of Eurodollars has not caused a reduction in the amount of bank deposits in the United States.

[4]Although most offshore deposits are denominated in dollars, some are denominated in other currencies. Collectively, these offshore deposits are referred to as Eurocurrencies. A Japanese yen-denominated deposit held in London, for example, is called a Euroyen.

Global Ironic Birth of the Eurodollar Market

One of capitalism's great ironies is that the Eurodollar market, one of the most important financial markets used by capitalists, was fathered by the Soviet Union. In the early 1950s, during the height of the Cold War, the Soviets had accumulated a substantial amount of dollar balances held by banks in the United States. Because the Russians feared that the U.S. government might freeze these assets in the United States, they wanted to move the deposits to Europe, where they would be safe from expropriation. (This fear was not unjustified—consider the U.S. freeze on Iranian assets in 1979 and Iraqi assets in 1990.) However, they also wanted to keep the deposits in dollars so that they could be used in their international transactions. The solution to the problem was to transfer the deposits to European banks but to keep the deposits denominated in dollars. When the Soviets did this, the Eurodollar was born.

Structure of U.S. Banking Overseas

U.S. banks have most of their foreign branches in Latin America, the Far East, the Caribbean, and London. The largest volume of assets is held by branches in London, because it is a major international financial center and the central location for the Eurodollar market. Latin America and the Far East have many branches because of the importance of U.S. trade with these regions. Parts of the Caribbean (especially the Bahamas and the Cayman Islands) have become important as tax havens, with minimal taxation and few restrictive regulations. In actuality, the bank branches in the Bahamas and the Cayman Islands are "shell operations" because they function primarily as bookkeeping centers and do not provide normal banking services.

An alternative corporate structure for U.S. banks that operate overseas is the **Edge Act corporation**, a special subsidiary engaged primarily in international banking. U.S. banks (through their holding companies) can also own a controlling interest in foreign banks and in foreign companies that provide financial services, such as finance companies. The international activities of U.S. banking organizations are governed primarily by the Federal Reserve's Regulation K.

In late 1981, the Federal Reserve approved the creation of **international banking facilities (IBFs)** within the United States that can accept time deposits from foreigners but are not subject to either reserve requirements or restrictions on interest payments. IBFs are also allowed to make loans to foreigners, but they are not allowed to make loans to domestic residents. States have encouraged the establishment of IBFs by exempting them from state and local taxes. In essence, IBFs are treated like foreign branches of U.S. banks and are not subject to domestic regulations and taxes. The purpose of establishing IBFs is to encourage American and foreign banks to do more banking business in the United States rather than abroad. From this point of view, IBFs were a success: Their assets climbed to nearly $200 billion in the first two years, and were $1.0 trillion at the end of 2004.

Foreign Banks in the United States

The growth in international trade has not only encouraged U.S. banks to open offices overseas, but has also encouraged foreign banks to establish offices in the United States. Foreign banks have been extremely successful in the United States. Currently, they hold more than 10% of total U.S. bank assets and do a large portion of all U.S. bank lending, with nearly a 16% market share for lending to U.S. corporations.

Foreign banks engage in banking activities in the United States by operating an agency office of the foreign bank, a subsidiary U.S. bank, or a branch of the foreign bank. An agency office can lend and transfer funds in the United States, but it cannot accept deposits from domestic residents. Agency offices have the advantage of not being subject to regulations that apply to full-service banking offices (such as requirements for FDIC insurance). A subsidiary U.S. bank is just like any other U.S. bank (it may even have an American-sounding name) and is subject to the same regulations, but it is owned by the foreign bank. A branch of a foreign bank bears the foreign bank's name and is usually a full-service office. Foreign banks may also form Edge Act corporations and IBFs.

Before 1978, foreign banks were not subject to many regulations that applied to domestic banks: They could open branches across state lines and were not expected to meet reserve requirements, for example. The passage of the International Banking Act of 1978, however, put foreign and domestic banks on a more equal footing. Now foreign banks may open new full-service branches only in the state they designate as their home state or in states that allow the entry of out-of-state banks. Limited-service branches and agency offices in any other state are permitted, however, and foreign banks are allowed to retain any full-service branches opened before ratification of the International Banking Act of 1978.

The internationalization of banking, both by U.S. banks going abroad and by foreign banks entering the United States, has meant that financial markets throughout the world have become more integrated. As a result, there is a growing trend toward international coordination of bank regulation, one example of which is the 1988 Basel Accord to standardize minimum capital requirements in industrialized countries, discussed in Chapter 11. Financial market integration has also encouraged bank consolidation abroad, culminating in the creation of the first trillion-dollar bank with the proposed merger of the Industrial Bank of Japan, Dai-Ichi Kangyo Bank, and Fuji Bank, announced in August 1999, but which took place in 2002. Another development has been the importance of foreign banks in international banking. As is shown in Table 3, in 2005, seven of the ten largest banking groups in the world were foreign. The implications of this financial market integration for the operation of our economy are examined further in Chapter 21 when we discuss the international financial system in more detail.

TABLE 3 Ten Largest Banks in the World, 2005

Bank	Assets (U.S. $ millions)
1. Citigroup, U.S.	1,484,100
2. Mizuho Financial, Japan	1,306,600
3. BNP Paribas, France	1,228,030
4. J. P. Morgan Chase, U.S.	1,138,470
5. Royal Bank of Scotland, Scotland	1,119,900
6. Bank of America, U.S.	1,110,460
7. HSBC Group, U.K.	1,031,290
8. Mitsubishi Tokyo Financial, Japan	1,014,560
9. Barclays, U.K.	1,002,090
10. Credit Agricole, France	987,790

Source: www.forbes.com/2005/03/30/05f2000land.html.

SUMMARY

1. The history of banking in the United States has left us with a dual banking system, with commercial banks chartered by the states and the federal government. Multiple agencies regulate commercial banks: the Office of the Comptroller, the Federal Reserve, the FDIC, and the state banking authorities.
2. A change in the economic environment will stimulate financial institutions to search for financial innovations. Changes in demand conditions, especially an increase in interest-rate risk; changes in supply conditions, especially improvements in information technology; and the desire to avoid costly regulations have been major driving forces behind financial innovation. Financial innovation has caused banks to suffer declines in cost advantages in acquiring funds and in income advantages on their assets. The resulting squeeze has hurt profitability in banks' traditional lines of business and has led to a decline in traditional banking.
3. Restrictive state branching regulations and the McFadden Act, which prohibited branching across state lines, led to a large number of small commercial banks. The large number of commercial banks in the United States reflected the past *lack* of competition, not the presence of vigorous competition. Bank holding companies and ATMs were important responses to branching restrictions that weakened the restrictions' anticompetitive effect.
4. Since the mid-1980s, bank consolidation has been occurring at a rapid pace. The first phase of bank consolidation was the result of bank failures and the reduced effectiveness of branching restrictions. The second phase has been stimulated by information technology and the Riegle-Neal Interstate Banking and Branching Efficiency Act of 1994, which establishes the basis for a nationwide banking system. Once banking consolidation has settled down, we are likely to be left with a banking system with several thousand banks. Most economists believe that the benefits of bank consolidation and nationwide banking will outweigh the costs.
5. The Glass-Steagall Act separated commercial banking from the securities industry. Legislation in 1999, however, repealed the Glass-Steagall Act, removing the separation of these industries.
6. The regulation and structure of the thrift industry (savings and loan associations, mutual savings banks, and credit unions) parallel closely the regulation and structure of the commercial banking industry. Savings and loans are primarily regulated by the Office of Thrift Supervision, and deposit insurance is administered by the FDIC. Mutual savings banks are regulated by the states, and federal deposit insurance is provided by the FDIC. Credit unions are regulated by the National Credit Union Administration, and deposit insurance is provided by the National Credit Union Share Insurance Fund.
7. With the rapid growth of world trade since 1960, international banking has grown dramatically. United States banks engage in international banking activities by opening branches abroad, owning controlling interests in foreign banks, forming Edge Act corporations, and operating international banking facilities (IBFs) located in the United States. Foreign banks operate in the United States by owning a subsidiary American bank or by operating branches or agency offices in the United States.

KEY TERMS

automated banking machine (ABM), p. 253
automated teller machine (ATM), p. 253
bank holding companies, p. 250
branches, p. 261
central bank, p. 248
deposit rate ceilings, p. 256
disintermediation, p. 256
dual banking system, p. 249
economies of scope, p. 265
Edge Act corporation, p. 273
financial derivatives, p. 251
financial engineering, p. 250
futures contracts, p. 251
hedge, p. 251
international banking facilities (IBFs), p. 273
large, complex banking organizations (LCBOs), p. 265
national banks, p. 249
securitization, p. 255
state banks, p. 249
superregional banks, p. 264
sweep account, p. 257
virtual bank, p. 253

QUESTIONS AND PROBLEMS

Questions marked with an asterisk are answered at the end of the book in an appendix, "Answers to Selected Questions and Problems." Questions marked with a blue circle indicate the question is available in MyEconLab at www.myeconlab.com/mishkin.

1. Why was the United States one of the last of the major industrialized countries to have a central bank?

*2. Which regulatory agency has the primary responsibility for supervising the following categories of commercial banks?
   a. National banks
   b. Bank holding companies
   c. Non–Federal Reserve state banks
   d. Federal Reserve member state banks

3. "The commercial banking industry in Canada is less competitive than the commercial banking industry in the United States because in Canada only a few large banks dominate the industry, while in the United States there are around 7,500 commercial banks." Is this statement true, false, or uncertain? Explain your answer.

*4. Why did new technology make it harder to enforce limitations on bank branching?

5. Why has there been such a dramatic increase in bank holding companies?

*6. Why is there a higher percentage of banks with less than $25 million of assets among commercial banks than among savings and loans and mutual savings banks?

7. Unlike commercial banks, savings and loans, and mutual savings banks, credit unions did not have restrictions on locating branches in other states. Why, then, are credit unions typically smaller than the other depository institutions?

*8. What incentives have regulatory agencies created to encourage international banking? Why have they done this?

9. How could the approval of international banking facilities (IBFs) by the Fed in 1981 have reduced employment in the banking industry in Europe?

*10. If the bank at which you keep your checking account is owned by Saudi Arabians, should you worry that your deposits are less safe than if the bank were owned by Americans?

11. If reserve requirements were eliminated in the future, as some economists advocate, what effects would this have on the size of money market mutual funds?

*12. Why have banks been losing cost advantages in acquiring funds in recent years?

13. "If inflation had not risen in the 1960s and 1970s, the banking industry might be healthier today." Is this statement true, false, or uncertain? Explain your answer.

*14. Why have banks been losing income advantages on their assets in recent years?

15. "The invention of the computer is the major factor behind the decline of the banking industry." Is this statement true, false, or uncertain? Explain your answer.

WEB EXERCISES

1. Go to www2.fdic.gov/SDI/SOB. Select "Historical Statistics on Banking," then "Commercial Bank Reports." Finally, choose "Number of Institutions, Branches, and Total Offices." Looking at the trend in bank branches, does the public appear to have more or less access to banking facilities? How many banks were there in 1934 and how many are there now? Does the graph indicate that the trend toward consolidation is continuing?

2. Despite the regulations that protect banks from failure, some do fail. Go to www2.fdic.gov/hsob/. Select the tab labeled "Bank and Thrift Failures." How many bank failures occurred in the United States during the most recent complete calendar year? What were the total assets held by the banks that failed? How many banks failed in 1937?

WEB REFERENCES

www.fdic.gov/bank/

The FDIC gathers data about individual financial institutions and the banking industry.

www.financialservicefacts.org/financial

Learn about the number of employees and the current profitability of commercial banks and saving institutions.

www2.fdic.gov/SDI/SOB

Visit this web site to gather statistics on the banking industry.

MyEconLab CAN HELP YOU GET A BETTER GRADE

CHAPTER

11 Economic Analysis of Banking Regulation

Preview

As we have seen in the previous chapters, the financial system is among the most heavily regulated sectors of the economy, and banks are among the most heavily regulated of financial institutions. In this chapter, we develop an economic analysis of why regulation of banking takes the form it does.

Unfortunately, the regulatory process may not always work very well, as evidenced by recent crises in the banking systems, not only in the United States but in many countries throughout the world. Here we also use our economic analysis of banking regulation to explain the worldwide crises in banking and to consider how the regulatory system can be reformed to prevent future disasters.

ASYMMETRIC INFORMATION AND BANKING REGULATION

In earlier chapters, we have seen how asymmetric information—the fact that different parties in a financial contract do not have the same information—leads to adverse selection and moral hazard problems that have an important impact on our financial system. The concepts of asymmetric information, adverse selection, and moral hazard are especially useful in understanding why government has chosen the form of banking regulation we see in the United States and in other countries. There are eight basic categories of banking regulation: the government safety net, restrictions on bank asset holdings, capital requirements, chartering and bank examination, assessment of risk management, disclosure requirements, consumer protection, and restrictions on competition.

Government Safety Net: Deposit Insurance and the FDIC

As we saw in Chapter 8, banks are particularly well suited to solving adverse selection and moral hazard problems because they make private loans that help avoid the free-rider problem. However, this solution to the free-rider problem creates another asymmetric information problem, because depositors lack information about the quality of these private loans. This asymmetric information problem leads to two reasons why the banking system might not function well.

First, before the FDIC started operations in 1934, a **bank failure** (in which a bank is unable to meet its obligations to pay its depositors and other creditors and so must go out of business) meant that depositors would have to wait to get their deposit funds until the bank was liquidated (until its assets had been turned into cash); at that time, they would be paid only a fraction of the value of their deposits. Unable to learn if bank managers were taking on too much risk or were outright crooks, depositors would be reluctant to put money in the bank, thus making banking institutions less viable. Second, depositors' lack of information about the quality of bank assets can lead to bank panics, which, as we saw in Chapter 8, can have serious harmful consequences for the economy. To see this, consider the following situation. There is no deposit insurance, and an adverse shock hits the economy. As a result of the shock, 5% of the banks have such large losses on loans that they become insolvent (have a negative net worth and so are bankrupt). Because of asymmetric information, depositors are unable to tell whether their bank is a good bank or one of the 5% that are insolvent. Depositors at bad *and* good banks recognize that they may not get back 100 cents on the dollar for their deposits and will want to withdraw them. Indeed, because banks operate on a "sequential service constraint" (a first-come, first-served basis), depositors have a very strong incentive to show up at the bank first, because if they are last in line, the bank may run out of funds and they will get nothing. Uncertainty about the health of the banking system in general can lead to runs on banks both good and bad, and the failure of one bank can hasten the failure of others (referred to as the *contagion effect*). If nothing is done to restore the public's confidence, a bank panic can ensue.

Indeed, bank panics were a fact of American life in the nineteenth and early twentieth centuries, with major ones occurring every 20 years or so in 1819, 1837, 1857, 1873, 1884, 1893, 1907, and 1930–1933. Bank failures were a serious problem even during the boom years of the 1920s, when the number of bank failures averaged around 600 per year.

A government safety net for depositors can short-circuit runs on banks and bank panics, and by providing protection for the depositor, it can overcome reluctance to put funds in the banking system. One form of the safety net is deposit insurance, a guarantee such as that provided by the Federal Deposit Insurance Corporation (FDIC) in the United States in which depositors are paid off in full on the first $100,000 they have deposited in a bank no matter what happens to the bank. With fully insured deposits, depositors don't need to run to the bank to make withdrawals—even if they are worried about the bank's health—because their deposits will be worth 100 cents on the dollar no matter what. From 1930 to 1933, the years immediately preceding the creation of the FDIC, the number of bank failures averaged more than 2,000 per year. After the establishment of the FDIC in 1934, bank failures averaged fewer than 15 per year until 1981.

The FDIC uses two primary methods to handle a failed bank. In the first, called the *payoff method*, the FDIC allows the bank to fail and pays off deposits up to the $100,000 insurance limit (with funds acquired from the insurance premiums paid by the banks who have bought FDIC insurance). After the bank has been liquidated, the FDIC lines up with other creditors of the bank and is paid its share of the proceeds from the liquidated assets. Typically, when the payoff method is used, account holders with deposits in excess of the $100,000 limit get back more than 90 cents on the dollar, although the process can take several years to complete.

In the second method, called the *purchase and assumption method*, the FDIC reorganizes the bank, typically by finding a willing merger partner who assumes (takes over) all of the failed bank's deposits so that no depositor loses a penny. The FDIC may help the merger partner by providing it with subsidized loans or by buying some of the failed bank's weaker loans. The net effect of the purchase and assumption method is that the FDIC has guaranteed *all* deposits, not just those under the $100,000 limit. The purchase and assumption method was the FDIC's most common procedure for dealing with a failed bank before new banking legislation in 1991.

Deposit insurance is not the only way in which governments provide a safety net for depositors. In other countries, governments have often stood ready to provide support to domestic banks when they face runs even in the absence of explicit deposit insurance. This support is sometimes provided by lending from the central bank to troubled institutions and is often referred to as the "lender of last resort" role of the central bank. In other cases, funds are provided directly by the government to troubled institutions, or these institutions are taken over by the government and the government then guarantees that depositors will receive their money in full. However, in recent years, government deposit insurance has been growing in popularity and has spread to many countries throughout the world. Whether this trend is desirable is discussed in the Global box, "The Spread of Government Deposit Insurance Throughout the World: Is This a Good Thing?".

Moral Hazard and the Government Safety Net. Although a government safety net has been successful at protecting depositors and preventing bank panics, it is a mixed blessing. The most serious drawback of the government safety net stems from moral hazard, the incentives of one party to a transaction to engage in activities detrimental to the other party. Moral hazard is an important concern in insurance arrangements in general because the existence of insurance provides increased incentives for taking risks that might result in an insurance payoff. For example, some drivers with automobile collision insurance that has a low deductible might be more likely to drive recklessly, because if they get into an accident, the insurance company pays most of the costs for damage and repairs.

Global **The Spread of Government Deposit Insurance Throughout the World: Is This a Good Thing?**

For the first 30 years after federal deposit insurance was established in the United States, only six countries emulated the United States and adopted deposit insurance. However, this began to change in the late 1960s, with the trend accelerating in the 1990s, when the number of countries adopting deposit insurance topped 70. Government deposit insurance has taken off throughout the world because of growing concern about the health of banking systems, particularly after the increasing number of banking crises in recent years (documented at the end of this chapter). Has this spread of deposit insurance been a good thing? Has it helped improve the performance of the financial system and prevent banking crises?

The answer seems to be no under many circumstances. Research at the World Bank has found that, on average, the adoption of explicit government deposit insurance is associated with less banking sector stability and a higher incidence of banking crises.* Furthermore, on average, it seems to retard financial development. However, the negative effects of deposit insurance appear only in countries with weak institutional environments: an absence of rule of law, ineffective regulation and supervision of the financial sector, and high corruption. This is exactly what might be expected because, as we will see later in this chapter, a strong institutional environment is needed to limit the moral hazard incentives for banks to engage in the excessively risky behavior encouraged by deposit insurance. The problem is that developing a strong institutional environment may be very difficult to achieve in many emerging market countries. This leaves us with the following conclusion: Adoption of deposit insurance may be exactly the wrong medicine for promoting stability and efficiency of banking systems in emerging market countries.

*See World Bank, *Finance for Growth: Policy Choices in a Volatile World* (Oxford: World Bank and Oxford University Press, 2001).

Moral hazard is a prominent concern in government arrangements to provide a safety net. Because with a safety net depositors know that they will not suffer losses if a bank fails, they do not impose the discipline of the marketplace on banks by withdrawing deposits when they suspect that the bank is taking on too much risk. Consequently, banks with a government safety net have an incentive to take on greater risks than they otherwise would, with taxpayers paying the bill if the bank subsequently goes belly up. Banks have been given the following bet: "Heads I win, tails the taxpayer loses."

Adverse Selection and the Government Safety Net. A further problem with a government safety net like deposit insurance arises because of adverse selection, the fact that the people who are most likely to produce the adverse outcome insured against (bank failure) are those who most want to take advantage of the insurance. For example, bad drivers are more likely than good drivers to take out automobile collision insurance with a low deductible. Because depositors protected by a government safety net have little reason to impose discipline on the bank, risk-loving entrepreneurs might find the banking industry a particularly attractive one to enter—they know that they will be able to engage in highly risky activities. Even worse, because protected depositors have so little reason to monitor the bank's activities, without government intervention outright crooks might also find banking an attractive industry for their activities because it is easy for them to get away with fraud and embezzlement.

"Too Big to Fail." The moral hazard created by a government safety net and the desire to prevent bank failures have presented bank regulators with a particular quandary. Because the failure of a very large bank makes it more likely that a major financial disruption will occur, bank regulators are naturally reluctant to allow a big bank to fail and cause losses to its depositors. Indeed, consider Continental Illinois, one of the ten largest banks in the United States when it became insolvent in May 1984. Not only did the FDIC guarantee depositors up to the $100,000 insurance limit, but it also guaranteed accounts exceeding $100,000 and even prevented losses for Continental Illinois bondholders. Shortly thereafter, the Comptroller of the Currency (the regulator of national banks) testified to Congress that eleven of the largest banks would receive a similar treatment to that of Continental Illinois. Although the Comptroller did not use the term "too big to fail" (it was actually used by Congressman McKinney in those hearings), this term is now applied to a policy in which the government provides guarantees of repayment of large uninsured creditors of the largest banks, so that no depositor or creditor suffers a loss, even when they are not automatically entitled to this guarantee. The FDIC would do this by using the purchase and assumption method, giving the insolvent bank a large infusion of capital and then finding a willing merger partner to take over the bank and its deposits. The too-big-to-fail policy was extended to big banks that were not even among the eleven largest. (Note that "too big to fail" is somewhat misleading because when a bank is closed or merged into another bank, the managers are usually fired and the stockholders in the bank lose their investment.)

One problem with the too-big-to-fail policy is that it increases the moral hazard incentives for big banks. If the FDIC were willing to close a bank using the payoff method, paying depositors only up to the $100,000 limit, large depositors with more than $100,000 would suffer losses if the bank failed. Thus they would have an incentive to monitor the bank by examining the bank's activities closely and pulling their money out if the bank was taking on too much risk. To prevent such a loss of deposits, the bank would be more likely to engage in less risky activities. However, once large depositors know that a bank is too big to fail, they have no incentive to monitor the bank and pull out their deposits when it takes on too much risk: No matter what the bank does, large depositors will not suffer any losses. The result of the too-big-to-fail policy is that big banks might take on even greater risks, thereby making bank failures more likely.[1]

Financial Consolidation and the Government Safety Net. With financial innovation and the passage of the Riegle-Neal Interstate Banking and Branching and Efficiency Act of 1994 and the Gramm-Leach-Bliley Financial Services Modernization Act in 1999, financial consolidation has been proceeding at a rapid pace, leading to both larger and more complex banking organizations. Financial consolidation poses two challenges to banking regulation because of the existence of the government safety net. First, the increased size of banks as a result of financial consolidation increases the too-big-to-fail problem, because there will now be more large institutions whose failure would expose the financial system to systemic (systemwide) risk. Thus more banking institutions are likely to be treated as too big to fail, and the increased moral hazard incentives for these large institutions to take on greater risk can then increase the fragility of the financial system. Second, financial consolidation of banks with other financial services firms means that the government safety net may be extended to new activities such as securities underwriting, insurance, or real estate activities, thereby increasing incentives for greater risk taking in these activities that can also weaken the fabric of the financial system. Limiting the moral hazard incentives for the larger, more complex financial organizations that are resulting from recent changes in legislation will be one of the key issues facing banking regulators in the future.

Restrictions on Asset Holdings and Bank Capital Requirements

As we have seen, the moral hazard associated with a government safety net encourages too much risk taking on the part of banks. Bank regulations that restrict asset holdings and bank capital requirements are directed at minimizing this moral hazard, which can cost the taxpayers dearly.

Even in the absence of a government safety net, banks still have the incentive to take on too much risk. Risky assets may provide the bank with higher earnings when they pay off; but if they do not pay off and the bank fails, depositors are left holding the bag. If depositors were able to monitor the bank easily by acquiring information on its risk-taking activities, they would immediately withdraw their deposits if the bank was taking on too much risk. To prevent such a loss of deposits, the bank would be more likely to reduce its risk-taking activities. Unfortunately, acquiring information on a bank's activities to learn how much risk the bank is taking can be a difficult task. Hence most depositors are incapable of imposing discipline that might prevent banks from engaging in risky activities. A strong rationale for government regulation to reduce risk taking on the part of banks therefore existed even before the establishment of federal deposit insurance.

Bank regulations that restrict banks from holding risky assets such as common stock are a direct means of making banks avoid too much risk. Bank regulations also promote diversification, which reduces risk by limiting the amount of loans in particular categories or to individual borrowers. Requirements that banks have sufficient bank capital are another way to reduce the bank's incentives to take on risk. When a bank is

---

[1]Evidence reveals, as our analysis predicts, that large banks took on riskier loans than smaller banks and that this led to higher loan losses for big banks; see John Boyd and Mark Gertler, "U.S. Commercial Banking: Trends, Cycles and Policy," *NBER Macroeconomics Annual*, 1993, pp. 319–368.

forced to hold a large amount of equity capital, the bank has more to lose if it fails and is thus more likely to pursue less risky activities.

Bank capital requirements take two forms. The first type is based on the **leverage ratio**, the amount of capital divided by the bank's total assets. To be classified as well capitalized, a bank's leverage ratio must exceed 5%; a lower leverage ratio, especially one below 3%, triggers increased regulatory restrictions on the bank. Through most of the 1980s, minimum bank capital in the United States was set solely by specifying a minimum leverage ratio.

In the wake of the Continental Illinois and savings and loans bailouts, regulators in the United States and the rest of the world have become increasingly worried about banks' holdings of risky assets and about the increase in banks' **off-balance-sheet activities**, activities that involve trading financial instruments and generating income from fees, which do not appear on bank balance sheets but nevertheless expose banks to risk. An agreement among banking officials from industrialized nations set up the **Basel Committee on Banking Supervision** (because it meets under the auspices of the Bank for International Settlements in Basel, Switzerland), which has implemented the **Basel Accord** dealing with a second type of capital requirements, risk-based capital requirements. The Basel Accord, which required that banks hold as capital at least 8% of their risk-weighted assets, has been adopted by more than 100 countries, including the United States. Assets and off-balance-sheet activities were allocated into four categories, each with a different weight to reflect the degree of credit risk. The first category carries a zero weight and includes items that have little default risk, such as reserves and government securities in the Organization for Economic Cooperation and Development (OECD—industrialized) countries. The second category has a 20% weight and includes claims on banks in OECD countries. The third category has a weight of 50% and includes municipal bonds and residential mortgages. The fourth category has the maximum weight of 100% and includes loans to consumers and corporations. Off-balance-sheet activities are treated in a similar manner by assigning a credit-equivalent percentage that converts them to on-balance-sheet items to which the appropriate risk weight applies. The 1996 Market Risk Amendment to the Basel Accord set minimum capital requirements for risks in banks' trading accounts.

Over time, limitations of the Basel Accord have become apparent, because the regulatory measure of bank risk as stipulated by the risk weights can differ substantially from the actual risk the bank faces. This has resulted in **regulatory arbitrage**, a practice in which banks keep on their books assets that have the same risk-based capital requirement but are relatively risky, such as a loan to a company with a very low credit rating, while taking off their books low-risk assets, such as a loan to a company with a very high credit rating. The Basel Accord could thus lead to increased risk taking, the opposite of its intent. To address these limitations, the Basel Committee on Bank Supervision has released proposals for a new capital accord, often referred to as Basel 2, but it is not clear if it is workable (see the Global box, "Basel 2: Is It Unworkable?").

The Basel Committee's work on bank capital requirements is never-ending. As the banking industry changes, the regulation of bank capital must change with it to ensure the safety and soundness of the banking institutions.

Bank Supervision: Chartering and Examination

Overseeing who operates banks and how they are operated, referred to as **bank supervision** or more generally as **prudential supervision**, is an important method for reducing adverse selection and moral hazard in the banking business. Because banks can be

Global Basel 2: Is It Unworkable?

Starting in June 1999, the Basel Committee on Banking Supervision released several proposals to reform the original 1988 Basel Accord. These efforts have culminated in what bank supervisors refer to as Basel 2, which is based on three pillars. Pillar 1 intends to link capital requirements for large, internationally active banks more closely to actual risk. It does so by specifying many more categories of risk with different weights in its standardized approach. Alternatively, it allows sophisticated banks to pursue instead an internal ratings–based approach that permits banks to use their own models of credit risk. Pillar 2 focuses on strengthening the supervisory process, particularly in assessing the quality of risk management in banking institutions and in evaluating whether these institutions have adequate procedures to determine how much capital they need. Pillar 3 focuses on improving market discipline through increased disclosure of details about the bank's credit exposures, its amount of reserves and capital, the officials who control the bank, and the effectiveness of its internal ratings system.

Although Basel 2 makes great strides toward limiting excessive risk taking by internationally active banking institutions, it has come at a cost of greatly increasing the complexity of the Accord. The document describing the original Basel Accord was 26 pages, while the second draft of Basel 2 issued in January 2001 exceeds 500 pages. The original timetable called for the completion of the final round of consultation by the end of May 2001, with the new rules taking effect by 2004. However, criticism from banks, trade associations, and national regulators led to several postponements. The final draft was not published until June of 2004, and Basel 2 is scheduled to be implemented at the beginning of 2008. Because of the increased complexity of the new Basel Accord, there are concerns that it might prove unworkable.

used by crooks or overambitious entrepreneurs to engage in highly speculative activities, such undesirable people would be eager to run a bank. Chartering banks is one method for preventing this adverse selection problem; through chartering, proposals for new banks are screened to prevent undesirable people from controlling them.

Regular on-site bank examinations, which allow regulators to monitor whether the bank is complying with capital requirements and restrictions on asset holdings, also function to limit moral hazard. Bank examiners give banks a *CAMELS rating.* The acronym is based on the six areas assessed: capital adequacy, asset quality, management, earnings, liquidity, and sensitivity to market risk. With this information about a bank's activities, regulators can enforce regulations by taking such formal actions as *cease and desist orders* to alter the bank's behavior or even close a bank if its CAMELS rating is sufficiently low. Actions taken to reduce moral hazard by restricting banks from taking on too much risk help reduce the adverse selection problem further, because with less opportunity for risk taking, risk-loving entrepreneurs will be less likely to be attracted to the banking industry. Note that the methods regulators use to cope with adverse selection and moral hazard have their counterparts in private financial markets (see Chapters 8 and 9). Chartering is similar to the screening of potential borrowers, regulations restricting risky asset holdings are similar to restrictive covenants that prevent borrowing firms from engaging in risky investment activities, bank capital requirements act like restrictive covenants that require minimum amounts of net worth for borrowing firms, and regular bank examinations are similar to the monitoring of borrowers by lending institutions.

A commercial bank obtains a charter either from the Comptroller of the Currency (in the case of a national bank) or from a state banking authority (in the case of a state bank). To obtain a charter, the people planning to organize the bank must submit an application that shows how they plan to operate the bank. In evaluating the application, the regulatory authority looks at whether the bank is likely to be sound by examining the quality of the bank's intended management, the likely earnings of the bank, and the amount of the bank's initial capital. Before 1980, the chartering agency typically explored the issue of whether the community needed a new bank. Often a new bank charter would not be granted if existing banks in a community would be hurt by its presence. Today this anticompetitive stance (justified by the desire to prevent failures of existing banks) is no longer as strong in the chartering agencies.

Once a bank has been chartered, it is required to file periodic (usually quarterly) *call reports* that reveal the bank's assets and liabilities, income and dividends, ownership, foreign exchange operations, and other details. The bank is also subject to examination by the bank regulatory agencies to ascertain its financial condition at least once a year. To avoid duplication of effort, the three federal agencies work together and usually accept each other's examinations. This means that, typically, national banks are examined by the Office of the Comptroller of the Currency, the state banks that are members of the Federal Reserve System are examined by the Fed, and insured nonmember state banks are examined by the FDIC.

Bank examinations are conducted by bank examiners, who sometimes make unannounced visits to the bank (so that nothing can be "swept under the rug" in anticipation of their examination). The examiners study a bank's books to see whether it is complying with the rules and regulations that apply to its holdings of assets. If a bank is holding securities or loans that are too risky, the bank examiner can force the bank to get rid of them. If a bank examiner decides that a loan is unlikely to be repaid, the examiner can force the bank to declare the loan worthless (to write off the loan, which reduces the bank's capital). If, after examining the bank, the examiner feels that it does not have sufficient capital or has engaged in dishonest practices, the bank can be declared a "problem bank" and will be subject to more frequent examinations.

Assessment of Risk Management

Traditionally, on-site bank examinations have focused primarily on assessment of the quality of the bank's balance sheet at a point in time and whether it complies with capital requirements and restrictions on asset holdings. Although the traditional focus is important for reducing excessive risk taking by banks, it is no longer felt to be adequate in today's world, in which financial innovation has produced new markets and instruments that make it easy for banks and their employees to make huge bets easily and quickly. In this new financial environment, a bank that is healthy at a particular point in time can be driven into insolvency extremely rapidly from trading losses, as forcefully demonstrated by the failure of Barings in 1995 (discussed in Chapter 9). Thus an examination that focuses only on a bank's position at a point in time may not be effective in indicating whether a bank will, in fact, be taking on excessive risk in the near future.

This change in the financial environment for banking institutions has resulted in a major shift in thinking about the bank supervisory process throughout the world. Bank examiners are now placing far greater emphasis on evaluating the soundness of a bank's management processes with regard to controlling risk. This shift in thinking was reflected in a new focus on risk management in the Federal Reserve System's 1993 guidelines to examiners on trading and derivatives activities. The focus was expanded and formalized in the Trading Activities Manual issued early in 1994, which provided bank examiners with tools to evaluate risk management systems. In late 1995, the Federal Reserve and the Comptroller of the Currency announced that they would be assessing risk management processes at the banks they supervise. Now bank examiners give a separate risk management rating from 1 to 5 that feeds into the overall management rating as part of the CAMELS system. Four elements of sound risk management are assessed to come up with the risk management rating: (1) the quality of oversight provided by the board of directors and senior management, (2) the adequacy of policies and limits for all activities that present significant risks, (3) the quality of the risk measurement and monitoring systems, and (4) the adequacy of internal controls to prevent fraud or unauthorized activities on the part of employees.

This shift toward focusing on management processes is also reflected in recent guidelines adopted by the U.S. bank regulatory authorities to deal with interest-rate risk. These guidelines require the bank's board of directors to establish interest-rate risk limits, appoint officials of the bank to manage this risk, and monitor the bank's risk exposure. The guidelines also require that senior management of a bank develop formal risk management policies and procedures to ensure that the board of director's risk limits are not violated and to implement internal controls to monitor interest-rate risk and compliance with the board's directives. Particularly important is the implementation of *stress testing*, which calculates losses under dire scenarios, or value-at-risk (VaR) calculations, which measure the size of the loss on a trading portfolio that might happen 1% of the time—say, over a two-week period. In addition to these guidelines, bank examiners will continue to consider interest-rate risk in deciding the bank's capital requirements.

Disclosure Requirements

The free-rider problem described in Chapter 8 indicates that individual depositors and other bank creditors will not have enough incentive to produce private information about the quality of a bank's assets. To ensure that there is better information for depositors and the marketplace, regulators can require that banks adhere to certain standard accounting principles and disclose a wide range of information that helps the market assess the quality of a bank's portfolio and the amount of the bank's exposure to risk. More public information about the risks incurred by banks and the quality of their portfolio can better enable stockholders, creditors, and depositors to evaluate and monitor banks and so act as a deterrent to excessive risk taking. This view is consistent with a position paper issued by the Eurocurrency Standing Committee of the G-10 Central Banks, which recommends that estimates of financial risk generated by firms' own internal risk management systems be adapted for public disclosure purposes.[2] Such information would supplement disclosures based on traditional accounting conventions by providing information about risk exposure and risk management that is not normally included in conventional balance sheet and income statement reports.

---

[2]See Eurocurrency Standing Committee of Central Banks of Group of Ten Countries (Fisher Group), "Discussion Paper on Public Disclosure of Markets and Credit Risks by Financial Intermediaries," September 1994, and a companion piece to this report, Federal Reserve Bank of New York, "A Discussion Paper on Public Disclosure of Risks Related to Market Activity," September 1994.

Consumer Protection

The existence of asymmetric information also suggests that consumers may not have enough information to protect themselves fully. Consumer protection regulation has taken several forms. First is "truth in lending," mandated under the Consumer Protection Act of 1969, which requires all lenders, not just banks, to provide information to consumers about the cost of borrowing including a standardized interest rate (called the *annual percentage rate*, or *APR*) and the total finance charges on the loan. The Fair Credit Billing Act of 1974 requires creditors, especially credit card issuers, to provide information on the method of assessing finance charges and requires that billing complaints be handled quickly. Both of these acts are administered by the Federal Reserve System under Regulation Z.

Congress has also passed legislation to reduce discrimination in credit markets. The Equal Credit Opportunity Act of 1974 and its extension in 1976 forbid discrimination by lenders based on race, gender, marital status, age, or national origin. It is administered by the Federal Reserve under Regulation B. The Community Reinvestment Act (CRA) of 1977 was enacted to prevent "redlining," a lender's refusal to lend in a particular area (marked off by a hypothetical red line on a map). The Community Reinvestment Act requires that banks show that they lend in all areas in which they take deposits, and if banks are found to be in noncompliance with the act, regulators can reject their applications for mergers, branching, or other new activities.

Restrictions on Competition

Increased competition can also increase moral hazard incentives for banks to take on more risk. Declining profitability as a result of increased competition could tip the incentives of bankers toward assuming greater risk in an effort to maintain former profit levels. Thus governments in many countries have instituted regulations to protect banks from competition. These regulations have taken two forms in the United States in the past. First were restrictions on branching, such as those described in Chapter 10, which reduced competition between banks, but were eliminated in 1994. The second form involved preventing nonbank institutions from competing with banks by engaging in banking business, as embodied in the Glass-Steagall Act, which was repealed in 1999.

Although restricting competition propped up the health of banks, restrictions on competition also had serious disadvantages: They led to higher charges to consumers and decreased the efficiency of banking institutions, which did not have to compete as vigorously. Thus, although the existence of asymmetric information provided a rationale for anticompetitive regulations, it did not mean that they would be beneficial. Indeed, in recent years, the impulse of governments in industrialized countries to restrict competition has been waning. Electronic banking has raised a new set of concerns for regulators to deal with. See the E-Finance box for a discussion of this challenge.

STUDY GUIDE

Because so many laws regulating banking have been passed in the United States, it is hard to keep track of them all. As a study aid, Table 1 lists the major banking legislation in the twentieth century and its key provisions.

E-Finance **Electronic Banking: New Challenges for Bank Regulation**

The advent of electronic banking has raised new concerns for banking regulation, specifically about security and privacy.

Worries about the security of electronic banking and e-money are an important barrier to their increased use. With electronic banking, you might worry that criminals might access your bank account and steal your money by moving your balances to someone else's account. Indeed, a notorious case of this happened in 1995, when a Russian computer programmer got access to Citibank's computers and moved funds electronically into his and his conspirators' accounts. Private solutions to deal with this problem have arisen with the development of more secure encryption technologies to prevent this kind of fraud. However, because bank customers are not knowledgeable about computer security issues, there is a role for the government to regulate electronic banking to make sure that encryption procedures are adequate. Similar encryption issues apply to e-money, so requirements that banks make it difficult for criminals to engage in digital counterfeiting make sense. To meet these challenges, bank examiners in the United States assess how a bank deals with the special security issues raised by electronic banking and also oversee third-party providers of electronic banking platforms. Also, because consumers want to know that electronic banking transactions are executed correctly, bank examiners assess the technical skills of banks in setting up electronic banking services and the bank's capabilities for dealing with problems. Another security issue of concern to bank customers is the validity of digital signatures. The Electronic Signatures in Global and National Commerce Act of 2000 makes electronic signatures as legally binding as written signatures in most circumstances.

Electronic banking also raises serious privacy concerns. Because electronic transactions can be stored on databases, banks are able to collect a huge amount of information about their customers—their assets, creditworthiness, purchases, and so on—that can be sold to other financial institutions and businesses. This potential invasion of our privacy rightfully makes us very nervous. To protect customers' privacy, the Gramm-Leach-Bliley Act of 1999 has limited the distribution of these data, but it does not go as far as the European Data Protection Directive, which prohibits the transfer of information about online transactions. How to protect consumers' privacy in our electronic age is one of the great challenges our society faces, so privacy regulations for electronic banking are likely to evolve over time.

TABLE 1 **Major Banking Legislation in the United States in the Twentieth Century**

Federal Reserve Act (1913)
Created the Federal Reserve System

McFadden Act of 1927
Effectively prohibited banks from branching across state lines
Put national and state banks on equal footing regarding branching

Banking Act of 1933 (Glass-Steagall) and 1935
Created the FDIC
Separated commercial banking from the securities industry
Prohibited interest on checkable deposits and restricted such deposits to commercial banks
Put interest-rate ceilings on other deposits

(continued)

TABLE 1 Major Banking Legislation in the United States in the Twentieth Century *(continued)*

Bank Holding Company Act and Douglas Amendment (1956)
Clarified the status of bank holding companies (BHCs)
Gave the Federal Reserve regulatory responsibility for BHCs

Depository Institutions Deregulation and Monetary Control Act (DIDMCA) of 1980
Gave thrift institutions wider latitude in activities
Approved NOW and sweep accounts nationwide
Phased out interest-rate ceilings on deposits
Imposed uniform reserve requirements on depository institutions
Eliminated usury ceilings on loans
Increased deposit insurance to $100,000 per account

Depository Institutions Act of 1982 (Garn–St. Germain)
Gave the FDIC and the FSLIC emergency powers to merge banks and thrifts across state lines
Allowed depository institutions to offer money market deposit accounts (MMDAs)
Granted thrifts wider latitude in commercial and consumer lending

Competitive Equality in Banking Act (CEBA) of 1987
Provided $10.8 billion to the FSLIC
Made provisions for regulatory forbearance in depressed areas

Financial Institutions Reform, Recovery, and Enforcement Act (FIRREA) of 1989
Provided funds to resolve S&L failures
Eliminated the FSLIC and the Federal Home Loan Bank Board
Created the Office of Thrift Supervision to regulate thrifts
Created the Resolution Trust Corporation to resolve insolvent thrifts
Raised deposit insurance premiums
Reimposed restrictions on S&L activities

Federal Deposit Insurance Corporation Improvement Act (FDICIA) of 1991
Recapitalized the FDIC
Limited brokered deposits and the too-big-to-fail policy
Set provisions for prompt corrective action
Instructed the FDIC to establish risk-based premiums
Increased examinations, capital requirements, and reporting requirements
Included the Foreign Bank Supervision Enhancement Act (FBSEA), which strengthened the Fed's authority to supervise foreign banks

Riegle-Neal Interstate Banking and Branching Efficiency Act of 1994
Overturned prohibition of interstate banking
Allowed branching across state lines

Gramm-Leach-Bliley Financial Services Modernization Act of 1999
Repealed Glass-Steagall and removed the separation of banking and securities industries

INTERNATIONAL BANKING REGULATION

Because asymmetric information problems in the banking industry are a fact of life throughout the world, bank regulation in other countries is similar to that in the United States. Banks are chartered and supervised by government regulators, just as they are in the United States. Deposit insurance is also a feature of the regulatory systems in most other developed countries, although its coverage is often smaller than in the United States and is intentionally not advertised. We have also seen that bank capital requirements are in the process of being standardized across countries with agreements like the Basel Accord.

Problems in Regulating International Banking

Particular problems in bank regulation occur when banks are engaged in international banking and thus can readily shift their business from one country to another. Bank regulators closely examine the domestic operations of banks in their country, but they often do not have the knowledge or ability to keep a close watch on bank operations in other countries, either by domestic banks' foreign affiliates or by foreign banks with domestic branches. In addition, when a bank operates in many countries, it is not always clear which national regulatory authority should have primary responsibility for keeping the bank from engaging in overly risky activities. The difficulties inherent in regulating international banking were highlighted by the collapse of the Bank of Credit and Commerce International (BCCI). BCCI, which was operating in more than 70 countries, including the United States and the United Kingdom, was supervised by Luxembourg, a tiny country unlikely to be up to the task. When massive fraud was discovered, the Bank of England closed BCCI down, but not before depositors and stockholders were exposed to huge losses. Cooperation among regulators in different countries and standardization of regulatory requirements provide potential solutions to the problems of regulating international banking. The world has been moving in this direction through agreements like the Basel Accord and oversight procedures announced by the Basel Committee in July 1992, which require a bank's worldwide operations to be under the scrutiny of a single home-country regulator with enhanced powers to acquire information on the bank's activities. Also, the Basel Committee ruled that regulators in other countries can restrict the operations of a foreign bank if they feel that it lacks effective oversight. Whether agreements of this type will solve the problem of regulating international banking in the future is an open question.

Summary

Asymmetric information analysis explains what types of banking regulations are needed to reduce moral hazard and adverse selection problems in the banking system. However, understanding the theory behind regulation does not mean that regulation and supervision of the banking system are easy in practice. Getting bank regulators and supervisors to do their job properly is difficult for several reasons. First, as we learned in the discussion of financial innovation in Chapter 10, in their search for profits, financial institutions have strong incentives to avoid existing regulations by loophole mining. Thus regulation applies to a moving target: Regulators are continually playing cat-and-mouse with financial institutions—financial institutions think up clever ways to avoid regulations, which then causes regulators to modify their regulation activities. Regulators continually face new challenges in a dynamically changing financial system, and unless they can respond rapidly to change, they may not be able to keep financial institutions from taking on excessive risk. This problem can be exacerbated if regulators and supervisors do not have the resources or expertise to keep up with clever people in financial institutions who think up ways to hide what they are doing or to get around the existing regulations.

Bank regulation and supervision are difficult for two other reasons. In the regulation and supervision game, the devil is in the details. Subtle differences in the details may have unintended consequences; unless regulators get the regulation and supervision just right, they may be unable to prevent excessive risk taking. In addition, regulators and supervisors may be subject to political pressure to not do their jobs properly. For all these reasons, there is no guarantee that bank regulators and supervisors will be successful in promoting a healthy financial system. Indeed, as we will see, bank regulation and supervision have not always worked well, leading to banking crises in the United States and throughout the world.

THE 1980s U.S. SAVINGS AND LOAN AND BANKING CRISIS: WHY?

Before the 1980s, federal deposit insurance seemed to work exceedingly well. In contrast to the pre-1934 period, when bank failures were common and depositors frequently suffered losses, the period from 1934 to 1980 was one in which bank failures were a rarity, averaging fifteen per year for commercial banks and fewer than five per year for savings and loans. After 1981, this rosy picture changed dramatically. Failures in both commercial banks and savings and loans climbed to levels more than ten times greater than in earlier years, as can be seen in Figure 1. Why did this happen? How did a deposit insurance system that seemed to be working well for half a century find itself in so much trouble?

Early Stages of the Crisis

The story starts with the burst of financial innovation in the 1960s, 1970s, and early 1980s. As we saw in Chapter 10, financial innovation decreased the profitability of certain traditional business for commercial banks. Banks now faced increased competition for their sources of funds from new financial institutions such as money market mutual funds even as they were losing commercial lending business to the commercial paper market and securitization.

With the decreasing profitability of their traditional business, by the mid-1980s commercial banks were forced to seek out new and potentially risky business to keep their profits up, by placing a greater percentage of their total loans in real estate and in credit extended to assist corporate takeovers and leveraged buyouts (called *highly leveraged transaction loans*).

The existence of deposit insurance increased moral hazard for banks because insured depositors had little incentive to keep the banks from taking on too much risk. Regardless of how much risk banks were taking, deposit insurance guaranteed that depositors would not suffer any losses.

Adding fuel to the fire, financial innovation produced new financial instruments that widened the scope for risk taking. New markets in financial futures, junk bonds, swaps, and other instruments made it easier for banks to take on extra risk—making the moral hazard problem more severe. New legislation that deregulated the banking

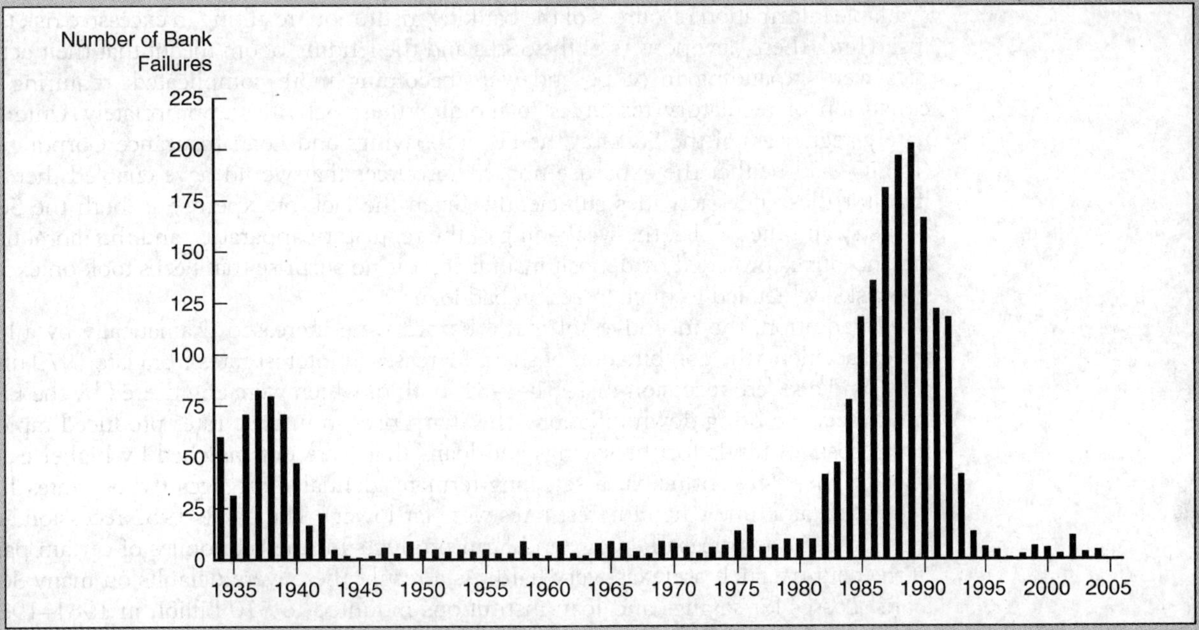

FIGURE 1 **Bank Failures in the United States, 1934–2005**

Source: www.fdic.gov/bank/historical/bank/index.html.

industry in the early 1980s, the Depository Institutions Deregulation and Monetary Control Act (DIDMCA) of 1980 and the Depository Institutions (Garn–St. Germain) Act of 1982, gave expanded powers to the S&Ls and mutual savings banks to engage in new risky activities. These thrift institutions, which had been restricted almost entirely to making loans for home mortgages, now were allowed to have up to 40% of their assets in commercial real estate loans, up to 30% in consumer lending, and up to 10% in commercial loans and leases. In the wake of this legislation, S&L regulators allowed up to 10% of assets to be in junk bonds or in direct investments (common stocks, real estate, service corporations, and operating subsidiaries).

In addition, DIDMCA increased the mandated amount of federal deposit insurance from $40,000 per account to $100,000 and phased out Regulation Q deposit-rate ceilings. Banks and S&Ls that wanted to pursue rapid growth and take on risky projects could now attract the necessary funds by issuing larger-denomination insured certificates of deposit with interest rates much higher than those being offered by their competitors. Without deposit insurance, high interest rates would not have induced depositors to provide the high-rolling banks with funds because of the realistic expectation that they might not get the funds back. But with deposit insurance, the government was guaranteeing that the deposits were safe, so depositors were more than happy to make deposits in banks with the highest interest rates.

Financial innovation and deregulation in the permissive atmosphere of the Reagan administration led to expanded powers for the S&L industry, which in turn led to several problems. First, many S&L managers did not have the required expertise to manage risk appropriately in these new lines of business. Second, the new expanded powers meant that there was a rapid growth in new lending, particularly to the real estate sector.

Even if the required expertise was available initially, rapid credit growth may outstrip the available information resources of the banking institution, resulting in excessive risk taking. Third, these new powers of the S&Ls and the lending boom meant that their activities were expanding in scope and were becoming more complicated, requiring an expansion of regulatory resources to monitor these activities appropriately. Unfortunately, regulators of the S&Ls at the Federal Savings and Loan Insurance Corporation (FSLIC) had neither the expertise nor the resources that would have enabled them to monitor these new activities sufficiently. Given the lack of expertise in both the S&L industry and the FSLIC, the weakening of the regulatory apparatus, and the moral hazard incentives provided by deposit insurance, it is no surprise that S&Ls took on excessive risks, which led to huge losses on bad loans.

In addition, the incentives of moral hazard were increased dramatically by a historical accident: the combination of sharp increases in interest rates from late 1979 until 1981 and a severe recession in 1981–1982, both of which were engineered by the Federal Reserve to bring down inflation. The sharp rises in interest rates produced rapidly rising costs of funds for the savings and loans that were not matched by higher earnings on the S&Ls' principal asset, long-term residential mortgages (whose rates had been fixed at a time when interest rates were far lower). The 1981–1982 recession and a collapse in the prices of energy and farm products hit the economies of certain parts of the country, such as Texas, very hard. As a result, there were defaults on many S&L loans. Losses for savings and loan institutions mounted to $10 billion in 1981–1982, and by some estimates more than half of the S&Ls in the United States had a negative net worth and were thus insolvent by the end of 1982.

Later Stages of the Crisis: Regulatory Forbearance

At this point, a logical step might have been for the S&L regulators—the Federal Home Loan Bank Board and its deposit insurance subsidiary, the Federal Savings and Loan Insurance Fund (FSLIC), both now abolished—to close the insolvent S&Ls. Instead, these regulators adopted a stance of **regulatory forbearance**: They refrained from exercising their regulatory right to put the insolvent S&Ls out of business. To sidestep their responsibility to close ailing S&Ls, they adopted irregular regulatory accounting principles that in effect substantially lowered capital requirements. For example, they allowed S&Ls to include in their capital calculations a high value for intangible capital, called **goodwill** (an accounting entry to reflect value to the firm of its having special expertise or a particularly profitable business line).

There were three main reasons why the Federal Home Loan Bank Board and FSLIC opted for regulatory forbearance. First, the FSLIC did not have sufficient funds in its insurance fund to close the insolvent S&Ls and pay off their deposits. Second, the Federal Home Loan Bank Board was established to encourage the growth of the savings and loan industry, so the regulators were probably too close to the people they were supposed to be regulating. Third, because bureaucrats do not like to admit that their own agency is in trouble, the Federal Home Loan Bank Board and the FSLIC preferred to sweep their problems under the rug in the hope that they would go away.

Regulatory forbearance increases moral hazard dramatically because an operating but insolvent S&L (nicknamed a "zombie S&L" by economist Edward Kane because it is the "living dead") has almost nothing to lose by taking on great risk and "betting the bank": If it gets lucky and its risky investments pay off, it gets out of insolvency. Unfortunately, if, as is likely, the risky investments don't pay off, the zombie S&L's losses will mount, and the deposit insurance agency will be left holding the bag.

This strategy is similar to the "long bomb" strategy in football. When a football team is almost hopelessly behind and time is running out, it often resorts to a high-risk play: the throwing of a long pass to try to score a touchdown. Of course, the long bomb is unlikely to be successful, but there is always a small chance that it will work. If it doesn't, the team has lost nothing, since it would have lost the game anyway.

Given the sequence of events we have discussed here, it should be no surprise that savings and loans began to take huge risks: They built shopping centers in the desert, bought manufacturing plants to convert manure to methane, and purchased billions of dollars of high-risk, high-yield junk bonds. The S&L industry was no longer the staid industry that once operated on the *3-6-3 rule*: You took in money at 3%, lent it at 6%, and played golf at 3 p.m. Although many savings and loans were making money, losses at other S&Ls were colossal.

Another outcome of regulatory forbearance was that with little to lose, zombie S&Ls attracted deposits away from healthy S&Ls by offering higher interest rates. Because there were so many zombie S&Ls in Texas pursuing this strategy, above-market interest rates on deposits at Texas S&Ls were said to have a "Texas premium." Potentially healthy S&Ls now found that to compete for deposits, they had to pay higher interest rates, which made their operations less profitable and frequently pushed them into the zombie category. Similarly, zombie S&Ls in pursuit of asset growth made loans at below-market interest rates, thereby lowering loan interest rates for healthy S&Ls, and again made them less profitable. The zombie S&Ls had actually taken on attributes of vampires—their willingness to pay above-market rates for deposits and take below-market interest rates on loans was sucking the lifeblood (profits) out of healthy S&Ls.

Competitive Equality in Banking Act of 1987

Toward the end of 1986, the growing losses in the savings and loan industry were bankrupting the insurance fund of the FSLIC. The Reagan administration sought $15 billion in funds for the FSLIC, a completely inadequate sum considering that many times this amount was needed to close down insolvent S&Ls. The legislation passed by Congress, the Competitive Equality in Banking Act (CEBA) of 1987, did not even meet the administration's requests. It allowed the FSLIC to borrow only $10.8 billion through a subsidiary corporation called Financing Corporation (FICO) and, what was worse, included provisions that directed the Federal Home Loan Bank Board to continue to pursue regulatory forbearance (allow insolvent institutions to keep operating), particularly in economically depressed areas such as Texas.

The failure of Congress to deal with the savings and loan crisis was not going to make the problem go away. Consistent with our analysis, the situation deteriorated rapidly. Losses in the savings and loan industry surpassed $10 billion in 1988 and approached $20 billion in 1989. The crisis was reaching epidemic proportions. The collapse of the real estate market in the late 1980s led to additional huge loan losses that greatly exacerbated the problem.

POLITICAL ECONOMY OF THE SAVINGS AND LOAN CRISIS

Although we now have a grasp of the regulatory and economic forces that created the S&L crisis, we still need to understand the political forces that produced the regulatory structure and activities that led to it. The key to understanding the political economy of the S&L crisis is to recognize that the relationship between voter-taxpayers and the regulators and politicians creates a particular type of moral hazard problem, discussed in Chapter 8: the *principal–agent problem*, which occurs when representatives (agents) such as managers have incentives that differ from those of their employer (the principal) and so act in their own interest rather than in the interest of the employer.

The Principal–Agent Problem for Regulators and Politicians

Regulators and politicians are ultimately agents for voter-taxpayers (principals), because in the final analysis, taxpayers bear the cost of any losses by the deposit insurance agency. The principal-agent problem occurs because the agent (a politician or regulator) does not have the same incentives to minimize costs to the economy as the principal (the taxpayer).

To act in the taxpayers' interest and lower costs to the deposit insurance agency, regulators have several tasks, as we have seen. They must set tight restrictions on holding assets that are too risky, must impose high capital requirements, and must not adopt a stance of regulatory forbearance, which allows insolvent institutions to continue to operate. However, because of the principal-agent problem, regulators have incentives to do the opposite. Indeed, as our sad saga of the S&L debacle indicates, they have at times loosened capital requirements and restrictions on risky asset holdings and pursued regulatory forbearance. One important incentive for regulators that explains this phenomenon is their desire to escape blame for poor performance by their agency. By loosening capital requirements and pursuing regulatory forbearance, regulators can hide the problem of an insolvent bank and hope that the situation will improve. Edward Kane characterizes such behavior on the part of regulators as "bureaucratic gambling."

Another important incentive for regulators is that they want to protect their careers by acceding to pressures from the people who most influence their careers. These people are not the taxpayers but the politicians who try to keep regulators from imposing tough regulations on institutions that are major campaign contributors. Members of Congress have often lobbied regulators to ease up on a particular S&L that contributed large sums to their campaigns. Regulatory agencies that have little independence from the political process are more vulnerable to these pressures.

In addition, both Congress and the presidential administration promoted banking legislation in 1980 and 1982 that made it easier for savings and loans to engage in risk-taking activities. After the legislation passed, the need for monitoring the S&L industry increased because of the expansion of permissible activities. The S&L regulatory agencies needed more resources to carry out their monitoring activities properly, but Congress (successfully lobbied by the S&L industry) was unwilling to allocate the necessary funds. As a result, the S&L regulatory agencies became so short-staffed that they actually had to cut back on their on-site examinations just when these were needed most. In the period from January 1984 to July 1986, for example, several hundred S&Ls were not examined even once. Even worse, spurred on by the intense lobbying efforts of the S&L industry, Congress passed the Competitive Equality in Banking Act of 1987, which, as we have seen, provided inadequate funding to close down the insolvent S&Ls and also hampered the S&L regulators from doing their job properly by including provisions encouraging regulatory forbearance.

As these examples indicate, the structure of our political system has created a serious principal-agent problem; politicians have strong incentives to act in their own interests rather than in the interests of taxpayers. Because of the high cost of running

FYI The Principal-Agent Problem in Action: Charles Keating and the Lincoln Savings and Loan Scandal

As we have seen, the principal-agent problem for regulators and politicians creates incentives that may cause excessive risk taking on the part of banking institutions, which then cause substantial losses to the taxpayer. The scandal associated with Charles H. Keating, Jr., and the Lincoln Savings and Loan Association provides a graphic example of the principal–agent problem at work. As Edwin Gray, a former chairman of the Federal Home Loan Bank Board, stated, "This is a story of incredible corruption. I can't call it anything else."*

Charles Keating was allowed to acquire Lincoln Savings and Loan of Irvine, California, in early 1984, even though he had been accused of fraud by the SEC less than five years earlier. For Keating, whose construction firm, American Continental, planned to build huge real estate developments in Arizona, the S&L was a gold mine: In the lax regulatory atmosphere at the time, controlling the S&L gave his firm easy access to funds without being scrutinized by outside bankers. Within days of acquiring control, Keating got rid of Lincoln's conservative lending officers and internal auditors, even though he had promised regulators he would keep them. Lincoln then plunged into high-risk investments such as currency futures, junk bonds, common stock, hotels, and vast tracts of desert land in Arizona.

Because of a shortage of savings and loan examiners at the time, Lincoln was able to escape a serious examination until 1986, whereupon examiners from the Federal Home Loan Bank of San Francisco discovered that Lincoln had exceeded the 10% limit on equity investments by $600 million. Because of these activities and some evidence that Lincoln was deliberately trying to mislead the examiners, the examiners recommended federal seizure of the bank and all its assets. Keating was not about to take this lying down; he engaged hordes of lawyers—eventually 77 law firms—and accused the bank examiners of bias. He also sued unsuccessfully to overturn the 10% equity limit. Keating is said to have bragged that he spent $50 million fighting regulators.

Lawyers were not Keating's only tactic for keeping regulators off his back. After receiving $1.3 million of contributions to their campaigns from Keating, five senators—Dennis De Concini and John McCain of Arizona, Alan Cranston of California, John Glenn of Ohio, and Donald Riegle of Michigan (subsequently nicknamed the "Keating Five")—met with Edwin Gray, the chairman of the Federal Home Loan Board, and later with four top regulators from San Francisco in April 1987. They complained that the regulators were being too tough on Lincoln and urged the regulators to quit dragging out the investigation. After Gray was replaced by M. Danny Wall, Wall took the unprecedented step of removing San Francisco examiners from the case in September 1987 and transferred the investigation to the bank board's headquarters in Washington. No examiners called on Lincoln for the next ten months, and as one of the San Francisco examiners described it, Lincoln dropped into a "regulatory black hole."

Lincoln Savings and Loan finally failed in April 1989, with estimated costs to taxpayers of $2.6 billion, making it possibly the most costly S&L failure in history. Keating was convicted for abuses (such as having Lincoln pay him and his family $34 million), but after serving four and a half years in jail, his conviction was overturned in 1996. Wall was forced to resign as head of the Office of Thrift Supervision because of his involvement in the Keating scandal. As a result of their activities on behalf of Keating, the Keating Five senators were made the object of a congressional ethics investigation, but given Congress's propensity to protect its own, they were subjected only to minor sanctions.

*Quoted in Tom Morganthau, Rich Thomas, and Eleanor Clift, "The S&L Scandal's Biggest Blowout," *Newsweek*, November 6, 1989, p. 35.

campaigns, American politicians must raise substantial contributions. This situation may provide lobbyists and other campaign contributors with the opportunity to influence politicians to act against the public interest, as we see in the FYI box on the previous page.

SAVINGS AND LOAN BAILOUT: THE FINANCIAL INSTITUTIONS REFORM, RECOVERY, AND ENFORCEMENT ACT OF 1989

Immediately after taking office, George H. W. Bush proposed new legislation to provide adequate funding to close down the insolvent S&Ls. The resulting legislation, the Financial Institutions Reform, Recovery, and Enforcement Act (FIRREA), was signed into law on August 9, 1989. It was the most significant legislation to affect the thrift industry since the 1930s. FIRREA's major provisions were as follows: The regulatory apparatus was significantly restructured, eliminating the Federal Home Loan Bank Board and the FSLIC, both of which had failed in their regulatory tasks. The regulatory role of the Federal Home Loan Bank Board was relegated to the Office of Thrift Supervision (OTS), a bureau within the U.S. Treasury Department whose responsibilities are similar to those that the Office of the Comptroller of the Currency has over the national banks. The regulatory responsibilities of the FSLIC were given to the FDIC, and the FDIC became the sole administrator of the federal deposit insurance system with two separate insurance funds: the Bank Insurance Fund (BIF) and the Savings Association Insurance Fund (SAIF). Another new agency, the Resolution Trust Corporation (RTC), was established to manage and resolve insolvent thrifts placed in conservatorship or receivership. It was assigned the task of selling more than $450 billion of real estate owned by failed institutions. After seizing the assets of about 750 insolvent S&Ls (more than 25% of the industry), the RTC sold over 95% of them, with a recovery rate exceeding 85%. After this success, the RTC went out of business on December 31, 1995.

The cost of the bailout ended up on the order of $150 billion. The funding for the bailout came partly from capital in the Federal Home Loan Banks (owned by the S&L industry), but mostly from the sale of government debt by both the Treasury and the Resolution Funding Corporation (RefCorp).

FIRREA also imposed new restrictions on thrift activities that in essence reregulated the S&L industry to the asset choices it had before 1982. It increased the core-capital leverage requirement from 3% to 8% and imposed the same risk-based capital standards imposed on commercial banks. FIRREA also enhanced the enforcement powers of thrift regulators by making it easier for them to remove managers, issue cease and desist orders, and impose civil monetary penalties.

FIRREA was a serious attempt to deal with some of the problems created by the S&L crisis in that it provided substantial funds to close insolvent thrifts. However, the losses that continued to mount for the FDIC in 1990 and 1991 would have depleted its Bank Insurance Fund by 1992, requiring that this fund be recapitalized. In addition, FIRREA did not focus on the underlying adverse selection and moral hazard problems created by deposit insurance. FIRREA did, however, mandate that the U.S. Treasury produce a comprehensive study and plan for reform of the federal deposit insurance system. After this study appeared in 1991, Congress passed the Federal Deposit Insurance Corporation Improvement Act (FDICIA), which engendered major reforms in the bank regulatory system.

FEDERAL DEPOSIT INSURANCE CORPORATION IMPROVEMENT ACT OF 1991

FDICIA's provisions were designed to serve two purposes: to recapitalize the Bank Insurance Fund of the FDIC and to reform the deposit insurance and regulatory system so that taxpayer losses would be minimized.

FDICIA recapitalized the Bank Insurance Fund by increasing the FDIC's ability to borrow from the Treasury and also mandated that the FDIC assess higher deposit insurance premiums until it could pay back its loans and achieve a level of reserves in its insurance funds that would equal 1.25% of insured deposits.

The bill reduced the scope of deposit insurance in several ways, but the most important one is that the too-big-to-fail doctrine has been substantially limited. The FDIC must now close failed banks using the least costly method, thus making it far more likely that uninsured depositors will suffer losses. An exception to this provision, whereby a bank would be declared too big to fail so that all depositors, both insured and uninsured, would be fully protected, would be allowed only if not doing so would "have serious adverse effects on economic conditions or financial stability." Furthermore, to invoke the too-big-to-fail policy, a two-thirds majority of both the Board of Governors of the Federal Reserve System and the directors of the FDIC, as well as the approval of the Secretary of the Treasury, are required. Furthermore, FDICIA requires that the Fed share the FDIC's losses if long-term Fed lending to a bank that fails increases the FDIC's losses.

Probably the most important feature of FDICIA is its prompt corrective action provisions, which require the FDIC to intervene earlier and more vigorously when a bank gets into trouble. Banks are now classified into five groups based on bank capital. Group 1, classified as "well capitalized," are banks that significantly exceed minimum capital requirements and are allowed privileges such as the ability to do some securities underwriting. Banks in group 2, classified as "adequately capitalized," meet minimum capital requirements and are not subject to corrective actions but are not allowed the privileges of the well-capitalized banks. Banks in group 3, "undercapitalized," fail to meet capital requirements. Banks in groups 4 and 5 are "significantly undercapitalized" and "critically undercapitalized," respectively, and are not allowed to pay interest on their deposits at rates that are higher than average. In addition, for group 3 banks, the FDIC is required to take prompt corrective actions such as requiring them to submit a capital restoration plan, restrict their asset growth, and seek regulatory approval to open new branches or develop new lines of business. Banks that are so undercapitalized as to have equity capital that amounts to less than 2% of assets fall into group 5, and the FDIC must take steps to close them down.

FDICIA also instructed the FDIC to come up with risk-based insurance premiums. The system that the FDIC has put in place, however, has not worked very well, because it resulted in more than 90% of the banks with over 95% of the deposits paying the same premium. Other provisions of FDICIA are listed in Table 1 earlier in this chapter.

FDICIA is an important step in the right direction, because it increases the incentives for banks to hold capital and decreases their incentives to take on excessive risk. However, concerns that it has not adequately addressed risk-based premiums or the too-big-to-fail problem have led economists to continue to search for further reforms that might help promote the safety and soundness of the banking system.[3]

[3]A further discussion of how well FDICIA has worked and other proposed reforms of the banking regulatory system appears in an appendix to this chapter that can be found on this book's web site at www.myeconlab.com/mishkin.

BANKING CRISES THROUGHOUT THE WORLD

Because misery loves company, it may make you feel better to know that the United States has by no means been alone in suffering a banking crisis. Indeed, as Table 2 and Figure 2 illustrate, banking crises have struck a large number of countries/regions throughout the world, and many of them have been substantially worse than ours. We will examine what took place in several of these other countries/regions and see that the same forces that produced a banking crisis in the United States have been at work elsewhere, too.

TABLE 2 The Cost of Rescuing Banks in Several Countries (regions)

Date	Country/region	Cost as a Percentage of GDP
1980–1982	Argentina	55
1997–2002	Indonesia	55
1990s–ongoing	China	47
1996–2000	Jamaica	44
1981–1983	Chile	42
1997–2002	Thailand	35
1993–1994	Macedonia	32
2000–ongoing	Turkey	31
1977–1983	Israel	30
1997–2002	South Korea	28
1988–1991	Cote d'Ivoire	25
1991–ongoing	Japan	24
1994–1995	Venezuela	22
1998–2001	Ecuador	20
1994–2000	Mexico	19
1997–2001	Malaysia	16
1992–1994	Slovenia	15
1998–ongoing	Philippines	13
1994–1999	Brazil	13
1995–2000	Paraguay	13
1989–1991	Czech Republic	12
1997–1998	Taiwan	12
1991–1994	Finland	11
1989–1990	Jordan	10
1991–1995	Hungary	10
1990–1993	Norway	8
1991–1994	Sweden	4
1988–1991	United States	3

Source: Gerard Caprio, Daniela Klingebiel, Luc Laeven, and Guillermo Noguera, *Banking Crises Database* (updated October 2003), http://www1.worldbank.org/finance/html/database_sfd.html.

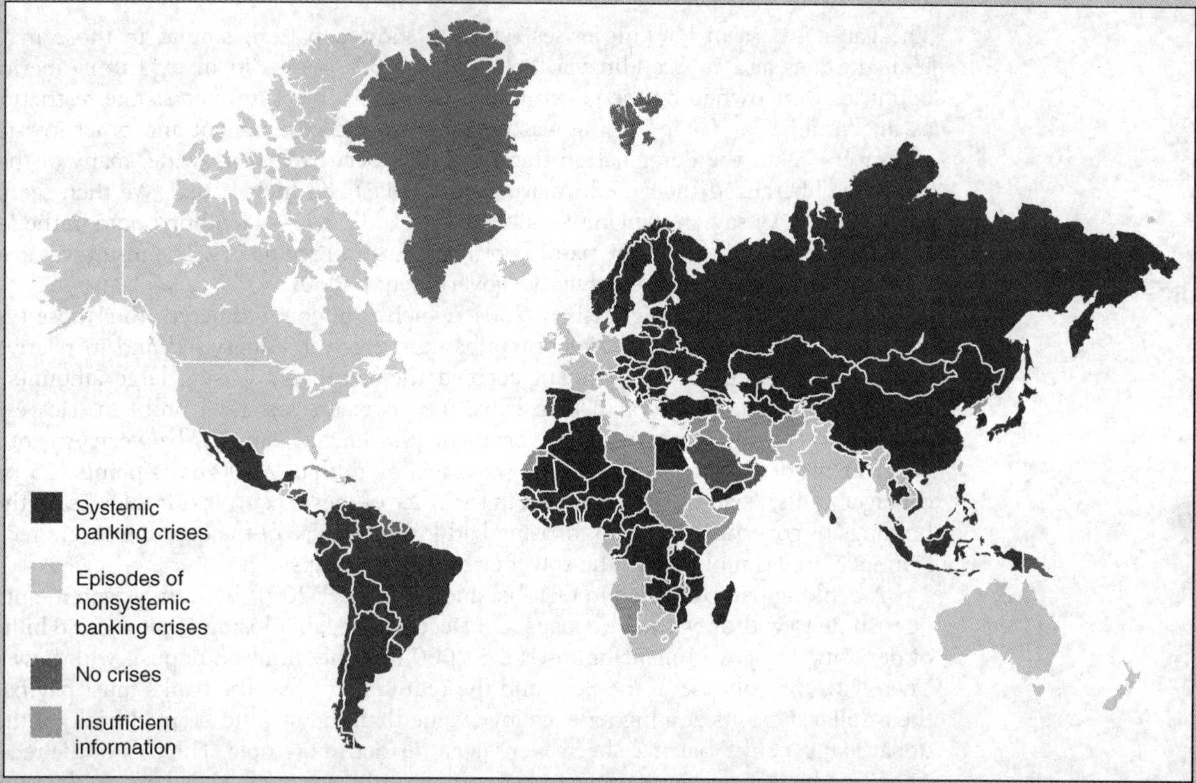

FIGURE 2 **Banking Crises Throughout the World Since 1970**

Source: Gerard Caprio and Daniela Klingebiel, "Episodes of Systemic and Borderline Financial Crises" mimeo., World Bank, October 1999.

Scandinavia

As in the United States, an important factor in the banking crises in Norway, Sweden, and Finland was the financial liberalization that occurred in the 1980s. Before the 1980s, banks in these Scandinavian countries were highly regulated and subject to restrictions on the interest rates they could pay to depositors and on the interest rates they could earn on loans. In this noncompetitive environment, and with artificially low rates on both deposits and loans, these banks lent only to the best credit risks, and both banks and their regulators had little need to develop expertise in screening and monitoring borrowers. With the deregulated environment, a lending boom ensued, particularly in the real estate sector. Given the lack of expertise in both the banking industry and its regulatory authorities in keeping risk taking in check, banks engaged in risky lending. When real estate prices collapsed in the late 1980s, massive loan losses resulted. The outcome of this process was similar to what happened in the savings and loan industry in the United States. The government was forced to bail out almost the entire banking industry in these countries in the late 1980s and early 1990s on a scale that was even larger relative to GDP than in the United States (see Table 2).

Latin America

The Latin American banking crises typically show a pattern similar to those in the United States and in Scandinavia. Before the 1980s, banks in many Latin American countries were owned by the government and were subject to interest-rate restrictions as in Scandinavia. Their lending was restricted to the government and other low-risk borrowers. With the deregulation trend that was occurring worldwide, many of these countries liberalized their credit markets and privatized their banks. We then see the same pattern we saw in the United States and Scandinavia—a lending boom in the face of inadequate expertise on the part of both bankers and regulators. The result was again massive loan losses and the inevitable government bailout.

The Argentine banking crisis of 2001, which is ongoing, differed from those typically seen in Latin America. Argentina's banks were well supervised and in relatively good shape before the government coerced them into purchasing large amounts of Argentine government debt to help solve the government's fiscal problem. However, when market confidence in the government plummeted, spreads between Argentine government debt and U.S. Treasuries soared to more than 2,500 basis points (25 percentage points), leading to a sharp fall in the price of these securities. The losses on their holdings of government debt and rising bad loans because of the ongoing severe recession increased doubts about the solvency of the banking system.

A banking panic erupted in October and November 2001, with the Argentine public rushing to withdraw their deposits. On December 1, after losing more than $8 billion of deposits, the government imposed a $1,000 monthly limit on deposit withdrawals. Then with the collapse of the peso and the requirement that the banks must pay back their dollar deposits at a higher exchange value than they would be paid back on their dollar loans, banks' balance sheets went even further in the hole. The cost of the recent Argentine banking crisis is not yet clear, but it could very well be as large as the previous banking crisis in Argentina in the 1980–1982 period listed in Table 2 and could exceed 50% of GDP.

What is particularly striking about the Latin American experience is that the cost of the bailouts relative to GDP dwarfs that in the United States. The cost to the taxpayer of the government bailouts in Latin America has been anywhere from around 20% to more than 50% of GDP, in contrast to the 3% figure for the United States.

Russia and Eastern Europe

Before the end of the Cold War, in the communist countries of Eastern Europe and the Soviet Union, banks were owned by the state. When the downfall of authorities occurred, banks in these countries had little expertise in screening and monitoring loans. Furthermore, a bank regulatory and supervisory apparatus that could rein in the banks and keep them from taking on excessive risk barely existed. Given the lack of expertise on the part of regulators and banks, not surprisingly substantial loan losses ensued, resulting in the failure or government bailout of many banks. For example, in the second half of 1993, eight banks in Hungary with 25% of the financial system's assets were insolvent, and in Bulgaria, an estimated 75% of all loans in the banking system were estimated to be substandard in 1995.

On August 24, 1995, a bank panic requiring government intervention occurred in Russia when the interbank loan market seized up and stopped functioning because of concern about the solvency of many new banks. This event was not the end of troubles in the Russian banking system. On August 17, 1998, the Russian government announced that Russia would impose a moratorium on the repayment of foreign debt because of insolvencies in the banking system. In November, the Russian central bank announced that nearly half of the country's 1,500 commercial banks might go under; the cost of the bailout was on the order of $15 billion.

Japan

Japan was a latecomer to the banking crisis game. Before 1990, the vaunted Japanese economy looked unstoppable. Unfortunately, it has recently experienced many of the same pathologies that we have seen in other countries. Before the 1980s, Japan's financial markets were among the most heavily regulated in the world, with very strict restrictions on the issuing of securities and interest rates. Financial deregulation and innovation produced a more competitive environment that set off a lending boom, with banks lending aggressively in the real estate sector. As in the other countries we have examined here, financial disclosure and monitoring by regulators did not keep pace with the new financial environment. The result was that banks could and did take on excessive risks. When property values collapsed in the early 1990s, the banks were left holding massive amounts of bad loans. For example, Japanese banks decided to get into the mortgage lending market by setting up *jusen*, home mortgage lending companies that raised funds by borrowing from banks and then lent these funds out to households. Seven of these *jusen* became insolvent, leaving banks with $60 billion or so of bad loans.

As a result the Japanese have experienced their first bank failures since World War II. In July 1995, Tokyo-based Cosmo Credit Corporation, Japan's fifth-largest credit union, failed. On August 30, 1995, the Osaka authorities announced the imminent closing of Kizu Credit Cooperative, Japan's second-largest credit union. (Kizu's story is remarkably similar to that of many U.S. savings and loans. Kizu, like many American S&Ls, began offering high rates on large time deposits and grew at a blistering pace, with deposits rising from $2.2 billion in 1988 to $12 billion by 1995 and real estate loans growing by a similar amount. When the property market collapsed, so did Kizu.) On the same day, the Ministry of Finance announced that it was liquidating Hyogo Bank, a midsize Kobe bank that was the first commercial bank to fail. Larger banks now began to follow the same path. In late 1996, the Hanwa Bank, a large regional bank, was liquidated, followed in 1997 by a government-assisted restructuring of the Nippon Credit Bank, Japan's seventeenth-largest bank. In November 1997, Hokkaido Takushoku Bank was forced to go out of business, making it the first city bank (a large commercial bank) to be closed during the crisis.

The Japanese went through a cycle of forbearance similar to the one that occurred in the United States in the 1980s. The Japanese regulators in the Ministry of Finance enabled banks to meet capital standards and to keep operating by allowing them to artificially inflate the value of their assets. For example, they were allowed to value their large holdings of equities at historical value, rather than market value, which was much lower. Inadequate amounts were allocated for recapitalization of the banking system, and the extent of the problem was grossly underestimated by government officials. Furthermore, until the closing of the Hokkaido Takushoku Bank, the bank regulators in the Ministry of Finance were unwilling to close down city banks and impose any losses on stockholders or any uninsured creditors.

By the middle of 1998, the Japanese government began to take some steps to attack these problems. In June, supervisory authority over financial institutions was taken away from the Ministry of Finance and transferred to the Financial Supervisory Agency (FSA), which reports directly to the prime minister. This was the first instance in half a century in which the all-powerful Ministry of Finance was stripped of some of its authority. In October, the parliament passed a bailout package of $500 billion (60 trillion yen). However, disbursement of the funds depended on the voluntary cooperation of the banks: The law did not require insolvent banks to close or to accept the funds. Indeed, acceptance of the funds required the bailed-out bank to open its books and reveal its true losses, and thus many banks remain very undercapitalized. The banking sector in Japan thus remained in very poor shape: It was burdened with bad loans and poor profitability. Indeed, many private sector analysts estimate that bad loans peaked at a level of more than $1 trillion.

There has been progress in cleaning up the banking mess. Immediately after the 1998 banking law was passed, one of the ailing city banks, Long-Term Credit Bank of Japan, was taken over by the government and declared insolvent. In December 1998, the Nippon Credit Bank was finally put out of its misery and closed down by the government. After this event, the cleanup process stalled. The Japanese economy remained weak, with a growth rate from 1991 to 2002 averaging an anemic 1%. A new, reform-oriented prime minister, Junichiro Koizumi, who pledged to clean up the banking system, came into office in 2001. Nevertheless, the Japanese government was slow to come to grips with the banking problem; indeed, the amount of nonperforming loans was still estimated to exceed $1 trillion in 2003. In 2003, the country's fifth-largest bank, Resona, was kept afloat only with a $17 billion (23 trillion yen) bailout, and a large regional bank, Ashigara, was declared insolvent and nationalized. However, with the pickup of the Japanese economy in 2003, the number of bad loans in Japanese banks finally began to decline and is now estimated to be below $200 billion. Another sign of optimism is the successful initial public offering of shares in Shinsei ("rebirth" in Japanese), which was formerly the Long Term Credit Bank; it had been nationalized in 1998 and then sold to a U.S. venture capital firm, Ripplewood.

China

Despite China's rapid economic growth (nearly 10% per year), China has a banking problem that is nearly as severe as that in Japan. Estimates of nonperforming loans are currently around $500 billion. In 1998, the Chinese government injected $30 billion into the country's four largest banks (the "Big Four"), all state-owned—Industrial and Commercial Bank of China, Agricultural Bank of China, Bank of China, and China Reconstruction Bank—with another $170 billion injection in 2000–2001. In 2004, the Chinese government entered into its third bailout, handing out a capital injection of more than $100 billion (which is expected to grow to as much as $200 billion).

The state-owned banks have gotten into trouble because they have lent massively to unprofitable state-owned enterprises and are notoriously inefficient: The Big Four have more than one million employees and more than 100,000 branches. The government hopes that its third try at a bailout will be a charm, and is attempting to handle this one differently. The new bailout is part of a plan to prepare the Big Four to become partially privatized by having them issue shares overseas. These banks are being encouraged to speed up their disposal of nonperforming loans, to close unprofitable branches, and to lay off unproductive employees. The Chinese government is aware that it needs to reform the banking sector so that capital can be allocated to private borrowers with good investment opportunities rather than to inefficient state-owned enterprises, but this is a daunting task. How successful the Chinese government will be in this endeavor remains far from clear.

East Asia

We discussed the banking and financial crisis in the East Asian countries (Thailand, Malaysia, Indonesia, the Philippines, and South Korea) in Chapter 8. Due to inadequate supervision of the banking system, the lending booms that arose in the aftermath of financial liberalization led to substantial loan losses, which became huge after the currency collapses that occurred in the summer of 1997. An estimated 15% to 35% of all bank loans turned sour in Thailand, Indonesia, Malaysia, and South Korea, and the cost of the bailout for the banking system was more than 15% of GDP in these countries and more than 50% of GDP in Indonesia. The Philippines fared somewhat better, with the cost being 13% of GDP.

"Déjà Vu All Over Again"

What we see in banking crises in these different countries is that history has kept repeating itself. The parallels between the banking crisis episodes in all these countries are remarkably similar, leaving us with a feeling of déjà vu. Although financial liberalization is generally a good thing because it promotes competition and can make a financial system more efficient, as we have seen in the countries examined here, it can lead to an increase in moral hazard, with more risk taking on the part of banks if there is lax regulation and supervision; the result can then be banking crises. However, these episodes do differ in that deposit insurance has not played an important role in many of the countries experiencing banking crises. For example, the size of the Japanese equivalent of the FDIC, the Deposit Insurance Corporation, was so tiny relative to the FDIC that it did not play a prominent role in the banking system and exhausted its resources almost immediately with the first bank failures. This means that deposit insurance is not to blame for some of these banking crises. However, what is common to all the countries discussed here is the existence of a government safety net, in which the government stands ready to bail out banks whether deposit insurance is an important feature of the regulatory environment or not. It is the existence of a government safety net, and not deposit insurance per se, that increases moral hazard incentives for excessive risk taking on the part of banks.

SUMMARY

1. The concepts of asymmetric information, adverse selection, and moral hazard help explain the eight types of banking regulation that we see in the United States and other countries: the government safety net, restrictions on bank asset holdings, capital requirements, bank supervision, assessment of risk management, disclosure requirements, consumer protection, and restrictions on competition.
2. Because asymmetric information problems in the banking industry are a fact of life throughout the world, bank regulation in other countries is similar to that in the United States. It is particularly problematic to regulate banks engaged in international banking, because they can readily shift their business from one country to another.
3. Because of financial innovation, deregulation, and a set of historical accidents, adverse selection and moral hazard problems increased in the 1980s and resulted in huge losses for the U.S. savings and loan industry and for taxpayers.

4. Regulators and politicians are subject to the principal-agent problem, meaning that they may not have sufficient incentives to minimize the costs of deposit insurance to taxpayers. As a result, regulators and politicians relaxed capital standards, removed restrictions on holdings of risky assets, and relied on regulatory forbearance, thereby increasing the costs of the S&L bailout.
5. The Financial Institutions Reform, Recovery, and Enforcement Act (FIRREA) of 1989 provided funds for the S&L bailout; created the Resolution Trust Corporation to manage the resolution of insolvent thrifts; eliminated the Federal Home Loan Bank Board and gave its regulatory role to the Office of Thrift Supervision; eliminated the FSLIC, whose insurance role and regulatory responsibilities were taken over by the FDIC; imposed restrictions on thrift activities similar to those in effect before 1982; increased the capital requirements to those adhered to by commercial banks; and increased the enforcement powers of thrift regulators.
6. The Federal Deposit Insurance Corporation Improvement Act (FDICIA) of 1991 recapitalized the Bank Insurance Fund of the FDIC and included reforms for the deposit insurance and regulatory system so that taxpayer losses would be minimized. This legislation limited brokered deposits and the use of the too-big-to-fail policy, mandated prompt corrective action to deal with troubled banks, and instituted risk-based deposit insurance premiums. These provisions have helped reduce the incentives of banks to take on excessive risk and so should help reduce taxpayer exposure in the future.
7. The parallels between the banking crisis episodes that have occurred in countries throughout the world are striking, indicating that similar forces are at work.

KEY TERMS

bank failure, p. 279
bank supervision (prudential supervision), p. 284
Basel Accord, p. 284
Basel Committee on Banking Supervision, p. 284
goodwill, p. 294
leverage ratio, p. 284
off-balance-sheet activities, p. 284
regulatory arbitrage, p. 284
regulatory forbearance, p. 294

QUESTIONS AND PROBLEMS

Questions marked with an asterisk are answered at the end of the book in an appendix, "Answers to Selected Questions and Problems." Questions marked with a blue circle indicate the question is available in MyEconLab at www.myeconlab.com/mishkin.

1. Give one example each of moral hazard and adverse selection in private insurance arrangements.
*2. If casualty insurance companies provided fire insurance without any restrictions, what kind of adverse selection and moral hazard problems might result?
3. What bank regulation is designed to reduce adverse selection problems for deposit insurance? Will it always work?
*4. What bank regulations are designed to reduce moral hazard problems created by deposit insurance? Will they completely eliminate the moral hazard problem?
5. What are the costs and benefits of a too-big-to-fail policy?
*6. Why did the S&L crisis not occur until the 1980s?
7. Why is regulatory forbearance a dangerous strategy for a deposit insurance agency?
*8. The FIRREA legislation of 1989 is the most comprehensive banking legislation since the 1930s. Describe its major features.
9. What steps were taken in the FDICIA of 1991 to improve the functioning of federal deposit insurance?
*10. Some advocates of campaign reform believe that government funding of political campaigns and restrictions on campaign spending might reduce the principal-agent problem in our political system. Do you agree? Explain your answer.

11. How can the S&L crisis be blamed on the principal-agent problem?

***12.** Do you think that eliminating or limiting the amount of deposit insurance would be a good idea? Explain your answer.

13. Do you think that removing the impediments to a nationwide banking system will be beneficial to the economy? Explain your answer.

***14.** How could higher deposit insurance premiums for banks with riskier assets benefit the economy?

15. How has the too-big-too-fail policy been limited in the FDICIA legislation? How might limiting the too-big-too-fail policy help reduce the risk of a future banking crisis?

WEB EXERCISES

1. Go to www.fdic.gov/regulations/laws/important/index.html. This site reports on the most significant pieces of legislation affecting banks since the 1800s. Summarize the most recently enacted bank regulation listed on this site.

2. The Office of the Comptroller of the Currency is responsible for many of the regulations affecting bank operations. Go to www.occ.treas.gov/. Click on "Legal and Regulatory" and then on "Law and Regulations." Now click on the 12 CFR Parts 1 to 199. What does Part 1 cover? How many parts are there in 12 CFR? Open Part 18. What topic does it cover? Summarize its purpose.

WEB REFERENCES

www.ny.frb.org/banking/supervisionregulate.html

View bank regulation information.

www.federalreserve.gov/Regulations/default.htm

Access regulatory publications of the Federal Reserve Board.

www.fdic.gov/regulations/laws/important/index.html

Describes the most important laws that have affected the banking industry in the United States.

www.fdic.gov/bank/historical/bank/index.html

Search for data on bank failures in any year.

CHAPTER

12 Nonbank Finance

Preview

Banking is not the only type of financial intermediation you are likely to encounter. You might decide to purchase insurance, take out an installment loan from a finance company, or buy a share of stock. In each of these transactions you will be engaged in nonbank finance and will deal with nonbank financial institutions. In our economy, nonbank finance also plays an important role in channeling funds from lender-savers to borrower-spenders. Furthermore, the process of financial innovation we discussed in Chapter 10 has increased the importance of nonbank finance and is blurring the distinction between different kinds of financial institutions. This chapter examines in more detail how institutions engaged in nonbank finance operate, how they are regulated, and what trends in nonbank finance have occurred recently.

INSURANCE

Every day we face the possibility of the occurrence of certain catastrophic events that could lead to large financial losses. A spouse's earnings might disappear due to death or illness; a car accident might result in costly repair bills or payments to an injured party. Because financial losses from crises could be large relative to our financial resources, we protect ourselves against them by purchasing insurance coverage that will pay a sum of money if catastrophic events occur. Life insurance companies sell policies that provide income if a person dies, is incapacitated by illness, or retires. Property and casualty companies specialize in policies that pay for losses incurred as a result of accidents, fire, or theft.

Life Insurance

The first life insurance company in the United States (Presbyterian Ministers' Fund in Philadelphia) was established in 1759 and is still in existence. There are currently about 1,700 life insurance companies, which are organized in two forms: as stock companies or as mutuals. Stock companies are owned by stockholders; mutuals are technically owned by the policyholders. Although more than 90% of life insurance companies are organized as stock companies, some of the largest ones are organized as mutuals.

Unlike commercial banks and other depository institutions, life insurance companies have never experienced widespread failures, so the federal government has not seen the need to regulate the industry. Instead, regulation is left to the states in which a company operates. State regulation is directed at sales practices, the provision of adequate liquid assets to cover losses, and restrictions on the amount of risky assets (such as common stock) that the companies can hold. The regulatory authority is typically a state insurance commissioner.

Because death rates for the population as a whole are predictable with a high degree of certainty, life insurance companies can accurately predict what their payouts to policyholders will be in the future. Consequently, they hold long-term assets that are not particularly liquid—corporate bonds and commercial mortgages as well as some corporate stock.

There are two principal forms of life insurance policies: permanent life insurance (such as whole, universal, and variable life) and temporary insurance (such as term). Permanent life insurance policies have a constant premium throughout the life of the policy. In the early years of the policy, the size of this premium exceeds the amount needed to insure against death because the probability of death is low. Thus the policy builds up a cash value in its early years, but in later years the cash value declines because the constant premium falls below the amount needed to insure against death, the probability of which is now higher. The policyholder can borrow against the cash value of the permanent life policy or can claim it by canceling the policy.

Term insurance, by contrast, has a premium that is matched every year to the amount needed to insure against death during the period of the term (such as one year or five years). As a result, term policies have premiums that rise over time as the probability of death rises (or level premiums with a decline in the amount of death benefits). Term policies have no cash value and thus, in contrast to permanent life policies, provide insurance only, with no savings aspect.

Weak investment returns on permanent life insurance in the 1970s led to slow growth of demand for life insurance products. The result was a shrinkage in the size of the life insurance industry relative to other financial intermediaries, with their share of total financial intermediary assets falling from 15.3% at the end of 1970 to 11.5% at the end of 1980. (See Table 1, which shows the relative shares of financial intermediary assets for each of the financial intermediaries discussed in this chapter.)

Beginning in the mid-1970s, life insurance companies began to restructure their business to become managers of assets for pension funds. An important factor behind this restructuring was 1974 legislation that encouraged pension funds to turn fund management over to life insurance companies. Now more than half of the assets managed by life insurance companies are for pension funds and not for life insurance. Insurance companies have also begun to sell investment vehicles for retirement such as **annuities**, arrangements whereby the customer pays an annual premium in exchange for a future stream of annual payments beginning at a set age, say 65, and continuing until death. The result of this new business has been that the market share of life insurance companies as a percentage of total financial intermediary assets has held steady since 1980.

Property and Casualty Insurance

There are on the order of 3,000 property and casualty insurance companies in the United States, the two largest of which are State Farm and Allstate. Property and casualty companies are organized as both stock and mutual companies and are regulated by the states in which they operate.

Although property and casualty insurance companies had a slight increase in their share of total financial intermediary assets from 1970 to 1990 (see Table 1), in recent years they have not fared well, and insurance premiums have skyrocketed. With the

TABLE 1 Relative Shares of Total Financial Intermediary Assets, 1970–2005 (percent)

	1970	1980	1990	2000	2005
Insurance Companies					
Life insurance	15.3	11.5	12.5	12.0	12.9
Property and casualty	3.8	4.5	4.9	3.3	3.7
Pension Funds					
Private	8.4	12.5	14.9	16.6	13.5
Public (state and local government)	4.6	4.9	6.7	8.8	8.0
Finance Companies	4.9	5.1	5.6	4.4	3.9
Mutual Funds					
Stock and bond	3.6	1.7	5.9	17.0	17.7
Money market	0.0	1.9	4.6	6.9	5.9
Depository Institutions (Banks)					
Commercial banks	38.5	36.7	30.4	24.7	27.1
S&Ls and mutual savings banks	19.4	19.6	12.5	4.7	5.2
Credit unions	1.4	1.6	2.0	1.7	2.0
Total	100.0	100.0	100.0	100.0	100.0

Source: Federal Reserve Flow of Funds Accounts.

high interest rates in the 1970s and 1980s, insurance companies had high investment income that enabled them to keep insurance rates low. Since then, however, investment income has fallen with the decline in interest rates, while the growth in lawsuits involving property and casualty insurance and the explosion in amounts awarded in such cases have produced substantial losses for companies.

To return to profitability, insurance companies have raised their rates dramatically—sometimes doubling or even tripling premiums—and have refused to provide coverage for some people. They have also campaigned actively for limits on insurance payouts, particularly for medical malpractice. In the search for profits, insurance companies are also branching out into uncharted territory by insuring the payment of interest on municipal and corporate bonds and on mortgage-backed securities. One worry is that the insurance companies may be taking on excessive risk in an attempt to boost their profits. One result of the concern about the health of the property and casualty insurance industry is that insurance regulators have proposed new rules that would impose risk-based capital requirements on these companies based on the riskiness of their assets and operations. Recent scandals have also come to the insurance industry (see the Conflicts of Interest box, "Insurance Behemoth Charged with Conflicts of Interest Violations"), which could result in increased insurance regulation.

The investment policies of these companies are affected by two basic facts. First, because they are subject to federal income taxes, the largest share of their assets is held in tax-exempt municipal bonds. Second, because property losses are more uncertain than the death rate in a population, these insurers are less able to predict how much they will have to pay policyholders than life insurance companies are. Natural and unnatural disasters such as the Los Angeles earthquake in 1994; Hurricane Katrina,

Conflicts of Interest Insurance Behemoth Charged with Conflicts of Interest Violations

In October 2004, New York Attorney General Eliot Spitzer charged Marsh & McLennan Cos. (MMC), a $12 billion financial services company, with fraud related to its insurance brokerage business. This legal attack is likely to have far-reaching effects on an industry that has so far remained removed from the scandals that have plagued other financial services firms.

Companies hire insurance brokers to help them control risk in a cost-effective manner. An insurance broker is expected to use its expertise and influence to search for the best possible prices from the insurance industry. The broker receives a fee for providing this service.

In the complaint filed against MMC, Spitzer charged that the insurance firm engaged in bid rigging and accepted payoffs from insurance companies in exchange for directing business their way. In practicing bid rigging, MMC required some insurance companies to submit abnormally high bids. This allowed another favored insurer to receive the business at a price fixed by MMC. The insurance companies were told by MMC that if they did not follow MMC's directions they would lose future business.

MMC also required insurers to pay contingent commissions—payments to MMC for steering clients to them. These pay-to-play revenues amounted to $800 million per year to MMC, or about half of the firm's 2003 net income. An e-mail Spitzer obtained from a senior MMC executive reads, "We need to place our business in 2004 with those that . . . pay us the most." MMC, along with other major insurance brokerage firms Aon and Willis Group Holdings, has halted all contingent commissions.

In the aftermath of these conflicts of interest scandals, MMC agreed to pay an $850 million fine, and Chairman and CEO Jeffery Greenberg and four other top executives left the firm. A number of other insurance firms and insurance brokerage companies have come under further scrutiny, including the huge insurance company American International Group (AIG), whose CEO, Maurice R. "Hank" Greenburg, is the father of Jeffrey Greenberg. The board of directors of AIG had to admit that the company had engaged in faulty accounting. The board then announced a reduction in the firm's net worth by nearly $3 billion and forced Greenberg, who had run the company for nearly 40 years, to resign in March 2005.

In the past, the insurance industry has been largely self-regulated. It is likely that the abuses uncovered by Spitzer and their clear costs to consumers will result in additional regulation and oversight.

which devastated New Orleans in 2005; and the September 11, 2001, destruction of the World Trade Center exposed the property and casualty insurance companies to billions of dollars of losses. Therefore, property and casualty insurance companies hold more liquid assets than life insurance companies; municipal bonds and U.S. government securities amount to over half their assets, and most of the remainder is held in corporate bonds and corporate stock.

Property and casualty insurance companies will insure against losses from almost any type of event, including fire, theft, negligence, malpractice, earthquakes, and automobile accidents. If a possible loss being insured is too large for any one firm, several firms may join together to write a policy and thus share the risk. Insurance companies may also reduce their risk exposure by obtaining **reinsurance**. Reinsurance allocates a portion of the risk to another company in exchange for a portion of the premium and is particularly important for small insurance companies. You can think of reinsurance as insurance for the insurance company. The most famous risk-sharing operation is Lloyd's of London, an association in which different insurance companies can underwrite a fraction of an insurance policy. Lloyd's of London has claimed that it will insure against any contingency—for a price.

The Competitive Threat from the Banking Industry

Until recently, banks have been restricted in their ability to sell life insurance products. This has been changing rapidly, however. More than two-thirds of the states allow banks to sell life insurance in one form or another. In recent years, the bank regulatory authorities, particularly the Office of the Comptroller of the Currency (OCC), have also encouraged banks to enter the insurance field because getting into insurance would help diversify banks' business, thereby improving their economic health and making bank failures less likely. For example, in 1990, the OCC ruled that selling annuities was a form of investment that was incidental to the banking business and so was a permissible banking activity. As a result, the banks' share of the annuities market has surpassed 20%. Currently, more than 60% of banks sell insurance products, and the number is expected to grow in the future.

Insurance companies and their agents reacted to this competitive threat with both lawsuits and lobbying actions to block banks from entering the insurance business. Their efforts were set back by several Supreme Court rulings that favored the banks. Particularly important was a ruling in favor of Barnett Bank in March 1996, which held that state laws to prevent banks from selling insurance can be superseded by federal rulings from banking regulators that allow banks to sell insurance. The decision gave banks a green light to further their insurance activities, and with the passage of the Gramm-Leach-Bliley Act of 1999, banking institutions will further engage in the insurance business, thus blurring the distinction between insurance companies and banks.

APPLICATION Insurance Management

Insurance, like banking, is in the financial intermediation business of transforming one type of asset into another for the public. Insurance providers use the premiums paid on policies to invest in assets such as bonds, stocks, mortgages, and other loans; the earnings from these assets are then used to pay out claims on the policies. In effect, insurers transform assets such as bonds, stocks, and loans into insurance policies that provide a set of services (for example, claim adjustments, savings plans, friendly insurance agents). If the insurer's production process of asset transformation efficiently provides its customers with adequate insurance services at low cost and if it can earn high returns on its investments, it will make profits; if not, it will suffer losses.

In Chapter 9 the economic concepts of adverse selection and moral hazard allowed us to understand principles of bank management related to managing credit risk; many of these same principles also apply to the lending activities of insurers. Here again we apply the adverse selection and moral hazard concepts to explain many management practices specific to insurance.

In the case of an insurance policy, moral hazard arises when the existence of insurance encourages the insured party to take risks that increase the likelihood of an insurance payoff. For example, a person covered by burglary insurance might not take as many precautions to prevent a burglary because the insurance company will reimburse most of the losses if a theft occurs. Adverse selection holds that the people most likely to receive large insurance payoffs are the ones who will want to purchase insurance the most. For example, a person suffering from a terminal disease would want to take out the biggest life and medical insurance policies possible, thereby exposing the insurance company to potentially large losses. Both adverse selection and moral hazard can result in large losses to insurance companies, because they lead to higher payouts on insurance claims. Lowering adverse selection and moral hazard to reduce these payouts is therefore an extremely important goal for insurance companies, and this goal explains the insurance practices we will discuss here.

Screening

To reduce adverse selection, insurance providers try to screen out good insurance risks from poor ones. Effective information collection procedures are therefore an important principle of insurance management.

When you apply for auto insurance, the first thing your insurance agent does is ask you questions about your driving record (number of speeding tickets and accidents), the type of car you are insuring, and certain personal matters (age, marital status). If you are applying for life insurance, you go through a similar grilling, but you are asked even more personal questions about such things as your health, smoking habits, and drug and alcohol use. The life insurer even orders a medical evaluation (usually done by an independent company) that involves taking blood and urine samples. Just as a bank calculates a credit score to evaluate a potential borrower, the insurers use the information you provide to allocate you to a risk class—a statistical estimate of how likely you are to have an insurance claim. Based on this information, the insurer can decide whether to accept you for the insurance or to turn you down because you pose too high a risk and thus would be an unprofitable customer.

Risk-Based Premiums

Charging insurance premiums on the basis of how much risk a policyholder poses for the insurance provider is a time-honored principle of insurance management. Adverse selection explains why this principle is so important to insurance company profitability.

To understand why an insurance provider finds it necessary to have risk-based premiums, let's examine an example of risk-based insurance premiums that at first glance seems unfair. Harry and Sally, both college students with no accidents or speeding tickets, apply for auto insurance. Normally, Harry will be charged a much higher premium than Sally. Insurance providers do this because young males have a much higher accident rate than young females. Suppose, though, that one insurer did not base its premiums on a risk classification but rather just charged a premium based on the average combined risk for males and females. Then Sally would be charged too much and Harry too little. Sally could go to another insurer and get a lower rate, while Harry would sign up for the insurance. Because Harry's premium isn't high enough to cover the accidents he is likely to have, on average the insurer would lose money on Harry. Only with a premium based on a risk classification, so that Harry is charged more, can the insurance provider make a profit.[1]

Restrictive Provisions

Restrictive provisions in policies are an insurance management tool for reducing moral hazard. Such provisions discourage policyholders from engaging in risky activities that make an insurance claim more likely. For example, life insurers have provisions in their policies that eliminate death benefits if the insured person commits suicide within the

[1]Note that the example here is, in fact, the lemons problem described in Chapter 8.

first two years that the policy is in effect. Restrictive provisions may also require certain behavior on the part of the insured. A company renting motor scooters may be required to provide helmets for renters to be covered for any liability associated with the rental. The role of restrictive provisions is not unlike that of restrictive covenants on debt contracts described in Chapter 8: Both serve to reduce moral hazard by ruling out undesirable behavior.

Prevention of Fraud

Insurance providers also face moral hazard because an insured person has an incentive to lie to the insurer and seek a claim even if the claim is not valid. For example, a person who has not complied with the restrictive provisions of an insurance contract may still submit a claim. Even worse, a person may file claims for events that did not actually occur. Thus an important management principle for insurance providers is conducting investigations to prevent fraud so that only policyholders with valid claims receive compensation.

Cancellation of Insurance

Being prepared to cancel policies is another insurance management tool. Insurers can discourage moral hazard by threatening to cancel a policy when the insured person engages in activities that make a claim more likely. If your auto insurance company makes it clear that coverage will be canceled if a driver gets too many speeding tickets, you will be less likely to speed.

Deductibles

The **deductible** is the fixed amount by which the insured's loss is reduced when a claim is paid off. A $250 deductible on an auto policy, for example, means that if you suffer a loss of $1,000 because of an accident, the insurer will pay you only $750. Deductibles are an additional management tool that helps insurance providers reduce moral hazard. With a deductible, you experience a loss along with the insurer when you make a claim. Because you also stand to lose when you have an accident, you have an incentive to drive more carefully. A deductible thus makes a policyholder act more in line with what is profitable for the insurer; moral hazard has been reduced. And because moral hazard has been reduced, the insurance provider can lower the premium by more than enough to compensate the policyholder for the existence of the deductible. Another function of the deductible is to eliminate the administrative costs of handling small claims by forcing the insured to bear these losses.

Coinsurance

When a policyholder shares a percentage of the losses along with the insurer, their arrangement is called **coinsurance**. For example, some medical insurance plans provide coverage for 80% of medical bills, and the insured person pays 20% after a certain deductible has been met. Coinsurance works to reduce moral hazard in exactly the same way that a deductible does. A policyholder who suffers a loss along with the insurer has less incentive to take actions, such as going to the doctor unnecessarily, that involve higher claims. Coinsurance is thus another useful management tool for insurance providers.

Limits on the Amount of Insurance

Another important principle of insurance management is that there should be limits on the amount of insurance provided, even though a customer is willing to pay for more coverage. The higher the insurance coverage, the more the insured person can gain from risky activities that make an insurance payoff more likely and hence the greater the moral hazard. For example, if Zelda's car were insured for more than its true value, she might not take proper precautions to prevent its theft, such as making sure that the key is always removed or putting in an alarm system. If it were stolen, she comes out ahead because the excessive insurance payment would allow her to buy an even better car. By contrast, when the insurance payments are lower than the value of her car, she will suffer a loss if it is stolen and will thus take precautions to prevent this from happening. Insurance providers must always make sure that their coverage is not so high that moral hazard leads to large losses.

Summary

Effective insurance management requires several practices: information collection and screening of potential policyholders, risk-based premiums, restrictive provisions, prevention of fraud, cancellation of insurance, deductibles, coinsurance, and limits on the amount of insurance. All of these practices reduce moral hazard and adverse selection by making it harder for policyholders to benefit from engaging in activities that increase the amount and likelihood of claims. With smaller benefits available, the poor insurance risks (those who are more likely to engage in the activities in the first place) see less benefit from the insurance and are thus less likely to seek it out.

PENSION FUNDS

In performing the financial intermediation function of asset transformation, pension funds provide the public with another kind of protection: regular income payments during retirement. Employers, unions, or private individuals can set up pension plans, which acquire funds through contributions paid in by the plan's participants. As we can see in Table 1, pension plans both public and private have grown in importance, with their share of total financial intermediary assets rising from 13% at the end of 1970 to 23.6% at the end of 2005. Federal tax policy has been a major factor behind the rapid growth of pension funds because employer contributions to employee pension plans are tax-deductible. Furthermore, tax policy has also encouraged employee contributions to pension funds by making them tax-deductible as well and enabling self-employed individuals to open up their own tax-sheltered pension plans, Keogh plans, and individual retirement accounts (IRAs).

Because the benefits paid out of the pension fund each year are highly predictable, pension funds invest in long-term securities, with the bulk of their asset holdings in bonds, stocks, and long-term mortgages. The key management issues for pension funds revolve around asset management: Pension fund managers try to hold assets with high expected returns and reduce risk through diversification. They also use techniques we discussed in Chapter 9 to manage credit and interest-rate risk. The investment strategies of pension plans have changed radically over time. In the aftermath of World War II, most pension fund assets were held in government bonds, with less than 1% held in stock. However, the strong performance of stocks in the 1950s and 1960s afforded pension plans higher returns, causing them to shift their portfolios into stocks, which currently account for approximately two-thirds of their assets. As a result, pension plans now have a much stronger presence in the stock market: In the early 1950s, they held on the order of 1% of corporate stock outstanding; currently they hold on the order of 19%. Pension funds, along with mutual funds, are now the dominant players in the stock market.

Although the purpose of all pension plans is the same, they can differ in a number of attributes. First is the method by which payments are made: If the benefits are determined by the contributions into the plan and their earnings, the pension is a **defined-contribution plan**; if future income payments (benefits) are set in advance, the pension is a **defined-benefit plan**. In the case of a defined-benefit plan, a further attribute is related to how the plan is funded. A defined-benefit plan is **fully funded** if the contributions into the plan and their earnings over the years are sufficient to pay out the defined benefits when they come due. If the contributions and earnings are not sufficient, the plan is **underfunded**. For example, if Jane Brown contributes $100 per year into her pension plan and the interest rate is 10%, after ten years the contributions and their earnings would be worth $1,753.[2] If the defined benefit on her pension plan pays her $1,753 or less after ten years, the plan is fully funded because her contributions and earnings will fully pay for this payment. But if the defined benefit is $2,000, the plan is underfunded, because her contributions and earnings do not cover this amount.

A second characteristic of pension plans is their *vesting*, the length of time that a person must be enrolled in the pension plan (by being a member of a union or an employee of a company) before being entitled to receive benefits. Typically, firms require that an employee work five years for the company before being vested and qualifying to receive pension benefits; if the employee leaves the firm before the five years are up, either by quitting or being fired, all rights to benefits are lost.

Private Pension Plans

Private pension plans are administered by a bank, a life insurance company, or a pension fund manager. In employer-sponsored pension plans, contributions are usually shared between employer and employee. Many companies' pension plans are underfunded because they plan to meet their pension obligations out of current earnings when the benefits come due. As long as companies have sufficient earnings, underfunding creates no problems, but if not, they may not be able to meet their pension obligations. Because of potential problems caused by corporate underfunding, mismanagement, fraudulent practices, and other abuses of private pension funds (Teamsters' pension funds are notorious in this regard), Congress enacted the Employee Retirement Income Security Act (ERISA) in 1974. This act established minimum standards for the reporting and disclosure of information, set rules for vesting and the degree of underfunding, placed restrictions on investment practices, and assigned the responsibility of regulatory oversight to the Department of Labor.

ERISA also created the Pension Benefit Guarantee Corporation (PBGC, called "Penny Benny"), which performs a role similar to that of the FDIC. It insures pension

[2]The $100 contributed in year 1 would become worth $\$100 \times (1 + 0.10)^{10} = \$259.37$ at the end of ten years; the $100 contributed in year 2 would become worth $\$100 \times (1 + 0.10)^{9} = \$235.79$; and so on until the $100 contributed in year 10 would become worth $\$100 \times (1 + 0.10) = \$110$. Adding these together, we get the total value of these contributions and their earnings at the end of ten years:

$$\$259.37 + \$235.79 + \$214.36 + \$194.87 + \$177.16$$
$$+ \$161.05 + \$146.41 + \$133.10 + \$121.00 + \$110.00 = \$1,753.11$$

FYI The Perils of Penny Benny: A Repeat of the S&L Bailout?

The current woes of "Penny Benny," the government pension insurance agency, unfortunately display many of the characteristics of the savings and loan crisis discussed in Chapter 11. When an insured company with an underfunded pension plan files for bankruptcy, Penny Benny must pay the company's workers their retirement benefits up to a limit of $47,000 per year per person. Once again we see the moral hazard principle at work: A company is more likely to risk underfunding its pension plan if Penny Benny will foot the pension bill if the firm goes bankrupt.

To keep the costs of government insurance programs from getting out of hand, the insurance agency must reduce moral hazard by monitoring the firms to assess the amount of the underfunding in their pension plans and charge higher premiums based on how much more underfunded the plans are. Unfortunately, Penny Benny has not been doing this, and since 2004 the liabilities arising from the responsibility for troubled pension plans have grown at an alarming rate. In 2004, these liabilities exceeded Penny Benny's assets by $23 billion. In 2005, the United Airlines bankruptcy resulted in Penny Benny taking over United's $6.6 billion liability to pay out pension benefits to its workers, even though Penny Benny took in only $1 billion in premiums that year. Congressional estimates suggest that Penny Benny may have to pay out $120 billion over the next decade to cover the pension liabilities of bankrupt companies. Taxpayers may be hit with another massive government bailout, the size of which will keep growing unless the government makes a concerted effort to reduce the underfunding of corporate pension plans.

The George W. Bush administration has proposed several measures to deal with the moral hazard problems created by the insurance provided by Penny Benny. It has suggested that premiums paid to Penny Benny should increase by more than 50% and that there should be a substantial increase in risk-based premiums, which would rise with greater underfunding of the pension plan. In addition, it has proposed tighter rules for calculating the degree of underfunding. Only time will tell whether these measures will be adequate to forestall a huge taxpayer bailout of Penny Benny.

benefits up to a limit (currently $47,000 per year per person) if a company with an underfunded pension plan goes bankrupt or is unable to meet its pension obligations for other reasons. Penny Benny charges pension plans premiums to pay for this insurance, and it can also borrow up to $100 million from the U.S. Treasury. Unfortunately, the problem of pension plan underfunding has been growing worse in recent years. Penny Benny has estimated that underfunding has reached levels in excess of $400 billion, with one company's pension plan alone, that of General Motors, being underfunded to the tune of $100 billion. As a result, Penny Benny, which ensures the pensions of one of every five workers, is encountering severe financial difficulties that may necessitate a federal bailout (see the FYI box, "The Perils of Penny Benny").

Public Pension Plans

The most important public pension plan is Social Security (Old Age and Survivors' Insurance Fund), which covers virtually all individuals employed in the private sector. Funds are obtained from workers through Federal Insurance Contribution Act (FICA) deductions from their paychecks and from employers through payroll taxes. Social Security benefits include retirement income, Medicare payments, and aid to the disabled.

When Social Security was established in 1935, the federal government intended to operate it like a private pension fund. However, unlike a private pension plan, benefits

FYI Should Social Security Be Privatized?

In recent years, public confidence in the Social Security system has reached a new low. Some surveys suggest that young people have more confidence in the existence of flying saucers than they do in the government's promise to pay them their Social Security benefits. Without some overhaul of the system, Social Security will not be able to meet its future obligations. The inability of the Social Security system to meet its future obligations is a problem that is not restricted to the United States, however. Indeed, European countries and Japan face an even greater problem because their populations are aging sooner than the U.S. population. What to do about social security has become a hotly debated political issue in recent years.

Currently, the assets of the U.S. Social Security system, which reside in a trust fund, are all invested in U.S. Treasury securities. Because stocks and corporate bonds have higher returns than Treasury securities, many proposals to save the Social Security system suggest investing part of the trust fund in corporate securities and thus partially privatizing the system. Suggestions for privatization take three basic forms:

1. *Government investment of trust fund assets in corporate securities.* This plan has the advantage of possibly improving the trust fund's overall return, while minimizing transactions costs because it exploits the economies of scale of the trust fund. Critics warn that government ownership of private assets could lead to increased government intervention in the private sector.

2. *Shift of trust fund assets to individual accounts that can be invested in private assets.* This option, advocated by the Bush administration, has the advantage of possibly increasing the return on investments and does not involve the government in the ownership of private assets. However, critics warn that it might expose individuals to greater risk and to transaction costs on individual accounts that might be very high because of the small size of many of these accounts.

3. *Individual accounts in addition to those in the trust fund.* This option has advantages and disadvantages similar to those of option 2 and may provide more funds to individuals at retirement. However, some increase in taxes would be required to fund these accounts.

Whether some privatization of the Social Security system occurs is an open question. In the short term, Social Security reform is likely to involve an increase in taxes, a reduction in benefits, or both. For example, the age at which benefits begin is already scheduled to increase from 65 to 67, and might be increased further to 70. It is also likely that the cap on wages subject to the Social Security tax will be raised further, thereby increasing taxes paid into the system.

are typically paid out from current contributions, not tied closely to a participant's past contributions. This "pay as you go" system at one point led to a massive underfunding, estimated at more than $1 trillion.

The problems of the Social Security system could become worse in the future because of the growth in the number of retired people relative to the working population. Congress has been grappling with the problems of the Social Security system for years, but the prospect of a huge bulge in new retirees when the 77 million baby boomers born between 1946 and 1964 start to retire in 2011 has resulted in calls for radical surgery on Social Security (see the FYI box, "Should Social Security Be Privatized?").

State and local governments and the federal government, like private employers, have also set up pension plans for their employees. These plans are almost identical in operation to private pension plans and hold similar assets. Underfunding of the plans is also prevalent, and some investors in municipal bonds worry that it may lead to future difficulties in the ability of state and local governments to meet their debt obligations.

FINANCE COMPANIES

Finance companies acquire funds by issuing commercial paper or stocks and bonds or borrowing from banks, and they use the proceeds to make loans (often for small amounts) that are particularly well suited to consumer and business needs. The financial intermediation process of finance companies can be described by saying that they borrow in large amounts but often lend in small amounts—a process quite different from that of banking institutions, which collect deposits in small amounts and then often make large loans.

A key feature of finance companies is that although they lend to many of the same customers that borrow from banks, they are virtually unregulated compared to commercial banks and thrift institutions. States regulate the maximum amount they can loan to individual consumers and the terms of the debt contract, but there are no restrictions on how they pursue branching, the assets they hold, or how they raise their funds. The lack of restrictions enables finance companies in many cases to tailor their loans to customer needs better than banking institutions can.

There are three types of finance companies: sales, consumer, and business.

1. *Sales finance companies* are owned by a particular retailing or manufacturing company and make loans to consumers to purchase items from that company. Sears Roebuck Acceptance Corporation, for example, finances consumer purchases of goods and services at Sears stores, and General Motors Acceptance Corporation finances purchases of GM cars. Sales finance companies compete directly with banks for consumer loans and are used by consumers because loans can frequently be obtained faster and more conveniently at the location where an item is purchased.

2. *Consumer finance companies* make loans to consumers to buy particular items such as furniture or home appliances, to make home improvements, or to help refinance small debts. Consumer finance companies are separate corporations (like Household Finance Corporation) or are owned by banks (Citigroup owns Person-to-Person Finance Company, which operates offices nationwide). Typically, these companies make loans to consumers who cannot obtain credit from other sources and charge higher interest rates.

3. *Business finance companies* provide specialized forms of credit to businesses by making loans and purchasing accounts receivable (bills owed to the firm) at a discount; this provision of credit is called *factoring*. For example, a dressmaking firm might have outstanding bills (accounts receivable) of $100,000 owed by the retail stores that have bought its dresses. If this firm needs cash to buy 100 new sewing machines, it can sell its accounts receivable for, say, $90,000 to a finance company, which is now entitled to collect the $100,000 owed to the firm. Besides factoring, business finance companies also specialize in leasing equipment (such as railroad cars, jet planes, and computers), which they purchase and then lease to businesses for a set number of years.

MUTUAL FUNDS

Mutual funds are financial intermediaries that pool the resources of many small investors by selling them shares and using the proceeds to buy securities. Through the asset transformation process of issuing shares in small denominations and buying large blocks of securities, mutual funds can take advantage of volume discounts on brokerage commissions and purchase diversified holdings (portfolios) of securities. Mutual funds allow the small investor to obtain the benefits of lower transaction costs in purchasing securities and to take advantage of the reduction of risk by diversifying the portfolio of securities held. Many mutual funds are run by brokerage firms, but others are run by banks or independent investment advisers such as Fidelity or Vanguard.

Mutual funds have seen a large increase in their market share since 1980 (see Table 1), due primarily to the then-booming stock market. Another source of growth has been mutual funds that specialize in debt instruments, which first appeared in the 1970s. Before 1970, mutual funds invested almost solely in common stocks. Funds that purchase common stocks may specialize even further and invest solely in foreign securities or in specialized industries, such as energy or high technology. Funds that purchase debt instruments may specialize further in corporate, U.S. government, or tax-exempt municipal bonds or in long-term or short-term securities.

Mutual funds are primarily held by households (around 80%) with the rest held by other financial institutions and nonfinancial businesses. Mutual funds have become increasingly important in household savings. In 1980, only 6% of households held mutual fund shares; this number has risen to around 50% in recent years. The age group with the greatest participation in mutual fund ownership includes individuals between 50 and 70, which makes sense because they are the most interested in saving for retirement. Interestingly, Generation X (ages 18–30) is the second most active age group in mutual fund ownership, suggesting that they have a greater tolerance for investment risk than those who are somewhat older. Generation X is also leading the way in Internet access to mutual funds (see the E-Finance box, "Mutual Funds and the Internet").

The growing importance of mutual funds and pension funds, known as *institutional investors*, has resulted in their controlling more than 50% of the outstanding stock in the United States. Thus institutional investors are the predominant players in the stock

E-Finance **Mutual Funds and the Internet**

The Investment Company Institute estimates that as of 2000, 68% of households owning mutual funds use the Internet, and nearly half of those online shareholders visit fund-related web sites. The Internet increases the attractiveness of mutual funds because it enables shareholders to review performance information and share prices and personal account information.

Of all U.S. households that conducted mutual funds transactions between April 1999 and March 2000, 18% bought or sold fund shares online. The median number of funds transactions conducted over the Internet during the twelve-month period was four, while the average number was eight, indicating that a high volume of online transactions were conducted by a small number of shareholders.

Online shareholders were typically younger, had greater household income, and were better educated than those not using the Internet. The median online shareholder was 42 years old, had a household income of $100,900, and was college-educated. The median shareholder not using the Internet was 51 years old, had a household income of $41,000, and did not have a college degree.

The use of the Internet to track and trade mutual funds is rapidly increasing. The number of shareholders who visited web sites offering fund shares nearly doubled between April 1999 and March 2000.

markets, with more than 70% of the total daily volume in the stock market due to their trading. Increased ownership of stocks has also meant that institutional investors have more clout with corporate boards, often forcing changes in leadership or in corporate policies.

Mutual funds are structured in two ways. The more common structure is an **open-end fund**, from which shares can be redeemed at any time at a price that is tied to the asset value of the fund. Mutual funds also can be structured as a **closed-end fund**, in which a fixed number of nonredeemable shares are sold at an initial offering and are then traded like a common stock. The market price of these shares fluctuates with the value of the assets held by the fund. In contrast to the open-end fund, however, the price of the shares may be above or below the value of the assets held by the fund, depending on factors such as the liquidity of the shares or the quality of the management. The greater popularity of the open-end funds is explained by the greater liquidity of their redeemable shares relative to the nonredeemable shares of closed-end funds.

Originally, shares of most open-end mutual funds were sold by salespeople (usually brokers) who were paid a commission. Because this commission is paid at the time of purchase and is immediately subtracted from the redemption value of the shares, these funds are called **load funds**. Most mutual funds are currently **no-load funds**; they are sold directly to the public with no sales commissions. In both types of funds, the managers earn their living from management fees paid by the shareholders. These fees amount to approximately 0.5% of the asset value of the fund per year.

Mutual funds are regulated by the Securities and Exchange Commission, which was given the ability to exercise almost complete control over them by the Investment Company Act of 1940. Regulations require periodic disclosure of information on these funds to the public and restrictions on the methods of soliciting business.

Until 2003, the mutual fund industry could brag that it had been "untainted by a major scandal for more than 60 years."[3] but that was soon to change. In the fall of 2003 Elliot Spitzer, the New York Attorney General, opened a probe into illegal trading practices in the mutual fund industry (see the Conflicts of Interest box, "The Mutual Fund Trading Scandal"), and there is now a trend toward increased regulation of this industry.

Money Market Mutual Funds

An important addition to the family of mutual funds resulting from the financial innovation process described in earlier chapters is the *money market mutual fund*. Recall that this type of mutual fund invests in short-term debt (money market) instruments of very high quality, such as Treasury bills, commercial paper, and bank certificates of deposit. There is some fluctuation in the market value of these securities, but because their maturity is typically less than six months, the change in the market value is small enough that these funds allow their shares to be redeemed at a fixed value. (Changes in the market value of the securities are figured into the interest paid out by the fund.) Because these shares can be redeemed at a fixed value, the funds allow shareholders to redeem shares by writing checks on the fund's account at a commercial bank. In this way, shares in money market mutual funds effectively function as checkable deposits that earn market interest rates on short-term debt securities.

---

[3]Terry Glenn, head of the mutual fund industry's Investment Company Institute, quoted in the *Wall Street Journal*, September 4, 2003, p. C1.

Conflicts of Interest **The Mutual Fund Trading Scandal**

In September 2003, New York Attorney General Eliot Spitzer accused a number of mutual funds of exploiting conflicts of interest in which they allowed favored customers to engage in illegal, late trades in the fund. These trades would be made after the fund's share value was set officially at 4 PM If the underlying value of the assets had changed after 4 PM, these customers could earn profits by buying the funds at a price below their market value or selling them at a price above the market value. (In Congressional testimony, Spitzer explained that "late trading is like betting on a horse race after the horses have crossed the finish line.") The profits from this activity were made at the expense of the general shareholders of the mutual fund.

Subsequent SEC investigations have found that illegal trading has been widespread in the mutual fund industry. As a result, more than 300 lawsuits have been filed against individual mutual funds, and the mutual fund industry has already paid out billions of dollars in settlements and fee reductions. In addition, some investment managers have been thrown in jail. Government regulators such as the SEC have addressed the scandals by insisting that directors of mutual funds be more independent from the funds' managers, requiring that trades after 4 PM be priced at the next day's net asset value, increasing enforcement of fees for redeeming mutual fund shares (which in effect makes it hard to profit from late trades), and increasing transparency of fund operating practices to the public.

In 1977, the assets in money market mutual funds were less than $4 billion; by 1980, they had climbed to more than $50 billion and now stand at $1.28 trillion, with a share of financial intermediary assets that has grown to nearly 6% (see Table 1). Currently, money market mutual funds account for around one-third of the asset value of all mutual funds.

Hedge Funds

Hedge funds are a special type of mutual fund, with estimated assets of more than $1 trillion. Hedge funds have received considerable attention recently due to the shock to the financial system resulting from the near collapse of Long-Term Capital Management, once one of the most important hedge funds (see the FYI box, "The Long-Term Capital Management Debacle"). Well-known hedge funds include Moore Capital Management and the Quantum Group of funds associated with George Soros. Like mutual funds, hedge funds accumulate money from many people and invest on their behalf, but several features distinguish them from traditional mutual funds. Hedge funds have a minimum investment requirement between $100,000 and $20 million, with the typical minimum investment being $1 million. Long-Term Capital Management required a $10 million minimum investment. Federal law limits hedge funds to have no more than 99 investors (limited partners) who must have steady annual incomes of $200,000 or more or a net worth of $1 million, excluding their homes. These restrictions are aimed at allowing hedge funds to be largely unregulated, on the theory that the rich can look out for themselves. Many of the 4,000 hedge funds are located offshore to escape regulatory restrictions.

Hedge funds also differ from traditional mutual funds in that they usually require that investors commit their money for long periods of time, often several years. The purpose of this requirement is to give managers breathing room to pursue long-run strategies. Hedge funds also typically charge large fees to investors. The typical fund

FYI The Long-Term Capital Management Debacle

Long-Term Capital Management (LTCM) was a hedge fund with a star cast of managers, including 25 PhDs, two Nobel Prize winners in economics (Myron Scholes and Robert Merton), a former vice-chairman of the Federal Reserve System (David Mullins), and one of Wall Street's most successful bond traders (John Meriwether). It made headlines in September 1998 because its near-collapse roiled markets and required a private rescue plan organized by the Federal Reserve Bank of New York.

The experience of Long-Term Capital demonstrates that hedge funds are far from risk-free, despite their use of market-neutral strategies. Long-Term Capital got into difficulties when it thought that the spread between prices on long-term Treasury bonds and long-term corporate bonds was too high, and bet that this "anomaly" would disappear and the spread would narrow. In the wake of the collapse of the Russian financial system in August 1998, investors increased their assessment of the riskiness of corporate securities and, as we saw in Chapter 6, the spread between corporates and Treasuries rose rather than narrowed as Long-Term Capital had predicted. The result was that Long-Term Capital took big losses on its positions, eating up much of its equity position.

By mid-September, Long-Term Capital was unable to raise sufficient funds to meet the demands of its creditors. With Long-Term Capital facing the potential need to liquidate its portfolio of $80 billion in securities and more than $1 trillion of notional value in derivatives, the Federal Reserve Bank of New York stepped in on September 23 and organized a rescue plan with Long-Term Capital's creditors. The Fed's rationale for stepping in was that a sudden liquidation of Long-Term Capital's portfolio would create unacceptable systemic risk. Tens of billions of dollars of illiquid securities would be dumped on an already jittery market, causing potentially huge losses to numerous lenders and other institutions. The rescue plan required creditors, banks, and investment banks to supply an additional $3.6 billion of funds to Long-Term Capital in exchange for much tighter management control of funds and a 90% reduction in the managers' equity stake. In the middle of 1999, John Meriwether began to wind down the fund's operations.

Even though no public funds were expended, the Fed's involvement in organizing the rescue of Long-Term Capital was highly controversial. Some critics argue that the Fed intervention increased moral hazard by weakening discipline imposed by the market on fund managers because future Fed interventions of this type would be expected. Others think that the Fed's action was necessary to prevent a major shock to the financial system that could have provoked a financial crisis. The debate on whether the Fed should have intervened is likely to go on for some time.

charges a 1% annual fee on the assets it manages plus 20% of profits, and some charge significantly more. Long-Term Capital, for example, charged investors a 2% asset management fee and took 25% of the profits.

The term *hedge fund* is highly misleading, because the word "hedge" typically indicates strategies to avoid risk. As the near-failure of Long-Term Capital illustrates, despite their name, these funds can and do take big risks. Many hedge funds engage in what are called "market-neutral" strategies where they buy a security, such as a bond, that seems cheap and sell an equivalent amount of a similar security that appears to be overvalued. If interest rates as a whole go up or down, the fund is hedged, because the decline in value of one security is matched by the rise in value of the other. However, the fund is speculating on whether the spread between the price on the two securities moves in the direction predicted by the fund managers. If the fund bets wrong, it can lose a lot of money, particularly if it has leveraged up its positions—that is, has borrowed heavily against these positions so that its equity stake is small relative to the size of its portfolio. When Long-Term Capital was rescued, it had a leverage ratio of 50 to 1; that is, its assets were 50 times larger than its equity, and even before it got into trouble, it was leveraged 20 to 1.

In the wake of the near collapse of Long-Term Capital, many U.S. politicians called for regulation of these funds, and the SEC has put in a new rule that hedge funds will have to register with the agency. However, because many of these funds operate offshore in places like the Cayman Islands and are outside of U.S. jurisdiction, they would be extremely difficult to regulate. What U.S. regulators can do is ensure that U.S. banks and investment banks have clear guidelines on the amount of lending they can provide to hedge funds and require that these institutions get the appropriate amount of disclosure from hedge funds as to the riskiness of their positions.

GOVERNMENT FINANCIAL INTERMEDIATION

The government has become involved in financial intermediation in two basic ways: by setting up federal credit agencies that directly engage in financial intermediation and by supplying government guarantees for private loans.

Federal Credit Agencies

To promote residential housing, the government has created three government agencies that provide funds to the mortgage market by selling bonds and using the proceeds to buy mortgages: the Government National Mortgage Association (GNMA, or "Ginnie Mae"), the Federal National Mortgage Association (FNMA, or "Fannie Mae"), and the Federal Home Loan Mortgage Corporation (FHLMC, or "Freddie Mac"). Except for Ginnie Mae, which is a federal agency and is thus an entity of the U.S. government, the other agencies are federally sponsored agencies that function as private corporations with close ties to the government. As a result, the debt of sponsored agencies is not explicitly backed by the U.S. government, as is the case for Treasury bonds. As a practical matter, however, it is unlikely that the federal government would allow a default on the debt of these sponsored agencies.

Agriculture is another area in which financial intermediation by government agencies plays an important role. The Farm Credit System (composed of Banks for Cooperatives, Farm Credit banks, and various farm credit associations) issues securities and then uses the proceeds to make loans to farmers.

In recent years, some government financial intermediaries have experienced financial difficulties. The Farm Credit System is one example. The rising tide of farm bankruptcies meant losses in the billions of dollars for the Farm Credit System, and as a result it required a bailout from the federal government in 1987. The agency was authorized to borrow up to $4 billion to be repaid over a fifteen-year period and received over $1 billion in assistance. There is growing concern in Washington about the health of the federal credit agencies. To head off government bailouts like that for the Farm Credit System, the Federal Credit Reform Act of 1990 set new rules that require such agencies to increase their capital to provide a greater cushion to offset any potential losses. However, there have been growing concerns about Fannie Mae and Freddie Mac (see the Conflicts of Interest box, "Are Fannie Mae and Freddie Mac Getting Too Big for Their Britches?").

Conflicts of Interest Are Fannie Mae and Freddie Mac Getting Too Big for Their Britches?

With the growth of Fannie Mae and Freddie Mac to immense proportions, there are rising concerns that these federally sponsored agencies could threaten the health of the financial system. Fannie Mae and Freddie Mac either own or insure the risk on roughly half of U.S. residential mortgages. In fact, their publicly issued debt of more than $2 trillion is nearly half that issued by the federal government. A failure of either of these institutions would therefore pose a grave shock to the financial system. Although the federal government would be unlikely to stand by and let them fail, in such a case the taxpayer would face substantial costs, as in the S&L crisis.

Concerns about the safety and soundness of these institutions arise because they have much smaller capital-to-asset ratios than banks. Critics also charge that Fannie Mae and Freddie Mac have become so large that they wield too much political influence. In addition, these federally sponsored agencies have conflicts of interest, because they have to serve two masters: As publicly traded corporations, they are supposed to maximize profits for the shareholders, but as government agencies, they are supposed to work in the interests of the public.

Both agencies have also experienced major accounting scandals recently. In 2003, Freddie Mac was accused by its regulator, the Office of Federal Housing Enterprise Oversight (OFHEO), of fiddling with its books in an effort to smooth out its earnings. The result was that Freddie Mac was forced to fire several of its top executives and pay a $125 million fine. Accounting irregularities at Fannie Mae also came to light in the fall of 2004, resulting in the resignation of Fannie Mae's CEO.

The accounting scandals and concerns about safety and soundness have led to calls for reform of these agencies. The George W. Bush administration and other government officials have argued that Congress should take steps to restrain the growth of Fannie Mae and Freddie Mac. One such approach would entail full privatization of these agencies, as was done voluntarily by the Student Loan Market Association ("Sallie Mae") in the mid-1990s. As private corporations they would lose the subsidies they receive as government-sponsored agencies and would be less likely to be bailed out, thereby increasing their cost of raising funds. Another approach would be to increase the ratio of capital to assets these agencies are required to hold—their regulator, the OFHEO, has recommended this route. Not only would an increase in the required capital ratio make Freddie Mac and Fannie Mae less likely to fail, but it would also require them to shrink the size of their asset base if they find it difficult to raise more capital. A third approach would be to directly limit the amount of certain assets they can hold. In February 2005, Alan Greenspan called for limits on the two agencies' holdings of mortgage securities, which expose them to substantial interest-rate risk, to around one-tenth of their current holdings.

Fannie Mae, which is legendary for its lobbying efforts in Congress, has argued that restricting its growth would lead to substantially higher housing costs for American homeowners. A study conducted at the Federal Reserve, however, estimates that the housing agencies probably save homeowners only about 0.07 of a percentage point, which comes out to $4.87 per month on a $100,000 mortgage—a trivial amount.

The recent accounting scandals have weakened Fannie Mae's and Freddie Mac's clout on Capital Hill, but it is not clear whether strong reforms will be enacted to cut them down to size.

SECURITIES MARKET OPERATIONS

The smooth functioning of securities markets, in which bonds and stocks are traded, involves several financial institutions, including securities brokers and dealers, investment banks, and organized exchanges. None of these institutions were included in our list of financial intermediaries in Chapter 2, because they do not perform the intermediation function of acquiring funds by issuing liabilities and then using the funds to acquire financial assets. Nonetheless, they are important in the process of channeling funds from savers to spenders and can be thought of as "financial facilitators."

First, however, we must recall the distinction between primary and secondary securities markets discussed in Chapter 2. In a primary market, new issues of a security are sold to buyers by the corporation or government agency borrowing the funds. A secondary market then trades the securities that have been sold in the primary market (and so are secondhand). *Investment banks* assist in the initial sale of securities in the primary market; *securities brokers* and *dealers* assist in the trading of securities in the secondary markets, some of which are organized into exchanges.

Investment Banking

When a corporation wishes to borrow (raise) funds, it normally hires the services of an investment banker to help sell its securities. (Despite its name, an investment bank is not a bank in the ordinary sense; that is, it is not engaged in financial intermediation that takes in deposits and then lends them out.) Some of the well-known U.S. investment banking firms are Merrill Lynch, Salomon Smith Barney, Morgan Stanley Dean Witter, Goldman Sachs, Lehman Brothers, and Credit Suisse First Boston, which have been very successful not only in the United States but outside it as well.

Investment bankers assist in the sale of securities as follows. First, they advise the corporation on whether it should issue bonds or stock. If they suggest that the corporation issue bonds, investment bankers give advice on what the maturity and interest payments on the bonds should be. If they suggest that the corporation should sell stock, they give advice on what the price should be. This is fairly easy to do if the firm has prior issues currently selling in the market, called **seasoned issues**. However, when a firm issues stock for the first time in an **initial public offering (IPO)**, it is more difficult to determine what the correct price should be. All the skills and expertise of the investment banking firm then need to be brought to bear to determine the most appropriate price. IPOs have become very important in the U.S. economy, because they are a major source of financing for Internet companies, which became all the rage on Wall Street in the late 1990s. Not only have IPOs helped these companies to acquire capital to substantially expand their operations, but they have also made the original owners of these firms very rich. Many a nerdy 20- to 30-year-old became an instant millionaire when his stake in his Internet company was given a high valuation after the initial public offering of shares in the company. However, with the bursting of the tech bubble in 2000, many of them lost much of their wealth when the value of their shares came tumbling down to earth.

When the corporation decides which kind of financial instrument it will issue, it offers the issue to **underwriters**—investment bankers that guarantee the corporation a price on the securities and then sell them to the public. If the issue is small, only one investment banking firm underwrites it (usually the original investment banking firm hired to provide advice on the issue). If the issue is large, several investment banking firms form a syndicate to underwrite the issue jointly, thus limiting the risk that any one investment bank must take. The underwriters sell the securities to the general public by contacting potential buyers, such as banks and insurance companies, directly.

The activities of investment bankers and the operation of primary markets are heavily regulated by the Securities and Exchange Commission (SEC), which was created by the Securities and Exchange Acts of 1933 and 1934 to ensure that adequate information reaches prospective investors. Issuers of new securities to the general public (for amounts greater than $1.5 million in a year with a maturity longer than 270 days) must file a registration statement with the SEC and must provide to potential investors a prospectus containing all relevant information on the securities. The issuer must then wait 20 days after the registration statement is filed with the SEC before it can sell any of the securities. If the SEC does not object during the 20-day waiting period, the securities can be sold.

Securities Brokers and Dealers

Securities brokers and dealers conduct trading in secondary markets. Brokers act as agents for investors in the purchase or sale of securities. Their function is to match buyers with sellers, a function for which they are paid brokerage commissions. In contrast to brokers, dealers link buyers and sellers by standing ready to buy and sell securities at given prices. Therefore, dealers hold inventories of securities and make their living by selling these securities for a slightly higher price than they paid for them—that is, on the "spread" between the asked price and the bid price. This can be a high-risk business because dealers hold securities that can rise or fall in price; in recent years, several firms specializing in bonds have collapsed. Brokers, by contrast, are not as exposed to risk because they do not own the securities involved in their business dealings.

Brokerage firms engage in all three securities market activities, acting as brokers, dealers, and investment bankers. The largest in the United States is Merrill Lynch; other well-known ones are UBSPaineWebber, Morgan Stanley Dean Witter, and Salomon Smith Barney. The SEC not only regulates the investment banking operation of the firms but also restricts brokers and dealers from misrepresenting securities and from trading on *insider information*, nonpublic information known only to the management of a corporation.

The forces of competition led to an important development: Brokerage firms started to engage in activities traditionally conducted by commercial banks. In 1977, Merrill Lynch developed the cash management account (CMA), which provides a package of financial services that includes credit cards, immediate loans, check-writing privileges, automatic investment of proceeds from the sale of securities into a money market mutual fund, and unified record keeping. CMAs were adopted by other brokerage firms and spread rapidly. The result is that the distinction between banking activities and the activities of nonbank financial institutions has become blurred. Another development is the growing importance of the Internet in securities markets (see the E-Finance box).

E-Finance The Internet Comes to Wall Street

An important development in recent years is the growing importance of the Internet in securities markets. Initial public offerings of stock are now being sold on the Internet, and many brokerage firms allow clients to conduct securities trades online or to transmit buy and sell orders via e-mail. In June 1999, Wall Street was rocked by the announcement that its largest full-service brokerage firm, Merrill Lynch, would begin offering online trading for as little as $29.95 per trade to its five million customers. Now online trading is ubiquitous. The brokerage business will never be the same.

Organized Exchanges

As discussed in Chapter 2, secondary markets can be organized either as over-the-counter markets, in which trades are conducted using dealers, or as organized exchanges, in which trades are conducted in one central location. The New York Stock Exchange (NYSE), trading thousands of securities, is the largest organized exchange in the world, and the American Stock Exchange (AMEX) is a distant second. A number of smaller regional exchanges, which trade only a small number of securities (fewer than 100), exist in places such as Boston and Los Angeles.

Organized stock exchanges actually function as a hybrid of an auction market (in which buyers and sellers trade with each other in a central location) and a dealer market (in which dealers make the market by buying and selling securities at given prices). Securities are traded on the floor of the exchange with the help of a special kind of dealer-broker called a **specialist**. A specialist matches buy and sell orders submitted at the same price and so performs a brokerage function. However, if buy and sell orders do not match up, the specialist buys stocks or sells from a personal inventory of securities, in this manner performing a dealer function. By assuming both functions, the specialist maintains orderly trading of the securities for which he or she is responsible.

Organized exchanges in which securities are traded are also regulated by the SEC. Not only does the SEC have the authority to impose regulations that govern the behavior of brokers and dealers involved with exchanges, but it also has the authority to alter the rules set by exchanges. In 1975, for example, the SEC disallowed rules that set minimum brokerage commission rates. The result was a sharp drop in brokerage commission rates, especially for institutional investors (mutual funds and pension funds), which purchase large blocks of stock. The Securities Amendments Act of 1975 confirmed the SEC's action by outlawing the setting of minimum brokerage commissions.

Furthermore, the Securities Amendments Act directed the SEC to facilitate a national market system that consolidates trading of all securities listed on the national and regional exchanges as well as those traded in the over-the-counter market using the National Association of Securities Dealers' automated quotation system (NASDAQ). Computers and advanced telecommunications, which reduce the costs of linking these markets, have encouraged the expansion of a national market system. We thus see that legislation and modern computer technology are leading the way to a more competitive securities industry.

The growing internationalization of capital markets has encouraged another trend in securities trading. Increasingly, foreign companies are being listed on U.S. stock exchanges, and the markets are moving toward trading stocks internationally, 24 hours a day.

SUMMARY

1. Insurance providers, which are regulated by the states, acquire funds by selling policies that pay out benefits if catastrophic events occur. Property and casualty insurance companies hold more liquid assets than life insurance companies because of greater uncertainty regarding the benefits they will have to pay out. All insurers face moral hazard and adverse selection problems that explain the use of insurance management tools, such as information collection and screening of potential policyholders, risk-based premiums, restrictive provisions, prevention of fraud, cancellation of insurance, deductibles, coinsurance, and limits on the amount of insurance.

2. Pension plans provide income payments to people when they retire after contributing to the plans for many years. Pension funds have experienced very rapid growth as a result of encouragement by federal tax policy and now play an important role in the stock market. Many pension plans are underfunded, which means that in future years they will have to pay out higher benefits than the value of their contributions and earnings. The problem of underfunding is especially acute for public pension plans such as Social Security. To prevent abuses, Congress enacted the Employee Retirement Income Security Act (ERISA), which established minimum standards for reporting, vesting, and degree of underfunding of private pension plans. This act also created the Pension Benefit Guarantee Corporation, which insures pension benefits.
3. Finance companies raise funds by issuing commercial paper and stocks and bonds and use the proceeds to make loans that are particularly suited to consumer and business needs. Virtually unregulated in comparison to commercial banks and thrift institutions, finance companies have been able to tailor their loans to customer needs very quickly and have grown rapidly.
4. Mutual funds sell shares and use the proceeds to buy securities. Open-end funds issue shares that can be redeemed at any time at a price tied to the asset value of the firm. Closed-end funds issue nonredeemable shares, which are traded like common stock. They are less popular than open-end funds because their shares are not as liquid. Money market mutual funds hold only short-term, high-quality securities, allowing shares to be redeemed at a fixed value using checks. Shares in these funds effectively function as checkable deposits that earn market interest rates. All mutual funds are regulated by the Securities and Exchange Commission (SEC).
5. Investment bankers assist in the initial sale of securities in primary markets, whereas securities brokers and dealers assist in the trading of securities in the secondary markets, some of which are organized into exchanges. The SEC regulates the financial institutions in the securities markets and ensures that adequate information reaches prospective investors.

KEY TERMS

annuities, p. 310
brokerage firms, p. 328
closed-end fund, p. 322
coinsurance, p. 315
deductible, p. 315
defined-benefit plan, p. 317
defined-contribution plan, p. 317
fully funded, p. 317
hedge fund, p. 323
initial public offering (IPO), p. 327
load funds, p. 322
no-load funds, p. 322
open-end fund, p. 322
reinsurance, p. 312
seasoned issue, p. 327
specialist, p. 329
underfunded, p. 317
underwriters, p. 327

QUESTIONS AND PROBLEMS

Questions marked with an asterisk are answered at the end of the book in an appendix, "Answers to Selected Questions and Problems." Questions marked with a blue circle indicate the question is available in MyEconLab at www.myeconlab.com/mishkin.

*1. If death rates were to become less predictable than they are, how would life insurance companies change the types of assets they hold?

2. Why do property and casualty insurance companies have large holdings of municipal bonds but life insurance companies do not?

*3. Why are all defined-contribution pension plans fully funded?

4. How can favorable tax treatment of pension plans encourage saving?

*5. "In contrast to private pension plans, government pension plans are rarely underfunded." Is this statement true, false, or uncertain? Explain your answer.

6. What explains the widespread use of deductibles in insurance policies?

*7. Why might insurance companies restrict the amount of insurance a policyholder can buy?

8. Why are restrictive provisions a necessary part of insurance policies?

*9. If you needed to take out a loan, why might you first go to your local bank rather than to a finance company?

10. Explain why shares in closed-end mutual funds typically sell for less than the market value of the stocks they hold.

*11. Why might you buy a no-load mutual fund instead of a load fund?

12. Why can a money market mutual fund allow its shareholders to redeem shares at a fixed price but other mutual funds cannot?

*13. Why might government loan guarantees be a high-cost way for the government to subsidize certain activities?

14. If you like to take risks, would you rather be a dealer, a broker, or a specialist? Why?

*15. Is investment banking a good career for someone who is afraid of taking risks? Why or why not?

WEB EXERCISES

1. Initial public offerings (IPOs) are where securities are sold to the public for the very first time. Go to http://www.ipohome.com. This site lists various statistics regarding the IPO market.
   a. What is the largest IPO year to date ranked by amount raised?
   b. What is the next IPO to be offered to the public?
   c. How many IPOs were priced this year?
2. The Federal Reserve maintains extensive data on finance companies. Go to www.federalreserve.gov/releases and scroll down until you find G.20 Finance Companies. Click on "Releases" and find the current release.
   a. Review the terms of credit for new car loans. What is the most recent average interest rate and what is the term to maturity? How much is the average new car loan offered by finance companies?
   b. Do finance companies make more consumer loans, real estate loans, or business loans?
   c. Which type of loan has grown most rapidly over the last five years?

WEB REFERENCES

www.iii.org

The Insurance Information Institute publishes facts and statistics about the insurance industry.

www.federalreserve.gov/releases/Z1/

The Flow of Funds Accounts of the United States reports details about the current state of the insurance industry. Scroll down through the table of contents to find the location of data on insurance companies.

www.pbgc.gov/

The web site for the Pension Benefit Guarantee Corporation contains information about pensions and the insurance that it provides.

www.ssa.gov/

The web site for the Social Security Administration contains information on your benefits available from Social Security.

www.federalreserve.gov/Releases/G20/current/default.htm

Federal Reserve information about finance companies.

www.ici.org/pdf/factbooks2.html

The Mutual Fund Fact Book published by Investment Company Institute includes information about the mutual funds industry's history, regulation, taxation, and shareholders.

www.ipohome.com

The site reports initial public offering news and information and includes advanced search tools for IPOs, venture capital research reports, and so on.

www.sec.gov

The Securities and Exchange Commission web site contains regulatory actions, concept releases, interpretive releases, and more.

www.nyse.com

At the New York Stock Exchange home page, you will find listed companies, member information, real-time market indices, and current stock quotes.

CHAPTER

13 Financial Derivatives

Preview

Starting in the 1970s and increasingly in the 1980s and 1990s, the world became a riskier place for the financial institutions described in this part of the book. Swings in interest rates widened, and the bond and stock markets went through some episodes of increased volatility. As a result of these developments, managers of financial institutions became more concerned with reducing the risk their institutions faced. Given the greater demand for risk reduction, the process of financial innovation described in Chapter 10 came to the rescue by producing new financial instruments that help financial institution managers manage risk better. These instruments, called **financial derivatives**, have payoffs that are linked to previously issued securities and are extremely useful risk reduction tools.

In this chapter, we look at the most important financial derivatives that managers of financial institutions use to reduce risk: forward contracts, financial futures, options, and swaps. We examine not only how markets for each of these financial derivatives work but also how they can be used by financial institutions to manage risk. We also study financial derivatives because they have become an important source of profits for financial institutions, particularly larger banks, which, as we saw in Chapter 10, have found their traditional business declining.

HEDGING

Financial derivatives are so effective in reducing risk because they enable financial institutions to **hedge**—that is, engage in a financial transaction that reduces or eliminates risk. When a financial institution has bought an asset, it is said to have taken a **long position**, and this exposes the institution to risk if the returns on the asset are uncertain. Conversely, if it has sold an asset that it has agreed to deliver to another party at a future date, it is said to have taken a **short position**, and this can also expose the institution to risk. Financial derivatives can be used to reduce risk by invoking the following basic principle of hedging: ***Hedging risk involves engaging in a financial transaction that offsets a long position by taking an additional short position, or offsets a short position by taking an additional long position***. In other words, if a financial institution has *bought* a security and has therefore taken a long position, it conducts a hedge by contracting to *sell* that security (take a short position) at some future date. Alternatively, if it has taken a short position by *selling* a security that it needs to deliver at a future date, then it conducts a hedge by contracting to *buy* that security (take a long position) at a future date. We look at how this principle can be applied using forward and futures contracts.

INTEREST-RATE FORWARD CONTRACTS

Forward contracts are agreements by two parties to engage in a financial transaction at a future (forward) point in time. Here we focus on forward contracts that are linked to debt instruments, called **interest-rate forward contracts**; later in the chapter, we discuss forward contracts for foreign currencies.

Interest-rate forward contracts involve the future sale (or purchase) of a debt instrument and have several dimensions: (1) specification of the actual debt instrument that will be delivered at a future date, (2) amount of the debt instrument to be delivered, (3) price (interest rate) on the debt instrument when it is delivered, and (4) date on which delivery will take place. An example of an interest-rate forward contract might be an agreement for the First National Bank to sell to the Rock Solid Insurance Company, one year from today, $5 million face value of the 6s of 2023 Treasury bonds (that is, coupon bonds with a 6% coupon rate that mature in 2023) at a price that yields the same interest rate on these bonds as today's, say 6%. Because Rock Solid will buy the securities at a future date, it is said to have taken a long position, while the First National Bank, which will sell the securities, has taken a short position.

APPLICATION Hedging with Interest-Rate Forward Contracts

Why would the First National Bank want to enter into this forward contract with Rock Solid Insurance Company in the first place?

To understand, suppose that you are the manager of the First National Bank and have bought $5 million of the 6s of 2023 Treasury bonds. The bonds are currently selling at par value, so their yield to maturity is 6%. Because these are long-term bonds, you recognize that you are exposed to substantial interest-rate risk: If interest rates rise in the future, the price of these bonds will fall and result in a substantial capital loss that may cost you your job. How do you hedge this risk?

Knowing the basic principle of hedging, you see that your long position in these bonds can be offset by an equal short position for the same bonds with a forward contract. That is, you need to contract to sell these bonds at a future date at the current par value price. As a result, you agree with another party—in this case, Rock Solid Insurance Company—to sell it the $5 million of the 6s of 2023 Treasury bonds at par one year from today. By entering into this forward contract, you have successfully hedged against interest-rate risk. By locking in the future price of the bonds, you have eliminated the price risk you face from interest-rate changes.

Why would Rock Solid Insurance Company want to enter into the futures contract with the First National Bank? Rock Solid expects to receive premiums of $5 million in one year's time that it will want to invest in the 6s of 2023, but worries that interest rates on these bonds will decline between now and next year. By using the forward contract, it is able to lock in the 6% interest rate on the Treasury bonds that will be sold to it by the First National Bank.

Pros and Cons of Forward Contracts

The advantage of forward contracts is that they can be as flexible as the parties involved want them to be. This means that an institution like the First National Bank may be able to hedge completely the interest-rate risk for the exact security it is holding in its portfolio, just as it has in our example.

However, forward contracts suffer from two problems that severely limit their usefulness. The first is that it may be very hard for an institution like the First National Bank to find another party (called a *counterparty*) to make the contract with. There are brokers to facilitate the matching up of parties like the First National Bank with the Rock Solid Insurance Company, but there may be few institutions that want to engage in a forward contract specifically for the 6s of 2023. This means that it may prove impossible to find a counterparty when a financial institution like the First National Bank wants to make a specific type of forward contract. Furthermore, even if the First National Bank finds a counterparty, it may not get as high a price as it wants because there may not be anyone else to make the deal with. A serious problem for the market in interest-rate forward contracts, then, is that it may be difficult to make the financial transaction or that it will have to be made at a disadvantageous price; in the parlance of financial economists, this market suffers from a *lack of liquidity*. (Note that this use of the term *liquidity* when it is applied to a market is somewhat broader than its use when it is applied to an asset. For an asset, liquidity refers to the ease with which the asset can be turned into cash; for a market, liquidity refers to the ease of carrying out financial transactions.)

The second problem with forward contracts is that they are subject to default risk. Suppose that in one year's time, interest rates rise so that the price of the 6s of 2023 falls. The Rock Solid Insurance Company might then decide that it would like to default on the forward contract with the First National Bank, because it can now buy the bonds at a price lower than the agreed price in the forward contract. Or perhaps Rock Solid may not have been rock solid after all, and may have gone bust during the year, and no longer be available to complete the terms of the forward contract. Because there is no outside organization guaranteeing the contract, the only recourse is for the First National Bank to go to the courts to sue Rock Solid, but this process will be costly. Furthermore, if Rock Solid is already bankrupt, the First National Bank will suffer a loss; the bank can no longer sell the 6s of 2023 at the price it had agreed on with Rock Solid, but instead will have to sell at a price well below that, because the price of these bonds has fallen.

The presence of default risk in forward contracts means that parties to these contracts must check each other out to be sure that the counterparty is both financially sound and likely to be honest and live up to its contractual obligations. Because this type of investigation is costly and because all the adverse selection and moral hazard problems discussed in earlier chapters apply, default risk is a major barrier to the use of interest-rate forward contracts. When the default risk problem is combined with a lack of liquidity, we see that these contracts may be of limited usefulness to financial institutions. Although there is a market for interest-rate forward contracts, particularly in Treasury and mortgage-backed securities, it is not nearly as large as the financial futures market, to which we turn next.

FINANCIAL FUTURES CONTRACTS AND MARKETS

Given the default risk and liquidity problems in the interest-rate forward market, another solution to hedging interest-rate risk was needed. This solution was provided by the development of financial futures contracts by the Chicago Board of Trade starting in 1975.

Following the Financial News **Financial Futures**

The prices for financial futures contracts for debt instruments are published daily. In the *Wall Street Journal*, these prices are found in the "Commodities" section under the "Interest Rate" heading of the "Future Prices" columns. An excerpt is reproduced here.

	OPEN	HIGH	LOW	SETTLE	CHG	LIFETIME HIGH	LIFETIME LOW	OPEN INT
Interest Rate Futures								
Treasury Bonds ((BT)-$100,000; pts 32nds of 100%)								
Mar	111-04	111-19	111-04	111-12	7	118-19	110-01	20,263
June	111-01	111-17	110-30	111-09	7	117-24	109-31	570,075

Information for each contract is presented in columns, as follows. (The Chicago Board of Trade's contract for delivery of long-term Treasury bonds in March 2006 is used as an example.)

Open: Opening price; each point corresponds to $1,000 of face value—111 4/32 is $111,125 for the March contract

High: Highest traded price that day—111 19/32 is $111,594 for the March contract

Low: Lowest traded price that day—111 4/32 is $111,125 for the March contract

Settle: Settlement price, the closing price that day—111 12/32 is $111,375 for the March contract

Chg: Change in the settlement price from the previous trading day—7/32 is $218.75 for the March contract

Lifetime High: Highest price ever—118 19/32 is $118,594 for the March contract

Lifetime Low: Lowest price ever—110 1/32 is $110,031 for the March contract

Open Interest: Number of contracts outstanding—20,263 for the March contract, with a face value of $2 billion (20,263 × $100,000)

Source: Wall Street Journal, March 21, 2006, p. C11.

A **financial futures contract** is similar to an interest-rate forward contract, in that it specifies that a financial instrument must be delivered by one party to another on a stated future date. However, it differs from an interest-rate forward contract in several ways that overcome some of the liquidity and default problems of forward markets.

To understand what financial futures contracts are all about, let's look at one of the most widely traded futures contracts—that for Treasury bonds, which are traded on the Chicago Board of Trade. (An illustration of how prices on these contracts are quoted can be found in the Following the Financial News box, "Financial Futures".) The contract value is for $100,000 face value of bonds. Prices are quoted in points, with each point equal to $1,000, and the smallest change in price is one thirty-second of a point ($31.25). This contract specifies that the bonds to be delivered must have at least fifteen years to maturity at the delivery date (and must also not be callable—that is, redeemable by the Treasury at its option—in less than fifteen years). If the Treasury bonds delivered to settle the futures contract have a coupon rate different from the 6% specified in the futures contract, the amount of bonds to be delivered is adjusted to reflect the difference in value between the delivered bonds and the 6% coupon bond. In line with the terminology used for forward contracts, parties who have bought a futures contract and thereby agreed to buy (take delivery of) the bonds are said to have taken a *long position*, and parties who have sold a futures contract and thereby agreed to sell (deliver) the bonds have taken a *short position*.

To make our understanding of this contract more concrete, let's consider what happens when you buy or sell a Treasury bond futures contract. Let's say that on February 1, you sell one $100,000 June contract at a price of 115 (that is, $115,000). By selling this contract, you agree to deliver $100,000 face value of the long-term Treasury bonds to the contract's counterparty at the end of June for $115,000. By buying the contract at a price of 115, the buyer has agreed to pay $115,000 for the $100,000 face value of bonds when you deliver them at the end of June. If interest rates on long-term bonds rise, so that when the contract matures at the end of June, the price of these bonds has fallen to 110 ($110,000 per $100,000 of face value), the buyer of the contract will have lost $5,000, because he or she paid $115,000 for the bonds but can sell them only for the market price of $110,000. But you, the seller of the contract, will have gained $5,000, because you can now sell the bonds to the buyer for $115,000 but have to pay only $110,000 for them in the market.

It is even easier to describe what happens to the parties who have purchased futures contracts and those who have sold futures contracts if we recognize the following fact: ***At the expiration date of a futures contract, the price of the contract is the same as the price of the underlying asset to be delivered.*** To see why this is the case, consider what happens on the expiration date of the June contract at the end of June when the price of the underlying $100,000 face value Treasury bond is 110 ($110,000). If the futures contract is selling below 110—say, at 109—a trader can buy the contract for $109,000, take delivery of the bond, and immediately sell it for $110,000, thereby earning a quick profit of $1,000. Because earning this profit involves no risk, it is a great deal that everyone would like to get in on. That means that everyone will try to buy the contract, and as a result, its price will rise. Only when the price rises to 110 will the profit opportunity cease to exist and the buying pressure disappear. Conversely, if the price of the futures contract is above 110—say, at 111—everyone will want to sell the contract. Now the sellers get $111,000 from selling the futures contract but have to pay only $110,000 for the Treasury bonds that they must deliver to the buyer of the contract, and the $1,000 difference is their profit. Because this profit involves no risk, traders will continue to sell the futures contract until its price falls back down to 110, at which price there are no longer any profits to be made. The elimination of riskless profit opportunities in the futures market is referred to as **arbitrage**, and it guarantees that the price of a futures contract at expiration equals the price of the underlying asset to be delivered.[1]

Armed with the fact that a futures contract at expiration equals the price of the underlying asset makes it even easier to see who profits and who loses from such a contract when interest rates change. When interest rates have risen so that the price of the Treasury bond is 110 on the expiration day at the end of June, the June Treasury bond futures contract will also have a price of 110. Thus, if you bought the contract for 115 in February, you have a loss of 5 points, or $5,000 (5% of $100,000). But if you sold the futures contract at 115 in February, the decline in price to 110 means that you have a profit of 5 points, or $5,000.

---

[1]In actuality, futures contracts sometimes set conditions for delivery of the underlying assets that cause the price of the contract at expiration to differ slightly from the price of the underlying assets. Because the difference in price is extremely small, we ignore it in this chapter.

APPLICATION Hedging with Financial Futures

First National Bank can also use financial futures contracts to hedge the interest rate risk on its holdings of $5 million of the 6s of 2023. To see how, suppose that in March 2007, the 6s of 2023 are the long-term bonds that would be delivered in the Chicago Board of Trade's T-bond futures contract expiring one year in the future, in March 2008. Also suppose that the interest rate on these bonds is expected to remain at 6% over the next year, so that both the 6s of 2023 and the futures contract are selling at par (i.e., the $5 million of bonds is selling for $5 million and the $100,000 futures contract is selling for $100,000). The basic principle of hedging indicates that you need to offset the long position in these bonds with a short position, so you have to sell the futures contract. But how many contracts should you sell? The number of contracts required to hedge the interest-rate risk is found by dividing the amount of the asset to be hedged by the dollar value of each contract, as is shown in Equation 1:

$$NC = VA/VC \tag{1}$$

where NC = number of contracts for the hedge
VA = value of the asset
VC = value of each contract

Given that the 6s of 2023 are the long-term bonds that would be delivered in the CBT T-bond futures contract expiring one year in the future and that the interest rate on these bonds is expected to remain at 6% over the next year, so that both the 6s of 2023 and the futures contract are selling at par, how many contracts must First National sell to remove its interest-rate exposure from its $5 million holdings of the 6s of 2023?[2] Since VA = $5 million and VC = $100,000,

$$NC = \$5 \text{ million}/\$100{,}000 = 50$$

You therefore hedge the interest-rate risk by selling 50 of the Treasury Bond futures contracts.

Now suppose that over the next year, interest rates increase to 8% due to an increased threat of inflation. The value of the 6s of 2023 that the First National Bank is holding will then fall to $4,039,640 in March 2008.[3] Thus the loss from the long position in these bonds is $960,360:

Value on March 2008 @ 8% interest rate	$4,144,052
Value on March 2007 @ 6% interest rate	−$5,000,000
Loss	−$ 855,948

However, the short position in the 50 futures contracts that obligate you to deliver $5 million of the 6s of 2023 on March 2007 has a value equal to $4,144,052, the value of the $5 million of bonds after the interest rate has risen to 8%, as we have seen before. Yet when you sold the futures contract, the buyer was obligated to pay you $5 million on the maturity date. Thus the gain from the short position on these contracts is also $855,948:

[2] In the real world, designing a hedge is somewhat more complicated than the example here, because the bond that is most likely to be delivered might not be a 6s of 2023.

[3] The value of the bonds can be calculated using a financial calculator as follows: FV = $5,000,000, PMT = $300,000, I = 8%, N = 15, PV = $4,144,052.

Amount paid to you on March 2008, agreed upon in March 2007	\$5,000,000
Value of bonds delivered on March 2008 @ 8% interest rate	−\$4,144,052
Gain	\$ 855,948

Therefore the net gain for the First National Bank is zero, indicating that the hedge has been conducted successfully.

The hedge just described is called a **micro hedge** because the financial institution is hedging the interest-rate risk for a specific asset it is holding. A second type of hedge that financial institutions engage in is called a **macro hedge**, in which the hedge is for the institution's entire portfolio. For example, if a bank has more rate-sensitive liabilities than assets, we have seen in Chapter 9 that a rise in interest rates will cause the value of the bank's net worth to decline. By selling interest-rate future contracts that will yield a profit when interest rates rise, the bank can offset the losses on its overall portfolio from an interest-rate rise and thereby hedge its interest-rate risk.

Organization of Trading in Financial Futures Markets

Financial futures contracts are traded in the United States on organized exchanges such as the Chicago Board of Trade, the Chicago Mercantile Exchange, the New York Futures Exchange, the MidAmerica Commodity Exchange, and the Kansas City Board of Trade. These exchanges are highly competitive with one another, and each organization tries to design contracts and set rules that will increase the amount of futures trading on its exchange.

The futures exchanges and all trades in financial futures in the United States are regulated by the Commodity Futures Trading Commission (CFTC), which was created in 1974 to take over the regulatory responsibilities for futures markets from the Department of Agriculture. The CFTC oversees futures trading and the futures exchanges to ensure that prices in the market are not being manipulated, and it also registers and audits the brokers, traders, and exchanges to prevent fraud and to ensure the financial soundness of the exchanges. In addition, the CFTC approves proposed futures contracts to make sure that they serve the public interest. The most widely traded financial futures contracts listed in the *Wall Street Journal* and the exchanges where they are traded (along with the number of contracts outstanding, called **open interest**, on March 20, 2006) are listed in Table 1.

Given the globalization of other financial markets in recent years, it is not surprising that increased competition from abroad has been occurring in financial futures markets as well.

The Globalization of Financial Futures Markets

Because American futures exchanges were the first to develop financial futures, they dominated the trading of financial futures in the early 1980s. For example, in 1985, all of the top ten futures contracts were traded on exchanges in the United States. With the rapid growth of financial futures markets and the resulting high profits made by the American exchanges, foreign exchanges saw a profit opportunity and began to enter this business. By the 1990s, Eurodollar contracts traded on the London International

TABLE 1 Widely Traded Financial Futures Contracts

Type of Contract	Contract Size	Exchange*	Open Interest March 20, 2006 Reflects March 2006 Futures
Interest Rate Contracts			
Treasury bonds	\$100,000	CBT	20,263
Treasury notes	\$100,000	CBT	35,929
Five-year Treasury notes	\$100,000	CBT	11,765
Two-year Treasury notes	\$200,000	CBT	17,989
Thirty-day Fed funds rate	\$5 million	CBT	90,122
One-month LIBOR	\$3 million	CME	22,068
Eurodollar	\$4 million	CME	139,936
Euroyen	\$100 million	CME	11,539
Sterling	£500,000	LIFFE	44,698
Long Gilt	£100,000	LIFFE	28,189
Three-month Euribor	€ 1 million	LIFFE	53,416
Euroswiss franc	SF 1 million	LIFFE	93,232
Stock Index Contracts			
Standard & Poor's 500 Index	\$250 × index	CME	646,296
Standard & Poor's MIDCAP 400	\$500 × index	CME	38,575
NASDAQ 100	\$100 × index	CME	55,342
Nikkei 225 Stock Average	\$5 × index	CME	53,435
Financial Times Stock Exchange 100 Index	£10 per index point	LIFFE	455,905
Currency Contracts			
Yen	12,500,000 yen	CME	159,182
Euro	125,000 euros	CME	132,925
Canadian dollar	100,000 Canadian \$	CME	83,061
British pound	100,000 pounds	CME	69,774
Swiss franc	125,000 francs	CME	76,630
Mexican peso	500,000 new pesos	CME	52,803

*Exchange abbreviations: CBT, Chicago Board of Trade; CME, Chicago Mercantile Exchange; LIFFE, London International Financial Futures Exchange.

Source: Wall Street Journal, March 21, 2006, p. C11; www.wsj.com/free.

Financial Futures Exchange, Japanese government bond contracts and Euroyen contracts traded on the Tokyo Stock Exchange, French government bond contracts traded on the Marché à Terme International de France, and Nikkei 225 contracts traded on the Osaka Securities Exchange all became among the most widely traded futures contracts in the world.

Foreign competition has also spurred knockoffs of the most popular financial futures contracts initially developed in the United States. These contracts traded on foreign exchanges are virtually identical to those traded in the United States and have the advantage that they can be traded when the American exchanges are closed. The movement to 24-hour-a-day trading in financial futures has been further stimulated by the development of the Globex electronic trading platform, which allows traders throughout the world to trade futures even when the exchanges are not officially open. Financial futures trading has thus become completely internationalized, and competition between U.S. and foreign exchanges is now intense.

Explaining the Success of Futures Markets

The tremendous success of the financial futures market in Treasury bonds is evident from the fact that the total open interest of Treasury bond contracts exceeded 20,000 on March 20, 2006, for a total value of more than $2 billion (20,000 × $100,000). There are several differences between financial futures and forward contracts and in the organization of their markets that help explain why financial futures markets such as those for Treasury bonds have been so successful.

Several features of futures contracts were designed to overcome the liquidity problem inherent in forward contracts. The first feature is that, in contrast to forward contracts, the quantities delivered and the delivery dates of futures contracts are standardized, making it more likely that different parties can be matched up in the futures market, thereby increasing the liquidity of the market. In the case of the Treasury bond contract, the quantity delivered is $100,000 face value of bonds, and the delivery dates are set to be the last business day of March, June, September, and December. The second feature is that after the futures contract has been bought or sold, it can be traded (bought or sold) again at any time until the delivery date. In contrast, once a forward contract is agreed on, it typically cannot be traded. The third feature is that in a futures contract, not just one specific type of Treasury bond is deliverable on the delivery date, as in a forward contract. Instead, any Treasury bond that matures in more than fifteen years and is not callable for fifteen years is eligible for delivery. Allowing continuous trading also increases the liquidity of the futures market, as does the ability to deliver a range of Treasury bonds rather than one specific bond.

Another reason why futures contracts specify that more than one bond is eligible for delivery is to limit the possibility that someone might corner the market and "squeeze" traders who have sold contracts. To corner the market, someone buys up all the deliverable securities so that investors with a short position cannot obtain from anyone else the securities that they contractually must deliver on the delivery date. As a result, the person who has cornered the market can set exorbitant prices for the securities that investors with a short position must buy to fulfill their obligations under the futures contract. The person who has cornered the market makes a fortune, but investors with a short position take a terrific loss. Clearly, the possibility that corners might occur in the market will discourage people from taking a short position and might therefore decrease the size of the market. By allowing many different securities to be delivered, the futures contract makes it harder for anyone to corner the market, because a much larger amount of securities would have to be purchased to establish the corner. Corners are a concern to both regulators and the organized exchanges that design futures contracts.

Trading in the futures market has been organized differently from trading in forward markets to overcome the default risk problems arising in forward contracts. In both types, for every contract, there must be a buyer who is taking a long position and a seller who is taking a short position. However, the buyer and seller of a futures contract make their contract not with each other but with the clearinghouse associated with the futures exchange. This setup means that the buyer of the futures contract does not need to worry about the financial health or trustworthiness of the seller, and vice versa, as in the forward market. As long as the clearinghouse is financially solid, buyers and sellers of futures contracts do not have to worry about default risk.

To make sure that the clearinghouse is financially sound and does not run into financial difficulties that might jeopardize its contracts, buyers or sellers of futures contracts must put an initial deposit, called a **margin requirement**, of perhaps $2,000 per Treasury bond contract into a margin account kept at their brokerage firm. Futures contracts are then **marked to market** every day. What this means is that at the end of every trading day, the change in the value of the futures contract is added to or subtracted from the margin account. Suppose that after you buy the Treasury bond contract at a price of 115 on Wednesday morning, its closing price at the end of the day, the *settlement price*, falls to 114. You now have a loss of 1 point, or $1,000, on the contract, and the seller who sold you the contract has a gain of 1 point, or $1,000. The $1,000 gain is added to the seller's margin account, making a total of $3,000 in that account, and the $1,000 loss is subtracted from your account, so you now have only $1,000 in your account. If the amount in this margin account falls below the maintenance margin requirement (which can be the same as the initial requirement but is usually a little less), the trader is required to add money to the account. For example, if the maintenance margin requirement is also $2,000, you would have to add $1,000 to your account to bring it up to $2,000. Margin requirements and marking to market make it far less likely that a trader will default on a contract, thus protecting the futures exchange from losses.

A final advantage that futures markets have over forward markets is that most futures contracts do not result in delivery of the underlying asset on the expiration date, whereas forward contracts do. A trader who sold a futures contract is allowed to avoid delivery on the expiration date by making an offsetting purchase of a futures contract. Because the simultaneous holding of the long and short positions means that the trader would in effect be delivering the bonds to itself, under the exchange rules the trader is allowed to cancel both contracts. Allowing traders to cancel their contracts in this way lowers the cost of conducting trades in the futures market relative to the forward market in that a futures trader can avoid the costs of physical delivery, which is not so easy with forward contracts.

APPLICATION Hedging Foreign Exchange Risk

As we discussed in Chapter 1, foreign exchange rates have been highly volatile in recent years. The large fluctuations in exchange rates subject financial institutions and other businesses to significant foreign exchange risk because they generate substantial gains and losses. Luckily for financial institution managers, the financial derivatives discussed in this chapter—forward and financial futures contracts—can be used to hedge foreign exchange risk.

To understand how financial institution managers manage foreign exchange risk, let's suppose that in January, the First National Bank's customer Frivolous Luxuries, Inc., is due a payment of 10 million euros in two months for $10 million worth of goods it has just sold in Germany. Frivolous Luxuries is concerned that if the value of the euro falls substantially from its current value of $1, the company might suffer a large loss because the 10 million euro payment will no longer be worth $10 million. So Sam, the CEO of Frivolous Luxuries, calls up his friend Mona, the manager of the First National Bank, and asks her to hedge this foreign exchange risk for his company. Let's see how the bank manager does this using forward and financial futures contracts.

Hedging Foreign Exchange Risk with Forward Contracts

Forward markets in foreign exchange have been highly developed by commercial banks and investment banking operations that engage in extensive foreign exchange trading and are widely used to hedge foreign exchange risk. Mona knows that she can use this market to hedge the foreign exchange risk for Frivolous Luxuries. Such a hedge is quite straightforward for her to execute. Because the payment of euros in two months means that at that time Sam would hold a long position in euros, Mona knows that the basic principle of hedging indicates that she should offset this long position by a short position. Thus she just enters a forward contract that obligates her to sell 10 million euros two months from now in exchange for dollars at the current forward rate of $1 per euro.[4]

In two months, when her customer receives the 10 million euros, the forward contract ensures that it is exchanged for dollars at an exchange rate of $1 per euro, thus yielding $10 million. No matter what happens to future exchange rates, Frivolous Luxuries will be guaranteed $10 million for the goods it sold in Germany. Mona calls up her friend Sam to let him know that his company is now protected from any foreign exchange movements, and he thanks her for her help.

Hedging Foreign Exchange Risk with Futures Contracts

As an alternative, Mona could have used the currency futures market to hedge the foreign exchange risk. In this case, she would see that the Chicago Mercantile Exchange has a euro contract with a contract amount of 125,000 euros and a price of $1 per euro. To do the hedge, Mona must sell euros as with the forward contract, to the tune of 10 million euros of the March futures. How many of the Chicago Mercantile Exchange March euro contracts must Mona sell to hedge the 10 million euro payment due in March?

Using Equation 1 with $VA = 10$ million euros and $VC = 125{,}000$ euros,

$$NC = 10 \text{ million}/125{,}000 = 80$$

Thus Mona does the hedge by selling 80 of the CME euro contracts. Given the $1-per-euro price, the sale of the contract yields 80 × 125,000 euros = $10 million. This

[4]The forward exchange rate will probably differ slightly from the current spot rate of $1 per euro because the interest rates in Germany and the United States may not be equal. In that case, as we will see in Equation 2 in Chapter 20, the future expected exchange rate will not equal the current spot rate and neither will the forward rate. However, since interest differentials have typically been less than 6% at an annual rate (1% bimonthly), the expected appreciation or depreciation of the euro over a two-month period has always been less than 1%. Thus the forward rate is always close to the current spot rate, and our assumption in the example that the forward rate and the spot rate are the same is a reasonable one.

futures hedge enables her to lock in the exchange rate for Frivolous Luxuries so that it gets its payment of $10 million.

One advantage of using the futures market is that the contract size of 125,000 euros, worth $125,000, is quite a bit smaller than the minimum size of a forward contract, which is usually $1 million or more. However, in this case, the bank manager is making a large enough transaction that she can use either the forward or the futures market. Her choice depends on whether the transaction costs are lower in one market than in the other. If the First National Bank is active in the forward market, that market would probably have the lower transaction costs. If First National rarely deals in foreign exchange forward contracts, the bank manager may do better by sticking with the futures market.

OPTIONS

Another vehicle for hedging interest-rate and stock market risk involves the use of options on financial instruments. **Options** are contracts that give the purchaser the option, or *right*, to buy or sell the underlying financial instrument at a specified price, called the **exercise price** or **strike price**, within a specific period of time (the *term to expiration*). The seller (sometimes called the *writer*) of the option is *obligated* to buy or sell the financial instrument to the purchaser if the owner of the option exercises the right to sell or buy. These option contract features are important enough to be emphasized: The *owner* or buyer of an option does not have to exercise the option; he or she can let the option expire without using it. Hence the owner of an option is not obligated to take any action, but rather has the *right* to exercise the contract if he or she so chooses. The seller of an option, by contrast, has no choice in the matter; he or she *must* buy or sell the financial instrument if the owner exercises the option.

Because the right to buy or sell a financial instrument at a specified price has value, the owner of an option is willing to pay an amount for it called a **premium**. There are two types of option contracts: **American options** can be exercised *at any time up to* the expiration date of the contract, and **European options** can be exercised only *on* the expiration date.

Option contracts are written on a number of financial instruments. Options on individual stocks are called **stock options**, and such options have existed for a long time. Option contracts on financial futures called **financial futures options** or, more commonly, **futures options**, were developed in 1982 and have become the most widely traded option contracts.

You might wonder why option contracts are more likely to be written on financial futures than on underlying debt instruments such as bonds or certificates of deposit. As you saw earlier in the chapter, at the expiration date, the price of the futures contract and of the deliverable debt instrument will be the same because of arbitrage. So it would seem that investors should be indifferent about having the option written on the debt instrument or on the futures contract. However, financial futures contracts have been so well designed that their markets are often more liquid than the markets in the underlying debt instruments. So investors would rather have the option contract written on the more liquid instrument—in this case, the futures contract. That explains why the most popular futures options are written on many of the same futures contracts listed in Table 1.

The regulation of option markets is split between the Securities and Exchange Commission (SEC), which regulates stock options, and the Commodity Futures Trading Commission (CFTC), which regulates futures options. Regulation focuses on ensuring that writers of options have enough capital to make good on their contractual obligations and on overseeing traders and exchanges to prevent fraud and ensure that the market is not being manipulated.

Option Contracts

A **call option** is a contract that gives the owner the right to buy a financial instrument at the exercise price within a specific period of time. A **put option** is a contract that gives the owner the right to sell a financial instrument at the exercise price within a specific period of time.

STUDY GUIDE

Remembering which is a call option and which is a put option is not always easy. To keep them straight, just remember that having a *call* option to buy a financial instrument is the same as having the option to *call* in the instrument for delivery at a specified price. Having a *put* option to sell a financial instrument is the same as having the option to *put* up an instrument for the other party to buy.

Profits and Losses on Option and Futures Contracts

To understand option contracts more fully, let's first examine the option on the same June Treasury bond futures contract that we looked at earlier in the chapter. Recall that if you buy this futures contract at a price of 115 (that is, $115,000), you have agreed to pay $115,000 for $100,000 face value of long-term Treasury bonds when they are delivered to you at the end of June. If you sold this futures contract at a price of 115, you agreed, in exchange for $115,000, to deliver $100,000 face value of the long-term Treasury bonds at the end of June. An option contract on the Treasury bond futures contract has several key features: (1) It has the same expiration date as the underlying futures contract, (2) it is an American option and so can be exercised at any time before the expiration date, and (3) the premium (price) of the option is quoted in points that are the same as in the futures contract, so each point corresponds to $1,000. If, for a premium of $2,000, you buy one call option contract on the June Treasury bond contract with an exercise price of 115, you have purchased the right to buy (call in) the June Treasury bond futures contract for a price of 115 ($115,000 per contract) at any time through the expiration date of this contract at the end of June. Similarly, when for $2,000 you buy a put option on the June Treasury bond contract with an exercise price of 115, you have the right to sell (put up) the June Treasury bond futures contract for a price of 115 ($115,000 per contract) at any time until the end of June.

Futures option contracts are somewhat complicated, so to explore how they work and how they can be used to hedge risk, let's first examine how profits and losses on the call option on the June Treasury bond futures contract occur. In February, our old friend Irving the Investor buys, for a $2,000 premium, a call option on the $100,000 June

Treasury bond futures contract with a strike price of 115. (We assume that if Irving exercises the option, it is on the expiration date at the end of June and not before.) On the expiration date at the end of June, suppose that the underlying Treasury bond for the futures contract has a price of 110. Recall that on the expiration date, arbitrage forces the price of the futures contract to be the same as the price of the underlying bond, so it too has a price of 110 on the expiration date at the end of June. If Irving exercises the call option and buys the futures contract at an exercise price of 115, he will lose money by buying at 115 and selling at the lower market price of 110. Because Irving is smart, he will not exercise the option, but he will be out the $2,000 premium he paid. In such a situation, in which the price of the underlying financial instrument is below the exercise price, a call option is said to be "out of the money." At the price of 110 (less than the exercise price), Irving thus suffers a loss on the option contract of the $2,000 premium he paid. This loss is plotted as point A in panel (a) of Figure 1.

On the expiration date, if the price of the futures contract is 115, the call option is "at the money," and Irving is indifferent whether he exercises his option to buy the futures contract, because exercising the option at 115 when the market price is also at 115 produces no gain or loss. Because he has paid the $2,000 premium, at the price of 115 his contract again has a net loss of $2,000, plotted as point B.

If the futures contract instead has a price of 120 on the expiration day, the option is "in the money," and Irving benefits from exercising the option: He would buy the futures contract at the exercise price of 115 and then sell it for 120, thereby earning a 5-point gain ($5,000 profit) on the $100,000 Treasury bond contract. Because Irving paid a $2,000 premium for the option contract, however, his net profit is $3,000 ($5,000 − $2,000). The $3,000 profit at a price of 120 is plotted as point C. Similarly, if the price of the futures contract rose to 125, the option contract would yield a net profit of $8,000 ($10,000 from exercising the option minus the $2,000 premium), plotted as point D. Plotting these points, we get the kinked profit curve for the call option that we see in panel (a).

Suppose that instead of purchasing the futures *option* contract in February, Irving decides instead to buy the $100,000 June Treasury bond *futures* contract at the price of 115. If the price of the bond on the expiration day at the end of June declines to 110, meaning that the price of the futures contract also falls to 110, Irving suffers a loss of 5 points, or $5,000. The loss of $5,000 on the futures contract at a price of 110 is plotted as point A′ in panel (a). At a price of 115 on the expiration date, Irving would have a zero profit on the futures contract, plotted as point B′. At a price of 120, Irving would have a profit on the contract of 5 points, or $5,000 (point C′), and at a price of 125, the profit would be 10 percentage points, or $10,000 (point D′). Plotting these points, we get the linear (straight-line) profit curve for the futures contract that appears in panel (a).

Now we can see the major difference between a futures contract and an option contract. As the profit curve for the futures contract in panel (a) indicates, the futures contract has a linear profit function: Profits grow by an equal dollar amount for every point increase in the price of the underlying financial instrument. By contrast, the kinked profit curve for the option contract is nonlinear, meaning that profits do not always grow by the same amount for a given change in the price of the underlying financial instrument. The reason for this nonlinearity is that the call option protects Irving from having losses that are greater than the amount of the $2,000 premium. In contrast, Irving's loss on the futures contract is $5,000 if the price on the expiration day falls to 110, and if the price falls even further, Irving's loss will be even greater. This insurance-like feature of option contracts explains why their purchase price is referred to as a premium. Once the underlying financial instrument's price rises above the exercise price, however,

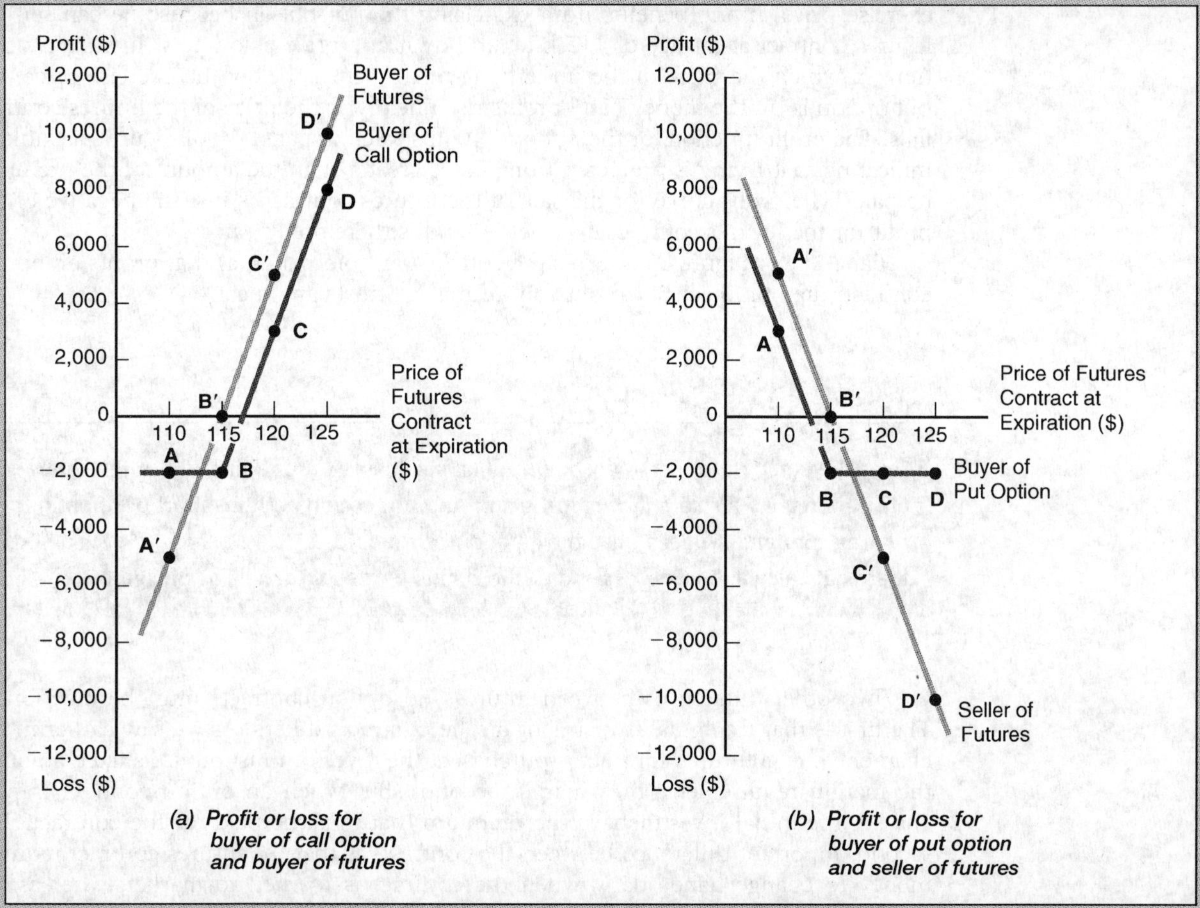

FIGURE 1 **Profits and Losses on Options Versus Futures Contracts**
The futures contract is the $100,000 June Treasury bond contract, and the option contracts are written on this futures contract with an exercise price of 115. Panel (a) shows the profits and losses for the buyer of the call option and the buyer of the futures contract, and panel (b) shows the profits and losses for the buyer of the put option and the seller of the futures contract.

Irving's profits grow linearly. Irving has given up something by buying an option rather than a futures contract. As we see in panel (a), when the price of the underlying financial instrument rises above the exercise price, Irving's profits are always less than that on the futures contract by exactly the $2,000 premium he paid.

Panel (b) plots the results of the same profit calculations if Irving buys not a call but a put option (an option to sell) with an exercise price of 115 for a premium of $2,000 and if he sells the futures contract rather than buying one. In this case, if on the expiration date the Treasury bond futures have a price above the 115 exercise price, the put option is "out of the money." Irving would not want to exercise the put option and then have to sell the futures contract he owns as a result at a price below the market price and lose money. He would not exercise his option, and he would be out only the

$2,000 premium he paid. Once the price of the futures contract falls below the 115 exercise price, Irving benefits from exercising the put option because he can sell the futures contract at a price of 115 but can buy it at a price below this. In such a situation, in which the price of the underlying instrument is below the exercise price, the put option is "in the money," and profits rise linearly as the price of the futures contract falls. The profit function for the put option illustrated in panel (b) of Figure 1 is kinked, indicating that Irving is protected from losses greater than the amount of the premium he paid. The profit curve for the sale of the futures contract is just the negative of the profit for the futures contract in panel (a) and is therefore linear.

Panel (b) of Figure 1 confirms the conclusion from panel (a) that profits on option contracts are nonlinear but profits on futures contracts are linear.

STUDY GUIDE

To make sure you understand how profits and losses on option and futures contracts are generated, calculate the net profits on the put option and the short position in the futures contract at prices on the expiration day of 110, 115, 120, and 125. Then verify that your calculations correspond to the points plotted in panel (b) of Figure 1.

Two other differences between futures and option contracts must be mentioned. The first is that the initial investment on the contracts differs. As we saw earlier in the chapter, when a futures contract is purchased, the investor must put up a fixed amount, the margin requirement, in a margin account. But when an option contract is purchased, the initial investment is the premium that must be paid for the contract. The second important difference between the contracts is that the futures contract requires money to change hands daily when the contract is marked to market, whereas the option contract requires money to change hands only when it is exercised.

APPLICATION Hedging with Futures Options

Earlier in the chapter, we saw how the First National Bank could hedge the interest-rate risk on its $5 million holdings of 6s of 2023 by selling $5 million of T-bond futures. A rise in interest rates and the resulting fall in bond prices and bond futures contracts would lead to profits on the bank's sale of the futures contracts that would exactly offset the losses on the 6s of 2023 the bank is holding.

As panel (b) of Figure 1 suggests, an alternative way for the manager to protect against a rise in interest rates and hence a decline in bond prices is to buy $5 million of put options written on the same Treasury bond futures. As long as the exercise price is not too far from the current price as in panel (b), the rise in interest rates and decline in bond prices will lead to profits on the futures and the futures put options, profits that will offset any losses on the $5 million of Treasury bonds.

The one problem with using options rather than futures is that the First National Bank will have to pay premiums on the options contracts, thereby lowering the bank's profits in an effort to hedge the interest-rate risk. Why might the bank manager be willing to use options rather than futures to conduct the hedge? The answer is that the option contract, unlike the futures contract, allows the First National Bank to gain if interest rates decline and bond prices rise. With the hedge using futures contracts, the First National Bank does not gain from increases in bond prices because the profits on the bonds it is holding are offset by the losses from the futures contracts it has sold. However, as panel (b) of Figure 1 indicates, the situation when the hedge is conducted with put options is quite different: Once bond prices rise above the exercise price, the bank does not suffer additional losses on the option contracts. At the same time, the value of the Treasury bonds the bank is holding will increase, thereby leading to a profit for the bank. Thus using options rather than futures to conduct the micro hedge allows the bank to protect itself from rises in interest rates but still allows the bank to benefit from interest-rate declines (although the profit is reduced by the amount of the premium).

Similar reasoning indicates that the bank manager might prefer to use options to conduct the macro hedge to immunize the entire bank portfolio from interest-rate risk. Again, the strategy of using options rather than futures has the disadvantage that the First National Bank has to pay the premiums on these contracts up front. By contrast, using options allows the bank to keep the gains from a decline in interest rates (which will raise the value of the bank's assets relative to its liabilities), because these gains will not be offset by large losses on the option contracts.

In the case of a macro hedge, there is another reason why the bank might prefer option contracts to futures contracts. Profits and losses on futures contracts can cause accounting problems for banks because such profits and losses are not allowed to be offset by unrealized changes in the value of the rest of the bank's portfolio. Consider what happens when interest rates fall. If First National sells futures contracts to conduct the macro hedge, then when interest rates fall and the prices of the Treasury bond futures contracts rise, it will have large losses on these contracts. Of course, these losses are offset by unrealized profits in the rest of the bank's portfolio, but the bank is not allowed to offset these losses in its accounting statements. So even though the macro hedge is serving its intended purpose of immunizing the bank's portfolio from interest-rate risk, the bank would experience large accounting losses when interest rates fall. Indeed, bank managers have lost their jobs when perfectly sound hedges with interest-rate futures have led to large accounting losses. Not surprisingly, bank managers might shrink from using financial futures to conduct macro hedges for this reason.

Futures options, however, can come to the rescue of the managers of banks and other financial institutions. Suppose that First National conducted the macro hedge by buying put options instead of selling Treasury bond futures. Now if interest rates fall and bond prices rise well above the exercise price, the bank will not have large losses on the option contracts, because it will just decide not to exercise its options. The bank will not suffer the accounting problems produced by hedging with financial futures. Because of the accounting advantages of using futures options to conduct macro hedges, option contracts have become important to financial institution managers as tools for hedging interest-rate risk.

Factors Affecting the Prices of Option Premiums

There are several interesting facts about how the premiums on option contracts are priced. The first fact is that when the strike (exercise) price for a contract is set at a higher level, the premium for the call option is lower and the premium for the put option is higher. For example, in going from a contract with a strike price of 112 to one with 115, the premium for a call option for the month of March might fall from 1 45/64 to 16/64, and the premium for the March put option might rise from 19/64 to 1 54/64.

Our understanding of the profit function for option contracts illustrated in Figure 1 helps explain this fact. As we saw in panel (a), a higher price for the underlying financial instrument (in this case a Treasury bond futures contract) relative to the option's exercise price results in higher profits on the call (buy) option. Thus, the lower the strike price, the higher the profits on the call option contract and the greater the premium that investors like Irving are willing to pay. Similarly, we saw in panel (b) that a higher price for the underlying financial instrument relative to the exercise price lowers profits on the put (sell) option, so that a higher strike price increases profits and thus causes the premium to increase.

The second fact is that as the period of time over which the option can be exercised (the term to expiration) gets longer, the premiums for both call and put options rise. For example, at a strike price of 112, the premium on a call option might increase from 1 45/64 in March to 1 50/64 in April and to 2 28/64 in May. Similarly, the premium on a put option might increase from 19/64 in March to 1 43/64 in April and to 2 22/64 in May. The fact that premiums increase with the term to expiration is also explained by the nonlinear profit function for option contracts. As the term to expiration lengthens, there is a greater chance that the price of the underlying financial instrument will be very high or very low by the expiration date. If the price becomes very high and goes well above the exercise price, the call (buy) option will yield a high profit; if the price becomes very low and goes well below the exercise price, the losses will be small because the owner of the call option will simply decide not to exercise the option. The possibility of greater variability of the underlying financial instrument as the term to expiration lengthens raises profits on average for the call option.

Similar reasoning tells us that the put (sell) option will become more valuable as the term to expiration increases, because the possibility of greater price variability of the underlying financial instrument increases as the term to expiration increases. The greater chance of a low price increases the chance that profits on the put option will be very high. But the greater chance of a high price does not produce substantial losses for the put option, because the owner will again just decide not to exercise the option.

Another way of thinking about this reasoning is to recognize that option contracts have an element of "Heads, I win; tails, I don't lose too badly." The greater variability of where the prices might be by the expiration date increases the value of both kinds of options. Because a longer term to the expiration date leads to greater variability of where the prices might be by the expiration date, a longer term to expiration raises the value of the option contract.

The reasoning that we have just developed also explains another important fact about option premiums. When the volatility of the price of the underlying instrument is great, the premiums for both call and put options will be higher. Higher volatility of prices means that for a given expiration date, there will again be greater variability of where the prices might be by the expiration date. The "Heads, I win; tails, I don't lose too badly" property of options then means that the greater variability of possible prices by the expiration date increases average profits for the option and thus increases the premium that investors are willing to pay.

Summary

Our analysis of how profits on options are affected by price movements for the underlying financial instrument leads to the following conclusions about the factors that determine the premium on an option contract:

1. The higher the strike price, everything else being equal, the lower the premium on call (buy) options and the higher the premium on put (sell) options.
2. The greater the term to expiration, everything else being equal, the higher the premiums for both call and put options.
3. The greater the volatility of prices of the underlying financial instrument, everything else being equal, the higher the premiums for both call and put options.

The results we have derived here appear in more formal models, such as the Black-Scholes model, which analyze how the premiums on options are priced. You might study such models in finance courses.

SWAPS

In addition to forwards, futures, and options, financial institutions use one other important financial derivative to manage risk. **Swaps** are financial contracts that obligate each party to the contract to exchange (swap) a set of payments (not assets) it owns for another set of payments owned by another party. There are two basic kinds of swaps. **Currency swaps** involve the exchange of a set of payments in one currency for a set of payments in another currency. **Interest-rate swaps** involve the exchange of one set of interest payments for another set of interest payments, all denominated in the same currency.

Interest-Rate Swap Contracts

Interest-rate swaps are an important tool for managing interest-rate risk, and they first appeared in the United States in 1982, when, as we have seen, there was an increase in the demand for financial instruments that could be used to reduce interest-rate risk. The most common type of interest-rate swap (called the *plain vanilla swap*) specifies (1) the interest rate on the payments that are being exchanged; (2) the type of interest payments (variable or fixed-rate); (3) the amount of **notional principal**, which is the amount on which the interest is being paid; and (4) the time period over which the exchanges continue to be made. There are many other more complicated versions of swaps, including forward swaps and swap options (called *swaptions*), but here we will look only at the plain vanilla swap. Figure 2 illustrates an interest-rate swap between the Midwest Savings Bank and the Friendly Finance Company. Midwest Savings agrees to pay Friendly Finance a fixed rate of 5% on $1 million of notional principal for the next ten years, and Friendly Finance agrees to pay Midwest Savings the one-year Treasury bill rate plus 1% on $1 million of notional principal for the same period. Thus, as shown in Figure 2, every year the Midwest Savings Bank would be paying the Friendly Finance Company 5% on $1 million, while Friendly Finance would be paying Midwest Savings the one-year T-bill rate plus 1% on $1 million.

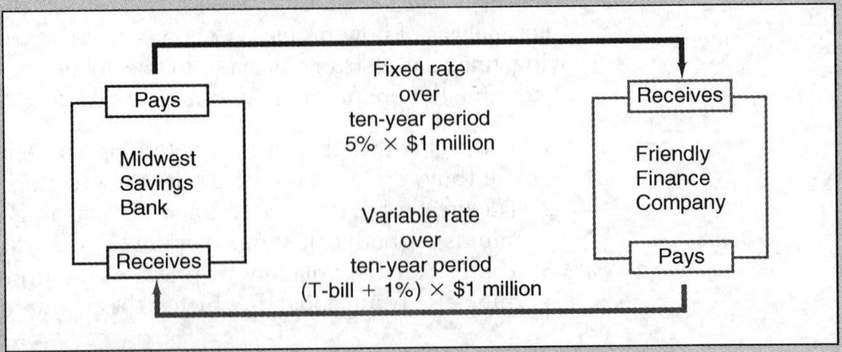

FIGURE 2
Interest-Rate Swap Payments
In this swap arrangement with a notional principal of $1 million and a term of ten years, the Midwest Savings Bank pays a fixed rate of 5% × $1 million to the Friendly Finance Company, which in turn agrees to pay the one-year Treasury bill rate plus 1% × $1 million to the Midwest Savings Bank.

APPLICATION Hedging with Interest-Rate Swaps

You might wonder why these two parties find it advantageous to enter into this swap agreement. The answer is that it may help both of them hedge interest-rate risk.

Suppose that the Midwest Savings Bank, which tends to borrow short-term and then lend long-term in the mortgage market, has $1 million less of rate-sensitive assets than it has of rate-sensitive liabilities. As we learned in Chapter 9, this situation means that as interest rates rise, the increase in the cost of funds (liabilities) is greater than the increase in interest payments it receives on its assets, many of which are fixed-rate. The result of rising interest rates is thus a shrinking of Midwest Savings' net interest margin and a decline in its profitability. As we saw in Chapter 9, to avoid this interest-rate risk, Midwest Savings would like to convert $1 million of its fixed-rate assets into $1 million of rate-sensitive assets, in effect making rate-sensitive assets equal rate-sensitive liabilities, thereby eliminating the gap. This is exactly what happens when it engages in the interest-rate swap. By taking $1 million of its fixed-rate income and exchanging it for $1 million of rate-sensitive Treasury bill income, it has converted income on $1 million of fixed-rate assets into income on $1 million of rate-sensitive assets. Now when interest rates rise, the increase in rate-sensitive income on its assets exactly matches the increase in the rate-sensitive cost of funds on its liabilities, leaving the net interest margin and bank profitability unchanged.

The Friendly Finance Company, which issues long-term bonds to raise funds and uses them to make short-term loans, finds that it is in exactly the opposite situation to Midwest Savings: It has $1 million more of rate-sensitive assets than of rate-sensitive liabilities. It is therefore concerned that a fall in interest rates, which will result in a larger drop in income from its assets than the decline in the cost of funds on its liabilities, will cause a decline in profits. By doing the interest-rate swap, it eliminates this interest-rate risk because it has converted $1 million of rate-sensitive income into $1 million of fixed-rate income. Now the Friendly Finance Company finds that when interest rates fall, the decline in rate-sensitive income is smaller and so is matched by the decline in the rate-sensitive cost of funds on its liabilities, leaving its profitability unchanged.

Advantages of Interest-Rate Swaps

To eliminate interest-rate risk, both the Midwest Savings Bank and the Friendly Finance Company could have rearranged their balance sheets by converting fixed-rate assets into rate-sensitive assets, and vice versa, instead of engaging in an interest-rate swap. However, this strategy would have been costly for both financial institutions for several reasons. The first is that financial institutions incur substantial transaction costs when they rearrange their balance sheets. Second, different financial institutions have informational advantages in making loans to certain customers who may prefer certain maturities. Thus adjusting the balance sheet to eliminate interest-rate risk might result in a loss of these informational advantages, which the financial institution is unwilling to give up. Interest-rate swaps solve these problems for financial institutions, because, in effect, they allow the institutions to convert fixed-rate assets into rate-sensitive assets without affecting the balance sheet. Large transaction costs are avoided, and the financial institutions can continue to make loans where they have an informational advantage.

We have seen that financial institutions can also hedge interest-rate risk with other financial derivatives such as futures contracts and futures options. Interest-rate swaps have one big advantage over hedging with these other derivatives: They can be written for very long horizons, sometimes as long as twenty years, whereas financial futures and futures options typically have much shorter horizons, not much more than a year. If a financial institution needs to hedge interest-rate risk for a long horizon, financial futures and option markets may not do it much good. Instead, it can turn to the swap market.

Disadvantages of Interest-Rate Swaps

Although interest-rate swaps have important advantages that make them very popular with financial institutions, they also have disadvantages that limit their usefulness. Swap markets, like forward markets, can suffer from a lack of liquidity. Let's return to looking at the swap between the Midwest Savings Bank and the Friendly Finance Company. As with a forward contract, it might be difficult for the Midwest Savings Bank to link up with the Friendly Finance Company to arrange the swap. In addition, even if the Midwest Savings Bank could find a counterparty like the Friendly Finance Company, it might not be able to negotiate a good deal because it cannot find any other institution with which to negotiate.

Swap contracts also are subject to the same default risk that we encountered for forward contracts. If interest rates rise, the Friendly Finance Company would love to get out of the swap contract, because the fixed-rate interest payments it receives are less than it could get in the open market. It might then default on the contract, exposing Midwest Savings to a loss. Alternatively, the Friendly Finance Company could go bust, meaning that the terms of the swap contract would not be fulfilled.

Financial Intermediaries in Interest-Rate Swaps

As we have just seen, financial institutions do have to be aware of the possibility of losses from a default on swaps. As with a forward contract, each party to a swap must have a lot of information about the other party to make sure that the contract is likely to be fulfilled. The need for information about counterparties and the liquidity problems in swap markets could limit the usefulness of these markets. However, as we saw in Chapter 8, when informational and liquidity problems crop up in a market, financial intermediaries come to the rescue. That is exactly what happens in swap markets. Intermediaries such as investment banks and especially large commercial banks have the ability to acquire information cheaply about the creditworthiness and reliability of parties to swap contracts and are also able to match up parties to a swap. Hence large commercial banks and investment banks have set up swap markets in which they act as intermediaries.

CREDIT DERIVATIVES

In recent years, a new type of derivatives has come on the scene to hedge credit risk. Like other derivatives, **credit derivatives** offer payoffs on previously issued securities, but ones that bear credit risk. In the past ten years, the markets in credit derivatives have grown at an astounding pace and the notional amounts of these derivatives now number in the trillions of dollars. These credit derivatives take several forms.

Credit Options

Credit options work just like the options discussed earlier in the chapter: For a fee, the purchaser gains the right to receive profits that are tied either to the price of an underlying security or to an interest rate. Suppose you buy $1 million of General Motors bonds but worry that a potential slowdown in the sale of SUVs might lead a credit-rating agency to *downgrade* (lower the credit rating on) GM bonds. As we saw in Chapter 5, such a downgrade would cause the price of GM bonds to fall. To protect yourself, you could buy an option for, say, $15,000, to sell the $1 million of bonds at a strike price that is the same as the current price. With this strategy, you would not suffer any losses if the value of the GM bonds declined because you could exercise the option and sell them at the price you paid for them. In addition, you would be able to reap any gains that occurred if GM bonds rose in value.

The second type of credit option ties profits to changes in an interest rate such as a credit spread (the interest rate on the average bond with a particular credit rating minus the interest rate on default-free bonds such as those issued by the U.S. Treasury). Suppose that your company, which has a Baa credit rating, plans to issue $10 million of one-year bonds in three months and expects to have a credit spread of 1 percentage point (i.e., it will pay an interest rate that is 1 percentage point higher than the one-year Treasury rate). You are concerned that the market might start to think that Baa companies in general will become riskier in the coming months. If this were to happen by the time you are ready to issue your bonds in three months, you would have to pay a higher interest rate than the 1 percentage point in excess of the Treasury rate and your cost of issuing the bonds would increase. To protect yourself against these higher costs, you could buy for, say, $20,000 a credit option on $10 million of Baa bonds that would pay you the difference between the average Baa credit spread in the market minus the 1 percentage point credit spread on $10 million. If the credit spread jumps to 2 percentage points, you would receive $100,000 from the option (= [2% − 1%] × $10 million), which would exactly offset the $100,000 higher interest costs from the 1 percentage point higher interest rate you would have to pay on your $10 million of bonds.

Credit Swaps

Suppose you manage a bank in Houston called Oil Drillers' Bank (ODB), which specializes in lending to a particular industry in your local area, oil drilling companies. Another bank, Potato Farmers Bank (PFB), specializes in lending to potato farmers in

Idaho. Both ODB and PFB have a problem because their loan portfolios are not sufficiently diversified. To protect ODB against a collapse in the oil market, which would result in defaults on most of its loans made to oil drillers, you could reach an agreement to have the loan payments on, say, $100 million worth of your loans to oil drillers paid to the PFB in exchange for PFB paying you the loan payments on $100 million of its loans to potato farmers. Such a transaction, in which risky payments on loans are swapped for each other, is called a **credit swap**. As a result of this swap, ODB and PFB have increased their diversification and lowered the overall risk of their loan portfolios because some of the loan payments to each bank are now coming from a different type of loans.

Another form of credit swap is, for arcane reasons, called a **credit default swap**, although it functions more like insurance. With a credit default swap, one party who wants to hedge credit risk pays a fixed payment on a regular basis, in return for a contingent payment that is triggered by a *credit event* such as the bankruptcy of a particular firm or the downgrading of the firm's credit rating by a credit-rating agency. For example, you could use a credit default swap to hedge the $1 million of General Motors bonds that you are holding by arranging to pay an annual fee of $1,000 in exchange for a payment of $10,000 if the GM bonds' credit rating is lowered. If a credit event happens and GM's bonds are downgraded so that their price falls, you will receive a payment that will offset some of the loss you suffer if you sell the bonds at this lower price.

Credit-Linked Notes

Another type of credit derivative, the **credit-linked note**, is a combination of a bond and a credit option. Just like any corporate bond, the credit-linked note makes periodic coupon (interest) payments and a final payment of the face value of the bond at maturity. If a key financial variable specified in the note changes, however, the issuer of the note has the right (option) to lower the payments on the note. For example, General Motors could issue a credit-linked note that pays a 5% coupon rate, with the specification that if a national index of SUV sales falls by 10%, then GM has the right to lower the coupon rate by 2 percentage points to 3%. In this way, GM can lower its risk because when it is losing money as SUV sales fall, it can offset some of these losses by making smaller payments on its credit-linked notes.

APPLICATION Are Financial Derivatives a Worldwide Time Bomb?

In recent years, politicians, the media, and regulators have become very concerned about the dangers of derivatives. Indeed, Warren Buffet has called financial derivatives "financial weapons of mass destruction." This concern is international and has spawned a slew of reports issued by such organizations as the Bank for International Settlements (BIS), the Bank of England, the Group of Thirty, the Office of the U.S. Comptroller of the Currency (OCC), the Commodity Futures Trading Commission (CFTC), and the Government Accounting Office (GAO). Particularly scary are the notional amounts of derivatives contracts—more than $100 trillion worldwide—and the facts that banks, which are subject to bank panics, are major players in the derivatives markets. As a result of these fears, some politicians have called for restrictions on banks' involvement in the derivatives markets. Are financial derivatives a time bomb that could bring down the world financial system?

There are three major concerns about financial derivatives. First is that financial derivatives allow financial institutions to increase their leverage; that is, they can in effect hold an amount of the underlying asset that is many times greater than the amount of money they have had to put up. Increasing their leverage enables them to take huge bets on currency and interest-rate movements, which if they are wrong can bring down the bank, as was the case for Barings in 1995. This concern is valid. As we saw earlier in the chapter, the amount of money placed in margin accounts is only a small fraction of the price of the futures contract, meaning that small movements in the price of a contract can produce losses that are many times the size of the initial amount put in the margin account. Thus, although financial derivatives can be used to hedge risk, they can also be used by financial institutions to take on excessive risk.

The second concern is that financial derivatives are too sophisticated for managers of financial institutions because they are so complicated. Although it is true that some financial derivatives can be so complex that some financial managers are not sophisticated enough to use them, this seems unlikely to apply to the big international financial institutions that are the major players in the derivatives markets. The Barings Bank collapse discussed in Chapter 9, which was due to trading in derivatives, looks like it might have been an exception, but recall that the bank was brought down not by trades in complex derivatives but rather by trades in one of the simplest derivatives, stock index futures. Furthermore, Barings's problem was more a lack of internal controls at the bank than a problem with derivatives per se.

A third concern is that banks have holdings of huge notional amounts of financial derivatives, particularly swaps, that greatly exceed the amount of bank capital, and so these derivatives expose the banks to serious risk of failure. Banks are indeed major players in the financial derivatives markets, particularly the swaps market, where our earlier analysis has shown that they are the natural market-makers because they can act as intermediaries between two counterparties who would not make the swap without their involvement. However, looking at the notional amount of swaps at banks gives a very misleading picture of their risk exposure. Because banks act as intermediaries in the swap markets, they are typically exposed only to credit risk—a default by one of their counterparties. Furthermore, swaps, unlike loans, do not involve payments of the notional amount but rather the much smaller interest payments based on the notional amounts. For example, in the case of a 7% interest rate, the payment is only $70,000 for the $1 million swap. Estimates of the credit exposure from swap contracts indicate that they are on the order of only 1% of the notional value of the contracts and that credit exposure at banks from derivatives is generally less than a quarter of their total credit exposure from loans. Banks' credit exposures from their derivatives activities are thus not out of line with other credit exposures they face. Furthermore, an analysis by the GAO indicates that actual credit losses incurred by banks in their derivatives contracts have been very small, on the order of 0.2% of their gross credit exposure.

The conclusion is that financial derivatives have their dangers for financial institutions, but some of these dangers have been overplayed. The biggest danger occurs in trading activities of financial institutions, and as discussed in Chapter 11, regulators have been paying increased attention to this danger and have issued new disclosure requirements and regulatory guidelines for how derivatives trading should be done. The credit risk exposure posed by derivatives, by contrasts, seems to be manageable with standard methods of dealing with credit risk, both by managers of financial institutions and by their regulators.

SUMMARY

1. Interest-rate forward contracts, which are agreements to sell a debt instrument at a future (forward) point in time, can be used to hedge interest-rate risk. The advantage of forward contracts is that they are flexible, but the disadvantages are that they are subject to default risk and their market is illiquid.
2. A financial futures contract is similar to an interest-rate forward contract, in that it specifies that a debt instrument must be delivered by one party to another on a stated future date. However, it has advantages over a forward contract in that it is not subject to default risk and is more liquid. Forward and futures contracts can be used by financial institutions to hedge (protect) against interest-rate risk.
3. An option contract gives the purchaser the right to buy (call option) or sell (put option) a security at the exercise (strike) price within a specific period of time. The profit function for options is nonlinear—profits do not always grow by the same amount for a given change in the price of the underlying financial instrument. The nonlinear profit function for options explains why their value (as reflected by the premium paid for them) is negatively related to the exercise price for call options, positively related to the exercise price for put options, positively related to the term to expiration for both call and put options, and positively related to the volatility of the prices of the underlying financial instrument for both call and put options. Financial institutions use futures options to hedge interest-rate risk in a similar fashion to the way they use financial futures and forward contracts. Futures options may be preferred for macro hedges because they suffer from fewer accounting problems than financial futures.
4. Interest-rate swaps involve the exchange of one set of interest payments for another set of interest payments and have default risk and liquidity problems similar to those of forward contracts. As a result, interest-rate swaps often involve intermediaries such as large commercial banks and investment banks that make a market in swaps. Financial institutions find thatinterest-rate swaps are useful ways to hedge interest-rate risk. Interest-rate swaps have one big advantage over financial futures and options: They can be written for very long horizons.
5. Credit derivatives are a new type of derivatives that offer payoffs on previously issued securities that have credit risk. These derivatives—credit options, credit swaps and credit linked notes—can be used to hedge credit risk.
6. There are three concerns about the dangers of derivatives: They allow financial institutions to more easily increase their leverage and take big bets (by effectively enabling them to hold a larger amount of the underlying assets than the amount of money put down), they are too complex for managers of financial institutions to understand, and they expose financial institutions to large credit risks because the huge notional amounts of derivative contracts greatly exceed the capital of these institutions. The second two dangers seem to be overplayed, but the danger from increased leverage using derivatives is real.

KEY TERMS

American option, p. 344
arbitrage, p. 337
call option, p. 345
credit default swap, p. 355
credit derivatives, p. 354
credit-linked note, p. 355
credit options, p. 354
credit swap, p. 355
currency swap, p. 351
European option, p. 344
exercise price (strike price), p. 344
financial derivatives, p. 333
financial futures contract, p. 336
financial futures option (futures option), p. 344
forward contract, p. 334
hedge, p. 333
interest-rate forward contract, p. 334
interest-rate swap, p. 352
long position, p. 333
macro hedge, p. 339
margin requirement, p. 342
marked to market, p. 342
micro hedge, p. 339
notional principal, p. 352
open interest, p. 339
option, p. 344
premium, p. 344
put option, p. 345
short position, p. 333
stock option, p. 344
swap, p. 352

QUESTIONS AND PROBLEMS

Questions marked with an asterisk are answered at the end of the book in an appendix, "Answers to Selected Questions and Problems." Questions marked with a blue circle indicate the question is available in MyEconLab at www.myeconlab.com/mishkin.

1. If the pension fund you manage expects to have an inflow of $120 million six months from now, what forward contract would you seek to enter into to lock in current interest rates?
*2. If the portfolio you manage is holding $25 million of 6s of 2023 Treasury bonds with a price of 110, what forward contract would you enter into to hedge the interest-rate risk on these bonds over the coming year?
3. If at the expiration date, the deliverable Treasury bond is selling for 101 but the Treasury bond futures contract is selling for 102, what will happen to the futures price? Explain your answer.
*4. If you buy a $100,000 June Treasury bond contract for 108 and the price of the deliverable Treasury bond at the expiration date is 102, what is your profit or loss on the contract?
5. Suppose that the pension fund you are managing is expecting an inflow of funds of $100 million next year and you want to make sure that you will earn the current interest rate of 8% when you invest the incoming funds in long-term bonds. How would you use the futures market to do this?
*6. How would you use the options market to accomplish the same thing as in Problem 5? What are the advantages and disadvantages of using an options contract rather than a futures contract?
7. If you buy a put option on a $100,000 Treasury bond futures contract with an exercise price of 95 and the price of the Treasury bond is 120 at expiration, is the contract in the money, out of the money, or at the money? What is your profit or loss on the contract if the premium was $4,000?
*8. Suppose that you buy a call option on a $100,000 Treasury bond futures contract with an exercise price of 110 for a premium of $1,500. If on expiration the futures contract has a price of 111, what is your profit or loss on the contract?
9. Explain why greater volatility or a longer term to maturity leads to a higher premium on both call and put options.
*10. Why does a lower strike price imply that a call option will have a higher premium and a put option a lower premium?
11. If the finance company you manage has a gap of +$5 million (rate-sensitive assets greater than rate-sensitive liabilities by $5 million), describe an interest-rate swap that would eliminate the company's income gap.
*12. If the savings and loan you manage has a gap of −$42 million, describe an interest-rate swap that would eliminate the S&L's income risk from changes in interest rates.
13. If your company has a payment of 200 million euros due one year from now, how would you hedge the foreign exchange risk in this payment with 125,000-euro futures contracts?
*14. If your company has to make a 10 million euro payment to a German company in June, three months from now, how would you hedge the foreign exchange risk in this payment with a 125,000-euro futures contract?
15. Suppose that your company will be receiving 30 million euros six months from now and the euro is currently selling for 1 euro per dollar. If you want to hedge the foreign exchange risk in this payment, what kind of forward contract would you want to enter into?

WEB EXERCISES

1. We have discussed the various stock markets in detail throughout this text. Another market that is less well known is the New York Mercantile Exchange. Here contracts on a wide variety of commodities are traded on a daily basis. Go to www.nymex.com/faq.aspx and read the discussion explaining the origin and purpose of the mercantile exchange. Write a one-page summary discussing this material.

2. The following site can be used to demonstrate how the features of an option affect the option's prices. Go to www.intrepid.com/~robertl/option-pricer4.html. What happens to the price of an option under each of the following situations?
   a. The strike price increases.
   b. Interest rates increase.
   c. Volatility increases.
   d. The time until the option matures increases.

WEB REFERENCES

www.rmahq.org

The web site of the Risk Management Association reports useful information such as annual statement studies, on-line publications, and so on.

www.usafutures.com/stockindexfutures.htm

Detailed information about stock index futures.

CHAPTER

14 Conflicts of Interest in the Financial Industry

Preview

Since the end of the stock market boom in 2000, financial markets have been jolted by one corporate scandal after another. The cycle began in December 2001 with the spectacular bankruptcy of Enron Corporation (once valued as the seventh-largest corporation in the United States) and the indictment of Enron's auditor, Arthur Andersen, one of the "Big Five" accounting firms. Subsequently, revelations of misleading accounting statements at numerous other corporations, including WorldCom, Tyco Industries, and Fannie Mae, have increased investors' doubts about the quality of information coming from the corporate sector. Criminal cases have been filed against all of the top investment banks (Morgan Stanley, J. P. Morgan, Merrill Lynch, Lehman Brothers, and Goldman Sachs, among others) that encouraged their stock analysts to hype dubious stocks, which later proved to be disastrous investments.

These scandals have attracted tremendous public attention for several reasons. First, the resulting bankruptcies cost employees of these firms their jobs, their pensions, or both. Second, these activities may have been a factor in the massive stock market decline that occurred from March 2000 to September 2002; during this downturn, the value of the S&P 500 index declined by 50% and NASDAQ's value declined by 75%. Third, the scandals have created doubts about the ethics of those working in the financial service industry.

Conflicts of interest, a type of moral hazard problem that occurs when a person or institution has multiple objectives (interests) and as a result has conflicts between them, may be responsible for the recent scandals. In each case, people who were supposed to act in the investing public's best interests by providing investors with reliable information had incentives to deceive the public and thereby benefit both themselves and their corporate clients. What are these conflicts of interest, and how serious are they? Where do they occur, and why have they been the source of the recent woes in financial markets ? What should, and can, we do about them?

This chapter provides a framework for answering these questions. It first explains what conflicts of interest are, why we should care about them, and why they raise ethical issues. It then surveys the different types of conflicts of interest in the financial industry and discusses policies to remedy them.[1]

---

[1]The analysis in this chapter is based on Andrew Crockett, Trevor Harris, Frederic S. Mishkin, and Eugene N. White, *Conflicts of Interest in the Financial Services Industry: What Should We Do About Them?* Geneva Reports on the World Economy 4 (Geneva and London: International Center for Monetary and Banking Studies and Centre for Economic Policy Research, 2003).

WHAT ARE CONFLICTS OF INTEREST AND WHY ARE THEY IMPORTANT?

In Chapter 8, we saw how how financial institutions play a key role in the financial system. Specifically, their expertise in interpreting signals and collecting information from their customers gives them a cost advantage in the production of information. Furthermore, because they collect, produce, and distribute this information, financial institutions can use the information over and over again in as many ways as they would like, thereby realizing economies of scale. By providing multiple financial services to their customers, they can also realize **economies of scope**—that is, they can lower the costs of information production for each service by applying one information resource to many different services. A bank, for example, can evaluate the creditworthiness of a corporation when making a loan to it, which then helps the bank decide whether it would be easy to sell the bonds of this corporation to the public. Additionally, by providing multiple financial services to their customers, financial institutions can develop broader and longer-term relationships with firms. These relationshiops further reduce the cost of producing information and, therefore, enhance economies of scope.

Although economies of scope may substantially benefit financial institutions, they also create potential costs in the form of conflicts of interest. Although conflicts of interest arise in almost all aspects of our lives, we need to be precise about the conflicts of interest that concern us here. Given the crucial role of information in financial markets, we focus on those conflicts of interest that arise when financial service firms or their employees have the opportunity to serve their own interests, rather than the interests of their customers, by misusing information, providing false information, or concealing information.

Conflicts of interest may occur within financial institutions that provide a specialized service, but they are most problematic when an institution provides multiple financial services to a given client or to many clients. The competing interests of these services may lead employees or a department of a financial institution to conceal information or disseminate misleading information to financial markets. Combinations of services that bring together any group of depository intermediaries, nondepository intermediaries, and brokers, or that allow any of these groups to invest directly in a business, are most likely to lead to conflicts of interest.

Why Do We Care About Conflicts of Interest?

Conflicts of interest can substantially reduce the quality of information in financial markets, thereby increasing asymmetric information problems. In turn, asymmetric information prevents financial markets from channeling funds into productive investment opportunities and causes financial markets and the economy to become less efficient.

ETHICS AND CONFLICTS OF INTEREST

Conflicts of interest raise ethical dilemmas for those engaged in the financial service business by generating incentives for financial service firms or their employees to conceal or provide misleading information, thereby hurting the customers for whom they work. The growing economies of scope in the financial industry that have led financial institutions to offer more services under one roof have increased conflicts of interest and, not surprisingly, led to more unethical behavior. One way to limit unethical behavior is to make those working in the financial industry aware of the ethical issues that arise when they exploit conflicts of interest; with this awareness, employees are less likely to engage in unethical behavior. To address this need to limit unethical behavior, business schools are now bringing the discussion of ethics into the classroom and firms are establishing policies (discussed later in this chapter) that make it harder for individuals to exploit conflicts of interest.

TYPES OF CONFLICTS OF INTEREST

Four areas of financial service activities harbor the greatest potential for generating conflicts of interest that ultimately reduce the amount of information available in financial markets:

- Underwriting and research in investment banking
- Auditing and consulting in accounting firms
- Credit assessment and consulting in credit-rating agencies
- Universal banking

Underwriting and Research in Investment Banking

Investment banks perform two tasks: They *research* corporations issuing securities, and they *underwrite* these securities by selling them to the public on behalf of the issuing corporation. Investment banks often combine research and underwriting because the information synergies created may lead to economies of scope. In other words, information that is produced for one task is also useful for another task. A conflict of interest arises between research and underwriting because the investment bank attempts to serve the needs of two client groups—the firms for which it is issuing the securities and the investors to whom it sells these securities.

These client groups have different information needs: Issuers benefit from optimistic research, whereas investors desire unbiased research. Due to economies of scope, however, both groups will receive the same information. When the potential revenues from underwriting greatly exceed brokerage commissions, the investment bank has a strong incentive to alter the information provided to both types of clients so as to favor the issuing firms' needs. If the information provided is not favorable to the issuing firm, it might take its business to a competitor that is willing to put out more positive information and thereby entice more people to buy the newly issued stock. For example, an internal Morgan Stanley memo excerpted in the *Wall Street Journal* on July 14, 1992, stated: "Our objective . . . is to adopt a policy, fully understood by the entire firm, including the Research Department, that we do not make negative or controversial comments about our clients as a matter of sound business practice."

Because of directives like this one, analysts in investment banks might be persuaded to distort their research to please the underwriting department of their bank and the corporations issuing the securities. Of course, such actions undermine the reliability of the information that investors use to make their financial decisions and, as a result, diminish the efficiency of securities markets. A similar chain of events precipitated the tech boom of the 1990s (see the Conflicts of Interest box, "The King, Queen, and Jack of the Internet").

Conflicts of Interest The King, Queen, and Jack of the Internet

The King, Queen, and Jack of the Internet are the nicknames of a trio of bullish technology analysts who were very influential during the tech boom of the late 1990s: Henry Blodgett at Merrill Lynch, Jack Grubman at Salomon Smith Barney (Citigroup), and Mary Meeker at Morgan Stanley. Their stories reveal a lot about how conflicts of interest may have influenced analysts' recommendations during this heady period.*

In late 1998, Henry Blodgett, then at Oppenheimer and Company, recommended a price target of $400 per share for Amazon.com. At the time, most analysts believed that Amazon.com was overvalued at $240 per share. In particular, Jonathan Cole of Merrill Lynch indicated that $50 was a more reasonable price. When the price of Amazon.com stock rose above $400 per share, Blodgett was hailed as a guru and hired by Merrill Lynch, while Cole left the firm. Clearly, Blodgett saw that he could reap benefits by hyping tech stocks. A subsequent investigation by the New York Attorney General's office found that Blodgett issued very positive reports on certain Internet stocks while privately deriding them in e-mails. Blodgett was accused of issuing favorable research reports for InfoSpace because he knew that it was planning to buy Go2Net, one of Merrill Lynch's clients. Similarly, Blodgett was alleged to have maintained a positive recommendation for GoTo.com, even though it was not doing well, at a time when Merrill Lynch was competing to manage a new stock issue for the company. He downgraded GoTo.com's rating only after it chose Credit Suisse First Boston as its underwriter instead.

The New York Attorney General's office accused Jack Grubman of engaging in similarly questionable behavior. Although he expressed doubts in private, Grubman made wildly bullish recommendations about several telecom companies—including WorldCom, Global Crossing, and Winstar Communications—that were spiraling toward bankruptcy. In 1999, he upgraded his rating of AT&T when Salomon Smith Barney was competing for a new issue of AT&T's spin-off of its cellular division. Six months after his firm, along with Goldman Sachs and Merrill Lynch, was awarded AT&T's business, Grubman downgraded AT&T's rating.

Blodgett and Grubman have faced criminal charges for their actions, whereas Mary Meeker has not. Like Blodgett and Grubman, Mary Meeker kept her ratings of tech stocks high after their prices plummeted. However, unlike Blodgett and Grubman, there was no evidence that Meeker did not believe her ratings, and she did discourage many Internet issues when the companies had poor outlooks. Morgan Stanley argued on her behalf that "research analysts helped screen out IPO candidates such that Morgan Stanley rejected five Internet IPOs for every one the firm underwrote. Mary Meeker was an integral part of this screening process, which benefited the firm's investor clients." Despite the New York Attorney General's office's criticisms of some of Morgan Stanley practices, Mary Meeker was not subjected to criminal charges because she did provide some screening and no exploitation of conflicts of interest was evident.

*For more detail, see Andrew Crockett, Trevor Harris, Frederic S. Mishkin, and Eugene N. White, *Conflicts of Interest in the Financial Services Industry: What Should We Do About Them?* Geneva Reports on the World Economy 4 (Geneva and London: International Center for Monetary and Banking Studies and Centre for Economic Policy Research, 2003).

Another practice that exploits conflicts of interest is **spinning**. Spinning occurs when investment banks allocate hot, but underpriced, **initial public offerings (IPOs)**, shares of newly issued stock, to executives of other companies that may potentially have business with the investment bank (see the Conflicts of Interest box, "Frank Quattrone and Spinning"). Because hot IPOs typically rise immediately in price after they are first purchased by investors, spinning is a form of kickback to other firms' executives, luring them to use that investment bank. When the executive's company plans to issue its own securities, he or she will be more likely to use as an underwriter the investment

Conflicts of Interest **Frank Quattrone and Spinning**

Frank Quattrone of Credit Suisse First Boston was a highly regarded investment banker specializing in technology companies. But his reputation took a big hit in March 2003, when the National Association of Securities Dealers (NASD) filed a complaint against him for improperly pressuring his analysts to provide favorable coverage in an effort to solicit customers for his firm. Allegedly, Quattrone linked his analysts' bonuses to their investment banking work and permitted executives of companies whose stock he handled to make changes in his staff's draft research reports.

NASD also accused Quattrone of spinning because he maintained more than 300 "Friends of Frank" accounts for executives of technology companies that were active or prospective clients of the bank. These "friends" were allocated hot shares at his discretion. Spinning was not isolated to Quattrone's firm; it was actually quite common on Wall Street. Salomon Smith Barney also allocated hard-to-get IPO shares to a number of executives, including Bernard Ebbers of WorldCom, Philip Anshutz and Joe Nacchio of Qwest, Stephen Garfalo of Metromedia, and Clark McLeod of McLeodUSA. The bank claimed that it issued shares to these executives because they were among the firm's best individual customers and not because it wanted to persuade these executives to channel their companies' investment banking business to Salomon Smith Barney. This claim was deemed dubious, at best. Quattrone was convicted in 2004 (but later overturned) of obstructing the investigation into his activities and was sentenced to eighteen months in prison.

bank that gave the executive the hot IPO shares, which is not necessarily the investment bank that could get the highest price for the firm's securities This action may raise the cost of capital for the firm, and therefore hinder the efficiency of the capital market.

Auditing and Consulting in Accounting Firms

Traditionally, an auditor reduces the information asymmetry between a firm's managers and its shareholders by checking the firm's books and monitoring the quality of the information the firm produces. Auditors play an important role in financial markets because they can reduce the inevitable information asymmetry between the firm's managers and its shareholders.

Threats to truthful reporting in an audit arise from several potential conflicts of interest. The conflict of interest that has received the most attention in the media occurs when an accounting firm provides its client with auditing services and nonaudit consulting services—commonly known as **management advisory services**—such as advice on taxes, accounting or management information systems, and business strategies. Accounting firms that provide multiple services enjoy economies of scale and scope, but have two potential sources of conflicts of interest. First, clients may pressure auditors into skewing their judgments and opinions by threatening to take their accounting and management services business to another accounting firm. Second, if auditors are analyzing information systems or examining tax and financial advice put in place by their nonaudit counterparts within the accounting firm, they may be reluctant to criticize the advice or systems. Both types of conflicts may potentially lead to biased audits. With less reliable information available to investors, it becomes more difficult for financial markets to allocate capital efficiently.

A third type of conflict of interest arises when an auditor provides an overly favorable audit in an effort to solicit or retain audit business. The unfortunate collapse of

Conflicts of Interest The Collapse of Arthur Andersen

In 1913, Arthur Andersen, a young accountant who had denounced the slipshod and deceptive practices that enabled companies to fool the investing public, founded his own firm. Until the early 1980s, auditing was the most important source of profits for this firm. By the late 1980s, however, the consulting part of the business began to experience high revenue growth with high profit margins, even as the audit profits slumped in a more competitive market. Consulting partners began to assume more power within the firm, and the resulting internal conflicts split the firm in two. Arthur Andersen (the auditing service) and Andersen Consulting were established as separate companies in 2000.

During the period of increasing conflict before the split, Andersen's audit partners had faced increasing pressure to focus on boosting revenue and profits from audit services. Many of Arthur Andersen's clients that later went bust—Enron, WorldCom, Qwest, and Global Crossing—were also the largest clients in Arthur Andersen's regional offices. The combination of intense pressure to generate revenue and profits from auditing and the fact that some clients dominated the business of regional offices translated into tremendous incentives for regional office managers to provide favorable audit stances for these large clients. The loss of a client such as Enron or WorldCom would have been devastating for a regional office and its partners, even if that client contributed only a small fraction of the overall revenue and profits for Arthur Andersen as a whole.

The Houston office of Arthur Andersen, for example, ignored many problems in Enron's reporting. Arthur Andersen was indicted in March 2002 and then convicted in June 2002 for obstruction of justice for impeding the SEC's investigation of the Enron collapse (the conviction was overturned by the Supreme Court in May 2005). Its conviction—the first ever against a major accounting firm—barred Arthur Andersen from conducting audits of publicly traded firms and so effectively put it out of business.

Arthur Andersen—once one of the five largest accounting firms in the United States—suggests that this may be the most dangerous conflict of interest (see the Conflicts of Interest box, "The Collapse of Arthur Andersen").

Credit Assessment and Consulting in Credit-Rating Agencies

Investors use credit ratings (e.g., Aaa or Baa) that reflect the probability of default to determine the creditworthiness of particular debt securities. As a consequence, debt ratings play a major role in the pricing of debt securities and in the regulatory process. Conflicts of interest can arise when multiple users with divergent interests (at least in the short term) depend on the credit ratings. Investors and regulators are seeking a well-researched, impartial assessment of credit quality; the issuer needs a favorable rating. In the credit-rating industry, the issuers of securities pay a rating firm such as Standard and Poor's or Moody's to have their securities rated (see the FYI box). Because the issuers are the parties paying the credit-rating agency, investors and regulators worry that the agency may bias its ratings upward to attract more business from the issuer.

Other conflicts of interest may arise when credit-rating agencies also provide ancillary consulting services. Debt issuers often ask rating agencies to advise them on how to structure their debt issues, usually with the goal of securing a favorable rating. In this situation, the credit-rating agencies would be auditing their own work and would experience a conflict of interest similar to the one found in accounting firms that provide both auditing and consulting services. Furthermore, credit-rating agencies may deliver

FYI Why Do Issuers of Securities Pay to Have Their Securities Rated?

Prior to the 1970s, credit-rating agencies earned revenues by having subscribers pay to receive information about securities ratings. In the early 1970s, however, the major rating agencies switched to having issuers of securities pay for their ratings. Why would they do this, given that it appears to set up an obvious conflict of interest?

The answer is provided by the asymmetric information framework, which was discussed in Chapter 8. By the early 1970s, technological changes, such as the advent of cheap photocopying, made it easier to disseminate information. Market participants were able to readily get information on securities ratings without paying for it. The free-rider problem became more widespread. As a result, the credit-rating agencies were no longer able to earn enough revenues by selling ratings information. The solution was to have the issuers of securities pay for the ratings, and this is the business model that we see currently.

favorable ratings to garner new clients for the ancillary consulting business. The possible decline in the quality of credit assessments issued by rating agencies could increase asymmetric information in financial markets, thereby diminishing their ability to allocate credit.

Universal Banking

Commercial banks, investment banks, and insurance companies were orginally created as distinct financial institutions that offered separate and distinct services. These institutions soon recognized, however, that combining these activities and services would provide economies of scope. In 1933, the Glass-Steagall Act halted the development of universal banking by banning the consolidation of these services under one organization. When the Glass-Steagall Act was repealed by Congress in 1999, universal banking reappeared. Given that the divisions within universal banks serve multiple clients, many potential conflicts of interest exist. If the potential for revenues in one department increases, employees in that department will have an incentive to distort information (or to pressure employees in another department to distort information) to the advantage of their clients and the profit of their department.

Several types of conflicts of interest can arise in universal banks:

- Securities issuers served by the underwriting department (and the underwriting department itself) will benefit from aggressive sales of the securities issue to customers of the bank, whereas the customers expect unbiased investment advice.
- A bank manager may push the issuing firm's securities to the disadvantage of the customer or may limit losses from a poor IPO by selling the firm's securities to the bank's managed trust accounts.
- A bank with an outstanding loan to a firm whose credit or bankruptcy risk has increased has private knowledge that may encourage the bank to use its underwriting department to sell bonds to the unsuspecting public, thereby paying off the loan and earning a fee.
- A bank may make loans to a firm on overly favorable terms to obtain fees from it for performing activities such as underwriting the firm's securities.
- To sell its insurance products, a bank may try to influence or coerce a borrowing or investing customer.

Conflicts of Interest Banksters

Just as in the aftermath of the collapse of the tech bubble in 2000, the stock market crash of 1929 prompted many investors to question why they had been encouraged to purchase so many securities that declined in value so quickly. The public blamed the universal banks for hyping securities, and bankers were pejoratively referred to as "banksters." Public pressure led the Senate Banking and Currency Committee to hold hearings to investigate potential abuses by the universal banks. These hearings, which became known as the Pecora hearings after the chief counsel who led them, were as famous in their day as the Watergate hearings that led to President Nixon's resignation in 1974 or the hearings of the 9/11 Commission in 2004.

The Pecora hearings turned up several cases of apparently severe abuses of conflicts of interest in the banking industry. An affiliate of National City Bank (the precursor to Citibank) was accused of selling "unsound and speculative securities" to the bank's customers, particularly bonds from the Republic of Peru that went into default. Chase National Bank and National City Bank were accused of converting bad loans to companies such as General Theaters and Equipment and the General Sugar Company into securities that were sold to the public and investment trusts managed by these banks. The president of National City Bank, Charles E. Mitchell, and the head of Chase National Bank, Albert H. Wiggin, were accused of setting up *pool operations*, in which resources from the banks were used to prop up the bank's stock price for the benefit of these executives and their associates.

The resulting scandals led to passage of the Glass-Steagall Act in 1933, which eliminated the possibility of these conflicts of interest by mandating complete separation of commercial banking from investment banking activities. It was not until 1999 that this act was repealed by Congress to enable banks to be more competitive.

All of these conflicts of interest may decrease the amount of accurate information production by the universal bank, thereby hindering its ability to promote efficient credit allocation. Although there have not been any recent banking scandals involving conflicts of interest, they did surface in the aftermath of the stock market crash of 1929 (see the Conflicts of Interest box, "Banksters").

CAN THE MARKET LIMIT EXPLOITATION OF CONFLICTS OF INTEREST?

Conflicts of interest become a problem for the financial system when they lead to a decrease in the flow of reliable information, either because information is concealed or because misleading information is disseminated. The decline in the flow of reliable information makes it harder for the financial system to solve adverse selection and moral hazard problems, which can slow the flow of credit to parties with productive investment opportunities.

Even though conflicts of interest exist, they do not necessarily reduce the flow of reliable information because the incentives to exploit the conflict of interest may not be very high. When an exploitation of a conflict of interest is visible to the market, it can punish a financial service firm by denying it business. Given the importance of maintaining and enhancing a financial firm's reputation, exploiting any conflicts of interest would decrease the firm's future profitability because it would have greater difficulty selling its services. In this way, the firm has incentives *not* to exploit a conflict of interest. These incentives limit conflicts of interest in the long run, but they may not be effective in the short run depending on structural factors within the firm, such as a lack of transparency and inappropriate monetary incentives.

One enlightening example of how the market can limit exploitation of conflicts of interest occurs in credit-rating agencies. At first glance, the fact that rating agencies are paid by the firms issuing securities to produce ratings for these securities looks like a serious conflict of interest. Rating agencies would seem to have powerful incentives to gain business by providing security-issuing firms with higher credit ratings than they deserve, making it easier for the firms to sell their securities at higher prices. In reality, little evidence suggests that rating agencies take advantage of this conflict of interest, despite prominent examples such as Enron.[2] Much research has shown that a reasonably close correlation exists between ratings and default probabilities. Ratings agencies do not exploit the conflict of interest because giving higher credit ratings to firms that pay for the ratings would lower the credibility of the ratings, making them less valuable to the market. The market is able to assess the quality of biased ratings because it can observe poorer performance by individual securities. Furthermore, credit-rating agencies themselves provide evidence on the relationship between their ratings and subsequent default history. If a rating agency continually gave high ratings to firms that eventually defaulted, investors in the market would no longer trust its ratings, its reputation would become tarnished, and good, nondefaulting firms would go elsewhere for their ratings. For this reason, the rating agency has an incentive not to exploit this conflict of interest and overrate the bonds of its customers.

Commercial banks that underwrote securities prior to the enactment of the Glass-Steagall Act do not appear to have exploited this conflict of interest. When a commercial bank underwrites securities, the bank may have an incentive to market the securities of financially troubled firms to the public because the firms will then be able to pay back the loans they owe to the bank, while at the same time the bank earns fees from the underwriting services. The evidence suggests that in the 1920s, markets found securities underwritten by bond departments within a commercial bank to be less attractive than securities underwritten in separate affiliates where the conflict of interest was more transparent. To maintain the bank's reputation, commercial banks shifted their underwriting to separate affiliates over time, with the result that securities underwritten by banks became valued as highly as those underwritten by independent investment banks.[3] When affiliates were unable to certify the absence of conflicts, they focused on underwriting securities from well-known firms, for which less of an information asymmetry existed and conflicts of interest were less pronounced. Again, the market provided incentives to control potential conflicts of interest. However, it is important to note that the market solution was not immediate, but took some time to develop.

---

[2]See the survey in Bank for International Settlements, "Credit Ratings and Complementary Sources of Credit Quality Information," Basel Committee on Banking Supervision Working Papers No. 3, August 2000, and the discussion in Andrew Crockett, Trevor Harris, Frederic S. Mishkin, and Eugene N. White, *Conflicts of Interest in the Financial Services Industry: What Should We Do About Them?* Geneva Reports on the World Economy 4 (Geneva and London: International Center for Monetary and Banking Studies and Centre for Economic Policy Research, 2003).

[3]See Randall S. Kroszner and Raghuram G. Rajan, "Is the Glass-Steagall Act Justified? A Study of the US Experience with Universal Banking Before 1933," *American Economic Review* 84 (1994): 810–832; Randall S. Kroszner and Raghuram G. Rajan, "Organization, Structure, and Credibility: Evidence from Commercial Bank Securities Activities Before the Glass-Steagall Act," *Journal of Monetary Economics* 39 (1997); James S. Ang and Terry Richardson, "The Underwriting Experience of Commercial Bank Affiliates Prior to the Glass-Steagall Act," *Journal of Banking and Finance* 18 (March 1994): 351–395; and Manu Pari, "Commercial Banks in Investment Banking: Conflict of Interest or Certification Role?" *Journal of Financial Economics* 40 (1996).

The responsiveness of the market is also evident in the apparent conflict of interest present in investment banks when underwriters who have incentives to favor issuers over investors pressure research analysts to provide more favorable assessments of issuers' securities. Analysts at an investment bank that is underwriting particular IPOs tend to make more "buy" recommendations for these IPOs than do analysts at other investment banks, and the market takes account of this tendency in pricing these securities. Over a two-year period, the performance of other analysts' recommended securities was 50% better than the performance of securities recommended by analysts at the investment banks that underwrote these IPOs. The market appears to recognize the difference in the quality of information when the potential for a conflict of interest exists.[4]

Fewer empirical studies have examined how the market addresses conflicts of interest that arise in accounting firms, but the limited evidence available does suggest that the market adjusts securities' prices to account for potential conflicts of interest. The evidence suggests that clients, who are concerned about the conflicts of interest that arise from the joint provision of auditing and management advisory services, ascribe less value to audit opinions and limit their nonaudit purchases from the accounting firms that have these conflicts of interest.[5]

Although the market can sometimes ameliorate the effects of conflicts of interest in financial service firms, it cannot always constrain the incentives to exploit conflicts of interest. For the market to prevent this type of exploitation, it needs to have enough information to assess whether an exploitation of conflicts of interest is actually occurring. In some cases, parties who want to take advantage of conflicts of interest will try to hide this information from the market. In other cases, alerting the market to potential conflicts of interest would reveal proprietary information that would help a financial firm's competitors, thus reducing the firm's incentives to reveal its true position.

The recent scandals described in this chapter demonstrate that the exploitation of a conflict of interest often leads to large gains for some members of the financial firm even while it reduces the value of the firm as a whole. Inappropriately designed compensation plans (the result of poor management), for example, may produce conflicts of interest that not only reduce the flow of reliable information to credit markets but also end up destroying the firm. Indeed, the collapse of Arthur Andersen illustrates how the compensation arrangements for one line of business, such as auditing, can create serious conflicts of interest. In the Arthur Andersen case, the partners in regional offices had incentives to please their largest clients even if their actions were detrimental to the firm as a whole. The conflict of interest problem can become even more hazardous when several lines of business are combined and the returns from one of the activities—such as underwriting or consulting—are very high for only a brief amount of time. Also, a compensation scheme that works reasonably well in the short term might become poorly aligned over time.

The extraordinary surge in the stock market created huge temporary rewards, making it possible for well-positioned analysts, underwriters, and audit firm partners to exploit the conflicts before incentives could be realigned. Often, these conflicts of interest were not readily visible to the market, and they may have been invisible even to the top management of a firm. In the most severe cases, opportunistic individuals were able to capture the firm's **reputational rents**, profits that the firm earns because it is trusted

---

[4]Rani Micaela and Kent L. Womack, "Conflict of Interest and the Credibility of Underwriter Analyst Recommendations," *Review of Financial Studies* 12 (Special Issue 1999): 653–686.

[5]Mohinder Parkas and Carol F. Venable, "Auditee Incentives for Auditor Independence: The Case of Non Audit Services," *Accounting Review* 68 (1993): 113–133.

by the marketplace. The exploitation of conflicts of interest clearly damaged the reputation of such investment banks as Merrill Lynch, Salomon Smith Barney of Citigroup, and Credit Suisse First Boston—and perhaps the credibility of analysts in general. Audit firms have lost much of their nonaudit business, while Arthur Andersen was destroyed.

WHAT HAS BEEN DONE TO REMEDY CONFLICTS OF INTEREST?

Two major policy measures have been implemented to deal with conflicts of interest in financial markets: the Sarbanes-Oxley Act and the Global Legal Settlement.

Sarbanes-Oxley Act of 2002

In 2002, the public outcry over the corporate and accounting scandals led to the passage of the Public Accounting Reform and Investor Protection Act, more commonly referred to as the Sarbanes-Oxley Act after its two principal authors in Congress. This act has four major components.

1. The act increases supervisory oversight to monitor and prevent conflicts of interest:
   - It establishes a Public Company Accounting Oversight Board (PCAOB), overseen by the SEC, to supervise accounting firms and ensure that audits are independent and controlled for quality.
   - It increases the SEC's budget to supervise securities markets.
2. Sarbanes-Oxley also directly reduces conflicts of interest:
   - The act makes it unlawful for a registered public accounting firm to provide any nonaudit service to a client contemporaneously with an impermissable audit (as determined by the PCAOB).
3. Sarbanes-Oxley provides incentives for investment banks not to exploit conflicts of interests:
   - It beefs up criminal charges for white-collar crime and obstruction of official investigations.
4. Sarbanes-Oxley also has measures to improve the quality of information in the financial markets:
   - It requires a corporation's chief executive officer (CEO) and chief financial officer (CFO) to certify that periodic financial statements and disclosures of the firm (especially regarding off-balance-sheet transactions) are accurate.
   - It requires members of the audit committee (the subcommittee of the board of directors that oversees the company's audit) to be "independent"—that is, they cannot be managers in the company or receive any consulting or advisory fee from the company.

Global Legal Settlement of 2002

The second policy arose out of a lawsuit brought by New York Attorney General Eliott Spitzer against the ten largest investment banks (Bear Stearns, Credit Suisse First Boston, Deutsche Bank, Goldman Sachs, J. P. Morgan, Lehman Brothers, Merrill Lynch, Morgan Stanley, Salomon Smith Barney, and UBS Warburg). Spitzer alleged that these firms allowed their investment banking departments to have inappropriate influence over their research analysts, thereby creating a conflict of interest. On December 20, 2002, the SEC, the New York Attorney General, NASD, NASAA, NYSE, and state regulators reached a global agreement with these investment banks. The agreement includes three key elements:

1. Like Sarbanes-Oxley, the Global Legal Settlement directly reduces conflicts of interest:
   - It requires investment banks to sever the links between research and securities underwriting.
   - It bans spinning.
2. The Global Legal Settlement provides incentives for investment banks not to exploit conflicts of interests:
   - It imposes $1.4 billion of fines on the accused investment banks.
3. The Global Legal Settlement has measures to improve the quality of information in financial markets:
   - It requires investment banks to make public their analysts' recommendations.
   - It requires investment banks for a five-year period to contract with no fewer than three independent research firms that would provide research to their brokerage customers.

A FRAMEWORK FOR EVALUATING POLICIES TO REMEDY CONFLICTS OF INTEREST

The information view of conflicts of interest developed in this chapter provides a framework for evaluating whether conflicts of interest require public policy actions to eliminate or reduce them. Some combination of financial service activities may result in incentives for agents to conceal information, but they may also result in synergies that make it easier to produce information. Thus preventing the combination of activities to eliminate the conflicts of interest may actually make financial markets less efficient. This reasoning suggests that two propositions are critical to evaluating what should be done about conflicts of interest:

1. *The existence of a conflict of interest does not mean that it will have serious adverse consequences.* Even though a conflict of interest exists, the incentives to exploit the conflict of interest may not be very high. An exploitation of a conflict of interest that is visible to the market will typically tarnish the reputation of the financial firm where it takes place. Given the importance of maintaining and enhancing its reputation, exploiting the conflict of interest would decrease the firm's future profitability because the firm would have greater difficulty selling its services. As a consequence, firms try to structure their salary and reward systems so as to include incentives to avoid the exploitation of the conflict of interest. Hence, the marketplace may be able to control conflicts of interest because a high value is placed on financial firms' reputations. When evaluating the need for remedies, this proposition raises the issue of whether the market has adequate information and incentives to control conflicts of interest.

2. *Even if incentives to exploit conflicts of interest remain strong, eliminating the economies of scope that create the conflicts of interest may be harmful because it will reduce*

the flow of reliable information. Thus, in evaluating possible remedies, we need to examine whether imposing the remedy will do more harm than good by curtailing the flow of reliable information in financial markets.

Approaches to Remedying Conflicts of Interest

In thinking about remedies for specific problematic situations, it is worthwhile to discuss five generic approaches to reconciling conflicts of interest. These approaches are discussed in the order of their intrusiveness, from least intrusive to most intrusive.

Leave It to the Market. This approach has a powerful appeal to many economists and may be a sufficient response in many cases. Market forces can work through two mechanisms. First, they can penalize the financial service firm if it exploits a conflict of interest. For example, a penalty may be imposed by the market in the form of higher funding costs or lower demand for the firm's services, in varying degrees, even to the point of forcing the demise of the firm. Second, market forces can promote new institutional means to contain conflicts of interest. For example, they can generate a demand for information from nonconflicted organizations. This is exactly what happened in the United States in the 1920s, when security affiliates took preeminence over in-house bond departments in universal banks.

One advantage of market-driven solutions is that they can hit where it hurts the most, through pecuniary penalties. Moreover, they may help avoid the risk of overreaction. It can be hard to resist the temptation to adopt nonmarket solutions to appease a public outcry that may reduce information production in financial markets. Conversely, market-based solutions may not always work if the market cannot obtain sufficient information to appropriately punish financial firms that are exploiting conflicts of interest. Memories may be short in financial markets, as is suggested by the new field of behavioral finance discussed in Chapter 7. Once a triggering event has faded from memory, conflicts may creep back in unless reforms have been "hard-wired" into the system.

Regulate for Transparency. A competitive market structure does not always adequately reduce information asymmetries. The gathering of information is costly, and any individual economic agent will gather information only if the private benefit outweighs the cost. When the information collected becomes available to the market immediately, the free-rider problem may reach serious levels. Information has the attribute of a public good, which will be undersupplied in the absence of some public intervention. To some extent, mandatory information disclosure can alleviate information asymmetries and is a key element of regulation of the financial system.

When mandatory disclosure of information reveals whether a conflict of interest exists, the market is able to discipline the financial firm that fails to ameliorate conflicts of interest. In addition, if a financial institution is required to provide information about potential conflicts of interest, the user of the institution's information services may be able to judge how much weight to place on the information this institution supplies.

At the same time, mandatory disclosure could create problems if it reveals so much proprietary information that the financial institution is unable to profitably engage in the information production business. The result could then be less information production, rather than more. Also, mandatory disclosure may not work if financial firms can successfully avoid the regulation and continue to hide relevant information about potential conflicts of interest. The free-rider problem might likewise result in insufficient monitoring of conflicts of interest because the benefits of monitoring and constraining these conflicts accrue only partially to the monitors. Finally, complying with regulations requiring information disclosure may be costly for financial firms—possibly exceeding the costs due to conflicts of interest.

Supervisory Oversight. If mandatory disclosure does not work because firms continue to hide relevant information, because the free-rider problem is severe, or because mandatory disclosure would reveal proprietary information, supervisory oversight can come to the rescue and contain conflicts of interest. Supervisors can observe proprietary information about conflicts of interest without revealing it to a financial firm's competitors so that the firm can continue to profitably engage in information production activities. Armed with this information, the supervisor can take actions to prevent financial firms from exploiting conflicts of interest. As part of this supervisory oversight, standards of practice can be developed, either by the supervisor or by the firms engaged in a specific information production activity. Enforcement of these standards would then be placed in the hands of the supervisor.

As we saw in Chapter 11, supervisory oversight of this type is very common in the banking industry. In recent years, bank supervisors have sharpened their focus on risk management. They now examine banks' risk management procedures to ensure that the appropriate internal controls on risk taking have been established at the bank. In a similar fashion, supervisors can examine banks' internal procedures and controls to restrict conflicts of interest. When they find weak internal controls, they can require the financial institution to modify them so that incentives to exploit conflicts of interest are eliminated.

Although supervisory oversight has proved successful in improving internal controls in financial firms in recent years, if the incentives to exploit conflicts of interest are sufficiently strong, financial institutions may still be able to hide conflicts of interest from the supervisors. Furthermore, supervisors have not always done their job well, as we saw in Chapter 11.

Separation of Functions. Where the market cannot obtain sufficient information to constrain conflicts of interest—because there is no satisfactory way of inducing information disclosure by market discipline or supervisory oversight—the incentives to exploit conflicts of interest may be reduced or eliminated by regulations enforcing separation of functions. Several degrees of separation are possible. First, activities may be separated into different in-house departments with firewalls between them. Second, the firm may restrict different activities to separately capitalized affiliates. Third, regulations may prohibit the combination of activities in any organizational form.

The goal of separation of functions is to ensure that agents are not placed in the position of responding to multiple principals. Moving from relaxed to more stringent separation of functions, conflicts of interest are reduced to an increasing degree. Of course, more stringent separation of functions also reduces synergies of information collection, thereby preventing financial firms from taking advantage of economies of scope in information production. The resulting increased cost of producing information could, in turn, lead to a decreased flow of reliable information because it becomes more expensive to produce it. Deciding on the appropriate amount of separation therefore involves a trade-off between the benefits of reducing conflicts of interest and the cost of reducing economies of scope in producing information.

Socialization of Information Production. The most radical response to conflicts generated by the existence of asymmetric information is the socialization of the provision or the funding source of the relevant information. For example, much macroeconomic information is provided by publicly funded agencies, because this particular public good is likely to be undersupplied if left to private provision. It is conceivable that other information-providing functions—for example, credit ratings and auditing—could also be publicly supplied. Alternatively, if the information-generating services are left to the private sector, they could be funded by public sources or by a publicly mandated levy to help ensure that information production is not tainted by obligations to fee-paying entities with special interests.

Of course, the problem with this approach is that a government agency or publicly funded entity may not have the same strong incentives as private financial institutions to produce high-quality information. Forcing information production to be conducted by a government or quasi-government entity—although it may diminish conflicts of interest—may reduce the flow of reliable information to financial markets. Furthermore, government agencies may have difficulty paying the market wages required to attract the best people. This problem may become even more serious if economies of scope are affected. For example, analysts in an investment banking firm are likely to receive additional compensation when their research has multiple uses. By contrast, a government agency that is interested in only one use of research may not provide a level of compensation sufficient to produce high-quality information. In addition, the government might not provide sufficient funds for information collection. Indeed, government provision of important series of macroeconomic data has already been discontinued because of a lack of funding.

APPLICATION Evaluating Sarbanes-Oxley and the Global Legal Settlement

Using the analytic framework discussed earlier, we now can turn to evaluating the Sarbanes-Oxley Act and the Global Legal Settlement.

We have seen that policies that regulate conflicts of interest can help to increase the amount of information in financial markets. Sarbanes-Oxley does exactly this when it requires that the CEO and the CFO certify the periodic financial statements and disclosures of the firm. It increases the likelihood that these statements will provide reliable information. In addition, Sarbanes-Oxley requires disclosure of off-balance-sheet transactions and other relationships with special-purpose entities. Again, this step can help increase information in the marketplace because these off-balance-sheet transactions were often used, as in the Enron case, to hide what was going on inside the firm. However, the costs of complying with the new regulations imposed by Sarbanes-Oxley are not cheap. Small firms are hit particularly hard: The estimated costs of complying with Sarbanes-Oxley exceed $800,000 for smaller firms with revenues of less than $100 million, which amounts to nearly 1.5% of their sales. Sarbanes-Oxley might severely hurt such companies' profitability and make it harder for them to make productive investments.

We have also seen that the market is often able to constrain conflicts of interest when it has sufficient information to do so. The Global Legal Settlement includes a provision that requires investment banking firms to make their analyst recommendations public. This policy will help the market to assess whether the analysts are acting in good faith. The SEC also requires increased disclosure by investment analysts, credit-rating agencies, and auditors, forcing them to reveal any interests they have in the firms they analyze. Provision of this information makes it more likely that financial institutions will develop internal rules to ensure that conflicts of interest are minimized, so that their reputations remain high and the firms profitable.

Of course, disclosure may not be enough to get markets to control conflicts of interest, because firms still have incentives to hide information so that they can profitably exploit conflicts of interest. Disclosure may also reveal so much proprietary information that the financial institution is unable to profitably engage in the information production business. In addition, some of the most damaging conflicts of interest have resulted from poorly designed internal compensation mechanisms, which are difficult for markets to observe. Supervisory oversight can focus on exactly these issues.

Increased supervisory oversight is a key feature of the Sarbanes-Oxley Act. First, the act establishes the PCAOB to supervise accounting firms. The PCAOB monitors compensation mechanisms to verify that they are in accord with best practices to control conflicts of interest. Second, Sarbanes-Oxley provides substantially more resources for the SEC. A supervisory agency cannot do its job properly without adequate resources. Indeed, one reason why the SEC may have failed to provide adequate supervisory oversight during the boom of the 1990s is because it was starved for resources. A similar problem occurred for the supervisors of the savings and loan industry, and it helped lead to scandals and a bailout that cost taxpayers more than $100 billion.

By keeping the audit committee independent of management, Sarbanes-Oxley eliminates the conflict of interest that occurs when the management of a firm hires its auditor. The PCAOB will be instrumental in writing the regulations to ensure that auditors will report to, be hired by, and be compensated by an independent audit committee that is supposed to represent shareholders other than management.

The Global Legal Settlement also directly eliminates one Wall Street practice that led to obvious conflicts of interest—spinning, in which executives received hot IPO shares in return for their companies' future business with the investment bank underwriting the new issue. The Global Legal Settlement punished investment banks that exploited conflicts of interest by imposing a fine of more than $1.4 billion. This tough punishment, along with the harsher criminal penalties established by Sarbanes-Oxley, provides incentives for investment banking firms to avoid taking advantage of conflicts of interest in the future.

The more radical parts of Sarbanes-Oxley and the Global Legal Settlement involve separation of functions and socialization of information. Sarbanes-Oxley makes it illegal for accounting firms to provide nonaudit consulting services to their audit customers. This law will potentially reduce the economies of scope available to auditing firms that also offer consulting services. It is unlikely that the proscription of nonauditing services in this situation, as envisioned by Sarbanes-Oxley, would have prevented the recent audit failures. However, greater transparency about the nature and role of nonaudit services would be a valuable aid to control a firm's temptation to exploit this conflict of interest. Similarly, the Global Legal Settlement requires investment banking firms to sever the link between research and investment banking. This divestiture also has the potential to eliminate economies of scope in information production. After all, analysts may be able to obtain much more information on firms they cover when the investment banking arm of the firm can share information with them.

The Global Legal Settlement requires that for a five-year period, brokerage firms contract with independent research firms to provide information to their customers. In addition, part of the $1.4 billion fine paid by the investment banks will be used to fund independent research and investor education. While it remains to be seen how the terms of this agreement will be implemented, there are both potentially positive and potentially negative features. Independent research may produce unbiased information.

However, by socializing research, firms can no longer compete for customers on the basis of the quality of their research. Because they are being taxed to fund independent research, firms may decrease their investment in their own research analysis. Indeed, this is exactly what has already happened, with research budgets at the seven largest securities firms being cut almost in half since 2000. If the investment banks do not control the information that they are being forced to acquire, the analysis produced may be of a lower quality.

SUMMARY

1. Conflicts of interest arise when financial service firms or their employees are serving multiple interests and develop incentives to misuse or conceal information needed for the effective functioning of financial markets. If taking advantage of conflicts of interest substantially reduces the amount of reliable information in financial markets, asymmetric information increases and prevents financial markets from channeling funds to those firms with the most productive investment opportunities.
2. Four types of financial service activities have the greatest potential for conflicts of interest that reduce reliable information in financial markets: (1) underwriting and research in investment banking, (2) auditing and consulting in accounting firms, (3) credit assessment and consulting in credit-rating agencies, and (4) universal banking.
3. Even though conflicts of interest may exist, they do not necessarily have to reduce the flow of reliable information, because the market provides strong incentives for financial service firms to avoid damaging their reputations. The evidence suggests that the market often succeeds in constraining the incentives to exploit conflicts of interest. However, conflicts of interest still pose a threat to the efficiency of financial markets.
4. Two major policy measures deal with conflicts of interest: the Sarbanes-Oxley Act of 2002 and the Global Legal Settlement arising from the lawsuit by the New York Attorney General against the ten largest investment banks.
5. Two basic propositions are critical to evaluating what should be done about conflicts of interest: (1) The fact that a conflict of interest exists does not mean that the conflict will necessarily have serious adverse consequences. (2) Even if incentives to exploit conflicts of interest remain strong, eliminating the conflict of interest may be harmful if it destroys economies of scope, thereby reducing the flow of reliable information. Five approaches to remedying conflicts of interest, going from least intrusive to most intrusive, have been suggested: (1) leave it to the market, (2) regulate for transparency, (3) provide supervisory oversight, (4) mandate separation of functions, and (5) require socialization of information.
6. Sarbanes-Oxley and the Global Legal Settlement help increase the flow of reliable information in financial markets by requiring the CEO and CFO to certify financial statements, corporations to disclose off-balance-sheet transactions and entities, and investment banks to make public their analysts' recommendations, and by requiring increased disclosure of potential conflicts of interest. Sarbanes-Oxley increases supervisory oversight by establishing the Public Company Accounting Oversight Board (PCAOB) and by increasing the resources available to the SEC. The act also reduces conflicts of interest in auditing by making the audit committee independent of management. The Global Legal Settlement eliminates the conflict of interest inherent in spinning. The $1.4 billion fine and harsher criminal penalties imposed by Sarbanes-Oxley provide incentives for investment banks not to exploit conflicts of interest in the future. The more radical parts of Sarbanes-Oxley and the Global Legal Settlement, which involve separation of functions (research from underwriting, and auditing from nonaudit consulting) and socialization of research information, may ultimately reduce the information available in financial markets.

KEY TERMS

conflicts of interest, p. 361
economies of scope, p. 362
initial public offerings (IPOs), p. 364
management advisory services, p. 365
reputational rents, p. 370
spinning, p. 364

QUESTIONS AND PROBLEMS

Questions marked with an asterisk are answered at the end of the book in an appendix, "Answers to Selected Questions and Problems." Questions marked with a blue circle indicate the question is available in MyEconLab at www.myeconlab.com/mishkin.

1. Why can provision of several types of financial services by one firm lead to a lower cost of information production?
*2. How does the provision of several types of financial services by one firm lead to conflicts of interest?
3. How can conflicts of interest make financial markets less efficient?
*4. How can conflicts of interest lead to unethical behavior?
5. Describe two conflicts of interest that occur when underwriting and research are provided by a single investment banking firm.
*6. How does spinning lead to a less efficient financial market?
7. Describe two conflicts of interest that occur in accounting firms.
*8. Some commentators have attributed the demise of Arthur Andersen to the combination of auditing and consulting activities in the firm. Is this assessment correct?
9. Describe two conflicts of interest that occur in credit-rating agencies.
*10. Describe two conflicts of interest that occur in universal banks.
11. "Conflicts of interest always reduce the flow of reliable information." Is this statement true, false, or uncertain? Explain your answer.
*12. Give two examples of conflicts of interest that do not seem to have been exploited and thus did not lead to a reduction of reliable information in the financial markets.
13. When is it more likely that conflicts of interest will be exploited?
*14. How can compensation schemes in financial service firms lead to conflicts of interest?
15. What are the advantages and disadvantages of mandatory disclosure in dealing with conflicts of interest?
*16. How can supervisory oversight help reduce conflicts of interest?
17. What are the disadvantages of separating financial activities into different firms in an effort to avoid conflicts of interest?
*18. What are the advantages and disadvantages of government provision of information as a solution to the problems created by conflicts of interest?
19. Which provisions of the Sarbanes-Oxley Act do you think are beneficial, and which are not?
*20. Which provisions of the Global Legal Settlement do you think are beneficial, and which are not?

WEB EXERCISES

1. Go to www.sarbanes-oxley.com/. This site tracks issues and news related to the Sarbanes-Oxley Act.
   a. Summarize in two or three sentences the primary reason for passage of the Sarbanes-Oxley Act.
   b. Summarize one of the articles discussed under the news/current events section. Address how this article relates to conflicts of interest in the financial markets.

2. Go to www.sec.gov/ and click on "Press releases."
   a. Summarize the major types of issues that the SEC addresses in these press releases.
   b. Review the last three months of releases, and count how many appear to be enforcement actions aimed at firms or individuals who have violated SEC regulations. From this review, does the SEC appear to be active in its effort to prevent fraud and misrepresentation in the securities industry?

WEB REFERENCES

http://stockcharts.com/charts/historical/

To review the timing of the stock market declines, this web site graphs a variety of stock market indexes for easy viewing.

www. moodys.com/cust/default.as

Moody's is a major rating agency for company debt. To view the Moody's website and learn more about how it evaluates company credit, you must register to view Moody's Web materials.

www.sarbanes-oxley.com/

A Web site devoted to discussion and dissemination of information about the Sarbanes-Oxley Act.

www.sec.gov/

The SEC is primarily responsible for preventing fraud in the securities markets. Click on "What we do" to learn what role the SEC envisions for itself in the securities industry.

PART

4

Central Banking and the Conduct of Monetary Policy

CHAPTER

15 Structure of Central Banks and the Federal Reserve System

Preview

Among the most important players in financial markets throughout the world are central banks, the government authorities in charge of monetary policy. Central banks' actions affect interest rates, the amount of credit, and the money supply, all of which have direct impacts not only on financial markets, but also on aggregate output and inflation. To understand the role that central banks play in financial markets and the overall economy, we need to understand how these organizations work. Who controls central banks and determines their actions? What motivates their behavior? Who holds the reins of power?

In this chapter, we look at the institutional structure of major central banks, and focus particularly on the Federal Reserve System, the most important central bank in the world. We start by focusing on the formal institutional structure of the Fed and then examine the more relevant informal structure that determines where the true power within the Federal Reserve System lies. By understanding who makes the decisions, we will have a better idea of how they are made. We then look at several other major central banks, particularly the European Central Bank, and see how they are organized. With this information, we will be more able to comprehend the actual conduct of monetary policy described in the following chapters.

ORIGINS OF THE FEDERAL RESERVE SYSTEM

Of all the central banks in the world, the Federal Reserve System probably has the most unusual structure. To understand why this structure arose, we must go back to before 1913, when the Federal Reserve System was created.

Before the twentieth century, a major characteristic of American politics was the fear of centralized power, as seen in the checks and balances of the Constitution and the preservation of states' rights. This fear of centralized power was one source of the American resistance to the establishment of a central bank (see Chapter 10). Another source was the traditional American distrust of moneyed interests, the most prominent symbol of which was a central bank. The open hostility of the American public to the existence of a central bank resulted in the demise of the first two experiments in central banking, whose function was to police the banking system: The First Bank of the United States was disbanded in 1811, and the national charter of the Second Bank of the United States expired in 1836 after its renewal was vetoed in 1832 by President Andrew Jackson.

Inside the Fed The Political Genius of the Founders of the Federal Reserve System

The history of the United States has been one of public hostility to banks and especially to a central bank. How were the politicians who founded the Federal Reserve able to design a system that has become one of the most prestigious institutions in the United States?

The answer is that the founders recognized that if power was too concentrated in either Washington, D.C., or New York, cities that Americans often love to hate, an American central bank might not have enough public support to operate effectively. They thus decided to set up a decentralized system with twelve Federal Reserve banks spread throughout the country to make sure that all regions of the country were represented in monetary policy deliberations. In addition, they made the Federal Reserve banks quasi-private institutions overseen by directors from the private sector living in each district who represent views from their region and are in close contact with the president of the Federal Reserve bank. The unusual structure of the Federal Reserve System has promoted a concern in the Fed with regional issues as is evident in Federal Reserve bank publications. Without this unusual structure, the Federal Reserve System might have been far less popular with the public, making the institution far less effective.

The termination of the Second Bank's national charter in 1836 created a severe problem for American financial markets, because there was no lender of last resort that could provide reserves to the banking system to avert a bank panic. Hence, in the nineteenth and early twentieth centuries, nationwide bank panics became a regular event, occurring every twenty years or so, culminating in the panic of 1907. The 1907 panic resulted in such widespread bank failures and such substantial losses to depositors that the public was finally convinced that a central bank was needed to prevent future panics.

The hostility of the American public to banks and centralized authority created great opposition to the establishment of a single central bank like the Bank of England. Fear was rampant that the moneyed interests on Wall Street (including the largest corporations and banks) would be able to manipulate such an institution to gain control over the economy and that federal operation of the central bank might result in too much government intervention in the affairs of private banks. Serious disagreements existed over whether the central bank should be a private bank or a government institution. Because of the heated debates on these issues, a compromise was struck. In the great American tradition, Congress wrote an elaborate system of checks and balances into the Federal Reserve Act of 1913, which created the Federal Reserve System with its twelve regional Federal Reserve banks (see the Inside the Fed box, "The Political Genius of the Founders of the Federal Reserve System").

STRUCTURE OF THE FEDERAL RESERVE SYSTEM

The writers of the Federal Reserve Act wanted to diffuse power along regional lines, between the private sector and the government, and among bankers, business people, and the public. This initial diffusion of power has resulted in the evolution of the Federal Reserve System to include the following entities: the **Federal Reserve banks**, the **Board of Governors of the Federal Reserve System**, the **Federal Open Market Committee (FOMC)**, the Federal Advisory Council, and around 2,800 member commercial

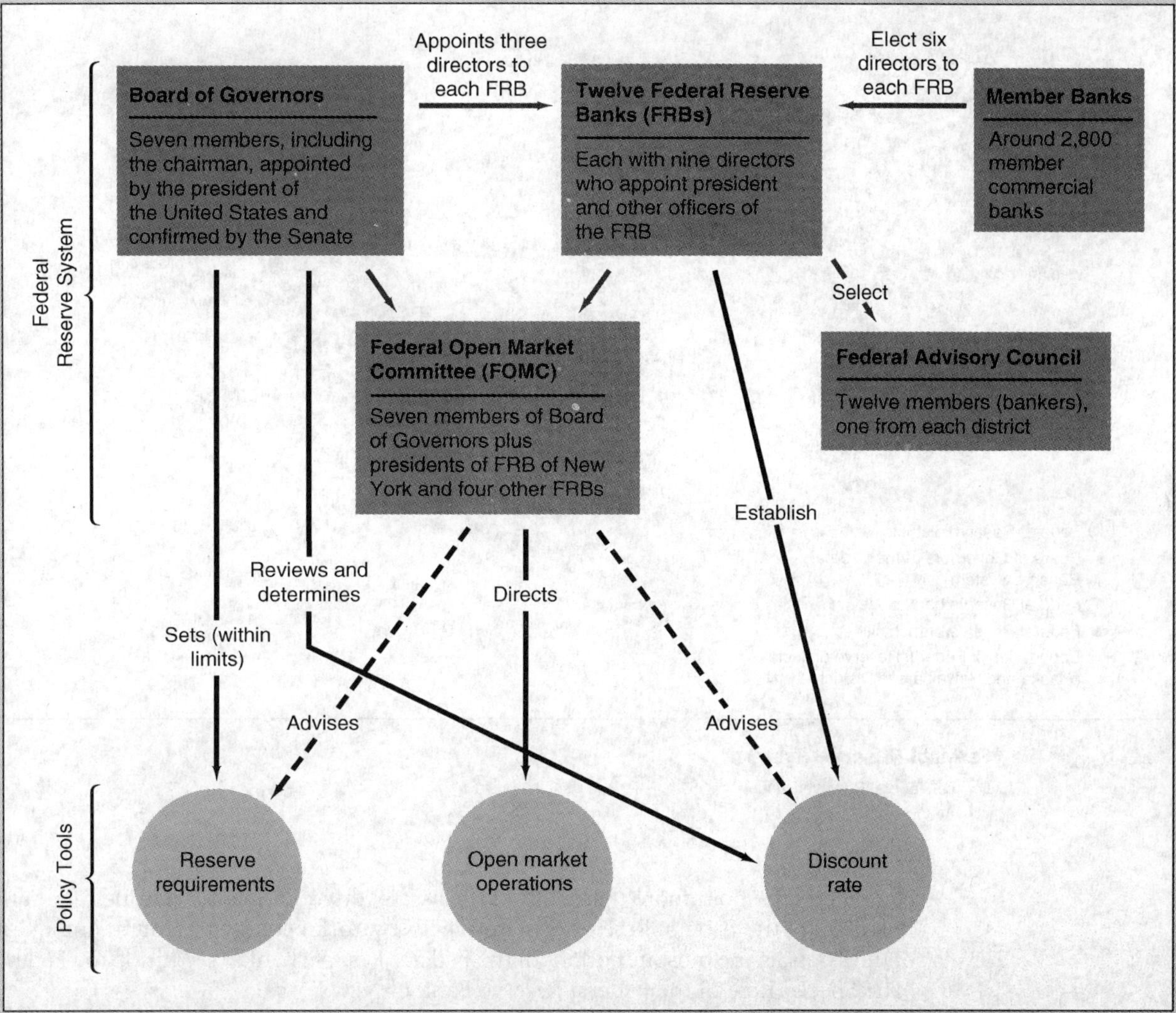

FIGURE 1 **Structure and Responsibility for Policy Tools in the Federal Reserve System**
Dashed lines indicate that the FOMC "advises" on the setting of reserve requirements and the discount rate.

banks. Figure 1 outlines the relationships of these entities to one another and to the three policy tools of the Fed (open market operations, the discount rate, and reserve requirements) discussed in Chapters 16 to 18.

Federal Reserve Banks

Each of the twelve Federal Reserve districts has one main Federal Reserve bank, which may have branches in other cities in the district. The locations of these districts, the Federal Reserve banks, and their branches are shown in Figure 2. The three largest Federal Reserve banks in terms of assets are those of New York, Chicago, and San Francisco—

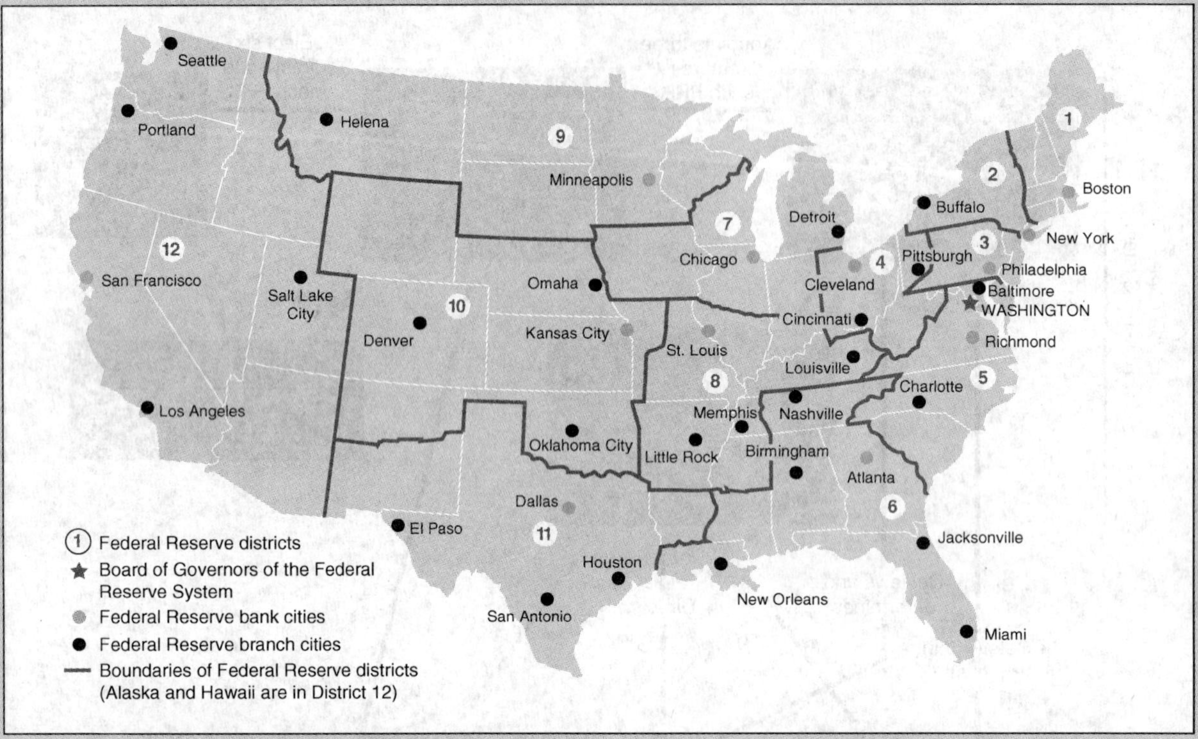

FIGURE 2 **Federal Reserve System**

Source: Federal Reserve *Bulletin.*

combined they hold more than 50% of the assets (discount loans, securities, and other holdings) of the Federal Reserve System. The New York bank, with around one-quarter of the assets, is the most important of the Federal Reserve banks (see Inside the Fed box, "The Special Role of the Federal Reserve Bank of New York").

Each of the Federal Reserve banks is a quasi-public (part private, part government) institution owned by the private commercial banks in the district that are members of the Federal Reserve System. These member banks have purchased stock in their district Federal Reserve bank (a requirement of membership), and the dividends paid by that stock are limited by law to 6% annually. The member banks elect six directors for each district bank; three more are appointed by the Board of Governors. Together, these nine directors appoint the president of the bank (subject to the approval of the Board of Governors).

The directors of a district bank are classified into three categories: A, B, and C. The three A directors (elected by the member banks) are professional bankers, and the three B directors (also elected by the member banks) are prominent leaders from industry, labor, agriculture, or the consumer sector. The three C directors, who are appointed by the Board of Governors to represent the public interest, are not allowed to be officers, employees, or stockholders of banks. This design for choosing directors was intended by the framers of the Federal Reserve Act to ensure that the directors of each Federal Reserve bank would reflect all constituencies of the American public.

Inside the Fed The Special Role of the Federal Reserve Bank of New York

The Federal Reserve Bank of New York plays a special role in the Federal Reserve System for several reasons. First, its district contains many of the largest commercial banks in the United States, the safety and soundness of which are paramount to the health of the U.S. financial system. The Federal Reserve Bank of New York conducts examinations of bank holding companies and state-chartered banks in its district, making it the supervisor of some of the most important financial institutions in our financial system. Not surprisingly, given this responsibility, the bank supervision group is one of the largest units of the New York Fed and is by far the largest bank supervision group in the Federal Reserve System.

The second reason for the New York Fed's special role is its active involvement in the bond and foreign exchange markets. The New York Fed houses the open market desk, which conducts open market operations—the purchase and sale of bonds—that determine the amount of reserves in the banking system. Because of this involvement in the Treasury securities market, as well as its walking-distance location near the New York and American Stock Exchanges, the officials at the Federal Reserve Bank of New York are in constant contact with the major domestic financial markets in the United States. In addition, the Federal Reserve Bank of New York houses the foreign exchange desk, which conducts foreign exchange interventions on behalf of the Federal Reserve System and the U.S. Treasury. Its involvement in these financial markets means that the New York Fed is an important source of information on what is happening in domestic and foreign financial markets, particularly during crisis periods, as well as a liaison between officials in the Federal Reserve System and private participants in the markets.

The third reason for the Federal Reserve Bank of New York's prominence is that it is the only Federal Reserve bank to be a member of the Bank for International Settlements (BIS). Thus the president of the New York Fed, along with the chairman of the Board of Governors, represents the Federal Reserve System in its regular monthly meetings with other major central bankers at the BIS. This close contact with foreign central bankers and interaction with foreign exchange markets means that the New York Fed has a special role in international relations, both with other central bankers and with private market participants. Adding to its prominence in international circles, the New York Fed is the repository for more than $100 billion of the world's gold, an amount greater than the gold at Fort Knox.

Finally, the president of the Federal Reserve Bank of New York is the only permanent member of the FOMC among the Federal Reserve bank presidents, serving as the vice-chairman of the committee. Thus he and the chairman and vice-chairman of the Board of Governors are the three most important officials in the Federal Reserve System.

The twelve Federal Reserve banks perform the following functions:

- Clear checks
- Issue new currency
- Withdraw damaged currency from circulation
- Administer and make discount loans to banks in their districts
- Evaluate proposed mergers and applications for banks to expand their activities
- Act as liaisons between the business community and the Federal Reserve System
- Examine bank holding companies and state-chartered member banks
- Collect data on local business conditions
- Use their staffs of professional economists to research topics related to the conduct of monetary policy

The twelve Federal Reserve banks are involved in monetary policy in several ways:

1. Their directors "establish" the discount rate (although the discount rate in each district is reviewed and determined by the Board of Governors).
2. They decide which banks, member and nonmember alike, can obtain discount loans from the Federal Reserve bank.
3. Their directors select one commercial banker from each bank's district to serve on the Federal Advisory Council, which consults with the Board of Governors and provides information that helps in the conduct of monetary policy.
4. Five of the twelve bank presidents each have a vote in the Federal Open Market Committee, which directs **open market operations** (the purchase and sale of government securities that affect both interest rates and the amount of reserves in the banking system). As explained in the Inside the Fed box, "The Special Role of the Federal Reserve Bank of New York," the president of the New York Fed always has a vote in the FOMC, making it the most important of the banks; the other four votes allocated to the district banks rotate annually among the remaining eleven presidents.

Member Banks

All *national banks* (commercial banks chartered by the Office of the Comptroller of the Currency) are required to be members of the Federal Reserve System. Commercial banks chartered by the states are not required to be members, but they can choose to join. Currently, 37% of the commercial banks in the United States are members of the Federal Reserve System, having declined from a peak figure of 49% in 1947.

Before 1980, only member banks were required to keep reserves as deposits at the Federal Reserve banks. Nonmember banks were subject to reserve requirements determined by their states, which typically allowed them to hold much of their reserves in interest-bearing securities. Because no interest is paid on reserves deposited at the Federal Reserve banks, it was costly to be a member of the system, and as interest rates rose, the relative cost of membership rose, and more and more banks left the system.

This decline in Fed membership was a major concern of the Board of Governors: one reason was that it lessened the Fed's control over the money supply, making it more difficult for the Fed to conduct monetary policy. The chairman of the Board of Governors repeatedly called for new legislation requiring all commercial banks to be members of the Federal Reserve System. One result of the Fed's pressure on Congress was a provision in the Depository Institutions Deregulation and Monetary Control Act of 1980: All depository institutions became subject (by 1987) to the same requirements to keep deposits at the Fed, so member and nonmember banks would be on an equal footing in terms of reserve requirements. In addition, all depository institutions were given access to the Federal Reserve facilities, such as the discount window (discussed in Chapter 18) and Fed check clearing, on an equal basis. These provisions ended the decline in Fed membership and reduced the distinction between member and nonmember banks.

Board of Governors of the Federal Reserve System

At the head of the Federal Reserve System is the seven-member Board of Governors, headquartered in Washington, D.C. Each governor is appointed by the president of the United States and confirmed by the Senate. To limit the president's control over the Fed and insulate the Fed from other political pressures, the governors can serve one full nonrenewable fourteen-year term plus part of another term, with one governor's term expiring every other January.[1] The governors (many are professional economists) are required to come from different Federal Reserve districts to prevent the interests of one region of the country from being overrepresented. The chairman of the Board of Governors is chosen from among the seven governors and serves a four-year, renewable term. It is expected that once a new chairman is chosen, the old chairman resigns from the Board of Governors, even if there are many years left to his or her term as a governor.

The Board of Governors is actively involved in decisions concerning the conduct of monetary policy. All seven governors are members of the FOMC and vote on the conduct of open market operations. Because there are only twelve voting members on this committee (seven governors and five presidents of the district banks), the Board has the majority of the votes. The Board also sets reserve requirements (within limits imposed by legislation) and effectively controls the discount rate by the "review and determination" process, whereby it approves or disapproves the discount rate "established" by the Federal Reserve banks. The chairman of the Board advises the president of the United States on economic policy, testifies in Congress, and speaks for the Federal Reserve System to the media. The chairman and other governors may also represent the United States in negotiations with foreign governments on economic matters. The Board has a staff of professional economists (larger than those of individual Federal Reserve banks), which provides economic analysis that the board uses in making its decisions. (See the Inside the Fed box, "The Role of the Research Staff.")

Through legislation, the Board of Governors has often been given duties not directly related to the conduct of monetary policy. In the past, for example, the Board set the maximum interest rates payable on certain types of deposits under Regulation Q. (After 1986, ceilings on time deposits were eliminated, but there is still a restriction on paying any interest on business demand deposits.) Under the Credit Control Act of 1969 (which expired in 1982), the Board had the ability to regulate and control credit once the president of the United States approved. The Board of Governors also sets margin requirements, the fraction of the purchase price of securities that has to be paid for with cash rather than borrowed funds. It also sets the salary of the president and all officers of each Federal Reserve bank and reviews each bank's budget. Finally, the Board has substantial bank regulatory functions: It approves bank mergers and applications for new activities, specifies the permissible activities of bank holding companies, and supervises the activities of foreign banks in the United States.

Federal Open Market Committee (FOMC)

The FOMC usually meets eight times a year (about every six weeks) and makes decisions regarding the conduct of open market operations, which influence the money supply and interest rates. Indeed, the FOMC is often referred to as the "Fed" in the press: For example, when the media say that the Fed is meeting, they actually mean that the FOMC is meeting. The committee consists of the seven members of the Board of Governors, the president of the Federal Reserve Bank of New York, and the presidents of four other Federal Reserve banks. The chairman of the Board of Governors also

[1]Although technically the governor's term is nonrenewable, a governor can resign just before the term expires and then be reappointed by the president. This explains how one governor, William McChesney Martin, Jr., served for 28 years. Since Martin, the chairman from 1951 to 1970, retired from the board in 1970, the practice of allowing a governor to in effect serve a second full term has not been done and this is why Alan Greenspan had to retire from the Board after his fourteen-year term expired in 2006.

Inside the Fed The Role of the Research Staff

The Federal Reserve System is the largest employer of economists not just in the United States, but in the world. The system's research staff has around 1,000 people, about half of whom are economists. Of these 500 economists, approximately 250 are at the Board of Governors, 100 are at the Federal Reserve Bank of New York, and the remainder are at the other Federal Reserve banks. What do all these economists do?

The most important task of the Fed's economists is to follow the incoming data from government agencies and private sector organizations on the economy and provide guidance to the policymakers on where the economy may be heading and what the impact of monetary policy actions on the economy might be. Before each FOMC meeting, the research staff at each Federal Reserve bank briefs its president and the senior management of the bank on its forecast for the U.S. economy and the issues that are likely to be discussed at the meeting. The research staff also provides briefing materials or a formal briefing on the economic outlook for the bank's region, something that each president discusses at the FOMC meeting. Meanwhile, at the Board of Governors, economists maintain a large econometric model (a model whose equations are estimated with statistical procedures) that helps them produce their forecasts of the national economy, and they, too, brief the governors on the national economic outlook.

The research staffers at the banks and the board also provide support for the bank supervisory staff, tracking developments in the banking sector and other financial markets and institutions and providing bank examiners with technical advice that they might need in the course of their examinations. Because the Board of Governors has to decide on whether to approve bank mergers, the research staff at both the board and the bank in whose district the merger is to take place prepare information on what effect the proposed merger might have on the competitive environment. To assure compliance with the Community Reinvestment Act, economists also analyze a bank's performance in its lending activities in different communities.

Because of the increased influence of developments in foreign countries on the U.S. economy, the members of the research staff, particularly at the New York Fed and the Board, produce reports on the major foreign economies. They also conduct research on developments in the foreign exchange market because of its growing importance in the monetary policy process and to support the activities of the foreign exchange desk. Economists help support the operation of the open market desk by projecting reserve growth and the growth of the monetary aggregates.

Staff economists also engage in basic research on the effects of monetary policy on output and inflation, developments in the labor markets, international trade, international capital markets, banking and other financial institutions, financial markets, and the regional economy, among other topics. This research is published widely in academic journals and in Reserve bank publications. (Federal Reserve bank reviews are a good source of supplemental material for money and banking students.)

Another important activity of the research staff primarily at the Reserve banks is in the public education area. Staff economists are called on frequently to make presentations to the board of directors at their banks or to make speeches to the public in their district.

presides as the chairman of the FOMC. Even though only the presidents of five of the Federal Reserve banks are voting members of the FOMC, the other seven presidents of the district banks attend FOMC meetings and participate in discussions. Hence they have some input into the committee's decisions.

Because open market operations are the most important policy tool that the Fed has for controlling the money supply, the FOMC is necessarily the focal point for policymaking in the Federal Reserve System. Although reserve requirements and the discount rate are not actually set by the FOMC, decisions in regard to these policy tools are effectively made there, and this is why Figure 1 has dashed lines indicating that the FOMC "advises" on the setting of reserve requirements and the discount rate. The FOMC does not actually carry out securities purchases or sales. Instead, it issues directives to the trading desk at the Federal Reserve Bank of New York, where the manager for domestic open market operations supervises a roomful of people who execute the purchases and sales of the government or agency securities. The manager communicates daily with the FOMC members and their staffs concerning the activities of the trading desk.

The FOMC Meeting

The FOMC meeting takes place in the boardroom on the second floor of the main building of the Board of Governors in Washington, D.C. The seven governors and the twelve Reserve Bank presidents, along with the secretary of the FOMC, the Board's director of the Research and Statistics Division and his deputy, and the directors of the Monetary Affairs and International Finance Divisions, sit around a massive conference table. Although only five of the Reserve Bank presidents have voting rights on the FOMC at any given time, all actively participate in the deliberations. Seated around the sides of the room are the directors of research at each of the Reserve banks and other senior board and Reserve Bank officials, who, by tradition, do not speak at the meeting.

Except for the meetings prior to the February and July testimony by the chairman of the Board of Governors before Congress, the meeting starts on Tuesday at 9:00 a.m. sharp with a quick approval of the minutes of the previous meeting of the FOMC. The first substantive agenda item is the report by the manager of system open market operations on foreign currency and domestic open market operations and other issues related to these topics. After the governors and Reserve Bank presidents finish asking questions and discussing these reports, a vote is taken to ratify them.

The next stage in the meeting is a presentation of the Board staff's national economic forecast, referred to as the "green book" forecast (see the Inside the Fed box, "Green, Blue, and Beige"), by the director of the Research and Statistics Division at the board. After the governors and Reserve Bank presidents have queried the division director about the forecast, the *go-round* occurs: Each bank president presents an overview of economic conditions in his or her district and the bank's assessment of the national outlook, and each governor, except for the chairman, gives a view of the national outlook. By tradition, remarks avoid the topic of monetary policy at this time.

After a coffee break, everyone returns to the boardroom and the agenda turns to current monetary policy and the domestic policy directive. The Board's director of the Monetary Affairs Division then leads off the discussion by outlining the different scenarios for monetary policy actions outlined in the "blue book" (see the aforementioned Inside the Fed box) and may describe an issue relating to how monetary policy should be conducted. After a question-and-answer period, the chairman (currently Ben Bernanke) sets the stage for the following discussion by presenting his views on the state of the economy and then typically makes a recommendation for what monetary policy action should be taken. Then each of the FOMC members as well as the nonvoting bank presidents expresses his or her views on monetary policy, and the chairman summarizes the discussion and proposes specific wording for the directive on the federal funds rate target transmitted to the open market desk. The secretary of the FOMC formally reads the proposed statement, and the members of the FOMC vote.[2]

[2]The decisions expressed in the directive may not be unanimous, and the dissenting views are made public. However, except in rare cases, the chairman's vote is always on the winning side.

Inside the Fed Green, Blue, and Beige: What Do These Colors Mean at the Fed?

Three research documents play an important role in the monetary policy process and at Federal Open Market Committee meetings. The national forecast for the next two years, generated by the Federal Reserve Board of Governors' Research and Statistics Division, is placed between green covers and is thus known as the "green book." It is provided to all who attend the FOMC meeting. The "blue book," in blue covers, also provided to all participants at the FOMC meeting, contains the projections for the monetary aggregates prepared by the Monetary Affairs Division at the Board of Governors and typically presents three alternative scenarios for the stance of monetary policy (labeled A, B, and C). The "beige book," with beige covers, is produced by the Reserve banks and details evidence gleaned either from surveys or from talks with key businesses and financial institutions on the state of the economy in each of the Federal Reserve districts. This is the only one of the three books that is distributed publicly, and it often receives a lot of attention in the press.

Then there is an informal buffet lunch, and while eating, the participants hear a presentation on the latest developments in Congress on banking legislation and other legislation relevant to the Federal Reserve. Around 2:15 p.m., the meeting breaks up and a public announcement is made about the outcome of the meeting: whether the federal funds rate target and discount rate have been raised, lowered, or left unchanged, and an assessment of the "balance of risks" in the future, whether toward higher inflation or toward a weaker economy.[3] The postmeeting announcement is an innovation initiated in 1994. Before then, no such announcement was made, and the markets had to guess what policy action was taken. The decision to announce this information was a step in the direction of greater openness by the Fed.

Why the Chairman of the Board of Governors Really Runs the Show

At first glance, the chairman of the Board of Governors is just one of twelve voting members of the FOMC and has no legal authority to exercise control over this body. So why does the media pay so much attention to every word the chairman speaks? Does the chairman really call the shots at the Fed? And if so, why does the chairman have so much power?

The chairman does indeed run the show. He is the spokesperson for the Fed and negotiates with Congress and the president of the United States. He also exercises control by setting the agenda of Board and FOMC meetings. For example, the fact that the agenda at the FOMC has the chairman speak and vote first about monetary policy enables him to have greater influence over what the policy action will be. The chairman also influences the Board through the force of stature and personality. Chairmen of the

[3]The meetings before the February and July chairman's testimony before Congress, in which the *Monetary Report to Congress* is presented, have a somewhat different format. Rather than start Tuesday morning at 9:00 a.m. like the other meetings, they start in the afternoon on Tuesday and go over to Wednesday, with the usual announcement around 2:15 p.m. These longer meetings consider the longer-term economic outlook as well as the current conduct of open market operations.

Board of Governors (including Marriner S. Eccles, William McChesney Martin, Jr., Arthur Burns, Paul A. Volcker, and Alan Greenspan) have typically had strong personalities and have wielded great power.

The chairman also exercises power by supervising the Board's staff of professional economists and advisers. Because the staff gathers information for the Board and conducts the analyses that the Board uses in its decisions, it has some influence over monetary policy. In addition, in the past, several appointments to the Board itself have come from within the ranks of its professional staff, making the chairman's influence even farther-reaching and longer-lasting than a four-year term.

HOW INDEPENDENT IS THE FED?

When we look, in the next four chapters, at how the Federal Reserve conducts monetary policy, we will want to know why it decides to take certain policy actions but not others. To understand its actions, we must understand the incentives that motivate the Fed's behavior. How free is the Fed from presidential and congressional pressures? Do economic, bureaucratic, or political considerations guide it? Is the Fed truly independent of outside pressures?

Stanley Fischer, who was a professor at MIT and then the Deputy Managing Director of the International Monetary Fund, has defined two different types of independence of central banks: **instrument independence**, the ability of the central bank to set monetary policy instruments, and **goal independence**, the ability of the central bank to set the goals of monetary policy. The Federal Reserve has both types of independence and is remarkably free of the political pressures that influence other government agencies. Not only are the members of the Board of Governors appointed for a fourteen-year term (and so cannot be ousted from office), but also the term is technically not renewable, eliminating some of the incentive for the governors to curry favor with the president and Congress.

Probably even more important to its independence from the whims of Congress is the Fed's independent and substantial source of revenue from its holdings of securities and, to a lesser extent, from its loans to banks. In recent years, for example, the Fed has had net earnings after expenses of around $18 billion per year—not a bad living if you can find it! Because it returns the bulk of these earnings to the Treasury, it does not get rich from its activities, but this income gives the Fed an important advantage over other government agencies: It is not subject to the appropriations process usually controlled by Congress. Indeed, the General Accounting Office, the auditing agency of the federal government, cannot audit the monetary policy or foreign exchange market functions of the Federal Reserve. Because the power to control the purse strings is usually synonymous with the power of overall control, this feature of the Federal Reserve System contributes to its independence more than any other factor.

Yet the Federal Reserve is still subject to the influence of Congress, because the legislation that structures it is written by Congress and is subject to change at any time. When legislators are upset with the Fed's conduct of monetary policy, they frequently threaten to take control of the Fed's finances and force it to submit a budget request like other government agencies. A recent example was the call by Senators Dorgan and Reid in 1996 for Congress to have budgetary authority over the nonmonetary activities of the Federal Reserve. This is a powerful club to wield, and it certainly has some effect in keeping the Fed from straying too far from congressional wishes.

Congress has also passed legislation to make the Federal Reserve more accountable for its actions. Under the Federal Reserve Act, the Federal Reserve is required to issue a *Moneary Policy Report to the Congress* semiannually, with accompanying testimony by the chairman of the Board of Governors, to explain how the conduct of monetary policy is consistent with the objectives given by the Federal Reserve Act.

The president can also influence the Federal Reserve. Because congressional legislation can affect the Fed directly or affect its ability to conduct monetary policy, the president can be a powerful ally through his influence on Congress. Second, although ostensibly a president might be able to appoint only one or two members to the Board of Governors during each presidential term, in actual practice the president appoints members far more often. One reason is that most governors do not serve out a full fourteen-year term. (Governors' salaries are substantially below what they can earn in the private sector, thus providing an incentive for them to take private sector jobs before their term expires.) In addition, the president is able to appoint a new chairman of the Board of Governors every four years, and a chairman who is not reappointed is expected to resign from the board so that a new member can be appointed.

The power that the president enjoys through his appointments to the Board of Governors is limited, however. Because the term of the chairman is not necessarily concurrent with that of the president, a president may have to deal with a chairman of the Board of Governors appointed by a previous administration. Alan Greenspan, for example, was appointed chairman in 1987 by President Ronald Reagan and was reappointed to another term by a Republican president, George H. W. Bush, in 1992. When Bill Clinton, a Democrat, became president in 1993, Greenspan had several years left to his term. Clinton was put under tremendous pressure to reappoint Greenspan when his term expired and did so in 1996 and again in 2000, even though Greenspan is a Republican.[4] George W. Bush, a Republican, then reappointed Greenspan in 2004.

You can see that the Federal Reserve has extraordinary independence for a government agency and is one of the most independent central banks in the world. Nonetheless, the Fed is not free from political pressures. Indeed, to understand the Fed's behavior, we must recognize that public support for the actions of the Federal Reserve plays a very important role.[5]

STRUCTURE AND INDEPENDENCE OF THE EUROPEAN CENTRAL BANK

Until recently, the Federal Reserve had no rivals in terms of its importance in the central banking world. However, this situation changed in January 1999 with the start-up of the European Central Bank (ECB) and European System of Central Banks (ESCB), which now conducts monetary policy for countries that are members of the European Monetary Union. These countries, taken together, have a population that exceeds that

[4]Similarly, William McChesney Martin, Jr., the chairman from 1951 to 1970, was appointed by President Truman (Dem.) but was reappointed by Presidents Eisenhower (Rep.), Kennedy (Dem.), Johnson (Dem.), and Nixon (Rep.). Also Paul Volcker, the chairman from 1979 to 1987, was appointed by President Carter (Dem.) but was reappointed by President Reagan (Rep.).

[5]An inside view of how the Fed interacts with the public and the politicians can be found in Bob Woodward, *Maestro: Greenspan's Fed and the American Boom* (New York: Simon and Schuster, 2000).

in the United States and a GDP comparable to that of the United States. The Maastricht Treaty, which established the ECB and ESCB, patterned these institutions after the Federal Reserve, in that central banks for each country (referred to as *National Central Banks*, or *NCBs*) have a similar role to that of the Federal Reserve Banks. The European Central Bank, which is housed in Frankfurt, Germany, has an Executive Board that is similar in structure to the Board of Governors of the Federal Reserve; it is made up of the president, the vice-president, and four other members, who are appointed to eight-year, nonrenewable terms. The Governing Council, which comprises the Executive Board and the presidents of the National Central Banks, is similar to the FOMC and makes the decisions on monetary policy. While the presidents of the National Central Banks are appointed by their countries' governments, the members of the Executive Board are appointed by a committee consisting of the heads of state of all the countries that are part of the European Monetary Union.

Differences Between the European System of Central Banks and the Federal Reserve System

In the popular press, the European System of Central Banks is usually referred to as the European Central Bank (ECB), even though it would be more accurate to refer to it as the *Eurosystem*, just as it would be more accurate to refer to the Federal Reserve System rather than the Fed. Although the structure of the Eurosystem is similar to that of the Federal Reserve System, some important differences distinguish the two. First, the budgets of the Federal Reserve Banks are controlled by the Board of Governors, while the National Central Banks control their own budgets *and* the budget of the ECB in Frankfurt. The ECB in the Eurosystem therefore has less power than does the Board of Governors in the Federal Reserve System. Second, the monetary operations of the Eurosystem are conducted by the National Central Banks in each country, so monetary operations are not centralized as they are in the Federal Reserve System. Third, in contrast to the Federal Reserve, the ECB is not involved in supervision and regulation of financial institutions; these tasks are left to the individual countries in the European Monetary Union.

Governing Council

Just as there is a focus on meetings of the FOMC in the United States, there is a similar focus in Europe on meetings of the Governing Council, which meets monthly at the ECB in Frankfurt to make decisions on monetary policy. Currently, twelve countries are members of the European Monetary Union, and the head of each of the twelve National Central Banks has one vote in the Governing Council; each of the six Executive Board Members also has one vote. In contrast to FOMC meeting, which staff from both the Board of Governors and individual Federal Reserve Banks attend, only the eighteen members of the Governing Council attend the meetings, with no staff present.

The Governing Council has decided that although its members have the legal right to vote, no formal vote will actually be taken; instead, the Council operates by consensus. One reason the Governing Council has decided not to take votes is because of worries that the casting of individual votes might lead the heads of National Central Banks to support a monetary policy that would be appropriate for their individual countries, but not necessarily for the countries in the European Monetary Union as a whole. This problem is less severe for the Federal Reserve: Although Federal Reserve Bank presidents do live in different regions of the country, all have the same nationality and are more likely to take a national view in monetary policy decisions rather than a regional view.

Just as the Federal Reserve releases the FOMC's decision on the setting of the policy interest rate (the federal funds rate) immediately after the meeting is over, the ECB does the same after the Governing Council meeting concludes (announcing the target for a similar short-term interest rate for interbank loans). However, whereas the Fed simply releases a statement about the setting of the monetary policy instruments, the ECB goes further by having a press conference in which the president and vice-president of the ECB take questions from the news media. Holding such a press conference so soon after the meeting is tricky because it requires the president and vice-president to be quick on their feet in dealing with the press. The first president of the ECB, Willem F. Duisenberg, put his foot in his mouth at some of these press conferences, and the ECB came under some sharp criticism. His successor, Jean-Claude Trichet, a more successful communicator, has encountered fewer problems in this regard.

Although currently only twelve countries in the European Monetary Union have representation on the Governing Council, this situation is likely to change in the future. Three countries in the European Community already qualify for entering the European Monetary Union: the United Kingdom, Sweden, and Denmark. Ten other countries entered the European Community in 2004 (Cyprus, the Czech Republic, Estonia, Hungary, Latvia, Lithuania, Malta, Poland, Slovakia, and Slovenia), and many of them plan to enter the European Monetary Union once they qualify, which will not be too far in the distant future. The possibly expansion of membership in the Eurosystem presents a particular dilemma. The current size of the Governing Council (eighteen voting members) is substantially larger than the FOMC (twelve voting members). Many commentators have wondered whether the Governing Council is already too unwieldy—a situation that would get considerably worse as more countries join the European Monetary Union. To deal with this potential problem, the Governing Council has decided on a complex system of rotation, somewhat like that for the FOMC, in which National Central Banks from the larger countries will vote more often than National Central Banks from the smaller countries.

How Independent Is the ECB?

Although the Federal Reserve is a highly independent central bank, the Maastricht Treaty, which established the Eurosystem, has made the latter the most independent central bank in the world. Like the Board of Governors, the members of the Executive Board have long terms (eight years), while heads of National Central Banks are required to have terms at least five years long. Like the Fed, the Eurosystem determines its own budget, and the governments of the member countries are not allowed to issue instructions to the ECB. These elements of the Maatricht Treaty make the ECB highly independent.

The Maastricht Treaty specifies that the overriding, long-term goal of the ECB is price stability, which means that the goal for the Eurosystem is more clearly specified than it is for the Federal Reserve System. However, the Maastricht Treaty did not specify exactly what "price stability" means. The Eurosystem has defined the quantitative goal for monetary policy to be an inflation rate slightly less than 2%, so from this perspective, the ECB is slightly less goal-independent than the Fed. The Eurosystem is, however, much more goal-independent than the Federal Reserve System in another way: The Eurosystem's charter cannot be changed by legislation; it can be changed only by revision of the Maastricht Treaty—a difficult process because *all* signatories to the treaty must agree to accept any proposed change.

STRUCTURE AND INDEPENDENCE OF OTHER FOREIGN CENTRAL BANKS

Here we examine the structure and degree of independence of three other important foreign central banks: the Bank of Canada, the Bank of England, and the Bank of Japan.

Bank of Canada

Canada was late in establishing a central bank: The Bank of Canada was founded in 1934. Its directors are appointed by the government to three-year terms, and they appoint the governor, who has a seven-year term. A governing council, consisting of the four deputy governors and the governor, is the policymaking body comparable to the FOMC that makes decisions about monetary policy.

The Bank Act was amended in 1967 to give the ultimate responsibility for monetary policy to the government. So on paper, the Bank of Canada is not as instrument-independent as the Federal Reserve. In practice, however, the Bank of Canada does essentially control monetary policy. In the event of a disagreement between the bank and the government, the minister of finance can issue a directive that the bank must follow. However, because the directive must be in writing and specific and applicable for a specified period, it is unlikely that such a directive would be issued, and none has been to date. The goal for monetary policy, a target for inflation, is set jointly by the Bank of Canada and the government, so the Bank of Canada has less goal independence than the Fed.

Bank of England

Founded in 1694, the Bank of England is one of the oldest central banks. The Bank Act of 1946 gave the government statutory authority over the Bank of England. The Court (equivalent to a board of directors) of the Bank of England is made up of the governor and two deputy governors, who are appointed for five-year terms, and sixteen non-executive directors, who are appointed for three-year terms.

Until 1997, the Bank of England was the least independent of the central banks examined in this chapter because the decision to raise or lower interest rates resided not within the Bank of England but with the chancellor of the Exchequer (the equivalent of the U.S. Secretary of the Treasury). All of this changed when the current Labour government came to power in May 1997. At this time, the chancellor of the Exchequer, Gordon Brown, made a surprise announcement that the Bank of England would henceforth have the power to set interest rates. However, the Bank was not granted total instrument independence: The government can overrule the Bank and set rates "in extreme economic circumstances" and "for a limited period." Nonetheless, as in Canada, because overruling the Bank would be so public and is supposed to occur only in highly unusual circumstances and for a limited time, it is likely to be a rare occurrence.

Because the United Kingdom is not a member of the European Monetary Union, the Bank of England makes its monetary policy decisions independently from the European Central Bank. The decision to set interest rates resides in the Monetary Policy Committee, made up of the governor, two deputy governors, two members appointed by the governor after consultation with the chancellor (normally central bank officials), plus four outside economic experts appointed by the chancellor. (Surprisingly, two of the four outside experts initially appointed to this committee were not British citizens—one was Dutch and the other American, although both were residents of the United Kingdom.) The inflation target for the Bank of England is set by the Chancellor of the Exchequer, so the Bank of England is also less goal-independent than the Fed.

Bank of Japan

The Bank of Japan (Nippon Ginko) was founded in 1882 during the Meiji Restoration. Monetary policy is determined by the Policy Board, which is composed of the governor; two vice-governors; and six outside members appointed by the cabinet and approved by the parliament, all of whom serve for five-year terms.

Until recently, the Bank of Japan was not formally independent of the government, with the ultimate power residing with the Ministry of Finance. However, the Bank of Japan Law, which took effect in April 1998 and was the first major change in the powers of the Bank of Japan in 55 years, changed this situation. In addition to stipulating that the objective of monetary policy is to attain price stability, the law granted greater instrument and goal independence to the Bank of Japan. Before this, the government had two voting members on the Policy Board, one from the Ministry of Finance and the other from the Economic Planning Agency. Now the government may send two representatives from these agencies to board meetings, but they no longer have voting rights, although they do have the ability to request delays in monetary policy decisions. In addition, the Ministry of Finance lost its authority to oversee many of the operations of the Bank of Japan, particularly the right to dismiss senior officials. However, the Ministry of Finance continues to have control over the part of the Bank's budget that is unrelated to monetary policy, which might limit its independence to some extent.

The Trend Toward Greater Independence

As our survey of the structure and independence of the major central banks indicates, in recent years we have been seeing a remarkable trend toward increasing independence. It used to be that the Federal Reserve was substantially more independent than almost all other central banks, with the exception of those in Germany and Switzerland. Now the newly established European Central Bank is far more independent than the Fed, and greater independence has been granted to central banks like the Bank of England and the Bank of Japan, putting them more on a par with the Fed, as well as to central banks in such diverse countries as New Zealand, Sweden, and the euro nations. Both theory and experience suggest that more independent central banks produce better monetary policy, thus providing an impetus for this trend.

EXPLAINING CENTRAL BANK BEHAVIOR

One view of government bureaucratic behavior is that bureaucracies serve the public interest (this is the *public interest view*). Yet some economists have developed a theory of bureaucratic behavior that suggests other factors that influence how bureaucracies operate. The *theory of bureaucratic behavior* suggests that the objective of a bureaucracy is to maximize its own welfare, just as a consumer's behavior is motivated by the maximization of personal welfare and a firm's behavior is motivated by the maximization of profits. The welfare of a bureaucracy is related to its power and prestige. Thus this theory

Inside the Fed **Federal Reserve Transparency**

As the theory of bureaucratic behavior predicts, the Fed has incentives to hide its actions from the public and from politicians to avoid conflicts with them. In the past, this motivation led to a penchant for secrecy in the Fed, about which one former Fed official remarked that "a lot of staffers would concede that [secrecy] is designed to shield the Fed from political oversight."* For example, the Fed pursued an active defense of delaying its release of FOMC directives to Congress and the public. However, as we have seen, in 1994, it began to reveal the FOMC directive immediately after each FOMC meeting. In 1999, it also began to immediately announce the "bias" toward which direction monetary policy was likely to go, later expressed as the balance of risks in the economy. In 2002, the Fed started to report the roll call vote on the federal funds rate target taken at the FOMC meeting. In December 2004, it moved up the release date of the minutes of FOMC meetings to three weeks after the meeting from six weeks, its previous policy. Obviously, the Fed has increased its transparency in recent years.

In contrast to the Fed, the European Central Bank has decided it will not make the minutes of the Governing Council meetings public for twenty years. In this regard the European Central Bank is much less transparent than the Fed. Yet even today, the Fed is not fully transparent: It does not publish its forecasts of the economy or its target for the inflation rate, as some other central banks do.

*Quoted in "Monetary Zeal: How the Federal Reserve Under Volcker Finally Slowed Down Inflation," *Wall Street Journal*, December 7, 1984, p. 23.

suggests that an important factor affecting a central bank's behavior is its attempt to increase its power and prestige.

What predictions does this view of a central bank like the Fed suggest? One is that the Federal Reserve will fight vigorously to preserve its autonomy, a prediction verified time and time again as the Fed has continually counterattacked congressional attempts to control its budget. In fact, it is extraordinary how effectively the Fed has been able to mobilize a lobby of bankers and business people to preserve its independence when threatened.

Another prediction is that the Federal Reserve will try to avoid conflict with powerful groups that might threaten to curtail its power and reduce its autonomy. The Fed's behavior may take several forms. One possible factor explaining why the Fed is sometimes slow to increase interest rates and so smooths out their fluctuations is that it wishes to avoid a conflict with the president and Congress over increases in interest rates. The desire to avoid conflict with Congress and the president may also explain why in the past the Fed was not at all transparent about its actions and is still not fully transparent (see the Inside the Fed box, "Federal Reserve Transparency").

The desire of the Fed to hold as much power as possible also explains why it vigorously pursued a campaign to gain control over more banks. The campaign culminated in legislation that expanded jurisdiction of the Fed's reserve requirements to *all* banks (not just the member commercial banks) by 1987.

The theory of bureaucratic behavior seems applicable to the Federal Reserve's actions, but we must recognize that this view of the Fed as being solely concerned with its own self-interest is too extreme. Maximizing one's welfare does not rule out altruism. (You might give generously to a charity because it makes you feel good about yourself, but in the process you are helping a worthy cause.) The Fed is surely concerned that it conduct monetary policy in the public interest. However, much uncertainty and disagreement exist over what monetary policy should be.[6] When it is unclear what is in the public interest, other motives may influence the Fed's behavior. In these situations, the theory of bureaucratic behavior may be a useful guide to predicting what motivates the Fed and other central banks.

SHOULD THE FED BE INDEPENDENT?

As we have seen, the Federal Reserve is probably the most independent government agency in the United States. Every few years, the question arises in Congress whether the independence of the Fed should be curtailed. Politicians who strongly oppose a Fed policy often want to bring it under their supervision so as to impose a policy more to their liking. Should the Fed be independent, or would we be better off with a central bank under the control of the president or Congress?

The Case for Independence

The strongest argument for an independent Federal Reserve rests on the view that subjecting the Fed to more political pressures would impart an inflationary bias to monetary policy. In the view of many observers, politicians in a democratic society are shortsighted because they are driven by the need to win their next election. With this as the primary goal, they are unlikely to focus on long-run objectives, such as promoting a stable price level. Instead, they will seek short-run solutions to problems, such as high unemployment and high interest rates, even if the short-run solutions have undesirable long-run consequences. For example, we saw in Chapter 5 that high money growth might lead initially to a drop in interest rates but might cause an increase later as inflation heats up. Would a Federal Reserve under the control of Congress or the president be more likely to pursue a policy of excessive money growth when interest rates are high, even though it would eventually lead to inflation and even higher interest rates in the future? The advocates of an independent Federal Reserve say yes. They believe that a politically insulated Fed is more likely to be concerned with long-run objectives and thus be a defender of a sound dollar and a stable price level.

A variation on the preceding argument is that the political process in America leads to the **political business cycle**, in which just before an election, expansionary policies are pursued to lower unemployment and interest rates. After the election, the bad effects of these policies—high inflation and high interest rates—come home to roost, requiring contractionary policies that politicians hope the public will forget before the next election. There is some evidence that such a political business cycle exists in the United States, and a Federal Reserve under the control of Congress or the president might make the cycle even more pronounced.

Putting the Fed under the control of the president (making it more subject to influence by the Treasury) is also considered dangerous because the Fed can be used to facil-

---

[6]One example of the uncertainty over how best to conduct monetary policy was discussed in Chapter 3: Economists are not sure how to measure money. So even if economists agreed that controlling the quantity of money is the appropriate way to conduct monetary policy (a controversial position, as we will see in later chapters), the Fed cannot be sure which monetary aggregate it should control.

itate Treasury financing of large budget deficits by its purchases of Treasury bonds.[7] Treasury pressure on the Fed to "help out" might lead to more inflation in the economy. An independent Fed is better able to resist this pressure from the Treasury.

Another argument for Fed independence is that control of monetary policy is too important to leave to politicians, a group that has repeatedly demonstrated a lack of expertise at making hard decisions on issues of great economic importance, such as reducing the budget deficit or reforming the banking system. Another way to state this argument is in terms of the principal-agent problem discussed in Chapters 8 and 11. Both the Federal Reserve and politicians are agents of the public (the principals), and as we have seen, both politicians and the Fed have incentives to act in their own interest rather than in the interest of the public. The argument supporting Federal Reserve independence is that the principal-agent problem is worse for politicians than for the Fed because politicians have fewer incentives to act in the public interest.

Indeed, some politicians may prefer to have an independent Fed, which can be used as a public "whipping boy" to take some of the heat off their backs. It is possible that a politician who in private opposes an inflationary monetary policy will be forced to support such a policy in public for fear of not being reelected. An independent Fed can pursue policies that are politically unpopular yet in the public interest.

The Case Against Independence

Proponents of a Fed under the control of the president or Congress argue that it is undemocratic to have monetary policy (which affects almost everyone in the economy) controlled by an elite group that is responsible to no one. The current lack of accountability of the Federal Reserve has serious consequences: If the Fed performs badly, there is no provision for replacing members (as there is with politicians). True, the Fed needs to pursue long-run objectives, but elected officials of Congress vote on long-run issues also (foreign policy, for example). If we push the argument further that policy is always performed better by elite groups like the Fed, we end up with such conclusions as the Joint Chiefs of Staff should determine military budgets or the IRS should set tax policies with no oversight from the president or Congress. Would you advocate this degree of independence for the Joint Chiefs or the IRS?

The public holds the president and Congress responsible for the economic well-being of the country, yet they lack control over the government agency that may well be the most important factor in determining the health of the economy. In addition, to achieve a cohesive program that will promote economic stability, monetary policy must be coordinated with fiscal policy (management of government spending and taxation). Only by placing monetary policy under the control of the politicians who also control fiscal policy can these two policies be prevented from working at cross-purposes.

Another argument against Federal Reserve independence is that an independent Fed has not always used its freedom successfully. The Fed failed miserably in its stated role as lender of last resort during the Great Depression, and its independence certainly didn't prevent it from pursuing an overly expansionary monetary policy in the 1960s and 1970s that contributed to rapid inflation in this period.

---

[7]The Federal Reserve Act prohibited the Fed from buying Treasury bonds directly from the Treasury (except to roll over maturing securities); instead, the Fed buys Treasury bonds on the open market. One possible reason for this prohibition is consistent with the foregoing argument: The Fed would find it harder to facilitate Treasury financing of large budget deficits.

Our earlier discussion also suggests that the Federal Reserve is not immune from political pressures.[8] Its independence may encourage it to pursue a course of narrow self-interest rather than the public interest.

There is yet no consensus on whether Federal Reserve independence is a good thing, although public support for independence of the central bank seems to have been growing in both the United States and abroad. As you might expect, people who like the Fed's policies are more likely to support its independence, while those who dislike its policies advocate a less independent Fed.

Central Bank Independence and Macroeconomic Performance Throughout The World

We have seen that advocates of an independent central bank believe that macroeconomic performance will be improved by making the central bank more independent. Recent research seems to support this conjecture: When central banks are ranked from least independent to most independent, inflation performance is found to be the best for countries with the most independent central banks.[9] Although a more independent central bank appears to lead to a lower inflation rate, this is not achieved at the expense of poorer real economic performance. Countries with independent central banks are no more likely to have high unemployment or greater output fluctuations than countries with less independent central banks.

---

[8] For evidence on this issue, see Robert E. Weintraub, "Congressional Supervision of Monetary Policy," *Journal of Monetary Economics* 4 (1978): 341–362. Some economists suggest that lessening the independence of the Fed might even reduce the incentive for politically motivated monetary policy; see Milton Friedman, "Monetary Policy: Theory and Practice," *Journal of Money, Credit and Banking* 14 (1982): 98–118.

[9] Alberto Alesina and Lawrence H. Summers, "Central Bank Independence and Macroeconomic Performance: Some Comparative Evidence," *Journal of Money, Credit and Banking* 25 (1993): 151–162. However, Adam Posen, "Central Bank Independence and Disinflationary Credibility: A Missing Link," Federal Reserve Bank of New York Staff Report No. 1, May 1995, has cast some doubt on whether the causality runs from central bank independence to improved inflation performance.

SUMMARY

1. The Federal Reserve System was created in 1913 to lessen the frequency of bank panics. Because of public hostility to central banks and the centralization of power, the Federal Reserve System was created with many checks and balances to diffuse power.
2. The formal structure of the Federal Reserve System consists of twelve regional Federal Reserve banks, around 2,800 member commercial banks, the Board of Governors of the Federal Reserve System, the Federal Open Market Committee (FOMC), and the Federal Advisory Council.
3. Although on paper the Federal Reserve System appears to be decentralized, in practice it has come to function as a unified central bank controlled by the Board of Governors, especially the board's chairman.
4. The Federal Reserve is more independent than most agencies of the U.S. government, but it is still subject to political pressures because the legislation that structures the Fed is written by Congress and can be changed at any time.
5. The European System of Central Banks has a similar structure to the Federal Reserve System, with each

member country having a National Central Bank, and an Executive Board of the European Central Bank being located in Frankfurt, Germany. The Governing Council, which is made up of the six members of the Executive Board (which includes the president of the European Central Bank) and the presidents of the National Central Banks, makes the decisions on monetary policy. The Eurosystem, which was established under the terms of the Maastricht Treaty, is even more independent than the Federal Reserve System because its charter cannot be changed by legislation. Indeed, it is the most independent central bank in the world.

6. There has been a remarkable trend toward increasing independence of central banks throughout the world. Greater independence has been granted to central banks such as the Bank of England and the Bank of Japan in recent years, as well as to other central banks in such diverse countries as New Zealand and Sweden. Both theory and experience suggest that more independent central banks produce better monetary policy.

7. The theory of bureaucratic behavior suggest that one factor driving central banks' behavior might be an attempt to increase their power and prestige. This view explains many central bank actions, although central banks may also act in the public interest.

8. The case for an independent Federal Reserve rests on the view that curtailing the Fed's independence and subjecting it to more political pressures would impart an inflationary bias to monetary policy. An independent Fed can afford to take the long view and not respond to short-run problems that will result in expansionary monetary policy and a political business cycle. The case against an independent Fed holds that it is undemocratic to have monetary policy (so important to the public) controlled by an elite that is not accountable to the public. An independent Fed also makes the coordination of monetary and fiscal policy difficult.

KEY TERMS

Board of Governors of the Federal Reserve System, p. 384

Federal Open Market Committee (FOMC), p. 384

Federal Reserve banks, p. 384

goal independence, p. 393

instrument independence, p. 393

open market operations, p. 388

political business cycle, p. 400

QUESTIONS AND PROBLEMS

Questions marked with an asterisk are answered at the end of the book in an appendix, "Answers to Selected Questions and Problems." Questions marked with a blue circle indicate the question is available in MyEconLab at www.myeconlab.com/mishkin.

*1. Why was the Federal Reserve System set up with twelve regional Federal Reserve banks rather than one central bank, as in other countries?

2. What political realities might explain why the Federal Reserve Act of 1913 placed two Federal Reserve banks in Missouri?

*3. "The Federal Reserve System resembles the U.S. Constitution in that it was designed with many checks and balances." Discuss.

4. In what ways can the regional Federal Reserve banks influence the conduct of monetary policy?

*5. Which entities in the Federal Reserve System control the discount rate? Reserve requirements? Open market operations?

6. Do you think that the fourteen-year nonrenewable terms for governors effectively insulate the Board of Governors from political pressure?

*7. Compare the structure and independence of the Federal Reserve System and the European System of Central Banks.

8. The Fed is the most independent of all U.S. government agencies. What is the main difference between it and other government agencies that explains the Fed's greater independence?

*9. What is the primary tool that Congress uses to exercise some control over the Fed?

10. In the 1960s and 1970s, the Federal Reserve System lost member banks at a rapid rate. How can the theory of bureaucratic behavior explain the Fed's campaign for legislation to require all commercial banks to become members? Was the Fed successful in this campaign?

*11. "The theory of bureaucratic behavior indicates that the Fed never operates in the public interest." Is this statement true, false, or uncertain? Explain your answer.

12. Why might eliminating the Fed's independence lead to a more pronounced political business cycle?

*13. "The independence of the Fed leaves it completely unaccountable for its actions." Is this statement true, false, or uncertain? Explain your answer.

14. "The independence of the Fed has meant that it takes the long view and not the short view." Is this statement true, false, or uncertain? Explain your answer.

*15. The Fed promotes secrecy by not releasing the minutes of the FOMC meetings to Congress or the public immediately. Discuss the pros and cons of this policy.

WEB EXERCISES

1. Go to www.federalreserve.gov/general.htm and click on the link to general information. Choose "Structure of the Federal Reserve." According to the Federal Reserve, what is the most important responsibility of the Board of Governors?

2. Go to the above site and click on "Monetary Policy" to find the beige book. According to the summary of the most recently published book, is the economy weakening or strengthening?

WEB REFERENCES

www.federalreserve.gov/pubs/frseries/frseri.htm

Information on the structure of the Federal Reserve System.

www.federalreserve.gov/otherfrb.htm

Addresses and phone numbers of Federal Reserve Banks, branches, and RCPCs and links to the main pages of the 12 reserve banks and Board of Governors.

www.federalreserve.gov/bios/boardmembership.htm

Lists all the members of the Board of Governors of the Federal Reserve since its inception.

www.federalreserve.gov/fomc

Find general information on the FOMC; its schedule of meetings, statements, minutes, and transcripts; information on its members; and the "beige book."

www.ecb.int

The web site for the European Central Bank.

www.bank-banque-canada.ca/

The web site for the Bank of Canada.

www.bankofengland.co.uk/index.htm

The web site for the Bank of England.

www.boj.or.jp/en/index.htm

The web site for the Bank of Japan.

CHAPTER

16 Multiple Deposit Creation and the Money Supply Process

Preview

As we saw in Chapter 5 and will see in later chapters on monetary theory, movements in the money supply affect interest rates and the overall health of the economy and thus affect us all. Because of its far-reaching effects on economic activity, it is important to understand how the money supply is determined. Who controls it? What causes it to change? How might control of it be improved? In this and subsequent chapters, we answer these questions by providing a detailed description of the *money supply process*, the mechanism that determines the level of the money supply.

Because deposits at banks are by far the largest component of the money supply, understanding how these deposits are created is the first step in understanding the money supply process. This chapter provides an overview of how the banking system creates deposits, and describes the basic principles of the money supply, needed to understand later chapters.

FOUR PLAYERS IN THE MONEY SUPPLY PROCESS

The "cast of characters" in the money supply story is as follows:

1. The *central bank*—the government agency that oversees the banking system and is responsible for the conduct of monetary policy; in the United States, it is called the Federal Reserve System
2. *Banks* (depository institutions)—the financial intermediaries that accept deposits from individuals and institutions and make loans: commercial banks, savings and loan associations, mutual savings banks, and credit unions
3. *Depositors*—individuals and institutions that hold deposits in banks
4. *Borrowers* from banks—individuals and institutions that borrow from the depository institutions and institutions that issue bonds that are purchased by the depository institutions

Of the four players, the central bank—the Federal Reserve System—is the most important. The Fed's conduct of monetary policy involves actions that affect its balance sheet (holdings of assets and liabilities), to which we turn now.

THE FED'S BALANCE SHEET

The operation of the Fed and its monetary policy involve actions that affect its balance sheet, its holdings of assets and liabilities. Here we discuss a simplified balance sheet that includes just four items that are essential to our understanding of the money supply process.[1]

Federal Reserve System

Assets	Liabilities
Government securities	Currency in circulation
Discount loans	Reserves

Liabilities

The two liabilities on the balance sheet, currency in circulation and reserves, are often referred to as the *monetary liabilities* of the Fed. They are an important part of the money supply story, because increases in either or both will lead to an increase in the money supply (everything else being constant). The sum of the Fed's monetary liabilities (currency in circulation and reserves) and the U.S. Treasury's monetary liabilities (Treasury currency in circulation, primarily coins) is called the **monetary base**. When discussing the monetary base, we will focus only on the monetary liabilities of the Fed because the monetary liabilities of the Treasury account for less than 10% of the base.[2]

1. *Currency in circulation*. The Fed issues currency (those green-and-gray pieces of paper in your wallet that say "Federal Reserve Note" at the top). Currency in circulation is the amount of currency in the hands of the public. Currency held by depository institutions is also a liability of the Fed, but is counted as part of the reserves.

Federal Reserve notes are IOUs from the Fed to the bearer and are also liabilities, but unlike most, they promise to pay back the bearer solely with Federal Reserve notes; that is, they pay off IOUs with other IOUs. Accordingly, if you bring a $100 bill to the Federal Reserve and demand payment, you will receive two $50s, five $20s, ten $10s, or one hundred $1 bills.

People are more willing to accept IOUs from the Fed than from you or me because Federal Reserve notes are a recognized medium of exchange; that is, they are accepted as a means of payment and so function as money. Unfortunately, neither you nor I can convince people that our IOUs are worth anything more than the paper they are written on.[3]

---

[1]A detailed discussion of the Fed's balance sheet and the factors that affect the monetary base can be found in the appendix to this chapter, which you can find on this book's web site at www.aw.com/mishkin.

[2]It is also safe to ignore the Treasury's monetary liabilities when discussing the monetary base because the Treasury cannot actively supply its monetary liabilities to the economy due to legal restrictions.

[3]The currency item on our balance sheet refers only to currency *in circulation*—that is, the amount in the hands of the public. Currency that has been printed by the U.S. Bureau of Engraving and Printing is not automatically a liability of the Fed. For example, consider the importance of having $1 million of your own IOUs printed up. You give out $100 worth to other people and keep the other $999,900 in your pocket. The $999,900 of IOUs does not make you richer or poorer and does not affect your indebtedness. You care only about the $100 of liabilities from the $100 of circulated IOUs. The same reasoning applies for the Fed in regard to its Federal Reserve notes.

For similar reasons, the currency component of the money supply, no matter how it is defined, includes only currency in circulation. It does not include any additional currency that is not yet in the hands of the public. The fact that currency has been printed but is not circulating means that it is not anyone's asset or liability and thus cannot affect anyone's behavior. Therefore, it makes sense not to include it in the money supply.

2. *Reserves*. All banks have an account at the Fed in which they hold deposits. **Reserves** consist of deposits at the Fed plus currency that is physically held by banks (called *vault cash* because it is stored in bank vaults). Reserves are assets for the banks but liabilities for the Fed, because the banks can demand payment on them at any time and the Fed is required to satisfy its obligation by paying Federal Reserve notes. As you will see, an increase in reserves leads to an increase in the level of deposits and hence in the money supply.

Total reserves can be divided into two categories: reserves that the Fed requires banks to hold (**required reserves**) and any additional reserves the banks choose to hold (**excess reserves**). For example, the Fed might require that for every dollar of deposits at a depository institution, a certain fraction (say, 10 cents) must be held as reserves. This fraction (10%) is called the **required reserve ratio**. Currently, the Fed pays no interest on reserves.

Assets

The two assets on the Fed's balance sheet are important for two reasons. First, changes in the asset items lead to changes in reserves and consequently to changes in the money supply. Second, because these assets (government securities and discount loans) earn interest while the liabilities (currency in circulation and reserves) do not, the Fed makes billions of dollars every year—its assets earn income, and its liabilities cost nothing. Although it returns most of its earnings to the federal government, the Fed does spend some of it on "worthy causes," such as supporting economic research.

1. *Government securities*. This category of assets covers the Fed's holdings of securities issued by the U.S. Treasury. As you will see, the Fed provides reserves to the banking system by purchasing securities, thereby increasing its holdings of these assets. An increase in government securities held by the Fed leads to an increase in the money supply.

2. *Discount loans*. The Fed can provide reserves to the banking system by making discount loans to banks. For these banks, the discount loans they have taken out are referred to as *borrowings from the Fed* or, alternatively, as *borrowed reserves*. These loans appear as a liability on banks' balance sheets. An increase in discount loans can also be the source of an increase in the money supply. The interest rate charged banks for these loans is called the **discount rate**.

CONTROL OF THE MONETARY BASE

The *monetary base* (also called **high-powered money**) equals currency in circulation C plus the total reserves in banking system R.[4] The monetary base MB can be expressed as

$$MB = C + R$$

The Federal Reserve exercises control over the monetary base through its purchases or sale of government securities in the open market, called **open market operations**, and through its extension of discount loans to banks.

[4]Here currency in circulation includes both Federal Reserve currency (Federal Reserve notes) and Treasury currency (primarily coins).

Federal Reserve Open Market Operations

The primary way in which the Fed causes changes in the monetary base is through its open market operations. A purchase of bonds by the Fed is called an **open market purchase**, and a sale of bonds by the Fed is called an **open market sale**.

Open Market Purchase from a Bank.

Suppose that the Fed purchases $100 of bonds from a bank and pays for them with a $100 check. To understand what occurs as a result of this transaction, we look at *T-accounts*, which list only the changes that occur in balance sheet items starting from the initial balance sheet position. The bank will either deposit the check in its account with the Fed or cash it in for currency, which will be counted as vault cash. Either action means that the bank will find itself with $100 more reserves and a reduction in its holdings of securities of $100. The T-account for the banking system, then, is

Banking System

Assets		Liabilities	
Securities	−$100		
Reserves	+$100		

The Fed, meanwhile, finds that its liabilities have increased by the additional $100 of reserves, while its assets have increased by the $100 of additional securities that it now holds. Its T-account is

Federal Reserve System

Assets		Liabilities	
Securities	+$100	Reserves	+$100

The net result of this open market purchase is that reserves have increased by $100, the amount of the open market purchase. Because there has been no change of currency in circulation, the monetary base has also risen by $100.

Open Market Purchase from the Nonbank Public.

To understand what happens when there is an open market purchase from the nonbank public, we must look at two cases. First, let's assume that the person or corporation that sells the $100 of bonds to the Fed deposits the Fed's check in the local bank. The nonbank public's T-account after this transaction is

Nonbank Public

Assets		Liabilities	
Securities	−$100		
Checkable deposits	+$100		

When the bank receives the check, it credits the depositor's account with the $100 and then deposits the check in its account with the Fed, thereby adding to its reserves. The banking system's T-account becomes

Banking System

Assets		Liabilities	
Reserves	+$100	Checkable deposits	+$100

The effect on the Fed's balance sheet is that it has gained $100 of securities in its assets column, while it has an increase of $100 of reserves in its liabilities column:

Federal Reserve System

Assets		Liabilities	
Securities	+$100	Reserves	+$100

As you can see in the above T-account, when the Fed's check is deposited in a bank, the net result of the Fed's open market purchase from the nonbank public is identical to the effect of its open market purchase from a bank: Reserves increase by the amount of the open market purchase, and the monetary base increases by the same amount.

If, however, the person or corporation selling the bonds to the Fed cashes the Fed's check either at a local bank or at a Federal Reserve bank for currency, the effect on reserves is different.[5] This seller will receive currency of $100 while reducing holdings of securities by $100. The bond seller's T-account will be

Nonbank Public

Assets		Liabilities	
Securities	−$100		
Currency	+$100		

The Fed now finds that it has exchanged $100 of currency for $100 of securities, so its T-account is

Federal Reserve System

Assets		Liabilities	
Securities	+$100	Currency in circulation	+$100

[5]If the bond seller cashes the check at the local bank, the bank's balance sheet will be unaffected, because the $100 of vault cash that it pays out will be exactly matched by the deposit of the $100 check at the Fed. Thus its reserves will remain the same, and there will be no effect on its T-account. That is why a T-account for the banking system does not appear here.

The net effect of the open market purchase in this case is that reserves are unchanged, while currency in circulation increases by the $100 of the open market purchase. Thus the monetary base increases by the $100 amount of the open market purchase, while reserves do not. This contrasts with the case in which the seller of the bonds deposits the Fed's check in a bank; in that case, reserves increase by $100, and so does the monetary base.

The analysis reveals that ***the effect of an open market purchase on reserves depends on whether the seller of the bonds keeps the proceeds from the sale in currency or in deposits***. If the proceeds are kept in currency, the open market purchase has no effect on reserves; if the proceeds are kept as deposits, reserves increase by the amount of the open market purchase.

The effect of an open market purchase on the monetary base, however, is always the same (the monetary base increases by the amount of the purchase) whether the seller of the bonds keeps the proceeds in deposits or in currency. The impact of an open market purchase on reserves is much more uncertain than its impact on the monetary base.

Open Market Sale. If the Fed sells $100 of bonds to a bank or the nonbank public, the monetary base will decrease by $100. For example, if the Fed sells the bonds to an individual who pays for them with currency, the buyer exchanges $100 of currency for $100 of bonds, and the resulting T-account is

Nonbank Public

Assets		Liabilities	
Securities	+$100		
Currency	−$100		

The Fed, for its part, has reduced its holdings of securities by $100 and has also lowered its monetary liability by accepting the currency as payment for its bonds, thereby reducing the amount of currency in circulation by $100:

Federal Reserve System

Assets		Liabilities	
Securities	−$100	Currency in circulation	−$100

The effect of the open market sale of $100 of bonds is to reduce the monetary base by an equal amount, although reserves remain unchanged. Manipulations of T-accounts in cases in which the buyer of the bonds is a bank or the buyer pays for the bonds with a check written on a checkable deposit account at a local bank lead to the same $100 reduction in the monetary base, although the reduction occurs because the level of reserves has fallen by $100.

STUDY GUIDE

The best way to learn how open market operations affect the monetary base is to use T-accounts. Using T-accounts, try to verify that an open market sale of $100 of bonds to a bank or to a person who pays with a check written on a bank account leads to a $100 reduction in the monetary base.

The following conclusion can now be drawn from our analysis of open market purchases and sales: ***The effect of open market operations on the monetary base is much more certain than the effect on reserves.*** Therefore, the Fed can control the monetary base with open market operations more effectively than it can control reserves.

Open market operations can also be done in other assets besides government bonds and have the same effects on the monetary base we have described here.

Shifts from Deposits into Currency

Even if the Fed does not conduct open market operations, a shift from deposits to currency will affect the reserves in the banking system. However, such a shift will have no effect on the monetary base, another reason why the Fed has more control over the monetary base than over reserves.

Let's suppose that Jane Brown (who opened a $100 checking account at the First National Bank in Chapter 9) decides that tellers are so abusive in all banks that she closes her account by withdrawing the $100 balance in cash and vows never to deposit it in a bank again. The effect on the T-account of the nonbank public is

Nonbank Public

Assets		Liabilities	
Checkable deposits	−$100		
Currency	+$100		

The banking system loses $100 of deposits and hence $100 of reserves:

Banking System

Assets		Liabilities	
Reserves	−$100	Checkable deposits	−$100

For the Fed, Jane Brown's action means that there is $100 of additional currency circulating in the hands of the public, while reserves in the banking system have fallen by $100. The Fed's T-account is

Federal Reserve System

Assets		Liabilities	
		Currency in circulation	+$100
		Reserves	−$100

The net effect on the monetary liabilities of the Fed is a wash; the monetary base is unaffected by Jane Brown's disgust at the banking system. But reserves are affected. Random fluctuations of reserves can occur as a result of random shifts into currency and out of deposits, and vice versa. The same is not true for the monetary base, making it a more stable variable.

Discount Loans

In this chapter so far we have seen changes in the monetary base solely as a result of open market operations. However, the monetary base is also affected when the Fed makes a discount loan to a bank. When the Fed makes a $100 discount loan to the First National Bank, the bank is credited with $100 of reserves from the proceeds of the loan. The effects on the balance sheets of the banking system and the Fed are illustrated by the following T-accounts:

Banking System

Assets		Liabilities	
Reserves	+$100	Discount loans (borrowings from the Fed)	+$100

Federal Reserve System

Assets		Liabilities	
Discount loans (borrowings from the Fed)	+$100	Reserves	+$100

The monetary liabilities of the Fed have now increased by $100, and the monetary base, too, has increased by this amount. However, if a bank pays off a loan from the Fed, thereby reducing its borrowings from the Fed by $100, the T-accounts of the banking system and the Fed are as follows:

Banking System

Assets		Liabilities	
Reserves	−$100	Discount loans (borrowings from the Fed)	−$100

Federal Reserve System

Assets		Liabilities	
Discount loans (borrowings from the Fed)	−$100	Reserves	−$100

The net effect on the monetary liabilities of the Fed, and hence on the monetary base, is a reduction of $100. We see that the monetary base changes one-for-one with the change in the borrowings from the Fed.

Other Factors That Affect the Monetary Base

So far in this chapter, it seems as though the Fed has complete control of the monetary base through its open market operations and discount loans. However, the world is a little bit more complicated for the Fed. Two important items that are not controlled by the Fed but affect the monetary base are *float* and *Treasury deposits at the Fed*. When the Fed clears checks for banks, it often credits the amount of the check to a bank that has deposited it (increases the bank's reserves) but only later debits (decreases the reserves of) the bank on which the check is drawn. The resulting temporary net increase in the total amount of reserves in the banking system (and hence in the monetary base) occurring from the Fed's check-clearing process is called **float**. When the U.S. Treasury moves deposits from commercial banks to its account at the Fed, leading to an increase in *Treasury deposits at the Fed*, it causes a deposit outflow at these banks like that shown in Chapter 9 and thus causes reserves in the banking system and the monetary base to decrease. Thus *float* (affected by random events such as the weather, which affects how quickly checks are presented for payment) and *Treasury deposits at the Fed* (determined by the U.S. Treasury's actions) both affect the monetary base but are not fully controlled by the Fed. Decisions by the U.S. Treasury to have the Fed intervene in the foreign exchange market also affect the monetary base.

Overview of the Fed's Ability to Control the Monetary Base

The factor that most affects the monetary base is the Fed's holdings of securities, which are completely controlled by the Fed through its open market operations. Factors not controlled by the Fed (for example, float and Treasury deposits with the Fed) undergo substantial short-run variations and can be important sources of fluctuations in the monetary base over time periods as short as a week. However, these fluctuations are usually predictable and so can be offset through open market operations. ***Although float and Treasury deposits with the Fed undergo substantial short-run fluctuations, which complicate control of the monetary base, they do not prevent the Fed from accurately controlling it.***

MULTIPLE DEPOSIT CREATION: A SIMPLE MODEL

With our understanding of how the Federal Reserve controls the monetary base and how banks operate (Chapter 9), we now have the tools necessary to explain how deposits are created. When the Fed supplies the banking system with $1 of additional reserves, deposits increase by a multiple of this amount—a process called **multiple deposit creation**.

Deposit Creation: The Single Bank

Suppose that the $100 open market purchase described earlier was conducted with the First National Bank. After the Fed has bought the $100 bond from the First National Bank, the bank finds that it has an increase in reserves of $100. To analyze what the bank will do with these additional reserves, assume that the bank does not want to hold excess reserves because it earns no interest on them. We begin the analysis with the following T-account:

First National Bank

Assets		Liabilities	
Securities	−$100		
Reserves	+$100		

Because the bank has no increase in its checkable deposits, required reserves remain the same, and the bank finds that its additional $100 of reserves means that its excess reserves have increased by $100. Let's say that the bank decides to make a loan equal in amount to the $100 increase in excess reserves. When the bank makes the loan, it sets up a checking account for the borrower and puts the proceeds of the loan into this account. In this way, the bank alters its balance sheet by increasing its liabilities with $100 of checkable deposits and at the same time increasing its assets with the $100 loan. The resulting T-account looks like this:

First National Bank

Assets		Liabilities	
Securities	−$100	Checkable deposits	+$100
Reserves	+$100		
Loans	+$100		

The bank has created checkable deposits by its act of lending. Because checkable deposits are part of the money supply, the bank's act of lending has, in fact, created money.

In its current balance sheet position, the First National Bank still has excess reserves and so might want to make additional loans. However, these reserves will not stay at the bank for very long. The borrower took out a loan not to leave $100 idle at the First National Bank but to purchase goods and services from other individuals and corporations. When the borrower makes these purchases by writing checks, they will be deposited at other banks, and the $100 of reserves will leave the First National Bank. ***A bank cannot safely make loans for an amount greater than the excess reserves it has before it makes the loan.***

The final T-account of the First National Bank is

First National Bank

Assets		Liabilities	
Securities	−$100		
Loans	+$100		

The increase in reserves of $100 has been converted into additional loans of $100 at the First National Bank, plus an additional $100 of deposits that have made their way to other banks. (All the checks written on accounts at the First National Bank are deposited in banks rather than converted into cash, because we are assuming that the public does not want to hold any additional currency.) Now let's see what happens to these deposits at the other banks.

Deposit Creation: The Banking System

To simplify the analysis, let us assume that the $100 of deposits created by First National Bank's loan is deposited at Bank A and that this bank and all other banks hold no excess reserves. Bank A's T-account becomes

Bank A

Assets		Liabilities	
Reserves	+$100	Checkable deposits	+$100

If the required reserve ratio is 10%, this bank will now find itself with a $10 increase in required reserves, leaving it $90 of excess reserves. Because Bank A (like the First National Bank) does not want to hold on to excess reserves, it will make loans for the entire amount. Its loans and checkable deposits will then increase by $90, but when the borrower spends the $90 of checkable deposits, they and the reserves at Bank A will fall back down by this same amount. The net result is that Bank A's T-account will look like this:

Bank A

Assets		Liabilities	
Reserves	+$10	Checkable deposits	+$100
Loans	+$90		

If the money spent by the borrower to whom Bank A lent the $90 is deposited in another bank, such as Bank B, the T-account for Bank B will be

Bank B

Assets		Liabilities	
Reserves	+$90	Checkable deposits	+$90

The checkable deposits in the banking system have increased by another $90, for a total increase of $190 ($100 at Bank A plus $90 at Bank B). In fact, the distinction between Bank A and Bank B is not necessary to obtain the same result on the overall expansion of deposits. If the borrower from Bank A writes checks to someone who deposits them at Bank A, the same change in deposits would occur. The T-accounts for Bank B would just apply to Bank A, and its checkable deposits would increase by the total amount of $190.

Bank B will want to modify its balance sheet further. It must keep 10% of $90 ($9) as required reserves and has 90% of $90 ($81) in excess reserves and so can make loans of this amount. Bank B will make an $81 loan to a borrower, who spends the proceeds from the loan. Bank B's T-account will be

Bank B

Assets		Liabilities	
Reserves	+$ 9	Checkable deposits	+$90
Loans	+$81		

The $81 spent by the borrower from Bank B will be deposited in another bank (Bank C). Consequently, from the initial $100 increase of reserves in the banking system, the total increase of checkable deposits in the system so far is $271 (= $100 + $90 + $81).

Following the same reasoning, if all banks make loans for the full amount of their excess reserves, further increments in checkable deposits will continue (at Banks C, D, E, and so on), as depicted in Table 1. Therefore, the total increase in deposits from the initial $100 increase in reserves will be $1,000: The increase is tenfold, the reciprocal of the 10% (0.10) reserve requirement.

If the banks choose to invest their excess reserves in securities, the result is the same. If Bank A had taken its excess reserves and purchased securities instead of making loans, its T-account would have looked like this:

Bank A

Assets		Liabilities	
Reserves	+$10	Checkable deposits	+$100
Securities	+$90		

When the bank buys $90 of securities, it writes a $90 check to the seller of the securities, who in turn deposits the $90 at a bank such as Bank B. Bank B's checkable deposits increase by $90, and the deposit expansion process is the same as before. ***Whether a bank chooses to use its excess reserves to make loans or to purchase securities, the effect on deposit expansion is the same.***

You can now see the difference in deposit creation for the single bank versus the banking system as a whole. Because a single bank can create deposits equal only to the amount of its excess reserves, it cannot by itself generate multiple deposit expansion. A single bank cannot make loans greater in amount than its excess reserves, because the bank will lose these reserves as the deposits created by the loan find their way to other banks. However, the banking system as a whole can generate a multiple expansion of deposits, because when a bank loses its excess reserves, these reserves do not leave the banking system even though they are lost to the individual bank. So as each bank makes a loan and creates deposits, the reserves find their way to another bank, which uses them to make additional loans and create additional deposits. As you have seen, this process continues until the initial increase in reserves results in a multiple increase in deposits.

TABLE 1 **Creation of Deposits (assuming 10% reserve requirement and a $100 increase in reserves)**

Bank	Increase in Deposits ($)	Increase in Loans ($)	Increase in Reserves ($)
First National	0.00	100.00	0.00
A	100.00	90.00	10.00
B	90.00	81.00	9.00
C	81.00	72.90	8.10
D	72.90	65.61	7.29
E	65.61	59.05	6.56
F	59.05	53.14	5.91
.	.	.	.
.	.	.	.
.	.	.	.
Total for all banks	1,000.00	1,000.00	100.00

The multiple increase in deposits generated from an increase in the banking system's reserves is called the **simple deposit multiplier**.[6] In our example with a 10% required reserve ratio, the simple deposit multiplier is 10. More generally, the simple deposit multiplier equals the reciprocal of the required reserve ratio, expressed as a fraction (10 = 1/0.10), so the formula for the multiple expansion of deposits can be written as follows:

$$\Delta D = \frac{1}{r} \times \Delta R \tag{1}$$

where ΔD = change in total checkable deposits in the banking system
r = required reserve ratio (0.10 in the example)
ΔR = change in reserves for the banking system ($100 in the example)[7]

Deriving the Formula for Multiple Deposit Creation

The formula for the multiple creation of deposits can also be derived directly using algebra. We obtain the same answer for the relationship between a change in deposits and a change in reserves, but more quickly.

[6]This multiplier should not be confused with the Keynesian multiplier, which is derived through a similar step-by-step analysis. That multiplier relates an increase in income to an increase in investment, whereas the simple deposit multiplier relates an increase in deposits to an increase in reserves.

[7]A formal derivation of this formula follows. Using the reasoning in the text, the change in checkable deposits is $100 (= $\Delta R \times 1$) plus $90 [= $\Delta R \times (1-r)$] plus $81 [= $\Delta R \times (1-r)^2$], and so on, which can be rewritten as

$$\Delta D = \Delta R \times [1 + (1-r) + (1-r)^2 + (1-r)^3 + \cdots]$$

Using the formula for the sum of an infinite series found in footnote 5 in Chapter 4, this can be rewritten as

$$\Delta D = \Delta R \times \frac{1}{1-(1-r)} = \frac{1}{r} \times \Delta R$$

Our assumption that banks do not hold on to any excess reserves means that the total amount of required reserves for the banking system RR will equal the total reserves in the banking system R:

$$RR = R$$

The total amount of required reserves equals the required reserve ratio r times the total amount of checkable deposits D:

$$RR = r \times D$$

Substituting $r \times D$ for RR in the first equation

$$r \times D = R$$

and dividing both sides of the preceding equation by r gives

$$D = \frac{1}{r} \times R$$

Taking the change in both sides of this equation and using delta to indicate a change gives

$$\Delta D = \frac{1}{r} \times \Delta R$$

which is the same formula for deposit creation found in Equation 1.

This derivation provides us with another way of looking at the multiple creation of deposits, because it forces us to look directly at the banking system as a whole rather than at one bank at a time. For the banking system as a whole, deposit creation (or contraction) will stop only when all excess reserves in the banking system are gone; that is, the banking system will be in equilibrium when the total amount of required reserves equals the total amount of reserves, as seen in the equation $RR = R$. When $r \times D$ is substituted for RR, the resulting equation $R = r \times D$ tells us how high checkable deposits will have to be for required reserves to equal total reserves. Accordingly, a given level of reserves in the banking system determines the level of checkable deposits when the banking system is in equilibrium (when $ER = 0$); put another way, the given level of reserves supports a given level of checkable deposits.

In our example, the required reserve ratio is 10%. If reserves increase by \$100, checkable deposits must rise by \$1,000 for total required reserves also to increase by \$100. If the increase in checkable deposits is less than this, say \$900, then the increase in required reserves of \$90 remains below the \$100 increase in reserves, so there are still excess reserves somewhere in the banking system. The banks with the excess reserves will now make additional loans, creating new deposits, and this process will continue until all reserves in the system are used up. This occurs when checkable deposits rise \$1,000.

We can also see this by looking at the T-account of the banking system as a whole (including the First National Bank) that results from this process:

Banking System

Assets		Liabilities	
Securities	−\$ 100	Checkable deposits	+\$1,000
Reserves	+\$ 100		
Loans	+\$1,000		

The procedure of eliminating excess reserves by loaning them out means that the banking system (First National Bank and Banks A, B, C, D, and so on) continues to make loans up to the \$1,000 amount until deposits have reached the \$1,000 level. In this way, \$100 of reserves supports \$1,000 (ten times the quantity) of deposits.

Critique of the Simple Model

Our model of multiple deposit creation seems to indicate that the Federal Reserve is able to exercise complete control over the level of checkable deposits by setting the required reserve ratio and the level of reserves. The actual creation of deposits is much less mechanical than the simple model indicates. If proceeds from Bank A's \$90 loan are not deposited but are kept in cash, nothing is deposited in Bank B, and the deposit creation process stops dead in its tracks. The total increase in checkable deposits is only \$100—considerably less than the \$1,000 we calculated. Thus, if some proceeds from loans are used to raise the holdings of currency, checkable deposits will not increase by as much as our simple model of multiple deposit creation tells us.

Another situation ignored in our model is one in which banks do not make loans or buy securities in the full amount of their excess reserves. If Bank A decides to hold on to all \$90 of its excess reserves, no deposits would be made in Bank B, and this would also stop the deposit creation process. The total increase in deposits would again be only \$100 and not the \$1,000 increase in our example. Hence, if banks choose to hold all or some of their excess reserves, the full expansion of deposits predicted by the simple model of multiple deposit creation does not occur.

Our examples rightly indicate that the Fed is not the only player whose behavior influences the level of deposits and therefore the money supply. Banks' decisions regarding the amount of excess reserves to hold, depositors' decisions regarding how much currency to hold, and borrowers' decisions on how much to borrow from banks can cause the money supply to change. In the next chapter, we stress the behavior and interactions of the four players in constructing a more realistic model of the money supply process.

SUMMARY

1. There are four players in the money supply process: the central bank, banks (depository institutions), depositors, and borrowers from banks.
2. Four items in the Fed's balance sheet are essential to our understanding of the money supply process: the two liability items, currency in circulation and reserves, which together make up the monetary base, and the two asset items, government securities and discount loans.
3. The Federal Reserve controls the monetary base through open market operations and extension of discount loans to banks and has better control over the monetary base than over reserves. Although float and Treasury deposits with the Fed undergo substantial short-run fluctuations, which complicate control of the monetary base, they do not prevent the Fed from accurately controlling it.
4. A single bank can make loans up to the amount of its excess reserves, thereby creating an equal amount of deposits. The banking system can create a multiple expansion of deposits, because as each bank makes a loan and creates deposits, the reserves find their way to another bank, which uses them to make loans and create additional deposits. In the simple model of multiple deposit creation in which banks do not hold on to excess reserves and the public holds no currency, the multiple increase in checkable deposits (simple deposit multiplier) equals the reciprocal of the required reserve ratio.

5. The simple model of multiple deposit creation has serious deficiencies. Decisions by depositors to increase their holdings of currency or of banks to hold excess reserves will result in a smaller expansion of deposits than the simple model predicts. All four players—the Fed, banks, depositors, and borrowers from banks—are important in the determination of the money supply.

KEY TERMS

discount rate, p. 407
excess reserves, p. 407
float, p. 413
high-powered money, p. 407
monetary base, p. 406
multiple deposit creation, p. 413
open market operations, p. 407
open market purchase, p. 408
open market sale, p. 408
required reserve ratio, p. 407
required reserves, p. 407
reserves, p. 407
simple deposit multiplier, p. 417

QUESTIONS AND PROBLEMS

Questions marked with an asterisk are answered at the end of the book in an appendix, "Answers to Selected Questions and Problems." Questions marked with a blue circle indicate the question is available in MyEconLab at www.myeconlab.com/mishkin.

1. If the Fed sells $2 million of bonds to the First National Bank, what happens to reserves and the monetary base? Use T-accounts to explain your answer.

*2. If the Fed sells $2 million of bonds to Irving the Investor, who pays for the bonds with a briefcase filled with currency, what happens to reserves and the monetary base? Use T-accounts to explain your answer.

*3. If the Fed lends five banks an additional total of $100 million but depositors withdraw $50 million and hold it as currency, what happens to reserves and the monetary base? Use T-accounts to explain your answer.

4. The First National Bank receives an extra $100 of reserves but decides not to lend any of these reserves out. How much deposit creation takes place for the entire banking system?

Unless otherwise noted, the following assumptions are made in all the remaining problems: The required reserve ratio on checkable deposits is 10%, banks do not hold any excess reserves, and the public's holdings of currency do not change.

*5. Using T-accounts, show what happens to checkable deposits in the banking system when the Fed lends an additional $1 million to the First National Bank.

6. Using T-accounts, show what happens to checkable deposits in the banking system when the Fed sells $2 million of bonds to the First National Bank.

*7. Suppose that the Fed buys $1 million of bonds from the First National Bank. If the First National Bank and all other banks use the resulting increase in reserves to purchase securities only and not to make loans, what will happen to checkable deposits?

8. If the Fed buys $1 million of bonds from the First National Bank, but an additional 10% of any deposit is held as excess reserves, what is the total increase in checkable deposits? (*Hint:* Use T-accounts to show what happens at each step of the multiple expansion process.)

*9. If a bank depositor withdraws $1,000 of currency from an account, what happens to reserves and checkable deposits?

10. If reserves in the banking system increase by $1 billion as a result of discount loans of $1 billion and checkable deposits increase by $9 billion, why isn't the banking system in equilibrium? What will continue to happen in the banking system until equilibrium is reached? Show the T-account for the banking system in equilibrium.

*11. If the Fed reduces reserves by selling $5 million worth of bonds to the banks, what will the T-account of the banking system look like when the banking system is in equilibrium? What will have happened to the level of checkable deposits?

12 If the required reserve ratio on checkable deposits increases to 20%, how much multiple deposit creation will take place when reserves are increased by $100?

*13 If a bank decides that it wants to hold $1 million of excess reserves, what effect will this have on checkable deposits in the banking system?

14 If a bank sells $10 million of bonds back to the Fed so as to pay back $10 million on the discount loan it owes, what will be the effect on the level of checkable deposits?

*15 If you decide to hold $100 less cash than usual and therefore deposit $100 in cash in the bank, what effect will this have on checkable deposits in the banking system if the rest of the public keeps its holdings of currency constant?

WEB EXERCISES

1. Go to www.federalreserve.gov/boarddocs/rptcongress/ and find the most recent annual report of the Federal Reserve. Read the first section of the annual report that summarizes Monetary Policy and the Economic Outlook. Write a one-page summary of this section of the report.
2. Go to www.federalreserve.gov/releases/h6/hist/ and find the historical report of M1, M2, and M3. Compute the growth rate in each aggregate over each of the last three years (it will be easier to do if you move the data into Excel as demonstrated in Chapter 1). Does it appear that the Fed has been increasing or decreasing the rate of growth of the money supply? Is this consistent with what you understand the economy needs? Why?

WEB REFERENCES

www.federalreserve.gov/boarddocs/rptcongress/annual04/default.htm

See the most recent Federal Reserve financial statement.

www.richmondfed.org/about_us/our_tours/money_museums/virtual_tour/index.cfm

A virtual tour of the Federal Reserve Bank of Richmond's money museum.

CHAPTER

17 Determinants of the Money Supply

Preview

In Chapter 16, we developed a simple model of multiple deposit creation that showed how the Fed can control the level of checkable deposits by setting the required reserve ratio and the level of reserves. Unfortunately for the Fed, life isn't that simple; control of the money supply is far more complicated. Our critique of this model indicated that decisions by depositors about their holdings of currency and by banks about their holdings of excess reserves also affect the money supply. To deal with this critique, in this chapter we develop a money supply model in which depositors and banks assume their important roles. The resulting framework provides an in-depth description of the money supply process to help you understand the complexity of the Fed's role.

To simplify the analysis, we separate the development of our model into several steps. First, because the Fed can exert more precise control over the monetary base (currency in circulation plus total reserves in the banking system) than it can over total reserves alone, our model links changes in the money supply to changes in the monetary base. This link is achieved by deriving a **money multiplier** (a ratio that relates the change in the money supply to a given change in the monetary base). Finally, we examine the determinants of the money multiplier.

STUDY GUIDE

One reason for breaking the money supply model into its component parts is to help you answer questions by using intuitive step-by-step logic rather than by memorizing how changes in the behavior of the Fed, depositors, or banks will affect the money supply.

In deriving a model of the money supply process, we focus here on a simple definition of *money* (currency plus checkable deposits), which corresponds to M1. Although broader definitions of money—particularly, M2—are frequently used in policymaking, we conduct the analysis with an M1 definition because it is less complicated and yet provides a basic understanding of the money supply process. Furthermore, all analyses and results using the M1 definition apply equally well to the M2 definition. A somewhat more complicated money supply model for the M2 definition is developed in an appendix to this chapter.

THE MONEY SUPPLY MODEL AND THE MONEY MULTIPLIER

Because, as we saw in Chapter 16, the Fed can control the monetary base better than it can control reserves, it makes sense to link the money supply M to the monetary base MB through a relationship such as the following:

$$M = m \times MB \tag{1}$$

The variable m is the money multiplier, which tells us how much the money supply changes for a given change in the monetary base MB. This multiplier tells us what multiple of the monetary base is transformed into the money supply. Because the money multiplier is larger than 1, the alternative name for the monetary base, *high-powered money*, is logical; a \$1 change in the monetary base leads to more than a \$1 change in the money supply.

The money multiplier reflects the effect on the money supply of other factors besides the monetary base, and the following model will explain the factors that determine the size of the money multiplier. Depositors' decisions about their holdings of currency and checkable deposits are one set of factors affecting the money multiplier. The reserve requirements imposed by the Fed on the banking system also affect the size of the multiplier, as do banks' decisions about excess reserves.

Deriving the Money Multiplier

In our model of multiple deposit creation in Chapter 16, we ignored the effects on deposit creation of changes in the public's holdings of currency and banks' holdings of excess reserves. Now we incorporate these changes into our model of the money supply process by assuming that the desired level of currency C and excess reserves ER grows proportionally with checkable deposits D; in other words, we assume that the ratios of these items to checkable deposits are constants in equilibrium, as the braces in the following expressions indicate:

$$c = \{C/D\} = \text{currency ratio}$$
$$e = \{ER/D\} = \text{excess reserves ratio}$$

We will now derive a formula that describes how the currency ratio desired by depositors, the excess reserves ratio desired by banks, and the required reserve ratio set by the Fed affect the multiplier m. We begin the derivation of the model of the money supply with the following equation:

$$R = RR + ER$$

which states that the total amount of reserves in the banking system R equals the sum of required reserves RR and excess reserves ER. (Note that this equation corresponds to the equilibrium condition $RR = R$ in Chapter 16, where excess reserves were assumed to be zero.)

The total amount of required reserves equals the required reserve ratio r times the amount of checkable deposits D:

$$RR = r \times D$$

Substituting $r \times D$ for RR in the first equation yields an equation that links reserves in the banking system to the amount of checkable deposits and excess reserves they can support:

$$R = (r \times D) + ER$$

A key point here is that the Fed sets the required reserve ratio r to less than 1. Thus \$1 of reserves can support more than \$1 of deposits, and the multiple expansion of deposits can occur.

Let's see how this works in practice. If excess reserves are held at zero ($ER = 0$), the required reserve ratio is set at $r = 0.10$, and the level of checkable deposits in the banking system is \$800 billion, then the amount of reserves needed to support these deposits is \$80 billion ($= 0.10 \times$ \$800 billion). The \$80 billion of reserves can support ten times this amount in checkable deposits, just as in Chapter 16, because multiple deposit creation will occur.

Because the monetary base MB equals currency C plus reserves R, we can generate an equation that links the amount of the monetary base to the levels of checkable deposits and currency by adding currency to both sides of the equation:

$$MB = R + C = (r \times D) + ER + C$$

Another way of thinking about this equation is to recognize that it reveals the amount of the monetary base needed to support the existing amounts of checkable deposits, currency, and excess reserves.

An important feature of this equation is that an additional dollar of MB that arises from an additional dollar of currency does not support any additional deposits. This occurs because such an increase leads to an identical increase in the right-hand side of the equation with no change occurring in D. The currency component of MB does not lead to multiple deposit creation as the reserves component does. Put another way, ***an increase in the monetary base that goes into currency is not multiplied, whereas an increase that goes into supporting deposits is multiplied.***

Another important feature of this equation is that an additional dollar of MB that goes into excess reserves ER does not support any additional deposits or currency. The reason for this is that when a bank decides to hold excess reserves, it does not make additional loans, so these excess reserves do not lead to the creation of deposits. Therefore, if the Fed injects reserves into the banking system and they are held as excess reserves, there will be no effect on deposits or currency and hence no effect on the money supply. In other words, you can think of excess reserves as an idle component of reserves that are not being used to support any deposits (although they are important for bank liquidity management, as we saw in Chapter 9). This means that for a given level of reserves, a higher amount of excess reserves implies that the banking system, in effect, has fewer reserves to support deposits.

To derive the money multiplier formula in terms of the currency ratio $c = \{C/D\}$ and the excess reserves ratio $e = \{ER/D\}$, we rewrite the last equation, specifying C as $c \times D$ and ER as $e \times D$:

$$MB = (r \times D) + (e \times D) + (c \times D) = (r + e + c) \times D$$

We next divide both sides of the equation by the term inside the parentheses to get an expression linking checkable deposits D to the monetary base MB:

$$D = \frac{1}{r + e + c} \times MB \qquad (2)$$

Using the definition of the money supply as currency plus checkable deposits ($M = D + C$) and again specifying C as $c \times D$,

$$M = D + (c \times D) = (1 + c) \times D$$

Substituting in this equation the expression for D from Equation 2, we have

$$M = \frac{1 + c}{r + e + c} \times MB \tag{3}$$

Finally, we have achieved our objective of deriving an expression in the form of our earlier Equation 1. As you can see, the ratio that multiplies MB is the money multiplier that tells how much the money supply changes in response to a given change in the monetary base (high-powered money). The money multiplier m is thus

$$m = \frac{1 + c}{r + e + c} \tag{4}$$

It is a function of the currency ratio set by depositors c, the excess reserves ratio set by banks e, and the required reserve ratio set by the Fed r.

Although the algebraic derivation we have just completed shows you how the money multiplier is constructed, you need to understand the basic intuition behind it to understand and apply the money multiplier concept without having to memorize it.

Intuition Behind the Money Multiplier

To get a feel for what the money multiplier means, let us again construct a numerical example with realistic numbers for the following variables:

r = required reserve ratio = 0.10
C = currency in circulation = \$400 billion
D = checkable deposits = \$800 billion
ER = excess reserves = \$0.8 billion
M = money supply (M1) = $C + D$ = \$1,200 billion

From these numbers we can calculate the values for the currency ratio c and the excess reserves ratio e:

$$c = \frac{\$400 \text{ billion}}{\$800 \text{ billion}} = 0.5$$

$$e = \frac{\$0.8 \text{ billion}}{\$800 \text{ billion}} = 0.001$$

The resulting value of the money multiplier is

$$m = \frac{1 + 0.5}{0.1 + 0.001 + 0.5} = \frac{1.5}{0.601} = 2.5$$

The money multiplier of 2.5 tells us that, given the required reserve ratio of 10% on checkable deposits and the behavior of depositors as represented by $c = 0.5$ and banks as represented by $e = 0.001$, a \$1 increase in the monetary base leads to a \$2.50 increase in the money supply (M1).

An important characteristic of the money multiplier is that it is less than the simple deposit multiplier of 10 found in Chapter 16. The key to understanding this result of our money supply model is to realize that ***although there is multiple expansion of***

deposits, there is no such expansion for currency. Thus, if some portion of the increase in high-powered money finds its way into currency, this portion does not undergo multiple deposit expansion. In our analysis in Chapter 16, we did not allow for this possibility, and so the increase in reserves led to the maximum amount of multiple deposit creation. However, in our current model of the money multiplier, the level of currency does increase when the monetary base *MB* and checkable deposits *D* increase because *c* is greater than zero. As previously stated, any increase in *MB* that goes into an increase in currency is not multiplied, so only part of the increase in *MB* is available to support checkable deposits that undergo multiple expansion. The overall level of multiple deposit expansion must be lower, meaning that the increase in *M*, given an increase in *MB*, is smaller than the simple model in Chapter 16 indicated.[1]

FACTORS THAT DETERMINE THE MONEY MULTIPLIER

To develop our intuition of the money multiplier even further, let us look at how this multiplier changes in response to changes in the variables in our model: *c*, *e*, and *r*. The "game" we are playing is a familiar one in economics: We ask what happens when one of these variables changes, leaving all other variables the same (*ceteris paribus*).

Changes in the Required Reserve Ratio *r*

If the required reserve ratio on checkable deposits increases while all the other variables stay the same, the same level of reserves cannot support as large an amount of checkable deposits; more reserves are needed because required reserves for these checkable deposits have increased. The resulting deficiency in reserves then means that banks must contract their loans, causing a decline in deposits and hence in the money supply. The reduced money supply relative to the level of *MB*, which has remained unchanged, indicates that the money multiplier has declined as well. Another way to see this is to realize that when *r* is higher, less multiple expansion of checkable deposits occurs. With less multiple deposit expansion, the money multiplier must decrease.[2]

We can verify that the foregoing analysis is correct by seeing what happens to the value of the money multiplier in our numerical example when *r* increases from 10% to 15% (leaving all the other variables unchanged). The money multiplier becomes

$$m = \frac{1 + 0.5}{0.15 + 0.001 + 0.5} = \frac{1.5}{0.651} = 2.3$$

which, as we would expect, is less than 2.5.

---

[1]Another reason the money multiplier is smaller is that *e* is a constant fraction greater than zero, indicating that an increase in *MB* and *D* leads to higher excess reserves. The resulting higher amount of excess reserves means that the amount of reserves used to support checkable deposits will not increase as much as it otherwise would. Hence the increase in checkable deposits and the money supply will be lower, and the money multiplier will be smaller. However, because *e* is currently so tiny—around 0.001—the impact of this ratio on the money multiplier is now quite small. But there have been periods when *e* has been much larger and so has had a more important role in lowering the money multiplier.

[2]This result can be demonstrated from the Equation 4 formula as follows: When *r* increases, the denominator of the money multiplier increases, and therefore the money multiplier must decrease.

The analysis just conducted can also be applied to the case in which the required reserve ratio falls. In this case, there will be more multiple expansion for checkable deposits because the same level of reserves can now support more checkable deposits, and the money multiplier will increase. For example, if r falls from 10% to 5%, plugging this value into our money multiplier formula (leaving all the other variables unchanged) yields a money multiplier of

$$m = \frac{1 + 0.5}{0.05 + 0.001 + 0.5} = \frac{1.5}{0.551} = 2.72$$

which is above the initial value of 2.5.

We can now state the following result: ***The money multiplier and the money supply are negatively related to the required reserve ratio r.*** In the past, the Fed sometimes used reserve requirements to affect the size of the money supply. In recent years, however, reserve requirements have become a less important factor in the determination of the money multiplier and the money supply (see the FYI box).

FYI The Declining Importance of Reserve Requirements

Two developments in recent years have led to the decreasing importance of reserve requirements in determining the money multiplier and the money supply.

We discussed in Chapter 10 how financial innovation led to the development of *sweep accounts*, in which any balances above a certain amount in a checking account at the end of a business day are "swept out" of the account and invested in overnight securities that pay interest and then redeposited the next morning. The resulting reduction in checking account balances has led to a substantial reduction in the amount of required reserves in recent years.

At the same time, banks have found that they need to put more cash in their ATMs to satisfy customer needs, particularly on the weekends and holidays when banks are closed. This cash is classified as vault cash, so it is counted as reserves. The Fed also allows banks to classify some of the reserves they hold as deposits at the Federal Reserve banks as *contractual clearing balances*, which earn credits that can be used to pay for Federal Reserve services such as check clearing and the use of Fedwire to transfer funds. The result is that approximately 70% of banks voluntarily have contractual clearing balances and vault cash that exceed the amount of their required reserves.* We describe this situation by saying that reserve requirement are not "binding"; in other words, higher reserve requirements would not change the banks' holdings of reserves because they already want to hold more than the required amount of reserves as vault cash in their ATMs and as contractual clearing balances.

A change in reserve requirements would have no effect on the bank's behavior for a bank for which reserve requirements are not binding: A change in reserve requirements would not cause the bank to change the amount of its reserves, which already exceed the reserve requirements. For the 70% of banks for which reserve requirements are not binding, a change in reserve requirements would have no effect on the amount of deposits and the money supply. It is only for the minority of banks for which reserve requirements are binding that changes in reserve requirements matter. Because reserve requirements have a much smaller effect on the money multiplier and the money supply than they did in the past, the Federal Reserve no longer views reserve requirements as a useful tool for controlling the money supply (see Chapter 18).

*See Paul Bennett and Stavros Peristiani, "Are U.S. Reserve Requirements Binding?" Federal Reserve Bank of New York, *Economic Policy Review* 8 (May 2002).

Changes in the Currency Ratio c

Next, what happens to the money multiplier when depositor behavior causes the currency ratio c to increase with all other variables unchanged? An increase in c means that depositors are converting some of their checkable deposits into currency. As shown before, checkable deposits undergo multiple expansion while currency does not. Hence, when checkable deposits are converted into currency, there is a switch from a component of the money supply that undergoes multiple expansion to one that does not. The overall level of multiple expansion declines, and so must the multiplier.[3]

This reasoning is confirmed by our numerical example, where c rises from 0.50 to 0.75. The money multiplier then falls from 2.5 to

$$m = \frac{1 + 0.75}{0.1 + 0.001 + 0.75} = \frac{1.75}{0.851} = 2.06$$

We have now demonstrated another result: ***The money multiplier and the money supply are negatively related to the currency ratio c.***

Changes in the Excess Reserves Ratio e

When banks increase their holdings of excess reserves relative to checkable deposits, the banking system, in effect, has fewer reserves to support checkable deposits. This means that given the same level of *MB*, banks will contract their loans, causing a decline in the level of checkable deposits and a decline in the money supply, and the money multiplier will decrease.[4]

This reasoning is supported in our numerical example when e rises from 0.001 to 0.005. The money multiplier declines from 2.5 to

$$m = \frac{1 + 0.5}{0.1 + 0.005 + 0.5} = \frac{1.5}{0.605} = 2.48$$

Note that although the excess reserves ratio has risen fivefold, there has been only a small decline in the money multiplier. This decline is small, because in recent years e has been extremely small, so changes in it have only a small impact on the money multiplier. However, there have been times, particularly during the Great Depression, when this ratio was far higher, and its movements had a substantial effect on the money supply and the money multiplier. Thus our final result is still an important one: ***The money multiplier and the money supply are negatively related to the excess reserves ratio e.***

To understand the factors that determine the level of e in the banking system, we must look at the costs and benefits to banks of holding excess reserves. When the costs of holding excess reserves rise, we would expect the level of excess reserves and hence e to fall; when the benefits of holding excess reserves rise, we would expect the level of excess reserves and e to rise. Two primary factors affect these costs and benefits

---

[3]As long as $r + e$ is less than 1 (as is the case using the realistic numbers we have used), an increase in c raises the denominator of the money multiplier proportionally by more than it raises the numerator. The increase in c causes the multiplier to fall. If you would like to know more about what explains movements in the currency ratio c, take a look at an appendix to this chapter on this topic, which can be found on this book's web site at www.myeconlab.com/mishkin. The appendix at the end of this chapter discusses how the money multiplier for *M2* is determined.

[4]This result can be demonstrated from the Equation 4 formula as follows: When e rises, the denominator of the money multiplier rises, and so the money multiplier must fall.

and hence affect the excess reserves ratio: market interest rates and expected deposit outflows.

Market Interest Rates. As you may recall from our analysis of bank management in Chapter 9, the cost to a bank of holding excess reserves is its opportunity cost, the interest that could have been earned on loans or securities if they had been held instead of excess reserves. For the sake of simplicity, we assume that loans and securities earn the same interest rate *i*, which we call the market interest rate. If *i* increases, the opportunity cost of holding excess reserves rises, and the desired ratio of excess reserves to deposits falls. A decrease in *i*, conversely, will reduce the opportunity cost of excess reserves, and *e* will rise. ***The banking system's excess reserves ratio e is negatively related to the market interest rate i.***

Another way of understanding the negative effect of market interest rates on *e* is to return to the theory of asset demand, which states that if the expected returns on alternative assets rise relative to the expected returns on a given asset, the demand for that asset will decrease. As the market interest rate increases, the expected return on loans and securities rises relative to the zero return on excess reserves, and the excess reserves ratio falls.

Figure 1 shows us (as the theory of asset demand predicts) that there is a negative relationship between the excess reserves ratio and a representative market interest rate, the federal funds rate. The period 1960–1981 saw an upward trend in the federal funds

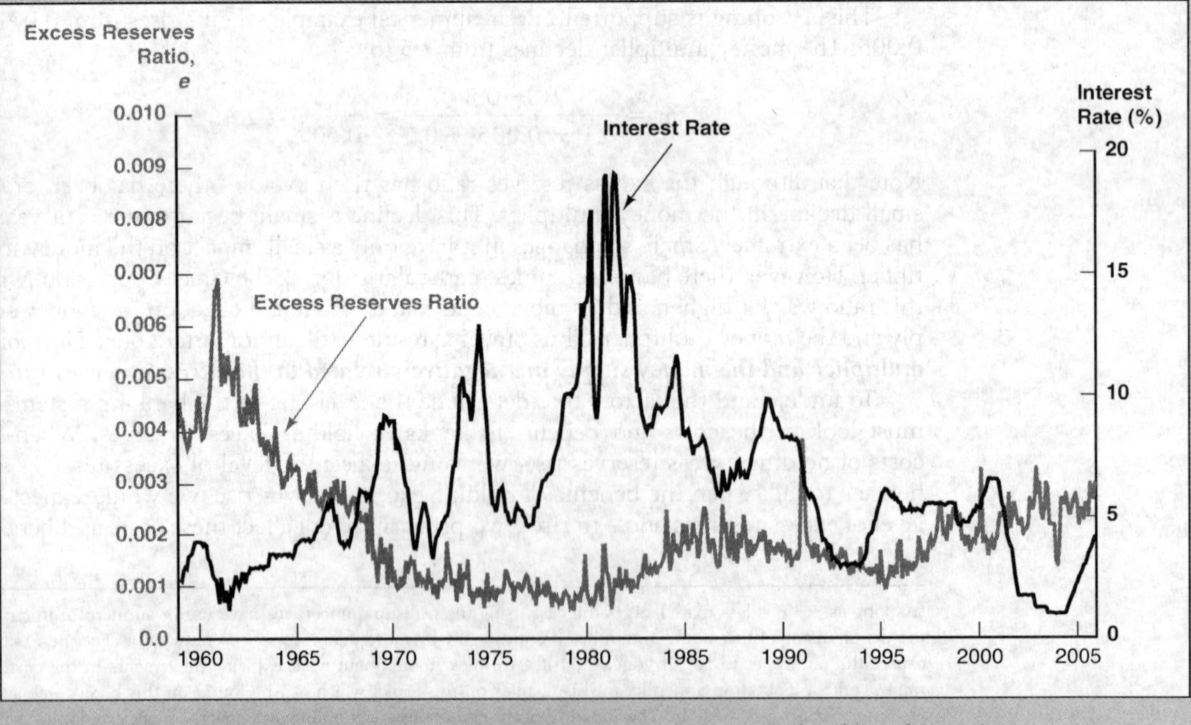

FIGURE 1 **The Excess Reserves Ratio e and the Interest Rate (Federal Funds Rate)**

Source: Federal Reserve: www.federalreserve.gov/releases/h3/hist/h3hist2.txt.

rate and a declining trend in e, whereas in the period 1981–2005, a decline in the federal funds rate is associated with a rise in e. The empirical evidence thus supports our analysis that the excess reserves ratio is negatively related to market interest rates.

Expected Deposit Outflows. Our analysis of bank management in Chapter 9 also indicated that the primary benefit to a bank of holding excess reserves is that they provide insurance against losses due to deposit outflows; that is, they enable the bank experiencing deposit outflows to escape the costs of calling in loans, selling securities, borrowing from the Fed or other corporations, or bank failure. If banks fear that deposit outflows are likely to increase (that is, if expected deposit outflows increase), they will want more insurance against this possibility and will increase the excess reserves ratio. Another way to put it is this: If expected deposit outflows rise, the expected benefits, and hence the expected returns for holding excess reserves, increase. As the theory of asset demand predicts, excess reserves will then rise. Conversely, a decline in expected deposit outflows will reduce the insurance benefit of excess reserves, and their level should fall. We have the following result: ***The excess reserves ratio e is positively related to expected deposit outflows.***

ADDITIONAL FACTORS THAT DETERMINE THE MONEY SUPPLY

So far we have been assuming that the Fed has accurate control over the monetary base. However, whereas the amount of open market purchases or sales is completely controlled by the Fed's placing orders with dealers in bond markets, the central bank cannot unilaterally determine, and therefore cannot perfectly predict, the amount of borrowing by banks from the Fed. The Federal Reserve sets the discount rate (interest rate on discount loans), and then banks make decisions about whether to borrow. The amount of discount loans, though influenced by the Fed's setting of the discount rate, is not completely controlled by the Fed; banks' decisions play a role, too.

Therefore, we might want to split the monetary base into two components: one that the Fed can control completely and another that is less tightly controlled. The less tightly controlled component is the amount of the base that is created by discount loans from the Fed. The remainder of the base (called the **nonborrowed monetary base**) is under the Fed's control, because it results primarily from open market operations.[5] The nonborrowed monetary base is formally defined as the monetary base minus banks' borrowings from the Fed (discount loans), which are referred to as **borrowed reserves**:

$$MB_n = MB - BR$$

where MB_n = nonborrowed monetary base
MB = monetary base
BR = borrowed reserves from the Fed

The reason for distinguishing the nonborrowed monetary base MB_n from the monetary base MB is that the nonborrowed monetary base, which is tied to open market

[5]Actually, there are other items on the Fed's balance sheet (discussed in the appendix on the web site) that affect the magnitude of the nonborrowed monetary base. Because their effects on the nonborrowed base relative to open market operations are both small and predictable, these other items do not present the Fed with difficulties in controlling the nonborrowed base.

operations, is directly under the control of the Fed, whereas the monetary base, which is also influenced by discount loans from the Fed, is not.

To complete the money supply model, we use $MB = MB_n + BR$ and rewrite the money supply model as

$$M = m \times (MB_n + BR) \quad (5)$$

where the money multiplier m is defined as in Equation 4. Thus, in addition to the effects on the money supply of the required reserve ratio, currency ratio, and excess reserves ratio, the expanded model stipulates that the money supply is also affected by changes in MB_n and BR. Because the money multiplier is positive, Equation 5 immediately tells us that the money supply is positively related to both the nonborrowed monetary base and borrowed reserves. However, it is still worth developing the intuition for these results.

Changes in the Nonborrowed Monetary Base MB_n

As shown in Chapter 16, the Fed's open market purchases increase the nonborrowed monetary base, and its open market sales decrease it. Holding all other variables constant, an increase in MB_n arising from an open market purchase increases the amount of the monetary base that is available to support currency and deposits, so the money supply will increase. Similarly, an open market sale that decreases MB_n shrinks the amount of the monetary base available to support currency and deposits, thereby causing the money supply to decrease.

We have the following result: ***The money supply is positively related to the nonborrowed monetary base*** MB_n.

Changes in Borrowed Reserves *BR* from the Fed

With the nonborrowed monetary base MB_n unchanged, more discount loans from the Fed provide additional borrowed reserves (and hence higher *MB*) to the banking system, and these are used to support more currency and deposits. As a result, the increase in *BR* will lead to a rise in the money supply. If banks reduce the level of their discount loans, with all other variables held constant, the amount of *MB* available to support currency and deposits will decline, causing the money supply to decline.

The result is this: ***The money supply is positively related to the level of borrowed reserves, BR, from the Fed.*** However, because the Federal Reserve now (since January 2003) keeps the interest rate on discount loans (the discount rate) above market interest rates at which banks can borrow from each other, banks usually have little incentive to take out discount loans. Borrowed reserves, *BR*, is thus very small except under exceptional circumstances that will be discussed in the next chapter.

OVERVIEW OF THE MONEY SUPPLY PROCESS

We now have a model of the money supply process in which all four of the players—the Federal Reserve System, depositors, banks, and borrowers from banks—directly influence the money supply. As a study aid, Table 1 charts the money supply (M1) response to the six variables discussed and gives a brief synopsis of the reasoning behind each result.

SUMMARY TABLE 1 Money Supply (M1) Response

Player	Variable	Change in Variable	Money Supply Response	Reason
Federal Reserve System	Required reserve ratio, r	↑	↓	Less multiple deposit expansion
	Nonborrowed monetary base, MB_n	↑	↑	More MB to support checkable deposits, D, and currency, C
	Borrowed reserves, BR	↑	↑	More MB to support D and C
Depositors	Currency ratio, c	↑	↓	Less multiple deposit expansion
Depositors and banks	Expected deposit outflows	↑	↓	Excess reserves, e, ↑ so fewer reserves to support D
Borrowers from banks and the other three players	Interest rate, i	↑	↑	e ↓ so more reserves to support D

Note: Only increases (↑) in the variables are shown. The effects of decreases on the money supply would be the opposite of those indicated in the "Money Supply Response" column.

STUDY GUIDE

To improve your understanding of the money supply process, slowly work through the logic behind the results in Table 1 rather than just memorizing the results. Then see if you can construct your own table in which all the variables decrease rather than increase.

The variables are grouped by the player or players who either influence the variable or are most influenced by it. The Federal Reserve, for example, influences the money supply by controlling the first three variables (called tools of the Fed)—r, MB_n, and BR. (How these tools are used is discussed in subsequent chapters.) Depositors influence the money supply through their decisions about the currency ratio c, while banks influence the money supply by their decisions about e, which are affected by their expectations about deposit outflows. Because depositors' behavior also influences bankers' expectations about deposit outflows, this variable also reflects the role of both depositors and bankers in the money supply process. Market interest rates, as represented by i, affect the money supply through the excess reserves ratio e. As shown in Chapter 5, the demand for loans by borrowers influences market interest rates, as does the supply of money. Therefore, all four players are important in the determination of i.

APPLICATION Explaining Movements in the Money Supply, 1980–2005

To make the theoretical analysis of this chapter more concrete, we need to see whether the model of the money supply process developed here helps us understand recent movements of the money supply. We look at money supply movements from 1980 to 2005—a particularly interesting period, because the growth rate of the money supply displayed unusually high variability.

Figure 2 shows the movements of the money supply (M1) from 1980 to 2005, with the percentage next to each bracket representing the annual growth rate for the bracketed period: From January 1980 to October 1984, for example, the money supply grew at a 7.2% annual rate. The variability of money growth in the 1980–2005 period is quite apparent, swinging from 7.2% to 13.1%, down to 3.3%, then up to 11.1% and finally back down to 1.6%. What explains these sharp swings in the growth rate of the money supply?

Our money supply model, as represented by Equation 5, suggests that the movements in the money supply that we see in Figure 2 are explained by either changes in $MB_n + BR$ (the nonborrowed monetary base plus borrowed reserves) or by changes in

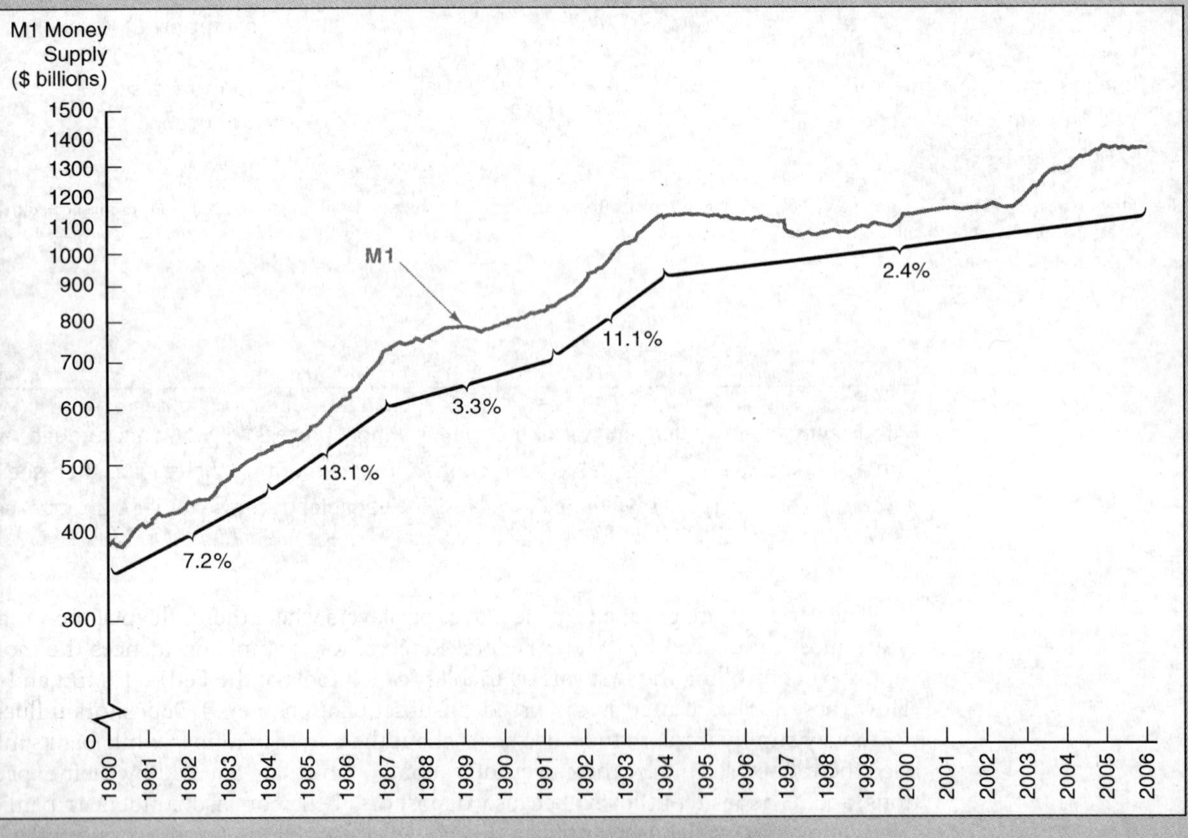

FIGURE 2 **Money Supply (M1), 1980–2005**
Percentage for each bracket indicates the annual growth rate of the money supply over the bracketed period.

Source: Federal Reserve: www.federalreserve.gov/releases/h6/hist/h6hist1.txt.

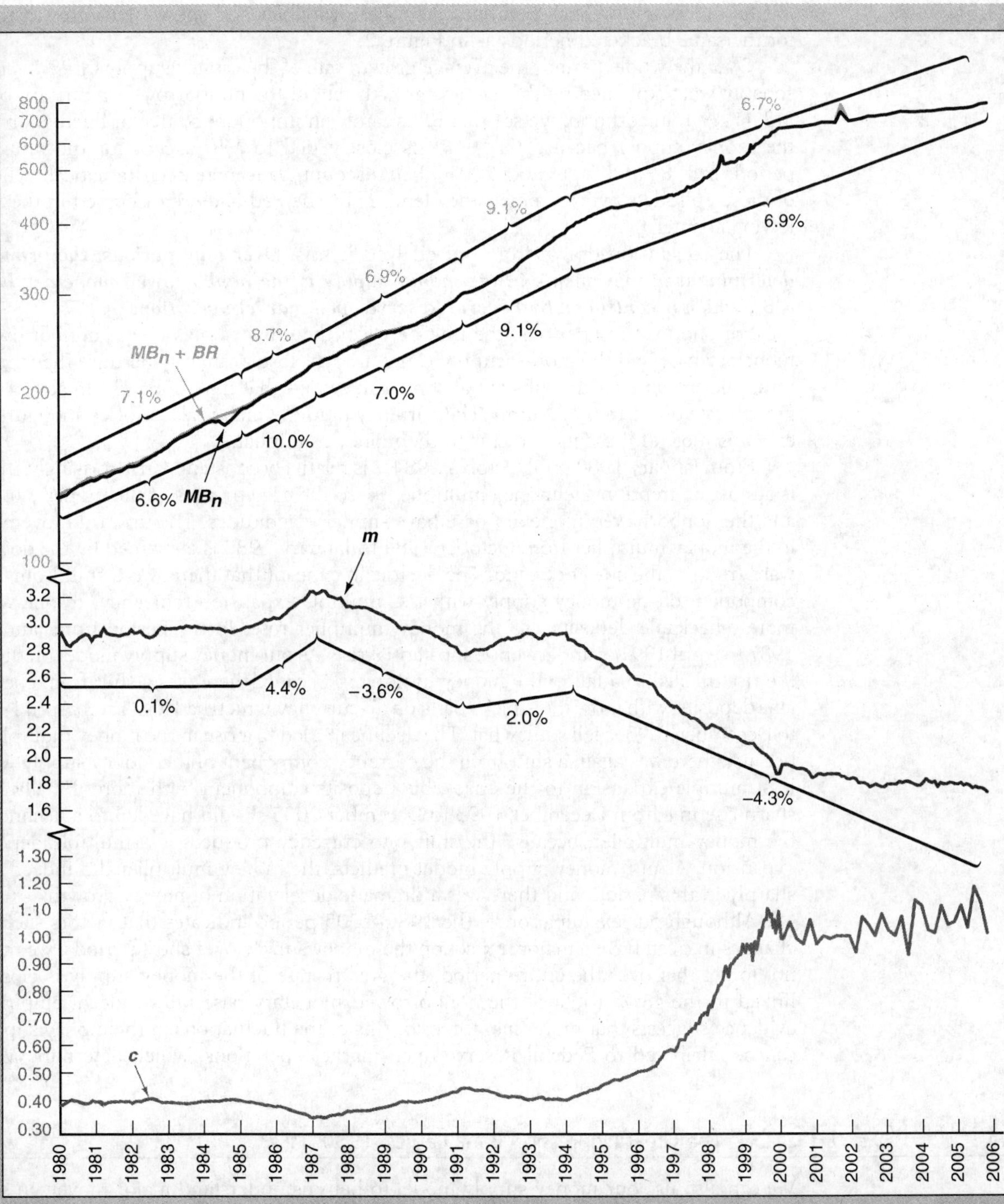

FIGURE 3 **Determinants of the Money Supply, 1980–2005**
Percentage for each bracket indicates the annual growth rate of the series over the bracketed period.

Source: Federal Reserve: www.federalreserve.gov/releases.

m (the money multiplier). Figure 3 plots these variables and shows their growth rates for the same bracketed periods as in Figure 2.

Over the whole period, the average growth rate of the money supply (4.9%) is reasonably well explained by the average growth rate of the nonborrowed monetary base MB_n (7.1%). In addition, we see that BR is rarely an important source of fluctuations in the money supply because $MB_n + BR$ is closely tied to MB_n except for the unusual periods in 1984 and September 2001 when discount loans increased dramatically. (Both of these episodes involved emergency lending by the Fed and are discussed in the following chapter.)

The conclusion drawn from our analysis is this: ***Over long periods, the primary determinant of movements in the money supply is the nonborrowed monetary base MB_n, which is controlled by Federal Reserve open market operations.***

For shorter time periods, the link between the growth rates of the nonborrowed monetary base and the money supply is not always close, primarily because the money multiplier m experiences substantial short-run swings that have a major impact on the growth rate of the money supply. The currency ratio c, which is also plotted in Figure 3, explains most of these movements in the money multiplier.

From January 1980 until October 1984, c is relatively constant. Unsurprisingly, there is almost no trend in the money multiplier m, so the growth rates of the money supply and the nonborrowed monetary base have similar magnitudes. The upward movement in the money multiplier from October 1984 to January 1987 is explained by the downward trend in the currency ratio. The decline in c meant that there was a shift from one component of the money supply with less multiple expansion (currency) to one with more (checkable deposits), so the money multiplier rose. In the period from January 1987 to April 1991, c underwent a substantial rise. As our money supply model predicts, the rise in c led to a fall in the money multiplier, because there was a shift from checkable deposits, with more multiple expansion, to currency, which had less. From April 1991 to December 1993, c fell somewhat. The decline in c led to a rise in the money multiplier, because there was again a shift from the currency component of the money supply with less multiple expansion to the checkable deposits component with more. Finally, the sharp rise in c from December 1993 to December 2005 should have led to a decline in the money multiplier, because the shift into currency produces less multiple deposit expansion. As our money supply model predicts, the money multiplier did indeed fall sharply in this period, and there was a dramatic deceleration of money growth.

Although our examination of the 1980–2005 period indicates that factors such as changes in c can have a major impact on the money supply over short periods, we must not forget that over the entire period, the growth rate of the money supply is closely linked to the growth rate of the nonborrowed monetary base MB_n. Indeed, empirical evidence suggests that more than three-fourths of the fluctuations in the money supply can be attributed to Federal Reserve open market operations, which determine MB_n.

APPLICATION The Great Depression Bank Panics, 1930–1933

We can also use our money supply model to help us understand major movements in the money supply that have occurred in the past. In this application, we use the model to explain the monetary contraction that occurred during the Great Depression, the worst economic downturn in U.S. history. In Chapter 8, we discussed bank panics and saw that they could harm the economy by making asymmetric information problems more severe in credit markets, as they did during the Great Depression. Here we can

FIGURE 4
Deposits of Failed Commercial Banks, 1929–1933

Source: Milton Friedman and Anna Jacobson Schwartz, *A Monetary History of the United States, 1867–1960* (Princeton, N.J.: Princeton University Press, 1963), p. 309.

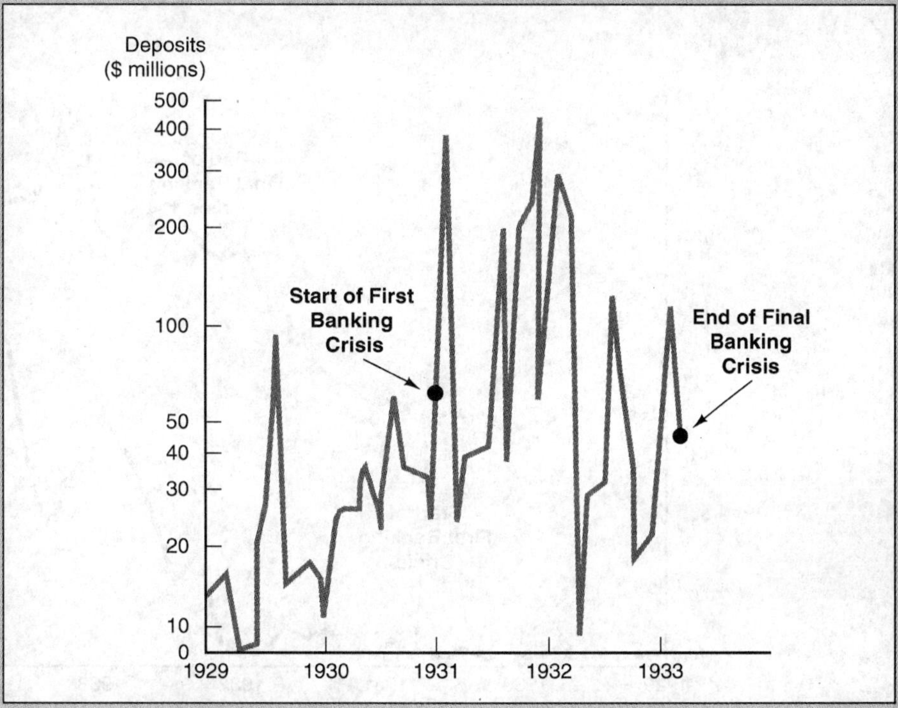

see that another consequence of bank panics is that they can cause a substantial reduction in the money supply. As we will see in the chapters on monetary theory later in the book, such reductions can also cause severe damage to the economy.

Figure 4 traces the bank crisis during the Great Depression by showing the volume of deposits at failed commercial banks from 1929 to 1933. In their classic book *A Monetary History of the United States, 1867–1960*, Milton Friedman and Anna Schwartz describe the onset of the first banking crisis in late 1930 as follows:

> Before October 1930, deposits of suspended [failed] commercial banks had been somewhat higher than during most of 1929 but not out of line with experience during the preceding decade. In November 1930, they were more than double the highest value recorded since the start of monthly data in 1921. A crop of bank failures, particularly in Missouri, Indiana, Illinois, Iowa, Arkansas, and North Carolina, led to widespread attempts to convert checkable and time deposits into currency, and also, to a much lesser extent, into postal savings deposits. A contagion of fear spread among depositors, starting from the agricultural areas, which had experienced the heaviest impact of bank failures in the twenties. But failure of 256 banks with $180 million of deposits in November 1930 was followed by the failure of 532 with over $370 million of deposits in December (all figures seasonally unadjusted), the most dramatic being the failure on December 11 of the Bank of United States with over $200 million of deposits. That failure was especially important. The Bank of United States was the largest commercial bank, as measured by volume of deposits, ever to have failed up to that time in U.S. history. Moreover, though it was just an ordinary commercial bank, the Bank of United

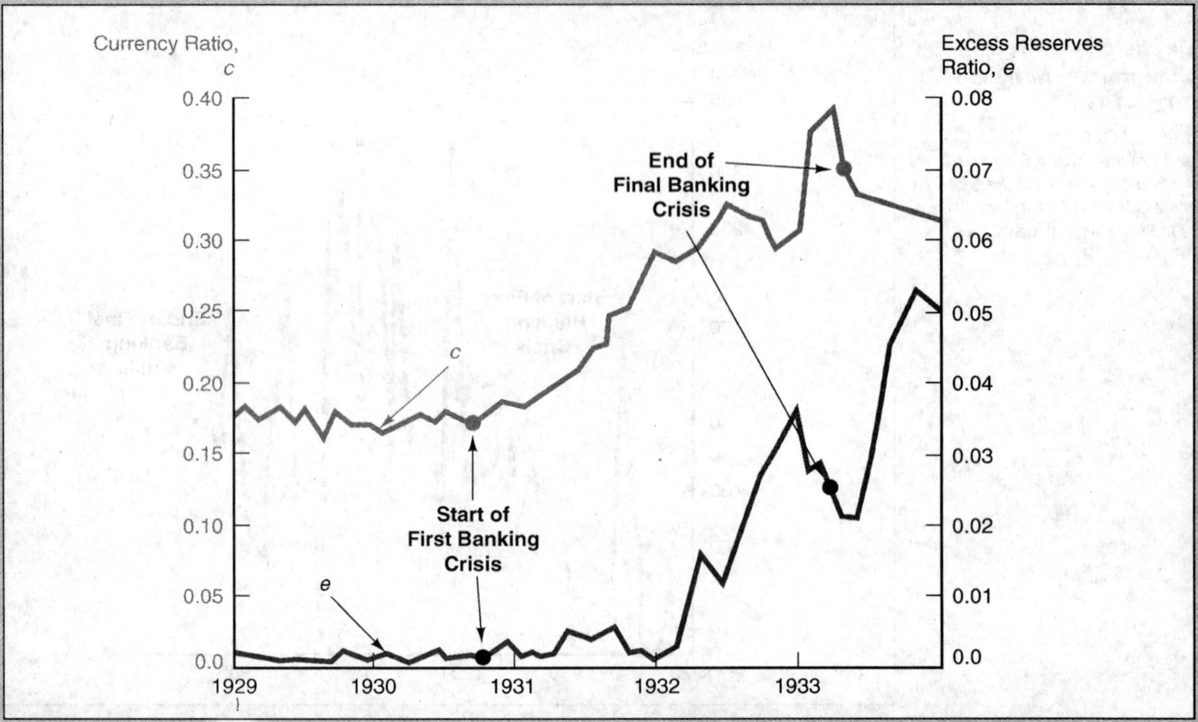

FIGURE 5 Excess Reserves Ratio and Currency Ratio, 1929–1933

Sources: Federal Reserve *Bulletin*; Milton Friedman and Anna Jacobson Schwartz, *A Monetary History of the United States, 1867–1960* (Princeton, N.J.: Princeton University Press, 1963), p. 333.

States's name had led many at home and abroad to regard it somehow as an official bank, hence its failure constituted more of a blow to confidence than would have been administered by the fall of a bank with a less distinctive name.[6]

The first bank panic, from October 1930 to January 1931, is clearly visible in Figure 4 at the end of 1930, when there is a rise in the amount of deposits at failed banks. Because there was no deposit insurance at the time (the FDIC wasn't established until 1934), when a bank failed, depositors would receive only partial repayment of their deposits. Therefore, when banks were failing during a bank panic, depositors knew that they would be likely to suffer substantial losses on deposits and thus the expected return on deposits would be negative. The theory of asset demand predicts that with the onset of the first bank crisis, depositors would shift their holdings from checkable deposits to currency by withdrawing currency from their bank accounts, and c would rise. Our earlier analysis of the excess reserves ratio suggests that the resulting surge in deposit outflows would cause the banks to protect themselves by substantially increasing their excess reserves ratio e. Both of these predictions are borne out by the

[6]Milton Friedman and Anna Jacobson Schwartz, *A Monetary History of the United States, 1867–1960* (Princeton, N.J.: Princeton University Press, 1963), pp. 308–311.

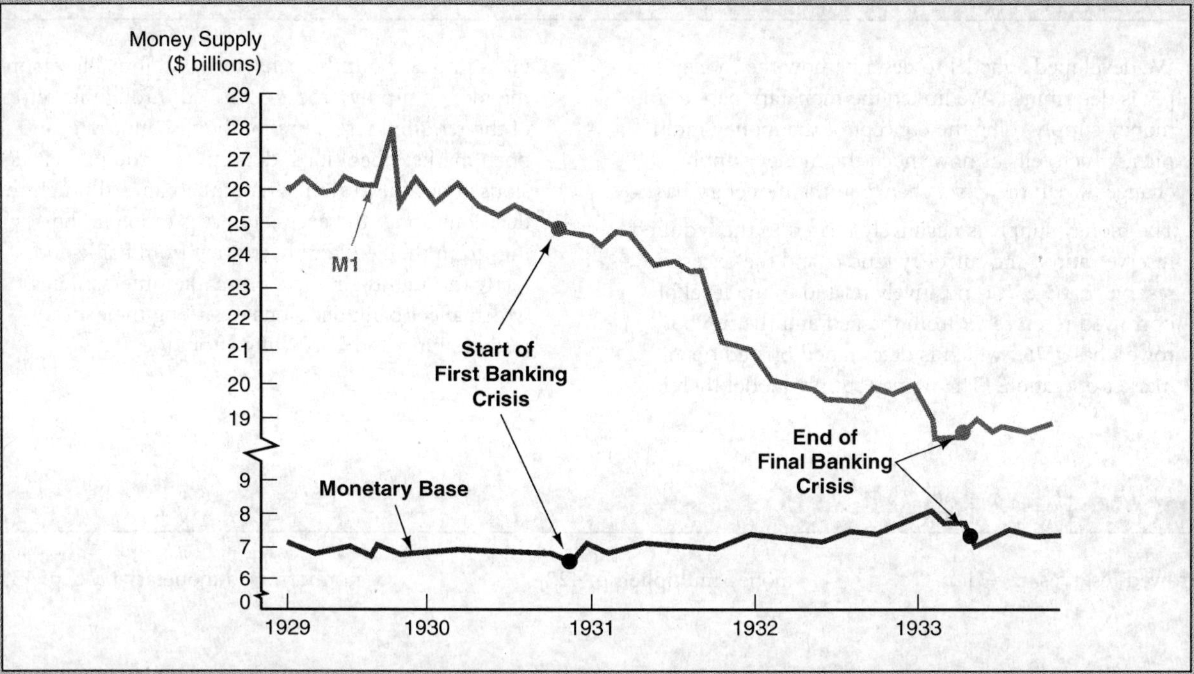

FIGURE 6 **M1 and the Monetary Base, 1929–1933**

Source: Milton Friedman and Anna Jacobson Schwartz, *A Monetary History of the United States, 1867–1960* (Princeton, N.J.: Princeton University Press, 1963), p. 333.

data in Figure 5. During the first bank panic (October 1930–January 1931) *c* began to climb. Even more striking is the behavior of *e*, which more than doubled from November 1930 to January 1931.

The money supply model predicts that when *e* and *c* increase, the money supply will contract. The rise in *c* results in a decline in the overall level of multiple deposit expansion, leading to a smaller money multiplier and a decline in the money supply, while the rise in *e* reduces the amount of reserves available to support deposits and also causes the money supply to decrease. Thus our model predicts that the rise in *e* and *c* after the onset of the first bank crisis would result in a decline in the money supply—a prediction borne out by the evidence in Figure 6.

Banking crises continued to occur from 1931 to 1933, and the pattern predicted by our model persisted: *c* continued to rise, and so did *e*. By the end of the crises in March 1933, the money supply (M1) had declined by over 25%—by far the largest decline in all of American history—and it coincided with the nation's worst economic contraction (see Chapter 8). Even more remarkable is that this decline occurred despite a 20% rise in the level of the monetary base—which illustrates how important the changes in *c* and *e* during bank panics can be in the determination of the money supply. It also illustrates that the Fed's job of conducting monetary policy can be complicated by depositor and bank behavior.

SUMMARY

1. We developed a model to describe how the money supply is determined. We linked the monetary base to the money supply using the concept of the money multiplier, which tells us how much the money supply changes when there is a change in the monetary base.
2. The money supply is negatively related to the required reserve ratio r, the currency ratio c, and the excess reserves ratio e. It is positively related to the level of borrowed reserves BR from the Fed and the nonborrowed base MB_n, which is determined by Fed open market operations. The money supply model therefore takes into account the behavior of all four players in the money supply process: the Fed through its setting of the required reserve ratio, the discount rate, and open market operations; depositors through their decisions about the currency ratio; the banks through their decisions about the excess reserves ratio and borrowings from the Fed; and borrowers from banks indirectly through their effect on market interest rates, which affect bank decisions regarding the excess reserves ratio and borrowings from the Fed.

KEY TERMS

borrowed reserves, p. 431

money multiplier, p. 423

nonborrowed monetary base, p. 431

QUESTIONS AND PROBLEMS

Questions marked with an asterisk are answered at the end of the book in an appendix, "Answers to Selected Questions and Problems." Questions marked with a blue circle indicate the question is available in MyEconLab at www.myeconlab.com/mishkin.

*1. "The money multiplier is necessarily greater than 1." Is this statement true, false, or uncertain? Explain your answer.

2. "If reserve requirements on checkable deposits were set at zero, the amount of multiple deposit expansion would go on indefinitely." Is this statement true, false, or uncertain? Explain.

*3. During the Great Depression years 1930–1933, the currency ratio c rose dramatically. What do you think happened to the money supply? Why?

4. During the Great Depression, the excess reserves ratio e rose dramatically. What do you think happened to the money supply? Why?

*5. Traveler's checks have no reserve requirements and are included in the M1 measure of the money supply. When people travel during the summer and convert some of their checking account deposits into traveler's checks, what happens to the money supply? Why?

6. If Jane Brown closes her account at the First National Bank and uses the money instead to open a money market mutual fund account, what happens to M1? Why?

*7. Some experts have suggested that reserve requirements on checkable deposits and time deposits should be set equal because this would improve control of M2. Does this argument make sense? (*Hint:* Look at the appendix to this chapter and think about what happens when checkable deposits are converted into time deposits, and vice versa.)

8. Why might the procyclical behavior of interest rates (rising during business cycle expansions and falling during recessions) lead to procyclical movements in the money supply?

Using Economic Analysis to Predict the Future

*9. The Fed buys $100 million of bonds from the public and also lowers r. What will happen to the money supply?

10. The Fed has been discussing the possibility of paying interest on excess reserves. If this occurred, what would happen to the level of e?

*11 If the Fed sells \$1 million of bonds and banks reduce their borrowings from the Fed by \$1 million, predict what will happen to the money supply.

12 Predict what will happen to the money supply if there is a sharp rise in the currency ratio.

*13 What do you predict would happen to the money supply if expected inflation suddenly increased?

14 If the economy starts to boom and loan demand picks up, what do you predict will happen to the money supply?

*15. Milton Friedman once suggested that Federal Reserve discount lending (and borrowed reserves) should be abolished. Predict what would happen to the money supply if Friedman's suggestion were put into practice.

WEB EXERCISES

1. An important aspect of the supply of money is reserve balances. Go to www.federalreserve.gov/Releases/h41/ and locate the most recent release. This site reports changes in factors that affect depository reserve balances.
   a. What is the current reserve balance?
   b. What is the change in reserve balances since a year ago?
   c. Based on parts a and b, does it appear that the money supply should be increasing or decreasing?
2. Refer to Figure 3, Determinants of the Money Supply, 1980–2005. Go to www.federalreserve.gov/Releases/h3/Current/ where the monetary base (*MB*) and borrowed reserves (*BR*) are reported. Compute the growth rate in $MB + BR$ since the end of 2005. How does this compare to previous periods reported on the graph?

WEB REFERENCES

www.federalreserve.gov/Releases/h3/

The Federal Reserve web site reports data about aggregate reserves and the monetary base. This site also reports on the volume of borrowings from the Fed.

www.federalreserve.gov/Releases/h6/

This site reports current and historical levels of M1, M2, and M3, and other data on the money supply.

APPENDIX TO CHAPTER 17

The M2 Money Multiplier

The derivation of a money multiplier for the M2 definition of money requires only slight modifications to the analysis in the chapter. The definition of M2 is

$$M2 = C + D + T + MMF$$

where C = currency in circulation
D = checkable deposits
T = time and savings deposits
MMF = primarily money market mutual fund shares and money market deposit accounts, plus overnight repurchase agreements and overnight Eurodollars

We again assume that all desired quantities of these variables rise proportionally with checkable deposits so that the equilibrium ratios c, $t = \{T/D\}$, and $mm = \{MMF/D\}$ set by depositors are treated as constants. Replacing C by $c \times D$, T by $t \times D$, and MMF by $mm \times D$ in the definition of M2 just given, we get

$$\begin{aligned} M2 &= D + (C \times D) + (t \times D) + (mm \times D) \\ &= (1 + c + t + mm) \times D \end{aligned}$$

Substituting in the expression for D from Equation 2 in the chapter,[1] we have

$$M2 = \frac{1 + c + t + mm}{r + e + c} \times MB \tag{1}$$

To see what this formula implies about the M2 money multiplier, we continue with the same numerical example in the chapter, with the additional information that $T =$ \$2,400 billion and $MMF =$ \$400 billion so that $t = 3$ and $mm = 0.5$. The resulting value of the multiplier for M2 is

$$m_2 = \frac{1 + 0.5 + 3 + 0.5}{0.10 + 0.001 + 0.5} = \frac{5.0}{0.601} = 8.32$$

[1]From the derivation here it is clear that the quantity of checkable deposits D is unaffected by the depositor ratios t and mm even though time deposits and money market mutual fund shares are included in M2. This is just a consequence of the absence of reserve requirements on time deposits and money market mutual fund shares, so T and MMF do not appear in any of the equations in the derivation of D in the chapter.

An important feature of the M2 multiplier is that it is substantially larger than the M1 multiplier of 2.5 that we found in the chapter. The crucial concept in understanding this difference is that a lower required reserve ratio for time deposits or money market mutual fund shares means that they undergo more multiple expansion because fewer reserves are needed to support the same amount of them. Time deposits and *MMFs* have a lower required reserve ratio than checkable deposits—zero—and they will therefore have more multiple expansion than checkable deposits will. Thus the overall multiple expansion for the sum of these deposits will be greater than for checkable deposits alone, so the M2 money multiplier will be greater than the M1 money multiplier.

FACTORS THAT DETERMINE THE M2 MONEY MULTIPLIER

Changes in r, c, and e

The economic reasoning analyzing the effect of changes in the required reserve ratio and the currency ratio on the M2 money multiplier is identical to that used for the M1 multiplier in the chapter. An increase in the required reserve ratio r will decrease the amount of multiple deposit expansion, thus lowering the M2 money multiplier. An increase in c means that depositors have shifted out of checkable deposits into currency. Because currency has no multiple deposit expansion, the overall level of multiple deposit expansion for M2 must also fall, lowering the M2 multiplier. An increase in the excess reserves ratio e means that banks use fewer reserves to support deposits, so deposits and the M2 money multiplier fall.

We thus have the same results we found for the M1 multiplier: ***The M2 money multiplier and M2 money supply are negatively related to the required reserve ratio r, the currency ratio c, and the excess reserves ratio e.***

Response to Changes in t and mm

An increase in either t or mm leads to an increase in the M2 multiplier because the required reserve ratios on time deposits and money market mutual fund shares are zero and hence are lower than the required reserve ratio on checkable deposits.

Both time deposits and money market mutual fund shares undergo more multiple expansion than checkable deposits. Thus a shift out of checkable deposits into time deposits or money market mutual funds, increasing t or mm, implies that the overall level of multiple expansion will increase, raising the M2 money multiplier.

A decline in t or mm will result in less overall multiple expansion, and the M2 money multiplier will decrease, leading to the following conclusion: ***The M2 money multiplier and M2 money supply are positively related to both the time deposit ratio t and the money market fund ratio mm.***

The response of the M2 money supply to all the depositor and required reserve ratios is summarized in Table 1.

SUMMARY TABLE 1 Response of the M2 Money Supply to Changes in MB_n, BR, r, e, c, t, and mm

Variable	Change in Variable	M2 Money Supply Response	Reason
MB_n	↑	↑	More *MB* to support *C* and *D*
BR	↑	↑	More *MB* to support *C* and *D*
r	↑	↓	Less multiple deposit expansion
e	↑	↓	Fewer reserves to support *D*
c	↑	↓	Less multiple deposit expansion
t	↑	↑	More multiple deposit expansion
mm	↑	↑	More multiple deposit expansion

Note: Only increases (↑) in the variables are shown; the effects of decreases in the variables on the M2 money supply would be the opposite of those indicated in the "Response" column.

CHAPTER

18 Tools of Monetary Policy

Preview

In the chapters describing the structure of the Federal Reserve System and the money supply process, we mentioned three policy tools that the Fed can use to manipulate the money supply and interest rates: open market operations, which affect the quantity of reserves and the monetary base; changes in borrowed reserves, which affect the monetary base; and changes in reserve requirements, which affect the money multiplier. Because the Fed's use of these policy tools has such an important impact on interest rates and economic activity, it is important to understand how the Fed wields them in practice and how relatively useful each tool is.

In recent years, the Federal Reserve has increasingly focused on the **federal funds rate** (the interest rate on overnight loans of reserves from one bank to another) as the primary indicator of the stance of monetary policy. Since February 1994, the Fed announces a federal funds rate target at each Federal Open Market Committee (FOMC) meeting, an announcement that is watched closely by market participants because it affects interest rates throughout the economy. Thus, to fully understand how the Fed's tools are used in the conduct of monetary policy, we must understand not only their effect on the money supply, but also their direct effects on the federal funds rate. The chapter therefore begins with a supply and demand analysis of the market for reserves to explain how the Fed's settings for the three tools of monetary policy determine the federal funds rate. We then go on to look in more detail at each of the three tools—open market operations, discount rate policy, and reserve requirements—to see how they are used in practice and to ask whether the use of these tools could be modified to improve the conduct of monetary policy. The chapter ends with a discussion of the tools of monetary policy used by other central banks besides the Federal Reserve.

THE MARKET FOR RESERVES AND THE FEDERAL FUNDS RATE

In Chapter 16, we saw how open market operations and discount lending (changes in borrowed reserves) affect the balance sheet of the Fed and the amount of reserves. The market for reserves is where the federal funds rate is determined, and this is why we turn to a supply and demand analysis of this market to analyze how all three tools of monetary policy affect the federal funds rate.

Supply and Demand in the Market for Reserves

The analysis of the market for reserves proceeds in a similar fashion to the analysis of the bond market we conducted in Chapter 5. We derive a demand and supply curve for reserves. Then the market equilibrium in which the quantity of reserves demanded equals the quantity of reserves supplied determines the federal funds rate, the interest rate charged on the loans of these reserves.

Demand Curve. To derive the demand curve for reserves, we need to ask what happens to the quantity of reserves demanded, holding everything else constant, as the federal funds rate changes. Recall from Chapter 17 that the amount of reserves can be split up into two components: (1) required reserves, which equal the required reserve ratio times the amount of deposits on which reserves are required, and (2) excess reserves, the additional reserves banks choose to hold. Therefore, the quantity of reserves demanded equals required reserves plus the quantity of excess reserves demanded. Excess reserves are insurance against deposit outflows, and the cost of holding these excess reserves is their opportunity cost, the interest rate that could have been earned on lending these reserves out, which is equivalent to the federal funds rate. Thus, as the federal funds rate decreases, the opportunity cost of holding excess reserves falls and, holding everything else constant, including the quantity of required reserves, the quantity of reserves demanded rises. Consequently, the demand curve for reserves, R^d, slopes downward in Figure 1.

Supply Curve. The supply of reserves, R^s, can be broken up into two components: the amount of reserves that are supplied by the Fed's open market operations, called nonborrowed reserves (*NBR*), and the amount of reserves borrowed from the Fed, called *borrowed reserves* (*BR*). The primary cost of borrowing from the Fed is the interest rate the Fed charges on these loans, the discount rate (i_d). Because borrowing fed-

myeconlab

FIGURE 1
Equilibrium in the Market for Reserves
Equilibrium occurs at the intersection of the supply curve R^s and the demand curve R^d at point 1 and an interest rate of i^*_{ff}.

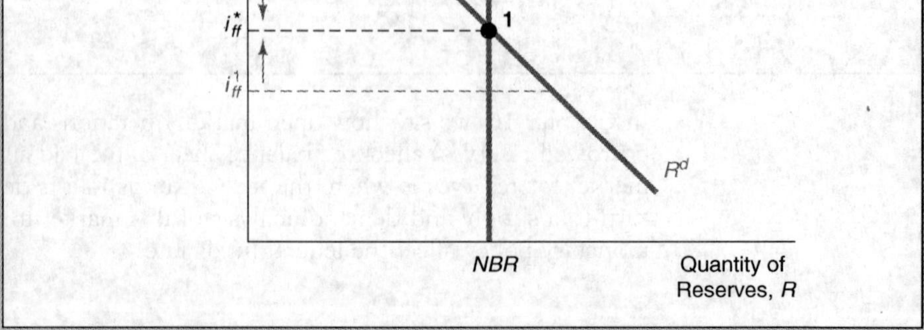

eral funds from other banks is a substitute for borrowing (taking out discount loans) from the Fed, if the federal funds rate i_{ff} is below the discount rate i_d, then banks will not borrow from the Fed and borrowed reserves will be zero because borrowing in the federal funds market is cheaper. Thus, as long as i_{ff} remains below i_d, the supply of reserves will just equal the amount of nonborrowed reserves supplied by the Fed, *NBR*, and so the supply curve will be vertical as shown in Figure 1. However, as the federal funds rate begins to rise above the discount rate, banks would want to keep borrowing more and more at i_d and then lending out the proceeds in the federal funds market at the higher rate, i_{ff}. The result is that the supply curve becomes flat (infinitely elastic) at i_d, as shown in Figure 1.

Market Equilibrium. Market equilibrium occurs where the quantity of reserves demanded equals the quantity supplied, $R^s = R^d$. Equilibrium therefore occurs at the intersection of the demand curve R^d and the supply curve R^s at point 1, with an equilibrium federal funds rate of i^*_{ff}. When the federal funds rate is above the equilibrium rate at i^2_{ff}, there are more reserves supplied than demanded (excess supply) and so the federal funds rate falls to i^*_{ff} as shown by the downward arrow. When the federal funds rate is below the equilibrium rate at i^1_{ff}, there are more reserves demanded than supplied (excess demand) and so the federal funds rate rises as shown by the upward arrow. (Note that Figure 1 is drawn so that i_d is above i^*_{ff} because the Federal Reserve now keeps the discount rate substantially above the target for the federal funds rate.)

How Changes in the Tools of Monetary Policy Affect the Federal Funds Rate

Now that we understand how the federal funds rate is determined, we can examine how changes in the three tools of monetary policy—open market operations, discount lending, and reserve requirements—affect the market for reserves and the equilibrium federal funds rate.

Open Market Operations. We have already seen that an open market purchase leads to a greater quantity of reserves supplied; this is true at any given federal funds rate because of the higher amount of nonborrowed reserves, which rises from NBR_1 to NBR_2. An open market purchase therefore shifts the supply curve to the right from R^s_1 to R^s_2 and moves the equilibrium from point 1 to point 2, lowering the federal funds rate from i^1_{ff} to i^2_{ff} (see Figure 2).[1] The same reasoning implies that an open market sale decreases the quantity of nonborrowed reserves supplied, shifts the supply curve to the left, and causes the federal funds rate to rise.

The result is that ***an open market purchase causes the federal funds rate to fall, whereas an open market sale causes the federal funds rate to rise***.

Discount Lending. The effect of a discount rate change depends on whether the demand curve intersects the supply curve in its vertical section versus its flat section. Panel (a) of Figure 3 shows what happens if the intersection occurs at the vertical section of the supply curve so there is no discount lending and borrowed reserves, *BR*, are

---

[1]We come to the same conclusion using the money supply framework in Chapter 17, along with the liquidity preference framework in Chapter 5. An open market purchase raises reserves and the money supply, and then the liquidity preference framework shows that interest rates fall.

FIGURE 2
Response to an Open Market Operation
An open market purchase increases nonborrowed reserves and hence the reserves supplied, and shifts the supply curve from R_1^s to R_2^s. The equilibrium moves from point 1 to point 2, lowering the federal funds rate from i_{ff}^1 to i_{ff}^2.

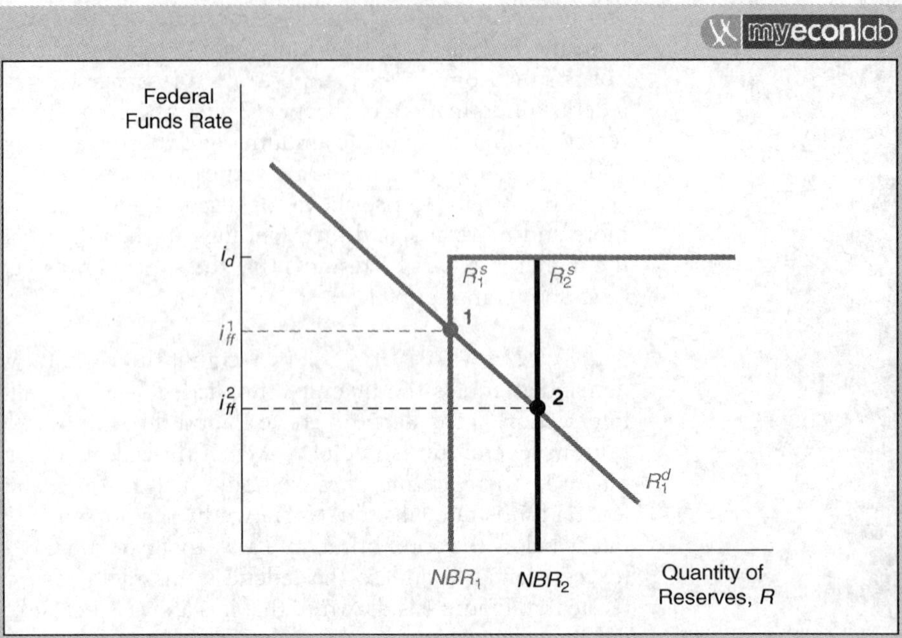

zero. In this case, when the discount rate is lowered by the Fed from i_d^1 to i_d^2, the vertical section of the supply curve where there is no discount lending just shortens, as in R_2^s, while the intersection of the supply and demand curve remains at the same point. Thus, in this case, there is no change in the equilibrium federal funds rate, which remains at i_{ff}^1. Because this is the typical situation—since the Fed now usually keeps the discount rate above its target for the federal funds rate—the conclusion is that ***most changes in the discount rate have no effect on the federal funds rate.***

However, if the demand curve intersects the supply curve on its flat section, so there is some discount lending, as in panel (b) of Figure 3, changes in the discount rate do affect the federal funds rate. In this case, initially discount lending is positive and the equilibrium federal funds rate equals the discount rate, $i_{ff}^1 = i_d^1$. When the discount rate is lowered by the Fed from i_d^1 to i_d^2, the horizontal section of the supply curve R_2^s falls, moving the equilibrium from point 1 to point 2, and the equilibrium federal funds rate falls from i_{ff}^1 to i_{ff}^2 $(= i_d^2)$ in panel (b).

Reserve Requirements. When the required reserve ratio increases, required reserves increase and hence the quantity of reserves demanded increases for any given interest rate. Thus a rise in the required reserve ratio shifts the demand curve to the right from R_1^d to R_2^d in Figure 4, moves the equilibrium from point 1 to point 2, and in turn raises the federal funds rate from i_{ff}^1 to i_{ff}^2.

The result is that ***when the Fed raises reserve requirements, the federal funds rate rises.***[2]

[2]Because an increase in the required reserve ratio means that the same amount of reserves is able to support a smaller amount of deposits, a rise in the required reserve ratio leads to a decline in the money supply. Using the liquidity preference framework, the fall in the money supply results in a rise in interest rates, yielding the same conclusion in the text—that raising reserve requirements leads to higher interest rates.

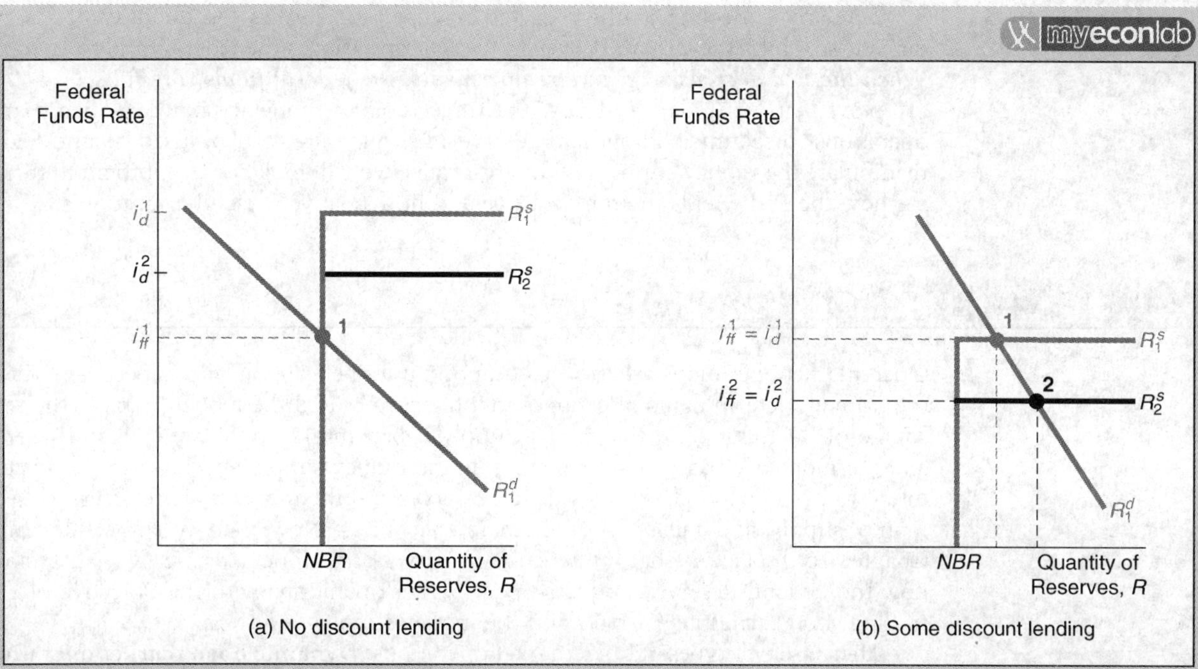

FIGURE 3 Response to a Change in the Discount Rate
In panel (a) when the discount rate is lowered by the Fed from i_d^1 to i_d^2, the vertical section of the supply curve just shortens, as in R_2^s, so that the equilibrium federal funds rate remains unchanged at i_{ff}^1. In panel (b) when the discount rate is lowered by the Fed from i_d^1 to i_d^2, the horizontal section of the supply curve R_2^s falls, and the equilibrium federal funds rate falls from i_{ff}^1 to i_{ff}^2.

FIGURE 4
Response to a Change in Required Reserves
When the Fed raises reserve requirements, required reserves increase, which increases the demand for reserves. The demand curve shifts from R_1^d to R_2^d, the equilibrium moves from point 1 to point 2, and the federal fund rate rises from i_{ff}^1 to i_{ff}^2.

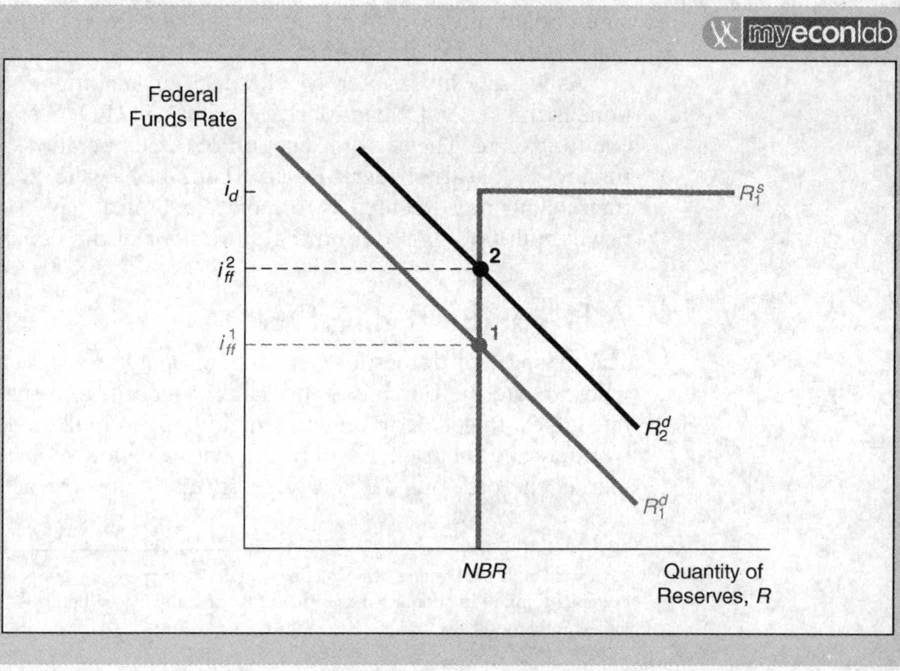

Similarly, a decline in the required reserve ratio lowers the quantity of reserves demanded, shifts the demand curve to the left, and causes the federal funds rate to fall. ***When the Fed decreases reserve requirements, the federal funds rate falls.***

Now that we understand how the three tools of monetary policy—open market operations, discount lending, and reserve requirements—can be used by the Fed to manipulate the money supply and interest rates, we will look at each of them in turn to see how the Fed wields them in practice and how relatively useful each tool is.

OPEN MARKET OPERATIONS

Open market operations are the most important monetary policy tool, because they are the primary determinants of changes in interest rates and the monetary base, the main source of fluctuations in the money supply. Open market purchases expand reserves and the monetary base, thereby increasing the money supply and lowering short-term interest rates. Open market sales shrink reserves and the monetary base, decreasing the money supply and raising short-term interest rates. Now that we understand from Chapter 16 the factors that influence the reserves and monetary base, we can examine how the Federal Reserve conducts open market operations with the objective of controlling short-term interest rates and the money supply.

There are two types of open market operations: **Dynamic open market operations** are intended to change the level of reserves and the monetary base, and **defensive open market operations** are intended to offset movements in other factors that affect reserves and the monetary base, such as changes in Treasury deposits with the Fed or changes in float. The Fed conducts open market operations in U.S. Treasury and government agency securities, especially U.S. Treasury bills.[3] The Fed conducts most of its open market operations in Treasury securities because the market for these securities is the most liquid and has the largest trading volume. It has the capacity to absorb the Fed's substantial volume of transactions without experiencing excessive price fluctuations that would disrupt the market.

As we saw in Chapter 15, the decision-making authority for open market operations is the Federal Open Market Committee (FOMC), which sets a target for the federal funds rate. The actual execution of these operations, however, is conducted by the trading desk at the Federal Reserve Bank of New York. The best way to see how these transactions are executed is to look at a typical day at the trading desk, located in a newly built trading room on the ninth floor of the Federal Reserve Bank of New York.

A Day at the Trading Desk

The manager of domestic open market operations supervises the analysts and traders who execute the purchases and sales of securities in the drive to hit the federal funds rate target. To get a grip on what might happen in the federal funds market that day, her workday and that of her staff begins with a review of developments in the federal funds market the previous day and with an update on the actual amount of reserves in the

[3]To avoid conflicts of interest, the Fed does not conduct open market operations in privately issued securities. (For example, think of the conflict if the Federal Reserve purchased bonds issued by a company owned by the chairman's brother-in-law.)

banking system the day before. Later in the morning, her staff issues updated reports that contain detailed forecasts of what will be happening to some of the short-term factors affecting the supply and demand of reserves (discussed in Chapter 16). For example, if float is predicted to decrease because good weather throughout the country is speeding up check delivery, the manager of domestic open market operations knows that she will have to conduct a defensive open market operation (in this case, a *purchase* of securities) to offset the expected decline in reserves and the monetary base from the decreased float. However, if Treasury deposits with the Fed are predicted to fall, a defensive open market *sale* would be needed to offset the expected increase in reserves. The report also predicts the change in the public's holding of currency. If currency holdings are expected to rise, then, as we have seen in Chapters 16 and 17, reserves fall, and an open market purchase is needed to raise reserves back up again.

This information will help the manager of domestic open market operations and her staff decide how large a change in nonborrowed reserves is needed to reach the federal funds rate target. If the amount of reserves in the banking system is too large, many banks will have excess reserves to lend that other banks may have little desire to hold, and the federal funds rate will fall. If the level of reserves is too low, banks seeking to borrow reserves from the few banks that have excess reserves to lend may push the funds rate higher than the desired level. Also during the morning, the staff will monitor the behavior of the federal funds rate and contact some of the major participants in the funds market, which may provide independent information about whether a change in reserves is needed to achieve the desired level of the federal funds rate. Early in the morning, members of the manager's staff contact several representatives of the **primary dealers**, government securities dealers (who operate out of private firms or commercial banks) that the open market desk trades with. Her staff finds out how the dealers view market conditions to get a feel for what may happen to the prices of the securities they trade in over the course of the day. They also call the Treasury to get updated information on the expected level of Treasury balances at the Fed to refine their estimates of the supply of reserves.

Shortly after 9 a.m., members of the Monetary Affairs Division at the Board of Governors are contacted, and the New York Fed's forecasts of reserve supply and demand are compared with the Board's. On the basis of these projections and the observed behavior of the federal funds market, the desk will formulate and propose a course of action to be taken that day, which may involve plans to add reserves to or drain reserves from the banking system through open market operations. If an operation is contemplated, the type, size, and maturity will be discussed.

At 9:20 a.m., a daily conference call is arranged linking the desk with the Office of the Director of Monetary Affairs at the Board of Governors and with one of the four voting Reserve Bank presidents outside of New York. During the call, a member of the open market operations unit will outline the desk's proposed reserve management strategy for the day. After the plan is approved, the desk is instructed to execute immediately any temporary open market operations that were planned for that day. (Outright operations, to be described shortly, may be conducted at other times of the day.)

The desk is linked electronically with its domestic open market trading counterparties by a computer system called TRAPS (Trading Room Automated Processing System), and all open market operations are now performed over this system. A message will be electronically transmitted simultaneously to all the primary dealers over TRAPS indicating the type and maturity of the operation being arranged. The dealers are given several minutes to respond via TRAPS with their propositions to buy or sell government securities. The propositions are then assembled and displayed on a computer screen for evaluation. The desk will select all propositions, beginning with the most attractively priced, up to the point where the desired amount is purchased or sold, and it will then notify each dealer via TRAPS which of its propositions have been chosen. The entire selection process is typically completed in a matter of minutes.

These temporary transactions are of two basic types. In a **repurchase agreement** (often called a **repo**), the Fed purchases securities with an agreement that the seller will repurchase them in a short period of time, anywhere from one to fifteen days from the original date of purchase. Because the effects on reserves of a repo are reversed on the day the agreement matures, a repo is actually a temporary open market purchase and is an especially desirable way of conducting a defensive open market purchase that will be reversed shortly. When the Fed wants to conduct a temporary open market sale, it engages in a **matched sale–purchase transaction** (sometimes called a **reverse repo**) in which the Fed sells securities and the buyer agrees to sell them back to the Fed in the near future.

At times, the desk may see the need to address a persistent reserve shortage or surplus and wish to arrange an operation that will have a more permanent impact on the supply of reserves. Outright transactions, which involve a purchase or sale of securities that is not self-reversing, are also conducted over TRAPS. These operations are traditionally executed at times of day when temporary operations are not being conducted.

Advantages of Open Market Operations

Open market operations have several advantages over the other tools of monetary policy.

1. Open market operations occur at the initiative of the Fed, which has complete control over their volume. This control is not found, for example, in discount operations, in which the Fed can encourage or discourage banks to borrow reserves by altering the discount rate but cannot directly control the volume of borrowed reserves.
2. Open market operations are flexible and precise; they can be used to any extent. No matter how small a change in reserves or the monetary base is desired, open market operations can achieve it with a small purchase or sale of securities. Conversely, if the desired change in reserves or the base is very large, the open market operations tool is strong enough to do the job through a very large purchase or sale of securities.
3. Open market operations are easily reversed. If a mistake is made in conducting an open market operation, the Fed can immediately reverse it. If the Fed decides that the federal funds rate is too low because it has made too many open market purchases, it can immediately make a correction by conducting open market sales.
4. Open market operations can be implemented quickly; they involve no administrative delays. When the Fed decides that it wants to change the monetary base or reserves, it just places orders with securities dealers, and the trades are executed immediately.

DISCOUNT POLICY

The facility at which banks can borrow reserves from the Federal Reserve is called the **discount window**. The easiest way to understand how the Fed affects the volume of borrowed reserves is by looking at how the discount window operates.

Operation of the Discount Window

The Fed's discount loans to banks are of three types: primary credit, secondary credit, and seasonal credit.[4] *Primary credit* is the discount lending that plays the most important role in monetary policy. Healthy banks are allowed to borrow all they want at very short maturities (usually overnight) from the primary credit facility, and it is therefore referred to as a **standing lending facility**. The interest rate on these loans is the discount rate, and as we mentioned before, it is set higher than the federal funds rate target, usually by 100 basis points (one percentage point), and thus in most circumstances the amount of discount lending under the primary credit facility is very small. If the amount is so small, why does the Fed have this facility?

The answer is that the facility is intended to be a backup source of liquidity for sound banks so that the federal funds rate never rises too far above the federal funds target set by the FOMC. To see how the primary credit facility works, let's see what happens if there is a large increase in the demand for reserves, say because deposits have surged unexpectedly and have led to an increase in required reserves. This situation is analyzed in Figure 5. Suppose that initially the demand and supply curves for reserves intersect at point 1 so that the federal funds rate is at its target level, i_{ff}^{T}. Now the increase in required reserves shifts the demand curve to R_2^d and the equilibrium moves to point 2. The result is that borrowed reserves increase from zero to *BR* and the federal funds rate rises to i_d and can rise no further. The primary credit facility has thus put a ceiling on the federal funds rate of i_d.

Secondary credit is given to banks that are in financial trouble and are experiencing severe liquidity problems. The interest rate on secondary credit is set at 50 basis points (0.5 percentage point) above the discount rate. The interest rate on these loans is set at a higher, penalty rate to reflect the less-sound condition of these borrowers. *Seasonal credit* is given to meet the needs of a limited number of small banks in vacation and agricultural areas that have a seasonal pattern of deposits. The interest rate charged on seasonal credit is tied to the average of the federal funds rate and certificate of deposit rates. The Federal Reserve has questioned the need for the seasonal credit facility because of improvements in credit markets and is thus contemplating eliminating it in the future.

Lender of Last Resort

In addition to its use as a tool to influence reserves, the monetary base, and the money supply, discounting is important in preventing financial panics. When the Federal Reserve System was created, its most important role was intended to be as the **lender of last resort**; to prevent bank failures from spinning out of control, it was to provide reserves to banks when no one else would, thereby preventing bank and financial panics. Discounting is a particularly effective way to provide reserves to the banking system during a banking crisis because reserves are immediately channeled to the banks that need them most.

Using the discount tool to avoid financial panics by performing the role of lender of last resort is an extremely important requirement of successful monetary policymaking. As we demonstrated with our money supply analysis in Chapter 17, the bank panics in

[4]The procedures for administering the discount window were changed in January 2003. The primary credit facility replaced an adjustment credit facility whose discount rate was typically set below market interest rates, so banks were restricted in their access to this credit. In contrast, now healthy banks can borrow all they want from the primary credit facility. The secondary credit facility replaced the extended credit facility, which focused somewhat more on longer-term credit extensions. The seasonal credit facility remains basically unchanged.

FIGURE 5

How the Primary Credit Facility Puts a Ceiling on the Federal Funds Rate

The rightward shift of the demand curve for reserves from R_1^d to R_2^d moves the equilibrium from point 1 to point 2 where $i_{ff}^2 = i_d$ and borrowed reserves increase from zero to BR.

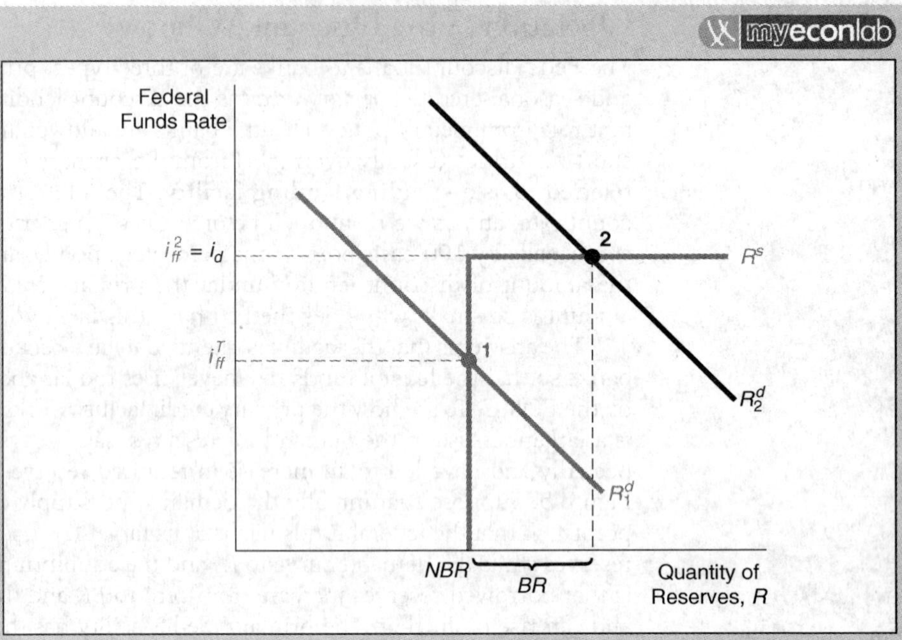

the 1930–1933 period were the cause of the sharpest decline in the money supply in U.S. history, which many economists see as the driving force behind the collapse of the economy during the Great Depression. Financial panics can also severely damage the economy because they interfere with the ability of financial intermediaries and markets to move funds to people with productive investment opportunities (see Chapter 8).

Unfortunately, the discount tool has not always been used by the Fed to prevent financial panics, as the massive failures during the Great Depression attest. The Fed learned from its mistakes of that period and has performed admirably in its role of lender of last resort in the post–World War II period. The Fed has used its discount lending weapon several times to avoid bank panics by extending loans to troubled banking institutions, thereby preventing further bank failures. The largest of these occurred in 1984, when the Fed lent Continental Illinois, at that time one of the ten largest banks in the United States, more than $5 billion.

At first glance, it might seem that the presence of the FDIC, which insures depositors up to a limit of $100,000 per account from losses due to a bank's failure, would make the lender-of-last-resort function of the Fed superfluous. There are two reasons why this is not the case. First, it is important to recognize that the FDIC's insurance fund amounts to around 1% of the amount of these deposits outstanding. If a large number of bank failures occurred, the FDIC would not be able to cover all the depositors' losses. Indeed, the large number of bank failures in the 1980s and early 1990s, described in Chapter 11, led to large losses and a shrinkage in the FDIC's insurance fund, which reduced the FDIC's ability to cover depositors' losses. This fact has not weakened the confidence of small depositors in the banking system because the Fed has been ready to stand behind the banks to provide whatever reserves are needed to prevent bank panics. Second, the nearly $1.8 trillion of large-denomination deposits in the banking system are not guaranteed by the FDIC, because they exceed the $100,000 limit. A loss of confidence in the banking system could still lead to runs on banks from the large-denomination depositors, and bank panics could still occur despite the existence of the FDIC. The importance of the Federal Reserve's role as lender of last resort is, if anything, more important today because of the high number of bank failures experienced in the 1980s and early 1990s.

Not only can the Fed be a lender of last resort to banks, but it can also play the same role for the financial system as a whole. The existence of the Fed's discount window can help prevent financial panics that are not triggered by bank failures, as was the case during the Black Monday stock market crash of 1987 and the terrorist destruction of the World Trade Center in September 2001 (see the Inside the Fed box).

Although the Fed's role as the lender of last resort has the benefit of preventing bank and financial panics, it does have a cost. If a bank expects that the Fed will provide it with discount loans when it gets into trouble, as occurred with Continental Illinois, it will be willing to take on more risk knowing that the Fed will come to the rescue. The Fed's lender-of-last-resort role has thus created a moral hazard problem similar to the one created by deposit insurance (discussed in Chapter 11): Banks take on more risk, thus exposing the deposit insurance agency, and hence taxpayers, to greater losses. The moral hazard problem is most severe for large banks, which may believe that the Fed and the FDIC view them as "too big to fail"; that is, they will always receive Fed loans when they are in trouble because their failure would be likely to precipitate a bank panic.

Similarly, Federal Reserve actions to prevent financial panic may encourage financial institutions other than banks to take on greater risk. They, too, expect the Fed to ensure that they could get loans if a financial panic seems imminent. When the Fed considers using the discount weapon to prevent panics, it therefore needs to consider the trade-off between the moral hazard cost of its role as lender of last resort and the benefit of preventing financial panics. This trade-off explains why the Fed must be careful not to perform its role as lender of last resort too frequently.

Advantages and Disadvantages of Discount Policy

The most important advantage of discount policy is that the Fed can use it to perform its role of lender of last resort. Experiences with Continental Illinois, the Black Monday crash, and September 11, 2001, indicate that this role has become more important in the past couple of decades. In the past, discount policy was used as a tool of monetary policy, with the discount rate changed to affect interest rates and the money supply. However, because the decisions to take out discount loans are made by banks and are therefore not completely controlled by the Fed, while open market operations are completely controlled by the Fed, the use of discount policy to conduct monetary policy has little to recommend it. This is why the Fed moved in January 2003 to the current system in which the discount facility is not used to set the federal funds rate, but is only a backup facility to prevent the federal funds rate from rising too far above its target.

RESERVE REQUIREMENTS

As we saw in Chapter 17, changes in reserve requirements affect the money supply by causing the money supply multiplier to change. A rise in reserve requirements reduces the amount of deposits that can be supported by a given level of the monetary base and will lead to a contraction of the money supply. A rise in reserve requirements also increases the demand for reserves and raises the federal funds rate. Conversely, a decline

Inside the Fed Using Discount Policy to Prevent a Financial Panic

The Black Monday Stock Market Crash of 1987 and the Terrorist Destruction of the World Trade Center in September 2001. Although October 19, 1987, dubbed "Black Monday," will go down in the history books as the largest one-day percentage decline in stock prices to date (the Dow Jones Industrial Average declined by more than 20%), it was on Tuesday, October 20, 1987, that financial markets almost stopped functioning. Felix Rohatyn, one of the most prominent men on Wall Street, stated flatly: "Tuesday was the most dangerous day we had in 50 years."* Much of the credit for prevention of a market meltdown after Black Monday must be given to the Federal Reserve System and the chairman of the Board of Governors, Alan Greenspan.

The stress of keeping markets functioning during the sharp decline in stock prices on Monday, October 19, meant that many brokerage houses and specialists (dealer-brokers who maintain orderly trading on the stock exchanges) were severely in need of additional funds to finance their activities. However, understandably enough, New York banks, as well as foreign and regional U.S. banks, growing very nervous about the financial health of securities firms, began to cut back credit to the securities industry at the very time when it was most needed. Panic was in the air. One chairman of a large specialist firm commented that on Monday, "from 2 p.m. on, there was total despair. The entire investment community fled the market. We were left alone on the field." It was time for the Fed, like the cavalry, to come to the rescue.

Upon learning of the plight of the securities industry, Alan Greenspan and E. Gerald Corrigan, then president of the Federal Reserve Bank of New York and the Fed official most closely in touch with Wall Street, became fearful of a spreading collapse of securities firms. To prevent this from occurring, Greenspan announced before the market opened on Tuesday, October 20, the Federal Reserve System's "readiness to serve as a source of liquidity to support the economic and financial system." In addition to this extraordinary announcement, the Fed made it clear that it would provide discount loans to any bank that would make loans to the securities industry, although this did not prove to be necessary. As one New York banker said, the Fed's message was, "We're here. Whatever you need, we'll give you."

The outcome of the Fed's timely action was that a financial panic was averted. The markets kept functioning on Tuesday, and a market rally ensued that day, with the Dow Jones Industrial Average climbing over 100 points.

A similar lender-of-last-resort operation was carried out in the aftermath of the destruction of the World Trade Center in New York City on Tuesday, September 11, 2001—the worst terrorist incident in U.S. history. Because of the disruption to the most important financial center in the world, the liquidity needs of the financial system skyrocketed. To satisfy these needs and to keep the financial system from seizing up, within a few hours of the incident, the Fed made an announcement similar to that made after the crash of 1987: "The Federal Reserve System is open and operating. The discount window is available to meet liquidity needs."** The Fed then proceeded to provide $45 billion to banks through the discount window, a 200-fold increase over the previous week. As a result of this action, along with the injection of as much as $80 billion of reserves into the banking system through open market operations, the financial system kept functioning. When the stock market reopened on Monday, September 17, trading was orderly, although the Dow Jones average did decline 7%.

The terrorists were able to bring down the twin towers of the World Trade Center, with nearly 3,000 dead. However, they were unable to bring down the U.S. financial system because of the timely actions of the Federal Reserve.

*"Terrible Tuesday: How the Stock Market Almost Disintegrated a Day After the Crash," *Wall Street Journal*, November 20, 1987, p. 1. This article provides a fascinating and more detailed view of the events described here and is the source of all the quotations cited.

**"Economic Front: How Policy Makers Regrouped to Defend the Financial System," *Wall Street Journal*, September 18, 2001, p. A1, provides more detail on this episode.

in reserve requirements leads to an expansion of the money supply and a fall in the federal funds rate. The Fed has had the authority to vary reserve requirements since the 1930s; this once was a powerful way of affecting the money supply and interest rates, but as we saw in Chapter 17 is less important now.

The Depository Institutions Deregulation and Monetary Control Act of 1980 provided a simpler scheme for setting reserve requirements. All depository institutions, including commercial banks, savings and loan associations, mutual savings banks, and credit unions, are subject to the same reserve requirements: Required reserves on all checkable deposits—including non-interest-bearing checking accounts, NOW accounts, super-NOW accounts, and ATS (automatic transfer savings) accounts—are equal to 3% of the bank's first $48.3 million of checkable deposits[5] and 10% of the checkable deposits over $48.3 million, and the percentage set initially at 10% can be varied between 8% and 14%, at the Fed's discretion. In extraordinary circumstances, the percentage can be raised as high as 18%.

Disadvantages of Reserve Requirements

As we saw in Chapter 17, reserve requirements are no longer binding for most banks, so this tool is much less effective than it once was. Another disadvantage of using reserve requirements to control the money supply and interest rates is that raising the requirements can cause immediate liquidity problems for banks where reserve requirements are binding. When the Fed increased these requirements in the past, it usually softened the blow by conducting open market purchases or by making the discount loan window (borrowed reserves) more available, thereby providing reserves to banks that needed them. Continually fluctuating reserve requirements would also create more uncertainty for banks and make their liquidity management more difficult.

The policy tool of changing reserve requirements does not have much to recommend it, and it is no longer used. Indeed, many economists advocate the elimination of reserve requirements in the United States, as has already been done in Canada, Australia, and New Zealand.

APPLICATION Why Have Reserve Requirements Been Declining Worldwide?

In recent years, central banks in many countries in the world have been reducing or eliminating their reserve requirements. In the United States, the Federal Reserve eliminated reserve requirements on time deposits in December 1990 and lowered reserve requirements on checkable deposits from 12% to 10% in April 1992. As a result, the majority of U.S. depository institutions find that reserve requirements are not binding: To service their depositors, many depository institutions need to keep sufficient vault cash on hand (which counts toward meeting reserve requirements) that they more than meet reserve requirements voluntarily. Canada has gone a step further: Financial market legislation that took effect in June 1992 eliminated all reserve requirements over a two-year period. The central banks of Switzerland, New Zealand, and Australia have also eliminated reserve requirements entirely. What explains the downward trend for reserve requirements in most countries?

---

[5]The $48.3 million figure is as of the end of 2005. Each year, the figure is adjusted upward by 80% of the percentage increase in checkable deposits in the United States.

You may recall from Chapter 9 that reserve requirements act as a tax on banks. Because central banks typically do not pay interest on reserves, the bank earns nothing on them and loses the interest that could have been earned if the bank held loans instead. The cost imposed on banks from reserve requirements means that banks, in effect, have a higher cost of funds than intermediaries not subject to reserve requirements, making them less competitive. We have already seen in Chapter 10 that additional market forces have been making banks less competitive, weakening the health of banking systems throughout the world. Central banks have thus been reducing reserve requirements to make banks more competitive and stronger.[6] The Federal Reserve was explicit about this rationale for its April 1992 reduction when it announced it on February 18, 1992, stating in its press release that the reduction "will reduce funding costs for depositories and strengthen their balance sheets. Over time, it is expected that most of these cost savings will be passed on to depositors and borrowers."

APPLICATION The Channel/Corridor System for Setting Interest Rates Used in Other Countries

The fall in reserve requirements has elicited the concern that if the demand for reserves falls to zero, then a central bank may not be able to exercise control over interest rates.[7] However, the *channel* or *corridor system* for conducting monetary policy—which has been adopted by Canada, Australia, and New Zealand, all of which have eliminated reserve requirements—shows that central banks can continue to effectively set overnight, interbank interest rates like the federal funds rate. How the channel/corridor system works is illustrated by Figure 6, which describes the market for reserves along the lines discussed at the beginning of this chapter.

In the channel/corridor system, the central bank sets up a standing lending facility, like the one currently in place in the United States and in most industrialized countries, in which the central bank stands ready to lend overnight any amount banks ask for at a fixed interest rate, i^l. This standing lending facility is commonly called a *lombard facility* and the interest rate charged on these loans is often called a *lombard rate*. (This name comes from Lombardy, a region in northern Italy that was an important center of banking in the Middle Ages.) As we saw at the beginning of the chapter, with a standing lending facility, the central bank does not limit the amount of borrowing by banks, but always stands ready to supply any amount the banks want at the lending rate i^l. Thus the quantity of reserves supplied is flat (infinitely elastic) at i^l as shown in Figure 6, because if the overnight interest rate, denoted by i_{ff}, begins to rise above i^l, banks would just keep borrowing discount loans indefinitely.

In the channel/corridor system the central bank sets up another standing facility that pays banks a fixed interest rate i^r on any reserves (deposits) they would like to keep at the central bank. (At this time, the Fed is not allowed to pay interest on reserves and so cannot set up this kind of facility, but this situation may change in the future because the U.S. Treasury has advocated legislation to permit the Fed to pay interest on reserves.)

[6]Many economists believe that the Fed should pay market interest rates on reserves, another suggestion for dealing with this problem.

[7]See Benjamin Friedman, "The Future of Monetary Policy: The Central Bank as an Army with Only a Signal Corps?" *International Finance* 2 (1999), pp. 321–338, and the rest of the symposium on this topic in the same journal.

FIGURE 6
The Channel/Corridor System for Setting Interest Rates
In the channel/corridor system standing facilities result in a step function supply curve, R^s. Then if the demand curve shifts between R_1^d and R_2^d, the overnight interest rate i_{ff} always remains between i^r and i^l.

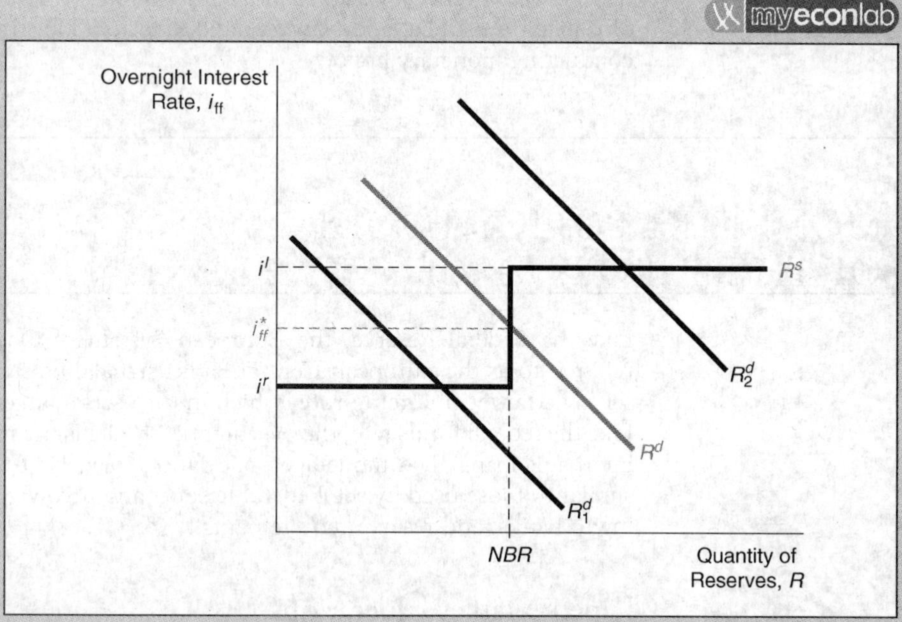

The quantity of reserves supplied is also flat at i^r, because if the overnight rate begins to fall below this rate, banks would not lend in the overnight market. Instead, they would keep increasing the amount of their deposits in the central bank (effectively lending to the central bank), and would thereby keep lowering the quantity of reserves supplied in the overnight loan market. In between i^r and i^l, the quantity of reserves supplied equals nonborrowed reserves *NBR*, which are determined by open market operations. Nonborrowed reserves are set to zero if the demand for reserves is also expected to be zero. The supply curve for reserves R^s is thus the step function depicted in Figure 6.

The demand curve for reserves R^d has the usual downward slope. As we can see in Figure 6, when the demand curve shifts to the left to R_1^d, the overnight interest rate never falls below i^r; if the demand curve shifts to the right to R_2^d, the overnight rate never rises above i^l. Thus the channel/corridor system enables the central bank to keep the overnight interest rate in between the narrow channel/corridor with an upper limit of i^l and lower limit of i^r. In Canada, Australia, and New Zealand the lending rate i^l is set 25 basis points (0.25 percentage point) above the announced target rate, while the inter- est rate paid on reserves kept at the central bank is set at 25 basis points below the target. More in-depth analysis shows that banks will set the demand for reserves so that the demand curve is expected to intersect the supply curve at the announced target overnight rate of i^*_{ff}, with the result that deviations from the announced target are fairly small.[8]

The important point of this analysis is that the channel/corridor approach enables the central bank to set the overnight policy rate, whatever the demand for reserves, including zero demand. Thus, in the future, continuing declines in the demand for

[8]See Michael Woodford, "Monetary Policy in the Information Economy," in *Symposium on Economic Policy for the Information Economy* (Federal Reserve Bank of Kansas City: 2001), pp. 297–370.

reserves may eventually lead central banks to follow in the footsteps of the central banks of Canada, Australia, and New Zealand, and to adopt the channel/corridor system for conducting monetary policy.

MONETARY POLICY TOOLS OF THE EUROPEAN CENTRAL BANK

Like the Federal Reserve, the European System of Central Banks (which is usually referred to as the European Central Bank) signals the stance of its monetary policy by setting a **target financing rate**, which in turn sets a target for the **overnight cash rate**. Like the federal funds rate, the overnight cash rate is the interest rate for very short-term interbank loans. The monetary policy tools used by the European Central Bank are similar to those used by the Federal Reserve and involve open market operations, lending to banks, and reserve requirements.

Open Market Operations

Like the Federal Reserve, the European Central Bank uses open market operations as its primary tool for conducting monetary policy and setting the overnight cash rate at the target financing rate. **Main refinancing operations** are the predominant form of open market operations and are similar to the Fed's repo transactions. They involve weekly **reverse transactions** (purchase or sale of eligible assets under repurchase or credit operations against eligible assets as collateral) that are reversed within two weeks. Credit institutions submit bids, and the European Central Bank decides which bids to accept. Like the Federal Reserve, the European Central Bank accepts the most attractively priced bids and makes purchases or sales to the point where the desired amount of reserves are supplied. In contrast to the Federal Reserve, which conducts open market operations in one location at the Federal Reserve Bank of New York, the European Central Bank decentralizes its open market operations by having them be conducted by the individual national central banks.

A second category of open market operations is the **longer-term refinancing operations**, which are a much smaller source of liquidity for the euro-area banking system and are similar to the Fed's outright purchases or sales of securities. These operations are carried out monthly and typically involve purchases or sales of securities with a maturity of three months. They are not used for signaling the monetary policy stance, but instead are aimed at providing euro-area banks with additional longer-term refinancing.

Lending to Banks

As for the Fed, the next most important tool of monetary policy for the European Central Bank involves lending to banking institutions, which is carried out by the national central banks, just as discount lending is performed by the individual Federal Reserve Banks. This lending takes place through a standing lending facility called the **marginal lending facility**. There banks can borrow (against eligible collateral) overnight loans from the national central banks at the **marginal lending rate**, which is set at 100 basis points above the target financing rate. The marginal lending rate provides a ceiling for the overnight market interest rate in the European Monetary Union, just as the discount rate does in the United States. In contrast to the U.S. system, but similar to the systems in Canada, Australia, and New Zealand, the Eurosystem has another standing facility, the **deposit facility**, in which banks are paid a fixed interest rate that is 100 basis points below the target financing rate. As with the corridor system, the prespecified interest rate on the deposit facility provides a floor for the overnight market interest rate, while the marginal lending rate sets a ceiling. This creates a channel/corridor, as in Canada, New Zealand, and Australia, but with a much wider range of 100 basis points on either side.

Reserve Requirements

Like the Federal Reserve, the European Central Bank imposes reserve requirements such that all deposit-taking institutions are required to hold 2% of the total amount of checking deposits and other short-term deposits in reserve accounts with national central banks. All institutions that are subject to minimum reserve requirements have access to the European Central Bank's standing lending facilities and participate in open market operations. Unlike the Federal Reserve, the European Central Bank pays interest on reserves. Consequently, the banks' cost of complying with reserve requirements is low.

SUMMARY

1. A supply and demand analysis of the market for reserves yields the following results: When the Fed makes an open market purchase or lowers reserve requirements, the federal funds rate declines. When the Fed makes an open market sale or raises reserve requirements, the federal funds rate rises. Changes in the discount rate may also affect the federal funds rate.
2. The amount of an open market operation conducted on any given day by the trading desk of the Federal Reserve Bank of New York is determined by the amount of the dynamic open market operation intended to change reserves and the monetary base and by the amount of the defensive open market operation used to offset other factors that affect reserves and the monetary base. Open market operations are the primary tool used by the Fed to control the money supply because they occur at the initiative of the Fed, are flexible, are easily reversed, and can be implemented quickly.
3. The volume of discount loans (borrowed reserves) is affected by the discount rate. Besides its effect on the monetary base and the money supply, discounting allows the Fed to perform its role as the lender of last resort. However, because the decisions by banks to take out discount loans (borrow reserves) are not controlled by the Fed, the use of discount policy to conduct monetary policy has little to recommend it.
4. Changing reserve requirements is too blunt a tool to use for controlling the money supply, and hence it is rarely used.
5. The monetary policy tools used by the European Central Bank are similar to those used by the Federal Reserve System and involve open market operations, lending to banks, and reserve requirements. Main financing operations—open market operations in repos that are typically reversed within two weeks—are the primary tool to set the overnight cash rate at the target financing rate. The European Central Bank also operates standing lending facilities that operate like the corridor system and ensure that the overnight cash rate remains within 100 basis points of the target financing rate.

KEY TERMS

defensive open market operations, p. 450
deposit facility, p. 461
discount window, p. 452
dynamic open market operations, p. 450
federal funds rate, p. 445
lender of last resort, p. 453
longer-term refinancing operations, p. 460
main refinancing operations, p. 460
marginal lending facility, p. 460
marginal lending rate, p. 460
matched sale–purchase transaction (reverse repo), p. 452
overnight cash rate, p. 460
primary dealers, p. 451
repurchase agreement (repo), p. 452
reverse transactions, p. 460
standing lending facility, p. 453
target financing rate, p. 460

QUESTIONS AND PROBLEMS

Questions marked with an asterisk are answered at the end of the book in an appendix, "Answers to Selected Questions and Problems." Questions marked with a blue circle indicate the question is available in MyEconLab at www.myeconlab.com/mishkin.

*1. If the manager of the open market desk hears that a snowstorm is about to strike New York City, making it difficult to present checks for payment there and so raising the float, what defensive open market operations will the manager undertake?

2. During Christmastime, when the public's holdings of currency increase, what defensive open market operations typically occur? Why?

*3. If the Treasury has just paid for a supercomputer and as a result its deposits with the Fed fall, what defensive open market operations will the manager of the open market desk undertake?

4. If float decreases below its normal level, why might the manager of domestic operations consider it more desirable to use repurchase agreements to affect the monetary base rather than an outright purchase of bonds?

*5. Most open market operations are currently repurchase agreements. What does this tell us about the likely volume of defensive open market operations relative to dynamic open market operations?

6. "The only way that the Fed can affect the level of borrowed reserves is by adjusting the discount rate." Is this statement true, false, or uncertain? Explain your answer.

*7. Using the supply and demand analysis of the market for reserves, show what happens to the federal funds rate, holding everything else constant, if the economy is surprisingly strong, leading to an increase in the amount of checkable deposits.

8. If there is a switch from deposits into currency, what happens to the federal funds rate? Use the supply and demand analysis of the market for reserves to explain your answer.

*9. "Discounting is no longer needed because the presence of the FDIC eliminates the possibility of bank panics." Discuss.

10. The benefits of using Fed discount operations to prevent bank panics are straightforward. What are the costs?

*11. You often read in the newspaper that the Fed has just lowered the discount rate. Does this signal that the Fed is moving to a more expansionary monetary policy? Why or why not?

12. How can the procyclical movement of interest rates (rising during business cycle expansions and falling during business cycle contractions) lead to a procyclical movement in the money supply as a result of Fed discounting? Why might this movement of the money supply be undesirable?

*13. "If reserve requirements were eliminated, it would be harder to control interest rates." True, false, or uncertain?

14. "Considering that raising reserve requirements to 100% makes complete control of the money supply possible, Congress should authorize the Fed to raise reserve requirements to this level." Discuss.

*15. Compare the use of open market operations, discounting, and changes in reserve requirements to control the money supply on the following criteria: flexibility, reversibility, effectiveness, and speed of implementation.

WEB EXERCISES

1. Go to www.federalreserve.gov/fomc/. This site reports activity by the FMOC. Scroll down to Calendar and click on the statement released after the last meeting. Summarize this statement in one paragraph. Be sure to note whether the committee has decided to increase or decrease the federal funds rate target. Now review the statements of the last two meetings. Has the stance of the committee changed?

2. Go to www.federalreserve.gov/releases/h15/update/. What is the current federal funds rate (define this rate as well)? What is the current Federal Reserve discount rate (define this rate as well)? Have short-term rates increased or declined since the end of 2005?

WEB REFERENCES

www.federalreserve.gov/fomc/fundsrate.htm

This site lists historical federal funds rates and discusses Federal Reserve targets.

www.frbdiscountwindow.org/

Information on the operation of the discount window and data on current and historical interest rates.

www.federalreserve.gov/monetarypolicy/reservereq.htm

Historical data and discussion about reserve requirements.

www.federalreserve.gov/fomc

A discussion about the Federal Open Market Committee, list of current members, meeting dates, and other current information.

CHAPTER

19 What Should Central Banks Do? Monetary Policy Goals, Strategy, and Tactics

Preview

Getting monetary policy right is crucial to the health of the economy. Overly expansionary monetary policy leads to high inflation, which decreases the efficiency of the economy and hampers economic growth. Monetary policy that is too tight can produce serious recessions in which output falls and unemployment rises. It can also lead to deflation, a fall in the price level, such as occurred in the United States during the Great Depression and in Japan more recently. As we saw in Chapter 8, deflation can be especially damaging to an economy, because it promotes financial instability and can trigger financial crises.

Now that we understand the tools that central banks such as the Federal Reserve use to conduct monetary policy, we can consider how central banks *should* conduct monetary policy. To explore this subject, we look at the goals that central banks have for monetary policy and the strategies and tactics for attaining them.

THE PRICE STABILITY GOAL AND THE NOMINAL ANCHOR

Over the past few decades, policymakers throughout the world have become increasingly aware of the social and economic costs of inflation and more concerned with maintaining a stable price level as a goal of economic policy. Indeed, **price stability**, which central bankers define as low and stable inflation, is increasingly viewed as the most important goal of monetary policy. Price stability is desirable because a rising price level (inflation) creates uncertainty in the economy, and that uncertainty might hamper economic growth. For example, when the overall level of prices is changing, the information conveyed by the prices of goods and services is harder to interpret, which complicates decision making for consumers, businesses, and government, thereby leading to a less efficient financial system.

Not only do public opinion surveys indicate that the public is hostile to inflation, but a growing body of evidence also suggests that inflation leads to lower economic growth.[1] The most extreme example of unstable prices is *hyperinflation*, such as Argentina, Brazil, and Russia have experienced in the recent past. Hyperinflation has proved to be very damaging to the workings of the economy.

---

[1] For example, see Stanley Fischer, "The Role of Macroeconomic Factors in Growth," *Journal of Monetary Economics* 32 (1993): 485–512.

Inflation also makes it difficult to plan for the future. For example, it is more difficult to decide how much to put aside to provide for a child's college education in an inflationary environment. Furthermore, inflation can strain a country's social fabric: Conflict might result, because each group in the society may compete with other groups to make sure that its income keeps up with the rising level of prices.

The Role of a Nominal Anchor

Because price stability is so crucial to the long-run health of an economy, a central element in successful monetary policy is the use of a **nominal anchor**, a nominal variable such as the inflation rate or the money supply, which ties down the price level to achieve price stability. Adherence to a nominal anchor that keeps the nominal variable within a narrow range promotes price stability by directly promoting low and stable inflation expectations. A more subtle reason for a nominal anchor's importance is that it can limit the **time-inconsistency problem**, in which monetary policy conducted on a discretionary, day-by-day basis leads to poor long-run outcomes.[2]

The Time-Inconsistency Problem

The time-inconsistency problem is something we deal with continually in everyday life. We often have a plan that we know will produce a good outcome in the long run, but when tomorrow comes, we just can't help ourselves and we renege on our plan because doing so has short-run gains. For example, we make a New Year's resolution to go on a diet, but soon thereafter we can't resist having one more bite of that rocky road ice cream—and then another bite, and then another bite—and the weight begins to pile back on. In other words, we find ourselves unable to *consistently* follow a good plan over *time;* the good plan is said to be *time-inconsistent* and will soon be abandoned.

Monetary policymakers also face the time-inconsistency problem. They are always tempted to pursue a discretionary monetary policy that is more expansionary than firms or people expect because such a policy would boost economic output (or lower unemployment) in the short run. The best policy, however, is *not* to pursue expansionary policy, because decisions about wages and prices reflect workers' and firms' expectations about policy; when they see a central bank pursuing expansionary policy, workers and firms will raise their expectations about inflation, driving wages and prices up. The rise in wages and prices will lead to higher inflation, but will not result in higher output on average.

A central bank will have better inflation performance in the long run if it does not try to surprise people with an unexpectedly expansionary policy, but instead keeps inflation under control. However, even if a central bank recognizes that discretionary policy will lead to a poor outcome (high inflation with no gains in output), it still may not be able to pursue the better policy of inflation control, because politicians are likely to apply pressure on the central bank to try to boost output with overly expansionary monetary policy.

---

[2]The time-inconsistency problem was first outlined in papers by Nobel Prize winners Finn Kydland and Edward Prescott, "Rules Rather Than Discretion: The Inconsistency of Optimal Plans," *Journal of Political Economy* 85 (1977): 473–491; Guillermo Calvo, "On the Time Consistency of Optimal Policy in the Monetary Economy," *Econometrica* 46 (November 1978): 1411–1428; and Robert J. Barro and David Gordon, "A Positive Theory of Monetary Policy in a Natural Rate Model," *Journal of Political Economy* 91 (August 1983): 589–610.

A clue as to how we should deal with the time-inconsistency problem comes from how-to books on parenting. Parents know that giving in to a child to keep him from acting up will produce a very spoiled child. Nevertheless, when a child throws a tantrum, many parents give him what he wants just to shut him up. Because parents don't stick to their "do not give in" plan, the child expects that he will get what he wants if he behaves badly, so he will throw tantrums over and over again. Parenting books suggest a solution to the time-inconsistency problem (although they don't call it that): Parents should set behavior rules for their children and stick to them.

A nominal anchor is like a behavior rule. Just as rules help to prevent the time-inconsistency problem in parenting by helping the adults to resist pursuing the discretionary policy of giving in, a nominal anchor can help prevent the time-inconsistency problem in monetary policy by providing an expected constraint on discretionary policy.

OTHER GOALS OF MONETARY POLICY

While price stability is the primary goal of most central banks, five other goals are continually mentioned by central bank officials when they discuss the objectives of monetary policy: (1) high employment, (2) economic growth, (3) stability of financial markets, (4) interest-rate stability, and (5) stability in foreign exchange markets.

High Employment

High employment is a worthy goal for two main reasons: (1) the alternative situation—high unemployment—causes much human misery, and (2) when unemployment is high, the economy has both idle workers and idle resources (closed factories and unused equipment), resulting in a loss of output (lower GDP).

Although it is clear that high employment is desirable, how high should it be? At what point can we say that the economy is at full employment? At first, it might seem that full employment is the point at which no worker is out of a job—that is, when unemployment is zero. But this definition ignores the fact that some unemployment, called *frictional unemployment*, which involves searches by workers and firms to find suitable matchups, is beneficial to the economy. For example, a worker who decides to look for a better job might be unemployed for a while during the job search. Workers often decide to leave work temporarily to pursue other activities (raising a family, travel, returning to school), and when they decide to reenter the job market, it may take some time for them to find the right job.

Another reason that unemployment is not zero when the economy is at full employment is *structural unemployment*, a mismatch between job requirements and the skills or availability of local workers. Clearly, this kind of unemployment is undesirable. Nonetheless, it is something that monetary policy can do little about.

This goal for high employment is not an unemployment level of zero but a level above zero consistent with full employment at which the demand for labor equals the supply of labor. This level is called the **natural rate of unemployment**.

Although this definition sounds neat and authoritative, it leaves a troublesome question unanswered: What unemployment rate is consistent with full employment? In some cases, it is obvious that the unemployment rate is too high: The unemployment rate in excess of 20% during the Great Depression, for example, was clearly far too high. In the early 1960s, on the other hand, policymakers thought that a reasonable goal was 4%, a level that was probably too low, because it led to accelerating inflation. Current estimates of the natural rate of unemployment place it between $4\frac{1}{2}$ and 6%, but even this estimate is subject to much uncertainty and disagreement. It is possible, for example, that appropriate government policy, such as the provision of better information about job vacancies or job training programs, might decrease the natural rate of unemployment.

Economic Growth

The goal of steady economic growth is closely related to the high-employment goal because businesses are more likely to invest in capital equipment to increase productivity and economic growth when unemployment is low. Conversely, if unemployment is high and factories are idle, it does not pay for a firm to invest in additional plants and equipment. Although the two goals are closely related, policies can be specifically aimed at promoting economic growth by directly encouraging firms to invest or by encouraging people to save, which provides more funds for firms to invest. In fact, this is the stated purpose of *supply-side economics* policies, which are intended to spur economic growth by providing tax incentives for businesses to invest in facilities and equipment and for taxpayers to save more. There is also an active debate over what role monetary policy can play in boosting growth.

Stability of Financial Markets

As our analysis in Chapter 8 showed, financial crises can interfere with the ability of financial markets to channel funds to people with productive investment opportunities and lead to a sharp contraction in economic activity. The promotion of a more stable financial system in which financial crises are avoided is thus an important goal for a central bank. Indeed, as discussed in Chapter 15, the Federal Reserve System was created in response to the bank panic of 1907 to promote financial stability.

Interest-Rate Stability

Interest-rate stability is desirable because fluctuations in interest rates can create uncertainty in the economy and make it harder to plan for the future. Fluctuations in interest rates that affect consumers' willingness to buy houses, for example, make it more difficult for consumers to decide when to purchase a house and for construction firms to plan how many houses to build. A central bank may also want to reduce upward movements in interest rates for the reasons we discussed in Chapter 15: Upward movements in interest rates generate hostility toward central banks and lead to demands that their power be curtailed.

The stability of financial markets is also fostered by interest-rate stability, because fluctuations in interest rates create great uncertainty for financial institutions. An increase in interest rates produces large capital losses on long-term bonds and mortgages, losses that can cause the failure of the financial institutions holding them. In recent years, more pronounced interest-rate fluctuations have been a particularly severe problem for savings and loan associations and mutual savings banks, many of which got into serious financial trouble in the 1980s and early 1990s (as we have seen in Chapter 11).

Stability in Foreign Exchange Markets

With the increasing importance of international trade to the U.S. economy, the value of the dollar relative to other currencies has become a major consideration for the Fed. A rise in the value of the dollar makes American industries less competitive with those abroad, and declines in the value of the dollar stimulate inflation in the United States. In addition, preventing large changes in the value of the dollar makes it easier for firms and individuals purchasing or selling goods abroad to plan ahead. Stabilizing extreme movements in the value of the dollar in foreign exchange markets is thus an important goal of monetary policy. In other countries, which are even more dependent on foreign trade, stability in foreign exchange markets takes on even greater importance.

SHOULD PRICE STABILITY BE THE PRIMARY GOAL OF MONETARY POLICY?

In the long run, there is no inconsistency between the price stability goal and the other goals mentioned earlier. The natural rate of unemployment is not lowered by high inflation, so higher inflation cannot produce lower unemployment or more employment in the long run. In other words, there is no long-run trade-off between inflation and employment. In the long run, price stability promotes economic growth as well as financial and interest-rate stability. Although price stability is consistent with the other goals in the long run, in the short run price stability often conflicts with the goals of high employment and interest-rate stability. For example, when the economy is expanding and unemployment is falling, the economy may become overheated, leading to a rise in inflation. To pursue the price stability goal, a central bank would prevent this overheating by raising interest rates, an action that would initially lower employment and increase interest-rate instability. How should a central bank resolve this conflict among goals?

Hierarchical Versus Dual Mandates

Because price stability is crucial to the long-run health of the economy, many countries have decided that price stability should be the primary, long-run goal for central banks. For example, the Maastricht Treaty, which created the European Central Bank, states, "The primary objective of the European System of Central Banks [ECSB] shall be to maintain price stability. Without prejudice to the objective of price stability, the ESCB shall support the general economic policies in the Community," which include objectives such as "a high level of employment" and "sustainable and non-inflationary growth." Mandates of this type, which put the goal of price stability first, and then say that as long as it is achieved other goals can be pursued, are known as **hierarchical mandates**. They are the directives governing the behavior of central banks such as the Bank of England, the Bank of Canada and the Reserve Bank of New Zealand, as well as for the European Central Bank.

In contrast, the legislation defining the mission of the Federal Reserve states, "The Board of Governors of the Federal Reserve System and the Federal Open Market Committee shall maintain long-run growth of the monetary and credit aggregates commensurate with the economy's long-run potential to increase production, so as to promote effectively the goals of maximum employment, stable prices, and moderate long-term interest rates." Because, as we learned in Chapter 5, long-term interest rates will be very high only if there is high inflation, this statement in practice is a **dual mandate** to achieve two co-equal objectives: price stability and maximum employment.

Is it better for an economy to operate under a hierarchical mandate or a dual mandate?

Price Stability as the Primary, Long-Run Goal of Monetary Policy

Because there is no inconsistency between achieving price stability in the long run and the natural rate of employment, these two types of mandates are not very different *if* maximum employment is defined as the natural rate of employment. In practice, however, there could be a substantial difference between these two mandates, because the public and politicians may believe that a hierarchical mandate puts too much emphasis on inflation control and not enough on reducing business-cycle fluctuations.

Because low and stable inflation rates promote economic growth, central bankers have come to realize that price stability should be the primary, long-run goal of monetary policy. Nevertheless, because output fluctuations should also be a concern of monetary policy, the goal of price stability should be seen as the primary goal only in the long run. Attempts to keep inflation at the same level in the short run no matter what would likely lead to excessive output fluctuations.

As long as price stability is a long-run goal, but not a short-run goal, central banks can focus on reducing output fluctuations by allowing inflation to deviate from the long-run goal for short periods of time and, therefore, can operate under a dual mandate. However, if a dual mandate leads a central bank to pursue short-run expansionary policies that increase output and employment without worrying about the long-run consequences for inflation, the time-consistency problem may recur. Concerns that a dual mandate might lead to overly expansionary policy is a key reason why central bankers often favor hierarchical mandates in which the pursuit of price stability takes precedence. Hierarchical mandates can also be a problem if they lead to a central bank behaving as what the Governor of the Bank of England, Mervyn King, has referred to as an "inflation nutter"—that is, a central bank that focuses solely on inflation control, even in the short run, and so undertakes policies that lead to large output fluctuations. The choice of which type of mandate is better for a central bank ultimately depends on the subtleties of how it will work in practice. Either type of mandate is acceptable as long as it operates to make price stability the primary goal in the long run, but not the short run.

In the following sections, we examine three monetary policy strategies by which policymakers can achieve price stability: monetary targeting, inflation targeting, and monetary policy with an implicit (not explicit) nominal anchor. All of these strategies feature a strong nominal anchor and have price stability as the primary, long-run goal of monetary policy.

MONETARY TARGETING

In pursuing a strategy of **monetary targeting**, the central bank announces that it will achieve a certain value (the target) of the annual growth rate of a monetary aggregate, such as a 5% growth rate of M1 or a 6% growth rate of M2. The central bank then is accountable for hitting the target.

Monetary Targeting in the United States, Japan, and Germany

In the 1970s, monetary targeting was adopted by several countries—most notably, Germany, Switzerland, Canada, the United Kingdom, Japan, and the United States. Monetary targeting as practiced during this decade was quite different from Milton Friedman's suggestion that the chosen monetary aggregate be targeted to grow at a constant rate. Indeed, in all of these countries, the central banks never adhered to strict, ironclad rules for monetary growth. In some of these countries, monetary targeting was not pursued very seriously.

United States. In 1970, Arthur Burns was appointed chairman of the Board of Governors of the Federal Reserve, and soon thereafter the Fed stated that it was committing itself to the use of monetary targets to guide monetary policy. In 1975, in response to a congressional resolution, the Fed began to announce publicly its targets for money supply growth, though it often missed them. In October 1979, two months after Paul Volcker became chairman of the Board of Governors, the Fed switched to an operating procedure that focused more on nonborrowed reserves and control of the monetary aggregates and less on the federal funds rate. Despite the change in focus, the performance in hitting monetary targets was even worse: In all three years of the 1979–1982 period, the Fed missed its M1 growth target ranges. What went wrong?

There are several possible answers to this question. The first is that the U.S. economy was exposed to several shocks during this period that made monetary control more difficult: the acceleration of financial innovation and deregulation, which added new categories of deposits such as NOW accounts to the measures of monetary aggregates; the imposition by the Fed of credit controls from March to July 1980, which restricted the growth of consumer and business loans; and the back-to-back recessions of 1980 and 1981–1982.[3]

A more persuasive explanation for poor monetary control, however, is that controlling the money supply was never really the intent of Volcker's policy shift. Despite Volcker's statements about the need to target monetary aggregates, he was not committed to these targets. Rather, he was far more concerned with using interest-rate movements to wring inflation out of the economy. Volcker's primary reason for changing the Fed's operating procedure was to free his hand to manipulate interest rates and thereby fight inflation. It was necessary to abandon interest-rate targets if Volcker were to be able to raise interest rates sharply when a slowdown in the economy was required to dampen inflation. This view of Volcker's strategy suggests that the Fed's announced attachment to monetary aggregate targets may have been a smokescreen to keep the Fed from being blamed for the high interest rates that would result from the new interest-rate policy.

In 1982, with inflation in check, the Fed decreased its emphasis on monetary targets. In July 1993, Board of Governors Chairman Alan Greenspan testified in Congress that the Fed would no longer use any monetary aggregates as a guide for conducting monetary policy.

The Bank of Canada and the Bank of England also made commitments to monetary targets around the same time as the Federal Reserve and had similar experiences to that in the United States. By the 1980s, they found that monetary aggregates were not a reliable guide to monetary policy and, like the Federal Reserve, abandoned monetary targeting. Gerald Bouey, the governor of the Bank of Canada, described his bank's experience colorfully by saying, "We didn't abandon monetary aggregates; they abandoned us."

---

[3]Another explanation focuses on the technical difficulties of monetary control when using a nonborrowed reserves operating target under a system of lagged reserve requirements, in which required reserves for a given week are calculated on the basis of the level of deposits two weeks earlier. See David Lindsey, "Nonborrowed Reserve Targeting and Monetary Control," in *Improving Money Stock Control*, ed. Laurence Meyer (Boston: Kluwer-Nijhoff, 1983), pp. 3–41.

Japan. The increase in oil prices in late 1973 was a major shock for Japan, which experienced a huge jump in the inflation rate, to greater than 20% in 1974—a surge facilitated by money growth in 1973 in excess of 20%. The Bank of Japan, like the other central banks discussed here, began to pay more attention to money supply growth rates. In 1978, the Bank of Japan began to announce "forecasts" at the beginning of each quarter for M2 + CDs. Although the Bank of Japan was not officially committed to monetary targeting, monetary policy appeared to be more money-focused after 1978. For example, after the second oil price shock in 1979, the Bank of Japan quickly reduced M2 + CDs growth, rather than allowing it to shoot up as occurred after the first oil shock. The Bank of Japan conducts monetary policy with operating procedures that are similar in many ways to those of the Federal Reserve. It uses the interest rate in the Japanese inter-bank market (similar to the federal funds market) as its daily operating target, just as the Fed does.

The Bank of Japan's monetary policy performance during the 1978–1987 period was much better than the Fed's. Money growth in Japan slowed gradually, beginning in the mid-1970s, and was much less variable than in the United States. The outcome was a more rapid braking of inflation and a lower average inflation rate. In addition, these excellent results on inflation were achieved with lower variability in real output than in the United States.

In parallel with the United States, financial innovation and deregulation in Japan began to reduce the usefulness of the M2 + CDs monetary aggregate as an indicator of monetary policy. Because of concerns about the appreciation of the yen, the Bank of Japan significantly increased the rate of money growth from 1987 to 1989. Many observers blame speculation in Japanese land and stock prices (the *bubble economy*) on the increase in money growth. To reduce this speculation, in 1989 the Bank of Japan switched to a tighter monetary policy aimed at slower money growth. The aftermath was a substantial decline in land and stock prices and the collapse of the bubble economy.

The Japanese economy was in a slump until quite recently. The collapse of land and stock prices helped provoke a severe banking crisis, discussed in Chapter 11, that was a severe drag on the economy. The resulting weakness of the economy even led to deflation, promoting further financial instability. The outcome has been an economy that has stagnated for over a decade. Many critics believe that the Bank of Japan has pursued overly tight monetary policy and needs to substantially increase money growth in order to lift the economy out of its stagnation.

Germany. Starting in the mid-1970s and continuing through the next two decades, both Germany and Switzerland engaged in monetary targeting. The success of monetary targeting in controlling inflation in these two countries explains why monetary targeting still has strong advocates and is an element of the official policy regime for the European Central Bank (see the Global box). Because the success of the German monetary targeting regime in producing low inflation has received the most attention, we'll concentrate on Germany's experience.

Germany's central bank, the Bundesbank, chose to focus on a narrow monetary aggregate called *central bank money*, the sum of currency in circulation and bank deposits weighted by the 1974 required reserve ratios. In 1988, the Bundesbank switched targets from central bank money to M3.

The key fact about the monetary targeting regime in Germany is that it was not a Friedman-type monetary targeting rule in which a monetary aggregate is kept on a constant-growth-rate path and is the primary focus of monetary policy. The Bundesbank allowed growth outside of its target ranges for periods of two to three years, and

Global The European Central Bank's Monetary Policy Strategy

The European Central Bank (ECB) pursues a hybrid monetary policy strategy that has elements in common with the monetary-targeting strategy previously used by the Bundesbank but also includes some elements of inflation targeting.* Like inflation targeting, the ECB has an announced goal for inflation over the medium term of "below, but close to, 2%." The ECB's strategy has two key "pillars." First, monetary and credit aggregates are assessed for "their implications for future inflation and economic growth." Second, many other economic variables are used to assess the future economic outlook. (Until 2003, the ECB employed something closer to a monetary target, setting a "reference value" for the growth rate of the M3 monetary aggregate.)

The ECB's strategy is somewhat unclear and has been subject to criticism for this reason. Although the "below, but close to, 2%" goal for inflation sounds like an inflation target, the ECB has repeatedly stated that it does not have an inflation target. This central bank seems to have decided to try to "have its cake and eat it, too" by not committing too strongly to either a monetary-targeting strategy or an inflation-targeting strategy. The resulting difficulty of assessing the ECB's strategy has the potential to reduce the accountability of the institution.

*For a description of the ECB's monetary policy strategy, go to the ECB's web site at www.ecb.int.

overshoots of its targets were subsequently reversed. Monetary targeting in Germany was instead primarily a method of communicating the strategy of monetary policy focused on long-run considerations and the control of inflation.

The calculation of monetary target ranges put great stress on making policy transparent (clear, simple, and understandable) and on regular communication with the public. First and foremost, a numerical inflation goal was prominently featured in the setting of target ranges. Second, monetary targeting, far from being a rigid policy rule, was flexible in practice. The target ranges for money growth were missed about 50% of the time in Germany, often because of the Bundesbank's concern about other objectives, including output and exchange rates. Furthermore, the Bundesbank demonstrated its flexibility by allowing its inflation goal to vary over time and to converge gradually to the long-run inflation goal.

The monetary targeting regime in Germany demonstrated a strong commitment to clear communication of the strategy to the general public. The money growth targets were continually used as a framework to explain the monetary policy strategy, and the Bundesbank expended tremendous effort in its publications and in frequent speeches by central bank officials to communicate to the public what the central bank was trying to achieve. Given that the Bundesbank frequently missed its money growth targets by significant amounts, its monetary targeting framework is best viewed as a mechanism for transparently communicating how monetary policy is being directed to achieve inflation goals and as a means for increasing the accountability of the central bank.

There are two key lessons to be learned from our discussion of German monetary targeting. First, a monetary targeting regime can restrain inflation in the longer run, even when the regime permits substantial target misses. Thus adherence to a rigid policy rule is not necessary to obtain good inflation outcomes. Second, the key reason why monetary targeting was reasonably successful, despite frequent target misses, is that the objectives of monetary policy were clearly stated and the central bank actively engaged in communicating the strategy of monetary policy to the public, thereby enhancing the transparency of monetary policy and the accountability of the central bank.

As we will see in the next section, these key elements of a successful monetary-targeting regime—flexibility, transparency, and accountability—are also important elements in inflation-targeting regimes. German monetary policy was actually closer in practice to inflation targeting than it was to Friedman-like monetary targeting, and thus might best be thought of as "hybrid" inflation targeting.

Advantages of Monetary Targeting

One advantage of monetary targeting is that information on whether the central bank is achieving its target is known almost immediately—figures for monetary aggregates are typically reported within a couple of weeks. Thus monetary targets can send almost immediate signals to the public and markets about the stance of monetary policy and the intentions of the policymakers to keep inflation in check. In turn, these signals help fix inflation expectations and produce less inflation. Monetary targets also allow almost immediate accountability for monetary policy to keep inflation low, thus helping to constrain the monetary policymaker from falling into the time-inconsistency trap.

Disadvantages of Monetary Targeting

All of the above advantages of monetary aggregate targeting depend on a big *if*: There must be a strong and reliable relationship between the goal variable (inflation or nominal income) and the targeted monetary aggregate. If the relationship between the monetary aggregate and the goal variable is weak, monetary aggregate targeting will not work; this seems to have been a serious problem in the United States and other countries that pursued monetary targets. The weak relationship implies that hitting the target will not produce the desired outcome on the goal variable and thus the monetary aggregate will no longer provide an adequate signal about the stance of monetary policy. As a result, monetary targeting will not help fix inflation expectations and will not be a good guide for assessing central bank accountability. In addition, an unreliable relationship between monetary aggregates and goal variables makes it difficult for monetary targeting to serve as a communications device that increases the transparency of monetary policy and makes the central bank accountable to the public.

INFLATION TARGETING

Given the breakdown of the relationship between monetary aggregates and goal variables such as inflation, many countries have recently adopted inflation targeting as their monetary policy strategy to achieve price stability. New Zealand was the first country to formally adopt inflation targeting in 1990, followed by Canada in 1991, the United Kingdom in 1992, Sweden and Finland in 1993, and Australia and Spain in 1994. Israel, Chile, and Brazil, among others, have also adopted a form of inflation targeting.

Inflation targeting involves several elements: (1) public announcement of medium-term numerical targets for inflation; (2) an institutional commitment to price stability as the primary, long-run goal of monetary policy and a commitment to achieve the inflation goal; (3) an information-inclusive approach in which many variables (not just monetary aggregates) are used in making decisions about monetary policy; (4) increased transparency of the monetary policy strategy through communication with the public and the markets about the plans and objectives of monetary policymakers; and (5) increased accountability of the central bank for attaining its inflation objectives.

Inflation Targeting in New Zealand, Canada, and the United Kingdom

We begin our look at inflation targeting with New Zealand, because it was the first country to adopt it. We then go on to look at the experiences in Canada and the United Kingdom, which were next to adopt this strategy.[4]

New Zealand. As part of a general reform of the government's role in the economy, the New Zealand parliament passed a new Reserve Bank of New Zealand Act in 1989, which became effective on February 1, 1990. Besides increasing the independence of the central bank, moving it from being one of the least independent to one of the most independent among the developed countries, the act committed the Reserve Bank to a sole objective of price stability. The act stipulated that the minister of finance and the governor of the Reserve Bank should negotiate and make public a Policy Targets Agreement, a statement that sets out the targets by which monetary policy performance will be evaluated, specifying numerical target ranges for inflation and the dates by which they are to be reached. An unusual feature of the New Zealand legislation is that the governor of the Reserve Bank is held highly accountable for the success of monetary policy. If the goals set forth in the Policy Targets Agreement are not satisfied, the governor is subject to dismissal.

The first Policy Targets Agreement, signed by the minister of finance and the governor of the Reserve Bank on March 2, 1990, directed the Reserve Bank to achieve an annual inflation rate within a 3–5% range. Subsequent agreements lowered the range to 0–2% until the end of 1996, when the range was changed to 0–3% and later to 1–3% in 2002. As a result of tight monetary policy, the inflation rate was brought down from above 5% to below 2% by the end of 1992 (see Figure 1, panel a), but at the cost of a deep recession and a sharp rise in unemployment. Since then, inflation has typically remained within the targeted range, with the exception of brief periods in 1995 and 2000 when it exceeded the range by a few tenths of a percentage point. (Under the Reserve Bank Act, the governor, Donald Brash, could have been dismissed, but after parliamentary debates he was retained in his job.) Since 1992, New Zealand's growth rate has generally been high, with some years exceeding 5%, and unemployment has come down significantly.

Canada. On February 26, 1991, a joint announcement by the minister of finance and the governor of the Bank of Canada established formal inflation targets. The target ranges were 2–4% by the end of 1992, 1.5–3.5% by June 1994, and 1–3% by December 1996. After the new government took office in late 1993, the target range was set at 1–3% from December 1995 until December 1998 and has been kept at this level. Canadian inflation has also fallen dramatically since the adoption of inflation targets,

---

[4]For further discussion of experiences with inflation targeting, particularly in other countries, see Leonardo Leiderman and Lars E. O. Svensson, *Inflation Targeting* (London: Centre for Economic Policy Research, 1995); Frederic S. Mishkin and Adam Posen, "Inflation Targeting: Lessons from Four Countries," Federal Reserve Bank of New York, *Economic Policy Review* 3 (August 1997), pp. 9–110; and Ben S. Bernanke, Thomas Laubach, Frederic S. Mishkin, and Adam S. Posen, *Inflation Targeting: Lessons from the International Experience* (Princeton: Princeton University Press, 1999).

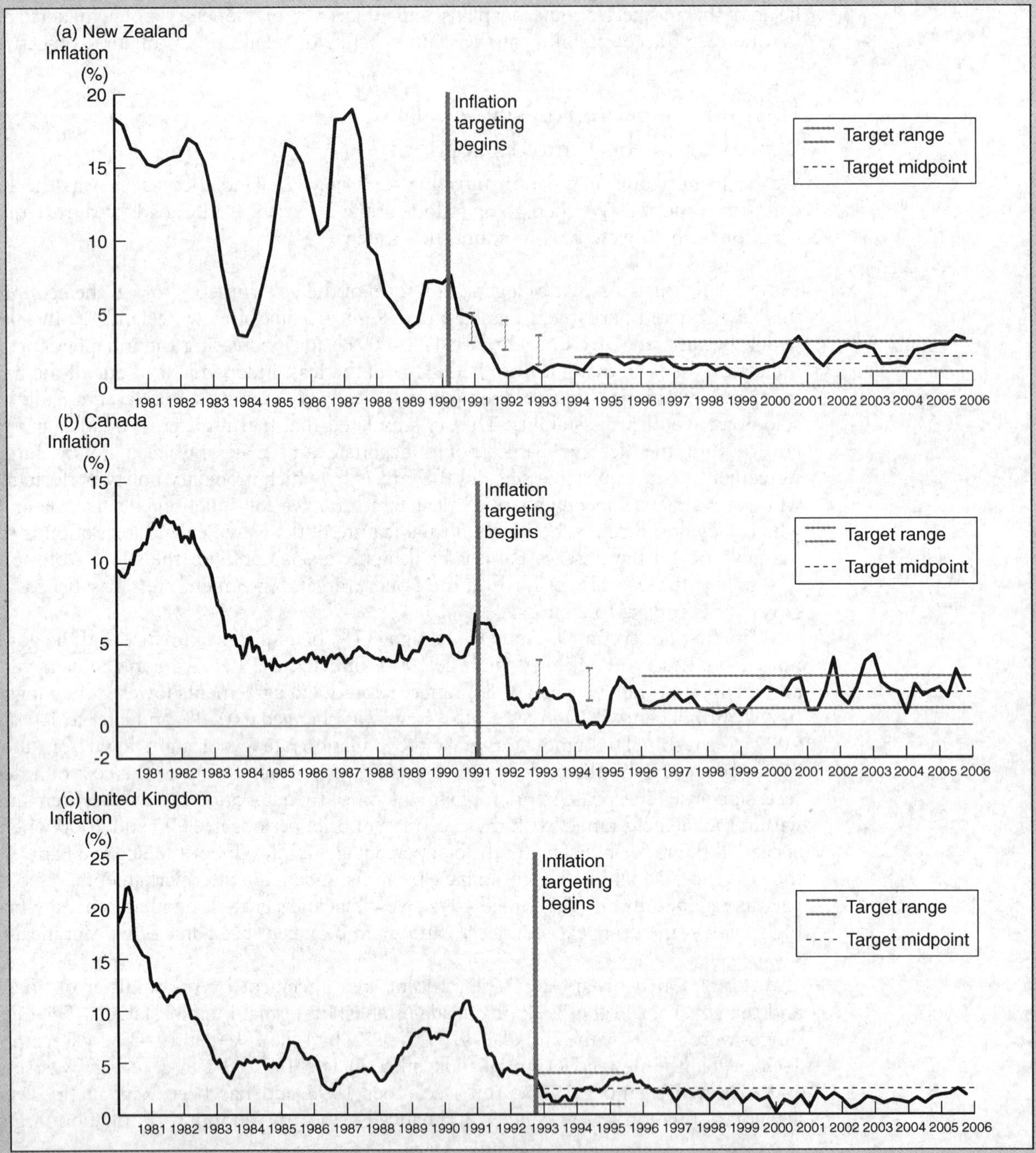

FIGURE 1 **Inflation Rates and Inflation Targets for New Zealand, Canada, and the United Kingdom, 1980–2005**
(a) New Zealand; (b) Canada; (c) United Kingdom

Source: Ben S. Bernanke, Thomas Laubach, Frederic S. Mishkin, and Adam S. Poson, *Inflation Targeting: Lessons from the International Experience* (Princeton: Princeton University Press, 1999), updates from the same sources, and www.rbnz.govt.nz/statistics/econind/a3/ha3.xls.

from above 5% in 1991, to a 0% rate in 1995, and to around 2% subsequently (see Figure 1, panel b). As was the case in New Zealand, however, this decline was not without cost: Unemployment soared to above 10% from 1991 until 1994, but then declined substantially.

United Kingdom. In October 1992, the United Kingdom adopted an inflation target as its nominal anchor, and the Bank of England began to produce an *Inflation Report*, a quarterly report on the progress being made in achieving that target. The inflation target range was initially set at 1–4% until the next election (spring 1997 at the latest), with the intent that the inflation rate should settle down to the lower half of the range (below 2.5%). In May 1997, the inflation target was set at 2.5% and the Bank of England was given the power to set interest rates henceforth, granting it a more independent role in monetary policy.

Before the adoption of inflation targets, inflation had already been falling in the United Kingdom, with a peak of 9% at the beginning of 1991 and a rate of 4% at the time of adoption (see Figure 1, panel c). By the third quarter of 1994, it was at 2.2%, within the intended range. Subsequently inflation rose, climbing slightly above the 2.5% level by the end of 1995, but then fell and has remained close to the target since then. In December 2003, the target was changed to 2.0% for a slightly different measure of inflation. Meanwhile, growth of the U.K. economy has been strong, causing a substantial reduction in the unemployment rate.

Advantages of Inflation Targeting

Inflation targeting has several advantages over monetary targeting as a strategy for the conduct of monetary policy. With inflation targeting, stability in the relationship between money and inflation is not critical to its success, because it does not rely on this relationship. An inflation target allows the monetary authorities to use all available information, not just one variable, to determine the best settings for monetary policy.

Inflation targeting also has the key advantage that it is readily understood by the public and is thus highly transparent. Monetary targets, in contrast, are less likely to be easily understood by the public, and if the relationship between the growth rates of monetary aggregates and the inflation goal variable is subject to unpredictable shifts, as has occurred in many countries, monetary targets lose their transparency because they are no longer able to accurately signal the stance of monetary policy.

Because an explicit numerical inflation target increases the accountability of the central bank, inflation targeting has the potential to reduce the likelihood that the central bank will fall into the time-inconsistency trap of trying to expand output and employment in the short run by pursuing overly expansionary monetary policy. A key advantage of inflation targeting is that it can help focus the political debate on what a central bank can do in the long run—that is, control inflation, rather than what it cannot do, permanently increase economic growth and the number of jobs through expansionary monetary policy. Thus inflation targeting has the potential to reduce political pressures on the central bank to pursue inflationary monetary policy and thereby to reduce the likelihood of the time inconsistency problem.

Inflation-targeting regimes also put great stress on making policy transparent and on regular communication with the public. Inflation-targeting central banks have frequent communications with the government, some mandated by law and some in response to informal inquiries, and their officials take every opportunity to make public speeches on their monetary policy strategy. While these techniques are also commonly used in countries that have not adopted inflation targeting, inflation-targeting central banks have taken public outreach a step further: Not only do they engage in extended public information campaigns, including the distribution of glossy brochures, but they also publish documents like the Bank of England's *Inflation Report*. The publication of these documents is particularly noteworthy, because they depart from the usual dull-looking, formal reports of central banks and use fancy graphics, boxes, and other eye-catching design elements to engage the public's interest.

The above channels of communication are used by central banks in inflation-targeting countries to explain the following concepts to the general public, financial market participants, and politicians: (1) the goals and limitations of monetary policy, including the rationale for inflation targets; (2) the numerical values of the inflation targets and how they were determined; (3) how the inflation targets are to be achieved, given current economic conditions; and (4) reasons for any deviations from targets. These communications have improved private sector planning by reducing uncertainty about monetary policy, interest rates, and inflation; they have promoted public debate of monetary policy, in part by educating the public about what a central bank can and cannot achieve; and they have helped clarify the responsibilities of the central bank and of politicians in the conduct of monetary policy.

Another key feature of inflation-targeting regimes is the tendency toward increased accountability of the central bank. Indeed, transparency and communication go hand in hand with increased accountability. The strongest case of accountability of a central bank in an inflation-targeting regime is in New Zealand, where the government has the right to dismiss the Reserve Bank's governor if the inflation targets are breached, even for one quarter. In other inflation-targeting countries, the central bank's accountability is less formalized. Nevertheless, the transparency of policy associated with inflation targeting has tended to make the central bank highly accountable to the public and the government. Sustained success in the conduct of monetary policy as measured against a pre-announced and well-defined inflation target can be instrumental in building public support for a central bank's independence and for its policies. This building of public support and accountability occurs even in the absence of a rigidly defined and legalistic standard of performance evaluation and punishment.

The performance of inflation-targeting regimes has been quite good. Inflation-targeting countries seem to have significantly reduced both the rate of inflation and inflation expectations beyond what would likely have occurred in the absence of inflation targets. Furthermore, once down, inflation in these countries has stayed down; following disinflations, the inflation rate in targeting countries has not bounced back up during subsequent cyclical expansions of the economy.

Disadvantages of Inflation Targeting

Critics of inflation targeting cite four disadvantages of this monetary policy strategy: delayed signaling, too much rigidity, the potential for increased output fluctuations, and low economic growth. We look at each in turn and examine the validity of these criticisms.

Delayed Signaling. In contrast to monetary aggregates, inflation is not easily controlled by the monetary authorities. Furthermore, because of the long lags in the effects of monetary policy, inflation outcomes are revealed only after a substantial lag. Thus an inflation target is unable to send immediate signals to both the public and markets about the stance of monetary policy. However, we have seen that the signals provided by monetary aggregates may not be very strong. Hence, it is not at all clear that monetary targeting is superior to inflation targeting on these grounds.

Too Much Rigidity. Some economists have criticized inflation targeting because they believe it imposes a rigid rule on monetary policymakers and limits their ability to respond to unforeseen circumstances. However, useful policy strategies exist that are "rule-like," in that they involve forward-looking behavior that limits policymakers from systematically engaging in policies with undesirable long-run consequences. Such policies avoid the time-inconsistency problem and would best be described as "constrained discretion."

Indeed, inflation targeting can be described exactly in this way. Inflation targeting, as actually practiced, is far from rigid and is better described as "flexible inflation targeting." First, inflation targeting does not prescribe simple and mechanical instructions on how the central bank should conduct monetary policy. Rather, it requires the central bank to use all available information to determine which policy actions are appropriate to achieve the inflation target. Unlike simple policy rules, inflation targeting never requires the central bank to focus solely on one key variable. Second, inflation targeting as practiced contains a substantial degree of policy discretion. Inflation targets have been modified depending on economic circumstances, as we have seen. Moreover, central banks under inflation-targeting regimes have left themselves considerable scope to respond to output growth and fluctuations through several devices.

Potential for Increased Output Fluctuations. An important criticism of inflation targeting is that a sole focus on inflation may lead to monetary policy that is too tight when inflation is above target and thus may lead to larger output fluctuations. Inflation targeting does not, however, require a sole focus on inflation—in fact, experience has shown that inflation targeters display substantial concern about output fluctuations. All the inflation targeters have set their inflation targets above zero.[5] For example, currently New Zealand has the lowest midpoint for an inflation target, 1.5%, while Canada and Sweden set the midpoint of their inflation target at 2%; and the United Kingdom and Australia currently have their midpoints at 2.5%.

The decision by inflation targeters to choose inflation targets above zero reflects the concern of monetary policymakers that particularly low inflation can have substantial negative effects on real economic activity. Deflation (negative inflation in which the price level actually falls) is especially to be feared because of the possibility that it may promote financial instability and precipitate a severe economic contraction (Chapter 8). The deflation in Japan in recent years has been an important factor in the weakening of the Japanese financial system and economy. Targeting inflation rates of above zero makes periods of deflation less likely. This is one reason why some economists both within and outside of Japan have been calling on the Bank of Japan to adopt an inflation target at levels of 2% or higher.

Inflation targeting also does not ignore traditional stabilization goals. Central bankers in inflation-targeting countries continue to express their concern about fluctuations in output and employment, and the ability to accommodate short-run stabilization goals to some degree is built into all inflation-targeting regimes. All inflation-targeting countries have been willing to minimize output declines by gradually lowering medium-term inflation targets toward the long-run goal.

---

[5]Consumer price indexes have been found to have an upward bias in the measurement of true inflation, so it is not surprising that inflation targets would be chosen to exceed zero. However, the actual targets have been set to exceed the estimates of this measurement bias, indicating that inflation targeters have decided to have targets for inflation that exceed zero even after measurement bias is accounted for.

Low Economic Growth. Another common concern about inflation targeting is that it will lead to low growth in output and employment. Although inflation reduction has been associated with below-normal output during disinflationary phases in inflation-targeting regimes, once low inflation levels were achieved, output and employment returned to levels at least as high as they were before. A conservative conclusion is that once low inflation is achieved, inflation targeting is not harmful to the real economy. Given the strong economic growth after disinflation in many countries (such as New Zealand) that have adopted inflation targets, a case can be made that inflation targeting promotes real economic growth, in addition to controlling inflation.

MONETARY POLICY WITH AN IMPLICIT NOMINAL ANCHOR

In recent years, the United States has achieved excellent macroeconomic performance (including low and stable inflation) without using an explicit nominal anchor such as a monetary aggregate or an inflation target. Although the Federal Reserve has not articulated an explicit strategy, a coherent strategy for the conduct of monetary policy exists nonetheless. This strategy involves an implicit but not an explicit nominal anchor in the form of an overriding concern by the Federal Reserve to control inflation in the long run. In addition, it involves forward-looking behavior in which there is careful monitoring for signs of future inflation using a wide range of information, coupled with periodic "preemptive strikes" by monetary policy against the threat of inflation.

As emphasized by Milton Friedman, monetary policy effects have long lags. In industrialized countries with a history of low inflation, the inflation process seems to have tremendous inertia: Estimates from large macroeconometric models of the U.S. economy, for example, suggest that monetary policy takes over a year to affect output and over two years to have a significant impact on inflation. For countries that have experienced highly variable inflation, and therefore have more flexible prices, the lags may be shorter.

The presence of long lags means that monetary policy cannot wait to respond until inflation has begun. If the central bank waits until overt signs of inflation appear, it will already be too late to maintain stable prices, at least not without a severe tightening of policy: Inflation expectations will already be embedded in the wage- and price-setting process, creating an inflation momentum that will be hard to halt. Inflation becomes much harder to control once it has been allowed to gather momentum, because higher inflation expectations become ingrained in various types of long-term contracts and pricing agreements.

To prevent inflation from getting started, therefore, monetary policy needs to be forward-looking and preemptive. That is, depending on the lags from monetary policy to inflation, monetary policy needs to act long before inflationary pressures appear in the economy. For example, suppose it takes roughly two years for monetary policy to have a significant impact on inflation. In this case, even if inflation is currently low but policymakers believe inflation will rise over the next two years with an unchanged stance of monetary policy, they must tighten monetary policy *now* to prevent the inflationary surge.

Under Alan Greenspan, the Federal Reserve was successful in pursuing a preemptive monetary policy. For example, the Fed raised interest rates from 1994 to 1995 before a rise in inflation got a toehold. As a result, inflation not only did not rise, but fell slightly. This preemptive, forward-looking monetary policy strategy is clearly also a feature of inflation-targeting regimes, because monetary policy instruments are adjusted to take account of the long lags in their effects in an effort to hit future inflation targets.

However, the Greenspan Fed's policy regime might best be described as a "just do it" policy, and differs from inflation targeting in that it does not officially have a nominal anchor and is much less transparent in its monetary policy strategy.

Advantages of the Fed's Approach

The Fed's "just do it" approach, which has some of the key elements of inflation targeting, has many of the same advantages. It also does not rely on a stable money–inflation relationship. As with inflation targeting, the central bank uses many sources of information to determine the best settings for monetary policy. The Fed's forward-looking behavior and stress on price stability also help to discourage overly expansionary monetary policy, thereby ameliorating the time-inconsistency problem.

Another key argument for the "just do it" strategy is its demonstrated success. The Federal Reserve has been able to reduce inflation in the United States from double-digit levels in 1980 to around the 3% level in 2005, which is arguably consistent with the price stability goal. From February 1994 until early 1995, the Fed conducted a successful preemptive strike against inflation when in several steps it raised the federal funds rate from 3% to 6% even though inflation was not increasing during this period. The business-cycle expansion from 1991 to 2001, the longest in U.S. history, brought unemployment down to around 4%, a level not seen since the 1960s, while CPI inflation fell to a level near 2%. The Fed engaged in a preemptive strike against a weakening economy when in January 2001, shortly before the start of the recession in March 2001, it began to sharply lower the federal funds rate from 6.5% to 1%. With the economy recovering, in June 2004, the Fed again moved preemptively to contain inflation and began raising the federal funds rate 25 basis points (0.25 percentage points) at each subsequent FOMC meeting. These preemptive strikes against both inflation and weakness in the economy enabled the United States to have steady growth with continuing low inflation. Indeed, the performance of the U.S. economy has become the envy of the industrialized world over the last decade.

Disadvantages of the Fed's Approach

Given the success of the "just do it" strategy in the United States, why should the United States consider other monetary policy strategies? (If it ain't broke, why fix it?) The answer is that the "just do it" strategy has some disadvantages that may cause it to work less well in the future.

One disadvantage of the strategy is its lack of transparency. The Fed's close-mouthed approach about its intentions gives rise to a constant guessing game about what it is going to do. This high level of uncertainty leads to unnecessary volatility in financial markets and creates doubt among producers and the general public about the future course of inflation and output. Furthermore, the opacity of its policymaking makes it hard to hold the Federal Reserve accountable to Congress and the general public: The Fed can't be held accountable if there are no predetermined criteria for judging its performance. Low accountability may make the central bank more susceptible to the time-inconsistency problem, whereby it may pursue short-term objectives at the expense of long-term ones.

Probably the most serious problem with the "just do it" approach is its strong dependence on the preferences, skills, and trustworthiness of the individuals in charge of the central bank. In recent years in the United States, Federal Reserve Chairman Alan Greenspan and other Federal Reserve officials have emphasized forward-looking policies and inflation control, with great success. The Fed's prestige and credibility with the public have risen accordingly. But the Fed's leadership will periodically change, and there is no guarantee that it will be committed to the same approach. Nor is there any guarantee that the relatively good working relationship that has existed between the Fed and the executive branch will always continue. In a different economic or political environment, the Fed might face strong pressure to engage in over-expansionary policies, raising the possibility that time inconsistency may become a more serious problem. In the past, after a successful period of low inflation, the Federal Reserve has reverted to inflationary monetary policy—the 1970s are one example—and without an explicit nominal anchor, this could certainly happen again.

Another disadvantage of the "just do it" approach is that it has some inconsistencies with democratic principles. As described in Chapter 15, there are good reasons—notably, insulation from short-term political pressures—for the central bank to have some degree of independence, as the Federal Reserve currently does, and the evidence does generally support central bank independence. Yet the practical economic arguments for central bank independence coexist uneasily with the presumption that government policies should be made democratically, rather than by an elite group.

In contrast, inflation targeting can make the institutional framework for the conduct of monetary policy more consistent with democratic principles and avoid some of the above problems. The inflation-targeting framework promotes the accountability of the central bank to elected officials, who are given some responsibility for setting the goals for monetary policy and then monitoring the economic outcomes. However, under inflation targeting as it has generally been practiced, the central bank has com-

Inside the Fed **The New Fed Chairman and Inflation Targeting**

Ben Bernanke, a former professor at Princeton University, became the new Federal Reserve Chairman in February 2006, after serving as a member of the Board of Governors from 2002–2005 and then the chairman of the Council of Economic Advisors. Bernanke is a world-renowned expert on monetary policy and while an academic wrote extensively on inflation targeting, including articles and a book written with the author of this text.*

Bernanke's writings suggest that he is a strong proponent of inflation targeting and increased transparency in central banks. In an important speech given at a conference at the Federal Reserve Bank of St. Louis in 2004 he described how the Federal Reserve might approach a movement toward inflation targeting.[†] Bernanke suggested that the Fed should announce a numerical value for its long-run inflation goal, which he labeled the *optimal level of the inflation rate* (OLIR). Bernanke emphasized that announcing the OLIR would be completely consistent with the Fed's dual mandate of achieving price stability and maximum employment because it would be set above zero to avoid deflations which have harmful effects on employment and would not be intended to be a short-run target that might lead to too tight control of inflation at the expense of overly high employment fluctuations.

Since becoming Fed Chairman, Bernanke has made it clear that any movement toward inflation targeting must result from a consensus within the Federal Reserve. Under Chairman Bernanke, some movement toward greater transparency about the Fed's inflation goals is likely, but how far the Fed will move toward inflation targeting is still uncertain.

*Ben S. Bernanke and Frederic S. Mishkin, "Inflation Targeting: A New Framework for Monetary Policy," *Journal of Economic Perspectives*, vol. 11, no. 2 (1997), Ben S. Bernanke, Frederic S. Mishkin and Adam S. Posen, "Inflation Targeting: Fed Policy After Greenspan," *Milken Institute Review*, (Fourth Quarter, 1999): 48-56, Ben S. Bernanke, Frederic S. Mishkin and Adam S. Posen, "What Happens When Greenspan is Gone," *Wall Street Journal*, January 5, 2000: p. A22, and Ben S. Bernanke, Thomas Laubach, Frederic S. Mishkin and Adam S. Posen, *Inflation Targeting: Lessosns from the International Experience* (Princeton, N.J.: Princeton University Press 1999).

†Ben S. Bernanke, "Inflation Targeting," Federal Reserve Bank of St. Louis, *Review*, vol 86, no. 4 (July/August 2004), pp. 165-168.

plete control over operational decisions, so that it can be held accountable for achieving its assigned objectives.

The Fed's monetary policy strategy may move more toward inflation targeting in the future, particularly with the appointment of a new chairman of the Fed, Ben Bernanke, who has been an advocate of inflation targeting. (See the Inside the Fed box, "The New Fed Chairman and Inflation Targeting".) Inflation targeting is not too far from the Fed's current policymaking philosophy, which has stressed the importance of price stability as the overriding, long-run goal of monetary policy. Also, a move to inflation targeting is consistent with recent steps by the Fed to increase the transparency of monetary policy, such as shortening the time before the minutes of the FOMC meeting are released, the practice of announcing the FOMC's decision about whether to change the target for the federal funds rates immediately after the conclusion of the FOMC meeting, and the announcement of the "balance of risks" in the future, whether toward higher inflation or toward a weaker economy.

STUDY GUIDE

As a study aid, the advantages and disadvantages of monetary targeting as well as the other monetary policy strategies are listed in Table 1.

SUMMARY TABLE 1 Advantages and Disadvantages of Different Monetary Policy Strategies

	Monetary Targeting	Inflation Targeting	Implicit Nominal Anchor
Advantages			
	Immediate signal on achievement of target	Simplicity and clarity of target	Does not rely on stable money–inflation relationship
		Does not rely on stable money–inflation relationship	Demonstrated success in United States
		Increased accountability of central bank	
		Reduced effects of inflationary shocks	
Disadvantages			
	Relies on stable money–inflation relationship	Delayed signal about achievement of target	Lack of transparency
		Could impose rigid rule (though has not in practice)	Success depends on individuals in charge
		Larger output fluctuations if sole focus on inflation (though not in practice)	Low accountability

TACTICS: CHOOSING THE POLICY INSTRUMENT

Now that we are familiar with the alternative strategies for monetary policy, let's look at how monetary policy is conducted on a day-to-day basis. Central banks directly control the tools of monetary policy—open market operations, reserve requirements, and the discount rate—but knowing the tools and the strategies for implementing a monetary policy does not tell us whether policy is easy or tight. The **policy instrument** (also called an **operating instrument**) is a variable that responds to the central bank's tools and indicates the stance (easy or tight) of monetary policy. A central bank like the Fed has at its disposal two basic types of policy instruments: reserve aggregates (total reserves, nonborrowed reserves, the monetary base, and the nonborrowed base) and interest rates (federal funds rate and other short-term interest rates). (Central banks in small countries can choose another policy instrument, the exchange rate, but we leave this topic to Chapter 21.) The policy instrument might be linked to an **intermediate target**, such as a monetary aggregate like M2 or a long-term interest rate. Intermediate targets stand between the policy instrument and the goals of monetary policy (e.g., price stability, output growth); they are not as directly affected by the tools of monetary policy, but might be more closely linked to the goals of monetary policy.

As an example, suppose the central bank's employment and inflation goals are consistent with a nominal GDP growth rate of 5%. The central bank might believe that the 5% nominal GDP growth rate will be achieved by a 4% growth rate for M2 (an intermediate target), which will in turn be achieved by a growth rate of 3% for nonborrowed reserves (the policy instrument). Alternatively, the central bank might believe that the best way to achieve its objectives would be to set the federal funds rate (a policy instrument) at, say, 4%. Can the central bank choose to target both the nonborrowed-reserves and the federal-funds-rate policy instruments at the same time? The answer is no. The application of supply and demand analysis to the market for reserves we developed in Chapter 15 explains why a central bank must choose one or the other.

Let's first see why an aggregate target involves losing control of the interest rate. Figure 2 contains a supply and demand diagram for the market for reserves. Although the central bank expects the demand curve for reserves to be a R^{d*}, it fluctuates between $R^{d'}$ and $R^{d''}$ because of unexpected fluctuations in deposits (and hence requires reserves) and changes in banks' desire to hold excess reserves. If the central bank has a nonborrowed reserves target of NBR^* (say, because it has a target growth rate of the money supply of 4%), it expects that the federal funds rate will be i_{ff}^*. However, as the figure indicates, the fluctuations in the reserves demand curve between $R^{d'}$ and $R^{d''}$ will result in a fluctuation in the federal funds rate between i_{ff}' and i_{ff}''. Pursuing an aggregate target implies that interest rates will fluctuate.

The supply and demand diagram in Figure 3 shows the consequences of an interest-rate target set at i_{ff}^*. Again the central bank expects the reserves demand curve to be at R^{d*}, but it fluctuates between $R^{d'}$ and $R^{d''}$ due to unexpected changes in deposits or banks' desire to hold excess reserves. If the demand curve rises to $R^{d''}$, the federal funds rate will begin to rise above i_{ff}^* and the central bank will engage in open market purchases of bonds until it raises the supply of nonborrowed reserves to NBR'', at which point the equilibrium federal funds rate is again at i_{ff}^*. Conversely, if the demand curve falls to $R^{d'}$ and lowers the federal funds rate, the central bank would keep making open market sales until nonborrowed reserves fall to NBR' and the federal funds rate returns to i_{ff}^*. The central bank's adherence to the interest-rate target thus leads to a fluctuating quantity of nonborrowed reserves and the money supply.

FIGURE 2
Result of Targeting on Nonborrowed Reserves
Targeting on nonborrowed reserves of NBR^* will lead to fluctuations in the federal funds rate between i'_{ff} and i''_{ff} because of fluctuations in the demand for reserves between $R^{d'}$ and $R^{d''}$.

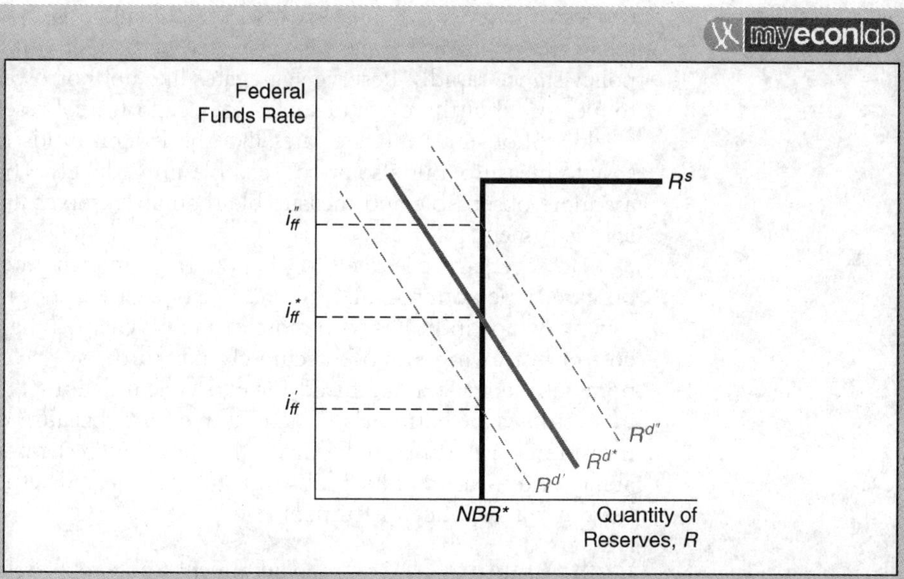

FIGURE 3
Result of Targeting on the Federal Funds Rate
Targeting on the interest rate i^*_{ff} will lead to fluctuation on nonborrowed reserves because of fluctuations in the demand for reserves between $R^{d'}$ and $R^{d''}$.

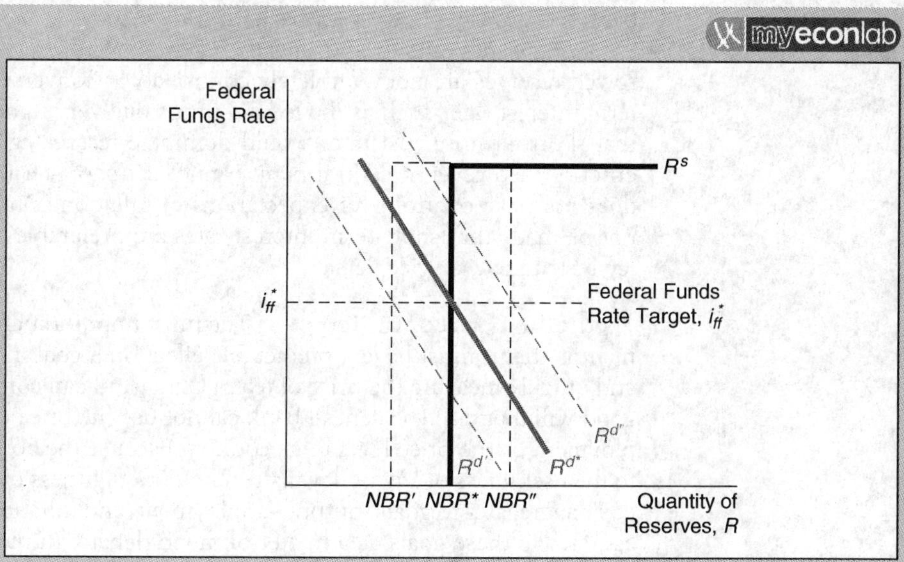

The conclusion from the supply and demand analysis is that interest-rate and reserve (monetary) aggregate targets are incompatible. A central bank can hit one or the other, but not both. Because a choice between them has to be made, we need to examine what criteria should be used to select a policy instrument.

Criteria for Choosing the Policy Instrument

Three criteria apply when choosing a policy instrument: The instrument must be observable and measurable, it must be controllable by the central bank, and it must have a predictable effect on the goals.

Observability and Measurability. Quick observability and accurate measurement of a policy instrument is necessary, because it will be useful only if it signals the policy stance rapidly. Reserve aggregates like nonborrowed reserves are straightforward to measure, but there is still some lag in reporting of reserve aggregates (a delay of two weeks). Short-term interest rates like the federal funds rate, by contrast, not only are easy to measure, but also are observable immediately. Thus, it seems that interest rates are more observable and measurable than are reserves and, therefore, are a better policy instrument.

However, as we learned in Chapter 4, the interest rate that is easiest to measure and observe is the nominal interest rate. It is typically a poor measure of the real cost of borrowing, which indicates with more certainty what will happen to the real GDP. This real cost of borrowing is more accurately measured by the real interest rate—that is, the nominal interest rate adjusted for expected inflation ($i_r = i - \pi^e$). Unfortunately, real interest rates are extremely difficult to measure, because we do not have a direct way to measure expected inflation. Given that both interest rates and aggregates have observability and measurability problems, it is not clear whether one should be preferred to the other as a policy instrument.

Controllability. A central bank must be able to exercise effective control over a variable if it is to function as a useful policy instrument. If the central bank cannot control the policy instrument, knowing that it is off track does little good, because the central bank has no way of getting it back on track.

Because of shifts in and out of currency, even reserve aggregates such as nonborrowed reserves are not completely controllable. Conversely, the Fed can control short-term interest rates such as the federal funds rate very tightly. It might appear, therefore, that short-term interest rates would dominate reserve aggregates on the controllability criterion. However, a central bank cannot set short-term real interest rates because it does not have control over expectations of inflation. Once again, a clear-cut case cannot be made that short-term interest rates are preferable to reserve aggregates as a policy instrument, or vice versa.

Predictable Effect on Goals. The most important characteristic of a policy instrument is that it must have a predictable effect on a goal. If a central bank can accurately and quickly measure the price of tea in China and can completely control its price, what good will that do? The central bank cannot use the price of tea in China to affect unemployment or the price level in its country. Because the ability to affect goals is so critical to the usefulness of any policy instrument, the tightness of the link from reserve or monetary aggregates to goals (output, employment, and inflation) or, alternatively, from interest rates to these goals, is a matter of much debate. In recent years, most central banks have concluded that the link between interest rates and goals such as inflation is tighter than the link between aggregates and inflation. For this reason, central banks throughout the world now generally use short-term interest rates as their policy instrument.

THE TAYLOR RULE, NAIRU, AND THE PHILLIPS CURVE

As we have seen, the Federal Reserve and most other central banks currently conduct monetary policy by setting a target for short-term interest rates like the federal funds rate. But how should this target be chosen?

John Taylor of Stanford University has come up with an answer, called the **Taylor rule**. The Taylor rule indicates that the federal (fed) funds rate should be set equal to the inflation rate plus an "equilibrium" real fed funds rate (the real fed funds rate that is consistent with full employment in the long run) plus a weighted average of two gaps: (1) an inflation gap, current inflation minus a target rate, and (2) an output gap, the percentage deviation of real GDP from an estimate of its potential full employment level.[6] This rule can be written as follows:

$$\text{Federal funds rate target} = \text{inflation rate} + \text{equilibrium real fed funds rate} + \tfrac{1}{2}\,(\text{inflation gap}) + \tfrac{1}{2}\,(\text{output gap})$$

Taylor has assumed that the equilibrium real fed funds rate is 2% and that an appropriate target for inflation would also be 2%, with equal weights of ½ on the inflation and output gaps. For an example of the Taylor rule in practice, suppose that the inflation rate were at 3%, leading to a positive inflation gap of 1% (= 3% − 2%), and real GDP was 1% above its potential, resulting in a positive output gap of 1%. Then the Taylor rule suggests that the federal funds rate should be set at 6% [= 3% inflation + 2% equilibrium real fed funds rate + ½ (1% inflation gap) + ½ (1% output gap)].

The presence of both an inflation gap and an output gap in the Taylor rule might indicate that the Fed should care not only about keeping inflation under control, but also about minimizing business-cycle fluctuations of output around its potential. Caring about both inflation and output fluctuations is consistent with many statements by Federal Reserve officials that controlling inflation and stabilizing real output are important concerns of the Fed.

An alternative interpretation of the presence of the output gap in the Taylor rule is that the output gap is an indicator of future inflation as stipulated in **Phillips curve theory**. Phillips curve theory indicates that changes in inflation are influenced by the state of the economy relative to its productive capacity, as well as to other factors. This productive capacity can be measured by potential GDP, which is a function of the natural rate of unemployment, the rate of unemployment consistent with full employment. A related concept is the **NAIRU**, the **nonaccelerating inflation rate of unemployment**, the rate of unemployment at which there is no tendency for inflation to change.[7] Simply put, the theory states that when the unemployment rate is above NAIRU with output below potential, inflation will come down, but if it is below NAIRU with output above potential, inflation will rise. Prior to 1995, the NAIRU was thought to reside around 6%. However, with the decline in unemployment to around the 4% level in the late 1990s, with no increase in inflation and even a slight decrease, some critics have questioned the value of Phillips curve theory. Either they claim that it just doesn't work any more or, alternatively, they believe that there is great uncertainty about the value of NAIRU, which may have fallen to below 5% for reasons that are not absolutely clear.

---

[6] John B. Taylor, "Discretion Versus Policy Rules in Practice," *Carnegie-Rochester Conference Series on Public Policy* 39 (1993): 195–214. A more intuitive discussion with a historical perspective can be found in John B. Taylor, "A Historical Analysis of Monetary Policy Rules," in *Monetary Policy Rules*, ed. John B. Taylor (Chicago: University of Chicago Press, 1999), pp. 319–341.

[7] There are, however, subtle differences between the two concepts, as is discussed in Arturo Estrella and Frederic S. Mishkin, "The Role of NAIRU in Monetary Policy: Implications of Uncertainty and Model Selection," in *Monetary Policy Rules*, ed. John Taylor (Chicago: University of Chicago Press, 1999): pp. 405–430.

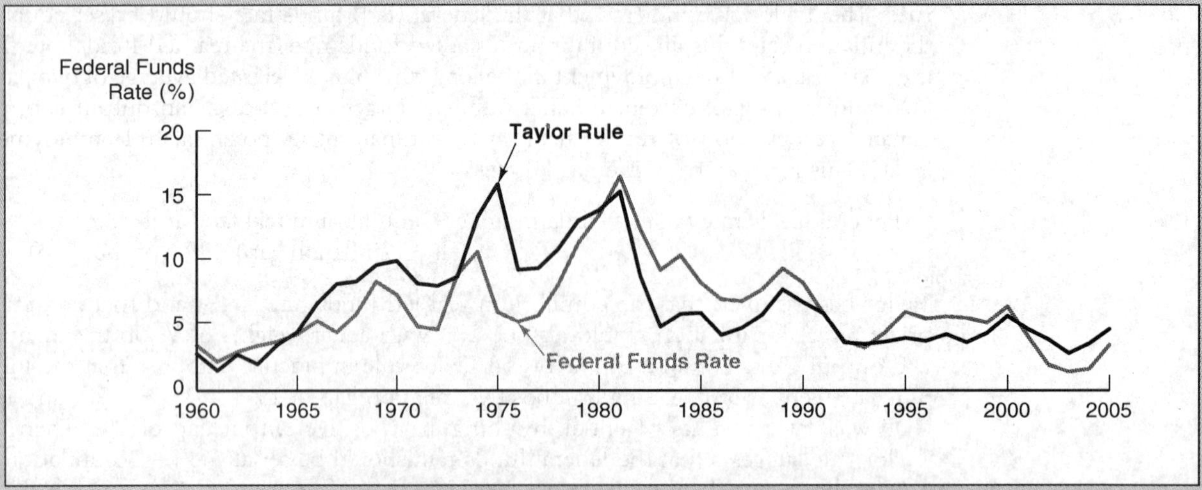

FIGURE 4 **The Taylor Rule for the Federal Funds Rate, 1970–2005**
Source: Federal Reserve: www.federalreserve.gov/releases and author's calculations.

Phillips curve theory is now highly controversial, and many economists believe that it should not be used as a guide for the conduct of monetary policy.

As Figure 4 shows, the Taylor rule does a pretty good job of describing the Fed's setting of the federal funds rate under Chairman Greenspan. (However, the Taylor rule does not explain all movements in the federal funds rate, which explains why financial institutions hire Fed watchers, as described in the Inside the Fed box.) It also provides

Inside the Fed **Fed Watchers**

As we have seen, the most important player in the determination of the U.S. money supply and interest rates is the Federal Reserve. When the Fed wants to inject reserves into the system, it conducts open market purchases of bonds, which cause bond prices to increase and their interest rates to fall, at least in the short term. If the Fed withdraws reserves from the system, it sells bonds, thereby depressing their price and raising their interest rates. From a longer-run perspective, if the Fed pursues an expansionary monetary policy with high money growth, inflation will rise and, as we saw in Chapter 5, interest rates will rise as well. Contractionary monetary policy is likely to lower inflation in the long run and lead to lower interest rates.

Knowing what actions the Fed might be taking can thus help investors and financial institutions to predict the future course of interest rates with greater accuracy. Because, as we have seen, changes in interest rates have a major impact on investors and financial institutions' profits, they are particularly interested in scrutinizing the Fed's behavior. To assist in this task, financial institutions hire *Fed watchers*, experts on Federal Reserve behavior who may have worked in the Federal Reserve System and so have an insider's view of Federal Reserve operations. A Fed watcher who can accurately predict the course of monetary policy is a very valuable commodity, and successful Fed watchers therefore often earn very high salaries, well into the six-figure range and sometimes even higher.

a perspective on the Fed's conduct of monetary policy under Chairmen Burns and Volcker. During the Burns period, from 1970 to 1979, the federal funds rate was consistently lower than that indicated by the Taylor rule. This fact helps explain why inflation rose during this period. During the Volcker period, from 1979 to 1987, when the Fed was trying to bring inflation down quickly, the funds rate was generally higher than that recommended by the Taylor rule. The closer correspondence between the actual funds rate and the Taylor rule recommendation during the Greenspan era may help explain why the Fed's performance has been so successful in recent years.

SUMMARY

1. The six basic goals of monetary policy are price stability (the primary goal), high employment, economic growth, interest-rate stability, stability of financial markets, and stability in foreign exchange markets.
2. A nominal anchor is a key element in monetary policy strategies. It helps promote price stability by tying down inflation expectations and limiting the time-inconsistency problem, in which monetary policymakers conduct monetary policy in a discretionary way that produces poor long-run outcomes.
3. Monetary targeting has the advantage that information on whether the central bank is achieving its target is known almost immediately. Monetary targeting suffers from the disadvantage that it works well only if there is a reliable relationship between the monetary aggregate and the goal variable, inflation—a relationship that has often not held in different countries.
4. Inflation targeting has several advantages: (1) It enables monetary policy to focus on domestic considerations; (2) stability in the relationship between money and inflation is not critical to its success; (3) it is readily understood by the public and is highly transparent; (4) it increases accountability of the central bank; and (5) it appears to ameliorate the effects of inflationary shocks. It does have some disadvantages, however: (1) Inflation is not easily controlled by the monetary authorities, so that an inflation target is unable to send immediate signals to both the public and markets; (2) it might impose a rigid rule on policymakers, although this has not been the case in practice; and (3) a sole focus on inflation may lead to larger output fluctuations, although this has also not been the case in practice.
5. In recent years, Federal Reserve has a strategy of having an implicit, not an explicit, nominal anchor. This strategy has the following advantages: (1) It enables monetary policy to focus on domestic considerations; (2) it does not rely on a stable money–inflation relationship; and (3) it has had a demonstrated success, producing low inflation with the longest business-cycle expansion in U.S. history. However, it does have some disadvantages: (1) It has a lack of transparency; (2) it is strongly dependent on the preferences, skills, and trustworthiness of individuals in the central bank and the government; and (3) it has some inconsistencies with democratic principles, because the central bank is not highly accountable.
6. Because interest-rate and aggregate policy instruments are incompatible, a central bank must choose between them on the basis of three criteria: measurability, controllability, and the ability to affect goal variables predictably. Central banks now typically use short-term interest rates as their policy instrument.
7. The Taylor rule indicates that the federal funds rate should be set equal to the inflation rate plus an "equilibrium" real funds rate plus a weighted average of two gaps: (1) an inflation gap, current inflation minus a target rate, and (2) an output gap, the percentage deviation of real GDP from an estimate of its potential full employment level. The output gap in the Taylor rule could represent an indicator of future inflation as stipulated in Phillips curve theory. However, this theory is controversial, because high output relative to potential as measured by low unemployment has not seemed to produce higher inflation in recent years.

KEY TERMS

dual mandate, p. 469
hierarchical mandate, p. 469
inflation targeting, p. 474
intermediate target, p. 484
international policy coordination, p. 500
monetary targeting, p. 470
natural rate of unemployment, p. 467
nominal anchor, p. 466
nonaccelerating inflation rate of unemployment (NAIRU), p. 487
operating instrument, p. 484
Phillips curve theory, p. 487
policy instrument, p. 484
price stability, p. 465
real bills doctrine, p. 492
Taylor rule, p. 487
time-inconsistency problem, p. 466

QUESTIONS AND PROBLEMS

Questions marked with an asterisk are answered at the end of the book in an appendix, "Answers to Selected Questions and Problems." Questions marked with a blue circle indicate the question is available in MyEconLab at www.myeconlab.com/mishkin.

*1. "Unemployment is a bad thing, and the government should make every effort to eliminate it." Do you agree or disagree? Explain your answer.

2. Classify each of the following as either a policy instrument or an intermediate target, and explain why.
   a. The ten-year Treasury bond rate
   b. The monetary base
   c. M2

*3. "If the demand for reserves did not fluctuate, the Fed could pursue both an aggregate target and an interest-rate target at the same time." Is this statement true, false, or uncertain? Explain your answer.

4. If the Fed has an interest-rate target, why will an increase in the demand for reserves lead to a rise in the money supply?

*5. What procedures can the Fed use to control the federal funds rate? Why does control of this interest rate imply that the Fed will lose control of nonborrowed reserves?

6. Compare the monetary base to M2 on the grounds of controllability and measurability. Which do you prefer as an intermediate target? Why?

*7. "Interest rates can be measured more accurately and more quickly than reserve aggregates. Hence an interest rate is preferred over the reserve aggregates as a policy instrument." Do you agree or disagree? Explain your answer.

8. What are the benefits of using a nominal anchor for the conduct of monetary policy?

9. Give an example of the time-inconsistency problem that you experience in your everyday life.

10. What incentives arise for a central bank to fall into the time-inconsistency trap of pursuing overly expansionary monetary policy?

*11. What are the advantages of monetary targeting as a strategy for the conduct of monetary policy?

12. What is the big *if* necessary for the success of monetary targeting? Does the experience with monetary targeting suggest that the big *if* is a problem?

*13. What methods have inflation-targeting central banks used to increase communication with the public and increase the transparency of monetary policymaking?

14. Why might inflation targeting increase support for the independence of the central bank to conduct monetary policy?

*15. "Because the public can see whether a central bank hits its monetary targets almost immediately, whereas it takes time before the public can see whether an inflation target is achieved, monetary targeting makes central banks more accountable than inflation targeting does." Is this statement true, false, or uncertain? Explain your answer.

16. "Because inflation targeting focuses on achieving the inflation target, it will lead to excessive output fluctuations." Is this statement true, false, or uncertain? Explain your answer.

*17. "A central bank with a dual mandate will achieve lower unemployment in the long run than a central bank with a hierarchical mandate in which price stability takes precedence." Is this statement true, false, or uncertain?

18. What are the key advantages and disadvantages of the monetary strategy used in the United States under Alan Greenspan in which the nominal anchor is only implicit?

***19.** What is the advantage that monetary targeting, inflation targeting, and a monetary strategy with an implicit, but not an explicit, nominal anchor have in common?

20. How can bank behavior and the Fed's behavior cause money supply growth to be procyclical (rising in booms and falling in recessions)?

WEB EXERCISES

1. The Federal Open Market Committee (FOMC) meets about every six weeks to assess the state of the economy and to decide what actions the central bank should take. The minutes of this meeting are released three weeks after the meeting; however, a brief press release is made available immediately. Find the schedule of minutes and press releases at www.federalreserve.gov/fomc/.
   a. When was the last scheduled meeting of the FOMC? When is the next meeting?
   b. Review the press release from the last meeting. What did the committee decide to do about short-term interest rates?
   c. Review the most recently published meeting minutes. What areas of the economy seemed to be of most concern to the committee members?

2. It is possible to access other central bank Web sites to learn about their structure. One example is the European Central bank. Go to www.ecb.int/index.html. On the ECB home page, find information about the ECB's strategy for monetary policy.

3. Many countries have central banks that are responsible for their nation's monetary policy. Go to www.bis.org/cbanks.htm and select one of the central banks (for example, Norway). Review that bank's Web site to determine its policies regarding application of monetary policy. How does this bank's policies compare to those of the U.S. central bank?

WEB REFERENCES

www.federalreserve.gov/pf/pf.htm

Review what the Federal Reserve reports as its primary purposes and functions.

www.economagic.com/

A comprehensive listing of sites that offer a wide variety of economic summary data and graphs.

www.federalreserve.gov/releases/H3

Historic and current data on the aggregate reserves of depository institutions and the monetary base.

www.federalreserve.gov/general.htm

The Federal Reserve provides links to other central bank webpages.

APPENDIX TO CHAPTER

19 Fed Policy Procedures: Historical Perspective

The well-known adage "The road to hell is paved with good intentions" applies as much to the Federal Reserve as it does to human beings. Understanding a central bank's goals and the strategies it can use to pursue them cannot tell us how monetary policy is actually conducted. To understand the practical results of the theoretical underpinnings, we have to look at how the Fed has actually conducted policy in the past. This historical perspective will not only show us how our central bank carries out its duties but will also help us interpret the Fed's activities and see where U.S. monetary policy may be heading in the future.

STUDY GUIDE

The following discussion of the Fed's policy procedures and their effect on the money supply provides an application of your understanding of the money supply process and how the Fed's policy tools work. If you have trouble understanding how the particular policies described affect the money supply, it might be helpful to review the material in Chapters 16 and 17.

THE EARLY YEARS: DISCOUNT POLICY AS THE PRIMARY TOOL

When the Fed was created, changing the discount rate was the primary tool of monetary policy—the Fed had not yet discovered that open market operations were a more powerful tool for influencing the money supply, and the Federal Reserve Act made no provisions for changes in reserve requirements. The guiding principle for the conduct of monetary policy was that as long as loans were being made for "productive" purposes—that is, to support the production of goods and services—providing reserves to the banking system to make these loans would not be inflationary. This theory, now thoroughly discredited, became known as the **real bills doctrine**. In practice, it meant that the Fed would make loans to member commercial banks when they showed up at the discount window with *eligible paper*, loans to facilitate the production and sale of goods and services. (Since the 1920s, the Fed has not conducted discount operations in this way.) The Fed's act of making loans to member banks was initially called *rediscounting*, because the original bank loans to businesses were made by discounting (loaning less than) the face value of the loan, and the Fed would be discounting them again.

(Over time, when the Fed's emphasis on eligible paper diminished, the Fed's loans to banks became known as *discounts*, and the interest rate on these loans the *discount rate*, which is the terminology we use today.)

By the end of World War I, the Fed's policy of rediscounting eligible paper and keeping interest rates low to help the Treasury finance the war had led to a raging inflation; in 1919 and 1920, the inflation rate averaged 14%. The Fed decided that it could no longer follow the passive policy prescribed by the real bills doctrine because it was inconsistent with the goal of price stability, and for the first time the Fed accepted the responsibility of playing an active role in influencing the economy. In January 1920, the Fed raised the discount rate from $4\frac{3}{4}\%$ to 6%, the largest jump in its history, and eventually raised it further, to 7% in June 1920, where it remained for nearly a year. The result of this policy was a sharp decline in the money supply and an especially sharp recession in 1920–1921. Although the blame for this severe recession can clearly be laid at the Fed's doorstep, in one sense the Fed's policy was very successful: After an initial decline in the price level, the inflation rate went to zero, paving the way for the prosperous Roaring Twenties.

DISCOVERY OF OPEN MARKET OPERATIONS

In the early 1920s, a particularly important event occurred: The Fed accidentally discovered open market operations. When the Fed was created, its revenue came exclusively from the interest it received on the discount loans it made to member banks. After the 1920–1921 recession, the volume of discount loans shrank dramatically, and the Fed was pressed for income. It solved this problem by purchasing income-earning securities. In doing so, the Fed noticed that reserves in the banking system grew and there was a multiple expansion of bank loans and deposits. This result is obvious to us now (we studied the multiple deposit creation process in Chapter 16), but to the Fed at that time it was a revelation. A new monetary policy tool was born, and by the end of the 1920s, it was the most important weapon in the Fed's arsenal.

THE GREAT DEPRESSION

The stock market boom in 1928 and 1929 created a dilemma for the Fed. It wanted to temper the boom by raising the discount rate, but it was reluctant to do so, because that would mean raising interest rates to businesses and individuals who had legitimate needs for credit. Finally, in August 1929, the Fed raised the discount rate, but by then it was too late; the speculative excesses of the market boom had already occurred, and the Fed's action merely hastened the stock market crash and pushed the economy into recession.

The weakness of the economy, particularly in the agricultural sector, led to what Milton Friedman and Anna Schwartz labeled a "contagion of fear" that triggered substantial withdrawals from banks, building to a full-fledged panic in November and December 1930. For the next two years, the Fed sat idly by while one bank panic after another occurred, culminating in the final panic in March 1933, at which point the new president, Franklin Delano Roosevelt, declared a bank holiday. (Why the Fed failed to engage in its lender-of-last-resort role during this period is discussed in the Inside the Fed box on bank panics.) The spate of bank panics from 1930 to 1933 were the most severe in U.S. history, and Roosevelt aptly summed up the problem in his statement,

Inside the Fed Bank Panics of 1930–1933: Why Did the Fed Let Them Happen?

The Federal Reserve System was totally passive during the bank panics of the Great Depression period and did not perform its intended role of lender of last resort to prevent them. In retrospect, the Fed's behavior seems quite extraordinary, but hindsight is always clearer than foresight.

The primary reason for the Fed's inaction was that Federal Reserve officials did not understand the negative impact that bank failures could have on the money supply and economic activity. Friedman and Schwartz report that the Federal Reserve officials "tended to regard bank failures as regrettable consequences of bank management or bad banking practices, or as inevitable reactions to prior speculative excesses, or as a consequence but hardly a cause of the financial and economic collapse in process." In addition, bank failures in the early stages of the bank panics "were concentrated among smaller banks and, since the most influential figures in the system were big-city bankers who deplored the existence of smaller banks, their disappearance may have been viewed with complacency."*

Friedman and Schwartz also point out that political infighting may have played an important role in the passivity of the Fed during this period. The Federal Reserve Bank of New York, which until 1928 was the dominant force in the Federal Reserve System, strongly advocated an active program of open market purchases to provide reserves to the banking system during the bank panics. However, other powerful figures in the Federal Reserve System opposed the New York bank's position, and the bank was outvoted. (Friedman and Schwartz's discussion of the politics of the Federal Reserve System during this period makes for fascinating reading, and you might enjoy their highly readable book.)

*Milton Friedman and Anna Jacobson Schwartz, *A Monetary History of the United States, 1867–1960* (Princeton, N.J.: Princeton University Press, 1963), p. 358.

"The only thing we have to fear is fear itself." By the time the panics were over in March 1933, more than one-third of the commercial banks in the United States had failed.

In Chapter 17, we examined how the bank panics of this period led to a decline in the money supply of more than 25%. The resulting unprecedented decline in the money supply during this period is thought by many economists, particularly monetarists, to have been the major contributing factor to the severity of the depression, never equaled before or since.

RESERVE REQUIREMENTS AS A POLICY TOOL

The Thomas Amendment to the Agricultural Adjustment Act of 1933 provided the Federal Reserve's Board of Governors with emergency power to alter reserve requirements with the approval of the president of the United States. In the Banking Act of 1935, this emergency power was expanded to allow the Fed to alter reserve requirements without the president's approval.

The first use of reserve requirements as a tool of monetary control proved that the Federal Reserve was capable of adding to the blunders that it had made during the bank panics of the early 1930s. By the end of 1935, banks had increased their holdings of excess reserves to unprecedented levels, a sensible strategy considering their discovery during the 1930–1933 period that the Fed would not always perform its intended role as lender of last resort. Bankers now understood that they would have to protect themselves against a bank run by holding substantial amounts of excess reserves. The Fed viewed these excess reserves as a nuisance that made it harder to exercise monetary control. Specifically, the Fed worried that these excess reserves might be lent out and would produce "an uncontrollable expansion of credit in the future."[1]

To improve monetary control, the Fed raised reserve requirements in three steps: August 1936, January 1937, and May 1937. The result of this action was, as we would expect from our money supply model, a slowdown of money growth toward the end of 1936 and an actual decline in 1937. The recession of 1937–1938, which commenced in May 1937, was a severe one and was especially upsetting to the American public because even at its outset unemployment was intolerably high. So not only does it appear that the Fed was at fault for the severity of the Great Depression contraction in 1929–1933, but, to add insult to injury, it was responsible for aborting the subsequent recovery. The Fed's disastrous experience with varying its reserve requirements made it far more cautious in the use of this policy tool in the future.

WAR FINANCE AND THE PEGGING OF INTEREST RATES: 1942–1951

With the entrance of the United States into World War II in late 1941, government spending skyrocketed, and to finance it, the Treasury issued huge amounts of bonds. The Fed agreed to help the Treasury finance the war cheaply by pegging interest rates at the low levels that had prevailed before the war: $\frac{3}{8}\%$ on Treasury bills and $2\frac{1}{2}\%$ on long-term Treasury bonds. Whenever interest rates rose above these levels and the price of bonds began to fall, the Fed would make open market purchases, thereby bidding up bond prices and driving interest rates down again. The result was a rapid growth in the monetary base and the money supply. The Fed had thus in effect relinquished its control of monetary policy to meet the financing needs of the government.

When the war ended, the Fed continued to peg interest rates, and because there was little pressure on them to rise, this policy did not result in an explosive growth in the money supply. When the Korean War broke out in 1950, however, interest rates began to climb, and the Fed found that it was again forced to expand the monetary base at a rapid rate. Because inflation began to heat up (the consumer price index rose 8% between 1950 and 1951), the Fed decided that it was time to reassert its control over monetary policy by abandoning the interest-rate peg. An often bitter debate ensued between the Fed and the Treasury, which wanted to keep its interest costs down and so favored a continued pegging of interest rates at low levels. In March 1951, the Fed and the Treasury came to an agreement known as the Accord, in which pegging was abandoned but the Fed promised that it would not allow interest rates to rise precipitously. After Eisenhower's election as president in 1952, the Fed was given complete freedom to pursue its monetary policy objectives.

TARGETING MONEY MARKET CONDITIONS: THE 1950s AND 1960s

With its freedom restored, the Federal Reserve, then under the chairmanship of William McChesney Martin, Jr., took the view that monetary policy should be grounded in intuitive judgment based on a feel for the money market. The policy procedure that resulted

[1]Milton Friedman and Anna Jacobson Schwartz, *A Monetary History of the United States, 1867–1960* (Princeton, N.J.: Princeton University Press, 1963), p. 524.

can be described as one in which the Fed targeted on money market conditions, and particularly on interest rates.

An important characteristic of this policy procedure was that it led to more rapid growth in the money supply when the economy was expanding and a slowing of money growth when the economy was in recession. The *procyclical monetary policy* (a positive association of money supply growth with the business cycle) is explained by the following step-by-step reasoning. As we learned in Chapter 5, a rise in national income ($Y\uparrow$) leads to a rise in market interest rates ($i\uparrow$). With the rise in interest rates, the Fed would purchase bonds to bid their price up and lower interest rates to their target level. The resulting increase in the monetary base caused the money supply to rise and the business-cycle expansion to be accompanied by a faster rate of money growth. In summary:

$$Y\uparrow \Rightarrow i\uparrow \Rightarrow MB\uparrow \Rightarrow M\uparrow$$

In a recession, the opposite sequence of events would occur, and the decline in income would be accompanied by a slower rate of growth in the money supply ($Y\downarrow \Rightarrow M\downarrow$).

A further problem with using interest rates as the primary operating instrument is that they may encourage an inflationary spiral to get out of control. As we saw in Chapter 5, when inflation and hence expected inflation rises, nominal interest rates rise via the Fisher effect. If the Fed attempted to prevent this increase by purchasing bonds, this would also lead to a rise in the monetary base and the money supply:

$$\pi\uparrow \Rightarrow \pi^e\uparrow \Rightarrow i\uparrow \Rightarrow MB\uparrow \Rightarrow M\uparrow$$

Higher inflation could thus lead to an increase in the money supply, which would increase inflationary pressures further.

By the late 1960s, the rising chorus of criticism of procyclical monetary policy by such prominent monetarist economists such as Milton Friedman, Karl Brunner, and Allan Meltzer and concerns about inflation finally led the Fed to abandon its focus on money market conditions.

TARGETING MONETARY AGGREGATES: THE 1970s

In 1970, after Arthur Burns was appointed chairman of the Board of Governors, the Fed committed itself to the use of monetary aggregates as intermediate targets. Did monetary policy cease to be procyclical? A glance at Figure 4 in Chapter 1 indicates that monetary policy was as procyclical in the 1970s as in the 1950s and 1960s. What went wrong? Why did the conduct of monetary policy not improve? The answers to these questions lie in the Fed's operating procedures during the period, which suggest that its commitment to targeting monetary aggregates was not very strong.

Every six weeks, the Federal Open Market Committee would set target ranges for the growth rates of various monetary aggregates and would determine what federal funds rate (the interest rate on funds loaned overnight between banks) it thought consistent with these aims. The target ranges for the growth in monetary aggregates were fairly broad—a typical range for M1 growth might be 3% to 6%; for M2, 4% to 7%—while the range for the federal funds rate was a narrow band, say, from $7\frac{1}{2}\%$ to $8\frac{1}{4}\%$. The trading desk at the Federal Reserve Bank of New York was then instructed to meet both sets of targets, but as we saw earlier, interest-rate targets and monetary aggregate targets might not be compatible. If the two targets were incompatible—say, the federal funds rate began to climb higher than the top of its target band when M1 was growing too rapidly—the trading desk was instructed to give precedence to the federal funds rate target. In the situation just described, this would mean that although M1 growth was too high, the trading desk would make open market purchases to keep the federal funds rate within its target range.

The Fed was actually using the federal funds rate as its operating instrument. During the six-week period between FOMC meetings, an unexpected rise in output (which would cause the federal funds rate to hit the top of its target band) would then induce open market purchases and a too-rapid growth of the money supply. When the FOMC met again, it would try to get money supply growth back on track by raising the target range on the federal funds rate. However, if income continued to rise unexpectedly, money growth would overshoot again. This is exactly what occurred from June 1972 to June 1973, when the economy boomed unexpectedly: M1 growth greatly exceeded its target, increasing at approximately an 8% rate, while the federal funds rate climbed from $4\frac{1}{2}$% to $8\frac{1}{2}$%. The economy soon became overheated, and inflationary pressures began to mount.

The opposite chain of events occurred at the end of 1974, when the economic contraction was far more severe than anyone had predicted. The federal funds rate fell dramatically, from over 12% to 5%, and persistently bumped against the bottom of its target range. The trading desk conducted open market sales to keep the federal funds rate from falling, and money growth dropped precipitously, actually turning negative by the beginning of 1975. Clearly, this sharp drop in money growth when the United States was experiencing one of the worst economic contractions of the postwar era was a serious mistake.

Using the federal funds rate as an operating instrument promoted a procyclical monetary policy despite the Fed's lip service to monetary aggregate targets. If the Federal Reserve really intended to pursue monetary aggregate targets, it seems peculiar that it would have chosen an interest rate for an operating instrument rather than a reserve aggregate. The explanation for the Fed's choice of an interest rate as an operating instrument is that it was still very concerned with achieving interest-rate stability and was reluctant to relinquish control over interest-rate movements. The incompatibility of the Fed's policy procedure with its stated intent of targeting on the monetary aggregates had become very clear by October 1979, when the Fed's policy procedures underwent drastic revision.

NEW FED OPERATING PROCEDURES: OCTOBER 1979–OCTOBER 1982

In October 1979, two months after Paul Volcker became chairman of the Board of Governors, the Fed finally de-emphasized the federal funds rate as an operating instrument by widening its target range more than fivefold: A typical range might be from 10% to 15%. The primary operating instrument became nonborrowed reserves, which the Fed would set after estimating the volume of discount loans the banks would borrow. Not surprisingly, the federal funds rate underwent much greater fluctuations after it was de-emphasized as an operating instrument. What is surprising, however, is that the deemphasis of the federal funds target did not result in improved monetary control: After October 1979, the fluctuations in the rate of money supply growth *increased* rather than decreased as would have been expected. In addition, the Fed missed its M1 growth target ranges in all three years of the 1979–1982 period.

In this chapter we saw that the likely reason for the target misses was that Volcker was not serious about controlling monetary aggregates, but rather wanted to avoid being blamed for the high interest rates that would be necessary to bring inflation down. Interest-rate movements during this period support this interpretation of Fed strategy. After the October 1979 announcement, short-term interest rates were driven up by nearly 5%, until in March 1980 they exceeded 15%. With the imposition of credit controls in March 1980 and the rapid decline in real GDP in the second quarter of 1980, the Fed eased up on its policy and allowed interest rates to decline sharply. When recovery began in July 1980, inflation remained persistent, still exceeding 10%. Because the inflation fight was not yet won, the Fed tightened the screws again, sending short-term rates above the 15% level for a second time. The 1981–1982 recession and its large decline in output and high unemployment began to bring inflation down. With inflationary psychology apparently broken, interest rates were allowed to fall.

The Fed's anti-inflation strategy during the October 1979–October 1982 period was neither intended nor likely to produce smooth growth in the monetary aggregates. Indeed, the large fluctuations in interest rates and the business cycle, along with financial innovation, helped generate volatile money growth.

DE-EMPHASIS OF MONETARY AGGREGATES: OCTOBER 1982–EARLY 1990s

In October 1982, with inflation in check, the Fed returned, in effect, to a policy of smoothing interest rates. It did this by placing less emphasis on monetary aggregate targets and shifting to borrowed reserves (discount loan borrowings) as an operating instrument. To see how a borrowed reserves target produces interest-rate smoothing, let's consider what happens when the economy expands ($Y\uparrow$) so that interest rates are driven up. The rise in interest rates ($i\uparrow$) increases the incentives for banks to borrow more from the Fed, so borrowed reserves rise ($DL\uparrow$). To prevent the resulting rise in borrowed reserves from exceeding the target level, the Fed must lower interest rates by bidding up the price of bonds through open market purchases. The outcome of targeting on borrowed reserves, then, is that the Fed prevents a rise in interest rates. In doing so, however, the Fed's open market purchases increase the monetary base ($MB\uparrow$) and lead to a rise in the money supply ($M\uparrow$), which produces a positive association of money and national income ($Y\uparrow \Rightarrow M\uparrow$). Schematically,

$$Y\uparrow \Rightarrow i\uparrow \Rightarrow DL\uparrow \Rightarrow MB\uparrow \Rightarrow M\uparrow$$

A recession causes the opposite chain of events: The borrowed reserves target prevents interest rates from falling and results in a drop in the monetary base, leading to a fall in the money supply ($Y\downarrow \Rightarrow M\downarrow$).

The de-emphasis on monetary aggregates and the change to a borrowed reserves target led to much smaller fluctuations in the federal funds rate after October 1982 but continued to have large fluctuations in money supply growth. Finally, in February 1987, the Fed announced that it would no longer even set M1 targets. The abandonment of M1 targets was defended on two grounds. The first was that the rapid pace of financial innovation and deregulation had made the definition and measurement of money very difficult. The second is that there had been a breakdown in the stable relationship between M1 and economic activity (discussed in Chapter 22). These two arguments suggested that a monetary aggregate such as M1 might no longer be a reliable guide for monetary policy. As a result, the Fed switched its focus to the broader monetary aggregate M2, which it felt had a more stable relationship with economic activity. However, in the early 1990s, this relationship also broke down, and in July 1993, Board of Governors Chairman Alan Greenspan testified in Congress that the Fed would no longer use any monetary targets, including M2, as a guide for conducting monetary policy. Finally, legislation in 2000 amending the Federal Reserve Act dropped the requirement that the Fed report target ranges for monetary aggregates to Congress.

FEDERAL FUNDS TARGETING AGAIN: EARLY 1990s AND BEYOND

Having abandoned monetary aggregates as a guide for monetary policy, the Federal Reserve returned to using a federal funds target in the early 1990s. Indeed, from late 1992 until February 1994, a period of a year and a half, the Fed kept the federal funds rate targeted at the constant rate of 3%, a low level last seen in the 1960s. The explanation for this unusual period of keeping the federal funds rate pegged so low for such a long period of time was fear on the part of the Federal Reserve that the credit crunch mentioned in Chapter 9 was putting a drag on the economy (the "headwinds" referred to by Greenspan) that was producing a sluggish recovery from the 1990–1991 recession. Starting in February 1994, after the economy returned to rapid growth, the Fed began a preemptive strike to head off any future inflationary pressures by raising the federal funds rate in steps to 6% by early 1995. The Fed not only has engaged in preemptive strikes against a rise in inflation, but it has acted preemptively against negative shocks to demand. It lowered the federal funds rate in early 1996 to deal with a possible slowing in the economy and took the dramatic step of reducing the federal funds rate by $\frac{3}{4}$ of a percentage point when the collapse of Long Term Capital Management in the fall of 1998 led to concerns about the health of the financial system. With the strong growth of the economy in 1999 and heightened concerns about inflation, the Fed reversed course and began to raise the federal funds rate again. The Fed's timely actions kept the economy on track, helping to produce the longest business-cycle expansion in U.S. history. With a weakening economy, in January 2001 (just before the start of the recession in March 2001) the Fed reversed course again and began to reduce sharply the federal funds rate from its height of 6.5% to near 1% eventually.

In February 1994, with the first change in the federal funds rate in a year and a half, the Fed adopted a new policy procedure. Instead of keeping the federal funds target secret, as it had done previously, the Fed now announced any federal funds rate target change. As mentioned in Chapter 15, around 2:15 p.m., after every FOMC meeting, the Fed now announces whether the federal funds rate target has been raised, lowered, or kept the same. This move to greater transparency of Fed policy was followed by another such move, when in February 1999 the Fed indicated that in the future it would announce the direction of bias to where the federal funds rate will head in the future. However, dissatisfaction with the confusion that the bias announcement created for market participants led the Fed to revise its policy, and starting in February 2000, the Fed switched to an announcement of a statement outlining the "balance of risks" in the future, whether toward higher inflation or toward a weaker economy. As a result of these announcements, the outcome of the FOMC meeting is now big news, and the media devote much more attention to FOMC meetings, because announced changes in the federal funds rate feeds into changes in other interest rates that affect consumers and businesses.

INTERNATIONAL CONSIDERATIONS

The increasing importance of international trade to the American economy has brought international considerations to the forefront of Federal Reserve policymaking in recent years. By 1985, the strength of the dollar had contributed to a deterioration in American competitiveness with foreign businesses. In public pronouncements, Chairman Volcker and other Fed officials made it clear that the dollar was at too high a value and needed to come down. Because, as we will see in Chapter 21, expansionary monetary policy is one way to lower the value of the dollar, it is no surprise that the Fed engineered an acceleration in the growth rates of the monetary aggregates in 1985 and 1986 and that the value of the dollar declined. By 1987, policymakers at the Fed agreed that the dollar had fallen sufficiently, and sure enough, monetary growth in the United States slowed. These monetary policy actions by the Fed were encouraged by the process of **international policy coordination** (agreements among countries to enact policies cooperatively) that led to the Plaza Agreement in 1985 and the Louvre Accord in 1987 (see the Global box).

International considerations also played a role in the Fed's decision to lower the federal funds rate by $\frac{3}{4}$ of a percentage point in the fall of 1998. Concerns about the potential for a worldwide financial crisis in the wake of the collapse of the Russian financial system at that time and weakness in economies abroad, particularly in Asia, stimulated the Fed to take a dramatic step to calm down markets. International considerations, although not the primary focus of the Federal Reserve, are likely to be a major factor in the conduct of U.S. monetary policy in the future.

Global International Policy Coordination: The Plaza Agreement and the Louvre Accord

By 1985, the decrease in the competitiveness of American corporations as a result of the strong dollar was raising strong sentiment in Congress for restricting imports. This protectionist threat to the international trading system stimulated finance ministers and the heads of central banks from the Group of Five (G-5) industrial countries—the United States, the United Kingdom, France, West Germany, and Japan—to reach an agreement at New York's Plaza Hotel in September 1985 to bring down the value of the dollar. From September 1985 until the beginning of 1987, the value of the dollar did indeed undergo a substantial decline, falling by 35% on average relative to foreign currencies. At this point, there was growing controversy over the decline in the dollar, and another meeting of policymakers from the G-5 countries plus Canada took place in February 1987 at the Louvre Museum in Paris. There the policymakers agreed that exchange rates should be stabilized around the levels currently prevailing. Although the value of the dollar did continue to fluctuate relative to foreign currencies after the Louvre Accord, its downward trend had been checked as intended.

Because subsequent exchange rate movements were pretty much in line with the Plaza Agreement and the Louvre Accord, these attempts at international policy coordination have been considered successful. However, other aspects of the agreements were not adhered to by all signatories. For example, West German and Japanese policymakers agreed that their countries should pursue more expansionary policies by increasing government spending and cutting taxes, and the United States agreed to try to bring down its budget deficit. At that time, the United States was not particularly successful in lowering its deficit, and the Germans were reluctant to pursue expansionary policies because of their concerns about inflation.

PART

5

International Finance and Monetary Policy

CHAPTER

20 The Foreign Exchange Market

Preview

In the mid-1980s, American businesses became less competitive with their foreign counterparts; subsequently, in the 1990s and 2000s, their competitiveness increased. Did this swing in competitiveness occur primarily because American management fell down on the job in the 1980s and then got its act together afterwards? Not really. American business became less competitive in the 1980s because American dollars become worth more in terms of foreign currencies, making American goods more expensive relative to foreign goods. By the 1990s and 2000s, the value of the U.S. dollar had fallen appreciably from its highs in the mid-1980s, making American goods cheaper and American businesses more competitive.

The price of one currency in terms of another is called the **exchange rate**. As you can see in Figure 1, exchange rates are highly volatile. The exchange rate affects the economy and our daily lives, because when the U.S. dollar becomes more valuable relative to foreign currencies, foreign goods become cheaper for Americans and American goods become more expensive for foreigners. When the U.S. dollar falls in value, foreign goods become more expensive for Americans and American goods become cheaper for foreigners.

Fluctuations in the exchange rate also affect both inflation and output, and are an important concern to monetary policymakers. When the U.S. dollar falls in value, the higher prices of imported goods feed directly into a higher price level and inflation. A declining U.S. dollar, which makes U.S. goods cheaper for foreigners, increases the demand for U.S. goods and leads to higher production and output.

We begin our study of international finance by examining the **foreign exchange market**, the financial market where exchange rates are determined.

FOREIGN EXCHANGE MARKET

Most countries of the world have their own currencies: The United States has its dollar; the European Monetary Union, the euro; Brazil, its real; and China, its yuan. Trade between countries involves the mutual exchange of different currencies (or, more usually, bank deposits denominated in different currencies). When an American firm buys foreign goods, services, or financial assets, for example, U.S. dollars (typically, bank deposits denominated in U.S. dollars) must be exchanged for foreign currency (bank deposits denominated in the foreign currency).

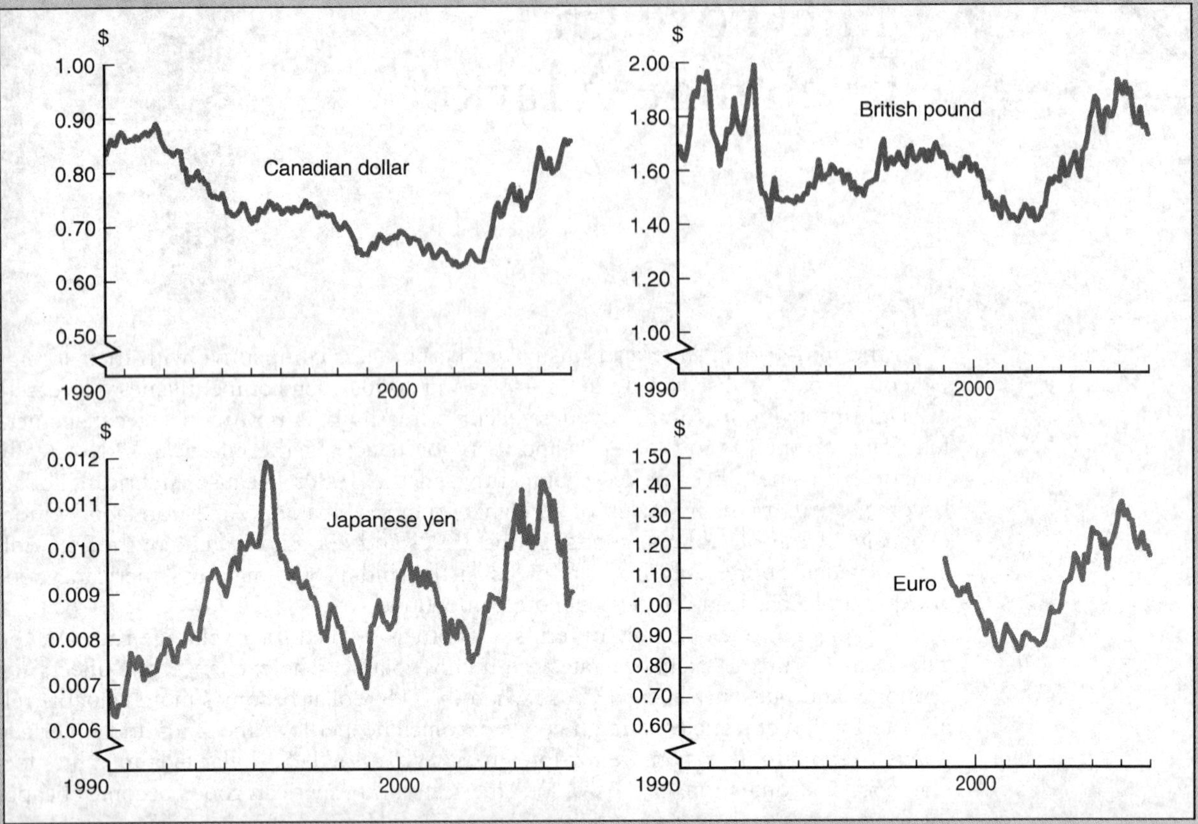

FIGURE 1 **Exchange Rates, 1990–2005**
Dollar prices of selected currencies. Note that a rise in these plots indicates a strengthening of the currency (weakening of the dollar).
Source: Federal Reserve: www.federalreserve.gov/releases/h10/hist.

The trading of currencies and bank deposits denominated in particular currencies takes place in the foreign exchange market. Transactions conducted in the foreign exchange market determine the rates at which currencies are exchanged, which in turn determine the cost of purchasing foreign goods and financial assets.

What Are Foreign Exchange Rates?

There are two kinds of exchange rate transactions. The predominant ones, called **spot transactions**, involve the immediate (two-day) exchange of bank deposits. **Forward transactions** involve the exchange of bank deposits at some specified future date. The **spot exchange rate** is the exchange rate for the spot transaction, and the **forward exchange rate** is the exchange rate for the forward transaction.

When a currency increases in value, it experiences **appreciation**; when it falls in value and is worth fewer U.S. dollars, it undergoes **depreciation**. At the beginning of 1999, for example, the euro was valued at 1.18 dollars; as indicated in the Following the Financial News box, "Foreign Exchange Rates", on February 23, 2006, it was

Following the Financial News Foreign Exchange Rates

Foreign exchange rates are published daily and appear in the "Currency Trading" column of the *Wall Street Journal*. The entries from one such column, shown here, are explained in the text.

The first entry for the euro lists the exchange rate for the spot transaction (the spot exchange rate) on February 23, 2006, and is quoted in two ways: $1.1919 per euro and 0.8390 euro per dollar. Americans generally regard the exchange rate with the euro as $1.1919 per euro, while Europeans think of it as 0.8390 euro per dollar. The three entries immediately below the spot exchange rates for some currencies give the rates for forward transactions (the forward exchange rates) that will take place one month, three months, and six months in the future.

Source: Reuters

Exchange Rates

February 23, 2006

The foreign exchange mid-range rates below apply to trading among banks in amounts of $1 million and more, as quoted at 4 p.m. Eastern time by Reuters and other sources. Retail transactions provide fewer units of foreign currency per dollar.

	U.S. $ EQUIVALENT		CURRENCY PER U.S. $	
Country/Region	**Thu**	**Wed**	**Thu**	**Wed**
Argentina (Peso)-y	.3253	.3256	3.0741	3.0713
Australia (Dollar)	.7385	.7364	1.3541	1.3580
Bahrain (Dinar)	2.6534	2.6529	.3769	.3769
Brazil (Real)	.4681	.4692	2.1363	2.1313
Canada (Dollar)	.8674	.8705	1.1529	1.1488
1-month forward	.8680	.8711	1.1521	1.1480
3-months forward	.8695	.8726	1.1501	1.1460
6-months forward	.8716	.8747	1.1473	1.1432
Chile (Peso)	.001933	.001926	517.33	519.21
China (Renminbi)	.1243	.1243	8.0475	8.0476
Colombia (Peso)	.0004447	.0004444	2248.71	2250.23
Czech. Rep. (Koruna)				
Commercial rate	.04198	.04170	23.821	23.981
Denmark (Krone)	.1597	.1595	6.2617	6.2696
Ecuador (US Dollar)	1.0000	1.0000	1.0000	1.0000
Egypt (Pound)-y	.1741	.1742	5.7425	5.7399
Hong Kong (Dollar)	.1289	.1288	7.7591	7.7611
Hungary (Forint)	.004705	.004689	212.54	213.27
India (Rupee)	.02254	.02245	44.366	44.543
Indonesia (Rupiah)	.0001079	.0001069	9268	9355
Israel (Shekel)	.2120	.2117	4.7170	4.7237
Japan (Yen)	.008535	.008435	117.16	118.55
1-month forward	.008565	.008465	116.75	118.13
3-months forward	.008638	.008534	115.77	117.18
6-months forward	.008745	.008641	114.35	115.73
Jordan (Dinar)	1.4098	1.4102	.7093	.7091
Kuwait (Dinar)	3.4230	3.4231	.2921	.2921
Lebanon (Pound)	.0006634	.0006634	1507.39	1507.39
Malaysia (Ringgit)-b	.2692	.2687	3.7147	3.7216
Malta (Lira)	2.7765	2.7730	.3602	.3606

	U.S. $ EQUIVALENT		CURRENCY PER U.S. $	
Country/Region	**Thu**	**Wed**	**Thu**	**Wed**
Mexico (Peso)				
Floating rate	.0954	.0955	10.4855	10.4668
New Zealand (Dollar)	.6609	.6587	1.5131	1.5181
Norway (Krone)	.1482	.1476	6.7476	6.7751
Pakistan (Rupee)	.01664	.01666	60.096	60.024
Peru (new Sol)	.3045	.3045	3.2841	3.2841
Philippines (Peso)	.01935	.01928	51.680	51.867
Poland (Zloty)	.3141	.3133	3.1837	3.1918
Russia (Ruble)-a	.03547	.03543	28.193	28.225
Saudi Arabia (Riyal)	2667	.2666	3.7495	3.7509
Singapore (Dollar)	.6154	.6128	1.6250	1.6319
Slovak Rep. (Koruna)	.03196	.03186	31.289	31.387
South Africa (Rand)	.1639	.1646	6.1013	6.0753
South Korea (Won)	.0010357	.0010261	965.53	974.56
Sweden (Krona)	.1269	.1271	7.8802	7.8678
Switzerland (Franc)	.7639	.7623	1.3091	1.3118
1-month forward	.7660	.7644	1.3055	1.3082
3-months forward	.7711	.7692	1.2968	1.3001
6-months forward	.7781	.7764	1.2852	1.2880
Taiwan (Dollar)	.03071	.03064	32.563	32.637
Thailand (Baht)	.02544	.02528	39.308	39.557
Turkey (New Lira)-d	.7568	.7553	1.3213	1.3240
U.K. (Pound)	1.7516	1.7435	.5709	.5736
1-month forward	1.7517	1.7436	.5709	.5735
3-months forward	1.7529	1.7447	.5705	.5732
6-months forward	1.7555	1.7473	.5696	.5723
United Arab (Dirham)	.2723	.2722	3.6724	3.6738
Uruguay (Peso)				
Financial	.04120	.04120	24.272	24.272
Venezuela (Bolivar)	.000466	.000466	2145.92	2145.92
SDR	1.4376	1.4310	.6956	.6988
Euro	1.1919	1.1903	.8390	.8401

Special Drawing Rights (SDR) are based on exchange rates for the U.S., British, and Japanese currencies. Source: International Monetary Fund.

a-Russian Central Bank rate. b-Government rate. d-Rebased as of Jan. 1, 2005. y-Floating rate.

Source: Wall Street Journal, February 23, 2006, p. C12.

valued at 1.19 dollars. The euro *appreciated* by 1%: (1.19 − 1.18)/1.18 = 0.01 = 1%. Equivalently, we could say that the U.S. dollar, which went from a value of 0.85 euro per dollar at the beginning of 1999 to a value of 0.84 euro per dollar on February 23, 2006, *depreciated* by 1%: (0.84 − 0.85)/0.85 = −0.01 = 1%.

Why Are Exchange Rates Important?

Exchange rates are important because they affect the relative price of domestic and foreign goods. The dollar price of French goods to an American is determined by the interaction of two factors: the price of French goods in euros and the euro/dollar exchange rate.

Suppose that Wanda the Winetaster, an American, decides to buy a bottle of 1961 (a very good year) Château Lafite Rothschild to complete her wine cellar. If the price of the wine in France is 1,000 euros and the exchange rate is $1.19 to the euro, the wine will cost Wanda $1,190 (= 1,000 euros × $1.19/euro). Now suppose that Wanda delays her purchase by two months, at which time the euro has appreciated to $1.40 per euro. If the domestic price of the bottle of Lafite Rothschild remains 1,000 euros, its dollar cost will have risen from $1,190 to $1,400.

The same currency appreciation, however, makes the price of foreign goods in that country less expensive. At an exchange rate of $1.19 per euro, a Dell computer priced at $2,000 costs Pierre the Programmer 1,681 euros; if the exchange rate increases to $1.40 per euro, the computer will cost only 1,429 euros.

A depreciation of the euro lowers the cost of French goods in America but raises the cost of American goods in France. If the euro drops in value to $1.00, Wanda's bottle of Lafite Rothschild will cost her only $1,000 instead of $1,190, and the Dell computer will cost Pierre 2,000 euros rather than 1,681.

Such reasoning leads to the following conclusion: ***When a country's currency appreciates (rises in value relative to other currencies), the country's goods abroad become more expensive and foreign goods in that country become cheaper (holding domestic prices constant in the two countries). Conversely, when a country's currency depreciates, its goods abroad become cheaper and foreign goods in that country become more expensive.***

Depreciation of a currency makes it easier for domestic manufacturers to sell their goods abroad and makes foreign goods less competitive in domestic markets. From 2002 to 2005, the depreciating dollar helped U.S. industries sell more goods, but it hurt American consumers because foreign goods were more expensive. The prices of French wine and cheese and the cost of vacationing abroad all rose as a result of the weak dollar.

How Is Foreign Exchange Traded?

You cannot go to a centralized location to watch exchange rates being determined; currencies are not traded on exchanges such as the New York Stock Exchange. Instead, the foreign exchange market is organized as an over-the-counter market in which several hundred dealers (mostly banks) stand ready to buy and sell deposits denominated in foreign currencies. Because these dealers are in constant telephone and computer contact, the market is very competitive; in effect, it functions no differently from a centralized market.

An important point to note is that while banks, companies, and governments talk about buying and selling currencies in foreign exchange markets, they do not take a fistful of dollar bills and sell them for British pound notes. Rather, most trades involve the buying and selling of bank deposits denominated in different currencies. So when we say that a bank is buying dollars in the foreign exchange market, what we actually mean is that the bank is buying *deposits denominated in dollars*. The volume in this market is colossal, exceeding $1 trillion per day.

Trades in the foreign exchange market consist of transactions in excess of $1 million. The market that determines the exchange rates in the Following the Financial News box is not where one would buy foreign currency for a trip abroad. Instead, we buy foreign currency in the retail market from dealers such as American Express or from banks. Because retail prices are higher than wholesale, when we buy foreign exchange, we obtain fewer units of foreign currency per dollar than exchange rates in the box indicate.

EXCHANGE RATES IN THE LONG RUN

Like the price of any good or asset in a free market, exchange rates are determined by the interaction of supply and demand. To simplify our analysis of exchange rates in a free market, we divide it into two parts. First, we examine how exchange rates are determined in the long run; then we use our knowledge of the long-run determinants of the exchange rate to help us understand how they are determined in the short run.

Law of One Price

The starting point for understanding how exchange rates are determined is a simple idea called the **law of one price**: If two countries produce an identical good, and transportation costs and trade barriers are very low, the price of the good should be the same throughout the world no matter which country produces it. Suppose that American steel costs $100 per ton and identical Japanese steel costs 10,000 yen per ton. For the law of one price to hold, the exchange rate between the yen and the dollar must be 100 yen per dollar ($0.01 per yen) so that one ton of American steel sells for 10,000 yen in Japan (the price of Japanese steel) and one ton of Japanese steel sells for $100 in the United States (the price of U.S. steel). If the exchange rate were 200 yen to the dollar, Japanese steel would sell for $50 per ton in the United States or half the price of American steel, and American steel would sell for 20,000 yen per ton in Japan, twice the price of Japanese steel. Because American steel would be more expensive than Japanese steel in both countries and is identical to Japanese steel, the demand for American steel would go to zero. Given a fixed dollar price for American steel, the resulting excess supply of American steel will be eliminated only if the exchange rate falls to 100 yen per dollar, making the price of American steel and Japanese steel the same in both countries.

Theory of Purchasing Power Parity

One of the most prominent theories of how exchange rates are determined is the **theory of purchasing power parity (PPP)**. It states that exchange rates between any two currencies will adjust to reflect changes in the price levels of the two countries. The theory of PPP is simply an application of the law of one price to national price levels rather than to individual prices. Suppose that the yen price of Japanese steel rises 10% (to 11,000 yen) relative to the dollar price of American steel (unchanged at $100). For the law of one price to hold, the exchange rate must rise to 110 yen to the dollar, a 10% appreciation of the dollar. Applying the law of one price to the price levels in the two countries

FIGURE 2
Purchasing Power Parity, United States/United Kingdom, 1973–2005 (Index: March 1973 = 100.)

Source: www.statistics.gov.uk/statbase/tsdataset2.asp.

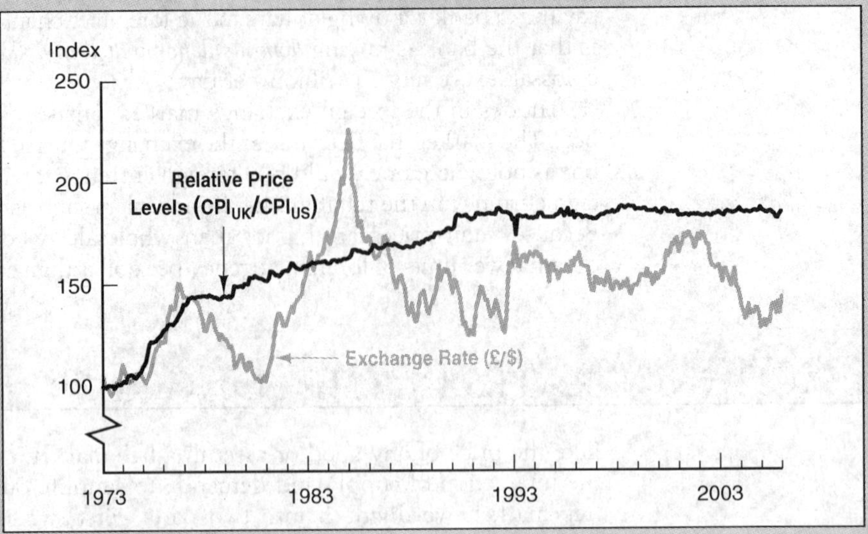

produces the theory of purchasing power parity, which maintains that if the Japanese price level rises 10% relative to the U.S. price level, the dollar will appreciate by 10%.

As our U.S./Japanese example demonstrates, the theory of PPP suggests that if one country's price level rises relative to another's, its currency should depreciate (the other country's currency should appreciate). As you can see in Figure 2, this prediction is borne out in the long run. From 1973 to the end of 2005, the British price level rose 84% relative to the U.S. price level, and as the theory of PPP predicts, the dollar appreciated against the pound—though by 43%, an amount smaller than the 84% increase predicted by PPP.

Yet, as the same figure indicates, PPP theory often has little predictive power in the short run. From early 1985 to the end of 1987, for example, the British price level rose relative to that of the United States. Instead of appreciating, as PPP theory predicts, the U.S. dollar actually depreciated by 40% against the pound. So even though PPP theory provides some guidance to the long-run movement of exchange rates, it is not perfect and in the short run is a particularly poor predictor. What explains PPP theory's failure to predict well?

Why the Theory of Purchasing Power Parity Cannot Fully Explain Exchange Rates

The PPP conclusion that exchange rates are determined solely by changes in relative price levels rests on the assumption that all goods are identical in both countries and that transportation costs and trade barriers are very low. When this assumption is true, the law of one price states that the relative prices of all these goods (that is, the relative price level between the two countries) will determine the exchange rate. The assumption that goods are identical may not be too unreasonable for American and Japanese steel, but is it a reasonable assumption for American and Japanese cars? Is a Toyota the equivalent of a Chevrolet?

Because Toyotas and Chevys are obviously not identical, their prices do not have to be equal. Toyotas can be more expensive relative to Chevys and both Americans and

Japanese will still purchase Toyotas. Because the law of one price does not hold for all goods, a rise in the price of Toyotas relative to Chevys will not necessarily mean that the yen must depreciate by the amount of the relative price increase of Toyotas over Chevys.

PPP theory furthermore does not take into account that many goods and services (whose prices are included in a measure of a country's price level) are not traded across borders. Housing, land, and services such as restaurant meals, haircuts, and golf lessons are not traded goods. So even though the prices of these items might rise and lead to a higher price level relative to another country's, there would be little direct effect on the exchange rate.

Factors That Affect Exchange Rates in the Long Run

In the long run, four major factors affect the exchange rate: relative price levels, tariffs and quotas, preferences for domestic versus foreign goods, and productivity. We examine how each of these factors affects the exchange rate while holding the others constant.

The basic reasoning proceeds along the following lines: Anything that increases the demand for domestically produced goods that are traded relative to foreign traded goods tends to appreciate the domestic currency because domestic goods will continue to sell well even when the value of the domestic currency is higher. Similarly, anything that increases the demand for foreign goods relative to domestic goods tends to depreciate the domestic currency because domestic goods will continue to sell well only if the value of the domestic currency is lower.

Relative Price Levels. In line with PPP theory, when prices of American goods rise (holding prices of foreign goods constant), the demand for American goods falls and the dollar tends to depreciate so that American goods can still sell well. By contrast, if prices of Japanese goods rise so that the relative prices of American goods fall, the demand for American goods increases, and the dollar tends to appreciate, because American goods will continue to sell well even with a higher value of the domestic currency. ***In the long run, a rise in a country's price level (relative to the foreign price level) causes its currency to depreciate, and a fall in the country's relative price level causes its currency to appreciate.***

Trade Barriers. Barriers to free trade such as **tariffs** (taxes on imported goods) and **quotas** (restrictions on the quantity of foreign goods that can be imported) can affect the exchange rate. Suppose that the United States increases its tariff or puts a lower quota on Japanese steel. These increases in trade barriers increase the demand for American steel, and the dollar tends to appreciate because American steel will still sell well even with a higher value of the dollar. ***Increasing trade barriers cause a country's currency to appreciate in the long run.***

Preferences for Domestic Versus Foreign Goods. If the Japanese develop an appetite for American goods—say, for Florida oranges and American movies—the increased demand for American goods (exports) tends to appreciate the dollar, because the American goods will continue to sell well even at a higher value for the dollar. Likewise, if Americans decide that they prefer Japanese cars to American cars, the increased demand for Japanese goods (imports) tends to depreciate the dollar. ***Increased demand for a country's exports causes its currency to appreciate in the long run; conversely, increased demand for imports causes the domestic currency to depreciate.***

Productivity When productivity in a country rises, it tends to rise in domestic sectors that produce traded goods rather than nontraded goods. Higher productivity, therefore, is associated with a decline in the price of domestically produced traded goods relative to foreign traded goods. As a result, the demand for domestic goods rises, and the domestic currency tends to appreciate. If, however, a country's productivity lags behind that of other countries, its traded goods become relatively more expensive, and the currency tends to depreciate. ***In the long run, as a country becomes more productive relative to other countries, its currency appreciates.***[1]

STUDY GUIDE

The trick to figuring out what long-run effect a factor has on the exchange rate is to remember the following: ***If a factor increases the demand for domestic goods relative to foreign goods, the domestic currency will appreciate; if a factor decreases the relative demand for domestic goods, the domestic currency will depreciate.*** See how this works by explaining what happens to the exchange rate when any of the factors in Table 1 decreases rather than increases.

Our long-run theory of exchange rate behavior is summarized in Table 1. We use the convention that the exchange rate E is quoted so that an appreciation of the currency corresponds to a rise in the exchange rate. In the case of the United States, this means that we are quoting the exchange rate as units of foreign currency per dollar (say, yen per dollar).[2]

EXCHANGE RATES IN THE SHORT RUN

We have developed a theory of the long-run behavior of exchange rates. However, because factors driving long-run changes in exchange rates move slowly over time, if we are to understand why exchange rates exhibit such large changes (sometimes several percent) from day to day, we must develop a theory of how current exchange rates (spot exchange rates) are determined in the short run.

The key to understanding the short-run behavior of exchange rates is to recognize that an exchange rate is the price of domestic assets (bank deposits, bonds, equities, etc., denominated in the domestic currency) in terms of foreign assets (similar assets denom-

[1]A country might be so small that a change in productivity or the preferences for domestic or foreign goods would have no effect on prices of these goods relative to foreign goods. In this case, changes in productivity or changes in preferences for domestic or foreign goods affect the country's income but will not necessarily affect the value of the currency. In our analysis, we are assuming that these factors can affect relative prices and consequently the exchange rate.

[2]Exchange rates can be quoted either as units of foreign currency per domestic currency or as units of domestic currency per foreign currency. In professional writing, many economists quote exchange rates as units of domestic currency per foreign currency so that an appreciation of the domestic currency is portrayed as a fall in the exchange rate. The opposite convention is used in the text here, because it is more intuitive to think of an appreciation of the domestic currency as a rise in the exchange rate.

SUMMARY TABLE 1 Factors That Affect Exchange Rates in the Long Run

Factor	Change in Factor	Response of the Exchange Rate, E^*
Domestic price level†	↑	↓
Trade barriers†	↑	↑
Import demand	↑	↓
Export demand	↑	↑
Productivity†	↑	↑

*Units of foreign currency per dollar: ↑ indicates domestic currency appreciation; ↓ , depreciation.

†Relative to other countries.

Note: Only increases (↑) in the factors are shown; the effects of decreases in the variables on the exchange rate are the opposite of those indicated in the "Response" column.

inated in the foreign currency). Because the exchange rate is the price of one asset in terms of another, the natural way to investigate the short-run determination of exchange rates is to use an asset market approach that relies heavily on the theory of asset demand developed in Chapter 5. As you will see, however, the long-run determinants of the exchange rate we have just outlined also play an important role in the short-run asset market approach.[3]

In the past, approaches to exchange rate determination emphasized the role of import and export demand. The more modern asset market approach used here emphasizes stocks of assets rather than the flows of exports and imports over short periods, because export and import transactions are small relative to the amount of domestic and foreign assets at any given time. For example, foreign exchange transactions in the United States each year are well over 25 times greater than the amount of U.S. exports and imports. Thus, over short periods, decisions to hold domestic or foreign assets play a much greater role in exchange rate determination than the demand for exports and imports does.

Comparing Expected Returns on Domestic and Foreign Assets

In this analysis, we treat the United States as the home country, so domestic assets are denominated in dollars. For simplicity, we use euros to stand for any foreign country's currency, so foreign assets are denominated in euros. The theory of asset demand suggests that the most important factor affecting the demand for domestic (dollar) assets and foreign (euro) assets is the expected return on these assets relative to each other. When Americans or foreigners expect the return on dollar assets to be high relative to the return on foreign assets, there is a higher demand for dollar assets and a correspondingly lower demand for euro assets. To understand how the demands for dollar and foreign assets change, we need to compare the expected returns on dollar assets and foreign assets.

[3]For a further description of the modern asset market approach to exchange rate determination that we use here, see Paul Krugman and Maurice Obstfeld, *International Economics*, 7th ed. (Boston.: Pearson Addison Wesley, 2006).

To illustrate further, suppose that dollar assets pay an interest rate of i^D and do not have any possible capital gains, so that they have an expected return payable in dollars of i^D. Similarly, foreign assets have an interest rate of i^F and an expected return payable in the foreign currency, euros, of i^F. To compare the expected returns on dollar assets and foreign assets, investors must convert the returns into the currency unit they use.

First let us examine how François the Foreigner compares the returns on dollar assets and foreign assets denominated in his currency, the euro. When he considers the expected return on dollar assets in terms of euros, he recognizes that it does not equal i^D; instead, the expected return must be adjusted for any expected appreciation or depreciation of the dollar. If François expects the dollar to appreciate by 3%, for example, the expected return on dollar assets in terms of euros would be 3% higher because the dollar is expected to become worth 3% more in terms of euros. Thus, if the interest rate on dollar assets is 4%, with an expected appreciation of the dollar of 3%, the expected return on dollar assets in terms of euros is 7%: the 4% interest rate plus the 3% expected appreciation of the dollar. Conversely, if the dollar were expected to depreciate by 3% over the year, the expected return on dollar assets in terms of euros would be only 1%: the 4% interest rate minus the 3% expected depreciation of the dollar.

Writing the current exchange rate (the spot exchange rate) as E_t and the expected exchange rate for the next period as E^e_{t+1}, we can write the expected rate of appreciation of the dollar as $(E^e_{t+1} - E_t)/E_t$. Our reasoning indicates that the expected return on dollar assets R^D in terms of foreign currency can be written as the sum of the interest rate on dollar assets plus the expected appreciation of the dollar:[4]

$$R^D \text{ in terms of euros} = i^D + \frac{E^e_{t+1} - E_t}{E_t}$$

However, François's expected return on foreign assets R^F in terms of euros is just i^F. Thus, in terms of euros, the relative expected return on dollar assets (that is, the difference between the expected return on dollar assets and euro assets) is calculated by subtracting i^F from the expression above to yield

$$\text{Relative } R^D = i^D - i^F + \frac{E^e_{t+1} - E_t}{E_t} \tag{1}$$

As the relative expected return on dollar assets increases, foreigners will want to hold more dollar assets and fewer foreign assets.

---

[4]This expression is actually an approximation of the expected return in terms of euros, which can be more precisely calculated by thinking how a foreigner invests in dollar assets. Suppose that François decides to put one euro into dollar assets. First he buys $1/E_t$ of U.S. dollar assets (recall that E_t, the exchange rate between dollar and euro assets, is quoted in euros per dollar), and at the end of the period he is paid $(1 + i^D)(1/E_t)$ in dollars. To convert this amount into the number of euros he expects to receive at the end of the period, he multiplies this quantity by E^e_{t+1}. François's expected return on his initial investment of one euro can thus be written as $(1 + i^D)(E^e_{t+1}/E_t)$ minus his initial investment of one euro:

$$(1 + i^D)\left(\frac{E^e_{t+1}}{E_t}\right) - 1$$

This expression can be rewritten as

$$i^D\left(\frac{E^e_{t+1}}{E_t}\right) + \frac{E^e_{t+1} - E_t}{E_t}$$

which is approximately equal to the expression in the text because E^e_{t+1}/E_t is typically close to 1. To see this, consider the example in the text in which $i^D = 0.04$; $(E^e_{t+1} - E_t)/E_t = 0.03$, so $E^e_{t+1}/E_t = 1.03$. Then François's expected return on dollar assets is $0.04 \times 1.03 + 0.03 = 0.0712 = 7.12\%$, rather than the 7% reported in the text.

Next let us look at the decision to hold dollar assets versus euro assets from Al the American's point of view. Following the same reasoning we used to evaluate the decision for François, we know that the expected return on foreign assets R^F in terms of dollars is the interest rate on foreign assets i^F plus the expected appreciation of the foreign currency, equal to minus the expected appreciation of the dollar, $-(E^e_{t+1} - E_t)/E_t$:

$$R^F \text{ in terms of dollars} = i^F - \frac{E^e_{t+1} - E_t}{E_t}$$

If the interest rate on euro assets is 5%, for example, and the dollar is expected to appreciate by 3%, then the expected return on euro assets in terms of dollars is 2%. Al earns the 5% interest rate, but he expects to lose 3% because he expects the euro to be worth 3% less in terms of dollars as a result of the dollar's appreciation.

Al's expected return on the dollar assets R^D in terms of dollars is just i^D. Hence, in terms of dollars, the relative expected return on dollar assets is calculated by subtracting the expression just given from i^D to obtain

$$\text{Relative } R^D = i^D - \left(i^F - \frac{E^e_{t+1} - E_t}{E_t}\right) = i^D - i^F + \frac{E^e_{t+1} - E_t}{E_t}$$

This equation is the same as the one describing François's relative expected return on dollar assets (calculated in terms of euros). The key point here is that the relative expected return on dollar assets is the same whether it is calculated by François in terms of euros or by Al in terms of dollars. Thus, as the relative expected return on dollar assets increases, both foreigners and domestic residents respond in exactly the same way—both will want to hold more dollar assets and fewer foreign assets.

Interest Parity Condition

We currently live in a world in which there is **capital mobility**: Foreigners can easily purchase American assets, and Americans can easily purchase foreign assets. If there are few impediments to capital mobility and we are looking at assets that have similar risk and liquidity—say, foreign and American bank deposits—then it is reasonable to assume that the assets are perfect substitutes (that is, equally desirable). When capital is mobile and when assets are perfect substitutes, if the expected return on dollar assets is above that on foreign assets, both foreigners and Americans will want to hold only dollar assets and will be unwilling to hold foreign assets. Conversely, if the expected return on foreign assets is higher than on dollar assets, both foreigners and Americans will not want to hold any dollar assets and will want to hold only foreign assets. For existing supplies of both dollar assets and foreign assets to be held, it must therefore be true that there is no difference in their expected returns; that is, the relative expected return in Equation 1 must equal zero. This condition can be rewritten as

$$i^D = i^F - \frac{E^e_{t+1} - E_t}{E_t} \qquad (2)$$

This equation, which is called the **interest parity condition**, states that the domestic interest rate equals the foreign interest rate minus the expected appreciation of the domestic currency. Equivalently, this condition can be stated in a more intuitive way: The domestic interest rate equals the foreign interest rate plus the expected appreciation of the foreign currency. If the domestic interest rate is higher than the foreign interest rate, this means that there is a positive expected appreciation of the foreign currency, which compensates for the lower foreign interest rate. A domestic interest rate of 5%

versus a foreign interest rate of 3% means that the expected appreciation of the foreign currency must be 2% (or, equivalently, that the expected depreciation of the dollar must be 2%).

There are several ways to look at the interest parity condition. First, we should recognize that interest parity means simply that the expected returns are the same on both dollar assets and foreign assets. To see this, note that the left side of the interest parity condition (Equation 2) is the expected return on dollar assets, while the right side is the expected return on foreign assets, both calculated in terms of a single currency, the U.S. dollar. Given our assumption that domestic and foreign assets are perfect substitutes (equally desirable), the interest parity condition is an equilibrium condition for the foreign exchange market. Only when the exchange rate is such that expected returns on domestic and foreign assets are equal—that is, when interest parity holds—will the domestic and foreign assets be willingly held.

The interest parity condition can be used to explain how the exchange rate is determined,[5] but in many circumstances it is not reasonable to assume that there is perfect capital mobility or that foreign and domestic assets are perfect substitutes. Here we develop a supply and demand analysis of the foreign exchange market that does not require us to make either of these assumptions.

Demand Curve for Domestic Assets

What determines the demand curve for domestic (dollar) assets is the relative expected return of domestic assets. This relative expected return equals the difference between the interest rate paid on dollar assets and the interest rate paid on foreign assets, plus the expected appreciation of the dollar: $i^D - i^F + (E^e_{t+1} - E_t)/E_t$. Suppose that the domestic and foreign interest rates are both 5% (so the expected interest differential is zero) and that the expected exchange rate next period E^e_{t+1} is 1.0 euro per dollar. When the current exchange rate is 1.05 euros per dollar, the expected appreciation of the dollar is $(1.00 - 1.05)/1.05 = -0.048 = -4.8\%$. The expected appreciation in this case is also the expected return on dollar assets relative to foreign assets because the interest differential is zero. In other words, holding dollar assets is not a very good deal because their relative expected return is negative; the quantity demanded of dollar assets will be low, as represented by point A in Figure 3. At a lower current exchange rate of $E_t = 1.0$ euro per dollar, the expected appreciation of the dollar is zero because E^e_{t+1} also equals 1.0 euro per dollar and the relative expected return is zero. Dollar assets are now a better deal, so the amount of dollar assets demanded is higher, as indicated by point B. At an even lower exchange rate of $E_t = 0.95$ euro per dollar, the expected appreciation and relative expected return of the dollar assets becomes $(1.00 - 0.95)/0.95 = 0.52 =$ 5.2%. With this higher expected return, the quantity of dollar assets demanded rises further, as indicated by point C. The resulting demand curve, *D*, which connects these points, is downward-sloping, indicating that at lower current values of the dollar (everything else equal), the quantity demanded of dollar assets is higher.

---

[5]By suitable algebraic manipulation, the interest parity condition in Equation 2 can be rewritten as

$$E_t = \frac{E^e_{t+1}}{i^F - i^D + 1}$$

This equation produces exactly the same results that we find in the supply and demand analysis to follow: If i^D rises, E_t rises; if i^F rises, E_t falls; and if E^e_{t+1} rises, E_t rises.

FIGURE 3
Equilibrium in the Foreign Exchange Market
Equilibrium in the foreign exchange market occurs at point B, the intersection of the demand curve *D* and the supply curve *S*. The equilibrium exchange rate is $E^* = 1$ euro per dollar.

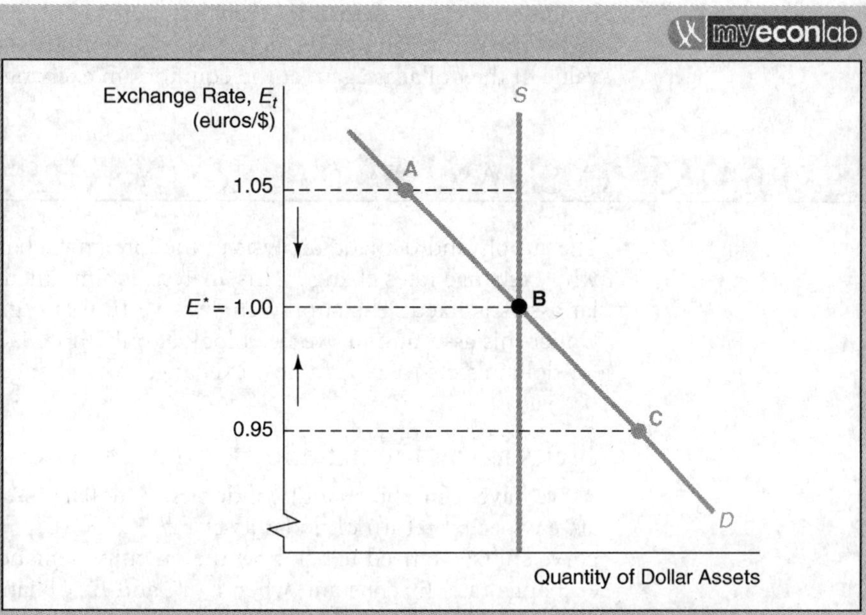

Another way of seeing that the demand curve is downward-sloping is to recognize that the lower the current exchange rate, E_t, the greater the expected appreciation of the dollar, $(E^e_{t+1} - E_t)/E_t$, and thus the higher the expected return on dollar assets relative to foreign assets. The lower the current exchange rate, the higher the quantity demanded of dollar assets (everything else held equal), so that the demand curve slopes down.

Supply Curve for Domestic Assets

Because the quantity of dollar assets supplied is primarily the amount of bank deposits, bonds, and equities in the United States, we will take this amount as fixed with respect to the exchange rate. The quantity supplied at any exchange rate does not change, so the supply curve, *S*, is vertical, as shown in Figure 3.

Equilibrium in the Foreign Exchange Market

As in the usual supply and demand analysis, the market is in equilibrium when the quantity of dollar assets demanded equals the quantity supplied. In Figure 3, equilibrium occurs at point B, the intersection of the demand and supply curves. At point B, the exchange rate is 1 euro per dollar.

Suppose that the exchange rate is 1.05 euros per dollar, which is higher than the equilibrium exchange rate. As we can see in Figure 3, the quantity of dollar assets supplied is then greater than the quantity demanded, a condition of excess supply. Given that more people want to sell dollar assets than want to buy them, the value of the dollar will fall. As long as the exchange rate remains above the equilibrium exchange rate, there will continue to be an excess supply of dollar assets, and the dollar will fall in value until it reaches the equilibrium exchange rate of 1 euro per dollar.

Similarly, if the exchange rate is less than the equilibrium exchange rate at 0.95 euro per dollar, the quantity of dollar assets demanded will exceed the quantity supplied, a condition of excess demand. Given that more people want to buy dollar assets than want to sell them, the value of the dollar will rise until the excess demand disappears and the value of the dollar is again at the equilibrium exchange rate of 1 euro per dollar.

EXPLAINING CHANGES IN EXCHANGE RATES

The supply and demand analysis of the foreign exchange market can explain how and why exchange rates change. This analysis is simplified by assuming the amount of dollar assets is fixed: The supply curve is vertical at a given quantity and does not shift. Under this assumption, we need look at only those factors that shift the demand curve for dollar assets to explain how exchange rates change over time.

Shifts in the Demand for Domestic Assets

As we have seen, the quantity of domestic (dollar) assets demanded depends on the relative expected return of dollar assets, $i^D - i^F + (E^e_{t+1} - E_t)/E_t$. To see how the demand curve shifts, we need to ask how the quantity demanded changes, holding the current exchange rate, E_t, constant, when i^D, i^F, and E^e_{t+1} changes.

Domestic Interest Rate, i^D.

When the domestic interest rate on dollar assets i^D rises, holding the current exchange rate E_t and everything else constant, the return on dollar assets increases relative to foreign assets, so people will want to hold more dollar assets. The quantity of dollar assets demanded increases at every value of the exchange rate, as shown by the rightward shift of the demand curve in Figure 4 from D_1 to D_2. The new equilibrium is reached at point 2, the intersection of D_2 and S, and the equilibrium exchange rate rises from E_1 to E_2. ***An increase in the domestic interest rate i^D***

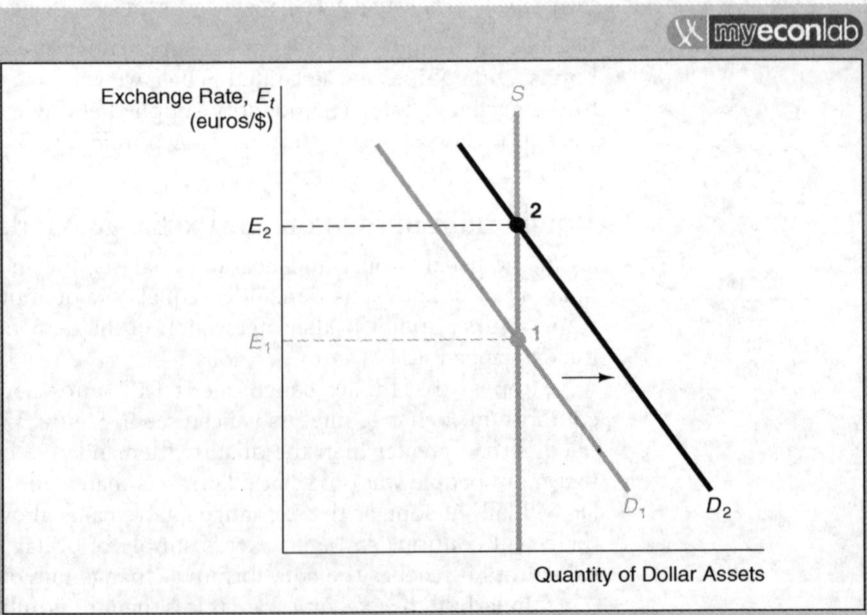

FIGURE 4
Response to an Increase in the Domestic Interest Rate, i^D
When the domestic interest rate i^D increases, the relative expected return on domestic (dollar) assets increases and the demand curve shifts to the right. The equilibrium exchange rate rises from E_1 to E_2.

shifts the demand curve for domestic assets, D, to the right and causes the domestic currency to appreciate (E ↑).

Conversely, if i^D falls, the relative expected return on dollar assets falls, the demand curve shifts to the left, and the exchange rate falls. ***A decrease in the domestic interest rate i^D shifts the demand curve for domestic assets, D, to the left and causes the domestic currency to depreciate (E ↓).***

STUDY GUIDE

To grasp how the demand curve shifts, just think of yourself as an investor who is considering putting funds into domestic (dollar) assets. When a variable changes (i^D, for example), decide whether at a given level of the current exchange rate, holding all other variables constant, you would earn a higher or lower expected return on dollar assets versus foreign assets. This decision tells you whether you want to hold more or less dollar assets and thus whether the quantity demanded increases or decreases at each level of the exchange rate. Knowing the direction of the change in the quantity demanded at each exchange rate then tells you which way the demand curve shifts.

Foreign Interest Rate, i^F. When the foreign interest rate i^F rises, holding the current exchange rate, E_{t+1}, and everything else constant, the return on foreign assets rises relative to dollar assets. Thus the relative expected return on dollar assets falls. Now people want to hold fewer dollar assets, and the quantity demanded decreases at every value of the exchange rate. This is shown by the leftward shift of the demand curve in Figure 5 from D_1 to D_2. The new equilibrium is reached at point 2, when the value of

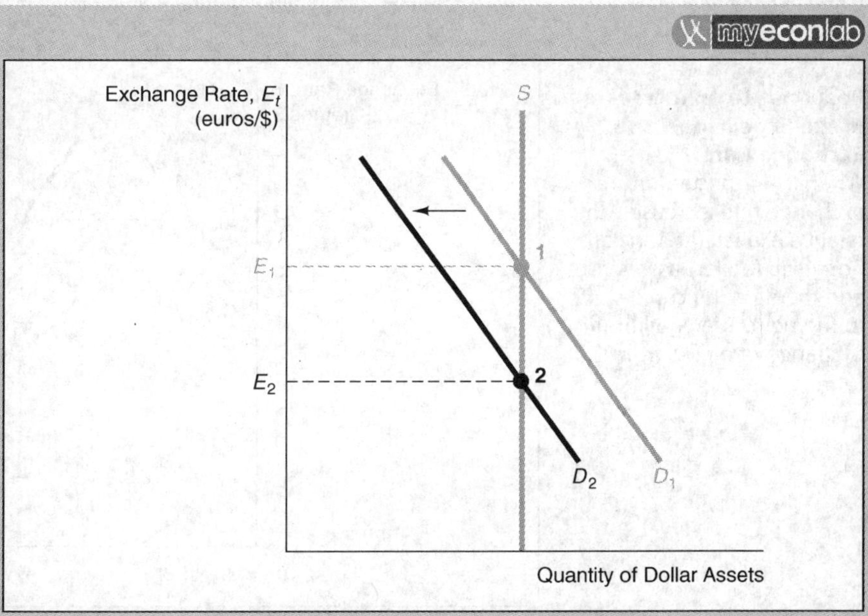

FIGURE 5
Response to an Increase in the Foreign Interest Rate, i^F
When the foreign interest rate i^F increases, the relative expected return on domestic (dollar) assets falls and the demand curve shifts to the left. The equilibrium exchange rate falls from E_1 to E_2.

the dollar has fallen. Conversely, a decrease in i^F raises the relative expected return on dollar assets, shifts the demand curve to the right, and raises the exchange rate. To summarize, ***an increase in the foreign interest rate i^F shifts the demand curve D to the left and causes the domestic currency to depreciate; a fall in the in the foreign interest rate i^F shifts the demand curve D to the right and causes the domestic currency to appreciate.***

Changes in the Expected Future Exchange Rate, E^e_{t+1}. Expectations about the future value of the exchange rate play an important role in shifting the current demand curve, because the demand for domestic assets, like the demand for any durable good, depends on the future resale price. Any factor that causes the expected future exchange rate, E^e_{t+1}, to rise increases the expected appreciation of the dollar. The result is a higher relative expected return on dollar assets, which increases the demand for dollar assets at every exchange rate, thereby shifting the demand curve to the right in Figure 6 from D_1 to D_2. The equilibrium exchange rate rises to point 2 at the intersection of the D_2 and S curves. ***A rise in the expected future exchange rate, E^e_{t+1}, shifts the demand curve to the right and causes an appreciation of the domestic currency.*** Using the same reasoning, ***a fall in the expected future exchange rate, E^e_{t+1}, shifts the demand curve to the left and causes a depreciation of the currency.***

Earlier in the chapter we discussed the determinants of the exchange rate in the long run: the relative price level, relative tariffs and quotas, import and export demand, and relative productivity (refer to Table 1). These four factors influence the expected future exchange rate. The theory of purchasing power parity suggests that if a higher American price level relative to the foreign price level is expected to persist, the dollar will depreciate in the long run. A higher expected relative American price level should thus have a tendency to lower E^e_{t+1}, lower the relative expected return on dollar assets, shift the demand curve to the left, and lower the current exchange rate.

FIGURE 6
Response to an Increase in the Expected Future Exchange Rate, E^e_{t+1}
When the expected future exchange rate increases, the relative expected return on domestic (dollar) assets rises and the demand curve shifts to the right. The equilibrium exchange rate rises from E_1 to E_2.

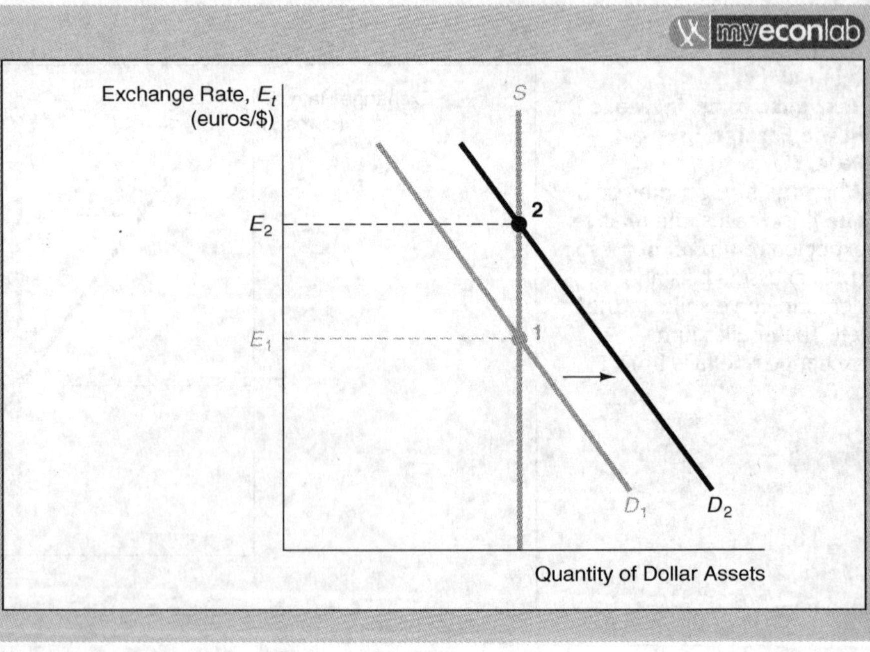

Similarly, the other long-run determinants of the exchange rate can influence the relative expected return on dollar assets and the current exchange rate. Briefly, the following changes, all of which increase the demand for domestic goods relative to foreign goods, will raise E^e_{t+1}: (1) expectations of a fall in the American price level relative to the foreign price level; (2) expectations of higher American trade barriers relative to foreign trade barriers; (3) expectations of lower American import demand; (4) expectations of higher foreign demand for American exports, and (5) expectations of higher American productivity relative to foreign productivity. By increasing E^e_{t+1}, all of these changes increase the relative expected return on dollar assets, shift the demand curve to the right, and cause an appreciation of the domestic currency, the dollar.

STUDY GUIDE

As a study aid, the factors that shift the demand curve D and lead to changes in the current exchange rate E_t are listed in Table 2. The table shows what happens to the exchange rate when each of the variables increases, holding everything else constant. To give yourself practice, try to work out what happens to the demand curve and the exchange rate if each of these factors falls rather than rises. Check your answers by seeing if you get the opposite changes in the exchange rate compared to the changes indicated in Table 2.

APPLICATION Changes in the Equilibrium Exchange Rate: Two Examples

Our analysis has revealed the factors that affect the value of the equilibrium exchange rate. Now we use this analysis to take a close look at the response of the exchange rate to changes in interest rates and money growth.

Changes in Interest Rates

Changes in domestic interest rates i^D are often cited as a major factor affecting exchange rates. For example, we see headlines in the financial press like this one: "Dollar Recovers as Interest Rates Edge Upward." But is the view presented in this headline always correct?

Not necessarily, because to analyze the effects of interest rate changes, we must carefully distinguish the sources of the changes. The Fisher equation (Chapter 4) states that a (nominal) interest rate equals the *real* interest rate plus expected inflation: $i = i_r + \pi^e$. The Fisher equation indicates that an interest rate i can change for two reasons: Either the real interest rate i_r changes or the expected inflation rate π^e changes. The effect on the exchange rate is quite different, depending on which of these two factors is the source of the change in the nominal interest rate.

Suppose that the domestic real interest rate increases so that the nominal interest rate i^D rises while expected inflation remains unchanged. In this case, it is reasonable to assume that the expected appreciation of the dollar will be unchanged because expected inflation is unchanged. In this case, the increase in i^D increases the relative expected return on dollar assets, increases the quantity of dollar assets demanded at each level of the exchange rate, and shifts the demand curve to the right. We end up with the situation depicted in Figure 4, which analyzes an increase in i^D, holding everything else

SUMMARY TABLE 2 Factors That Shift the Demand Curve for Domestic Assets and Affect the Exchange Rate

Factor	Change in Factor	Change in Quantity Demanded of Domestic Assets at Each Exchange Rate	Response of Exchange Rate, E_t	
Domestic interest rate, i^D	↑	↑	↑	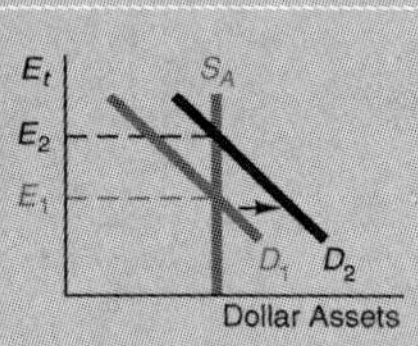
Foreign interest rate, i^F	↑	↓	↓	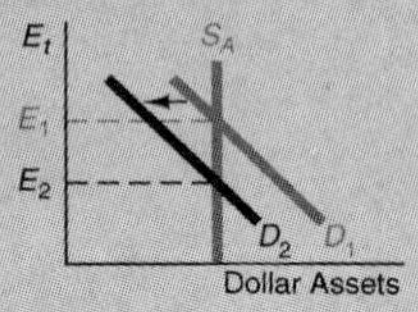
Expected domestic price level*	↑	↓	↓	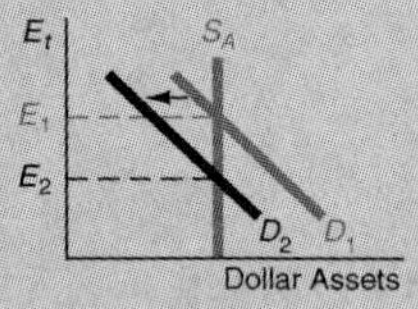
Expected trade barriers*	↑	↑	↑	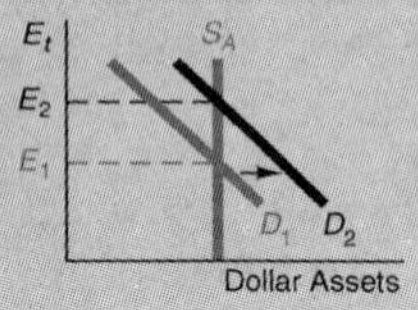
Expected import demand	↑	↓	↓	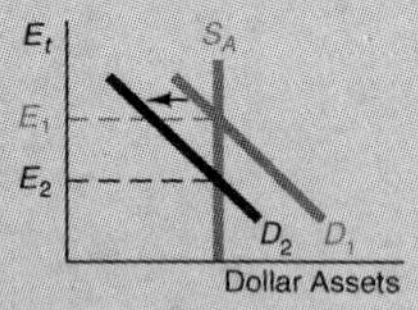
Expected export demand	↑	↑	↑	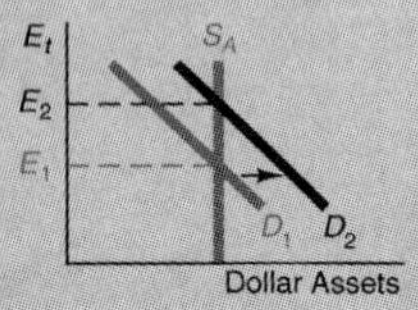
Expected productivity*	↑	↑	↑	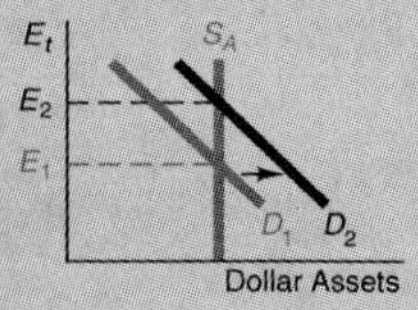

*Relative to other countries.

Note: Only increases (↑) in the factors are shown; the effects of decreases in the variables on the exchange rate are the opposite of those indicated in the "Response" column.

constant. Our model of the foreign exchange market produces the following result: ***When domestic real interest rates rise, the domestic currency appreciates.***

When the nominal interest rate rises because of an increase in expected inflation, we get a different result from the one shown in Figure 4. The rise in expected domestic inflation leads to a decline in the expected appreciation of the dollar, which is typically thought to be larger than the increase in the domestic interest rate i^D.[6] As a result, at any given exchange rate, the relative expected return on domestic (dollar) assets falls, the demand curve shifts to the left, and the exchange rate falls from E_1 to E_2 as shown in Figure 7. Our analysis leads to this conclusion: ***When domestic interest rates rise due to an expected increase in inflation, the domestic currency depreciates.***

Because this conclusion is completely different from the one reached when the rise in the domestic interest rate is associated with a higher real interest rate, we must always distinguish between *real* and *nominal* measures when analyzing the effects of interest rates on exchange rates.

Changes in the Money Supply

Suppose that the Federal Reserve decides to increase the level of the money supply in an attempt to reduce unemployment, which it believes to be excessive. The higher money supply will lead to a higher American price level in the long run (as we will see

FIGURE 7

Effect of a Rise in the Domestic Interest Rate as a Result of an Increase in Expected Inflation

Because a rise in domestic expected inflation leads to a decline in expected dollar appreciation that is larger than the increase in the domestic interest rate, the relative expected return on domestic (dollar) assets falls. The demand curve shifts to the left, and the equilibrium exchange rate falls from E_1 to E_2.

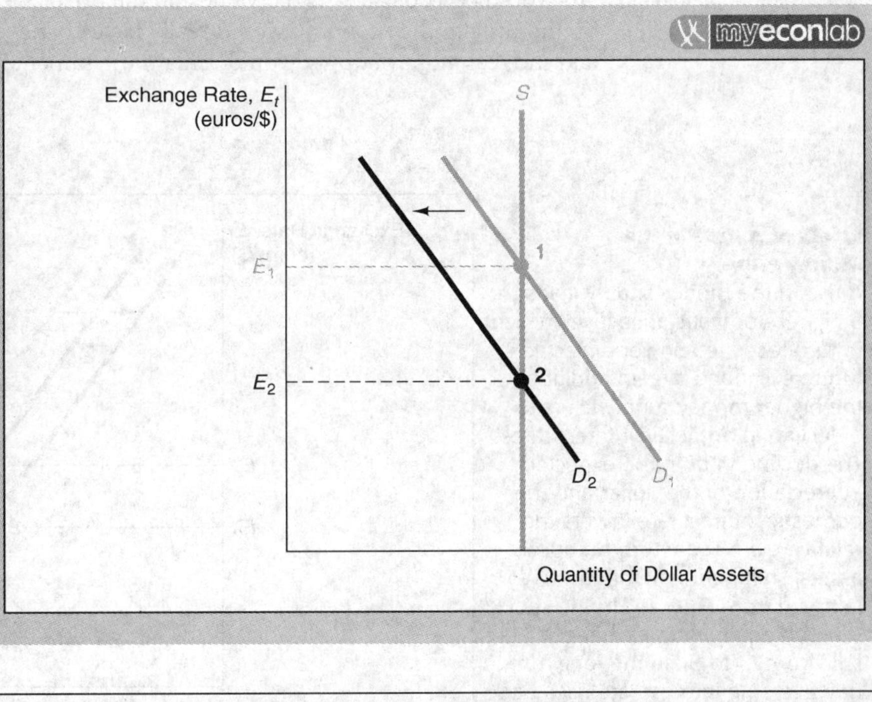

[6]This conclusion is standard in asset market models of exchange rate determination; see Rudiger Dornbusch, "Expectations and Exchange Rate Dynamics," *Journal of Political Economy* 84 (1976): 1061–1076. It is also consistent with empirical evidence that suggests that nominal interest rates do not rise one-for-one with increases in expected inflation. See Frederic S. Mishkin, "The Real Interest Rate: An Empirical Investigation," *Carnegie-Rochester Conference Series on Public Policy* 15 (1981): 151–200; and Lawrence Summers, "The Nonadjustment of Nominal Interest Rates: A Study of the Fisher Effect," in *Macroeconomics, Prices and Quantities*, ed. James Tobin (Washington, D.C.: Brookings Institution, 1983), pp. 201–240.

in Chapter 23) and hence to a lower expected future exchange rate. The resulting decline in the expected appreciation of the dollar lowers the quantity of dollar assets demanded at each level of the exchange rate and shifts the demand curve to the left. In addition, the higher money supply will lead to a higher real money supply *M/P*, because the price level does not immediately increase in the short run. As suggested in Chapter 5, the resulting rise in the real money supply causes the domestic interest rate to fall, which also lowers the relative expected return on dollar assets, providing a further reason why the demand curve shifts to the left. As we can see in Figure 8, the demand curve shifts to D_2, and the exchange rate declines from E_1 to E_2. The conclusion: ***A higher domestic money supply causes the domestic currency to depreciate.***

Exchange Rate Overshooting

Our analysis of the effect of an increase in the money supply on the exchange rate is not yet over—we still need to look at what happens to the exchange rate in the long run. A basic proposition in monetary theory, called **monetary neutrality**, states that in the long run, a one-time percentage rise in the money supply is matched by the same one-time percentage rise in the price level, leaving unchanged the real money supply and all other economic variables such as interest rates. An intuitive way to understand this proposition is to think of what would happen if our government announced overnight that an old dollar would now be worth 100 new dollars. The money supply in new dollars would be 100 times its old value and the price level would also be 100 times higher, but nothing in the economy would really have changed: Real and nominal interest rates and the real money supply would remain the same. Monetary neutrality tells us that in

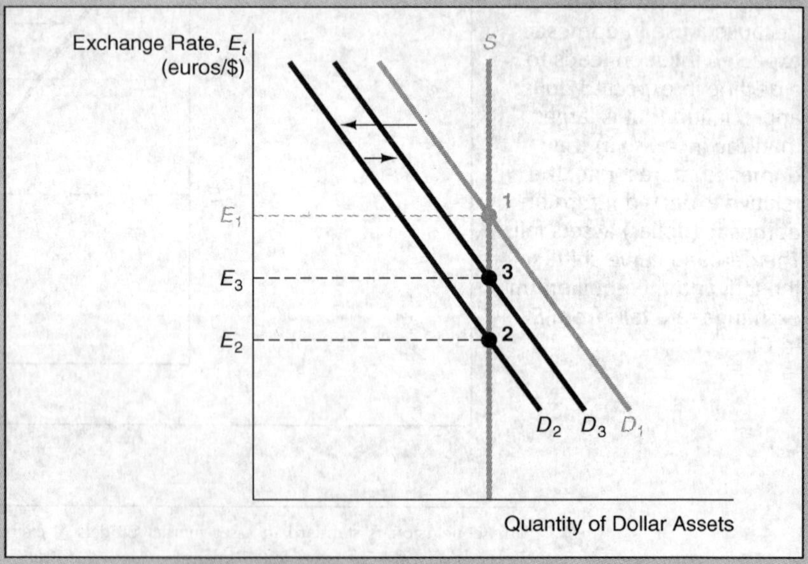

FIGURE 8
Effect of a Rise in the Money Supply
A rise in the money supply leads to a higher domestic price level, which in turn leads to a lower expected future exchange rate. In addition, the higher money supply leads to a decline in domestic interest rates. The decline in both the expected appreciation of the dollar and the domestic interest rate lowers the relative expected return on dollar assets, shifting the demand curve leftward from D_1 to D_2. In the short run, the equilibrium exchange rate falls from E_1 to E_2. In the long run, however, the interest rate rises back up again to its initial level and the demand curve shifts rightward to D_3. The exchange rate rises from E_2 to E_3 in the long run.

the long run, the rise in the money supply would not lead to a change in the domestic interest rate so it would rise back to its old level. The demand curve would shift to the right to D_3, but not all the way back to D_1, because the price level will still be higher in the long run. As we can see in Figure 8, this means that the exchange rate would rise from E_2 to E_3 in the long run.

The phenomenon we have described here in which the exchange rate falls by more in the short run than it does in the long run when the money supply increases is called **exchange rate overshooting**. It is important because, as we will see in the following application, it can help explain why exchange rates exhibit so much volatility.

Another way of thinking about why exchange rate overshooting occurs is to recognize that when the domestic interest rate falls in the short run, equilibrium in the foreign exchange market means that the expected return on foreign deposits must be lower. With the foreign interest rate given, this lower expected return on foreign deposits means that there must be an expected appreciation of the dollar (depreciation of the euro) for the expected return on foreign deposits to decline when the domestic interest rate falls. This can occur only if the current exchange rate falls below its long-run value.

APPLICATION Why Are Exchange Rates So Volatile?

The high volatility of foreign exchange rates surprises many people. Thirty or so years ago, economists generally believed that allowing exchange rates to be determined in the free market would not lead to large fluctuations in their values. Recent experience has proved them wrong. If we return to Figure 1, we see that exchange rates over the 1980–2005 period have been very volatile.

The asset market approach to exchange rate determination that we have outlined in this chapter gives a straightforward explanation of volatile exchange rates. Because expected appreciation of the domestic currency affects the expected return on foreign deposits, expectations about the price level, inflation, trade barriers, productivity, import demand, export demand, and the money supply play important roles in determining the exchange rate. When expectations about any of these variables change, as they do—and often at that—our model indicates that there will be an immediate effect on the expected return on foreign deposits and therefore on the exchange rate. Because expectations on all these variables change with just about every bit of news that appears, it is not surprising that the exchange rate is volatile. In addition, we have seen that our exchange rate analysis produces exchange rate overshooting when the money supply increases. Exchange rate overshooting is an additional reason for the high volatility of exchange rates.

Because earlier models of exchange rate behavior focused on goods markets rather than asset markets, they did not emphasize changing expectations as a source of exchange rate movements, and so these earlier models could not predict substantial fluctuations in exchange rates. The failure of earlier models to explain volatility is one reason why they are no longer so popular. The more modern approach developed here emphasizes that the foreign exchange market is like any other asset market in which expectations of the future matter. The foreign exchange market, like other asset markets such as the stock market, displays substantial price volatility, and foreign exchange rates are notoriously hard to forecast.

APPLICATION The Dollar and Interest Rates, 1973–2005

In the chapter preview, we mentioned that the dollar was weak in the late 1970s, rose substantially from 1980 to 1985, and declined thereafter. We can use our analysis of the foreign exchange market to understand exchange rate movements and help explain the dollar's rise and fall in the 1980s.

Some important information for tracing the dollar's changing value is presented in Figure 9, which plots measures of real and nominal interest rates and the value of the dollar in terms of a basket of foreign currencies (called an **effective exchange rate index**). We can see that the value of the dollar and the measure of real interest rates tend to rise and fall together. In the late 1970s, real interest rates were at low levels, and so was the value of the dollar. Beginning in 1980, however, real interest rates in the United States began to climb sharply, and at the same time so did the dollar. After 1984, the real interest rate declined substantially, as did the dollar.

Our model of exchange rate determination helps explain the rise and fall in the dollar in the 1980s. As Figure 4 indicates, a rise in the U.S. real interest rate raises the relative expected return on dollar assets, which leads to purchases of dollar assets that

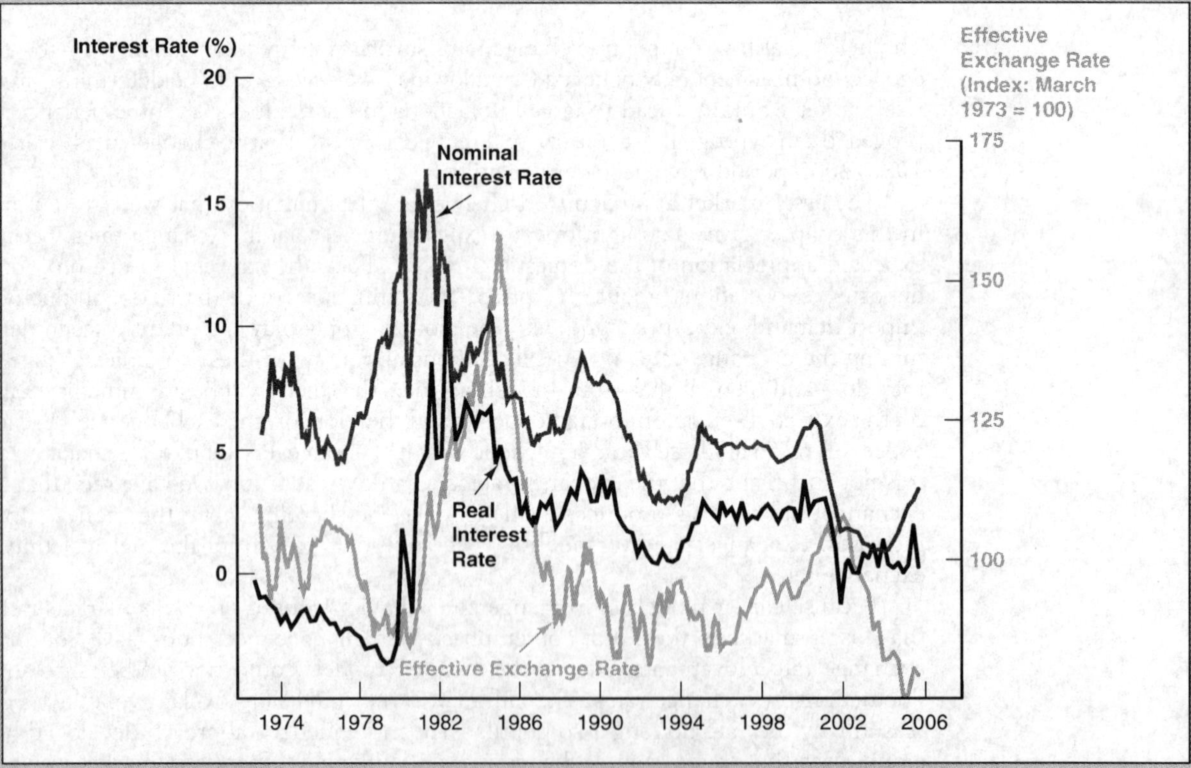

FIGURE 9 **Value of the Dollar and Interest Rates, 1973–2005**

Sources: Federal Reserve: www.federalreserve.gov/releases/h10/summary/indexn_m.txt; real interest rate from Figure 1 in Chapter 4.

raise the exchange rate. This is exactly what happened in the 1980–1984 period. The subsequent fall in U.S. real interest rates then lowered the relative expected return on dollar assets, which lowered the demand for them and thus lowered the exchange rate.

The plot of *nominal* interest rates in Figure 9 also demonstrates that the correspondence between nominal interest rates and exchange rate movements is not nearly as close as that between *real* interest rates and exchange rate movements. This is also exactly what our analysis predicts. The rise in nominal interest rates in the late 1970s was not reflected in a corresponding rise in the value of the dollar; indeed, the dollar actually fell in the late 1970s. Figure 9 explains why the rise in nominal rates in the late 1970s did not produce a rise in the dollar. As a comparison of the real and nominal interest rates in the late 1970s indicates, the rise in nominal interest rates reflected an increase in expected inflation and not an increase in real interest rates. As our analysis in Figure 7 demonstrates, the rise in nominal interest rates stemming from a rise in expected inflation should lead to a decline in the dollar, and that is exactly what happened.

If there is a moral to the story, it is that a failure to distinguish between real and nominal interest rates can lead to poor predictions of exchange rate movements: The weakness of the dollar in the late 1970s and the strength of the dollar in the early 1980s can be explained by movements in *real* interest rates but not by movements in *nominal* interest rates.

APPLICATION The Euro's First Seven Years

With much fanfare, the euro debuted on January 1, 1999, at an exchange rate of 1.18 dollars per euro. Despite early hopes that the euro would be a strong currency, it initially proved to be weak. It declined 30% to a low of 83 cents per euro in October 2000, and then began a steady recovery to around the $1.20 level by the end of 2005. What explains the weakness of the euro in its first two years, and the subsequent recovery thereafter?

The previous application showed that changes in real interest rates are an important factor determining the exchange rate. When the domestic real interest rate falls relative to the foreign real interest rate, the domestic currency declines in value. While the euro was coming into existence, European economies were experiencing slow recoveries from recessions which had caused both real and nominal interest rates to fall. In contrast, the United States experienced very rapid growth in 1999 and 2000, substantially higher than the growth in its European counterparts. As in the analysis of the previous application, low real interest rates in Europe relative to those in the United States drove down the value of the euro.

With the slowing of the U.S. economy, after the recession started in the spring of 2001, both real and nominal U.S. interest rates began to fall to low levels, thereby weakening the dollar relative to the euro.

APPLICATION Reading the *Wall Street Journal*: The "Currency Trading" Column

Now that we have an understanding of how exchange rates are determined, we can use our analysis to understand discussions about developments in the foreign exchange market reported in the financial press.

Following the Financial News The "Currency Trading" Column

The "Currency Trading" column appears daily in the *Wall Street Journal*; an example is presented here. It is usually found in the third section, "Money and Investing."

Dollar Rises on Deficit Report, European Bank's Rate Message

BY LAURENCE NORMAN AND STEVEN VAMES

Dow Jones Newswires

The dollar rose against the euro, boosted by a smaller-than expected U.S. trade deficit and a signal from the European Central Bank that it hasn't changed its cautious approach to policy tightening.

The dollar also climbed significantly against the Swiss franc and the pound, though it rose only very slightly against the yen. Euro losses took it to a three-month low versus the yen.

CURRENCY TRADING

Late yesterday afternoon in New York, the euro was at $1,2033 from $1,2126 late Wednesday. The dollar was at 114.26 yen from 114.13 yen, and at 1.2857 Swiss francs from 1.2753 francs, The euro was at 137.43 yen from 138.38 yen.

The pound slipped to $1.7598 from $1.7642, but rose against the euro after the Bank of England kept rates steady at 4.5% for the fifth month running.

The dollar came into the U.S. session little changed versus the euro and slightly lower against the yen after calm overnight trading.

However, the U.S. currency snapped higher when the Commerce Department reported that the November trade deficit contracted to $64.21 billion from a revised record $68.13 billion in October.

Lower oil prices and stronger exports helped the trade gap narrow more than economists' forecast of a $66.5 billion deficit. A smaller-than-predicted rise in weekly jobless claims also helped.

The dollar received an additional nudge higher as the ECB, which earlier in the day had left rates unchanged at 2.25%, held a news conference after the rates meeting. The message from ECB President Jean-Claude Trichet was that despite stronger regional data, the bank didn't see the December rate increase—its first in five years—as the start of a protracted rate-tightening cycle.

Elsewhere, the Canadian dollar ended slightly lower, after falling back following the U.S. trade deficit and after Canada reported that its trade surplus for November was C$6.88 billion, a touch under the consensus. A 2$ monthly drop in exports was responsible for the decline.

Late in New York, the dollar was fetching C$1.1628 from C$1.1585 a day earlier.

Source: Wall Street Journal, Friday, January 13, 2006, p. C3.

Every day, the *Wall Street Journal* reports on developments in the foreign exchange market on the previous business day in its "Currency Trading" column, an example of which is presented in the Following the Financial News box, "The 'Currency Trading' Column."

The column states that the dollar rose on a smaller-than-expected U.S. trade deficit and a message from the ECB president that it was unlikely to raise interest rates substantially in the near future. Our analysis of the foreign exchange market explains why these devlopments led to a stronger dollar.

The announcement of the smaller-than-expected U.S. trade deficit indicates the demand for American goods relative to foreign good is higher than expected and so American goods will continue to sell well even if the dollar is higher in the long run. The smaller-than-expected trade deficit therefore leads to a higher expected future value of the dollar and a higher expected appreciation of the dollar, which in turn leads to an increase in the relative expected return for dollar assets and an increase in the quantity demanded of dollar assets at each exchange rate. The outcome is the one depicted in Figure 6 in which the demand curve shifts to the right and the dollar appreciates today.

The message sent by ECB president Jean-Claude Trichet that the ECB did not see the previous month's rate increase as the start of a protracted rate-tightening cycle suggests that real interest rates in the euro zone are likely to be lower than markets were expecting. Lower euro zone real interest rates mean that the relative expected return on dollar assets has risen, which increases the demand for dollar assets, shifts the demand curve to the right, and also leads to an appreciation of the dollar.

SUMMARY

1. Foreign exchange rates (the price of one country's currency in terms of another's) are important because they affect the price of domestically produced goods sold abroad and the cost of foreign goods bought domestically.
2. The theory of purchasing power parity suggests that long-run changes in the exchange rate between two countries are determined by changes in the relative price levels in the two countries. Other factors that affect exchange rates in the long run are tariffs and quotas, import demand, export demand, and productivity.
3. In the short run, exchange rates are determined by changes in the relative expected return on domestic assets, which cause the demand curve to shift. Any factor that changes the relative expected return on domestic assets will lead to changes in the exchange rate. Such factors include changes in the interest rates on domestic and foreign assets as well as changes in any of the factors that affect the long-run exchange rate and hence the expected future exchange rate. Changes in the money supply lead to exchange rate overshooting, causing the exchange rate to change by more in the short run than in the long run.
4. The asset market approach to exchange rate determination can explain both the volatility of exchange rates and the rise of the dollar in the 1980–1984 period and its subsequent fall.

KEY TERMS

appreciation, p. 504
capital mobility, p. 513
depreciation, p. 504
effective exchange rate index, p. 524
exchange rate, p. 503
exchange rate overshooting, p. 523
foreign exchange market, p. 503
forward exchange rate, p. 504
forward transaction, p. 504
interest parity condition, p. 513
law of one price, p. 507
monetary neutrality, p. 522
quotas, p. 509
spot exchange rate, p. 504
spot transaction, p. 504
tariffs, p. 509
theory of purchasing power parity (PPP), p. 507

QUESTIONS AND PROBLEMS

Questions marked with an asterisk are answered at the end of the book in an appendix, "Answers to Selected Questions and Problems." Questions marked with a blue circle indicate the question is available in MyEconLab at www.myeconlab.com/mishkin.

1. When the euro appreciates, are you more likely to drink California or French wine?

*2. "A country is always worse off when its currency is weak (falls in value)." Is this statement true, false, or uncertain? Explain your answer.

3. In a newspaper, check the exchange rates for the foreign currencies listed in the Following the Financial News box on page 433. Which of these currencies have appreciated and which have depreciated since February 23, 2006?

*4. If the Japanese price level rises by 5% relative to the price level in the United States, what does the theory of purchasing power parity predict will happen to the value of the Japanese yen in terms of dollars?

5. If the demand for a country's exports falls at the same time that tariffs on imports are raised, will the country's currency tend to appreciate or depreciate in the long run?

*6. In the mid- to late 1970s, the yen appreciated relative to the dollar even though Japan's inflation rate was higher than America's. How can this be explained by an improvement in the productivity of Japanese industry relative to American industry?

Using Economic Analysis to Predict the Future

Answer the remaining questions by drawing the appropriate exchange market diagrams.

7. The president of the United States announces that he will reduce inflation with a new anti-inflation program. If the public believes him, predict what will happen to the U.S. exchange rate.

*8. If the British central bank prints money to reduce unemployment, what will happen to the value of the pound in the short run and the long run?

9. If the Indian government unexpectedly announces that it will be imposing higher tariffs on foreign goods one year from now, what will happen to the value of the Indian rupee today?

*10. If nominal interest rates in America rise but real interest rates fall, predict what will happen to the U.S. exchange rate.

11. If American auto companies make a breakthrough in automobile technology and are able to produce a car that gets 60 miles to the gallon, what will happen to the U.S. exchange rate?

*12. If Mexicans go on a spending spree and buy twice as much French perfume, Japanese TVs, English sweaters, Swiss watches, and Italian wine, what will happen to the value of the Mexican peso?

13. If expected inflation drops in Europe so that interest rates fall there, predict what will happen to the exchange rate for the U.S. dollar?

*14. If the European central bank decides to contract the money supply to fight inflation, what will happen to the value of the U.S. dollar?

15. If there is a strike in France, making it harder to buy French goods, what will happen to the value of the euro?

WEB EXERCISES

1. The Federal Reserve maintains a web site that lists the exchange rates between the U.S. dollar and many other currencies. Go to www.newyorkfed.org/markets/foreignex.html. Go to the historical data from 1999 and later and find the euro.
   a. What has the percentage change in the euro–dollar exchange rate been between introduction and now?
   b. What has been the annual percentage change in the euro–dollar exchange rate for each year since the euro's introduction?

2. International travelers and business people frequently need to accurately convert from one currency to another. It is often easy to find the rate needed to convert the U.S. dollar into another currency. It can be more difficult to find exchange rates between two non-U.S. currencies. Go to www.oanda.com/convert/classic. This site lets you convert from any currency into any other currency. How many Lithuanian litas can you currently buy with one Chilean peso?

WEB REFERENCES

www.newyorkfed.org/markets/foreignex.html

Get detailed information about the foreign exchange market in the United States.

http://quotes.ino.com/chart/

Go to this web site and click on "Foreign Exchange" to get market rates and time charts for the exchange rate of the U.S. dollar to major world currencies.

www.oecd.org/department/0,2688,en_2649_34357_1_1_1_1_1,00.html

The purchasing power parities home page includes the PPP program overview, statistics, research, publications, and OECD meetings on PPP.

www.federalreserve.gov/releases/

The Federal Reserve reports current and historical exchange rates for many countries.

http://fx.sauder.ubc.ca

The Pacific Exchange Rate Service at the University of British Columbia's Sauder School of Business provides information on how market conditions are affecting exchange rates and allows easy plotting of exchange rate data.

CHAPTER

21 The International Financial System

Preview

As the U.S. economy and the economies of the rest of the world grow more independent, a country's monetary policy can no longer be conducted without taking international considerations into account. In this chapter, we examine how international financial transactions and the structure of the international financial system affect monetary policy. We also examine the evolution of the international financial system during the past half century and consider where it may be heading in the future.

INTERVENTION IN THE FOREIGN EXCHANGE MARKET

In Chapter 20, we analyzed the foreign exchange market as if it were a completely free market that responds to all market pressures. Like many other markets, however, the foreign exchange market is not free of government intervention; central banks regularly engage in international financial transactions called **foreign exchange interventions** to influence exchange rates. In our current international environment, exchange rates fluctuate from day to day, but central banks attempt to influence their countries' exchange rates by buying and selling currencies. We can use the exchange rate analysis we developed in Chapter 20 to explain the impact of central bank intervention on the foreign exchange market.

Foreign Exchange Intervention and the Money Supply

The first step in understanding how central bank intervention in the foreign exchange market affects exchange rates is to see the impact on the monetary base from a central bank sale in the foreign exchange market of some of its holdings of assets denominated in a foreign currency (called **international reserves**). Suppose that the Fed decides to sell $1 billion of its foreign assets in exchange for $1 billion of U.S. currency. (This transaction is conducted at the foreign exchange desk at the Federal Reserve Bank of New York—see the Inside the Fed box.) The Fed's purchase of dollars has two effects. First, it reduces the Fed's holding of international reserves by $1 billion. Second, because the Fed's purchase of currency removes it from the hands of the public,

Inside the Fed A Day at the Federal Reserve Bank of New York's Foreign Exchange Desk

Although the U.S. Treasury is primarily responsible for foreign exchange policy, decisions to intervene in the foreign exchange market are made jointly by the U.S. Treasury and the Federal Reserve's FOMC (Federal Open Market Committee). The actual conduct of foreign exchange intervention is the responsibility of the foreign exchange desk at the Federal Reserve Bank of New York, which is right next to the open market desk.

The manager of foreign exchange operations at the New York Fed supervises the traders and analysts who follow developments in the foreign exchange market. Every morning at 7:30, a trader on staff who has arrived at the New York Fed in the predawn hours speaks on the telephone with counterparts at the U.S. Treasury and provides an update on overnight activity in overseas financial and foreign exchange markets. Later in the morning, at 9:30, the manager and his or her staff hold a conference call with senior staff at the Board of Governors of the Federal Reserve in Washington. In the afternoon, at 2:30, they have a second conference call, which is a joint briefing of officials at the board and the Treasury. Although by statute the Treasury has the lead role in setting foreign exchange policy, it strives to reach a consensus among all three parties—the Treasury, the Board of Governors, and the Federal Reserve Bank of New York. If they decide that a foreign exchange intervention is necessary that day—an unusual occurrence, as a year may go by without a U.S. foreign exchange intervention—the manager instructs his traders to carry out the agreed-on purchase or sale of foreign currencies. Because funds for exchange rate intervention are held separately by the Treasury (in its Exchange Stabilization Fund) and the Federal Reserve, the manager and his or her staff are not trading the funds of the Federal Reserve Bank of New York; rather, they act as an agent for the Treasury and the FOMC in conducting these transactions.

As part of their duties, before every FOMC meeting, the staff help prepare a lengthy document full of data for the FOMC members, other Reserve bank presidents, and Treasury officials. It describes developments in the domestic and foreign markets over the previous five or six weeks, a task that keeps them especially busy right before the FOMC meeting.

currency in circulation falls by $1 billion. We can see this in the following T-account for the Federal Reserve:

Federal Reserve System

Assets		Liabilities	
Foreign assets (international reserves)	−$1 billion	Currency in circulation	−$1 billion

Because the monetary base is made up of currency in circulation plus reserves, this decline in currency implies that the monetary base has fallen by $1 billion.

If instead of paying for the foreign assets sold by the Fed with currency, the persons buying the foreign assets pay for them by checks written on accounts at domestic banks, then the Fed deducts the $1 billion from the reserve deposits it holds for these banks. The result is that deposits with the Fed (reserves) decline by $1 billion, as shown in the following T-account:

Federal Reserve System

Assets		Liabilities	
Foreign assets (international reserves)	−$1 billion	Deposits with the Fed (reserves)	−$1 billion

In this case, the outcome of the Fed sale of foreign assets and the purchase of dollar deposits is a $1 billion decline in reserves and a $1 billion decline in the monetary base because reserves are also a component of the monetary base.

We now see that the outcome for the monetary base is exactly the same when a central bank sells foreign assets to purchase domestic bank deposits or domestic currency. This is why when we say that a central bank has purchased its domestic currency, we do not have to distinguish whether it actually purchased currency or bank deposits denominated in the domestic currency. We have thus reached an important conclusion: ***A central bank's purchase of domestic currency and corresponding sale of foreign assets in the foreign exchange market leads to an equal decline in its international reserves and the monetary base.***

We could have reached the same conclusion by a more direct route. A central bank sale of a foreign asset is no different from an open market sale of a government bond. We learned in our exploration of the money supply process that an open market sale leads to an equal decline in the monetary base; therefore, a sale of foreign assets also leads to an equal decline in the monetary base. By similar reasoning, a central bank purchase of foreign assets paid for by selling domestic currency, like an open market purchase, leads to an equal rise in the monetary base. Thus we reach the following conclusion: ***A central bank's sale of domestic currency to purchase foreign assets in the foreign exchange market results in an equal rise in its international reserves and the monetary base.***

The intervention we have just described, in which a central bank allows the purchase or sale of domestic currency to have an effect on the monetary base, is called an **unsterilized foreign exchange intervention**. But what if the central bank does not want the purchase or sale of domestic currency to affect the monetary base? All it has to do is to counter the effect of the foreign exchange intervention by conducting an offsetting open market operation in the government bond market. For example, in the case of a $1 billion purchase of dollars by the Fed and a corresponding $1 billion sale of foreign assets, which, as we have seen, would decrease the monetary base by $1 billion, the Fed can conduct an open market purchase of $1 billion of government bonds, which would increase the monetary base by $1 billion. The resulting T-account for the foreign exchange intervention and the offsetting open market operation leaves the monetary base unchanged:

Federal Reserve System

Assets		Liabilities	
Foreign assets (international reserves)	−$1 billion	Monetary base (reserves)	0
Government bonds	+$1 billion		

A foreign exchange intervention with an offsetting open market operation that leaves the monetary base unchanged is called a **sterilized foreign exchange intervention**.

Now that we understand that there are two types of foreign exchange interventions—unsterilized and sterilized—let's look at how each affects the exchange rate.

Unsterilized Intervention

Your intuition might lead you to suspect that if a central bank wants to lower the value of the domestic currency, it should sell its currency in the foreign exchange market and purchase foreign assets. Indeed, this intuition is correct for the case of an unsterilized intervention.

Recall that in an unsterilized intervention, if the Federal Reserve decides to sell dollars so that it can buy foreign assets in the foreign exchange market, this works just like an open market purchase of bonds to increase the monetary base. Hence the sale of dollars leads to an increase in the money supply, and we find ourselves analyzing a similar situation to that described in Figure 8 of Chapter 20, which is reproduced here as Figure 1.[1] The higher money supply leads to a higher U.S. price level in the long run

FIGURE 1

Effect of a Sale of Dollars and a Purchase of Foreign Assets

A sale of dollars and the consequent open market purchase of foreign assets increase the monetary base. The resulting rise in the money supply leads to a decline in domestic interest rates and a higher domestic price level in the long run, which produces a lower expected future exchange rate. The decline in both the expected appreciation of the dollar and the domestic interest rate lowers the relative expected return on dollar assets, shifting the demand curve leftward from D_1 to D_2. In the short run, the equilibrium exchange rate falls from E_1 to E_2. In the long run, the interest rate rises back to its initial level and the demand curve shifts rightward to D_3. The exchange rate rises from E_2 to E_3 in the long run.

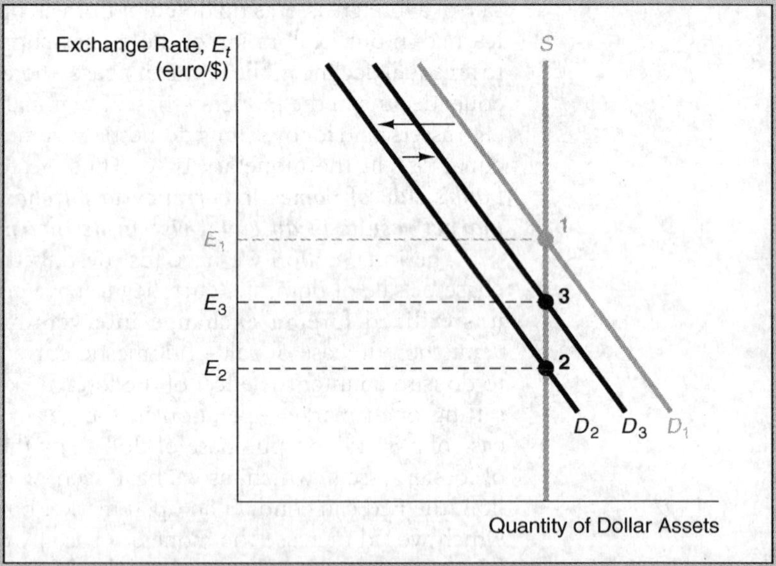

[1]An unsterilized intervention in which the Fed sells dollars increases the amount of dollar assets slightly because it leads to an increase in the monetary base while leaving the amount of government bonds in the hands of the public unchanged. The curve depicting the supply of dollar assets would thus shift to the right slightly, which also works toward lowering the exchange rate, yielding the same conclusion derived from Figure 1. Because the resulting increase in the monetary base would be only a minuscule fraction of the total amount of dollar assets outstanding, the supply curve would shift by an imperceptible amount. This is why Figure 1 is drawn with the supply curve unchanged.

and so to a lower expected future exchange rate. The resulting decline in the expected appreciation of the dollar lowers the relative expected return on dollar assets and shifts the demand curve to the left. In addition, the increase in the money supply will lead to a higher real money supply in the short run, which causes the interest rate on dollar assets to fall, also lowering the relative expected return on dollar assets, and providing another reason for the demand curve to shift to the left. The demand curve shifts from D_1 to D_2, and the exchange rate falls to E_2. Because the domestic interest rate will rise back to its initial level in the long run, the relative expected return of dollar assets will increase somewhat, sending the demand curve to D_3 but not all the way back to D_1 because the price level will still be higher in the long run. The exchange rate thus rises from E_2 to E_3, which is still below the initial value of E_1. The result is the same we found in the previous chapter, in which there is exchange rate overshooting—that is, the exchange rate falls by more in the short run than in the long run.

Our analysis leads us to the following conclusion about unsterilized interventions in the foreign exchange market: ***An unsterilized intervention in which domestic currency is sold to purchase foreign assets leads to a gain in international reserves, an increase in the money supply, and a depreciation of the domestic currency.***

The reverse result is found for an unsterilized intervention in which domestic currency is purchased by selling foreign assets. The purchase of domestic currency by selling foreign assets (reducing international reserves) works like an open market sale to reduce the monetary base and the money supply. The decrease in the money supply raises the interest rate on dollar assets and lowers the long-run price level, thereby increasing the future expected exchange rate. The resulting increase in the relative expected return on dollar assets means that people will buy more dollar assets, so the demand curve shifts to the right and the exchange rate rises. ***An unsterilized intervention in which domestic currency is purchased by selling foreign assets leads to a drop in international reserves, a decrease in the money supply, and an appreciation of the domestic currency.***

Sterilized Intervention

The key point to remember about a sterilized intervention is that the central bank engages in offsetting open market operations, so that there is no impact on the monetary base and the money supply. In the context of the model of exchange rate determination we have developed here, it is straightforward to show that a sterilized intervention has almost *no effect* on the exchange rate. A sterilized intervention leaves the money supply unchanged and so has no direct way of affecting interest rates or the expected future exchange rate.[2] Because the relative expected return on dollar assets is unaffected, the demand curve would remain at D_1 in Figure 1, and the exchange rate would remain unchanged at E_1.

---

[2]A sterilized intervention changes the amount of foreign securities relative to domestic securities in the hands of the public, called a *portfolio balance effect*. Through this effect, the central bank might be able to affect the interest differential between domestic and foreign assets, which in turn affects the relative expected return of domestic assets. Empirical evidence has not revealed this portfolio balance effect to be significant. However, a sterilized intervention *could* indicate what central banks want to happen to the future exchange rate and so might provide a signal about the course of future monetary policy. In this way a sterilized intervention could lead to shifts in the demand curve for domestic assets and ultimately affect the exchange rate. However, the future change in monetary policy—not the sterilized intervention—is the source of the exchange rate effect. For a further discussion of the signaling and portfolio balance effects and the possible differential effects of sterilized versus unsterilized intervention, see Paul Krugman and Maurice Obstfeld, *International Economics*, 7th ed. (Boston: Addison-Wesley, 2006).

At first it might seem puzzling that a central bank purchase or sale of domestic currency that is sterilized does not lead to a change in the exchange rate. A central bank purchase of domestic currency cannot raise the exchange rate, because with no effect on the domestic money supply or interest rates, any resulting rise in the exchange rate would mean that there would be an excess supply of dollar assets. With more people willing to sell dollar assets than to buy them, the exchange rate would have to fall back to its initial equilibrium level, where the demand and supply curves intersect.

BALANCE OF PAYMENTS

Because international financial transactions such as foreign exchange interventions have considerable effects on monetary policy, it is worth knowing how these transactions are measured. The **balance of payments** is a bookkeeping system for recording all receipts and payments that have a direct bearing on the movement of funds between a nation (private sector and government) and foreign countries.

Here we examine the key items in the balance of payments that you often hear about in the media.

The **current account** shows international transactions that involve currently produced goods and services. The difference between merchandise exports and imports, the net receipts from trade, is called the **trade balance**. When merchandise imports are greater than exports (by \$665 billion in 2004), we have a trade deficit; if exports are greater than imports, we have a trade surplus.

Additional items included in the current account are the net receipts (cash flows received from abroad minus cash flows sent abroad) from three categories: investment income, service transactions, and unilateral transfers (gifts, pensions, and foreign aid). In 2004, for example, net investment income was \$30 billion for the United States because Americans received more investment income from abroad than they paid out. Americans bought less in services from foreigners than foreigners bought from Americans, so net services generated \$48 billion in receipts. Because Americans made more unilateral transfers to foreign countries (especially foreign aid) than foreigners made to the United States, net unilateral transfers were negative \$81 billion. The sum of the previous three items plus the trade balance is the current account balance, which in 2004 showed a deficit of \$668 billion ($-\$665 + \$30 + \$48 - \$81 = -\$668$ billion).

Another important item in the balance of payments is the **capital account**, the net receipts from capital transactions (e.g., purchases of stocks and bonds, bank loans, etc.). In 2004 the capital account was $-\$2$ billion, indicating that \$2 billion more capital flowed out of the United States than came in. Another way of saying this is that the United States had a net capital outflow of \$2 billion.[3] The sum of the current account and the capital account equals the **official reserve transactions balance** (net change in government international reserves), which was negative \$670.1 billion in 2004 ($-\$670 - \$2 = -\$670$ billion). When economists refer to a surplus or deficit in the balance of payments, they actually mean a surplus or deficit in the official reserve transactions balance.

Because the balance of payments must balance, the official reserve transactions balance, which equals the current account plus the capital account, tells us the net amount

[3]The capital account balance number reported here includes a statistical discrepancy item that represents errors due to unrecorded transactions involving smuggling and other capital flows ($-\$39$ billion in 2004). Many experts believe that the statistical discrepancy item, which keeps the balance of payments in balance, is primarily the result of large hidden capital flows, and this is why it is included in the capital account balance.

Global Why the Large U.S. Current Account Deficit Worries Economists

The massive U.S. current account deficits in recent years, which now exceed 6% of GDP (the highest level reached over the past century), worries economists for several reasons. First, it indicates that at current exchange rate values, foreigners' demand for U.S. exports is far less than Americans' demand for imports. As we saw in the previous chapter, low demand for U.S. exports and high U.S. demand for imports may lead to a future decline in the value of the U.S. dollar. Some economists estimate that this decline could be very large, with the U.S. dollar depreciating by as much as 50%.

Second, the current account deficit means that foreigners' claims on U.S. assets are growing, and these claims will have to be paid back at some point. Americans are mortgaging their future to foreigners; when the bill comes due, Americans will be poorer. Furthermore, if Americans have a greater preference for dollar assets than foreigners do, the movement of American wealth to foreigners could decrease the demand for dollar assets over time, also causing the dollar to depreciate.

The hope is that the eventual decline in the dollar resulting from the large U.S. current account deficits will be a gradual one, occurring over a period of several years. If the decline is precipitous, however, it could poetentially disrupt financial markets and hurt the U.S. economy.

of international reserves that must move between governments (as represented by their central banks) to finance international transactions: i.e.,

$$\text{Current account} + \text{capital account} = \text{net change in government international reserves}$$

This equation shows us why the current account receives so much attention from economists and the media. The current account balance tells us whether the United States (private sector and government combined) is increasing or decreasing its claims on foreign wealth. A surplus indicates that America is increasing its claims on foreign wealth and thus is increasing its holdings of foreign capital (both good things for Americans); a deficit (as in 2005) indicates that the United States is reducing its holdings of foreign capital and foreign countries are increasing their claims on the United States.[4] The rapid growth in the U.S. current account deficit in recent years, which is now near $1 trillion, has raised serious concerns that these large deficits may have negative consequences for the U.S. economy (see the Global box, "Why the Large U.S. Current Account Deficit Worries Economists").

EXCHANGE RATE REGIMES IN THE INTERNATIONAL FINANCIAL SYSTEM

Exchange rate regimes in the international financial system are classified into two basic types: fixed and floating. In a **fixed exchange rate regime**, the value of a currency is pegged relative to the value of one other currency (called the **anchor currency**) so that

[4]The current account balance can also be viewed as showing the amount by which total saving exceeds private sector and government investment in the United States. Total U.S. saving equals the increase in total wealth held by the U.S. private sector and government. Total investment equals the increase in the U.S. capital stock (wealth physically in the United States). The difference between them is the increase in U.S. claims on foreign wealth.

exchange rate is fixed. In a **floating exchange rate regime**, the value of a currency is allowed to fluctuate against all other currencies. When countries attempt to influence their exchange rates by buying and selling currencies, the regime is referred to as a **managed float regime** (or a **dirty float**).

In examining past exchange rate regimes, we start with the gold standard of the late nineteenth and early twentieth centuries.

Gold Standard

Before World War I, the world economy operated under the **gold standard**, a fixed exchange rate regime in which the currency of most countries was convertible directly into gold at fixed rates, so exchange rates between currencies were also fixed. American dollar bills, for example, could be turned in to the U.S. Treasury and exchanged for approximately $\frac{1}{20}$ ounce of gold. Likewise, the British Treasury would exchange $\frac{1}{4}$ ounce of gold for £1 sterling. Because an American could convert $20 into 1 ounce of gold, which could be used to buy £4, the exchange rate between the pound and the dollar was effectively fixed at $5 to the pound. The fixed exchange rates under the gold standard had the important advantage of encouraging world trade by eliminating the uncertainty that occurs when exchange rates fluctuate.

As long as countries abided by the rules under the gold standard and kept their currencies backed by and convertible into gold, exchange rates remained fixed. However, adherence to the gold standard meant that a country had no control over its monetary policy, because its money supply was determined by gold flows between countries. Furthermore, monetary policy throughout the world was greatly influenced by the production of gold and gold discoveries. When gold production was low in the 1870s and 1880s, the money supply throughout the world grew slowly and did not keep pace with the growth of the world economy. The result was deflation (falling price levels). Gold discoveries in Alaska and South Africa in the 1890s greatly expanded gold production, causing money supplies to increase rapidly and price levels to rise (inflation) until World War I.

The Bretton Woods System

After World War II, the victors set up a fixed exchange rate system that became known as the **Bretton Woods system**, after the New Hampshire town in which the agreement was negotiated in 1944. The Bretton Woods system remained in effect until 1971.

The Bretton Woods agreement created the **International Monetary Fund (IMF)**, headquartered in Washington, D.C., which had 30 original member countries in 1945 and currently has over 180. The IMF was given the task of promoting the growth of world trade by setting rules for the maintenance of fixed exchange rates and by making loans to countries that were experiencing balance-of-payments difficulties. As part of its role of monitoring the compliance of member countries with its rules, the IMF also took on the job of collecting and standardizing international economic data.

The Bretton Woods agreement also set up the International Bank for Reconstruction and Development, commonly referred to as the **World Bank**. Headquartered in Washington, D.C., it provides long-term loans to help developing countries build dams, roads, and other physical capital that would contribute to their economic development. The funds for these loans are obtained primarily by issuing World Bank bonds, which are sold in the capital markets of the developed countries. In addition, the General Agreement on Tariffs and Trade (GATT), headquartered in Geneva, Switzerland, was set

Global The Euro's Challenge to the Dollar

With the creation of the European Monetary System and the euro in 1999, the U.S. dollar is facing a challenge to its position as the key reserve currency in international financial transactions. Adoption of the euro increases integration of Europe's financial markets, which could help them rival those in the United States. The resulting increase in the use of euros in financial markets will make it more likely that international transactions are carried out in the euro. The economic clout of the European Union rivals that of the United States: Both have a similar share of world GDP (around 20%) and world exports (around 15%). If the European Central Bank can make sure that inflation remains low so that the euro becomes a sound currency, this should bode well for the euro.

However, for the euro to eat into the dollar's position as a reserve currency, the European Union must function as a cohesive political entity that can exert its influence on the world stage. There are serious doubts on this score, however, particularly with the "no" votes on the European constitution by France and the Netherlands in 2005. Most analysts think it will be a long time before the euro beats out the dollar in international financial transactions.

up to monitor rules for the conduct of trade between countries (tariffs and quotas). The GATT has since evolved into the **World Trade Organization (WTO)**.

Because the United States emerged from World War II as the world's largest economic power, with over half of the world's manufacturing capacity and the greater part of the world's gold, the Bretton Woods system of fixed exchange rates was based on the convertibility of U.S. dollars into gold (for foreign governments and central banks only) at $35 per ounce. The fixed exchange rates were to be maintained by intervention in the foreign exchange market by central banks in countries besides the United States that bought and sold dollar assets, which they held as international reserves. The U.S. dollar, which was used by other countries to denominate the assets that they held as international reserves, was called the **reserve currency**. Thus an important feature of the Bretton Woods system was the establishment of the United States as the reserve currency country. Even after the breakup of the Bretton Woods system, the U.S. dollar has kept its position as the reserve currency in which most international financial transactions are conducted. However, with the creation of the euro in 1999, the supremacy of the U.S. dollar may be subject to a serious challenge (see the Global box, "The Euro's Challenge to the Dollar").

The fixed exchange rate, dictated by the Bretton Woods system was abandoned in 1971. From 1979 to 1990, however, the European Union instituted among its members its own fixed exchange rate system, the European Monetary System (EMS). In the *exchange rate mechanism (ERM)* in this system, the exchange rate between any pair of currencies of the participating countries was not supposed to fluctuate outside narrow limits, called the "snake." In practice, all of the countries in the EMS pegged their currencies to the German mark.

How a Fixed Exchange Rate Regime Works

Figure 2 shows how a fixed exchange rate regime works in practice by using the supply and demand analysis of the foreign exchange market we learned in the previous chapter. Panel (a) describes a situation in which the domestic currency is fixed relative

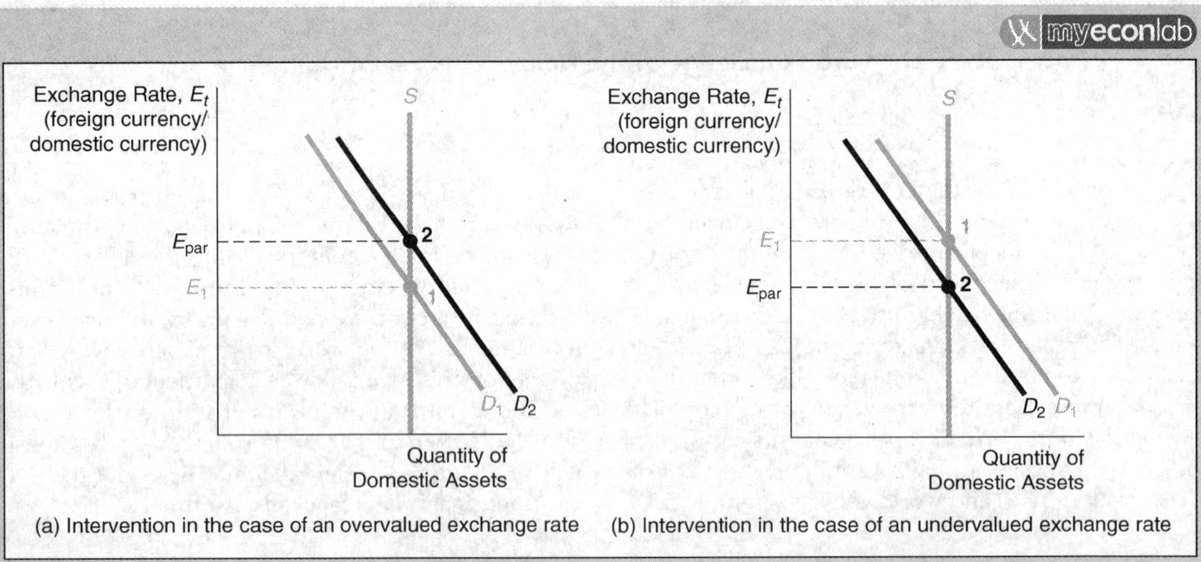

FIGURE 2 **Intervention in the Foreign Exchange Market Under a Fixed Exchange Rate Regime**
In panel (a), the exchange rate at E_{par} is overvalued. To keep the exchange rate at E_{par} (point 2), the central bank must purchase domestic currency to shift the demand curve to D_2. In panel (b), the exchange rate at E_{par} is undervalued, so the central bank must sell domestic currency to shift the demand curve to D_2 and keep the exchange rate at E_{par} (point 2).

to an anchor currency, while the demand curve has shifted left to D_1, perhaps because foreign interest rates have risen, thereby lowering the relative expected return of domestic assets. The exchange rate is now *overvalued:* The demand curve D_1 intersects the supply curve at an exchange rate E_1, which is lower than the fixed (par) value of the exchange rate E_{par}. To keep the exchange rate at E_{par}, the central bank must intervene in the foreign exchange market to purchase domestic currency by selling foreign assets. This action, like an open market sale, means that both the monetary base and the money supply decline, driving up the interest rate on domestic assets, i^D.[5] This increase in the domestic interest rate raises the relative expected return on domestic assets, shifting the demand curve to the right. The central bank will continue purchasing domestic currency until the demand curve reaches D_2 and the equilibrium exchange rate is at E_{par} at point 2 in panel (a).

We have thus come to the conclusion that ***when the domestic currency is overvalued, the central bank must purchase domestic currency to keep the exchange rate fixed, but as a result it loses international reserves.***

Panel (b) in Figure 2 describes the situation in which the demand curve has shifted to the right to D_1 because the relative expected return on domestic assets has risen and hence the exchange rate is undervalued: The initial demand curve D_1 intersects the supply curve at exchange rate E_1, which is above E_{par}. In this situation, the central bank must sell domestic currency and purchase foreign assets. This action works like an open market purchase to increase the money supply and lower the interest rate on domestic

[5]Because the exchange rate will continue to be fixed at E_{par}, the expected future exchange rate remains unchanged and so does not need to be addressed in the analysis.

assets i^D. The central bank keeps selling domestic currency and lowering i^D until the demand curve shifts all the way to D_2, where the equilibrium exchange rate is at E_{par}—point 2 in panel (b). Our analysis thus leads us to the following result: ***When the domestic currency is undervalued, the central bank must sell domestic currency to keep the exchange rate fixed, but as a result, it gains international reserves.***

As we have seen, if a country's currency is overvalued, its central bank's attempts to keep the currency from depreciating will result in a loss of international reserves. If the country's central bank eventually runs out of international reserves, it cannot keep its currency from depreciating, and a **devaluation** must occur, in which the par exchange rate is reset at a lower level.

If, by contrast, a country's currency is undervalued, its central bank's intervention to keep the currency from appreciating leads to a gain of international reserves. As we will see shortly, the central bank might not want to acquire these international reserves, and so it might want to reset the par value of its exchange rate at a higher level (a **revaluation**).

If there is perfect capital mobility—that is, if there are no barriers to domestic residents purchasing foreign assets or foreigners purchasing domestic assets—then a sterilized exchange rate intervention cannot keep the exchange rate at E_{par} because, as we saw earlier in the chapter, the relative expected return of domestic assets is unaffected. For example, if the exchange rate is overvalued, a sterilized purchase of domestic currency will leave the relative expected return and the demand curve unchanged—so pressure for a depreciation of the domestic currency is not removed. If the central bank keeps purchasing its domestic currency but continues to sterilize, it will just keep losing international reserves until it finally runs out of them and is forced to let the value of the currency seek a lower level.

One implication of the foregoing analysis is that a country that ties its exchange rate to an anchor currency of a larger country loses control of its monetary policy. If the larger country pursues a more contractionary monetary policy and decreases its money supply, this would lead to lower expected inflation in the larger country, thus causing an appreciation of the larger country's currency and a depreciation of the smaller country's currency. The smaller country, having locked in its exchange rate to the anchor currency, will now find its currency overvalued and will therefore have to sell the anchor currency and buy its own to keep its currency from depreciating. The result of this foreign exchange intervention will then be a decline in the smaller country's international reserves, a contraction of its monetary base, and thus a decline in its money supply. Sterilization of this foreign exchange intervention is not an option because this would just lead to a continuing loss of international reserves until the smaller country was forced to devalue its currency. The smaller country no longer controls its monetary policy, because movements in its money supply are completely determined by movements in the larger country's money supply.

Another way to see that when a country fixes its exchange rate to a larger country's currency it loses control of its monetary policy is through the interest parity condition discussed in the previous chapter. There we saw that when there is capital mobility, the domestic interest rate equals the foreign interest rate minus the expected appreciation of the domestic currency. With a fixed exchange rate, expected appreciation of the domestic currency is zero, so that the domestic interest rate equals the foreign interest rate. Therefore changes in the monetary policy in the large anchor country that affect its interest rate are directly transmitted to interest rates in the small country. Furthermore, because the monetary authorities in the small country cannot make their interest rate deviate from that of the larger country, they have no way to use monetary policy to affect their economy.

APPLICATION How Did China Accumulate Nearly $1 Trillion of International Reserves?

By the end of 2005, China had accumulated more than $700 billion of international reserves, and its international reserves are expected to top $1 trillion in the near future. How did the Chinese get their hands on this vast amount of foreign assets? After all, China is not yet a rich country.

The answer is that China pegged its exchange rate to the U.S. dollar at a fixed rate of 8.28 yuan (also called renminbi) to the dollar in 1994. Because of China's rapidly growing productivity and an inflation rate that is lower than in the United States, the long-run value of the yuan has increased, leading to a higher relative expected return for yuan assets and a rightward shift of the demand for yuan assets. As a result, the Chinese have found themselves in the situation depicted in panel (b) of Figure 2, in which the yuan is undervalued. To keep the yuan from appreciating above E_{par} to E_1 in the figure, the Chinese central bank has been engaging in massive purchases of U.S. dollar assets. Today the Chinese government is one of the largest holders of U.S. government bonds in the world.

The pegging of the yuan to the U.S. dollar has created several problems for Chinese authorities. First, the Chinese now own a lot of U.S. assets, particularly U.S. Treasury securities, which have very low returns. Second, the undervaluation of the yuan has meant that Chinese goods are so cheap abroad that many countries have threatened to erect trade barriers against these goods if the Chinese government does not allow an upward revaluation of the yuan. Third, as we learned earlier in the chapter, the Chinese purchase of dollar assets has resulted in a substantial increase in the Chinese monetary base and money supply, which has the potential to produce high inflation in the future. Because the Chinese authorities have created substantial roadblocks to capital mobility, they have been able to sterilize most of their exchange rate interventions while maintaining the exchange rate peg. Nevertheless, they still worry about inflationary pressures. In July 2005, China finally made its peg somewhat more flexible by letting the value of the yuan rise 2.1%. The central bank also indicated that it would no longer fix the yuan to the U.S. dollar, but would instead maintain its value relative to a basket of currencies.

Why did the Chinese authorities maintain this exchange rate peg for so long despite the problems? One answer is that they wanted to keep their export sector humming by keeping the prices of their export goods low. A second answer might be that they wanted to accumulate a large amount of international reserves as a "war chest" that could be sold to buy yuan in the event of a speculative attack against the yuan at some future date. Given the pressure on the Chinese government to further revalue its currency from government officials in the United States and Europe, there are likely to be further adjustments in China's exchange rate policy in the future.

How the Bretton Woods System Worked. Under the Bretton Woods system, exchange rates were supposed to change only when a country was experiencing a "fundamental disequilibrium"—that is, large persistent deficits or surpluses in its balance of payments. To maintain fixed exchange rates when countries had balance-of-payments deficits and were losing international reserves, the IMF would loan deficit countries international reserves contributed by other members. As a result of its power to dictate loan terms to borrowing countries, the IMF could encourage deficit countries to pursue contractionary monetary policies that would strengthen their currency or eliminate their balance-of-payments deficits. If the IMF loans were not sufficient to prevent depreciation of a currency, the country was allowed to devalue its currency by setting a new, lower exchange rate.

A notable weakness of the Bretton Woods system was that although deficit countries losing international reserves could be pressured into devaluing their currencies or pursuing contractionary policies, the IMF had no way to force surplus countries to revise their exchange rates upward or pursue more expansionary policies. Particularly troublesome in this regard was the fact that the reserve currency country, the United States, could not devalue its currency under the Bretton Woods system even if the dollar was overvalued. When the United States attempted to reduce domestic unemployment in the 1960s by pursuing an inflationary monetary policy, a fundamental disequilibrium of an overvalued dollar developed. Because surplus countries were not willing to revise their exchange rates upward, adjustment in the Bretton Woods system did not take place, and the system collapsed in 1971. Attempts to patch up the Bretton Woods system with the Smithsonian Agreement in December 1971 proved unsuccessful, and by 1973, America and its trading partners had agreed to allow exchange rates to float.

Managed Float

Although exchange rates are currently allowed to change daily in response to market forces, central banks have not been willing to give up their option of intervening in the foreign exchange market. Preventing large changes in exchange rates makes it easier for firms and individuals purchasing or selling goods abroad to plan into the future. Furthermore, countries with surpluses in their balance of payments frequently do not want to see their currencies appreciate, because it makes their goods more expensive abroad and foreign goods cheaper in their country. Because an appreciation might hurt sales for domestic businesses and increase unemployment, surplus countries have often sold their currency in the foreign exchange market and acquired international reserves.

Countries with balance-of-payments deficits do not want to see their currency lose value, because it makes foreign goods more expensive for domestic consumers and can stimulate inflation. To keep the value of the domestic currency high, deficit countries have often bought their own currency in the foreign exchange market and given up international reserves.

The current international financial system is a hybrid of a fixed and a flexible exchange rate system. Rates fluctuate in response to market forces but are not determined solely by them. Furthermore, many countries continue to keep the value of their currency fixed against other currencies, as was the case in the European Monetary System before the introduction of the euro (to be described shortly).

Another important feature of the current system is the continuing de-emphasis of gold in international financial transactions. Not only has the United States suspended convertibility of dollars into gold for foreign central banks, but since 1970 the IMF has been issuing a paper substitute for gold, called **special drawing rights (SDRs)**. Like gold in the Bretton Woods system, SDRs function as international reserves. Unlike gold, whose quantity is determined by gold discoveries and the rate of production, SDRs can be created by the IMF whenever it decides that there is a need for additional international reserves to promote world trade and economic growth.

The use of gold in international transactions was further de-emphasized by the IMF's elimination of the official gold price in 1975 and by the sale of gold by the U.S. Treasury and the IMF to private investors in an effort to demonetize it. Currently, the price of gold is determined in a free market. Investors who want to speculate in it are able to purchase and sell gold at will, as are jewelers and dentists who use gold in their businesses.

European Monetary System (EMS)

In March 1979, eight members of the European Economic Community (Germany, France, Italy, the Netherlands, Belgium, Luxembourg, Denmark, and Ireland) set up the European Monetary System (EMS), in which they agreed to fix their exchange rates vis-à-vis one another and to float jointly against the U.S. dollar. Spain joined the EMS in June 1989, the United Kingdom in October 1990, and Portugal in April 1992. The EMS created a new monetary unit, the *European currency unit* (ECU), whose value was tied to a basket of specified amounts of European currencies.

The exchange rate mechanism (ERM) of the European Monetary System worked as follows. The exchange rate between every pair of currencies of the participating countries was not allowed to fluctuate outside narrow limits around a fixed exchange rate. (The limits were typically ±2.25% but were raised to ±15% in August 1993.) When the exchange rate between two countries' currencies moved outside these limits, the central banks of both countries were supposed to intervene in the foreign exchange market. If, for example, the French franc depreciated below its lower limit against the German mark, the Bank of France was required to buy francs and sell marks, thereby giving up international reserves. Similarly, the German central bank was required to intervene to sell marks and buy francs and consequently increase its international reserves. The EMS thus required that intervention be symmetric when a currency fell outside the limits, with the central bank with the weak currency giving up international reserves and the one with the strong currency gaining them. Central bank intervention was also very common even when the exchange rate was within the limits, but in this case, if one central bank intervened, no others were required to intervene as well.

A serious shortcoming of fixed exchange rate systems such as the Bretton Woods system or the European Monetary System is that they can lead to foreign exchange crises involving a "speculative attack" on a currency—massive sales of a weak currency or purchases of a strong currency to cause a sharp change in the exchange rate. In the following application, we use our model of exchange rate determination to understand how the September 1992 exchange rate crisis that rocked the European Monetary System came about.

APPLICATION The Foreign Exchange Crisis of September 1992

In the aftermath of German reunification in October 1990, the German central bank, the Bundesbank, faced rising inflationary pressures, with inflation having accelerated from below 3% in 1990 to near 5% by 1992. To get monetary growth under control and to dampen inflation, the Bundesbank raised German interest rates to near double-digit levels. Figure 3 shows the consequences of these actions by the Bundesbank in the foreign exchange market for British pounds. Note that in the diagram, the pound is the domestic currency and the German mark (deutsche mark, DM) is the foreign currency.

The increase in German interest rates i^F lowered the relative expected return of British pound assets and shifted the demand curve to D_2 in Figure 3. The intersection of the supply and demand curves at point 2 was now below the lower exchange rate

FIGURE 3

Foreign Exchange Market for British Pounds in 1992

The realization by speculators that the United Kingdom would soon devalue the pound decreased the relative expected return on British pound assets, resulting in a leftward shift of the demand curve from D_2 to D_3. The result was the need for a much greater purchase of pounds by the British central bank to raise the interest rate so that the demand curve would shift back to D_1 and keep the exchange rate E_{par} at 2.778 German marks per pound.

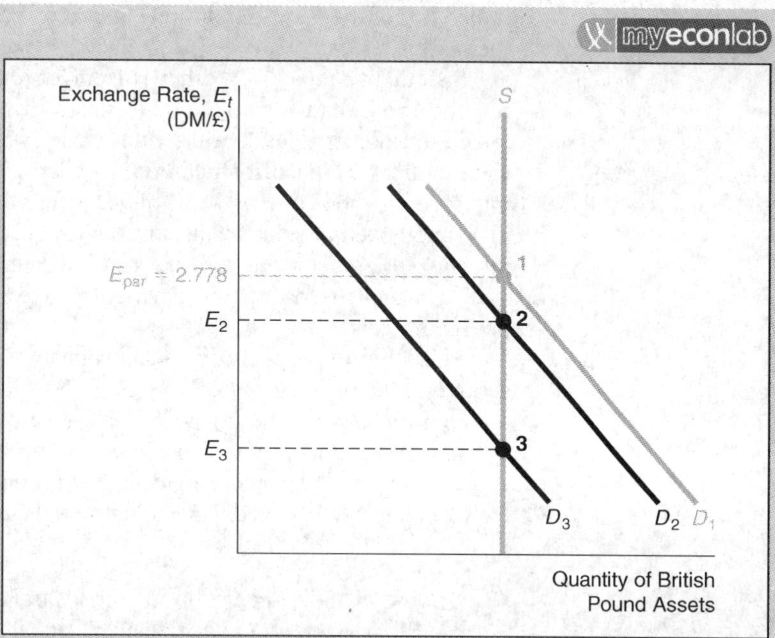

limit at that time (2.778 marks per pound, denoted E_{par}). To increase the value of the pound relative to the mark and to restore the mark/pound exchange rate to within the exchange rate mechanism limits, one of two things had to happen. The Bank of England would have to pursue a contractionary monetary policy, thereby raising British interest rates sufficiently to shift the demand curve back to D_1 so that the equilibrium would remain at point 1, where the exchange rate would remain at E_{par}. Alternatively, the Bundesbank would have to pursue an expansionary monetary policy, thereby lowering German interest rates. Lower German interest rates would raise the relative expected return on British assets and shift the demand curve back to D_1 so the exchange rate would be at E_{par}.

The catch was that the Bundesbank, whose primary goal was fighting inflation, was unwilling to pursue an expansionary monetary policy, and the British, who were facing their worst recession in the postwar period, were unwilling to pursue a contractionary monetary policy to prop up the pound. This impasse became clear when in response to great pressure from other members of the EMS, the Bundesbank was willing to lower its lending rates by only a token amount on September 14 after a speculative attack was mounted on the currencies of the Scandinavian countries. So at some point in the near future, the value of the pound would have to decline to point 2. Speculators now knew that the depreciation of the pound was imminent. As a result, the relative expected return of the pound fell sharply, shifting the demand curve left to D_3 in Figure 3.

As a result of the large leftward shift of the demand curve, there was now a huge excess supply of pound assets at the par exchange rate E_{par}, which caused a massive sell-off of pounds (and purchases of marks) by speculators. The need for the British central bank to intervene to raise the value of the pound now became much greater and required a huge rise in British interest rates. After a major intervention effort on the part of the Bank of England, which included a rise in its lending rate from 10% to 15%, which still wasn't enough, the British were finally forced to give up on September 16: They pulled out of the ERM indefinitely and allowed the pound to depreciate by 10% against the mark.

Speculative attacks on other currencies forced devaluation of the Spanish peseta by 5% and the Italian lira by 15%. To defend its currency, the Swedish central bank was forced to raise its daily lending rate to the astronomical level of 500%! By the time the crisis was over, the British, French, Italian, Spanish, and Swedish central banks had intervened to the tune of $100 billion; the Bundesbank alone had laid out $50 billion for foreign exchange intervention. Because foreign exchange crises lead to large changes in central banks' holdings of international reserves and thus affect the official reserve asset items in the balance of payments, these crises are also referred to as **balance-of-payments crises**.

The attempt to prop up the European Monetary System was not cheap for these central banks. It is estimated that they lost $4 to $6 billion as a result of exchange rate intervention during the crisis. What the central banks lost, the speculators gained. A speculative fund run by George Soros ran up $1 billion of profits during the crisis, and Citibank traders reportedly made $200 million. When an exchange rate crisis comes, life can certainly be sweet for exchange rate speculators.

APPLICATION Recent Foreign Exchange Crises in Emerging Market Countries: Mexico 1994, East Asia 1997, Brazil 1999, and Argentina 2002

Major currency crises in emerging market countries have been a common occurrence in recent years. We can use Figure 3 to understand the sequence of events during the currency crises in Mexico in 1994, East Asia in 1997, Brazil in 1999, and Argentina in 2002. To do so, we just need to recognize that dollars are the foreign currency, while the domestic currency was either pesos, baht, or reals. (Note that the exchange rate label on the vertical axis would be in terms of dollars/domestic currency and that the label on the horizontal axis would be the quantity of domestic currency (say, pesos) assets.

In Mexico in March 1994, political instability (the assassination of the ruling party's presidential candidate) sparked investors' concerns that the peso might be devalued. The result was that the relative expected return on peso assets fell, thus moving the demand curve from D_1 to D_2 in Figure 3. In the case of Thailand in May 1997, the large current account deficit and the weakness of the Thai financial system raised similar concerns about the devaluation of the domestic currency, with the same effect on the demand curve. In Brazil in late 1998 and Argentina in 2001, concerns about fiscal situations that could lead to the printing of money to finance the deficit, and thereby raise inflation, also meant that a devaluation was more likely to occur. The concerns thus lowered the relative expected return on peso assets and shifted the demand curve from D_1 to D_2. In all of these cases, the result was that the intersection of the supply and demand curves was below the pegged value of the domestic currency at E_{par}.

To keep their domestic currencies from falling below E_{par}, these countries' central banks needed to buy the domestic currency and sell dollars to raise interest rates and shift the demand curve to the right, in the process losing international reserves. At first, the central banks were successful in containing this speculative attack. However, when more bad news broke, speculators became even more confident that these countries could not defend their currencies. (The bad news was everywhere: In Mexico, there was an uprising in Chiappas and revelations about problems in the banking system; in Thailand, there was a major failure of a financial institution; Brazil had a worsening fiscal situation, along with a threat by a governor to default on his state's debt; and in Argentina, a full-scale bank panic and an actual default on the government debt occurred.) As a result, the relative expected returns on domestic assets fell further, and the demand curve moved much farther to the left to D_3, and the central banks lost even more international reserves. Given the stress on the economy from rising interest rates and the loss of reserves, eventually the monetary authorities could no longer continue to defend the currency and were forced to give up and let their currencies depreciate. This scenario happened in Mexico in December 1994, in Thailand in July 1997, in Brazil in January 1999, and in Argentina in January 2002.

Concerns about similar problems in other countries then triggered speculative attacks against them as well. This contagion occurred in the aftermath of the Mexican crisis (jauntily referred to as the "Tequila effect") with speculative attacks on other Latin American currencies, but there were no further currency collapses. In the East Asian crisis, however, fears of devaluation spread throughout the region, leading to a scenario akin to that depicted in Figure 3. Consequently, one by one, Indonesia, Malaysia, South Korea, and the Philippines were forced to devalue sharply. Even Hong Kong, Singapore, and Taiwan were subjected to speculative attacks, but because these countries/regions had healthy financial systems, the attacks were successfully averted.

As we saw in Chapter 8, the sharp depreciations in Mexico, East Asia, and Argentina led to full-scale financial crises that severely damaged these countries' economies. The foreign exchange crisis that shocked the European Monetary System in September 1992 cost central banks a lot of money, but the public in European countries were not seriously affected. By contrast, the public in Mexico, Argentina, and the crisis countries of East Asia were not so lucky: The collapse of these currencies triggered by speculative attacks led to the financial crises described in Chapter 8, producing severe depressions that caused hardship and political unrest.

CAPITAL CONTROLS

Because capital flows have been an important element in the currency crises in Mexico and East Asia, politicians and some economists have advocated that emerging market countries avoid financial instability by restricting capital mobility. Are capital controls a good idea?

Controls on Capital Outflows

Capital outflows can promote financial instability in emerging market countries, because when domestic residents and foreigners pull their capital out of a country, the resulting capital outflow forces a country to devalue its currency. This is why some politicians in emerging market countries have recently found capital controls particularly attractive. For example, Prime Minister Mahathir of Malaysia instituted capital controls in 1998 to restrict outflows in the aftermath of the East Asian crisis.

Although these controls sound like a good idea, they suffer from several disadvantages. First, empirical evidence indicates that controls on capital outflows are seldom effective during a crisis because the private sector finds ingenious ways to evade them and has little difficulty moving funds out of the country.[6] Second, the evidence suggests

[6]See Sebastian Edwards, "How Effective are Capital Controls?," *Journal of Economic Perspectives* 13, (Winter 2000): pp. 65–84.

that capital flight may even increase after controls are put into place, because confidence in the government is weakened. Third, controls on capital outflows often lead to corruption, as government officials get paid off to look the other way when domestic residents are trying to move funds abroad. Fourth, controls on capital outflows may lull governments into thinking they do not have to take the steps to reform their financial systems to deal with the crisis, with the result that opportunities are lost to improve the functioning of the economy.

Controls on Capital Inflows

Although most economists find the arguments against controls on capital outflows persuasive, controls on capital inflows receive more support. Supporters reason that if speculative capital cannot come in, then it cannot go out suddenly and create a crisis. Our analysis of the financial crises in East Asia in Chapter 8 provides support for this view by suggesting that capital inflows can lead to a lending boom and excessive risk taking on the part of banks, which then helps trigger a financial crisis.

However, controls on capital inflows have the undesirable feature that they may block from entering a country funds that would be used for productive investment opportunities. Although such controls may limit the fuel supplied to lending booms through capital flows, over time they produce substantial distortions and misallocation of resources as households and businesses try to get around them. Indeed, just as with controls on capital outflows, controls on capital inflows can lead to corruption. There are serious doubts whether capital controls can be effective in today's environment, in which trade is open and where there are many financial instruments that make it easier to get around these controls.

On the other hand, there is a strong case for improving bank regulation and supervision so that capital inflows are less likely to produce a lending boom and encourage excessive risk taking by banking institutions. For example, restricting banks in how fast their borrowing can grow might substantially limit capital inflows. Supervisory controls that focus on the sources of financial fragility, rather than the symptoms, can enhance the efficiency of the financial system, rather than hampering it.

THE ROLE OF THE IMF

The International Monetary Fund was originally set up under the Bretton Woods system to help countries deal with balance-of-payments problems and stay with the fixed exchange rate by lending to deficit countries. When the Bretton Woods system of fixed exchange rates collapsed in 1971, the IMF took on new roles.

The IMF continues to function as a data collector and provide technical assistance to its member countries. Although the IMF no longer attempts to encourage fixed exchange rates, its role as an international lender has become more important recently. This role first came to the fore in the 1980s during the Third World debt crisis, in which the IMF assisted developing countries in repaying their loans. The financial crises in Mexico in 1994–1995 and in East Asia in 1997–1998 led to huge loans by the IMF to these and other affected countries to help them recover from their financial crises and to prevent the spread of these crises to other countries. This role, in which the IMF acts like an international lender of last resort to cope with financial instability, is indeed highly controversial.

Should the IMF Be an International Lender of Last Resort?

As we saw in Chapter 18, in industrialized countries when a financial crisis occurs and the financial system threatens to seize up, domestic central banks can address matters with a lender-of-last-resort operation to limit the degree of instability in the banking system. In emerging market countries, however, where the credibility of the central bank as an inflation-fighter may be in doubt and debt contracts are typically short-term and denominated in foreign currencies, a lender-of-last-resort operation becomes a double-edged sword—as likely to exacerbate the financial crisis as to alleviate it. For example, when the U.S. Federal Reserve engaged in a lender-of-last-resort operation during the 1987 stock market crash (Chapter 18), there was almost no sentiment in the markets that there would be substantially higher inflation. However, for a central bank with less inflation-fighting credibility than the Fed, central bank lending to the financial system in the wake of a financial crisis—even under the lender-of-last-resort rhetoric—may well arouse fears of inflation spiraling out of control, causing an even greater currency depreciation and still greater deterioration of balance sheets. The resulting increase in moral hazard and adverse selection problems in financial markets, along the lines discussed in Chapter 8, would only worsen the financial crisis.

Central banks in emerging market countries therefore have only a very limited ability to successfully engage in a lender-of-last-resort operation. However, liquidity provided by an international lender of last resort does not have these undesirable consequences, and in helping to stabilize the value of the domestic currency, it strengthens domestic balance sheets. Moreover, an international lender of last resort may be able to prevent contagion, the situation in which a successful speculative attack on one emerging market currency leads to attacks on other emerging market currencies, spreading financial and economic disruption as it goes. Because a lender of last resort for emerging market countries is needed at times, and because it cannot be provided domestically, there is a strong rationale for an international institution to fill this role. Indeed, since Mexico's financial crisis in 1994, the International Monetary Fund and other international agencies have stepped into the lender-of-last-resort role and provided emergency lending to countries threatened by financial instability.

However, support from an international lender of last resort brings risks of its own, especially the risk that the perception it is standing ready to bail out irresponsible financial institutions may lead to excessive risk taking of the sort that makes financial crises more likely. In the Mexican and East Asian crises, governments in the crisis countries used IMF support to protect depositors and other creditors of banking institutions from losses. This safety net creates a well-known moral hazard problem because the depositors and other creditors have less incentive to monitor these banking institutions and withdraw their deposits if the institutions are taking on too much risk. The result is that these institutions are encouraged to take on excessive risks. Indeed, critics of the IMF—most prominently, the Congressional Commission headed by Professor Alan Meltzer of Carnegie-Mellon University—contend that IMF lending in the Mexican crisis, which was used to bail out foreign lenders, set the stage for the East Asian crisis, because these lenders expected to be bailed out if things went wrong, and thus provided funds that were used to fuel excessive risk taking.[7]

An international lender of last resort must find ways to limit this moral hazard problem, or it can actually make the situation worse. The international lender of last resort can make it clear that it will extend liquidity only to governments that put the

---

[7]See International Financial Institution Advisory Commission, *Report* (IFIAC: Washington, D.C., 2000).

proper measures in place to prevent excessive risk taking. In addition, it can reduce the incentives for risk taking by restricting the ability of governments to bail out stockholders and large uninsured creditors of domestic financial institutions. Some critics of the IMF believe that the IMF has not put enough pressure on the governments to which it lends to contain the moral hazard problem.

One problem that arises for international organizations like the IMF engaged in lender-of-last-resort operations is that they know that if they don't come to the rescue, the emerging market country will suffer extreme hardship and possible political instability. Politicians in the crisis country may exploit these concerns and engage in a game of chicken with the international lender of last resort: They resist necessary reforms, hoping that the IMF will cave in. Elements of this game were present in the Mexican crisis of 1994 and were also a particularly important feature of the negotiations between the IMF and Indonesia during the Asian crisis.

How Should the IMF Operate?

The IMF would produce better outcomes if it made clear that it will not play this game. Just as giving in to ill-behaved children may be the easy way out in the short run, but supports a pattern of poor behavior in the long run, some critics worry that the IMF may not be tough enough when confronted by short-run humanitarian concerns. For example, these critics have been particularly critical of the IMF's lending to the Russian government, which resisted adopting appropriate reforms to stabilize its financial system.

The IMF has also been criticized for imposing on the East Asian countries so-called austerity programs that focus on tight macroeconomic policies rather than on microeconomic policies to fix the crisis-causing problems in the financial sector. Such programs are likely to increase resistance to IMF recommendations, particularly in emerging market countries. Austerity programs allow these politicians to label institutions such as the IMF as being anti-growth, rhetoric that helps the politicians mobilize the public against the IMF and avoid doing what they really need to do to reform the financial system in their country. IMF programs focused instead on reforms of the financial sector would increase the likelihood that the IMF will be seen as a helping hand in the creation of a more efficient financial system.

An important historical feature of successful lender-of-last-resort operations is that the faster the lending is done, the lower the amount that actually has to be lent. An excellent example occurred in the aftermath of the stock market crash on October 19, 1987 (Chapter 18). At the end of that day, to service their customers' accounts, securities firms needed to borrow several billion dollars to maintain orderly trading. However, given the unprecedented developments, banks were nervous about extending further loans to these firms. Upon learning this, the Federal Reserve engaged in an immediate lender-of-last-resort operation, making it clear that it would provide liquidity to banks making loans to the securities industry. What is striking about this episode is that the extremely quick intervention of the Fed not only resulted in a negligible impact of the stock market crash on the economy, but also meant that the amount of liquidity that the Fed needed to supply to the economy was not very large.

The ability of the Fed to engage in a lender-of-last-resort operation within a day of a substantial shock to the financial system stands in sharp contrast to the amount of time it has taken the IMF to supply liquidity during the recent crises in emerging market countries. Because IMF lending facilities were originally designed to provide funds after a country was experiencing a balance-of-payments crisis and because the conditions for the loan had to be negotiated, it took several months before the IMF made funds available. By this time, the crises had gotten much worse—and much larger sums of funds were needed to cope with the crisis, often stretching the resources of the IMF. One reason central banks can lend so much more quickly than the IMF is that they have set up procedures in advance to provide loans, with the terms and conditions for this lending agreed upon beforehand. The need for quick provision of liquidity, to keep the loan amount manageable, argues for similar credit facilities at the international lender of last resort, so that funds can be provided quickly, as long as the borrower meets conditions such as properly supervising its banks or keeping budget deficits low. A step in this direction was made in 1999 when the IMF set up a new lending facility, the Contingent Credit Line, so that it can provide liquidity faster during a crisis.

The debate on whether the world will be better off with the IMF operating as an international lender of last resort is currently a hot one. Much attention is being focused on making the IMF more effective in performing this role, and redesign of the IMF is at the center of proposals for a new international financial architecture to help reduce international financial instability.

INTERNATIONAL CONSIDERATIONS AND MONETARY POLICY

Our analysis in this chapter so far has suggested several ways in which monetary policy can be affected by international matters. Awareness of these effects can have significant implications for the way monetary policy is conducted.

Direct Effects of the Foreign Exchange Market on the Money Supply

When central banks intervene in the foreign exchange market, they acquire or sell off international reserves, and their monetary base is affected. When a central bank intervenes in the foreign exchange market, it gives up some control of its money supply. For example, in the early 1970s, the German central bank faced a dilemma. In attempting to keep the German mark from appreciating too much against the U.S. dollar, the Germans acquired huge quantities of international reserves, leading to a rate of money growth that the German central bank considered inflationary.

The Bundesbank could have tried to halt the growth of the money supply by stopping its intervention in the foreign exchange market and reasserting control over its own money supply. Such a strategy has a major drawback when the central bank is under pressure not to allow its currency to appreciate: The lower price of imports and higher price of exports as a result of an appreciation in its currency will hurt domestic producers and increase unemployment.

Because the U.S. dollar has been a reserve currency, the U.S. monetary base and money supply have been less affected by developments in the foreign exchange market. As long as foreign central banks, rather than the Fed, intervene to keep the value of the dollar from changing, American holdings of international reserves are unaffected. The ability to conduct monetary policy is typically easier when a country's currency is a reserve currency.[8]

[8]However, the central bank of a reserve currency country must worry about a shift away from the use of its currency for international reserves.

Balance-of-Payments Considerations

Under the Bretton Woods system, balance-of-payments considerations were more important than they are under the current managed float regime. When a nonreserve currency country is running balance-of-payments deficits, it necessarily gives up international reserves. To keep from running out of these reserves, under the Bretton Woods system it had to implement contractionary monetary policy to strengthen its currency—exactly what occurred in the United Kingdom before its devaluation of the pound in 1967. When policy became expansionary, the balance of payments deteriorated, and the British were forced to "slam on the brakes" by implementing a contractionary policy. Once the balance of payments improved, policy became more expansionary until the deteriorating balance of payments again forced the British to pursue a contractionary policy. Such on-again, off-again actions became known as a "stop-go" policy, and the domestic instability it created was criticized severely.

Because the United States is a major reserve currency country, it can run large balance-of-payments deficits without losing huge amounts of international reserves. This does not mean, however, that the Federal Reserve is never influenced by developments in the U.S. balance of payments. Current account deficits in the United States suggest that American businesses may be losing some of their ability to compete because the value of the dollar is too high. In addition, large U.S. balance-of-payments deficits lead to balance-of-payments surpluses in other countries, which can in turn lead to large increases in their holdings of international reserves (this was especially true under the Bretton Woods system). Because such increases put a strain on the international financial system and may stimulate world inflation, the Fed worries about U.S. balance-of-payments and current account deficits. To help shrink these deficits, the Fed might pursue a more contractionary monetary policy.

Exchange Rate Considerations

Unlike balance-of-payments considerations, which have become less important under the current managed float system, exchange rate considerations now play a greater role in the conduct of monetary policy. If a central bank does not want to see its currency fall in value, it may pursue a more contractionary monetary policy of reducing the money supply to raise the domestic interest rate, thereby strengthening its currency. Similarly, if a country experiences an appreciation in its currency, its domestic industry may suffer from increased foreign competition and may pressure the central bank to pursue a higher rate of money growth so as to lower the exchange rate.

The pressure to manipulate exchange rates seems to be greater for central banks in countries other than the United States, but even the Federal Reserve is not completely immune. The growing tide of protectionism stemming from the inability of American firms to compete with foreign firms because of the strengthening dollar from 1980 to early 1985 stimulated congressional critics of the Fed to call for a more expansionary monetary policy to lower the value of the dollar. As we saw in the appendix to Chapter 19, the Fed let money growth surge. A policy to bring the dollar down was confirmed in the Plaza Agreement of September 1985, in which the finance ministers from the five most important industrial nations in the free world (the United States, Japan, West Germany, the United Kingdom, and France) agreed to intervene in foreign exchange markets to achieve a decline in the dollar. The dollar continued to fall rapidly after the Plaza Agreement, and the Fed played an important role in this decline by continuing to expand the money supply at a rapid rate.

TO PEG OR NOT TO PEG: EXCHANGE-RATE TARGETING AS AN ALTERNATIVE MONETARY POLICY STRATEGY

In Chapter 19, we discussed several monetary policy strategies that could be followed to promote price stability: monetary targeting, inflation targeting, and monetary policy with an implicit (not explicit) nominal anchor. One other strategy also uses a strong nominal anchor to promote price stability: *exchange-rate targeting* (sometimes referred to as an *exchange rate peg*).

Targeting the exchange rate is a monetary policy strategy with a long history. It can take the form of fixing the value of the domestic currency to a commodity such as gold, the key feature of the gold standard described earlier in the chapter. More recently, fixed exchange rate regimes have involved fixing the value of the domestic currency to that of a large, low-inflation country like the United States or Germany (the *anchor country*). Another alternative is to adopt a *crawling target* or *peg*, in which a currency is allowed to depreciate at a steady rate so that the inflation rate in the pegging country can be higher than that of the anchor country.

Advantages of Exchange-Rate Targeting

Exchange-rate targeting has several advantages. First, the nominal anchor of an exchange-rate target directly contributes to keeping inflation under control by tying the inflation rate for internationally traded goods to that found in the anchor country. It does this because the foreign price of internationally traded goods is set by the world market, while the domestic price of these goods is fixed by the exchange-rate target. For example, until 2002 in Argentina the exchange rate for the Argentine peso was exactly one to the dollar, so that a bushel of wheat traded internationally at five dollars had its price set at five pesos. If the exchange-rate target is credible (i.e., expected to be adhered to), the exchange-rate target has the added benefit of anchoring inflation expectations to the inflation rate in the anchor country.

Second, an exchange-rate target provides an automatic rule for the conduct of monetary policy that helps mitigate the time-inconsistency problem described in Chapter 19. As we saw earlier in the chapter, an exchange-rate target forces a tightening of monetary policy when there is a tendency for the domestic currency to depreciate or a loosening of policy when there is a tendency for the domestic currency to appreciate, so that discretionary monetary policy is less of an option. The central bank will therefore be constrained from falling into the time-inconsistency trap of trying to expand output and employment in the short-run by pursuing overly expansionary monetary policy.

Third, an exchange-rate target has the advantage of simplicity and clarity, which makes it easily understood by the public. A "sound currency" is an easy-to-understand rallying cry for monetary policy. In the past, for example, this aspect was important in France, where an appeal to the "franc fort" (strong franc) was often used to justify tight monetary policy.

Given its advantages, it is not surprising that exchange-rate targeting has been used successfully to control inflation in industrialized countries. Both France and the United Kingdom, for example, successfully used exchange-rate targeting to lower inflation by tying the values of their currencies to the German mark. In 1987, when France first pegged its exchange rate to the mark, its inflation rate was 3%, two percentage points above the German inflation rate. By 1992, its inflation rate had fallen to 2%, a level that can be argued is consistent with price stability, and was even below that in Germany. By 1996, the French and German inflation rates had converged, to a number slightly below 2%. Similarly, after pegging to the German mark in 1990, the United Kingdom was able to lower its inflation rate from 10% to 3% by 1992, when it was forced to abandon the exchange rate mechanism (ERM).

Exchange-rate targeting has also been an effective means of reducing inflation quickly in emerging market countries. For example, before the devaluation in Mexico in 1994, its exchange-rate target enabled it to bring inflation down from levels above 100% in 1988 to below 10% in 1994.

Disadvantages of Exchange-Rate Targeting

Despite the inherent advantages of exchange-rate targeting, there are several serious criticisms of this strategy. The problem (as we saw earlier in the chapter) is that with capital mobility the targeting country can no longer pursue its own independent monetary policy and use it to respond to domestic shocks that are independent of those hitting the anchor country. Furthermore, an exchange-rate target means that shocks to the anchor country are directly transmitted to the targeting country, because changes in interest rates in the anchor country lead to a corresponding change in interest rates in the targeting country.

A striking example of these problems occurred when Germany was reunified in 1990. In response to concerns about inflationary pressures arising from reunification and the massive fiscal expansion required to rebuild East Germany, long-term German interest rates rose until February 1991 and short-term rates rose until December 1991. This shock to the anchor country in the exchange rate mechanism (ERM) was transmitted directly to the other countries in the ERM whose currencies were pegged to the mark, and their interest rates rose in tandem with those in Germany. Continuing adherence to the exchange-rate target slowed economic growth and increased unemployment in countries such as France that remained in the ERM and adhered to the exchange-rate peg.

A second problem with exchange-rate targets is that they leave countries open to speculative attacks on their currencies. Indeed, one aftermath of German reunification was the foreign exchange crisis of September 1992. As we saw earlier, the tight monetary policy in Germany following reunification meant that the countries in the ERM were subjected to a negative demand shock that led to a decline in economic growth and a rise in unemployment. It was certainly feasible for the governments of these countries to keep their exchange rates fixed relative to the mark in these circumstances, but speculators began to question whether these countries' commitment to the exchange-rate peg would weaken. Speculators reasoned that these countries would not tolerate the rise in unemployment resulting from keeping interest rates high enough to fend off attacks on their currencies.

At this stage, speculators were, in effect, presented with a one-way bet, because the currencies of countries like France, Spain, Sweden, Italy, and the United Kingdom could go in only one direction and depreciate against the mark. Selling these currencies before the likely depreciation occurred gave speculators an attractive profit opportunity with potentially high expected returns. The result was the speculative attack in September 1992. Only in France was the commitment to the fixed exchange rate strong enough so that France did not devalue. The governments in the other countries were unwilling to defend their currencies at all costs and eventually allowed their currencies to fall in value.

The different responses of France and the United Kingdom after the September 1992 exchange-rate crisis illustrates the potential cost of an exchange-rate target. France, which continued to peg its currency to the mark and was thus unable to use monetary policy to respond to domestic conditions, found that economic growth remained slow after 1992 and unemployment increased. The United Kingdom, on the other hand, which dropped out of the ERM exchange-rate peg and adopted inflation targeting, had much better economic performance: Economic growth was higher, the unemployment rate fell, and yet its inflation was not much worse than France's.

In contrast to industrialized countries, emerging market countries (including the transition countries of Eastern Europe) may not lose much by giving up an independent monetary policy when they target exchange rates. Because many emerging market countries have not developed the political or monetary institutions that allow the successful use of discretionary monetary policy, they may have little to gain from an independent monetary policy, but a lot to lose. Thus they would be better off by, in effect, adopting the monetary policy of a country like the United States through targeting exchange rates than by pursuing their own independent policy. This is one of the reasons that so many emerging market countries have adopted exchange-rate targeting.

Nonetheless, exchange-rate targeting is highly dangerous for these countries, because it leaves them open to speculative attacks that can have far more serious consequences for their economies than for the economies of industrialized countries. Indeed, the successful speculative attacks in Mexico in 1994, East Asia in 1997, and Argentina in 2002 plunged their economies into full-scale financial crises that devastated their economies.

An additional disadvantage of an exchange-rate target is that it can weaken the accountability of policymakers, particularly in emerging market countries. Because exchange-rate targeting fixes the exchange rate, it eliminates an important signal that can help constrain monetary policy from becoming too expansionary and thereby limit the time-inconsistency problem. In industrialized countries, particularly in the United States, the bond market provides an important signal about the stance of monetary policy. Overly expansionary monetary policy or strong political pressure to engage in overly expansionary monetary policy produces an inflation scare in which inflation expectations surge, interest rates rise because of the Fisher effect (described in Chapter 5), and there is a sharp decline in long-term bond prices. Because both central banks and the politicians want to avoid this kind of scenario, overly expansionary monetary policy will be less likely.

In many countries, particularly emerging market countries, the long-term bond market is essentially nonexistent. Under a floating exchange rate regime, however, if monetary policy is too expansionary, the exchange rate will depreciate. In these countries the daily fluctuations of the exchange rate can, like the bond market in the United States, provide an early warning signal that monetary policy is too expansionary. Just as the fear of a visible inflation scare in the bond market constrains central bankers from pursuing overly expansionary monetary policy and constrains politicians from putting pressure on the central bank to engage in overly expansionary monetary policy, fear of exchange-rate depreciations can make overly expansionary monetary policy, and the time-inconsistency problem, less likely.

The need for signals from the foreign exchange market may be even more acute for emerging market countries, because the balance sheets and actions of their central banks are not as transparent as they are in industrialized countries. Targeting the exchange rate can make it even harder to ascertain the central bank's policy actions. The public is less able to keep a watch on the central bank and the politicians pressuring it, which makes it easier for monetary policy to become too expansionary.

When Is Exchange-Rate Targeting Desirable for Industrialized Countries?

Given the above disadvantages with exchange-rate targeting, when might it make sense?

In industrialized countries, the biggest cost to exchange-rate targeting is the loss of an independent monetary policy to deal with domestic considerations. If an independent, domestic monetary policy can be conducted responsibly, this can be a serious cost indeed, as the comparison between the post-1992 experiences of France and the United Kingdom indicates. However, not all industrialized countries have found that they are capable of conducting their own monetary policy successfully, either because the central bank is not independent or because political pressures on the central bank lead to an inflationary bias in monetary policy. In these cases, giving up independent control of domestic monetary policy may not be a great loss, while the gain of having monetary policy determined by a better-performing central bank in the anchor country can be substantial.

Italy provides an example: It was not a coincidence that the Italian public had the most favorable attitude of all those in Europe toward the European Monetary Union. The past record of Italian monetary policy was not good, and the Italian public recognized that having monetary policy controlled by more responsible outsiders had benefits that far outweighed the costs of losing the ability to focus monetary policy on domestic considerations.

A second reason why industrialized countries might find targeting exchange rates useful is that it encourages integration of the domestic economy with its neighbors. Clearly this was the rationale for long-standing pegging of the exchange rate to the deutsche mark by countries such as Austria and the Netherlands, and the more recent exchange-rate pegs that preceded the European Monetary Union.

To sum up, exchange-rate targeting for industrialized countries is probably not the best monetary policy strategy to control the overall economy unless (1) domestic monetary and political institutions are not conducive to good monetary policymaking or (2) there are other important benefits of an exchange-rate target that have nothing to do with monetary policy.

When Is Exchange-Rate Targeting Desirable for Emerging Market Countries?

In countries whose political and monetary institutions are particularly weak and who therefore have been experiencing continued bouts of hyperinflation, a characterization that applies to many emerging market (including transition) countries, exchange-rate targeting may be the only way to break inflationary psychology and stabilize the economy. In this situation, exchange-rate targeting is the stabilization policy of last resort. However, if the exchange-rate targeting regimes in emerging market countries are not always transparent, they are more likely to break down, often resulting in disastrous financial crises.

Are there exchange-rate strategies that make it less likely that the exchange-rate regime will break down in emerging market countries? Two such strategies that have received increasing attention in recent years are currency boards and dollarization.

Currency Boards

One solution to the problem of lack of transparency and commitment to the exchange-rate target is the adoption of a **currency board**, in which the domestic currency is backed 100% by a foreign currency (say, dollars) and in which the note-issuing authority, whether the central bank or the government, establishes a fixed exchange rate to this foreign currency and stands ready to exchange domestic currency for the foreign currency at this rate whenever the public requests it. A currency board is just a variant of a fixed exchange-rate target in which the commitment to the fixed exchange rate is especially strong because the conduct of monetary policy is in effect put on autopilot, taken completely out of the hands of the central bank and the government. In contrast, the typical fixed or pegged exchange-rate regime does allow the monetary authorities some discretion in their conduct of monetary policy because they can still adjust interest rates or print money.

A currency board arrangement thus has important advantages over a monetary policy strategy that just uses an exchange-rate target. First, the money supply can expand only when foreign currency is exchanged for domestic currency at the central bank. Thus the increased amount of domestic currency is matched by an equal increase in foreign exchange reserves. The central bank no longer has the ability to print money and thereby cause inflation. Second, the currency board involves a stronger commitment by the central bank to the fixed exchange rate and may therefore be effective in bringing down inflation quickly and in decreasing the likelihood of a successful speculative attack against the currency.

Although they solve the transparency and commitment problems inherent in an exchange-rate target regime, currency boards suffer from some of the same shortcomings: the loss of an independent monetary policy and increased exposure of the economy to shocks from the anchor country, and the loss of the central bank's ability to create money and act as a lender of last resort. Other means must therefore be used to cope with potential banking crises. Also, if there is a speculative attack on a currency board, the exchange of the domestic currency for foreign currency leads to a sharp contraction of the money supply, which can be highly damaging to the economy.

Currency boards have been established in countries such as Hong Kong (1983), Argentina (1991), Estonia (1992), Lithuania (1994), Bulgaria (1997), and Bosnia (1998). Argentina's currency board, which operated from 1991 to 2002 and required the central bank to exchange U.S. dollars for new pesos at a fixed exchange rate of 1 to 1, is one of the most interesting. For more on this subject, see the Global box, "Argentina's Currency Board."

Dollarization

Another solution to the problems created by a lack of transparency and commitment to the exchange-rate target is **dollarization**, the adoption of a sound currency, like the U.S. dollar, as a country's money. Indeed, dollarization is just another variant of a fixed exchange-rate target with an even stronger commitment mechanism than a currency board provides. A currency board can be abandoned, allowing a change in the value of the currency, but a change of value is impossible with dollarization: A dollar bill is always worth one dollar, whether it is held in the United States or outside of it.

Dollarization has been advocated as a monetary policy strategy for emerging market countries: It was discussed actively by Argentine officials in the aftermath of the devaluation of the Brazilian real in January 1999 and was adopted by Ecuador in March

Global Argentina's Currency Board

Argentina has had a long history of monetary instability, with inflation rates fluctuating dramatically and sometimes surging to beyond 1,000% per year. To end this cycle of inflationary surges, Argentina decided to adopt a currency board in April 1991. The Argentine currency board worked as follows. Under Argentina's convertibility law, the peso/dollar exchange rate was fixed at one to one, and a member of the public could go to the Argentine central bank and exchange a peso for a dollar, or vice versa, at any time.

The early years of Argentina's currency board looked stunningly successful. Inflation, which had been running at an 800% annual rate in 1990, fell to less than 5% by the end of 1994, and economic growth was rapid, averaging almost 8% per year from 1991 to 1994. In the aftermath of the Mexican peso crisis, however, concern about the health of the Argentine economy resulted in the public pulling money out of the banks (deposits fell by 18%) and exchanging pesos for dollars, thus causing a contraction of the Argentine money supply. The result was a sharp drop in Argentine economic activity, with real GDP shrinking by more than 5% in 1995 and the unemployment rate jumping above 15%. Only in 1996 did the economy begin to recover.

Because the central bank of Argentina had no control over monetary policy under the currency board system, it was relatively helpless to counteract the contractionary monetary policy stemming from the public's behavior. Furthermore, because the currency board did not allow the central bank to create pesos and lend them to the banks, it had very little capability to act as a lender of last resort. With help from international agencies, such as the IMF, the World Bank, and the Interamerican Development Bank, which lent Argentina more than $5 billion in 1995 to help shore up its banking system, the currency board survived.

However, in 1998 Argentina entered another recession, which was both severe and very long lasting. By the end of 2001, unemployment reached nearly 20%, a level comparable to that experienced in the United States during the Great Depression of the 1930s. The result has been civil unrest and the fall of the elected government, as well as a major banking crisis and a default on nearly $150 billion of government debt. Because the Central Bank of Argentina had no control over monetary policy under the currency board system, it was unable to use monetary policy to expand the economy and get out of its recession. Furthermore, because the currency board did not allow the central bank to create pesos and lend them to banks, it had very little capability to act as a lender of last resort. In January 2002, the currency board finally collapsed and the peso depreciated by more than 70%. The result was the full-scale financial crisis described in Chapter 8, with inflation shooting up and an extremely severe depression. Clearly, the Argentine public is not as enamored of its currency board as it once was.

2000. Dollarization's key advantage is that it completely avoids the possibility of a speculative attack on the domestic currency (because there is none). (Such an attack is still a danger even under a currency board arrangement.)

Dollarization is subject to the usual disadvantages of an exchange-rate target (the loss of an independent monetary policy, increased exposure of the economy to shocks from the anchor country, and the inability of the central bank to create money and act as a lender of last resort). Dollarization has one additional disadvantage not characteristic of currency boards or other exchange-rate target regimes. Because a country adopting dollarization no longer has its own currency, it loses the revenue that a government receives by issuing money, which is called **seignorage**. Because governments (or their central banks) do not have to pay interest on their currency, they earn revenue (seignorage) by using this currency to purchase income-earning assets such as bonds. In the case of the Federal Reserve in the United States, this revenue is on the order of $30 billion per year. If an emerging market country dollarizes and gives up its currency, it needs to make up this loss of revenue somewhere, which is not always easy for a poor country.

SUMMARY

1. An unsterilized central bank intervention in which the domestic currency is sold to purchase foreign assets leads to a gain in international reserves, an increase in the money supply, and a depreciation of the domestic currency. Available evidence suggests, however, that sterilized central bank interventions have little long-term effect on the exchange rate.
2. The balance of payments is a bookkeeping system for recording all payments between a country and foreign countries that have a direct bearing on the movement of funds between them. The official reserve transactions balance is the sum of the current account balance plus the items in the capital account. It indicates the amount of international reserves that must be moved between countries to finance international transactions.
3. Before World War I, the gold standard was predominant. Currencies were convertible into gold, thus fixing exchange rates between countries. After World War II, the Bretton Woods system and the IMF were established to promote a fixed exchange rate system in which the U.S. dollar was convertible into gold. The Bretton Woods system collapsed in 1971. We now have an international financial system that has elements of a managed float and a fixed exchange rate system. Some exchange rates fluctuate from day to day, although central banks intervene in the foreign exchange market, while other exchange rates are fixed.
4. Controls on capital outflows receive support because they may prevent domestic residents and foreigners from pulling capital out of a country during a crisis and make devaluation less likely. Controls on capital inflows make sense under the theory that if speculative capital cannot flow in, then it cannot go out suddenly and create a crisis. However, capital controls suffer from several disadvantages: They are seldom effective, they lead to corruption, and they may allow governments to avoid taking the steps needed to reform their financial systems to deal with the crisis.
5. The IMF has recently taken on the role of an international lender of last resort. Because central banks in emerging market countries are unlikely to be able to perform a lender-of-last-resort operation successfully, an international lender of last resort like the IMF is needed to prevent financial instability. However, the IMF's role as an international lender of last resort creates a serious moral hazard problem that can encourage excessive risk taking and make a financial crisis more likely, but refusing to lend may be politically hard to do. In addition, it needs to be able to provide liquidity quickly during a crisis to keep manageable the amount of funds lent.
6. Three international considerations affect the conduct of monetary policy: direct effects of the foreign exchange market on the money supply, balance-of-payments considerations, and exchange rate considerations. Inasmuch as the United States has been a reserve currency country in the post–World War II period, U.S. monetary policy has been less affected by developments in the foreign exchange market and its balance of payments than is true for other countries. However, in recent years, exchange rate considerations have been playing a more prominent role in influencing U.S. monetary policy.
7. Exchange-rate targeting has the following advantages as a monetary policy strategy: (1) It directly keeps inflation under control by tying the inflation rate for internationally traded goods to that found in the anchor country to whom its currency is pegged; (2) it provides an automatic rule for the conduct of monetary policy that helps mitigate the time-inconsistency problem; and (3) it is simple and clear. Exchange-rate targeting also has serious disadvantages: (1) It results in a loss of independent monetary policy; (2) it leaves the country open to speculative attacks; and (3) it can weaken the accountability of policymakers because the exchange-rate signal is lost. Two strategies that make it less likely that the exchange-rate regime will break down are currency boards, in which the central bank stands ready to automatically exchange domestic for foreign currency at a fixed rate, and dollarization, in which a sound currency like the U.S. dollar is adopted as the country's money.

KEY TERMS

anchor currency, p. 537
balance of payments, p. 536
balance-of-payments crisis, p. 546
Bretton Woods system, p. 538
capital account, p. 536
currency board, p. 557
current account, p. 536
devaluation, p. 541
dollarization, p. 557
fixed exchange rate regime, p. 537
floating exchange rate regime, p. 538
foreign exchange interventions, p. 531
gold standard, p. 538
International Monetary Fund (IMF), p. 538
international reserves, p. 531
managed float regime (dirty float), p. 538
official reserve transactions balance, p. 536
reserve currency, p. 539
revaluation, p. 541
seignorage, p. 558
special drawing rights (SDRs), p. 543
sterilized foreign exchange intervention, p. 534
trade balance, p. 536
unsterilized foreign exchange intervention, p. 533
World Bank, p. 538
World Trade Organization (WTO), p. 539

QUESTIONS AND PROBLEMS

Questions marked with an asterisk are answered at the end of the book in an appendix, "Answers to Selected Questions and Problems." Questions marked with a blue circle indicate the question is available in MyEconLab at www.myeconlab.com/mishkin.

1. If the Federal Reserve buys dollars in the foreign exchange market but conducts an offsetting open market operation to sterilize the intervention, what will be the impact on international reserves, the money supply, and the exchange rate?

*2. If the Federal Reserve buys dollars in the foreign exchange market but does not sterilize the intervention, what will be the impact on international reserves, the money supply, and the exchange rate?

3. For each of the following, identify in which part of the balance-of-payments account it appears (current account, capital account, or net change in international reserves) and whether it is a receipt or a payment.
   a. A British subject's purchase of a share of Johnson & Johnson stock
   b. An American's purchase of an airline ticket from Air France
   c. The Swiss government's purchase of U.S. Treasury bills
   d. A Japanese's purchase of California oranges
   e. $50 million of foreign aid to Honduras
   f. A loan by an American bank to Mexico
   g. An American bank's borrowing of Eurodollars

*4. Why does a balance-of-payments deficit for the United States have a different effect on its international reserves than a balance-of-payments deficit for the Netherlands?

5. Under the gold standard, if Britain became more productive relative to the United States, what would happen to the money supply in the two countries? Why would the changes in the money supply help preserve a fixed exchange rate between the United States and Britain?

*6. What is the exchange rate between dollars and Swiss francs if one dollar is convertible into $\frac{1}{20}$ ounce of gold and one Swiss franc is convertible into $\frac{1}{40}$ ounce of gold?

7. If a country's par exchange rate was undervalued during the Bretton Woods fixed exchange rate regime, what kind of intervention would that country's central bank be forced to undertake, and what effect would it have on its international reserves and the money supply?

*8. How can a large balance-of-payments surplus contribute to the country's inflation rate?

9. "If a country wants to keep its exchange rate from changing, it must give up some control over its money supply." Is this statement true, false, or uncertain? Explain your answer.

*10. Why can balance-of-payments deficits force some countries to implement a contractionary monetary policy?

11. "Balance-of-payments deficits always cause a country to lose international reserves." Is this statement true, false, or uncertain? Explain your answer.

*12. How can persistent U.S. balance-of-payments deficits stimulate world inflation?

13. "Inflation is not possible under the gold standard." Is this statement true, false, or uncertain? Explain your answer.

*14. Why is it that in a pure flexible exchange rate system, the foreign exchange market has no direct effects on the money supply? Does this mean that the foreign exchange market has no effect on monetary policy?

15. "The abandonment of fixed exchange rates after 1973 has meant that countries have pursued more independent monetary policies." Is this statement true, false, or uncertain? Explain your answer.

*16. What are the key advantages of exchange-rate targeting as a monetary policy strategy?

17. Why did the exchange-rate peg lead to difficulties for the countries in the ERM when German reunification occurred?

*18. How can exchange-rate targets lead to a speculative attack on a currency?

19. Why may the disadvantage of exchange-rate targeting of not having an independent monetary policy be less of an issue for emerging market countries than for industrialized countries?

*20. How can the long-term bond market help reduce the time-inconsistency problem for monetary policy? Can the foreign exchange market also perform this role?

21. When is exchange-rate targeting likely to be a sensible strategy for industrialized countries? When is exchange-rate targeting likely to be a sensible strategy for emerging market countries?

*22. What are the advantages and disadvantages of a currency board over a monetary policy that just uses an exchange-rate target?

23. What are the key advantages and disadvantages of dollarization over other forms of exchange-rate targeting?

WEB EXERCISES

1. The Federal Reserve publishes information online that explains the workings of the foreign exchange market. One such publication can be found at www.ny.frb.org/pihome/addpub/usfxm/. Review the table of contents and open Chapter 10, the evolution of the international monetary system. Read this chapter and write a one-page summary that discusses why each monetary standard was dropped in favor of the succeeding one.

2. The International Monetary Fund stands ready to help nations facing monetary crises. Go to www.imf.org. Click on the tab labeled "About IMF." What is the stated purpose of the IMF? How many nations participate and when was it established?

WEB REFERENCES

http://research.stlouisfed.org/fred2

This web site contains exchange rates, balance of payments, and trade data.

www.imf.org/external/np/exr/facts/sdr.htm

Find information about special drawing rights, allocation, valuation, and SDR users' guide.

http://users.erols.com/kurrency/intro.htm

A detailed discussion of the history, purpose, and function of currency boards.

PART 6

Monetary Theory

CHAPTER

22 The Demand for Money

Preview

In earlier chapters, we spent a lot of time and effort learning what the money supply is, how it is determined, and what role the Federal Reserve System plays in it. Now we are ready to explore the role of the money supply in determining the price level and total production of goods and services (aggregate output) in the economy. The study of the effect of money on the economy is called **monetary theory**, and we examine this branch of economics in the chapters of Part VI.

When economists mention *supply*, the word *demand* is sure to follow, and the discussion of money is no exception. The supply of money is an essential building block in understanding how monetary policy affects the economy, because it suggests the factors that influence the quantity of money in the economy. Not surprisingly, another essential part of monetary theory is the demand for money.

This chapter describes how the theories of the demand for money have evolved. We begin with the classical theories refined at the start of the twentieth century by economists such as Irving Fisher, Alfred Marshall, and A. C. Pigou; then we move on to the Keynesian theories of the demand for money. We end with Milton Friedman's modern quantity theory.

A central question in monetary theory is whether or to what extent the quantity of money demanded is affected by changes in interest rates. Because this issue is crucial to how we view money's effects on aggregate economic activity, we focus on the role of interest rates in the demand for money.

QUANTITY THEORY OF MONEY

Developed by the classical economists in the nineteenth and early twentieth centuries, the quantity theory of money is a theory of how the nominal value of aggregate income is determined. Because it also tells us how much money is held for a given amount of aggregate income, it is a theory of the demand for money. The most important feature of this theory is that it suggests that interest rates have no effect on the demand for money.

Velocity of Money and Equation of Exchange

The clearest exposition of the classical quantity theory approach is found in the work of the American economist Irving Fisher, in his influential book *The Purchasing Power of Money*, published in 1911. Fisher wanted to examine the link between the total quantity of money M (the money supply) and the total amount of spending on final goods and services produced in the economy $P \times Y$, where P is the price level and Y is aggregate output (income). (Total spending $P \times Y$ is also thought of as aggregate nominal income for the economy or as nominal GDP.) The concept that provides the link between M and $P \times Y$ is called the **velocity of money** (often reduced to *velocity*), the average number of times per year (turnover) that a dollar is spent in buying the total amount of goods and services produced in the economy. Velocity V is defined more precisely as total spending $P \times Y$ divided by the quantity of money M:

$$V = \frac{P \times Y}{M} \tag{1}$$

If, for example, nominal GDP ($P \times Y$) in a year is \$5 trillion and the quantity of money is \$1 trillion, velocity is 5, meaning that the average dollar bill is spent five times in purchasing final goods and services in the economy.

By multiplying both sides of this definition by M, we obtain the **equation of exchange**, which relates nominal income to the quantity of money and velocity:

$$M \times V = P \times Y \tag{2}$$

The equation of exchange thus states that the quantity of money multiplied by the number of times that this money is spent in a given year must equal nominal income (the total nominal amount spent on goods and services in that year).[1]

As it stands, Equation 2 is nothing more than an identity—a relationship that is true by definition. It does not tell us, for instance, that when the money supply M changes, nominal income ($P \times Y$) changes in the same direction; a rise in M, for example, could be offset by a fall in V that leaves $M \times V$ (and therefore $P \times Y$) unchanged. To convert the equation of exchange (an *identity*) into a *theory* of how nominal income is determined requires an understanding of the factors that determine velocity.

Irving Fisher reasoned that velocity is determined by the institutions in an economy that affect the way individuals conduct transactions. If people use charge accounts and credit cards to conduct their transactions, as they can today, and consequently use money less often when making purchases, less money is required to conduct the transactions generated by nominal income (M falls relative to $P \times Y$), and velocity $(P \times Y)/M$ will increase. Conversely, if it is more convenient for purchases to be paid for with cash or checks (both of which are money), more money is used to conduct the transactions generated by the same level of nominal income, and velocity will fall. Fisher took the

---

[1]Fisher actually first formulated the equation of exchange in terms of the nominal value of transactions in the economy PT:

$$MV_T = PT$$

where P = average price per transaction
T = number of transactions conducted in a year.
$V_T = PT/M$ = transactions velocity of money

Because the nominal value of transactions T is difficult to measure, the quantity theory has been formulated in terms of aggregate output Y as follows: T is assumed to be proportional to Y so that $T = vY$, where v is a constant of proportionality. Substituting vY for T in Fisher's equation of exchange yields $MV_T = vPY$, which can be written as Equation 2 in the text, in which $V = V_T/v$.

view that the institutional and technological features of the economy would affect velocity only slowly over time, so velocity would normally be reasonably constant in the short run.

Quantity Theory

Fisher's view that velocity is fairly constant in the short run transforms the equation of exchange into the **quantity theory of money**, which states that nominal income is determined solely by movements in the quantity of money: When the quantity of money M doubles, $M \times V$ doubles and so must $P \times Y$, the value of nominal income. To see how this works, let's assume that velocity is 5, nominal income (GDP) is initially \$5 trillion, and the money supply is \$1 trillion. If the money supply doubles to \$2 trillion, the quantity theory of money tells us that nominal income will double to \$10 trillion (= 5 × \$2 trillion).

Because the classical economists (including Fisher) thought that wages and prices were completely flexible, they believed that the level of aggregate output Y produced in the economy during normal times would remain at the full-employment level, so Y in the equation of exchange could also be treated as reasonably constant in the short run. The quantity theory of money then implies that if M doubles, P must also double in the short run, because V and Y are constant. In our example, if aggregate output is \$5 trillion, the velocity of 5 and a money supply of \$1 trillion indicate that the price level equals 1 because 1 times \$5 trillion equals the nominal income of \$5 trillion. When the money supply doubles to \$2 trillion, the price level must also double to 2 because 2 times \$5 trillion equals the nominal income of \$10 trillion.

For the classical economists, the quantity theory of money provided an explanation of movements in the price level: ***Movements in the price level result solely from changes in the quantity of money.***

Quantity Theory of Money Demand

Because the quantity theory of money tells us how much money is held for a given amount of aggregate income, it is, in fact, a theory of the demand for money. We can see this by dividing both sides of the equation of exchange by V, thus rewriting it as

$$M = \frac{1}{V} \times PY$$

where nominal income $P \times Y$ is written as PY. When the money market is in equilibrium, the quantity of money M that people hold equals the quantity of money demanded M^d, so we can replace M in the equation by M^d. Using k to represent the quantity $1/V$ (a constant, because V is a constant), we can rewrite the equation as

$$M^d = k \times PY \tag{3}$$

Equation 3 tells us that because k is a constant, the level of transactions generated by a fixed level of nominal income PY determines the quantity of money M^d that people demand. Therefore, Fisher's quantity theory of money suggests that the demand for money is purely a function of income, and interest rates have no effect on the demand for money.[2]

[2]While Fisher was developing his quantity theory approach to the demand for money, a group of classical economists in Cambridge, England led by Alfred Marshall and A. C. Pigou, came to similar conclusions, although with slightly different reasoning. They derived Equation 3 by recognizing that two properties of money motivate people to hold it: its utility as a medium of exchange and as a store of wealth.

Fisher came to this conclusion because he believed that people hold money only to conduct transactions and have no freedom of action in terms of the amount they want to hold. The demand for money is determined (1) by the level of transactions generated by the level of nominal income *PY* and (2) by the institutions in the economy that affect the way people conduct transactions and thus determine velocity and hence *k*.

IS VELOCITY A CONSTANT?

The classical economists' conclusion that nominal income is determined by movements in the money supply rested on their belief that velocity *PY/M* could be treated as reasonably constant.[3] Is it reasonable to assume that velocity is constant? To answer this, let's look at Figure 1, which shows the year-to-year changes in velocity from 1915 to 2005 (nominal income is represented by nominal GDP and the money supply by M1 and M2).

What we see in Figure 1 is that even in the short run, velocity fluctuates too much to be viewed as a constant. Prior to 1950, velocity exhibited large swings up and down. This may reflect the substantial instability of the economy in this period, which included two world wars and the Great Depression. (Velocity actually falls, or at least its rate of growth declines, in years when recessions are taking place.) After 1950, veloc-

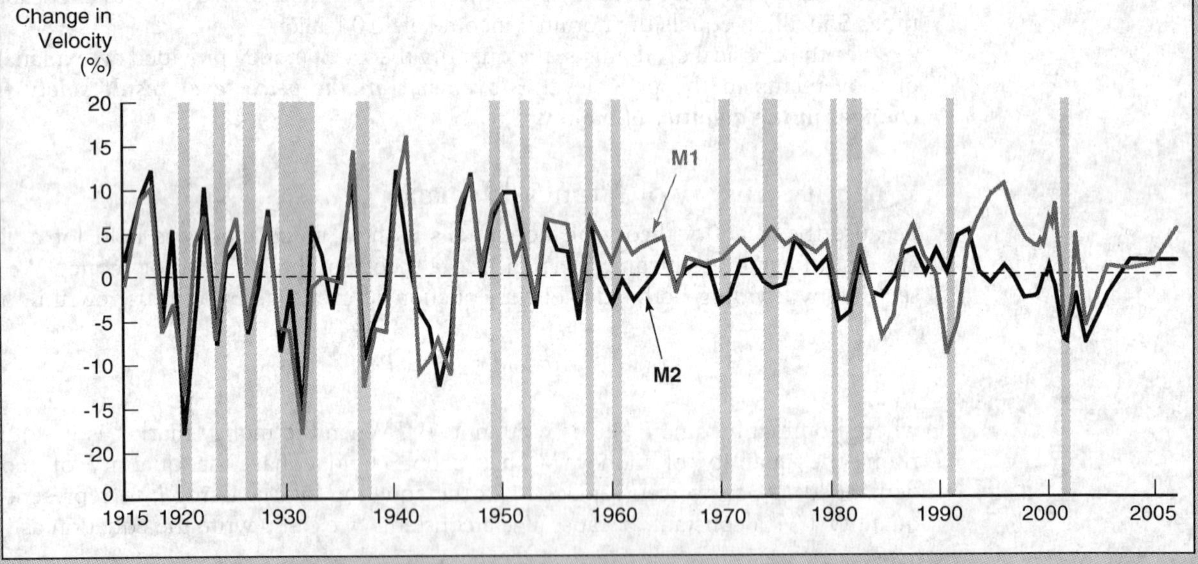

FIGURE 1 **Change in the Velocity of M1 and M2 from Year to Year, 1915–2005**
Shaded areas indicate recessions. Velocities are calculated using nominal GNP before 1959 and nominal GDP thereafter.

Sources: Economic Report of the President; Banking and Monetary Statistics; www.federalreserve.gov/releases/h6/.

[3]Actually, the classical conclusion still holds if velocity grows at some uniform rate over time that reflects changes in transaction technology. Hence the concept of a constant velocity should more accurately be thought of here as a lack of upward and downward fluctuations in velocity.

ity appears to have more moderate fluctuations, yet there are large differences in the growth rate of velocity from year to year. The percentage change in M1 velocity (GDP/M1) from 1981 to 1982, for example, was −2.5%, whereas from 1980 to 1981 velocity grew at a rate of 4.2%. This difference of 6.7% means that nominal GDP was 6.7% lower than it would have been if velocity had kept growing at the same rate as in 1980–1981.[4] The drop is enough to account for the severe recession that took place in 1981–1982. After 1982, M1 velocity appears to have become even more volatile, a fact that has puzzled researchers when they examine the empirical evidence on the demand for money (discussed later in this chapter). M2 velocity remained more stable than M1 velocity after 1982, with the result that the Federal Reserve dropped its M1 targets in 1987 and began to focus more on M2 targets. However, instability of M2 velocity in the early 1990s resulted in the Fed's announcement in July 1993 that it no longer felt that any of the monetary aggregates, including M2, was a reliable guide for monetary policy.

Until the Great Depression, economists did not recognize that velocity declines sharply during severe economic contractions. Why did the classical economists not recognize this fact when it is easy to see in the pre-Depression period in Figure 1? Unfortunately, accurate data on GDP and the money supply did not exist before World War II. (Only after the war did the government start to collect these data.) Economists had no way of knowing that their view of velocity as a constant was demonstrably false. The decline in velocity during the Great Depression years was so great, however, that even the crude data available to economists at that time suggested that velocity was not constant. This explains why, after the Great Depression, economists began to search for other factors influencing the demand for money that might help explain the large fluctuations in velocity.

Let us now examine the theories of money demand that arose from this search for a better explanation of the behavior of velocity.

KEYNES'S LIQUIDITY PREFERENCE THEORY

In his famous 1936 book *The General Theory of Employment, Interest, and Money*, John Maynard Keynes abandoned the classical view that velocity was a constant and developed a theory of money demand that emphasized the importance of interest rates. His theory of the demand for money, which he called the **liquidity preference theory**, asked the question: Why do individuals hold money? He postulated that there are three motives behind the demand for money: the transactions motive, the precautionary motive, and the speculative motive.

Transactions Motive

In the classical approach, individuals are assumed to hold money because it is a medium of exchange that can be used to carry out everyday transactions. Following the classical tradition, Keynes emphasized that this component of the demand for money is determined primarily by the level of people's transactions. Because he believed that these transactions were proportional to income, like the classical economists, he took the transactions component of the demand for money to be proportional to income.

[4]We reach a similar conclusion if we use M2 velocity. The percentage change in M2 velocity (GDP/M2) from 1981 to 1982 was −5.0%, whereas from 1980 to 1981 it was +2.3%. This difference of 7.3% means that nominal GDP was 7.3% lower than it would have been if M2 velocity had kept growing at the same rate as in 1980–1981.

Precautionary Motive

Keynes went beyond the classical analysis by recognizing that in addition to holding money to carry out current transactions, people hold money as a cushion against an unexpected need. Suppose that you've been thinking about buying a fancy stereo; you walk by a store that is having a 50%-off sale on the one you want. If you are holding money as a precaution for just such an occurrence, you can purchase the stereo right away; if you are not holding precautionary money balances, you cannot take advantage of the sale. Precautionary money balances also come in handy if you are hit with an unexpected bill—say, for car repair or hospitalization.

Keynes believed that the precautionary money balances people want to hold are determined primarily by the level of transactions that they expect to make in the future and that these transactions are proportional to income. Therefore, he postulated, the demand for precautionary money balances is proportional to income.

Speculative Motive

If Keynes had ended his theory with the transactions and precautionary motives, income would be the only important determinant of the demand for money, and he would not have added much to the classical approach. However, Keynes took the view that people also hold money as a store of wealth. He called this reason for holding money the *speculative motive*. Because he believed that wealth is tied closely to income, the speculative component of money demand would be related to income. However, Keynes looked more carefully at other factors that influence the decisions regarding how much money to hold as a store of wealth, especially interest rates.

Keynes divided the assets that can be used to store wealth into two categories: money and bonds. He then asked the following question: Why would individuals decide to hold their wealth in the form of money rather than bonds?

Thinking back to the discussion of the theory of asset demand (Chapter 5), you would want to hold money if its expected return was greater than the expected return from holding bonds. Keynes assumed that the expected return on money was zero because in his time, unlike today, most checkable deposits did not earn interest. For bonds, there are two components of the expected return: the interest payment and the *expected* rate of capital gains.

You learned in Chapter 4 that when interest rates rise, the price of a bond falls. If you expect interest rates to rise, you expect the price of the bond to fall and therefore suffer a negative capital gain—that is, a capital loss. If you expect the rise in interest rates to be substantial enough, the capital loss might outweigh the interest payment, and your *expected* return on the bond would be negative. In this case, you would want to store your wealth as money because its expected return is higher; its zero return exceeds the negative return on the bond.

Keynes assumed that individuals believe that interest rates gravitate to some normal value (an assumption less plausible in today's world). If interest rates are below this normal value, individuals expect the interest rate on bonds to rise in the future and so expect to suffer capital losses on them. As a result, individuals will be more likely to hold their wealth as money rather than bonds, and the demand for money will be high.

What would you expect to happen to the demand for money when interest rates are above the normal value? In general, people will expect interest rates to fall, bond prices to rise, and capital gains to be realized. At higher interest rates, they are more likely to expect the return from holding a bond to be positive, thus exceeding the expected return from holding money. They will be more likely to hold bonds than money, and the demand for money will be quite low. From Keynes's reasoning, we can conclude that as interest rates rise, the demand for money falls, and therefore ***money demand is negatively related to the level of interest rates***.

Putting the Three Motives Together

In putting the three motives for holding money balances together into a demand for money equation, Keynes was careful to distinguish between nominal quantities and real quantities. Money is valued in terms of what it can buy. If, for example, all prices in the economy double (the price level doubles), the same nominal quantity of money will be able to buy only half as many goods. Keynes thus reasoned that people want to hold a certain amount of **real money balances** (the quantity of money in real terms)—an amount that his three motives indicated would be related to real income Y and to interest rates i. Keynes wrote down the following demand for money equation, known as the *liquidity preference function*, which says that the demand for real money balances M^d/P is a function of (related to) i and Y:[5]

$$\frac{M^d}{P} = f(\underset{-}{i}, \underset{+}{Y}) \tag{4}$$

The minus sign below i in the liquidity preference function means that the demand for real money balances is negatively related to the interest rate i, and the plus sign below Y means that the demand for real money balances and real income Y are positively related. This money demand function is the same one used in our analysis of money demand in Chapter 5. Keynes's conclusion that the demand for money is related not only to income but also to interest rates is a major departure from Fisher's view of money demand, in which interest rates have no effect on the demand for money.

By deriving the liquidity preference function for velocity PY/M, we can see that Keynes's theory of the demand for money implies that velocity is not constant, but instead fluctuates with movements in interest rates. The liquidity preference equation can be rewritten as

$$\frac{P}{M^d} = \frac{1}{f(i, Y)}$$

Multiplying both sides of this equation by Y and recognizing that M^d can be replaced by M because they must be equal in money market equilibrium, we solve for velocity:

$$V = \frac{PY}{M} = \frac{Y}{f(i, Y)} \tag{5}$$

We know that the demand for money is negatively related to interest rates; when i goes up, $f(i, Y)$ declines, and therefore velocity rises. In other words, a rise in interest rates encourages people to hold lower real money balances for a given level of income; therefore, the rate at which money turns over (velocity) must be higher. This reasoning

---

[5]The classical economists' money demand equation can also be written in terms of real money balances by dividing both sides of Equation 3 by the price level P to obtain:

$$\frac{M^d}{P} = k \times Y$$

implies that because interest rates have substantial fluctuations, the liquidity preference theory of the demand for money indicates that velocity has substantial fluctuations as well.

An interesting feature of Equation 5 is that it explains some of the velocity movements in Figure 1, in which we noted that when recessions occur, velocity falls or its rate of growth declines. What fact regarding the cyclical behavior of interest rates (discussed in Chapter 5) might help us explain this phenomenon? You might recall that interest rates are procyclical, rising in expansions and falling in recessions. The liquidity preference theory indicates that a rise in interest rates will cause velocity to rise also. The procyclical movements of interest rates should induce procyclical movements in velocity, and that is exactly what we see in Figure 1.

Keynes's model of the speculative demand for money provides another reason why velocity might show substantial fluctuations. What would happen to the demand for money if the view of the normal level to which interest rates gravitate changes? For example, what if people expect the future normal interest rate to be higher than the current normal interest rate? Because interest rates are then expected to be higher in the future, more people will expect the prices of bonds to fall and will anticipate capital losses. The expected returns from holding bonds will decline, and money will become more attractive relative to bonds. As a result, the demand for money will increase. This means that $f(i, Y)$ will increase and so velocity will fall. Velocity will change as expectations about future normal levels of interest rates change, and unstable expectations about future movements in normal interest rates can lead to instability of velocity. This is one more reason why Keynes rejected the view that velocity could be treated as a constant.

STUDY GUIDE

Keynes's explanation of how interest rates affect the demand for money will be easier to understand if you think of yourself as an investor who is trying to decide whether to invest in bonds or to hold money. Ask yourself what you would do if you expected the normal interest rate to be lower in the future than it is currently. Would you rather be holding bonds or money?

In summary, Keynes's liquidity preference theory postulated three motives for holding money: the transactions motive, the precautionary motive, and the speculative motive. Although Keynes took the transactions and precautionary components of the demand for money to be proportional to income, he reasoned that the speculative motive would be negatively related to the level of interest rates.

Keynes's model of the demand for money has the important implication that velocity is not constant, but instead is positively related to interest rates, which fluctuate substantially. His theory also rejected the constancy of velocity, because changes in people's expectations about the normal level of interest rates would cause shifts in the demand for money that would cause velocity to shift as well. Thus Keynes's liquidity preference theory casts doubt on the classical quantity theory that nominal income is determined primarily by movements in the quantity of money.

FURTHER DEVELOPMENTS IN THE KEYNESIAN APPROACH

After World War II, economists began to take the Keynesian approach to the demand for money even further by developing more precise theories to explain the three Keynesian motives for holding money. Because interest rates were viewed as a crucial element in monetary theory, a key focus of this research was to understand better the role of interest rates in the demand for money.

Transactions Demand

William Baumol and James Tobin independently developed similar demand for money models, which demonstrated that even money balances held for transactions purposes are sensitive to the level of interest rates.[6] In developing their models, they considered a hypothetical individual who receives a payment once a period and spends it over the course of this period. In their model, money, which earns zero interest, is held only because it can be used to carry out transactions.

To refine this analysis, let's say that Grant Smith receives $1,000 at the beginning of the month and spends it on transactions that occur at a constant rate during the course of the month. If Grant keeps the $1,000 in cash to carry out his transactions, his money balances follow the sawtooth pattern displayed in panel (a) of Figure 2. At the beginning of the month he has $1,000, and by the end of the month he has no cash left because he has spent it all. Over the course of the month, his holdings of money will on average be $500 (his holdings at the beginning of the month, $1,000, plus his holdings at the end of the month, $0, divided by 2).

At the beginning of the next month, Grant receives another $1,000 payment, which he holds as cash, and the same decline in money balances begins again. This process repeats monthly, and his average money balance during the course of the year is $500. Since his yearly nominal income is $12,000 and his holdings of money average $500, the velocity of money ($V = PY/M$) is $12,000/$500 = 24.

Suppose that as a result of taking a money and banking course, Grant realizes that he can improve his situation by not always holding cash. In January, then, he decides to hold part of his $1,000 in cash and puts part of it into an income-earning security such as bonds. At the beginning of each month, Grant keeps $500 in cash and uses the other $500 to buy a Treasury bond. As you can see in panel (b), he starts out each month with $500 of cash, and by the middle of the month, his cash balance has run down to zero. Because bonds cannot be used directly to carry out transactions, Grant must sell them and turn them into cash so that he can carry out the rest of the month's transactions. At the middle of the month, then, Grant's cash balance rises back up to $500. By the end of the month, the cash is gone. When he again receives his next $1,000 monthly payment, he again divides it into $500 of cash and $500 of bonds, and the process continues. The net result of this process is that the average cash balance held during the month is $500/2 = $250—just half of what it was before. Velocity has doubled to $12,000/$250 = 48.

[6]William J. Baumol, "The Transactions Demand for Cash: An Inventory Theoretic Approach," *Quarterly Journal of Economics* 66 (1952): 545–556; James Tobin, "The Interest Elasticity of the Transactions Demand for Cash," *Review of Economics and Statistics* 38 (1956): 241–247.

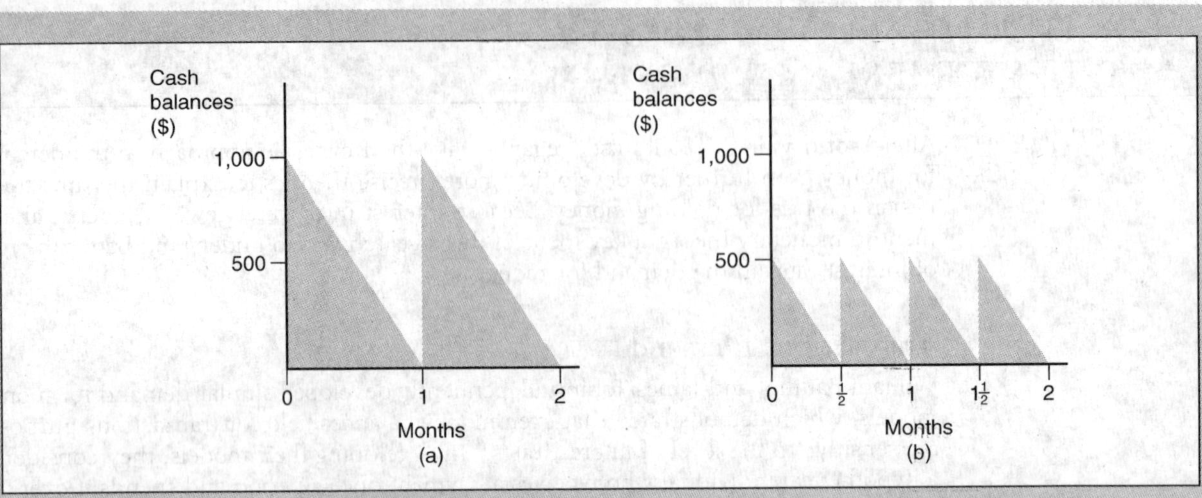

FIGURE 2 **Cash Balances in the Baumol-Tobin Model**
In panel (a), the $1,000 payment at the beginning of the month is held entirely in cash and is spent at a constant rate until it is exhausted by the end of the month. In panel (b), half of the monthly payment is put into cash and the other half into bonds. At the middle of the month, cash balances reach zero and bonds must be sold to bring balances up to $500. By the end of the month, cash balances again dwindle to zero.

What has Grant Smith gained from his new strategy? He has earned interest on $500 of bonds that he held for half the month. If the interest rate is 1% per month, he has earned an additional $2.50 (= $^1/_2$ × $500 × 1%) per month.

Sounds like a pretty good deal, doesn't it? In fact, if he had kept $333.33 in cash at the beginning of the month, he would have been able to hold $666.67 in bonds for the first third of the month. Then he could have sold $333.33 of bonds and held on to $333.34 of bonds for the next third of the month. Finally, two-thirds of the way through the month, he would have had to sell the remaining bonds to raise cash. The net result of this is that Grant would have earned $3.33 per month [= ($^1/_3$ × $666.67 × 1%) + ($^1/_3$ × $333.34 × 1%)]. This is an even better deal. His average cash holdings in this case would be $333.33/2 = $166.67. Clearly, the lower his average cash balance, the more interest he will earn.

As you might expect, there is a catch to all this. In buying bonds, Grant incurs transaction costs of two types. First, he must pay a straight brokerage fee for the buying and selling of the bonds. These fees increase when average cash balances are lower because Grant will be buying and selling bonds more often. Second, by holding less cash, he will have to take time to sell the bonds to get the cash. Because time is money, this must also be counted as part of the transaction costs.

Grant faces a trade-off. If he holds very little cash, he can earn a lot of interest on bonds, but he will incur greater transaction costs. If the interest rate is high, the benefits of holding bonds will be high relative to the transaction costs, and he will hold more bonds and less cash. Conversely, if interest rates are low, the transaction costs involved in holding a lot of bonds may outweigh the interest payments, and Grant would then be better off holding more cash and fewer bonds.

The conclusion of the Baumol-Tobin analysis may be stated as follows: As interest rates increase, the amount of cash held for transactions purposes will decline, which in turn means that velocity will increase as interest rates increase.[7] Put another way, the ***transactions component of the demand for money is negatively related to the level of interest rates***.

The basic idea in the Baumol-Tobin analysis is that there is an opportunity cost of holding money—the interest that can be earned on other assets. There is also a benefit to holding money—the avoidance of transaction costs. When interest rates increase, people will try to economize on their holdings of money for transactions purposes, because the opportunity cost of holding money has increased. By using simple models, Baumol and Tobin revealed something that we might not otherwise have seen: that the transactions demand for money, and not just the speculative demand, will be sensitive to interest rates. The Baumol-Tobin analysis presents a nice demonstration of the value of economic modeling.[8]

STUDY GUIDE

The idea that as interest rates increase, the opportunity cost of holding money increases so that the demand for money falls, can be stated equivalently with the terminology of expected returns used in Chapter 5. As interest rates increase, the expected return on the other asset, bonds, increases, causing the relative expected return on money to fall, thereby lowering the demand for money. These two explanations are in fact identical, because as we saw in Chapter 5, changes in the opportunity cost of an asset are just a description of what is happening to the relative expected return. Baumol and Tobin used opportunity cost terminology in their work on the transactions demand for money, and that is why we used this terminology in the text. To make sure you understand the equivalence of the two terminologies, try to translate the reasoning in the precautionary demand discussion from opportunity cost terminology to expected returns terminology.

Precautionary Demand

Models that explore the precautionary motive of the demand for money have been developed along lines similar to the Baumol-Tobin framework, so we will not go into great detail about them here. We have already discussed the benefits of holding precautionary money balances, but weighed against these benefits must be the opportunity cost of the interest forgone by holding money. We therefore have a trade-off similar to the one for transactions balances. As interest rates rise, the opportunity cost of holding

[7]Similar reasoning leads to the conclusion that as brokerage fees increase, the demand for transactions money balances increases as well. When these fees rise, the benefits from holding transactions money balances increase because by holding these balances, an individual will not have to sell bonds as often, thereby avoiding these higher brokerage costs. The greater benefits to holding money balances relative to the opportunity cost of interest forgone, then, lead to a higher demand for transactions balances.

[8]The mathematics behind the Baumol-Tobin model can be found in an appendix to this chapter on this book's web site at www.myeconlab.com/mishkin.

precautionary balances rises, so the holdings of these money balances fall. We then have a result similar to the one found for the Baumol-Tobin analysis.[9] ***The precautionary demand for money is negatively related to interest rates.***

Speculative Demand

Keynes's analysis of the speculative demand for money was open to several serious criticisms. It indicated that an individual holds only money as a store of wealth when the expected return on bonds is less than the expected return on money and holds only bonds when the expected return on bonds is greater than the expected return on money. Only when people have expected returns on bonds and money that are exactly equal (a rare instance) would they hold both. Keynes's analysis therefore implies that practically no one holds a diversified portfolio of bonds and money simultaneously as a store of wealth. Because diversification is apparently a sensible strategy for choosing which assets to hold, the fact that it rarely occurs in Keynes's analysis is a serious shortcoming of his theory of the speculative demand for money.

Tobin developed a model of the speculative demand for money that attempted to avoid this criticism of Keynes's analysis.[10] His basic idea was that not only do people care about the expected return on one asset versus another when they decide what to hold in their portfolio, but they also care about the riskiness of the returns from each asset. Specifically, Tobin assumed that most people are risk-averse—that they would be willing to hold an asset with a lower expected return if it is less risky. An important characteristic of money is that its return is certain; Tobin assumed it to be zero. Bonds, by contrast, can have substantial fluctuations in price, and their returns can be quite risky and sometimes negative. So even if the expected returns on bonds exceed the expected return on money, people might still want to hold money as a store of wealth because it has less risk associated with its return than bonds do.

The Tobin analysis also shows that people can reduce the total amount of risk in a portfolio by diversifying—that is, by holding both bonds and money. The model suggests that individuals will hold bonds and money simultaneously as stores of wealth. Because this is probably a more realistic description of people's behavior than Keynes's, Tobin's rationale for the speculative demand for money seems to rest on more solid ground.

Tobin's attempt to improve on Keynes's rationale for the speculative demand for money was only partly successful, however. It is still not clear that the speculative demand even exists. What if there are assets that have no risk—like money—but earn a higher return? Will there be any speculative demand for money? No, because an individual will always be better off holding such an asset rather than money. The resulting portfolio will enjoy a higher expected return yet has no higher risk. Do such assets exist in the American economy? The answer is yes. U.S. Treasury bills and other assets that have no default risk provide certain returns that are greater than those available on money. Therefore, why would anyone want to hold money balances as a store of wealth (ignoring for the moment transactions and precautionary reasons)?

---

[9]These models of the precautionary demand for money also reveal that as uncertainty about the level of future transactions grows, the precautionary demand for money increases. This is so because greater uncertainty means that individuals are more likely to incur transaction costs if they are not holding precautionary balances. The benefit of holding such balances then increases relative to the opportunity cost of forgone interest, and so the demand for them rises.

[10]James Tobin, "Liquidity Preference as Behavior Towards Risk," *Review of Economic Studies* 25 (1958): 65–86.

Although Tobin's analysis did not explain why money is held as a store of wealth, it was an important development in our understanding of how people should choose among assets. Indeed, his analysis was an important step in the development of the academic field of finance, which examines asset pricing and portfolio choice (the decision to buy one asset over another).

To sum up, further developments of the Keynesian approach have attempted to give a more precise explanation for the transactions, precautionary, and speculative demand for money. The attempt to improve Keynes's rationale for the speculative demand for money has been only partly successful; it is still not clear that this demand even exists. However, the models of the transactions and precautionary demand for money indicate that these components of money demand are negatively related to interest rates. Hence Keynes's proposition that the demand for money is sensitive to interest rates—suggesting that velocity is not constant and that nominal income might be affected by factors other than the quantity of money—is still supported.

FRIEDMAN'S MODERN QUANTITY THEORY OF MONEY

In 1956, Milton Friedman developed a theory of the demand for money in a famous article, "The Quantity Theory of Money: A Restatement."[11] Although Friedman frequently refers to Irving Fisher and the quantity theory, his analysis of the demand for money is actually closer to that of Keynes.

Like his predecessors, Friedman pursued the question of why people choose to hold money. Instead of analyzing the specific motives for holding money, as Keynes did, Friedman simply stated that the demand for money must be influenced by the same factors that influence the demand for any asset. Friedman then applied the theory of asset demand to money.

The theory of asset demand (Chapter 5) indicates that the demand for money should be a function of the resources available to individuals (their wealth) and the expected returns on other assets relative to the expected return on money. Like Keynes, Friedman recognized that people want to hold a certain amount of real money balances (the quantity of money in real terms). From this reasoning, Friedman expressed his formulation of the demand for money as follows:

$$\frac{M^d}{P} = f(\underset{+}{Y_p}, \underset{-}{r_b - r_m}, \underset{-}{r_e - r_m}, \underset{-}{\pi^e - r_m}) \tag{6}$$

where M^d/P = demand for real money balances

Y_p = Friedman's measure of wealth, known as *permanent income* (technically, the present discounted value of all expected future income, but more easily described as expected average long-run income)

r_m = expected return on money

r_b = expected return on bonds

r_e = expected return on equity (common stocks)

π^e = expected inflation rate

[11]Milton Friedman, "The Quantity Theory of Money: A Restatement," in *Studies in the Quantity Theory of Money*, ed. Milton Friedman (Chicago: University of Chicago Press, 1956), pp. 3–21.

The signs underneath the equation indicate whether the demand for money is positively (+) related or negatively (−) related to the terms that are immediately above them.[12]

Let us look in more detail at the variables in Friedman's money demand function and what they imply for the demand for money.

Because the demand for an asset is positively related to wealth, money demand is positively related to Friedman's wealth concept, permanent income (indicated by the plus sign beneath it). Unlike our usual concept of income, permanent income (which can be thought of as expected average long-run income) has much smaller short-run fluctuations, because many movements of income are transitory (short-lived). For example, in a business cycle expansion, income increases rapidly, but because some of this increase is temporary, average long-run income does not change very much. Hence in a boom, permanent income rises much less than income. During a recession, much of the income decline is transitory, and average long-run income (hence permanent income) falls less than income. One implication of Friedman's use of the concept of permanent income as a determinant of the demand for money is that the demand for money will not fluctuate much with business cycle movements.

An individual can hold wealth in several forms besides money. Friedman categorized them into three types of assets: bonds, equity (common stocks), and goods. The incentives for holding these assets rather than money are represented by the expected return on each of these assets relative to the expected return on money, the last three terms in the money demand function. The minus sign beneath each indicates that as each term rises, the demand for money will fall.

The expected return on money r_m, which appears in all three terms, is influenced by two factors:

1. The services provided by banks on deposits included in the money supply, such as provision of receipts in the form of canceled checks or the automatic paying of bills. When these services are increased, the expected return from holding money rises.
2. The interest payments on money balances. NOW accounts and other deposits that are included in the money supply currently pay interest. As these interest payments rise, the expected return on money rises.

The terms $r_b - r_m$ and $r_e - r_m$ represent the expected return on bonds and equity relative to money; as they rise, the relative expected return on money falls, and the demand for money falls. The final term, $\pi^e - r_m$, represents the expected return on goods relative to money. The expected return from holding goods is the expected rate of capital gains that occurs when their prices rise and hence is equal to the expected inflation rate π^e. If the expected inflation rate is 10%, for example, then goods' prices are expected to rise at a 10% rate, and their expected return is 10%. When $\pi^e - r_m$ rises, the expected return on goods relative to money rises, and the demand for money falls.

---

[12]Friedman also added to his formulation a term h that represented the ratio of human to nonhuman wealth. He reasoned that if people had more permanent income coming from labor income and thus from their human capital, they would be less liquid than if they were receiving income from financial assets. In this case, they might want to hold more money because it is a more liquid asset than the alternatives. The term h plays no essential role in Friedman's theory and has no important implications for monetary theory. That is why we ignore it in the money demand function.

DISTINGUISHING BETWEEN THE FRIEDMAN AND KEYNESIAN THEORIES

There are several differences between Friedman's theory of the demand for money and the Keynesian theories. One is that by including many assets as alternatives to money, Friedman recognized that more than one interest rate is important to the operation of the aggregate economy. Keynes, for his part, lumped financial assets other than money into one big category—bonds—because he felt that their returns generally move together. If this is so, the expected return on bonds will be a good indicator of the expected return on other financial assets, and there will be no need to include them separately in the money demand function.

Also in contrast to Keynes, Friedman viewed money and goods as substitutes; that is, people choose between them when deciding how much money to hold. That is why Friedman included the expected return on goods relative to money as a term in his money demand function. The assumption that money and goods are substitutes indicates that changes in the quantity of money may have a direct effect on aggregate spending.

In addition, Friedman stressed two issues in discussing his demand for money function that distinguish it from Keynes's liquidity preference theory. First, Friedman did not take the expected return on money to be a constant, as Keynes did. When interest rates rise in the economy, banks make more profits on their loans, and they want to attract more deposits to increase the volume of their now more profitable loans. If there are no restrictions on interest payments on deposits, banks attract deposits by paying higher interest rates on them. Because the industry is competitive, the expected return on money held as bank deposits then rises with the higher interest rates on bonds and loans. The banks compete to get deposits until there are no excess profits, and in doing so they close the gap between interest earned on loans and interest paid on deposits. The net result of this competition in the banking industry is that $r_b - r_m$ stays relatively constant when the interest rate i rises.[13]

What if there are restrictions on the amount of interest that banks can pay on their deposits? Will the expected return on money be a constant? As interest rates rise, will $r_b - r_m$ rise as well? Friedman thought not. He argued that although banks might be restricted from making pecuniary payments on their deposits, they can still compete on the quality dimension. For example, they can provide more services to depositors by hiring more tellers, paying bills automatically, or making more cash machines available at more accessible locations. The result of these improvements in money services is that the expected return from holding deposits will rise. So despite the restrictions on pecuniary interest payments, we might still find that a rise in market interest rates will raise the expected return on money sufficiently so that $r_b - r_m$ will remain relatively constant. ***Unlike Keynes's theory, which indicates that interest rates are an important determinant of the demand for money, Friedman's theory suggests that changes in interest rates should have little effect on the demand for money.***

[13]Friedman does suggest that there is some increase in $r_b - r_m$ when i rises because part of the money supply (especially currency) is held in forms that cannot pay interest in a pecuniary or nonpecuniary form. See, for example, Milton Friedman, "Why a Surge of Inflation Is Likely Next Year," *Wall Street Journal*, September 1, 1983, p. 24.

Therefore, Friedman's money demand function is essentially one in which permanent income is the primary determinant of money demand, and his money demand equation can be approximated by

$$\frac{M^d}{P} = f(Y_p) \tag{7}$$

In Friedman's view, the demand for money is insensitive to interest rates—not because he viewed the demand for money as insensitive to changes in the incentives for holding other assets relative to money, but rather because changes in interest rates should have little effect on these incentive terms in the money demand function. The incentive terms remain relatively constant, because any rise in the expected returns on other assets as a result of the rise in interest rates would be matched by a rise in the expected return on money.

The second issue Friedman stressed is the stability of the demand for money function. In contrast to Keynes, Friedman suggested that random fluctuations in the demand for money are small and that the demand for money can be predicted accurately by the money demand function. When combined with his view that the demand for money is insensitive to changes in interest rates, this means that velocity is highly predictable. We can see this by writing down the velocity that is implied by the money demand equation (Equation 7):

$$V = \frac{Y}{f(Y_p)} \tag{8}$$

Because the relationship between Y and Y_p is usually quite predictable, a stable money demand function (one that does not undergo pronounced shifts, so that it predicts the demand for money accurately) implies that velocity is predictable as well. If we can predict what velocity will be in the next period, a change in the quantity of money will produce a predictable change in aggregate spending. Even though velocity is no longer assumed to be constant, the money supply continues to be the primary determinant of nominal income as in the quantity theory of money. Therefore, Friedman's theory of money demand is indeed a restatement of the quantity theory, because it leads to the same conclusion about the importance of money to aggregate spending.

You may recall that we said that the Keynesian liquidity preference function (in which interest rates are an important determinant of the demand for money) is able to explain the procyclical movements of velocity that we find in the data. Can Friedman's money demand formulation explain this procyclical velocity phenomenon as well?

The key clue to answering this question is the presence of permanent income rather than measured income in the money demand function. What happens to permanent income in a business cycle expansion? Because much of the increase in income will be transitory, permanent income rises much less than income. Friedman's money demand function then indicates that the demand for money rises only a small amount relative to the rise in measured income, and as Equation 8 indicates, velocity rises. Similarly, in a recession, the demand for money falls less than income, because the decline in permanent income is small relative to income, and velocity falls. In this way, we have the procyclical movement in velocity.

To summarize, Friedman's theory of the demand for money used a similar approach to that of Keynes but did not go into detail about the motives for holding money. Instead, Friedman made use of the theory of asset demand to indicate that the demand for money will be a function of permanent income and the expected returns on alternative assets relative to the expected return on money. There are two major differences between Friedman's theory and Keynes's. Friedman believed that changes in interest rates have little effect on the expected returns on other assets relative to money. Thus, in contrast to Keynes, he viewed the demand for money as insensitive to interest rates. In addition, he differed from Keynes in stressing that the money demand function does not undergo substantial shifts and is therefore stable. These two differences also indicate that velocity is predictable, yielding a quantity theory conclusion that money is the primary determinant of aggregate spending.

EMPIRICAL EVIDENCE ON THE DEMAND FOR MONEY

As we have seen, the alternative theories of the demand for money can have very different implications for our view of the role of money in the economy. Which of these theories is an accurate description of the real world is an important question, and it is the reason why evidence on the demand for money has been at the center of many debates on the effects of monetary policy on aggregate economic activity. Here we examine the empirical evidence on the two primary issues that distinguish the different theories of money demand and affect their conclusions about whether the quantity of money is the primary determinant of aggregate spending: Is the demand for money sensitive to changes in interest rates, and is the demand for money function stable over time?[14]

Interest Rates and Money Demand

Earlier in the chapter, we saw that if interest rates do not affect the demand for money, velocity is more likely to be a constant—or at least predictable—so that the quantity theory view that aggregate spending is determined by the quantity of money is more likely to be true. However, the more sensitive the demand for money is to interest rates, the more unpredictable velocity will be, and the less clear the link between the money supply and aggregate spending will be. Indeed, there is an extreme case of ultrasensitivity of the demand for money to interest rates, called the *liquidity trap*, in which monetary policy has no direct effect on aggregate spending, because a change in the money supply has no effect on interest rates. (If the demand for money is ultrasensitive to interest rates, a tiny change in interest rates produces a very large change in the quantity of money demanded. Hence, in this case, the demand for money is completely flat in the supply and demand diagrams of Chapter 5. Therefore, a change in the money supply that shifts the money supply curve to the right or left results in it intersecting the flat money demand curve at the same unchanged interest rate.)

The evidence on the interest sensitivity of the demand for money found by different researchers is remarkably consistent. Neither extreme case is supported by the data: In situations in which nominal interest rates have not hit a floor of zero, the demand for money is sensitive to interest rates, and there is little evidence that a liquidity trap has ever existed. However, as we saw in Chapter 4, when interest rates fall to zero, they can go no lower. In this situation, a liquidity trap has occurred because the demand for

[14]If you are interested in a more detailed discussion of the empirical research on the demand for money, you can find it in an appendix to this chapter on this book's web site at www.myeconlab.com/mishkin.

money is now completely flat. Indeed, Japan has been experiencing a liquidity trap of this type in recent years, which is one reason why it has been difficult for Japanese monetary authorities to stimulate the economy.

Stability of Money Demand

If the money demand function, like Equation 4 or 6, is unstable and undergoes substantial unpredictable shifts, as Keynes thought, then velocity is unpredictable, and the quantity of money may not be tightly linked to aggregate spending, as it is in the modern quantity theory. The stability of the money demand function is also crucial to whether the Federal Reserve should target interest rates or the money supply (see Chapter 19). Thus it is important to look at the question of whether the money demand function is stable, because it has important implications for how monetary policy should be conducted.

By the early 1970s, evidence strongly supported the stability of the money demand function. However, after 1973, the rapid pace of financial innovation, which changed which items could be used as money, led to substantial instability in estimated money demand functions. The recent instability of the money demand function calls into question whether our theories and empirical analyses are adequate. It also has important implications for the way monetary policy should be conducted, because it casts doubt on the usefulness of the money demand function as a tool to provide guidance to policymakers. In particular, because the money demand function has become unstable, velocity is now harder to predict, and as discussed in Chapter 19, setting rigid money supply targets to control aggregate spending in the economy may not be an effective way to conduct monetary policy.

SUMMARY

1. Irving Fisher developed a transactions-based theory of the demand for money in which the demand for real balances is proportional to real income and is insensitive to interest-rate movements. An implication of his theory is that velocity, the rate at which money turns over, is constant. This generates the quantity theory of money, which implies that aggregate spending is determined solely by movements in the quantity of money.
2. The classical view that velocity can be effectively treated as a constant is not supported by the data. The nonconstancy of velocity became especially clear to the economics profession after the sharp drop in velocity during the years of the Great Depression.
3. John Maynard Keynes suggested three motives for holding money: the transactions motive, the precautionary motive, and the speculative motive. His resulting liquidity preference theory views the transactions and precautionary components of money demand as proportional to income. However, the speculative component of money demand is viewed as sensitive to interest rates as well as to expectations about the future movements of interest rates. This theory, then, implies that velocity is unstable and cannot be treated as a constant.
4. Further developments in the Keynesian approach provided a better rationale for the three Keynesian motives for holding money. Interest rates were found to be important to the transactions and precautionary components of money demand as well as to the speculative component.
5. Milton Friedman's theory of money demand used a similar approach to that of Keynes. Treating money like any other asset, Friedman used the theory of asset demand to derive a demand for money that is a function of the expected returns on other assets relative to the expected return on money and permanent income. In contrast to Keynes, Friedman believed that the demand for money is stable and insensitive to interest-rate movements. His belief that velocity is predictable

(though not constant) in turn leads to the quantity theory conclusion that money is the primary determinant of aggregate spending.

6. There are two main conclusions from the research on the demand for money: The demand for money is sensitive to interest rates, but there is little evidence that it is or has been ultrasensitive (liquidity trap). Since 1973, money demand has been found to be unstable, with the most likely source of the instability being the rapid pace of financial innovation.

KEY TERMS

equation of exchange, p. 566
liquidity preference theory, p. 569
monetary theory, p. 565
quantity theory of money, p. 567
real money balances, p. 571
velocity of money, p. 566

QUESTIONS AND PROBLEMS

Questions marked with an asterisk are answered at the end of the book in an appendix, "Answers to Selected Questions and Problems." Questions marked with a blue circle indicate the question is available in MyEconLab at www.myeconlab.com/mishkin.

*1. Suppose the money supply M has been growing at 10% per year, and nominal GDP PY has been growing at 20% per year. The data are as follows (in billions of dollars):

	2004	2005	2006
M	100	110	121
PY	1,000	1,200	1,440

Calculate the velocity in each year. At what rate is velocity growing?

2. Calculate what happens to nominal GDP if velocity remains constant at 5 and the money supply increases from $200 billion to $300 billion.

*3. What happens to nominal GDP if the money supply grows by 20% but velocity declines by 30%?

4. If credit cards were made illegal by congressional legislation, what would happen to velocity? Explain your answer.

*5. If velocity and aggregate output are reasonably constant (as the classical economists believed), what happens to the price level when the money supply increases from $1 trillion to $4 trillion?

6. If velocity and aggregate output remain constant at 5 and 1,000, respectively, what happens to the price level if the money supply declines from $400 billion to $300 billion?

*7. Looking at Figure 1 in the chapter, when were the two largest falls in velocity? What do declines like this suggest about how velocity moves with the business cycle? Given the data in Figure 1, is it reasonable to assume, as the classical economists did, that declines in aggregate spending are caused by declines in the quantity of money?

8. Using data from the *Economic Report of the President*, calculate velocity for the M2 definition of the money supply for each of the past five years. Does velocity appear to be constant?

*9. In Keynes's analysis of the speculative demand for money, what will happen to money demand if people suddenly decide that the normal level of the interest rate has declined? Why?

10. Why is Keynes's analysis of the speculative demand for money important to his view that velocity will undergo substantial fluctuations and thus cannot be treated as constant?

*11. If interest rates on bonds go to zero, what does the Baumol-Tobin analysis suggest Grant Smith's average holdings of money balances should be?

12. If brokerage fees go to zero, what does the Baumol-Tobin analysis suggest Grant Smith's average holdings of money should be?

*13. "In Tobin's analysis of the speculative demand for money, people will hold both money and bonds, even if bonds are expected to earn a positive return." Is this statement true, false, or uncertain? Explain your answer.

14. Both Keynes's and Friedman's theories of the demand for money suggest that as the relative expected return on money falls, demand for it will fall. Why does Friedman think that money demand is unaffected by changes in interest rates? Why did Keynes think that money demand is affected by changes in interest rates?

*15. Why does Friedman's view of the demand for money suggest that velocity is predictable, whereas Keynes's view suggests the opposite?

WEB EXERCISES

1. Refer to Figure 1. The formula for computing the velocity of money is GDP/M1. Go to www.research.stlouisfed.org/fred2 and look up the GDP. Next go to www.federalreserve.gov/Releases/h6/Current/ and find M1. Compute the most recent year's velocity of money and compare it to its level in 2002. Has it risen or fallen? Suggest reasons for its change since that time.

2. John Maynard Keynes is among the most well-known economic theorists. Go to cepa.newschool.edu/het/profiles/keynes.htm and write a one-page summary of his life and contributions.

WEB REFERENCES

www.usagold.com/gildedopinion/puplava/20020614.html

A summary of how various factors affect the velocity of money.

cepa.newschool.edu/het/ profiles/keynes.htm

A brief history of John Maynard Keynes.

CHAPTER

23 Aggregate Demand and Supply Analysis

Preview

In earlier chapters, we focused considerable attention on monetary policy, because it touches our everyday lives by affecting the prices of the goods we buy and the quantity of available jobs. In this chapter, we develop a basic tool, aggregate demand and supply analysis, that will enable us to study the effects of monetary policy on output and prices. **Aggregate demand** is the total quantity of an economy's final goods and services demanded at different price levels. **Aggregate supply** is the total quantity of final goods and services that firms in the economy want to sell at different price levels. As with other supply and demand analyses, the actual quantity of output and the price level are determined by equating aggregate demand and aggregate supply.

Aggregate demand and supply analysis will enable us to explore how aggregate output and the price level are determined. (The Following the Financial News box indicates where and how often data on aggregate output and the price level are published.) Not only will the analysis help us interpret recent episodes in the business cycle, but it will also enable us to understand the debates on how economic policy should be conducted.

AGGREGATE DEMAND

The first building block of aggregate supply and demand analysis is the **aggregate demand curve**, which describes the relationship between the quantity of aggregate output demanded and the price level when all other variables are held constant. There are two ways to derive the aggregate demand curve. The first, and simplest, approach is based on the quantity theory of money, in which aggregate demand is determined solely by the quantity of money. The second approach is based on an examination of the behavior of the component parts of aggregate demand: consumption, investment, government spending, and net exports. The components approach also takes into account the role of the quantity of money in determining aggregate demand, but it does so indirectly, by considering how changes in the quantity of money affect the components of aggregate demand.

Quantity Theory of Money Approach to Aggregate Demand

The quantity theory of money links the quantity of money M with total nominal spending on goods and services $P \times Y$ (P = price level and Y = aggregate real output or, equivalently, aggregate real income). To obtain this linkage it uses the concept of the **velocity of money**: the average number of times per year that a dollar is spent on final

Following the Financial News Aggregate Output, Unemployment, and the Price Level

Newspapers and Internet sites periodically report data that provide information on the level of aggregate output, unemployment, and the price level. Here is a list of the relevant data series, their frequency, and when they are published.

Aggregate Output and Unemployment

Real GDP: Quarterly (January–March, April–June, July–September, October–December); published three to four weeks after the end of a quarter.

Industrial production: Monthly. Industrial production is not as comprehensive a measure of aggregate ouput as real GDP, because it measures only manufacturing output; the estimate for the previous month is reported in the middle of the following month.

Unemployment rate: Monthly; previous month's figure is usually published on the Friday of the first week of the following month.

Price Level

GDP deflator: Quarterly. This comprehensive measure of the price level (described in the appendix to Chapter 1) is published at the same time as the real GDP data.

Consumer price index (CPI): Monthly. The CPI is a measure of the price level for consumers (also described in the appendix to Chapter 1); the value for the previous month is published in the third or fourth week of the following month.

Producer price index (PPI): Monthly. The PPI is a measure of the average level of wholesale prices charged by producers and is published at the same time as industrial production data.

goods and services. More formally, velocity V is calculated by dividing nominal spending $P \times Y$ by the money supply M:

$$V = \frac{P \times Y}{M}$$

Suppose that the total nominal spending in a year was \$2 trillion and the money supply was \$1 trillion; velocity would then be \$2 trillion/\$1 trillion = 2. On average, the money supply supports a level of transactions associated with 2 times its value in final goods and services in the course of a year. By multiplying both sides by M, we obtain the **equation of exchange**, which relates the money supply to aggregate spending:

$$M \times V = P \times Y \tag{1}$$

At this point, the equation of exchange is nothing more than an identity; that is, it is true by definition. It does not tell us that when M rises, aggregate spending will rise as well. For example, the rise in M could be offset by a fall in V, with the result that $M \times V$ does not rise. However, the quantity theory of money demand developed by Milton Friedman (discussed in detail in Chapter 22) suggests that velocity varies over time in a predictable manner unrelated to changes in the money supply. With this analysis, the equation of exchange is transformed into a theory of how aggregate spending is determined and is called the **quantity theory of money**.

To see how the theory works, let's look at an example. If velocity is predicted to be 5 and the money supply is \$1 trillion, the equation of exchange tells us that aggregate spending will be \$5 trillion (5 × \$1 trillion). If the money supply doubles to \$2 trillion, the quantity theory suggests that velocity will continue to be 5 and aggregate spending will double to \$10 trillion (5 × \$2 trillion). Thus the quantity theory of money concludes that ***changes in aggregate spending are determined primarily by changes in the money supply***.

Deriving the Aggregate Demand Curve. To learn how the quantity theory of money generates the aggregate demand curve, let's look at an example in which we measure aggregate output in trillions of 2000 dollars, with the price level in 2000 having a value of 1.0. As just shown, with a predicted velocity of 5 and a money supply of \$1 trillion, aggregate spending will be \$5 trillion. If the price level is given at 2.0, the quantity of aggregate output demanded is \$2.5 trillion because aggregate spending $P \times Y$ then continues to equal 2.0 × \$2.5 trillion = \$5 trillion, the value of $M \times V$. This combination of a price level of 2.0 and aggregate output of 2.5 is marked as point A in Figure 1. If the price level is given as 1.0 instead, aggregate output demanded is \$5 trillion (point B), so aggregate spending continues to equal \$5 trillion (= 1.0 × 5 trillion). Similarly, at an even lower price level of 0.5, the quantity of output demanded rises to \$10 trillion, shown by point C. The curve connecting these points, marked AD_1, is the aggregate demand curve, given a money supply of \$1 trillion. As you can see, it has the usual downward slope of a demand curve, indicating that as the price level falls (everything else held constant), the quantity of output demanded rises.

Shifts in the Aggregate Demand Curve. In the quantity theory, changes in the money supply are the primary source of the changes in aggregate spending, which shifts in the aggregate demand curve. To see how a change in the money supply shifts the aggregate demand curve in Figure 1, let's look at what happens when the money supply increases to \$2 trillion. Now aggregate spending rises to 5 × \$2 trillion = \$10 trillion, and at a price level of 2.0, the quantity of aggregate output demanded will rise to \$5 trillion so that 2.0 × 5 trillion = \$10 trillion. Therefore, at a price level of 2.0, the quantity of output demanded moves from point A to A′. At a price level of 1.0, the quantity of output demanded rises from \$5 to \$10 trillion (from point B to B′), and at a price level of 0.5, output demanded rises from \$10 to \$20 trillion (from point C to C′). The result is that the rise in the money supply to \$2 trillion shifts the aggregate demand curve outward to AD_2.

myeconlab

FIGURE 1
Aggregate Demand Curve
An aggregate demand curve is drawn for a *fixed* level of the money supply. A rise in the money supply from \$1 trillion to \$2 trillion leads to a shift in the aggregate demand curve from AD_1 to AD_2.

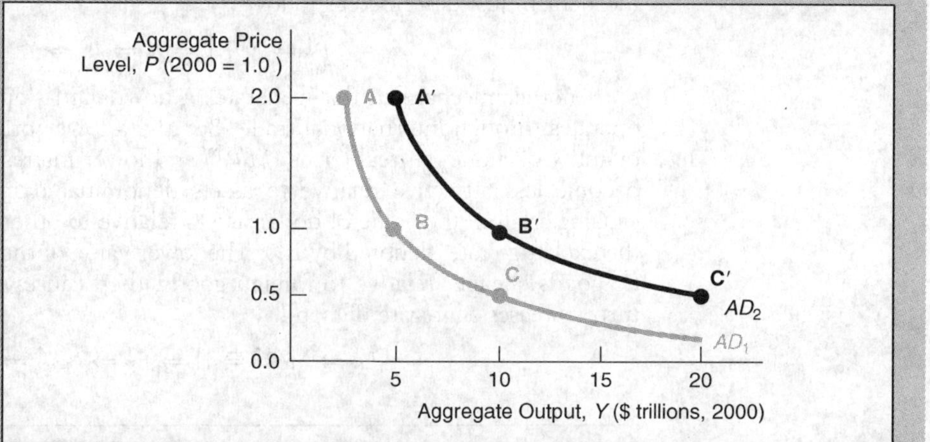

Similar reasoning indicates that a decline in the money supply lowers aggregate spending proportionally and reduces the quantity of aggregate output demanded at each price level. Thus a decline in the money supply shifts the aggregate demand curve to the left.

Deriving Aggregate Demand from the Behavior of Its Component Parts

Rather than determining aggregate demand by looking at how money affects the total amount of aggregate demand, we can derive the aggregate demand curve by examining its four component parts: **consumer expenditure**, the total demand for consumer goods and services; **planned investment spending**,[1] the total planned spending by business firms on new machines, factories, and other capital goods, plus planned spending on new homes; **government spending**, spending by all levels of government (federal, state, and local) on goods and services (paper clips, computers, computer programming, missiles, government workers, and so on); and **net exports**, the net foreign spending on domestic goods and services, equal to exports minus imports. Using the symbols C for consumer expenditure, I for planned investment spending, G for government spending, and NX for net exports, we can write the following expression for aggregate demand Y^{ad}:

$$Y^{ad} = C + I + G + NX \tag{2}$$

Deriving the Aggregate Demand Curve. The components approach, like the quantity theory approach, suggests that the aggregate demand curve is downward-sloping because a lower price level ($P\downarrow$), holding the nominal quantity of money (M) constant, leads to a larger quantity of money in real terms (in terms of the goods and services that it can buy, $M/P\uparrow$). The larger quantity of money in real terms ($M/P\uparrow$) that results from the lower price level causes interest rates to fall ($i\downarrow$), as suggested in Chapter 5. The resulting lower cost of financing purchases of new physical capital makes investment more profitable and stimulates planned investment spending ($I\uparrow$). Because, as shown in Equation 2, the increase in planned investment spending adds directly to aggregate demand ($Y^{ad}\uparrow$), the lower price level leads to a higher level of the quantity of aggregate output demanded ($P\downarrow \Rightarrow Y^{ad}\uparrow$). Schematically, we can write the mechanism just described as follows:

$$P\downarrow \Rightarrow M/P\uparrow \Rightarrow i\downarrow \Rightarrow I\uparrow \Rightarrow Y^{ad}\uparrow$$

Another mechanism that generates a downward-sloping aggregate demand curve operates through international trade. Because a lower price level ($P\downarrow$) leads to a larger quantity of money in real terms ($M/P\uparrow$) and lower interest rates ($i\downarrow$), U.S. dollar assets become less attractive relative to assets denominated in foreign currencies, thereby causing a fall in the value of dollar assets relative to other currency assets (a decline in the exchange rate, denoted by $E\downarrow$). The lower value of the dollar, which makes domestic goods cheaper relative to foreign goods, then causes net exports to rise, which in turn increases aggregate demand:

$$P\downarrow \Rightarrow M/P\uparrow \Rightarrow i\downarrow \Rightarrow E\downarrow \Rightarrow NX\uparrow \Rightarrow Y^{ad}\uparrow$$

---

[1]Recall that economists restrict use of the word *investment* to the purchase of new physical capital, such as a new machine or a new house, that adds to expenditure.

Factors That Shift the Aggregate Demand Curve.

The mechanisms described also indicate why the components approach suggests that changes in the money supply shift the aggregate demand curve. For a given price level, a rise in the money supply causes the real money supply to increase ($M/P\uparrow$), which leads to an increase in aggregate demand. Thus an increase in the money supply shifts the aggregate demand curve to the right (as in Figure 1), because it lowers interest rates and stimulates planned investment spending and net exports. Similarly, a decline in the money supply shifts the aggregate demand curve to the left.

In contrast to the quantity theory, the components approach suggests that other factors (manipulation of government spending and taxes, changes in net exports, and changes in consumer and business spending) are also important causes of shifts in the aggregate demand curve. For instance, if the government spends more ($G\uparrow$) or net exports increase ($NX\uparrow$), the quantity of aggregate output demanded at each price level rises, and the aggregate demand curve shifts to the right. A decrease in government taxes ($T\downarrow$) leaves consumers with more income to spend, so consumer expenditure rises ($C\uparrow$). The quantity of aggregate output demanded at each price level also rises, and the aggregate demand curve shifts to the right. Finally, if consumer and business optimism increases, consumer expenditure and planned investment spending rise ($C\uparrow$, $I\uparrow$), again shifting the aggregate demand curve to the right. John Maynard Keynes described waves of optimism and pessimism as **"animal spirits"** and considered them a major factor affecting the aggregate demand curve and an important source of business cycle fluctuations.

Summary.

Both the quantity theory and the components approach to aggregate demand agree that the aggregate demand curve slopes downward and shifts in response to changes in the money supply. However, in the quantity theory approach, there is only one important source of movements in the aggregate demand curve—changes in the money supply. The components approach suggests that other factors—fiscal policy, net exports, and "animal spirits"—are equally important sources of shifts in the aggregate demand curve. Our discussion of the quantity theory and the components approach indicate that six factors can shift the aggregate demand curve: the money supply, government spending, net exports, taxes, consumer optimism, and business optimism. The last two ("animal spirits") affect willingness to spend. The possible effect on the aggregate demand curve of these six factors (often referred to as **demand shocks**) is summarized in Table 1.

AGGREGATE SUPPLY

To complete our analysis we need to derive an **aggregate supply curve**, the relationship between the quantity of output supplied and the price level. In the typical supply and demand analysis, we have only one supply curve, but because prices and wages take time to adjust to their long-run level, the aggregate supply curve differs in the short and the long runs. First, we examine the long-run aggregate supply curve. We then derive the short-run aggregate supply curve and see how it shifts over time as the economy moves from the short run to the long run.

SUMMARY TABLE 1 Factors That Shift the Aggregate Demand Curve

Factor	Change	Shift in the Aggregate Demand Curve
Money supply, M	↑	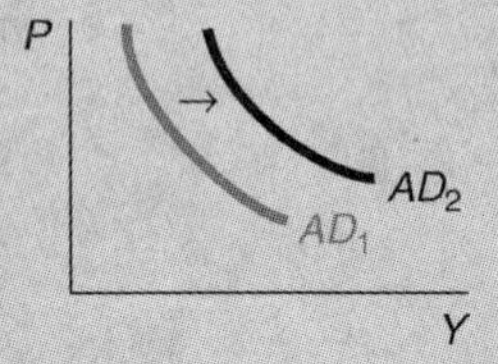
Government spending, G	↑	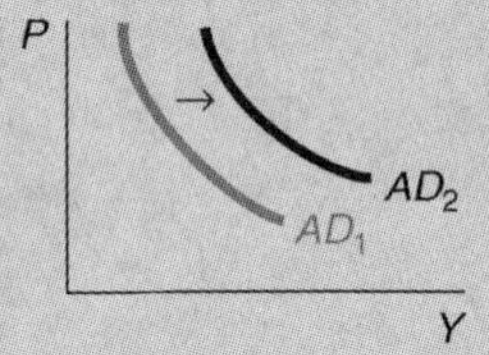
Taxes, T	↑	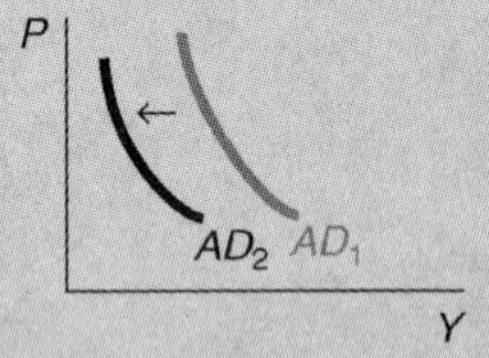
Net exports, NX	↑	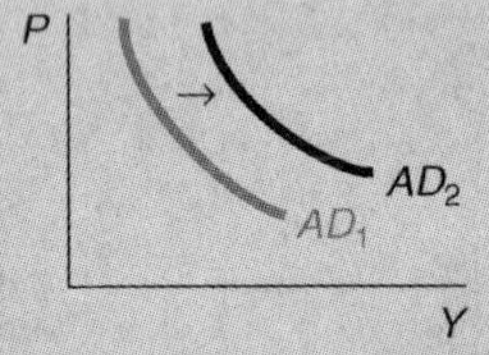
Consumer optimism, C	↑	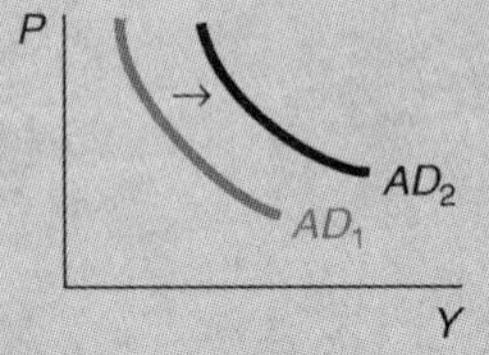
Business optimism, I	↑	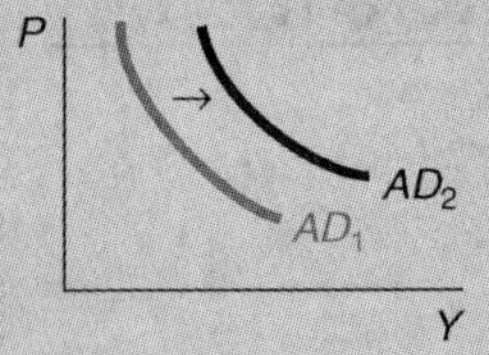

Note: Only increases (↑) in the factors are shown. The effect of decreases in the factors would be the opposite of those indicated in the "Shift" column. Note that the quantity theory approach views the money supply as the only important cause of shifts in the aggregate demand curve.

Long-Run Aggregate Supply Curve

The amount of output that can be produced in the economy in the long run is determined by the amount of capital in the economy, the amount of labor supplied at full employment, and the available technology. As discussed in Chapter 19, some unemployment cannot be helped because it is either frictional or structural. Thus at full employment, unemployment is not at zero, but is rather at a level above zero at which the demand for labor equals the supply of labor. This **natural rate of unemployment** is where the economy gravitates to in the long run.[2] Many economists believe that the natural rate of unemployment is currently around 5%.

The level of aggregate output produced at the natural rate of unemployment is called the **natural rate of output**; it is where the economy settles in the long run for any price level. Hence the long-run aggregate supply curve (LRAS) is vertical at the natural rate of output, denoted by Y_n, as drawn in Figure 2.

Short-Run Aggregate Supply Curve

Because wages and prices take time to adjust to economic conditions, a process described by saying that wages and prices are *sticky*, the aggregate supply curve (AS_1) in the short run is upward-sloping, as depicted in Figure 3. To understand why the short-run aggregate supply curve is upward-sloping, we have to look at the factors that cause the quantity of output supplied to change. Because the goal of business firms is to maximize profits, the quantity of output supplied is determined by the profit made on each unit of output. If profit rises, more aggregate output will be produced, and the quantity of output supplied will increase; if it falls, less output will be produced, and the quantity of aggregate output supplied will fall.

FIGURE 2
Long-Run Aggregate Supply Curve
The amount of aggregate output supplied at any given price level goes to the natural rate level of output in the long run, so that the long-run aggregate supply curve *LRAS* is a vertical line at Y_n.

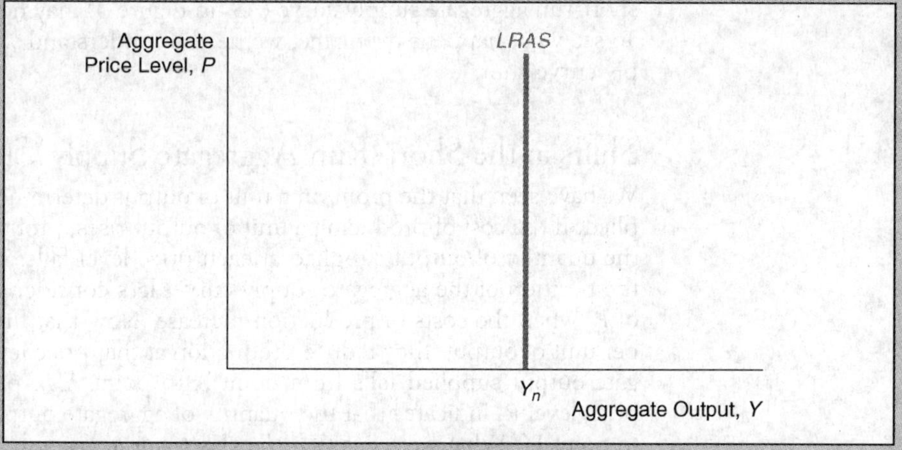

[2]A related concept is the *nonaccelerating inflation rate of unemployment* (NAIRU), the rate of unemployment at which there is no tendency for the inflation rate to change.

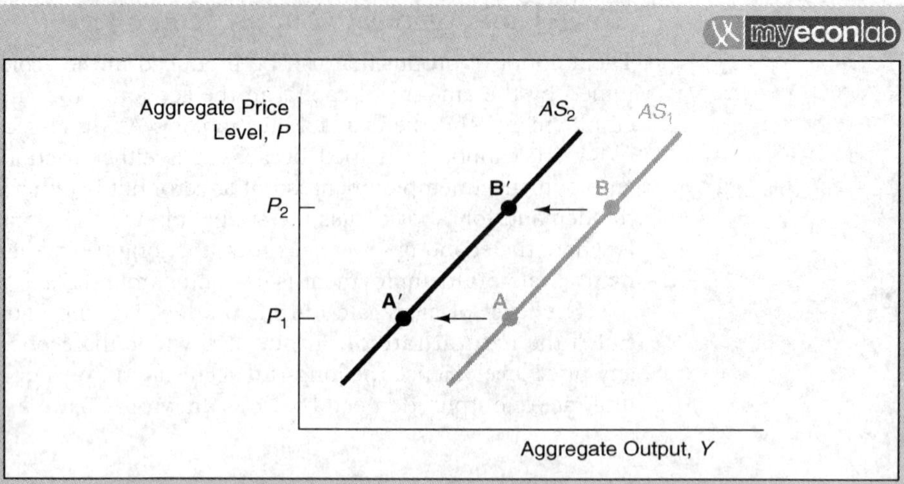

FIGURE 3
Aggregate Supply Curve in the Short Run
A rise in the costs of production shifts the short-run supply curve leftward from AS_1 to AS_2.

Profit on a unit of output equals the price for the unit minus the costs of producing it. In the short run, costs of many factors that go into producing goods and services are fixed; wages, for example, are often fixed for periods of time by labor contracts, and raw materials are often bought by firms under long-term contracts that fix the price. Because these costs of production are fixed in the short run, when the overall price level rises, the price for a unit of output will rise relative to the costs of producing it, and the profit per unit will rise. Because the higher price level results in higher profits in the short run, firms increase production, and the quantity of aggregate output supplied rises, resulting in an upward-sloping short-run aggregate supply curve.

Frequent mention of the *short run* in the preceding paragraph hints that the relationship between the price level and aggregate output embodied in the upward-sloping, short-run aggregate supply curve (AS_1 in Figure 3) may not remain fixed as time passes. To see what happens over time, we need to understand what makes the aggregate supply curve shift.[3]

Shifts in the Short-Run Aggregate Supply Curve

We have seen that the profit on a unit of output determines the quantity of output supplied. If the cost of producing a unit of output rises, profit on a unit of output falls, and the quantity of output supplied at each price level falls. To learn what this implies for the position of the aggregate supply curve, let's consider what happens at a price level of P_1 when the costs of production increase. Now that firms are earning a lower profit per unit of output, they reduce production at that price level, and the quantity of aggregate output supplied falls from point A to point A′. Applying the same reasoning at price level P_2 indicates that the quantity of aggregate output supplied falls from point B to point B′. What we see is that ***the short-run aggregate supply curve shifts to the left when costs of production increase and to the right when costs decrease***.

[3]The aggregate supply curve is closely linked to the Phillips curve discussed in Chapter 19. More information on the Phillips and aggregate supply curve can be found in an appendix to this chapter, which is on this book's web site at www.myeconlab.com/mishkin.

Factors That Shift the Short-Run Aggregate Supply Curve

The factors that cause the short-run aggregate supply curve to shift are ones that affect the costs of production: (1) tightness of the labor market, (2) expectations of inflation, (3) workers' attempts to push up their real wages, and (4) changes in the production costs that are unrelated to wages (such as energy costs). The first three factors shift the short-run aggregate supply curve by affecting wage costs; the fourth affects other costs of production.

Tightness of the Labor Market. If the economy is booming and the labor market is tight ($Y > Y_n$), employers may have difficulty hiring qualified workers and may even have a hard time keeping their present employees. Because the demand for labor now exceeds supply in this tight labor market, employers will raise wages to attract needed workers, and the costs of production will rise. The higher costs of production lower the profit per unit of output at each price level, and the short-run aggregate supply curve shifts to the left. (See Figure 3.)

By contrast, if the economy enters a recession and the labor market is slack ($Y < Y_n$), because the demand for labor is less than the supply, workers who cannot find jobs will be willing to work for lower wages. In addition, employed workers may be willing to make wage concessions to keep their jobs. Therefore, in a slack labor market in which the quantity of labor demanded is less than the quantity supplied, wages and hence costs of production will fall, the profit per unit of output will rise, and the short-run aggregate supply curve will shift to the right.

The effects of tightness of the labor market on the short-run aggregate supply curve can be summarized as follows: ***When aggregate output is above the natural rate, the short-run aggregate supply curve shifts to the left; when aggregate output is below the natural rate, the short-run aggregate supply curve shifts to the right.***

Expected Price Level. Workers and firms care about wages in real terms—that is, in terms of the goods and services that wages can buy. When the price level increases, a worker earning the same nominal wage will be able to buy fewer goods and services. A worker who expects the price level to rise will thus demand a higher nominal wage to keep the real wage from falling. For example, if Chuck the Construction Worker expects prices to increase by 5%, he will want a wage increase of at least 5% (more, if he thinks he deserves an increase in real wages). Similarly, if Chuck's employer knows that the houses he is building will rise in value at the same rate as inflation (5%), his employer will be willing to pay Chuck 5% more. An increase in the expected price level leads to higher wages, which in turn raise the costs of production, lower the profit per unit of output at each price level, and shift the aggregate supply curve to the left (see Figure 3). Therefore, ***a rise in the expected price level causes the aggregate supply curve to shift to the left; the greater the expected increase in price level (that is, the higher the expected inflation), the larger the shift***.

Wage Push. Suppose that Chuck and his fellow construction workers decide to strike and succeed in obtaining higher real wages. This wage push will then raise the costs of production, and the aggregate supply curve will shift leftward. ***A successful wage push by workers will cause the aggregate supply curve to shift to the left.***

Changes in Production Costs Unrelated to Wages. Changes in technology and in the supply of raw materials (called **supply shocks**) can also shift the aggregate supply curve. A negative supply shock, such as a reduction in the availability of raw materials (like oil), which raises their price, increases production costs and shifts the aggregate supply curve leftward. A positive supply shock, such as unusually good weather that leads to a bountiful harvest and lowers the cost of food, will reduce production costs and shift the aggregate supply curve rightward. Similarly, the development of a new technology that lowers production costs, perhaps by raising worker productivity, can be considered a positive supply shock that shifts the aggregate supply curve to the right.

The effect on the aggregate supply curve of changes in production costs unrelated to wages (supply shocks) can be summarized as follows: ***A negative supply shock that raises production costs shifts the aggregate supply curve to the left; a positive supply shock that lowers production costs shifts the aggregate supply curve to the right.***[4]

STUDY GUIDE

As a study aid, factors that shift the short-run aggregate supply curve are listed in Table 2.

EQUILIBRIUM IN AGGREGATE SUPPLY AND DEMAND ANALYSIS

The equilibrium level of aggregate output and the price level will occur at the point where the quantity of aggregate output demanded equals the quantity of aggregate output supplied. However, in the context of aggregate supply and demand analysis, there are two types of equilibrium: short-run and long-run.

Equilibrium in the Short Run

Figure 4 illustrates a short-run equilibrium in which the quantity of aggregate output demanded equals the quantity of output supplied—that is, where the short-run aggregate demand curve *AD* and the aggregate supply curve *AS* intersect at point E. The equilibrium level of aggregate output equals Y^*, and the equilibrium price level equals P^*.

As in our earlier supply and demand analyses, equilibrium is a useful concept only if there is a tendency for the economy to head toward it. We can see that the economy heads toward the equilibrium at point E by first looking at what happens when we are at a price level above the equilibrium price level P^*. If the price level is at P'', the quan-

[4]Developments in the foreign exchange market can also shift the aggregate supply curve by changing domestic production costs. As discussed in more detail in Chapter 20, an increase in the value of the dollar makes foreign goods cheaper in the United States. The decline in prices of foreign goods and hence foreign factors of production lowers U.S. production costs and thus raises the profit per unit of output at each price level in the United States. An increase in the value of the dollar therefore shifts the aggregate supply curve to the right. Conversely, a decline in the value of the dollar, which makes foreign factors of production more expensive, shifts the aggregate supply curve to the left.

SUMMARY TABLE 2 Factors That Shift the Short-Run Aggregate Supply Curve

Factor	Shifts in the Short-Run Aggregate Supply Curve	Factor	Shifts in the Short-Run Aggregate Supply Curve
$Y > Y_n$	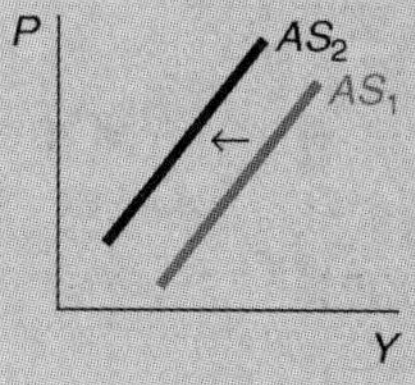	Wage push	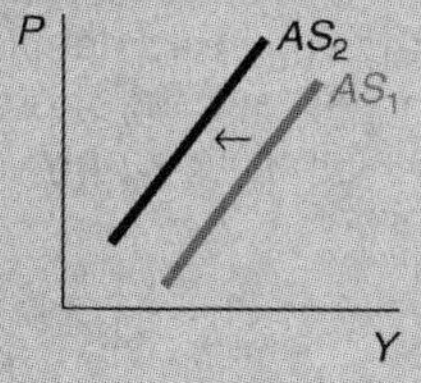
$Y < Y_n$	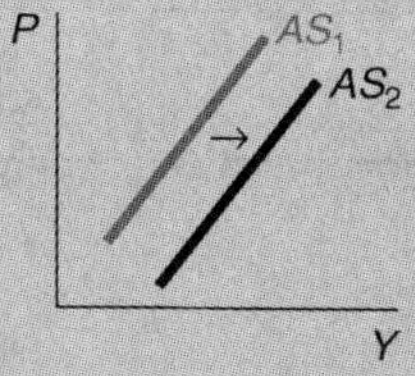	Positive supply shock	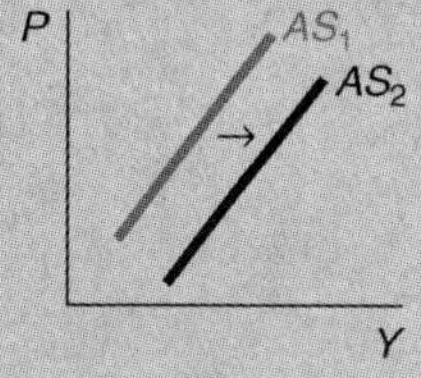
Rise in expected price level	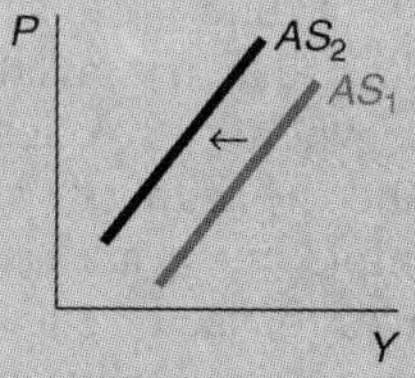	Negative supply shock	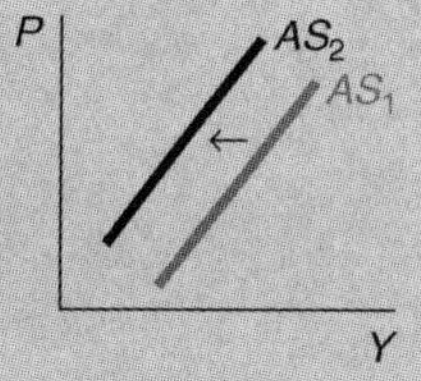

tity of aggregate output supplied at point D is greater than the quantity of aggregate output demanded at point A. Because people want to sell more goods and services than others want to buy (a condition of *excess supply*), the prices of goods and services will fall, and the aggregate price level will drop, as shown by the downward arrow. This decline in the price level will continue until it has reached its equilibrium level of P^* at point E.

When the price level is below the equilibrium price level, say at P', the quantity of output demanded is greater than the quantity of output supplied. Now the price level will rise, as shown by the upward arrow, because people want to buy more goods than others want to sell (a condition of *excess demand*). This rise in the price level will continue until it has again reached its equilibrium level of P^* at point E.

Equilibrium in the Long Run

Usually in supply and demand analysis, once we find the equilibrium at which the quantity demanded equals the quantity supplied, there is no need for additional discussion. In *aggregate* supply and demand analysis, however, that is not the case. Even when the quantity of aggregate output demanded equals the quantity supplied, forces operate that can cause the equilibrium to move over time if $Y^* \neq Y_n$. To understand why, we must remember that if costs of production change, the aggregate supply curve will shift.

FIGURE 4
Equilibrium in the Short Run
Equilibrium occurs at point E at the intersection of the aggregate demand curve *AD* and the short-run aggregate supply curve *AS*.

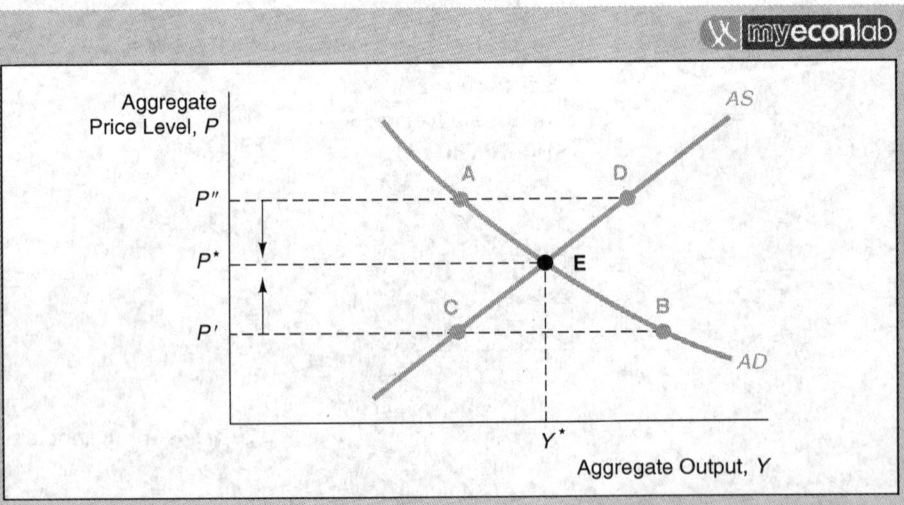

As we saw earlier, the short-run aggregate supply curve will not remain stationary when aggregate output and unemployment differ from their natural rate: When $Y > Y_n$, labor markets are tight, production costs rise at any given price level, and the short-run aggregate supply curve shifts to the left; when $Y < Y_n$, labor markets are slack, production costs fall at any given price level, and the aggregate supply curve shifts to the right. Only when aggregate output and unemployment are at their natural rates is there no pressure from the labor market for wages to rise or fall. Under these conditions, there is no reason for the short-run aggregate supply to shift.

We look at how the short-run equilibrium changes over time in response to two situations: when short-run equilibrium is initially below the natural rate level and when it is initially above the natural rate level.

In panel (a) of Figure 5, the initial equilibrium occurs at point 1, the intersection of the aggregate demand curve *AD* and the initial short-run aggregate supply curve AS_1. Because the level of equilibrium output Y_1 is greater than the natural rate level Y_n, unemployment is less than its natural rate, and excessive tightness exists in the labor market. This tightness drives wages up, raises production costs, and shifts the aggregate supply curve to AS_2. The equilibrium is now at point 2, and output falls to Y_2. Because aggregate output Y_2 is still above the natural rate level, Y_n, wages continue to be driven up, eventually shifting the aggregate supply curve to AS_3. The equilibrium reached at point 3 is on the vertical long-run aggregate supply curve (*LRAS*) at Y_n and is a long-run equilibrium. Because output is at the natural rate level, there is no further pressure on wages to rise and thus no further tendency for the aggregate supply curve to shift.

The movements in panel (a) indicate that the economy will not remain at a level of output higher than the natural rate level because the short-run aggregate supply curve will shift to the left, raise the price level, and cause the economy (equilibrium) to slide upward along the aggregate demand curve until it comes to rest at a point on the long-run aggregate supply curve at the natural rate level of output Y_n.

In panel (b), the initial equilibrium at point 1 is one at which output Y_1 is below the natural rate level. Because unemployment is higher than its natural rate, wages begin to fall, shifting the short-run aggregate supply curve rightward until it comes to rest at AS_3. The economy (equilibrium) slides downward along the aggregate demand curve until it

FIGURE 5

Adjustment to Long-Run Equilibrium in Aggregate Supply and Demand Analysis

In both panels, the initial short-run equilibrium is at point 1 at the intersection of AD and AS_1. In panel (a), $Y_1 > Y_n$, so the short-run aggregate supply curve keeps shifting to the left until it reaches AS_3, where output has returned to Y_n. In panel (b), $Y_1 < Y_n$, so the short-run aggregate supply curve keeps shifting to the right until output is again returned to Y_n. Hence in both cases, the economy displays a self-correcting mechanism that returns it to the natural rate level of output.

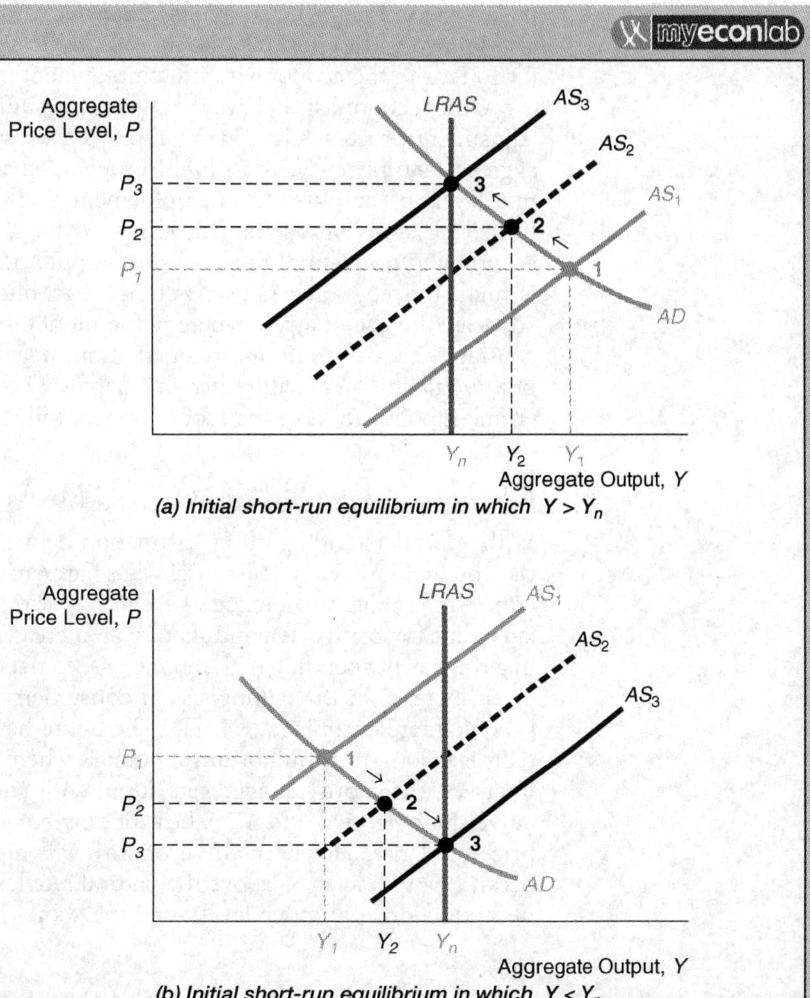

(a) Initial short-run equilibrium in which $Y > Y_n$

(b) Initial short-run equilibrium in which $Y < Y_n$

reaches the long-run equilibrium point 3, the intersection of the aggregate demand curve (AD) and the long-run aggregate supply curve ($LRAS$) at Y_n. Here, as in panel (a), the economy comes to rest when output has again returned to the natural rate level.

A striking feature of both panels of Figure 5 is that regardless of where output is initially, it returns eventually to the natural rate level. This feature is described by saying that the economy has a **self-correcting mechanism**.

An important issue for policymakers is how rapidly this self-correcting mechanism works. Many economists believe that the self-correcting mechanism takes a long time, so the approach to long-run equilibrium is slow. This view is reflected in Keynes's often quoted remark, "In the long run, we are all dead." These economists view the self-correcting mechanism as slow, because wages are inflexible, particularly in the downward direction when unemployment is high. The resulting slow wage and price adjustments mean that the aggregate supply curve does not move quickly to restore the economy to the natural rate of unemployment. Hence when unemployment is high, these economists (called **activists**), many of whom are followers of Keynes and are thus also known as **Keynesians**, are more likely to see the need for active government policy to restore the economy to full employment.

Other economists believe that wages are sufficiently flexible that the wage and price adjustment process is reasonably rapid. As a result of this flexibility, adjustment of the aggregate supply curve to its long-run position and the economy's return to the natural rate levels of output and unemployment will occur quickly. Thus these economists (called **nonactivists**) see much less need for active government policy to restore the economy to the natural rate levels of output and unemployment when unemployment is high. Indeed, some nonactivists led by Milton Friedman, known as **monetarists**, advocate the use of a rule whereby the money supply or the monetary base grows at a constant rate so as to minimize fluctuations in aggregate demand that might lead to output fluctuations. We will return in Chapter 24 to the debate about whether active government policy to keep the economy near full employment is beneficial.

Changes in Equilibrium Caused by Aggregate Demand Shocks

With an understanding of the distinction between the short-run and long-run equilibria, you are now ready to analyze what happens when an economy's aggregate demand curve shifts. Figure 6 depicts the effect of a rightward shift in the aggregate demand curve due to positive demand shocks: an increase in the money supply ($M\uparrow$), an increase in government spending ($G\uparrow$), an increase in net exports ($NX\uparrow$), a decrease in taxes ($T\downarrow$), or an increase in the willingness of consumers and businesses to spend because they become more optimistic ($C\uparrow$, $I\uparrow$). The figure has been drawn so that the economy initially is in long-run equilibrium at point 1, where the initial aggregate demand curve AD_1 intersects the short-run aggregate supply AS_1 curve at Y_n. When the aggregate demand curve shifts rightward to AD_2, the economy moves to point 1′, and both output and the price level rise. However, the economy will not remain at point 1′ in the long run, because output at $Y_{1'}$ is above the natural rate level. Wages will rise, increasing the cost of production at all price levels, and the short-run aggregate supply curve will eventu-

FIGURE 6

Response of Output and the Price Level to a Shift in the Aggregate Demand Curve

A shift in the aggregate demand curve from AD_1 to AD_2 moves the economy from point 1 to point 1′. Because $Y_{1'} > Y_n$, the short-run aggregate supply curve begins to shift leftward, eventually reaching AS_2, where output returns to Y_n and the price level has risen to P_2.

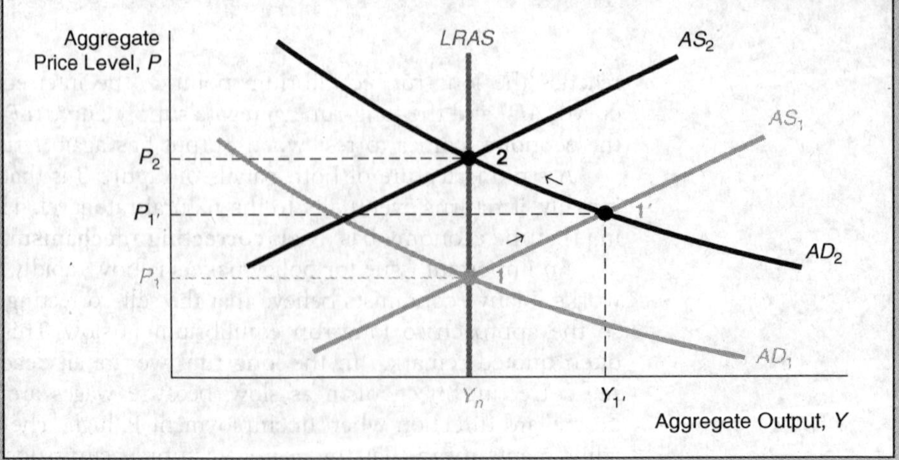

ally shift leftward to AS_2, where it finally comes to rest. The economy (equilibrium) thus slides up the aggregate demand curve from point 1′ to point 2, which is the point of long-run equilibrium at the intersection of AD_2 and the long-run aggregate supply curve (*LRAS*) at Y_n. ***Although the initial short-run effect of the rightward shift in the aggregate demand curve is a rise in both the price level and output, the ultimate long-run effect is only a rise in the price level.***

Changes in Equilibrium Caused by Aggregate Supply Shocks

Our understanding of the distinction between short-run and long-run equilibria allows us to analyze what happens when aggregate supply shocks shift the short-run aggregate supply curve. Suppose that the economy is initially at the natural rate level of output at point 1 when the short-run aggregate supply curve shifts from AS_1 to AS_2 in Figure 7 because of a negative supply shock (a sharp rise in energy prices, for example). The economy will move from point 1 to point 2, where the price level rises but aggregate output *falls*. A situation of a rising price level but a falling level of aggregate output, as pictured in Figure 7, has been labeled *stagflation* (a combination of words *stagnation* and *inflation*). At point 2, output is below the natural rate level, so wages fall and shift the short-run aggregate supply curve back to where it was initially at AS_1. The result is that the economy (equilibrium) slides down the aggregate demand curve AD_1 (assuming that the aggregate demand curve remains in the same position) and returns to the long-run equilibrium at point 1. ***Although a leftward shift in the short-run aggregate supply curve initially raises the price level and lowers output, the ultimate effect is that output and price level are unchanged (holding the aggregate demand curve constant).***

Shifts in the Long-Run Aggregate Supply Curve: Real Business Cycle Theory and Hysteresis

To this point, we have assumed that the natural rate level of output Y_n and hence the long-run aggregate supply curve are given. However, over time, the natural rate level of output increases as a result of economic growth. If the productive capacity of the

myeconlab

FIGURE 7
Response of Output and the Price Level to a Shift in Short-Run Aggregate Supply
A shift in the short-run aggregate supply curve from AS_1 to AS_2 moves the economy from point 1 to point 2. Because $Y_2 < Y_n$, the short-run aggregate supply curve begins to shift back to the right, eventually returning to AS_1, where the economy is again at point 1.

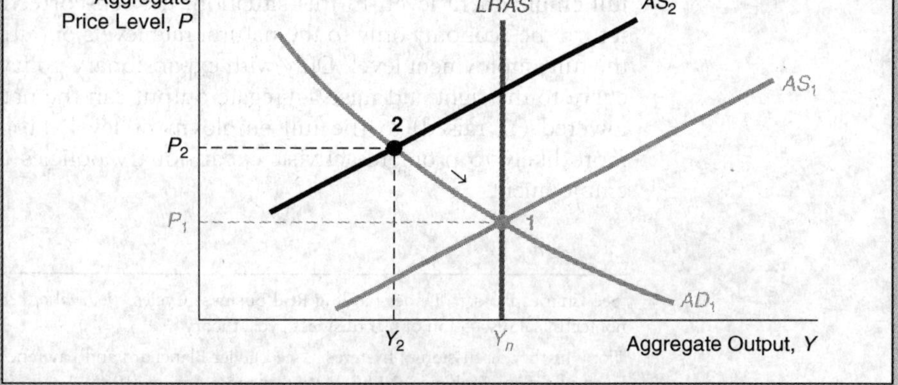

economy is growing at a steady rate of 3% per year, for example, every year Y_n will grow by 3% and the long-run aggregate supply curve at Y_n will shift to the right by 3%. To simplify the analysis when Y_n grows at a steady rate, Y_n and the long-run aggregate supply curve are drawn as fixed in the aggregate demand and supply diagrams. Keep in mind, however, that the level of aggregate output pictured in these diagrams is actually best thought of as the level of aggregate output relative to its normal rate of growth (trend).

The usual assumption when conducting aggregate demand and supply analysis is that shifts in either the aggregate demand curve or the aggregate supply curve have no effect on the natural rate level of output (which grows at a steady rate). Movements of aggregate output around the Y_n level in the diagram then describe short-run (business cycle) fluctuations in aggregate output. However, some economists take issue with the assumption that Y_n is unaffected by aggregate demand and supply shocks.

One group, led by Edward Prescott of the University of Minnesota, has developed a theory of aggregate economic fluctuations called **real business cycle theory**, in which aggregate supply (real) shocks do affect the natural rate level of output Y_n. This theory views shocks to tastes (workers' willingness to work, for example) and technology (productivity) as the major driving forces behind short-run fluctuations in the business cycle, because these shocks lead to substantial short-run fluctuations in Y_n. Shifts in the aggregate demand curve, perhaps as a result of changes in monetary policy, by contrast are not viewed as being particularly important to aggregate output fluctuations. Because real business cycle theory views most business cycle fluctuations as resulting from fluctuations in the natural rate level of output, it does not see much need for activist policy to eliminate high unemployment. Real business cycle theory is highly controversial and is the subject of intensive research.[5]

Another group of economists disagrees with the assumption that the natural rate level of output Y_n is always at the full employment level and is unaffected by aggregate demand shocks. These economists contend that the natural rate level of unemployment and output are subject to **hysteresis**, a departure from full employment levels as a result of past high unemployment.[6] When unemployment rises because of a reduction of aggregate demand that shifts the *AD* curve inward, the natural rate of unemployment is viewed as rising above the full employment level. This could occur because the unemployed become discouraged and fail to look hard for work or because employers may be reluctant to hire workers who have been unemployed for a long time, seeing it as a signal that the worker is undesirable. The outcome is that the natural rate of unemployment shifts upward after unemployment has become high, and Y_n falls below the full employment level. In this situation, the self-correcting mechanism will be able to return the economy only to the natural rate levels of output and unemployment, not to the full employment level. Only with expansionary policy to shift the aggregate demand curve to the right and raise aggregate output can the natural rate of unemployment be lowered (Y_n raised) to the full employment level. Proponents of hysteresis are thus more likely to promote activist, expansionary policies to restore the economy to full employment.

---

[5]See Charles Plosser, "Understanding Real Business Cycles," *Journal of Economic Perspectives* (1989): 51–77, for a nontechnical discussion of real business cycle theory.

[6]For a further discussion of hysteresis, see Olivier Blanchard and Lawrence Summers, "Hysteresis in the European Unemployment Problem," *NBER Macroeconomics Annual*, 1986, 1, ed. Stanley Fischer (Cambridge, Mass.: MIT Press, 1986), pp. 15–78.

STUDY GUIDE

Aggregate supply and demand analysis are best learned by practicing applications. In this section, we have traced out what happens to aggregate output when there is an increase in the money supply or a negative supply shock. Make sure you can also draw the appropriate shifts in the aggregate demand and supply curves and analyze what happens when other variables such as taxes or the expected price level change.

Conclusions

Aggregate demand and supply analysis yields the following conclusions (under the usual assumption that the natural rate level of output is unaffected by aggregate demand and supply shocks):

1. A shift in the aggregate demand curve—which can be caused by changes in monetary policy (the money supply), fiscal policy (government spending or taxes), international trade (net exports), or "animal spirits" (business and consumer optimism)—affects output only in the short run and has no effect in the long run. Furthermore, the initial change in the price level is less than is achieved in the long run, when the aggregate supply curve has fully adjusted.

2. A shift in the aggregate supply curve—which can be caused by changes in expected inflation, workers' attempts to push up real wages, or a supply shock—affects output and prices only in the short run and has no effect in the long run (holding the aggregate demand curve constant).

3. The economy has a self-correcting mechanism, which will return it to the natural rate levels of unemployment and aggregate output over time.

APPLICATION Explaining Past Business Cycle Episodes

Aggregate supply and demand analysis is an extremely useful tool for analyzing aggregate economic activity; we will apply it to several business cycle episodes. To simplify our analysis, we always assume in all four examples that aggregate output is initially at the natural rate level.

Vietnam War Buildup, 1964–1970

America's involvement in Vietnam began to escalate in the early 1960s, and after 1964, the United States was fighting a full-scale war. Beginning in 1965, the resulting increases in military expenditure raised government spending, while at the same time the Federal Reserve increased the rate of money growth in an attempt to keep interest rates from rising. What does aggregate supply and demand analysis suggest should have happened to aggregate output and the price level as a result of the Vietnam War buildup?

The rise in government spending and the higher rate of money growth would shift the aggregate demand curve to the right (shown in Figure 6). As a result, aggregate output would rise, unemployment would fall, and the price level would rise. Table 3 demonstrates that this is exactly what happened: The unemployment rate fell steadily from

TABLE 3 Unemployment and Inflation During the Vietnam War Buildup, 1964–1970

Year	Unemployment Rate (%)	Inflation (Year to Year) (%)
1964	5.0	1.3
1965	4.4	1.6
1966	3.7	2.9
1967	3.7	3.1
1968	3.5	4.2
1969	3.4	5.5
1970	4.8	5.7

Source: Economic Report of the President.

1964 to 1969, remaining well below what economists now think was the natural rate of unemployment during that period (around 5%), and inflation began to rise. As Figure 6 predicts, unemployment would eventually begin to return to the natural rate level because of the economy's self-correcting mechanism. This is exactly what we saw occurring in 1970, when the inflation rate rose even higher and unemployment increased.

Negative Supply Shocks, 1973–1975 and 1978–1980

In 1973, the U.S. economy was hit by a series of negative supply shocks. As a result of the oil embargo stemming from the Arab–Israeli war of 1973, the Organization of Petroleum Exporting Countries (OPEC) was able to engineer a quadrupling of oil prices by restricting oil production. In addition, a series of crop failures throughout the world led to a sharp increase in food prices. Another factor was the termination of U.S. wage and price controls in 1973 and 1974, which led to a push by workers to obtain wage increases that had been prevented by the controls. The triple thrust of these events caused the aggregate supply curve to shift sharply leftward, and as the aggregate demand and supply diagram in Figure 7 predicts, both the price level and unemployment began to rise dramatically (see Table 4).

The 1978–1980 period was almost an exact replay of the 1973–1975 period. By 1978, the economy had just about fully recovered from the 1973–1975 supply shocks,

TABLE 4 Unemployment and Inflation During the Negative Supply Shock Periods, 1973–1975 and 1978–1980

Year	Unemployment Rate (%)	Inflation (Year to Year) (%)	Year	Unemployment Rate (%)	Inflation (Year to Year) (%)
1973	4.8	6.2	1978	6.0	7.6
1974	5.5	11.0	1979	5.8	11.3
1975	8.3	9.1	1980	7.0	13.5

Source: Economic Report of the President.

TABLE 5 Unemployment and Inflation During the Favorable Supply Shock Period, 1995–1999

Year	Unemployment Rate (%)	Inflation (Year to Year) (%)
1995	5.6	2.8
1996	5.4	3.0
1997	4.9	2.3
1998	4.5	1.6
1999	4.2	2.2

Source: Economic Report of the President.

when poor harvests and a doubling of oil prices (as a result of the overthrow of the Shah of Iran) again led to another sharp leftward shift of the aggregate supply curve. The pattern predicted by Figure 7 played itself out again—inflation and unemployment both shot upward (see Table 4).

Favorable Supply Shocks, 1995–1999

In February 1994, the Federal Reserve began to raise interest rates, because it believed the economy would be reaching the natural rate of output and unemployment in 1995 and might become overheated thereafter. As we can see in Table 5, however, the economy continued to grow rapidly, with unemployment falling to below 5%, well below what many economists believed to be the natural rate level, and yet inflation continued to fall, declining to around 2%. Can aggregate demand and supply analysis explain what happened?

The answer is yes. Two favorable supply shocks hit the economy in the late 1990s. First, changes in the health care industry, such as the emergence of health maintenance organizations (HMOs), reduced medical care costs substantially relative to other goods and services. Second, the computer revolution finally began to have a favorable impact on productivity, raising the potential growth rate of the economy (which journalists have dubbed the "new economy"). The outcome was a rightward shift in the aggregate supply curve, producing the opposite result depicted in Figure 7: Aggregate output rose, and unemployment fell, while inflation also declined.

Negative Demand Shocks, 2001–2004

In 2000, the U.S. economy was experiencing a business cycle boom when it was hit by a series of negative shocks to aggregate demand. First, the "tech bubble" burst in March 2000 and the stock market fell sharply. Second, the September 11, 2001, terrorist attacks weakened both consumer and business confidence. Third, the Enron bankruptcy in late 2001 and other corporate accounting scandals in 2002 revealed that corporate financial data were not to be trusted. The result was that interest rates on corporate bonds rose (see Chapter 6), making it more expensive for corporations to finance their investments.

All of these shocks decreased household and business spending, causing a drop in aggregate demand and a shift of the aggregate demand curve to the left. The situation

TABLE 6 Unemployment and Inflation During the Negative Demand Shock Period , 2000–2004

Year	Unemployment Rate (%)	Inflation (Year to Year) (%)
2000	4.0	3.4
2001	4.7	2.8
2002	5.8	1.6
2003	6.0	2.3
2004	5.5	2.7

Source: Economic Report of the President.

was exactly the opposite to that shown in Figure 6, and our aggregate demand and supply analysis predicts that unemployment would rise and inflation would fall. As we can see in Table 6, this prediction is what came to pass. Unemployment, which had been at 4% in 2000, rose to 6% in 2003, while the annual rate of inflation fell from 3.4% to 1.6%. By 2004, the self-correcting mechanism feature of aggregate demand and supply analysis began to come into play, with the unemployment rate dropping back to 5.5%.

SUMMARY

1. The aggregate demand curve indicates the quantity of aggregate output demanded at each price level, and it is downward-sloping. The primary sources of shifts in the aggregate demand curve are changes in the money supply, fiscal policy (government spending and taxes), net exports, and the willingness of consumers and businesses to spend ("animal spirits").
2. The long-run aggregate supply curve is vertical at the natural rate level of output. The short-run aggregate supply curve slopes upward, because a rise in the price level raises the profit earned on each unit of production, and the quantity of output supplied rises. Four factors can cause the aggregate supply curve to shift: tightness of the labor market as represented by unemployment relative to the natural rate, expectations of inflation, workers' attempts to push up their real wages, and supply shocks unrelated to wages that affect production costs.
3. Equilibrium in the short run occurs at the point where the aggregate demand curve intersects the short-run aggregate supply curve. Although this is where the economy heads temporarily, it has a self-correcting mechanism, which leads it to settle permanently at the long-run equilibrium where aggregate output is at its natural rate level. Shifts in either the aggregate demand or the short-run aggregate supply curve can produce changes in aggregate output and the price level in the short run.

KEY TERMS

activists, p. 598
aggregate demand, p. 585
aggregate demand curve, p. 585
aggregate supply, p. 585
aggregate supply curve, p. 589
"animal spirits," p. 589

consumer expenditure, p. 588
demand shocks, p. 589
equation of exchange, p. 586
government spending, p. 588
hysteresis, p. 600
Keynesians, p. 598
monetarists, p. 598
natural rate of output, p. 591
natural rate of unemployment, p. 591
net exports, p. 588
nonactivists, p. 598
planned investment spending, p. 588
quantity theory of money, p. 586
real business cycle theory, p. 600
self-correcting mechanism, p. 597
supply shocks, p. 593
velocity of money, p. 585

QUESTIONS AND PROBLEMS

Questions marked with an asterisk are answered at the end of the book in an appendix, "Answers to Selected Questions and Problems." Questions marked with a blue circle indicate the question is available in MyEconLab at www.myeconlab.com/mishkin.

1. Given that the quantity theory predicts velocity to be 5, graph the aggregate demand curve that results if the money supply is $400 billion. If the money supply falls to $50 billion, what happens to the position of the aggregate demand curve?

*2. Milton Friedman states, "Money is all that matters to nominal income." How is this statement built into the aggregate demand curve in the quantity theory framework?

3. Suppose that government spending is raised at the same time that the money supply is lowered. What will happen to the position of the aggregate demand curve?

*4. Why does the aggregate demand curve shift when "animal spirits" change?

5. If the dollar increases in value relative to foreign currencies so that foreign goods become cheaper in the United States, what will happen to the position of the short-run aggregate supply curve? The aggregate demand curve?

*6. "Profit-maximizing behavior on the part of firms explains why the short-run aggregate supply curve is upward-sloping." Is this statement true, false, or uncertain? Explain your answer.

7. If huge budget deficits cause the public to think that there will be higher inflation in the future, what is likely to happen to the short-run aggregate supply curve when budget deficits rise?

*8. If a pill were invented that made workers twice as productive but their wages did not change, what would happen to the position of the short-run aggregate supply curve?

9. When aggregate output is below the natural rate level, what will happen to the price level over time if the aggregate demand curve remains unchanged? Why?

*10. Show how aggregate supply and demand analysis can explain why both aggregate output and the price level fell sharply when investment spending collapsed during the Great Depression.

11. "An important difference between activists and nonactivists rests on how long they think the long run actually is." Is this statement true, false, or uncertain? Explain your answer.

Using Economic Analysis to Predict the Future

*12. Predict what will happen to aggregate output and the price level if the Federal Reserve increases the money supply at the same time that Congress implements an income tax cut.

13. Suppose that the public believes that a newly announced anti-inflation program will work and so lowers its expectations of future inflation. What will happen to aggregate output and the price level in the short run?

*14. Proposals have come before Congress that advocate the implementation of a national sales tax. Predict the effect of such a tax on both the aggregate supply and demand curves and on aggregate output and the price level.

15. When there is a decline in the value of the dollar, some experts expect it to lead to a dramatic improvement in the ability of American firms to compete abroad. Predict what would happen to output and the price level in the United States as a result.

WEB EXERCISES

1. As this book goes to press, the United States has had high growth and relatively low unemployment. Go to www.whitehouse.gov/fsbr/esbr.html and follow the link to unemployment statistics. What has happened to unemployment since the last reported figure in Table 6?
2. As the economy stalled toward the end of 2002, Fed policymakers were beginning to be concerned about deflation. Go to www.whitehouse.gov/fsbr/esbr.html and follow the link to prices. What has happened to prices since the last reported figure in Table 5? Does deflation still appear to be a threat?

WEB REFERENCES

www.bls.gov/data/home.htm

The home page of the Bureau of Labor Statistics lists information on unemployment and price levels.

www.census.gov/statab/www/

Statistics on the U.S. economy in an easy-to-understand format.

www.whitehouse.gov/fsbr/esbr.html

The White House sponsors an economic statistics briefing room that reports a wide variety of interesting data dealing with the state of the economy.

CHAPTER

24 Transmission Mechanisms of Monetary Policy: The Evidence

Preview

Since 1980, the U.S. economy has been on a roller coaster, with output, unemployment, and inflation undergoing drastic fluctuations. At the start of the 1980s, inflation was running at double-digit levels, and the recession of 1980 was followed by one of the shortest economic expansions on record. After a year, the economy plunged into the 1981–1982 recession, the most severe economic contraction in the postwar era—the unemployment rate climbed to over 10%, and only then did the inflation rate begin to come down to below the 5% level. The 1981–1982 recession was then followed by a long economic expansion that reduced the unemployment rate to below 6% in the 1987–1990 period. With Iraq's invasion of Kuwait and a rise in oil prices in the second half of 1990, the economy again plunged into recession. Subsequent growth in the economy was sluggish at first but eventually sped up, lowering the unemployment rate to below 5% in the late 1990s. In March 2001, the economy slipped into recession, with the unemployment rate climbing to around 6%. By 2005, a recovery brought the unemployment rate down to 5%. In light of large fluctuations in aggregate output (reflected in the unemployment rate) and inflation, and the economic instability that accompanies them, policymakers face the following dilemma: What policy or policies, if any, should be implemented to reduce fluctuations in output and inflation in the future?

To answer this question, monetary policymakers must have an accurate assessment of the timing and effect of their policies on the economy. To make this assessment, they need to understand the mechanisms through which monetary policy affects the economy. In this chapter, we examine empirical evidence on the effect of monetary policy on economic activity. We first look at a framework for evaluating empirical evidence and then use this framework to understand why there are still deep disagreements on the importance of monetary policy to the economy. We then go on to examine the transmission mechanisms of monetary policy and evaluate the empirical evidence on them to better understand the role that monetary policy plays in the economy. We will see that these monetary transmission mechanisms emphasize the link between the financial system (which we studied in the first three parts of this book) and monetary theory, the subject of this part.

FRAMEWORK FOR EVALUATING EMPIRICAL EVIDENCE

To develop a framework for understanding how to evaluate empirical evidence, we need to recognize that there are two basic types of empirical evidence in economics and other scientific disciplines: **Structural model evidence** examines whether one variable affects another by using data to build a model that explains the channels through which this variable affects the other; **reduced-form evidence** examines whether one variable has an effect on another simply by looking directly at the relationship between the two variables.

Suppose that you were interested in whether drinking coffee leads to heart disease. Structural model evidence would involve developing a model that analyzed data on how coffee is metabolized by the human body, how it affects the operation of the heart, and how its effects on the heart lead to heart attacks. Reduced-form evidence would involve looking directly at whether coffee drinkers tend to experience heart attacks more frequently than non–coffee drinkers.

How you look at evidence—whether you focus on structural model evidence or reduced-form evidence—can lead to different conclusions. This is particularly true for the debate on the importance of monetary policy to economic fluctuations.

Structural Model Evidence

The components analysis of aggregate demand discussed in Chapter 23 is specific about the channels through which the money supply affects economic activity (called the **transmission mechanisms of monetary policy**). This approach examines the effect of changes in the money supply on economic activity by building a **structural model**, a description of how the economy operates using a collection of equations that describe the behavior of firms and consumers in many sectors of the economy. These equations then show the channels through which monetary and fiscal policy affect aggregate output and spending. A structural model might have behavioral equations that describe the workings of monetary policy with the following schematic diagram:

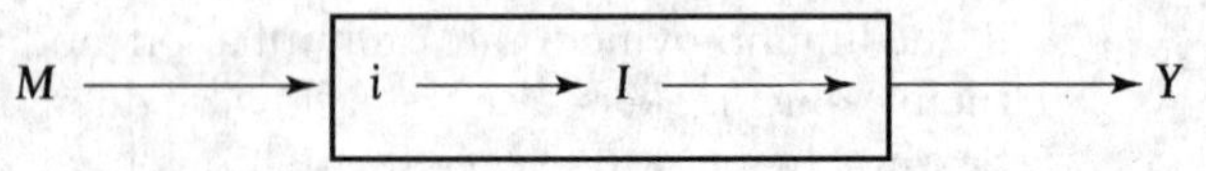

The model describes the transmission mechanism of monetary policy as follows: The change in the money supply M affects interest rates i, which in turn affect investment spending I, which in turn affects aggregate output or aggregate spending Y. Structural model evidence on the relationship between M and Y looks at empirical evidence on the specific channels of monetary influence, such as the link between interest rates and investment spending.

Reduced-Form Evidence

The quantity theory approach to aggregate demand does not describe specific ways in which the money supply affects aggregate spending. Instead, it suggests that the effect of money on economic activity should be examined by looking at whether movements in Y are tightly linked to (have a high correlation with) movements in M. Reduced-form evidence analyzes the effect of changes in M on Y as if the economy were a black box whose workings cannot be seen. The reduced-form way of looking at the evidence can be represented by the following schematic diagram, in which the economy is drawn as a black box with a question mark:

Advantages and Disadvantages of Structural Model Evidence

The structural model approach has the advantage of giving us an understanding of how the economy works. If the structure is correct—if it contains all the transmission mechanisms and channels through which monetary policy can affect economic activity—the structural model approach has three major advantages over the reduced-form approach.

1. Because we can evaluate each transmission mechanism separately to see whether it is plausible, we can gather more evidence on whether monetary policy has an important effect on economic activity. If we find that monetary policy significantly affects economic activity, for example, we will have more confidence that changes in monetary policy actually cause the changes in economic activity; that is, we will have more confidence on the direction of causation between *M* and *Y*.

2. Knowing how changes in monetary policy affect economic activity may help us predict the effect of changes in *M* on *Y* more accurately. For example, expansions in the money supply might be found to be less effective when interest rates are low. Then, when interest rates are higher, we would be able to predict that an expansion in the money supply would have a larger impact on *Y* than would otherwise be the case.

3. By knowing how the economy operates, we may be able to predict how institutional changes in the economy might affect the link between changes in *M* and *Y*. For instance, before 1980, when Regulation Q was still in effect, restrictions on interest payments on savings deposits meant that the average consumer would not earn more on savings when interest rates rose. Since the termination of Regulation Q, the average consumer now earns more on savings when interest rates rise. If we understand how changes in the interest rates paid on savings affect consumer spending, we might be able to say that a change in monetary policy, which affects interest rates, will have a different effect today than it would have had before 1980. Because of the rapid pace of financial innovation, the advantage of being able to predict how institutional changes affect the link between changes in *M* and *Y* may be more important now than in the past.

These three advantages of the structural model approach suggest that it is better than the reduced-form approach *if we know the correct structure of the model.* Put another way, structural model evidence is only as good as the structural model it is based on; it is best only if all the transmission mechanisms are fully understood. This is a big *if*, as failing to include one or two relevant transmission mechanisms for monetary policy in the structural model might result in a serious misjudgment about the impact of changes in *M* on *Y*.

However, structural models may ignore the transmission mechanisms for monetary policy that are most important. For example, if the most important monetary transmission mechanisms involve consumer spending rather than investment spending, the structural model (such as the $M\uparrow \Rightarrow i\downarrow \Rightarrow I\uparrow \Rightarrow Y\uparrow$ model we used earlier), which focuses on investment spending for its monetary transmission mechanism, may underestimate the importance of an increase in the money supply to economic activity.

Advantages and Disadvantages of Reduced-Form Evidence

The main advantage of reduced-form evidence over structural model evidence is that no restrictions are imposed on the way monetary policy affects the economy. If we are not sure that we know what all the monetary transmission mechanisms are, we may be more likely to spot the full effect of changes in *M* on *Y* by looking at whether movements in *Y* correlate highly with movements in *M*.

FYI Perils of Reverse Causation: A Russian Folk Tale

A Russian folk tale illustrates the problems that can arise from reverse causation. As the story goes, there once was a severe epidemic in the Russian countryside and many doctors were sent to the towns where the epidemic was at its worst. The peasants in the towns noticed that wherever doctors went, many people were dying. So to reduce the death rate, they killed all the doctors.

Were the peasants better off? Clearly not.

The most notable objection to reduced-form evidence is that it may misleadingly suggest that changes in *M* cause changes in *Y* when that is not the case. A basic principle applicable to all scientific disciplines, including economics, states that ***correlation does not necessarily imply causation.*** That movement of one variable is linked to another doesn't necessarily mean that one variable *causes* the other.

Suppose, for example, you notice that wherever criminal activity abounds, more police patrol the street. Should you conclude from this evidence that police patrols cause criminal activity and recommend pulling police off the street to lower the crime rate? The answer is clearly no, because police patrols do not cause criminal activity; criminal activity causes police patrols. This situation is called **reverse causation** and can produce misleading conclusions when interpreting correlations (see the FYI box, "Perils of Reverse Causation: A Russian Folk Tale").

The reverse causation problem may be present when examining the link between changes in money and aggregate output or spending. Our discussion of the conduct of monetary policy in Chapter 19 suggested that when the Federal Reserve has an interest-rate target, higher output may lead to a higher money supply. If most of the correlation between *M* and *Y* occurs because of the Fed's interest-rate target, controlling the money supply will not help control aggregate output, because it is actually changes in *Y* that are causing changes in *M*, rather than the other way around.

Another facet of the correlation–causation question is that an outside factor, yet unknown, could be the driving force behind two variables that move together. Coffee drinking might be associated with heart disease not because coffee drinking causes heart attacks but because coffee drinkers tend to be people who are under a lot of stress and the stress causes heart attacks. Getting people to stop drinking coffee, then, would not lower the incidence of heart disease. Similarly, if there is an unknown outside factor that causes *M* and *Y* to move together, controlling *M* will not improve control of *Y*. (See the FYI box, "Perils of Ignoring an Outside Driving Factor: How to Lose a Presidential Election".)

Conclusions

No clear-cut case can be made that reduced-form evidence is preferable to structural model evidence, or vice versa. The structural model approach offers an understanding of how the economy works. If the structure is correct, it predicts the effect of monetary policy more accurately, allows predictions of the effect of monetary policy when institutions change, and provides more confidence in the direction of causation between *M* and *Y*. If the structure of the model is not correctly specified because it leaves out important transmission mechanisms of monetary policy, it could be very misleading.

The reduced-form approach does not restrict the way monetary policy affects the economy and may be more likely to spot the full effect of changes in *M* on *Y*. However,

FYI Perils of Ignoring an Outside Driving Factor: How to Lose a Presidential Election

Ever since Muncie, Indiana, was dubbed "Middletown" by two sociology studies over half a century ago, it has produced a vote for president that closely mirrors the national vote; that is, in every election, there has been a very high correlation between Muncie's vote and the national vote. Noticing this, a political adviser to a presidential candidate recommends that the candidate's election will be assured if *all* the candidate's campaign funds are spent in Muncie. Should the presidential candidate promote or fire this adviser? Why?

It is very unlikely that the vote in a small town like Muncie drives the vote in a national election. Rather, it is more likely that national preferences are a third driving factor that determines the vote in Muncie and also determines the vote in the national election. Changing the vote in Muncie will thus only break the relationship between that town's vote and national preferences and will have almost no impact on the election. Spending all the campaign money on this town will therefore be a waste of money.

The presidential candidate should definitely fire the adviser.

reduced-form evidence cannot rule out reverse causation, whereby changes in output cause changes in money, or the possibility that an outside factor drives changes in both output and money. A high correlation of money and output might then be misleading, because controlling the money supply would not help control the level of output.

Armed with the framework to evaluate empirical evidence we have outlined here, we can now use it to evaluate the empirical debate on the importance of monetary policy to economic fluctuations.

APPLICATION The Debate on the Importance of Monetary Policy to Economic Fluctuations

We can apply our understanding of the advantages and disadvantages of structural model versus reduced-form evidence to a debate that has been going on for more than 70 years: How important is monetary policy to economic fluctuations? The followers of Milton Friedman, known as **monetarists**, tended to focus on reduced-form evidence and found that changes in the money supply are very important to economic fluctuations. Early followers of John Maynard Keynes, known as **Keynesians**, focused on structural model evidence based on the components approach to determination of aggregate demand, which was less likely to find that monetary policy is important. We evaluate the evidence that monetarists and Keynesians brought to bear on the importance of monetary policy using the analysis we developed in the previous section.

Early Keynesian Evidence on the Importance of Money

Although Keynes proposed his theory for analyzing aggregate economic activity in 1936, his views reached their peak of popularity among economists in the 1950s and early 1960s, when the majority of economists had accepted his framework. Although most Keynesians currently believe that monetary policy has important effects on economic activity, the early Keynesians of the 1950s and early 1960s characteristically held the view that *monetary policy does not matter at all* to movements in aggregate output and hence to the business cycle.

Their belief in the ineffectiveness of monetary policy stemmed from three pieces of structural model evidence:

1. During the Great Depression, interest rates on U.S. Treasury securities fell to extremely low levels; the three-month Treasury bill rate, for example, declined to below 1%. Early Keynesians believed monetary policy affected aggregate demand solely through its effect on nominal interest rates, which in turn affected investment spending; they believed that low interest rates during the Great Depression indicated that monetary policy was easy (expansionary) because it encouraged investment spending and so could not have played a contractionary role during this period. Because monetary policy was not capable of explaining why the worst economic contraction in U.S. history had taken place, early Keynesians concluded that changes in the money supply have no effect on aggregate output—in other words, money doesn't matter.

2. Early empirical studies found no linkage between movements in nominal interest rates and investment spending. Because early Keynesians saw this link as the channel through which changes in the money supply affect aggregate demand, finding that the link was weak also led them to the conclusion that changes in the money supply have no effect on aggregate output.

3. Surveys of business people revealed that their decisions on how much to invest in new physical capital were not influenced by market interest rates. This evidence further confirmed that the link between interest rates and investment spending was weak, strengthening the conclusion that money doesn't matter. The result of this interpretation of the evidence was that most economists paid only scant attention to monetary policy before the mid-1960s.

STUDY GUIDE

Before reading about the objections that were raised against early Keynesian interpretations of the evidence, use the ideas on the disadvantages of structural model evidence to see if you can come up with some objections yourself. This will help you learn to apply the principles of evaluating evidence discussed earlier.

Objections to Early Keynesian Evidence

While Keynesian economics was reaching its ascendancy in the 1950s and 1960s, a small group of economists at the University of Chicago, led by Milton Friedman, adopted what was then the unfashionable view that money *does* matter to aggregate demand. Friedman and his disciples, who later became known as monetarists, objected to the early Keynesian interpretation of the evidence on the grounds that the structural model used by the early Keynesians was severely flawed. Because structural model evidence is only as good as the model it is based on, the monetarist critique of this evidence needs to be taken seriously.

In 1963, Friedman and Anna Schwartz, a researcher at the National Bureau of Economic Research, published their classic monetary history of the United States, which showed that contrary to the early Keynesian beliefs, monetary policy during the Great Depression was not easy; indeed, it had never been more contractionary.[1] Friedman and Schwartz documented the massive bank failures of this period and the resulting decline in the money supply—the largest ever experienced in the United States (see Chapter 17). Hence monetary policy could explain the worst economic contraction in U.S. history, and the Great Depression could not be singled out as a period that demonstrates the ineffectiveness of monetary policy.

A Keynesian could still counter Friedman and Schwartz's argument that monetary policy was contractionary during the Great Depression by citing the low level of interest rates. But were these interest rates really so low? Referring to Figure 1 in Chapter 6, you will note that although interest rates on U.S. Treasury securities and high-grade corporate bonds were low during the Great Depression, interest rates on lower-grade bonds, such as Baa corporate bonds, rose to unprecedented high levels during the sharpest part of the contraction phase (1930–1933). By the standard of these lower-grade bonds, then, interest rates were high and monetary policy was tight.

There is a moral to this story. Although much aggregate economic analysis proceeds as though there is only *one* interest rate, we must always be aware that there are *many* interest rates, which may tell different stories. During normal times, most interest rates move in tandem, so lumping them all together and looking at one representative interest rate may not be too misleading. But that is not always so. Unusual periods (like the Great Depression), when interest rates on different securities begin to diverge, do occur. This is exactly the kind of situation in which a structural model (like the early Keynesians') that looks at only the interest rates on a low-risk security such as a U.S. Treasury bill or bond can be very misleading.

There is a second, potentially more important reason why the early Keynesian structural model's focus on nominal interest rates provides a misleading picture of the tightness of monetary policy during the Great Depression. In a period of deflation, when there is a declining price level, low *nominal* interest rates do not necessarily indicate that the cost of borrowing is low and that monetary policy is easy—in fact, the cost of borrowing could be quite high. If, for example, the public expects the price level to decline at a 10% rate, then even though nominal interest rates are at zero, the real cost of borrowing would be as high as 10%. (Recall from Chapter 4 that the real interest rate equals the nominal interest rate, 0, minus the expected rate of inflation, -10%, so the real interest rate equals $0 - (-10\%) = 10\%$.)

You can see in Figure 1 that this is exactly what happened during the Great Depression: Real interest rates on U.S. Treasury bills were far higher during the 1931–1933 contraction phase of the depression than was the case throughout the next 40 years.[2] As a result, movements of *real* interest rates indicate that, contrary to the early Keynesians' beliefs, monetary policy was extremely tight during the Great Depression. Because

---

[1]Milton Friedman and Anna Jacobson Schwartz, *A Monetary History of the United States, 1867–1960* (Princeton, N.J.: Princeton University Press, 1963).

[2]In the 1980s, real interest rates rose to exceedingly high levels, approaching those of the Great Depression period. Research has tried to explain this phenomenon, some of which points to monetary policy as the source of high real rates in the 1980s. For example, see Oliver J. Blanchard and Lawrence H. Summers, "Perspectives on High World Interest Rates," *Brookings Papers on Economic Activity* 2 (1984): 273–324; and John Huizinga and Frederic S. Mishkin, "Monetary Policy Regime Shifts and the Unusual Behavior of Real Interest Rates," *Carnegie-Rochester Conference Series on Public Policy* 24 (1986): 231–274.

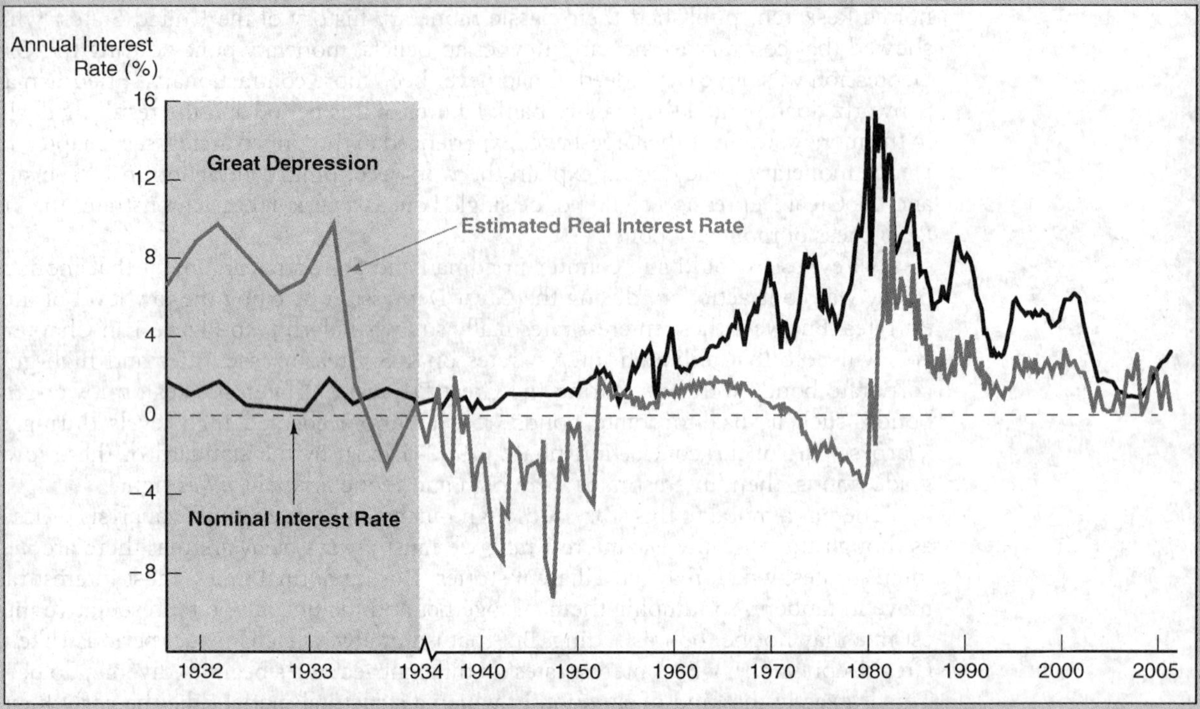

FIGURE 1 Real and Nominal Interest Rates on Three-Month Treasury Bills, 1931–2005

Sources: Nominal rates from www.federalreserve.gov/releases/h15/update/. The real rate is constructed using the procedure outlined in Frederic S. Mishkin, "The Real Interest Rate: An Empirical Investigation," *Carnegie-Rochester Conference Series on Public Policy* 15 (1981): 151–200. This involves estimating expected inflation as a function of past interest rates, inflation, and time trends and then subtracting the expected inflation measure from the nominal interest rate.

an important role for monetary policy during this depressed period could no longer be ruled out, most economists were forced to rethink their position regarding whether money matters.

Monetarists also objected to the early Keynesian structural model's view that a weak link between nominal interest rates and investment spending indicates that investment spending is unaffected by monetary policy. A weak link between *nominal* interest rates and investment spending does not rule out a strong link between *real* interest rates and investment spending. As depicted in Figure 1, nominal interest rates are often a very misleading indicator of real interest rates—not only during the Great Depression, but in later periods as well. Because real interest rates more accurately reflect the true cost of borrowing, they should be more relevant to investment decisions than nominal interest rates. Accordingly, the two pieces of early Keynesian evidence indicating that nominal interest rates have little effect on investment spending do not rule out a strong effect of changes in the money supply on investment spending and hence on aggregate demand.

Monetarists also asserted that interest-rate effects on investment spending might be only one of many channels through which monetary policy affects aggregate demand. Monetary policy could then have a major impact on aggregate demand even if interest-rate effects on investment spending are small, as was suggested by the early Keynesians.

STUDY GUIDE

As you read the monetarist evidence presented in the next section, again try to think of objections to the evidence. This time use the ideas on the disadvantages of reduced-form evidence.

Early Monetarist Evidence on the Importance of Money

In the early 1960s, Milton Friedman and his followers published a series of studies based on reduced-form evidence that promoted the case for a strong effect of money on economic activity. In general, reduced-form evidence can be broken down into three categories: *timing evidence*, which looks at whether the movements in one variable typically occur before another; *statistical evidence*, which performs formal statistical tests on the correlation of the movements of one variable with another; and *historical evidence*, which examines specific past episodes to see whether movements in one variable appear to cause another. Let's look at the monetarist evidence on the importance of money that falls into each of these three categories.

Timing Evidence. Monetarist timing evidence reveals how the rate of money supply growth moves relative to the business cycle. The evidence on this relationship was first presented by Friedman and Schwartz in a famous paper published in 1963.[3] Friedman and Schwartz found that in every business cycle over nearly a century that they studied, the money growth rate always declined before output did. On average, the peak in the rate of money growth occurred 16 months before the peak in the level of output. However, this lead time could vary, ranging from a few months to more than two years. The conclusion that these authors reached on the basis of this evidence is that money growth causes business cycle fluctuations, but its effect on the business cycle operates with "long and variable lags."

Timing evidence is based on the philosophical principle first stated in Latin as *post hoc, ergo propter hoc*, which means that if one event occurs after another, the second event must have been caused by the first. This principle is valid only if we know that the first event is an *exogenous* event, an event occurring as a result of an independent action that could not possibly be caused by the event following it or by some outside factor that might affect both events. If the first event is exogenous, when the second event follows the first we can be more confident that the first event is causing the second.

An example of an exogenous event is a controlled experiment. A chemist mixes two chemicals; suddenly his lab blows up and he with it. We can be absolutely sure that the cause of his demise was the act of mixing the two chemicals together. The principle of *post hoc, ergo propter hoc* is extremely useful in scientific experimentation.

Unfortunately, economics does not enjoy the precision of hard sciences like physics or chemistry. Often we cannot be sure that an economic event, such as a decline in the rate of money growth, is an exogenous event—it could have been caused by an outside factor or by the event it is supposedly causing. When another event (such as a decline in

[3]Milton Friedman and Anna Jacobson Schwartz, "Money and Business Cycles," *Review of Economics and Statistics* 45, Suppl. (1963): 32–64.

output) typically follows the first event (a decline in money growth), we cannot conclude with certainty that one caused the other. Timing evidence is clearly of a reduced-form nature because it looks directly at the relationship of the movements of two variables. Money growth could lead output, or both could be driven by an outside factor.

Because timing evidence is of a reduced-form nature, there is also the possibility of reverse causation, in which output growth causes money growth. How can this reverse causation occur while money growth still leads output? There are several ways in which this can happen, but we will deal with just one example.[4]

Suppose that you are in a hypothetical economy with a very regular business cycle movement, plotted in panel (a) of Figure 2, that is four years long (four years from peak to peak). Let's assume that in our hypothetical economy, there is reverse causation from output to the money supply and movements in the money supply and output are perfectly correlated; that is, the money supply M and output Y move upward and downward at the same time. The result is that the peaks and troughs of the M and Y series in panels (a) and (b) occur at exactly the same time. Therefore, no lead or lag relationship exists between them.

Now let's construct the rate of money supply growth from the money supply series in panel (b). This is done in panel (c). What is the rate of growth of the money supply at its peaks in years 1 and 5? At these points, it is not growing at all; the rate of growth is zero. Similarly, at the trough in year 3, the growth rate is zero. When the money supply is declining from its peak in year 1 to its trough in year 3, it has a negative growth rate, and its decline is fastest sometime between years 1 and 3 (year 2). Translating to panel (c), the rate of money growth is below zero from years 1 to 3, with its most negative value reached at year 2. By similar reasoning, you can see that the growth rate of money is positive in years 0 to 1 and 3 to 5, with the highest values reached in years 0 and 4. When we connect all these points together, we get the money growth series in panel (c), in which the peaks are at years 0 and 4, with a trough in year 2.

Now let's look at the relationship of the money growth series of panel (c) with the level of output in panel (a). As you can see, the money growth series consistently has its peaks and troughs exactly one year before the peaks and troughs of the output series. We conclude that in our hypothetical economy, the rate of money growth always decreases one year before output does. This evidence does not, however, imply that money growth *drives* output. In fact, by assumption, we know that this economy is one in which causation actually runs from output to the level of money supply, and there is no lead or lag relationship between the two. Only by our judicious choice of using the *growth rate* of the money supply rather than its *level* have we found a leading relationship.

This example shows how easy it is to misinterpret timing relationships. Furthermore, by searching for what we hope to find, we might focus on a variable, such as a growth rate, rather than a level, which suggests a misleading relationship. Timing evidence can be a dangerous tool for deciding on causation.

Stated even more forcefully, "one person's lead is another person's lag." For example, you could just as easily interpret the relationship of money growth and output in Figure 2 to say that the money growth rate lags output by three years—after all, the peaks in the money growth series occur three years after the peaks in the output series. In short, you could say that output leads money growth.

[4]A famous article by James Tobin, "Money and Income: *Post Hoc, Ergo Propter Hoc*," *Quarterly Journal of Economics* 84 (1970): 301–317, describes an economic system in which changes in aggregate output cause changes in the growth rate of money but changes in the growth rate of money have no effect on output. Tobin shows that such a system with reverse causation could yield timing evidence similar to that found by Friedman and Schwartz.

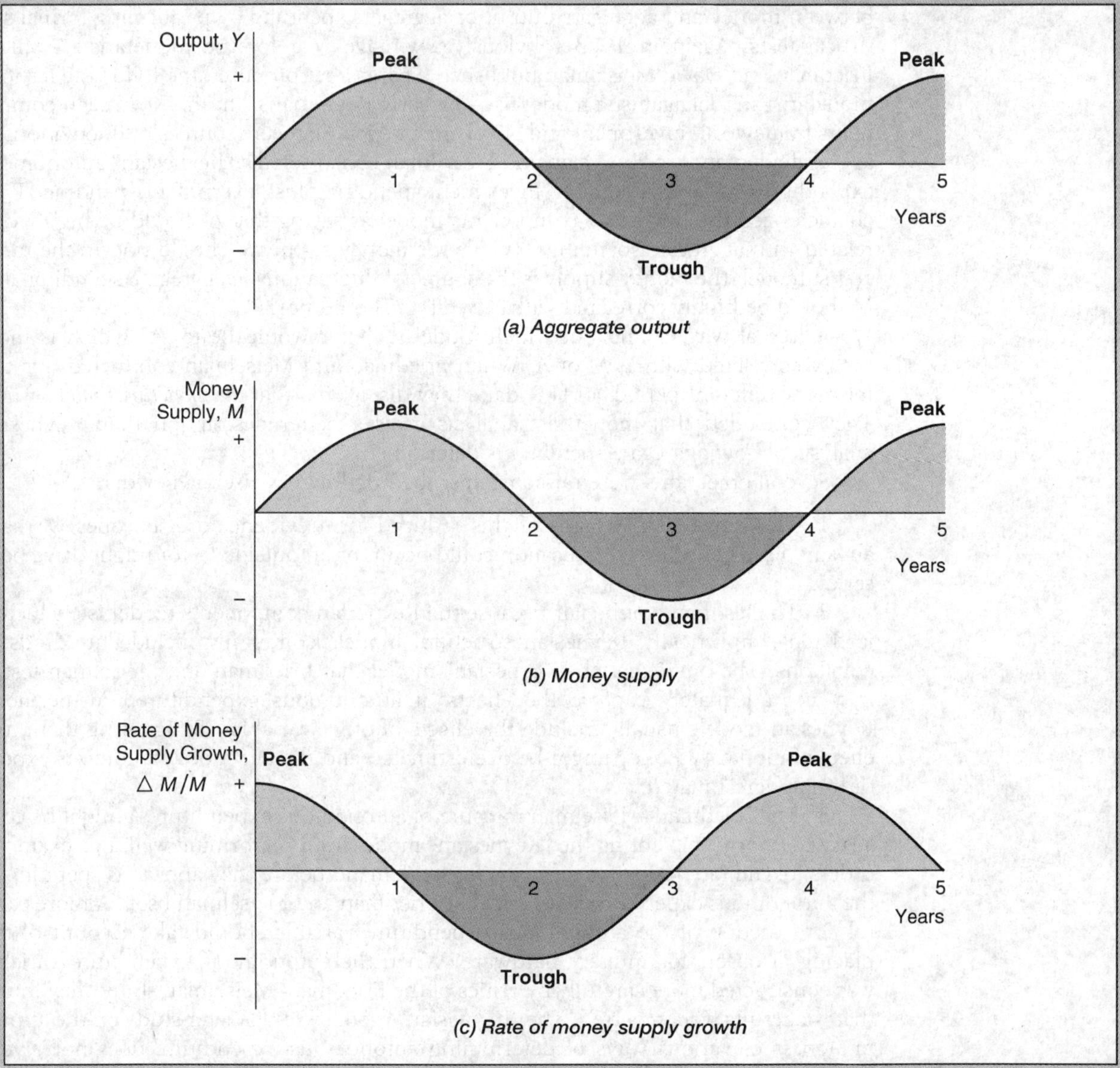

FIGURE 2 **Hypothetical Example in Which Money Growth Leads Output**
Although neither M nor Y in panels (a) and (b) leads the other (that is, their peaks and troughs coincide), $\Delta M/M$ has its peaks and troughs one year ahead of M and Y, thus leading both series. (Note that M and Y in the panels are drawn as movements around a positive average value; a plus sign indicates a value above the average, and a minus sign indicates a value below the average, not a negative value.)

We have seen that timing evidence is extremely hard to interpret. Unless we can be sure that changes in the leading variable are exogenous events, we cannot be sure that the leading variable is actually causing the following variable. And it is all too easy to find what we seek when looking for timing evidence. Perhaps the best way of describing this danger is to say that "timing evidence may be in the eyes of the beholder."

Statistical Evidence. Monetarist statistical evidence examined the correlations between money and aggregate output or aggregate spending by performing formal statistical tests. Again in 1963 (obviously a vintage year for the monetarists), Milton Friedman and David Meiselman published a paper that proposed the following test of a monetarist model against a model used by early Keynesians.[5] In the Keynesian components framework, investment and government spending were sources of fluctuations in aggregate demand, so Friedman and Meiselman constructed a "Keynesian" autonomous expenditure variable A equal to investment spending plus government spending. They characterized the Keynesian components model as saying that A should be highly correlated with aggregate spending Y, while the money supply M should not. In the monetarist model, the money supply is the source of fluctuations in aggregate spending, and M should be highly correlated with Y, while A should not.

A logical way to find out which model is better would be to see which is more highly correlated with Y: M or A. When Friedman and Meiselman conducted this test for many different periods of U.S. data, they discovered that *the monetarist model wins!*[6] They concluded that monetarist analysis gives a better description than Keynesian analysis of how aggregate spending is determined.

Several objections were raised against the Friedman–Meiselman evidence:

1. The standard criticisms of this reduced-form evidence are the ones we have already discussed: Reverse causation could occur, or an outside factor might drive both series.

2. The test may not be fair because the Keynesian components model is characterized too simplistically. Keynesian structural models commonly include hundreds of equations. The one-equation "Keynesian" model that Friedman and Meiselman tested may not adequately capture the effects of autonomous expenditure. Furthermore, Keynesian models usually include the effects of other variables. By ignoring them, the effect of monetary policy might be overestimated and the effect of autonomous expenditure underestimated.

3. The Friedman–Meiselman measure of autonomous expenditure A might be constructed poorly, preventing the "Keynesian" model from performing well. For example, orders for military hardware affect aggregate demand before they appear as spending in the autonomous expenditure variable that Friedman and Meiselman used. A more careful construction of the autonomous expenditure variable should take account of the placing of orders for military hardware. When the autonomous expenditure variable was constructed more carefully by critics of the Friedman–Meiselman study, they found that the results were reversed: The "Keynesian" model won.[7] A later study on the appropriateness of various ways of determining autonomous expenditure does not give a clear-cut victory to either the "Keynesian" or the monetarist model.[8]

---

[5]Milton Friedman and David Meiselman, "The Relative Stability of Monetary Velocity and the Investment Multiplier," in *Stabilization Policies*, ed. Commission on Money and Credit (Upper Saddle River, N.J.: Prentice-Hall, 1963), pp. 165–268.

[6]Friedman and Meiselman did not actually run their tests using the Y variable because they felt that this gave an unfair advantage to the Keynesian model in that A is included in Y. Instead, they subtracted A from Y and tested for the correlation of $Y - A$ with M or A.

[7]See, for example, Albert Ando and Franco Modigliani, "The Relative Stability of Monetary Velocity and the Investment Multiplier," *American Economic Review* 55 (1965): 693–728.

[8]See William Poole and Edith Kornblith, "The Friedman-Meiselman CMC Paper: New Evidence on an Old Controversy," *American Economic Review* 63 (1973): 908–917.

Historical Evidence. The monetarist historical evidence found in Friedman and Schwartz's *A Monetary History* has been very influential in gaining support for the monetarist position. We have already seen that the book was extremely important as a criticism of early Keynesian thinking, showing as it did that the Great Depression was not a period of easy monetary policy and that the depression could be attributed to the sharp decline in the money supply from 1930 to 1933 resulting from bank panics. In addition, the book documented in great detail that the growth rate of money leads business cycles, because it declines before every recession. This timing evidence is, of course, subject to all the criticisms raised earlier.

The historical evidence contains one feature, however, that makes it different from other monetarist evidence we have discussed so far. Several episodes occur in which changes in the money supply appear to be exogenous events. These episodes are almost like controlled experiments, so the *post hoc, ergo propter hoc* principle is far more likely to be valid: If the decline in the growth rate of the money supply is soon followed by a decline in output in these episodes, much stronger evidence is presented that money growth is the driving force behind the business cycle.

One of the best examples of such an episode is the increase in reserve requirements in 1936–1937 (discussed in the appendix to Chapter 19), which led to a sharp decline in the money supply and in its rate of growth. The increase in reserve requirements was implemented because the Federal Reserve wanted to improve its control of monetary policy; it was not implemented in response to economic conditions. We can thus rule out reverse causation from output to the money supply. Also, it is hard to think of an outside factor that could have driven the Fed to increase reserve requirements and that could also have directly affected output. Therefore, the decline in the money supply in this episode can probably be classified as an exogenous event with the characteristics of a controlled experiment. Soon after this experiment, the very severe recession of 1937–1938 occurred. We can conclude with confidence that in this episode, the change in the money supply due to the Fed's increase in reserve requirements was indeed the source of the business cycle contraction that followed.

A Monetary History also documented other historical episodes, such as the bank panics of 1907 and other years in which the decline in money growth again appears to have been an exogenous event. The fact that recessions have frequently followed apparently exogenous declines in money growth is very strong evidence that changes in the growth rate of the money supply do have an impact on aggregate output. Recent work by Christina and David Romer, both of the University of California, Berkeley, applies the historical approach to more recent data using more sophisticated statistical techniques and also finds that monetary policy shifts have had an important impact on the aggregate economy.[9]

Overview of the Monetarist Evidence

Where does this discussion of the monetarist evidence leave us? We have seen that because of reverse causation and outside-factor possibilities, there are some serious doubts about the conclusions that can be drawn from timing and statistical evidence alone. However, some of the historical evidence in which exogenous declines in money growth are followed by business cycle contractions does provide stronger support for

[9]Christina Romer and David Romer, "Does Monetary Policy Matter? A New Test in the Spirit of Friedman and Schwartz," *NBER Macroeconomics Annual, 1989*, 4, ed. Stanley Fischer (Cambridge, Mass.: MIT Press, 1989), pp. 121–170.

FYI Real Business Cycle Theory and the Debate on Money and Economic Activity

New entrants to the debate on money and economic activity are advocates of *real business cycle theory*, which states that real shocks to tastes and technology (rather than monetary shocks) are the driving forces behind business cycles. Proponents of this theory are critical of the monetarist view that money matters to business cycles because they believe that the correlation of output with money reflects reverse causation; that is, the business cycle drives money, rather than the other way around. An important piece of evidence they offer to support the reverse causation argument is that almost none of the correlation between money and output comes from the monetary base, which is controlled by the monetary authorities.* Instead, the money–output correlation stems from other sources of money supply movements that, as we saw in Chapters 16 and 17, are affected by the actions of banks, depositors, and borrowers from banks and are more likely to be influenced by the business cycle.

*Robert King and Charles Plosser, "Money, Credit and Prices in a Real Business Cycle," *American Economic Review* 74 (1984): 363–380; Charles Plosser, "Understanding Real Business Cycles," *Journal of Economic Perspectives* 3 (Summer 1989): 51–78.

the monetarist position. When historical evidence is combined with timing and statistical evidence, the conclusion that monetary policy does matter seems warranted.

As you can imagine, the economics profession was shaken by the appearance of the monetarist evidence, because up to that time most economists believed that money does not matter at all. Monetarists had demonstrated that this early Keynesian position was probably wrong, and it won them a lot of converts. Recognizing the fallacy of the position that money does not matter does not necessarily mean that we must accept the position that money is *all* that matters. Many Keynesian economists shifted their views toward the monetarist position, but not all the way. Instead, they adopted an intermediate position: They allowed that money, fiscal policy, net exports, and "animal spirits" all contributed to fluctuations in aggregate demand. The result has been a convergence of the views on the importance of monetary policy to economic activity. However, proponents of a new theory of aggregate fluctuations called *real business cycle theory* are more critical of the monetarist reduced-form evidence that money is important to business cycle fluctuations because they believe there is reverse causation from the business cycle to money (see the FYI box, "Real Business Cycle Theory and the Debate on Money and Economic Activity").

TRANSMISSION MECHANISMS OF MONETARY POLICY

After the successful monetarist attack on the early Keynesian position, economic research went in two directions. One direction was to use more sophisticated monetarist reduced-form models to test for the importance of money to economic activity.[10]

[10]The most prominent example of more sophisticated reduced-form research is the St. Louis model, which was developed at the Federal Reserve Bank of St. Louis in the late 1960s and early 1970s. It provided support for the monetarist position, but is subject to the same criticisms of reduced-form evidence outlined in the text. The St. Louis model was first outlined in Leonall Andersen and Jerry Jordan, "Monetary and Fiscal Actions: A Test of Their Relative Importance in Economic Stabilization," Federal Reserve Bank of St. Louis *Review* 50 (November 1968): 11–23.

The second direction was to pursue a structural model approach and to develop a better understanding of channels (other than interest-rate effects on investment) through which monetary policy affects aggregate demand. In this section we examine some of these channels, or *transmission mechanisms*, beginning with interest-rate channels, because they are the key monetary transmission mechanism in the *ISLM* and *AD/AS* models you have seen in Chapter 23.

Traditional Interest-Rate Channels

The traditional components view of the monetary transmission mechanism can be characterized by the following schematic, which shows the effect of an expansionary monetary policy:

$$\text{Expansionary monetary policy} \Rightarrow i_r\downarrow \Rightarrow I\uparrow \Rightarrow Y\uparrow \qquad (1)$$

where an expansionary monetary policy leads to a fall in real interest rates ($i_r\downarrow$), which in turn lowers the cost of capital, causing a rise in investment spending ($I\uparrow$), thereby leading to an increase in aggregate demand and a rise in output ($Y\uparrow$).

Although Keynes originally emphasized this channel as operating through businesses' decisions about investment spending, the search for new monetary transmission mechanisms recognized that consumers' decisions about housing and **consumer durable expenditure** (spending by consumers on durable items such as automobiles and refrigerators) also are investment decisions. Thus the interest-rate channel of monetary transmission outlined in Equation 1 applies equally to consumer spending, in which *I* also represents residential housing and consumer durable expenditure.

An important feature of the interest-rate transmission mechanism is its emphasis on the *real* (rather than the nominal) interest rate as the rate that affects consumer and business decisions. In addition, it is often the real *long*-term interest rate (not the real short-term interest rate) that is viewed as having the major impact on spending. How is it that changes in the short-term nominal interest rate induced by a central bank result in a corresponding change in the real interest rate on both short- and long-term bonds? The key is the phenomenon known as *sticky prices*, the fact that the aggregate price level adjusts slowly over time, meaning that expansionary monetary policy, which lowers the short-term nominal interest rate, also lowers the short-term *real* interest rate. The expectations hypothesis of the term structure described in Chapter 6, which states that the long-term interest rate is an average of expected future short-term interest rates, suggests that a lower real short-term interest rate, as long as it persists, leads to a fall in the real long-term interest rate. These lower real interest rates then lead to rises in business fixed investment, residential housing investment, inventory investment, and consumer durable expenditure, all of which produce the rise in aggregate output.

That the real interest rate rather than the nominal rate affects spending provides an important mechanism for how monetary policy can stimulate the economy, even if nominal interest rates hit a floor of zero during a deflationary episode. With nominal interest rates at a floor of zero, a commitment to future expansionary monetary policy can raise the expected price level ($P^e\uparrow$) and hence expected inflation ($\pi^e\uparrow$), thereby lowering the real interest rate ($i_r = [i - \pi^e]\downarrow$) even when the nominal interest rate is fixed at zero and stimulating spending through the interest-rate channel:

$$\text{Expansionary monetary policy} \Rightarrow P^e\uparrow \Rightarrow \pi^e\uparrow \Rightarrow i_r\downarrow \Rightarrow I\uparrow \Rightarrow Y\uparrow \qquad (2)$$

This mechanism thus indicates that monetary policy can still be effective even when nominal interest rates have already been driven down to zero by the monetary authorities. Indeed, this mechanism is a key element in monetarist discussions of why the U.S.

economy was not stuck in a liquidity trap (in which increases in the money supply might be unable to lower interest rates during the Great Depression and why expansionary monetary policy could have prevented the sharp decline in output during that period.

Some economists, such as John Taylor of Stanford University, take the position that there is strong empirical evidence for substantial interest-rate effects on consumer and investment spending through the cost of capital, making the interest-rate monetary transmission mechanism a strong one. His position is highly controversial, and many researchers, including Ben Bernanke, now the chairman of the Fed, and Mark Gertler of New York University, believe that the empirical evidence does not support strong interest-rate effects operating through the cost of capital.[11] Indeed, these researchers see the empirical failure of traditional interest-rate monetary transmission mechanisms as having provided the stimulus for the search for other transmission mechanisms of monetary policy.

These other transmission mechanisms fall into two basic categories: those operating through asset prices other than interest rates and those operating through asymmetric information effects on credit markets (the **credit view**). (These mechanisms are summarized in the schematic diagram in Figure 3.)

Other Asset Price Channels

As we saw earlier in the chapter, a key monetarist objection to the Keynesian analysis of monetary policy effects on the economy is that it focuses on only one asset price, the interest rate, rather than on many asset prices. Monetarists envision a transmission mechanism in which other relative asset prices and real wealth transmit monetary effects onto the economy. In addition to bond prices, two other asset prices receive substantial attention as channels for monetary policy effects: foreign exchange rates and the prices of equities (stocks).

Exchange Rate Effects on Net Exports.

With the growing internationalization of economies throughout the world and the advent of flexible exchange rates, more attention has been paid to how monetary policy affects exchange rates, which in turn affect net exports and aggregate output.

This channel also involves interest-rate effects, because, as we saw in Chapter 20, when domestic real interest rates fall, domestic dollar assets become less attractive relative to assets denominated in foreign currencies. As a result, the value of dollar assets relative to other currency assets falls, and the dollar depreciates (denoted by $E\downarrow$). The lower value of the domestic currency makes domestic goods cheaper than foreign goods, thereby causing a rise in net exports ($NX\uparrow$) and hence in aggregate output ($Y\uparrow$). The schematic for the monetary transmission mechanism that operates through the exchange rate is

$$\text{Expansionary monetary policy} \Rightarrow i_r\downarrow \Rightarrow E\downarrow \Rightarrow NX\uparrow \Rightarrow Y\uparrow \qquad (3)$$

Recent research has found that this exchange rate channel plays an important role in how monetary policy affects the domestic economy.[12]

---

[11]See John Taylor, "The Monetary Transmission Mechanism: An Empirical Framework," *Journal of Economic Perspectives* 9 (Fall 1995): 11–26, and Ben Bernanke and Mark Gertler, "Inside the Black Box: The Credit Channel of Monetary Policy Transmission," *Journal of Economic Perspectives* 9 (Fall 1995): 27–48.

[12]For example, see Ralph Bryant, Peter Hooper, and Catherine Mann, *Evaluating Policy Regimes: New Empirical Research in Empirical Macroeconomics* (Washington, D.C.: Brookings Institution, 1993); and John B. Taylor, *Macroeconomic Policy in a World Economy: From Econometric Design to Practical Operation* (New York: Norton, 1993).

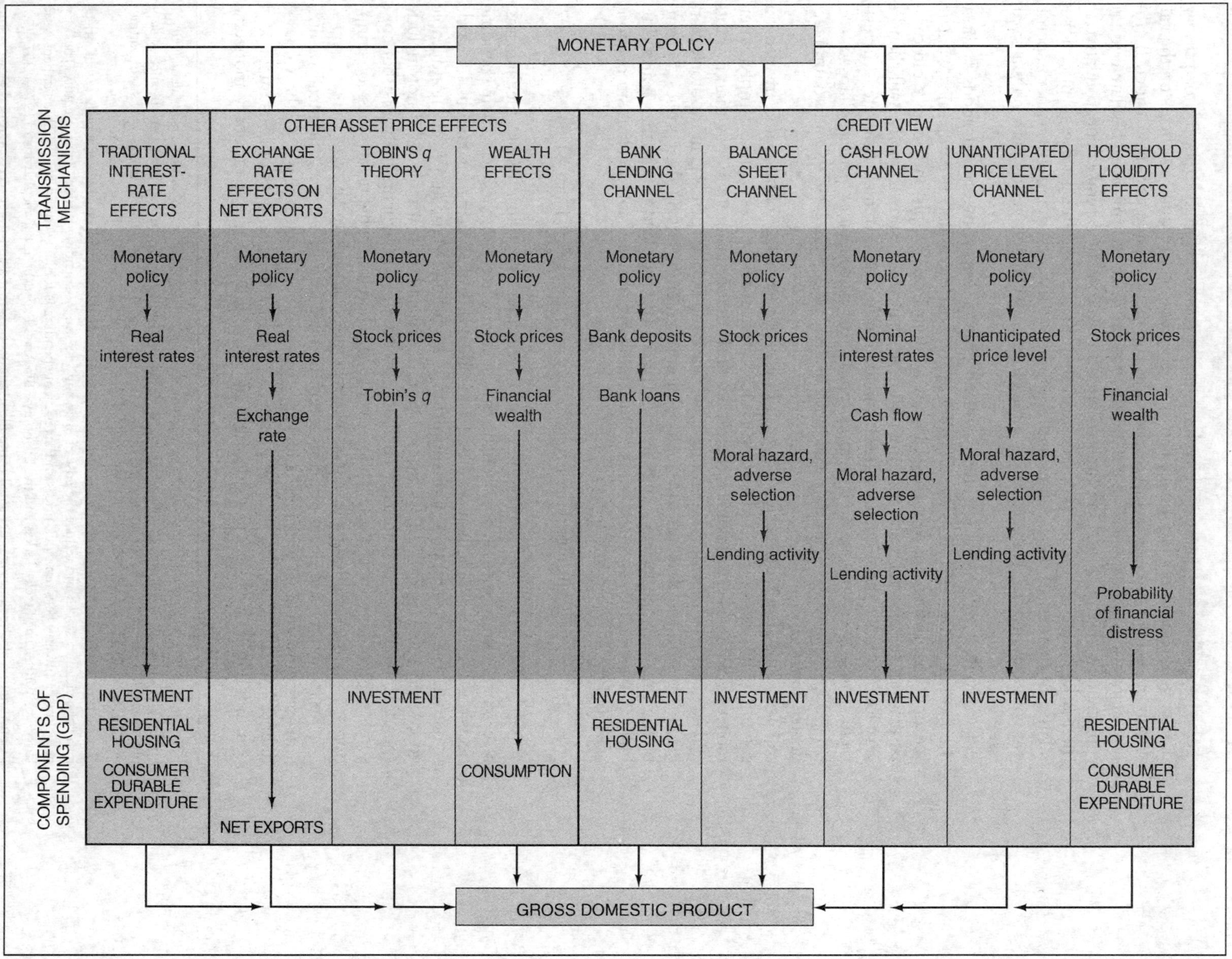

FIGURE 3 **The Link Between Monetary Policy and GDP: Monetary Transmission Mechanisms**

Tobin's *q* Theory. James Tobin developed a theory, referred to as *Tobin's q theory*, that explains how monetary policy can affect the economy through its effects on the valuation of equities (stock). Tobin defines q as the market value of firms divided by the replacement cost of capital. If q is high, the market price of firms is high relative to the replacement cost of capital, and new plant and equipment capital is cheap relative to the market value of firms. Companies can then issue stock and get a high price for it relative to the cost of the facilities and equipment they are buying. Investment spending will rise, because firms can buy a lot of new investment goods with only a small issue of stock.

Conversely, when q is low, firms will not purchase *new* investment goods because the market value of firms is low relative to the cost of capital. If companies want to acquire capital when q is low, they can buy another firm cheaply and acquire old capital instead. Investment spending, the purchase of new investment goods, will then be very low. Tobin's q theory gives a good explanation for the extremely low rate of investment spending during the Great Depression. In that period, stock prices collapsed, and by 1933, stocks were worth only one-tenth of their value in late 1929; q fell to unprecedented low levels.

The crux of this discussion is that a link exists between Tobin's q and investment spending. But how might monetary policy affect stock prices? Quite simply, when monetary policy is expansionary, the public finds that it has more money than it wants and so gets rid of it through spending. One place the public spends is in the stock market, increasing the demand for stocks and consequently raising their prices.[13] Combining this with the fact that higher stock prices (P_s) will lead to a higher q and thus higher investment spending I leads to the following transmission mechanism of monetary policy:[14]

$$\text{Expansionary monetary policy} \Rightarrow P_s\uparrow \Rightarrow q\uparrow \Rightarrow I\uparrow \Rightarrow Y\uparrow \tag{4}$$

Wealth Effects. In their search for new monetary transmission mechanisms, researchers also looked at how consumers' balance sheets might affect their spending decisions. Franco Modigliani was the first to take this tack, using his famous life cycle hypothesis of consumption. **Consumption** is spending by consumers on nondurable goods and services.[15] It differs from *consumer expenditure* in that it does not include spending on consumer durables. The basic premise of Modigliani's theory is that consumers smooth out their consumption over time. Therefore, what determines consumption spending is the lifetime resources of consumers, not just today's income.

An important component of consumers' lifetime resources is their financial wealth, a major component of which is common stocks. When stock prices rise, the value of financial wealth increases, thereby increasing the lifetime resources of consumers, and consumption should rise. Considering that, as we have seen, expansionary monetary

---

[13]See James Tobin, "A General Equilibrium Approach to Monetary Theory," *Journal of Money, Credit, and Banking* 1 (1969): 15–29. A somewhat more Keynesian story with the same outcome is that the increase in the money supply lowers interest rates on bonds so that the yields on alternatives to stocks fall. This makes stocks more attractive relative to bonds, so demand for them increases, raises their price, and thereby lowers their yield.

[14]An alternative way of looking at the link between stock prices and investment spending is that higher stock prices lower the yield on stocks and reduce the cost of financing investment spending through issuing equity. This way of looking at the link between stock prices and investment spending is formally equivalent to Tobin's q theory; see Barry Bosworth, "The Stock Market and the Economy," *Brookings Papers on Economic Activity* 2 (1975): 257–290.

[15]Consumption also includes another small component, the services that a consumer receives from the ownership of housing and consumer durables.

policy can lead to a rise in stock prices, we now have another monetary transmission mechanism:

$$\text{Expansionary monetary policy} \Rightarrow P_s\uparrow \Rightarrow \text{wealth}\uparrow \Rightarrow \text{consumption}\uparrow \Rightarrow Y\uparrow \quad (5)$$

Modigliani's research found this relationship to be an extremely powerful mechanism that adds substantially to the potency of monetary policy.[16]

The wealth and Tobin's q channels allow for a general definition of equity, so they can also be applied to the housing market, where housing is equity. An increase in house prices, which raises their prices relative to replacement cost, leads to a rise in Tobin's q for housing, thereby stimulating its production. Similarly, housing and land prices are extremely important components of wealth, so rises in these prices increase wealth, thereby raising consumption. Monetary expansion, which raises land and housing prices through the Tobin's q and wealth mechanisms described here, thus leads to a rise in aggregate demand.

Credit View

Dissatisfaction with the conventional stories that interest-rate effects explain the impact of monetary policy on expenditures on durable assets has led to a new explanation based on the problem of asymmetric information in financial markets (see Chapter 8). This explanation, referred to as the *credit view*, proposes that two types of monetary transmission channels arise as a result of information problems in credit markets: those that operate through effects on bank lending and those that operate through effects on firms' and households' balance sheets.[17]

Bank Lending Channel. The bank lending channel is based on the analysis in Chapter 8, which demonstrated that banks play a special role in the financial system because they are especially well suited to solve asymmetric information problems in credit markets. Because of banks' special role, certain borrowers will not have access to the credit markets unless they borrow from banks. As long as there is no perfect substitutability of retail bank deposits with other sources of funds, the bank lending channel of monetary transmission operates as follows. Expansionary monetary policy, which increases bank reserves and bank deposits, increases the quantity of bank loans available. Because many borrowers are dependent on bank loans to finance their activities, this increase in loans will cause investment (and possibly consumer) spending to rise. Schematically, the monetary policy effect is

$$\begin{aligned}\text{Expansionary monetary policy} &\Rightarrow \text{bank deposits}\uparrow \\ &\Rightarrow \text{bank loans}\uparrow \Rightarrow I\uparrow \Rightarrow Y\uparrow \quad (6)\end{aligned}$$

An important implication of the credit view is that monetary policy will have a greater effect on expenditure by smaller firms, which are more dependent on bank loans, than

[16]See Franco Modigliani, "Monetary Policy and Consumption," in *Consumer Spending and Money Policy: The Linkages* (Boston: Federal Reserve Bank, 1971), pp. 9–84.

[17]Surveys of the credit view can be found in Ben Bernanke, "Credit in the Macroeconomy," Federal Reserve Bank of New York *Quarterly Review* (Spring 1993): 50–70; Ben Bernanke and Mark Gertler, "Inside the Black Box: The Credit Channel of Monetary Policy Transmission," *Journal of Economic Perspectives* 9 (Fall 1995): 27–48; Stephen G. Cecchetti, "Distinguishing Theories of the Monetary Transmission Mechanism," Federal Reserve Bank of St. Louis *Review* 77 (May–June 1995): 83–97; and R. Glenn Hubbard, "Is There a 'Credit Channel' for Monetary Policy?" Federal Reserve Bank of St. Louis *Review* 77 (May–June 1995): 63–74.

it will on large firms, which can get funds directly through stock and bond markets (and not only through banks).

Though this result has been confirmed by researchers, doubts about the bank lending channel have been raised in the literature, and there are reasons to suspect that the bank lending channel in the United States may not be as powerful as it once was.[18] The first reason this channel is not as powerful is that current U.S. regulations no longer impose restrictions on banks that hinder their ability to raise funds (see Chapter 9). Prior to the mid-1980s, certificates of deposit (CDs) were subjected to reserve requirements and Regulation Q deposit rate ceilings, which made it hard for banks to replace deposits that flowed out of the banking system during a monetary contraction. With these regulatory restrictions abolished, banks can more easily respond to a decline in bank reserves and a loss of retail deposits by issuing CDs at market interest rates that do not have to be backed up by required reserves. Second, the worldwide decline of the traditional bank lending business (see Chapter 10) has rendered the bank lending channel less potent. Nonetheless, many economists believe that the bank lending channel played an important role in the slow recovery in the U.S. from the 1990–1991 recession.

Balance Sheet Channel. Even though the bank lending channel may be declining in importance, it is by no means clear that this is the case for the other credit channel, the balance sheet channel. Like the bank lending channel, the balance sheet channel arises from the presence of asymmetric information problems in credit markets. In Chapter 8, we saw that the lower the net worth of business firms, the more severe the adverse selection and moral hazard problems in lending to these firms. Lower net worth means that lenders in effect have less collateral for their loans, so their potential losses from adverse selection are higher. A decline in net worth, which raises the adverse selection problem, thus leads to decreased lending to finance investment spending. The lower net worth of businesses also increases the moral hazard problem because it means that owners have a lower equity stake in their firms, giving them more incentive to engage in risky investment projects. Because taking on riskier investment projects makes it more likely that lenders will not be paid back, a decrease in businesses' net worth leads to a decrease in lending and hence in investment spending.

Monetary policy can affect firms' balance sheets in several ways. Expansionary monetary policy, which causes a rise in stock prices ($P_s\uparrow$) along the lines described earlier, raises the net worth of firms and so leads to higher investment spending ($I\uparrow$) and aggregate demand ($Y\uparrow$) because of the decrease in adverse selection and moral hazard problems. This leads to the following schematic for one balance sheet channel of monetary transmission:

$$\begin{aligned}\text{Expansionary monetary policy} \Rightarrow P_s\uparrow \Rightarrow \text{net worth}\uparrow \Rightarrow \text{adverse selection}\downarrow,\\ \text{moral hazard}\downarrow \Rightarrow \text{lending}\uparrow \Rightarrow I\uparrow \Rightarrow Y\uparrow\end{aligned} \quad (7)$$

Cash Flow Channel. Another balance sheet channel operates by affecting *cash flow*, the difference between cash receipts and cash expenditures. Expansionary monetary policy, which lowers nominal interest rates, also causes an improvement in firms' balance sheets because it raises cash flow. The rise in cash flow causes an improvement in the balance sheet because it increases the liquidity of the firm (or household) and

---

[18]For example, see Valerie Ramey, "How Important Is the Credit Channel in the Transmission of Monetary Policy?" *Carnegie-Rochester Conference Series on Public Policy* 39 (1993): 1–45; and Allan H. Meltzer, "Monetary, Credit (and Other) Transmission Processes: A Monetarist Perspective," *Journal of Economic Perspectives* 9 (Fall 1995): 49–72.

thus makes it easier for lenders to know whether the firm (or household) will be able to pay its bills. The result is that adverse selection and moral hazard problems become less severe, leading to an increase in lending and economic activity. The following schematic describes this additional balance sheet channel:

$$\begin{aligned}\text{Expansionary monetary policy} \Rightarrow i\downarrow \Rightarrow \text{cash flow}\uparrow \Rightarrow \text{adverse selection}\downarrow,\\ \text{moral hazard}\downarrow \Rightarrow \text{lending}\uparrow \Rightarrow I\uparrow \Rightarrow Y\uparrow\end{aligned} \quad (8)$$

An important feature of this transmission mechanism is that *nominal* interest rates affect firms' cash flow. Thus this interest-rate mechanism differs from the traditional interest-rate mechanism discussed earlier, in which the real interest rate affects investment. Furthermore, the short-term interest rate plays a special role in this transmission mechanism, because interest payments on short-term (rather than long-term) debt typically have the greatest impact on households' and firms' cash flow.

A related mechanism involving adverse selection through which expansionary monetary policy that lowers interest rates can stimulate aggregate output involves the credit-rationing phenomenon. As discussed in Chapter 9, credit rationing occurs in cases where borrowers are denied loans even when they are willing to pay a higher interest rate. This is because individuals and firms with the riskiest investment projects are exactly the ones who are willing to pay the highest interest rates, for if the high-risk investment succeeds, they will be the primary beneficiaries. Thus higher interest rates increase the adverse selection problem, and lower interest rates reduce it. When expansionary monetary policy lowers interest rates, less risk-prone borrowers make up a higher fraction of those demanding loans, so lenders are more willing to lend, raising both investment and output, along the lines of parts of the schematic in Equation 8.

Unanticipated Price Level Channel. A third balance sheet channel operates through monetary policy effects on the general price level. Because in industrialized countries debt payments are contractually fixed in nominal terms, an unanticipated rise in the price level lowers the value of firms' liabilities in real terms (decreases the burden of the debt) but should not lower the real value of the firms' assets. Monetary expansion that leads to an unanticipated rise in the price level ($P\uparrow$) therefore raises real net worth, which lowers adverse selection and moral hazard problems, thereby leading to a rise in investment spending and aggregate output as in the following schematic:

$$\begin{aligned}\text{Expanionary monetary policy} \Rightarrow \text{unanticipated } P\uparrow \Rightarrow \text{real net worth}\uparrow\\ \Rightarrow \text{adverse selection}\downarrow, \text{moral hazard}\downarrow \Rightarrow \text{lending}\uparrow \Rightarrow I\uparrow \Rightarrow Y\uparrow\end{aligned} \quad (9)$$

The view that unanticipated movements in the price level affect aggregate output has a long tradition in economics: It is the key feature in the debt-deflation view of the Great Depression outlined in Chapter 8.

Household Liquidity Effects. Although most of the literature on the credit channel focuses on spending by businesses, the credit view should apply equally well to consumer spending, particularly on consumer durables and housing. Declines in bank lending induced by a monetary contraction should cause a decline in durables and housing purchases by consumers who do not have access to other sources of credit. Similarly, increases in interest rates cause a deterioration in household balance sheets, because consumers' cash flow is adversely affected.

Another way of looking at how the balance sheet channel may operate through consumers is to consider liquidity effects on consumer durable and housing expenditures, which were found to be important factors during the Great Depression (see the FYI box, "Consumers' Balance Sheets and the Great Depression"). In the liquidity effects view,

FYI Consumers' Balance Sheets and the Great Depression

The years between 1929 and 1933 witnessed the worst deterioration in consumers' balance sheets ever seen in the United States. The stock market crash in 1929, which caused a slump that lasted until 1933, reduced the value of consumers' wealth by $737 billion (in 2000 dollars), and as expected, consumption dropped sharply (by over $100 billion). Because of the decline in the price level in that period, the level of real debt consumers owed also increased sharply (by over 20%). Consequently, the value of financial assets relative to the amount of debt declined sharply, increasing the likelihood of financial distress. Not surprisingly, spending on consumer durables and housing fell precipitously: From 1929 to 1933, consumer durable expenditure declined by over 50%, while expenditure on housing declined by 80%.*

*For further discussion of the effect of consumers' balance sheets on spending during the Great Depression, see Frederic S. Mishkin, "The Household Balance Sheet and the Great Depression," *Journal of Economic History* 38 (1978): 918–937.

balance sheet effects work through their impact on consumers' desire to spend rather than on lenders' desire to lend. Because of asymmetric information about their quality, consumer durables and housing are very illiquid assets. If, as a result of a bad income shock, consumers needed to sell their consumer durables or housing to raise money, they would expect a big loss because they could not get the full value of these assets in a distress sale. (This is just a manifestation of the lemons problem described in Chapter 8.) In contrast, if consumers held financial assets (such as money in the bank, stocks, or bonds), they could easily sell them quickly for their full market value and raise the cash. Hence, if consumers expect a higher likelihood of finding themselves in financial distress, they would rather hold fewer illiquid consumer durable or housing assets and more liquid financial assets.

A consumer's balance sheet should be an important influence on his or her estimate of the likelihood of suffering financial distress. Specifically, when consumers have a large amount of financial assets relative to their debts, their estimate of the probability of financial distress is low, and they will be more willing to purchase consumer durables or housing. When stock prices rise, the value of financial assets rises as well; consumer durable expenditure will also rise because consumers have a more secure financial position and a lower estimate of the likelihood of suffering financial distress. This leads to another transmission mechanism for monetary policy, operating through the link between money and stock prices:[19]

$$\begin{aligned}\text{Expansionary monetary policy} &\Rightarrow P_s\uparrow \Rightarrow \text{value of financial assets}\uparrow\\ &\Rightarrow \text{likelihood of financial distress}\downarrow\\ &\Rightarrow \text{consumer durable and housing expenditure}\uparrow \Rightarrow Y\uparrow\end{aligned} \tag{10}$$

The illiquidity of consumer durable and housing assets provides another reason why a monetary expansion, which lowers interest rates and thereby raises cash flow to consumers, leads to a rise in spending on consumer durables and housing. A rise in consumer cash flow decreases the likelihood of financial distress, which increases the desire of consumers to hold durable goods or housing, thus increasing spending on

[19]See Frederic S. Mishkin, "What Depressed the Consumer? The Household Balance Sheet and the 1973–1975 Recession," *Brookings Papers on Economic Activity* 1 (1977): 123–164.

them and hence aggregate output. The only difference between this view of cash flow effects and that outlined in Equation 8 is that it is not the willingness of lenders to lend to consumers that causes expenditure to rise but the willingness of consumers to spend.

Why Are Credit Channels Likely to Be Important?

There are three reasons to believe that credit channels are important monetary transmission mechanisms. First, a large body of evidence on the behavior of individual firms supports the view that credit market imperfections of the type crucial to the operation of credit channels do affect firms' employment and spending decisions.[20] Second, there is evidence that small firms (which are more likely to be credit-constrained) are hurt more by tight monetary policy than large firms, which are unlikely to be credit-constrained.[21] Third, and maybe most compelling, the asymmetric information view of credit market imperfections at the core of the credit channel analysis is a theoretical construct that has proved useful in explaining many other important phenomena, such as why many of our financial institutions exist, why our financial system has the structure that it has, and why financial crises are so damaging to the economy (all topics discussed in Chapter 8). The best support for a theory is its demonstrated usefulness in a wide range of applications. By this standard, the asymmetric information theory supporting the existence of credit channels as an important monetary transmission mechanism has much to recommend it.

APPLICATION Corporate Scandals and the Slow Recovery from the March 2001 Recession

The collapse of the tech boom and the stock market slump led to a decline in investment spending that triggered a recession starting in March 2001. Just as the recession got under way, the Fed rapidly lowered the federal funds rate. At first it appeared that the Fed's actions would keep the recession mild and stimulate a recovery. However, the economy did not bounce back as quickly as the Fed had hoped. Why was the recovery from the recession so sluggish?

One explanation is that corporate scandals at Enron, Arthur Andersen, and several other large firms caused investors to doubt the quality of the financed information they were receiving about corporations. Doubts about the quality of corporate information meant that asymmetric information problems worsened, so that it became harder for an investor to screen out good firms from bad firms when making investment decisions. Because of the potential for increased adverse selection, as described in the credit view, individuals and financial institutions were less willing to lend. This reluctance to lend in turn led to a decline in investment and aggregate output.

In addition, as we saw in Chapter 7, the corporate scandals caused investors to be less optimistic about earnings growth and to think that stocks were riskier, an effect leading to a further drop in the stock market. The decline in the stock market also weakened the economy, because it lowered household wealth. In turn, the decrease in household wealth led not only to restrained consumer spending, but also to weaker

[20] For a survey of this evidence, see Hubbard, "Is There a 'Credit Channel' for Monetary Policy?" (note 17).

[21] See Mark Gertler and Simon Gilchrist, "Monetary Policy, Business Cycles, and the Behavior of Small Manufacturing Firms," *Quarterly Journal of Economics* 109 (May 1994): 309–340.

investment, because of the resulting drop in Tobin's q. In addition, the stock market decline weakened corporate balance sheets. This weakening increased asymmetric information problems and decreased lending and investment spending.

LESSONS FOR MONETARY POLICY

What useful implications for central banks' conduct of monetary policy can we draw from the analysis in this chapter? There are four basic lessons to be learned.

1. ***It is dangerous always to associate the easing or the tightening of monetary policy with a fall or a rise in short-term nominal interest rates.*** Because most central banks use short-term nominal interest rates—typically, the interbank rate—as the key operating instrument for monetary policy, there is a danger that central banks and the public will focus too much on short-term nominal interest rates as an indicator of the stance of monetary policy. Indeed, it is quite common to see statements that always associate monetary tightenings with a rise in the interbank rate and monetary easings with a decline in the rate. This view is highly problematic, because—as we have seen in our discussion of the Great Depression period—movements in nominal interest rates do not always correspond to movements in real interest rates, yet it is typically the real and not the nominal interest rate that is an element in the channel of monetary policy transmission. For example, we have seen that during the contraction phase of the Great Depression in the United States, short-term interest rates fell to near zero, yet real interest rates were extremely high. Short-term interest rates that are near zero therefore do not indicate that monetary policy is easy if the economy is undergoing deflation, as was true during the contraction phase of the Great Depression. As Milton Friedman and Anna Schwartz have emphasized, the period of near-zero short-term interest rates during the contraction phase of the Great Depression was one of highly contractionary monetary policy, rather than the reverse.

2. ***Other asset prices besides those on short-term debt instruments contain important information about the stance of monetary policy because they are important elements in various monetary policy transmission mechanisms.*** As we have seen in this chapter, economists have come a long way in understanding that other asset prices besides interest rates have major effects on aggregate demand. As we saw in Figure 3, other asset prices, such as stock prices, foreign exchange rates, and housing and land prices, play an important role in monetary transmission mechanisms. Furthermore, the discussion of such additional channels as those operating through the exchange rate, Tobin's q, and wealth effects provides additional reasons why other asset prices play such an important role in the monetary transmission mechanisms. Although there are strong disagreements among economists about which channels of monetary transmission are the most important—not surprising, given that economists, particularly those in academia, always like to disagree—they do agree that other asset prices play an important role in the way monetary policy affects the economy.

The view that other asset prices besides short-term interest rates matter has important implications for monetary policy. When we try to assess the stance of policy, it is critical that we look at other asset prices in addition to short-term interest rates. For example, if short-term interest rates are low or even zero and yet stock prices are low, land prices are low, and the value of the domestic currency is high, monetary policy is clearly tight, *not* easy.

3. ***Monetary policy can be highly effective in reviving a weak economy even if short-term interest rates are already near zero.*** We have recently entered a world where inflation is not always the norm. Japan, for example, recently experienced a period of deflation when the price level was actually falling. One common view is that when a central bank has driven down short-term nominal interest rates to near zero, there is nothing more that monetary policy can do to stimulate the economy. The transmission mechanisms of monetary policy described here indicate that this view is false. As our discussion of the factors that affect the monetary base in Chapter 16 indicated, expansionary monetary policy to increase liquidity in the economy can be conducted with open market purchases, which do not have to be solely in short-term government securities. For example, purchases of foreign currencies, like purchases of government bonds, lead to an increase in the monetary base and in the money supply. This increased liquidity and a commitment to future expansionary monetary policy helps revive the economy by raising general price-level expectations and by reflating other asset prices, which then stimulate aggregate demand through the channels outlined here. Therefore, monetary policy can be a potent force for reviving economies that are undergoing deflation and have short-term interest rates near zero. Indeed, because of the lags inherent in fiscal policy and the political constraints on its use, expansionary monetary policy is the key policy action required to revive an economy experiencing deflation.

4. ***Avoiding unanticipated fluctuations in the price level is an important objective of monetary policy, thus providing a rationale for price stability as the primary long-run goal for monetary policy.*** As we saw in Chapter 19, central banks in recent years have been putting greater emphasis on price stability as the primary long-run goal for monetary policy. Several rationales have been proposed for this goal, including the undesirable effects of uncertainty about the future price level on business decisions and hence on productivity, distortions associated with the interaction of nominal contracts and the tax system with inflation, and increased social conflict stemming from inflation. The discussion here of monetary transmission mechanisms provides an additional reason why price stability is so important. As we have seen, unanticipated movements in the price level can cause unanticipated fluctuations in output, an undesirable outcome. Particularly important in this regard is the knowledge that, as we saw in Chapter 8, price deflation can be an important factor leading to a prolonged financial crisis, as occurred during the Great Depression. An understanding of the monetary transmission mechanisms thus makes it clear that the goal of price stability is desirable, because it reduces uncertainty about the future price level. Thus the price stability goal implies that a negative inflation rate is at least as undesirable as too high an inflation rate. Indeed, because of the threat of financial crises, central banks must work very hard to prevent price deflation.

APPLICATION Applying the Monetary Policy Lessons to Japan

Until 1990, it looked as if Japan might overtake the United States in per capita income. Since then, the Japanese economy has been stagnating, with deflation and low growth. As a result, Japanese living standards have been falling further and further behind those in the United States. Many economists take the view that Japanese monetary policy is in part to blame for the poor performance of the Japanese economy. Could applying the four lessons outlined in the previous section have helped Japanese monetary policy perform better?

The first lesson suggests that it is dangerous to think that declines in interest rates always mean that monetary policy has been easing. In the mid-1990s, when short-term interest rates began to decline, falling to near zero in the late 1990s and early 2000s, the monetary authorities in Japan took the view that monetary policy was sufficiently expansionary. Now it is widely recognized that this view was incorrect, because the falling and eventually negative inflation rates in Japan meant that real interest rates were actually quite high and that monetary policy was tight, not easy. If the monetary authorities in Japan had followed the advice of the first lesson, they might have pursued a more expansionary monetary policy, which would have helped boost the economy.

The second lesson suggests that monetary policymakers should pay attention to other asset prices in assessing the stance of monetary policy. At the same time interest rates were falling in Japan, stock and real estate prices were collapsing, thus providing another indication that Japanese monetary policy was not easy. Recognizing the second lesson might have led Japanese monetary policymakers to recognize sooner that they needed a more expansionary monetary policy.

The third lesson indicates that monetary policy can still be effective even if short-term interest rates are near zero. Officials at the Bank of Japan have frequently claimed that they have been helpless in stimulating the economy, because short-term interest rates had fallen to near zero. Recognizing that monetary policy can still be effective even when interest rates are near zero, as the third lesson suggests, would have helped them to take monetary policy actions that would have stimulated aggregate demand by raising other asset prices and inflationary expectations.

The fourth lesson indicates that unanticipated fluctuations in the price level should be avoided. If the Japanese monetary authorities had adhered to this lesson, they might have recognized that allowing deflation to occur could be very damaging to the economy and would be inconsistent with the goal of price stability. Indeed, critics of the Bank of Japan have suggested that the bank should announce an inflation target to promote the price stability objective, but the bank has resisted this suggestion.

Heeding the advice from the four lessons in the previous section might have led to a far more successful conduct of monetary policy in Japan in recent years.[22]

[22]For a more detailed critique of recent monetary policy in Japan, see Takatoshi Ito and Frederic S. Mishkin, "Two Decades of Japanese Monetary Policy and the Deflation Problem," *National Bureau of Economic Research Working Paper No. 10878* (November 2004).

SUMMARY

1. There are two basic types of empirical evidence: reduced-form evidence and structural model evidence. Both have advantages and disadvantages. The main advantage of structural model evidence is that it provides us with an understanding of how the economy works and gives us more confidence in the direction of causation between money and output. However, if the structure is not correctly specified, because it ignores important monetary transmission mechanisms, it could seriously underestimate the effectiveness of monetary policy. Reduced-form evidence has the advantage of not restricting the way monetary policy affects economic activity and so may be more likely to capture the full effects of monetary policy. However, reduced-form evidence cannot rule out the possibility of reverse causation or an outside driving factor, which could lead to misleading conclusions about the importance of money.

2. The early Keynesians believed that money does not matter, because they found weak links between interest rates and investment and because low interest rates on Treasury securities convinced them that monetary policy was easy during the worst economic contraction in U.S. history, the Great Depression. Monetarists objected to this interpretation of the evidence on the grounds that (a) the focus on nominal rather than real interest rates may have obscured any link between interest rates and investment, (b) interest-rate effects on investment might be only one of many channels through which monetary policy affects aggregate demand, and (c) by the standards of real interest rates and interest rates on lower-grade bonds, monetary policy was extremely contractionary during the Great Depression.
3. Early monetarist evidence falls into three categories: timing, statistical, and historical. Because of reverse causation and outside-factor possibilities, some serious doubts exist regarding conclusions that can be drawn from timing and statistical evidence alone. However, some of the historical evidence in which exogenous declines in money growth are followed by recessions provides stronger support for the monetarist position that money matters. As a result of empirical research, Keynesian and monetarist opinion has converged to the view that money does matter to aggregate economic activity and the price level. However, Keynesians do not agree with the monetarist position that money is *all* that matters.
4. The transmission mechanisms of monetary policy include traditional interest-rate channels that operate through the cost of capital and affect investment; other asset price channels such as exchange rate effects, Tobin's q theory, and wealth effects; and the credit view channels—the bank lending channel, the balance sheet channel, the cash flow channel, the unanticipated price level channel, and household liquidity effects.
5. Four lessons for monetary policy can be drawn from this chapter: (a) It is dangerous always to associate monetary policy easing or tightening with a fall or a rise in short-term nominal interest rates; (b) other asset prices besides those on short-term debt instruments contain important information about the stance of monetary policy because they are important elements in the monetary policy transmission mechanisms; (c) monetary policy can be highly effective in reviving a weak economy even if short-term interest rates are already near zero; and (d) avoiding unanticipated fluctuations in the price level is an important objective of monetary policy, thus providing a rationale for price stability as the primary long-run goal for monetary policy.

KEY TERMS

consumer durable expenditure, p. 621
consumption, p. 624
credit view, p. 622
Keynesians, p. 611
monetarists, p. 611
reduced-form evidence, p. 608
reverse causation, p. 610
structural model, p. 608
structural model evidence, p. 607
transmission mechanisms of monetary policy, p. 608

QUESTIONS AND PROBLEMS

Questions marked with an asterisk are answered at the end of the book in an appendix, "Answers to Selected Questions and Problems." Questions marked with a blue circle indicate the question is available in MyEconLab at www.myeconlab.com/mishkin.

1. Suppose that a researcher is trying to determine whether jogging is good for a person's health. She examines this question in two ways. In method A, she examines whether joggers live longer than nonjoggers. In method B, she examines whether jogging reduces cholesterol in the bloodstream and lowers blood pressure; then she asks whether lower cholesterol and blood pressure prolong life. Which of these two methods will produce reduced-form evidence and which will produce structural model evidence?
2. If research indicates that joggers do not have lower cholesterol and blood pressure than nonjoggers, is it still possible that jogging is good for your health? Give a concrete example.

3. If research indicates that joggers live longer than nonjoggers, is it possible that jogging is not good for your health? Give a concrete example.

*4. Suppose that you plan to buy a car and want to know whether a General Motors car is more reliable than a Ford. One way to find out is to ask owners of both cars how often their cars go into the shop for repairs. Another way is to visit the factory producing the cars and see which one is built better. Which procedure will provide reduced-form evidence and which structural model evidence?

*5. If the GM car you plan to buy has a better repair record than a Ford, does this mean that the GM car is necessarily more reliable? (GM car owners might, for example, change their oil more frequently than Ford owners.)

*6. Suppose that when you visit the Ford and GM car factories to examine how the cars are built, you have time only to see how well the engine is put together. If Ford engines are better built than GM engines, does that mean that the Ford will be more reliable than the GM car?

7. How might bank behavior (described in Chapter 17) lead to causation running from output to the money supply? What does this say about evidence that finds a strong correlation between money and output?

*8. What operating procedures of the Fed (described in the Appendix to Chapter 19) might explain how movements in output might cause movements in the money supply?

9. "In every business cycle in the past 100 years, the rate at which the money supply is growing always decreases before output does. Therefore, the money supply causes business cycle movements." Do you agree? What objections can you raise against this argument?

*10. How did the research strategies of Keynesian and monetarist economists differ after they were exposed to the earliest monetarist evidence?

11. In the 1973–1975 recession, the value of common stocks in real terms fell by nearly 50%. How might this decline in the stock market have affected aggregate demand and thus contributed to the severity of this recession? Be specific about the mechanisms through which the stock market decline affected the economy.

*12. "The cost of financing investment is related only to interest rates; therefore, the only way that monetary policy can affect investment spending is through its effects on interest rates." Is this statement true, false, or uncertain? Explain your answer.

13. Predict what will happen to stock prices if the money supply rises. Explain why you are making this prediction.

*14. Franco Modigliani found that the most important transmission mechanisms of monetary policy involve consumer expenditure. Describe how at least two of these mechanisms work.

15. "The monetarists have demonstrated that the early Keynesians were wrong in saying that money doesn't matter at all to economic activity. Therefore, we should accept the monetarist position that money is all that matters." Do you agree? Why or why not?

WEB EXERCISES

1. Figure 1 shows the relationship between estimated real interest rates and nominal interest rates. Go to www.martincapital.com/ and click on "charts and data," then on "nominal versus real market rates" to find data showing the spread between real interest rates and nominal interest rates. Discuss how the current spread differs from that shown most recently in Figure 1. What are the implications of this change?

2. Figure 2 discusses business cycles. Go to www.econlib.org/library/Enc/Recessions.html and review the material reported on recessions.
   a. What is the formal definition of a recession?
   b. What are the problems with the definition?
   c. What are the three D's used by the National Bureau of Economic Research (NBER) to define a recession?
   d. Review Chart 1. What trend is apparent about the length of recessions?

WEB REFERENCES

www.martincapital.com/

Click on "charts and data," then on "nominal versus real market rates" to find up-to-the-minute data showing the spread between real rates and nominal rates.

www.conference-board.org/economics/bci

A site with extensive data on the factors that define business cycles.

CHAPTER

25 Money and Inflation

Preview

Since the early 1960s, when the inflation rate hovered between 1% and 2%, the economy has suffered from higher and more variable rates of inflation. By the late 1960s, the inflation rate had climbed beyond 5%, and by 1974, it reached the double-digit level. After moderating somewhat during the 1975–1978 period, it shot above 10% in 1979 and 1980, slowed to around 5% from 1982 to 1990, declined further to around 2% in the late 1990s, and remained around that level through 2005. Inflation, the condition of a continually rising price level, has become a major concern of politicians and the public, and how to control it frequently dominates the discussion of economic policy.

How do we prevent the inflationary fire from igniting and end the roller-coaster ride in the inflation rate of the past 40 years? Milton Friedman provides an answer in his famous proposition that "Inflation is always and everywhere a monetary phenomenon." He postulates that the source of all inflation episodes is a high growth rate of the money supply: Simply by reducing the growth rate of the money supply to low levels, inflation can be prevented.

In this chapter, we use aggregate demand and supply analysis from Chapter 23 to reveal the role of monetary policy in creating inflation. You will find that as long as inflation is defined as the condition of a continually and rapidly rising price level, almost all economists agree with Friedman's proposition that inflation is a monetary phenomenon.

But what *causes* inflation? How does inflationary monetary policy come about? You will see that inflationary monetary policy is an offshoot of other government policies: the attempt to hit high employment targets or the running of large budget deficits. Examining how these policies lead to inflation will point us toward ways of preventing it at minimum cost in terms of unemployment and output loss.

MONEY AND INFLATION: EVIDENCE

The evidence for Friedman's statement is straightforward. ***Whenever a country's inflation rate is extremely high for a sustained period of time, its rate of money supply growth is also extremely high.*** Indeed, this is exactly what we saw in Figure 6 in Chapter 1, which shows that the countries with the highest inflation rates have also had the highest rates of money growth.

Evidence of this type seems to support the proposition that extremely high inflation is the result of a high rate of money growth. Keep in mind, however, that you are looking at reduced-form evidence, which focuses solely on the correlation of two variables:

money growth and the inflation rate. As with all reduced-form evidence, reverse causation (inflation causing money supply growth) or an outside factor that drives both money growth and inflation could be involved.

How might you rule out these possibilities? First, you might look for historical episodes in which an increase in money growth appears to be an exogenous event; a high inflation rate for a sustained period following the increase in money growth would provide strong evidence that high money growth is the driving force behind the inflation. Luckily for our analysis, such clear-cut episodes—hyperinflations (extremely rapid inflations with inflation rates exceeding 50% per month)—have occurred, the most notorious being the German hyperinflation of 1921–1923.

German Hyperinflation, 1921–1923

In 1921, the need to make reparations and reconstruct the economy after World War I caused the German government's expenditures to greatly exceed revenues. The government could have obtained revenues to cover these increased expenditures by raising taxes, but that solution was, as always, politically unpopular and would have taken much time to implement. The government could also have financed the expenditure by borrowing from the public, but the amount needed was far in excess of its capacity to borrow. There was only one route left: the printing press. The government could pay for its expenditures simply by printing more currency (increasing the money supply) and using it to make payments to the individuals and companies that were providing it with goods and services. As shown in Figure 1, this is exactly what the German government did; in late 1921, the money supply began to increase rapidly, and so did the price level.

In 1923, the budgetary situation of the German government deteriorated even further. Early that year, the French invaded the Ruhr, because Germany had failed to make its scheduled reparations payments. A general strike in the region then ensued to protest the French action, and the German government actively supported this "passive resistance" by making payments to striking workers. As a result, government expenditures climbed dramatically, and the government printed currency at an even faster rate to finance this spending. As displayed in Figure 1, the result of the explosion in the money supply was that the price level blasted off, leading to an inflation rate for 1923 that exceeded 1 million percent!

The invasion of the Ruhr and the printing of currency to pay striking workers fit the characteristics of an exogenous event. Reverse causation (that the rise in the price level caused the French to invade the Ruhr) is highly implausible, and it is hard to imagine a third factor that could have been a driving force behind both inflation and the explosion in the money supply. Therefore, the German hyperinflation qualifies as a "controlled experiment" that supports Friedman's proposition that inflation is a monetary phenomenon.

Recent Episodes of Rapid Inflation

Although recent rapid inflations have not been as dramatic as the German hyperinflation, many countries in the 1980s and 1990s experienced rapid inflations in which the high rates of money growth can also be classified as exogenous events. For example, of all Latin American countries in the decade from 1980 to 1990, Argentina, Brazil, and Peru had both the highest rates of money growth and the highest average inflation rates. However, in recent years, inflation in these countries has been brought down considerably.

FIGURE 1
Money Supply and Price Level in the German Hyperinflation

Source: Frank D. Graham, *Exchange, Prices and Production in Hyperinflation: Germany, 1920–25* (Princeton, N.J.: Princeton University Press, 1930), pp. 105–106.

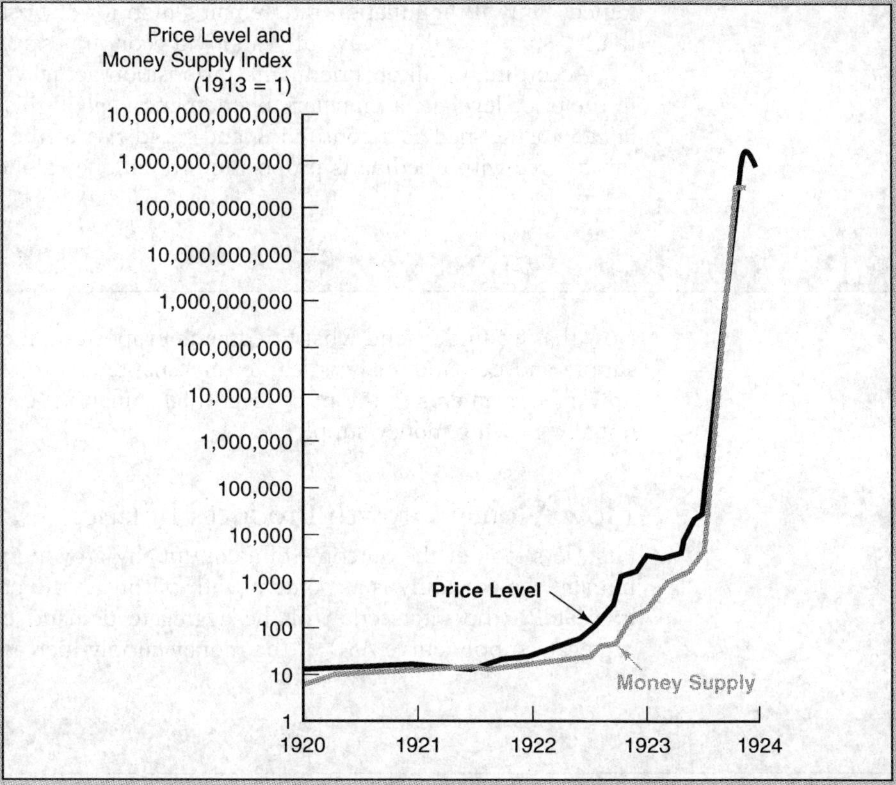

The explanation for the high rates of money growth in these countries is similar to the explanation for Germany during its hyperinflation: The unwillingness of Argentina, Brazil, and Peru to finance government expenditures by raising taxes led to large budget deficits (sometimes over 15% of GDP), which were financed by money creation.

That the inflation rate is high in all cases in which the high rate of money growth can be classified as an exogenous event (including episodes in Argentina, Brazil, Peru, and Germany) is strong evidence that high money growth causes high inflation.

MEANING OF INFLATION

You may have noticed that all the empirical evidence on the relationship of money growth and inflation discussed so far looks only at cases in which the price level is continually rising at a rapid rate. It is this definition of inflation that Friedman and other economists use when they make statements such as "Inflation is always and everywhere a monetary phenomenon." This is not what your friendly newscaster means when reporting the monthly inflation rate on the nightly news. The newscaster is only telling you how much, in percentage terms, the price level has changed from the previous month. For example, when you hear that the monthly inflation rate is 1% (12% annual rate), this indicates only that the price level has risen by 1% in that month. This could be a one-shot change, in which the high inflation rate is merely temporary, not sustained. Only if the inflation rate remains high for a substantial period of time (greater than 1% per month for several years) will economists say that inflation has been high.

Accordingly, Milton Friedman's proposition actually says that upward movements in the price level are a monetary phenomenon *only* if this is a sustained process. When *inflation* is defined as a continuing and rapid rise in the price level, almost all economists agree with Friedman's proposition that money alone is to blame.

VIEWS OF INFLATION

Now that we understand what Friedman's proposition means, we can use the aggregate supply and demand analysis learned in Chapter 23 to show that large and persistent upward movements in the price level (high inflation) can occur only if there is a continually growing money supply.

How Money Growth Produces Inflation

First, let's look at the outcome of a continually growing money supply (see Figure 2). Initially, the economy is at point 1, with output at the natural rate level and the price level at P_1 (the intersection of the aggregate demand curve AD_1 and the short-run aggregate supply curve AS_1). If the money supply increases steadily over the course of

myeconlab

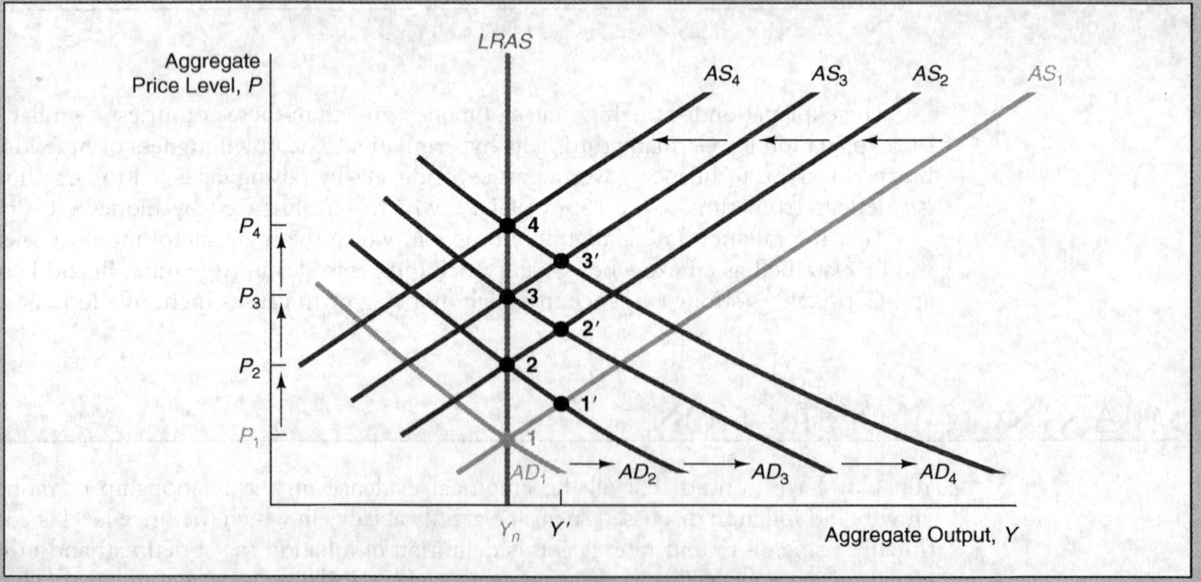

FIGURE 2 **Response to a Continually Rising Money Supply**
A continually rising money supply shifts the aggregate demand curve to the right from AD_1 to AD_2 to AD_3 to AD_4, while the short-run aggregate supply curve shifts to the left from AS_1 to AS_2 to AS_3 to AS_4. The result is that the price level rises continually from P_1 to P_2 to P_3 to P_4.

the year, the aggregate demand curve shifts rightward to AD_2. At first, for a very brief time, the economy may move to point 1′ and output may increase above the natural rate level to Y', but the resulting decline in unemployment below the natural rate level will cause wages to rise, and the short-run aggregate supply curve will quickly begin to shift leftward. It will stop shifting only when it reaches AS_2, at which time the economy has returned to the natural rate level of output on the long-run aggregate supply curve.[1] At the new equilibrium, point 2, the price level has increased from P_1 to P_2.

If the money supply increases the next year, the aggregate demand curve will shift to the right again to AD_3, and the short-run aggregate supply curve will shift from AS_2 to AS_3; the economy will move to point 2′ and then to point 3, where the price level has risen to P_3. If the money supply continues to grow in subsequent years, the economy will continue to move to higher and higher price levels. As long as the money supply grows, this process will continue, and inflation will occur. ***High money growth produces high inflation.***

Can Other Factors Besides Money Growth Produce a Sustained Inflation?

In the aggregate demand and supply analysis in Chapter 23, you learned that other factors besides changes in the money supply (such as fiscal policy and supply shocks) can affect the aggregate demand and supply curves. Doesn't this suggest that these other factors can generate high inflation? The answer, surprisingly, is no. To see why high inflation is always a monetary phenomenon, let's dig a little deeper into aggregate demand and supply analysis to see whether other factors can generate high inflation in the absence of a high rate of money growth.

Can Fiscal Policy by Itself Produce Inflation? To examine this question, let's look at Figure 3, which demonstrates the effect of a one-shot permanent increase in government expenditure (say, from \$500 billion to \$600 billion) on aggregate output and the price level. Initially, we are at point 1, where output is at the natural rate level and the price level is P_1. The increase in government expenditure shifts the aggregate demand curve to AD_2, and we move to point 1′, where output is above the natural rate level at $Y_{1'}$. Because of this, the short-run aggregate supply curve will begin to shift leftward, eventually reaching AS_2, where it intersects the aggregate demand curve AD_2 at point 2, at which output is again at the natural rate level and the price level has risen to P_2.

The net result of a one-shot permanent increase in government expenditure is a one-shot permanent increase in the price level. What happens to the inflation rate? When we move from point 1 to 1′ to 2, the price level rises, and we have a positive inflation rate. But when we finally get to point 2, the inflation rate returns to zero. We see that the one-shot increase in government expenditure leads to only a *temporary* increase in the inflation rate, not to an inflation in which the price level is continually rising.

If government spending increases continually, however, we *could* get a continuing rise in the price level. It appears, then, that aggregate demand and supply analysis could reject Friedman's proposition that inflation is always the result of money growth. The

---

[1]There is a possibility that the short-run aggregate supply curve may immediately shift in toward AS_2, because workers and firms may expect the increase in the money supply, so expected inflation will be higher. In this case, the movement to point 2 will be very rapid, and output need not rise above the natural rate level. (Some support for this scenario from the theory of rational expectations is discussed in Chapter 25.)

FIGURE 3

Response to a One-Shot Permanent Increase in Government Expenditure

A one-shot permanent increase in government expenditure shifts the aggregate demand curve rightward from AD_1 to AD_2, moving the economy from point 1 to point 1′. Because output now exceeds the natural rate level Y_n, the short-run aggregate supply curve eventually shifts leftward to AS_2, and the price level rises from P_1 to P_2, a one-shot permanent increase but not a continuing increase.

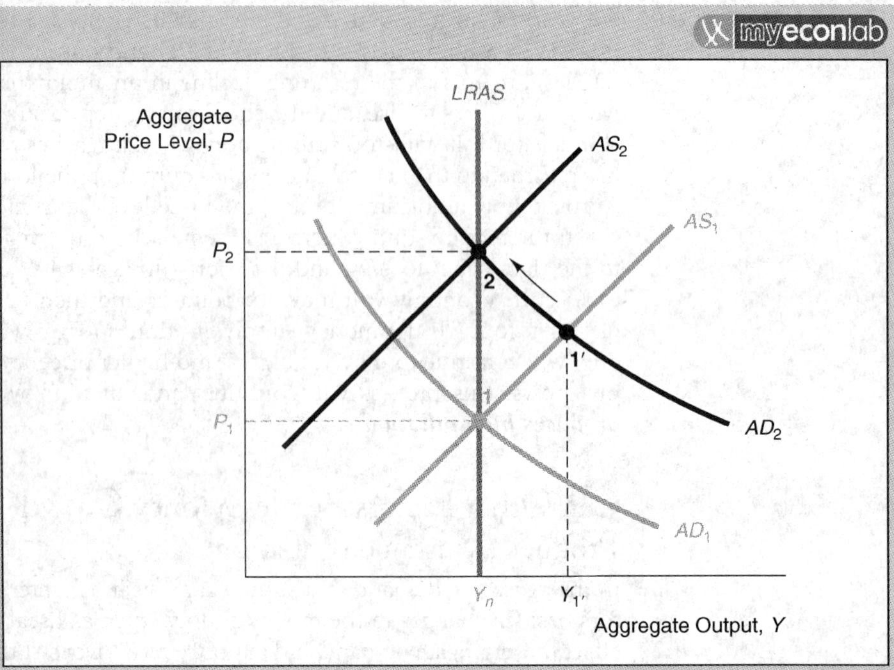

problem with this argument is that a continually increasing level of government expenditure is not a feasible policy. There is a limit on the total amount of possible government expenditure; the government cannot spend more than 100% of GDP. In fact, well before this limit is reached, the political process would stop the increases in government spending. As revealed in the continual debates in Congress over balanced budgets and government spending, both the public and politicians have a particular target level of government spending they deem appropriate; although small deviations from this level might be tolerated, large deviations would not. Indeed, public and political perceptions impose tight limits on the degree to which government expenditures can increase.

What about the other side of fiscal policy—taxes? Could continual tax cuts generate an inflation? Again the answer is no. The analysis in Figure 3 also describes the price and output response to a one-shot decrease in taxes. There will be a one-shot increase in the price level, but the increase in the inflation rate will be only temporary. We can increase the price level by cutting taxes even more, but this process would have to stop—once taxes reach zero, they can't be reduced further. We must conclude, then, that ***high inflation cannot be driven by fiscal policy alone.***[2]

Can Supply-Side Phenomena by Themselves Produce Inflation?

Because supply shocks and workers' attempts to increase their wages can shift the short-run aggregate supply curve leftward, you might suspect that these supply-side phenomena

[2]The argument here demonstrates that "animal spirits" also cannot be the source of inflation. Although consumer and business optimism, which stimulates these groups' spending, can produce a one-shot shift in the aggregate demand curve and a temporary inflation, it cannot produce continuing shifts in the aggregate demand curve and inflation in which the price level rises continually. The reasoning is the same as before: Consumers and businesses cannot continue to raise their spending without limit because their spending cannot exceed 100% of GDP.

FIGURE 4
Response to a Supply Shock
A negative supply shock (or a wage push) shifts the short-run aggregate supply curve leftward to AS_2 and results in high unemployment at point 1′. As a result, the short-run aggregate supply curve shifts back to the right to AS_1, and the economy returns to point 1, where the price level has returned to P_1.

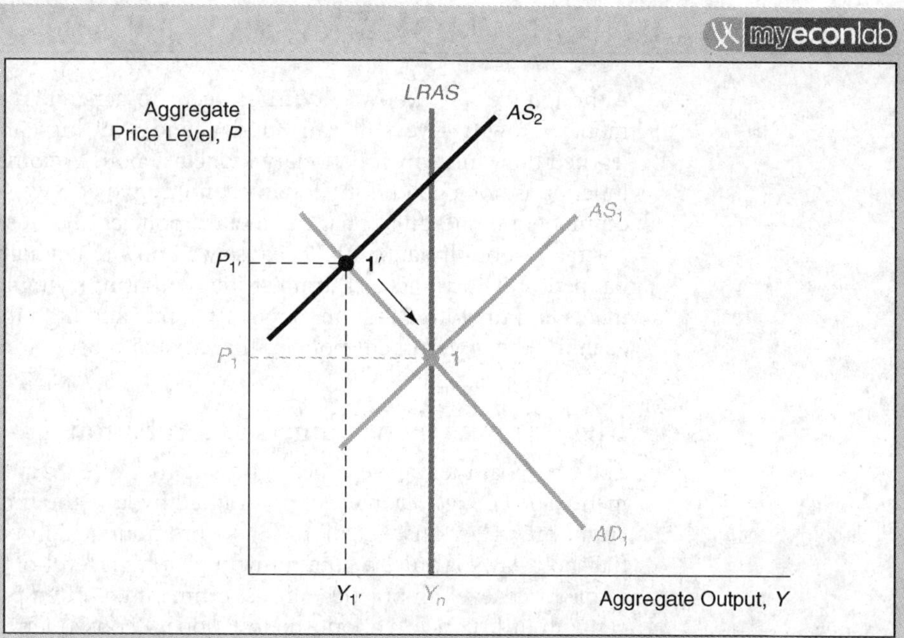

by themselves could stimulate inflation. Again, we can show that this suspicion is incorrect.

Suppose that a negative supply shock—for example, an oil embargo—raises oil prices (or workers could have successfully pushed up their wages). As displayed in Figure 4, the negative supply shock shifts the short-run aggregate supply curve from AS_1 to AS_2. If the money supply remains unchanged, leaving the aggregate demand curve at AD_1, we move to point 1′, where output $Y_{1'}$ is below the natural rate level and the price level $P_{1'}$ is higher. The short-run aggregate supply curve will now shift back to AS_1, because unemployment is above the natural rate, and the economy slides down AD_1 from point 1′ to point 1. The net result of the supply shock is that we return to full employment at the initial price level, and there is no continuing inflation. Additional negative supply shocks that again shift the short-run aggregate supply curve leftward will lead to the same outcome: The price level will rise temporarily, but inflation will not result. The conclusion that we have reached is the following: ***Supply-side phenomena cannot be the source of high inflation.***[3]

Summary

Our aggregate demand and supply analysis shows that high inflation can occur only with a high rate of money growth. As long as we recognize that inflation refers to a continuing increase in the price level at a rapid rate, we now see why Milton Friedman was correct when he said that "Inflation is always and everywhere a monetary phenomenon."

[3]Supply-side phenomena that alter the natural rate level of output (and shift the long-run aggregate supply curve at Y_n) can produce a permanent one-shot change in the price level. However, this resulting one-shot change results in only a temporary inflation, not a continuing rise in the price level.

ORIGINS OF INFLATIONARY MONETARY POLICY

Although we now know *what* must occur to generate a rapid inflation—a high rate of money growth—we still can't understand *why* high inflation occurs until we have learned how and why inflationary monetary policies come about. If everyone agrees that inflation is not a good thing for an economy, why do we see so much of it? Why do governments pursue inflationary monetary policies? Because there is nothing intrinsically desirable about inflation and because we know that a high rate of money growth doesn't happen of its own accord, it must follow that in trying to achieve other goals, governments end up with a high money growth rate and high inflation. In this section, we will examine the government policies that are the most common sources of inflation.

High Employment Targets and Inflation

The first goal most governments pursue that often results in inflation is high employment. The U.S. government is committed by law (the Employment Act of 1946 and the Humphrey-Hawkins Act of 1978) to promoting high employment. Though it is true that both laws require a commitment to a high level of employment consistent with a stable price level, in practice our government has often pursued a high employment target with little concern about the inflationary consequences of its policies. This was true especially in the mid-1960s and 1970s, when the government began to take a more active role in attempting to stabilize unemployment.

Two types of inflation can result from an activist stabilization policy to promote high employment: **cost-push inflation**, which occurs because of negative supply shocks or a push by workers to get higher wages, and **demand-pull inflation**, which results when policymakers pursue policies that shift the aggregate demand curve to the right. We will now use aggregate demand and supply analysis to examine how a high employment target can lead to both types of inflation.

Cost-Push Inflation.

In Figure 5, the economy is initially at point 1, the intersection of the aggregate demand curve AD_1 and the short-run aggregate supply curve AS_1. Suppose that workers decide to seek higher wages, either because they want to increase their real wages (wages in terms of the goods and services they can buy) or because they expect inflation to be high and wish to keep up with inflation. The effect of such an increase (similar to a negative supply shock) is to shift the short-run aggregate supply curve leftward to AS_2.[4] If government fiscal and monetary policy remains unchanged, the economy would move to point 1′ at the intersection of the new short-run aggregate supply curve AS_2 and the aggregate demand curve AD_1. Output would decline to below its natural rate level Y_n, and the price level would rise to $P_{1'}$.

What would activist policymakers with a high employment target do if this situation developed? Because of the drop in output and resulting increase in unemployment, they would implement policies to raise the aggregate demand curve to AD_2, so that we would return to the natural rate level of output at point 2 and price level P_2. The workers who have increased their wages have not fared too badly. The government has stepped in to make sure that there is no excessive unemployment, and they have achieved their goal of higher wages. Because the government has, in effect, given in to the demands of workers

[4]The cost-push inflation we describe here might also occur as a result either of firms' attempts to obtain higher prices or of negative supply shocks.

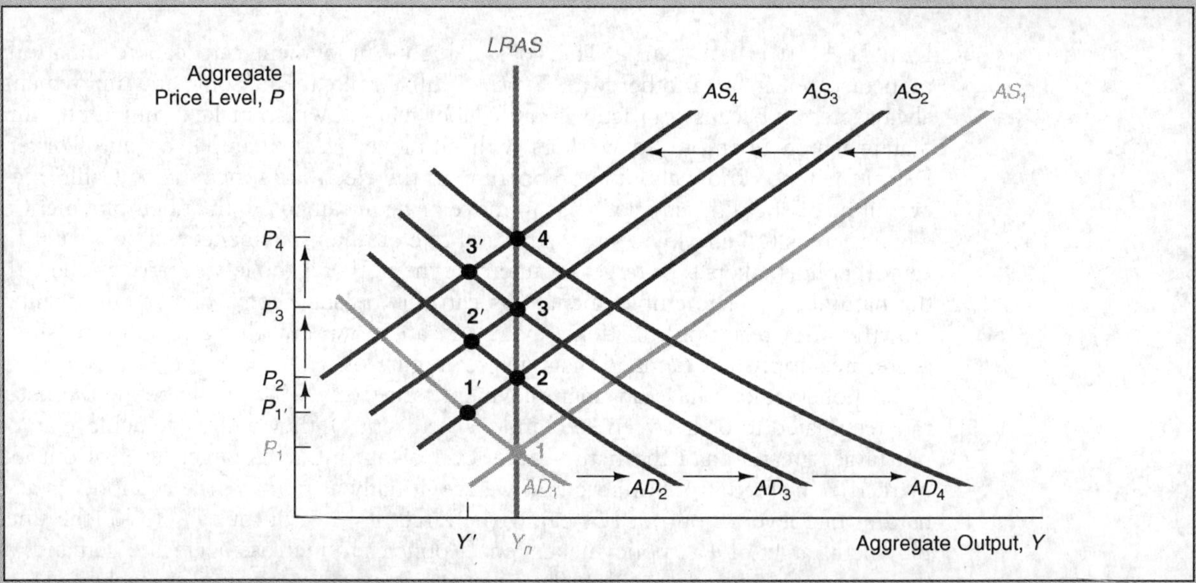

FIGURE 5 **Cost-Push Inflation with an Activist Policy to Promote High Employment**
In a cost-push inflation, the leftward shifts of the short-run aggregate supply curve from AS_1 to AS_2 to AS_3 and so on cause a government with a high employment target to shift the aggregate demand curve to the right continually to keep unemployment and output at their natural rate levels. The result is a continuing rise in the price level from P_1 to P_2 to P_3 and so on.

for higher wages, an activist policy with a high employment target is often referred to as an **accommodating policy**.

The workers, having eaten their cake and had it too, might be encouraged to seek even higher wages. In addition, other workers might now realize that their wages have fallen relative to their fellow workers', and because they don't want to be left behind, these workers will seek to increase their wages. The result is that the short-run aggregate supply curve shifts leftward again, to AS_3. Unemployment develops again when we move to point 2′, and the activist policies will once more be used to shift the aggregate demand curve rightward to AD_3 and return the economy to full employment at a price level of P_3. If this process continues, the result will be a continuing increase in the price level—a cost-push inflation.

What role does monetary policy play in a cost-push inflation? A cost-push inflation can occur only if the aggregate demand curve is shifted continually to the right. The first shift of the aggregate demand curve to AD_2 could be achieved by a one-shot increase in government expenditure or a one-shot decrease in taxes. But what about the next required rightward shift of the aggregate demand curve to AD_3, and the next, and the next? The limits on the maximum level of government expenditure and the minimum level of taxes would prevent the use of this expansionary fiscal policy for very long. Hence it cannot be used continually to shift the aggregate demand curve to the right. But the aggregate demand curve *can* be shifted continually rightward by continually increasing the money supply—that is, by going to a higher rate of money growth. Therefore, ***a cost-push inflation is a monetary phenomenon because it cannot occur***

without the monetary authorities pursuing an accommodating policy of a higher rate of money growth.

Demand-Pull Inflation. The goal of high employment can lead to inflationary monetary policy in another way. Even at full employment, some unemployment is always present because of frictions in the labor market, which make it difficult to immediately match unemployed workers with employers. An unemployed autoworker in Detroit may not know about a job opening in the electronics industry in California or, even if he or she did, may not want to move or be retrained. So the unemployment rate when there is full employment (the natural rate of unemployment) will be greater than zero. If policymakers set a target for unemployment that is too low because it is less than the natural rate of unemployment, this can set the stage for a higher rate of money growth and a resulting inflation. Again we can show how this can happen using an aggregate supply and demand diagram (see Figure 6).

If policymakers have an unemployment target (say, 4%) that is below the natural rate (estimated to be between $4\frac{1}{2}\%$ and $5\frac{1}{2}\%$ currently), they will try to achieve an output target greater than the natural rate level of output. This target level of output is marked Y_T in Figure 6. Suppose that we are initially at point 1; the economy is at the natural rate level of output but below the target level of output Y_T. To hit the unemployment target of 4%, policymakers enact policies to increase aggregate demand, and the effects of these policies shift the aggregate demand curve until it reaches AD_2 and

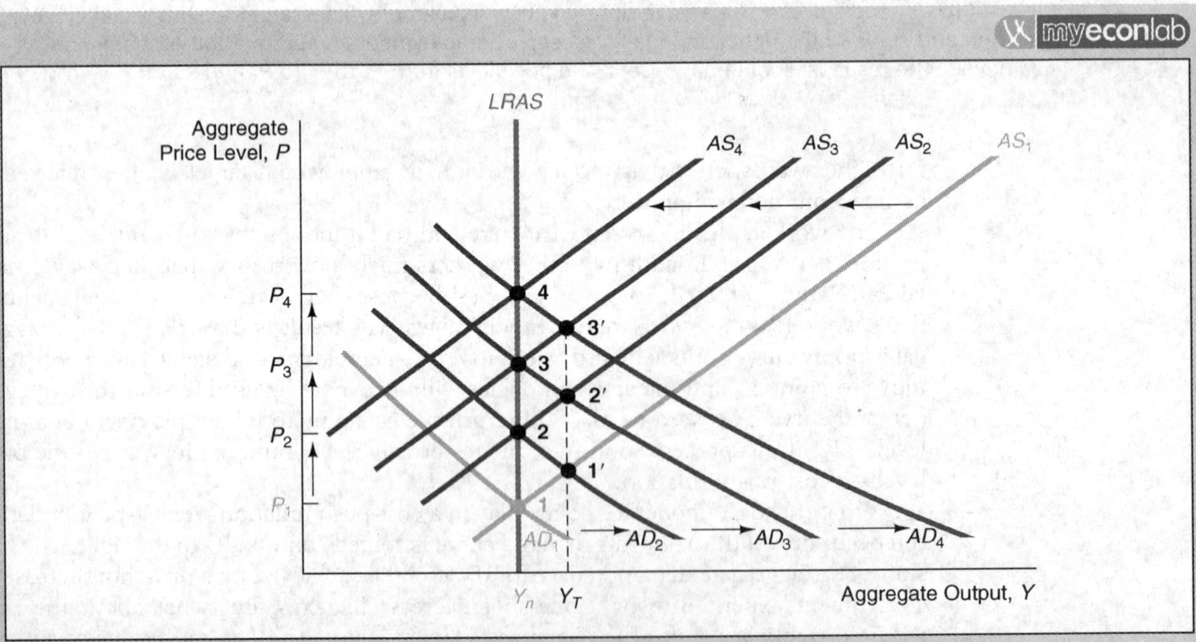

FIGURE 6 **Demand-Pull Inflation: The Consequence of Setting Too Low an Unemployment Target**
Too low an unemployment target (too high an output target of Y_T) causes the government to shift the aggregate demand curve rightward from AD_1 to AD_2 to AD_3 and so on, while the short-run aggregate supply curve shifts leftward from AS_1 to AS_2 to AS_3 and so on. The result is a continuing rise in the price level known as a demand-pull inflation.

the economy moves to point 1′. Output is at Y_T, and the 4% unemployment rate goal has been reached.

If the targeted unemployment rate was at the natural rate level between $4\frac{1}{2}\%$ and $5\frac{1}{2}\%$, there would be no problem. However, because at Y_T the 4% unemployment rate is below the natural rate level, wages will rise and the short-run aggregate supply curve will shift in to AS_2, moving the economy from point 1′ to point 2. The economy is back at the natural rate of unemployment, but at a higher price level of P_2. We could stop there, but because unemployment is again higher than the target level, policymakers would again shift the aggregate demand curve rightward to AD_3 to hit the output target at point 2′, and the whole process would continue to drive the economy to point 3 and beyond. The overall result is a steadily rising price level—an inflation.

How can policymakers continually shift the aggregate demand curve rightward? We have already seen that they cannot do it through fiscal policy, because of the limits on raising government expenditures and reducing taxes. Instead they will have to resort to expansionary monetary policy: a continuing increase in the money supply and hence a high money growth rate.

Pursuing too low an unemployment rate target or, equivalently, too high an output target is the source of inflationary monetary policy in this situation, but it seems senseless for policymakers to do this. They have not gained the benefit of a permanently higher level of output but have generated the burden of an inflation. If, however, they do not realize that the target rate of unemployment is below the natural rate, the process that we see in Figure 6 will be well under way before they realize their mistake.

Because the inflation described results from policymakers' pursuing policies that shift the aggregate demand curve to the right, it is called a *demand-pull inflation*. In contrast, a *cost-push inflation* occurs when workers push their wages up. Is it easy to distinguish between them in practice? The answer is no. We have seen that both types of inflation will be associated with higher money growth, so we cannot distinguish between them on this basis. Yet as Figures 5 and 6 demonstrate, demand-pull inflation will be associated with periods when unemployment is below the natural rate level, whereas cost-push inflation is associated with periods when unemployment is above the natural rate level. To decide which type of inflation has occurred, we can look at whether unemployment has been above or below its natural rate level. This would be easy if economists and policymakers actually knew how to measure the natural rate of unemployment; unfortunately, this difficult research question is still not fully resolved by the economics profession. In addition, the distinction between cost-push and demand-pull inflation is blurred, because a cost-push inflation can be initiated by a demand-pull inflation: When a demand-pull inflation produces higher inflation rates, expected inflation will eventually rise and cause workers to demand higher wages so that their real wages do not fall. In this way, demand-pull inflation can eventually trigger cost-push inflation.

Budget Deficits and Inflation

Our discussion of the evidence on money and inflation suggested that budget deficits are another possible source of inflationary monetary policy. To see if this could be the case, we need to look at how a government finances its budget deficits.

Government Budget Constraint.

Because the government has to pay its bills just as we do, it has a budget constraint. There are two ways we can pay for our spending: raise revenue (by working) or borrow. The government also enjoys these two options: raise revenue by levying taxes or go into debt by issuing government bonds. Unlike us, however, it has a third option: The government can create money and use it to pay for the goods and services it buys.

Methods of financing government spending are described by an expression called the **government budget constraint**, which states the following: The government budget deficit DEF, which equals the excess of government spending G over tax revenue T, must equal the sum of the change in the monetary base ΔMB and the change in government bonds held by the public ΔB. Algebraically, this expression can be written as follows:

$$DEF = G - T = \Delta MB + \Delta B \tag{1}$$

To see what the government budget constraint means in practice, let's look at the case in which the only government purchase is a $100 million supercomputer. If the government convinces the electorate that such a computer is worth paying for, it will probably be able to raise the $100 million in taxes to pay for it, and the budget deficit will equal zero. The government budget constraint then tells us that no issue of money or bonds is needed to pay for the computer, because the budget is balanced. If taxpayers think that supercomputers are too expensive and refuse to pay taxes for them, the budget constraint indicates that the government must pay for it by selling $100 million of new bonds to the public or by, in effect, printing $100 million of currency to pay for the computer. In either case, the budget constraint is satisfied; the $100 million deficit is balanced by the change in the stock of government bonds held by the public ($\Delta B =$ $100 million) or by the change in the monetary base ($\Delta MB =$ $100 million).

The government budget constraint thus reveals two important facts: ***If the government deficit is financed by an increase in bond holdings by the public, there is no effect on the monetary base and hence on the money supply. But, if the deficit is not financed by increased bond holdings by the public, the monetary base and the money supply increase.***

There are several ways to understand why a deficit leads to an increase in the monetary base when the public's bond holdings do not increase. The simplest case is when the government's treasury has the legal right to issue currency to finance its deficit. Financing the deficit is then very straightforward: The government just pays for the spending that is in excess of its tax revenues with new currency. Because this increase in currency adds directly to the monetary base, the monetary base rises and the money supply with it through the process of multiple deposit creation described in Chapters 16 and 17.

In the United States, however, and in many other countries, the government does not have the right to issue currency to pay for its bills. In this case, the government must finance its deficit by first issuing bonds to the public to acquire the extra funds to pay its bills. Yet if these bonds do not end up in the hands of the public, the only alternative is that they are purchased by the central bank. For the government bonds not to end up in the hands of the public, the central bank must conduct an open market purchase, which, as we saw in Chapters 16 and 17, leads to an increase in the monetary base and in the money supply. This method of financing government spending is called **monetizing the debt** because, as the two-step process described indicates, government debt issued to finance government spending has been removed from the hands of the public and has been replaced by high-powered money. This method of financing, or the more direct method when a government just issues the currency directly, is also, somewhat inaccurately, referred to as **printing money** because high-powered money (the monetary base) is created in the process. The use of the word *printing* is misleading because what is essential to this method of financing government spending is that the monetary base increases when the central bank conducts open market purchases, just as it would if more currency is put in circulation.

We thus see that a budget deficit can lead to an increase in the money supply if it is financed by the creation of high-powered money. However, earlier in this chapter you have seen that inflation can develop only when the stock of money grows continually. Can a budget deficit financed by printing money do this? The answer is yes, if the budget deficit persists for a substantial period of time. In the first period, if the deficit is financed by money creation, the money supply will rise, shifting the aggregate demand curve to the right and leading to a rise in the price level (see Figure 2). If the budget deficit is still present in the next period, it has to be financed all over again. The money supply will rise again, and the aggregate demand curve will again shift to the right, causing the price level to rise further. As long as the deficit persists and the government resorts to printing money to pay for it, this process will continue. ***Financing a persistent deficit by money creation will lead to a sustained inflation.***

A critical element in this process is that the deficit is persistent. If temporary, it would not produce an inflation because the situation would then be similar to that shown in Figure 3, in which there is a one-shot increase in government expenditure. In the period when the deficit occurs, there will be an increase in money to finance it, and the resulting rightward shift of the aggregate demand curve will raise the price level. If the deficit disappears in the next period, there is no longer a need to print money. The aggregate demand curve will not shift further, and the price level will not continue to rise. Hence the one-shot increase in the money supply from the temporary deficit generates only a one-shot increase in the price level, and no inflation develops.

To summarize, ***a deficit can be the source of a sustained inflation only if it is persistent rather than temporary and if the government finances it by creating money rather than by issuing bonds to the public***.

If inflation is the result, why do governments frequently finance persistent deficits by creating money? The answer is the key to understanding how budget deficits may lead to inflation.

Budget Deficits and Money Creation in Other Countries.

Although the United States has well-developed money and capital markets in which huge quantities of its government bonds, both short- and long-term, can be sold, this is not the situation in many developing countries. If developing countries run budget deficits, they cannot finance them by issuing bonds and must resort to their only other alternative, printing money. As a result, when they run large deficits relative to GDP, the money supply grows at substantial rates, and inflation results.

Earlier we cited Latin American countries that had high inflation rates and high money growth as evidence that inflation is a monetary phenomenon. The Latin American countries that had high money growth are precisely the ones that had persistent and extremely large budget deficits relative to GDP. The only way to finance the deficits was to print more money, so the ultimate source of their high inflation rates was their large budget deficits.

In all episodes of hyperinflation, huge government budget deficits are also the ultimate source of inflationary monetary policies. The budget deficits during hyperinflations are so large that even if a capital market exists to issue government bonds, it does not have sufficient capacity to handle the quantity of bonds that the government wishes to sell. In this situation, the government must also resort to the printing press to finance the deficits.

Budget Deficits and Money Creation in the United States. So far we have seen why budget deficits in some countries must lead to money creation and inflation. Either the deficit is huge, or the country does not have sufficient access to capital markets in which it can sell government bonds. But neither of these scenarios seems to describe the situation in the United States. True, the United States' deficits were large in the 1980s, early 1990s and mid-2000s, but even so, the magnitude of these deficits relative to GDP was small compared to the deficits of countries that have experienced hyperinflations: The U.S. deficit as a percentage of GDP reached a peak of 6% in 1983, whereas Argentina's budget deficit sometimes exceeded 15% of GDP. Furthermore, because the United States has the best-developed government bond market of any country in the world, it can issue large quantities of bonds when it needs to finance its deficit.

Whether the budget deficit can influence the monetary base and the money supply depends critically on how the Federal Reserve chooses to conduct monetary policy. If the Fed pursues a policy goal of preventing high interest rates (a possibility, as we have seen in Chapter 19), many economists contend that a budget deficit will lead to the printing of money. Their reasoning, using the supply and demand analysis of the bond market in Chapter 5, is as follows: When the Treasury issues bonds to the public, the supply of bonds rises (from B_1^s to B_2^s in Figure 7), causing bond prices to fall from P_1 to P_2 and hence interest rates to rise. If the Fed considers the rise in interest rates undesirable, it will buy bonds to prop up bond prices and reduce interest rates. The net result is that the government budget deficit can lead to Federal Reserve open market purchases, which raise the monetary base (create high-powered money) and raise the money supply. If the budget deficit persists so that the quantity of bonds supplied keeps on growing, the upward pressure on interest rates will continue, the Fed will purchase bonds again and again, and the money supply will continually rise, resulting in an inflation.

Economists such as Robert Barro of Harvard University, however, do not agree that budget deficits influence the monetary base in the manner just described. Their analy-

myeconlab

FIGURE 7
Interest Rates and the Government Budget Deficit
When the Treasury issues bonds to finance the budget deficit, the supply curve for bonds shifts rightward from B_1^s to B_2^s. Many economists take the position that the equilibrium moves to point 2 because the bond demand curve remains unchanged, with the result that the bond price falls from P_1 to P_2 and the interest rate rises. Adherents of Ricardian equivalence, however, suggest that the demand curve for bonds also increases to B_R^d, moving the equilibrium to point 2′, where the bond price is unchanged at P_1, so that the interest rate does not rise and there is no need for the Fed to buy bonds and increase the money supply.

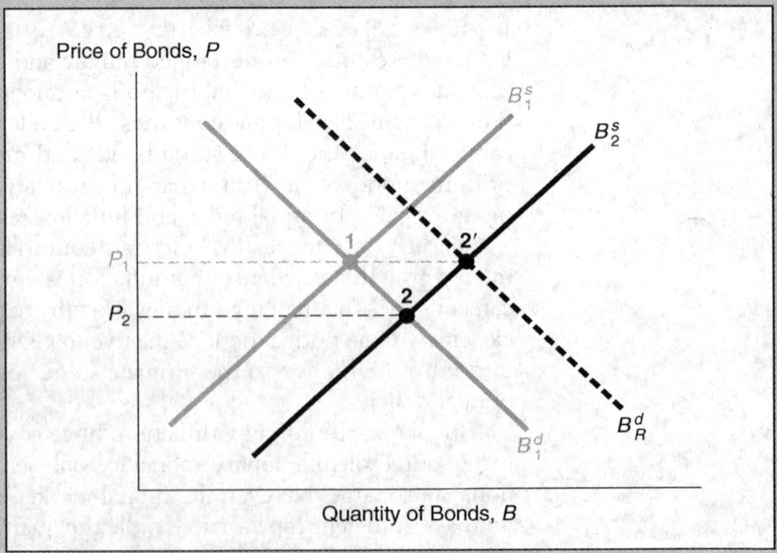

sis (which Barro named **Ricardian equivalence** after the nineteenth-century British economist David Ricardo) contends that when the government runs deficits and issues bonds, the public recognizes that it will be subject to higher taxes in the future to pay off these bonds. The public then saves more in anticipation of these future taxes, with the net result that the public demand for bonds increases to match the increased supply. The demand curve for bonds shifts rightward to B^d_R in Figure 7, leaving the bond price and interest rate unchanged. There is now no need for the Fed to purchase bonds to keep the interest rate from rising.

To sum up, although high inflation is "always and everywhere a monetary phenomenon" in the sense that it cannot occur without a high rate of money growth, there are reasons why this inflationary monetary policy might come about. The two underlying reasons are the adherence of policymakers to a high employment target and the presence of persistent government budget deficits.

APPLICATION Explaining the Rise in U.S. Inflation, 1960–1980

Now that we have examined the underlying sources of inflation, let's apply this knowledge to understanding the causes of the rise in U.S. inflation from 1960 to 1980.

Figure 8 documents the rise in inflation in those years. At the beginning of the period, the inflation rate is close to 1% at an annual rate; by the late 1970s, it is averaging around 8%. How does the analysis of this chapter explain this rise in inflation?

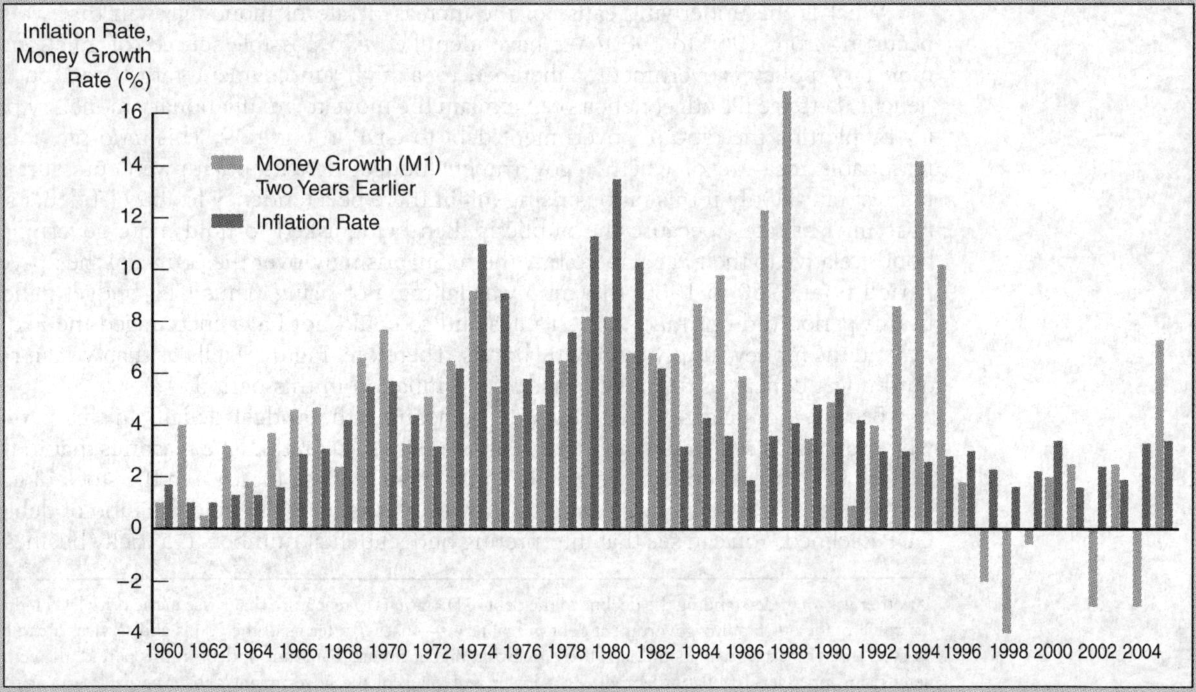

FIGURE 8 **Inflation and Money Growth, 1960–2005**

Source: Economic Report of the President; www.federalreserve.gov/releases/h6/hist/h6hist1.txt.

The conclusion that inflation is a monetary phenomenon is given a fair amount of support by the period from 1960 through 1980. As Figure 8 shows, in this period, there is a close correspondence between movements in the inflation rate and the monetary growth rate from two years earlier. (The money growth rates are from two years earlier, because research indicates that a change in money growth takes that long to affect the inflation rate.) The rise in inflation from 1960 to 1980 can be attributed to the rise in the money growth rate over this period. But you have probably noticed that in 1974–1975 and 1979–1980, the inflation rate is well above the money growth rate from two years earlier. You may recall from Chapter 23 that temporary upward bursts of the inflation rate in those years can be attributed to supply shocks from oil and food price increases that occurred in 1973–1975 and 1978–1980.

However, the linkage between money growth and inflation after 1980 is not at all evident in Figure 8, which explains why in 1982 the Fed announced that it would no longer use M1 as a basis to set monetary policy (see the appendix to Chapter 19). The breakdown of the relationship between money growth and inflation is the result of substantial gyrations in velocity in the 1980s and 1990s (documented in Chapter 22). For example, the early 1980s was a period of rapid disinflation (a substantial fall in the inflation rate), yet the money growth rates in Figure 8 do not display a visible downward trend until after the disinflation was over. (The disinflationary process in the 1980s will be discussed in another application later in this chapter.) Although some economists see the 1980s and 1990s as evidence against the money–inflation link, others view this as an unusual period characterized by large fluctuations in interest rates and by rapid financial innovation that made the correct measurement of money far more difficult (see Chapter 3). In their view, this period was an aberration, and the close correspondence of money and inflation is sure to reassert itself. However, this has not yet occurred.

What is the underlying cause of the increased rate of money growth that we see occurring from 1960 to 1980? We have identified two possible sources of inflationary monetary policy: government adherence to a high employment target and budget deficits. Let's see if budget deficits can explain the move to an inflationary monetary policy by plotting the ratio of government debt to GDP in Figure 9. This ratio provides a reasonable measure of whether government budget deficits put upward pressure on interest rates. Only if this ratio is rising might there be a tendency for budget deficits to raise interest rates, because the public is then being asked to hold more government bonds relative to their capacity to buy them. Surprisingly, over the course of the 20-year period from 1960 to 1980, this ratio was falling, not rising. Thus U.S. budget deficits in this period did not raise interest rates and so could not have encouraged the Fed to expand the money supply by buying bonds. Therefore, Figure 9 tells us that we can rule out budget deficits as a source of the rise in inflation in this period.

Because politicians were frequently bemoaning the budget deficits in this period, why did deficits not lead to an increase in the debt–GDP ratio? The reason is that in this period, U.S. budget deficits were sufficiently small that the increase in the stock of government debt was still slower than the growth in nominal GDP, and the ratio of debt to GDP declined. You can see that interpreting budget deficit numbers is a tricky business.[5]

---

[5]Another way of understanding the decline in the debt–GDP ratio is to recognize that a rise in the price level reduces the value of the outstanding government debt in real terms—that is, in terms of the goods and services it can buy. So even though budget deficits did lead to a somewhat higher nominal amount of debt in this period, the continually rising price level (inflation) produced a lower real value of the government debt. The decline in the real amount of debt at the same time that real GDP was rising in this period then resulted in the decline in the debt–GDP ratio. For a fascinating discussion of how tricky it is to interpret deficit numbers, see Robert Eisner and Paul J. Pieper, "A New View of the Federal Debt and Budget Deficits," *American Economic Review* 74 (1984): 11–29.

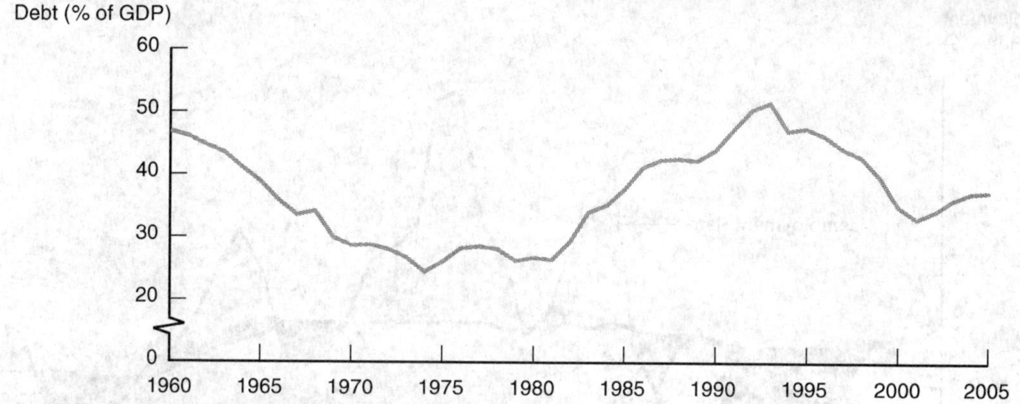

FIGURE 9 **Government Debt-to-GDP Ratio, 1960–2005**
Source: Economic Report of the President.

We have ruled out budget deficits as the instigator; what else could be the underlying cause of the higher rate of money growth and more rapid inflation in the 1960s and 1970s? Figure 10, which compares the actual unemployment rate to the natural rate of unemployment, shows that the economy was experiencing unemployment below the natural rate in all but one year between 1965 and 1973. This suggests that in 1965–1973, the American economy was experiencing the demand-pull inflation described in Figure 6.

Policymakers apparently pursued policies that continually shifted the aggregate demand curve to the right in trying to achieve an output target that was too high, thus causing the continual rise in the price level outlined in Figure 6. This occurred because policymakers, economists, and politicians had become committed in the mid-1960s to a target unemployment rate of 4%, the level of unemployment they thought was consistent with price stability. In hindsight, most economists today agree that the natural rate of unemployment was substantially higher in this period, on the order of 5% to 6%, as shown in Figure 10. The result of the inappropriate 4% unemployment target was the beginning of the most sustained inflationary episode in American history.

After 1975, the unemployment rate was regularly above the natural rate of unemployment, yet inflation continued. It appears that we have the phenomenon of a cost-push inflation described in Figure 5 (the impetus for which was the earlier demand-pull inflation). The persistence of inflation can be explained by the public's knowledge that government policy continued to be concerned with achieving high employment. With a higher rate of expected inflation arising initially from the demand-pull inflation, the aggregate supply curve in Figure 5 continued to shift leftward, causing a rise in unemployment that policymakers would try to eliminate by shifting the aggregate demand curve to the right. The result was a continuation of the inflation that had started in the 1960s.

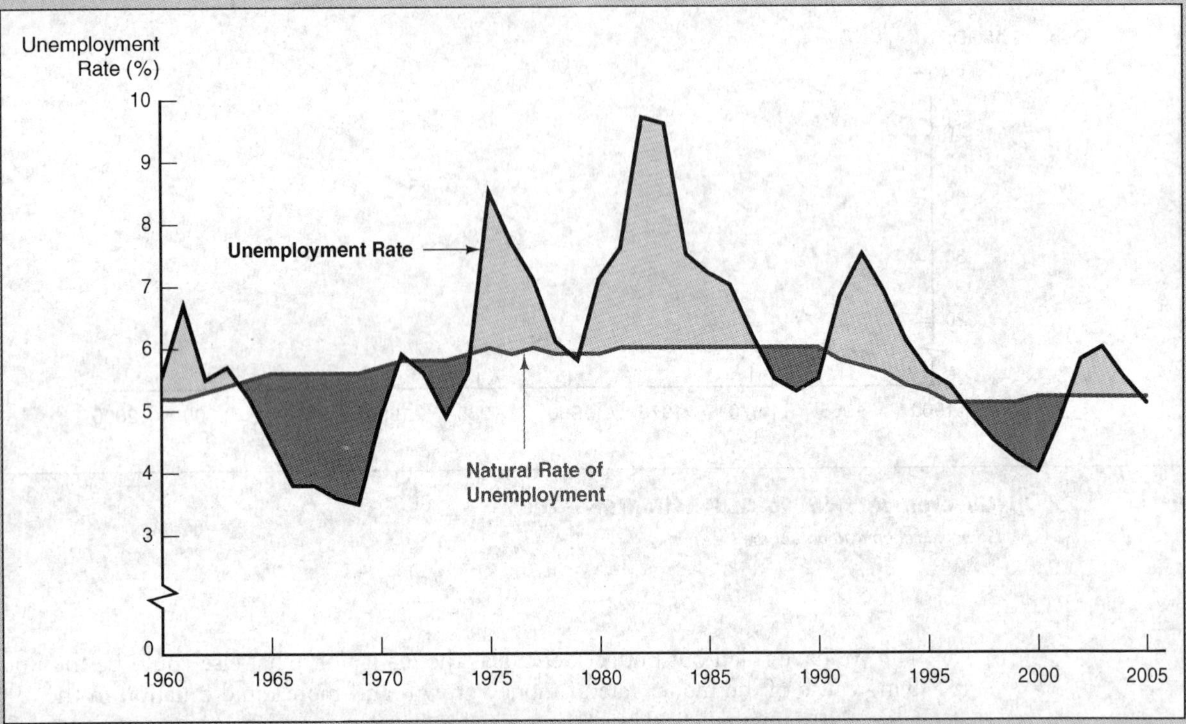

FIGURE 10 **Unemployment and the Natural Rate of Unemployment, 1960–2005**

Sources: Economic Report of the President and Congressional Budget Office.

ACTIVIST/NONACTIVIST POLICY DEBATE

All economists have similar policy goals—they want to promote high employment and price stability—and yet they often have very different views on how policy should be conducted. Activists regard the self-correcting mechanism through wage and price adjustment (see Chapter 23) as very slow and hence see the need for the government to pursue active, accommodating, discretionary policy to eliminate high unemployment whenever it develops. Nonactivists, by contrast, believe that the performance of the economy would be improved if the government avoided active policy to eliminate unemployment. We will explore the activist/nonactivist policy debate by first looking at what the policy responses might be when the economy experiences high unemployment.

Responses to High Unemployment

Suppose that policymakers confront an economy that has moved to point 1′ in Figure 11. At this point, aggregate output $Y_{1'}$ is lower than the natural rate level, and the economy is suffering from high unemployment. Policymakers have two viable choices: If they are nonactivists and do nothing, the short-run aggregate supply curve will eventually shift rightward over time, driving the economy from point 1′ to point 1, where

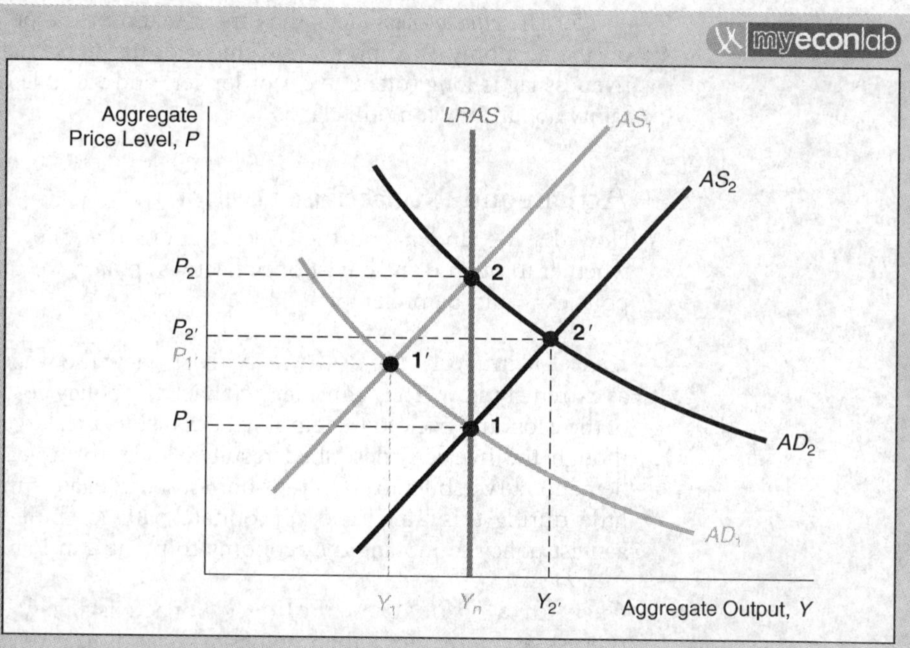

FIGURE 11
The Choice Between Activist and Nonactivist Policy
When the economy has moved to point 1′, the policymaker has two choices of policy: the nonactivist policy of doing nothing and letting the economy return to point 1 or the activist policy of shifting the aggregate demand curve to AD_2 to move the economy to point 2.

full employment is restored. The accommodating, activist alternative is to try to eliminate the high unemployment by attempting to shift the aggregate demand curve rightward to AD_2 by pursuing expansionary policy (an increase in the money supply, increase in government spending, or lowering of taxes). If policymakers could shift the aggregate demand curve to AD_2 instantaneously, the economy would immediately move to point 2, where there is full employment. However, several types of lags prevent this immediate movement from occurring.

1. The *data lag* is the time it takes for policymakers to obtain the data that tell them what is happening in the economy. Accurate data on GDP, for example, are not available until several months after a given quarter is over.

2. The *recognition lag* is the time it takes for policymakers to be sure of what the data are signaling about the future course of the economy. For example, to minimize errors, the National Bureau of Economic Research (the organization that officially dates business cycles) will not declare the economy to be in recession until at least six months after it has determined that one has begun.

3. The *legislative lag* represents the time it takes to pass legislation to implement a particular policy. The legislative lag does not exist for most monetary policy actions such as open market operations. It is, however, important for the implementation of fiscal policy, when it can sometimes take six months to a year to get legislation passed to change taxes or government spending.

4. The *implementation lag* is the time it takes for policymakers to change policy instruments once they have decided on the new policy. Again, this lag is unimportant for the conduct of open market operations because the Fed's trading desk can purchase or sell bonds almost immediately upon being told to do so by the Federal Open Market Committee. Actually implementing fiscal policy may take time, however; for example, getting government agencies to change their spending habits takes time, as does changing tax tables.

5. The *effectiveness lag* is the time it takes for the policy actually to have an impact on the economy. An important element of the nonactivist viewpoint is that the effectiveness lag is long (often a year or longer) and variable (i.e., there is substantial uncertainty about how long this lag is).

Activist and Nonactivist Positions

Now that we understand the considerations that affect decisions by policymakers on whether to pursue an activist or nonactivist policy, we can examine when each of these policies would be preferable.

Case for an Activist Policy. Activists view the wage and price adjustment process as extremely slow. They consider a nonactivist policy costly, because the slow movement of the economy back to full employment results in a large loss of output. However, even though the five lags described result in delay of a year or two before the aggregate demand curve shifts to AD_2, the short-run aggregate supply curve likewise moves very little during this time. The appropriate path for policymakers to pursue is thus an activist policy of moving the economy to point 2 in Figure 11.

Case for a Nonactivist Policy. Nonactivists view the wage and price adjustment process as more rapid than activists do and consider nonactivist policy less costly because output is soon back at the natural rate level. They suggest that an activist, accommodating policy of shifting the aggregate demand curve to AD_2 is costly, because it produces more volatility in both the price level and output. The reason for this volatility is that the time it takes to shift the aggregate demand curve to AD_2 is substantial, whereas the wage and price adjustment process is more rapid. Hence, before the aggregate demand curve shifts to the right, the short-run aggregate supply curve will have shifted rightward to AS_2, and the economy will have moved from point 1′ to point 1, where it has returned to the natural rate level of output Y_n. After adjustment to the AS_2 curve is complete, the shift of the aggregate demand curve to AD_2 finally takes effect, leading the economy to point 2′ at the intersection of AD_2 and AS_2. Aggregate output at $Y_{2'}$ is now greater than the natural rate level ($Y_{2'} > Y_n$), so the short-run aggregate supply curve will now shift leftward back to AS_1, moving the economy to point 2, where output is again at the natural rate level.

Although the activist policy eventually moves the economy to point 2 as policymakers intended, it leads to a sequence of equilibrium points—1′, 1, 2′, and 2—at which both output and the price level have been highly variable: Output overshoots its target level of Y_n, and the price level falls from $P_{1'}$ to P_1 and then rises to $P_{2'}$ and eventually to P_2. Because this variability is undesirable, policymakers would be better off pursuing the nonactivist policy, which moved the economy to point 1 and left it there.

Expectations and the Activist/Nonactivist Debate

Our analysis of inflation in the 1970s demonstrated that expectations about policy can be an important element in the inflation process. Allowing for expectations about policy to affect how wages are set (the wage-setting process) provides an additional reason for pursuing a nonactivist policy.

Do Expectations Favor a Nonactivist Approach? Does the possibility that expectations about policy matter to the wage-setting process strengthen the case for a nonactivist policy? The case for an activist policy states that with slow wage and price adjustment, the activist policy returns the economy to full employment at point 2 far more quickly than it takes to get to full employment at point 1 under nonactivist policy. However, the activist argument does not allow for the possibility (1) that expectations about policy matter to the wage-setting process and (2) that the economy might initially have moved from point 1 to point 1′ because an attempt by workers to raise their wages or a negative supply shock shifted the short-run aggregate supply curve from AS_2 to AS_1. We must therefore ask the following question about activist policy: Will the short-run aggregate supply curve continue to shift to the left after the economy has reached point 2, leading to cost-push inflation?

The answer to this question is yes *if* expectations about policy matter. Our discussion of cost-push inflation in Figure 5 suggested that if workers know that policy will be accommodating in the future, they will continue to push their wages up, and the short-run aggregate supply curve will keep shifting leftward. As a result, policymakers are forced to accommodate the cost push by continuing to shift the aggregate demand curve to the right to eliminate the unemployment that develops. The accommodating, activist policy with its high employment target has the hidden cost or disadvantage that it may well lead to inflation.[6]

The main advantage of a nonaccommodating, nonactivist policy, in which policymakers do not try to shift the aggregate demand curve in response to the cost push, is that it will prevent inflation. As depicted in Figure 4, the result of an upward push on wages in the face of a nonaccommodating, nonactivist policy will be a period of unemployment above the natural rate level, which will eventually shift the short-run aggregate supply curve and the price level back to their initial positions. The main criticism of this nonactivist policy is that the economy will suffer protracted periods of unemployment when the short-run aggregate supply curve shifts leftward. Workers, however, would probably not push for higher wages to begin with if they knew that policy would be nonaccommodating, because their wage gains will lead to a protracted period of unemployment. A nonaccommodating, nonactivist policy may have not only the advantage of preventing inflation but also the hidden benefit of discouraging leftward shifts in the short-run aggregate supply curve that lead to excessive unemployment.

In conclusion, ***if workers' opinions about whether policy is accommodating or nonaccommodating matter to the wage-setting process, the case for a nonactivist policy is much stronger***.

Do Expectations About Policy Matter to the Wage-Setting Process?

The answer to this question is crucial to deciding whether activist or nonactivist policy is preferred and so has become a major topic of current research for economists, but the evidence is not yet conclusive. We can ask, however, whether expectations about policy do affect people's behavior in other contexts. This information will help us know if expectations regarding whether policy is accommodating are important to the wage-setting process.

As any good negotiator knows, convincing your opponent that you will be nonaccommodating is crucial to getting a good deal. If you are bargaining with a car dealer over price, for example, you must convince him that you can just as easily walk away from the deal and buy a car from a dealer on the other side of town. This principle also applies to conducting foreign policy—it is to your advantage to convince your opponent that you will go to war (be nonaccommodating) if your demands are not met. Similarly, if your opponent thinks that you will be accommodating, he will almost certainly

[6]The issue that is being described here is the time-inconsistency problem described in Chapter 19.

take advantage of you. Finally, anyone who has dealt with a two-year-old child knows that the more you give in (pursue an accommodating policy), the more demanding the child becomes. People's expectations about policy *do* affect their behavior. Consequently, it is quite plausible that expectations about policy also affect the wage-setting process.[7]

Activist Versus Nonactivist: Conclusions

The following conclusions can be generated from our analysis: Activists believe in the use of discretionary policy to eliminate excessive unemployment whenever it develops, because they view the wage and price adjustment process as sluggish and unresponsive to expectations about policy. Nonactivists, by contrast, believe that a discretionary policy that reacts to excessive unemployment is counterproductive, because wage and price adjustment is rapid and because expectations about policy can matter to the wage-setting process. Nonactivists thus advocate the use of a policy rule to keep the aggregate demand curve from fluctuating away from the trend rate of growth of the natural rate level of output. Monetarists, who adhere to the nonactivist position and who also see money as the sole source of fluctuations in the aggregate demand curve, in the past advocated a policy rule whereby the Federal Reserve keeps the money supply growing at a constant rate. This monetarist rule is referred to as a **constant-money-growth-rate rule**. Because of the unstable velocity of M1 and M2, monetarists such as Bennett McCallum and Alan Meltzer of Carnegie-Mellon University have advocated a rule for the growth of the monetary base that is adjusted for past velocity changes.

As our analysis indicates, an important element for the success of a nonaccommodating policy rule is that it be *credible*: The public must believe that policymakers will be tough and not accede to a cost push by shifting the aggregate demand curve to the right to eliminate unemployment. In other words, government policymakers need credibility as inflation-fighters in the eyes of the public. Otherwise, workers will be more likely to push for higher wages, which will shift the aggregate supply curve leftward after the economy reaches full employment at a point such as point 2 in Figure 11 and will lead to unemployment or inflation (or both). Alternatively, a credible, nonaccommodating policy rule has the benefit that it makes a cost push less likely and thus helps prevent inflation and potential increases in unemployment. The following application suggests that recent historical experience is consistent with the importance of credibility to successful policymaking.

APPLICATION Importance of Credibility to Volcker's Victory over Inflation

In the period from 1965 through the 1970s, policymakers had little credibility as inflation-fighters—a well-deserved reputation, as they pursued an accommodating policy to achieve high employment. As we have seen, the outcome was not a happy one.

[7]A recent development in monetary theory, new classical macroeconomics, strongly suggests that expectations about policy are crucial to the wage-setting process and the movements of the aggregate supply curve.

Inflation soared to double-digit levels, while the unemployment rate remained high. To wring inflation out of the system, the Federal Reserve under Chairman Paul Volcker put the economy through two back-to-back recessions in 1980 and 1981–1982 (see the appendix to Chapter 19). (The data on inflation, money growth, and unemployment in this period are shown in Figures 8 and 10.) Only after the 1981–1982 recession—the most severe in the postwar period, with unemployment above the 10% level—did Volcker establish credibility for the Fed's anti-inflation policy. By the end of 1982, inflation was running at a rate of less than 5%.

One indication of Volcker's credibility came in 1983, when the money growth rate accelerated dramatically and yet inflation did not rise. Workers and firms were convinced that if inflation reared its head, Volcker would pursue a nonaccommodating policy of quashing it. They did not raise wages and prices, which would have shifted the aggregate supply curve leftward and would have led to both inflation and unemployment. The success of Volcker's anti-inflation policy continued throughout the rest of his term as chairman, which ended in 1987; unemployment fell steadily, while the inflation rate remained below 5%. Volcker's triumph over inflation was achieved because he obtained credibility the hard way—he earned it.

SUMMARY

1. Milton Friedman's famous proposition that "Inflation is always and everywhere a monetary phenomenon" is supported by the following evidence: Every country that has experienced a sustained, high inflation has also experienced a high rate of money growth.
2. Aggregate demand and supply analysis shows that high inflation can occur only if there is a high rate of money growth. As long as we recognize that by inflation we mean a rapid and continuing increase in the price level, almost all economists agree with Friedman's proposition.
3. Although high inflation is "always and everywhere a monetary phenomenon" in the sense that it cannot occur without a high rate of money growth, there are reasons why inflationary monetary policy comes about. The two underlying reasons are the adherence of policymakers to a high employment target and the presence of persistent government budget deficits.
4. Activists believe in the use of discretionary policy to eliminate excessive unemployment whenever it occurs because they view wage and price adjustment as sluggish and unresponsive to expectations about policy. Nonactivists take the opposite view and believe that discretionary policy is counterproductive. In addition, they regard the credibility of a nonaccommodating (nonactivist) anti-inflation policy as crucial to its success.

KEY TERMS

accommodating policy, p. 645
constant-money-growth-rate rule, p. 658
cost-push inflation, p. 644
demand-pull inflation, p. 644
government budget constraint, p. 648
monetizing the debt, p. 648
printing money, p. 648
Ricardian equivalence, p. 651

QUESTIONS AND PROBLEMS

Questions marked with an asterisk are answered at the end of the book in an appendix, "Answers to Selected Questions and Problems." Questions marked with a blue circle indicate the question is available in MyEconLab at www.myeconlab.com/mishkin.

1. "There are frequently years when the inflation rate is high and yet money growth is quite low. Therefore, the statement that inflation is a monetary phenomenon cannot be correct." Comment.

*2. Why do economists focus on historical episodes of hyperinflation to decide whether inflation is a monetary phenomenon?

3. "Because increases in government spending raise the aggregate demand curve, fiscal policy by itself can be the source of inflation." Is this statement true, false, or uncertain? Explain your answer.

*4. "A cost-push inflation occurs as a result of workers' attempts to push up their wages. Therefore, inflation does not have to be a monetary phenomenon." Is this statement true, false, or uncertain? Explain your answer.

5. "Because government policymakers do not consider inflation desirable, their policies cannot be the source of inflation." Is this statement true, false, or uncertain? Explain your answer.

*6. "A budget deficit that is only temporary cannot be the source of inflation." Is this statement true, false, or uncertain? Explain your answer.

7. How can the Fed's desire to prevent high interest rates lead to inflation?

*8. "If the data and recognition lags could be reduced, activist policy would more likely be beneficial to the economy." Is this statement true, false, or uncertain? Explain your answer.

9. "The more sluggish wage and price adjustment is, the more variable output and the price level are when an activist policy is pursued." Is this statement true, false, or uncertain? Explain your answer.

*10. "If the public believes that the monetary authorities will pursue an accommodating policy, a cost-push inflation is more likely to develop." Is this statement true, false, or uncertain? Explain your answer.

11. Why are activist policies to eliminate unemployment more likely to lead to inflation than nonactivist policies?

*12. "The less important expectations about policy are to movements of the aggregate supply curve, the stronger the case is for activist policy to eliminate unemployment." Is this statement true, false, or uncertain? Explain your answer.

13. If the economy's self-correcting mechanism works slowly, should the government necessarily pursue an activist policy to eliminate unemployment?

*14. "To prevent inflation, the Fed should follow Teddy Roosevelt's advice: 'Speak softly and carry a big stick.'" What would the Fed's "big stick" be? What is the statement trying to say?

15. In a speech early in the Iraq–Kuwait crisis in 1990, President George H. W. Bush stated that although his heart went out to the hostages held by Saddam Hussein, he would not let this hostage-taking deter the United States from insisting on the withdrawal of Iraq from Kuwait. Do you think that Bush's position made sense? Explain why or why not.

WEB EXERCISES

1. Figure 8 reports the inflation rate from 1960 to 2005. As this chapter states, inflation continues to be a major factor in economic policy. Go to ftp://ftp.bls.gov/pub/special.requests/cpi/cpiai.txt. Move data into Excel using the method described at the end of Chapter 1. Delete all but the first and last column (date and annual CPI). Graph this data and compare it to Figure 8.
   a. Has inflation increased or decreased since the end of 2005?
   b. When was inflation at its highest?
   c. When was inflation at its lowest?
   d. Have we ever had a period of deflation? If so, when?
   e. Have we ever had a period of hyperinflation? If so, when?

2. It can be an interesting exercise to compare the purchasing power of the dollar over different periods in history. Go to www.bls.gov/cpi/ and scroll down to the link to the "inflation calculator." Use this calculator to compute the following:
   a. If a new home cost $125,000 in 2005, what would it have cost in 1950?
   b. The average household income in 2005 was about $37,000. How much would this have been in 1945?
   c. An average new car cost about $18,000 in 2005. What would this have cost in 1945?
   d. Using the results you found in Exercises b and c, does a car consume more or less of average household income in 2005 than in 1945?

WEB REFERENCES

www.bls.gov/cpi/

The home page of the Bureau of Labor Statistics, which reports inflation numbers.

ftp://ftp.bls.gov/pub/special.requests/cpi/cpiai.txt

Download historical inflation statistics going back to 1913. This data can easily be moved into Microsoft Excel using the procedure discussed at the end of Chapter 1.

http://www.gpoaccess.gov/eop

The *Economic Report of the President* reports debt levels and gross domestic product, along with many other economic statistics.

GLOSSARY

accommodating policy An activist policy in pursuit of a high employment target. **645**

activist An economist who views the self-correcting mechanism through wage and price adjustment to be very slow and hence sees the need for the government to pursue active, discretionary policy to eliminate high unemployment whenever it develops. **598**

adaptive expectations Expectations of a variable based on an average of past values of the variable. **157**

adverse selection The problem created by asymmetric information *before* a transaction occurs: The people who are the most undesirable from the other party's point of view are the ones who are most likely to want to engage in the financial transaction. **37**

agency theory The analysis of how asymmetric information problems affect economic behavior. **188, 204**

aggregate demand The total quantity of output demanded in the economy at different price levels. **585**

aggregate demand curve A relationship between the price level and the quantity of aggregate output demanded when the goods and money markets are in equilibrium. **585**

aggregate income The total income of factors of production (land, labor, capital) in the economy. **20**

aggregate output The total production of final goods and services in the economy. **8**

aggregate price level The average price of goods and services in an economy. **10**

aggregate supply The quantity of aggregate output supplied by the economy at different price levels. **585**

aggregate supply curve The relationship between the quantity of output supplied and the price level. **589**

American option An option contract that can be exercised at any time up to the expiration date of the contract. **344**

anchor currency A currency to which other countries' currencies are pegged. **537**

"animal spirits" Waves of optimism and pessimism that affect consumers' and businesses' willingness to spend. **589**

annuities Financial contracts under which a customer pays an annual premium in exchange for a future stream of annual payments beginning at a set age, say 65, and ending when the person dies. **310**

appreciation Increase in a currency's value. **504**

arbitrage Elimination of a riskless profit opportunity in a market. **337**

asset A financial claim or piece of property that is a store of value. **3**

asset management The acquisition of assets that have a low rate of default and diversification of asset holdings to increase profits. **226**

asset transformation The process of turning risky assets into safer assets for investors by creating and selling assets with risk characteristics that people are comfortable with and then using the funds acquired by selling these assets to purchase other assets that may have far more risk. **37**

asset market approach An approach to determine asset prices using stocks of assets rather than flows. **99**

asymmetric information The unequal knowledge that each party to a transaction has about the other party. **37**

automated bank machine (ABM) One location that provides an automated teller machine (ATM), an Internet connection to the bank's Web site, and a telephone link to customer service. **253**

automated teller machine (ATM) An electronic machine that provides banking services 24-hours a day. **253**

balance of payments A bookkeeping system for recording all payments that have a direct bearing on the movement of funds between a country and foreign countries. **536**

balance-of-payments crisis A foreign exchange crisis stemming from problems in a country's balance of payments. **546**

balance sheet A list of the assets and liabilities of a bank (or firm) that balances: Total assets equal total liabilities plus capital. **219**

bank failure A situation in which a bank cannot satisfy its obligations to pay its depositors and other creditors and so goes out of business. **279**

bank holding companies Companies that own one or more banks. **250**

bank panic The simultaneous failure of many banks, as during a financial crisis. **206**

banks Financial institutions that accept money deposits and make loans (such as commercial banks, savings and loan associations, and credit unions). **8**

bank supervision (prudetial supervision) Overseeing who operates banks and how they are operated. **284**

Basel Accord An agreement that required that banks hold as capital at least 8% of their risk-weighted assets. **284**

Basel Committee on Banking Supervision An international committee of bank supervisors that meets under the auspices of the Bank for International Settlements in Basel, Switzerland. **284**

basis point One one-hundredth of a percentage point. **82**

behavioral finance A subfield of finance that applies concepts from other social sciences such as anthropology, sociology, and, particularly, psychology to understand the behavior of securities prices. **173**

Board of Governors of the Federal Reserve System A board with seven governors (including the chairman) that plays an essential role in decision making within the Federal Reserve System. **384**

bond A debt security that promises to make payments periodically for a specified period of time. **3**

borrowed reserves A bank's borrowings from the Fed **431**

branches Additional offices of banks that conduct banking operations. **261**

Bretton Woods system The international monetary system in use from 1945 to 1971 in which exchange rates were fixed and the U.S. dollar was freely convertible into gold (by foreign governments and central banks only). **538**

brokerage firms Firms that participate in securities markets as brokers, dealers, and investment bankers. **328**

brokers Agents for investors; they match buyers with sellers. **26**

bubble A situation in which the price of an asset differs from its fundamental market value. **173**

budget deficit The excess of government expenditure over tax revenues. **12**

budget surplus The excess of tax revenues over government expenditures. **12**

business cycles The upward and downward movement of aggregate output produced in the economy. **9**

call option An option contract that provides the right to buy a security at a specified price. **345**

capital account An account that describes the flow of capital between a country and other countries. **536**

capital adequacy management A bank's decision about the amount of capital it should maintain and then acquisition of the needed capital. **226**

capital market A financial market in which longer-term debt (generally with original maturity of greater than one year) and equity instruments are traded. **27**

capital mobility A situation in which foreigners can easily purchase a country's assets and the country's residents can easily purchase foreign assets. **513**

cash flow The difference between cash receipts and cash expenditures. **206**

cash flows Cash payments to the holder of a security. **67, 151**

central bank The government agency that oversees the banking system and is responsible for the amount of money and credit supplied in the economy; in the United States, the Federal Reserve System. **12, 248**

closed-end fund A mutual fund in which a fixed number of nonredeemable shares are sold at an initial offering, then traded in the over-the-counter market like common stock. **322**

coinsurance A situation in which only a portion of losses are covered by insurance, so that the insured suffers a percentage of the losses along with the insurance agency. **315**

collateral Property that is pledged to the lender to guarantee payment in the event that the borrower is unable to make debt payments. **185**

commodity money Money made up of precious metals or another valuable commodity. **53**

common stock A security that is a claim on the earnings and assets of a company. **5**

compensating balance A required minimum amount of funds that a firm receiving a loan must keep in a checking account at the lending bank. **237**

conflicts of interest A manifestation of the moral hazard problem, particularly when a financial institution provides multiple services and the potentially competing interests of those services may lead to a concealment of information or dissemination of misleading information. **202, 378**

consol A perpetual bond with no maturity date and no repayment of principal that periodically makes fixed coupon payments. **75**

constant-money-growth-rate rule A policy rule advocated by monetarists, whereby the Federal Reserve keeps the money supply growing at a constant rate. **658**

consumer durable expenditure Spending by consumers on durable items such as automobiles and household appliances. **621**

consumer expenditure The total demand for (spending on) consumer goods and services. **588**

consumption Spending by consumers on nondurable goods and services (including services related to the ownership of homes and consumer durables). **624**

costly state verification Monitoring a firm's activities, an expensive process in both time and money. **195**

cost-push inflation Inflation that occurs because of the push by workers to obtain higher wages. **644**

coupon bond A credit market instrument that pays the owner a fixed interest payment every year until the maturity date, when a specified final amount is repaid. **70**

coupon rate The dollar amount of the yearly coupon payment expressed as a percentage of the face value of a coupon bond. **70**

credit default swap A transaction in which one party who wants to hedge credit risk pays a fixed payment on a regular basis, in return for a contingent payment that is triggered by a credit event such as the bankruptcy of a particular firm, or the downgrading of the firm's credit rating by a credit rating agency. **355**

credit derivatives Derivatives that have payoffs to previously issued securities, but ones that bear credit risk. **354**

credit rationing A lender's refusal to make loans even though borrowers are willing to pay the stated interest rate or even a higher rate or restriction of the size of loans made to less than the full amount sought. **238**

credit-linked note A type of credit derivative that combines a bond and a credit option. **355**

credit options Options in which for a fee, the purchaser has the right to get profits that are tied either to the price of an underlying risky security or to an interest rate. **354**

credit-rating agencies Investment advisory firms that rate the quality of corporate and municipal bonds in terms of the probability of default. **130**

credit risk The risk arising from the possibility that the borrower will default. **226**

credit swap A transaction in which risky payments on loans are swapped for each other. **352**

credit view Monetary transmission mechanisms operating through asymmetric information effects on credit markets. **622**

currency Paper money (such as dollar bills) and coins. **29, 49**

currency board A monetary regime in which the domestic currency is backed 100% by a foreign currency (say, dollars) and in which the note-issuing authority, whether the central bank or the government, establishes a fixed exchange rate to this foreign currency and stands ready to exchange domestic currency at this rate whenever the public requests it. **557**

currency swap The exchange of a set of payments in one currency for a set of payments in another currency. **351**

current account An account that shows international transactions involving currently produced goods and services. **536**

current yield An approximation of the yield to maturity that equals the yearly coupon payment divided by the price of a coupon bond. **77**

dealers People who link buyers with sellers by buying and selling securities at stated prices. **26**

debt deflation A situation in which a substantial decline in the price level sets in, leading to a further deterioration in firms' net worth because of the increased burden of indebtedness. **209**

deductible The fixed amount by which the insured's loss is reduced when a claim is paid off. **315**

default A situation in which the party issuing a debt instrument is unable to make interest payments or pay off the amount owed when the instrument matures. **29, 127**

default-free bonds Bonds with no default risk, such as U.S. government bonds. **128**

default risk The chance that the issuer of a debt instrument will be unable to make interest payments or pay off the face value when the instrument matures. **127**

defensive open market operations Open market operations intended to offset movements in other factors that affect the monetary base (such as changes in Treasury deposits with the Fed or changes in float). **450**

defined-benefit plan A pension plan in which benefits are set in advance. **317**

defined-contribution plan A pension plan in which benefits are determined by the contributions into the plan and their earnings. **317**

demand curve A curve depicting the relationship between quantity demanded and price when all other economic variables are held constant. **96**

demand-pull inflation Inflation that results when policymakers pursue policies that shift the aggregate demand curve. **644**

demand shocks Shocks that can shift the aggregate demand curve, including changes in the money supply, changes in government expenditure and taxes, changes in net exports, and changes in consumer and business spending. **589**

deposit facility The European Central Bank's standing facility in which banks are paid a fixed interest rate 100 basis points below the target financing rate. **461**

deposit outflows Losses of deposits when depositors make withdrawals or demand payment. **226**

deposit rate ceiling Restriction on the maximum interest rate payable on deposits. **256**

depreciation Decrease in a currency's value. **504**

devaluation Resetting of the fixed value of a currency at a lower level. **541**

dirty float An exchange rate regime in which countries attempt to influence their exchange rates by buying and selling currencies (also called a *managed float*). **538**

discount bond A credit market instrument that is bought at a price below its face value and whose face value is repaid at the maturity date; it does not make any interest payments. Also called a zero-coupon bond. **70**

discount loans A bank's borrowings from the Federal Reserve System; also known as advances. **221**

discount rate The interest rate that the Federal Reserve charges banks on discount loans. **228, 407**

discount window The Federal Reserve facility at which discount loans are made to banks. **452**

discount yield See *yield on a discount basis*. **79**

disintermediation A reduction in the flow of funds into the banking system that causes the amount of financial intermediation to decline. **256**

diversification Investing in a collection (**portfolio**) of assets whose returns do not always move together, with the result that overall risk is lower than for individual assets. **37**

dividends Periodic payments made by equities to shareholders. **26, 152**

dollarization The adoption of a sound currency, like the U.S. dollar, as a country's money. **557**

dual banking system The system in the United States in which banks supervised by the federal government and banks supervised by the states operate side by side. **249**

dual mandate A central bank mandate that features two co-equal objectives: price stability and maximum employment. **469**

duration analysis A measurement of the sensitivity of the market value of a bank's assets and liabilities to changes in interest rates. **239**

dynamic open market operations Open market operations that are intended to change the level of reserves and the monetary base. **450**

e-cash Electronic money that is used on the Internet to purchase goods or services. **55**

economies of scale The reduction in transaction costs per dollar of transaction as the size (scale) of transactions increases. **35**

economies of scope The ability to use one resource to provide many different products and services. **201, 265, 362**

Edge Act corporation A special subsidiary of a U.S. bank that is engaged primarily in international banking. **273**

effective exchange rate index An index reflecting the value of a basket of representative foreign currencies. **524**

efficient market hypothesis The application of the theory of rational expectations to financial markets. **159**

e-finance A new means of delivering financial services electronically. **8**

electronic money (e-money) Money that exists only in electronic form and substitutes for cash as well. **54**

equation of exchange The equation $MV = PY$, which relates nominal income to the quantity of money. **566, 586**

equities Claims to share in the net income and assets of a corporation (such as common stock). **26**

equity capital See *net worth*. **193**

equity multiplier (*EM*) The amount of assets per dollar of equity capital. **232**

Eurobonds Bonds denominated in a currency other than that of the country in which they are sold. **33**

Eurocurrencies A variant of the Eurobond; foreign currencies deposited in banks outside the home country. **33**

Eurodollars U.S. dollars that are deposited in foreign banks outside the United States or in foreign branches of U.S. banks. **33**

European option An option that can be exercised only at the expiration date of the contract. **344**

excess demand A situation in which quantity demanded is greater than quantity supplied. **98**

excess reserves Reserves in excess of required reserves. **222, 407**

excess supply A situation in which quantity supplied is greater than quantity demanded. **98**

exchange rate The price of one currency stated in terms of another currency. **503**

exchange rate overshooting A phenomenon whereby the exchange rate changes by more in the short run than it does in the long run when the money supply changes. **523**

exchanges Secondary markets in which buyers and sellers of securities (or their agents or brokers) meet in one central location to conduct trades. **27**

exercise price (strike price) The price at which the purchaser of an option has the right to buy or sell the underlying financial instrument. Also known as the strike price. **344**

expectations theory The proposition that the interest rate on a long-term bond will equal the average of the short-term interest rates that people expect to occur over the life of the long-term bond. **136**

expected return The return on an asset expected over the next period. **93**

face value A specified final amount paid to the owner of a coupon bond at the maturity date. Also called par value. **70**

federal funds rate The interest rate on overnight loans of deposits at the Federal Reserve. **31, 445**

Federal Open Market Committee (FOMC) The committee that makes decisions regarding the conduct of open market operations; composed of the seven members of the Board of Governors of the Federal Reserve System, the president of the Federal Reserve Bank of New York, and the presidents of four other Federal Reserve banks on a rotating basis. **384**

Federal Reserve banks The 12 district banks in the Federal Reserve System. **384**

Federal Reserve System (the Fed) The central banking authority responsible for monetary policy in the United States. **12**

fiat money Paper currency decreed by a government as legal tender but not convertible into coins or precious metal. **53**

financial crisis A major disruption in financial markets that is characterized by sharp declines in asset prices and the failures of many financial and nonfinancial firms. **204**

financial derivatives Instruments that have payoffs that are linked to previously issued securities, used as risk reduction tools. **251, 333**

financial engineering The process of researching and developing new financial products and services that would meet customer needs and prove profitable. **250**

financial futures contract A futures contract in which the standardized commodity is a particular type of financial instrument. **336**

financial futures option (futures option) An option in which the underlying instrument is a *futures contract*. Also called a futures option. **344**

financial intermediaries Institutions (such as banks, insurance companies, mutual funds, pension funds, and finance companies) that borrow funds from people who have saved and then make loans to others. **7**

financial intermediation The process of indirect finance whereby financial intermediaries link lender-savers and borrower-spenders. **35**

financial markets Markets in which funds are transferred from people who have a surplus of available funds to people who have a shortage of available funds. **3**

financial panic The widespread collapse of financial markets and intermediaries in an economy. **44**

fiscal policy Policy that involves decisions about government spending and taxation. **12**

Fisher effect The outcome that when expected inflation occurs, interest rates will rise; named after economist Irving Fisher. **106**

fixed exchange rate regime A regime in which central banks buy and sell their own currencies to keep their exchange rates fixed at a certain level. **537**

fixed-payment loan A credit market instrument that provides a borrower with an amount of money that is repaid by making a fixed payment periodically (usually monthly) for a set number of years. **70**

float Cash items in process of collection at the Fed minus deferred-availability cash items. **413**

floating exchange rate regime An exchange rate regime in which the value of currencies are allowed to fluctuate against one another. **538**

foreign bonds Bonds sold in a foreign country and denominated in that country's currency. **33**

foreign exchange intervention An international financial transaction in which a central bank buys or sells currency to influence foreign exchange rates. **531**

foreign exchange market The market in which exchange rates are determined. **5, 503**

foreign exchange rate See *exchange rate*. **5**

forward contract An agreement by two parties to engage in a financial transaction at a future (forward) point in time. **334**

forward exchange rate The exchange rate for a forward transaction. **504**

forward transaction A transaction that involves the exchange of bank deposits denominated in different currencies at some specified future date. **504**

free-rider problem The problem that occurs when people who do not pay for information take advantage of the information that other people have paid for. **190**

fully-amortized loan See *fixed-payment loan*. **70**

fully funded Describing a pension plan in which the contributions to the plan and their earnings over the years are sufficient to pay out the defined benefits when they come due. **317**

futures contract A contract in which the seller agrees to provide a certain standardized commodity to the buyer on a specific future date at an agreed-on price. **251**

futures option See *financial futures option*. **344**

gap analysis A measurement of the sensitivity of bank profits to changes in interest rates, calculated by subtracting the amount of rate-sensitive liabilities from the amount of rate-sensitive assets. **239**

generalized dividend model Calculates that the price of a stock is determined only by the present value of the dividends. **153**

goal independence The ability of the central bank to set the goals of monetary policy. **393**

gold standard A fixed exchange rate regime under which a currency is directly convertible into gold. **538**

goodwill An accounting entry to reflect value to the firm of its having special expertise or a particularly profitable business line. **294**

Gordon growth model A simplified model to compute the value of a stock by assuming constant dividend growth. **153**

government budget constraint The requirement that the government budget deficit equal the sum of the change in the monetary base and the change in government bonds held by the public. **648**

government spending Spending by all levels of government on goods and services. **588**

gross domestic product (GDP) The value of all final goods and services produced in the economy during the course of a year. **12, 20**

hedge To protect oneself against risk. **251, 333**

hedge fund A special type of mutual fund that engages in "market-neutral strategies." **323**

hierarchical mandate A mandate for the central bank that puts the goal of price stability first, but as long as it is achieved other goals can be pursued. **469**

high-powered money The monetary base. **407**

hyperinflation An extreme inflation in which the inflation rate exceeds 50% per month. **52**

hysteresis A departure from full-employment levels as a result of past high unemployment. **600**

incentive-compatible Having the incentives of both parties to a contract in alignment. **198**

income The flow of earnings. **50**

indexed bond A bond whose interest and principal payments are adjusted for changes in the price level, and whose interest rate thus provides a direct measure of a real interest rate. **89**

inflation The condition of a continually rising price level. **10**

inflation rate The rate of change of the price level, usually measured as a percentage change per year. **11**

inflation targeting A monetary policy strategy to achieve price stability. **474**

initial public offering (IPO) Shares of newly issued stock. **327, 364**

insolvent A situation in which the value of a firm's or bank's assets has fallen below its liabilities; bankrupt. **209**

instrument independence The ability of the central bank to set monetary policy instruments. **393**

interest parity condition The observation that the domestic interest rate equals the foreign interest rate plus the expected appreciation in the foreign currency. **513**

interest rate The cost of borrowing or the price paid for the rental of funds (usually expressed as a percentage per year). **4**

interest-rate forward contract A forward contract that is linked to a debt instrument. **334**

interest-rate risk The possible reduction in returns associated with changes in interest rates. **85, 226**

interest-rate swap A financial contract that allows one party to exchange (swap) a set of interest payments for another set of interest payments owned by another party. **352**

intermediate target Any of a number of variables, such as monetary aggregates or interest rates, that have a direct effect on employment and the price level and that the Fed seeks to influence. **484**

intermediate-term With reference to a debt instrument, having a maturity of between one and ten years. **26**

international banking facilities (IBFs) Banking establishments in the United States that can accept time deposits from foreigners but are not subject to either reserve requirements or restrictions on interest payments. **273**

International Monetary Fund (IMF) The international organization created by the Bretton Woods agreement whose objective is to promote the growth of world trade by making loans to countries experiencing balance-of-payments difficulties. **538**

international policy coordination Agreements among countries to enact policies cooperatively. **500**

international reserves Central bank holdings of assets denominated in foreign currencies. **531**

inventory investment Spending by firms on additional holdings of raw materials, parts, and finished goods. **539**

inverted yield curve A yield curve that is downward-sloping. **130**

investment banks Firms that assist in the initial sale of securities in the primary market. **26**

January effect An abnormal rise in stock prices from December to January. **166**

junk bonds Bonds with ratings below Baa (or BBB) that have a high default risk. **130**

Keynesian A follower of John Maynard Keynes who believes that movements in the price level and aggregate output are driven by changes not only in the money supply but also in government spending and fiscal policy and who does not regard the economy as inherently stable. **598, 611**

large, complex banking organizations (LCBOs) Large companies that provide banking as well as many other financial services. **265**

law of one price The principle that if two countries produce an identical good, the price of this good should be the same throughout the world no matter which country produces it. **507**

lender of last resort Provider of reserves to financial institutions when no one else would provide them to prevent a financial crisis. **453**

leverage ratio A bank's capital divided by its assets. **284**

liabilities IOUs or debts. **24**

liability management The acquisition of funds at low cost to increase profits. **226**

liquid Easily converted into cash. **27**

liquidity The relative ease and speed with which an asset can be converted into cash. **52, 94**

liquidity management The decisions made by a bank to maintain sufficient liquid assets to meet the bank's obligations to depositors. **226**

liquidity preference framework A model developed by John Maynard Keynes that predicts the equilibrium interest rate on the basis of the supply of and demand for money. **111**

liquidity preference theory John Maynard Keynes's theory of the demand for money. **569**

liquidity premium theory The theory that the interest rate on a long-term bond will equal an average of short-term interest rates expected to occur over the life of the long-term bond plus a positive term (liquidity) premium. **140**

liquidity services Services financial intermediaries provide to their customers to make it easier for them to conduct their transactions. **36**

load funds Open-end mutual funds sold by salespeople who receive a commission that is paid at the time of purchase and is immediately subtracted from the redemption value of the shares. **322**

loan commitment A bank's commitment (for a specified future period of time) to provide a firm with loans up to a given amount at an interest rate that is tied to some market interest rate. **237**

loan sale The sale under a contract (also called a secondary loan participation) of all or part of the cash stream from a specific loan, thereby removing the loan from the bank's balance sheet. **241**

longer-term refinancing operations A category of open market operations by the European Central Bank that are similar to the Fed's outright purchases or sales of securities. **460**

long position A contractual obligation to take delivery of an underlying financial instrument. **333**

long-run monetary neutrality See *monetary neutrality*. **522**

long-term With reference to a debt instrument, having a maturity of ten years or more. **26**

M1 A measure of money that includes currency, traveler's checks, and checkable deposits. **57**

M2 A measure of money that adds to M1: money market deposit accounts, money market mutual fund shares, small-denomination time deposits, savings deposits, overnight repurchase agreements, and overnight Eurodollars. **57**

macro hedge A hedge of interest-rate risk for a financial institution's entire portfolio. **339**

main refinancing operations Weekly reverse transactions (purchase or sale of eligible assets under repurchase agreements or credit operations against eligible assets as collateral) that are reversed within two weeks and are the primary monetary policy tool of the European Central Bank. **460**

managed float regime An exchange rate regime in which countries attempt to influence their exchange rates by buying and selling currencies (also called a dirty float). **538**

management advisory services When an accounting firm provides its client with auditing services and nonaudit consulting services creating a potential conflict of interest problem. **365**

marginal lending facility The European Central Bank's standing lending facility in which banks can borrow (against eligible collateral) overnight loans from the national central bank at a rate 100 basis points above the target financing rate. **460**

marginal lending rate The interest rate charged by the European Central Bank for borrowing at its marginal lending facility. **460**

margin requirement A sum of money that must be kept in an account (the margin account) at a brokerage firm. **342**

marked to market Repriced and settled in the margin account at the end of every trading day to reflect any change in the value of the futures contract. **342**

market equilibrium A situation occurring when the quantity that people are willing to buy (demand) equals the quantity that people are willing to sell (supply). **98**

market fundamentals Items that have a direct impact on future income streams of a security. **162**

matched sale–purchase transaction An arrangement whereby the Fed sells securities and the buyer agrees to sell them back to the Fed in the near future; sometimes called a reverse repo. **452**

maturity Time to the expiration date (maturity date) of a debt instrument. **25**

mean reversion The phenomenon that stocks with low returns today tend to have high returns in the future, and vice versa. **167**

medium of exchange Anything that is used to pay for goods and services. **50**

micro hedge A hedge for a specific asset. **339**

monetarist A follower of Milton Friedman who sees changes in the money supply as the primary source of movements in the price level and aggregate output and who views the economy as inherently stable. **598, 611**

monetary aggregates The measures of the money supply used by the Federal Reserve System (M1 and M2). **57**

monetary base The sum of the Fed's monetary liabilities (currency in circulation and reserves) and the U.S. Treasury's monetary liabilities (Treasury currency in circulation, primarily coins). **406**

monetary neutrality A proposition that in the long run, a percentage rise in the money supply is matched by the same percentage rise in the price level, leaving unchanged the real money supply and all other economic variables such as interest rates. **522**

monetary policy The management of the money supply and interest rates. **12**

monetary targeting A monetary policy strategy in which the central bank announces that it will achieve a certain value (the target) of the annual growth rate of a monetary aggregate. **470**

monetary theory The theory that relates changes in the quantity of money to changes in economic activity. **9, 565**

monetizing the debt A method of financing government spending whereby the government debt issued to finance government spending is removed from the hands of the public and is replaced by high-powered money instead. Also called *printing money*. **648**

money Anything that is generally accepted in payment for goods or services or in the repayment of debts. **8**

money center banks Large banks in key financial centers (New York, Chicago, San Francisco). **230**

money market A financial market in which only short-term debt instruments (generally those with original maturity of less than one year) are traded. **27**

money multiplier A ratio that relates the change in the money supply to a given change in the monetary base. **423**

money supply The quantity of money. **8**

moral hazard The risk that one party to a transaction will engage in behavior that is undesirable from the other party's point of view. **38**

multiple deposit creation The process whereby, when the Fed supplies the banking system with $1 of additional reserves, deposits increase by a multiple of this amount. **413**

NAIRU (nonaccelerating inflation rate of unemployment) The rate of unemployment when demand for labor equals supply, consequently eliminating the tendency for the inflation rate to change. **487, 590**

national banks Federally chartered banks. **249**

natural rate of output The level of aggregate output produced at the natural rate of unemployment at which there is no tendency for wages or prices to change. **591**

natural rate of unemployment The rate of unemployment consistent with full employment at which the demand for labor equals the supply of labor. **467, 591**

net exports Net foreign spending on domestic goods and services, equal to exports minus imports. 588

net worth The difference between a firm's assets (what it owns or is owed) and its liabilities (what it owes). Also called *equity capital*. 193

no-load funds Mutual funds sold directly to the public on which no sales commissions are charged. 322

nominal anchor A nominal variable such as the inflation rate, an exchange rate, or the money supply that monetary policymakers use to tie down the price level. 466

nominal interest rate An interest rate that does not take inflation into account. 87

nonaccelerating inflation rate of unemployment See *NAIRU*. 487

nonactivist An economist who believes that the performance of the economy would be improved if the government avoided active policy to eliminate unemployment. 598

nonborrowed monetary base The monetary base minus discount loans (borrowed reserves). 431

notional principal The amount on which interest is being paid in a swap arrangement. 352

off-balance-sheet activities Bank activities that involve trading financial instruments and the generation of income from fees and loan sales, all of which affect bank profits but are not visible on bank balance sheets. 241, 284

official reserve transactions balance The current account balance plus items in the capital account. 536

open-end fund A mutual fund in which shares can be redeemed at any time at a price that is tied to the asset value of the fund. 322

open interest The number of contracts outstanding. 339

open market operations The Fed's buying or selling of bonds in the open market. 388, 407

open market purchase A purchase of bonds by the Fed. 408

open market sale A sale of bonds by the Fed. 408

operating instrument A variable that is very responsive to the central bank's tools and indicates the stance of monetary policy (also called a policy instrument). 484

opportunity cost The amount of interest (expected return) sacrificed by not holding an alternative asset. 112

optimal forecast The best guess of the future using all available information. 157

option A contract that gives the purchaser the option (right) to buy or sell the underlying financial instrument at a specified price, called the exercise price or strike price, within a specific period of time (the term to expiration). 344

over-the-counter (OTC) market A secondary market in which dealers at different locations who have an inventory of securities stand ready to buy and sell securities "over the counter" to anyone who comes to them and is willing to accept their prices. 27

overnight cash rate The interest rate for very-short-term interbank loans in the euro area. 460

par value See *face value*. 70

payments system The method of conducting transactions in the economy. 53

perpetuity See *consol*. 75

Phillips curve theory A theory suggesting that changes in inflation are influenced by the state of the economy relative to its production capacity, as well as to other factors. 487

planned investment spending Total planned spending by businesses on new physical capital (e.g., machines, computers, apartment buildings) plus planned spending on new homes. 588

policy instrument A variable that is very responsive to the central bank's tools and indicates the stance of monetary policy (also called an operating instrument). 484

political business cycle A business cycle caused by expansionary policies before an election. 400

portfolio A collection or group of assets. 37

preferred habitat theory A theory that is closely related to liquidity premium theory, in which the interest rate on a long-term bond equals an average of short-term interest rates expected to occur over the life of the long-term bond plus a positive term premium. 141

premium The amount paid for an option contract. 344

present discounted value See *present value*. 67

present value Today's value of a payment to be received in the future when the interest rate is *i*. Also called *present discounted value*. 67

price stability Low and stable inflation. 465

primary dealers Government securities dealers, operating out of private firms or commercial banks, with whom the Fed's open market desk trades. 451

primary market A financial market in which new issues of a security are sold to initial buyers. 26

principal–agent problem A moral hazard problem that occurs when the managers in control (the agents) act in their own interest rather than in the interest of the owners (the principals) due to different sets of incentives. 194

printing money See *monetizing the debt*. 648

prudential supervision See *bank supervision*. 284

put option An option contract that provides the right to sell a security at a specified price. 345

quantity theory of money The theory that nominal income is determined solely by movements in the quantity of money. 567, 586

quotas Restrictions on the quantity of foreign goods that can be imported. 509

random walk The movements of a variable whose future changes cannot be predicted (are random) because the variable is just as likely to fall as to rise from today's value. 163

rate of capital gain The change in a security's price relative to the initial purchase price. 83

rate of return See *return*. 82

rational expectations Expectations that reflect optimal forecasts (the best guess of the future) using all available information. 157

real bills doctrine A guiding principle (now discredited) for the conduct of monetary policy that states that as long as loans are made to support the production of goods and services, providing reserves to the banking system to make these loans will not be inflationary. 492

real business cycle theory A theory that views real shocks to tastes and technology as the major driving force behind short-run business cycle fluctuations. 600

real interest rate The interest rate adjusted for expected changes in the price level (inflation) so that it more accurately reflects the true cost of borrowing. 87

real money balances The quantity of money in real terms. 571

real terms Terms reflecting actual goods and services one can buy. 87

recession A period when aggregate output is declining. 9

reduced-form evidence Evidence that examines whether one variable has an effect on another by simply looking directly at the relationship between the two variables. 608

regulatory arbitrage A process in which banks keep on their books assets that have the same risk-based capital requirement but are relatively risky, such as a loan to a company with a very low credit rating, while taking off their books low-risk assets, such as a loan to a company with a very high credit rating. 284

regulatory forbearance Regulators' refraining from exercising their right to put an insolvent bank out of business. 294

reinsurance An allocation of a portion of the insurance risk to another company in exchange for a portion of the insurance premium. 312

repurchase agreement (repo) An arrangement whereby the Fed, or another party, purchases securities with the understanding that the seller will repurchase them in a short period of time, usually less than a week. 452

reputational rents Profits that a firm earns because it is trusted by the marketplace. 370

required reserve ratio The fraction of deposits that the Fed requires be kept as reserves. 222, 407

required reserves Reserves that are held to meet the Fed's requirement that for every dollar of deposits at a bank, a certain fraction must be kept as reserves. 222, 407

reserve currency A currency, such as the U.S. dollar, that is used by other countries to denominate the assets they hold as international reserves. 539

reserve requirements Regulation making it obligatory for depository institutions to keep a certain fraction of their deposits in accounts with the Fed. 222

reserves Banks' holding of deposits in accounts with the Fed plus currency that is physically held by banks (vault cash). 222, 407

residual claimant The right as a stockholder to receive whatever remains after all other claims against the firm's assets have been satisfied. 151

restrictive covenants Provisions that restrict and specify certain activities that a borrower can engage in. 185

return The payments to the owner of a security plus the change in the security's value, expressed as a fraction of its purchase price. More precisely called the *rate of return*. 82

return on assets (ROA) Net profit after taxes per dollar of assets. 232

return on equity (ROE) Net profit after taxes per dollar of equity capital. 232

revaluation Resetting of the fixed value of a currency at a higher level. 541

reverse causation A situation in which one variable is said to cause another variable, when in reality the reverse is true. 610

reverse repo See *matched sale–purchase transaction*. 452

reverse transactions Purchase or sale of eligible assets by the European Central Bank under repurchase agreements or credit operations against eligible assets as collateral that are reversed within two weeks. 460

Ricardian equivalence Named after the nineteenth-century British economist David Ricardo, it contends that when the government runs deficits and issues bonds, the public recognizes that it will be subject to higher taxes in the future to pay off these bonds. 651

risk The degree of uncertainty associated with the return on an asset. 36, 94

risk premium The spread between the interest rate on bonds with default risk and the interest rate on default-free bonds. 128

risk sharing The process of creating and selling assets with risk characteristics that people are comfortable with and then using the funds acquired by selling these assets to purchase other assets that may have far more risk. 36

risk structure of interest rates The relationship among the interest rates on various bonds with the same term to maturity. 127

seasoned issue A stock issued for sale for which prior issues currently sell in the market. 327

secondary market A financial market in which securities that have previously been issued (and are thus secondhand) can be resold. **26**

secondary reserves Short-term U.S. government and agency securities held by banks. **222**

secured debt Debt guaranteed by collateral. **185**

securitization The process of transforming illiquid financial assets into marketable capital market instruments. **255**

security A claim on the borrower's future income that is sold by the borrower to the lender. Also called a financial instrument. **3**

segmented markets theory A theory of term structure that sees markets for different-maturity bonds as completely separated and segmented such that the interest rate for bonds of a given maturity is determined solely by supply of and demand for bonds of that maturity. **139**

seignorage The revenue a government receives by issuing money. **558**

self-correcting mechanism A characteristic of the economy that causes output to return eventually to the natural rate level regardless of where it is initially. **597**

short position A contractual obligation to deliver an underlying financial instrument. **333**

short sales Borrowing stock from brokers and then selling the stock in the market, with the hope that a profit will be earned by buying the stock back again ("covering the short") after it has fallen in price. **173**

short-term With reference to a debt instrument, having a maturity of one year or less. **26**

simple deposit multiplier The multiple increase in deposits generated from an increase in the banking system's reserves in a simple model in which the behavior of depositors and banks plays no role. **417**

simple loan A credit market instrument providing the borrower with an amount of funds that must be repaid to the lender at the maturity date along with an additional payment (interest). **68**

smart card A stored-value card that contains a computer chip that lets it be loaded with digital cash from the owner's bank account whenever needed. **55**

special drawing rights (SDRs) An IMF-issued paper substitute for gold that functions as international reserves. **543**

specialist A dealer-broker operating in an exchange who maintains orderly trading of the securities for which he or she is responsible. **329**

spinning When an investment bank allocates shares of hot, but underpriced initial public offerings to executives of other companies in return for their companies' future business with the investment bank. **364**

spot exchange rate The exchange rate for a spot transaction. **504**

spot transaction The predominant type of exchange rate transaction, involving the immediate exchange of bank deposits denominated in different currencies. **504**

standing lending facility A lending facility in which healthy banks are allowed to borrow all they want from a central bank. **453**

state banks State-chartered banks. **249**

state-owned banks Banks that are owned by governments. **203**

sterilized foreign exchange intervention A foreign exchange intervention with an offsetting open market operation that leaves the monetary base unchanged. **534**

stock A security that is a claim on the earnings and assets of a company. **5**

stock option An option on an individual stock. **344**

stockholders Those who hold stock in a corporation. **151**

store of value A repository of purchasing power over time. **52**

strike price See *exercise price*. **344**

structural model A description of how the economy operates, using a collection of equations that describe the behavior of firms and consumers in many sectors of the economy. **608**

structural model evidence Evidence that examines whether one variable affects another by using data to build a model illustrating the channels through which this variable affects the other. **607**

superregional banks Bank holding companies similar in size to money center banks, but whose headquarters are not based in one of the money center cities (New York, Chicago, San Francisco). **264**

supply curve A curve depicting the relationship between quantity supplied and price when all other economic variables are held constant. **98**

supply shocks Any change in technology or the supply of raw materials that can shift the aggregate supply curve. **593**

swap A financial contract that obligates one party to exchange (swap) a set of payments it owns for a set of payments owned by another party. **352**

sweep account An arrangement in which any balances above a certain amount in a corporation's checking account at the end of a business day are "swept out" of the account and invested in overnight repos that pay the corporation interest. **257**

T-account A simplified balance sheet with lines in the form of a T that lists only the changes that occur in balance sheet items starting from some initial balance sheet position. **223**

target financing rate The European Central Bank's target for the overnight cash rate, the interest rate for very-short-term interbank loans in the euro area. **460**

tariffs Taxes on imported goods. **509**

Taylor rule Economist John Taylor's monetary policy rule that explains how the federal funds rate target is set. **487**

term structure of interest rates The relationship among interest rates on bonds with different terms to maturity. **127**

theory of asset demand The theory that the quantity demanded of an asset is (1) usually positively related to wealth, (2) positively related to its expected return relative to alternative assets, (3) negatively related to the risk of its return relative to alternative assets, and (4) positively related to its liquidity relative to alternative assets. **95**

theory of efficient capital markets See *efficient market hypothesis*. **159**

theory of purchasing power parity (PPP) The theory that exchange rates between any two currencies will adjust to reflect changes in the price levels of the two countries. **507**

thrift institutions (thrifts) Savings and loan associations, mutual savings banks, and credit unions. **39**

time-inconsistency problem The problem that occurs when monetary policymakers conduct monetary policy in a discretionary way and pursue expansionary policies that are attractive in the short run but lead to bad long-run outcomes. **466**

trade balance The difference between merchandise exports and imports. **536**

transaction costs The time and money spent trying to exchange financial assets, goods, or services. **35**

transmission mechanisms of monetary policy The channels through which the money supply affects economic activity. **608**

underfunded Describing a pension plan in which the contributions and their earnings are not sufficient to pay out the defined benefits when they come due. **317**

underwriting Purchase securities from a corporation at a predetermined price and then resell them in the market. **26**

underwriters Investment banks that guarantee prices on securities to corporations and then sell the securities to the public. **327**

unemployment rate The percentage of the labor force not working. **8**

unexploited profit opportunity A situation in which an investor can earn a higher than normal return. **161**

unit of account Anything used to measure value in an economy. **51**

unsecured debt Debt not guaranteed by collateral. **185**

unsterilized foreign exchange intervention A foreign exchange intervention in which a central bank allows the purchase or sale of domestic currency to affect the monetary base. **533**

vault cash Currency that is physically held by banks and stored in vaults overnight. **222**

velocity See *velocity of money*. **566, 585**

velocity of money The rate of turnover of money; the average number of times per year that a dollar is spent in buying the total amount of final goods and services produced in the economy. **566, 585**

venture capital firm A financial intermediary that pools the resources of its partners and uses the funds to help entrepreneurs start up new businesses. **196**

virtual bank A bank that has no building but rather exists only in cyberspace. **253**

wealth All resources owned by an individual, including all assets. **50, 93**

World Bank The International Bank for Reconstruction and Redevelopment, an international organization that provides long-term loans to assist developing countries in building dams, roads, and other physical capital that would contribute to their economic development. **538**

World Trade Organization (WTO) An organization headquartered in Geneva, Switzerland, that monitors rules for the conduct of trade between countries (tariffs and quotas). **539**

yield curve A plot of the interest rates for particular types of bonds with different terms to maturity. **134**

yield on a discount basis The measure of interest rates by which dealers in bill markets quote the interest rate on U.S. Treasury bills; formally defined in Equation 8 of Chapter 4. Also known as the *discount yield*. **79**

yield to maturity The interest rate that equates the present value of payments received from a credit market instrument with its value today. **71**

zero-coupon bond See *discount bond*. **70**

ANSWERS TO SELECTED QUESTIONS AND PROBLEMS

Chapter 1 Why Study Money, Banking, and Financial Markets?

2. The data in Figures 1, 2, 3, and 4 suggest that real output, the inflation rate, and interest rates would all fall.
4. You might be more likely to buy a house or a car because the cost of financing them would fall, or you might be less likely to save because you earn less on your savings.
6. No. It is true that people who borrow to purchase a house or a car are worse off because it costs them more to finance their purchase; however, savers benefit because they can earn higher interest rates on their savings.
8. They channel funds from people who do not have a productive use for them to people who do, thereby resulting in higher economic efficiency.
10. The lower price for a firm's shares means that it can raise a smaller amount of funds, so investment in facilities and equipment will fall.
12. It makes foreign goods more expensive, so British consumers will buy fewer foreign goods and more domestic goods.
14. In the mid- to late 1970s and in the late 1980s and early 1990s, the value of the dollar was low, making travel abroad relatively more expensive; thus it was a good time to vacation in the United States and see the Grand Canyon. With the rise in the dollar's value in the early 1980s, travel abroad became relatively cheaper, making it a good time to visit the Tower of London.

Chapter 2 An Overview of the Financial System

1. The share of Microsoft stock is an asset for its owner, because it entitles the owner to a share of the earnings and assets of Microsoft. The share is a liability for Microsoft, because it is a claim on its earnings and assets by the owner of the share.
3. Yes, because the absence of financial markets means that funds cannot be channeled to people who have the most productive use for them. Entrepreneurs then cannot acquire funds to set up businesses that would help the economy grow rapidly.
5. This statement is false. Prices in secondary markets determine the prices that firms issuing securities receive in primary markets. In addition, secondary markets make securities more liquid and thus easier to sell in the primary markets. Therefore, secondary markets are, if anything, more important than primary markets.
7. Because you know your family member better than a stranger, you know more about the borrower's honesty, propensity for risk taking, and other traits. There is less asymmetric information than with a stranger and less likelihood of an adverse selection problem, with the result that you are more likely to lend to the family member.
9. Loan sharks can threaten their borrowers with bodily harm if borrowers take actions that might jeopardize their paying off the loan. Hence borrowers from a loan shark are less likely to increase moral hazard.
11. Yes, because even if you know that a borrower is taking actions that might jeopardize paying off the loan, you must still stop the borrower from doing so. Because that may be costly, you may not spend the time and effort to reduce moral hazard, and so the problem of moral hazard still exists.
13. Because the costs of making the loan to your neighbor are high (legal fees, fees for a credit check, and so on), you will probably not be able to earn 5% on the loan after your expenses even though it has a 10% interest rate. You are better off depositing your savings with a financial intermediary and earning 5% interest. In addition, you are likely to bear less risk by depositing your savings at the bank rather than lending them to your neighbor.
15. Increased discussion of foreign financial markets in the U.S. press and the growth in markets for international financial instruments such as Eurodollars and Eurobonds.

Chapter 3 What Is Money?

2. Because the orchard owner likes only bananas but the banana grower doesn't like apples, the banana grower will not want apples in exchange for his bananas, and they will not trade. Similarly, the chocolatier will not be willing to trade with the banana grower because she does not like bananas. The orchard owner will not trade with the chocolatier because he doesn't like chocolate. Hence, in a barter economy, trade among these three people may well not take place, because in no case is there a double coincidence of wants. However, if money is introduced into the economy, the orchard owner can sell his apples to the chocolatier and then use the money to buy bananas from the banana grower. Similarly, the banana grower can use the money she receives from the orchard owner to buy chocolate from the chocolatier, and the chocolatier can use the money to buy apples from the orchard owner. The result is that the need for a double coincidence of wants is eliminated, and everyone is better off because all three producers are now able to eat what they like best.
4. Because a check was so much easier to transport than gold, people would frequently rather be paid by check even if there was a possibility that the check might bounce. In other words, the lower transactions costs involved in handling checks made people more willing to accept them.
6. Because money was losing value at a slower rate (the inflation rate was lower) in the 1950s than in the 1970s, it was then a better store of value, and you would have been willing to hold more of it.

9. Money loses its value at an extremely rapid rate in hyperinflation, so you want to hold it for as short a time as possible. Thus money is like a hot potato that is quickly passed from one person to another.
11. Not necessarily. Although the total amount of debt has predicted inflation and the business cycle better than M1 or M2, it may not be a better predictor in the future. Without some theoretical reason for believing that the total amount of debt will continue to predict well in the future, we may not want to define money as the total amount of debt.
13. M1 contains the most liquid assets. M2 is the largest measure.
15. Revisions are not a serious problem for long-run movements of the money supply, because revisions for short-run (one-month) movements tend to cancel out. Revisions for long-run movements, such as one-year growth rates, are thus typically quite small.

Chapter 4 Understanding Interest Rates

1. Less. It would be worth $1/(1 + 0.20) = \$0.83$ when the interest rate is 20%, rather than $1/(1 + 0.10) = \$0.91$ when the interest rate is 10%.
3. $\$1{,}100/(1 + 0.10) + \$1{,}210/(1 + 0.10)^2 + \$1{,}331/(1 + 0.10)^3 = \$3{,}000$.
5. $\$2{,}000 = \$100/(1 + i) + \$100/(1 + i)^2 + \cdots + \$100/(1 + i)^{20} + \$1{,}000/(1 + i)^{20}$.
7. 14.9%, derived as follows: The present value of the \$2 million payment five years from now is $\$2/(1 + i)^5$ million, which equals the \$1 million loan. Thus $1 = 2/(1 + i)^5$. Solving for i, $(1 + i)^5 = 2$, so that $i = \sqrt[5]{2} - 1 = 0.149 = 14.9\%$.
9. If the one-year bond did not have a coupon payment, its yield to maturity would be $(\$1{,}000 - \$800)/\$800 = \$200/\$800 = 0.25 = 25\%$. Because it does have a coupon payment, its yield to maturity must be greater than 25%. However, because the current yield is a good approximation of the yield to maturity for a twenty-year bond, we know that the yield to maturity on this bond is approximately 15%. Therefore, the one-year bond has a higher yield to maturity.
11. You would rather own the Treasury bill, because it has a higher yield to maturity. As the example in the text indicates, the discount yield's understatement of the yield to maturity for a one-year bill is substantial, exceeding one percentage point. Thus the yield to maturity on the one-year bill would be greater than 9%, the yield to maturity on the one-year Treasury bond.
13. No. If interest rates rise sharply in the future, long-term bonds may suffer such a sharp fall in price that their return might be quite low—possibly even negative.
15. The economists are right. They reason that nominal interest rates were below expected rates of inflation in the late 1970s, making real interest rates negative. The expected inflation rate, however, fell much faster than nominal interest rates in the mid-1980s, so nominal interest rates were above the expected inflation rate and real rates became positive.

Chapter 5 The Behavior of Interest Rates

2. (a) More, because your wealth has increased; (b) more, because the house has become more liquid; (c) less, because its expected return has fallen relative to Microsoft stock; (d) more, because it has become less risky relative to stocks; (e) less, because its expected return has fallen.
4. (a) More, because the bonds have become more liquid; (b) more, because their expected return has risen relative to stocks;
(c) less, because they have become less liquid relative to stocks; (d) less, because their expected return has fallen; (e) more, because they have become more liquid.
6. When the Fed sells bonds to the public, it increases the supply of bonds, thus shifting the supply curve B^s to the right. The result is that the intersection of the supply and demand curves B^s and B^d occurs at a lower price and a higher equilibrium interest rate, and the interest rate rises. With the liquidity preference framework, the decrease in the money supply shifts the money supply curve M^s to the left, and the equilibrium interest rate rises. The answer from the bond supply and demand analysis is consistent with the answer from the liquidity preference framework.
8. When the price level rises, the quantity of money in real terms falls (holding the nominal supply of money constant); to restore their holdings of money in real terms to their former level, people will want to hold a greater nominal quantity of money. Thus the money demand curve M^d shifts to the right, and the interest rate rises.
11. Interest rates would rise. A sudden increase in people's expectations of future real estate prices raises the expected return on real estate relative to bonds, so the demand for bonds falls. The demand curve B^d shifts to the left, bond prices fall, and the equilibrium interest rate rises.
13. In bond supply and demand analysis, the increased riskiness of bonds lowers the demand for bonds. The demand curve B^d shifts to the left, bond prices fall, and the equilibrium interest rate rises. The same answer is found in the liquidity preference framework. The increased riskiness of bonds relative to money increases the demand for money. The money demand curve M^d shifts to the right, and the equilibrium interest rate rises.
15. Yes, interest rates will rise. The lower commission on stocks makes them more liquid than bonds, and the demand for bonds will fall. The demand curve B^d will therefore shift to the left, and the equilibrium interest rate will rise.
17. The interest rate on the AT&T bonds will rise. Because people now expect interest rates to rise, the expected return on long-term bonds such as the $8\frac{1}{8}$s of 2022 will fall, and the demand for these bonds will decline. The demand curve B^d will therefore shift to the left, the price will fall, and the equilibrium interest rate will rise.

19. Interest rates will rise. When bond prices become volatile and bonds become riskier, the demand for bonds will fall. The demand curve B^d will shift to the left, the price will fall, and the equilibrium interest rate will rise.

Chapter 6 The Risk and Term Structure of Interest Rates

2. U.S. Treasury bills have lower default risk and more liquidity than negotiable CDs. Consequently, the demand for Treasury bills is higher, and they have a lower interest rate.
4. True. When bonds of different maturities are close substitutes, a rise in interest rates for one bond causes the interest rates for others to rise because the expected returns on bonds of different maturities cannot get too far out of line.
6. (a) The yield to maturity would be 5% for a one-year bond, 6% for a two-year bond, 6.33% for a three-year bond, 6.5% for a four-year bond, and 6.6% for a five-year bond. (b) The yield to maturity would be 5% for a one-year bond, 4.5% for a two-year bond, 4.33% for a three-year bond, 4.25% for a four-year bond, and 4.2% for a five-year bond. The upward-sloping yield curve in (a) would be even steeper if people preferred short-term bonds over long-term bonds, because long-term bonds would then have a positive liquidity premium. The downward-sloping yield curve in (b) would be less steep and might even have a slight positive upward slope if the long-term bonds have a positive liquidity premium.
8. The flat yield curve at shorter maturities suggests that short-term interest rates are expected to fall moderately in the near future, while the steep upward slope of the yield curve at longer maturities indicates that interest rates further into the future are expected to rise. Because interest rates and expected inflation move together, the yield curve suggests that the market expects inflation to fall moderately in the near future but to rise later on.
10. The reduction in income tax rates would make the tax-exempt privilege for municipal bonds less valuable, and they would be less desirable than taxable Treasury bonds. The resulting decline in the demand for municipal bonds and increase in demand for Treasury bonds would raise interest rates on municipal bonds while causing interest rates on Treasury bonds to fall.
12. Lower brokerage commissions for corporate bonds would make them more liquid and thus increase their demand, which would lower their risk premium.
14. You would raise your predictions of future interest rates, because the higher long-term rates imply that the average of the expected future short-term rates is higher.

Chapter 7 The Stock Market, the Theory of Rational Expectations, and the Efficient Market Hypothesis

2. There are two cash flows from stock, periodic dividends and a future sales price. Dividends are frequently changed when firm earnings either rise or fall. The future sales price is also difficult to estimate, because it depends on the dividends that will be paid at some date even further in the future. Bond cash flows also consist of two parts, periodic interest payments and a final maturity payment. These payments are established in writing at the time the bonds are issued and cannot be changed without the firm defaulting and being subject to bankruptcy. Stock prices tend to be more volatile, because their cash flows are more subject to change.
4. $P_0 = \dfrac{\$3 \times (1.07)}{0.18 - 0.07} = \$29.18$
6. False. Expectations can be highly inaccurate and still be rational, because optimal forecasts are not necessarily accurate: A forecast is optimal if it is the best possible even if the forecast errors are large.
8. No, because he could improve the accuracy of his forecasts by predicting that tomorrow's interest rates will be identical to today's. His forecasts are therefore not optimal, and he does not have rational expectations.
10. No, you shouldn't buy stocks, because the rise in the money supply is publicly available information that will be already incorporated into stock prices. Hence you cannot expect to earn more than the equilibrium return on stocks by acting on the money supply information.
12. No, because this is publicly available information and is already reflected in stock prices. The optimal forecast of stock returns will equal the equilibrium return, so there is no benefit from selling your stocks.
14. No, if the person has no better information than the rest of the market. An expected price rise of 10% over the next month implies over a 100% annual return on Google stock, which certainly exceeds its equilibrium return. This would mean that there is an unexploited profit opportunity in the market, which would have been eliminated in an efficient market. The only time that the person's expectations could be rational is if the person had information unavailable to the market that allowed him or her to beat the market.
16. False. The people with better information are exactly those who make the market more efficient by eliminating unexploited profit opportunities. These people can profit from their better information.
18. True, in principle. Foreign exchange rates are a random walk over a short interval such as a week, because changes in the exchange rate are unpredictable. If a change were predictable, large unexploited profit opportunities would exist in the foreign exchange market. If the foreign exchange market is efficient, these unexploited profit opportunities cannot exist and so the foreign exchange rate will approximately follow a random walk.
20. False. Although human fear may be the source of stock market crashes, that does not imply that there are unexploited profit opportunities in the market. Nothing in rational expectations theory rules out large changes in stock prices as a result of fears on the part of the investing public.

Chapter 8 An Economic Analysis of Financial Structure

2. Financial intermediaries develop expertise in such areas as computer technology so that they can inexpensively provide liquidity services such as checking accounts that lower transaction costs for depositors. Financial intermediaries can also take advantage of economies of scale and engage in large transactions that have a lower cost per dollar of transaction.
4. Standard accounting principles make profit verification easier, thereby reducing adverse selection and moral hazard problems in financial markets and hence making them operate better. Standard accounting principles make it easier for investors to screen out good firms from bad firms, thereby reducing the adverse selection problem in financial markets. In addition, they make it harder for managers to understate profits, thereby reducing the principal–agent (moral hazard) problem.
6. Smaller firms that are not well known are the most likely to use bank financing. Because it is harder for investors to acquire information about these firms, it will be hard for the firms to sell securities in the financial markets. Banks that specialize in collecting information about smaller firms will then be the only outlet these firms have for financing their activities.
8. Yes. The person who is putting her life savings into her business has more to lose if she takes on too much risk or engages in personally beneficial activities that don't lead to higher profits. So she will act more in the interest of the lender, making it more likely that the loan will be paid off.
10. True. If the borrower turns out to be a bad credit risk and goes broke, the lender loses less, because the collateral can be sold to make up any losses on the loan. Thus adverse selection is not as severe a problem.
12. The separation of ownership and control creates a principal–agent problem. The managers (the agents) do not have as strong an incentive to maximize profits as the owners (the principals). Thus the managers might not work hard, might engage in wasteful spending on personal perks, or might pursue business strategies that enhance their personal power but do not increase profits.
14. A stock market crash reduces the net worth of firms and so increases the moral hazard problem. With less of an equity stake, owners have a greater incentive to take on risky projects and spend corporate funds on items that benefit them personally. A stock market crash, which increases the moral hazard problem, thus makes it less likely that lenders will be paid back. So lending and investment will decline, creating a financial crisis in which financial markets do not work well and the economy suffers.

Chapter 9 Banking and the Management of Financial Institutions

2. The rank from most to least liquid is (c), (b), (a), (d).
4. Reserves drop by $500. The T-account for the First National Bank is as follows:

First National Bank

Assets		Liabilities	
Reserves	−$500	Checkable deposits	−$500

6. The bank would rather have the balance sheet shown in this problem, because after it loses $50 million due to deposit outflow, the bank would still have excess reserves of $5 million: $50 million in reserves minus required reserves of $45 million (10% of the $450 million of deposits). Thus the bank would not have to alter its balance sheet further and would not incur any costs as a result of the deposit outflow. By contrast, with the balance sheet in Problem 5, the bank would have a shortfall of reserves of $20 million ($25 million in reserves minus the required reserves of $45 million). In this case, the bank will incur costs when it raises the necessary reserves through the methods described in the text.
8. No. When you turn a customer down, you may lose that customer's business forever, which is extremely costly. Instead, you might go out and borrow from other banks, corporations, or the Fed to obtain funds so that you can make the customer loans. Alternatively, you might sell negotiable CDs or some of your securities to acquire the necessary funds.
10. It can raise $1 million of capital by issuing new stock. It can cut its dividend payments by $1 million, thereby increasing its retained earnings by $1 million. It can decrease the amount of its assets so that the amount of its capital relative to its assets increases, thereby meeting the capital requirements.
12. Compensating balances can act as collateral. They also help establish long-term customer relationships, which make it easier for the bank to collect information about prospective borrowers, thus reducing the adverse selection problem. Compensating balances help the bank monitor the activities of a borrowing firm so that it can prevent the firm from taking on too much risk, thereby not acting in the interest of the bank.
14. The assets fall in value by $8 million (= $100 million × −2% × 4 years) while the liabilities fall in value by $10.8 million (= $90 million × −2% × 6 years). Because the liabilities fall in value by $2.8 million more than the assets do, the net worth of the bank rises by $2.8 million. The interest-rate risk can be reduced by shortening the maturity of the liabilities to a duration of four years or lengthening the maturity of the assets to a duration of six years. Alternatively, you could engage in an interest-rate swap, in which you swap the interest earned on your assets with the interest on another bank's assets that have a duration of six years.

Chapter 10 Banking Industry: Structure and Competition

2. (a) Office of the Comptroller of the Currency; (b) the Federal Reserve; (c) state banking authorities and the FDIC; (d) the Federal Reserve.
4. New technologies such as electronic banking facilities are frequently shared by several banks, so these facilities are not classified as branches. Thus they can be used by banks to escape limitations on offering services in other states and, in effect, to escape limitations from restrictions on branching.
6. Because restrictions on branching are stricter for commercial banks than for savings and loans. Thus small commercial banks have greater protection from competition and are more likely to survive than small savings and loans.
8. International banking has been encouraged by giving special tax treatment and relaxed branching regulations to Edge Act corporations and to international banking facilities (IBFs); this was done to make American banks more competitive with foreign banks. The hope is that it will create more banking jobs in the United States.
10. No, because the Saudi-owned bank is subject to the same regulations as the American-owned bank.
12. The rise in inflation and the resulting higher interest rates on alternatives to checkable deposits meant that banks had a big shrinkage in this low-cost way of raising funds. The innovation of money market mutual funds also meant that the banks lost checking account business. The abolishment of Regulation Q and the appearance of NOW accounts did help decrease disintermediation, but raised the cost of funds for American banks, which now had to pay higher interest rates on checkable and other deposits. Foreign banks were also able to tap a large pool of domestic savings, thereby lowering their cost of funds relative to American banks.
14. The growth of the commercial paper market and the development of the junk bond market meant that corporations were now able to issue securities rather than borrow from banks, thus eroding the competitive advantage of banks on the lending side. Securitization has enabled other financial institutions to originate loans, again taking away some of the banks' loan business.

Chapter 11 Economic Analysis of Banking Regulation

2. There would be adverse selection, because people who might want to burn their property for some personal gain would actively try to obtain substantial fire insurance policies. Moral hazard could also be a problem, because a person with a fire insurance policy has less incentive to take measures to prevent a fire.
4. Regulations that restrict banks from holding risky assets directly decrease the moral hazard of risk taking by the bank. Requirements that force banks to have a large amount of capital also decrease the banks' incentives for risk taking, because banks now have more to lose if they fail. Such regulations will not completely eliminate the moral hazard problem, because bankers have incentives to hide their holdings of risky assets from the regulators and to overstate the amount of their capital.
6. The S&L crisis did not occur until the 1980s, because interest rates stayed low before then, so S&Ls were not subjected to losses from high interest rates. Also, the opportunities for risk taking were not available until the 1980s, when legislation and financial innovation made it easier for S&Ls to take on more risk, thereby greatly increasing the adverse selection and moral hazard problems.
8. FIRREA provided funds for the S&L bailout, created the Resolution Trust Corporation to manage the resolution of insolvent thrifts, eliminated the Federal Home Loan Bank Board and gave its regulatory role to the Office of Thrift Supervision, eliminated the FSLIC and turned its insurance role and regulatory responsibilities over to the FDIC, imposed restrictions on thrift activities similar to those in effect before 1982, increased the capital requirements to those adhered to by commercial banks, and increased the enforcement powers of thrift regulators.
10. If political candidates receive campaign funds from the government and are restricted in the amount they spend, they will have less need to satisfy lobbyists to win elections. As a result, they may have greater incentives to act in the interest of taxpayers (the principals), and so the political process might improve.
12. Eliminating or limiting the amount of deposit insurance would help reduce the moral hazard of excessive risk taking on the part of banks. It would, however, make bank failures and panics more likely, so it might not be a very good idea.
14. The economy would benefit from reduced moral hazard; that is, banks would not want to take on too much risk, because doing so would increase their deposit insurance premiums. The problem is, however, that it is difficult to monitor the degree of risk in bank assets because often only the bank making the loans knows how risky they are.

Chapter 12 Nonbank Finance

1. Because there would be more uncertainty about how much they would have to pay out in any given year, life insurance companies would tend to hold shorter-term assets that are more liquid.
3. Because benefits paid out are set to equal contributions to the plan and their earnings.
5. False. Government pension plans are often underfunded. Many pension plans for both federal and state employees are not fully funded.
7. Because the bigger the policy, the greater the moral hazard—the incentive for the policyholder to engage in activities that make the insurance payoff more likely. Because payoffs are costly, the insurance company will want to reduce moral hazard by limiting the amount of insurance.

9. Because interest rates on loans are typically lower at banks than at finance companies.
11. Because you do not have to pay a commission on a no-load fund, it is cheaper than a load fund, which does require a commission.
13. Government loan guarantees may be very costly, because, like any insurance, they increase moral hazard. Because the banks and other institutions making the guaranteed loans do not suffer any losses if the borrowers default on these loans, these institutions have little incentive not to make bad loans. The resulting losses to the government can be substantial, as was true in past years.
15. No. Investment banking is a risky business, because if the investment bank cannot sell a security it is underwriting for the price it promised to pay the issuing firm, the investment bank can suffer substantial losses.

Chapter 13 Financial Derivatives

2. You would enter into a contract that specifies that you will sell the $25 million of 6s of 2015 at a price of 110 one year from now.
4. You have a loss of 6 points, or $6,000, per contract.
6. You would buy $100 million worth (1,000 contracts) of the call long-term bond option with a delivery date of one year in the future and with a strike price that corresponds to a yield of 8%. This means that you would have the option to buy the long bond with the 8% interest rate, thereby making sure that you can earn the 8%. The disadvantage of the options contract is that you have to pay a premium that you would not have to pay with a futures contract. The advantage of the options contract is that if the interest rate rises and the bond price falls during the next year, you do not have to exercise the option and so will be able to earn a higher rate than 8% when the funds come in next year, whereas with the futures contract, you have to take delivery of the bond and will earn only 8%.
8. You have a profit of 1 point ($1,000) when you exercise the contract, but you have paid a premium of $1,500 for the call option, so your net profit is −$500, a loss of $500.
10. Because for any given price at expiration, a lower strike price means a higher profit for a call option and a lower profit for a put option. A lower strike price makes a call option more desirable and raises its premium and makes a put option less desirable and lowers its premium.
12. It would swap the interest on $42 million of fixed-rate assets for the interest on $42 million of variable-rate assets, thereby eliminating its income gap.
14. You would hedge the risk by buying 80 euro futures contracts that mature three months from now.

Chapter 14 Conflicts of Interest in the Financial Industry

2. Conflicts of interest arise because higher profits might arise in providing one kind of service if the service provider misuses infomation, provides false information, or conceals information when providing another kind of service.
4. Unethical behavior can arise because conflicts of interest generate incentives for service providers to lie or conceal information, thereby hurting the customers they work for.
6. Spinning makes financial markets less efficiant because it might influence executives to not use the lowest-cost investment bank when issuing securities. The result would be a higher cost of capital and hence lower efficiency.
8. The source of Arthur Andersen's demise was not that the company combined its auditing and consulting activities, but rather that the Houston office succumbed to tremendous pressure to give favorable opinions about Enron because Enron was such a large client and the Houston office could not afford to lose Enron's business.
10. The underwriting department may aggeseeively sell bad securities to the bank's customers; the bank may use its underwriting department to sell bonds of a troubled firm so that the firm can pay off its loans to the bank; a bank may make loans at overly favorable terms to get the firm's underwriting business; or a bank may lean on its customers to purchase insurance that they may not need from the bank.
12. (1) Credit-rating agencies seem to give acurate appraisals of credit risk even though they are paid by the firms that are issuing the securities. (2) Commercial banks that underwrote securities before the Glass-Steagall Act was enacted did not seem to push bad securities they had underwritten onto their customers. (3) The market can often figure out which research analysts not to trust if they are subject to stong conflicts of interest. (4) Clients of accounting firms limit the use on nonaudit services if the conflicts of interest lead to a decrease in trust of the audit.
14. If the compensation scheme for one acivity is very high relative to the compensation scheme for another activity, then employees might conceal or misuse information when engaging in the lower-paying activity to get more business in the higher-paying activity.
16. Supervisory oversight can reduce conflicts of interest because the supervisor might have better access to information about whether a conflict of interest exists and is being exploited and can then take actions to stop it.
18. The government agency is less likely to have the conflict of interest than the private sector. In addition, information may be a public good that is undersupplied, so government provision of this information might make the markets more efficient. Conversely, the government may not have as good incentives as the private sector to provide good-quality information. Also, government agencies have trouble paying high salaries to get the best people, so the quality of information they provide might not be very good.
20. The Global Settlement has increased disclosure of analysts' recommendations, which can help increase information in financial markets. Also, it requires increased disclosure of potential conflicts of interest, which can help the market to constrain them. The Global Settlement bans spinning, which

might otherwise encourage executives to choose high-cost investment banks to underwrite their securities: banning spinning makes it more likely that lower-cost and more efficient underwriting will take place. The fines imposed by the Global Settlement also provide incentives for investment banks to avoid exploiting conflicts of interest in the future. The negative side of the Global Settlement is that it separates activitites and so may mean that economies of scope in information production are lost. The Global Settlement also requires that part of the $1.4 billion fine be used to fund independent research, but it is not clear that the quality of this research will be high.

Chapter 15 Structure of Central Banks and the Federal Reserve System

1. Because of traditional American hostility to a central bank and centralized authority, the system of 12 regional banks was set up to diffuse power along regional lines.
3. Like the U.S. Constitution, the Federal Reserve System, originally established by the Federal Reserve Act, has many checks and balances and is a peculiarly American institution. The ability of the twelve regional banks to affect discount policy was viewed as a check on the centralized power of the Board of Governors, just as states' rights are a check on the centralized power of the federal government. The provision that there be three types of directors (A, B, and C) representing different groups (professional bankers, business people, and the public) was again intended to prevent any group from dominating the Fed. The Fed's independence from the federal government and the setting up of the Federal Reserve banks as incorporated institutions were further intended to restrict government power over the banking industry.
5. The Board of Governors sets reserve requirements and the discount rate; the FOMC directs open market operations. In practice, however, the FOMC helps make decisions about reserve requirements and the discount rate.
7. The structure of the European System of Central Banks (ECSB) is similar to that of the Federal Reserve: the National Central Banks (NCBs) have a similar role to the Federal Reserve Banks and the Executive Board is similar to the Board of Governors. The Governing Council has a similar role to the FOMC and its voting members include the presidents of the NCBs and the Executive Board members, just as the FOMC has as its voting members Federal Reserve Bank presidents and members of the Board of Governors. There are some differences however. First, the budgets of the Federal Reserve Banks are controlled by the Board of Governors, while the NCBs control their own budgets and the budget of the ECB in Frankfurt. Second, the monetary operations of the Eurosystem are conducted by the NCBs in each country, so monetary operations are not centralized as they are in the Federal Reserve System. Third, in contrast to the Fed, the ECB is not involved in supervision and regulation of financial institutions. The ECSB is more independent than the Fed because its charter can only be changed by revision of the Maastricht Treaty, a very difficult process because all signatories to the treaty must agree to accept any proposed change, while the Fed's charter can be changed by legislation which is much easier to do. On the other hand, the goal for the ECSB is more clearly specified than it is for the Fed because the Maastricht Treaty states that the overriding long-run goal of the ECSB is price stability, although it doesn't specify exactly what "price stability" means.
9. The threat that Congress will acquire greater control over the Fed's finances and budget.
11. False. Maximizing one's welfare does not rule out altruism. Operating in the public interest is clearly one objective of the Fed. The theory of bureaucratic behavior merely points out that other objectives, such as maximizing power, also influence Fed decision making.
13. False. The Fed is still subject to political pressure, because Congress can pass legislation limiting the Fed's power. If the Fed is performing badly, Congress can make the Fed accountable by passing legislation that the Fed does not like.
15. The argument for not releasing the FOMC directives immediately is that it keeps Congress off the Fed's back, thus enabling the Fed to pursue an independent monetary policy that is less subject to inflation and political business cycles. The argument for releasing the directive immediately is that it would make the Fed more accountable.

Chapter 16 Multiple Deposit Creation and the Money Supply Process

2. Reserves are unchanged, but the monetary base falls by $2 million, as indicated by the following T-accounts:

Irving the Investor

Assets		Liabilities	
Currency	−$2 million		
Securities	+$2 million		

Federal Reserve System

Assets		Liabilities	
Securities	−$2 million	Currency	−$2 million

3. Reserves increase by $50 million, but the monetary base increases by $100 million, as the T-accounts for the five banks and the Fed indicate:

Five Banks

Assets		Liabilities	
Reserves	+$50 million	Discount loans	+$100 million
		Deposits	−$50 million

Federal Reserve System

Assets		Liabilities	
Discount loans	+$100 million	Reserves	+$50 million
		Currency	+$50 million

5. The T-accounts are identical to those in the sections "Deposit Creation: The Single Bank" and "Deposit Creation: The Banking System" except that all the entries are multiplied by 10,000 (that is, $100 becomes $1 million). The net result is that checkable deposits rise by $10 million.
7. The $1 million Fed purchase of bonds increases reserves in the banking system by $1 million, and the total increase in checkable deposits is $10 million. The fact that banks buy securities rather than make loans with their excess reserves makes no difference in the multiple deposit creation process.
9. Reserves in the banking system fall by $1,000, and a multiple contraction occurs, reducing checkable deposits by $10,000.
11. The level of checkable deposits falls by $50 million. The T-account of the banking system in equilibrium is as follows:

Banking System

Assets		Liabilities	
Reserves	−$5 million	Checkable deposits	−$50 million
Securities	+$5 million		
Loans	−$50 million		

13. The $1 million holdings of excess reserves means that the bank has to reduce its holdings of loans or securities, thus starting the multiple contraction process. Because the required reserve ratio is 10%, checkable deposits must decline by $10 million.
15. The deposit of $100 in the bank increases its reserves by $100. This starts the process of multiple deposit expansion, leading to an increase in checkable deposits of $1,000.

Chapter 17 Determinants of the Money Supply

1. Uncertain. As the formula in Equation 4 indicates, if $r + e$ is greater than 1, the money multiplier can be less than 1. In practice, however, e is so small that $r + e$ is less than 1 and the money multiplier is greater than 1.
3. The money supply fell sharply because when c rose, there was a shift from one component of the money supply (checkable deposits) with more multiple expansion to another (currency) with less. Overall multiple deposit expansion fell, leading to a decline in the money supply.
5. There is a shift from one component of the money supply (checkable deposits) with less multiple expansion to another (traveler's checks) with more multiple expansion. Multiple expansion therefore increases, and the money supply increases.
7. Yes, because with no reserve requirements on time deposits, a shift from checkable deposits (with less multiple expansion) to time deposits (with more multiple expansion) increases the total amount of deposits and raises M2. However, if reserve requirements were equal for both types of deposits, they would both undergo the same amount of multiple expansion, and a shift from one to the other would have no effect on M2. Thus control of M2 would be better because random shifts from time deposits to checkable deposits, or vice versa, would not affect M2.
9. Both the Fed's purchase of $100 million of bonds (which raises the monetary base) and the lowering of r (which increases the amount of multiple expansion and raises the money multiplier) lead to a rise in the money supply.
11. The Fed's sale of $1 million of bonds shrinks the monetary base by $1 million, and the reduction of borrowings from the Federal Reserve lowers the monetary base by another $1 million. The resulting $2 million decline in the monetary base leads to a decline in the money supply.
13. A rise in expected inflation would increase interest rates (through the Fisher effect), which would in turn cause e to fall and the volume of borrowed researves to rise. The fall in e increases the amount of reserves available to support checkable deposits so that deposits and the money multiplier will rise. The rise in borrowed reserves causes the monetary base to rise. The resulting increase in the money multiplier and the monetary base leads to an increase in the money supply.
15. The money supply would fall, because if the discount window were eliminated, banks would need to hold more excess reserves, making fewer reserves available to support deposits. Moreover, abolishing discounting would reduce the volume of borrowed reserves, which would also cause the monetary base and the money supply to fall.

Chapter 18 Tools of Monetary Policy

1. The snowstorm would cause float to increase, which would increase the monetary base. To counteract this effect, the manager will undertake a defensive open market sale.
3. As we saw in Chapter 16, when the Treasury's deposits at the Fed fall, the monetary base increases. To counteract this increase, the manager would undertake an open market sale.
5. It suggests that defensive open market operations are far more common than dynamic operations because repurchase agreements are used primarily to conduct defensive operations to counteract temporary changes in the monetary base.
7. A rise in checkable deposits leads to a rise in required reserves at any given interest rate and thus shifts the demand curve to the right. If the federal funds rate is initially below the discount rate, this then leads to a rise in the federal funds rate. If the federal funds rate is initially at the discount

rate, then the federal funds rate will just remain at the discount rate.

9. This statement is incorrect. The FDIC would not be effective in eliminating bank panics without Fed discounting to troubled banks to keep bank failures from spreading.
11. Most likely not. If the federal funds rate target is initially below the discount rate and the decline in the discount rate still leaves it above the federal funds target, then the shift in the supply curve has no effect on the federal funds rate. Furthermore, the Fed usually moves the discount rate in line with changes in the federal funds rate target, so that changes in the discount rate provide no additional information about the direction of monetary policy.
13. False. As the analysis of the channel/corridor approach to setting interest rates demonstrates, central banks can still tightly control interest rates by putting in place standing facilities where the difference between the interest rate paid on reserves kept at the central bank and the interest rate charged in central bank loans to banks is kept small.
15. Open market operations are more flexible, reversible, and faster to implement than the other two tools. Discount policy is more flexible, reversible, and faster to implement than changing reserve requirements, but it is less effective than either of the other two tools.

Chapter 19 What Should Central Banks Do? Monetary Policy Goals, Strategy, and Tactics

1. Disagree. Some unemployment is beneficial to the economy because the availability of vacant jobs makes it more likely that a worker will find the right job and that the employer will find the right worker for the job.
3. True. In such a world, hitting a reserves target would mean that the Fed would also hit its interest-rate target, or vice versa. Thus the Fed could pursue both a reserves target and an interest-rate target at the same time.
5. The Fed can control the interest rate on federal funds by buying and selling bonds in the open market. When the fed funds rate rises above the target level, the Fed would buy bonds, which would increase nonborrowed reserves and lower the interest rate to its target level. Similarly, when the fed funds rate falls below the target level, the Fed would sell bonds to raise the interest rate to the target level. The resulting open market operations would of course affect the quantity of reserves and the money supply and cause it to change. The Fed would be giving up control of reserves and the money supply to pursue its interest-rate target.
7. Disagree. Although *nominal* interest rates are measured more accurately and more quickly than the money supply, the interest-rate variable that is of more concern to policymakers is the *real* interest rate. Because the measurement of real interest rates requires estimates of expected inflation, it is not true that real interest rates are necessarily measured more accurately and more quickly than the money supply. Interest-rate targets are therefore not necessarily better than money supply targets.
11. Monetary targeting has the advantage that it enables a central bank to adjust its monetary policy to cope with domestic considerations. Furthermore, information on whether the central bank is achieving its target is known almost immediately.
13. Inflation-targeting central banks engage in extensive public information campaigns that include the distribution of glossy brochures, the publication of *Inflation Report*–type documents, making speeches to the public, and continual communication with the elected government.
15. Uncertain. If the relationship between monetary aggregates and the goal variable—say, inflation—is unstable, then the signal provided by the monetary aggregates is not very useful and is not a good indicator of whether the stance of monetary policy is correct.
17. False. There is no long-run trade-off between inflation and unemployment, so in the long run a central bank with a dual mandate that attempts to promote maximum employment by pursuing inflationary policies would have no more success at reducing unemployment than one whose primary goal is price stability.
19. All allow a central bank to pursue an independent monetary policy that can focus on domestic considerations.

Chapter 20 The Foreign Exchange Market

2. False. Although a weak currency has the negative effect of making it more expensive to buy foreign goods or to travel abroad, it may help domestic industry. Domestic goods become cheaper relative to foreign goods, and the demand for domestically produced goods increases. The resulting higher sales of domestic products may lead to higher employment, a beneficial effect on the economy.
4. It predicts that the value of the yen will fall 5% in terms of dollars.
6. Even though the Japanese price level rose relative to the American, the yen appreciated because the increase in Japanese productivity relative to American productivity made it possible for the Japanese to continue to sell their goods at a profit at a high value of the yen.
8. The pound depreciates but overshoots, declining by more in the short run than in the long run. Consider Britain to be the domestic country. The rise in the money supply leads to a higher domestic price level in the long run, which leads to a lower expected future exchange rate. In addition, the rise in the money supply lowers the domestic interest rate on pound assets. Both of these changes lower the expected return on pound assets at any given exchange rate, thus shifting the demand curve to the left. The short-run outcome is a lower value of the pound. However, in the long run, the domestic interest rate returns to its previous value, and the demand curve shifts back to the right somewhat. The exchange rate rises to some extent, but still remains below its initial level.

10. The dollar will depreciate. A rise in nominal interest rates but a decline in the real rate implies a rise in expected inflation that produces an expected depreciation of the dollar that is larger than the increase in the domestic interest rate. As a result, the expected return on dollar assets falls at any exchange rate, shifting the demand curve to the left and leading to a fall in the exchange rate.
12. The peso will depreciate. Consider Mexico to be the domestic country. An increased demand for imports would lower the expected future exchange rate and result in a lower expected appreciation of the peso. The resulting lower expected return on peso assets at any given exchange rate would then shift the demand curve to the left, leading to a rise in the peso exchange rate.
14. The contraction of the European money supply will increase European interest rates and raise the future value of the euro, both of which will decrease the relative expected return on dollar assets. The demand curve will then shift to the left, and the dollar will depreciate.

Chapter 21 The International Financial System

2. The purchase of dollar assets involves a sale of foreign assets, which means that international reserves fall and the monetary base decreases. The resulting fall in the money supply causes domestic interest rates to rise and lowers the future price level, thereby raising the future expected exchange rate. Both of these effects raise the expected return on dollar assets at any given exchange rate, shifting the demand curve to the right and raising the equilibrium exchange rate.
4. Because other countries often intervene in the foreign exchange market when the United States has a deficit so that U.S. holdings of international reserves do not change. By contrast, when the Netherlands has a deficit, it must intervene in the foreign exchange market and buy euros, which results in a reduction of international reserves for the Netherlands and Euroland.
6. Two francs per dollar.
8. A large balance-of-payments surplus may require a country to finance the surplus by selling its currency in the foreign exchange market, thereby gaining international reserves. The result is that the central bank will have supplied more of its currency to the public, and the monetary base will rise. The resulting rise in the money supply can cause the price level to rise, leading to a higher inflation rate.
10. To finance the deficits, the central banks in these countries might intervene in the foreign exchange market and buy domestic currency, thereby implementing a contractionary monetary policy. The result is that they sell off international reserves and their monetary base falls, leading to a decline in the money supply.
12. When other countries buy U.S. dollars to keep their exchange rates from changing vis-à-vis the dollar because of the U.S. deficits, they gain international reserves and their monetary base increases. The outcome is that the money supply in these countries grows faster and leads to higher inflation throughout the world.
14. There are no direct effects on the money supply, because there is no central bank intervention in a pure flexible exchange rate regime; therefore, changes in international reserves that affect the monetary base do not occur. However, monetary policy can be affected by the foreign exchange market, because monetary authorities may want to manipulate exchange rates by changing the money supply and interest rates.
16. First is that the exchange-rate target directly keeps inflation under control by tying the inflation rate for internationally traded goods to that found in the anchor country to which its currency is pegged. Second is that it provides an automatic rule for the conduct of monetary policy that helps mitigate the time-inconsistency problem. Third, it has the advantage of simplicity and clarity.
18. With a pegged exchange rate, speculators are sometimes presented with a one-way bet in which the only direction for a currency to go is down in value. In this case, selling the currency before the likely depreciation gives speculators an attractive profit opportunity with potentially high expected returns. As a result, they jump on board and attack the currency.
20. The long-term bond market can help reduce the time-inconsistency problem because politicians and central banks will realize that pursuing an overly expansionary policy will lead to an inflation scare in which inflation expectations surge, interest rates rise, and there is a sharp fall in long-term bond prices. Similarly, they will realize that overly expansionary monetary policy will result in a sharp fall in the value of the currency. Avoiding these outcomes constrains policymakers and politicians so time-inconsistent monetary policy is less likely to occur.
22. A currency board has the advantage that the central bank no longer can print money to create inflation, and so it is a stronger commitment to a fixed exchange rate. The disadvantage is that it is still subject to a speculative attack, which can lead to a sharp contraction of the money supply. In addition, a currency board limits the ability of the central bank to play a lender-of-last-resort role.

Chapter 22 The Demand for Money

1. Velocity is approximately 10 in 2004, 11 in 2005, and 12 in 2006. The rate of velocity growth is approximately 10% per year.
3. Nominal GDP declines by approximately 10%.
5. The price level quadruples.
7. The two largest declines are during the recession in 1920 and the Great Depression of 1929–1933. These declines suggest that velocity is procyclical—that is, it rises in business cycle upturns and falls in business cycle downturns. The data in Figure 1 indicate that it is not reasonable to assume that

declines in the quantity of money cause declines in aggregate spending because when aggregate spending declines it could just reflect the fact that velocity declines at that time.

9. The demand for money will decrease. People would be more likely to expect interest rates to fall and therefore more likely to expect bond prices to rise. The increase in the expected return on bonds relative to money will then mean that people would demand less money.
11. Money balances should average one-half of Grant's monthly income, because he would hold no bonds, because holding them would entail additional brokerage costs but would not provide him with any interest income.
13. True. Because bonds are riskier than money, risk-averse people would be likely to want to hold both.
15. In Keynes's view, velocity is unpredictable because interest rates, which have large fluctuations, affect the demand for money and hence velocity. In addition, Keynes's analysis suggests that if people's expectations of the normal level of interest rates change, the demand for money changes. Keynes thought that these expectations moved unpredictably, meaning that money demand and velocity are also unpredictable. Friedman sees the demand for money as stable, and because he also believes that changes in interest rates have only small effects on the demand for money, his position is that the demand for money, and hence velocity, is predictable.

Chapter 23 Aggregate Demand and Supply Analysis

2. Because the position of the aggregate demand curve is fixed if nominal income ($P \times Y$) is fixed, Friedman's statement implies that the position of the aggregate demand curve is completely determined by the quantity of money. This is built into the monetarist aggregate demand curve because it shifts only when the money supply changes.
4. The aggregate demand curve shifts because a change in "animal spirits" causes consumer expenditure or planned investment spending to change, which then causes the quantity of aggregate output demanded to change at any given price level.
6. True. Given fixed production costs in the short run, firms can earn higher profits by producing more when prices are higher. Profit-maximizing behavior on the part of firms thus leads them to increase production when prices are higher.
8. The short-run aggregate supply curve would shift to the right because production costs would fall, and the long-run aggregate supply curve would also shift to the right because productivity would be higher.
10. The collapse in investment spending during the Great Depression reduced the quantity of output demanded at any given price level and shifted the aggregate demand curve to the left. In an aggregate demand and supply diagram, the equilibrium price level and aggregate output would then fall, which explains the decline in aggregate output and the price level that occurred during the Great Depression.
12. Both the increase in the money supply and the income tax cut will increase the quantity of output demanded at any given price level and so will shift the aggregate demand curve to the right. The intersection of the aggregate demand and short-run aggregate supply curve will be at a higher level of both output and price level in the short run. However, in the long run, the short-run aggregate supply curve will shift leftward, leaving output at the natural rate level, but the price level will be even higher.
14. Because goods would cost more, the national sales tax would raise production costs, and the short-run aggregate supply curve would shift to the left. The intersection of the short-run aggregate supply curve with the aggregate demand curve would then be at a higher level of prices and a lower level of aggregate output; aggregate output would fall, and the price level would rise.

Chapter 24 Transmission Mechanisms of Monetary Policy: The Evidence

4. Seeing which car is built better produces structural model evidence, because it explains why one car is better than the other (that is, how the car is built). Asking owners how often their cars undergo repairs produces reduced-form evidence, because it looks only at the correlation of reliability with the manufacturer of the car.
5. Not necessarily. If GM car owners change their oil more frequently than Ford owners, GM cars would have better repair records, even though they are not more reliable cars. In this case, it is a third factor, the frequency of oil changes, that leads to the better repair record for GM cars.
6. Not necessarily. Although the Ford engine might be built better than the GM engine, the rest of the GM car might be better made than the Ford. The result could be that the GM car is more reliable than the Ford.
8. If the Fed has interest-rate targets, a rise in output that raises interest rates might cause the Fed to buy bonds and bid up their price so as to drive interest rates back down to their target level (see Chapter 5). The result of these open market purchases would be that the increase in output would cause an increase in the monetary base and hence an increase in the money supply. In addition, a rise in output and interest rates would cause free reserves to fall (because excess reserves would fall and the volume of discount loans would rise). If the Fed has a free reserves target, the increase in aggregate output will then cause the Fed to increase the money supply because it believes that money is tight.
10. Monetarists went on to refine their reduced-form models with more sophisticated statistical procedures, one outcome of which was the St. Louis model. Keynesians began to look for transmission mechanisms of monetary policy that they may have ignored.

12. False. Monetary policy can affect stock prices, which affect Tobin's *q*, thereby affecting investment spending. In addition, monetary policy can affect loan availability, which may influence investment spending.
14. There are three mechanisms involving consumer expenditure. First, a rise in the money supply lowers interest rates and reduces the cost of financing purchases of consumer durables, and consumer durable expenditure rises. Second, a rise in the money supply causes stock prices and wealth to rise, leading to greater lifetime resources for consumers and causing them to increase their consumption. Third, a rise in the money supply that causes stock prices and the value of financial assets to rise also lowers people's probability of financial distress, so they spend more on consumer durables.

Chapter 25 Money and Inflation

2. Because hyperinflations appear to be examples in which the increase in money supply growth is an exogenous event, the fact that hyperinflation occurs when money growth is high is powerful evidence that a high rate of money growth causes inflation.
4. False. Although workers' attempts to push up their wages can lead to inflation if the government has a high employment target, inflation is still a monetary phenomenon, because it cannot occur without accommodating monetary policy.
6. True. If financed with money creation, a temporary budget deficit can lead to a one-time rightward shift in the aggregate demand curve and hence to a one-time increase in the price level. However, once the budget deficit disappears, there is no longer any reason for the aggregate demand curve to shift. Thus a temporary deficit cannot lead to a continuing rightward shift of the aggregate demand curve and therefore cannot produce inflation, a continuing increase in the price level.
8. True. The monetarist objection to activist policy would no longer be as serious. The aggregate demand curve could be more quickly moved to AD_2 in Figure 11, and the economy would move more quickly to point 2 because the short-run aggregate supply curve would not have as much time to shift. The scenario of a highly variable price level and output would not occur, making an activist policy more desirable.
10. True, if expectations about policy affect the wage-setting process. In this case, workers and firms are more likely to push up wages and prices because they know that if they do so and unemployment develops as a result, the government will pursue expansionary policies to eliminate the unemployment. Therefore, the cost of pushing up wages and prices is lower, and workers and firms will be more likely to do it.
12. True. If expectations about policy have no effect on the short-run aggregate supply curve, a cost-push inflation is less likely to develop when policymakers pursue an activist accommodating policy. Furthermore, if expectations about policy do not matter, pursuing a nonaccommodating, nonactivist policy does not have the hidden benefit of making it less likely that workers will push up their wages and create unemployment. The case for an activist policy is therefore stronger.
14. The Fed's big stick is the ability to let unemployment develop as a result of a wage push by not trying to eliminate unemployment with expansionary monetary policy. The statement proposes that the Fed should pursue a nonaccommodating policy because this will prevent cost-push inflation and make it less likely that unemployment develops because of workers' attempts to push up their wages.

CREDITS

Page 16. Figure 10: Excel Spreadsheet with Interest-Rate Data. Microsoft Excel® screen shot reprinted with permission from Microsoft Corp.

Page 17. Figure 11: Excel Graph of Interest-Rate Data. Microsoft Excel® screen shot reprinted with permission from Microsoft Corp.

Page 110. Following the Financial News: The "Credit Markets" Column. "Treasury Prices Edge Higher Amid Stock-Market Weakness" from *The Wall Street Journal*, January 21-22, 2006, p. B6. Reprinted with permission of *The Wall Street Journal*, Copyright © 2006 Dow Jones & Company, Inc. All Rights Reserved Worldwide.

Pages 122–123. Following the Financial News: Forecasting Interest Rates. "*The Wall Street Journal* Forecasting Survey for 2006" from *The Wall Street Journal*, January 3, 2006, p. A2. Reprinted with permission of *The Wall Street Journal*, Copyright © 2006 Dow Jones & Company, Inc. All Rights Reserved Worldwide. Page 136. Following the Financial News: Yield Curves. "Treasury Yield Curve" from *The Wall Street Journal*, January 22, 2003, p. C2. Reprinted with permission of *The Wall Street Journal*, Copyright © 2006 Dow Jones & Company, Inc. All Rights Reserved Worldwide.

Page 301. Figure 2: Banking Crisis throughout the World Since 1970. Reprinted with permission of Gerard Caprio and Daniela Klingebiel, "Episodes of Systemic and Borderline Financial Crises" mimeo. © World Bank, October 1999.

Pages 437–438. Excerpt from *A Monetary History of the United States, 1867-1960* (Princeton, NJ: Princeton University Press, 1963, pp. 308-311), by Milton Friedman and Anna Jacobson Schwartz. © 1963 NBER, 1991 renewed. Reprinted with permission of Princeton University Press.

Page 505. Following the Financial News: Foreign Exchange Rates. "Exchange Rates" from *The Wall Street Journal*, February 23, 2006, p. C12. Reprinted with permission of *The Wall Street Journal*, Copyright © 2006 Dow Jones & Company, Inc. All Rights Reserved Worldwide.

Page 526. Following the Financial News: The "Currency Trading" Column. "Dollar Rises on Deficit Report, European Bank's Rate Message" from *The Wall Street Journal*, January 13, 2006, p. C3. Reprinted with permission of *The Wall Street Journal*, Copyright © 2006 Dow Jones & Company, Inc. All Rights Reserved Worldwide.

图书在版编目（CIP）数据

货币金融学：英文/米什金著.
北京：中国人民大学出版社，2010
高等院校双语教材·经济系列
ISBN 978-7-300-12082-9

Ⅰ. ①货…
Ⅱ. ①米…
Ⅲ. ①货币和银行经济学-双语教学-高等学校-教材-英文
Ⅳ. ①F820

中国版本图书馆 CIP 数据核字（2010）第 077129 号

高等院校双语教材·经济系列
货币金融学
弗雷德里克·S·米什金　著
Huobi Jinrongxue

出版发行	中国人民大学出版社		
社　址	北京中关村大街 31 号	**邮政编码**	100080
电　话	010－62511242（总编室）		010－62511398（质管部）
	010－82501766（邮购部）		010－62514148（门市部）
	010－62515195（发行公司）		010－62515275（盗版举报）
网　址	http：//www. crup. com. cn		
	http：//www. ttrnet. com（人大教研网）		
经　销	新华书店		
印　刷	涿州星河印刷有限公司		
规　格	203 mm×255 mm　16 开本	**版　次**	2010 年 5 月第 1 版
印　张	44.5 插页 1	**印　次**	2017 年 9 月第 6 次印刷
字　数	936 000	**定　价**	69.00 元

PEARSON ALWAYS LEARNING

尊敬的老师：

您好！

为了确保您及时有效地申请培生整体教学资源，请您务必完整填写如下表格，加盖学院的公章后传真给我们，我们将会在2~3个工作日内为您处理。

请填写所需教辅的开课信息：

采用教材			□中文版 □英文版 □双语版
作　者		出版社	
版　次		ISBN	
课程时间	始于　年　月　日	学生人数	
	止于　年　月　日	学生年级	□专科　□本科1/2年级 □研究生　□本科3/4年级

请填写您的个人信息：

学　校			
院系/专业			
姓　名		职　称	□助教 □讲师 □副教授 □教授
通信地址/邮编			
手　机		电　话	
传　真			
official email(必填) (eg:XXX@ruc.edu.cn)		email (eg:XXX@163.com)	
是否愿意接受我们定期的新书讯息通知：　□是　□否			

系 / 院主任：________（签字）

（系 / 院办公室章）

____年____月____日

资源介绍：

--教材、常规教辅（PPT、教师手册、题库等）资源：请访问 **www.pearsonhighered.com/educator**；（免费）

--MyLabs/Mastering 系列在线平台：适合老师和学生共同使用；访问需要 **Access Code**；（付费）

100013　北京市东城区北三环东路36号环球贸易中心D座1208室

电话：(8610)57355169　　传真：(8610)58257961

Please send this form to: **Service.CN@pearson.com**